THE GOLD COOK BOOK

THE
GOLD
COOK
BOOK

by Master Chef
LOUIS P. DE GOUY

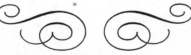

introduction by Oscar of the Waldorf

GALAHAD BOOKS
NEW YORK CITY

INTRODUCTION BY
OSCAR OF THE WALDORF-ASTORIA

THE TASTY SAVORINESS OF FINE FOOD, PROPERLY PREPARED. The appetizing blend of flavors to which we are accustomed. The appeal of the truly good things to eat, that knows no boundary of race, creed, or country. These are the universal pleasures of the gourmet.

For many years it was necessary for the gourmet to travel extensively in order to acquaint himself with the delights of foreign diets. It is the ambition of this book, written by Louis P. DeGouy, a professional Chef whom I have known for more than 40 years, to enable him to do this at home.

The history of cookery is part of the history of civilization. At some remote period—too remote to be gauged—primitive man discovered that the flesh of his captures became less tough and more palatable when subjected to the action of fire, and from this the art of cookery evolved, slowly and laboriously like all arts, and progressed from a simple to an elaborate process.

The preparation of food is geographic. Basically, this geographical limitation was simply the natural tendency of each separate nation to consume only the foods that could easily be produced within its own borders.

It is curious that although the various arts, music, drama, painting, and the like, have become international in scope, each country, in the matter of food, seems to prefer to isolate itself. This is indeed a happy situation for the gourmet. The nations of the world have not blended their cuisines. They prefer apparently, to remain at home and raise to perfection the crude dishes that nourished their people generations ago. So we have today a different style of cooking in each country, even in each of the forty-eight states of this great country.

American homemakers are increasingly aware of their rich heritage of cooking, of its wide variety as a result of its regional origins. We have the fine culinary traditions of those who settled in Louisiana, Virginia, New England, the South, the North, the East, and the West. No statement of the excellence of the cooking of American homemakers, who are representative of every race of mankind, is complete without a reference to the fine cooking of the Negroes of the South, who are natural gourmets. They seem to have inherited a sort of tradition of good cooking, and it may be that this will have a large place in the final development of a real American type of cookery.

Monotony needs no longer harass the gourmet. He may choose not only the foods of his own country but those of the entire world in these United States of America. In fact, he is missing a great deal if he permits himself to be limited by geographical considerations that no longer really exist. Perhaps the true gourmet or gourmand may see in international cookery in America a sure step to permanent understanding among the nations and a way to eventual peace. It is unnecessary, though, to propound any such remote defense of the gourmet, for his is the joyous appreciation of one of the most essential phases of our existence.

The author of this book is an old personal friend of mine and a real professional and practising Chef who learned his chosen profession from the bottom up under his father who was Esquire of Cuisine at the Court of Austria and Belgium. He has emphasized throughout this book the art of seasoning food, which is essential in good cooking, as certain seasonings lift up certain foods. In using them, however, the homemaker must be careful not to over-season or under-season, but rather to obtain a delicious blend which will bring out the flavor of the predominant ingredient in the dish and add that elusive aroma, so subtle that even the gourmet hesitates to name it.

In culinary combinations of food, the spices and other stimulants are used not merely for the purpose of imparting their own flavor but with the aim of exciting the organ of taste to a heightened perception of the flavor of the meat, soup, poultry, game, vegetables, sauces, etc. It is not the biting quality of pepper alone that is valued; and wine is not used in sauces or soups for the purpose of making the wine taste stand out.

The perfection of the art of making culinary combinations is the production of a happy combination, in which the elementary flavors are all lost and indistinguishable in the new one created by their combined effect on the palate. The palate must never be excited by powerful stimuli when some food with a delicate flavor is about to be consumed. Food properly seasoned is an art in itself. Salt and pepper are the basic seasonings and should be used during the cooking of the food, not after the food is cooked, no matter the method of cooking.

All the recipes contained in this book, many of them hitherto unpublished, have been tested and tasted by the author during his sixty years of practical cooking. Louis De Gouy is already well known among both homemakers and gourmets for his dozen or so superb cook books.

Oscar
of the Waldorf

AUTHOR'S INTRODUCTION

GASTRONOMISTS, MASTERS OF THE ART OF GOOD EATING, NEVER consider food in terms of calories, mineral salts, proteins, carbohydrates or vitamins. They leave to the cook who prepares the food the task of retaining all of its nutritive substances. The elements and aliments in good cookery should be varied and numerous; they should be tasted and savored slowly, with pleasure and moderation. There is delight in eating good dishes prepared with interest on the part of the cook, but not in eating those that are thrown together and served with an attitude of "Here it is—eat!"

The delight of eating is the only enjoyment that belongs to all weathers, to all conditions, and to all ages. The impressions of a good dinner are always durable and comforting. A good menu is not a long list of chemical formulas and laboratory analyses, but a list of dishes, agreeable to the eye and the tongue, dishes that tempt and awaken the laggard appetite by exciting the gastric juices and by repairing the loss that the human body sustains.

The true gourmet considers a good, even a simple, dinner as a period of relaxation. It is the culminating point in the events of the day; for, in good company, one may pass in review a new play or motion picture, a new book or musical composition; he may discuss new ideas or turn with pleasure to the old—in short, all that is gay—while savoring dishes which delight the appetite. But as soon as a dinner turns to gluttony, voracity, or debauchery, it loses its good name and its advantages, and falls into the hands of moralists . . . and doctors.

Good cooking is represented by savory dishes of good taste, and nothing can better define the term "good cooking" than the inscription we find in the big gold book of the Grand Council of Gourmets of Paris, in the language that never changes: *Urcumque ferculum, eximii et bene noti saporis, appositum fuerit, fiat autopsia convivos, et nisi ejus ac oculi vertantur ad extasis, notetur ut indignus*—"Every time that a special dish of excellent savor is presented at the table, the guests should be carefully observed, and those whose silent approbation does not make them radiate with ecstasy should be marked as unworthy."

The ultimate purpose of good cooking is to contribute to the preservation of man by the means of good, healthy, and agreeable nourishment. In the exercise of this virtue, cooking embraces all aspects of human life, from cradle to grave, and sustains a long list of human activities: Agriculture, which produces; Commerce, which trades; Chemistry, which analyzes; Industry, which prepares; Medicine, which studies and examines; Political Economy, which furnishes resources; and General Satisfaction, which is attained by a judicious combination of all of these.

Good cooking, by its modifications, transformations, preparations and concoctions, classifies all edible substances according to their diverse qualities. There are those that go well together; those that have a certain affinity; those that nourish; those that form the base of our daily diet; and those which, as accessories, are yet necessary to excite the lazy and sleepy appetite—hence often the necessary concomitants of convivial reunions. Good cooking, therefore, raises the sum total of contentment and of the joy of living.

One must be precise in calculation if one is to excell in this art. By *good* cooking we mean the conscientious preparation of the simple food of everyday life, not the more or less skillful concoctions of idle feasts and rare dishes. Good cooking is that into which the cook puts all his or her soul, art, and culinary knowledge, in order to attain from simple ingredients a masterpiece worthy of presentation at table.

Good cooking is always associated with good living. Like marriage, it consists of two elements which should blend in harmony: the aliment and the seasoning. Conscientious cooking, by rendering easy the processes of digestion, promotes that serenity of mind, graciousness of thought, and indulgent view of our neighbor's failings, which is the only genuine form of optimism. No virtues will fully promote happiness if the art of cooking be neglected by the national conscience. We owe much to the fruitful meditations of our sages, but a sane view of life is, after all, initiated mainly in the kitchen—the kitchen of the small house, the abode of the great majority of the people.

"Of all books produced," said Joseph Conrad, "since the most remote ages by human talents and industry, those only that treat of cooking are, from a moral point of view, above suspicion. The intention of every other piece of prose may be discussed and even mistrusted; but the purpose of a cookery book is one and unmistakable. Its object can conceivably be no other than to increase the happiness of mankind."

NOTE: Since the last printing of *The Gold Cook Book*, Pique Seasoning mentioned in recipes has been concentrated in strength. Therefore, if desired, quantities suggested by the Author may be reduced accordingly.

CONTENTS

PAGE

INTRODUCTION BY OSCAR OF THE WALDORF VII

AUTHOR'S INTRODUCTION IX

Chapter One

HORS D'OEUVRES I

Hot and Cold—Raw and Cooked. Canapés: Seafood, Cheese, Meat, Vegetable. Cocktails: Fruit, Fruit Juices, Vegetable Juices, Seafood. Frozen Specialties. Cheeses—Aspics—Crunches—Pick-ups—Relishes— Smörgasbord—Snacks—Tidbits.

Chapter Two

BEVERAGES 47

Beer—Punches—Flips—Wassail Bowls—Holiday Drinks—Chocolate and Malted Drinks—Shakes—Sodas—Cocoa—Eggnogs—Cider—Fruit Drinks. Coffee: Varieties, Preparation and Uses. Milk and Milk Drinks. Tea: Varieties, Preparation and Uses. Wines.

Chapter Three

SOUPS AND SOUP GARNISHES 87

Bouillons—Consommés—Broths—Light Cream and Heavy Cream Soups—Chowders. Soup Stocks: Brown Stock, White Stock, Vegetable Stock and Fish Stock. Clarifying the Stock. Garnishes: Dumplings, Bread Garnishes, Floats, Custards, Egg Garnishes, Toasts and Crackers. Soup Sauces.

Chapter Four

EGGS 143

Eggs and Nutrition. How to Buy Them. Variety Uses in Cooking. Rules for Egg Cookery. Omelettes—Soufflés—Scrambled Eggs (with Cheese, Seafood, and Vegetables)—Eggs in Casserole—Fritters—Poached Egg Dishes—Stuffed Eggs. Garnishes.

Chapter Five

FISH AND SHELLFISH

PAGE
189

Rules for Fish Cookery. Guide to Purchase and Preparation of Fish and
Shellfish.   Baked—Fried—Grilled—Broiled—Boiled—Stewed   Fish
Dishes. Fish Dinners. Fish Roe. Clams—Crabs—Eels—Frog's Legs—
Lobster—Mussels—Oysters—Snails—Turtle.

Chapter Six

MEATS

307

Beef—Veal—Lamb—Mutton—Pork—Ham. Rules for Meat Cookery.
Beef: Guide to Purchase and Preparation. Steaks—Filets—Roasts—
Barbecues—Stews—Goulashes—Beef Loaf—Beef Pies—Corned Beef—
Hamburgers—Casserole Dishes. *Veal:* Guide to Purchase and Prepara-
tion. Roasts—Veal Stews—Curried Veal—Veal Loaf—Potted Veal—
Veal Chops—Veal Cutlets. *Lamb:* Facts About Lamb—Roasts—Barbe-
cued Lamb—Stews—Cutlets—Chops—Curries—Shish Kabab. Mutton
Dishes. *Pork:* Guide to Purchase and Preparation. Roasts—Chops—
Roast Pig—Loin—Pig's Knuckles—Pig's Feet—Pork Pies. Ham (Fresh
and Cured). Scrapple.

Chapter Seven

VARIETY MEATS

425

Guide to Purchase and Preparation. Brains—Feet—Heart—Kidneys—
Livers—Sausages (Fresh, Smoked, Summer). Specialties—Sweetbreads.

Chapter Eight

POULTRY

475

Poultry Preparation and Hints. Guide to Purchase of Poultry. Chicken
Dishes: Capon—Broiler or Fowl—Fryer—Roaster. Squabs and Pigeons
—Duck—Goose—Guinea Hen and Turkey. Jellied Dishes—Stuffings—
Pies—Curries.

Chapter Nine

COMPOUND BUTTERS, SAUCES AND GRAVIES

547

Seafood Butters—Vegetable Butters—Horseradish, Spice, and Herb
Butters. Sauces: Barbecue—Béchamel—Brown—Cheese—Cocktail—
Curry—Fruit—Hollandaise—Mustard—Onion—Vegetable—Wine
Sauces.

Chapter Ten

VEGETABLES

PAGE
591

Rules for Vegetable Cookery. Frying—Boiling—Broiling—Stewing—
Baking—Mashed—Creamed—Stuffed. With Sauces. Vegetable Pies.
Hints on Cabbage. The World of the Onion. Potato Dishes. Specialties.

Chapter Eleven

CEREALS, ALIMENTARY PASTES
AND RICE   745

Corn Meal and Polenta Dishes—Hominy—Rice and Wild Rice. Macaroni—Noodles—Spaghetti—Ravioli. Sauces.

Chapter Twelve

FRIED BREADS, DUMPLINGS AND STUFFINGS 777

Doughnuts—Crullers. Dumplings: Egg—Meat—Vegetable. Rivvles.
Stuffings. Pancakes and Griddle Cakes. Waffles.

Chapter Thirteen

SALADS, DRESSINGS AND SANDWICHES 809

Salad-Making Hints. Fruit Salads—Vegetable Salads—Aspics—Cheese
Salads. Salad Dressings: French Dressings—Cheese Dressings—Mayon-
naise. First Aid to Mayonnaise. Sweet and Sour Cream Dressings.
Specialty Dressings. Sandwich Hints. Tea and Cocktail Sandwiches.
Three-Decker Sandwiches. Sandwich Fillings.

Chapter Fourteen

DESSERT AND DESSERT SAUCES   857

The Climax of the Meal. Fruit and Berry Desserts. Puddings—Whips—
Creams—Crêpes—Custards—Gelatins—Meringues. Fruit Sauces—
Rum, Wine and Brandy Sauces—Hard Sauces.

Chapter Fifteen

CAKES AND COOKIES   899

Baking Techniques. Common Causes and Remedies in Cake Baking
Failures. Sponge Cakes—Fruit Cakes—Berry Cakes—Bride's Cakes—
Chocolate and Cream Cakes—Spice Cakes—Holiday Specialty Cakes.
Cookies—Macaroons—Petits Fours.

Chapter Sixteen

PIES AND PASTRIES

PAGE 935

Pie-Baking Techniques. Types of Pastry—Puff Paste. Hot and Cold Pies—Fruit and Berry Pies—Cream Pies—Meringues. Deep-Dish Pies. Use of Nuts. Tarts and Tartlets.

Chapter Seventeen

CANDY

965

Candy-Making Techniques. Temperatures. Pralines—Crunches— Kisses—Brittle—Fudge—Marshmallow Candies—Carmels—Fondants —Bonbons—Marzipan—Lollypops—Taffy.

Chapter Eighteen

GENERAL INFORMATION

981

Methods of Cooking. Braising—Broiling or Grilling—Deep Fat Frying— Pan Broiling—Pan Frying—Pot Roasting—Roasting—Searing—Simmering—Stewing—Sautéeing—Steaming—Carving. Seasoning—Herb and Spice Chart. Frozen Foods. Guide for Cooking Time. Thawing Meats. Table of Measurements and Equivalents. How to Prepare, Cook and Use Nuts. Nut Chart for Weight and Measure.

Chapter Nineteen

BISCUITS, BREAD, MUFFINS AND ROLLS

1033

Baking Terms and Methods—Baking Powder Biscuits—Nut Breads— Fruit Breads—Brown Bread—Corn Bread—Molasses Bread—Short Breads—Buns—Muffins, Gems and Johnny Cakes—Gingerbread— Popovers—Rolls—Toasts

Chapter Twenty

ICE CREAM DESSERTS

1111

Ices—Ice Cream Recipes—Mousses—Parfaits—Sherbets

Chapter Twenty-One

PRESSURE COOKERY

1157

Do's and Don't's in Pressure Cookery. Pressure Chart. Chart of Altitude Corrections to Time Tables. Detailed Chart for Cooking Fresh Vegetables.

INDEX

1177

Chapter One

HORS D'OEUVRES

APPETIZERS—COCKTAILS (Fruit, Seafood, and Vegetable Juices)
—CANAPES—COCKTAIL ESCORTS—CRUNCHES—HORS
D'OEUVRES—PICK-UPS—RELISHES—SMÖRGASBORD—
SNACKS—TIDBITS, etc.

When gourmets to the board propel
Their paunchy selves for tasty fare,
Most nostrils quiver at the smell
Of food that master chefs prepare;
But if you wish that you were there,
Hold on—Lucullan tables lack
The virtues found when you prepare
The pleasures of a midnight snack.
At witching hour, when all is well,
A hungry man steals down the stair
Into the cook's own citadel,
To gather morsels extra rare
And strip unguarded cupboards bare;
Then to the bedroom creeping back,
Thus adding to adventure's flair
The pleasures of a midnight snack.

—Prince, would you forget your thinning hair,
Your troubles state and cardiac?
Then try, for liberty from care,
The pleasures of a midnight snack.

—The Poète Cuisinier

HORS D'OEUVRES

IT IS BECOMING THE MODISH THING THESE DAYS TO PREFACE even a simple family dinner with a cocktail and a few tasty snacks. The cocktail may be tomato juice, citrus fruit juice, sauerkraut juice, seafood juice or something of that nature, or again it may be the conventional alcoholic appetizer or a glass of sherry, Madeira or a dry wine. Service for this is usually in the living room, which gives the family and guests a chance to assemble for a few moments of conversational exchange. The living room service has another advantage, for the main course of the meal can then be brought to the table without the need of jumping up to remove the glasses and bring in the plates.

The snack that goes with the cocktail must be of the sort that will put a sharp edge on the appetite, which means that it must have distinctive flavor. Nothing is more attractive to the eye nor more tempting to the palate than a tray of canapés with contrasting shapes and garnishes. And as every hostess knows, nothing takes more time to prepare. An hour to make, a few moments of display, and they are gone, if they are as good as they look. And they *must* be, to justify the time they take to make. A snack used to mean something pillaged from the refrigerator for a midnight supper in the kitchen. It might have been a slice of cold chicken or a piece of cake or apple pie. Today the demand for snacks is leading the food industry to new inventiveness. The modern snack is anything from a diminutive sausage to a fluffy kernel of popcorn covered with melted cheese; the classifications between these two are legion, the purpose of all is to appear at the cocktail hour before dinner is served.

A good start gives a guest a sense of confidence in coming dishes—but start off with tepid, tasteless canapés or first course and even your best main dish trick will fail.

Tidbits, snacks, canapés, and appetizers—acrobatic imps in harlequin motley—have reappeared since the war, with their fantastic condiments, as accompaniments for cocktails. The mustard pot, the walnut and mushroom catsup and all the other catsups of the world have come back. They are more and more in evidence and clown with oysters, fresh or smoked, little neck clams, shrimps, anchovy paste, lobster paste, liver paste, and filets of anchovies, filets of smoked trout, with puff paste, crackers, celery, potato, parsnip and Brazil nut chips loaded with cheese or some delicious concoction. Cocktail parties have given rise to little round, square or oblong canapés filled with all kinds of mixtures of every color, taste, and fancy; to tidbits flavored with caraway seeds, poppy seeds, celery seeds, and whatnot. Cheese baked in hollowed crackers has made its reappearance. So have new pastes, such as bloater, sardine, curried pickled paste, liver paste of all kinds of edible birds and animals from chicken, goose, guinea hen or duck to reindeer.

Potted meats of domestic or wild animals also are growing in popularity. Caviar—red, blond, black, auburn—and the true pâté made of duck and goose liver with white and black truffles, stand alone as two of the most luxurious spreads for the mouthfuls which everyone enjoys at a cocktail party, a buffet party, a family party or a wedding party.

The Swedish *smörgasbord*, the Italian *antipasti*, the Spanish *gaspachio*, the French *hors d'oeuvres*, the Hindu *dumpoke*, the Russian *akrochka* of chicken moistened with *kwass* (a fermented drink made from wheat, etc.), the English *savoury*, the French *salmagundi*, are more conspicuous than before the war because our heroes who have been abroad have tasted them and want them at home.

And for all this multitude of tidbits there are no methods, no basic standard recipes. All is left to the innate talent, the ingenuity, taste, and economic situation of the "artist."

An appetizer is a teaser or rouser of the appetite, but not enough to satisfy the hunger. Its primary object is to stimulate the flow of gastric juice, tickle the papillae of the palate. Its nature, therefore, is zestful and snappy.

Following are a few hot and cold appetizers to be served with cocktails, or on a buffet table.

AIGRETTES D'ANCHOIS   [2]
Anchovy Aigrettes (Hot)

Wash, dry, trim neatly, then cut into narrow strips lengthwise, 12 anchovy filets. Have ready ½ cup of hot cream sauce (No. 258), stir in 1 teaspoon of grated Parmesan cheese and anchovy paste the size of a pea, then add the anchovy strips. Stir well to coat thoroughly with the sauce. Take the anchovy strips one by one, drop them into hot, deep fat, and cook until strips are crisp and lightly browned. Drain on absorbent paper and dress in pyramidal form upon a napkin or paper doily. Sprinkle with a little grated Parmesan cheese, then finally with a little paprika. Serve as hot as possible.

AIGRETTES AU PARMESAN   [3]
Parmesan Cheese Aigrettes (Hot)

Heat ¼ cup of sweet butter in a small saucepan together with 1 cup of beef bouillon, ¼ cup of flour and ¼ teaspoon salt, stirring briskly over a bright flame until mixture follows the spoon. Remove from the fire and, when cool, beat in 3 fresh egg yolks, one at a time, beating briskly after each addition, adding with the last egg yolk 3 ounces of grated Parmesan cheese and a few grains of cayenne pepper. When quite cold, fold in 3 stiffly beaten egg whites, beaten with a few grains each of salt and nutmeg. Spread preparation upon a cold platter. When ready to serve, drop by small rough pieces, about the size of a small walnut, into hot deep fat, and cook until delicately browned, turning the pieces with a wooden spoon that they may brown evenly. Drain on absorbent paper; dress the aigrettes in a pyramidal form upon a folded napkin or paper doily placed on a hot platter; sprinkle lightly with a little grated Parmesan cheese, then, finally, with a little paprika. Serve at once.

CANAPÉS [4]

Canapés, which are quite different from sandwiches, are thin slices of bread, either fried in butter, toasted or left plain. The toasted bread is most usual. The bread—toasted, fried, or not—may be cut in fancy shapes. Their garnishing may be of one or several ingredients harmoniously, appetizingly and tastefully combined. Toast used for canapés is usually toasted on one side only, the untoasted side being the recipient of the spread, or vice-versa, according to fancy. The side used is generally spread with plain butter or any one of the compounded butters (Nos. 978–1006). The use of a pastry bag with a small fancy tube is a clean and rapid method of decorating or garnishing canapés whenever a purée of fish, meat, game, poultry, or a compounded butter, or other food is indicated or selected for its appropriateness; and allows one to make fancy and decorative designs and effects.

Important as this first course is, you must not run away with the idea that it's the principal course of a repast. There is a subtle distinction here between "important" and "principal," and the two qualities are not to be confused with each other. The *importance* of the first course should lie in its delicate deliciousness; it should be carefully thought out and executed, and above all it should give a fillip to the appetite. The *principal* course on the other hand is the dish to which one looks for satisfaction of quite another sort. It is, and should be, a more substantial enjoyment, but one which all the same can be made or marred by a good or a bad start.

ANCHOVY CANAPÉ FINGERS [5]
(*Hot*)

Wash 12 anchovy filets in several changes of cold water, the last one being lukewarm, and dry them thoroughly. Sprinkle over them 1 tablespoon of lemon juice, 1 teaspoon of finely chopped parsley and about 1 teaspoon of finely chopped shallots. Toast 4 slices of bread on both sides; decrust and cut them into finger strips, each large enough to accommodate 2 anchovy filets; lay the drained filets on the toast fingers, sprinkle over each a few drops of the marinade, then a little melted butter, arrange the fingers on a baking sheet, and heat thoroughly in a hot oven (450° F.) but do not let them brown. Serve on a napkin placed on a hot platter and garnish with lemon quarters and fresh, crisp parsley.

ANCHOVY CANAPÉ LOZENGES   [6]
(Cold)

Arrange on freshly made and buttered toast cut in lozenge shapes, enough filets of anchovies, previously washed and sponged dry to cover entirely, slightly overlapping one another. Smooth with a wet spatula; trim neatly and surround the edges with anchovy butter forced through a pastry bag with a very small fancy tube.

ANCHOVY CANAPÉ ROUNDS   [7]
(Cold)

Spread small rounds of bread toasted on one side only, with anchovy butter. Place a smaller round of plum tomato over each and top the tomato slice with a tiny cream cheese ball rolled in finely chopped nut meats.

ANCHOVY CANAPÉS NANTAIS   [8]
(Cold)

Toast small rounds of white bread on one side only; spread untoasted sides with Lobster Butter (No. 991) and place in center of each a thin slice of cucumber, previously dipped in tomato catsup and well drained. Surround the edges with anchovy filets, trim neatly, and place on the cucumber slices 3 tiny balls of cream cheese or Roquefort cheese, each ball colored in a different color as follows: Roll 1 cheese ball in paprika, another in finely chopped parsley or chives and the third one in finely ground toasted almonds, and press in center of each cheese ball a small stuffed olive.

ANCHOVY CANAPÉS ODETTE   [9]
(Cold)

Stamp from fresh bread (using a cookie cutter) as many small crescents as required; toast on one side; spread untoasted side with Anchovy Butter (No. 979). Garnish the borders with Salmon Butter (No. 999) forced through a pastry bag with a small fancy rose tube, and place in center of each canapé a small olive stuffed with a tiny bit of anchovy filet topping, the olive topped with a little tuft of Salmon Butter forced through a pastry bag with a small rose tube.

ANCHOVY CANAPÉS PATRICIA [10]
(Cold).

Toast small rounds of white bread on one side only; spread the un-toasted sides with Chivry Butter (No. 984); lay some filets of anchovy over the butter, each filet overlapping another, and smooth with a spatula dipped in cold water. Trim neatly, and criss-cross each canapé with narrow strips of red canned pimiento. Place on each tiny lozenge a dot of Green Butter (No. 987) as tastefully as possible.

ANCHOVY CANAPÉS À LA ROYALE [11]
(Cold)

Rub 6 ounces (12 tablespoons) of sweet butter into 6 ounces (1½ cups) of sifted cake flour, previously sifted with a few grains of cayenne and curry powder, until thoroughly blended. Moisten with 1 slightly beaten egg into which 1 teaspoon anchovy essence or anchovy paste and a drop or two of red vegetable coloring have been beaten. The dough should be stiff; if not, add a little more sifted cake flour. Roll out as thinly as possible on a lightly floured board; cut into rounds about the size of a small baking powder biscuit with a fluted cutter; arrange the rounds on a buttered baking sheet and bake in a moderate oven (350° F.) about 4 or 5 minutes or until crisp, then let cool. Wash thoroughly in several changes of cold water and a last one of lukewarm water, 8 anchovy filets and dry well; chop, then pound (or put them through food chopper, using the finest blade 2 or 3 times) together with 2 hard-cooked egg yolks, ¼ cup of sweet butter, a pinch of cayenne pepper and nutmeg to taste. Again rub this preparation through a fine-meshed sieve, then beat in 6 tablespoons of heavy cream which has been whipped with a little finely-grated lemon rind (about ¼ teaspoon). Fill a wet pastry bag having a small star tube with the mixture and spread the baked, cold rounds of pastry in the form of a small cone or cornucopia; decorate tastefully with a few grains of caviar scattered here and there and serve at once.

ANCHOVY [12]
The Epicure's Debt to the Anchovy
Subtle Influence of the Midget Fish Found in the Kitchens of the World

The pounding of one boned anchovy to a paste with mortar and pestle is the first step in the composition of many a delectable sauce, etc., that may apparently have nothing in the world to do with fish, but the master cook is a practitioner of white magic, and the subtlety of his or her art is based on a knowledge of peculiar affinities. The filet of anchovy, figuring variously in hors d'oeuvres, antipasto and smörgasbord, sharpens the appetite for both meat and drink; and when used judiciously in conjunction with certain fish, flesh and fowl, it mysteriously, inexplicably enhances flavors and gives accent to elusive nuances of taste.

The salted bummaloe fish of India, known generally as Bombay ducks, are strong and crude in comparison with the delicate anchovy in oil, but they are as inseparable from curried meats and chutney sauces as is the anchovy from certain milder viands, and the affinity is just as puzzling. Shakespeare knew his anchovies and his caviar, and there's little doubt that he had good reasons for charging Sir John Falstaff two and six pence for anchovies on the tavern chit, when the other items were one capon, some sauce, bread and two gallons of sack.

Your practical cook would scarcely associate anchovies with veal cutlets or a Wiener schnitzel, yet some distinguished American and European chefs specify in their recipes that boned filets of anchovy shall be used in garnishing the cutlets; and a world-famous schnitzel is identified by a rolled filet and a slice of lemon in its center. It is expected that the diner-out will pop the bit of anchovy into his mouth first of all, and thereby prepare his palate for the veal and its delicate sauce.

Anchovy butter is a staple kept in stock jars in the refrigerator by experienced cooks, ready to be spread lightly on a steak for broiling, or rubbed into a piquant sauce or a salad dressing; and it is made simply enough by pounding boned and skinned anchovies in a mortar and mixing one part of the smooth paste with two parts of sweet butter. If one has no mortar and pestle, however, the prepared anchovy paste can be used in the mixture, but it should be the rich, heavy paste that comes in small earthen or glass jars. That same paste is the very soul of half the exquisite tidbits of the smörgasbord, however it may be disguised, and one of the fine old Boston hotels had as one of its many specialties a renowned canapé that was nothing more than skillfully blended anchovy paste and tomato paste spread on bits of crisp toast. (See No. 13.)

A delicious salad dressing or artichoke or broccoli dressing is made by pounding two whole anchovies, boned and skinned, to a paste and mixing with olive oil, tarragon white wine vinegar, a dash of English mustard, one fresh egg yolk, and minced parsley, chives, capers and chervil, seasoned with salt and mignonette pepper or freshly ground black pepper. This dressing is also very good for oysters on the half-shell. Anchovy, regarded as a seasoning rather than a major ingredient, is effective in sauces for cold meats, poultry and game; and some of the geniuses of the kitchen incorporate the essence in Béarnaise, Ravigote, Remoulade, Hollandaise, and the standard basic Espagnole and Demi-Glace sauce. In Europe, the bland, delicate fishes for boiling and baking are stepped up to a keener piquancy with dashes of anchovy; but mature judgment and the practiced hand are required or the original delicacy is lost.

The confirmed anchovy addict doesn't stop short of the larding needle, but draws thin strips of anchovy through roasts or meat or game, fowl and wild birds, to impart a tang of salt and a mysterious flavor; and, if it is not overdone, the effect is both puzzling and pleasing. As in all things, there are anchovies and anchovies, and they must be bought with care. Some of the most tasty anchovies for the snack bar, well pickled and spiced with bay, clove and pepper, are naught but sprats, pilchards, alewives, or other country cousins of the herring family.

ANCHOVY CANAPÉS À LA STATLER [13]
(Cold)

Toast small rounds of white bread on one side only; spread on the untoasted sides a mixture of equal parts of anchovy paste and heavy chili sauce or ketchup; arrange over the spread, 3 cold, cooked mussels, and cover the entire surface with mayonnaise forced through a pastry bag with a small rose tube. When ready to serve, scatter all over the mayonnaise some washed, dried small capers, then dust with a tiny film of paprika.

Variations. (1) Use cold cooked shrimps instead of mussels. (2) Use slices of cooked lobster instead of mussels. (3) Use whole anchovy filets instead of mussels. (4) Use slices of hard-cooked eggs instead of mussels. (5) Use grilled walnuts instead of mussels. (6) Use sardine filets instead of mussels.

ANCHOVY FRITOTS IN PYRAMID [14]
(Hot)

Wash and dry 10 anchovy filets and chop coarsely. Have ready a scant half cup of thick, cold Mornay Sauce (No. 1088); stir in the chopped anchovies and let stand 1 hour in refrigerator. When ready to serve, drop by teaspoonfuls into hot, deep fat, and cook until crisp and delicately browned. Drain on absorbent paper; dress in pyramidal form on a folded napkin or paper doily; garnish with quartered lemon and scatter over all deep-fat-fried parsley. Serve as hot as possible.

ANGELS ON HORSEBACK [15]
(Hot)

Trim and clean—but do not wash—1 dozen fresh, plump oysters; half-cook 6 strips of bacon, then cut them in two, crosswise; fry 1 dozen small rounds of white bread in butter until golden brown on both sides. Place 1 oyster on a piece of bacon; season with a little paprika and a little finely chopped shallot and parsley; add a few tears of lemon juice and roll tightly, securing the bacon with a couple of wooden toothpicks. Place the prepared angels on a pie plate or small baking sheet and grill under the flame of the broiling oven, having the pan about 6 inches from the gentle flame, broiling just long enough to crisp the bacon, and turning the angels twice during the broiling process. Further broiling would toughen the oysters. Dress the angels on the hot fried rounds of bread. Remove toothpicks carefully, without damaging the angels, and serve at once as hot as possible the angels dressed on a hot platter in crown fashion, filling the center with a cleaned bunch of crisp, green watercress.

ASPERGES DES PAUVRES VINAIGRETTE   [16]
Leeks à la Vinaigrette (Cold)

Cut the white portion of a large bunch of leeks (about 3–3½ inches long), and tie in bunches of 3 or 4; cook in salted water until tender. Drain, then place the cooked leeks in a colander and run cold water from the faucet over them for at least 30 minutes; dry on a cloth and store in refrigerator to chill thoroughly. Two hours before serving, pour over them a well-seasoned French Vinaigrette (No. 1133) and let marinate for 2 hours in refrigerator.

ASPIC   [17]

Aspic probably was used a century or two before Gallic pigs rooted up the first truffle for appreciative gourmets; and every patron of the more formal hotels and restaurants has seen it glittering on plates and platters; yet the word scarcely occurs in the working vocabulary of the average man, and the average housewife has never dreamed of bothering with such a frivolous bit of culinary affectation.

You scan the restaurant carte du jour (menu) and languidly order some mildly alluring entrée, or decide to vary the formal monotony by treating yourself to savory "Chicken-Ham Pie" or a dainty assortment of cold cuts; then along comes a silver trencher on which good things are laid out with artful little scenic effects, and your eyes dwell for an instant with casual indifference—perhaps with momentary curiosity—on one or two little pyramids of sparkling amber or topaz jewels cut in cubes, lozenges or prismatic forms; but in another second your ruthless fork has toppled the pyramids and swept the jewels aside.

However, in the sardonic irony of unresting and relentless Fate, those amber and topaz gems may have caused some brother man a sleepless night, or another man his job. An underchef or a probationary candidate for a post of responsibility in the metropolitan kitchen should be well able to turn out a day's supply of aspic at the word of command, but his savory crystals may lack the glitter of jewels or, worse still, they may rest on the critical tongue for a fatal instant with an acrid or a bitter tang—even with no tang at all—and a white-capped Rhadamanthus glowers on the luckless wretch and thunders, "Off with his head! He can't make aspic!"

And the irony of such a tragi-comic situation is bitter enough, and silly enough, too, in all conscience!—for aspic is nothing more nor less than jellied soup. Yet it *has* to have flavor and piquancy as well as crystal clarity and sparkle, for the eleventh man or woman in the dining room may spear a jewel off the platter and test it on a tongue attuned to the subtleties and refinements of sophisticated taste. Otherwise, you perceive, aspic might as well be made of barley sugar, or even the ubiquitous and versatile celluloid of commerce.

A change is perhaps impending, however, in the historic course of aspic, for at last it is flirting with the fickle jade Popularity, who leads her victims on to fame or quite as often down to the dismal depths of the eternal commonplace. Aspic, after all these years and centuries, actually is being advertised, is being introduced to the classes and the masses; and deadly peril lurks in the certain menace to its charm of mystery and elegance. For aspic—tender, fragile, delicate aspic—comes now in packages and is talked about on the air waves with that familiarity that fairly courts contempt. Yes, in packages, with directions printed on the cover, and the housewife-cook and the June bride fetch measuring cups and spoons, and in a jiffy there is aspic sparkling in the kitchenette and in the dinette alcove. All this, mind you, while head chefs still puzzle over formulas and work frantically with the crucibles and mortars, pounding herbs and essences to liquid paste, adding a dash of this elixir and a spot of that—and savoring the brew on sensitive tongues and under quivering nostrils for bouquet and aroma and the elusive charm of piquancy and pep.

But why should not the masses have their aspic, after all, and why should it have been so long like caviar to the general? For aspic certainly is good, and worthy to be loved, else how could it have survived the long, long march of time and the search tests of age and custom?

Try it yourself, not in the restaurant but in the kitchenette, and out of the package, if you like—for you may not have the skill and patience to make a topaz consommé and clarify it till not a cloud or flaw remains in the crystal. It casts the aura of class about a salad for a party, for a buffet. It makes the children cry out, "O boy!" when the platter of cold boiled tongue and Virginia ham or snow-white hard-cooked eggs, or tiny tomato bijou comes on. Molded in graceful forms about choice tidbits of game or chicken, it elevates you, the creator, to the realm of the culinary art.

BARQUETTES OF BEEF MARROW   [18]
(*Warm*)

Prepare a flaky pie crust or, if preferred, a puff paste or semi-puff paste and shape into small individual boats, using special molds which are easy to find and purchase in any good house-furnishing store, alongside of the tartlet or other fancy individual molds. Have some fresh beef marrow, parboil—do not boil—in a little beef stock; drain well and cut into small cubes, and combine these hot cubes with a little seasoned Madeira Sauce (No. 1076) and fill the barquettes or small boats, previously baked and warm, sprinkle with finely chopped chervil or parsley and serve warm, not really hot.

Variations. The baked barqettes may also be filled with a purée of either clams, oysters, mushrooms, chicken, turkey, smoked turkey or tongue, or any kind of game purée desired.

BLINIS   [19]
(*Hot*)

Sometimes called "bleeny," these popular Russian pancakes are practically always made with buckwheat flour in Russia, but can also be made with ordinary sifted flour. As with the ordinary pancake, there are various recipes for the making of blinis. These tiny pancakes are served with melted butter, sour cream or caviar.

Dissolve 1 yeast cake in 1 cup of lukewarm milk and add enough flour to make a sponge, seasoning with $\frac{1}{4}$ teaspoon of salt. Let stand, covered with a light cloth in a warm place for 2 hours. Punch down and gradually add $\frac{3}{4}$ pound of buckwheat flour (less what was added to the dissolved yeast and milk) alternately with 3 fresh egg yolks, slightly beaten, and 2 cups of sweet milk. Mix throughout, but do not allow mixture to get too thick. Cover and let rise for $1\frac{1}{2}$ hours, covered and in a warm place. Punch down, then fold in gently but thoroughly 3 stiffly beaten egg whites. Cover and let stand 30–35 minutes, in a warm place. Then proceed in the same manner as when making little French pancakes, (No. 1919, Batter only) using a buttered individual frying pan. NOTE. You may use half buckwheat and pastry flour instead of all buckwheat flour, and substitute 6 tablespoons of rich, sweet cream for 6 tablespoons of sweet milk and proceed as directed.

BRAZIL NUT CHIPS [20]

Cover 1 pound of shelled Brazil nuts with water. Bring to a boil, and let simmer gently for 5 minutes. Cut into slices lengthwise, with a very sharp knife. Spread in shallow pans; add 2 tablespoons of butter, salt well and toast in a moderate oven (350° F.) until the chips are light brown and crisp. Drain on absorbent paper.

There are about 45 Brazil nuts, with shell on, to a pound. That will produce about 2 cups of shaved or coarsely ground nut meat. To remove Brazil nuts from the shells whole without breaking the meats, stick the nuts in a hot oven (400° F.) for about 20 minutes. Remove, cool, crack and shell. You'll find they come forth whole with the greatest of ease and the flavor is fine and toasty.

The pods grow in clusters at the top of the tallest Amazon jungle trees, about 150 feet high. When they are ripe they are shaken loose by the rain or wind storms. They vary in size from 3 to 8 inches in diameter and weigh all the way up to 8 pounds. And inside each pod are 14 to 28 "seeds," which are the Brazil nuts that we crack and enjoy eating in hundreds of different ways, in breads, cakes, cookies, salads, appetizers, hot, cold and frozen desserts and main course dishes.

CALF'S FEET BUDAPEST [21]
(*Cold*)

Wash and scald 2 calf's feet, bone the upper part, remove the shank-bone, split them in two and soak them in cold water for 2 hours. Put them in a soup kettle, cover with water slightly seasoned with salt, bring to a boil, and drain. Return to the kettle with as much cold water as will cover the feet, add 6 peppercorns, gently bruised, 1 medium-sized onion, sliced, 1 medium-sized carrot, scraped, then sliced, 1 bouquet garni composed of 1 large bay leaf, 8 sprigs of parsley, and 1 sprig of thyme all tied together with kitchen thread, ½ teaspoon of salt, 2 whole cloves and 1 clove of garlic, mashed to a pulp. Bring to a boil; lower the flame, and let simmer gently until the meat is tender and falls from the bones, or about 3–3½ hours. Drain, reserving the stock for a base for a soup or sauce. Cool the calf's feet to lukewarm, then cut the meat in julienne fashion. Place the cut-up meat into a bowl, pour over enough Vinaigrette Sauce (No. 1133) to generously cover and let marinate in refrigerator for at least 2 hours. When ready to serve, drain the vinaigrette sauce, which reserve. To 1 cup of this vinaigrette, add ½ generous cup of mayonnaise and mix thoroughly; toss the calf's meat julienne into this, turn mixture into a serving dish, decorate all around with overlapping slices of hard-cooked eggs, dusting the egg slices with paprika, and sprinkle over all 1 generous tablespoon of finely chopped parsley. Serve as cold as possible.

NOTE. Lamb, mutton, pork and beef feet may be prepared in the same manner, and make an excellent and delicious hors d'oeuvre dish appropriate for any cold buffet or summer luncheon.

CANAPÉS ARISTOCRATES   [22]
(Hot)

Spread 6 rounds of pumpernickel with a thin film of Mustard Butter (No. 992). Place a thin slice of peeled tomato on each round, and over the tomato slice, pile up flaked crabmeat moistened with mayonnaise flavored with a little curry powder. Cover the entire surface of the rounds with stiffly beaten egg-white, flavored with salt and a few grains of saffron powder; place the prepared rounds on a baking sheet and set in a slow oven (300° F.) to delicately brown. Serve at once.

CANAPÉS POUR BRIDGE   [23]
Bridge Canapés (Cold)

Hearts. Use heart-shaped cookie cutter. Cut hearts from thin slices of freshly-made toast. Spread with highly seasoned mayonnaise, then chopped red pimiento, and a thin slice of smoked salmon, also cut heart-fashion. Brush the salmon with soft Sherry Aspic Coating Jelly (No. 82) and while the coating jelly is still soft, sprinkle with finely chopped pistachio nuts.

Diamond. Use a diamond-shaped cookie cutter. Cut diamonds from thin slices of fresh rye bread; spread with chopped hard-cooked egg white moistened with mayonnaise, then cover with chopped well-drained black olives mixed with equal parts of finely chopped pickled beets, which have been gently squeezed in the corner of a piece of cheese-cloth to remove all excess moisture.

Spade. Use a spade-shaped cookie cutter. Cut spades from thin slices of day-old white bread and fry in butter until brown on both sides. Cool a little and spread with mustard mayonnaise, then cover with finely chopped cooked shrimps mixed with finely chopped capers. Outline each spade near the edge with a thin ribbon of caviar, and arrange a rolled anchovy around a small stuffed olive in center, topped with a little tuft of mayonnaise forced through a pastry bag with a rose tube and sprinkled with a few grains of caviar.

Club. Use a club-shaped cookie cutter. Cut clubs from thin slices of fresh Boston brown bread; spread with a film of Horseradish Butter (No. 988). Border with cream cheese worked with a little cream until smooth but still firm, forced through a wet pastry bag with a small fancy tube.

CANAPÉS CAMILLE   [24]
(Cold)

Spread over thin circles of freshly made toast some Almond Butter (No. 980 or 981). Surround the edges with purée of cooked, smoked tongue rubbed through a fine-meshed sieve, mixed with enough heavy cream to make of a spreading consistency and tinted with a few drops of yellow vegetable coloring then forced through a pastry bag with a small rose tube. Garnish center with a small ball of pâté de foie gras, and the space between the ball and the border of tongue purée with softened cream cheese forced through a pastry bag with a small fancy tube. Sprinkle the cream cheese with a few grains of caviar and finely chopped parsley.

CANAPÉS CANNIBAL   [25]
(Cold)

Proceed as indicated for Canapés Camille (No. 24), substituting a small ball of chopped or ground raw beef rolled in finely chopped, toasted almonds, for the balls of pâté de foie gras.

CANAPÉS DE CAVIAR VOISIN   [26]
(Cold)

NOTE. Although Caviar is now imported from Russia, in the Eighteen Eighties we exported it to that country from the Sacramento River. Like the grape, with its various vintages, caviar has its differences of quality and flavor. Four kinds of sturgeon give their eggs for caviar. *Beluga* is the largest, and it's only the finest of the beluga eggs which are packed fresh. The average beluga sturgeon weighs around 1,000 pounds and usually 10% of this weight represents the eggs. *Ocetrina sturgeon* is the next size. A still smaller type is the *Sebruga sturgeon*, and the smallest is the *Sterlet sturgeon*, weighing less than 25 pounds.

The flavor of real caviar is so individual and piquant that a little goes a long way in the preparation of canapés. The height of luxury, however, is to offer caviar in its original container, surrounded by cracked ice. With this, fingers of hot toast, or brown bread and butter finger sandwiches, a dish of minced onions, minced egg white and sieved egg yolk are usually offered.

Tiny Russian pancakes, known as Blinis (No. 19), may be served hot with melted butter, sour cream, minced onions, minced hard-cooked egg whites and caviar. Any very thin pancakes, like the French crêpes, however, may be used.

Prepare thin slices of brown bread and butter; cut from them a dozen small rounds about 1¾ inches in diameter and cover these with very thin slices of lemon trimmed to the size of the rounds. To about 2½–3 ounces of fresh caviar, add ½ of a shallot, very finely chopped, a few drops of lemon juice and a few grains of cayenne pepper, and stir with a wooden spoon, to blend well. Pile this on the prepared bread rounds, then, with the point of a wooden skewer, hollow the center down to the lemon, and fill first with a very little, very finely chopped onion, then with a little finely chopped hard-cooked egg white, and finally with a few capers which have been rolled in olive oil. Decorate with 4 cooked, shelled small shrimps in a nearly upright equidistant position, then serve each canapé in a crisp lettuce cup, the lettuce part dusted with sieved, hard-cooked egg yolk. This is the acme of eye-appeal . . . and delicious, too.

CAVIAR CANAPÉS MA FAÇON   [26-A]
(Cold)

Cut small circles from freshly made French pancakes, using a cookie cutter. Spread on these circles a little highly flavored softened fish gelatine, and sprinkle generously with caviar. Place these small rounds of pancake on small rounds of very thin, fresh brown bread first covered with a thin slice of smoked salmon. The brown bread rounds should be a little larger than the pancake rounds. Near the edge of the outstanding brown bread, spread finely chopped hard-cooked egg seasoned with finely chopped onion. Surround the very edge of the brown bread with a thin circle of Smoked Salmon Butter (No. 999) forced through a pastry bag with a very small straight tube.

CAVIAR CANAPÉS SA FAÇON   [27]
(Cold)

Garnish buttered thin finger slices of toasted white bread with caviar; arrange a cavity in the center, in which place a small fresh oyster, previously poached in a little fish stock until edges curl. Sprinkle a few grains of freshly ground black pepper over the oyster, then a few tears of lemon juice. Garnish with a border of Tarragon Butter (No. 1002).

CAVIAR CANAPÉS LEUR FAÇON   [28]
(Cold)

Place thin slices of peeled tomato on rounds of fresh pumpernickel which has been spread with Horseradish Butter (No. 988). Over the tomato slices pile (in center) small mounds of caviar. Surround the edges of the tomato with thick mayonnaise forced through a pastry bag with a rose tube. Sprinkle over this a little finely chopped onion, mixed with a little finely chopped hard-cooked egg white, and cover the caviar mounds with sieved hard-cooked egg yolk. (This should be done just before serving, as the moisture of the caviar will smear the egg yolk.)

CANAPÉS DE CREVETTES CREOLE   [29]
Shrimp Canapés Creole (Cold)

Toast 6 rounds of white bread on one side. Spread the untoasted sides with a rather thick layer of Shrimp Butter (No. 1001) and press over, as tastefully as possible, small cooked, shelled shrimps to cover the entire mound. Garnish with a narrow border of Salmon Butter (No. 999) forced through a pastry bag with a small tube and sprinkle finely chopped chives over all.

Three kinds of shrimps come to market, but only one in quantity, the *common* shrimp. There is also the *grooved* shrimp and the *sea bob* shrimp. To bring out the flavor, shrimps are best boiled in sea water. If this is impossible, use strongly salted water, adding thyme, bay leaf, peppercorns and 7 or 8 sprigs of fresh parsley.

CANAPÉS FLAMANDS   [30]
Flemish Canapés (Cold)

Cut rounds of fresh brown bread, butter generously, then spread with the following mixture:

Mix 1 cup of cottage cheese, ½ cup of deviled ham (the prepared kind), 1 tablespoon of drained, then ground prepared horseradish, ¼ cup of thick sour cream, salt and pepper to taste and a few grains of cayenne pepper, ½ cup of finely chopped watercress, 2 tablespoons of finely chopped chives and 1 teaspoon of grated onion, piling the spread in dome-fashion. Cover with mayonnaise, then criss-cross the mayonnaise with very narrow strips of anchovy, previously washed and dried. Press into each tiny lozenge formed by the anchovy strips a well-drained caper. Serve in lettuce cups.

To Make Lettuce Cups from Head of Lettuce. Cut out center core, run cold water at a fairly good force into the open center and gently separate the leaves.

CANAPÉS DE FOIE GRAS   [31]
Goose Liver Pâté (Cold)

A pleasant by-product of the French Revolution is the fact that during those fateful years of turmoil and change, foie gras moved over into the democratic column and became available to Tom, Dick and Harry, regardless of class or condition.

Before 1789, foie gras had been the privilege of a select few. It was enjoyed by the aristocrats of Alsace who were fortunate enough to be invited to the Prefect's table. Invented in Strassburg about 1762, pâté de foie gras (goose liver loaf) had been served there regularly for more than two decades before the Revolution, invariably provoking surprise and admiration. All the while the formula for preparing it was as jealously guarded as a State secret.

Then, a century and a half ago, Jean Pierre Clause (it is also spelled Close, Klotz, and Claude), inventor of the delicious pâté, left the service of his noble master, the Maréchal de Contades, Royal Chamberlain and Prefect of Alsace, to embark upon a business career. He opened a restaurant in Strassburg, with pâté de foie gras as its specialty. Popularity and success came at once. No wonder!—When a man dined Chez Clause, no embarrassing questions were asked about his rank or pedigree; he was not required to show his coat of arms or his birth certificate. Everybody who was able to pay was served, which heretofore had been the privilege of nobility. And that is why pâté de foie gras became the food of commoners, peasants and tradesfolk—a minor yet significant triumph of the French Revolution that no gourmet will belittle.

The motto of Clause's restaurant was *"Moult foie, moult espoir"*—literally, "Much liver, much hope." However, it includes a play on words which defies translation, since *foie* (liver) and *foi* (faith) are pronounced exactly the same way. Had an American invented pâté de foie gras, he might have chosen as his slogan that triple play on words so appreciated by William James: "Is life worth living? It all depends on the liver!"

A short time after Clause opened his restaurant, another and vitally important event influenced the destiny of foie gras. This was its "marriage" with Mademoiselle Truffle, the function of the latter being to heighten the flavor of foie gras and so make it even more palatable and more delicious. This felicitous union was engineered by no less a person than the famous Nicholas François Doyen, a Paris-born chef who had first settled in Bordeaux, then come to Paris, where he opened his famous Restaurant Doyen.

The Revolution uprooted Doyen, as it did many others, and he moved to Strassburg, where, in 1792, he joined the truffles of Perigord with the foie gras of Alsace, then opened his famous restaurant in Paris.

For many decades experts have disagreed as to the proper place of foie gras in a well-balanced and well-ordained repast. Curnonsky, who has the title of "Prince des Gastronomes" in Paris and throughout France, asserts that foie gras should be served at the beginning of a meal, when the diner is still hungry and can fully appreciate its delicacy. Many French chefs and hostesses are of his opinion, and they frequently serve the foie gras with the hors d'oeuvres. Curnonsky also declares that under no circumstances should a salad be served with the foie gras because of the vinegar it contains; the salad, he insists, should always come after.

Monsieur Prosper Montagné, master caterer and prolific writer on gastronomic subjects, states his opposing viewpoint as follows:

"Foie gras is the summit of gastronomy. Eating a meal is like mountain-climbing—you always begin at the bottom and move upward. For this reason, foie gras should always come after the fowl, and at big banquets it should be the fifth dish. Oysters (if in season) should be first; then the consommé, the fish, the turkey, and only then the foie gras. After that, the salad, the cheese with the fruits, and the desserts. This is the traditional order, and I see no reason for changing it."

Both Curnonsky and Montagné have their followers in this dispute. Each hostess does as she thinks best. Curnonsky's advice is usually accepted for small, private dinners; the Montagné rule is followed at great, official banquets.

For the canapés of foie gras, there is no fast rule. The choice is unlimited. You may use small squares, triangles, oblongs, crescents, lozenges, etc., of bread toasted or sautéed on one side and spread either side with a good thickness of foie gras. Dip the sides in melted butter and at once press sides of canapés into finely chopped parsley, chervil, finely chopped hard-cooked eggs, finely chopped black truffles, finely chopped chives, almond, nuts, etc. Do not garnish centers.

CANAPÉS DE HADDOCK FUMÉ [32]
Finnan Haddie Canapés (Hot)

Pour boiling water over 1 pound of finnan haddie filets and let stand for 10 minutes; drain, remove the skin and bones, then flake the fish filet. Place the flakes in a saucepan, pour over 1 cup of milk, or enough to barely cover, and simmer very gently for 15 minutes, stirring occasionally, then strain, reserving the milk. Put the fish flakes through the food chopper using the finest blade, and grind. Heat 2 tablespoons of butter in a saucepan, stir in 1 teaspoon of finely chopped shallot without browning, then add the ground fish and 1½ teaspoons of very finely chopped parsley. Mix well and when thoroughly heated stir in 3 fresh egg yolks, previously beaten with 2 tablespoons of the reserved milk in which the fish was cooked: season to taste with white pepper and nutmeg, and stir over a gentle flame until just beginning to thicken. Remove from the fire and stir in 2 tablespoons of good sherry wine. Keep hot over hot water while preparing the following brown bread croustades:

Croustades for Mousses, Aspic Jelly and Fish Cream Appetizers. From slices of brown or white bread of about ¼–¾ inch in thickness, cut or stamp out small rounds, ovals, or squares, 2 inches in diameter. With a smaller cutter, make an inner circle, oval, or square, ⅓ of an inch from the outer edge of the croustade. Fry them in clarified butter until lightly browned, then with the point of a small sharp knife lift out the inner ring, remove all moist crumbs, set croustades on a cookie sheet, then place in a moderate oven (325° F.) to become crisp and dry. Fill with the creamed finnan haddie, decorate the border with Anchovy Butter (No. 979) forced through a pastry bag or paper cornet with a tiny fancy tube. Serve as hot as possible, sprinkling the top, lightly with paprika.

For cold fillings, such as caviar, jellied mixtures, etc., cool the croustades before filling.

CANAPÉS DE HOMARD I   [33]
Lobster Canapés (Cold)

Toast small squares of bread on one side, then spread Lobster Butter (No. 991) on the untoasted sides; dip the edges in melted butter and press them into finely chopped hard-cooked egg whites.

CANAPÉS DE HOMARD II   [34]
Lobster Canapés (Cold)

Toast small rounds of rye bread on one side and butter the other side with Lobster Butter (No. 991). Arrange thin slices of cooked lobster meat over the surface; trim neatly; garnish with a small border of Lobster Butter forced through a pastry bag with a small fancy tube, and top the center with a rosette of Lobster Butter on which place a caper.

CANAPÉS D'HUITRES   [35]
Oyster Canapés (Hot)

Pick over as many fresh oysters as desired, place them with their own liquor and a little sweet butter between 2 plates and warm them in the oven or over hot water. Spread untoasted brown bread fingers with a tiny film of anchovy paste, cover with a strip of cooked bacon, trimming neatly, and place 2 or 3 oysters on top of the bacon; sprinkle with lemon juice and paprika, and serve as hot as possible.

CANAPÉS DE JAMBON I   [36]
Ham Canapés (Cold)

Use small rounds, squares, lozenges, rectangles, finger strips, and so forth of bread, the more assorted shapes the better. Toast on one side, then butter the other side. On buttered side spread a little potted ham or ground cooked ham, seasoned highly with pepper and a few drops of Worcestershire sauce; garnish with a border of mustard mayonnaise forced through a pastry bag with a small fancy tube, and place in center a half stuffed olive topped with a rosette of mustard mayonnaise.

CANAPÉS DE JAMBON II [37]
Ham Canapés (Cold)

Spread 6 finger-strips of white bread with Mustard Butter (No. 992); cover each with a thin slice of cold, lean cooked ham, cut in the same shape as the bread. Dip the sides of each canapé into clarified butter, then press into sieved hard-cooked egg yolks. Make a border of Mustard Butter forced through a pastry bag with a small fancy tube, and top center with a thin slice of sweet-sour gherkin topped with a tuft of mayonnaise.

CANAPÉS DE JAMBON III [38]
Ham Canapés (Cold)

Toast 6 squares of fresh Boston brown bread on one side; butter the other side. Heap on each some ground, cooked cold ham moistened with a little mayonnaise forced through a pastry bag with a small fancy tube, making small fancy puffs. Using another bag, place between the puffs a little mustard mayonnaise. Dip edges in melted butter and press them into finely chopped chives.

CANAPÉS DE JAMBON EN BEIGNETS FRITS [39]
Fried Ham Canapés (Hot)

Spread 20 small rounds of fresh brown bread or Boston brown bread with butter. Over the butter spread a layer of chutney sauce; over the chutney sauce, place a thin round of cold, lean cooked ham, shaped in the same size as the bread rounds, then top each with another round of white bread, also buttered and of the same diameter as the brown bread rounds, placing this buttered side down and pressing the whole lightly together. When ready to serve, dip them into a frying batter and fry in hot, deep fat until golden-brown. Drain on absorbent paper and serve on a folded napkin placed on a hot round platter. Arrange the canapés pyramid-fashion, and scatter fried parsley over all. Serve hot.

CANAPÉS DE LAITANCES DE HARENG [40]
Herring Roe Canapés (Hot)

Cut into finger-lengths fresh toast which has been spread with melted butter, then with a little film of anchovy paste. Melt 2 tablespoons of butter in a frying pan, and add a can of herring roes, previously drained and well separated. Cook until lightly browned, shaking the pan frequently. Dress on prepared toasts, sprinkle with a little lemon juice and a few grains of cayenne pepper, dress on a hot platter; garnish with lemon quarters and fried crisp parsley. Serve hot.

CANAPÉS LORENZO   [41]
Original Recipe (Hot)

Cook without browning 2 tablespoons of chopped onions in 2 table-spoons of butter; stir in 1 tablespoon of flour, and let this cook for a few minutes, over a low flame, stirring constantly with a wooden spoon, still without browning, then stir in 1 pint of fresh cream, season with salt, cayenne pepper and nutmeg to taste and cook over a gentle flame until thickened, stirring constantly. Now toss in 1 pound of picked, canned or fresh flaked crabmeat, and stir until thoroughly heated. Remove from the fire and let cool. Cut a dozen slices of white bread ¼ inch thick; toast, then cut into rounds about 4 inches in diameter. Split these rounds of bread through the center to make 2 even-sized rounds, then cover with a good thick layer of crabmeat mixture. Now with the hands work in a mixing bowl ½ pound of sweet butter, add to it ¼ pound of grated parmesan cheese, and season highly with cayenne and white pepper. No salt; cream until thoroughly mixed, adding gradually while creaming another ¼ pound of grated parmesan cheese so as to form a thick paste. Cover the entire canapés with a good layer of this butter-cheese mixture; arrange on a buttered baking sheet and bake in a hot oven (400° F.) until golden brown and slightly puffed. Serve immediately, simply garnished with lemon quarters and crisp watercress, this last dipped in cold water, shaken, then dipped into plenty of paprika, shaking a little to remove excess of paprika.

CANAPÉS MARQUIS   [41-A]
(Lukewarm)

This delicious canapé is the creation of Arthur Marchisio, brother of Ercole Marchisio, Caterer of the Marguery Restaurant on Park Avenue, New York City, and is in great favor throughout the Americas, including the West Indies.

Chop finely but do not grind 2 hard-cooked shelled eggs, 1 large green pepper, 8 filets of anchovy, ½ cup of canned, picked, drained tuna fish; season to taste with cayenne pepper and a few grains of nutmeg, but no salt. Trim the crusts from a dozen small rounds of bread (about 3 inches in diameter), and fry in plenty of sweet butter until delicately brown on both sides. Divide the chopped mixture among the hot, fried rounds of bread. Sprinkle over each canapé a generous teaspoon of Russian dressing flavored with a few drops of Worcestershire sauce and serve on a hot platter.

CANAPÉS MÉPHISTO [42]
(Hot)

Cream together ¼ pound of grated American cheese, ¼ pound of grated parmesan cheese and ¼ pound of sweet butter until smooth. Season with ¼ teaspoon of tabasco sauce, a little salt, plenty of black pepper and about 1 teaspoon of paprika. Spread on small rounds of bread, toasted on one side, the spreading done on the toasted side; place on a baking sheet and bake in a very hot oven (425° F.) until nicely browned and bubbling. Serve as quickly as possible after removing from the oven.

With cocktails or tea, as a first course at dinner or luncheon, at bridge evening parties or buffets, it's the appetizers that set the pace.

CANAPÉS MEURICE [43]
(Hot)

Heat 2 tablespoons of sweet butter, stir in ¼ cup of peeled, thinly sliced, then ground fresh mushrooms, 1 ground green pepper, freed from seeds and white ribs, and cook gently without coloring, until tender, stirring constantly over a gentle flame, then stir in 2 cups of fresh or canned crabmeat, previously picked and flaked, alternately with ¼ cup of Béchamel Sauce (No. 259), flavored with ¼ cup of sherry wine; season with salt, cayenne pepper, a few grains of nutmeg and a tiny pinch of powdered thyme. Toast 6 rounds of white bread on one side, spread the untoasted sides with Salmon Butter (No. 999), then lay on each a round of Swiss cheese, cut the same diameter as the toasted rounds of bread. Top in dome-shape with the crab-meat mixture; cover with another thin round of Swiss cheese, place the canapés upon a buttered baking sheet and bake in a very hot oven (425° F.) until cheese is melted, dripping all over the canapés and nicely browned. Serve as soon as removed from the oven, garnished with lemon quarters and watercress, first carefully trimming from the canapés any cheese which may have run over the baking sheet.

CANAPÉS À LA MÖELLE DE BOEUF [44]
Beef Marrow Canapés (Hot)

Soak the marrow from 2 large beef bones in lukewarm beef bouillon for about 1 hour, placing container over hot water. About 15 minutes before serving, cut the marrow into inch lengths; place them in cold beef bouillon to barely cover; bring to the boiling point, and drain at once. Have ready 6 rounds of bread toasted on one side and buttered on the untoasted side. Dress the pieces of marrow on the untoasted sides of the toast rounds. Arrange on a pie plate or small baking sheet; place in a hot oven (400° F.) until marrow is melted but not running. Serve as hot as possible, each toast sprinkled with a little chopped chives, parsley or chervil, then with a few drops of lemon juice. Serve at once.

CANAPÉS MONTE CRISTO   [45]
(*Hot*)

Toast small rounds of white bread on one side; spread untoasted sides with butter, then cover with a ham purée (cooked ham ground with a little sweet cream to make a mixture of spreadable consistency, and highly seasoned with prepared mustard, cayenne, nutmeg and salt to taste). Place a thin slice of Cheddar cheese over the ham purée, having the cheese cut the shape and size of the toast rounds; place on a baking sheet, dust with a little paprika and glaze quickly under the flame of the broiling oven. Serve as hot as possible.

CANAPÉS RICHARDIN   [46]
(*Hot*)

Rub through a fine-meshed sieve ⅓ cup of foie gras. Cook in 1 tablespoon of sweet butter ¼ cup of peeled, ground fresh mushroom, stirring constantly, over a low flame, until mushrooms are tender but not brown; stir in 2 tablespoons of good Madeira wine; season highly with salt, a few grains of cayenne and nutmeg, then stir in the foie gras. Stir until preparation is almost to the boiling point, but do not allow it to actually boil. Toast 6 or 8 small rounds of white bread on one side only; rub the untoasted side with shallot, then dip in melted butter. Spread the foie preparation as evenly as possible over the butter side, then top each canapé with an egg yolk freshly poached in milk and well drained, dust with paprika and serve at once.

COEURS D'ARTICHAUTS POMPADOUR   [47]
Artichoke Bottom Pompadour Manner (*Hot*)

Drain a can of artichoke hearts; trim so that the artichoke hearts (also called bottoms) may stand level. Fill the cavities with a little foie gras previously rubbed through a fine sieve, sprinkle tops with equal parts of sieved bread crumbs and finely grated Gruyère cheese, and brown quickly under the flame of the broiling oven. Serve as hot as possible on small rounds of baked flaky pie crust.

CORNETS D'ABONDANCE [48]
Horns of Plenty (Cold)

(a) Cut thin slices of lean cooked ham into 3-inches squares. Roll into cornucopia shape and fill with well-seasoned cole slaw, marinated first in Pique seasoning and squeezed very gently, but thoroughly, then marinated in French dressing and again squeezed gently.

(b) Do likewise with thin slices of smoked turkey, and fill with chopped Sherry Aspic Coating Jelly or Port Wine Aspic Coating Jelly (No. 82 and No. 78, respectively).

(c) Do likewise with thin slices of smoked salmon, and fill with Chopped Tomato Aspic Jelly (No. 87).

(d) Do likewise with thin slices of cooked smoked tongue and fill with watercress.

(e) Do likewise with thin slices of cooked breast of chicken and fill with curled parsley.

NOTE. All these cornucopias or cornets d'abondance may be brushed with melted gelatine to glaze them.

COURONNES DE CONCOMBRE EN GELÉE [49]
Individual Cucumber Rings in Jelly (Cold)

Pare 4 large fresh cucumbers, slice thinly and place in a saucepan with ½ cup of cold water and ½ cup of Pique seasoning; 1 clove of garlic, left whole; 1 large bay leaf, tied with 4 sprigs of fresh parsley; no salt; 3 whole peppercorns, crushed. Gradually bring to a boil and let simmer gently until tender. Empty the entire contents of the saucepan into a fine-meshed sieve, and rub through into a saucepan. Then stir in 1 tablespoon of granulated gelatine, previously sprinkled on top of ¾ cup of clear beef bouillon and allowed to stand ten minutes, mixed with ¾ cup of sherry wine, and stir until gelatine is dissolved. Now stir in 1 tablespoon of tarragon white wine vinegar, 2 tablespoons of washed, dried, coarsely chopped fresh mint leaves, and again rub through a fine-meshed sieve. Fill 6 individual wet ring molds and, when cold, store in refrigerator to chill for at least 1½ hours. When ready to serve unmold on a round, cold platter and fill centers of each ring with thick mayonnaise mixed with a little finely chopped black truffle, 1 teaspoon of caviar, 1 teaspoon of tomato paste, 2 teaspoons of capers, previously washed and drained, all blended, then forced through a pastry bag with a straight tube. Garnish center of platter with a crisp bunch of green watercress. Serve at once.

French cookery is no more for French people alone than Sousa's music is the music of one country exclusively. French cookery doesn't take the place of provincial or local cookery in various parts of the

world; local supplies and local demands and local customs always have
the place of honor, but French cookery brings to every civilized land a
welcome element of cultured traditionalism, a pattern of harmony, of
balance and beauty, sometimes in the simplest form imaginable and
sometimes in the most elaborate.

CRABMEAT CRUNCHES   [50]
(Cold)

Select as many large potato chips as required, allowing 2 per person.
Flake, bone and moisten canned or cooked crabmeat with mayonnaise
blended with tomato paste in equal parts. Sandwich the crabmeat mixture between 2 large potato chips, previously lightly brushed with
anchovy paste. Serve on a bed of crisp lettuce leaves.

CRABMEAT REMICK   [51]
(Hot)

Line as many small tartlet molds as required with your favorite
flaky pastry. Set aside. Mix, for a dozen tartlets, 1 cup of flaked, picked
fresh or canned crabmeat with the following sauce:

Sauce Remick. Mix ½ cup of mayonnaise with 1 tablespoon of chili
sauce, ½ teaspoon of paprika, and season with a dash of Tabasco sauce
and a dash of celery salt. Fill tartlets with crabmeat mixture, place
on a baking sheet and bake in a moderate oven (375° F.) about 18-20
minutes. Serve hot.

CROQUETTES DOMINICAINES   [52]
Dominican Oyster Croquettes (Hot)

To ½ cup of hot, thick cream sauce (No. 258) add 2 tablespoons of
cooked, sieved onions, and rub through a fine-meshed sieve. Poach
12 plump fresh oysters in their own liquor until edges curl; chop them
fine and add to the cream sauce with the hot liquor. Peel and cook 1 large
fresh mushroom cap in a little butter gently until tender; pass through
food chopper and add to the sauce with the butter left in the pan.
Season with a few grains each of cayenne and nutmeg, mixing well, then
spread on a platter to cool. When quite cold, divide into portions about
the size of a walnut, form into small cork shapes, roll in seasoned flour,
then in sieved bread crumbs and chill for 1 hour in refrigerator. When
ready to serve, place the "corks" in a frying basket, plunge the basket
into hot, clear, deep fat 375°-390° F. and let brown. Drain on absorbent
paper and serve on a paper doily placed on a hot, round platter.
Garnish simply with fried parsley.

CUMBERLAND SNACKS [53]
(Cold)

Originally produced as a family delicacy to celebrate the birth of a baby, these snacks have gradually extended their sphere throughout England in every hotel and refreshment house, and are fine with any kind of cocktail.

Slightly melt ½ pound of sweet butter; add 1 pound of brown sugar; stir well over a gentle flame until thoroughly blended, then stir in ½ cup of the best rum. Season with freshly ground nutmeg to taste and a few grains of cayenne pepper and when of pouring consistency, pour into small glass cups and let set and cool. Serve with bread and butter finger sandwiches.

ECLAIRS D'ANCHOIS [54]
Anchovy Eclairs (Hot)

These éclairs should have the appearance of miniature sausage rolls.

Roll puff paste trimmings (See Puff Paste, No. 2076-77-78) out as thinly as possible; cut into oblong pieces. Lay on each a well-washed, well-dried and trimmed anchovy filet slightly shorter than the paste, fold together and seal the edge over with a little cold water or slightly beaten.egg white. Sprinkle each éclair with a little grated parmesan cheese; arrange on an ungreased baking sheet and bake in a very hot oven (425–450° F.) for a few minutes, or until nicely browned and glazed. Serve at once.

NOTE. Small cooked or canned sardines may also prepared in the same manner.

FRIAR'S FRIANDISES PLATTER [55]
(Cold)

This is a platter arranged with slices of stuffed cucumber, stuffed green pepper, large dill pickles stuffed with cheese, around a glass dish containing Lentil Relish, (No. 74) and another glass dish of Maquereaux au Vin Blanc (Mackerel in White Wine (No. 76) plus one of Roses d'Hiver Armenonville (No. 79).

Stuffed Cucumber Slices. Scoop out the pulp of medium-sized fresh cucumbers without peeling; fill the hollow part with a mixture of equal parts of creamed Blue cheese and sweet butter, seasoning with a few grains of cayenne pepper. Chill for several hours, then slice in thin slices. Serve on round crackers first spread with a tiny film of Anchovy Butter (No. 979).

Stuffed Dill Slices. Proceed as for Stuffed Cucumber Slices, using Roquefort cheese instead of Blue cheese, and dress each slice on a small round of fresh brown bread slightly filmed with Smoked Salmon Butter (No. 999).

Stuffed Green Pepper Slices. Remove stems and seeds from smooth green peppers through openings made in both ends; fill centers as compactly as possible with cream cheese softened with a little sour cream, leaving a hole down through the center of the cheese. Fill this cavity with an anchovy filet rolled around a slice of red, canned pimiento. Chill well before slicing.

Arrange these different slices tastefully around the dishes of Lentil Relish, Mackerel in White Wine and Pickled Mushrooms, decorating with small bouquets of crisp watercress dipped into paprika and shake slightly to remove excess paprika.

For a refreshing "Pick-me-Up" when tired, Dutch housewives of the seventeenth century served their menfolk a glass of hot water in which small pieces of cheese had been melted.

FRIED PARMESAN KISSES [56]
(Hot)

Beat 2 egg whites until stiff; season with a few grains of cayenne pepper and ¼ teaspoon of salt; then stir in 3 ounces of grated parmesan cheese, mixing thoroughly. When ready to serve, drop by teaspoonfuls into hot, clear, deep fat (360°–375° F.) and cook until delicately browned on all sides. Drain on absorbent paper or a towel, and serve as hot as possible on a folded napkin, dusted with a little paprika.

FRITTO MISTO [57]
(Hot)

There is a surprise in every mouthful of this Italian Kitchen favorite.

Fritto Misto, the mixed fry of all Italy and of Italians wherever they may be, comes to the table in infinite variety, limited only by human imagination. It may be a one-plate banquet for the vegetarian, a spectacular platter of richness and delicacy for the gourmet, or a glorified fish fry for the seafood lover, but always shrouded in mystery.

According to the theory or the taste of the cook, the delectable morsels may be fried in crumbs, but quite as often they appear in a puffy golden jacket of fritter batter, and it's hard to say whether one is better than the other. You may go marketing for fritto misto, and buy anything or everything that fancy suggests; or you can prepare it on the impulse of the moment if you have an emergency shelf in the pantry and a reserve stock of snacks.

(1) Take a cup of cold boiled rice and mix it lightly with a tablespoon of grated parmesan cheese, salt and white pepper, a slight grating of nutmeg, and a beaten whole egg. Form into balls the size of a walnut, dip in beaten egg and roll in finely grated or sieved bread crumbs. You have, perhaps, some cold mashed potatoes. Add a little minced parsley with salt, pepper and nutmeg to taste and 1 beaten whole egg for each cup of potato; then form into balls, the same size as the rice balls, dredge them lightly with flour, then roll in egg and fine crumbs. Pick the left-overs of cold meats—chicken, turkey, capon, beef, veal, pork, lamb, tongue, ham or feathered or furred game—and mince them together or separately, making a composite hash or as many varieties of balls as you have meats, poultry or game. Season with salt and black pepper, minced parsley, a little minced green pepper, and a little grated onion; mix with beaten egg or eggs (according to the amount of ingredients, using 1 egg per cup of food), mold into balls or ovals, and roll in beaten egg and fine crumbs. Some of the meat or poultry, or game, may be left whole and trimmed into symmetrical shapes for frying in egg and crumbs, but never larger than a walnut size; and whatever you may find of calf's liver, lamb's kidneys, sweetbreads, calf's brains, or chicken, turkey or feathered birds livers will add novelty to the ensemble.

Cauliflower is found on most of the plates of fritto misto or mixed fry, broken into flowerets and shaped nicely for the frying; and there is a wide range of selection in artichoke hearts or bottoms, bulbs of fennel, eggplant squares, vegetable marrow, summer or winter squash, asparagus tips, small white onions, pieces of ripe, peeled tomatoes, ripe cucumbers, gherkins, and so forth. In fact, you may run the entire gamut of all the edible solid foods.

(2) Heat a frying kettle of olive oil to 375°–390° F., submerge the frying basket in it, then plump in the small balls or ovals one by one, to keep them from sticking together. Let them fry to a rich golden brown. Then drain on absorbent paper. Many cooks will use lard, in spite of all that may be said, and the results will be highly gratifying, yet a book might be written on the superiority of olive oil in all frying, and the incidental advantages to digestion, flavor, and even practical economy.

Some Italians will tell you that fritto misto should always be in batter, and there's much to be said on that side of the question. There are few things more luscious than light and digestible fritters, and the method opens the way for an even greater variety of materials.

The orthodox Italian batter is all eggs and without baking powder, yet some of the most distinguished French and Italian chefs use baking powder, and with it one can be a little more certain of results.

To Prepare Frying Batter for Fritto Misto. Sift half a cup of flour with 1 teaspoon of baking powder, ½ teaspoon of salt, ⅛ teaspoon of white pepper, a grating of nutmeg and a few grains of cayenne pepper into a mixing bowl. Make a hollow in center, pour in 3 well-beaten whole eggs and 2 tablespoons of olive oil or, if desired, use melted (lukewarm) butter. Gradually bring the flour mixture into the egg-oil (or butter) mixture and, when well moistened, beat briskly with a wire whisk or egg beater. Be sure mixture is thoroughly blended and smooth. Let stand for 30 minutes, covered with a cheesecloth. Then, before using, beat again briskly.

Dip all your rice and potato balls or what have you in the line of fritto, and then drop quickly into the smoking-hot oil. As soon as they puff up and get nicely brown, lift them out of the basket and drain on absorbent paper.

A platter of fritters made by this method may reveal to the astonished and delighted guests such prizes as lobster, prawns, scallops, crab meat, oysters, clams, mussels, and bits of salmon, fresh or smoked, bits of smoked trout and shad roe, accompanied by brown-crusted rice, potato, cauliflowers, artichoke hearts, mushrooms, broccoli, Brussels sprouts, chestnuts, okra, oysterplant, and balls of green corn and minced green peppers.

NOTE. In preparing the batter for meats, poultry, game shellfish, crustaceans, and fish, a tablespoon or two of sherry or brandy adds piquancy and distinction. Be sure to serve these fritter-appetizers (they may also be used as a main dish) sizzling-hot, crackling-crisp and well mixed.

FRUIT, FRUIT JUICE, VEGETABLE JUICE, [58] AND SEAFOOD COCKTAIL SUGGESTIONS

It turns out that fresh grass is not to be sneezed at as an aid to health. When Nebuchadnezzar of biblical fame went out with the beasts of the fields to "eat grass as the oxen," everyone thought he was crazy, but instead, he or his physician may have been extremely wise. In this day of vegetable and fruit cocktails, when friends gather round and drink their carrots, cabbage and spinach as well as most other garden favorites, the farmer in the grassy dell has something to contribute also. This is fresh grass juice.

As yet there is no report that babies cry for it but certain professors have found that guinea pigs die for the lack of it. In recent experiments laboratory guinea pigs were fed on winter cows' milk, which, of course, didn't have any fresh grass juice in it because the cow had not had any fresh grass to eat. The guinea pigs, previously perfectly healthy, got sick and died on this diet. This is not surprising because the milk lacked many of the elements which science now knows to be necessary for health. To remedy this, the professors added iron and other mineral salts, liver extract and various vitamins to the milk. Even this addition of materials known to be beneficial to health did not keep the guinea pigs from dying.

Then new-mown hay was called in. The lucky animals who lived to quaff this potion came out of the doldrums and grew fat and sassy. In short, the grass juice was a life-saver.

Now the questions which scientists ask are, first, what powerful ingredients does grass juice have in addition to ordinary vitamins that make all the difference between life and death to guinea pigs? And, second, how important is this to human beings?

Man has made wonderful strides in his ability to duplicate Nature's aids to health. Vitamins, either concentrated from natural sources, or synthetic, are available to meet many needs. But the experiment with the guinea pigs seems to indicate that Nature may be better at con-cocting the proper foods than man is, and while she doesn't take out any patents on her inventions, she does stick to the old-fashioned way of keeping the formula a secret.

Man undoubtedly will search until the secret of the grass juice also is discovered but until then it might be a good idea, not only for guinea pigs, but for human beings as well, to eat grass or sip its juice now and then in order to reap its mysterious benefits.

In pursuit of this health-giving elixir it even may be possible for a person to better the old feat of killing two birds with one stone and make it three birds. A man getting up early enough in the morning can mow the lawn, thereby getting in his daily dozen and keeping the grass short. But he can at the same time lay in a supply of liquid vim and vigor when he takes the green blades to the kitchen and asks Mary to squeeze them, to see himself and the family through the day.

Such a "fad," as some people might call it, would be another of the many things to bear out the saying that there is nothing new except that which is forgotten. Grass, or its equivalent in green leaves, often has been used in the past to cure human ills. An historic example of grass playing an important part in saving the lives of men has to do with one of the early visits to this continent. In the year 1619, Denmark sent out, under the command of a man named Jens Munk, an expedition of sixty-four men searching for the suspected Northwest Passage between the Atlantic and the Pacific. Landing on the west coast of Hudson Bay, Jens Munk and his men spent a winter of misery during which most of the men sickened and died. The epidemic which took this toll of lives probably was scurvy, a disease which medical science now knows to be due to lack of vitamin C.

According to the story, food grew shorter and shorter and when spring came Jens Munk and the miserable few who were left started eating the green shoots and grass which they found on the shore. These men, who had expected to die just as had their comrades, were surprised to find their health returning and soon were able to go back to Denmark.

Another expedition to the polar regions, about two hundred years later, probably was saved from similar discomfort and death because its leader, Sir W. Edward Parry, knew the value of greens in preventing the dread scurvy which threatened sailors everywhere. Captain Parry raised cress and mustard greens on shipboard in boxes of earth which he brought along for the purpose, and so the sailors had plenty of greens to eat.

In the case of Nebuchadnezzar, he seems to have been suffering from bad dreams and a "mightier than thou" attitude, which may have indicated some nervous disorder bordering on the actual insanity of which he was suspected. Many such nervous disorders are helped by diet. Perhaps some wise doctor of that age knew what science has now rediscovered, that grass contains mysterious health-giving properties, and helped to cure the king by its use. What seemed to the people of Babylon the act of a madman may have been nothing but obedience to the orders of a progressive doctor.

Newcomers in the never-ending procession of juices, fruit and vegetables, take their places in the phalanx already lined up on grocery shelves. They are pure carrot juice and a combination of carrots with celery and parsley as well as fig juice, apple juice, sauerkraut juice, etc. Different from the usual juice is fig juice, since, instead of being extracted from the fresh fruit, it is the liquid resulting from cooking dried figs in water. No sugar, preservative or flavoring is added.

Approved mixtures are listed in the newest cook books and in books devoted especially to raw dieting. The whole line of humble garden products from cabbage up is used. Usually those who drink the raw juices are also devoted to the raw vegetable plate. As many as six colorful garden products may be assembled on such plates as they are now served on home tables and in restaurants.

Better than tonics or "cures" are tangy fruit juices and similar foods attractively served just for the purpose of tempting lagging appetites and stimulating the flow of the digestive juices. Fruit juice cocktails and a number of other inexpensive but very tasty concoctions have decided value in this line and they also add to that enjoyment of eating that makes food better digested and more easily assimilated. For variation, serve them in small glasses, the rims of which have been rubbed in a slice of lemon and then dipped in powdered sugar. This makes a frosted rim around the edge and is very attractive—do not use any sugar in the fruit juice mixtures.

ARTICHOKE COCKTAIL [59]

Cut artichoke bottoms, cooked or canned, in small cubes and marinate with French dressing made with lime juice instead of vinegar. Serve in chilled cocktail glasses with a piece of lime on the side.

AVOCADO CRABMEAT COCKTAIL [60]

Pare and cube 1 avocado. Mix with 1 pound of picked, flaked, fresh or canned crabmeat and 1 grated medium-sized onion. Serve in sherbet glass topped with Russian Dressing (No. 1800) and pass a plate of lemon quarters dressed on a bed of crisp watercress.

Variation. (a) Substitute cooked or canned shrimps for crabmeat. (b) Or parboiled sliced sea scallops for crabmeat. (c) Or cooked or canned lobster meat for crabmeat. (d) Or cooked, flaked, boned white-fleshed fish for crabmeat.

CRABMEAT COCKTAIL KNICKERBOCKER MANNER [61]

Put thoroughly chilled, picked, boned and flaked fresh or canned crabmeat in cocktail glasses. Pour over the following sauce: $\frac{1}{3}$ cup of tomato catsup, 2 tablespoons of lemon juice, 2 tablespoons of sherry wine, 1 tablespoon of drained prepared horseradish, $\frac{1}{2}$ teaspoon of prepared mustard, 4 or 5 drops of Tabasco sauce, 1 teaspoon of Worcestershire sauce, $\frac{1}{4}$ cup of mayonnaise and 1 teaspoon of grated lemon rind. Mix thoroughly and chill before using.

CRANBERRY JUICE COCKTAIL [62]

Cook 1 pound (4 cups) of picked, washed, sound cranberries and 1 quart of water, very slightly salted, until all the skins pop open, using only a gentle flame. Strain through double thickness of cheesecloth. Heat, stir in $\frac{1}{2}$ cup of sugar and let boil for 2 minutes, no more. Chill well before serving.

NOTE. Lemon, orange, grapefruit or pineapple juice combine well with this cocktail.

FROSTED RASPBERRY COCKTAIL [63]

Combine 2 cups of canned raspberry juice, 2 tablespoons of lime juice, $\frac{1}{2}$ cup of pineapple juice in a shaker. Add $\frac{1}{2}$ cup of crushed ice and the slightly beaten whites of 2 eggs. Shake until frothy and strain into chilled cocktail glasses. Garnish each glass with a fresh mint leaf.

NOTE. Strawberry juice and orange juice may be prepared in the same manner.

FROZEN TOMATO COCKTAIL [64]

Soften 1 teaspoon of granulated gelatine in 2 tablespoons of lemon juice; dissolve over hot water. Combine with 2 tablespoons of sugar, a tiny pinch of salt, 1 tablespoon of grated onion, a dash of cayenne, and 2 cups of tomato juice. Mix well, cool, then turn preparation to freezing tray of refrigerator and freeze until firm or about 3 hours.

When ready to serve, empty the frozen tomato juice into a shallow pan and chop coarsely. Fill 6 chilled cocktail glasses or sherbet glasses and serve at once with a mint leaf topping each cocktail.

NOTE. Any other kind of vegetable juice may also be prepared in this manner.

GRAPEFRUIT MINT COCKTAIL   [65]

Halve 3 sound grapefruits, remove cores and seeds and notch the edges. Over the top sprinkle crushed after-dinner mints in place of the usual addition of sugar. Top with green minted cherries or other cherries. Serve well chilled.

Upon seeing grapefruit for the first time an Irishman said: "Thim's pretty big oranges and it wouldn't take many of them to make a dozen."

HONEY COCKTAIL   [66]

Beat the yolks of 4 eggs until thick and lemon-colored. Gradually add 4 tablespoons of strained honey, beating briskly or whipping with rotary beater, alternately with 3 cups of cold, rich milk and a few grains of salt. Fold in the stiffly beaten whites of 4 eggs, beaten with ¼ teaspoon of salt and a dash of nutmeg. Fill 6 chilled cocktail or sherbet glasses and dust tops with a little grated lemon rind.

LOBSTER COCKTAIL GOURMET   [67]

Allow ¼-⅓ cup of cooked lobster meat cut in about ⅓-½-inch pieces. Moisten with a good mayonnaise dressing blended with enough tomato catsup to give a delicate pink color. Fill chilled cocktail glass with the mixture, and pour over the following cocktail sauce:

Cocktail Sauce for Shellfish. Mix the following ingredients thoroughly and chill before using: ½ cup of tomato catsup, ⅓ cup of sherry wine, 4 tablespoons of lemon juice, 6 drops of Tabasco sauce, 1 tablespoon of drained, finely chopped prepared horseradish, a dash of salt and ½ teaspoon of prepared mustard.

MELON BALL COCKTAIL EPICURE   [68]

Scoop out Cantaloupe, Honey Dew Melon, Honey Ball Melon, Casaba Melon, Cranshaw Melon of Persian (Santa Claus) Melon into little balls with French potato ball cutter, being sure to have the selected melon thoroughly chilled. Put the balls into a mixing bowl; pour over the following sauce:

Epicure Cocktail Sauce. Combine 1 cup of good red wine, 1 cup of good Port wine and 2 ounces of good brandy (¼ cup) and sugar to taste. Pour over the melon balls and let stand at least 2 hours in the refrigerator, stirring occasionally. When ready to serve, fill chilled sherbet glasses with melon balls and sauce and place over top with a thin slice of lime.

Variation. (a) Cover with chilled ginger ale instead of the Epicure Cocktail sauce. (b) Cover with sauterne wine and top each cocktail with a little ground ginger. (c) Or, combine equal parts of melon balls and orange sections (carefully seeded and rind cut off) and pour over the Epicure Cocktail Sauce. Buy melons way ahead—give them a chance to chill through. Forty-eight hours is none too much. That goes for *any* melon.

Alexandre Dumas presented the French town of Cavaillon with a set of his works on condition that each year it would send him some of its famous melons.

MUSSEL COCKTAIL   [69]

Allow 6–7 cooked, shelled mussels per portion. Place them in a bowl and pour over (for 6 cocktails) 1 cup of the following sauce:

Horseradish Cream Cocktail Sauce. Whip ½ cup of heavy cream, until stiff; season with ⅓ teaspoon of salt and a few grains each of cayenne pepper and nutmeg, then stir in 3 tablespoons of freshly grated horseradish, 1 teaspoon of prepared mustard, 1 teaspoon of Worcestershire sauce and 1 tablespoon of tomato paste. Serve very well chilled.

PALMER HOUSE CLAM JUICE COCKTAIL   [70]

Combine the juice of 30 large clams, minced, with the juice of ½ lemon (about 1 tablespoonful), 6 drops of Tabasco sauce and 1 cupful of tomato catsup. Chill and divide in glasses surrounded by ice. Dust with a little celery salt before serving.

PICKLED OYSTER COCKTAIL   [71]

Cook very slowly 1 quart of picked fresh oysters in their own liquor till edges curl. Remove oysters from the liquor; drop in bowl of cold water, and let stand 20 minutes with cold water running over them. Drain, set aside. Put into an enameled saucepan 1 cup of tarragon vinegar, 1 spice bag containing 1 teaspoon of allspice, 6 whole cloves, 1 leaf of mace, 1 large bay leaf, 1 inch piece of grated parsley root and 10 whole peppercorns. Strain the reserved oyster liquor; and 1¾ cups of it to the vinegar mixture, and let boil gently for 5 minutes. Drop in the oysters; remove from the fire and let stand until cold. Store in refrigerator in a closed jar to chill well. When ready to serve, place 6 or 7 well drained oysters in each chilled sherbet glass, and pour over the following sauce:

Oyster Cocktail Sauce. ¼ cup of tomato catsup, ¼ cup of chili sauce, ¼ cup of mayonnaise, 1½ tablespoons of prepared horseradish, drained and ground, 1 teaspoon of finely chopped shallots, 1 tablespoon of finely chopped chives, 1 teaspoon of grated onion, 10 drops of Tabasco sauce, 1 teaspoon of grated lemon rind and 1 tablespoon of finely minced parsley. Combine all ingredients and chill thoroughly, then pour over oysters and serve surrounded by ice.

RAW FISH COCKTAIL FISHERMAN MANNER [72]

Flake with 2 forks 1¾ cups of uncooked white fish filets, separating the flakes carefully and picking any bone which may be left in. Pour over ¾ cup of lime juice, 1 teaspoon of finely-grated lemon rind, 1 large bay leaf, 3 whole cloves, 8 whole peppercorns, 8 drops of Tabasco sauce, ½ teaspoon of salt and ⅛ teaspoon of freshly grated nutmeg. Cover with a double-thickness of cheesecloth, and let stand at room temperature overnight. Next day, drain, squeezing gently, but thoroughly and discard the whole seasoning and spices. Divide among 6 sherbet or cocktail glasses surrounded by ice and spoon over each glass the following cocktail sauce:

Fisherman's Fish Cocktail Sauce. ¾ cup of mayonnaise, 2 teaspoons of finely chopped capers, 1 tablespoon of finely chopped parsley, 1 tablespoon of grated onion, ½ small clove of garlic, finely chopped, 1 tablespoon of finely chopped dill pickles, 1 teaspoon of prepared mustard, 2 tablespoons of chili sauce and 1 teaspoon of drained, ground prepared horseradish. Mix well, then chill thoroughly.

TOMATO JUICE COCKTAIL GEORGIA   [73]
MANNER

To the grated pulp of 2 medium-sized onions, add the juice of 2 lemons; let stand 4 minutes, then squeeze off the juice and add to 1 cup of mayonnaise, beating in thoroughly. In serving, add 2 teaspoons of the mayonnaise to each glass of tomato juice, fresh or canned, but thoroughly chilled. Stir in and garnish with a sprig of parsley or mint.

Second Version. Substitute 1 teaspoon of freshly grated horseradish for the mayonnaise, and beat well. Top each glass with a bruised mint leaf.

Third Version. Instead of mayonnaise or horseradish, drop into each glass 3 or 4 pearl onions (canned or bottled).

LENTIL RELISH PARISIENNE [74]

Mix thoroughly the following ingredients: 2 cups of cooked, well drained lentils, 4 small green apples, peeled, cored, cubed small, 2 medium-sized onions, finely chopped, 1 clove of garlic, finely chopped, 1 pickled herring, peeled, bones carefully removed then cubed small, 2 tablespoons of capers, 1 tablespoon each of finely chopped parsley and chives, and pour over 1 cup of French dressing. Store in refrigerator to thoroughly chill before serving, stirring occasionally.

LONDON CELERY CENTERPIECE [75]

This unusual hors d'oeuvre centerpiece makes an amusing decoration. The material for this creation is easily obtained. Needless to say it is more appropriate for informal lunches. It is especially useful when flowers are not available.

Select a firm and perfect stalk of celery. Be sure that the leaves are fresh, green and crisp. If not, crisp them in refrigerator, wrapped into a wet cloth. A bunch of nice red radishes is also needed. Separate the celery stalks and clean them. Leave the foliage on half of the stalks, but cut off the leaves on the rest. Be sure to cut off only the leaves of these stalks, allowing the branches to remain.

Clean radishes; slice them six or eight times sidewise almost through. Drop in ice-water for an hour to crisp and spread the "petals." Drain, hollow out the ends of the radishes to fit the celery branches. Just before serving time, arrange the celery stalks as a bouquet in a wire frog and place in a shallow bowl filled with ice water. Then stick the radishes onto the branches of celery, and you'll have a clever, edible centerpiece which your guests will eat with pleasure.

MAQUEREAUX MARINÉS AU VIN BLANC [76]
Marinated Filets of Mackerel in White Wine

Select a dozen fresh mackerel, weighing about ½ pound each; remove the filets carefully and place them in a large, shallow pan; season to taste with salt, freshly ground black pepper, and sprinkle over 1 medium-sized, thinly sliced onion, 1 sprig of thyme, 6 sprigs of fresh parsley, 1 large bay leaf, ¼ cup of unstrained lemon juice, and enough dry white wine to cover. Place over a gentle flame. Bring slowly to the boiling point; lower the flame, cover and let simmer gently for 5 or 6 minutes. Remove the pan from the stove and allow the fish filets to cool in their own liquid overnight. Next day, lift up the filets very carefully, using a broad spatula; place them in a cold, large, shallow serving dish; discard the thyme, parsley and bay leaf from the cooking stock, and strain stock over the filets. Chill thoroughly before serving.

NOTE. Herring filets, large sardine filets and any kind of small fish having the fat distributed throughout the body may be prepared in the same manner. The fish stock should be semi-jellied if directions are followed.

OYSTERS A LA ROCKEFELLER   [77]

Lo! and behold, ye gourmets, one and all, far and wide, here at last is one of the sacred recipes that have lured discriminating palates to New Orleans, where far-famed alchemists of the kitchen prepare comestibles that are beyond criticism.

Proceeding in alphabetical order, I confer the cordon bleu upon the chefs of Antoine, Arnaud, Brussard, Galatoire, Kolb, La Louisiane Maylie—and upon the composite genius who assembled that mysterious triumph, Oysters à la Rockefeller.

Be it known that Monsieur Alciatore, the living descendant of the wizard who first brought this delectable dish to the attention of the Christian world, exacted on his deathbed a promise that the exact proportions of the ingredients be kept forever a secret, adding: "They must be mixed with brains to achieve perfection. To all those who comprehend the subtle suggestion embodied in the quoted line—to those who put mind into matter, this legacy is laid bare."

Take selected oysters, open them and leave them on the deep half shell. Place the shells containing the oysters on a bed of rock salt in a pie pan. The sauce for the oysters is compounded as follows:

Take the tail and tips of small green onions. Take celery, take chervil, take tarragon leaves and the crumbs of stale bread. Take Tabasco sauce and the best of butter obtainable. Pound all these into a mixture in a mortar, so that all the fragrant flavorings are blended. Add a dash of absinthe.

Force the mixture through a fine-meshed sieve. Place 1 spoonful on each oyster as it rests on its own shell and in its own juice on the crushed rock salt, the purpose of which is to keep the oyster piping hot. Then place them in an oven with overhead heat and cook until brown. Serve immediately. Thus spoke Monsieur Alciatore to your humble servant.

> *Tom, whom today no noise stirs,*
> *Lies buried in these cloisters;*
> *If at the last trump*
> *He does not quickly jump,*
> *Only cry, "OYSTERS."*
> *—Epitaph on a Colchester*
> *(England) Man's Grave*

PORT WINE ASPIC COATING JELLY [78]

Proceed as indicated for Sherry Wine Aspic Coating Jelly (No. 82), substituting port wine for sherry wine.

ROSES D'HIVER ARMENONVILLE [79]
Stuffed Radishes Armenonville

Select bright red-radishes of uniform size. Soak them in ice-water for 2 hours. Drain and dry them. Cut the red peeling down in sections as for making radish roses and with a sharp pointed knife remove the inner part, leaving only the "petals." Drop them again in ice-water while preparing the stuffing as follows: Mash—for each dozen large radishes—⅓ cup of Roquefort cheese with a little port wine, then rub through a fine-meshed sieve. Place the cheese mixture in a pastry bag with a small rose tube and fill the cavity of each radish after draining and drying them thoroughly, by holding the radish by a small piece of green stem between the thumb and first finger while with the other hand pressing the cheese into the cavity. Sprinkle each radish "rose" with paprika and arrange in bouquet fashion in center of a bunch of crisp watercress, placed upon a cold crystal platter. Any other kind of cheese may be substituted for Roquefort cheese.

SALMAGUNDI [80]

Always a distinguished hodge-podge whether in abstract or concrete form.

"As everybody knows, or ought to know, what a salmagundi is, we shall spare ourselves the trouble of an explanation," wrote the editors in their introduction to No. 1 of the journal *Salmagundi*, dated New York, January 24, 1807. And Washington Irving and his brother, William, and James K. Paulding, and their contemporaries in young New York knew what a salmagundi was, but a century and a quarter later New Yorkers rarely heard the word except as the name of a venerable and distinguished club on the avenue.

In that same introduction, Irving and his colleagues proclaimed themselves "critics, amateurs, dilettanti and cognoscenti," and in 1870 a group of critics, amateurs, dilettanti and cognoscenti in all the fine arts organized a club that has made history in artistic America, and whimsically assumed the title that Irving had made famous in literature.

Salmagundi is disposed of in the dictionaries as a hodge-podge of almost anything, animal, vegetable or mineral; a pot-pourri, an olio podrido, an olla podrida. Most of the dictionaries dismiss the origin of the term as obscure, but it appears to be a corruption of the French *salmigondis*. The French *salmis* is usually a chaudfroid of left-over meats or game or poultry, and there is a story extant that a French chef of

Paris in the eighteenth century served a special salmis of a savor so rich and piquant that it made him internationally famous; and there's some doubt whether his name was Gondis or Gonde, but creditable authorities have maintained that salmis de Gonde, or salmis de Gondis, was one of the popular viands among Continental gourmets for a century or more, and it is said to have been a combination of game and chicken with filets of anchovies, in a sauce of eggs, shallots, garlic, fine herbs, and white wine.

Today the authority of the dictionaries is taken as sufficient warrant for applying the term to any mixture, hot or cold, sweet, sour or savory. Several delectable dishes have been served at the famous club under the name, and one of them was a simple, refreshing and delicious chilled cup of little balls cut with a French cutter from very red watermelon, and Casaba melons and cantaloupes of various shades of jade green, salmon pink, and white, dressed with a fruit syrup flavored with maraschino liqueur, curaçao or other cordial.

Adapting salmagundi to the salad course, as a heavy salad for a buffet luncheon or supper, chicken, veal or lamb is cut into neat half-inch cubes and mixed with smaller quantities of similar dice of cooked potato, carrot and eggplant, and small green peas and haricot beans. The mixture is marinated in oil and vinegar or lemon juice, some sliced onion, salt, pepper and a touch of tarragon vinegar; then well drained, tossed lightly with fresh mayonnaise, and served with hearts of lettuce and crisp watercress. Small filets of anchovy might be added to the salad with good effect, and would be in keeping with the original formula.

A picturesque and delicious cold platter for the midsummer buffet is made with those brands of chicken which come in glass, with the white meat cut in round wafers about the size of a half-dollar. Arrange the wafers in a design with thinly sliced small tomatoes and hard-cooked eggs and young cucumbers, then decorate with filets of anchovy, small wafers of imported cervelat or mortadella sausage, cubes of fancy forms of aspic, a few small capers, and bouquets of watercress, parsley or chervil. Dress very lightly with a mild French dressing in which there is a mere soupçon of tarragon. This dish, or something very nearly its counterpart, has been served by many a hostess as a salmagundi.

Thus anyone is at liberty to invent or compose his or her salmagundi and make it hot or cold, and as bland and delicate or as pungent and piquant as he or she may desire. Grimod de la Reynière, in his *Almanach des Gourmands*, 1803, tantalizes the reader with a reference to a salmis of wild duck, partridge, woodcock, and other dark-fleshed game, served with a "poignant" sauce the formula of which was reserved for his most intimate friends. Frantic gourmets of the time tried to discover the mysterious formula in vain, but the tang of anchovy was in it, without a doubt, and there must have been truffles, and possibly cock's combs, and some excellent wine; perhaps the equally mysterious chef, Gondis or Gonde, had that formula, and the root of a tradition that owes its life to American literature. These salmagundis are also very appropriate for hors d'oeuvres and buffets.

SCHNITZELBANK CHEESE POT   [81]

There is a quaint Alsatian folk song sung with the guidance of a Schnitzelbank. Before this song may be properly done by a mixed chorus of adult voices, there must be appropriate food and drink. As to the food, a pot of cottage cheese made up earlier in the day and set away to grow cold is "just about what the doctor ordered." And here is the prescription therefor:

Scrape clean and free from outer skin 2 Camembert cheeses and 1 Liederkranz, and put into a copper stew pan with ¼ pound Roquefort cheese, ½ pound of butter, ¼ pound of cottage cheese, 2 tablespoons of flour and 1 pint of rich sweet cream. Boil until melted into a smooth mass, stirring almost constantly. Strain, or rather rub, through a fine-meshed sieve and then stir into this strained cheese 1 cup of finely chopped olive meat, and ½ cup of chopped red pimiento. Season this indefinable mixture highly with cayenne; pack into a pot to chill, and when well chilled, have your guests seated around the table, a table loaded with thinly sliced fresh brown bread, freshly made finger toasts and several pitchers of cool beer. . . . "*Ei, du schöene, ei, du schöne, ei, du schöene Schnitzelbank!*"

SHERRY ASPIC COATING JELLY   [82]
(*Cold*)

NOTE. The following coating jelly uses a little more gelatine than for a jellied dessert. It may be used for coating any kind of molded or unmolded cold dessert. If used for coating a molded cold dessert, use the thinly pared rind and juice of 4 lemons, orange, lime, grapefruit, etc., and ¾ cup of sugar. For fish, meat, poultry or game, omit the sugar. This coating jelly may be kept in the refrigerator for several months when sealed in a container.

Combine, in a saucepan, 2¼ cups of cold water, the finely-pared rind and juice of 2 lemons, 1 large bay leaf, 1 whole clove, ½ teaspoon of salt, and ⅛ teaspoon of white pepper in a saucepan; the slightly beaten whites and crushed shells of 2 eggs, and 1¾ tablespoons of granulated gelatine, previously soaked in 2 tablespoons of cold water. Bring gradually to boiling point, whisking the mixture constantly, but do not actually boil. When the boiling point seems to be reached, lower the flame as low as possible, and simmer very, very gently for 5 minutes, without stirring. Then strain through a fine-meshed sieve or muslin bag or cloth into a porcelain or enameled bowl, and stir in ¼–⅓ cup of good sherry wine. Use for coating, and store the remainder, carefully sealed, in the colder part of your refrigerator.

STUFFED CELERY CLUB STYLE   [83]
(*Cold*)

Separate 1 nice bunch of celery and wash, then scrape carefully.
Dry. Have ready ¾ cup of minced cooked or canned lobster, carefully
picked and put through food chopper, using the finest blade. To this
ground lobster add 2–3 tablespoons of Mustard Butter (No. 992),
3 drops of Tabasco sauce, 1 teaspoon of Worcestershire sauce, 1 teaspoon of finely chopped shallots, and work to a smooth paste. Turn
into a pastry bag having a small rose tube and fill celery stalk hollows
with the mixture. Dust with paprika and serve as cold as possible on
a bed of shredded lettuce.

Variations. Substitute creamed Roquefort cheese with a little butter
for lobster meat, or use any other type of creamed cheese, such as cream
cheese, cottage cheese, etc. Or substitute crabmeat paste, shrimp paste,
fish paste, etc., for lobster purée.

STUFFED EGGS   [84]
(*Cold*)

There is no definite or established rule for the preparation and
making of stuffed eggs for service as appetizers, this being left to the
creative imagination, availability of material and taste of the cook.
The following suggestions and ideas have all been tested by the author,
and afford the possibilities of using almost any kind of left-over which
otherwise would not be sufficient to prepare a dish. For good effect, and
at the same time to provide a choice variety and obviate monotony,
it is suggested that an appetizer tray be garnished with different stuffed
eggs arranged in nests of shredded lettuce or crisp, green watercress.
They may be arranged in as many "nests" as required, thus providing
a diversity of colors, schemes, designs, flavors, etc., and also tempting
looking morsels. The hard-cooked eggs may be halved crosswise or
lengthwise.

Filling No. 1. Six hard-cooked eggs, cut in two lengthwise. Remove
the yolks, rub them through a sieve then combine with a few drops of
lemon or onion juice a package of cream cheese, a teaspoon of finely
chopped chives and just enough cream to moisten. Force mixture
(thoroughly creamed) through a pastry bag with a small fancy tube into
the hard-cooked egg white cavities, dust with paprika and chill.

Filling No. 2. Six hard-cooked eggs, halved crosswise, the yolks
creamed with a little mayonnaise tinted with a little tomato paste,
the shells filled with an anchovy filet rolled around a stuffed olive,

and the surface entirely covered with yolk mixture forced through a pastry bag with a rose tube, and topped with a few grains of cinnamon.

Filling No. 3. Six hard-cooked eggs, halved lengthwise, yolks removed and the white shells filled with a mixture of creamed Roquefort cheese blended with finely chopped gherkins, then completely covered with the yolks sieved and mixed with a little fresh, sweet cream, and tomato paste, the whole highly seasoned with cayenne pepper and forced through a pastry bag with a small fancy tube, then dusted with finely chopped chives.

Filling No. 4. Six hard-cooked eggs, halved crosswise, yolks removed, the egg-white shells filled with prepared fish paste mixed with a little mayonnaise forced through a pastry bag with a small fancy tube, then dusted with a little caviar and paprika.

Filling No. 5. Six hard-cooked eggs, halved crosswise, yolks removed, sieved and mixed with a little chili sauce; the egg-white cavities filled with small balls of pâté de foie gras rolled in finely chopped black truffle and surrounded with a narrow ribbon of the egg yolk mixture forced through a pastry bag with a small fancy tube.

Filling No. 6. Six hard-cooked eggs, halved lengthwise, yolks removed and sieved, the white of egg cavities filled with a green, pitted olive, stuffed with caviar, and on both sides of the olive a narrow strip of anchovy filet wraped around a small ball of cream cheese, previously blended with some of the sieved hard-cooked egg yolks; the olive surrounded (not covered) with a narrow ribbon of Caviar Butter (No. 983) and the cheese balls with a narrow ribbon of Salmon Butter (No. 999) both forced through a pastry bag with a small fancy tube.

Filling No. 7. Six hard-cooked eggs, halved lengthwise, yolks removed and egg white cavities filled with the following deviled mixture: Mash the yolks and blend with 1 tablespoon of French dressing, 1 teaspoon of prepared mustard, 1 teaspoon of finely chopped parsley, ½ teaspoon of finely minced pickles, ½ teaspoon of grated onions with celery salt and cayenne pepper to taste. Refill egg-white cavities and chill. Top filling with a thin slice of black olive.

Filling No. 8. Six hard-cooked eggs, halved lengthwise, yolks removed and mixed with ½ teaspoon of anchovy paste and 1 teaspoon of sweet butter, then worked until completely smooth, seasoning while working the paste with a dash of Tabasco sauce and a dash of Worcestershire sauce. Fill the egg white cavities with this paste and reshape to original form. Serve on a bed of crisp, young watercress, and serve with toasted crackers, made as follows: Spread as many crackers as desired generously with salted butter and sprinkle the tops lightly with equal parts cinnamon and paprika. Toast as they are needed so that there will always be a supply warm and crisp. (Fine with cocktails.)

TAMALES [85]

The Spanish-American tamale, that delicious edible cigarette in a corn-husk wrapper, has preserved its identity even when jammed into tin cans, though its distant cousin, the dolma of the Near East, has been brought to ignominious disaster by American cook books. If vine leaves are not obtainable, say the cook books, parboiled cabbage leaves will do as well—and did they not say, also, under prohibition, that a little Worcestershire sauce would do as well as a glass of sherry for a Newburg, and that milk was better than beer for a rarebit?

However, the tragedy of the dolma is another story, and the hot tamale is yours for the making, in New York, Philadelphia, Boston, Palm Beach, Chicago as well as in Mexico City, without makeshifts or apologies. But corn husks, you say, come only with the green corn and the watermelon for July 4. Aye, but thousands of people make and eat tamales, and husks are harvested by proper husbandmen and stored away against the lean days of winter, when piping hot tamales fill empty stomachs and warm the cockles of fainting hearts.

Preparing the Corn Husks. Go to the Spanish and Latin-American shops and you'll find the thin, tender husks of corn tied in neat bundles hanging on walls or packed in bins and boxes. Buy yourself a liberal supply and procure at the same time some of the best chili powder and a sack of Mexican corn meal, finely ground for tortillas.

Soak the husks in water till they are soft and pliant, then select the best ones and trim them neatly to rectangles about 6 inches long and 3 inches wide.

The Filling. Scald about 4 cups of corn meal with boiling stock of chicken, veal or beef and, if it is not rich, replace 1 cup of the stock with 1 cup of Pique seasoning and stir in 2 tablespoons of melted butter. Stir vigorously to make a soft but firm and workable paste and season with enough chili powder to make it as hot as you desire it. Do not salt if you have added Pique seasoning.

Your meat may be chicken, veal, beef or pork, or a mixture of beef and pork; and it may be cooked or raw; but at any rate you will grind or chop it coarsely, then brown it in a skillet with a medium-sized onion, grated, a clove of garlic, mashed, a green pepper, finely chopped white seeds and white ribs carefully removed and 1 tablespoon of finely chopped parsley. Season generously with chili powder again, adding a little of the stock if the mixture seems too dry.

Rolling the Tamales. Spread your corn husk wrappers on a board and line each one with a thin layer of the corn meal paste, leaving a margin all around. On the corn meal paste place a spoonful of the meat mixture, then roll up carefully, folding in the ends as you complete the cylinder. Some cooks tie them with kitchen thread, but it is better to place them side by side, horizontally or vertically, in a steamer, so that they will bind one another. Steam for 2 long hours over boiling water, and when they are done they will stay rolled and keep their shape. Like the lamented dolmas, they are good hot or cold, and packed hot in a vacuum jar they will create a sensation as a cocktail, a picnic, or a buffet snack.

TAMALES CARIBBEAN STYLE   [86]

When summer rolls around and brings green corn, you can make another kind of tamale, familiar to travelers in the Caribbean, by grating sweet corn right down to the cob, pressing the pulp through a sieve if the hulls are tough. Using no other moisture, cook the pulp with your meat mixture as described in the above recipe (No. 85) and add a tomato or a little tomato paste. In this form no corn meal is used, and the filling is applied to the fresh husks in a single layer. If the white meat of chicken is used and the mixture is enriched with crushed almonds and pistachios and minced ripe olives, all lightly seasoned, the result is delicate and entrancing.

With the vogue of the cocktail hour and the progression of hors d'oeuvres into the cosmopolitan mazes of smörgasbord, thrills and innovations are coveted, and the sudden appearance of well-molded tamales among the sausages, filets and canapés is sure to be a little startling. Hot or cold, in winter or summer, they are generally well received—if not too fiery—and if those made from green corn are well iced or chilled in the refrigerator the filling will become a soft and delectable jelly, savory and refreshing.

TOMATO ASPIC PLAZA   [87]
(Cold)

Sprinkle 2½ tablespoons of granulated gelatine in ½ cup of cold, dry white wine for 5 minutes. Place in a saucepan 1 quart of stewed or canned tomatoes, add 2 bay leaves, 6 sprigs of parsley, 2 dill leaves, 1 medium-sized onion, thinly sliced, 4 freshly crushed peppercorns, 1 blade of garlic, ½ teaspoon of salt, 2 teaspoons of sugar, and the slightly beaten whites of 2 eggs with their crushed shells. Gradually bring to the boiling point, whisking constantly with a wire whisk; lower the flame and let simmer gently for 10 minutes. Then remove from the fire and stir in the gelatine mixture, stirring until gelatine is dissolved. Rub through a fine-meshed sieve, taste for seasoning and pour mixture into 6 individual molds, previously rinsed in cold water. When cold, place in the refrigerator to chill for at least 2 hours. Unmold on cold individual plates on a bed of finely shredded green lettuce and garnish with lemon quarters. Serve at once.

Chapter Two

BEVERAGES

Where dwells the wretch, beneath what zone,
To every elegance unknown;
Whose soul ne'er felt the genial fire,
That coffee's subtle fumes inspire.
When thou'rt infus'd with nicest art,
New life to all thy dreams impart,
If Cynthia's hand the task assumes,
Ambrosia yields to thy perfumes,
Thy fragrant scent alone shall gain.

—"Ode to Coffee" (Author unknown)

Two GALLONS OF BEER IS NO GREAT QUANTITY TO DIVIDE among 32 thirsty persons. But considering that the beer is free; that each portion is accompanied by a slice of bread; and that this beer and bread have been doled out 365 days of the year for the past 810 years, anyone can readily appreciate the magnitude and the magnanimity of the Wayfarer's Dole. For the statistically minded, this means that 18,748 barrels, 590,570 gallons, or 18,898,240 portions of beer have been thirstily consumed by weary wanderers—and by the grace of the good Bishop Henry de Blois.

At the hospital of St. Cross near Winchester, in the county of Hampshire, England, any traveler who happens by before the 32 daily portions are exhausted, may rap at the door of a gray stone building situated hard by the Itchem River, ask for his portion of beer and bread and it will not be denied him. It all goes back to the year 1136, when the philanthropic and kindly Bishop Henry de Blois, grandson of William the Conqueror, founded the Hospital of St. Cross, to shelter "13 poor men, feeble and so reduced in strength that they can hardly or with difficulty support themselves without another's aid." These unfortunates were to be provided "with garments and beds suitable to their infirmities, good wheaten bread daily of the weight of five marks, and three dishes at dinner and one at supper suitable to the day, and drink of good stuff."

In addition to this, the hospice was to give food and drink to poor wanderers who came to its gates. This has been going on for eight long centuries, making St. Cross the oldest almshouse in England.

At the beginning of the Christian era, the Germanic tribes brewed beer from barley, wheat and oats . . . and mead, that romantic beverage of medieval legend, out of honey and water. They connected their omnipotent Donar, the god of thunder, closely with the juice of barley grain, believing that in his capacity as the donor of light and growth, he took care of beer's main components, the hops and the malt. In northern European countries, the well-guarded thunder stones which the aboriginals believed had come down with Thor's lightning, are still sprinkled with beer every Christmas Eve to increase their magic power. Brewing was so important that it engaged the attention of Charlemagne, King of the Franks (742–814 A. D.), and he issued an order that all able beer masters should be sent to his court, where he gave directions himself on best brewing methods. He selected his brew masters with the same care that he chose his counselors and leaders.

The pyramids were a thousand years old and beginning to show their age when Greek civilization began. In the beginning it did not amount to much, but after centuries piled on centuries, we find in Greece, the little land of broken valleys and seaswept cliffs, that ancient civilization had climbed to its zenith. Naturally we are interested in what they chose to eat and drink. The Greeks, above everybody else, wanted to be free in spirit and to live in moderation. Their meals were as simple as possible: a little bread, a little meat, some green vegetables and Zythos (beer) as reported by Sophocles—also wine and barley. The Romans had their Cerevisia (beer), the expression pointing to the name of the classic goddess Ceres, goddess of the cereal kingdom. Again and again one finds mention of beer in the works of the old writers. Xenophon, in his account of the Retreat of the Ten Thousand, written about 400 B. C., mentions that the inhabitants of Armenia used a fermented drink from barley. Herodotus and Strabo both wrote that in Abyssinia and Nubia the people lived on millet and barley, "whereof they made a beverage." There is reference to a beer made from germinated millet by the Langonassis in the Congo. In the South the Kaffirs have made beer according to their own account from time immemorial, just as they do today. In China there are records of a beer made from millet several centuries before Christ. Records of fermented cereal beverage among the classical writers include such countries as Thracia, Illyria, Pannonia, all northern Europe and the British Isles.

"Beer and bread make the cheeks red," runs the old German adage. Beer is one of the delicate beverages, more capricious than champagne. Once out of its container, treat it with the gentleness of a new-born babe. Protect it from evil influences. Beer is easily corrupted, taking up with wayward odors as eagerly as a fresh-churned butter ball. Light is its bugaboo. So, keep the bottles in a dark place, right side up. Store the bottles in the refrigerator, on the bottom shelf away from the cooling unit. Beer is not only a beverage, but is also a food. Beer is also greatly used in cookery.

Egyptians, in 5000 B. C., drank beer, but not from bottles. They carried their beer supply with them in small, convenient-sized cakes. They devised the unique method of preparing their "boozan" by drying barley, crushing it, making it into a paste, and baking until firm. Boozan or boozah cakes were dropped in water to make beer on the spot.

BEER SYLLABUB   [89]

This is a great drink to prepare for summer country house guests. Making it is great fun for the crowd.

Get ready a handful of dried currants which have been washed and allowed to swell up nice and plump in boiling water, then seed them. Into a large punch bowl, put 1 pint bottle of beer and the same quantity of hard cider—using light beer and good bottled cider. Sweeten to taste and add a dash or so of nutmeg. Now have your cow set and ready —able and willing—and the expert milker on the job. Hold the bowl at a safe and convenient distance from the cow and milk directly into the bowl about three pints of milk.

Milk infused in this way is creamy and frothy and the syllabub is a picturesque drink.

BLACK CHAMPAGNE VELVET   [90]

Choose 1 quart of the finest stout and 1 quart of a fine champagne brandy and, both chilled in their bottles, pour them together into the same pitcher and then out into champagne goblets. (An appropriate beverage for a large crowd in the summer.)

"A tavern is the busy man's recreation, the idle man's business, the melancholy man's sanctuary, the stranger's welcome, the scholar's kindness, and the citizen's courtesy."—*Earle.*

PORTER PUNCH   [91]
(Serves 6)

Have a pitcher ready and into it pour 1 bottle of porter, ½ pint of claret or similar dry red wine, 1 pony glass of dry sherry, a little grated nutmeg and, if desired, a little sugar to sweeten to taste. You may start this mixture with well chilled ingredients and have it sufficiently cold to serve as soon as prepared. Or you may drop a lump or a cube of ice or two, about the size of a grapefruit, into the pitcher. You may also float a slice of lemon or a slice of cucumber on top of each glass when serving.

SHANDYGAFF   [92]

This is another very interesting summer drink, popular in India, all over Asia, and in England. It is made by pouring a pint of light beer and a pint of ginger ale into a pitcher together, then pour into glasses immediately. Of course, both bottles must have been well chilled.

> *For what this house affords us,*
> *Come, praise the brewer most—*
> *Who caught into a bottle*
> *The barley's gentle ghost*
> *Until our parching throttles*
> *In silence we employ*
> *Like geese that drink a mouthful*
> *Then stretch their necks with joy!*
> *—Higgins, "Grace Before Beer."*

TAVERN BEER BISHOP   [93]
(Serves 4)

Pumpernickel is grated on a grater and put in a tureen; mix with it ¼ pound of powdered sugar, ¼ pound of seedless raisins, 1 teaspoon of ground cinnamon, and 1 unpeeled lemon, cut into small pieces and seeded. Pour over a quart of chilled beer, stir and serve at once, in tall glasses.

WALDORF BEER FLIP   [94]
(*Serves 6*)

Pour into a saucepan 3 pint bottles of beer and add 1 tablespoon of sugar, the grated rind of half a small lemon or, still better, the rind cut into small pieces, a pinch of mace, 1 whole clove, head removed, and ½ teaspoon of sweet butter. Bring to boiling point and remove from the fire. Beat the white of 1 egg and yolks of 2 eggs with 3 tablespoons of beer, and gradually stir briskly into the hot beer mixture, which has been strained, beating until frothy with rotary beater. Serve at once in heated punch cups.

English schoolboys of the eighteenth century were fed beer, bread and cheese both for breakfast and supper. Their luncheon consisted of beef and wheat boiled in milk with sugar and egg yolks.

WASSAIL ALE BOWL   [95]
(*Serves 6*) (*Hot*)

Games grew up around the Yuletide bowl. For centuries Snapdragon has been played on Christmas Eve in every English shire. Remember the party at Dingley Bell and the great game of Snapdragon where fingers were burned aplenty? A handful of raisins are placed in a shallow dish, brandy is poured over, then ignited. The trick is to pick up the raisins through the flames. A hearty laugh goes round if the blue lapping tongue of the fire dragon sears a player's finger. While the game proceeds, the song of the Snapdragon is sung by the circle of guests:

> " . . . *Here be comes with a flaming bowl,*
> *Don't be mean to take his toll!*
> *Snap! Snap! Dragon!* . . . "

and so on with infinite verses all to the honor of the dragon, traditional guardian spirit of the Wassail Bowl.

Put 1 quart of ale in a saucepan and bring next to boiling, or until it foams; remove from the flame and stir in ¼ ounce each of grated nutmeg, ginger and cinnamon, ½ fifth-bottle of sherry wine, 1 lemon juice and thinly pared peel, cut into small pieces, and sugar to taste. When sugar is dissolved, cover the pan tightly and let infuse, over a very, very low flame, but do not boil at all. Pour into a punch bowl. Float in the Wassail bowl 2 slices of toasted bread, each ½ inch thick and 2 well-baked apples. Serve in heated cups.

WASSAIL BEER BOWL [96]
(*Serves 16–18*) (*Hot*)

Put into a quart of hot beer (not boiling) 1 pound of powdered sugar, a freshly grated whole nutmeg, ½–¾ teaspoon of powdered ginger, 1 cup of sherry wine, and 2 more quarts of hot beer with 4 or 5 thin slices of seeded lemon. Bring almost to boiling point, when the surface will look pearly. Remove from the fire; taste for sweetening, and pour into a large heated bowl containing 6 slices of freshly made toast. Serve as hot as possible in punch glasses.

CHOCOLATE AND COCOA [97]

The first settlers in America were imbued with the lust of gold. In that epoch, mineral products were valued above all else. Agriculture and commerce were in their infancy, and political economy was as yet unknown. The Spaniards also found precious metals. The land further South, where a very warm sun produced in the ground an extreme fertility, were found suited for the cultivation of sugar, coffee, cocoa, and other food products. Just when the cacao bean was discovered, we are not exactly sure; however, the story of cocoa and chocolate is a fascinating one! Cortez discovered it in Mexico in 1519, where it was used as a beverage by the Aztecs; later it was drunk by the Spanish ladies of the New World, who, passionately fond of chocolate, were not satisfied with taking it several times a day—they even brought it to church. This indulgence often brought on them the censure of their bishops, who, however, at last shut their eyes to it.

Chocolate was introduced into Spain about the XVIIth century and subsequently taken to France, then to England. "The devil has erected a new university," stated Roger North, in criticizing an English public house of the day—not because of a new-fangled drink known as chocolate, but because of the spirits which lost ground.

Chocolate is manufactured from the husked, dried, ground and fermented seeds of a tree indigenous to South America, which are roasted and made into a paste, then compressed into cakes by moderate pressure. To increase the flavor and nutrient power of the cakes more or less sugar (but at least 50% for sweet chocolate) is added, and various flavoring extracts are blended with the paste before compressing it.

The value of chocolate as a concentrated food is in part derived from the sugar which is added, but it is in itself very nutritious. Like cocoa, if pure and carefully prepared, its ingredients are easily digested and absorbed. It is also, according to medical authorities, mildly stimulating and exhilarating to the nervous system when the nervous system is exhausted through overwork or worry. Chocolate possesses the advantage over tea and coffee that it doesn't produce wakefulness.

Chocolate or cocoa owes these various properties to its being nothing but oleosaccharus, so that there are few other substances which contain in the same proportions more nutrition or more alimentary particles, in such a manner that nearly everything can be assimilated. Tested during the World Wars I and II, a chocolate ration was found to equal five times its weight of beef.

In preparing recipes calling for chocolate, it is well to remember that chocolate tends to burn easily, so it should be melted over hot water.

If cocoa is used to replace chocolate in a pudding, cakes or candies, as well as a beverage, it should be first blended with cold water for beverages, and for desserts with sugar or flour used in the recipe.

BRAZILIAN CHOCOLATE   [98]
(Serves 4)

Add 2 squares of grated unsweetened chocolate to 1 cup of strong coffee in top of double boiler; place directly over a low flame and stir till thoroughly blended; stir in 3 tablespoons of sugar (more or less according to taste) and a dash of salt and bring to a boil. Let boil 3 or 4 times, removing the pan quickly as soon as mixture rises. Place over boiling water; add 3 cups of scalded milk, stirring constantly. Remove from hot water; beat with rotary beater until light and frothy, and top each cup with a tuft of whipped cream, whipped with a little finely chopped mint and serve at once.

CHOCOLATE EGGNOG PLAIN   [99]
(Serves 1)

Add 1 cup of chilled milk slowly to 3 tablespoons of chocolate syrup (No. 105), stirring constantly till smooth; add 1 well-beaten fresh egg and beat or shake well. Pour into tall glass. Serve at once.

CHOCOLATE EGGNOG FLUFFY   [100]
(Serves 1)

Proceed as indicated above (No. 99), beating egg yolk and white separately; fold in egg white last. Flavor with a dash of cinnamon or nutmeg. Serve at once.

CHOCOLATE ICEBERG   [101]
(Serves 6)

Add 4 tablespoons of sugar to 2 cups of strong coffee; blend well and freeze as for coffee cubes. Combine in a saucepan 1 cup of boiling water, ½ teaspoon of vanilla extract, 4 tablespoons of sugar and 2 squares of grated unsweetened chocolate. Cook without stirring till mixture comes to boil. Remove from heat immediately, stir in 3 cups of hot milk, and blend well. Chill. To serve, place 2 coffee cubes in each glass, pour in chilled mixture, and top with stiffly-whipped cream, then sprinkle the cream with a few grains of cinnamon or nutmeg.

CHOCOLATE ICE CREAM SHAKE   [102]
(Serves 1)

Place 2 generous tablespoons of chocolate syrup (No. 105) in ¾ cup of chilled rich milk, or half milk and half undiluted, evaporated milk, or thin cream, 1 teaspoon of sugar (more or less, according to taste) and 4 tablespoons of vanilla ice cream in a shaker or jar with a cover and shake vigorously. Pour into chilled tall glass and serve at once, the top covered with a tablespoon of whipped cream.

> *Pity me, God! for I die of thirst;*
> *Take me out of this land accurst;*
> *And if ever I reach my home again,*
> *Where earth has springs, and the sky has rain,*
> *I will dig a well for the passersby.*
> *And none shall suffer from thirst as I . . .*
> *—John Greenleaf Whittier*

CHOCOLATE MALTED MILK   [103]
(Serves 1)

Combine 1 cup of rich milk, 2 tablespoons of malted milk powder (commercial) and 2 tablespoons of chocolate or cocoa syrup. Shake in shaker or in a jar with a cover and serve very cold.

CHOCOLATE SODA   [104]

Add ½ cup each of chilled milk and carbonated water or ginger ale to 2 generous tablespoons of chocolate or cocoa syrup (No. 105 and No. 107, respectively), add 3 or 4 tablespoons of vanilla ice cream, and serve immediately.

CHOCOLATE SYRUP   [105]
(Makes 1 pint)

Combine 2 or 3 squares of unsweetened chocolate cut into small pieces in top of double boiler with 1 cup of sugar and scant ¼ teaspoon of salt; gradually add 1¼ cups of boiling water, and cook over direct low flame for 5 minutes, stirring constantly. Place over hot water and let simmer gently for 10 minutes. Now beat hard with rotary beater; pour into a sterilized pint jar having a tight fitting cover. Chill and store in refrigerator until wanted. Keeps for months.

COCOA EGGNOG   [106]
(*Serves 1*)

Beat 1 egg white stiff, then gradually beat in 1 teaspoon of sugar (more or less, according to taste), mixed with 1 teaspoon of powdered cocoa, a few grains of salt, and a dash of ground nutmeg. When thoroughly blended, beat in ¾ cup of rich, chilled sweet milk and serve dusted with a little nutmeg.

A soft drink made of fruit juices mixed with water was sold in the Roman stadiums in the first century B. C. There was a choice of two lemon flavors, one tart and one very sweet.

COCOA SYRUP   [107]
(*Makes 2 pints*)

Like chocolate syrup (No. 105) this syrup may be used as a basis for any number of cold or hot drinks. Keeps indefinitely.

Put 1 cup of cocoa and 2 cups of cold water into a large saucepan and stir till thoroughly blended. Place over a low flame and cook, stirring almost constantly, till mixture is thick and smooth. Stir in 2 cups of sugar and ¼ teaspoon of salt; let boil steadily, but gently for 3 minutes: stir in, off the fire, 1 teaspoon of vanilla extract, and pour into 2 sterilized pint jars. Seal and, when cold, store in a cool, dry dark place.

Cocoa should always be cooked with a small amount of water before the milk is added in order to cook the starch and give a smooth well-blended mixture.

FRENCH CHOCOLATE   [108]
(*Serves 6*)

This is especially suitable for entertaining when the serving is done by the hostess at such parties as bridge, luncheon, afternoon tea, or after-theatre parties. Accompaniments or escortes should be light and dainty, thin bread and butter sandwiches, unsweetened wafers, lady fingers or sponge drops.

Add 2½ squares (2½ ounces) of grated, unsweetened chocolate to ½ cup of cold water and stir till blended. Place over a very low flame and cook, stirring constantly till chocolate is melted. Stir in ¼ cup of sugar and a dash of salt; bring to a boil, remove from the fire and repeat this boiling process 4 times stirring constantly. Cool. When quite cold, fold in ¼ cup of sweet, chilled heavy cream, whipped. Chill. This will keep a month under refrigeration. When ready to serve, place 1 generous tablespoon of chocolate preparation in each serving cup, and pour scalded milk (6 cups in all) over to fill up the cups; dust with nutmeg or cinnamon, if desired.

ICED CHOCOLATE [109]
(Serves 2)

Combine in a saucepan 4 tablespoons of cocoa (or 2 squares of unsweetened grated chocolate), 2–4 tablespoons of sugar (more or less, according to taste), ½ cup of boiling water, and a few grains of salt. Stir till smooth, and cook 2 minutes. Stir in 2 cups of scalded milk; blend well, but do not boil after adding the milk. Pour over shaved ice. Top with whipped cream. Serve with straws. Or use 2 generous tablespoons of chocolate or cocoa syrup (No. 105 and No. 107, respectively); pour over ice, then fill with cold milk.

MINTED CHOCOLATE [110]
(Serves 1)

Add 1 cup of chilled milk slowly to 3 tablespoons of chocolate or cocoa syrup (No. 105 and No. 107, respectively), stirring constantly, pour into shaker and shake well. Strain into tall, chilled glass; top with whipped or plain cream, and serve with 1 or 2 sprigs of fresh mint. Serve at once.

The Aztecs used cocoa beans as a medium of exchange. A slave cost about a hundred beans.

MOCHA MILK SHAKE I [111]
(Serves 4)

Grate a square of unsweetened chocolate, then melt over hot water; stir in ½ teaspoon of ground cinnamon, 5 tablespoons of sugar and a dash of salt; blend well, then stir in ½ cup of cold water. When thoroughly blended, cook over a low flame, stirring almost constantly to the boiling point; let simmer very gently for 5 or 6 minutes. Chill. When ready to serve, add 2 cups of chilled thin cream or undiluted evaporated milk and 2 cups of very strong coffee, also well chilled. Serve in chilled tall glasses with straws.

MOCHA MILK SHAKE II [112]
Special Newport Manner (Serves 4)

Combine 4 tablespoons of ground coffee, 2 squares unsweetened, crated chocolate, 6 whole cloves (heads removed), 1 four-inch stick of cinnamon bark and a dash of salt with 1 quart of rich milk, and blend well. Cook over hot water (double boiler) till chocolate is melted; then strain through a fine cloth into a saucepan. Combine 1 tablespoon of flour and ¾ cup of sugar; stir into milk mixture, and cook over a gentle flame for 15 minutes or until thickened, stirring constantly. Remove from fire; cool slightly, and pour over 1 well-beaten fresh egg, beating briskly. Chill. Pour over cracked ice in tall glasses; top each with a tuft of whipped cream sweetened and flavored with powdered ginger. Serve with straws.

SPICED COCOA [113]
(*Serves 6*)

This is a breakfast for chilly mornings. Mix in a saucepan ⅛ cup of cocoa, ⅛ cup of sugar, a few grains of salt, ½ teaspoon of ground cinnamon and a dash each of nutmeg and cloves. Stir in 2 cups of cold water and, when thoroughly blended and sugar is dissolved, bring to a boil and let boil for 3 minutes; then, stir in 2 cups of thin cream or undiluted evaporated milk; boil once more; remove from the fire and beat with rotary beater till frothy, adding, while beating, ½ teaspoon of vanilla extract. Serve as hot as possible, each cup topped with whipped cream.

CIDER [114]

Among the early New England farmers, cider, cider brandy, beer and rum were the popular beverages. The Dutch were partial to beer, and after landing on the shores of the New World, they lost little time in establishing breweries in New York and Albany. New Englanders, however, abandoned the steady drinking of beer and ale for cider. It was cheap and cost but a few shillings a barrel. The thrifty farmer sometimes laid in a supply of from ten to thirty barrels of cider against the winter. A keg or puncheon of rum would usually lie beside the cider barrels in the cellar, left there to ripen with age. Thirsty travelers needed go thirsty only between farmhouses, for every farmer kept a liberal supply of cider and proffered it without remuneration.

It is said that President John Adams, although an earnest wisher for temperance reform, drank a large tankard of cider every morning on getting up from bed, to the end of his life. Perhaps this contributed to his reaching the age of ninety-one. Cider lovers would probably argue that it did. It may be recalled that another President, William Henry Harrison, was elected after one of the most spectacular campaigns in our political history, known as "The Log Cabin and Hard Cider" campaign.

Cider-making is about as natural a process as the making of anything can be. After pressing the juice from the apples, nature does the rest of the work, only requiring a little time. If one doesn't want his cider hard, he must step in and prevent the natural process of fermentation from taking place by the use of chemicals or by the process of pasteurization. The United States Department of Agriculture recommends the pasteurization method, which doesn't employ chemicals at all. If one wishes really hard cider, he may raise its potency by freezing it. This separates the water from the alcoholic portion and, by chipping off the ice formed from the water, the remaining liquid is truly a strong man's drink.

The process of making cider consists of three main operations: the collection of the fruit; the expression and fermentation of the juice, and the storing and care of the fermented liquor.

"Sweet Cider" is the juice before fermentation has begun; as it ferments it becomes "hard," and the longer it is allowed to ferment, the harder it gets.

When thoroughly fermented, it can become just as potent as any liquor made from fruit or grain.

Three sorts of apples may be used in the process: the sour, the sweet, the bitter; late apples are said to make better cider than early ones. After the fruit has been crushed, the pulp, to which a little water has been added, is placed in canvas bags to drain into vats. The juice is allowed to flow through a strainer, which, in the old days, was always made of straw. The barrels are bunged up and removed to a cool cellar, where the bungs are removed and the cider left to ferment.

Cider which has been submitted to distillation becomes applejack, also known as cider brandy, and frequently called "Jersey Lightning."

> " . . . Should good old cider be despised
> And ever neglected more.
> Should plain log cabin be despised
> Our fathers built of yore . . . "

Although it is one of the oldest beverages known, the exact place of cider in the nomenclature of beverages is uncertain. At first thought, its place would seem to be under the classification of wines, but in some of its more alcoholic forms, such as hard cider, cider brandy, apple whisky, and applejack, it belongs more properly with the more potent liquors.

The name is related to the Hebrew word "shekar" or "shakar," and the Greek word "sikera," meaning "strong drink." In Wycliffe's version of the Bible, he translated Luke I:15: "He shall be great before the Lord, and he shall not drink wyne ne sider." The precise origin of the drink has never been determined, but it is fair to assume that it has always been manufactured wherever apples are found. Tertullian (A. D. 220) and Augustine (A. D. 325) both mention it.

CIDER COOLER [115]
(Serves 6–8)

Combine in a large bowl or pitcher ½ cup of lemon juice, ½ cup of orange juice, ⅓ cup of grenadine syrup, 1 pint of ginger ale, 1 quart hard cider, and ½ cup of brandy. Mix well; add a large chunk of ice and whirl the ice till mixture is well chilled. Serve in tall glasses with straws.

CIDER CUP I [116]
(Serves 4–6)

Place in a crystal bowl a large piece of ice, and pour over it 1 quart of sweet cider, 1 bottle of soda water, ⅓ cup of sherry wine, ¼ cup of brandy, 2 tablespoons of lemon juice, peel of a quarter of a lemon, cut into thin, narrow strips, sugar to taste. Whirl the piece of ice till the mixture is well-chilled. Discard ice and serve in glasses, each one dusted with a little nutmeg.

CIDER CUP II [117]
(Serves 4–6)

Place in a crystal or silver bowl a large piece of ice, and pour over it ⅓ cup of lemon juice, ½ cup of orange juice, ⅓ cup of grenadine syrup, 1 pint of ginger ale, 1½ pints of hard cider, ⅓ cup of brandy, and a few pieces of cucumber rind. Whirl the piece of ice till mixture is thoroughly chilled. Discard ice and serve in chilled cup glasses, or goblets.

Beneath these stones repose the bones of Theodosius Grimm;
He took his hard cider from year to year, and then his cider took him.
—Old English Epitaph

CIDER CUP III [118]
(Serves 12)

Infuse the peel of 2 and the juice of 4 oranges with ¾ pound of sugar in 1 quart of boiling water for 35–40 minutes; strain into a bowl containing a large piece of ice; when cold, remove any small remaining piece of ice and add a large fresh one, then pour over 1 quart of hard cider, ⅓ cup of maraschino liquor, 1 cup of applejack, and whirl till well chilled. Serve in chilled goblets each containing 1 red maraschino cherry.

CIDER FRAPPE [119]
(Serves 6)

Serve this in orange cups for Halloween, in red apple cups for Noël and New Year's Evening.

To 4 cups of sweet cider, add 1¼ cups each of water and orange juice,

½ cup of lemon juice, 1¼ cup of sugar and freeze to a mush in refrigerator tray. Remove from refrigerator and beat quickly with rotary beater, adding, while beating, ½ cup of applejack. Return to refrigerator tray and again freeze to a mush and serve at once in chilled sherbet glasses.

For children, omit the applejack.

CIDER FRUIT PUNCH Ā LA NORMANDE [120]
(Serves 18–20)

For this cup or punch, have all the ingredients well chilled in advance. Combine 2 quarts of sparkling cider and 1 pint of carbonated water in a large mixing bowl; add a large chunk of ice, and pour over the ice ½ cup of Benedictine and ½ cup of applejack. Whirl the ice chunk till mixture is well-chilled; discard the ice and add 1 dozen thinly sliced orange slices, halved, 1 cup of hulled, washed fresh small strawberries, and ⅓ cup of coarsely chopped red maraschino cherries. Serve in chilled punch glasses.

CIDER AND ORANGE COOLER [121]
(Serves 12)

Fill tall glasses half full of hard cider and add a large scoop of orange ice. Serve at once.

Variations. Substitute lemon, pineapple or any kind of fruit ice for orange ice.

> *What makes the cider blow its cork*
> *With such a merry din?*
> *What makes those little bubbles rise*
> *And dance like harlequin?*
> *It is the fatal apple, boys,*
> *The fruit of human sin.*
>   *—Author unknown*

CIDER WASSAIL [122]
Spiced (Hot or Cold) (Serves 8–10)

Place the following ingredients in a large enameled saucepan: 2 quarts of sweet cider, 2 cups of orange juice, 1 cup of lemon juice, juice from 2 cans of sliced pineapple, ¼-inch stick of cinnamon bark, 1 teaspoon whole cloves, heads removed, and sugar to taste. Bring to a boil; reduce the flame and simmer very gently 12–15 minutes. Strain into a heated punch bowl, and stir in 1 cup of applejack. Serve as hot as possible in heated punch goblets.

For children, omit the applejack. In summer, chill thoroughly before serving.

ENGLISH CIDER CUP [123]
(*Serves 6–8*)

Put a piece of toasted white bread in a large bowl; grate half a small nutmeg over it and lay on it 3 thin slices of lemon rind and 6 lumps of sugar. Pour in ½ generous cup of sherry wine, 1 wine glass of brandy, 2 tablespoons of lemon juice, 1 bottle of well-chilled club soda and a quart of chilled sweet cider. Mix well. Put a large piece of ice in the bowl and whirl it till mixture is chilled and blended. Discard ice and serve immediately in chilled cups.

> *At all your feasts, remember too,*
> *When cups are sparkling to the brim*
> *That there is one who drinks to you,*
> *And oh! as warmly drink to him.*
> —*French Toast*

HOT BUTTERED RUM PUNCH [124]
(*Serves 8–10*)

Heat 2 quarts of hard cider till you see beads over the surface, but do not let it actually boil; remove from the fire; add ½ cup of brown or maple sugar, a dash of salt, and ½ cup of sweet butter. Stir till dissolved and thoroughly blended. Into each punch glass put 2 tablespoons (1 ounce) of good rum; fill with the hot cider mixture and sprinkle with powdered cinnamon. Serve at once.

MULLED CIDER [125]
(*Serves 12*)

Boil 3 quarts of hard cider with 1 teaspoon of whole cloves, heads removed, ⅓ teaspoon of freshly grated nutmeg and ½ scant cup of sugar together for 5 minutes. Strain and serve at once in heated goblets.

For adults, add ½–¾ cup of applejack, and call it Spiced Cider Punch.

PEACH CIDER PUNCH [126]
(*Cold*) (*Serves 8–10*)

Put a dozen ripe peaches, peeled, stoned and sliced, in a punch bowl; sprinkle freely with sugar (the amount depending on taste and sweetness of the fruit) and let stand, covered with a cloth, for 2 hours; then pour on 1 bottle of light red wine, 1 of dry white wine, and add 1 large piece of ice. Whirl till liquid is well-chilled and, just before serving, discard the ice and add 1 quart of sparkling cider. Serve at once in chilled punch glasses. To insure success of this fine punch, all the ingredients should be well chilled.

SPICY CIDER BOWL [127]
(Hot) (Serves 12–15)

Put the following ingredients in a large enameled saucepan: 1 gallon sweet cider, 1½ pounds brown sugar, 6-inch stick of cinnamon bark, 1 blade mace, 1 tablespoon whole cloves, head removed, 1 tablespoon whole spice, ½ teaspoon salt and 2 tablespoons crystallized ginger; bring to a boil, but do not let boil. Lower the flame and let simmer gently for 10 minutes. Strain through fine cheesecloth into a large bowl; stir in 1½ cups grapefruit juice, fresh or canned, but strained, ½ cup strained orange juice and ¼ cup strained lemon juice; both juices heated, but not boiled. Serve steaming hot.

THANKSGIVING CIDER PUNCH [128]
(Cold) (Serves 12–15)

Combine 3 cups of canned or bottled apricot juice, juice of 3 large oranges, and 3 lemons, 1½ quarts of sweet cider, 1 dozen or so green maraschino cherries and 1 dozen red maraschino cherries. Chill thoroughly, and serve in tall glasses over crushed ice with a couple of cherries (red and green) in each glass.

COFFEE [129]

> *Where dwells the wretch, beneath what zone,*
> *To every elegance unknown;*
> *Whose soul ne'er felt the genial fire,*
> *That coffee' subtile fumes inspire.*
> *When thou'rt infus'd with nicest art,*
> *New life to all thy dreams impart,*
> *If Cynthia's hand the task assumes,*
> *Ambrosia yields to thy perfumes,*
> *Thy fragrant scent alone shall gain*
> *—Ode to Coffee—Author unknown.*

There are in the neighborhood of 5,000 brands of coffee on the country's markets, and together they account for sales of more than a billion and a half pounds a year. That figures out to something like 13 pounds for every man, woman and child in the United States, or, roughly, 500 cups. If the decaffeinated coffee ads speak the truth, so much coffee must be turning the United States into a nation of Mr. and Mrs. Coffee Nerves, haggard from sleepless nights, unable to hold their

jobs or their spouses. But the medical investigators are not so pessi-
mistic. They reassure coffee drinkers that if they limit themselves to
moderate amounts (two or three cups a day) most of them need fear
no ill effects.

The amount of caffeine in ordinary coffee (about two grains to a cup)
produces, in the great majority of people, no more than a slight and
rather pleasant stimulation.

A good cup of coffee is sheer black magic. Indeed, I am convinced
that it must have been an early coffee conjurer who introduced the
term "black magic" to an appreciative world. Fragrant, full-flavored,
clear coffee brings a three-fold appeal to the senses—an exciting aroma,
a thrilling taste and an exhilarating effect. It is surprising to note how
much coffee affects us. Most of us receive both an emotional and physical
stimulus from this dark-clear liquid. Full-flavored and pungent, a fine
cup of coffee is one of the spirit-lifting things in this old world. When
we drink it—whether at breakfast or after dinner, we have a feeling
of well-being, of better spirits, sometimes even of gaiety. In some of us,
good coffee produces a mood of restful dignity, in others a gay animation,
in still others a gamut of pleasant moods in between. Yet—unlike many
exciting drinks—it is good for us as well as good to drink, when properly
brewed. Fresh coffee, freshly made, with its mellow flavor and friendly
fragrance, is a wholesome, healthful drink which commands the loyalty
of many when served full strength in the usual way.

In the year 1720, a French naval officer, Monsieur Gabriel Mathieu
de Clieu, sailed for the Caribbean island of Martinique with three small
coffee bushes he had obtained from the Paris Botanical Gardens. The
voyage was a hard one. Supplies ran short and it was necessary for
Monsieur de Clieu to share his water ration with his precious plants in
order to keep them alive. Only one bush survived the voyage. It was
planted in Martinique and began the coffee industry in the New World.

The history of coffee is romantic enough to discourage any attempt
to defile the beverage with adulterants. All the mysticism of the Far
East and Near East is bound up in its oriental fragrance.

Legend has it that an Arabian herdsman in upper Egypt or Abyssinia
(legend is allowed to approximate) discovered that after his goats fed
on the red berries of a certain evergreen shrub, they started to cut
capers. The herdsman complained of this behavior to the abbot of a
nearby monastery. The abbot decided to try the berries himself and
became slightly exhilarated. He ordered that they be boiled and served
to his monks. Thereafter, so the story goes, the monks had no difficulty
in keeping awake during nightly religious services and the fame of the
"wakeful" monastery spread so widely that the magic berry was soon
much in demand.

In the more than 1,000 years of its development, coffee has been the
subject of fierce political opposition as well as of injust taxation. At one
time, in Germany, it was necessary to get a license to roast it. In England,
Charles II tried to suppress coffee houses, prominent in literary, social
and economic activity, as centers of political agitation. In America, the
importance of coffee was attested as early as January 1, 1791. That

New Year's Day, The New York *Packet*, a newspaper, carried the famous ode to coffee seen at the beginning of this section.

Coffee drinking was forbidden in sixteenth-century Constantinople. The ruling dictator believed that coffee stimulated thinking among the common people. The first offense was punished by a beating; the second offense by death.

TO INSURE GOOD COFFEE—A FEW DO'S AND DON'T'S [130]

(1) Be accurate in your measurements of water and dry coffee. Guess at nothing.

(2) Be sure the coffee is correctly ground for your special method of brewing: FINE for DRIP POT; MEDIUM for PERCOLATOR; COARSE for POT; EXTRA FINE for VACUUM-TYPE COFFEE MAKER.

(3) Be sure the coffee maker is clean; scald with boiling water before each using.

(4) Use 2 level tablespoons, or 1 rounded tablespoon of ground coffee for each coffee cup of water. If you like stronger coffee, use more of it—longer brewing will not make it stronger without ruining the flavor.

(5) Coffee loses its flavor when exposed to the air.

(6) If the inside of your coffee pot burns dry, see that it is thoroughly scoured out with steel wool or a stiff brush before the next use. Unless this is done the coffee may have a slightly burned flavor.

(7) Coffee is like conversation. It's good or it isn't; it sparkles or it's flat. Look out! Tried and tested and found to work wonders is the idea of keeping coffee in glass—it comes in glass, too—and storing it in the refrigerator. These two points help immeasurably to retain both flavor and aroma.

(8) For efficiency and best flavor of coffee, the electric percolator should be frequently given a soap and water bath. Fill with hot soapy water with 2 teaspoons of soda added. "Perk" 10 minutes, drain, refill with hot water and boil 5 minutes. NEVER immerse an electric percolator in water or the electric unit will be injured.

(9) Removing grounds from coffee as soon as it is made helps to avoid bitter flavors.

(10) To keep a vacuum coffee maker spotless, so that the brew has a fresh, true flavor, rinse the filter cloths in clear cold water after each use and allow them to soak in cold water until next using. Empty the grounds from the upper bowl as soon as the coffee has returned to the lower section. Rinse bowl in warm water. Wash in clear, fresh suds, rinse thoroughly and dry with a clean towel. Use a flexible brush to cleanse funnel and any sections not easily accessible.

(11) Chicory is the most common adulterant of coffee. One test for detecting chicory in ground coffee is made by placing a good pinch of the material on a piece of white paper. Examine the individual particles with a hand lens, though you can tell the difference between coffee and chicory without this aid. Coffee grounds are usually light brown and granular, while those of chicory, being made from a root, are fibrous and darker in color.

The water tests shows up the difference more distinctly. When half a teaspoon of coffee is placed in a quarter of a glass of water, most of the true coffee will stay on top for a time, but grains of chicory or other fibrous vegetable material quickly become water-logged and sink to the bottom, often coloring the water brown. After allowing the mixture to soak for 10 minutes, drain off the water and spread the grains out on a dish or piece of white paper. If, on prodding with a match stick or tweezers, a granule appears hard and resilient and jumps away, it is probably coffee. However, if it is plastic, almost like gelatine in consistency, it is a foreign substance, probably chicory. Coffee substitutes and coffee blends may contain chicory, soybean, roasted barley, Mexican chickpeas or garbanzos, roasted rye cereal, rolled wheat flour, molasses, or corn meal.

(12) Milk used in coffee as a substitute for cream will taste much richer if it is scalded and poured into the cup while it is still very hot.

POT METHOD [131]

Measure 1 rounded tablespoon of coarsely ground coffee for each cup into scalded pot; add 1 extra measure of coffee. Measure briskly boiling water and pour over coffee. Stir, cover, and let simmer (not boil) 5–6 minutes—2 or 3 minutes longer if coffee is desired stronger. Settle with a dash of cold water and serve at once.

DRIP POT METHOD [132]

Measure 1 rounded tablespoon of finely ground coffee for each cup into dripper. If filter paper is required, measure coffee on top of filter paper. Insert water spreader. Measure briskly boiling water and pour into dripper. Cover and allow coffee to drip into pot. Remove dripper as soon as water has filtered through coffee. Cover pot and serve.

PERCOLATOR METHOD [133]

Measure water into freshly scalded percolator. Use cold water for percolator without valve; use boiling water for percolator with valve.

Measure into basket, 1 rounded tablespoon of medium ground coffee for each cup, place in percolator, insert water spreader, and cover. Percolate 6–9 minutes (less if desired weaker). Serve at once. Long percolating will spoil the flavor.

Catherine the Great, Empress of Russia, drank five big cups of coffee for breakfast daily. To make them, the palace chef used an entire pound of coffee.

VACUUM METHOD [134]

Measure water into bottom section. Put top section in place. Measure 1 rounded tablespoon extra finely ground coffee for each cup into upper section, place on stove. When all but thin layer of water has been forced into upper section, turn off heat or remove from stove. Stir just once. As soon as coffee has filtered back into bottom section, remove top. Serve at once while still piping hot.

> " . . . Black as the devil;
>   Hot as hell;
> Pure as an angel!"—
>   Note these well.
> Then—"Sweet as love!"
>   Writes Talleyrand.
>   I've tried it and
>   My coffee's grand!

ARABIAN MOCHA [135]
(Serves 2)

Place 4 tablespoons of powdered, burnt mocha coffee (commercial) in a small saucepan and pour over it 2 cups of briskly boiling water. Cover and let simmer (not boil) 4–5 minutes, covered. Lift up the cover, add 1 tiny pinch of saffron and 3 whole cloves; let stand 2 minutes and pour in a copper jug or kettle. Sweeten to taste after pouring into tiny fancy cups.

ARCTIC COOLER [136]
(Serves 4)

Prepare double-strength coffee and chill quickly. To each 4 cups of coffee, add 6 tablespoons of powdered sugar and 2½ teaspoons of vanilla extract. Stir to dissolve. Pour into chilled glasses and fill up with a couple of coffee ice cubes. Top each glass with whipped cream.

ARMENIAN COFFEE   [137]
(*Serves 12*)

This brew requires a special pot, a racquie, carried by Armenian or Syrian stores. These pots are of copper, nickel-lined, urn-shaped, with a long handle at the side.

Fill the racquie with cold water to within 2 inches of the top. Measure in 6 teaspoons of powdered sugar for the 12 cups. Place the sweetened water over a chafing dish flame, electric table stove, or "canned heat" and bring to a brisk boil. Now measure in 1 teaspoon of powdered coffee for each cup and add 1 or 2 cardamom seeds, slightly cracked. Let the brew come to a froth; at once lift the coffee pot—the racquie—from the heat, tap the pot once—twice, to settle the brew, then return to the flame instantly. Again the brew bubbles, and again you remove it from the flame. Tap, and repeat the above procedure, once or even twice again. Now dip off the "skim" from the pot and divide among the 12 cups. Each cup must have its portion of the brown froth. Into the pot shake a drop or two of orange flower water, splash in cold water— about 1 teaspoon—to compel the unruly grounds to settle, and pour.

Ladies in the time of Louis XIV of France were wary of drinking too much of the new beverages coffee and chocolate, believing that over-indulgence would darken the skin.

BRAZILIAN MOCHA I   [138]
(*Serves 4*)

Place 2 squares (2 ounces) of unsweetened chocolate, cut into small pieces or scraped, and 1 cup of strong coffee in top of double boiler over direct heat. Stir until chocolate is blended and thoroughly melted, then stir in a few grains of salt and 3 tablespoons of sugar. Boil 4 or 5 minutes, stirring constantly. Place over hot water; gradually stir in 3 cups of scalded milk, stirring well, and when near the boiling point, beat with rotary beater until light and frothy. Serve hot in cups, topped with whipped cream. Should you wish a richer mocha, use undiluted evaporated milk or thin cream instead of plain milk.

BRAZILIAN MOCHA II   [139]
(*Serves 6*)

Combine 5 tablespoons of cocoa, a generous pinch of salt and 5 tablespoons of sugar with ½ cup of cold water and stir till smooth, then cook over direct low flame for 2 or 3 minutes, stirring frequently. Gradually add 1 cup of boiling water, alternately with 1½ cups of strong hot coffee, mixed with 1½ cups of undiluted evaporated milk. Bring to a boil; remove from the fire and beat with rotary beater until slightly frothy. Serve in heated cups, topped, or not, with whipped cream.

CAFÉ BRÛLOT CREOLE MANNER [140]
(Serves 6)

The Café Brûlot ceremony can be made as fascinating to your guests as an exhibition of black magic. But as any magician, you must perform the tricks with a deft, sure grace. Perform your coffee trick on a fireside table with tray and brûlot-bowl at hand. These bowls, a sheer luxury, resemble a baptismal font in silver or in copper; an alcohol flame burns below. Lacking a real brûlot bowl, the chafing dish will do a brûlot beautifully.

Place in a metal bowl the outer rind of ½ orange cut into 5 or 6 pieces, and the thin peel of a quarter lemon. Add 2 sticks of broken cinnamon bark, 10 whole cloves, heads removed, 8 lumps of sugar and 2 demi-tasses of Cognac. Light the burner under the bowl or chafing dish, stir constantly with a punch ladle or gravy ladle, till the contents are warm, then ignite. A spectral flame in the darkened room ensues. Burn about a long minute, then slowly pour over the blaze 5 demi-tasses of freshly made double-strength black coffee. Ladle out at once into demi-tasse cups.

CAFÉ DIABOLIQUE CREOLE MANNER [141]
Deviled Coffee (Serves 6)

Café Diabolique, also called Café Diable, is a Creole ceremonial brew slightly more elaborate than the brûlot but similar in taste.

Have ready 1 broken stick cinnamon bark, 1 tablespoon whole cloves, heads removed, 2 teaspoons coriander seeds, 1 tablespoon whole roasted coffee beans, grated rind 1 orange, and 12 lumps of sugar. Standing at hand are the cognac bottle and enough freshly made after-dinner coffee for 6 persons. Now the host is ready for the dinner's epilogue. It's a better show if you lower the lights or stage the act by candle power. Light the flame beneath the chafing dish and let the bowl warm slightly before dropping in cinnamon stick, headless cloves, coffee beans, coriander, sugar and orange rind. Let all warm together cosily a minute or so, then stir in ⅓ cup cognac, and get the cognac hot, then touch it with a match. The ice-blue flames have greedy little tongues that lick around the bowl while the guests admire. Ladle the liquid fire gently to mix well, then add 1 quart of hot, strong coffee. Wait! it's not ready yet. Next pour a little brandy into the coffee ladle, let it burn a moment, then dip this up and down in the coffee till the flames are extinguished. Add more brandy to the ladle and repeat the performance till another

⅓ cup of cognac has been added and well blended through the deviled brew. Serve hot in demi-tasse cups, if you don't possess the very sophisticated diable (devil) cups designed for the purpose.

CAFÉ EGGNOG SOUTHERN MANNER [142]
(*Serves 2*)

To 2 well-beaten egg yolks, add 2 tablespoons of powdered sugar, the more the better, then beat in brandy or whisky, so strong that it not only cooks these eggs but is plainly discernible when the stiffly beaten whites (2) are added. Now, beat together, then add enough pure, sweet cream to fill 2 good-sized tumblers. Dust a little freshly grated nutmeg on top.

CAFÉ ÉPICÉ [143]
(*Serves 8*)

Place 3 two-inch sticks of cinnamon bark and 12 whole cloves, heads removed, in the bowl of a vacuum coffee maker, in the cold water of a percolator, or in the pot of a drip maker. Make 1 quart of coffee double strength—2 heaping tablespoons of coffee to each cup of water. Serve in heated demi-tasse cups either black or with cream plain or whipped.

Eighteenth-century settlers in Maine flavored their crude coffee with powdered mustard. Later the "mustarded coffee" was used to spice meat gravy.

CAFÉ ESSENCE [144]
Essence of Coffee (Makes about 2 quarts)

Melt 1 cup of granulated sugar in a heavy saucepan; stir constantly till it becomes a light brown; then add 2½ quarts of hot water; stir until mixture boils; then stir in 1½ pounds of medium-ground coffee. Let boil 2 minutes; strain through a flannel cloth into clean glass jars; cover tightly, and store in refrigerator till wanted. Two tablespoons of the essence is sufficient for a cup of coffee. For a cold drink, use cold milk; for a hot drink, add the coffee essence to the scalded milk and sweeten to taste.

CAFÉ EXPRESSO [145]
(*Serves 6*)

This Italian coffee specialty is served only in well-equipped restaurants, as the steam-pressure apparatus for its production costs a thousand dollars. But here is a recipe for a good imitation Coffee Expresso to make at home:

Use that practically charred pulverized coffee roasted black as midnight (22% roast) preferred by Italians and French. The novice had better start with ⅓ black roast blended with ⅔ American roast until accustomed to the flavor of the black roast. Take ⅓ cup of the coffee and prepare by the usual drip method. Beat 1 egg white till foamy, then beat in 2 tablespoons of powdered sugar. Whip ½ cup of sweet, heavy cream lightly but not stiff. Fold sweetened egg white and cream together and use this as a fluffy night cap to peak the surface of the brew, which is served in demi-tasse cups. Before pouring the coffee, drop a lump of sugar into each cup.

CAFÉ FLAMAND [146]
Old-Fashioned Belgian Coffee

Use 1 heaping tablespoon of strong, fragrant coffee for each cup and 2 additional for the pot (pot method). Beat 1 egg lightly, add to the coffee grounds, fill the pot ¾ full with briskly boiling water, and let boil up; stir down, then boil for 5 minutes. Fill the pot to the top with boiling water, keep hot for 10 minutes to brew, to mellow. Just before serving in heated cups, beat 2 egg whites stiff, slowly add 2 cups of thick sweet cream, sweeten to taste. Put a quantity of this in each cup and add the hot coffee. Serve as hot as possible.

CAFÉ GLORIA [147]
Also known as Café Royal

This French after-dinner coffee is very popular and easy to prepare. Drop a lump of sugar into each little after-dinner coffee cup, then fill but half way with double-strength coffee. Fill up with good cognac poured in very slowly and carefully. Touch it with a lighted match and let it burn a few seconds, never too long or the flame destroys all the alcohol and love's labor is lost. Stir and drink it as hot as the mouth will stand without making faces!

CAFÉ AU LAIT [148]
Also known as Café Viennois

For each serving, use 1½ heaping tablespoons of ground coffee to each cup (½ pint) water. Make by any method desired. Have ready a pot of hot, rich milk, or equal parts of milk and cream. When serving, pour milk and coffee together into hot coffee cup in equal amounts or to taste.

CAFÉ MAZAGRAN [149]

Consists of double-strength black coffee mixed with equal parts of red wine, and is always served very hot, sweetened to taste.

In the seventeenth century many southern Europeans believed that a dark complexion was a sign of manliness and bathed their faces in black coffee twice a day, hoping to achieve the desired results. Although ignorant of antiseptics as such, Arabian physicians in A. D. 1200 used black coffee to wash their patients' wounds.

CAFÉ MEXICAIN [150]
Mexican Coffee (Serves 6)

Ingredients are 6 cups of strong black coffee as hot as possible, ½ cup of whipped cream, ⅛ generous teaspoon each of ground cinnamon and nutmeg. Top each cup of coffee with a generous tablespoonful of whipped cream into which has been folded the mixed cinnamon and nutmeg. Sweeten or not, as preferred.

CAFÉ SYRIEN [151]
Syrian Coffee

This consists of demi-tasse, or after-dinner coffee, very strong and black, served with 2 or 3 cracked cardamom seeds in each cup and sweetened to taste.

CAFÉ TURQUE [152]
Turkish Coffee (Serves 2)

This can be made best with a lidless Turkish copper coffeepot. Lacking this, proceed as follows: Place 4 generous tablespoons of pulverized (powdered) coffee, and 4 tablespoons of sugar in a coffeepot, stir in 2 cups of cold water. Heat and stir till mixture comes to a brisk boil and is very frothy. Remove from the fire and let the froth subside; replace pot (a pan may be used, too) on a very hot flame. Repeat the process three times. Before serving, settle by adding a little cold water. If desired, add a few drops of rosewater to each cup.

COFFEE FLOAT [153]
(Serves 6–8)

This is a combination of frozen coffee custard or ice cream. Here's how:

In a double boiler, scald ¼ cup of ground coffee with 1½ cups of rich milk. Keep at scalding point 5 minutes, then strain. Mix thoroughly ⅔ cup of sugar with 2 tablespoons of flour, ½ cup of milk, 2 well-beaten egg yolks and a dash of salt, add to milk and cook, stirring constantly until thickened. Strain through a fine sieve, cool, then fold in 2 egg whites stiffly beaten, together with 1 cup of heavy, sweet cream, whipped stiff with a few grains of salt. Add 2 or 3 drops of oil of cloves, turn into refrigerator tray and freeze till firm. Serve in tall glasses, putting a large spoonful of the mixture into each glass and, filling up with regular strength chilled black coffee or double-strength hot coffee. Stir till mixture is partly blended, then top with an additional spoon of the frozen custard and serve at once.

In the seventeenth century most Italian apothecaries sold a stomach medicine consisting of brewed coffee diluted with sugar syrup.

COFFEE SHAKE [154]
(*Serves 2*)

Pour freshly made, strong coffee over cracked ice or ice cubes in shaker; add 2 or 3 tablespoons of sugar (more or less, according to sweetness desired), ½ cup of heavy cream, a few grains of salt and a few drops of vanilla extract, and shake vigorously until foamy. Strain into chilled tall glasses and top with whipped cream, the cream dusted with a little nutmeg or cinnamon.

FROSTED COFFEE [155]
(*Serves 6*)

Pour 3½ cups of extra strong black coffee over cracked ice in a tall pitcher and stir thoroughly till well chilled. Pour half of the coffee into a shaker, add 4 or 5 heaping tablespoons of vanilla ice cream and shake till ice cream is dissolved. Top with a float of ice cream. Repeat process with remaining coffee.

ICED COFFEE [156]

Make double-strength black coffee infusion, allowing 1½–1¾ tablespoons of finely ground coffee to each cup of water, and make by any preferred method. Have coffee clear and well settled, then pour, hot, over ice cubes or crushed ice. Add a large spoonful of whipped cream just before serving. Sweeten to taste while coffee is still hot.

Before 1850, hotels west of Chicago served no coffee but furnished pot, hot water and stove for guests who brought their own coffee beans along with their luggage.

IMPERIAL COFFEE CREAM   [157]
(*Serves 6*)

Add 4 one-inch sticks of cinnamon bark to 6 cups of strong hot coffee, cover and let stand 1 hour. Remove cinnamon sticks; stir in ¼–⅓ cup of sugar (more or less according to taste), and ¾ cup of heavy sweet cream. Chill in refrigerator. When thoroughly chilled, pour preparation into 6 chilled tall glasses and fill with shaved ice. Top each glass with a tuft of whipped cream sweetened to taste and flavored with vanilla extract. Serve immediately with straws.

LOUISIANA PETIT BRÛLOT   [158]

Select thin-skinned oranges, one for each guest. Cut round the oranges, then with a spoon-handle loosen the peel from the oranges almost to the end and turn it inside out, making a cup. Now cut the orange from the cup, leaving half of the fruit, with the cup on top. Then place the orange in a plate or saucer. Into the cup put 1 whole clove, a tiny bit of bay leaf, a tiny bit of cinnamon bark and 1 lump of sugar, pouring over all 2 tablespoons of the best cognac. The oranges are now brought to the table, the brandy is lighted, the lights are extinguished, and the spirit is left burning away. To serve, the contents are poured into demi-tasse coffee cups not quite filled. The burning of the cognac in the orange peels gives a most delicious flavor.

> *Tom runs from his wife to get rid of his trouble—*
> *He drinks, and he drinks, till he sees all things double;*
> *But when he has ceased wine and brandy to mingle,*
> *Oh! what would he give to see himself single!*
> *   —From an Old Joke Booklet*

MILK   [159]

Take it any way you like it—on breakfast cereal, as a chocolate malted at the noon lunch, or as ice cream or other chilled or frozen desserts at dinner—and you find milk is an economical and nourishing food. All nutrition experts agree that milk in some form must be included in every diet, every day. How much milk, depends partly on the age of the person, on the make-up of the other dishes in the diet, and on the season; but between three and five quarts per person (adult) per week is the accepted average.

Milk owes its importance in the diet to the fine, easy digestibility of its proteins, to the completeness of its assortment of mineral elements, and to the excellent proportions in which they occur; to the high content of its calcium (food lime), to the liberal amounts of vitamins A and B; and to the presence of vitamin D in association with phosphorus as is most favorable to the calcification of bones and teeth. In short, milk is the ideal growth and stabilizer food.

And when we ask the question as to how much milk should be allowed per person, we must include milk in all its forms, not merely straight or fresh milk. "Milk" in this sense includes buttermilk, cheese, sour or clabbered milk, cottage or soft freshly-made cheeses, ice cream, and every type of milk as offered to the cook: whole fresh milk, dry milk, evaporated milk, and sweetened condensed milk as well as milk taken at the soda fountain, in the lunchroom, at the beach, in an ice cream cone, or from a glass at the home table, or eaten in solid form in a delicious dessert, custard, soufflé, floating island, cream dessert, or dish featuring a milk or cream gravy.

Sometimes nationality and race make a difference in milk habits. Sometimes the need of counting pennies in the food budget affects the amount of milk consumed in certain families. However, milk is always an inexpensive food, when its cost and its value to the diet are taken into account. The reason for a hold-back on milk consumption is not always to be found in a low income, but because of a failure on the part of the homemaker, or mother or cook, to understand the true value of milk as a staple or essential food.

Milk is, first of all, a protein or "meat food." That is why a generous amount of milk should be used in the summer and in all hot weather, when many interesting milk dishes may well replace some of the hot and more expensive dishes.

DIFFERENT KINDS OF MILK [160]

While most cooks are familiar with the following points on milk, it may be well to talk briefly about the different kinds of milk.

Whole Fresh Milk. One of the best sources of vitamin A; a good source of vitamin B; builds new muscle tissue just as meat does; contains abundant calcium and phosphorus; its fat is easily digested.

Evaporated Milk. Exactly the same as fresh whole milk, reduced to half the water content of fresh milk.

Condensed Milk. Identical with fresh whole milk, with the additional high sugar content of the "sweetened" factor.

Skim Milk. Just as valuable as whole fresh milk for its protein, its calcium and its vitamin B; but doesn't supply the same abundance of vitamin A; less fats.

Buttermilk. Has the same food value as skim milk. Its casein (solids) is easily digested because it is clotted or soured before entering the stomach.

Cottage Cheese. Valuable as a meat equivalent or protein food.

Cheese. Rich in both protein and fat. Also high in calcium, phosphorus and vitamin A.

Cream. Cream (including butter and ice cream and sour cream) has vitamins A and D, plus the high energy value of the fat it contains.

Pasteurized Milk. Milk which has been heated for 30 minutes at 145° F. to destroy any harmful bacteria.

Irradiated Milk. Milk which has been treated by means of the ultra-violet rays of sunshine lamps so as to increase or give extra vitamin D.

Certified Milk. Milk which must meet very exacting standards as to cleanliness, sanitation, etc., and counts as to chemical analysis. Three quarts of milk are required to give the food total of 1 pound of butter; but one pound of butter is equal to 5 quarts of milk in energy value alone.

Yoghurt. See No. 162.

Goat's Milk. This requires a lengthy explanation. See No. 163.

Dry Milk. This milk provides all the calcium, phosphorus, protein and milk sugar of fluid milk at a cost of about 5–6 cents a quart when liquefied. It is made from fresh fluid milk with only the water, fat and vitamin A removed. By restoring the water, you have a product which can be used in all kinds of cooking and baking and in beverages, just as you would use fluid milk. Extra tablespoons of skim milk added in dry form to any cooked dish can be counted on to improve flavor and texture in addition to stepping up nutritive values.

MILK IS NOT FATTENING [161]

Many cooks, homemakers and hostesses who would gladly enjoy milk dishes and beverages refrain from doing so because they think that milk is fattening. True, we always find milk used generously in the diet of those who are underweight or trying to recover from illness. But that doesn't mean that milk *in itself* is fattening. The question is: What else does the person eat?

The average daily calorie intake of a normal person is between 2500 and 3000 calories or food units. Even in the most severe diet, one should seldom go below 1800 or 1500 calories. Now it is well to recall that one glass of whole fresh milk contains 170 calories. Thus, if the person dieting takes one glass of milk at each of the two main meals, he is using 340 calories of his total daily supply, which is one-fifth of his entire supply allowed for the whole day. If kept at this figure—two glasses of milk per day, and the other foods balanced accordingly—milk will not be fattening. Also, milk seems to be one of those balancing foods which tend to keep nerves relaxed and less irritated—another special advantage to dieters.

YOGHURT [162]

It is a long story from the discovery of the original culture of yoghurt in the VIIth century in Southern Bulgaria to the present day.

Professor Elya Metchnikoff, eminent Russian bacteriologist, isolated the germ and proved it an original culture. He was searching for years for the reasons of early senility in people and found that in the Rodope Mountains of Southern Bulgaria the greatest number of aged people in proportion to population lived, some attaining the age of 150 years and over, and remaining unusually healthy and active. Practically all of them made their main diet the cultured milk, fermented with "bisselo mleko"—the Bulgarian name for the pure culture.

Unlike other milk ferments, yoghurt culture must be kept scientifically pure to remain active; the Bulgarians knew that centuries ago, and have kept the strain pure and virulent, using it as needed in their daily preparation of the Bulgarian Health Drink, and according to the strict formula, the secret of the Bulgarians for centuries.

Yoghurt is a tasty, refreshing milk food of custard consistency, made from fresh, pasteurized whole milk and selected pure lactic cultures; these cultures and the lactic acid they produce are, when taken regularly and in sufficient quantities, of recognized value in helping to maintain or restore normal intestinal conditions. Yoghurt is not just a clabber and is entirely different from sour cream or buttermilk. It contains all the vitamins, minerals and nutritive values of fresh, whole, pasteurized milk but is more easily digested even by many who are allergic to milk, and it is as good for children as for adults.

There is only one way in which yoghurt shouldn't be used. It should *never* be combined with anything hot and should *never* be heated because then it loses its efficacy.

One bottle of milk can endanger the earth! The bacteria in a bottle of milk reproduce so rapidly that if none died, in 24 hours they would grow into a mass the size of the earth.

GOAT'S MILK [163]

For infant or invalid feeding, the milk from a good, healthy milk-type of goat has been found exceedingly useful. Several people have told this writer goat's milk helped them to overcome stomach ulcers. Families with small children have found goat's milk very nourishing and, with infants it seems to take the place of mother's milk.

All told, there are in the United States nearly 5,000,000 goats, with about 150,000 of them used for milk production and the great bulk for the production of mohair. The most common breeds of milk goats in this country are the Toggenburg, the Saanen, the Nubian and the American. Goat farms in the United States are certified, and the milk is handled under the same specifications as those which obtain for certified cow's milk.

There is very little difference in the inorganic constituents of cow's and goat's milk. Goat's milk, however, is higher in vitamin B, as well as in albumen, while the butter, although as white as the milk, is as high in vitamin A as the yellow butter from Holstein milk. In goat's milk, there is a softer curd and less fat.

GOAT'S MILK WITH VICHY WATER [164]

Drunk half and half with Vichy water goat's milk is an old French cure after too much wining and dining. Have you ever tried it in coffee, in chocolate, with tomato, carrot, spinach or cabbage juice? For a nightcap, try tossing it down slugged with rum, brandy, applejack, etc.

In many European countries, baby goat (*cordero*) is roasted in exactly the same manner as we roast a young piglet or a baby lamb, and is usually served with a wine sauce highly flavored with spices and sage.

So that the quality of their products would never lessen, fifteenth-century Persian merchants who sold goat meat and goat milk were not permitted to handle anything else under threat of severe prison terms, sometimes for life, and a heavy fine of money.

Milk is everybody's food, not just for children. Milk contains 34 of the 36 food-elements needed every day by everybody to maintain health and fitness.

MILK FACTS   [165]

Whey. Whey is obtained from milk after the fat and protein have been removed. It contains milk, sugar, and some minerals. At one time its use was as popular as soda water is today. It is a valuable drink for invalids.

Milk in Coffee, Tea, etc. Milk impedes the effect of caffein, according to medical authorities, whose findings confirm the popular serving of half milk and half coffee, as in the French Café au Lait (Coffee with Milk).

Calcium. This essential element is present in milk in much larger quantity than in any other food. For example, a pint of milk daily will supply almost the entire calcium requirement of the average adult, but it takes nearly 20 servings of common vegetables and fruits to satisfy the daily calcium need.

Causes of Souring. Certainly, milk may sour during a thunderstorm but not because of the meteorological disturbance. The souring is caused by the multiplication of bacteria in inadequately refrigerated milk in hot weather. Keep milk cold, and there's no need to worry about thunderstorms.

Refrigeration. Coldest spot of the refrigerator should be dedicated to dairy products and meat. Both demand a temperature of 45° F., or below, especially if they are to be kept more than 24 hours.

Cooking with Milk. Cooking cereals in milk or equal parts of water and milk increases the milk consumption. This is especially advised for those underweight people or for children who balk at drinking milk.

Souring. Milk going sour is no calamity. It may be a blessing in disguise. It may not serve the purpose for which it was purchased, but it should never go down the sink. It can form the basis of delicious, tasty foods which are made even more delicate by the addition of spices and herbs.

Constipation. Those who find milk constipating should try boiled milk. Or they may dilute their milk with carbonated water. This combination makes a most palatable beverage.

Stale Milk. This is worse—far worse—than sour milk. Sour milk and sour cream are valuable commodities. Stale milk will upset the stomach—and certainly any recipe.

Fallacies. Some people consider it dangerous to eat ice cream and milk at the same meal; others believe that milk and fish don't agree. These are only two of many persistent fallacies regarding food. Superstitions die hard, though, and recent researches indicate that even the well educated are guided by fallacies that food experts long ago consigned to limbo. Fish baked in milk is highly prized by gourmets and epicures.

To Sour Milk or Cream. Remove chill from milk or cream by keeping at room temperature 15–20 minutes; add 1½ tablespoons of lemon juice or vinegar for each cup of milk or cream; let stand 20–25 minutes before using.

Emergency Milk. Use extended evaporated milk for cooking. It costs less than fresh milk. When extended equally with water, it has the same food values as a like quantity of fresh milk.

To Prevent Curdling. Milk, even fresh milk, curdles when cooked, for a various number of reasons; sometimes salt will do it, sometimes heat; sometimes the natural acids present in vegetables will cause the curdling to take place. This curdling is most easily prevented by using some form of thickener. Since skim milk curdles more rapidly than whole milk made thicker and heavier by the presence of fat in the form of cream, the easiest means of preventing curdling is to mix the milk with a small amount of heavy cream (½ cup cream to each pint of milk), or to blend ½ cup evaporated milk into 1 pint of fresh milk, and use this mixture in cooking.

In making cream of tomato soup, it is important to add the tomato to the milk; but if half cream is used, or if the milk is slightly thickened, the danger of curdling is definitely lessened.

Bread crumbs are a good milk thickener and that is why so many casserole dishes cooked with milk call for "bread crumbs sprinkled between the layers."

Drinking Milk. If milk is *drunk quickly*, it is curdled into one large mass, forming a particularly tough curd. The stomach digestive juices have a harder time digesting such a curd than if it were divided into many small portions.

Scalding Milk for Baby's Formula. Stir the milk while it is heating. If not stirred, a coating of milk forms on the bottom and sides of the saucepan and this coating contains part of the precious calcium.

Getting More Cream. You can get more cream from your milk by heating it to lukewarm, then chilling it suddenly. More cream will come to the surface.

Fooling Children. Add berry juices to color milk if children will not drink it without. Raspberry or grape juice may be added to give color.

Digestibility of Milk. Some persons believe they digest milk better if they stir a tablespoon or so of lime water into each glassful just before drinking it. *To make lime water,* put a lump of unslaked (live) lime the size of a walnut, into a quart of water in a crock. Let it stand a few hours; pour off the clear upper water—*that* is lime water.

To Prevent Souring. Cold weather keeps milk from souring on porches or in apartment entry ways . . . but it's not just the souring that you want to prevent. One hour in the sun, even in winter, can destroy 40% of the riboflavin . . . that's one of the B complex group of vitamins. Ask your milkman to leave your milk in the shade.

Home Pasteurization. Health authorities are constantly reminding us of the importance of pasteurizing all milk, especially if we are to drink the milk. It is a little trouble but less than nursing a sick child or adult. Pasteurized milk must still be kept clean and cool and used while fresh and good.

Heat the milk in a double boiler to about 145° F., and then allow it to stand covered for 30 minutes, during which time the temperature should be kept between 142–145° F. It is then cooled as quickly as possible. This method requires a thermometer.

Another procedure which assures safe milk is to heat it to the boiling point and then cool immediately. To some persons, this milk has a cooked flavor, but it is absolutely safe.

Buttermilk. This may be substituted for sour milk in any recipe calling for sour milk. Use in equal amounts.

Whipping Evaporated Milk. All contentions to the contrary notwithstanding, evaporated milk will whip. Pour the contents of the can into the freezing tray of refrigerator turned as low as possible, and leave for about 10 minutes or until particles of ice begin to form about the edges. Remove and whip briskly with a chilled rotary beater and all will be well for your whipped cream. This is the quickest way. Another way is as follows:

Soften 1 teaspoon of unflavored gelatine in 2 tablespoons of cold water. Dissolve over hot water. Have milk thoroughly chilled; add dissolved gelatine and whip until stiff.

Another way is to add 1 level teaspoon of any of 4 vegetable gums— karaya, gum acacia, gum tragacanth or locust bean gum—to 1 cup of cold, light cream or evaporated milk, to make it whip.

One ounce of any of the above gums, which are easily obtained in drug stores, will do 8 batches of cream. Pure food products, the gums act as water-absorbent and emulsifying agents. To use, mix the gum with 2 tablespoons of sugar, add slowly to cold cream or evaporated milk and whip at once with rotary beater. It should take only 2 or 3 minutes to thicken.

Baking Soda. This is essential in any recipe calling for sour milk, sour cream or buttermilk. Add ½ teaspoon of baking soda for each cup of sour milk and deduct 2 teaspoons of baking powder, if this is indicated in the recipe. But always sift the soda with the dry ingredients.

Sweetness of Cream. When the sweetness of cream is a bit doubtful and there is no more at hand, and it must be used, add a pinch of baking soda to it. It will prevent curdling even in hot coffee and therefore save you embarrassment.

Sour Milk in Baking. Sour cream is not so acid as sour milk and, when making pastry, breads, muffins or biscuits, if you use ⅛ teaspoon of soda with the usual amount of baking powder and reduce the shortening one-fifth, you will get good results. If you are making sour milk or buttermilk replace sweet milk, allow ½ teaspoon of soda to each cup of milk. A little baking powder with any recipe using sour milk and soda is a great improvement. This is also true when using molasses, which contains a natural acid with which soda is a necessary ingredient. Honey also needs a very small amount of soda, and so do corn syrup, maple syrup, and treacle.

TEA [166]

" . . . I did send for a cup of tea (a China drink) of which I had never drank before . . . "writes Samuel Pepys in his diary in the year 1660. At this period it is recorded that the best quality "Tcha, Tay, alias Tee"—tea for you—sold for four guineas a pound. We find this novel beverage advertised on a handbill in almost a modern way. ". . . Tea removeth lassitude, vanquisheth heavy dreams, easeth the frame and lassitude and strengtheneth the memory. It is of great avail to men and women of corpulent bodies and to such as eat much flesh . . . "writes Brillat-Savarin in his *Handbook of Gastronomy*.

The English taste for tea naturally came to America with the ever-increasing number of colonists. It might have remained our national beverage except for the tax which resulted in the famous Boston Tea Party and was one of the causes of the American Revolution.

The early history of tea is shrouded in antiquity. The precise date and place of origin is not known. While the earliest authentic written references to the subject are fairly easily established, it is equally certain that the knowledge of tea antedates these references. It is generally accepted that the use of tea as a beverage had its genesis in China. There is considerable doubt among authorities, however, that its botanical history began there. Some researches claim that the tea plant was imported into China from India and that its early growth in China was slowed by the transplanting of the tree to unfavorable fields.

The earliest written records, both trustworthy and otherwise, are Chinese. The Chinese have ascribed the vague origin of the plant to the time of a legendary emperor, Shen Nung, the "Divine Healer," who is said to have lived about 2737 B. C. Support for this belief is claimed in a reference to the subject in Shen Nung's book, *Pen Ts'ao*. This legend is effectively disposed of, however, by the fact that Shen Nung's book actually was not written until the Neo-Han dynasty, in A. D. 25–221, thirty-four hundred years later.

A more widely circulated report ascribes the first reference to tea to the Book of Odes, edited by Confucius about 550 B. C. Orientalists are agreed now that the character *t'u*, which is said to mean tea, was written to describe a "sow thistle" and has nothing to do with the subject of tea.

The earliest credible written mention of the subject, which is accepted by authorities, occurs in A. D. 317 in a letter from Liu Kun, a general of the Chin dynasty, to his nephew Liu Yen, the governor of Yenchow in the province of Shantung, in which the general said he felt aged and depressed and wanted some real *t'u*.

One of the most intriguing legends about the origin of tea is contained in Japanese mythology. It is related the Bodhidharma, a Buddhist saint in China, fell asleep one day after having taken a vow of perpetual wakefulness. When he awoke he was so abashed by his sin that forthwith he cut off his eyelids and cast them on the ground, where they took root and grew up as tea plants.

One point upon which science is agreed, however, is that tea had its genesis in the monsoon district of Southeastern Asia. Specimens of the original jungle, or wild, tea plant are still to be found in the forests of the Shan states of Northern Siam (where this writer collected the above documentation), Eastern Burma, Yunnan, Upper Indo-China and British India.

" . . . Be kind and courteous to all, even the stranger from afar. If he say to thee that he thirsteth, give unto him a cup of hot tea, and ask for no payment thereof." So sang the great Chinese poet Lu-wuh eleven centuries ago. (Some attribute this to Confucius.)

The tea plant belongs to the camellia family of vegetation. There are several varieties of plants, principal among them being the Assam and the China. Historically, tea has played an important part in advancing social graces. In 1664, Queen Catherine of England, wife of Charles II, received a present of tea from the English East India Company. She liked it so well she introduced it into society, and it became the fashionable drink.

In Tibet, just across the mountain border of India, the favorite tea concoction is hot, buttered tea, made by boiling tea leaves with rancid butter. The Persian prefers his half and half, which is a glass of tea half filled with sugar and half with tea. The English never deviate from cream and sugar in their tea. In Japan, tea-drinking is always a ceremonial. Each person sits on the floor in the small room reached through the garden, and the bowl of tea is drained in three and a half sips, the last sip being inhaled loudly. And while they sip, the tea-drinkers think upon the beautiful in everyday living. The Russians are also lovers of tea. They add lemon to it and sweeten it with jelly and, on occasions, a drop . . . or two of vodka.

The Chinese have a saying that only water which is aërated should be used in tea-making. That is why water which has been boiled a long time will not make tea of a fine flavor. So the first law of tea-making, according to the Chinese, is freshly boiling water.

The second law of the brewing is to warm the teapot with scalding water. The third is a level teaspoon of tea for each teacup and one for the pot. The fourth is to pour the boiling water on the tea leaves, and replace the teapot cover, and the fifth is to brew the tea three to five minutes—*no more*. To paraphrase Kipling:

> *Now these are the law of the brewing*
> *And many and mighty are they*
> *But the rim and the lid of the law*
> *And the handle and spout is—OBEY!*
> *And you'll have a cup that cheers!*

AROMATIC TEA, RUSSIAN MANNER [167]

Scald the teapot with rapidly boiling water. Put 1 rounded teaspoon of your favorite blend of tea in the pot for each cup desired, plus 1 for the pot for good measure. Measure freshly drawn cold water and bring it to a bubbling boil before pouring it on the tea leaves. Steep the tea, covered, 3–5 minutes, add 1 bay leaf, 1 whole clove and a few grains of thyme leaves, and immediately strain into a clean, heated teapot. Serve at once, sweetening it with a teaspoon (more or less) of currant jelly.

Practically all teas will "cream down" or cloud when the infusion is chilled. This doesn't mean, however, that the tea is inferior. Tea experts prize very highly teas that "cream down," since it is often indicative of quality, especially body. The chemical reason for this cloudiness or "creaming down," lies in the precipitation of the caffein and tannin in the tea in the form of caffein tannate. This caffein tannate content is the element which makes tea vitalizing and cooling. It varies in different blends of tea but the average has been found to be 1 part caffein to 3 parts tannin. When tea that has been brewed in boiling water is chilled, the tannin in the caffein tannate content turns cloudy. This has nothing to do with the taste or refreshing quality of the tea but does detract from its clear, sparkling appearance. There are ways to avoid this. One is to select a brand of tea containing the smallest possible amount of tannin. A number of such blends are on the market, made for exclusive use in making iced tea. The smaller amount of tannin in these iced tea blends reduces imperceptibly the tang which is most appealing to connoisseurs of a cup of tea but assures a clear, sparkling drink.

Another way to avoid cloudiness or "creaming down" without using a special iced tea blend, is to use the cold-water method, a method indorsed by all the experts. The recipe for this method follows:

ICED TEA, COLD-WATER METHOD [168]

Use 2 teaspoons of your favorite blend of tea for each glass of water. Allow the cold water to remain on the tea leaves in a glass, china or pottery container 12–18 hours or overnight. Strain the liquid from the tea leaves before serving. This method saves ice and a quantity of iced tea can always be available. Sweeten to taste and serve as ordinary iced tea.

Tea made by this recipe will not cloud at all, because the tannin in the leaves is not as soluble in cold water as the caffein and other properties. It will carry the same bouquet and stimulating qualities as a hot brew. *Important:* Never allow this kind of brew to stand in a metal container.

NUTMEG TEA [169]
(*Serves 1*)

Put 1 teaspoon of sweet butter, 1 teaspoon of sugar and ⅛ of a teaspoon of freshly grated nutmeg in heated cup. Pour in freshly boiling water until cup is ⅔ full. Stir till butter is melted, then fill the cup with milk or cream.

SPICED TEA [170]
(*Serves 6–8 generously*)

Dissolve ¾ cup of sugar in ½ cup of cold water; when quite dissolved, bring to boiling point; remove from the fire and add the juice of 1 orange, the juice of 4 juicy lemons, 10 whole cloves, heads removed, 1 teaspoon of cinnamon, and mix well. Have ready 5 cups of furiously boiling water; pour over 5 heaping teaspoons of tea in a heated teapot; let brew and steep for 5 minutes; strain over the fruit juice mixture, which has been placed in a crystal bowl, and serve immediately in punch or tea cups, each cup containing a thin slice of lemon studded with a whole clove.

TEA PUNCH [171]
(*Cold*)

Have ready 1 pint of strong and freshly made tea, chilled. Mix it with 1 cup of apricot juice (from canned apricots), 1 cup of canned pineapple juice, 1 cup of orange juice, ½ cup of lemon juice, 1 pint of chilled club soda; add sugar to taste; add a block of ice to the bowl, and whirl it till punch is chilled and well mixed. Serve at once in glass goblets.

WHAT WITH TEA? [172]

If you are addicted to that pleasant afternoon tea custom, nothing is better for service with the tea itself than thin bread and butter finger sandwiches, or crisp toast. With the latter, you will like orange marmalade, plum jam or some other type of preserves. Cinnamon toast is one of our American favorites for tea service. There is also a whole range of dainty sandwiches, which belong to the tea hour. These may be supplemented, but not replaced, by a sweet in the form of cake, cookies or dainty pastries. Note, however, that the tea itself is more important than its accompaniments.

When the Dutch introduced tea into Europe, people used it for seasoning instead of for beverage purposes.

HOW TO DRINK GOOD WINES [173-4]

The best set of rules ever written regarding the drinking and serving of wine is by Dr. Louis Mathieu, a professor in Bordeaux, France.

"Pure wine plays a very important part in human nutrition. It is to facts, rather than laboratories, that we must turn in such matters in order to carry conviction. Liebig, the famous chemist, relates that, at the time of the foundation of the temperance societies in England and Germany, many persons who had substituted a payment in money for the wine they used to supply to their servants, noticed that the latters' consumption of bread and other eatables was noticeably on the increase, so that their masters actually had to pay twice for their wine: first in cash and secondly in the form of extra food."

As for the temperature, *white wines* should be a few degrees colder than the room, and in hot weather full-bodied wines may even be iced. *Red wines*, on the other hand, should have had time to take the temperature of the room, a matter of 3 or 4 hours, and there is no objection to their being a degree or two above it. If used, the decanter, which is to receive the wine, must be in winter very slightly warmed. As for the wine, nothing must be done to it. None of the varied gadgets or instruments invented for decanting wine is equal to the precaution of not stirring the dregs, and of handling the bottle with due care and surety of hand. But it must be remembered that if wine is at too high a temperature, all its finer qualities will disappear and the particles which it gives off will be so loaded with alcohol that perfume, bouquet and aroma will become indistinguishable.

The following rule, which is not a rigid prescription, is to be followed in order to keep an exact concordance between the wines and the dishes they are served with. *White wines* should accompany fish and shellfish as well as crustaceans; and generous *red wines* go with meat, poultry and game. The progressive order to be followed with red wines places first the youngest and the least famous. After white and red wines it is still possible to taste the sweet sauternes and to empty a few foaming glasses of champagne.

Cooking with Wines. To cook successfully with wines, here's all you need to know: Shellfish and creamed dishes are natural flavor-mates with *sherry wine.* Add the wine just a few minutes before removing from the heat.

A *dry white wine* enhances the delicate flavor of chicken and fish.

Red meats, on the other hand, require the richness of a dry *red wine* like Burgundy or Bordeaux to bring out their full-bodied flavor. For instance, use a cup of *red wine* to replace part of the liquid you ordinarily add to potroast or stew, proceeding as indicated by the directions in the recipe. Roasts have extra zest when you baste them with red or white wine.

In warm weather, an opened bottle of dry wine keeps better when you add two or three drops of olive oil, which seals it from the air. Of course, you do this only to wines you use for cooking.

Wine gives an elusive, subtle flavor to even the simplest dishes. What you taste is not the flavor of wine. It's an unsuspected goodness which wine discovers for you in the food itself! Wine in cooking acts as a flavoring only; the alcohol evaporates as heat is applied. Remember that alcohol makes sugar available in the human system. With no thought of going into it technically, consider that the use of wines in cooking conserves sugar. Ask anybody who knows, if there is any doubt in your mind.

Chapter Three

SOUPS AND SOUP GARNISHES

To make a good chowder and have it quite nice
Dispense with sweet marjoram, parsley and spice;
Mace, pepper and salt are now wanted alone.
To make the stew eat well and stick to the bone,
Some pork is sliced thin and put into the pot;
Some say you must turn it, some say you must not;
And when it is brown, take it out of the fat,
And add it again when you add this and that.
A layer of potatoes, sliced quarter inch thick,
Should be placed in the bottom to make it eat slick;
A layer of onions now over this place,
Then season with pepper and salt and some mace.
Split open your crackers and give them a soak;
In eating you'll find this the cream of the joke.
On the top of all this, now comply with my wish
And put in large chunks, all your pieces of fish;
Then put on the pieces of pork you have fried
I mean those from which all the fat has been tried.
In seasoning I pray you, don't spare the cayenne;
'Tis this makes it fit to be eaten by men.
After adding these things in their regular rotation
You'll have a dish fit for the best of the nation.

—*Author Unknown, "Chowder" (1834)*

GOOD SOUP HAS BEEN CELEBRATED IN VERSE AND STORY almost as reverently as the first signs of Spring, for there is nothing like a plate of hot soup, its wisp of aromatic steam making the nostrils quiver with anticipation, to dispel the depressing effects of a gruelling day at the office, at the shop, in the fields, or rain or snow in the streets. Good soup is one of the prime ingredients of good living. For soup can do more to lift the spirits and stimulate the appetite than any other one dish. Soups challenge us, because an enticing flavorful soup can be as different from the thin, watery beverage sometimes erroneously called soup as a genuine green turtle is from the mock turtle.

Perhaps one of the surest tests of a good cook is the choice of soup in relation to the rest of the meal. The purpose of soup in the meal is twofold: First, to stimulate appetite; second, to provide nourishment. Light soups serve as appetizers, heavier ones may be a main course. Men, we notice, have always been partial to soups that "fill you up"— those rich with chunks of meat or chicken, hearty with vegetables, alimentary pastes, barley or rice.

Brillat-Savarin once made the remark that a woman who couldn't make soups should not be allowed to marry. Soups were important in his world, and they still are important to us all, young and ex-young. In fact, soup is to the meal what the hostess' smile of welcome is to the party. Steaming hot soup, sipped in leisurely manner, may be as refreshing on hot days as crisp salads, and iced beverages served in cold glasses. From the clear, well-seasoned bouillon, or the more "herbal" consommé which starts everything off amiably, to the thick vegetable, tomato, bean or pea soup or purée that make a lunch in themselves— all have a place in year-round menus. One whiff of a savory, aromatic soup, and appetites come to attention. The steaming fragrance of a tempting soup is a prelude to the goodness to come. An inspired soup puts family and guests into a receptive mood for the rest of the menu.

Meals, like everything else, are better when they get off to the right start. The first course is vastly important, for hungry people are apt to notice what they eat. If you begin the repast with a comforting chowder or a pungent consommé, you can relax even if the roast is not as tenderly browned as you had hoped. But if your soup lacks flavor and distinction, the rest of the menu must be superb to distract attention from the bad start. Though many first course favorites such as canapés, fruit or vegetable juices and all the gamut of hors d'oeuvres have strayed from the table to the living-room, soup must be served at the table. Consequently, it requires more attention than tidbits nibbled informally. Definitely, the soup is the curtain-raiser for the meal, and must be good.

CLASSIFICATION OF SOUPS [177]

In planning menus, the cook must reckon with his or her soups. This is especially true if the food budget is to run on economical lines, for there are many ways of using soups, and many types of soups which will do much to bolster up an otherwise scanty meal.

All soup recipes may generally be classified into three main groups, as follows: (1) Thin, clear soups which stimulate appetite (consommé, bouillon, broth); (2) thin, light, delicate cream soups, bisques, vegetable broth; (3) Heavy, thick soups or chowders (pepper-pot, Scotch broth, minestrone, mulligatawny, thick vegetable soups, thick cream soups, etc.).

Bouillon, Consommé and Broth. Bouillon is the clarified liquid in which meat, poultry or vegetables have been cooked. Clear consommé, or clarified bouillon, flavored with sherry, bitters, etc., can almost be regarded as a "cocktail." Broth is the unclarified liquid in which meats, poultry, game or vegetables are cooked. It, like the consommé, is frequently garnished, but lightly.

Light Cream Soup. This is ideal as the preface to a meal, or as the main supper dish, particularly for growing children.

Heavy Soup. This is the hearty soup whose general characteristic is that it is a whole meal in itself.

Another group comprises the cold, chilled or jellied soups, usually called summer soups, of which more later.

Then we have the soup stocks, of which there are six variants: Brown stock, fish stock, gravy stock, vegetable stock, and white stock, which all need to be clarified before using for either soup base or sauce base. Any kind of stock should be well-seasoned and well-flavored by means of spices, condiments or herbs.

Aside from its use in soup-making, the stock which many cooks keep on hand gives flavor to sauces and to many made dishes. Scraps of meat, bones of chops, outside leaves of lettuce, celery tops and the water in which vegetables are boiled are only some of the items which go into the soup pot, contributing their savors to the stock. Careful cooks see that bones and trimmings of roasts are sent from the market, also chicken feet—to be scalded and scraped for the soup pot.

Stock forms the basis of all meat or fish soups. It is therefore essential to the success of these culinary operations to know the most complete and economical method of extracting from a certain quantity of meat the best possible stock or bouillon, or broth. Fresh uncooked beef makes the best stock, with the addition of cracked bones, as the glutinous matter contained in them renders it important that they should be boiled with the meat, which adds to the strength and thickness of the soup. They are composed of an earthy substance—to which they owe their solidity—of gelatine, and a fatty fluid called marrow. Two ounces of them contain as much gelatine as one pound of meat; but, in them, this is so encased in the earthy substance that boiling water can dissolve only the surface of the whole bones. When there is an abundance of it, it causes the stock, when cold, to become a jelly. The flesh of old animals contains more flavor than the flesh of young ones. Red meats contain more flavor than white.

Some cooks use meat that has once been cooked; this renders little nourishment and destroys the flavor. It might answer for ready soup, but for stock to keep, it is not so good, unless it should be roasted meats. Those contain higher fragrant properties; so by putting the remains of roast meats in the stock-pot you obtain a better flavor.

The shin bone is generally used, but the neck or "sticking," as the butchers call it, contains more of the substance that you want to extract, makes a stronger and more nutritious soup than any other part of the animal. Meats for soup *should always* be put on to cook in *cold water*, in a covered soup kettle or pot, and allowed to simmer slowly for several hours, in order that the essence of the meat may be drawn out thoroughly. The cooking stock should be carefully skimmed to prevent it from becoming turbid; never allow it to boil fast *at any time*, and if more water is needed, use boiling water from the tea-kettle; cold or lukewarm water spoils the flavor. Stock will be as good the second, third, fourth or fifth day if kept in the refrigerator, as the first day if heated to the boiling point before using.

COLORING THE SOUP [178]

Coloring, the chief of which is brown burnt sugar, known by French cooks as caramel, is used in some brown soups.

Pounded spinach leaves give a fine green color to certain soups. Parsley, or the green leaves of celery, put in soup will also serve instead of spinach; or use a few drops of green vegetable coloring. Pound a large handful of spinach in a mortar, then tie it in cheesecloth, and wring out all the juice; add this to the soup you wish to color, 5 minutes before taking it up. Mock turtle, and sometimes lamb or veal soups, should be this color.

To color red, skin 6 red tomatoes, squeeze out the seeds and put the pulp into the soup with the other vegetables, or take the juice only, as directed for spinach, or use a few drops of red vegetable coloring or cochineal.

BROWN STOCK HOME MANNER [179]
(Makes about 6 quarts)

Cut up 2 pounds of shin or neck of beef; break 1 pound of knuckle of veal into small pieces (about 3 or 4 pounds of bones all together); cover with cold water (about 8 quarts), add 1 tablespoon of salt, and let stand for an hour, then bring gently to the boiling point, skimming the scum as it rises. When quite clear, add 2 carrots, scraped and cut into inch pieces, 2 medium-sized onions, halved, 1 half stuck with 2 whole cloves. 1 medium-sized white turnip peeled and quartered, 1 stalk of celery, well-washed and cut into inch pieces, a bouquet garni composed of 2 large bay leaves, 1 large sprig of thyme, 12 sprigs of fresh parsley, all tied together with kitchen thread, add also 15 whole peppercorns, gently bruised. Again bring to the boiling point, skim well, then cover, lower the flame and let simmer gently, very gently; let it "smile" 4½–5½ hours without disturbing, except skimming occasionally any fat or scum. Strain through a fine meshed hair sieve and, when cold, remove the cake of fat from the surface. This can be clarified and used for frying. Store in refrigerator until wanted. If you desire a "second" stock, cover the meat and vegetables with cold water and let it boil down until reduced to half, over a gentle flame, and use as a base for soup, sauce or to cook vegetables in.

Among the 4 pounds of bones indicated for this stock, you may use the cleaned feet and gizzards of chickens, turkey or any kind of domestic bird. The above brown stock made according to this recipe could, after being cleared, be used for any clear soup, which would take its name from the garnish served with it.

BROWNING THE STOCK [180]

The best method of assuring a dark brown stock is to sear the meat and bones in their own fat, or to add a few drops of caramel (No. 181).

CARAMEL FOR SOUP COLORING [181]

Boil ½ pound of granulated sugar with ⅓ cup of cold water until it is dark brown, almost black, then add another ⅓ cup of cold water and boil again till it acquires the consistency of thick syrup. Strain bottle, cork and use as required. Fine for coloring stews, goulashes, gravies and sauces.

FISH STOCK HOME MANNER [182]
(Makes about 1½ quarts)

Put 2 pounds of any inexpensive white-fleshed fish with bones and trimmings into a saucepan, add 1 medium-sized onion, thinly sliced, 1 blade of mace, 12 white peppercorns, gently bruised, 1 teaspoon of salt, 1 bouquet garni composed of 1 large bay leaf, 1 large sprig of thyme, and 10 sprigs of fresh parsley, tied together with kitchen thread, 1 medium-sized carrot, scraped and thinly sliced and 2 whole cloves; bring to a boil, lower the flame and let simmer gently for about 1 hour from the time the stock begins to simmer. Further cooking sometimes imparts a disagreeable bitter taste to the stock. Skim carefully, strain through a fine-meshed sieve and, when cold, store in the refrigerator until needed.

GRAVY STOCK HOME MANNER   [183]

Crack rather small, some bones from roast meat, and fry them until well browned in a baking pan with a little meat drippings; pour off all the fat, and add enough Pique Seasoning and water in equal parts to cover the bones generously, season with a little pepper, but no salt, and let simmer very, very gently 35–40 minutes. Strain through cheesecloth and keep in refrigerator until required. This stock will keep several weeks in a good refrigerator, when tightly sealed in a glass jar.

VEGETABLE STOCK HOME MANNER   [184]
(Makes about 2 quarts)

Cut 2 medium-sized onions, 3 medium-sized carrots, 1 medium-sized white turnip, 1 stalk of celery, 1 small head of lettuce into small pieces; wash quickly, drain and dry well. Heat ¼ cup of butter or margarine in a soup kettle, stir in the prepared vegetables and cook very gently, over a low flame, having the kettle covered, for about 25 minutes, stirring frequently with a wooden spoon; then add 2 large fresh tomatoes, peeled and quartered, 1 bouquet garni, composed of 1 large bay leaf, 8 sprigs of fresh parsley, and 1 sprig of thyme, tied together with kitchen thread, 1 blade of mace, 10 whole peppercorns, gently bruised, 1 small blade of garlic, 2 whole cloves and ½ teaspoon of salt. Now stir in 1½ quarts of boiling water and 2 cups of Pique Seasoning, mixing well. Gradually bring to a rolling boil, lower the flame and allow to simmer very gently, covered, for 1½ hours, skimming as the scum rises. Strain through cheesecloth, and it is ready for use. If not needed at once, cool, then store in glass jars in the refrigerator until needed. This stock will keep more than 2 weeks in the refrigerator when kept sealed in glass jar or jars.

In eighteenth-century Russia it was an insult to the host or hostess to sip soup with a spoon. This implied that the guest found it too disagreable to drink from the cup or bowl.

WHITE or VEAL STOCK HOME MANNER   [185]

Cut up the meat from 4 pounds of veal knuckle and break the bones into small pieces; place in a soup kettle, with the neck and cleaned feet of a chicken; pour over 1 quart of cold water for each pound of meat and bones, or about 4 quarts in all, cover and let stand in a cool place for a full hour. Then place the kettle over a low flame and bring slowly to a gentle boil, skimming as the scum rises to the surface. Simmer very gently, over a low flame, until quite clear. Now, add 2 medium-sized onions, quartered, 2 medium-sized carrots, scraped and cut into inch pieces after being halved lengthwise. 1 medium-sized white turnip, peeled and quartered, 1 stalk of celery, scraped, then cut into inch pieces, 1 bouquet garni composed of 12 sprigs of fresh parsley, 1 sprig of thyme, 2 large bay leavs, 4 whole cloves, tied together with kitchen thread, 12 peppercorns, freshly bruised, 1 tablespoon of salt and 1 blade each of mace and garlic. Bring slowly to a boil, skim again as the scum rises and, when clear, cover and simmer gently 4–4½ hours, skimming occasionally as the fat and scum rise. Remove from the fire, strain through a cheesecloth, cool and, when cold, remove the cake of fat from the surface. Keep in refrigerator until wanted. This stock will keep 2 weeks in the refrigerator if stored in a closely sealed container.

CLARIFYING ANY KIND OF STOCK   [186]
HOME MANNER
(For each 3 quarts of stock)

Wash and cut small ½ medium-sized onion or ½ small leek, 1 small carrot and 3 sprigs of green celery leaves, first peeling the onion or leek, and scraping the carrot. Place the prepared vegetables in a clean saucepan, add a small bouquet garni composed of 1 small bay leaf, 1 small sprig of thyme, 2 sprigs or leaflet of tarragon herb, 6 sprigs of chervil or parsley and 1 whole clove, all tied together with kitchen thread, 6 peppercorns, the white and shell of 1 egg, 1 scant teaspoon of lemon juice and 1 tablespoon of white wine vinegar; stir with a wire whisk and, when mixed, add ½ pound of finely chopped or ground lean, raw beef, previously moistened with 1 tablespoon of cold water. Gradually bring mixture to a boil, while whisking steadily until the boiling point is reached. Then lower the flame and let simmer very, very gently, uncovered and without stirring, 25–30 minutes. Taste for seasoning, strain through a fine-meshed sieve, the sieve covered with a cheesecloth, and, when cold, store in refrigerator or use at once for clear soup or consommé. This clear stock will keep about 2 weeks in the refrigerator when kept in a sealed container.

SOUP GARNISHES   [187]

Garnishing and decorating the soup challenges any cook who desires to create something beautiful and appetizing. Inspiration may come from the colorful array of greens, croutons, tiny dumplings, etc. Wherever a woman is in charge of activities in a kitchen, half the monotony and drudgery is eliminated by allowing her imagination and natural artistry to have full play in the careful arrangement of the simplest meal. The keynote to happiness within the four walls that make any home is plain, wholesome, well-cooked food attractively served. A sprig of parsley or a bit of tender celery top garnishing the serving dish, a few delicately golden-browned croutons floating on top of the soup, will go a long way toward raising dejected spirits, stimulating poor or laggard appetites, and creating an atmosphere of contentment and well-being. It is surprising and oftentimes amusing to see how easily a clever cook can train her household into accepting the most ordinary foods when a little forethought is given to the serving.

Dress up your soups; serve them with different garnishes and accompaniments such as: croutons, noodles, spaghetti and vermicelli, rice, barley, grated cheese, tiny forcemeat balls or dumplings such as liver dumplings, bread dumplings, etc.; marrow balls, sliced frankfurter, sliced hard-cooked eggs, sieved egg yolk over a slice of lemon, a poached egg, a round of toasted bread, salted whipped cream plain or dusted with a film of paprika or cinnamon, shredded salami, chiffonade (thinly shredded salad greens), vegetable julienne, bread sticks, Melba toasts, crackers, cheese straws, savory cheese puffs, tiny egg balls, bread crumb balls, puffed crackers, chicken or other meat, tiny custard cubes, nutmeg dumplings as made in Connecticut, farina dumplings, tiny cornmeal dumplings, toast floats, cheese and olive floats, toasted popcorn, shredded toasted almonds, burger balls, baking powder dumplings, matzo knoedel, etc.

A FEW GOOD SOUP GARNISH HINTS   [188]

Chopped, blanched, toasted almonds are the perfect last touch in a cream or chicken soup. . . . Have you tried adding a tablespoonful of salted whipped cream as a garnish for a plate of tomato soup, or any cream soup? It adds not only taste but elegance; you may tint the whipped cream with a little paprika, saffron, or a few drops of green vegetable coloring; also a little curry powder. Butter crackers spread with a mixture of butter and a little curry powder or paprika, then heated under the flame of the broiling oven, form an appetizing accompaniment to fish soup, oyster stew, and fish chowder. Add thin little rounds of frankfurters to the split pea soup, lentil soup or cream soup by way of an edible garnish. A few rounds of these with squares of browned bread look pretty and appetizing together. Cut bread or pastry dough into short, slender sticks; brush with beaten egg white; dust with salt and caraway seeds and bake quickly; these go well with salad, too. . . . Grate American cheese on to salted crackers, dust with paprika, curry powder, nutmeg or cinnamon and brown in the oven under flame of broiling oven; these, too, are fine with salads.

Foods colored yellow were highly regarded as luxurious eating in Roman times. Foods were colored with saffron, one of the most costly products obtainable. Imitations were used by hosts in the lower income brackets—false saffron, which imparted a reddish tint, and marigold.

ALL-BRAN THIMBLE-SIZE DUMPLINGS   [189]

Sift 1½ cups of bread flour once, measure, add 1 scant teaspoon of salt, 3 teaspoons of baking powder and a tiny pinch of curry powder

and resift into a mixing bowl. Beat 1 large fresh egg until light; add
1 tablespoon of bacon drippings, melted and cooled to lukewarm, with
½ cup of All-Bran, alternately with about ¾ cup of cold, rich milk.
Stir into the flour mixture, blending thoroughly. Drop by scant teaspoons into boiling soup; cover and cook a few minutes before serving.

BACON CRUMBS   [190]

Fry bacon until crisp, or broil under the flame of the broiling oven;
drain on absorbent paper; crumble into fine particles, and sprinkle on
soup before serving.

BAKING POWDER THIMBLE-SIZE   [191]
DUMPLINGS

Mix and sift 2 cups of all-purpose flour, 4 teaspoons of baking powder,
½ teaspoon of ground cinnamon and 1 scant teaspoon of salt; work in
1 tablespoon of bacon or ham drippings; add 1 scant cup of cold, rich
milk and mix lightly. Drop from teaspoon on top of the soup (or stew),
or roll very gently on lightly-floured board, shape with a very small
biscuit-cutter or with a tiny glass, and drop on top of boiling soup or
stew, cover and cook for a few minutes, or until dumplings rise.

BREAD CRUMB BALLS   [192]

Mix 2 tablespoons of sieved stale bread crumbs, 1 tablespoon of
beef marrow, 1 teaspoon of grated lemon rind, salt and pepper to taste,
1 teaspoon each of finely chopped parsley, grated onion and chives,
and add just enough unbeaten egg white to moisten. Form into very
small balls and, just before serving, drop into hot soup or stew and cook
until the balls rise. Serve immediately.

BREAD STICKS   [193]

Slice bread ¾ inch thick, remove crusts; cut each slice into 3 or 4
finger strips; arrange on baking sheet and dry in very slow oven (200° F.)
until lightly browned throughout.

BRUNOISE   [194]

This term implies fresh vegetables cut in tiny squares, rounds, or
lozenge pellets, cooked in beef, poultry or fish stock, and used for garnishing clear consommé of beef or poultry, then well drained before
adding to the soup.

BURGER BALLS WITH MARJORAM [195]

To ½ pound of finely ground lean raw meat (beef, lamb, mutton, pork, ham, or veal) add 1 teaspoon of grated onion, ½ teaspoon of grated lemon rind, ¼ teaspoon of dried marjoram, salt, pepper, nutmeg to taste, and sufficient moistened crackers to "bind." Mix thoroughly, roll into balls, the size of a small walnut, and 10 minutes before serving, drop them into gently boiling soup (clear or otherwise). Cook 10 minutes and serve at once.

CHEESE AND CHIVE FLOATS [196]

Beat 1 egg white until stiff; fold in 2 tablespoons of flour and beat again, season with a drop or two of Tabasco sauce, a pinch each of salt, pepper, nutmeg and clove, and 1 tablespoon each of grated cheese and finely chopped chives. Drop by teaspoonfuls on top of boiling soup; cover, lower the heat and let simmer gently for 3 or 4 minutes.

CHEESE POPCORN [197]

Pop 1 cup of corn (packaged). While still hot, sprinkle with grated American cheese, shaking and rocking the pan. Cool, store in tightly covered container and float a few on soup in tureen just before serving or put a few into each bowl or plate. If preferred omit the cheese.

CHEESE STICKS [198]

Remove crust from loaf of unsliced bread; cut into slices, ½ inch thick, then cut the slices into ½ inch strips. Cream ¼ cup of butter until light, add ¼ cup of grated cheese (any desired kind), and beat until creamy with a few grains each of cayenne and nutmeg; spread cheese mixture on strips of bread; sprinkle with paprika and set in oven or place under the flame of the broiling oven to melt the cheese. Remove from oven or broiler, trim neatly with a sharp knife, and serve as hot as possible.

NOTE. Bread may be cut in any desired fancy shapes, as hearts, lozenges, rounds, squares, ovals, etc., instead of strips.

CHICKEN CUSTARD CUBES [199]

Grind or finely chop cooked white meat of chicken, then rub through a fine-meshed sieve. To ¼ cup of the sieved chicken, add ¼ cup of chicken stock and season to taste with salt, celery salt, paprika and nutmeg, then beat in 1 slightly beaten egg or 2 slightly beaten egg yolks.

Turn into a buttered shallow pan; set in a pan of hot water, and bake in a slow oven (250–375° F.) until firm. Cool, and cut in tiny cubes.

CHICKEN FORCEMEAT BALLS [200]

Finely chop, pound and sieve 2 raw chicken breasts. This will yield about 1 cup of meat. Season to taste with salt, pepper, a few grains each of nutmeg and clove, and set aside. Scald 1 cup of dry, sieved, white bread crumbs with 1 cup of rich milk and a pinch of mace. Remove from heat, stir in 3 tablespoons of butter and the ground, seasoned chicken. Now, fold in 2 well-beaten egg whites, mixing gently but thoroughly. Form into balls, the size of a small walnut, dip in beaten egg yolks and fry in hot, deep, clear fat (360° F.) or brown in the oven. Drain on absorbent paper. Or form into very small balls, the size of an ordinary marble and drop into boiling soup stock, cook for a few minutes, or until balls rise to the surface. Serve very hot.

NOTE. These delicate and delicious balls may be served as a main dish in which case arrange them on hot cooked spinach, mashed potatoes, mashed carrots or turnips, or any preferred cooked green vegetable accompanied by either tomato, mushroom or egg sauce.

Any kind of raw meat, raw game or raw fish may be prepared in the same manner, and served with a sauce appropriate to the kind of meat, game or fish used.

CHIFFONADE GARNISH [201]

Almost all vegetables except the pods may be used as a garnish either for clear or thick soup. They may be cut julienne, that is, in thin, narrow strips, matchlike, put in ice-cold water as soon as scraped and cut, cooked in salt water or meat or fish or game stock until tender yet firm, and kept in lukewarm stock until used. Vegetables used for soup garnish may be of one kind only or a composite of several kinds. However, as a rule, no more than a teaspoon or thereabouts should be used for each serving.

CORNMEAL THIMBLE-SIZE DUMPLINGS [202]

These dumplings make a wonderful addition to a soup, be it clear or thick.

Sprinkle ¼ cup of yellow, white or blue cornmeal into ½ cup of boiling water mixed with ¼ cup of Pique Seasoning and stir until it thickens. Do not season at all; cook in a double boiler for 25–30 minutes or until thick, stirring frequently. Remove from hot water and scrape the mush out into a mixing bowl; stir in 1 teaspoon of grated onion,

1 tablespoon each of finely minced chives and parsley and 1 small, well beaten egg; spread upon a cold platter to chill. When quite cold, take portions the size of a very large marble, roll in flour, drop into simmering soup, cover and boil very gently for about 8–10 minutes. Serve the soup with the thimble-size dumplings. They are fine with stew, too. They may be deep fried, drained and served as a main dish by doubling the amount of ingredients and serving them scattered over cooked macaroni, noodles or spaghetti with a side dish of rich tomato sauce.

The blue cornmeal is sacred to the Indians of the West. It is blessed by their medicine men and has a part in tribal ceremonials.

CROUTONS   [203]

(1) Remove the crusts from thinly sliced stale bread, cut in tiny cubes, and brown lightly in a little melted butter, bacon or ham drippings.

(2) Prepare croutons as above, having the cubes cut into about ¼-inch squares; dip quickly in and out of milk; roll in grated dry cheese; place on a greased baking sheet in a single layer and bake in a hot oven (425° F.) until the cheese is melted and the croutons delicately browned, shaking the pan frequently. Or place under the flame of the broiling oven, about 4 inches under the flame, and brown delicately, shaking the pan frequently, until cheese is browned.

(3) Cut the bread as indicated above, place on ungreased baking sheet, and brown or toast under the flame of the broiling oven until croutons are crisp.

(4) Cut the bread as indicated, dip quickly into Pique Seasoning, drain well, place on to a dry baking sheet, and brown delicately under the flame of the broiling oven, shaking the pan frequently.

These croutons may be prepared in advance, stored in a closed tin and kept in a cool, dry place, where they will keep for a fortnight.

CURRIED POTATO THIMBLE-SIZE   [204]
NOCKERLN (DUMPLINGS)

Cream 4 tablespoons of butter until light and fluffy; add 1 slightly-beaten egg yolk, continuing creaming and beating at the same time until well blended; season to taste with salt, nutmeg and ½ teaspoon of powdered curry powder, then mix in about ¾ cup of cooked, riced potatoes (freshly cooked or left-over), alternately with 4 tablespoons of flour. Beat until very smooth and free from lumps; shape into balls, the size of a large marble and, about 8 minutes before serving, drop the nockerln or dumplings into simmering meat, fish or vegetable stock, depending on kind of soup used, cover and simmer very gently for about 6–8 minutes. Drain and serve at once in the soup.

DUMPLING FLOATS   [205]

Blend 1 egg, slightly beaten, with ¼ teaspoon of salt, ½ teaspoon of paprika, a few grains of pepper and 2 tablespoons of Pique Seasoning. Gradually add ¾ cup of bread flour, previously sifted with ¾ teaspoon of baking powder and a generous pinch of nutmeg powder, beating well after each addition, and lastly beat in 1 generous teaspoon of melted butter or margarine. About 15 minutes before serving, drop batter by half teaspoon into boiling soup; lower the flame, cover with the lid, and let simmer gently 12–15 minutes without removing the lid. Serve the soup at once.

EGG BALLS   [206]

Rub 4 hard-cooked egg yolks through a sieve; season to taste with salt, pepper and a few grains of thyme and nutmeg and mix in enough uncooked and unbeaten egg white to moisten. Shape into small balls, the size of a marble; roll in flour, and brown in 4 tablespoons of butter over a low flame, rocking the pan frequently to brown on all sides. Drain on absorbent paper and add to hot, clear soup. Serve at once as a side dish, each guest helping himself.

EGG FLAKES   [207]

Beat 1 egg as for an omelet with a pinch of pepper, no salt, and a few grains of nutmeg, then beat in 2 tablespoons of Pique Seasoning. Just when ready to serve a clear soup, which should be boiling, pour egg mixture into a not too fine sieve and let drop egg mixture all over the boiling soup. Serve at once.

FARINA THIMBLE-SIZE DUMPLINGS   [208]

Cream well 1 tablespoon of butter, then add 2 well-beaten eggs gradually, alternately with 5 ounces of farina, about ⅛ teaspoon of sugar, a dash of salt and white pepper to taste, mixing thoroughly. Drop by small teaspoonfuls into boiling meat stock; lower the flame and let simmer very, very gently, uncovered, 30–35 minutes. Remove from the fire, cover with the lid, and let stand for 2 minutes without simmering before serving with any kind of clear meat, poultry or fish soup.

HOMINY

Grandmother's stanch standby, hominy, has shortened its skirts and bobbed its hair, figuratively speaking, and now steps out in most up-to-date guise. The cooks of today buy this "vegetable-cereal" in convenient tins or packages instead of making it in their own backyards. Furthermore, hominy is no longer reserved for the breakfast table alone. Oh, no! It appears with meats, game and vegetables, it pops up in muffins, in gems, in cheese timbales, in fritters, scalloped, flaked, creamed, au gratin, cooked with sherry, in filled squares with meats, poultry or game. Use left-over cooked hominy fried golden brown for garnishing meat, poultry or game platters, cook it with cheese, serve in croquettes, in a ring, and as croutons for garnishing soups. Excellent though the homemade product was, that made under scientifically controlled conditions is far better and available at a moment's notice. As most of us know, hominy is made from corn; the whole kernels are soaked in lye to remove the husks, and are then cooked until tender. There are several excellent brands of both canned and flaked hominy from which to choose, the latter both packaged and sold in bulk. In the South, there is the finer form, called "grits."

HOMINY CROUTONS [209]

Pack left-over cooked hominy in buttered ¼-pound baking powder can or similar empty, clean can. Chill. Remove from can, cut in ¼-inch slices, then into tiny cubes. Dip in sieved bread crumbs, seasoned to taste with salt, white pepper, and a few grains each of powdered thyme and nutmeg, then roll in slightly beaten egg, diluted with a little cold milk, and again in crumbs. Fry in hot, deep fat (360–370° F.) until delicately browned, drain on absorbent paper, and serve with any clear or semi-clear hot soup.

JEWISH KRAPLACH [210]

During Passover, the Jewish cook prepares the traditional specialties of the holiday, such as the dry, crumbly sponge cake made with matzoth meal, gefüllte fish with its dressing of wine-red horseradish and the famous kraplach, triangles of dough stuffed with seasoned meat. These dishes are so delectable and have become so popular that many restaurants throughout the country serve them to gourmets of all religions during Passover as well as at other times of the year.

Sift 2 cups of pastry flour once, return to sifter, add ¼ generous teaspoon of salt and sift into a mixing bowl. Make a hole in center of the flour, drop in 1 well-beaten egg and 1 teaspoon of creamed, soft butter. Mix well, starting from the center, adding just enough ice-cold water to make a stiff dough. Roll the dough out very, very thin, then cut into neat 3- or 4-inch squares.

Combine 1 pound of lean boiled beef, finely chopped or ground, 1 large onion, grated, 1 scant teaspoon of salt, ¼ teaspoon of pepper and 2 teaspoons of Worcestershire sauce. Place a portion of the meat mixture on each of the dough squares, then fold the dough over the meat to make pastry triangles; close the edges by pinching firmly together and, when ready to serve, drop the kraplach into rapidly boiling salted water, or into equal parts of rapidly boiling water and Pique Seasoning, boiling for about 6–7 minutes. Serve these light meat puffs in clear, rich chicken broth or bouillon or consommé.

Fifteenth-century European women dined frequently on calves' liver boiled in milk as a beauty tonic.

LIVER THIMBLE-SIZE DUMPLINGS   [211]
New England Manner

Rub ¼ pound of beef, calf, lamb or pork liver through a fine-meshed sieve with 1 tablespoon of chopped raw fat salt pork. Add 1 teaspoon of grated onion, 1 teaspoon each of finely chopped chives and parsley, 1 fresh egg, slightly beaten, ½ cup of soft bread crumbs, salt, pepper, thyme and nutmeg to taste and mix thoroughly. Chill for several hours in refrigerator and, when ready to serve, drop by scant teaspoons into boiling clear, semi-clear or thick soup. Serve at once.

MARROW BALLS   [212]

Strain 2 tablespoons of melted beef marrow through a fine sieve, and beat until creamy, then add 1 well-beaten fresh egg, season to taste with salt and pepper, and add ½ cup of soft bread crumbs moistened with a little Pique Seasoning. Form into balls, the size of a marble, and poach in boiling salted beef stock. When cooked, the tiny balls rise to the surface. You may, if desired, add 1 scant teaspoon of grated lemon rind to the mixture before forming into balls. Or use 1 unbeaten egg white or more to bind the mixture instead of Pique Seasoning.

MATZOTH BALLS or MATZOTH KNOEDEL   [213]

Soak 6 matzoths in boiling water for a minute, then squeeze them dry and crumble well. Heat 2 tablespoons of chicken fat, stir in 1 medium-sized onion, grated, and cook until delicately browned, over a gentle flame, stirring constantly, then stir in the matzoth and cook for a few minutes longer, stirring constantly, over a low flame. Season with 1 scant teaspoon of salt, a dash of pepper, ¼ teaspoon of powdered ginger,

1 tablespoon of finely chopped parsley and 3 fresh egg yolks, slightly beaten. Beat all together and lastly fold in 3 stiffly beaten egg whites. Form into small balls by rolling portions in a little matzoth meal and, when ready to serve the soup, drop the balls into boiling salted water and let boil gently 12–15 minutes. Serve very hot.

Matzoth or matzoh, the oldest and the simplest bread known to man, is made by billions of pounds before Passover. The eating of the matzoth is the most symbolic feature of this Jewish festival commemorating the Hebrews' liberation from Egyptian bondage. Fleeing Egypt hurriedly, the Jews had no time to leaven the bread. This they have eaten for thousands of years, remembering it as the bread of affliction.

MELBA TOAST [214]

It is from Escoffier himself that I learned the origin of Melba Toast. One afternoon, Mrs. Marie Louise Ritz, very capable and devoted wife of Cesar Ritz, complained about toast which was never thin enough to suit her, and asked Escoffier in front of me, "Can't you do something about it?"
As usual, Escoffier and Ritz took such a remark with absolute seriousness. They discussed the problem of thin toast. "Why not," said Ritz, "toast the thin slices of bread once, then cut it through again, and again toast it?" And with Escoffier he retired to the kitchens to see if it could not be done. The result was Escoffier's justly famous Toast Melba. When they brought out on the lawn of the Carlton a silver tray full of thin, crisp curled wafers, Escoffier said, "Behold! a new dish, and it is called Toast Marie." But, as Mrs. Ritz ate it, she tried to think up another name. "Marie" was far too anonymous to suit her.
During that year, Nellie Melba, the famous prima donna, had returned from America very ill. She was staying at the Savoy in London, where she was a much-indulged invalid, and Mrs. Ritz had heard Escoffier discuss her régime. Dry toast figured in it. "Call it Toast Melba," said Madame Ritz. And so it was done, and the name remains for posterity.
This recipe is as follows:

Cut stale bread as thinly as possible, into squares or long pieces; arrange on a baking sheet and bake in a very slow oven (200–250° F.) until very crisp and evenly colored, turning the pieces frequently. Store in a cool, dry place in a container covered with waxed paper. Handle with care as these fragile toasts break easily.

NUTMEG THIMBLE-SIZE DUMPLINGS [215]

Cream ½ cup of butter until light and fluffy; gradually add 2 fresh eggs, one at a time, beating well after each addition. Sift ¾ cup of cake flour once, return to sifter, add ¼ teaspoon of salt, a few grains of pepper and about ¼ teaspoon of freshly grated nutmeg (more or less according to taste), and sift again into a bowl; make a hole in center, add the butter mixture, and cut in the flour till well blended and flour is all dampened. Then fold in gently but thoroughly 1 stiffly beaten egg white; shape into balls about the size of a large marble and, when ready to serve a clear soup (bouillon, consommé, broth, or clear vegetable soup), drop the balls into the boiling soup, cover closely and let simmer very gently for about 5 minutes. Serve at once.

PARSLEY CRACKERS   [216]

Cream 2 tablespoons of butter until light and fluffy; gradually add 2 tablespoons of finely chopped parsley; spread on crackers and heat under the flame of the broiling oven for 2 minutes, or until tops just begin to bubble and take on color. Serve as hot as possible. These are fine with salad, too.

PIMIENTO WHIP   [217]

A fluff of this whipped cream forced through a pastry bag with a small rose fancy tube over chilled or jellied consommé, bouillon, broth or any kind of cold soup gives an appetite appeal and stimulates the gastric juices.

Whip ½ cup of sweet, heavy cream, top of the bottle or undiluted evaporated milk chilled until stiff; gradually add 2 tablespoons of lemon juice and continue whipping until very stiff; fold in 1 drained canned red pimiento, previously rubbed through a fine-meshed sieve, and when ready to serve, force a pompon of this preparation through a pastry bag with a small fancy tube. Serve at once. This preparation may be used for decorating any kind of cold mousse or aspic or jellied foods.

PUFFED CRACKERS   [218]

Soak soda crackers in cold Pique Seasoning diluted with an equal amount of cold water for 12–15 minutes; lift very carefully with a broad spatula or slotted pancake turner so the liquid can drain off. Place on a baking sheet, far enough apart to allow the crackers to expand; put a teaspoon of melted butter on each cracker and bake in a hot oven (425° F.) about 25 minutes or until light brown and crisp. Serve as hot as possible with any kind of soup.

PULLED BREAD   [219]

Remove the crusts from French bread. Tear into thin strips, but do not cut with a knife. Place on a baking sheet, and bake in a very slow oven (250° F.) until crisp and delicately browned, turning the bread occasionally. Serve hot or cold.

ROYAL CUSTARD CUBES [220]

Beat 2 fresh egg yolks slightly; then beat in 1 slightly beaten whole egg, alternately with ½ cup of cream, sweet or sour (if sour cream is used, add ⅛ teaspoon of soda), rich beef or chicken bouillon or consommé. Season to taste with salt and pepper; pour into a buttered shallow pan; set this in another pan of hot water and bake in a slow oven (300° F.) until firm. When quite cold, cut in small cubes or fancy shapes with French vegetable cutter. Serve in clear soup, hot or cold.

ALE (or BEER) SOUP [221]

Put 1½ quarts of ale in a saucepan with 1-inch stick of cinnamon bark and 1½ tablespoons of lemon juice; season with a scant ¼ teaspoon of salt, a few grains of cayenne pepper and 1 teaspoon of sugar (more or less according to taste); bring almost to boiling point, when beads will appear on the surface; then stir in 1 tablespoon of flour, previously moistened with a little cold ale or beer, let simmer gently for 5 minutes, stirring frequently, taste for seasoning, and serve very hot with salted crackers.

ALMOND CREAM OF LETTUCE SOUP [222]
Also called Cream of Lettuce Soup Amandine

Proceed as indicated for Cream of Spinach Soup (No. 278), substituting lettuce for spinach and cooking in exactly the same manner. When ready to serve, stir in ⅓ of a cup of blanched, thinly sliced, toasted almonds. Serve hot.

ALMOND MINTED MUTTON SOUP [223]

Wipe with a damp cloth 2¼ pounds of breast and neck of mutton, put in a soup kettle and add 2 quarts of cold water. Bring almost to boiling point, drain, add 2 quarts of fresh water; 2 large, fresh peeled tomatoes cut into quarters; 3 medium-sized onions, previously sliced and cooked golden brown in a little butter or fat, ¼ cup chopped celery stalks; 2 tablespoons finely chopped fresh mint; 1 small bouquet garni composed of 1 small bay leaf, 1 small sprig of thyme and 6 sprigs of fresh parsley, tied together with kitchen thread; a very little salt and pepper; and gradually bring to a boil. Lower the flame, let simmer very gently, covered for 3–3¼ hours, and, when ready to serve, cut the meat into small cubes, discard the bones, place the cubed meat in a heated soup tureen, strain the broth over, then stir in ½ cup of blanched, thinly sliced, toasted almonds. Serve with freshly made toast.

APPLE GINGER SOUP   [224]
India

Peel, quarter and core 2 pounds of cooking apples; cut up coarsely. Have ready 2 quarts of rapidly boiling meat stock; drop the apples in all at once and add 3 whole cloves and ¼ of an inch of root ginger. Simmer very, very gently until apples are tender; strain through a fine-meshed sieve. Season to taste with salt and white pepper, reheat and serve in hot soup plates with a side dish of small croutons (No. 203).

As early as A. D. 800, good children in North Africa were treated to apples dipped in honey, somewhat like our own popular "apples on a stick." In India, the home cook has used apples in soup for more than 1000 years.

APPLE SOUP POLISH STYLE   [225]
(Cold)

Pare, core, and slice 5 large apples and put in a saucepan with enough cold water to cover, add ⅛ teaspoon of powdered cinnamon, the finely-pared rind of 1 lemon and 2 tablespoons of white bread crumbs. Bring slowly to a boil, lower the flame, and simmer gently until apples are tender, then rub through a fine-meshed sieve and let cool. When quite cold, stir in 1 bottle of red wine, mixed with 2 tablespoons of lemon juice, 1 tablespoon of black-currant jelly and 2 tablespoons of sugar, stir thoroughly and, when well blended, place in refrigerator to chill. Serve in chilled bouillon cups, adding to each cup a tiny twist of lemon and a little ground cinnamon.

BARLEY SOUP   [226]
English

Combine in a soup kettle 1 quart of white stock and 2 cups of rich milk. Bring to boiling point and cook 3 or 4 minutes. Heat 1 tablespoon of butter and blend in 1 tablespoon of flour; stir constantly over a low flame without browning. Now, still stirring, add a cup of the stock-milk mixture and, when bubbling, add to remaining stock and milk in the soup kettle. Stir until boiling and add 2½ tablespoons of finely crushed barley. Continue boiling with frequent stirring until barley is clear and thoroughly cooked. Season to taste with salt and pepper and serve with fried croutons (No. 203).

BEET SOUP THAT IS BORTSCH [227]
A mess of pottage from Northern lands to cheer the wayworn traveler

Your confirmed vegetarian is earnest, but never emotional, dramatic, or passionate in his madness. The omnivorous gourmet, on the other hand, can extol the delicacy or flavor of vegetables, and apostrophize artichokes, cèpes, or truffles in hexameters or sprightly jingles. But has anyone, anywhere, ever risen to lyrical heights over the turnip or the blood-red beet?

The turnip? No! there is no poetry in a turnip, unless it has been conjured into wine, as it sometimes is in rural America and Britain, and then there's no telling what might happen. But the humble beet is not without its occasions, when it may rise and spurn the turnip, the parsnip and other lowly neighbors of the garden patch. Here we drag it from the dry ground of harvest time and fling it into the root cellar, then bring it out indifferently enough to add bulk to a dish of hash (red flannel hash of New England), or color and variety to a New England Boiled Dinner.

Even in the cook books it is disposed of in a paragraph or two. It seems that there is nothing to do but butter it or pickle it, and trust to luck that some one will eat it. There are times and places, however, when and where the beet is treated with tender consideration, even as the purple grape is treated in the vineyard. For the beet is the essence, the spirit, the alpha and omega, of one of the world's great classic soups: B-o-r-t-s-c-h, or b-o-r-s-h, or however you may have a fancy for spelling it.

Bortsch ranks with all the aristocracy of the soup tureen, holding its title with clear green turtle, petite marmite, Madrilène, pot-au-feu and potage à la Reine. It is national in Russia and in Poland, and in Russia you must swear on your life that it's Russian, but in Poland you must salute it as the symbol of Poland's life blood. There are recipes without number, and some are simple and easy, but native cooks and gourmets are inclined to go about it with ceremony and ritual. To study an elaborate formula is to have misgivings, for the beets are set away in their juice to undergo chemical change and, after days and days, the scum and the mold are scraped from the surface of the brew, and bubbles rise and give off noxious vapors, and the process goes on—one thinks of Chinese eggs that are buried for years and years—and when the mess has reached a state which would cause any good Yankee cook to pour it down the drain, and good riddance, it is ready for the making of the soup, and your Polish friends will tell you, smacking their lips, that that is *bortsch!*

However it is made it is undeniably good, and a taste for it is not hard to cultivate. It was, for long years, a rare novelty in large restaurants, but fallen majesty brought Russian restaurants to us, and now you may see tired business men slipping into Russian and Polish and Jewish restaurants at noontime to refresh themselves with a bowl of cold bortsch, and they will add a liberal dash of thick sour cream in the orthodox manner and go to it with the gusto of Muscovites.

Bortsch Polonaise. Roast a whole, cleaned domestic duck of about 6 pounds in a hot oven (450° F.) until well browned (seared). Drain, put it in a soup kettle with 1 pound of beef bone, and ¼ pound bacon in 1 piece. Add 3 quarts of cold, salted water, the pulp of 12 medium-sized fresh beets, the pulp of 2 small carrots, 5 small leeks, carefully washed and passed through food chopper, 1 bouquet garni composed of 1 large bay leaf, 12 sprigs of fresh parsley, 1 large sprig of thyme, tied together with kitchen thread, 2 stalks of celery, scraped and chopped, 2 medium-sized onions, quartered, 2 quarters being stuck with 2 cloves each, 1 large clove of garlic, 12 whole peppercorns, gently bruised, and a grating of nutmeg. Bring slowly to a boil, skimming off all scum carefully. When boiling, lower the flame, let simmer gently (covered) over a very low flame for about 4 hours without disturbing. When done and tender, strain the bouillon through a fine-meshed sieve or fine cheesecloth into another soup kettle. Add 3 egg whites and their crushed shells, gradually bring to a boil, stiring and beating at the same time gently but thoroughly. When the boiling point is reached, simmer very gently for 12–15 minutes, but do not stir or beat any more. Strain through a fine cheesecloth placed over a sieve, taste for seasoning, and serve either very hot or very cold, but always with plenty of rich sour cream on the side. When served cold, sour cream, whipped with a few grains of salt, may be forced through a pastry bag with a small fancy tube to decorate the top of each cup with fancy designs.

BEET SOUP   [228]
American

Put 1 cup of cooked or canned beet pulp and any available juice into a soup kettle with 1 cup of raw potato cubes, ¼ cup of chopped green celery leaves, 1 small onion chopped, 1 bay leaf, ⅛ teaspoon of thyme leaves, and 1 quart of cold water. Cover, bring slowly to boiling point, lower the flame and let simmer gently for 20 minutes. Then rub mixture through a coarse sieve into a fresh soup kettle. Combine with 2 cups of scalded milk, to which has been added 2½ tablespoons of butter, season to taste with salt, pepper and a dash of powdered nutmeg. Reheat to the boiling point, remove from the fire, and stir in 3 slightly beaten egg yolks. Return again to the fire and cook 2 or 3 minutes, stirring constantly. Serve hot with a side dish of popcorn.

Variation. (1) Stir in, just before serving, ½ cup of hot split pea soup. (2) Stir in, just before serving ½ cup of boiled rice. (3) Stir in, just before serving, ½ cup of cooked. chopped vermicelli. (4) Stir in, just before serving, ½ cup of cooked, finely shredded spinach, lettuce or cabbage.

BLACK BEAN SOUP I [229]
American Home Style (Serves 10 persons)

Heat ¼ cup of sweet butter; stir in ¼ cup of chopped onion and ⅓ cup of chopped carrots and cook over a low flame until mixture just begins to brown. Add 2½ quarts of hot water mixed with 1 cup of Pique Seasoning, then 1½ pounds of black beans which have been soaked in water overnight and well drained, 1 bouquet garni, composed of 1 small bay leaf, tied with kitchen thread with 1 sprig of thyme and 1 sprig of very green celery leaves, season to taste with pepper only. Bring slowly to a boil; lower the flame and simmer gently 2¼–2½ hours or until beans are tender (the exact time cannot be determined, it depends on the age and quality of the beans). Discard the bouquet garni, rub liquid and solid through a fine sieve into a fresh soup kettle, and stir in 1 quart of Cream of Chicken Soup (No. 268). Taste for seasoning, adding salt and black pepper as needed. Heat to boiling point and, when ready to serve, stir in 1 cup of scalded heavy cream, 2 tablespoons of sweet butter and 2 hard-cooked eggs finely chopped.
NOTE. If desired, garnish each serving with a thin slice of seeded lemon.

BLACK BEAN SOUP II [230]
French Style (Serves about 10 persons)

Soak 1½ cups of carefully picked black beans overnight in cold water. Next day, drain, rejecting any which float on the surface of the water. Place the beans in a soup kettle, add 1 quart of cold water and gradually bring to boiling point. Meantime, cook in 1½ tablespoons of sweet butter ¼ cup of chopped onions, ¼ cup of finely chopped green celery leaves, 1 small carrot, scraped and chopped, 1 small leek, halved lengthwise and carefully washed in several changes of cold water, then drained and finely chopped, cooking until just beginning to brown and stirring frequently, over a gentle flame. Add to the beans and stir well. Season with 1 teaspoon of celery salt, ¼ teaspoon of black pepper, freshly crushed or milled, 4 or 5 grains of mustard seeds, and continue simmering 3¼–3½ hours, or until beans are tender, adding more boiling water as it boils away. Rub through a fine-meshed sieve, reheat to boiling point, taste for seasoning, stir in 3 tablespoons of sherry wine and ¾ cup of scalded sweet cream. When ready to serve, sprinkle over the soup 2 hard-cooked eggs, finely chopped and mixed with 1 teaspoon of finely chopped parsley. Serve at once with a side dish of thin slices of lemon, half of them dipped or pressed in finely chopped parsley, the other half in paprika.

Variations. (1) *Guatemala Style:* Substitute coarsely chopped alligator pear for chopped eggs. (2) *Country Style:* Substitute 3 tablespoons of cooked rice for chopped eggs. (3) *Fermière Style:* Substitute ¼ cup of cooked, chopped vermicelli for chopped eggs. (4) *Grandmother Style:* Substitute croutons fried in butter for chopped eggs.

BOHEMIAN RYE BREAD SOUP   [231]

Heat ¼ cup of sweet butter in a soup kettle; stir in half a loaf of grated rye bread and brown slightly over a low flame, stirring constantly; then add ¼ cup of grated onions and 2 tablespoons of finely chopped parsley, and continue cooking for 2 minutes longer, stirring almost constantly. Pour over 2¼ quarts of boiling water, previously mixed with 1 cup of Pique Seasoning. Do not season with salt and pepper as yet, but sprinkle over a generous grating of nutmeg. Cook very gently over a low flame for about 1 hour. Strain the soup through a fine-meshed sieve into a fresh soup kettle or sauce pan. Stir in 1 cup of cooked mixed vegetables (peas, potato cubes, carrot cubes, celery cubes, green pepper cubes and finely chopped leeks, in equal parts), also 2 or 3 skinned, thinly sliced frankfurters, and heat to boiling point. Taste for seasoning, adding salt and pepper as needed. Stir in 3 well-beaten fresh egg yolks. Serve at once.

"Appulmoy," a popular soup of the fourteenth century which contained almond milk, apples and honey, is still being eaten in some parts of Germany today. Another of the same period, "Snow Pottage," made of rice and milk, was revived in England in 1753 and is still popular.

BORTSCH SOUP   [232]
See No. 227, Beet Soup That is Bortsch.

BREAD SOUP   [233]

Grate the crusts of 3 stale rolls into a saucepan; pour over 1¾ quarts of boiling water and 1 cup of Pique Seasoning; add 1 bouquet garni composed of 1 large bay leaf, 1 sprig of thyme and 8 sprigs of fresh parsley, tied with kitchen thread, and let simmer very gently for 25 minutes. Discard the bouquet garni and, when ready to serve, stir in 3 slightly beaten egg yolks, beaten with a grating of nutmeg, stirring briskly and constantly to prevent curdling. Serve at once with thin slices of brown bread, generously buttered.

CALF'S HEAD SOUP I   [234]
Virginia Method

Wash and scald 1 calf's head. Put it into 4 quarts of cold water and simmer gently 4–4½ hours, skimming off all scum as it rises. Add during the last hour, 1 large onion, quartered; 1 bouquet garni composed of 2 bay leaves, 3 sprigs of green celery leaves, about 15 sprigs of fresh parsley, 1 large sprig of thyme, 3 or 4 sprigs of marjoram, all tied together with kitchen thread; 1 tablespoon of peppercorns, 4 whole cloves, and salt to taste. Remove the head. Strain the stock through a fine sieve into a saucepan and keep hot. Reserve the rest of the calf's head for an excellent dish of Calf's Head Vinaigrette (No. 624).

Take about 1 pound of the meat from the head and with it, make small forcemeat balls as indicated for Chicken Forcemeat Balls (No. 200) and fry them in butter until delicately browned. Place the balls in a heated soup tureen. Pour 2 quarts of the head stock, seasoned to taste, over them, stir in ½ cup of good sherry wine or Madeira wine and serve as hot as possible, each plate garnished with a thin slice of lemon, topped with a little finely chopped parsley. Serve a side dish of chopped hard-cooked eggs and plenty of toast.

CALF'S HEAD SOUP II   [235]
French (Clear) (Serves about 10–12)

Soak ½ calf's head overnight in slightly salted cold water to generously cover. Next day, drain, dry and bone the head, setting aside the brains and tongue for other service. Tie the meat in a cheesecloth; break the bones into small pieces and put them, with the meat, into a soup kettle. Cover with cold salted water, bring to a boil, strain, and wash the head in cold water. Return the meat and bones to the kettle, put in 5 quarts of clear beef stock, add ½ teaspoons of salt; bring to a boil and skim off very carefully all scum as it rises. Now add 2 medium-sized onions, quartered; 2 medium-sized carrots, scraped and cut into inch pieces; 1 small white turnip, peeled and quartered; 1 stalk of celery, cut into inch pieces, 1 bouquet garni composed of 10 sprigs of fresh parsley, 2 large bay leaves, 3 sprigs of marjoram, 2 sprigs of sweet basil, and 1 sprig of thyme all tied together with kitchen thread; ¼ teaspoon of mace, 4 whole cloves, and 12 peppercorns. Bring gradually to boiling point, skimming off all scum as it rises; cover and simmer very gently over a low flame for about 3 hours, or until the meat is tender.

Strain through a fine-meshed sieve into an earthenware or porcelain bowl and, when cold, remove every particle of fat from the surface. Reserve the meat and discard the bones. Pour the clear stock into a saucepan, add ¼ pound of lean, chopped beef, ½ pound of chopped lean veal, 3 egg whites and their crushed shells, and gradually bring to a boil, stirring and beating with a wire whisk. When near the boiling point, stop stirring and beating and let simmer very gently for 15 minutes, uncovered. Strain the stock through a wet cheese cloth placed over a strainer into a fresh saucepan; reheat to boiling point, stir in

¾ cup of good sherry wine, 1 tablespoon of strained lemon juice and about 1 cup of the meat of the head, cubed very small. Taste for seasoning and serve as hot as possible. The remainder of the calf's head may be used for a delicious entrée. If desired, thicken the soup with a little flour rubbed smooth with cold water.

CANADIAN PEA SOUP   [236]
Soupe aux Pois à l'Habitant

The cuisine of the Canadian shows its spiritual descent from French gastronomy by its rich and recondite sauces, by its slow simmerings (so as to extract all the nourishing parts of the foods), and by the refinements which make a meal an act of delicate sensuality.

To make the genuine Canadian pea soup, the soup of the habitant, soak 2 cups (1 pound) of washed, dried whole green or yellow peas overnight in 1½ quarts of cold water. Next day, discard the water and rinse the peas several times in cold running water. Turn them into a soup kettle with 6 cups of fresh, cold water, and add 2 small onions, each stuck with a whole clove; ½ pound of salt pork; 8 whole peppercorns, slightly bruised; 1 generous teaspoon of salt; and the real *herbes salées* or, if the latter is unobtainable, a bouquet garni made of 8 sprigs of parsley, 2 sprigs of green celery tops, 1 large bay leaf, and 1 sprig of thyme, tied with kitchen thread. Gradually bring these to a boil, reduce the flame, and allow to simmer very, very gently 2½–3 hours, the kettle being only half covered with the lid. Remove the salt pork and keep it hot. Then turn the contents of the kettle into a fine-meshed sieve and rub till all liquid and peas and onions have been forced through into a fresh soup kettle. Return the soup to the fire, taste for seasoning, reheat to boiling point, then serve in hot soup plates, dropping into each plate a small square of the salt pork and a few croutons.

> *He's like a brother of his wares,*
> *Brown-shelled, and burred with bristle.*
> *His only advertisement is*
> *A steam-escaping whistle. . . .*
> *He'll pull your chestnuts from the fire,*
> *No extra charge for burns,*
> *So let Pierre roast you some—*
> *He gives more than he earns.*
> *'Round the corner, down the street*
> *The whistle's growing fainter—*
> *He'll never know that he has been*
> *A model for a painter. . . .*
> *—L. P. De Gouy, "The Chestnut Man"*

CHESTNUT SOUP AUVERGNATE MANNER [237]

Wash and dry 1¾ pounds of sound chestnuts, then criss-cross the rounded sides of their shells with a sharp-pointed knife and roast the nuts 12–15 minutes on a pan containing 1 tablespoon of good cooking oil in a very hot oven (450–475° F.), shaking the pan occasionally. Remove the chestnuts from the oven, and when cool enough to handle, peel them; the inner skin should come off with the outer one. Place the chestnuts in a saucepan and add a bouquet garni consisting of 3 sprigs of green celery tops, 8 sprigs of fresh parsley, 1 large bay leaf, 1 sprig of thyme, and 2 whole cloves, all tied together with kitchen thread. Pour over the nuts enough boiling salted water to cover, then let them boil gently 20–25 minutes, or until tender. Discard the bouquet garni, drain the chestnuts thoroughly, and rub them through a ricer into a fresh soup kettle, easing the rubbing by adding a few tablespoons of thin cream or undiluted evaporated milk to the chestnuts in the ricer (or sieve). Measure the resulting chestnut purée; there should be 4 generous cups.

Add to the purée 1 quart of rich chicken broth (No. 238), season to taste with salt, white pepper, and a few grains of paprika, and bring to boiling point. Stir in 1 cup of scalded cream seasoned with a tiny pinch of dry mustard and a pinch of salt. Let the soup boil once, remove it from the fire, and stir in a generous ⅓ cup of sherry wine. Divide the soup among 6 heated bouillon cups and top each cup with meringue. For this, beat 2 egg whites very stiffly with a few grains of salt, and fold into them 3 tablespoons of coarsely ground nut meats. Set the cups under the flame of the broiling oven 5 inches from the flame, and delicately brown the meringue. Serve at once.

According to Xenophon, the Greek historian, the children of the Persian nobility ate large quantities of chestnuts and thrived on them.

CHICKEN BROTH PARISIAN STYLE [238]

Clean a 4–4½ pound fowl carefully; if you can get a few chicken feet and necks, so much the better—this will reinforce your broth. Place fowl with feet and necks in a soup kettle; bring to a boil as slowly as possible, skimming off all scum as it rises. When quite clear and there is no more scum on the surface, add 2 well washed small leeks split in two, tied with 1 large bay leaf, 10 sprigs of fresh parsley, 2 sprigs of green celery leaves (the greener the better) 1 sprig of thyme and 2 whole cloves, 1 medium-sized carrot, scraped then quartered, 1 large onion, peeled and quartered, 1 small white turnip, peeled and quartered, 7 or

8 peppercorns, gently bruised, 2 teaspoons of salt and a small parsnip, about the size of an egg halved. Bring to a boil, lower the flame, and simmer gently for 3 hours, covered. Strain through fine, wet cheese-cloth, placed over a strainer, into a bowl, cool and, when cold, remove carefully all fat from the surface. Reheat and serve with any desired garnish or use in any recipes which require chicken broth or stock. Use the chicken for an entrée, croquettes, cutlets, hash, etc. Keep the broth in a glass jar, hermetically sealed and in the refrigerator until wanted. This broth will keep for 2 weeks in a good refrigerator.

COCK-A-LEEKIE SOUP   [239]
England (Original Recipe)

Put into a soup kettle 2 quarts of Chicken Broth Parisian Style (No. 238) and bring to a boil. Let simmer gently while preparing the following ingredients: Wash very carefully in several changes of water 8 small leeks, roots and outside leaves trimmed off, and halved length-wise. Drain, then blanch in boiling water to cover, drain again and dry, then add to the chicken broth with 2 tablespoons of washed, un-cooked rice. Bring slowly to a boil, lower the flame, cover and let simmer gently 35–40 minutes. When ready to serve, add 1 cup of small chicken cubes, using the chicken meat from the broth. Heat well and serve, topping each portion with a little finely chopped parsley.

CONSOMMÉ A L'AURORE   [240]

Consommé, and in fact any kind of good soup, is cuisine's "kindest" course. It breathes reassurance; it steams consolation; it promotes sociability as successfully as the 5 o'clock cup of tea, or the 6 o'clock cocktail hour. But it must be good. Good consommé must have body and clarity and it must be greaseless when served.

Why were the Scots such good soup-makers? Leaving aside the pleasantry that they were thrifty and stingy (they had to be) and thus conserved every morsel of left-overs, the real reason dates back to their queen, the ill-fated Mary of Scotland. She was reared at the French Courts, and when she returned to Edinburgh, she brought with her a train of French chefs and cooks, and it is due to their culinary skill that the Scots became noted for their fine soups, their pastries or meat pies, and their various cakes and sweetmeats.

Put into a saucepan 2 quarts of rich beef consommé (No. 301); bring to a boil and when at a full, rolling boil let drop in rainlike, 1/4 cup of Minute Tapioca, being careful that the consommé doesn't stop boiling. Let boil for about 15 minutes, stir in 2 tablespoons of tomato paste, taste for seasoning and serve in heated bouillon cups.

CONSOMMÉ ALEXANDRA   [241]

Cook in a little salted water ¼ cup of tapioca until tender. Strain through a fine cloth and add to 1½ quarts of chicken consommé (No. 301); bring to a boil and serve in hot bouillon cups, each cup garnished with 3 or 4 tiny sticks of cooked chicken meat, 1 tiny Chicken Force-meat Ball (No. 200) and 5 or 6 pieces of finely shredded lettuce previously parboiled.

CONSOMMÉ ARGENTEUIL   [242]

Bring to a boil 1½ quarts of beef consommé (No. 301). When ready to serve, add ½ cup of asparagus tips, cooked or canned, and taste for seasoning. Serve in heated bouillon cups.

CONSOMMÉ ANDALOUSE   [243]

This consommé is what is known in France and the United States as Consommé Madrilène, the difference being as follows. In the French recipe it is made with chicken stock, strongly flavored with celery and tomato juice. It is quite clear and when served hot is garnished with small tomato cubes, but when served cold it is ungarnished. In Spain, however, ordinary beef consommé is used, the tomato purée thickens it slightly, and it is garnished with 3 or 4 tablespoons of cooked vermicelli.

Bring 1½ quarts of beef consommé (No. 301) to a boil, stir in 3 or 4 tablespoons of tomato purée, and 5 minutes before serving, add the vermicelli.

CONSOMMÉ CENDRILLON   [244]

This is a very rich and expensive consommé. Bring 2 quarts of clear chicken consommé (No. 301) to a boil. Remove from the fire and stir in 1 black truffle, previously cooked in Marsala wine, then cut into fine julienne strips (matchlike), and ½ cup of cooked rice. Serve in heated bouillon cups.

CONSOMMÉ AUX CHEVEUX D'ANGE   [245]
Consommé with Vermicelli

Bring to a rolling boil 1¾ quarts of rich beef consommé (No. 301). When ready to serve, drop in ¼ cup of the smallest vermicelli you can get. Cook 5 minutes and serve in heated bouillon cups.

CONSOMMÉ IVAN   [246]

Heat to boiling point 1½ quarts of chicken consommé (No. 301), stir in ¼ cup of beet juice (fresh or canned) and, when ready to serve, stir in ½ cup of boiled rice.

CONSOMMÉ LORETTE   [247]

Bring to a boil 1½ quarts of chicken consommé and, when ready to serve, stir in 1 black truffle, peeled and cut julienne-fashion, ¼ cup of asparagus tips (fresh cooked or canned) and a teaspoon of finely chopped chervil or parsley.

CONSOMMÉ LUCETTE   [248]

Bring to a rapid boil 2 quarts of beef consommé, then gradually, in rainlike fashion, drop in ⅓ cup of alimentary paste (alphabet) and cook for 5 or 6 minutes or until alphabet paste is tender. When ready to serve, stir in 1 tablespoon of small pieces of tomato pulp (raw). Serve in soup plates, each plate garnished with a poached egg.

CONSOMMÉ MIDINETTE   [249]

Heat 1½ quarts of chicken consommé to the boiling point. Cook in a small saucepan 6 poached eggs and set aside. To the consommé brought to a rapid boil, add gradually, in rainlike fashion, ¼ cup of minute tapioca and cook until tender. Pour the consommé into a heated soup tureen and float the 6 poached eggs on top.

CONSOMMÉ MILLE FEUILLES   [250]

Combine, mixing thoroughly, ⅓ cup of soft bread crumbs and 3 tablespoons of grated Gruyère cheese or Swiss cheese; add 2 fresh eggs, a dash of nutmeg, salt and a few grains of cayenne, and beat briskly for at least 2 minutes. Have ready at a rolling boil 1¾ quarts of clear beef consommé (No. 301). Drop the preparation by means of a small funnel into the boiling consommé; allow it to simmer gently for 5 minutes. By this time the broth will become clear again. Serve in heated bouillon cups with toasted, buttered finger strips.

A Southern European custom of the thirteenth century was for the bride to prepare a pot of soup which she took to her wedding, stirring it continuously. After the ceremony the groom tasted it—but if she was a poor cook it was too late for him to do anything about it.

CONSOMMÉ MURAT [251]

Bring to a boil 1½ quarts of beef consommé (No. 301) and let simmer. When ready to serve, pour the consommé into a heated soup tureen and add 12 freshly made or canned raviolis. Serve with a side dish of grated parmesan cheese.

CONSOMMÉ NANA [252]

This consommé is very substantial and nourishing. Arrange in bottom of a heated soup tureen a layer of tiny toasted rounds of long French bread called "flute," or ordinary bread cut with the smallest cookie cutter and toasted; cover these rounds with a layer of grated Gruyère cheese. Add another layer of toasted bread rounds, and spread with grated parmesan cheese. Cover these with more small toasted rounds, and top them with 6 poached eggs, neatly trimmed, with just a narrow border of white. When ready to serve, pour over very gently and carefully 2 quarts of boiling rich chicken consommé.
NOTE. If desired, serve the poached eggs separately, thus preventing breaking them when ladling the consommé.

CONSOMMÉ OLGA [253]

Bring to boiling point 1½ quarts of rich beef consommé (No. 301), but do not let it actually boil. When ready to serve, stir in 1 scant cup of port wine and 2 tablespoons each of cooked celery-root, cut julienne-fashion, and caviar, previously rinsed in hot stock to remove the brine. Serve in heated bouillon cups.

CONSOMMÉ PAULETTE [254]

Bring to a boil 1½ quarts of chicken consommé (No. 301), and serve in heated bouillon cups each cup garnished with 2 or 3 tiny cubes of Chicken Custard Cubes (No. 199) and 4 or 5 canned pimiento stars, cut from drained, canned pimientos with a tiny French star cutter. Serve in heated bouillon cups with Cheese Sticks (No. 198).

CONSOMMÉ SAINT QUENTIN [255]

Heat 1½ quarts of beef consommé to the boiling point, stir in ¼ cup of sherry wine, and serve in heated cups garnished with 2 Egg Bails (No. 206).

Whenever Giuseppi Verdi, the famous composer, needed inspiration, he found it in a large bowl of noodle soup. He also rewarded himself with a bowlful when he completed a composition.

CORN CHOWDER   [256]
American

Brown lightly ½ cup of salt pork, cut in small dice; stir in 3 or 4 thin slices of onion, and cook 2 or 3 minutes, stirring frequently, over a gentle flame. Then add 1 small bay leaf tied with 5 or 6 sprigs of fresh parsley and 1 small sprig of thyme. Season to taste with salt, pepper and a dash of sage, then stir in 1 cup of raw potatoes, diced small, and 2 cups of hot water. Cook until the potatoes are tender. Thicken the mixture with 3 tablespoons of flour mixed smoothly with a little cold water or milk. Add 2½ cups of canned or freshly cooked whole kernel corn and 2 cups of scalded rich milk, and stir well. Bring the whole to a boil; remove from the fire and, just before serving, stir in 2 fresh egg yolks, slightly beaten, and 1 tablespoon of butter. Dust with finely chopped parsley or chives, and serve very hot.

CREAM SOUPS   [257]

Cream soups made with fresh milk, thin cream, heavy cream, butter, flour and seasonings, and either a cooked and sieved vegetable, meat, fish, crustacean or shellfish are a substantial, nourishing and delicious part of any meal, except, of course, breakfast. They should be distinctive in flavor. The vegetables are cooked, strained, then sieved in a kind of purée before being added to the basic sauce, which is the base of almost all cream soups. They must be well seasoned, and the addition of a little onion cooked with the vegetables, meat, fish, etc., will always enhance and add flavor.

Four kinds of basic standard cream sauces are used in the making of cream soups. These basic cream sauces are also used for sauces to accompany fish, meats, poultry, game, vegetables, crustacea and shellfish.

As a rule, any kind of vegetable, legume, meat, fish, fowl—in fact, almost any kind of edible food which may be sieved—may be used for cream soup. Or, a combination of two or three different foods may be used.

BASIC STANDARD RECIPES FOR CREAM   [258]
SAUCES

THIN	MEDIUM	THICK
1 tablespoon butter	2 tablespoons butter	3 tablespoons butter
1 tablespoon flour	2 tablespoons flour	3 tablespoons flour
1 cup of milk, or thin cream, or heavy cream	1 cup of milk, or thin cream, or heavy cream	1 cup of milk, or thin cream, or heavy cream
½ scant teaspoon salt	½ scant teaspoon salt	½ scant teaspoon salt
⅛ teaspoon white pepper	⅛ teaspoon white pepper	⅛ teaspoon white pepper
1 beaten egg yolk	1 beaten egg yolk	1 beaten egg yolk

Directions. In any one of the three basic sauces, melt the butter; stir in the flour and blend thoroughly, but do not let brown, over a gentle flame. Add seasonings, then gradually, while stirring constantly, stir in the milk, thin cream or heavy cream, previously scalded with 2 thin slices of onion, a bit of bay leaf, 2 sprigs of parsley, and 1 whole clove. Keep stirring, still over a low flame, until mixture thickens and bubbles. Let bubble for 3 or 4 minutes. Remove from the fire and briskly stir in the egg yolk. Do not boil any more, unless you stir briskly and from the bottom of the pan, lest mixture curdle. This makes 1 cup of cream sauce.

Just as every good soup maker has little tricks that are all his or her own, so nearly every dish requires a different technique to bring the basic part to just the right consistency and flavor. For instance, when making the basic cream sauce for a cream soup, you may fry a little onion—oh, not much!—in the butter before stirring in the flour, or you may use a little finely chopped shallot, or a soupçon of garlic instead of the onion, and let all blend together slowly to get the full flavor. To this you add the scalded milk, thin cream or heavy cream, and the seasonings. Or, you may use any one of the compounded (creamed) butters corresponding to the food ingredient or ingredients which are to be added to the basic sauce. Above all, a cream soup should be smooth, light without being liquid, glossy to the eye and definite as to taste.

The ambrosia, which the Greeks and the Romans insisted was the food of their gods, was probably only a clever way with garlic. A little rubbing of a cut clove of garlic in the pan will do. If a cream soup must stand after being made, place it in a double boiler over hot, but not boiling, water. It is absolutely impossible to keep it hot over a direct heat without scorching.

Notice that I call the basic sauce for cream soups "Cream sauce." "White sauce" (a most unattractive title) is usually badly made, incorrectly served, cool when it should be hot, sticky when it should be "creamy," and the less said about it the better—until numerous cooks really learn to make it.

For delicate cream soups, the milk in the basic recipe for cream sauce may be partly replaced by chicken or veal stock. And, a little—very little—grated cheese added to a basic sauce for cream soup gives it much more flavor than if it were served plain. These basic cream sauces may also be used for creamy chowders.

There is a fourth basic standard cream sauce—a master-key sauce—which may be used for cream soups, compounded sauces, and as a base or a foundation for any kind of rich cream sauce for fish, meat, poultry, game or vegetables. It is called Béchamel Sauce, a velvety, smooth, rich cream sauce, one of the creamiest white sauces. It was named and created by Louis de Béchamel, Marquis de Nointel, Lord Steward and Maître d'Hôtel of the Household at the Court of Louis XIV.

BÉCHAMEL SAUCE FOR CREAM SOUP   [259]

Bring 1 quart of milk to the scalding point with 1 large bay leaf. Meantime, heat ¼ cup of butter, stir in 1½ tablespoons of grated onion and cook, but do not let it brown, stirring almost constantly over a very low flame. Stir in ¼ cup of flour. Gradually add the strained, scalded rich milk, cooking until smooth and free from any lumps or clots, still stirring constantly. Set over hot water and keep hot. In another saucepan, heat 2 tablespoons of butter; stir in ¼ pound of coarsely chopped lean raw veal and cook, without letting it take on color, stirring constantly; season to taste with salt, white pepper and a dash of nutmeg. Now, slowly, very slowly, pour the scalded milk mixture over the veal and cook, over a very low flame (placing an asbestos under the saucepan) for an hour, stirring frequently from the bottom of the pan. Strain this sauce through a fine-meshed sieve and spread over it bit by bit 1 tablespoon of sweet butter, to prevent the forming of a film or thin crust on the top.

For each quart of this hot sauce, have ready 1½ cups of cooked, sieved and well drained fish, meat, fowl, game vegetable or a combination of vegetables and, when ready to serve, stir in 2 well-beaten egg yolks. Taste for seasoning, and serve as hot as possible.

NOTE. This sauce will keep for a whole week in a sealed jar in the refrigerator and needs only to be heated over hot water, and the desired purée of food added to make a smooth, rich cream soup; or it may be used as a cream sauce.

Soup à La Squirt. The "Soup Syringe," a clever gadget used to serve the poor in eighteenth-century Paris, guaranteed no free meals. An attendant squirted soup from an oversize syringe into a basin nailed to the table—and unless payment was immediately forthcoming the soup was vacuumed back into the syringe!

CREAM OF ASPARAGUS SOUP [260]

Trim the end butts from a bunch of asparagus; cut off tips and stems and boil both in 1 quart of salted boiling water until tender. Drain. Set aside tips and 2 cups of asparagus stock. Cook 1 tablespoon of butter and 1 tablespoon of flour, together, stirring constantly until cream colored but not brown. Gradually add 3 cups of scalded rich milk, mixed with the 2 cups of reserved asparagus stock and 1 small ham bone, or its equivalent in cooked lean ham, and cook gently 25–30 minutes, stirring occasionally. Strain through a fine sieve; season to taste with salt, pepper and a dash of nutmeg. Again bring to a boil; remove from the fire and beat in 2 or 3 slightly beaten egg yolks. Taste for seasoning, and, when ready to serve, add the reserved asparagus tips and 1 tablespoon of butter.

CREAM OF BARLEY SOUP [261]

Simmer 1 veal knuckle, or left-over chicken or turkey carcass broken into pieces, in 2 quarts of slightly salted, cold water very gently for

2½ hours, skimming off all scum as it rises to the surface. Strain through a fine sieve. Wash ½ cup of barley in cold water; drain, add to the strained stock, with 1 large bay leaf, 1 whole clove and 4 thin slices of onion; cover the kettle and cook until barley is tender. Remove about half of the barley from the soup and set it aside. Rub the soup through a fine-meshed sieve; return the reserved barley, stir in 1 can of undiluted evaporated milk or thin cream, season to taste with salt and white pepper; bring to a boil and let simmer gently for 20 minutes. Just before serving, stir in 1 tablespoon of butter and serve in hot soup plates, each plate garnished with 2 or 3 Burger Balls with Marjoram Dumplings (No. 195).

The ancient Romans had a triple use for milk—as a beverage, a cosmetic, and as bath "water."

CREAM OF BEAN SOUP FRENCH MANNER   [262]

Soak 2 cups of carefully picked red kidney beans in cold water overnight. Next day, drain, place in a soup kettle, add 1 small cooked leg of lamb bone, cracked, 1 medium-sized onion stuck with 2 whole cloves, 1 bouquet garni composed of 6 or 7 sprigs of parsley, tied with 1 large bay leaf and 1 sprig of thyme; 8 whole peppercorns, fresh crushed, 1 teaspoon of salt, 3 cups of cold water and 3 cups of cold milk. Bring to a boil and cook very gently until beans are tender. Empty the whole contents of the soup kettle except bone into a fine-meshed sieve and rub through, into a fresh saucepan. Return to the fire, adding more scalded milk if mixture is too thick; taste for seasoning; bring to boiling point; remove from the fire and beat in 2 well-beaten egg yolks and 1 tablespoon of sweet butter. Serve in soup plate, with a side dish of freshly made Melba Toast (No. 214).

CREAM OF BUTTERMILK ALMOND SOUP   [263]

Bring ¾ quart of buttermilk to which has been added ½-inch stick of cinnamon to a boil over a gentle flame, stirring occasionally. Combine 1 cup of cold buttermilk and 2 tablespoons of rice flour until smooth, then stir in 3 tablespoons of sugar and ⅓ cup of blanched, ground almonds; add to the hot buttermilk; bring to a boil, season to taste with salt and a few grains of white pepper and, when ready to serve, stir in 1 cup of thin cream or undiluted evaporated milk. Serve in hot soup plates, dusting with a little paprika.

CREAM (SOUR) OF CABBAGE SOUP   [264]

Shred 1 medium-sized head of fresh green cabbage (Savoy cabbage, if possible) together with 3 large onions in a soup kettle, as for slaw.

Mince 1 green pepper very fine and add. Cover generously with boiling water and add 2 slices of canned pimiento, chopped, 1 large bouquet garni, composed of 1 large bay leaf, 6 sprigs of fresh parsley and 1 sprig of thyme, tied together with kitchen thread; no salt, but pepper to taste. Cover and allow to boil gently until the cabbage is tender, the onions nearly dissolved and the water is boiled down to half. Then add 3 cups of scalded sweet milk, mixed with 1 pint of scalded sour cream. Season to taste with salt and a dash of nutmeg, and thicken with 2 tablespoons of butter kneaded with 2 teaspoons of flour. When ready to serve, add to the soup 3 strips of bacon, broiled crisp and coarsely chopped. Serve with a side dish of grated Swiss cheese.

CREAM OF CAULIFLOWER SOUP [265]
SOUTHERN MANNER

Clean a small head of cauliflower and separate into small flowerets. Blanch 3 or 4 minutes in slightly salted boiling water; drain, and reserve the water. Cook the blanched cauliflower flowerets 6–8 minutes in 2 generous tablespoons of butter, over a gentle flame, but do not let brown; sprinkle with 2 tablespoons of flour, mix well, then gradually stir in the reserved cauliflower water, and cook gently for 25 minutes. Strain through a fine-meshed sieve into a fresh saucepan. Return to the fire and stir in 1 quart of scalded rich sweet milk, and continue cooking gently for 10 minutes. Remove from the fire, season to taste with salt, white pepper and a dash of nutmeg, then beat in 2 slightly beaten egg yolks, alternately with ⅓ cup of freshly cooked, drained rice. You may reserve a few cauliflower flowerets before rubbing and add them to the finished soup. Serve as hot as possible.

CREAM OF CELERY SOUP [266]

Boil 1 minced medium-sized onion, 1½ cups of finely diced celery stalk and leaves, 1 small bouquet garni composed of 1 small bay leaf, 4 sprigs of fresh parsley and 1 sprig of thyme, tied together with kitchen thread, and 1 whole clove in cold salted water to cover for about 30–35 minutes, or until tender. Cream 1 tablespoon of butter and 1 tablespoon of flour, and stir into 1 pint of scalded milk till thoroughly blended, then add to the celery mixture and cook 10 minutes longer. Turn all into a fine meshed sieve and rub through into a saucepan; return to the fire, season to taste with mixed salt, pepper and a dash of nutmeg; remove from the fire; stir in 1 well-beaten egg yolk, mixed with 2 cups of scalded thin cream or undiluted evaporated milk; heat to boiling point; taste for seasoning, and serve in hot soup plates, garnishing with fried croutons (No. 203).

Long before celery became a food, it was used as a medicine. Its very name, from the Latin *celeri*, means quick or fast. Ah-Pang Su, a famous Chinese epicure, declared that he could prepare 326 distinctly different recipes or dishes using only celery, water and salt.

CREAM OF CHESTNUT SOUP   [267]
FRENCH STYLE

Wipe with a damp cloth 1 small veal knuckle, split in two or three; place in a large soup kettle and add 5 or 6 bruised peppercorns, 1 small blade of garlic, 1 bay leaf tied with 6 sprigs of fresh parsley, 2 teaspoons of onion juice, 2 whole cloves and 1 scant teaspoon of salt, 1/3 cup of chopped celery leaves, and pour over all 5 cups of cold water. Bring slowly to a boil, then simmer gently, closely covered for 1½–1¾ hours. Turn the entire contents of the kettle into a fine-meshed sieve placed over a clean saucepan; discard the veal knuckle and bay leaf and rub remaining ingredients through sieve; return to the fire and let mixture reduce over a bright flame, until there is about 1½ cups of liquid left, then add ¾ cup of medium white sauce (No. 258), 2 cups of boiled, peeled, chopped chestnuts, alternately with 1 can of undiluted evaporated milk, or equivalent of thin cream, previously scalded. Bring to a boil, empty the contents into a very fine sieve and rub through into a fresh saucepan, taste for seasoning; reheat to boiling point, remove from the fire and stir in 2 slightly beaten egg yolks. Serve in heated soup plates, each plate garnished with a little popcorn lightly toasted.

CREME VICHYSSOISE also called   [268]
"CREME GAULOISE"
(*Cold*)

Wash and slice finely the white part of 4 leeks and 1 medium-sized onion, and brown lightly in ¼ cup butter; then add 5 medium-sized potatoes, thinly sliced. Moisten with 1 quart of chicken broth or water, season to taste with salt and white pepper. Let this mixture boil about 30 minutes until tender enough to mash and strain through a fine sieve. Stir in 2 cups scalded rich milk and 2 cups medium sweet cream. Bring the mixture to a rapid boil and taste for seasoning, adding salt and white pepper if necessary. Let cool and pass through a very fine sieve or muslin cloth. Stir in 1 cup heavy plain sweet cream. Chill thoroughly. When ready to serve, sprinkle each serving with finely minced chives.

In 1941, during the war, a group of French chefs in the U.S. decided to name it *Crème Gauloise*, as the name *Vichyssoise* had become unsavory to them.

CREAM OF CHICKEN SOUP A LA REINE   [269]
FAÇON BOURGEOISE
Home Method

Put into a large soup kettle, ¼ pound of bacon cut into small cubes, 1 three-pound chicken, cleaned and trussed as for roasting; 1 medium-sized onion, left whole and stuck with 1 whole clove; 1 medium-sized carrot, quartered; 1 bouquet garni composed of 8 sprigs of fresh parsley, 1 extra large bay leaf or 2 medium-sized ones, 1 sprig of thyme, and 1 sprig of green celery leaves (top), all tied together with kitchen thread, 2 teaspoons of salt, 8 whole peppercorns, gently bruised; and 1 quart of white stock (No. 185), chicken stock (No. 301), or canned chicken bouillon. Bring to a boil; skim very carefully and when bouillon is clear, cover and let simmer as gently as possible until the stock is reduced to about 2 cups, turning the chicken occasionally to prevent the part uncovered by the stock or liquid from becoming dry. Add 2 quarts more of similar hot stock to that used previously, and simmer gently, skimming frequently until chicken meat falls from the carcass. Carefully remove the chicken from the kettle and, when cool enough to handle, remove skin and bones very carefully and put the white meat alternately with ¼ pound of soft bread crumbs twice through food chopper, using the finest blade. Then rub chicken and crumb mixture through a fine-meshed wire sieve. Return this purée to the strained stock, add 1 ounce of blanched, peeled, then twice ground almonds, cooked 2 or 3 minutes in a little milk. Taste for seasoning, adding salt, pepper, if needed, with a tiny dish of nutmeg. Bring to a boil, let boil 2 minutes, and strain again through a fine-meshed wire sieve. When ready to serve, pour into a heated soup tureen containing a dozen Chicken Forcemeat Balls (No. 200), 3 tablespoons of freshly cooked green peas, a dozen freshly cooked or canned asparagus tips, and 2 tablespoons of sweet butter.

CREAM OF CORN FARMER STYLE   [270]

Melt 2 tablespoons of butter in saucepan; add 1 tablespoon of flour and, when thoroughly blended, but not brown, stir in 2 cups of boiling water. Cook until mixture begins to thicken, stirring almost constantly. Now add 1 medium sized can of corn cream style, 1 pint of scalded milk, 1 bay leaf, 4 thin slices of onion, 1 whole clove, and a little salt and pepper, and continue cooking 15 minutes longer. Empty the contents of the saucepan into a fine-meshed wire sieve and rub through into a fresh saucepan. Return this purée to the fire, stir in 1 cup of sweet cream, previously scalded; bring to a boil; taste for seasoning, and serve in hot soup plates, garnishing each with a dozen or so freshly popped kernels of corn.

CREAM OF CUCUMBER SOUP   [271]

Peel 3 medium-sized cucumbers and split lengthwise; remove the seeds; slice very thin, and cook, stirring constantly, but without browning, in 3 tablespoons of butter. Sprinkle 1 tablespoon of flour over and blend well. Gradually stir in 1½ quarts of scalded sweet milk, bring again to boiling point, stirring constantly, and simmer gently for 15 minutes, stirring frequently. Empty the whole contents of the saucepan or kettle into a fine-meshed wire sieve and rub through into a saucepan. Return to the fire; bring once more to a boil; season to taste with salt, pepper and a generous dash of freshly ground nutmeg; remove from the fire and beat in 2 or 3 beaten egg yolks, one at a time, beating briskly after each addition and adding with the last egg yolk 1 tablespoon of sweet butter. Finally, stir in ½ cup of blanched toasted and shredded almonds, and pass a side dish of fried croutons (No. 203).

CREAM OF GIBLET SOUP NEW ENGLAND   [272]
STYLE

This soup is very good and very inexpensive. It is an excellent imitation of mock turtle soup.

Melt 2 tablespoons of butter; stir in 1 medium-sized onion, diced; 1 small carrot, finely chopped; and ½ small white turnip, chopped. Cook until tender and light brown over a medium flame, stirring frequently. Then add the giblets of 4 chickens or 2 turkeys, first carefully washed and dried, then cut in small pieces. Cook 2 or 3 minutes, stirring constantly, then sprinkle in 1 tablespoon of flour and stir until thoroughly blended. Turn into a soup kettle; add 2 quarts of boiling water or equal parts of water and white stock (No. 185); bring to a boil, lower the flame and simmer gently for 2½ hours, or until giblets are tender. Rub through a fine sieve the 4 chicken livers or 2 turkey livers and add to contents of soup kettle together with 1 tablespoon of butter and 1 tablespoon of flour browned together. Bring to boiling point and cook 3 minutes. Season to taste with salt and pepper and, when ready to serve, stir in 3 hard-cooked eggs, coarsely chopped. Serve in hot soup plates with freshly made toast.

CREAM OF KIDNEY SOUP HUNTER STYLE   [273]

Cut 2 large veal kidneys in thin slices and brown in 2 tablespoons of butter over a low flame, stirring almost constantly, then stir in 1½ cups of water or beef stock, and cook until kidneys are tender, or about 10–12 minutes, skimming carefully. Turn into a fine-meshed wire sieve and rub through, into a fresh saucepan; return to the fire and simmer very gently for 25 minutes. Moisten ½ ounce of freshly ground polished rice with 1 cup of cold milk, and add to the soup, alternately with 1 quart of scalded sweet milk and ½ cup of finely chopped raw, fresh mushrooms; season to taste with salt, pepper and a dash of mace; cover and simmer gently for 20 minutes. Then add 1 tablespoon of butter, kneaded with 2 teaspoons of flour, bring to a boil, cook 3 or 4 minutes, and remove from the fire. Finally, stir in 2 egg yolks, well beaten with 2 or 3 tablespoons of Madeira wine. Taste for seasoning, and serve in heated soup plates, each containing 2 egg balls (No. 206).

Because the Greeks believed that lettuce induced sleep, they served it at the end of the meal. This custom was followed by the Romans, but the cruel Emperor Domitian reversed the custom, serving lettuce and eggs at the beginning of feasts, intending to torture the guests by forcing them to keep awake in the presence of the Emperor.

CREAM OF LETTUCE SOUP   [274]

Wash 2 heads of crisp lettuce, the greener the better, first picking carefully and discarding any wilted leaves. Shred very fine, wash again and drain; then dry by patting between 2 dry towels. Blanch in 2 cups of slightly salted water. Blend 2 tablespoons of butter and 1 tablespoon of flour, over a gentle flame. When beginning to bubble, stir in 1 quart of sweet milk, which has been scalded with 3 thin slices of onion, 3 sprigs of fresh parsley, 1 whole clove, and 1 small bay leaf, then strained. Stir almost constantly over a low flame until mixture boils and thickens slightly. Then add the shredded lettuce, and continue simmering gently 30–35 minutes, stirring occasionally. Season to taste with salt, pepper and a dash of nutmeg. Turn into a fine-meshed wire sieve and rub through into a fresh saucepan. Return to the fire; bring again to a boil and stir in 2 egg yolks, beaten with 1 cup of thin cream or undiluted evaporated milk; finally stir in 1 tablespoon of sweet butter. Taste for seasoning, and serve in heated soup plates, garnishing each with a sprinkling of chopped parsley or chervil. Serve with croutons (No. 203).

CREAM OF MUSHROOM SOUP   [275]

Peel 1 pound of fresh mushrooms; cut the rough ends of the stems and chop coarsely, then put through food chopper. Melt ¼ cup of butter in top of double boiler; add 1 medium-sized onion, finely chopped, also the ground mushrooms and cook for 5 minutes, over direct flame, stirring frequently. Sprinkle in 1½ tablespoons of flour and blend well.

Gradually stir in 1½ quarts of sweet milk (previously scalded with 1 large bay leaf, 4 sprigs of fresh parsley and 1 whole clove, then strained) and cook, stirring almost constantly, until mixture thickens and boils. Season to taste with salt, pepper, a dash of cayenne and one of mace; place top of boiler over hot water and let simmer gently for 20 minutes, stirring frequently. Turn into a fine-meshed wire sieve and rub through into a fresh saucepan; return to the fire, taste for seasoning, stir in ½ cup of sweet, scalded heavy cream, to which has been added 2 well beaten egg yolks. Stir briskly. Serve in heated soup plates with croutons(No. 203).

CREAM OF PEA PODS [276]

Boil 2 quarts of carefully picked, cleaned and washed pea pods in 1 quart of slightly salted water with 1 generous cup of well-packed shredded lettuce and 1 large onion, minced. When the liquid is reduced to a pint, rub through a fine-meshed wire sieve into a fresh saucepan; return to the fire and stir in 1 quart of milk, scalded with 1 bay leaf and 4 sprigs of fresh parsley, then strained; bring to a boil, season to taste with salt, pepper and a dash of nutmeg, and remove from the fire. Beat in 2 egg yolks, one at a time, beating well after each addition, alternately with 1 tablespoon of butter, kneaded with 1 teaspoon of flour. Return to the fire, bring almost to a boil, stirring constantly, and serve in heated soup plates with croutons (No. 203).

CREAM OF PUMPKIN SOUP FRENCH STYLE [277]

Of the honesty and the sincerity of our sentimental fondness for the pumpkin there is no doubt. It is impossible, indeed, that the aura of sanctity with which we have surrounded that gourd has limited our desire to find new culinary uses for it; for the French, who have no emotion one way or the other about the pumpkin, which they call "potiron," have gone far beyond pumpkin pie. On a cold winter night, for instance, warmth and comfort that penetrate to the soul can be yours when a rich, creamy pumpkin soup is on the table.

Cook 3½ pounds of peeled and diced pumpkin in 1½ quarts of salted water until the pumpkin is tender. Empty the entire contents of the kettle into a fine-meshed wire sieve and rub through into a saucepan. Stir in 1 quart of milk which has been boiled with 1 bay leaf, 4 thin slices of onion and 3 sprigs of fresh parsley, then strained; return to the fire, stir in 1 teaspoon of sugar (more or less, according to taste), and a pinch of freshly grated nutmeg. Keep the mixture over hot water. Then cook until tender 3 tablespoons of quick-cooking tapioca in 2 cups of chicken or beef stock (No. 301) and add to the soup. Taste for seasoning and, when ready to serve, stir in 1 pint of scalded fresh sweet cream. Serve with croutons (No. 203).

CREAM OF SPINACH SOUP HOME STYLE   [278]

Wash, pick and chop 2 quarts of spinach. Wash once more and cook in a large soup kettle without water, cooking gently and slowly until the juice is drawn out, then boil until tender and chop. Rub the spinach through a fine-meshed wire sieve, into a saucepan; stir in 1 quart of chicken stock (No. 301), and set over a hot fire. When boiling, lower the flame and let simmer gently for about 15 minutes. Blend 1 tablespoon of butter and flour together over a low flame; stir in 1 cup of heavy cream, which has been scalded with a small bay leaf, 4 thin slices of onion, 3 sprigs of parsley and 1 whole clove, then strained, and cook gently for 10 minutes, stirring frequently. Season to taste with salt and pepper; boil up once; remove from the fire, and beat in 2 egg yolks, added one at a time, beating well after each addition. Serve very hot in heated soup plates, each topped with a spoonful of whipped cream dusted with finely chopped parsley and a film of paprika.

CREAM OF TOMATO SOUP CLUB STYLE   [279]

Put 2 cups of canned tomatoes in a soup kettle, add 1 tablespoon of finely minced onion, 1 tablespoon of chopped celery leaves and 1 teaspoon of sugar. Cook gently 15–20 minutes, stirring occasionally, then rub through a fine-meshed sieve, into a saucepan. Blend 2 tablespoons of butter and 2 tablespoons of flour over a gentle flame, stirring constantly; gradually stir in 1½ quarts of milk, previously scalded with 1 large bay leaf, 4 sprigs of fresh parsley and 1 whole clove, then strained, still stirring constantly, and cook until mixture thickens and boils. Combine with the tomato mixture; then let boil up once or twice; season to taste with salt and white pepper; remove from the fire; stir in 2 well-beaten egg yolks, alternately with 1 tablespoon of sweet butter, and serve in heated soup plates, each plate garnished with 1 tablespoon of salted whipped cream, topped with a little finely chopped parsley or chervil.

CHOWDERS   [280]

Following food trails in quest of food origins is always adventurous and, as often as not, the trail itself comes to an end at a picturesque but totally unexpected source.

Whence comes our chowder—that hot, savory and substantial dish that heartens us on those chill days of early fall and winter? Is chowder an Indian name, like so many others borne by our native dishes—the samp, the succotash?

No, the trail in quest of chowder origins leads us over the vast waters of the Atlantic, and begins first in the little hamlets and villages of Brittany, famed fishing sea-coast of France. There, in those so-specialized fishing villages, originated a community enterprise in the shape of *faire la chaudiere*, or "prepare the cauldron."

After a fishing expedition, when the men were back home from the sea with their catches, it became the custom to celebrate with a huge pot or cauldron of soup or stew, to which each man or family contributed some ingredients. Some brought fish, others vegetables, still others seasonings and spices—and everything went into the pot, all together and at once.

In return, each family participated equally in this steaming pot, around which gathered, too, much festivity, quite after our own fashion of a village fair or festival, or perhaps like our first Thanksgiving dinner.

Step number two along this interesting trail occurred when many of these French fisherfolk crossed the Atlantic to settle in Newfoundland, bringing, of course, their chaudière with them.

Step number three is only a little distance farther on, either in New England or across that narrow link of water called Long Island Sound, each claimed as the original home of the chowder. For by this time the French word meaning "big stew pot" had been contracted and modified into the more Yankeefied "chowder."

Naturally the New Englander, with an abundance of seafood at his very doorstep, continued mightily in the chowder tradition. He made it of fish, he made it of clams, he made it of oysters—or he made it of all three, and added other little seasoning tidbits, such as diced salt pork, chopped bacon, thyme and other fragrances out of the spice cabinet. Now and again he added milk—or, still later, and lower down the Middle Atlantic seaboard, he began to add tomatoes. Thus started the famous food controversy, still—if ever—to be settled, as to whether chowder should be made with tomatoes.

Alas, what crimes have been committed in the name of chowder! Dainty chintz-draped tea rooms, charity bazaars, church suppers, summer hotels, canning factories—all have shamelessly travestied one of America's noblest institutions; yet while clams and onions last, the chowder shall not die, neither shall it sink into the limbo of denatured, emasculated forgotten things.

Clam chowder, mind you, is not a bisque, not a Parisian potage, not a delicate broth for invalids. It matters not whether you belong to the milk or the water party in the chowder cult—clams and onions and salt pork are the fundamentals on which to concentrate. Much has been said about onions, and much must be said of onions and clams when chowder is in the balance.

MASSACHUSETTS BAY CLAM CHOWDER   [281]
Also called New England Clam Chowder

"Take a dozen clams and 1 small onion," says a certain undeservedly popular cook book, taking the name of clam chowder in vain.

A dozen clams, forsooth! Take 4 or 5 dozen good soft clams, if your family is a small one. Men and women of Rhode Island and Massachusetts Bay never sat down to less than a peck of clams apiece. Then take 6 large onions and ½ pound of the finest salt pork. Cut the pork in half-inch dice and brown them slowly in an iron skillet, then add the sliced onions to the pork fat and let them turn to golden-brown rings. Meanwhile wash the live clams, using a brush to get rid of all sand, and heat them slowly in a pan till the shells open. Save the juice, cut off the long necks and remove the coarse membrane, then chop half of the clams, not too finely, and keep the rest whole. Put pork, onions, clam juice, and 1 quart of boiling water in a kettle, add 3 large peeled tomatoes, 1 bunch of leeks cut finely, 2 stalks of celery, finely minced, 2 young carrots, diced, 1 tablespoon of chopped parsley, ½ teaspoon of thyme leaves, 2 large bay leaves, 1 teaspoon of salt, ½ generous teaspoon of freshly ground black pepper, a slight grating of nutmeg, and let the mixture boil up smartly. Then reduce to the simmering point, and put in 3 large potatoes, peeled and cut in neat small dice. Prepare a roux by browning 2 rounded tablespoons of flour in 2 rounded tablespoons of butter, and make it creamy and smooth by stirring in broth from the kettle. Put all the clams into the kettle before the potatoes begin to soften, and simmer slowly until the potatoes are just tender, then stir in the roux and 2 large pilot biscuits coarsely crumbled, and add 1 tablespoon of Worcestershire sauce and a dash of Tabasco sauce. Serve sizzling hot.

If preferred, omit the tomatoes and add instead 1 cup of scalded sweet cream.

CLEAR TURTLE SOUP IN THE MANNER OF DROUANT   [282]

Soak ½ pound of the best sun-dried turtle in cold water for 3 days, changing the water frequently. Put 5 quarts of rich, clear beef stock (No. 301), the drained, rinsed piece of turtle and 1 tablespoon of salt (less if stock is salty), in a large soup kettle; bring to a boil, and boil steadily for 5 minutes, then skim off all scum as it rises to the surface. When quite clear, add 2 large onions, thinly sliced, 3 medium-sized carrots, chopped, 1 medium-sized white turnip, peeled and quartered, 2 stalks of celery, cut into inch lengths, 10 whole peppercorns, left whole and tied in a spice bag with 3 whole cloves, ½ teaspoon each of marjoram, mace, basil and dried leaves of fennel. Let simmer gently 7–8 hours—the longer the better—adding more boiling stock as it evaporates. Strain through a fine-meshed sieve; put the piece of turtle aside; then strain the stock through fine muslin into a large earthenware or porcelain container. When thoroughly cold, skim off the cake of fat from the surface, transfer the stock to a soup kettle, and let simmer very, very gently while preparing the ingredients to clarify it, as follows:

Put ½ pound of boned, lean neck of beef, together with ½ pound of lean, raw veal through food chopper 2 or 3 times, using the finest blade; add to the turtle stock; bring to a boil, beating with a wire whisk, the while and, as soon as boiling, add the crushed shells and the stiffly beaten whites of 3 eggs. Let boil up steadily two or three times; lower the flame and simmer gently for 30 minutes, then strain through fine muslin into a soup kettle. Add the reserved turtle meat, cubed small and 1 small can (optional) of turtle fat (commercial), ¾ cup of the best sherry wine you can get, 1 tablespoon of strained lemon juice, and simmer gently, but do not actually boil, lest the flavor of the wine be impaired, for 5 minutes, or just enough to heat well, over a low flame. Taste for seasoning, and serve at once in heated bouillon cups or soup plates with a side dish of lemon quarters neatly dressed on a bed of crisp, green watercress.

Next to herring, cod is the world's most important economic fish. By the sea faring folk of New England, particularly Massachusetts and of Newfoundland and Nova Scotia, it is often referred to as "sacred."

CODFISH CHOWDER NEWFOUNDLAND STYLE [283]

Wipe 3–3½ pounds of codfish with a damp cloth and place in a heavy soup kettle with 5 cups of cold water and ¾ teaspoon of salt, 1 bouquet garni composed of 1 large bay leaf, 8 sprigs of fresh parsley, 1 sprig of thyme, and 1 sprig of green celery leaves (top), tied together with kitchen thread, 1 whole clove, 1 blade of garlic, and 8 whole peppercorns. Bring slowly to a boil; lower the flame and simmer very gently for about 25 minutes. Strain the broth through a fine-meshed wire sieve into a soup kettle. Skin and carefully bone the fish, and set it aside to keep hot. Fry 2¾–3-inch cube of salt port fat back, cut into small cubes, add 2 medium-sized onions, thinly sliced, and add to the fish broth with 2 cups of diced small potatoes. Cook until potatoes are almost tender (about 10 minutes). Return the shredded, boned, skinned fish to the chowder; stir in 2 cups of scalded thin cream or undiluted evaporated milk; bring to a boil; taste for seasoning, and when ready to serve stir in 1 tablespoon of minced parsley and 1½ tablespoons of butter. Serve in hot plates each containing a toasted cracker.

Any kind of fresh, uncooked white-fleshed fish may be prepared in this manner.

CRAB MEAT AND CORN CHOWDER   [284]

Combine 2½ cups of fresh grated corn, or cream style canned corn, 3 thin slices of onion, 2½ cups of scalded sweet milk, and cook over boiling water 20–25 minutes. Take out the onion slices, if you wish, then force liquid and corn through a coarse sieve. Add to it 2½ cups of thin white or cream sauce (No. 258) and bring the whole to the boiling point. Stir in 2 beaten egg yolks, one at a time, beating briskly after each addition, and season to taste with salt, white pepper and a grating of nutmeg. Just before serving, stir in 1 cup of flaked crabmeat, either freshly cooked or canned, but carefully boned. Serve very hot with salted crackers.

HALIBUT SOUP WITH SAFFRON   [285]

Cut into serving pieces 2–2½ pounds of fresh halibut, previously cleaned and washed quickly in cold running water. Now place the fish in a saucepan and barely cover with boiling hot white wine court-bouillon (No. 1037). Place the kettle over a low flame and simmer very gently 8–10 minutes, covered. Meanwhile, sauté until light brown in 3 tablespoons of butter 1 medium-sized onion, finely chopped, and 1 clove of garlic, mashed. Add to the fish with 1 cup of fresh tomatoes, peeled and gently pressed to remove the seeds, then chopped, 1 tablespoon each of parsley and chives, finely chopped, and a bouquet garni made with 1 small bay leaf, 4 or 5 sprigs of fresh parsley, 2 sprigs of green celery tops, 1 sprig of thyme and 1 whole clove tied with white kitchen thread. Season to taste with salt, white pepper, and a small pinch of nutmeg, and continue simmering very gently, over a low flame, for about 25 minutes.

Strain through a fine sieve into a fresh saucepan; carefully remove the bones from the pieces of fish, keeping the meat hot. Place the strained broth over a gentle flame and, as soon as it boils, add a small pinch of saffron and 1 quart of rich, creamy, scalded milk, or 2 cups of milk and 2 cups of undiluted evaporated milk. Boil up once; let simmer 5 minutes; remove from the fire; return the pieces of fish to the stock, and taste for seasoning. Serve very hot, with a piece of fish in each plate and a side dish of fresh toast spread with parsley sauce (No. 1101).

The life span of the halibut is about the same as that of human. The largest halibut are forty to sixty years of age or older. Halibuts do not reproduce until they are about ten years old.

HUDSON RIVER CHOWDER   [286]

Heat slowly until they begin to crisp 4 slices of bacon cut into small pieces, stirring occasionally, over a low flame. Pour off most of the fat, leaving only about 2 tablespoons in the kettle, and sprinkle over this 1 rounded tablespoon of flour. Blend well, and add 1 large onion, thinly sliced, and 1 large potato, cubed small, cook for about 5 minutes, stirring frequently, or until the potato cubes and onion slices begin to take on color. Moisten gradually with 2 cups of dry white wine and 2 cups of boiling water, stirring constantly; then add ½ cup of carrots, cubed small, ½ cup of celery, chopped fine, ½ seeded green pepper, chopped, 1 bouquet garni made with 4 sprigs of fresh parsley, 1 sprig of thyme, and 1 bay leaf, tied with kitchen thread, 1 generous pinch each of mace, sage, marjoram and 2 large tomatoes, peeled, then cut into small pieces, and lastly a tiny pinch of soda. Cook, covered, for 30 minutes over a gentle flame, then add 2 cups of boiling water and 2–2½ pounds. of either striped bass, mullet, or catfish, cleaned and cut into pieces the size of a large nut. Season to taste with salt and 8 whole peppercorns, gently bruised, and continue cooking very slowly about 15–20 minutes. Discard the bouquet garni, taste for seasoning, then thicken with 2 egg yolks slightly beaten, mixed with 1 cup of scalded heavy cream and poured slowly into the chowder, stirring gently while pouring. Heat thoroughly but do not actually boil. Serve at once with toasted and buttered saltine crackers.

LOBSTER CHOWDER MAINE STYLE [287]

The chowder family is as full of surprises as a grab-bag at a country fair, but a chowder is always nourishing and full of flavor, no matter what turns up in it. This is no fish story. Perhaps one of the most famous gastronomic controversies in American history arose when Assemblyman Seeder introduced into the Maine legislature in February, 1939, a bill to make the entrance of a tomato into clam chowder illegal! God forbid that the man who likes the roseate glow of a tomato in his soup be deprived of it. If, however, tomatoes make you see red, here is a chowder virgin of them:

Remove the meat from a cooked 2½ pound lobster and cut in small dice. Cream 2 tablespoons of butter; add the liver of the lobster (green part), and 2 ordinary soda crackers finely rolled. Mix well. Scald 1 quart of milk with 1 cup of cream with a small slice of onion, a tiny pinch of powdered thyme, a small bay leaf, 1 whole clove, 4 crushed peppercorns, a sprig of parsley and a blade of garlic and strain over the creamed butter and lobster liver mixture, stirring constantly while pouring slowly. Cook the crushed shells of the lobster in 1 cup of cold water for 10 minutes over a very hot flame, and strain through cheese cloth over the milk mixture. Season to taste with salt, generously with paprika and a few grains of freshly grated nutmeg, then beat in 2 egg yolks, slightly beaten with 2 tablespoons of sherry wine, stirring briskly. Last of all, stir in the diced lobster meat; heat well but do not boil, and serve with toast.

OYSTER GUMBO [288]

Clean, pick over and parboil in their own liquor 1 pint of shucked or canned oysters until the edges curl. Drain and add the oyster liquor to 1 quart of fish stock (No. 182). Cook 2 tablespoons of grated onion in 2 tablespoons of butter over a low flame, until it just takes on a light color, stirring occasionally, then add to the stock, butter and all, together with 1 cup of cooked or canned, drained okra, 2 cups of tomatoes, cooked or canned (in either case chopped and well drained), season to taste with salt, pepper and thyme leaves; heat to the boiling point; remove from the fire; stir in the oysters and 2 tablespoons of sweet butter. Serve with toasted crackers or buttered toast.

FRIMSEL SOUP [289]

Add a little salt to 3 eggs and beat in as much bread flour as needed to make a dough sufficiently stiff to roll out as thin as a wafer, and divide it into 3 strips. Set aside until thoroughly dry, then place the strips one above the other, and shred very finely, vermicelli-fashion. Bring to a rolling boil 1½ quarts of rich beef stock; gradually add the shredded strips of frimsel, and simmer very gently for 20 minutes, skimming carefully, so as to obtain a clear broth. Taste for seasoning, and serve boiling hot in hot soup plates.

GARLIC SOUP MADRILENE [290]

One of the most famous soups in Spain, and each province has its own and special way of making it. This is how it is made in Madrid:

Fry, for each person, 1 clove of garlic in a little olive oil over a gentle flame until it begins to take on color, stirring occasionally, then add 1 thin slice of bread, season to taste with salt and pepper, pour over ¾ cup of boiling water, let boil 1 minute and serve after stirring into it 1 well-beaten egg.

HOCHEPOT [291]

The Belgian Hochepot is a variation of the French Pot-au-Feu. It is a meal in itself, because the soup or stock is served in the soup tureen at the same time as the meat—as a separate course, but at the same time.

Put 1½ pounds of brisket of beef, 1½ pounds of shoulder and breast of mutton in equal parts, 1½ pounds of shoulder of veal, 1½ pounds of cleaned pigs' feet, ½ pound of pigs' tails in a large earthenware deep casserole called "pot-au-feu," cover with cold water, bring very slowly to a boil and skim thoroughly. When the scum has ceased to rise and the stock is quite clear, add the following vegetables, coarsely chopped: ¼ pound of carrots, 4 leeks, 2 small turnips, 3 celery stalks, a dozen of small white onions, left whole, 2 of which are each stuck with 1 whole clove, 1 small head of green cabbage, cut into quarters. Season to taste with salt and pepper, add a bouquet garni composed of 1 large bay leaf, 8 sprigs of fresh parsley, and 1 sprig of thyme, all tied together with white kitchen thread, and lastly a dozen (2 per person) of small chipolata sausage or, lacking them, 1 pound of hard sausage. Cover and simmer very, very gently for 3 hours. If using soft sausages, add them only ¾ hour before serving. When ready to serve, put the meats and sausages on a hot dish in the center; drain the vegetables and garnish the meat platter with them and pour a little of the strained stock over them and the meat after tasting for seasoning, and serve the broth in the soup tureen with a side dish of very coarse salt.

LENTIL SOUP ARMENIAN STYLE   [292]

Also called Potage Esaü, this is a 3500-year-old recipe. It is probably Arabic in origin, for it is the main dish throughout North Africa and Arabia. They keep the stock pot on the fire, throwing in with the lentils whatever vegetables they have in season, with chunks of goat meat or mutton, but never, never any pork. This "potage" is warmed up as many times as necessary until it is all eaten, and we find that we like it better when warmed up than we do the first time, though it is extra delicious the first time. The following recipe is from Armenia, and is very popular in America.

Pick over carefully and wash 1 generous cup of lentils and soak overnight in ½ pint of cold water. Heat 1 tablespoon of ham or bacon drippings and in it cook ¼–⅓ cup of finely chopped onions until delicately brown, stirring almost constantly. Turn onion and fat into a soup kettle; add 1 bouquet garni, composed of 1 bay leaf, 8 sprigs of fresh parsley and 1 sprig of thyme, tied together with kitchen thread, then the soaked lentils and whatever water is left with them. Gradually bring to boiling point, cover, lower the flame, and simmer very gently 1½–1¾ hours, or until lentils are tender but not mashed. Taste for seasoning, discard the bouquet garni, and about 4 or 5 minutes before serving, stir in 3 tablespoons of finely chopped parsley and 5 or 6 fresh mint leaves also finely chopped. Serve in heated soup plates with crackers and, if desired (this is not Armenian) garnish each plate with 4 or 5 thin slices of frankfurters, slightly heated in beef broth.

MADRILENE (JELLIED)   [293]

Consommé Madrilène, usually called Madrilène for short, is served either hot or cold, but it is always liquid. The jellied soup, on the other hand, is made with consommé Madrilène in the following manner:

Add to the finished clear consommé (No. 301) a small quantity of lean raw beef (⅓ pound for each quart), chopped, a few tomatoes in pieces and an egg white well-beaten. Bring to a boil, lower the flame and let simmer about 30 minutes. Strain several times through a fine cloth. To each quart of Madrilène add 2 tablespoons of granulated, unflavored gelatine, first softened 5 minutes in 3 tablespoons of cold water or consommé; after this add 1 cup of hot consommé and stir until the gelatine is dissolved, then stir in 3 cups of consommé and turn into cold, individual bouillon cups; chill until firm or jellied. This will serve 4.

MINESTRONE MILANAISE   [294]

As in America, soups and their innumerable "trimmings" in the way of ravioli, gnocchi, spaghetti and all manner of appetizing delicacies are very popular in Italy. Each province, each city, small town, or even village, seems to boast of its own particular soup or of some special and characteristic accompaniment to it. Minestrone soup is the great spring and summer soup, made with fresh, young vegetables, and may be served hot or cold. In any case, this soup should be very thick.

Put 1½ quarts of good beef stock (No. 301) in a large saucepan, bring to the boiling point, and add ¼ pound of salt pork, cut in inch lengths; ½ pound of fresh kidney beans; ½ pound of new peas; 1 stalk of celery, scraped and diced; ½ pound of young cabbage, shredded; ⅓ pound of fresh spinach, stemmed, the leaves shredded; 1 small onion, thinly sliced; ¼ cup of chopped carrots; 2 medium-sized fresh tomatoes, peeled and chopped; 1 sprig of sage; ¼ cup of uncooked rice, and salt and pepper to taste. Bring again to a boil, lower the flame and let simmer very gently, as slowly as possible, until vegetables are tender and have nearly absorbed the beef stock. Taste for seasoning, add 2 or 3 cups of hot beef stock, and serve in heated soup plates, or bowls, passing a dish of grated parmesan cheese on the side.

Variations. You may add, before cooking the vegetables, ½ cup of uncooked macaroni, spaghetti or vermicelli, broken small.

MOCK TURTLE SOUP COUNTRY STYLE   [295]

That versatile viand, veal, masquerading around the civilized world in chicken croquettes and salad, game pasties, galantine of turkey, turtle soup, terrapin stew, and even, it is charged, in pâté de foie gras, is a mystery meat throughout its brief career. Lamb is so much like mutton—young pig so much like pork—but it's always hard to think that a pale veal cutlet would have been in a few more months a ruddy and rugged beefsteak, or that its head will masquerade as turtle soup.

Scald a calf's head with the skin on; split it and take out the brains and bones of the nose (the butcher will do it for you); blanch it well in several waters. Place in a large kettle and cover with cold water; bring it to a boil and skim as often as any scum rises. When the head has boiled gently till tender, take it out, and as soon as cool enough to handle, cut off the skin and fat parts, and cut some of the fleshy parts into cubes 1½ inches square. Peel the tongue and cut it up in the same way.

Meanwhile, put the broken bones and trimmings back into the water they were boiled in, with 1 pound of lean beef, some knuckle of veal (about half of a knuckle), with only a little of the meat left on (but not cooked bones), and let it stew for 4 consecutive hours as slowly as possible. Now strain through a fine cloth into an earthenware container and, when quite cold and the fat has formed a cake over, remove this fat carefully. If the directions have been followed, the stock will be a stiff jelly, or nearly so. Put this jelly again into a soup kettle with a dozen small white onions first sliced and browned in a little butter. Thicken with a little mixed flour and butter as needed; season highly, with white pepper, cloves, cayenne, mace, and basil, sage and lemon thyme or lemon peel to taste. When all are well cooked together, strain through a fine-meshed wire or hair sieve into a fresh pan, and add the meat, ¼ cup of Madeira wine or sherry (more or less, according to taste); about 2 dozen Chicken Forcemeat Balls (No. 200), as many Egg Balls (No. 206) and the juice of a large lemon, strained. Serve at once.

Before making a broth of sheeps' heads, the Arabs of Morocco send them to the blacksmith to be singed.

MULLIGATAWNY SOUP [296]
Also called Potage à l'Indienne

Cut the fat from 2 pounds of mutton and melt it in the soup kettle. Have ready peeled and chopped 2 green apples, 2 medium-sized onions, 2 young carrots, and 1 small white turnip. Drain all but 2 or 3 tablespoons of the mutton fat from the kettle and in this cook the vegetables, over a low flame, stirring frequently for about 12–15 minutes, or until vegetables are almost tender. Sprinkle 2 tablespoons of flour over and blend well, stirring constantly. Now stir in the mutton, previously cut into small cubes and rolled in mixed salt and pepper and 1 tablespoon of curry powder. Pour over 2 quarts of boiling water, add 6 or 7 whole peppercorns, gently bruised, 1 bouquet garni composed of 1 large bay leaf, 8 sprigs of fresh parsley or a 2-inch piece of scraped parsley root, and 1 sprig of thyme, all tied together with white kitchen thread. Bring to a boil, skim off all scum as it rises, as carefully as possible, then cover and allow to simmer very gently for 3 hours, stirring occasionally. Strain through a fine-meshed wire sieve, rubbing the meat and vegetables through into a fresh pan; return to the fire; bring to a boil; add 2 tablespoons of strained lemon juice; taste for seasoning and serve in hot soup plates or bowls with a side dish of hot boiled rice.

NOTE. The bones and remains of any kind of uncooked meat or poultry, even game, may be used instead of mutton. The soup would take its name from the materials employed.

ONION SOUP AU GRATIN   [297]

Cook in 4 tablespoons of sweet butter over a gentle flame, 3 large onions, finely sliced until golden brown, stirring frequently; sprinkle over them 1 tablespoon of flour, if the soup is desired thick. Gradually stir in 2 quarts of beef stock (No. 301); season to taste with salt and pepper, cover and cook gently for 20 minutes. Serve in heated soup plates, each plate garnished with a toasted round of French bread topped with grated Swiss, Parmesan or plain American grated cheese.

"I am small but I am mighty; they speak of my virility and strength. I am known from ocean to ocean as the giver of health and happiness. I provide for earth its first beautiful mantle in the spring. I am hardy yet mild. Women shun me—yet love me, while men glory in my friendship, especially with a juicy steak. I bless the sleepless eye with the kind caress of slumber; while often I am smothered with heat of flame. Some weep for me; all desire me—yet denounce me when among friends. I travel 'round the globe, yet often I am content to live my life in some lone sequestered spot. I was the sustaining power and inspiration to those who reared the pyramids and the Chinese Wall. I helped the doughboys win the war. I am the truest friend of the poor, yet I am in the favor of mighty kings. The fragrance of my spirit pervades alike the humble cottage and the palace. I am as old as the world's history but my youth bursts forth each spring to a waiting and expectant multitude. I am derided and made a jest—yet I am loved by the universe. I AM AN ONION."

OXTAIL SOUP   [298]

Cut 1 large oxtail in scant ½-inch pieces, wash quickly in cold water and dry. Season with salt and pepper, then roll the pieces in flour. Cook 10 minutes in 1 tablespoon of fat; transfer to soup kettle; add ½ cup each of carrot, onions, leeks and celery, cut into small pieces or fancy shapes, 1 bouquet garni composed of 1 bay leaf, 8 sprigs of fresh parsley and 1 sprig of thyme, tied with white kitchen thread; cover with 1½ quarts of beef stock or water; bring to a boil, and allow to simmer gently for 3 hours, or until oxtail pieces are tender. Discard the bouquet garni; taste for seasoning, adding salt, pepper and powdered cloves to taste. When ready to serve, stir in 1 generous teaspoon of lemon juice and one of Worcestershire sauce. Serve as hot as possible.

During the Terror in Paris in 1793, many of the nobility were starving. It was the custom those days for the abattoirs of Paris to send their hides, as soon as the animals were killed, to the tanneries without cleaning them, even leaving on the tails, subsequently discarded during cleaning. One of the nobles asked for a tail, which was willingly given him, and with it he created the first oxtail soup. Hearing of this, the tanners, annoyed by the great and constant demand for oxtails, put a price on them.

PETITE MARMITE [299]
French Little Pot (Serves 10–12)

Place in a 10-quart earthenware pot 2 pounds of lean beef plate, 1 5-pound young fowl, and about 5½–6 quarts of cold water with salt to taste. Bring very slowly to a boil; lower the flame and let simmer very gently, until tender, or about 3–3½ hours, the longer the better, skimming off all scum as it rises to the surface. Then add 2 medium-sized leeks, carefully washed and cut into inch strips; 3 or 4 medium-sized carrots, cut into inch pieces; 2 white turnips, quartered; 3 stalks of celery, scraped, then cut into inch pieces; half a very small green cabbage, quartered, 1 medium-sized onion, halved, each half stuck with 1 clove—the onions slightly browned in a little fat, to impart color to the bouillon, and give it a delicate flavor. Season to taste with salt and black pepper, and finally add 1 bouquet garni composed of 1 large bay leaf, 8 sprigs of fresh parsley and 1 sprig of thyme, tied with white kitchen thread. Allow the whole to cook slowly for 1½ hours longer, removing the beef and chicken after ½ hour of this further slow cooking. Cool slightly, then cut the meat into cubes or strips (except the chicken legs, which may be used otherwise). Return to the kettle, and continue cooking till vegetables are tender. Just before serving, add 8 slices of raw, beef marrow and a generous teaspoon of minced chervil or parsley; discard the onion, and serve in individual earthenware soup tureens with a side dish of toasted bread and grated cheese. The remainder of the soup keeps well for a week in refrigerator.

PHILADELPHIA PEPPER POT [300]

Cook 2 pounds of honeycomb tripe the day before using. Wash thoroughly, place in kettle and cover with cold water. Bring to a boil and let simmer gently for at least 8 hours. Remove the tripe and, when cool, cut into pieces about ½ inch square. The next day wash 1 veal knuckle in cold water; cover with 3 quarts of cold water, gradually bring to a boil, skimming off very carefully all scum as it rises to the surface, then add 1 bouquet garni, composed of 2 bay leaves, 10 sprigs of parsley and 2 sprigs of green celery leaves, tied together with white kitchen thread, and let simmer gently for 3 hours, adding, after 2 hours of simmering, 1½ teaspoons of salt and 12 peppercorns, slightly bruised. Remove the meat from the bones and cut into small pieces; strain the broth and return to the kettle, then add 2 medium-sized onions, each stuck with 1 whole clove; simmer for 1 hour, then add 4 medium-sized potatoes, peeled and cubed, also the meat and tripe pieces, taste for seasoning, and let simmer gently while making the following:

Suet Dumplings. Combine 1 cup of beef suet, previously put through food chopper, 2 cups of flour, ½ generous teaspoon of salt, and enough ice-cold water to allow the rolling of the dough into dumplings, about the size of marbles; flour well to prevent sticking and drop into the simmering soup. Cook about 8–10 minutes; stir some chopped parsley into the soup and serve in heated soup plates with brown bread and butterfinger sandwiches.

Pepper-y Pot, piping hot! In Colonial days the pepper-pot vendor plodded Philadelphia's twisted and twisting streets and alleyways chanting the pepper-pot call:

> *"All hot! All hot!*
> *Pepper pot! Pepper pot!*
> *Makes back strong,*
> *Makes live long,*
> *All hot! Pepper pot!"*

The vendor and her cart have gone but pepper pot lives on as one of America's favorite soups in midwinter and even in the spring.

POT-AU-FEU or CLEAR BEEF SOUP or CONSOMMÉ   [301]
Home Style

The "pot-au-feu," or pot on the fire, is as much of a national institution in France as tea-drinking is in England and coffee-drinking is in America. It is made at least once a week in every bourgeois home. Start as follows:

For each quart of cold water take 1½ pounds of beef.

For each pound of beef add ½ pound of beef bone (no other bones but beef bones). Salt to taste, usually ½ teaspoon of salt for each quart of cold water, finishing the seasoning after the consommé is clear.

Wash the meat and cracked bones quickly in cold water and place in a soup kettle. Then pour in the cold water. Gradually and slowly bring to a boil, and let boil gently for 3 or 4 minutes, while skimming very carefully. Then add the following vegetables but only when the scum has completely disappeared from the surface: For each 2 quarts of liquid, add 2 medium-sized young carrots, scraped, then cut into inch pieces; 1 medium-sized white turnip, pared and quartered; 1 large onion, peeled, left whole, and studded with 3 whole cloves; 1 thin slice of garlic; parsnip, the size of a large egg, pared and cut into small pieces; 1 stalk of celery, scraped, then cut into inch pieces; 1 bouquet garni composed of 1 extra large or 2 small bay leaves, 2 small leeks, trimmed, halved, carefully washed in several changes of cold water, and folded in two or three, then tied with 12 sprigs of fresh parsley and 1 sprig of thyme; and finally 12 whole peppercorns. Again bring to a boil, lower the heat as low as possible and let simmer very slowly, allowing the liquid to "smile" for at least 3–3½ hours, the pot not quite covered.

Strain the necessary hot soup for the meal into a soup tureen, add a few of the vegetables and serve as hot as possible.

To Make Clear Consommé. Strain the soup into a clean container. Let cool, then carefully remove the cake of fat on the surface, and you have a clear consommé without using commercial gelatine. If the consommé is not to be used at once, then do not remove the cake of fat from the top. Put both soup and fat into a saucepan, heat enough to melt the fat, then pour into quart jars and, when cold, store in refrigerator. The fat will form a good seal and the consommé may be kept for weeks.

To Make Chicken Consommé. Proceed as for Pot-au-Feu, or Clear Beef Soup or Consommé, substituting a cleaned, plump fowl weighing 5–5½ pounds, adding the vegetables after all scum is completely removed from the top of the kettle.

SPLIT PEA SOUP   [302]

Wash and soak overnight 1 cup of yellow or green split peas in cold water to generously cover. In the morning drain off the water and cover the peas with 3 quarts of fresh water. Add the ham bone left over from a baked or boiled ham; 3 tablespoons of chopped onions; 1 bouquet garni composed of 1 large bay leaf, 8 sprigs of fresh parsley, 2 sprigs of fresh green celery leaves (tops), and 1 sprig of thyme, all tied together with white kitchen thread; season to taste with salt, and 8 freshly crushed peppercorns. Bring slowly to a boil; lower the heat and simmer very gently until peas are tender, placing an asbestos pad under the kettle, as peas are liable to scorch or burn when slowly cooked. Empty the mixture into a fine sieve, discard the ham bone and the bouquet garni, and rub through a fine-meshed wire sieve, into a fresh saucepan. Keep hot. Melt 2 tablespoons of butter, stir in 1½ tablespoons of flour and stir over a low flame until thoroughly blended, but not browned; then stir in gradually 2 cups of scalded milk, stirring constantly until mixture boils and thickens slightly. Combine the mixtures, taste for seasoning, let boil up 2 or 3 times and serve at once with croutons (No. 203).

SPRING SOUP FRENCH STYLE   [303]

Cook ¼ cup of chopped onions in 3 tablespoons of butter over a very low heat, stirring frequently until onion is tender but not brown; gradually add 1 quart of White or Veal Stock (No. 185) with ½ cup of small pieces of stale bread, and simmer gently for 35 minutes; then rub through a fine-meshed sieve into a fresh saucepan, and add 2 cups of scalded thin cream or undiluted evaporated milk, thickened with 1½ tablespoons of flour blended with 1 tablespoon of sweet butter. Taste for seasoning, let boil gently for 3 minutes and serve at once, each plate sprinkled with finely chopped parsley.

TOMATO SOUP COUNTRY STYLE   [304]

Heat 2 tablespoons of butter, stir in 2 tablespoons of flour and, when bubbling, stir in 2 cups of Brown Stock (No. 179) and add 2 tablespoons each of finely chopped carrots, celery, turnip and leeks; ¼ cup of finely chopped cooked lean ham; 1 bouquet garni composed of 1 large bay leaf, 6 sprigs of fresh parsley, and 2 whole cloves, all tied together with white kitchen thread; and cook gently for 30 minutes. Season lightly with salt and generously with black pepper, and add 2 cups of canned tomatoes. Mix well, bring to a boil, lower the flame and let cook gently for 20 minutes longer. Rub mixture through a fine-meshed wire sieve into a fresh saucepan. Taste for seasoning, stir in 1 tablespoon of butter and 1 tablespoon of finely chopped chives and serve at once with croutons (No. 203).

VEGETABLE CHOWDER SOUTHERN STYLE   [305]

Cook 4 slices of bacon, chopped, until crisp but not burned; stir in 2 cups of canned tomatoes; ½ cup of shelled peas and ½ cup of cleaned pea pods, ⅓ cup of thinly sliced onions; ⅓ cup each of diced celery and green pepper; ½ cup of cleaned string beans cut in small pieces; ½ cup of thinly shredded cabbage, ½ cup of thinly sliced carrots; 2 quarts of Brown Stock (No. 179); 1 bay leaf, 1 cup of sliced okra, cooked or canned; and salt and pepper to taste. Cook gently until vegetables are tender, taste for seasoning and serve at once.

Chapter Four

EGGS

*In 1506, the dark-skinned Infanta Juanita
of Spain was told that hard-cooked eggs
would lighten her complexion. After that
she would eat nothing else.*

" . . . If a bird's nest chance to be before thee in the way in any tree, or on the ground, whether they be young ones, or eggs, and the dam sitting upon the young, or upon the eggs, thou shalt not take the dam with the young . . . "   *Deuteronomy XXII:6*

ABOUT TWENTY-SEVEN BILLION EGGS ARE PRODUCED ANNUALLY in the United States alone. They give immeasurable strength and health to the American people.

The elements which afford energy are found in the yolk of the egg in the form of protein and fat; the growth elements exist in the white or albumen, in the form of protein. The protein of the egg white contains little that cannot be obtained from the protein of milk, but the yolk has qualities which milk lacks. It has more iron than milk; its proteins are of high quality and easily utilized, it is as rich a source of vitamin A and B as milk, and it also contains vitamin D. Protein, fat, minerals (especially iron) and vitamins are found in the egg. These elements place it among the essential foods for young and old and include it among many invalid diets.

The yolk of an egg is very complex. Besides the proteid vitellin, it contains three fats, coloring matter, nuclein, lecithin and salts of iron, calcium, magnesium and potassium.

Like milk, eggs constitute a complete food, for out of an egg the entire structure of the bird—its bones, nerves, muscles, viscera, and in the case of some birds even the feathers—are developed previous to hatching.

STRUCTURE OF EGGS [307]

Eggs are essentially interesting food because they contain all the elements necessary to the development of life. The structure of the egg is familiar, with its division into the yolk and white, and it is interesting to note the details of this structure. Break a fresh egg carefully into a saucer. The shell is porous, allowing water to evaporate from the egg, and air to enter. To this porosity is due the fact that other substances may enter the egg, giving it an unnatural flavor and even hastening its deterioration. Within the shell is a fine membrane which protects the white. The yolk is also divided from the white by a more delicate membrane which enables one to separate the yolk from the white of a fresh egg.

A careful examination reveals at each end of the yolk a continuation of this membrane in the form of small cords which are attached to each end of the shell, holding the yolk entirely and evenly suspended in the center of the shell. Rough handling or jolting breaks this membrane, and the yolk drops to one side.

Lift the white carefully with a fork, and notice its elasticity. This cohesive property makes it possible to beat air into the white until the whole mass becomes porous, full of air bubbles.

The egg white is in three, sometimes four layers: An inner watery part, next to the yolk; one or two jelly-like layers; and an outer watery white section. The yolk is creamy rather than light when beaten, and a bit of the yolk mixed with the white prevents the latter from becoming light and dry when beaten.

RELATIVE DIGESTIBILITY OF SOFT AND HARD COOKED EGGS [308]

The fact must be recalled that to digest is to dissolve, and the digestion of food means a dissolving by the digestive juices, aided by water. When we speak of the digestibility of food we may mean the ease and comfort of digestion, or the length of time taken by the process, or the completeness of the process. If we take the third of these meanings, the hard-cooked egg is as digestible as the soft-cooked or the raw egg, because it is completely dissolved in digestion in the course of time. If the second meaning of digestion is taken, the hard-cooked egg may be slightly less digestible, for a slightly longer time is consumed in the process.

The latest researches, however, show that the digestive process is longer with any food than was formerly supposed, and the difference in this case is not especially important. Indeed, we must accept the conclusion of the scientist and frankly admit that the differences of temperature in cooking an egg do not have any great effect upon its digestibility. Why, then, the popular idea that a hard-cooked egg is absolutely indigestible? A hard-cooked egg, or two hard-cooked eggs eaten rapidly, without mastication, at a picnic, and with much sweet food at an unusual hour, may interfere with the "ease and comfort" associated with such a meal. But if the whites of the hard-cooked eggs are chopped fine, the yolk mashed, and the two served upon bread or toast, thus insuring mastication, a dish is produced that is of average digestibility and that may be used for breakfast or luncheon without indigestion.

Albumen, or the white of an egg, is altered physically but not chemically by process of cooking. At about 134° F., delicate fibrillae of coagulated albuminous material begin to stretch through the substance, and they increase with the temperature up to 160° F. The fibrillae are so numerous that the entire mass is coagulated, but is still of soft or gelatinous consistency. Eggs baked in pudding or in any other manner form one of the most insoluble varieties of albumen possible. A raw egg is ordinarily digested in the stomach in $1\frac{1}{2}$ hours, but a baked egg requires from $3\frac{1}{4}$ to 4 hours.

The principle involved in this account of the cooking of an egg is further illustrated by the process of overcooking beefsteak. When strong heat is too long applied in the process of broiling, the albumen of the meat becomes dried, shriveled, and comparatively tasteless; and eggs cooked for persons with delicate digestions, instead of being boiled in water at 212° F., should be coddled, that is, placed in water at a temperature between 170 and 180° F., and immersed for fully ten minutes;

at the end of which time they will be found of a uniform gelatinous consistency, very palatable, and not too tough to be readily acted upon by the gastric juices.

The yolk really coagulates at a lower temperature than the white, although as eggs are commonly cooked it does not have an opportunity to coagulate first. In the ordinary rapid cooking of eggs in boiling water, the white is firmly set before there is time for the temperature of the interior of the egg to be thoroughly raised; consequently, the yolk is softer than the white. The shell of the egg facilitates the process of slow cooking of the albumen by protecting the interior and preventing the escape of the contents through solution, just as, in the cooking of fish or meat in water, the latter should be hot enough to immediately form an external coagulum of albumen sufficiently dense to prevent the diffusion of albuminous material and mineral salts into the water, or indicated liquid.

HOW TO BUY EGGS [309]

The retail grades represent four classes of edible hen's eggs:

Fancy Grade. The top grade is known as the *fancy grade* and includes the selection of the finest quality of eggs of the day's lay. This grade is seldom available in retail stores, unless ordered in advance.

Grade A. The next highest grade is *grade A*, and any egg which falls below the standard for grade A cannot legally be sold as fresh. This grade is limited, and for that reason commands a high price.

Grade B. The next grade is known as *grade B*. Sometimes the question arises whether in buying grade B eggs the cook has bought the poorest quality eggs on the market. This is not so, for a grade B egg is a United States standard and is of good table quality, and the great bulk of eggs in commercial channels is of this grade. Grade B eggs are suitable for baking, frying, scrambling, omelet in any style, poaching, and all similar uses. They differ from grade A in that a little more of their water content has evaporated from the grade B egg, the air cell in the egg has become slightly tremulous, and the white of the egg has become less firm than that of the grade A.

As to food value—strictly grade B eggs have qualities nearly equal to eggs sold under the grade A classification. There should be no discrimination against the grade B, for that grade is considered a good egg which is satisfactory for almost any use.

The coloration of eggs bears no fixed relation to the species of bird which lays them—the degree of light in which the eggs are incubated *has much* to do with determining their coloring, which does not alter the nutritive value of an egg. In other words, the color of the shell is not a criterion of its quality. The preferred shell color is a matter of individual taste, varying, strangely enough, with locality. In Boston and vicinity, brown eggs are considered choice and fetch the highest prices, while in New York and elsewhere, white eggs are favored.

But, like the meat for which they are substituted, eggs have a tendency to putrefaction in the intestinal tract, and this should be coun-- teracted by serving them with vegetable foods. Egg yolk is acid in reaction after digestion, and this undesirable after-effect should also be guarded against. Eggs cooked by any method and served with potatoes for alkalinity, and spinach or any other green vegetable to give them bulk, make an acceptable main course.

USEFULNESS OF EGGS [310]

Eggs are one of the most useful of the staple food products. They can be used for any meal during the day and will find a place in every course from appetizer to dessert. As main luncheon dishes, they are difficult to surpass, for they are quickly and easily prepared.

Eggs are used as a thickening for sauces, soups, pie fillings, stuffings, salad dressings, custards and hundreds of other dishes. They are a coating agent when used for dipping croquettes, cutlets and other foods for frying.

For muffins, cookies, croquettes, and some kinds of cakes, they are used as a binder to hold the other ingredients together.

They improve the texture of frozen mixtures, because they act as a sort of wrapper around the crystals, preventing them from collecting in lumps.

In soups they act as a clarifier.

Mayonnaise, Hollandaise, and similar emulsions demand eggs as a stabilizer.

As a garnish for salads, cold meats, hot or cold fish, as well as for numerous vegetables, eggs have no rival.

Eggs enhance the flavor, color and texture of the products in which they are used, giving them more nutritive powers.

Eggs are the cement that holds the castles of cookery together.

Eggs are especially rich in all the necessary elements required by the human body.

EGGS ARE USED FOR THICKENING [311]

Do you ever wonder why eggs are able to *thicken* sauces, soups and custards? Though the reason is scientific, it is very simple to understand. Let us suppose you are making a custard. After beating the eggs, you combine them thoroughly with the milk until each tiny milk particle is covered with egg; then you cook the blended mixture after flavoring to taste or according to given directions. You have seen how a poached egg "sets" when you drop it into hot liquid; the same thing happens here. The protein (albumen) of the eggs quickly begins to coagulate or "set"; naturally the milk must "set," or thicken, too, because your beating has made "the twain one."

EGGS ARE A LEAVENING AGENT [312]

Eggs are a source of leavening. Chemists call it "viscosity" or "adhesiveness." If you have ever tried to pick up a dropped egg, you know just how adhesive it is. Annoying as this characteristic can be under ordinary circumstances, it is one of the reasons why eggs are so valuable as a cooking ingredient. Just as soap suds, when beaten, turn into bubbles, so eggs develop multitudes of tiny air sacs as we beat them. How many uses these sacs have, you will soon see.

As a matter of fact, only the whites of eggs possess the power of leavening. You have often seen them perform in sponge cake. First they gently and firmly entangle some air in their tiny sacs; then as the heat of the oven is applied, this air expands, stretching the walls of the sacs until they puff out like small balloons. It is these balloons that raise your cake.

Since the walls of these sacs are made of albumen, which is toughened by too much heat, egg mixtures *must be cooked at a low or moderate heat* if you want them to be tender. But your oven must not be too cool, because the little balloons collapse unless their albumen walls are hardened ever so little, by cooking.

When you beat egg whites for leavening, the rule is: Beat the whites until they are stiff enough to stand up and hold their shape, but *do not* beat them until they lose their glossy appearance. Egg whites beaten too much allow small bits to fly from the beater and the fluffy mass loses its shininess. This is the "dry" stage and it is not satisfactory as a leavener.

In a frozen mixture these balloon-like sacs wrap themselves around the single crystals and prevent them from forming colonies. This film-forming property of eggs is especially valuable when you want to freeze desserts without stirring them, in a mechanical refrigerator, for instance, or by packing them in ice and salt.

EGGS ARE A STABILIZER [313]

When we add eggs to our mayonnaise, we are again calling these little air sacs to our aid. Just as their filmy walls close around the crystals in a frozen mixture, so they wrap drops of oil in their embrace to keep them from running together. When eggs are used in this way, they are called stabilizers.

EGGS ARE A BINDER [314]

Eggs are a binder externally and internally. They are an external binder when used for croquettes, cutlets and fritters (batter), for unless the food material is dipped in egg, the crumbs used will float off and drop to the bottom of the frying kettle.

We often use eggs to hold together the ingredients in fish balls, meat balls, hamburgers, lamburgers, vealburgers, croquettes, loaves, desserts, ice cream, beverages, etc., and all similar preparations requiring a binder. This is an internal binder, and though the eggs bind the ingredients together, they also push them apart. By slipping their little films between the other particles of food, eggs prevent those particles from packing together into a hard lump.

EGGS ARE A CLARIFIER   [315]

We depend on an egg or egg shells to clear soup, coffee, sugar syrup, or whatever food is to be clarified. Here is what happens: As heat is applied, the albumen of the egg or eggs coagulates, catching all the little undesirable particles that are floating around loose in the pan, pot or kettle. This is called clarifying.

There are about a dozen methods of preparing and cooking eggs, such as: (1) Baking; (2) boiling; (3) broiling; (4) coddling; (5) deep-frying; (6) hard-cooking; (7) mollet; (8) omelet; (9) poaching; (10) scrambling; (11) shirring; (12) short-frying.

Ab ovo ad mala, from eggs to apples, was the Roman equivalent for our modern "from soup to nuts." Roman banquets always began with eggs and ended with apples. The grandeur of service in those days was quite unlike the simplicity of today. Nevertheless, eggs still play a highly significant part in the preparation of good food.

Eggs are a very important food in that they may be used as a meat substitute. They are plentiful and inexpensive. They are rich in vitamins A and D, riboflavin, thiamin and minerals. One egg a day (or at least 4 a week) is recommended for the average diet. It is not necessary to include them as "eggs"; they may appear as custards, cakes, appetizers, sauces, salads, etc.

Eggs simplify meal-planning since they can be served alone in a variety of ways, or combined with just about any food you have on hand. Moreover, they simplify meal-getting because egg dishes that are substantial meals in themselves can be prepared quickly and easily.

One way of announcing a new baby in China is to send a basket of eggs to relatives and friends.

HEN ALONE CAN MAKE AN EGG   [316]

An old recipe for making chicken fricassee began, "First catch the chicken." Our recipe for making an egg begins, "First catch a germ." Then drop the germ in about two-thirds of an ounce of the golden emulsion called egg yolk. Incase this in a transparent balloon of albumen, leaving no seam. Drop the yolk balloon into a bath of thin white of egg, or albumen. Wrap all this in about two-thirds of an ounce of viscid albumen, heavy enough to cut with a knife. Cover this with another layer of thin albumen. Then prepare another balloon as thin and tough as the gossamer of the spider web. Over this, wrap another seamless balloon of fibrous cretin, the tough material out of which fingernails are made. You are now ready for the shell.

Now take about one-quarter of an ounce of powdered marble, or oyster shell, and plaster it evenly over your balloon. First shape the plaster into a round ball. Then roll this lightly so that it becomes oval. Then make the oval blunter at one end than at the other. This shape keeps the egg from rolling far away from the nest, and also from rolling off the breakfast table. Now let the plaster set until it is dry, hard, solid, limestone rock.

The shell is now chalk-white. You may tint it any color you like, provided you are making an Easter egg. Otherwise, good taste limits you to buff, brown, or possibly blue, as there *is* a breed of chicken which lay eggs with blue shells. If, however, you are making the egg for the New York market, you'll do better to leave it white. New Yorkers prefer platinum blondes and no one has figured out why. But if you are making the egg for the Boston market, you'll do better to tint it brown. Bostonians prefer brunettes, possibly because they match the beloved brown bread and Boston baked beans. Finally lightly shellac the surface with a thin albuminous veneer. Then you have it: The perfect food, the perfect package. This is the way to make an egg. But only a hen can do it. You had better buy them. If you have them, there are some very definite rules in egg cookery, some of which follow:

EGG COOKERY RULES—DO'S AND DON'T'S [317]

DO NOT wash an egg until you are ready to use it, as there is a natural coating that to some degree protects the pores.

DO NOT rush egg cooking. Eggs are like some people—rush them and they get tough. Cook eggs slowly.

DO NOT use eggs that are just taken from the refrigerator. Very cold eggs sometimes crack after you slip them into the boiling water to cook. You easily can prevent this by puncturing the rounded end of each egg with a needle or pin before it goes into the water. Also, you'll find it much easier to remove the shells smoothly from hard-cooked eggs if you plunge them into cold water as soon as they are cooked. To prevent a cracked egg from breaking when cooking, add a few drops of vinegar or lemon juice to the water in which it is boiled.

DO NOT differentiate between white and brown eggs. Color makes little difference. Eggs can be brown, white or speckled and still be good. The shell must be clean, sound and normal. Grading is based on appearance and interior quality, and has nothing to do with size. Large eggs are good for table service. Medium-sized eggs are best for baking purposes, as most recipes are built with the medium-sized egg in mind. An average medium-sized egg weighs 1¾ ounces. Small eggs are good for soft cooking, but should be weighed for use in baking to make sure enough are used.

DO NOT handle eggs roughly. An egg left in the warm nest all day, then kept in a warm place at night, will be less fresh at the end of twenty-four hours than an older egg that has been kept cool.

DO NOT judge quality by a glance at the shell. Only one point is worth noting. If the shell looks dull, that means the natural "bloom" is still there. Once this covering is rubbed off, the air goes through the shell easily and the egg's moisture is lost rapidly.

DO NOT beat egg whites in an aluminum pan as it will darken them.

DO NOT despise powdered eggs. They are just as good as fresh

ones. One-half pound of powdered eggs represents $1\frac{1}{2}$ dozen eggs. For
1 egg, combine 2 level tablespoons of the powder with 2 tablespoons of
water and mix well. The egg mixture may then be scrambled, used in
an omelet or in cake and pudding recipes.

DO NOT let eggs that are to be stuffed stand except in cold water.
As soon as they are boiled, plunge them in cold water until ready to
stuff. They will not, then, discolor.

DO NOT let fresh eggs stand at a temperature of 65°. Eight days
at this temperature will reduce the white of an egg to a watery state.
It pays to keep eggs in a cool place and to buy them frequently.

DO NOT split eggs. If you are making something that calls for only
one egg, don't try to divide the egg. Too much is better than too little,
and the egg serves a thickening purpose.

DO remove any yolk which gets into the white when you are breaking an egg. Take a piece of the shell and lightly touch the yolk with it.
The yolk will adhere and can be easily removed.

DO add a pinch of curry powder to eggs before scrambling them.
This gives them a new and interesting flavor.

DO break eggs separately (when using several) into a small dish.
Examine each egg for freshness before adding it to the rest.

DO add chopped parsley or chives to beaten egg used as a coating
for breaded chops, etc. This imparts a delicious taste and fragrance.

DO use a double boiler for scrambling eggs when the breakfasters
do not rise at the same time. Not only do the eggs remain hot, but they
also keep moist and creamy.

DO poach eggs in hot milk, hot consommé, hot tomato soup, etc.,
instead of in water, and they will be tastier.

DO keep left-over egg yolks in the refrigerator. Beat yolks with a
fork; add 1 teaspoon cold water for each 2 yolks; and store, covered,
in the refrigerator. The yolks will not dry out or have film form.

DO always be sure that an omelet is loosened from the sides of the
pan before turning it out. Hold omelet pan firmly while slipping omelet
onto platter.

DO you know that when you buy a dozen standard size eggs you
are buying $1\frac{1}{2}$ pounds of finest quality protein, or "egg meat"—not to
mention their vitamin and mineral values?

DO remove scrambled eggs from the heat while they are still a little
on the soft side because the heat retained by the utensil and also within
the mass of egg itself will complete the cooking before they can be
served.

DO keep eggs on the lower shelf of the refrigerator.

DO poach the left-over egg yolks, when a recipe calls just for egg
whites. Poach the yolks until firm and then put them through a sieve.
Then add them as a protein garnish to green salads, soups or cooked
greens.

DO stir the boiling water in one direction when poaching an egg,
and the egg will not spread.

DO peel the hard-cooked eggs like onions, under cold running water,

so that the yolks have no dark circles. Do you ever forget which eggs
are hard boiled and which are uncooked . . . and, if so, you spin them
on their ends to see? A raw egg won't spin.

DO store hard-cooked eggs in their shells in the refrigerator until
they are to be served. If shelled, they sometimes darken if left any
length of time . . . In slicing hard-cooked eggs, dip your knife in cold
water and the yolk won't crumble.

DO break a freshly-laid egg, and see the two twisted, somewhat
dense appearing portions of the egg white. These ropy portions of the
white are located on opposite sides of the yolk and are called the "chala-
zac." These twisted portions of the egg white are believed to be formed
in the egg to support the yolk and protect it against sudden jars.

DO add a generous pinch of soda to the egg whites before they are
beaten. They'll stand up better when beaten for a meringue.

BAKED EGGS SAN SEBASTIAN [318]

Pour a half inch of undiluted cream of tomato soup into a buttered
earthenware baking dish (or individual custard cups or ramekins);
drop in 6 fresh eggs carefully; sprinkle with salt, pepper and a few
grains of cayenne and nutmeg, and a little grated Swiss cheese mixed in
equal parts with grated parmesan cheese. Add another layer of cream
of tomato soup; repeat the sprinkling of mixed cheese; sprinkle over about
1 teaspoon of finely minced parsley or chives, mixed with 1 teaspoon of
finely minced or grated onion, and bake in a very moderate oven (300–
325° F.) for about 20–25 minutes, or until eggs are set. Serve immediately
from the baking dish.

BREAD CRUMB OMELET [319]

This recipe is for an individual omelet. For more, increase amount
of ingredients accordingly.

Pour ½ cup of boiling milk over ½ cup of soft bread crumbs, add
2 well-beaten egg yolks seasoned to taste with salt, pepper and a few
grains of powdered cloves, and beat with rotary beater until smooth.
Beat the 2 egg whites until stiff, together with 1 teaspoon of finely
chopped chives and a few grains of salt, fold into egg yolk mixture. Heat
1 scant tablespoon of butter in hot individual light frying pan; pour in
the egg preparation all at once, and cook over a gentle flame until
browned on bottom and well puffed. Place in a slow oven until top is
dry; fold over on to a hot platter, and serve immediately.

CLAM OMELET [320]

Remove the necks, and use only the bellies of 1 pint of soft clams
carefully picked and drained. Heat 1 tablespoon of butter in a light,

large saucepan, stir in 1 teaspoon of minced shallots, and just before it begins to brown, stir in the clams, and let cook 2 minutes, stirring constantly. Pour in ½ cup of scalded cream, seasoned with salt and pepper to taste, and cook 2 minutes longer, stirring frequently. Break 8 eggs into a bowl; add ¾ teaspoon of salt, a dash of pepper and nutmeg, and 2 tablespoons of cream, and beat with a fork for a full minute. Melt 3 tablespoons of butter in a large, light frying pan and, when at the foaming stage, pour in the eggs. Allow to set, making holes with a fork or a knife so that the uncooked eggs will come in contact with the bottom of the frying pan. Pour clam mixture over half the omelet, let brown a few seconds longer, then fold the plain half over the clam filling, and turn out onto a hot platter. Serve immediately, garnished with crisp watercress.

CODDLED EGGS [321]

Drop as many fresh eggs as required into rapidly boiling water. Remove from the flame, cover, and let stand undisturbed for 10 minutes. Remove from water and turn from shell into serving dish. They will be jellied all through, with no noticeable difference in firmness between the white and yolk.

Although Napoleon had many talents he was an awkward amateur cook as Empress Marie-Louise discovered one day. Napoleon tried to turn an omelet, and it flipped on the floor.

CODFISH OMELET PORTUGUESE STYLE [322]
A He-man Omelet

Combine ¾ cup of left-over cooked codfish and ¼ cup of cooked rice; season with a blade of garlic, finely chopped, 1 teaspoon of grated onion, and 1 teaspoon of finely minced parsley. Beat 8 eggs with the codfish mixture, seasoned to taste with salt, pepper and a dash of nutmeg. Melt 3 tablespoons of butter in a large, light frying pan and, when at the foaming stage, pour in the egg mixture. Allow to set, making holes with a fork or a knife so that the uncooked part will come in contact with bottom of the frying pan. Pour 1 cup of freshly stewed or drained canned tomatoes, previously heated and seasoned with salt and pepper to taste, over half the omelet; let brown a minute longer, then fold the plain half over the tomato filling. Turn the omelet out on to a hot platter; brush top with melted butter, and lightly brown under the flame of the broiling oven. Serve at once, garnished with smothered onions.

CORN AND EGG SCRAMBLE KENTUCKY STYLE [323]

Take 1 cup of drained canned whole grain corn, or fresh boiled corn cut from the cob, and brown in heavy skillet in 4 tablespoons of bacon drippings, with 1 small green pepper, chopped, 1 tablespoon of chopped parsley, and 2 tablespoons of chopped canned pimiento; stirring to keep it from sticking. When done, and just before serving, add 5 or 6 whole eggs, salt and pepper to taste and scramble all until eggs are set but not dry.

COTTAGE CHEESE OMELET PAYSANNE [324]

Beat 6 fresh egg yolks until thick, seasoning as you beat with ¾ teaspoon of salt mixed with ¼ teaspoon of nutmeg and ⅛ generous teaspoon of white pepper, then beat in ¾ cup of sieved cottage cheese well mixed with ⅓ cup (more or less) of cold milk, 3 tablespoons of finely chopped green pepper, 1 tablespoon each of finely chopped parsley, onion and chives. Then fold in 5 stiffly beaten egg whites. Heat 2 tablespoons of butter, spreading it all over the sides of a large, light frying pan; pour in the egg mixture and cook as an ordinary omelet, folding when mixture just begins to solidify and bottom is delicately browned. Invert upon a hot, long platter, brush top with melted butter, sprinkle over 3 tablespoons of grated cheese, and put the platter under the flame of the broiling oven to melt the cheese. Sprinkle with a little paprika and serve at once, the platter garnished with crisp, green watercress.

The egg dance was once a popular diversion in many parts of Europe It is now confined chiefly to Spain, among the people of Valencia. A number of eggs are arranged in a prescribed form upon the dancing floor, and among them a blindfolded dancer moves as best he may, to music, the object being to execute an intricate dance without breaking the eggs.

CRABMEAT OMELET A LA NEWBURG [325]
The Favorite Dish of the Late Baron Selmer Fougnier

Sauté ½ pound of flaked, picked fresh or canned crabmeat in 2 tablespoons of butter over a gentle flame until well heated, but not browned, stirring almost constantly; stir in ½ teaspoon of paprika and 2 tablespoons of sherry wine, mixed with ¾ cup of scalded cream, and continue cooking for 3 or 4 minutes. Remove from the fire, and stir in 2 well-beaten egg yolks, seasoned with salt and pepper. Keep hot but do not let boil. Make an omelet of 8 eggs in the usual way and, when almost set, make some holes with a fork so that the uncooked eggs will come in contact with bottom of the frying pan. Pour crabmeat preparation over half the omelet, let brown a few seconds longer, then fold the plain half over the crabmeat filling; turn out onto a hot, long platter, and serve at once garnished with crisp, green watercress, first brushing the omelet top with melted butter. Lobster, shrimps, mussels, and any kind of cooked, carefully boned fish may also be prepared in this delicious way.

## CREAMED EGGS IN SPINACH RING					[326]

Clean, wash in several changes of cold water, then cook 2 pounds of spinach in its own juice until tender, seasoning with salt. Drain thoroughly and put the spinach through food chopper. Add then $\frac{1}{2}$ cup of hot milk, 3 tablespoons of fine dry bread crumbs, $\frac{1}{3}$ cup of butter, 1 tablespoon of grated onion, pepper and nutmeg to taste, and mix well. Pack into a buttered ring mold and place the mold in a pan of hot water. Bake in a moderate oven (325°–350° F.) about 15–20 minutes. Turn out onto a large, round, hot platter and fill the center with the following preparation: To 2 cups of medium cream sauce, add 6 hard-cooked, sliced eggs; $\frac{1}{2}$ cup of sliced, cooked mushrooms and 1 teaspoon each of grated onion, minced parsley and chives. Serve at once.

## CREOLE OMELET					[327]

Beat 8 eggs in a bowl with 4 tablespoons of cold water, seasoning, while beating, with 1 scant teaspoon of salt, a little pepper and paprika. Heat $2\frac{1}{2}$ tablespoons of butter to a very light brown, and turn in the eggs. As they brown, lift the edges with a spatula and let the uncooked part run under. When the omelet is lightly browned underneath and creamy on top, fold one half over the other and slip onto a hot platter. Surround with Creole sauce, the genuine one, made as follows:

Slice 4 large onions thinly into a well-buttered pan, and stir them about till the rings are separated. Don't be niggardly with the butter, use $\frac{1}{2}$ cup. Cover the pan and smother slowly till every shred of onion is tender and translucent, then add 1 green and 1 red pepper, cut in slivers, and 3 peeled and sliced tomatoes, or a tin of tomato paste. Peel $\frac{1}{2}$ pound of fresh mushrooms, and put the minced stems into the cooking sauce. Sauté the caps until brown and tender, in another pan containing 3–4 tablespoons of hot butter. When the pepper and tomatoes are done, add 1 tablespoon of Worcestershire sauce, salt and pepper to taste, and 1 tablespoon of minced parsley to the sauce, and mix contents of both pans, except the mushroom caps, which should be arranged along the top of the omelet in a ridge. Garnish with watercress and serve at once.

CURRIED HARD-COOKED EGGS WITH NOODLES [328]

Hard-cook 6 eggs; remove the shells and quarter the eggs. Melt ¼ cup of butter in a saucepan; stir in 1 tablespoon of finely chopped green pepper, mixed with 2 tablespoons of grated onion and 2 tablespoons of finely chopped celery, and cook over a low flame for 3 or 4 minutes, or until vegetables turn yellow, but not brown, stirring constantly; sprinkle over 2½ tablespoons of flour and, when well blended, stir in 2 cups of milk which has been scalded with a large bay leaf and 3 sprigs of parsley, then strained. Stir constantly until mixture is smooth and just begins to thicken, then season with 2 tablespoons of curry powder, moistened in a little cold water, 3 or 4 drops of tabasco sauce, ¾ teaspoon salt and 1 teaspoon of Pique Seasoning, mixing thoroughly. Let simmer gently for 5 or 6 minutes, then pour into a ring of cooked noodles. Sprinkle top with paprika and a little finely minced parsley and serve at once.

CURRIED SCRAMBLED EGGS WITH LOBSTER [329]

Heat ¾ cup of cooked, shredded lobster meat, fresh or canned, in 3 tablespoons of butter, stirring almost constantly, but do not let boil; season with a dash of paprika mixed with 1½–2 teaspoons of curry powder and ¼ teaspoon of salt. Beat 7 fresh eggs as for an omelet, with ⅓ cup of heavy cream or thin cream sauce, and pour all at once over the lobster mixture, stirring gently but thoroughly over a low flame until eggs just begin to set. Serve on a hot platter, over freshly made buttered toast, garnish with crisp, green parsley or cress and lemon quarters, and serve at once.

Many of us think of ham and eggs as a typical American dish but the Egyptians of 1500 B. C. were partial to it and praised it in a cookbook of that period.

EGGS BENEDICT [330]

For 6 servings, split, toast and butter 3 English muffins. Sauté 6 thin, round slices of cooked, lean ham. Poach 6 fresh eggs. Place 1 round slice of hot ham on each toasted, hot English muffin half; cover with a poached egg; dress on very hot platter, and cover each egg with Hollandaise sauce (No. 1062) slightly thinned with hot, heavy sweet cream to pouring consistency; top each with a thin slice of black truffle, and garnish platter with parsley. Serve at once.

EGGS CASSEROLE CHARCUTIÈRE   [331]

Cook 1 pound of small link pork sausage (24 sausages) 15 minutes in their own fat (covered) over a low flame. Arrange 4 sausages in each of 6 au gratin dishes or custard cups, and sprinkle over each portion ½ teaspoon of Pique Seasoning, ½ teaspoon of finely chopped shallots, as much of finely chopped parsley and set aside. Beat 6 egg whites until stiff, season with a few grains of cayenne, nutmeg and salt. Pile the egg whites over the sausages; make a hollow in center, and in it drop 1 unbroken egg yolk. Dust the yolks with a little paprika, and bake in a moderate oven (325–350° F.) about 15–20 minutes, or until yolks are set and whites delicately browned. Serve immediately.

EGGS CELESTINE   [332]

Cut 6 hard-cooked eggs in half lengthwise and place in a well-buttered baking dish. Cook 1 medium-sized onion, finely chopped or grated in 3 tablespoons of butter 2 minutes, stirring constantly; sprinkle with 2 tablespoons of flour; season to taste with salt, white pepper and a few grains of nutmeg, and blend well until mixture just begins to bubble still stirring constantly; then pour over gradually 1 cup of thin cream or undiluted evaporated milk, previously mixed with a small can of French peas and cook, still stirring until mixture thickens. Pour over the eggs. Trim 6 slices of freshly made toast and with a doughnut cutter, cut into rings; dip the toasted rings in melted butter, then in grated American cheese, and place on top of the egg mixture. Brown lightly under the flame of the broiling oven and serve at once from the baking dish.

EGG DIETETIC   [333]

Take a strictly fresh egg; break it into a cold egg-glass; squeeze a few drops (the more the better) of lemon juice over, add a tiny pinch of salt, mix it, and drink at once. Very comforting when tired or the appetite is laggard.

EGGS FLORIDA   [334]

The Fountain of Youth wasn't the only thing that Ponce de Leon failed to find when he browsed around St. Augustine, Florida. The delicious egg dish of Eggs Florida, although credited to him by some natives of the sunshine peninsula, probably came much later. Just when it was created has been lost in the annals of culinary history. Its recipe, however, was not. Here is the way it's prepared:

Mash the yolks of 6 hard-cooked eggs and chop the whites. Brown
1 medium-sized onion in 2 tablespoons of butter; sprinkle over 1 tablespoon of flour, and blend well. Then stir in ½–⅔ cup of cream, scalded
with a bay leaf and 1 whole clove, then strained, stirring constantly,
alternately with 2 cups of tomato juice, and cook until mixture just
begins to thicken. Now stir in ½ cup of chopped, cooked mushrooms,
celery and green pepper, 1 finely chopped small clove of garlic, salt and
pepper to taste. Finally stir in the chopped eggs. Turn mixture into 6
buttered individual baking casseroles, sprinkle with buttered bread
crumbs and brown under the flame of the broiling oven. Serve at once.

EGG FRITTERS A LA MILANAISE   [335]

Halve 6 hard-cooked eggs lengthwise and remove the yolks. Heat
1¾ tablespoons of butter in a saucepan; stir in 1 tablespoon of flour,
blend well without browning, then add gradually ¼ cup of scalded milk
and cook very gently with constant stirring for a minute or so, or until
preparation is of the consistency of thick cream. Now stir in the sieved
hard-cooked yolks, blending well; then 3 tablespoons of ground cooked
chicken, ham or tongue, mixed with 1 teaspoon each of finely chopped
chervil, shallots, and lemon juice. Season to taste with salt, pepper and
nutmeg. Fill cavities of the egg whites with this stuffing; roll in beaten,
seasoned eggs, then in fine bread crumbs and, when ready to serve,
place the prepared eggs in a wire basket and plunge the basket into hot,
deep, clear fat (360°–375° F.), cooking until eggs are nicely browned.
Drain on absorbent paper; dress on a hot platter covered with cooked
spaghetti mixed with rich tomato sauce; scatter over all plenty of fresh
parsley fried in deep fat (375°–390° F.) and well drained. Serve at once.

EGG FRITTERS À LA ROYALE   [336]

Beat 7 strictly fresh eggs with 3 tablespoons of cold sweet cream;
season to taste with salt, pepper, nutmeg and powdered thyme, and
turn mixture into a buttered square, shallow baking dish. Place the
dish in a pan of hot water and bake until the custard is set. Cool and,
when thoroughly cold, cut into strips about 2 inches long and ⅓ inch
thick. Have ready a special frying batter made as follows and called:

Royal Frying Batter. Sift ¼ cup of bread flour with a dash of salt
into a bowl; stir in 1 tablespoon of olive oil, alternately with 2 tablespoons of lukewarm water, mixed with 2 tablespoons of sherry wine,
adding gradually and beating briskly until batter is of the consistency
of heavy cream, then continue to beat briskly for 5 minutes, adding
while beating 1 blade of garlic, finely chopped, and 1 teaspoon each of
finely chopped parsley and chives. Set aside to mellow 25–30 minutes

and, when ready to use, fold in 2 stiffly beaten egg whites with a few grains of salt and a dash each of nutmeg and cayenne pepper.

Dip egg strips into this flavorful frying batter; place a few strips at a time in a wire frying basket, plunge the basket into hot, deep, clear fat (375°–390° F.) and fry until crisp and delicately browned. Drain on absorbent paper and serve on a folded napkin with a side dish of rich tomato sauce to which has been added a tablespoon or two of chopped capers.

EGGS AU GRATIN CELIA [337]

Sprinkle the bottom of a generously buttered earthenware baking dish, which should be decorative enough to be presented at table, with a thin layer of cracker crumbs. Arrange over the crumbs a layer of 3 hard-cooked, sliced eggs; sprinkle the egg slices with ¼ cup of grated cheese (any kind), then arrange a thin layer of finely chopped green pepper, mixed with 2 finely chopped canned red pimientos, well drained, 1 teaspoon of grated onion and 1 teaspoon of finely chopped parsley, seasoning to taste with mixed salt, pepper, nutmeg and marjoram (powdered). Pour over all 1 cup of medium cream sauce, and repeat with 3 more eggs, sliced, green pepper mixture and another ½ cup of cream sauce. Sprinkle top with ½ cup of fine bread crumbs, mixed with ¼ cup of grated cheese, and bake 15–20 minutes in a moderate oven (350° F.), or until the crumb-cheese mixture bubbles and is nicely browned. Serve from the baking dish.

EGG AND HAM CROQUETTES [338]

Scramble 8 eggs in the usual way, seasoning to taste with salt and white pepper. When eggs just begin to set, stir in 1 cup of finely chopped or ground, cold, lean, cooked ham, 1 teaspoon of grated onion, 2 teaspoons of finely chopped parsley, mixing thoroughly. Remove from the fire; spread over a cold platter to cool and, when quite cold, shape into croquettes, cones or egg-shapes. Roll in beaten seasoned egg, then in fine bread crumbs; again in beaten egg and fine bread crumbs. Chill well. When ready to serve, place a few croquettes at a time in a wire basket, plunge it into hot, deep, clear fat (375°–390° F.) and fry until delicately browned. Drain on absorbent paper and serve on a hot platter covered with a folded napkin or paper doily; garnish with parsley or watercress and small bouquets or mounds of shoestring potatoes, and serve at once with a side dish of tomato, mushroom, or cream sauce. NOTE. Any kind of left-over cooked fish, crustaceans, meat, game or vegetables may be prepared in this manner.

EGGS MOLLET [339]

Eggs Mollet are eggs which are related both to poached eggs and those cooked in the shell. They are soft-cooked in hot water, then plunged into cold water. Just before they are used or served, the shells are removed and the eggs are reheated in hot water, wine, milk, fish stock, meat stock, game stock or vegetable stock, and may be prepared exactly as poached eggs, hot or cold.

EGGS OX EYES [340]
Oeufs à l'Oeil de Boeuf (Formula of the Auberge of the Old Mill of Dijon, France)

Cut 6 slices of stale bread ¾ of an inch in thickness. Toast on both sides and stamp them into rounds about 3 inches in diameter, then remove the middle of each round with a 1½-inch cutter. Place the rings in a generously buttered baking dish; pour over them gradually as much sour cream as they will absorb without becoming sodden; then break a fresh egg carefully into each ring. Sprinkle lightly with mixed salt and white pepper; cover each egg with 1 generous teaspoon of rich, sweet milk; place in a slow oven (300° F.), and bake until eggs are set but not hard. Serve on hot, individual plates, surrounding each egg with a ribbon of tomato sauce to which has been added thinly sliced fresh mushrooms cooked in butter.

EGG PIE FRENCH STYLE [341]

Brush the bottom of a 9-inch pie plate generously with anchovy butter (sweet butter creamed with anchovy paste, using a pea-size bit of paste to each tablespoon of butter). Spread over this, as evenly as possible, 1 cup of cooked, sliced fresh mushrooms. Over the mushrooms, break 6 large fresh eggs, without breaking the yolks, keeping each egg apart. Between the eggs arrange 6 small cooked pork sausage, and dust the eggs with mixed salt and a few grains each of cayenne and powdered clove. Combine ½ cup of rich cream sauce with ⅓ teaspoon of dry mustard, and carefully pour this between the eggs. Cover with your favorite flaky pie crust, as you would for an ordinary pie; prick well with the tines of a fork to let the steam escape; make a hole the size of a dime in center top of crust; brush the crust with cold milk and bake in a very moderate oven (300–325° F.) until crust is delicately golden brown. Remove from oven, and through the hole in center, by means of a small funnel or paper funnel, pour in 2 or 3 tablespoons of good sherry wine. Return to the oven for 5 minutes, and serve at once. The eggs should be poached soft and the sherry wine distributed throughout the sauce. A fine luncheon dish.

EGG PATTIES BOURGEOISE [342]

Brown ½ cup of finely chopped onions in 2 tablespoons of butter over a very gentle flame, stirring almost constantly, then stir in 2 cups of soft bread crumbs, alternately with ¾ cup of rich milk, previously scalded with 1 bay leaf, 1 clove of garlic, left whole, 3 sprigs of parsley and 1 tablespoon of chopped green celery leaves, then strained. Cook very slowly until mixture is thoroughly blended and thick; season to taste with mixed salt, pepper and nutmeg, then stir in 6 hard-cooked eggs, finely chopped. Spread mixture on a cold platter to cool. When quite cold, shape into 6 individual patties or cakes; dip in seasoned beaten egg, then roll in fine bread crumbs. Chill. When ready to serve, fry in plenty of butter till golden brown on both sides. Serve on a hot, round platter covered with fluffy mashed potatoes, the potatoes sprinkled with small cubes of bread fried in butter and well drained; the cakes or patties should surround the edge of the mashed potatoes, crown-fashion.

EGG AND POTATO SCALLOP [343]

Heat 3 tablespoons of butter; stir in 3 tablespoons of flour until thoroughly blended, stirring constantly over a gentle flame. When mixture just begins to bubble, stir in 2 cups of rich milk, previously scalded with 4 slices of onion, a blade of garlic, a blade of mace, and 3 sprigs of fresh parsley, then drained. Stir constantly until thickened; season with mixed salt, pepper, nutmeg and a few grains of cayenne pepper. Have ready cooked and sliced 5 medium-sized peeled potatoes and 6 hard-cooked eggs, also sliced. Place alternate layers of potato, white sauce, and hard-cooked egg, in a buttered baking dish, separating each layer with ⅓ cup of soft bread crumbs, mixed with 1 scant teaspoon each of finely chopped parsley and chives, having top layer of bread crumb mixture. Sprinkle over the top 1 generous tablespoon of melted butter, and bake in a moderate oven (350° F.) for about 20 minutes, or until top is delicately brown. Serve at once from the baking dish.

Variations. Substitute for potato slices 2 cups of cooked peas or 2 cups of cooked and cut string beans, or 2 cups of cooked spinach, or 2 cups of cooked macaroni, spaghetti or noodles.

EGG RAMEKINS FLORENTINE [344]

Cook a generous half pound of fresh spinach till tender, strain and rub through a fine-meshed sieve. Line 6 individual buttered ramekins with the spinach, previously buttered; pour over the spinach 1 table-spoon of scalded, seasoned, heavy cream; break a fresh egg into each prepared ramekin; place the ramekins on a baking sheet, and bake 7 or 8 minutes in a moderate oven (325–350° F.) or until eggs are set. Dust the eggs with a little paprika and serve at once.

EGG RAMEKINS RENVERSÉS   [345]
Upside-down Eggs in Ramekins or Muffin Tins

Butter 6 individual ramekins or muffin tins generously with anchovy butter (No. 979), then coat them rather thickly with fine bread crumbs. Into each break a fresh egg; sprinkle lightly with mixed salt and white pepper; place the ramekins or muffin tins on a baking sheet, and bake in a very moderate oven (300–325° F.) 8–10 minutes, or until eggs are set. Pass the blade of a knife or a small spatula around the inside edge, invert very carefully on to a buttered round of toast, top each egg with a small fresh mushroom cap, freshly broiled and rolled in melted butter, and surround the base all around with Mornay sauce (No. 1088). Serve at once.

EGG RAMEKINS YVONNE   [346]

Chop or grind the cooked breast or left-over portions of a guinea hen, add 2 teaspoons of very finely chopped chervil (parsley if chervil is not available); season to taste with mixed salt and white pepper and a tiny pinch of powdered juniper berries. Butter generously 6 individual ramekins, then coat bottom and sides of each ramekin with the guinea hen preparation. Break a fresh egg into each ramekin without breaking the yolk; sprinkle the eggs with a dash of salt and cayenne pepper, and pour over each egg 1 tablespoon of cold, heavy, sweet cream. Dot with a little butter, using a piece about the size of a marble for each ramekin. Place the ramekins in a deep baking dish; carefully fill the baking dish with hot (not boiling) water to half the depth of the ramekins, and bake in a slow oven (275–300° F.) about 12–15 minutes, or until eggs are set. Have ready 6 rounds of freshly made toast, cut the size of the rame-kins and spread with a little melted butter, then with a thin spread of creamed, finely chopped ham; unmold the eggs onto the prepared rounds of toast. Pour around the bottom a neat ribbon of rich tomato sauce to which has been added a few drained, washed, dried capers, and serve immediately.

After eating eggs or snails the ancient Romans would carefully break the shells to destroy any lurking evil spirits.

EGG AND RICE PATTIES IN WATERCRESS [347] NESTS

Combine and blend thoroughly 6 hard-cooked eggs, shelled and finely chopped, 1 well-beaten whole egg, beaten with 1 additional egg yolk, ¾ cup of cold, cooked rice, well "in grains," 1 tablespoon of tomato catsup, 1 teaspoon of Pique Seasoning, 2 tablespoons of grated onion, salt and pepper to taste with a dash each of paprika and cayenne. Shape into small patties, the size of a silver dollar; roll in sieved bread crumbs and fry in plenty of butter until golden brown on both sides. Drain and serve in a large nest of crisp, green watercress, the cress dipped in cold water, well shaken, then dipped in paprika and shaken to remove excess. A side dish of sliced cucumber in sour cream and a dish of baked potatoes will complete a fine Lenten meal.

EGG RING PARISIENNE [348]

Butter a ring mold generously with salmon butter (No. 999). Beat 6 eggs slightly and season with salt, paprika and a few grains of cayenne, then stir in 1½ cups of rich, sweet, cold milk, mixing thoroughly. Fill the prepared ring mold with this preparation; cover with waxed or buttered paper; place the mold in a pan containing hot (not boiling) water to half the depth of the egg mixture and bake in a slow even oven (300° F.) until knife inserted in the custard comes away almost clean. At no time should the water reach the boiling point, and the custard should be cooked in about 20 minutes. Remove from the oven, lift the ring from the water, let stand 5 minutes to complete the cooking by stored heat. Loosen the custard from the mold with a knife or spatula, and invert upon a heated, round platter. Carefully lift off the mold; fill center with creamed sweetbreads, creamed chicken, creamed turkey, creamed mushrooms, creamed potatoes, etc. Dust the creamed mixture with finely chopped parsley mixed with paprika, and surround the base of the ring with tomato sauce.

EGG SHORT CAKE HOME STYLE [349]
(*Individual*)

Sift 2 cups of flour once; return to sifter, add 4 teaspoons of baking powder and ½ teaspoon of salt and sift in a mixing bowl; cut in ¼ cup of shortening, then mix in 1 cup of grated American cheese and a generous pinch each of pepper and nutmeg, mixing thoroughly. Now add 1 large fresh egg, beaten, then combined with about ½ cup of cold milk, or enough to form a soft dough. Roll out on a lightly floured board, to about ½ inch in thickness; cut into rounds or squares, and bake in a very hot oven (450° F.) until brown. Split the hot shortcakes and put them together with 2 cups of cream sauce (No. 258) to which 8 sliced hard-cooked eggs and 1 teaspoon of grated onion, 1 teaspoon each of finely chopped parsley and chives with a little salt and pepper have been added. Sprinkle with paprika and serve as hot as possible.

In the fifteenth century in England, a diner requesting white meat was given food prepared from milk, butter and eggs. According to Cogan, a writer of that time, "The third kind of meat, which is neither fish nor fleshe, is called 'white meate,' as eggs, milk and so on."

EGG SOUFFLÉ BERNARDINE [350]

Combine 3 cups of cooked and ground chicken with 1½ cups of bread crumbs; heat 3 generous tablespoons of butter; blend in 3 tablespoons of flour, mixed with ½ teaspoon salt, a few grains of pepper and a tiny pinch of powdered marjoram, and stir until smooth over a low flame but do not let brown; gradually stir in 1 cup of rich milk, mixed with ½ cup of thin cream (or undiluted evaporated milk), previously scalded with 1 small bay leaf, 3 sprigs of parsley, 1 whole clove, and 4 thin slices of onion, then strained, stirring constantly until thick and smooth. Remove from the fire and beat in 3 fresh egg yolks, adding one at a time and beating briskly after each addition. Stir in the chicken-crumb mixture, mixing well. Lastly fold in 4 stiffly beaten egg whites, beaten with a few grains of salt and 2 teaspoons of curry powder. Fill 6 buttered shirred egg dishes, previously sprinkled with 2 tablespoons each of chopped, cooked mushrooms; make a depression in center; drop 1 uncooked fresh egg into each; place the dishes on a baking sheet, and bake in a moderate oven (350° F.) for about 20 minutes or until eggs are set and chicken mixture puffed. Serve immediately.

NOTE. Left-over cooked meat, ham or fish or crustaceans may also be prepared in the same manner.

EGG STEW MOTHER KATE TURNER'S STYLE [351]

Hard-cook 7 or 8 eggs. Shell and drop them in cold water. Set aside. Slice 2 medium-sized onions and sauté in 2 tablespoons of butter until just beginning to brown, stirring frequently; stir in ¾ cup of dry white wine; cover and let simmer gently until the wine is half evaporated; then stir in 2½ cups of canned tomato sauce, 1 bay leaf, 2 blades of fresh dill, or a generous pinch of powdered dill, 1 whole clove of garlic, 2 whole cloves, head removed, and a 1-inch piece of scraped parsley root; season to taste with salt and pepper, cover and let simmer gently for 25 minutes, stirring occasionally. Drain the eggs, quarter them, and gently put them into the sauce. Let heat thoroughly without boiling;

discard bay leaf parsley root, garlic and clove and serve at once in a
hot deep dish garnished with small triangles of bread fried in butter.

EGGS A LA TRIPE   [352]

Boil 7 or 8 eggs until hard; place in a colander and let cold water
run over them until quite cold; shell, then slice or quarter them. Have
ready 1¾ cups of rich cream sauce or, better still, Béchamel sauce
(No. 258 and No. 259, respectively), and stir in 3 tablespoons of scalded
sweet, heavy cream. Arrange the prepared eggs in 6 china individual
casseroles or coquille shells or, failing these, in a shallow baking dish;
pour over them the hot sauce, first tasted for seasoning, and sprinkle
with finely chopped parsley. Serve immediately.

When an egg rattles if shaken, it is not fresh. The air space inside the
shell has become large through slow evaporation—hence the rattle.

EGGS IN WHITE WINE WITH CHEESE   [353]

Heat 2 tablespoons of butter in a saucepan; stir in 1 tablespoon of
chopped shallots and 1 tablespoon of finely chopped parsley, and cook
2 minutes, stirring constantly; then stir in ½–¾ cup of dry white wine,
season to taste with salt and cayenne, and stir till well blended and
mixture just begins to bubble. Break in 6 whole eggs and ½ cup cheese
Stir constantly over a very low flame until eggs and cheese are blended.
Serve on 6 slices of freshly made toast, each criss-crossed with trimmed
anchovy filets.

ENGLISH EGG SAUSAGE   [354]
A Lenten Dish

This preparation requires a little care, but if the directions are
strictly followed, the results will amply repay the trouble.

Procure from the delicatessen store some sausage casings such as are
used for ordinary sausages. Wash well and ascertain, by filling them with
water, that there are no holes in them, as a single pinhole might cause
the failure of the operation. Tie 1 of the ends of the skins (casing) with
thread. Now break 8 fresh eggs in a bowl, season with salt and pepper
to taste, then add 1 teaspoon each of chives, onion, parsley, green pepper
and canned red pimiento all finely chopped, and 1 teaspoon of black
olives finely chopped, and mix thoroughly. Then add 1 cup of fresh,
heavy cream or Béchamel sauce (No. 259), or rich cream sauce (No.
258), and beat with rotary beater. Fill the skins or casing through a
small funnel, leaving 2 inches to allow space for the swelling while
cooking. Plunge the "sausage" into a pan containing water brought to

the boiling point; turn off the gas or remove from the fire and let stand 25 minutes. Do not allow to boil; stir occasionally with a wooden spoon or wooden stick, to prevent the mixture in the skins from separating. Lift out the sausages and plunge immediately into cold water to cool.

Serve hot or cold. If hot, peel off the skin, warm the sausage or sausages in meat, chicken or vegetable stock, or in canned bouillon or consommé and serve over a bed of creamed or whole spinach, mashed potatoes, mashed peas, mashed turnips, or over noodles, macaroni or spaghetti. If served cold, slice as ordinary sausage (first removing the skin) and serve with a green salad.

FLUFFY AVOCADO OMELET AU CURRY   [355]

The avocado, or alligator pear, or ahuacatl, is as old as history and may be even older. Yet many of us still think of it merely as something upon which to sprinkle French dressing, or lemon juice, or to flavor with a dab of mayonnaise. And some of us do not think of it at all, which is a great pity. Natives of tropical lands lush with avocados may not know a protein from a fat or a mineral from a vitamin, but they have long fed themselves all those valued elements via the avocado. Whatever the alias—alligator pear, avocado, calavo, midshipman's butter, etc.— the avocado is no rarity here and now. We grow our own chiefly in California and Florida. Ever try an avocado omelet as they do in Miami? Here's how:

Beat 6 egg yolks separately. Do likewise with the 6 whites, but to the whites add ½ teaspoon of salt, ¼ teaspoon of white pepper and 2 teaspoons of curry powder. Combine the yolks and whites very gently. Heat 2 generous tablespoons of butter in a light frying pan, spreading it all over the bottom and edges and removing any excess of butter. Drop egg mixture in it all at once, and cook the omelet in the usual way. When lightly browned on the bottom and just beginning to set, place on one side of the omelet 1 cup of small cubes of avocado; fold, slide onto a hot platter: brush top with meat glaze (meat extract, slightly melted) and glaze under the flame of the broiling oven. Garnish with crisp watercress and serve at once.

> *Alas! My child, where is the Pen*
> *That can do justice to the Hen?*
> *Like Royalty she goes her way,*
> *Laying Foundations every day.*
> *Though not for Public Buildings yet—*
> *For Custard, Cake, and Omelette.*
> *No wonder, Child, we prize the hen*
> *Whose egg is mightier than the Pen. . . .*
>   *—Oliver Herpid*

FRIED EGG BURGER LUNCHEON   [356]

Combine 1 pound of finely chopped (not ground) hamburger meat with 1 tablespoon each of finely chopped green pepper, cooked in butter and drained, 1 tablespoon of finely chopped parsley and 1 tablespoon of finely chopped or grated onion, 3 tablespoons of bread crumbs, 1 whole, large egg or 2 small eggs, salt, pepper, nutmeg and thyme to taste, mixing thoroughly. Divide mixture into 6 equal parts and make 6 flat patties, the size of a fried egg, and cook in butter until patties are brown on both sides. Serve patties on 6 slices of toast, topping each patty with a fried egg. Surround with tomato sauce. Serve at once.

FRIED EGGS SCOTCH STYLE   [357]
Oeufs Frits à l'Ecossaise

Hard-cook eggs and, when cold, remove the shells and cover each egg completely with seasoned pork sausage. Roll each egg in beaten egg, then in fine, seasoned bread crumbs and, when ready to serve, place half of the eggs in a wire basket and plunge in hot, deep, clear fat (360°–375° F.) letting brown nicely. Drain on absorbent paper and repeat for the 3 remaining prepared eggs. Serve at once on a dish of cooked, generously buttered kale.

FRIED STUFFED EGGS MONTFERMEIL   [358]

Have ready 6 hard-cooked eggs; shell and cut them in halves lengthwise; remove the yolks (which reserve for other use) and fill each half with the following stuffing: Heat 2 tablespoons of butter in a saucepan; stir in the size of an extra large pea-size of anchovy paste, then 1 cup of ground, fresh mushrooms, mixed with 1 teaspoon of grated onion, and cook 2 or 3 minutes over a very low flame, stirring constantly; moisten with 1 generous teaspoon of sherry wine and 2 tablespoons of scalded heavy cream. Do not salt, but stir in 1 pinch of pepper and 1 of nutmeg, blending thoroughly. Fill the egg white cavities with the mixture, having mushroom mixture rounded up to represent a whole egg; dip each egg thus prepared in seasoned beaten egg, then in plenty of fine bread crumbs. Chill. When ready to serve, place a few stuffed eggs in a wire basket, plunge in hot, deep, clear fat (375°–390° F.) and fry as for croquettes. Drain on absorbent paper; serve on a folded napkin on a hot platter, strewing generously with fried watercress sprigs these dipped in frying batter and fried in hot deep fat (380° F.), and serve at once with a side dish of Poivrade sauce (No. 1104).

MONSIEUR PIQUE'S EGG PANCAKE TURNOVERS [359]

Beat 6 fresh eggs with ½ teaspoon of curry powder, very little salt, and a dash of pepper, and strain through a fine sieve or let stand until most of the foam settles.

Cook 2 tablespoons each of finely chopped onion, green pepper and pimiento in 1½–2 tablespoons of bacon or ham drippings until lightly colored; stir in 1 cup of ground, carefully picked crabmeat, fresh or canned, 1 tablespoon of Victoria sauce (commercial), 1 teaspoon of Pique seasoning and ⅓ cup of heavy cream, and heat to the boiling point but do not let boil. The mixture should be of dropping consistency similar to that of pancakes. Drop the egg mixture by tablespoons on hot, greased griddle and, when half cooked, place a heaping teaspoon of crabmeat filling on each pancake, folding in half and patting edges together gently with a broad spatula. Be careful to fold before the egg pancake sets completely and turn each pancake once. Serve hot with a side dish of rich tomato sauce to which have been added 2 tablespoons of finely chopped dill pickles. Very nourishing.

MUSHROOM OMELET WITH SHERRY [360]

Fry ¼ pound of peeled, sliced fresh mushrooms in 3 tablespoons of butter or margarine until tender; stir in 1½ tablespoons of sherry wine, and let simmer very gently over a very low flame. Make an omelet with 8 eggs in the ordinary way and, when slightly brown underneath and top is just beginning to set, place the undrained mushrooms on one side and fold over the uncovered part of the omelet. Cook 1 minute, slide the omelet onto a hot, long platter, brush top with melted butter, and brown delicately under the flame of the broiling oven. Remove as soon as browned and top the omelet with 6 caps of fresh mushrooms freshly broiled and brushed with melted butter. Garnish the platter with plenty of crisp watercress, and serve at once.

NOTE. If preferred, stir the cooked mushrooms into the eggs when beating them, and cook the omelet as directed.

MUSSEL OMELET DIEPPOISE [361]

Make an ordinary omelet in the usual way, using 7 or 8 eggs for 6 servings. When ready to fold the omelet, spread in the center 2–2½ dozens nice, plump but small mussels, previously boiled and shelled, then sautéed in butter until golden brown. Fold the omelet, slide it on to a hot, long platter; brush the top with melted clarified butter; sprinkle all over with grated cheese (any desired kind) and place the platter under the flame of the broiling oven to melt and brown the cheese. Surround the base of the omelet with tomato sauce and scatter over the sauce 2 dozen cooked, shelled mussels.

OMELET [362]

Most of us know, or think we know, how to make an omelet. Yet, to make an omelet requires a certain practice, for, to be successful, an omelet must be mellow inside, of an oval shape, pointed at both ends, plump in the middle and of a golden color all over. The best method, the one practiced by most good cooks, is as follows:

Break the eggs into a bowl and beat thoroughly—the more beating, the lighter the omelet—then season to taste with salt and white pepper. Place a light frying pan (not a skillet) containing 1 scant tablespoon of butter on a hot fire and let it become well heated, but not browned; pour the eggs *all at once* into it and with a fork quickly and gently press the edges back towards the centre as soon as they just begin to thicken. The soft part will run immediately to fill the space thus left vacant. Repeat until the eggs do not run easily. Bring the contents of the pan to the side nearest you. Then let slide toward the other side, and have a hot oval platter ready to receive the unctuous preparation. After doing this 2 or 3 times you'll be an expert and obtain an omelet of nice shape, appetizing, golden brown and soft inside. The main point to success is to operate *rapidly*, so I advise you to try first with 2 eggs; the fewer the eggs the easier they are to handle.

If it is a composite omelet—that is, with an inside filling—have the ingredients all prepared before starting the omelet, and when the eggs are beginning to set and do not run easily any more, place the garnishing or filling in the center and fold one side over carefully so as to form a pouch, let slide toward the edge. Brown a little and turn over onto a hot oval platter.

You may add a tablespoon or two of cream, evaporated milk or plain milk, or water for the sake of economy, yet the real omelet is made without the addition of these ingredients.

OMELET AUX FINES HERBES [363]

Beat 8 eggs in the usual way; season to taste with salt and white pepper, then beat in 4 tablespoons of finely mixed herbs in equal parts such as parsley, chervil, tarragon, chives, mixed together. Proceed as directed for (No. 362).

OMELET MASCOTTE [364]

Mince 12 canned or freshly cooked artichoke bottoms, and sauté in 3 tablespoons of butter for about 5 minutes, stirring frequently.

Then stir in ½ generous cup of Béchamel sauce (No. 259), or a thick, rich cream sauce (No. 258). Cook an omelet of 8 eggs in the ordinary way and, when just beginning to set, place the artichoke bottom mixture in the center. Fold the omelet and slide it onto a hot, oval platter the bottom of which has been spread with some of the sauce already used. Garnish both ends of the platter with small triangles of bread fried in butter, and both sides with crisp watercress bouquets.

OMELET A LA MERE POULARD [365]

Probably no dish has ever been so wrapped in legend as "Mother Poulard's Omelet," and surely none has ever been eaten by more millions of people. Every tourist who ever visited Mont St. Michel, that medieval marvel of marvels, and stayed long enough to eat a meal on the Mount, has tasted it, for it is the unvarying pièce de résistance of every repast served in any one of the dozen restaurants that line the winding street that climbs up to the ancient monastery.

All these restaurants lay claim to being the "original" or the "true" or the "genuine" Mother Poulard's, or at least to be the depositories of the secret of making the famous omelet. Probably there is some basis for all the claims, as Mont St. Michel boasts only 240 inhabitants, and the prolific Poulard family has been established there for three generations. Almost any native you meet can justly claim to be a nephew or a niece or a grandchild of "Mère Poulard."

This writer visited the rector of the parish, Monsieur Couillard, who recently completed a study of the Poulard genealogy. After patient research he learned that the "original Mère Poulard" was a certain Annette Boutiaut of Nevers. She married the Norman, Victor Poulard, and together they opened a modest inn on the Mount in 1873, calling it St. Michel la Tête d'Or, or St. Michael the Golden Head, probably using a gilded bust of the saint as their shop sign.

Birth of the Omelet. The beginnings were difficult, and more than once the young couple were tempted to give up in despair, but in 1877 the bishop of the diocese authorized the resumption of pilgrimages to the Mount, and the Tête d'Or began to flourish. But "Mère Poulard" found herself with a serious problem on her hands. One never knew how many pilgrims and tourists were going to arrive on any given day. One had to have a large advance supply of provisions, and moreover one had to offer a menu that could be quickly prepared, for the time of the visitors was limited, especially in the case of those who came over the sands between tides. She hit on the idea of making her main dish an omelet, and whether because she really did have a special recipe or simply because the travelers, after their climb to the topmost chapel, were particularly hungry, the fame of that omelet spread. All over northern France the word went round that there was no omelet equal to Mother Poulard's.

Crowned heads went there as much to satisfy their curiosity about the cuisine as to see the architectural wonders of the Mount. Leopold II of Belgium one day took his place patiently in the queue that lined up for tables at the Tête d'Or. King Oscar of Sweden, on his visit there, wagered, after tasting the omelet, that he could duplicate it. Mère Poulard handed him the frying pan, but he made a mess of the job, much to the amusement of his entourage. Georges Clemenceau, the Tiger of France, visited the Mount and the famous restaurant shortly after the victory of 1918 and was embraced by the proprietress. He was the last famous visitor she lived to welcome.

Conjectures about the Secret. Some, including no less a personage than Escoffier, say the secret of the omelet was that she used more yolk than whites. Some say it was in the dosage of butter. Some maintain that it resided in a slight admixture of fresh cream.

The kitchen in the Tête d'Or, which is run today by descendants of Mère Poulard, as are many other of the restaurants, is right at the entrance, and guests pass through it to reach their tables. They can see the omelet being made. But all they see is an immense bowl of beaten eggs, from which the cook dips a ladleful of the golden fluid and tosses it into the well-buttered light frying pan. The mixture is stirred vigorously until it sets, then it is seasoned, deftly rolled and slid off onto a sizzling oval platter.

Possibly there is something in the fact that it is cooked on a fire of blazing logs in an open fireplace. The faint perfume of wood smoke never did an omelet any harm. At any rate, I watched several makings of this famous omelet, tasted several, and my deduction is that it is made as follows:

Allow 2 strictly fresh eggs for each person. Break one egg at a time in a saucer and slide it into a bowl. Repeat this for each egg. Allow 1 tablespoon of heavy sweet cream for each egg. Beat well with a wooden fork (no metal allowed, even silver) and season with a little salt and white pepper. Let stand for 15 minutes, then beat again briskly, and pour entire mixture at once into a light frying pan, containing enough butter to cover the entire bottom and sides of the frying pan. Tilt the pan, as it is important to have the sides buttered also, as already said. The fire should be very bright. There is a wrist motion in shaking the frying pan don't use a skillet) so the liquid part of the omelet will run over to the sides and under the bottom, thereby making a very light omelet. If this motion hasn't been mastered or seems difficult, use a narrow spatula and lift the edge of the omelet, letting the liquid part run under. Cook only until omelet is set at the bottom; the top should be like heavy cream. Over that "cream" pour *in the center* a teaspoon of heavy sweet cream for each 2 eggs, taking care not to let the cream reach the edge of the pan. Take a spatula and with a quick turn fold the soft omelet and transfer to a hot, oval platter. Garnish with parsley or cress and serve at once.

Important. Never serve an omelet nor, in fact, any kind of cooked eggs upon a silver or metal platter. Porcelain is the thing.

PARSLEY OMELET SOUFFLÉE [366]

Beat 6 fresh eggs lightly; add 6 tablespoons of sweet heavy cream with salt and white pepper to taste, and ½ cup of very finely chopped parsley, then beat briskly until foamy. Let stand until foam has almost disappeared, then beat slightly and pour all at once in a frying pan containing 1½ tablespoons of butter. Cook as an ordinary omelet. Fold, increase the heat to brown the underpart; slide onto a hot, oval platter and garnish with freshly cooked or canned asparagus tips covered with hot brown butter.

Eggs are sold by the "meter" (about 39⅓ inches) in the interior of Brazil. There are 18–20 eggs in a meter.

ONION OMELET COUNTRY STYLE [367]

Slice 3 large Bermuda onions thinly; separate the rings, and cook covered in 4 tablespoons of butter, with 4 tablespoons of beef or chicken stock, over a gentle flame, stirring frequently until soft and tender, or about 10–12 minutes. Keep hot. Prepare an ordinary omelet of 8 eggs in the usual way and, when eggs are set, drain the onions and place in center of the soft omelet; fold, raise the flame to brown the underside for about a half minute and slide the omelet onto a hot, oval platter. Garnish each end of the platter with a bouquet of watercress and on both sides with thick slices of broiled tomatoes. Serve at once.

OMELET A LA ROMAINE [368]
Roman Omelet

Rub with garlic, to taste, the bowl into which you are going to break and beat the eggs (2 for each serving). Make the omelet as usual; when ready to fold it, place in the center some hot cooked spinach en branche, that is, cooked with stems and unchopped, but thoroughly drained, and generously buttered. Fold the omelet, brush with butter, and arrange across the top 2 anchovy filets for each serving. Surround the omelet with a ribbon of hot tomato sauce (No. 1130), and serve at once.

OMELET SANTÉ [369]
Health Omelet

Wash and drain 1 bunch of crisp, green, young watercress and discard the stems. Break enough tips and leaves to make 1 cup (well-packed). Separate 8 eggs; beat the yolks slightly and stir in 6 tablespoons of thin cream (undiluted evaporated milk may be used) and season to taste with salt, white pepper and nutmeg. Beat briskly for a minute. Beat the whites until stiff with a few grains of salt and ½–¾ cup of parsley leaves, or half parsley and half chives, both finely chopped. Combine the yolks and whites and make the omelet in the usual way. Slide it onto a hot, oval platter; brush top with melted butter and garnish it with 6 cups of fresh mushrooms sautéed in butter and well drained, garnish both ends with crisp watercress and the sides with rather thick tomato stew. Serve at once.

OMELET SOUFFLÉE [370]
Puffed Omelet

Separate 8 fresh eggs; beat the whites until stiff with ½ teaspoon of salt and ¼ scant teaspoon of white pepper. Beat the yolks until creamy, then beat in them 5 tablespoons of hot water, and fold in the stiffly beaten whites. Heat a light frying pan; add 2 tablespoons of butter and spread it all over the bottom and sides, discarding the excess of melted butter. Pour in egg mixture all at once and cook over a gentle flame until bottom is brown and top creamy, then fold it in the usual way and slide onto a hot, oval platter; brush with melted butter and brown lightly under the flame of the broiling oven. Garnish with parsley or cress and serve immediately.

A temperature of 104° F., sustained for a period of three weeks, is necessary to hatch the egg of a hen.

OMELET DES SPORTS [371]
Sportive Omelet (Formula of the Café des Sports, Porte Maillot, Paris, France)

Separate 7 or 8 eggs. Beat the whites until stiff with ½ teaspoon of salt. Then, gradually beat in 2 tablespoons of whipped cream mixed with 2 tablespoons of tomato catsup, a few grains of cayenne and nutmeg. Beat the egg yolks until creamy and light, then stir in 1 tablespoon of grated onion. Combine whites and yolks very lightly. Heat 2 tablespoons of sweet butter until foamy in a light frying pan, and spread it all over the bottom and sides, then pour in the egg mixture all at once, and cook like an ordinary omelet. When bottom is lightly brown, and top is rather soft, spread on one side 1 cup of kidneys sautéed in red wine, having the sauce rather thick and the kidneys thinly sliced. Fold the omelet in the usual way. Let brown a minute, and slide the unctuous omelet onto a hot, oval platter. Brush with melted butter, place under the flame of the broiling oven to glaze and surround the omelet with more kidneys sautéed in red wine. Garnish both ends with watercress. The acme in omelets!

If a Borneo tribe looks upon a visitor with approval, it presents him with an egg, like our key to the city.

PLANKED EGGS IN NEST MY WAY   [372]

Cooking by means of the plank is our only distinctive American method, the one culinary delight that we have been able to teach the French masters of cuisine. It was invented by the Indians long before Christopher Columbus discovered the New World, and the early settlers, finding it convenient and delicious, adopted it. But along with the disappearance of the big open fireplace and the evolution of the range, the plank vanished for years, only to be revived two or three score years ago in hotel and restaurant cookery. Planking is really practical, inexpensive and adaptable to any home. The plank itself should be made of well-seasoned hard wood—maple, oak or hickory—and either oblong or oval in shape. It should be grooved so that the juices can be retained, and not lost in the oven. Any fish, meat, chicken, eggs and game may be cooked on a plank. In using the plank, first heat it in the oven, oil thoroughly or rub it with melted butter. The plates are served right from the plank; in the case of individual planks, each guest gets one on a dinner plate. Wash the plank after each use in hot soap suds, rinse it well, don't soak it; dry it, then wrap it in waxed paper to keep it clean for next time. For use, set it in a hot oven to warm it. Have the vegetables used for garnishing the plank cooked and ready. This dish of my own creation, which is really a one-dish meal, and very appetizing as well as economical, is prepared as follows:

Heat 2 generous tablespoons of bacon or ham drippings; stir in 3 cups of hamburger (1½ pounds) mixed with 2 tablespoons of finely chopped or grated onion, 1½ tablespoons of finely chopped parsley, seasoned to taste with mixed salt, pepper, nutmeg and thyme, and 2 slightly beaten fresh eggs, all well blended, and cook over a gentle flame until the meat is almost done, stirring frequently with a fork to separate the meat lumps. Divide the mixture into 6 equal parts, and press each part into a greased individual ring mold. Unmold the rings upon a heated, greased large plank, separating them so as to be able to fill the spaces with vegetables later on. Pour into each ring 1 tablespoon of Victoria sauce (commercial); over this sauce break a large fresh egg without breaking the yolk, and dust the egg with a little salt mixed with white pepper. Using a wet pastry bag with a rose tube, the pastry bag filled with creamy, rich Duchesse Potatoes (No. 1419—Variation), force a narrow border all along the edge of the plank; brush the potato with beaten egg yolk, and the hamburger rings with melted meat glaze or melted meat extract (commercial). Do not touch the egg. Place the plank thus prepared in a moderate oven (350° F.) and bake until eggs are set or about 12–15 minutes. Meantime, heat separately in small casserole or saucepan 1 cup each of any 3 preferred canned vegetables in ½ cup of hot water to which has been added 1 teaspoon of Pique Seasoning. Remove the plank from the oven, place it on a larger platter; drain each vegetable separately, and into each stir 1 tablespoon of butter and season to taste with salt and pepper. Arrange small mounds of these vegetables in between hamburger rings, dust each with finely chopped parsley, place mounds of freshly made French fried potatoes at both ends of the plank, and decorate tastefully with small bouquets of green, crisp watercress. Serve immediately. Make this really good one-meal dish a star performer and give it an effective entrance. It's worth while.

As regards wholesomeness, there is no well-founded objection to cold storage eggs as such. In general, storage eggs may be regarded as less desirable than those which are in reality "strictly fresh," but superior to many of the so-called "fresh" eggs which have not had the benefit of refrigeration.

POACHED EGGS AMANDINE   [373]

To poach an egg, select a fairly deep pan with slanting rim and have the water at least 2 inches deep. For each quart of water, add 2 teaspoons of salt or 1 tablespoon of good vinegar, or a little of both. The vinegar helps to harden the egg white while the salt gives flavor and helps to set the white. The eggs should be broken separately in a saucer and then slipped into the pan of boiling water. The water should cover the eggs but *should not* boil after the eggs are put in. Let stand until the white becomes opaque (about 5 minutes). Remove eggs from water with perforated spoon or perforated cake turner. Drain off water thoroughly. This is the American method.

The French method is to poach the eggs so that they are round. A deep pan is used, with boiling water to which salt and vinegar have been added. The water is stirred in a circular motion until a hollow is formed in the middle, into which the egg is carefully slipped. The heat should be reduced and the water constantly stirred to keep it in motion. Only 1 egg can be done at a time. Eggs may be poached in other liquids besides water, such as milk, any kind of clear or cream soup, tomato juice, meat or poultry stock or vegetable stock, beer and wine, and the liquid may be thickened and used as a sauce. Now for the Poached Eggs Amandine:

Poach 6 fresh eggs in boiling chicken stock for 5 or 6 minutes. Drain and place the poached eggs on freshly made rounds of toast, spread with Salmon Butter (No. 999). Keep hot. Heat 4 tablespoons of sweet butter, stir in ¼ cup of blanched, shredded and toasted almonds, and pour bubbling hot over the poached eggs. Garnish the platter with watercress.

POACHED EGGS IN ASPIC I AND II [374]

Poach 6 fresh eggs in the usual way. Cool. Soften 1 tablespoon of granulated gelatine in ¼ cup cold, clear chicken or beef consommé, and stir into 1¾ cups of hot clear chicken or beef consommé, to which have been added 2 tablespoons of good sherry wine. Arrange the 6 cold poached eggs, neatly trimmed, upon a cold platter and, when gelatine mixture is almost cold, pour 2 or 3 tablespoons of it over the eggs, which may be decorated with fresh parsley or tarragon leaves. Set the platter in refrigerator to congeal, then pour some more cold gelatine over the eggs, let congeal, and repeat until eggs are completely covered with the gelatine. Trim neatly and chill. When ready to serve, place each egg on a round of cold toast or bread and serve garnished with watercress. A fine summer appetizer or luncheon dish.

Another method is to cut in halves 6 hard-cooked eggs, remove the yolks, make a stuffing with the yolks, 1 tablespoon of finely chopped chives, ½ teaspoon of dry mustard, 1 teaspoon of tarragon vinegar, 1 teaspoon of finely chopped capers or gherkins, salt and pepper to taste. When smooth, add enough mayonnaise to make a soft filling, fill the egg whites with this mixture and put the 2 halves together. Then put 1 generous tablespoon of the gelatine mixture into each of 6 custard cups and set the cups in refrigerator until congealed. Put 1 egg on each layer of jelly, and fill each cup with the gelatine. Chill well; unmold and serve on crisp lettuce with a garnish of highly spiced mayonnaise.

POACHED EGGS BOULANGERE [375]

Cut 3 long, narrow, raw potatoes into thin slices; sauté them in 4 generous tablespoons of butter until tender and nicely browned on both sides, stirring frequently over a gentle flame and seasoning to taste with mixed salt, pepper and a dash of nutmeg. Spread the cooked potatoes in the bottom of a generously buttered baking dish, as evenly as possible; sprinkle with a generous ⅓ cup of grated cheese (any desired kind). On top of the cheese, break 6 fresh eggs, each apart from one another; dust with mixed salt and pepper; cover the eggs with fresh cream, and bake 10–12 minutes in a moderate oven (375° F.) or until eggs are set. Serve right from the baking dish.

POACHED EGGS BOURDALOUE [376]

Pour into 6 individual casseroles 2 tablespoons of hot brown sauce (No. 1018), to which has been added 1 teaspoon of finely chopped gherkins. Break 1 egg into each casserole, cover each egg with 2 more tablespoons of the same sauce; sprinkle tops with bread crumbs mixed in equal parts with grated cheese (any kind), and place the casseroles on a baking sheet. Bake 8–10 minutes in a moderate oven (375° F.) and serve immediately.

Yugoslavian peasants probably paint the most colorful of all Easter eggs. To leave them white is a sign of mourning.

POACHED EGGS CARACAS [377]

Cook 2½ tablespoons onions, finely chopped, with a generous blade of garlic in 2 tablespoons of butter until tender but not browned, over a very low flame, stirring frequently; then stir in 3 tablespoons of tomato paste, combined with 1 cup of sour cream, and stir until thoroughly blended and mixture begins to bubble; season to taste with salt and a few grains of cayenne, and stir in 1 tablespoon each of finely minced parsley, chives and capers. Stir in 3 cups of hot, freshly boiled, well-drained rice and dress preparation on a hot platter. Top the rice with 6 poached eggs, sprinkle over ¼ cup of grated cheese mixed with ¼ cup of soft bread crumbs; dust with paprika, and brown under the flame of the boiling oven. Serve at once.

POACHED EGGS COLETTE [378]

Spread in bottom of 6 buttered shirred egg dishes 3 tablespoons of hot creamed smoked turkey; over the turkey, sprinkle 1½ tablespoons each of sieved bread crumbs and grated American cheese mixed. Using a pastry bag filled with smooth Potato Duchesse (No. 1419—Variation) mixture, making a nice border around the inner edges of the dish; place the dishes on a baking sheet, then set the baking sheet under the flame of the broiling oven to delicately brown the Potato Duchesse. Have the crumb and cheese mixture bubbling, place a poached egg in center of each dish; cover the entire surface (except the Potato Duchesse) with cheese sauce (No. 1027) dust with a little paprika and serve at once.

POACHED EGGS COQUETTE [379]

Butter generously 6 individual ramekins; place in center of each a small ball, the size of a marble, of anchovy butter (No. 979), then 2 teaspoons of sweet, heavy cream, a dash of nutmeg and a little salt mixed with a little white pepper. Be careful with the salt; remember that the anchovy butter is a little salty. Place the ramekins on a baking sheet and place under the flame of the broiling oven about 6 inches from the flame. When mixture begins to bubble, at once break a fresh egg into each ramekin; dust tops with a little paprika, and bake in a very moderate oven (325° F.) until eggs are set. Remove from the oven and immediately sprinkle the edge of the white part only with finely chopped, cooked lean ham, tongue or white meat of chicken, taking care not to put any over the place where the yolk is. Serve immediately.

POACHED EGGS A LA FRISSAC [380]

Wash in several changes of cold water 3 small heads of lettuce, having the final water lukewarm. Then parboil in slightly salted water, drain well and cool. Split in two lengthwise. Lay them in a saucepan, and cover with 1½ cups of boiling water to which has been added 1 tablespoon of Pique Seasoning, and cook until lettuce stems are tender. Drain well, squeezing gently but thoroughly. Arrange the lettuce halves on a hot serving platter, top each one with a poached egg; cover the eggs with rich cream sauce; then sprinkle generously with grated Swiss cheese, and brown quickly under the flame of the broiling oven. Serve at once, the platter garnished with crisp, green watercress.

A famous king, Frederick the Great, once asked a peasant,"How much do you want for fresh eggs?" "A dollar a dozen, Your Majesty," said the peasant. "That seems too much. Are eggs so scarce?" "No, Your Majesty, but kings are," came the quick reply.

POACHED EGGS LUCETTE [381]

Poach 6 fresh eggs in milk in the usual way; arrange the eggs on small rounds of bread fried on both sides in melted anchovy butter (No. 979); cover them with a rich cream sauce or a Béchamel sauce (Nos. 258 and 259 respectively); sprinkle with a little grated cheese (any desired kind) and brown quickly under the flame of the boiling oven. Serve garnished with 1 grilled mushroom cap for each egg, and crisp watercress.

POACHED EGGS MONGOLE [382]

Spread cooked, mashed or sieved green split peas in bottoms of 6 individual casseroles, coquilles or ramekins; make a little nest in center of the peas and, into each depression drop 1 tablespoon of creamed, curried chicken; place a freshly poached egg over the chicken; dust the egg with paprika, then with finely chopped chives and serve at once.

POACHED EGGS MORNAY [383]

Place 1 poached egg on a round of buttered toast for each serving; cover with Mornay sauce (No. 1088); sprinkle each egg with grated

cheese and brown quickly under the flame of the broiling oven. Serve
at once.

POACHED EGGS NINON   [384]

Place 6 poached eggs on 6 rounds of toast, the same size as the egg.
Top each egg with Hollandaise sauce (No. 1062), then with a thin slice
of truffle. Arrange on a round, hot platter, in a circle and well separated.
Garnish between the eggs with asparagus tips which have been dipped
in melted butter, and in the center with a large bunch of crisp, green
watercress. Serve at once.

POACHED EGGS PARMENTIER   [385]

Wash and scrub 3 large potatoes of about the same size and bake
in oven until tender. Cut them in halves lengthwise, scoop out the greater
part of the inside; pour into each shell a generous tablespoon of Béchamel sauce (No. 259), top with a freshly poached egg; cover the entire
surface of the potato with Béchamel sauce to which has been added a
little grated cheese to taste; sprinkle with fine buttered bread crumbs
and brown quickly under the flame of the broiling oven. Serve at once.

POACHED EGGS IN POTATO NESTS   [386]
JACQUELINE

Add to 2 rounded or 2½ level cups of hot mashed potatoes the following ingredients: 2 tablespoons of anchovy butter (No. 979), ½ teaspoon of salt, a few grains of white pepper and nutmeg, with a generous
¼ cup of scalded thin cream or undiluted evaporated milk, scalded
with a small piece of bay leaf, 1 whole clove, a blade of garlic and 2 thin
slices of onion, then strained; beat briskly until fluffy, then beat in
½ cup of canned pimientos, well drained, then sieved, also ¼ cup of
blanched, shredded and toasted almonds. Butter 6 custard cups; fill
¾ full of potato mixture, having a well in center of each. Drop an egg
in each well; sprinkle with a little grated cheese, place the cups on a
baking sheet, and bake in a moderate oven (350° F.) 12–15 minutes or
until the eggs are set. Serve at once.

POACHED EGGS COMTE POTOCKI   [387]

Fry 6 thick slices of large tomatoes in olive oil with a whole clove of
garlic till brown on both sides. Arrange each slice on a round of toast,
the size of the tomato slice; top each tomato slice with a poached egg;
cover entirely with thick tomato sauce, sprinkle all over with grated

cheese (any kind desired) and serve at once with an extra side dish of grated cheese and French fried potatoes. Garnish with watercress and serve at once.

POACHED EGGS À LA REINE [388]

Place rounds of buttered toast in bottoms of 6 shirred egg dishes; cover the toast with fresh mushrooms, sautéed in garlic butter (No. 986) and moistened with a little scalded heavy cream; place a freshly poached egg over each dish; cover the eggs with Béchamel sauce (No. 259) to which has been added a little grated cheese; place the dishes on a baking sheet and brown under the flame of the broiling oven. Serve at once.

POACHED EGGS IN RICE RING [389] A L'ORIENTAL

Break 2 fresh eggs in a bowl, season with salt and pepper to taste and beat as for an omelet; stir in 1½ cups of hot cream sauce seasoned with a generous pinch of saffron, alternately with 1½ cups of hot cooked rice. Pack mixture in 6 buttered individual ring molds, having the rings ¾ full. Place in a pan of hot water and bake in a moderate oven (325–350° F.) until firm, or about 20–25 minutes. Remove from the oven; let stand 3 or 4 minutes, and very carefully unmold on individual hot plates; drop in center of each ring 1 tablespoon of hot creamed mushrooms; put a poached egg on top of each; dust with a little mixed salt, white pepper and paprika; surround the base of each poached egg with a ring of rich brown sauce (No. 1018) and serve immediately garnished with watercress dipped in paprika.

POACHED EGGS RODRIGUEZ [390]

Brown lightly 3 large, thinly sliced onions in ½ cup of bacon or ham drippings. Wash, peel, core and slice 3 tart apples and add to onions; cover and cook very, very gently, over a very low flame, until almost tender, shaking the pan gently and occasionally (but do not stir, lest mixture become a mush). Remove cover, season to taste with salt and white pepper, and sprinkle 2½ tablespoons of granulated sugar over the whole. Continue cooking until lightly glazed. Divide mixture among 6 buttered shirred egg dishes; make a nest in center of each; place a poached egg in each nest; cover with Mornay sauce (No. 1088); sprinkle with grated cheese and place the dishes on a baking sheet. Glaze quickly under the flame of the broiling oven and serve at once.

POACHED EGGS A LA ROTONDE   [391]

Poach 6 fresh eggs in the usual way; dress each egg on a freshly made round of toast, the size of the egg, spread with smoked salmon butter (No. 999) and keep hot. Melt 4 tablespoons of sweet butter; stir in 2 tablespoons of sherry wine, 1 teaspoon of finely chopped shallots, 1 teaspoon of finely chopped black truffles, 4 tablespoons of finely chopped fresh, peeled mushrooms, and season highly with salt, a few grains of cayenne and a generous pinch of paprika. Blend thoroughly, then stir in ½ cup of fresh sweet cream, previously scalded with a small bit of bay leaf, 1 whole clove and 1 thin slice of onion and strained. Heat until mixture begins to thicken. Taste for seasoning, divide this sauce over the poached eggs, and serve at once, the dish simply garnished with crisp watercress.

Both the acute odor of a badly shopworn egg and the discoloration of a spoon with which egg has been eaten are due to the sulphur which forms part of the composition of the egg.

POACHED EGGS STRASBOURGEOIS   [392]

Have ready 2 cups of rich cream sauce (No. 258) flavored with 1 tablespoon of onion juice. Fry 6 slices of toast, crust removed, in butter until brown on both sides. Spread each slice of toast with pâté de foie gras (using about a 2-ounce jar). Top the foie gras with a freshly poached egg, cover both egg and toast with the hot cream sauce, dust with paprika and serve immediately.

POACHED EGGS A LA SUISSESSE   [393]
Poached Eggs in the Swiss Style

Butter a fireproof earthenware baking dish generously; sprinkle over it 3 ounces of grated Swiss cheese; break 6 strictly fresh eggs over the cheese, keeping the yolks whole; season to taste with mixed salt and white pepper, then scatter over all ⅓ cup of grated Swiss cheese mixed with 1 tablespoon each of parsley, chives, chervil and onion, all finely chopped and mixed together. Dot the top with 1½ tablespoons of sweet butter and bake 10–12 minutes in a moderate oven (350–375° F.) or until top bubbles and is nicely browned. Serve at once. These eggs may also be cooked in individual ramekins.

POACHED EGGS SUZANNE   [394]

Peel an eggplant; cut in slices of about the same size, using a large biscuit cutter. There should be 6 nice slices. Cover the slices with cold water, sprinkle over 1 generous teaspoon of salt; weight down with a plate, placing a heavy weight on top of the plate and let stand at least 2 hours. Drain and dry carefully; dip each slice into seasoned flour and fry in ⅓ cup of butter until delicately brown on both sides. Arrange the hot brown eggplant slices on a hot platter, top each slice with a thin slice of grilled ham, cut the size of the eggplant; top with an egg, freshly poached in tomato juice or tomato sauce, and cover entirely with Hollandaise sauce (No. 1062). Serve immediately, garnished with 6 fresh mushroom caps sautéed in clarified butter and crisp watercress.

SCRAMBLED EGGS À LA BUCKINGHAM   [395]

It is as easy to scramble eggs as it is hard to unscramble them. The art is knowing what not to do. First, do not overcook; have your scrambled eggs on the soft side. Second, do not add much liquid. If you like scrambles with milk, cream, or tomato juice, be careful not to add so much as to make the dish watery. A double boiler or frying pan may be used over low heat. Beat eggs until yolks and whites are mixed; add the indicated liquid or not, as well as seasonings. If you use a frying pan, have it generously buttered before the egg mixture is put in it. As the egg sets, it should be stirred until the mixture is the consistency of soft custard, rather on the soft side because the stored heat continues the cooking.

Beat 7 eggs until well blended, stir in 2 tablespoons of tomato paste, season to taste with salt and white pepper and cook in a generously buttered frying pan, stirring with a fork from the bottom of the pan, letting the soft part run freely. Divide the mixture among 6 slices of buttered toast, free of crust and cut diagonally; make a little nest in the center of the eggs and put 1 tablespoon of thick tomato purée in it. Place a sautéed chicken liver on top of the tomato purée and garnish the platter with a dozen bacon curls and watercress. Serve immediately.

SCRAMBLED EGGS WITH CHEESE ON TOAST   [396]
Also called Squiggled Eggs

Break and beat 1 dozen fresh eggs in a bowl; season to taste with salt, pepper, a few grains of cayenne, a dash of nutmeg and one of powdered sage; beat as for an omelet. Heat ¼ cup of butter in a large frying pan and, when it is heated to the foamy stage, turn in the eggs all at one time, then very quickly sprinkle all over the eggs ½–¾ cup of grated sharp dairy cheese; stir all together briskly with a fork, and at the same time pour in ¼ cup of sweet, heavy, scalded cream. Divide mixture among 6 freshly made and buttered slices of toast and serve at once.

> *"Woe is me," said Hen-Fruit,*
> *"Existence is a shamble.*
> *Someday I'll be hard-boiled*
> *Or wind up in a scramble."*

SCRAMBLED EGGS MILANAISE   [397]

Melt 3 tablespoons of butter in a saucepan over a low flame. Stir in 4 ounces of grated parmesan cheese alternately with 1 tablespoon of finely minced shallot, mixed with 1 tablespoon of finely minced chives. Gradually stir in 1 cup of dry white wine and, when smooth, pour in all at once 8 well-beaten eggs seasoned to taste with salt, white pepper and nutmeg. When eggs just begin to set, serve on a hot platter garnished with small triangles of bread fried in butter.

SCRAMBLED EGGS IN BREAD NESTS   [398]

Cut a thin slice from tops of as many long rolls as needed, having 1 roll for each serving; remove the crumb from inside; brush inside and out with anchovy butter (No. 979) and toast in a slow oven (250–275° F.). Keep hot. Scramble as many eggs as needed, allowing 2 eggs per person, with 2 tablespoons of thin cream (undiluted evaporated milk may be used) for each egg; season to taste with salt and white pepper; scrambling the eggs in the usual way, but very soft. Fill each toasted roll with egg mixture; sprinkle tops with a mixture of fine (sieved) bread crumbs and grated cheese in equal parts, and brown quickly under the flame of the broiling oven. Serve at once.

SCRAMBLED EGGS SPANISH STYLE   [399]

Cook ½ cup of thinly sliced onions, ½ cup of thinly sliced green peppers, ½ cup of thinly sliced mushrooms, and ½ cup of thinly sliced black olives in ⅓ cup of butter over a very low flame until tender, stirring frequently; then stir in ½ cup of tomato purée, and let simmer, covered, for 5 minutes. When ready to serve, pour in, all at once, 6 well-beaten eggs, seasoned to taste with salt and cayenne, and scramble until eggs just begin to set. Pack mixture into an oiled ring mold; unmold on a hot, round platter, and fill center with creamed potatoes. Serve at once.

SHIRRED EGGS   [400]

Eggs prepared in this way have a particular resemblance to poached eggs, with the difference that the right amount of cooking time enhances their flavor. The exact proportions established for this method of cooking eggs are as follows: ½ tablespoon of butter to each egg, of which half is heated and spread all over the bottom of the shirred egg dish, ordinarily a flat earthenware dish, the other half being poured, when melted, over the yolks only. The cooking process should be slow to permit egg whites to coagulate gradually and preserve their milky appearance, and at the same time prevent scorching or burning. These eggs are usually served in the dish.

The following recipes and formulas for shirred eggs are for 1 person only, unless otherwise indicated. As a rule 2 eggs are used for each person.

SHIRRED EGGS AU BEURRE NOIR [401]
(*Black Butter*)

Melt 1½ teaspoons of butter in a shirred egg dish and spread it all over by tilting the dish. Break in 2 fresh eggs and cook over an extremely low flame after seasoning to taste with salt and white pepper, basting frequently and gradually with 1½ teaspoons of melted butter. Meantime, melt and heat 1 tablespoon of butter in a small frying pan until brown, immediately stir in 1 scant teaspoon of tarragon vinegar, and pour, sizzling hot, all over the eggs. Serve immediately.

Variations. Sprinkle the eggs with a teaspoon of small capers before adding the brown butter-vinegar mixture. Or, sprinkle eggs with finely chopped chives before pouring on the brown butter-vinegar mixture.

SHIRRED EGGS BOULEVARDIER [402]

Heat 1½ tablespoons of butter in a shirred egg dish; slide in 2 eggs; season to taste with salt and pepper and cook very slowly, over a very low flame, until eggs are set. Meantime, cook 2 strips of salt pork until done. Keep hot. In a small frying pan melt and heat 1½ tablespoons of butter until brown, stir in ½–¾ teaspoon of lemon juice and, when ready to serve, sprinkle over the eggs 1 scant teaspoon of fines herbes (tarragon, chervil, parsley and chives, finely chopped and in equal parts) and pour over the sizzling hot butter-lemon mixture, taking care to keep your face far from the shirred egg dish, as the butter splashes. Garnish with the 2 strips of cooked, well-drained salt pork and serve at once.

SHIRRED EGGS CECILE [403]

Force through a pastry bag about ¾ cup of hot Potatoes Duchesse (No. 1419–Variation), making a narrow border all around the inside of a buttered shirred egg dish. Melt in center 1 teaspoon of butter, break in 2 fresh eggs, and cook very gently over a low flame until eggs just begin to set; season lightly with mixed salt and pepper, remove from the fire; sprinkle over the eggs 2 teaspoons of grated Gruyère cheese, dust with a little paprika and brush the potatoes with egg yolk; place the dish under the flame of the broiling oven to brown. Remove from the broiling oven, surround the potato border with a thin ribbon of Madeira sauce (No. 1076), crown-fashion. Serve at once.

SHIRRED EGGS Ā L'ESTRAGON   [404]
(*Tarragon Leaves*)

Spread over the bottom of a shirred egg dish 1 tablespoon of Brown Sauce (No. 1018); sprinkle over ½ generous teaspoon of dried tarragon leaves; break 2 eggs, one at a time, over the sauce; sprinkle the top with a little additional Brown Sauce, and cook over a very low flame until eggs are set. Decorate each yolk with a fresh leaflet of tarragon herb. Serve immediately.

In various primitive religions, the egg has symbolized life, or the source of life. This ancient belief is expressed in the Latin proverb *Omne vivum ex ovo*—"All life comes from an egg."

SHIRRED EGGS MIDINETTE   [405]

Line a buttered shirred egg dish with 2 tablespoons of fine buttered bread crumbs. Break 2 eggs into each dish, being very careful not to break the yolks; cover the whites with 2 generous tablespoons of cooked, chopped mushrooms; again with 2 tablespoons of fine buttered bread crumbs, and bake in a slow oven (250–275° F.) for about 15–20 minutes. Remove from the oven and surround the border with a ribbon of rich tomato sauce.

SHIRRED EGGS TETRAZZINI   [406]

Cover the buttered bottom of a shirred egg dish with a thin layer of pâté de foie gras; sprinkle over 1 teaspoon of finely chopped green olives and 1 teaspoon of finely chopped chives. Break 2 fresh eggs over this, one at a time; season to taste with mixed salt and white pepper, and cook over a very low flame until the eggs are set. Garnish each side with a teaspoon of creamed artichoke bottom diced fine. Serve at once.

SOUTHERN FLEECE   [407]

Break ¾ pound of cream cheese with a fork; spread it in a buttered earthenware baking dish; place the dish in a slow oven (275° F.) and heat until soft. Remove from the oven, stir in 1½ cups of thin cream or evaporated milk, and season to taste with mixed salt and cayenne pepper. Break 6 fresh eggs on top of the cheese and beat until thoroughly blended; cover the dish, heat well; remove again from the oven; break 2 fresh eggs on top of cheese mixture; season them with salt and white pepper and cook until the whites begin to set, then beat briskly for several minutes. It should be light and fluffy like an omelet. Serve at once with hot toast points.

STUFFED EGGS IN ASPIC   [408]

Cut 6 hard-cooked eggs in halves, lengthwise, remove yolks and mash them. Add to the mashed yolks 3 tablespoons of melted butter, 2 teaspoons of tarragon vinegar, 1 tablespoon of French prepared mustard, ½ teaspoon of paprika, a few grains of cayenne and 1 scant teaspoon of salt. Mix thoroughly. Fill egg white cavities with this mixture; press halves together, place the eggs an inch apart in a narrow, shallow platter, and pour a little of the following aspic over. (The eggs may be placed in custard cups or timbale molds).

Sprinkle over ½ cup of cold water 1½ tablespoons of granulated, unflavored gelatine and let stand 5 minutes. Meanwhile, pour into a small saucepan 1½ cups of boiling water, the rind and juice of a half lemon, a dash of salt and a very few grains of cayenne pepper. Stir in the soaked gelatine mixture; bring to the boiling point, then stir in 1 egg white, slightly beaten, also its cracked shell. Let this simmer very gently for 10 minutes, then strain through a fine flannel cloth into a clean container. Let cool a little, then stir in 2½ tablespoons of good sherry wine.

When aspic is just beginning to congeal, pour a little over the eggs and, when sufficiently firm, pour some more and continue to do so until eggs are completely covered with the aspic. Let chill in refrigerator several hours, and serve with sliced tomatoes, crisp lettuce, and French dressing, if desired.

STUFFED EGGS A LA BÉCHAMEL SUPRÊME   [409]

Prepare a special Béchamel sauce as follows: Bring 2 cups of rich sweet milk to the scalding point. In a separate pan, heat 1 tablespoon of butter and cook in it 1½ teaspoons of finely crushed or rather, mashed shallot for 1 minute, stirring constantly, but do not let brown; add 1 tablespoon flour then stir in the hot scalded milk gradually, stirring until smooth and free from lumps. Strain this through a fine-meshed sieve, pressing gently but thoroughly, so as to incorporate the entire shallot pulp. In another saucepan heat 1 tablespoon of sweet butter; stir in a tiny pinch of powdered thyme, a dash of white pepper and one of freshly grated nutmeg. Now stir in 2 ounces of chopped, lean raw veal and cook 1 minute, stirring constantly, over a gentle flame. Add this to the milk mixture and mix thoroughly. Cook over a gentle flame for 1 hour, placing an asbestos pad under the saucepan to prevent scorching, stirring frequently. Strain through a fine flannel cloth into a clean saucepan and keep hot, after testing for seasoning.

Cut 6 hard-cooked eggs in halves remove the yolks and blend them with 3 tablespoons of pâté de foie gras, 1 teaspoon of very finely chopped black truffle, 1 teaspoon of butter, ½ teaspoon of finely chopped chervil, and blend well. Fill egg white cavities with this Suprême stuffing; adjust 2 halves together and place 1 egg in each of 6 individual earthenware casseroles, ramekins or custard cups, previously buttered. Divide the sauce into 6 equal portions. To one, add a drop or two of red vegetable coloring; to another a drop or two of green vegetable coloring; to another a drop or two of yellow vegetable coloring; and so on, adding to each portion of Béchamel sauce a different vegetable coloring and mixing thoroughly. Fill each of the 6 casseroles or ramekins with a different color of sauce; sprinkle over each casserole or ramekin a tiny pinch of powdered tarragon herb, then top all the casseroles with grated Swiss or Parmesan cheese, and brown quickly under the flame of the broiling oven. Serve very hot, on individual plates covered with lace paper doilies, and garnish simply with a sprig or two of watercress. The ultimum in egg cookery!

Byron is said to have remarked a century ago: "The greatest trial to a woman's beauty is the ungraceful act of eating eggs." Since Byron was all the rage at the time, especially among women, his rather cheap dictum created a profound stir in the English society world.

CHEESE SOUFFLÉ   [409—A]
(Serves 4-5)

Melt 3 tablespoons of butter in a saucepan over a low flame. Blend in 3 tablespoons of flour. Then add 1 cup of warm milk gradually, stirring constantly, and cook until smooth and thickened. Now season with ½ teaspoon each of salt and dry mustard, a pinch of cayenne pepper and 1 cup of grated American or Cheddar cheese. Mix well, remove from the stove. Beat 3 egg yolks until thick and lemon colored. Add them to the mixture, stirring constantly. Then fold in the 3 stiffly beaten egg whites slowly but thoroughly; blend well. Pour into a well-buttered baking dish and bake in a moderate oven (350–375° F.) for about 30 to 35 minutes. Serve at once.

Chapter Five

FISH AND SHELLFISH

Don't talk to me o' bacon fat,
Or taters, coon, or 'possum;
Fo' when I'se hooked a yaller cat,
I'se got a meal to boss 'em. . . .

—*"The Darkey and the Catfish"*

Fish is an excellent source of menu variety. Light in texture, delicate of flavor and tender to the extent that it takes a very short cooking period, fish is different from meat, yet it brings approximately the same amount of protein to a meal.

Though not a source of iron as red meat is, fish, be it fresh, frozen, or smoked or salted, gives calcium and iodine to help maintain the health of the family.

Technically, fish is flesh, old sayings and obdurate appetites notwithstanding. But numbers of people apparently refuse to abide by the technicalities. Moreover, lots of folk really like fish as a regular item of diet, not just as an occasional novelty. King Neptune's bottomless larder is chock-full of edible material. Out of that bountiful monarch's salty realms or out of fresh-water lakes or streams, fishermen can, if it is necessary and remunerative, haul in enough provender to defy the worst meat shortage that ever was or ever could be.

Fish cookery is really very simple, yet many cooks run into difficulties with baking and broiling, having had experience only in frying fish, or vice-versa. Dried out or tasteless fish is the result of overcooking or use of too high temperature. There is no such thing as a tough-meated fish. All fish are naturally tender-meated, and should come to the table that way. Only oily or fat fish should be broiled, unless fat is added, for a dry meated steak or filet will inevitably become drier under the broiler without protection such as fat affords.

Baking is a suitable preparation for almost any kind of fish. It may be accomplished in a very hot oven for a very, very short time, or in a moderate oven for a somewhat longer period. The hot oven has the advantage of keeping fish odors from permeating the kitchen atmosphere, but a close watch must be kept or overcooking will take place. A whole stuffed fish is better off in a moderate oven, about 350–375° F., and will, of course, take longer than that which is grilled.

The most important advice to give about fish is that it be strictly fresh. A fresh fish looks you in the eye with a brilliant stare, not a dulled one. Its gills are a fresh pink, and the body is stiff and firm, not limp.

If the fish is to be *broiled*, the grill for that purpose should be piping hot and well greased, as otherwise the skin will stick. The fish should be dusted with mixed salt and pepper, then brushed with fat, and several times during the grilling process it must be brushed over with cooking oil or butter.

"Boiled" fish should be a manner of speaking and not of cooking, since fish ought *never* to be actually boiled, but poached. Highly seasoned water, known in culinary parlance as court-bouillon, should be allowed to boil 15–20 minutes, and the fish should be laid in and cooked in the very gently simmering white wine court-bouillon (No. 1037) which is kept just below the boiling point. Strained, this court-bouillon makes the best possible base for all fish sauces.

Pan-frying is an excellent way of cooking smaller fish or filets, such as butterfish, small trout, flounders or thin slices of fish. The fish is sprinkled with mixed salt and pepper, sometimes with seasoned flour, or dipped into a batter, highly seasoned, and laid in a hot frying pan where a little butter or margarine has been brought to the foaming stage. It should be cooked over a gentle flame and turned to brown on both sides. The butter in which it is cooked should *never* be served with a fish, but extra butter should be melted for that purpose, to which is added lemon, lime juice or other ingredients, according to the recipe.

Above all, a sauce, no matter how fine a one, should never be used to mask a poor fish. Rather, study the best points of your fish (see Guide to the Purchase and Preparation of Fish No. 411) and make a sauce which will bring out its consistency or flavor. Certain extremely delicate fish, such as pompano or shad for example, lose something of their own fine flavor by being served with anything more elaborate than a plain but fine sauce; but, on the other hand, equally fine specimens, like salmon and sole (flounder), adapt themselves wonderfully to all kinds of complicated variations. The point is that every single step in the cooking of fish has to be done with care and skill, so that a shad, perfectly grilled, is as great a work of art as any bouillabaisse or fish cooked *en papillote.*

The secrets of professional cooks are the secrets of home cooks. They should tune in, one on the other, because their object in life is the same—to please those they feed. The difference is just one: A professional cook can concentrate on one fish and learn by both study and experience to produce it exactly right each time. The dangers of it, he knows. The success of it, he has mastered. Any time a home cook can speak to a chef, she should. He will give sound advice, and often confirm her own viewpoint. Or settle forever a cooking question, as for instance one of the following in fish cookery:

FISH COOKERY—DO'S AND DON'T'S

DO when purchasing fish allow a generous half pound for each person to be served.

DO invert a colander over the pan when frying fish spatters. This will prevent a nasty burn, yet the small holes will allow the steam to escape and keep the fish crisp. The reason fried fish spatters is because the fish has not been dried properly after washing.

DO always tightly cover fish stored in the refrigerator to prevent its flavor from penetrating other foods. As soon as the fish is received, remove from its paper wrappings, wipe off with a damp cloth and place in a covered dish or securely roll up in waxed paper. Store in the coldest part of the refrigerator.

DO line the baking pan with greaseproof paper when cooking fish in the oven. It is not only to easier remove the fish when cooked, but the pan or dish is left comparatively clean and will not need scraping when it is washed.

(These hints are continued at end of Fish Chart.)

GUIDE TO THE PURCHASE AND [411]
PREPARATION OF FISH

NAME OF FISH SEASON TYPE: Fat or Lean	OTHER NAME (According to locality)	SPECIFICATIONS	SIZE and WEIGHT (average) MARKET UNIT	HOW TO COOK (Methods)
BARRA-CUDA† All year Fat	Guachanche	Commonly known as a reef fish, the Barracuda is long and slim, with a long head, the lower jaw projecting. The sharp teeth are large. It is a tasty food fish, but the skin should be removed before the fish is cooked. The smaller fish is seldom used for food. It has the same color and shape as the mackerel.	7 feet; 25–65 lbs. Filets, steaks, chunks	Bake, broil, fry, steam, sauté
BASS† Black Sea Summer Lean	Channel bass Sea-Wolf Brigue	Small-mouthed and large-mouthed; stout bodied fish, about 3 times long as deep; high back, flat head, moderately pointed nose, eye set high up, sharp flat spine; scales large, top of head naked; color—smoky-gray to dusky brown or almost black, sometimes bluish cast, usually mottled; belly slightly paler than sides. Plenty of small bones.	¾ lb. to 5 lbs. Whole, filets	Bake, broil, fry, steam, sauté, boil
BASS† Striped January to June Fat		About 7 narrow, continuous black stripes lengthwise of body; larger than black sea bass; dark back, paler on sides and silvery on belly. Plenty of small bones.	2–5 lbs. Whole, filets	Bake, broil, fry, steam, sauté
BASS† California White Sea Summer Fat	Totuava Croaker	Is more a croaker than a sea bass; no scales on fins; no stripes or bars on body. Tail slightly concave; color—steel blue, silvery sides and belly white. Plenty of bones.	12–90 lbs. Filets, steaks, chunks	Bake, broil, pan-fry, steam, sauté, boil
BASS* White Winter Lean	Silver Bass Striped Lake Bass	Fresh-water edition of the striped or rock bass. Except in size, resembles closely its sea-going cousin. Compressed body and arched back. Color—silver, sides horizontal stripes. Plenty of bones.	18 inches; 1–3 lbs. Whole, filets	Bake, broil, fry, steam, sauté

* Fresh water.   † Salt water.

GUIDE TO THE PURCHASE AND PREPARATION OF FISH [411]

NAME OF FISH SEASON TYPE: Fat or Lean	OTHER NAME (According to locality)	SPECIFICATIONS	SIZE and WEIGHT (average) MARKET UNIT	HOW TO COOK (Methods)
BASS*— ROCK Winter Fat	Sunfish Bass, Goggle-eye Bass, Red-eye Perch, Red-eye Bass	Body and fins somewhat resemble those of black bass. Color—golden brown, slightly barred with green; head mottled brown with a black spot on the gill cover; mouth large, the lower jaw projects slightly.	1–2 lbs.; 1 foot Whole, filets	Bake, broil, fry, steam, sauté
BLACK-FISH* All year Lean	Bowfin, Mudfish, Lawyer, Cottonfish, Speckled Cat, Scaled Ling, Grindle, Choupiquel, Dogfish	Most interesting and venerable of all American fishes. It's a *living fossil*, the sole surviving species of a once numerous order that lived in very early geologic times. Its survival, unchanged over practically all other forms of life of that time shows that it has remarkable qualities of endurance. Male marked with a dark spot at base of tail.	1–2 feet (male being smaller than female) Whole, filets	Bake, broil, fry, steam, sauté
BLUEFISH† May to October Medium lean		Bluish color, tinged with green and silvery below; flesh firm, sweet and delicate, close to pompano and Spanish mackerel in taste; long, with deeply forked tail, large mouth, projecting lower jaw with doglike teeth around both jaws; although flesh contains little oil, oily condition more than white-fleshed fish.	3–6 lbs. (average); up to 25 lbs. Steaks, filets, whole (when small), chunks	Bake, stuff, broil, fry, sauté, steam, stew
BLUEGILL* Winter Lean	Blue Sunfish, Blue Perch, Bream, Coppernosed Bream, Dollardee, Gold Perch, Chainside	Flesh, flaky firm, and delicious, somewhat resembling trout. Roundish flat, with gill pale blue. Body striped vertically with 6 to 8 stripes on greenish blue, with golden belly.	12–22 inches; 1–3 lbs. Whole, filets	Bake, broil, fry, steam, sauté
BONITO† Summer Fall Little fat	Pacific Coast Bonito, Chilean Bonito, Atlantic Bonito	Blue on top, with numerous dark, narrow stripes running obliquely downward and forward from back; under part silvery white.	3 feet 3–16 lbs. Whole (when small), steaks, chunks	Bake, broil, fry, steam, sauté

* Fresh water.   † Salt water.

GUIDE TO THE PURCHASE AND PREPARATION OF FISH [411]

NAME OF FISH SEASON TYPE: Fat or Lean	OTHER NAME (According to locality)	SPECIFICATIONS	SIZE and WEIGHT (average) MARKET UNIT	HOW TO COOK (Methods)
CARP* All year (better from August to spring) Lean	Winter Carp, Buffalo Fish, Golden Carp	Of yellowish tinge on sides, shading to bronze above, with scales of considerable size. In summer, flesh has muddy flavor, which is eliminated by keeping live fish in fresh water for a time, or by skinning and soaking in cold water. Soft-roed carp more delicate than hard-roed ones.	Average: 12–20 inches; 2½–8 lbs. Whole, filets, fresh or smoked	Au bleu, in beer, in wine, bake, boil, fry, steam, stew, in honey
CATFISH* All year Lean	Bull-head, Easter or Holy Cross, Horned pout, Channel Catfish, Blue Cat, Mud Catfish, Tadpole, Mad Tomcat	Has long, fleshy feelers (whiskers), smooth scaleless skin and its small, fleshy fin to the rear of the dorsal fin, exactly as in salmon and trout. Consists mostly of head; it's a toothsome morsel when properly cooked. Of different varieties: Black, white, or brown and usually without mottles or spots. The smaller the fish, the better.	1 foot 1–40 lbs. Whole, filets, steaks, chunks	Bake, boil, pan-fry, steam, stew
CAVALLA† Winter Fat	Jack Crevalle, Toro, Jackfish, Skipjack	This member of the Pompano family is golden-olive with iridescent shades of grayish-blue, purple and green. The black spots on the gill cover distinguish it from its relatives.	3½–40 lbs. Whole, filets, steaks, chunks	Bake, boil, stew, filet in wine
COBIA† All year little fat	Black Salmon, Lemon Fish, Black Bonito, Crab-eater, Sergeant Fish	Slender, with a large mouth, projecting lower jaw and forked caudal fin. Color: Brown on the back, shading to yellow-brown on the sides, and white below. Because the dark lateral band resembles the stripe on military trousers, is best known as the "Sergeant Fish." Below this band is a narrower one. The fins are mostly black. Has the flavor of bonito.	6 feet and up Average: 20 lbs. Maximum: 90 lbs. Steaks, chunks	Bake, boil, broil, stew in wine, sauté

* Fresh water.   † Salt water.

GUIDE TO THE PURCHASE AND PREPARATION OF FISH

NAME OF FISH SEASON TYPE: Fat or Lean	OTHER NAME (According to locality)	SPECIFICATIONS	SIZE and WEIGHT (average) MARKET UNIT	HOW TO COOK (Methods)
CODFISH† All year (best from Sept. to middle Dec.) Lean	Rock Cod, Offshore Cod, Scrod, Cabillaud, Green Cod (when salted but not dried), Stockfish (when dried but not salted)	This migratory fish is greenish or brownish, the back and sides having numerous rounded brownish spots, and the lateral line being pale. Both eyes on upper side; flesh—white, flaky, rather sweet, contains little fat.	3–3⅓ feet 4–100 lbs. Steaks, chunks, filets, whole (when small), fresh, salted, canned	Bake, stuff, boil, fry, steam, cakes, kedgeree
DAB†		See "Lemon Sole"		See "Lemon Sole"
DRUM-FISH† Winter Lean	Common Drum, Black Drum, Red Drum, Redfish, Channel Bass	Has taller dorsal fins and grows larger than its relatives the fresh-water species, but has all the same specifications. Both make a loud drumming noise, especially the males during spawning season. Very sweet flesh.	4 feet 20–75 lbs. Chunks, steaks, pounds, canned	Same preparation as for codfish
DRUM-FISH* Fall and Winter Lean	Sheepshead in Great Lakes region; Gasperou in the South; Crocus in Indiana; Thunder-Pumper in Louisiana, etc.	It is grayish-green and silvery in color, dark above with oblique streaks on both sides. Fishermen who catch drum form the habit of looking for the "lucky stones," which are white bonelike stones found in both temples of this fish. Fibrous but sweet flesh.	4 feet 25–60 lbs. Chunks, steaks, or pound, canned	Same preparation as for codfish, but needs much seasoning
EEL*²† All year (but better in winter around Christmas and New Year) Fat	Capitone, Anguilla, Shoestring	Long, greenish-brown, snake-like fresh-water fish and salt-water fish with a dorsal fin that continues around the tail, meeting with the anal fin. Its scales, finely embedded in the skin, are at right angles to one another. The Eel has small teeth, small eyes and a projecting lower jaw. They spawn	Average: 2 feet Maximum: 5 feet Average weight: 1–2 lbs. Maximum weight: 10 lbs.	Broil, boil, fry, fines herbes casserole, bake, in jelly, cream, white wine etc.,

* Fresh water.   † Salt water.

GUIDE TO THE PURCHASE AND PREPARATION OF FISH [411]

NAME OF FISH SEASON TYPE: Fat or Lean	OTHER NAME (According to locality)	SPECIFICATIONS	SIZE and WEIGHT (average) MARKET UNIT	HOW TO COOK (Methods)
EEL— (*Continued*)		in salt water, and there die. It is very important to distinguish between Eels which have been taken in running water and those which come from stagnant water. The first may be recognized by the greenish reflex on the back, and the belly is silvery; while the second has a brown skin, and the belly is yellowish. Whatever its use in cookery, an Eel must be freshly killed and skinned at once. To skin, make an incision on the skin, near the head, hold the head with a towel and pull down skin bluntly. Clean and wash at once.	Shoestring Eels average ¼ lb. Fresh, smoked, pickled, by the lb.	filets à la Orly, matelote, Provençale, tartare
EEL— CONGER† Winter Fat	Sea Eel	Common on both coasts of the Atlantic and very popular food-fish. With a long dorsal fin, scaleless skin, depressed and pointed head, deeply cleft mouth, projecting underjaw, closely set teeth, dark brown color above, dirty white beneath. In the transparent larval state, it is called the "Morris." The flesh is sweet and firm and snow-white. The uninitiated assume that Eel, fresh or salt-water, are indigestible: NONSENSE!	4–10 feet and a weight of 100 lbs. Fresh, pickled, smoked, by the lb.	Same as fresh-water Eel
EEL— SAND† All year (but better in Winter) Fat	Sand Launce, Sand Boy	These sharp-pointed nosed Eels swim in immense schools on sandy shores and frequently embed themselves in the sand —hence their name—where they remain above low-water mark while the tide is out. The flesh is firm and sweet, similar to that of the smelt. Abundant on both oceans.	6–8 inches Same as fresh-water Eels	Same as fresh-water Eels

* Fresh water.   † Salt water.

GUIDE TO THE PURCHASE AND PREPARATION OF FISH [411

NAME OF FISH SEASON TYPE: Fat or Lean	OTHER NAME (According to locality)	SPECIFICATIONS	SIZE and WEIGHT (average) MARKET UNIT	HOW TO COOK (Methods
FINNAN HADDIE† All year Lean		Finnan Haddie, Haddock smoked and salted, takes its name from the town of Findon, Scotland, where it was first prepared. It was formerly called "Findon Haddie." Part of the enormous catch of the Grand Banks each year undergoes salting and smoking to become Finnan Haddie. This fish needs almost no preliminary treatment.	By the pound or whole, filets	Steam, in cream, Delmonic scallop, various sauces, or butter, in puddin soufflé, et
FLOUN-DER† All year Lean	Summer Flounder, Winter Flounder, Four-spotted Flounder of Cape Cod, Arctic or Bering Sea; Eel-Back of Labrador; Starry from California to the Arctic; Pale or Craig Fluke Flounder of New England	The Summer Flounder is flat and oval, with both eyes on the same side when old. The young fish has an eye on each side. The Winter Flounder, flavorsome and common, rarely exceeds 24 inches and 6 lbs. It is on the market in winter and spring. Both have the teeth on the blind side, color on right side, scales comparatively large. Both have flaky, white flesh.	½–6 lbs. Fresh, whole, filets	Bake, broil, fry. All methods cooking filets of sole in filets or whole
FLUKE† All year Lean	Carrelet in certain parts of New England	Small Flounder also called Craig Fluke.	½–4 lbs. Fresh, whole, filets	Same as Flounder
FROST-FISH* Spring, Summer, Fall Fat		Name given to the Whitefish in the Adirondack lakes.	Same as Whitefish	Same as Whitefish
GRAY-LING* Spring, Summer, Fall Fat	Trout	As a food fish, Grayling is superior to Trout. It lives only in clear icy water of fresh-water of mountains. It is delicately colored, has a huge dorsal fin, and is more than often sold as Trout.	1–4 lbs. Fresh, whole, smoked, filets	Same as Trout

* Fresh water.   † Salt water.

GUIDE TO THE PURCHASE AND   [411]
PREPARATION OF FISH

NAME OF FISH SEASON TYPE: Fat or Lean	OTHER NAME (According to locality)	SPECIFICATIONS	SIZE and WEIGHT (average) MARKET UNIT	HOW TO COOK (Methods)
GRINDLE* all and Winter an	Dogfish, Bowfin, Mudfish, Layer, Blackfish, Cottonfish, Speckled Cat, or Scaled Ling in New York. Grindle in Virginia, and Choupiquel in Louisiana	The sole surviving species of a once numerous order that lived in very early geological times, yet is very abundant especially in Middle West lakes and rivers.	1½–2 feet, the male being smaller than the female Fresh, whole, steaks	Same as Bass
GROUPER† year an	Nassau Grouper, Red Grouper, Black Grouper, Snowy Grouper, etc.	The Nassau Grouper is a large compressed, colorful Sea Bass with a rounded tail. It varies in color, being a light gray, brown, or green, with irregular, vertical dark brown bands on its sides. The cheeks are light brown, with horizontal bands of gray. The Red Grouper is a handsome common fish. It is known also as the Cherna, Mero and Jaboncillo in Florida and the Gulf States, and adapts its colors to the surroundings. Gaily colored is the beautiful red kind of the Florida Keys. Black Grouper is very popular in Florida. Snowy Grouper is a rare species.	2–90 lbs. Fresh, whole, steaks	Bake, broil, boil, fry, steam
GRUNT† year ut best Summer) t	Roncos, Margaret Grunt, Gray Grunt, Striped Grunt, Bastard, Boar Grunt, Common Grunt, White Grunt, French Grunt,	Many species (about 55). All valued as food fish. Abundant in Florida and on the Pacific Coast. Chiefly in warm seas. Body oblong, with variegated colors. Utters a hoglike sound, hence the name Grunt.	Average: 4–5 lbs., but as high as 10 lbs. Fresh, whole, filets, smoked, steaks or chunks	Same as Pompano and similar fish

* Fresh water.   † Salt water.

GUIDE TO THE PURCHASE AND PREPARATION OF FISH   [411

NAME OF FISH SEASON TYPE: Fat or Lean	OTHER NAME (According to locality)	SPECIFICATIONS	SIZE and WEIGHT (average) MARKET UNIT	HOW T COOK (Method
GRUNT†— (*Continued*)	Open-Mouther Grunt, Boca Colorado or Cachicato in Puerto Rico, etc.			
GUACA-MAIA† All year (but best in Summer) Lean	Parrot-Fish; Cotoros in Florida; Lauia and Palukaluka in Hawaii	Member of a large family of herbivorous, oblong, and compressed fish of more than 100 species found in warm seas, especially in Florida, the Pacific Coast and Guacamaia. Has soft, sweet, and somewhat pasty flesh. In Hawaii, the Guacamaia is eaten raw as an appetizer. It is highly esteemed and rather expensive.	6–20 lbs. Fresh, whole, filets, steaks	Same as Weakfish and simil fish. Delicious when stuffed and bake
HADDOCK† All year Lean	Haddock to French-speaking inhabitants of New England, also Aiglefin; Shellfish in many parts of Pennsylvania Dutch; Finnan Haddie when smoked	Closely related to the Cod and like it in appearance and habits. Is easily distinguished by the black lateral line and by the spot above each pectoral fin. Haddock is extremely popular as a food fish. Smaller than the Cod, and found only in the North Atlantic. Colors: Dark gray above, whitish below. During some years it abounds, while in others it is very scarce, the cause of which is not understood. Smoked, it is called Finnan Haddie or Smoked Haddock, which names are derived from the town of Findon, Scotland, where it originated. In England and in America a pretty legend is attached to the Haddock. It is said to be the fish for which St. Peter received the tribute-money. Indeed, on some of the large Haddocks have been seen finger marks according to the legend, attributed to that Old Saint. Be that as it may, fishermen believe firmly in this old legend.	Average: 3–4 lbs. When 8 years old, frequently grows as heavy as 25 lbs. Fresh, smoked, whole, slices, steaks, filets, frozen, canned as Finnan Haddie	Bake, casserole, pie, boil, broil, in kedge chowders loaf, croquett roe patti stuff, pudding, soufflé, scallop, cream, sauté wi various sauces, poach in white wi milk, or tomato juice.

* Fresh water.   † Salt water.

GUIDE TO THE PURCHASE AND   [411]
PREPARATION OF FISH

NAME OF FISH SEASON TYPE: Fat or Lean	OTHER NAME (According to locality)	SPECIFICATIONS	SIZE and WEIGHT (average) MARKET UNIT	HOW TO COOK (Methods)
HAKE† year (better Summer) Lean	Codling, White Hake, Silver Hake, Silver Fish, Whiting, Merluche in many parts of New England	A fish moderately elongated, with small, smooth scales. Head elongated with strong teeth. Voracious habits. The Silver Hake, also called New England Hake or Whiting, is common from Newfoundland to Cape Cod. It is also found on the Pacific Coast from Santa Catalina to Puget Sound. It has considerable food value and is considered superior to any other small fish of the Cod family, to which it belongs.	3–8 lbs. Fresh, whole, filets, steaks, salted, smoked	Boil, broil, filets with various sauces, bake, stuff. Also same as codfish, halibut and similar fish
HALF-BEAK† summer Lean	Balaos, Juniper, Common Half-Beak in Rhode Island	A Florida and warm-seas fish which leaps in the air when near shore. Swims in large schools. Also found during the summer along the New England coast. It has a snout the shape of a half-beak, hence its name. It has a long compressed body, with sweet, flaky flesh.	Average 10 inches to a foot Fresh, whole, filets	Same as Flounder or Grey Sole
HALIBUT† year	Halibut or Fletan in Canada, Elbot in Pennsylvania Dutch, Greenland Halibut, Bastard Halibut, Common Halibut, Arrow-Toothed Halibut, Little Halibut, Monterey Halibut, King of the Sea almost anywhere	The largest of all flat fish in the coldest waters of the Atlantic, Pacific and Arctic Oceans. An upright swimmer with eyes placed on either side of the head. When a few months old it becomes a side swimmer, the under eye migrating across the forehead to a place alongside the upper eye. The eyes of the adult Halibut are always on the right. This is characteristic of all northern species of flat fish. Rich in vitamins A and D. Prized for its firm white flesh and absence of small bones.	Common Halibut, 200–350 lbs., but large ones run as heavy as 700 lbs. Arrow-Toothed, 10–25 lbs. Monterey, 1 lb. Fletan, 4½–10 lbs. Average: 4½–5 lbs. Whole, pound, steak, fresh, smoked, filets	Bake in wine, cream, stock, tomato juice, poach, various sauces, mousse, grill, poulette, in cutlets, jelly, braise, plank, soufflé, stuff, boil, pie, curry, pan-fry, loaf, pudding, hash, timbales, croquettes

* Fresh water.   † Salt water.

GUIDE TO THE PURCHASE AND PREPARATION OF FISH

NAME OF FISH SEASON TYPE: Fat or Lean	OTHER NAME (According to locality)	SPECIFICATIONS	SIZE and WEIGHT (average) MARKET UNIT	HOW T COOK (Method
HER- RING*† All year (but better in winter) Fat	Common Herring, California, Blue, Freshwater or Lake Michigan. Sawbelly in Lake Erie. Taylor, Fall, Matto Wacca by the Indians, meaning "Long Island." Taylor Shad in the Potomac River. Alewife, "Wall-Eyed," Big-Eyed, Spring, Gaspereau, Glut, Blueback, Kyack in the Carolinas	This fish belongs to a large family of about 150 species and inhabits all seas. Many of the species are anadromous, ascending freshwater streams to spawn, where they remain permanently. The common Herring is a small, compressed, bluish-silver fish with a single dorsal fin. Unlike other fish, it is particularly delicious at spawning time. For this reason most of the herring fisheries are carried on when the fish are in full roe. New York and surrounding territory receive quantities of the fish direct from Newfoundland while those caught on the New England coast are smoked, salted or pickled and packed as sardines. The California Herring is generally packed as sardines or frozen. Lake Herring is generally found on the market in fall and winter. It is prepared like the salt-water Herring. The Red Herring is a special grade of heavily salted species. It gets its rich brown color from long smoking. Kipper is first gutted then lightly salted and cured for 12 hours over a smouldering fire of oak chips. It is then canned in oil and shipped to the four corners of the world.	¾–1½ lbs. Fresh, smoked, salted, pickled, canned in brine or sauce	Poach in wine, cream or tomato juice, marinate grill, bake, boil, en papill
KINGFISH† Spring Lean and Fat (equal parts)	Whiting in California, Sierra in Gulf of Mexico, Pintado, Cero in Florida, Kingfish elsewhere,	This fish is found from Cape Cod to Texas. It belongs to the Mackerel family. It appears early in spring along with the Weakfish. The flesh is firm and of delicate flavor.	10–100 lbs. Average: 12 lbs. Length: Up to 6 feet Fresh, whole, steaks, filets	Same as Mackere Stuff, grill, bake, sauté

* Fresh water.   † Salt water.

GUIDE TO THE PURCHASE AND PREPARATION OF FISH [411]

NAME OF FISH SEASON TYPE: Fat or Lean	OTHER NAME (According to locality)	SPECIFICATIONS	SIZE and WEIGHT (average) MARKET UNIT	HOW TO COOK (Methods)
INGFISH† (Continued)	King Mackerel down South, also Cavalla			
EMON OLE† ll year an	Sand Dab, Rough Dab, Alaska Dab, Rusty Dab, Smear Dab, Limande in New England and Canada, Common Flatfish, Cimanda	Popular name of several species of flat fish found on the Atlantic and North Pacific coasts. Resembles the Flounder except that the dark side is of a more brownish color. It has a relatively short head of light yellowish-brown color with a lemon cast, hence its name. Although an all-year-round fish, it is in season in January and February. Found off the New England coast in deep water. The Alaska Lemon Sole or Alaska Dab is generally common in Northern Pacific waters. Limande is the French-Canadian name for this fish.	1–1½ lbs. Fresh, filets, whole	Sauté, grill, bake, cream, various sauces
OTE† ll year ut best in nter) t	Ocean Pout in Boston, Eel Pout elsewhere, Gulper Eel	A fish with an eel-like body and common all along the Atlantic coastline from New England south to the Carolinas. Like any other eel-shaped fish, it is best when smoked. The smoking is usually done in an oak pickle barrel set up on four bricks over a fire of hickory wood, from which rows of eels hang.	18–20 inches Fresh, smoked, brined, whole, filets, steaks	Bake, grill, stew, marinate, pie, chowder
ACK-REL† l year ut best in mmer) t	Common Mackerel, Chub, also called Tinker; Frigate, Horse, Spanish, Monterey	The Mackerel is a member of a wandering streamlined race which includes the Tunny, Bonito, Albacore, Kingfish, Sardine and similar fish. It appears in the spring off Cape Hatteras and later reaches the shores of the Middle and New England States and Canada.	1–6 lbs., but as heavy as 10 lbs. Average: 1–2 lbs. Whole, filets, steaks	Bake, grill, boil in milk, tomato juice, and water, court-bouillon of wine or

* Fresh water.   † Salt water.

GUIDE TO THE PURCHASE AND PREPARATION OF FISH [411]

NAME OF FISH SEASON TYPE: Fat or Lean	OTHER NAME (According to locality)	SPECIFICATIONS	SIZE and WEIGHT (average) MARKET UNIT	HOW TO COOK (Methods)
MACK-EREL†— (*Continued*)	Spanish; Boston, which is the summer Mackerel	There are about 60 species of this well-known food fish. The flesh is firm and oily. The common Mackerel, when taken out of salt water, is a beautiful metallic blue color, changing immediately on contact with the air to an iris-green, reflecting gold and purple. Mackerel caught for the freezing process is hauled in, in autumn, rushed to refrigerating plants right off the docks. To defrost frozen Mackerel: Immerse in cold water and clean as soon as defrosted. Cook immediately at a moderate temperature. High temperature toughens the protein of any kind of fish, whether fresh, frozen or salted. Salt Mackerel must be freshened before cooking for at least 24 hours in a large amount of cold water. Place on a rack, meat side down, a few inches from the bottom of the vessel so that the salt drops away from the fish. Change water several times. For broiling or frying, freshen the fish more than for boiling with milk as milk covers up some of the salty flavor.	when fresh, pickled, salted, smoked, canned	vinegar; casserole, Beurre noir various sauces, hash, pan, plank, pan-fry, scallop
MARI-POSA† All year Fat	Opah, Moonfish, San Pedro, Cravo, Soho, Jerusalem Haddock, Glancefish, Gudlax, Poisson Lune in Canada	Fish of large size and brilliant silver coloration inhabiting the open sea of the Atlantic and Pacific. Has high food value. The flesh, resembling the Red Salmon, is firm, rich and of delicious flavor. Body oval, compressed and elevated, covered with minute cycloid scales. Small, rather pointed head and small mouth.	3–6 feet 10–400 lbs. Fresh, canned, smoked, brined, steaks, pound, frozen	Bake, roast, boil, broil, in loaves

* Fresh water.   † Salt water.

GUIDE TO THE PURCHASE AND PREPARATION OF FISH   [411]

NAME OF FISH SEASON TYPE: Fat or Lean	OTHER NAME (According to locality)	SPECIFICATIONS	SIZE and WEIGHT (average) MARKET UNIT	HOW TO COOK (Methods)
MARLIN† All year Lean	Marlin and Striped in California; White in Florida; Black in California; and Blue in West Indies	A large fish of the Spearfish family with a long first dorsal fin extending the length of the back; long narrow scales buried just below the surface of the skin. It resembles the Sword-fish, except that it has a short, rounded spear, resembling a marlin spike, hence its name. Methods of preparation for the swordfish may be applied to the Marlin.	White, 170 lbs. Blue, 700 lbs. Black, 950 lbs. Striped, 1000 lbs. Fresh, brined, smoked, steaks, pound, frozen	Bake, boil, skewer, then broil; scallop, pan fry, sauté, also loaves, cakes, burgers, cutlets, pies
MULLET*·† All year Fat	Common, Striped, Galapagos, White, Red-Eye, Oeil de Perdrix, meaning "Partridge eye" in French	Many species—about 100. The common Mullet is a fish of wide distribution and is found in both the Atlantic and Pacific Oceans. Its color is dark blue above, with sides silvery and a dark stripe along each row of scales; underpart yellowish. The White Mullet is found from Cape Cod to Brazil, and in the Pacific, south of California. All species are small and enter fresh-water as do the Salmon and Shad.	Common: 1–5 lbs.; Striped: 1–6 lbs.; Galapagos: 1–4 lbs. Fresh, filets, steaks, smoked, brined	Same as Herring. Smaller ones are usually lightly veiled in seasoned flour, and sautéed in butter
MUSKEL-LUNGE* All year but best in spring) Lean	Muskellunge along the border of Canada and Great Lakes; Musky popular nickname; Chautauqua or Ohio; Salmon-Pike; White Pike; Jack White; Pickerel; Picareau Blanc in	Resembles the Pike family but has distinguishing markings above the eye, back of the eye and along the cheeks. Found in the Great Lake regions, Canada and Mississippi Valley. Color: Dark gray with round or squarish black spots of vary-ing size on a ground of grayish silver. Musky (as it is popu-larly called) fishing is com-parable to elephant hunting. The man who belittles this most ferocious of American fresh-water fish shouldn't be granted a license.	15–40 lbs. Average: 12 lbs. Fresh, whole, pound, steaks, filets	Boil, bake, broil, roast, steam, grill, in aspic. May be prepared and cooked the same as pike, pickerel, bass, salmon and similar fish,

* Fresh water.   † Salt water.

GUIDE TO THE PURCHASE AND PREPARATION OF FISH

[411]

NAME OF FISH SEASON TYPE: Fat or Lean	OTHER NAME (According to locality)	SPECIFICATIONS	SIZE and WEIGHT (average) MARKET UNIT	HOW TO COOK (Methods)
MUSKEL-LUNGE*— (*Continued*)	Missouri. Muskellunge signifies "deformed pike" to Indians; French Canadians call it "Masque allonge," meaning "elongated mask"	The flesh of the Musky is delicate and divides easily as does the Salmon. It is considered by epicurians one of the best fish of the West and Middlewest. Flesh is juicy and of better flavor after a day or two on ice.		cold or ho
PERCH*,† All year Lean	Yellow, also known as American; Racoon; Striped; Ringed; Black, also known as Surf-fish; Blue; Chinquapin, also known as Crappie; Gray, also known as Fresh-water Drum; Sheepshead in Great Lakes; Gaspergou in Louisiana; Red; White, also called Porgie on the Pacific Coast	The Yellow Perch is abundant in the Great Lakes and in the larger coastwise streams and lakes from Nova Scotia down to the Carolinas. It is the fish par excellence as a fresh-water pan fish. Color: Back, olive; sides, golden yellow with 6 or 8 broad dark bars extending from back to below axis. The Red Perch, also called the Rosefish, Redfish, or Ocean Perch, has the flavor of the Mullet. All Perch weigh about the same, except the Gray Perch, which is as heavy as 50 or 60 pounds and is 5 feet in length. The perch has a light, flaky and delicious flavored flesh. The word "perch" comes from the Latin perca, meaning "black blotched." The roe are delicious, especially when grilled and served with thin slices of brown bread—lavishly buttered. The body is large, and the jaws about equal. All perch are of the carnivorous type. This fish has a high food value.	Yellow, 10–15 inches; weight, ¾–2 lbs. Black, Blue and Chinquapin, 1 foot; Gray, 50–60 lbs.; length, 5 feet. Other species average 2 lbs. Whole, fresh, smoked, frozen, filets. Large ones such as the Gray, by the pound in steak or chunk	Bake, boil with various sauces, grill, poach, stuff, steam, pan-fry. Cold in aspic, salad; smoked as an appetizer; hot or cold, Delmonico style
PICKEREL* All year Lean	Grass, Chain, Common, Jackfish,	The pickerel is the smallest member of the pike family. Its color is green, with shades varying to golden brown and	2½–20 lbs. Fresh, frozen, filets,	Same methods as for Perch

* Fresh water.   † Salt water.

GUIDE TO THE PURCHASE AND PREPARATION OF FISH [411]

NAME OF FISH SEASON TYPE: Fat or Lean	OTHER NAME (According to locality)	SPECIFICATIONS	SIZE and WEIGHT (average) MARKET UNIT	HOW TO COOK (Methods)
PICKEREL* —(Continued)	Snake, Little Banded, Small, Muskellunge	it is marked with horizontal streaks on the sides; dark band below the eyes, and the fins plain. This fish is found in creeks, rivers, ponds and lakes from Maine to Florida and up the Mississippi River. It is quite common in the northeastern States and Canada.	steak, pound	
PIKE* All year Lean	Wall-Eyed; Yellow; Dore or Dory among the Great Lakes; Pickerel in places where the true Pike (Esox Lucius) is found. Salmon or Jack Salmon in Northern Indiana; Jack in Mississippi, elsewhere it is called Okow; Blowfish or Green; Sauger in Montana, Tennessee and Arkansas; Pike-Perch in many localities	The flesh is firm, flaky and of delicious flavor. It is dark olive, has a finely mottled brassy sheen, the latter color forming indistinct oblique bars. The lower jaw is flesh colored, the belly and lower fins pinkish. The spinal dorsal is marked with a large, jet-black blotch. The color of the pike is variable as is indicated by some of its names—Yellow, Gray, and the like. This fish is found in almost all fresh waters of North America, Europe and Asia. The French call it "Brochet" while the British know it as Pike-Perch. The Common Pike is easily distinguished from all other of its species in that each scale has a grayish V-shaped marking.	3 feet. Average weight: 1–5 lbs. Maximum: 20 lbs. Sauger Pike: 1–2 lbs. Whole, fresh, frozen, pound, filet	Same methods as for Perch
POLLOCK† All year Lean	Coalfish, Green Cod	The Common Pollock is a member of the Cod family and is highly esteemed. The liver yields a valuable oil which is used extensively in adulterating true cod liver oil. The flesh is white, firm and fairly dry.	3 feet. 4–25 lbs. Fresh, salted, corned, filets, steaks	Bake, stuff, boil, fry, steam, cakes, kedgeree

* Fresh water.   † Salt water.

GUIDE TO THE PURCHASE AND PREPARATION OF FISH [411]

NAME OF FISH SEASON TYPE: Fat or Lean	OTHER NAME (According to locality)	SPECIFICATIONS	SIZE and WEIGHT (average) MARKET UNIT	HOW TO COOK (Methods)
POLLOCK† —(*Continued*)		This fish swims in large schools in the North Atlantic. It is more active than its relatives the Cod and Haddock. The Alaska Pollock, found in the Bering Sea, is the chief food of the seals.		
POMPANO† Winter Fat	Common, Gaff-Topsail, Irish, Permit, Great, Round, Silver	Pompano, which means "Grape Leaf" in Spanish, is a warm-water dweller found all along the Coast of Florida and Gulf of Mexico. It is sometimes found as far north as Maryland. Body oblong and compressed; small, smooth scales. The flesh is flaky, sweet and delicious. The body color is metallic gray with a yellowish breast, while the head is blue, yellow and silver. The Silver Pompano is rare and very expensive. The Permit is the largest of this species.	1½–3 lbs. Permit or Great, 20–25 lbs., some reaching 30 lbs. Fresh, filet, steak	Same as for mackerel, herring or shad
PORGIES† All year, (but best in summer) Lean	Saucer-Eye and Little-Head in Florida, Jolt-Head, Grass, Little-Mouth, Scup or Scuppang in New England, Pargo or Red in Gulf of Mexico, Paugy in N.Y., Fairmaid in the South	Many species—about 100—all having high food value. Very abundant in the North and South Atlantic in the summer. The Common Porgie has brown and silver colorings. An inexpensive food fish with a white, flaky flesh and delicate flavor. The greatest source of supply of this year-round fish seems to be the region off the Jersey Coast. The fish should be cooked until brown and the flesh firm. Overcooking detracts from its flavor.	1–3 lbs. Fresh, whole	Bake, boil, grill, pan-fry, sauté, in aspic, salads
REDFISH† All year,	Channel Bass, Red Drum,	A member of the Croaker family, this popular fish is found	3–40 lbs. Whole,	Same as Salmon,

* Fresh water.   † Salt water.

GUIDE TO THE PURCHASE AND PREPARATION OF FISH [411]

NAME OF FISH SEASON TYPE: Fat or Lean	OTHER NAME (According to locality)	SPECIFICATIONS	SIZE and WEIGHT (average) MARKET UNIT	HOW TO COOK (Methods)
REDFISH † –(Continued) but best in summer and fall) Lean	Reef Bass, Ocean-Perch, Red Perch, Bull Redfish, Pescado, Colorado	in coastal waters from Cape Cod to the Gulf of Mexico. It has copper-red scales—hence its name—and a lateral line that runs to the tail, which is almost square. The most recognizable marking is the black spot at the base of the tail, California Redfish, or Fathead, is very common on the Pacific Coast. It weighs 12–15 lbs. and is 3 feet in length. This species is salted immediately after being caught. All Redfish are large in size, the largest coming from the waters off Virginia and the Carolinas.	steak, pound, filet, smoked, fresh, frozen	Pompano, Snappers, Herring, Mackerel
SALMON *, † Fresh: summer and fall Fat	Atlantic or Common, Blueback, also known as Little Redfish, Kernnerly's or Walla in Idaho and British Columbia, Chinook also known as Quinnat, King, Columbia River or Sacramento, Dog, also known as Calico, Hayo or Lekai, Humpback also known as the Lost Salmon, Haddo, Holia, Dog Salmon (although it is not the	The Atlantic, or Common Salmon, is perhaps the best and most widely known. It inhabits both coasts of the North Atlantic. The color, as well as the form of the head and body, varies with age and food. The black spots in the adult are often X-shaped or XX-shaped, The Blueback is found in the Pacific from Oregon up to Alaska rivers. It is one of the most beautiful of the species, Its flesh is attractive in color, rich in oil and of superior quality when canned. The Chinook is found in the Pacific from Monterey Bay up to the Bering Sea, Chinook or King Salmon usually commands a higher price than any other because its quantity is limited. It is generally packed in flat cans. Color is from red to white. Rich in oil. Separates into large flakes. The Dog is found from Sacramento northward to Kamchatka and Bering Sea or	Atlantic: 8–10 lbs.; maximum; 20 lbs. Blueback: 3–7 lbs. Chino 4–20 lbs.; average: 7–8 lbs. Dog: 8–12 lbs. Humpback: 3–6 lbs. Ouananiche: 3–6 lbs. Red: 3½–8 lbs. Sebago: 2–4 lbs. Silver: 3½–8 lbs. Sockeye: 3–7 lbs. Inconnu: 6–25 lbs. Fresh, smoked, steak, canned	Bake, boil, grill, poach, barbecue, loaves, kedgeree, casserole, cream, curry, creole, pie, patties, croquettes, fry, sauté, mousse, sandwich, jelly, mixed-grill, pickle, rarebit, cakes, fritters, chops, soufflé, custard, à la King, chowder,

* Fresh water.   † Salt water.

GUIDE TO THE PURCHASE AND PREPARATION OF FISH   [411]

NAME OF FISH SEASON TYPE: Fat or Lean	OTHER NAME (According to locality)	SPECIFICATIONS	SIZE and WEIGHT (average) MARKET UNIT	HOW TO COOK (Methods
SALMON*,† —(Continued)	real Dog Salmon), Negro, Ouananiche or Wisconsin, Winnonish, Red or Coho, Sebago also known as Presumpscot River, Schoodic Lake, Landlocked, Silver also known as Hoopid, Coho, Kisutch, etc.; Sockeye, which is spelled in different ways; Inconnu, Gaspe	Straits rivers. It is one of the species often packed under a fictitious name. Its flesh is pinkish white. When packed it is labeled "Pink Salmon." The Humpback is the smallest of the genus and is found on the Pacific Coast. Color is bluish, sides silvery with numerous black spots. Its flesh is pink, and when packed is also labelled "Pink Salmon." The Ouananiche is a landlocked relative of the North Atlantic Salmon which it resembles. The name "Ouananiche," an Indian name, means "little Salmon." The Red Salmon is a genus from Alaska, and is better known as Coho or Red. It has large medium flakes. The Sebago is a fine Maine Lakes' fish and resembles the Atlantic or Common Salmon. The Silver Salmon is blessed with a large number of names. It is a delicious, flaky, oily fish, found in large quantities on the Pacific Coast from San Francisco, Oregon and up to Alaska. It resembles the Chinook but is easily distinguished from it by its fewer scales. The Sockeye, which is identical to the Blueback in quality, flakes and oil, has a delicious flavor. It is often called Blueback in the Columbia River, while in the Fraser River it is called Sockeye, Sawkeye, or Sau-Qui. In Alaska it is called the Redfish. The Inconnu inhabits the larger streams of Alaska and northwestern British Columbia. It is		meuniere, ring

* Fresh water.   † Salt water.

GUIDE TO THE PURCHASE AND PREPARATION OF FISH [411]

NAME OF FISH SEASON TYPE: Fat or Lean	OTHER NAME (According to locality)	SPECIFICATIONS	SIZE and WEIGHT (average) MARKET UNIT	HOW TO COOK (Methods)
SALMON *·† (Continued)		found in abundance in the Yukon and Mackenzie Rivers. Its large size renders this fish of considerable commercial importance. It is also canned and labeled "Pink Salmon."		
SARDINES† year Fat	California, Spanish or Sardines de España as they are called on the Pacific Coast. Imported from Norway; when smoked they are called Brisling, Sprat or Sild. They are also brined and canned. Menhaden (which is not a true Sardine but is sold as such)	This excellent American food fish is found on the Pacific Coast from Puget Sound southward to Magdalena Bay. It is abundant on the California Coast and spawns in the open sea. It resembles the European Sardine. However, it is much bigger, has no teeth, and the belly is less strongly notched. Where did the sardine get its name? Those who enjoy knowing little facts in food history recall that originally the term was applied to the young fish of the Pilchard family, caught off the island of Sardinia. Color is dark bluish above, silvery below; a series of round black spots running backward from level to eye, bounding the dark color of the back; similar smaller spots above. Flesh darker and more oily than that of the herring. The Spanish Sardine, also called Maine Sardine, is found from Cape Cod down to the Gulf Stream, and it closely resembles the European Sardine. It is distinguished by the absence of radiating stripes on the gills; is unspotted on sides and has minute teeth.	California: up to 1 foot. Spanish or Maine: 6–8 inches Fresh, smoked, brined, canned	NOTE: Fresh or canned sardines: broil, sauté, casserole, cream, stuff, bake. Where canned and brined, they are also served as hors d'oeuvres and in salads
SCROD† year Lean		Originally, in New England, Scrod was the name applied to a young codfish prepared for	Maximum weight: 2½ lbs.	Bake, boil, broil,

---

* Fresh water.   † Salt water.

GUIDE TO THE PURCHASE AND PREPARATION OF FISH   [411

NAME OF FISH SEASON TYPE: Fat or Lean	OTHER NAME (According to locality)	SPECIFICATIONS	SIZE and WEIGHT (average) MARKET UNIT	HOW TO COOK (Methods
SCROD†— (*Continued*)		frying or broiling by "scrodding." This means splitting and cutting into strips convenient for cooking. Later the name Scrod was also applied to young Haddock and then to almost any small fish similarly prepared for the pan, and weighing 2½ lbs. or less.	Fresh, whole, filets, frozen	pan-fry, casserole, plank
SHAD*,† Almost all year, according to locality Fat	Common Shad, as well as the names of the various rivers where they are taken	The Shad is found on the Atlantic Coast from Florida to Newfoundland, its chief abundance being from North Carolina to Long Island, N.Y. The principal Shad rivers are: Potomac, Susquehanna, Delaware and Hudson. The fish passes most of its life in the sea, performing annual migrations from the sea to the rivers for the sole purpose of reproduction, ascending rivers when the water temperature is 56–66° F. Shad Roe has been considered a great delicacy since the days of Washington. There is but one species of Shad on our Atlantic Coast, but it has received almost as many vernacular names as there are rivers, and people on each particular stream regard theirs as the best. The sweetness and delicate flavor of the Shad depend upon its freshness. Body comparatively deep; mouth rather large, jaws about equal. Color is bluish above, sides silvery white: a dark spot behind gill-cover. Shad is really a salt-water fish. The male spends 2–5 years at sea and the female 4–6 years before moving into the rivers to spawn. What they need for	2–2½ feet, average weight; less than 4 lbs. Fresh, frozen, pound, boned, roe, canned roes	Bake, plank, boil, grill, steam, sauté, pan-fry, loaves, shad roe in croquettes sauté, broil

* Fresh water.   † Salt water.

GUIDE TO THE PURCHASE AND PREPARATION OF FISH [411]

NAME OF FISH SEASON TYPE: Fat or Lean	OTHER NAME (According to locality)	SPECIFICATIONS	SIZE and WEIGHT (average) MARKET UNIT	HOW TO COOK (Methods)
SHAD*,† (continued)		spawning is not fresh water, but warm water. They swim back to the open sea after spawning is over.		
SHARK† All year Slightly oily	White, Blue, Hammer-headed, Porbeagle, Thresher, Mako, Tiger, Sand, Soupfin Mackerel, Shark Pilot which is not a Shark	This voracious fish has lateral bronchial clefts, fan-shaped pectoral fins and an elongated, tapering body. An interesting fact is that when a Shark loses a front tooth, the lost member is soon replaced by another tooth from an inner row. This fish has been eaten for centuries but has suddenly increased so greatly in popularity that fishermen are unable to fill the orders. It is comparable to the Swordfish in texture, and the Haddock in flavor; and with almost no small bones. Slow cooking is essential to prevent the meat from toughening. Fins of the Soupfish Shark are sold to Chinese chefs for producing Shark's Fin Soup, a delicacy of the Orient. Once imported in America in considerable quantity from Hongkong and Shanghai, it is now prepared on the Pacific Coast. The Shark Pilot, which is not a Shark but a small fish found from Cape Hatteras up to Cape Cod, as well as on the Pacific Coast, is a good food fish.	10–700 lbs. or more. Shark Pilot: 2–3 ft. Fresh, frozen, pound, steak, filet, gutted, head off, fins removed	Same as Swordfish, Marlin and similar large fish
SHEEPS-HEAD† Fall and winter Lean	Salema; in the Great Lakes, the fresh-water Drum; in the lakes of Indiana, the Crovens, evidently a corruption of croaker; in Ohio, the White Perch	The Common Sheepshead, one of our best fish, is found from Cape Cod down to the Gulf of Mexico and Texas. Though a salt-water fish, it often runs far up fresh-water rivers. This fish is a cross between a Black-fish and a Porgy. Sheepshead Bay, Long Island, N.Y., received its name because of the teeming millions of Sheeps-head that inhabited its waters years ago. For some unknown reason it left Sheepshead Bay almost 50 years ago.	2–15 lbs., average: 3–4 lbs. Whole, filets, steak, fresh	Bake, boil, grill, pan-fry, chowder

* Fresh water.   † Salt water.

GUIDE TO THE PURCHASE AND PREPARATION OF FISH [411]

NAME OF FISH SEASON TYPE: Fat or Lean	OTHER NAME (According to locality)	SPECIFICATIONS	SIZE and WEIGHT (average) MARKET UNIT	HOW TO COOK (Methods)
SKATE† Almost all year, but in the fresh state from October to April Medium fat	Laevis, Smooth, Erenacca, Tobacco, Sting or Sting Ray, Raie in certain parts of New England and Canada; Turbot, Buckled, Sand	There are over 50 species and subspecies of Skate, also called Raie or Ray in American coastal waters. All are flat, large-bodied fish having a pointed snout. This genus is six-sided, having highly developed fins. However, only the fins or wings are eaten, the rest being discarded. The wings are always cooked in salted water with either vinegar, lemon or dry white wine before being prepared in a number of delicious ways. Then the pieces are drained and scraped and the extremities cut off, for they consist of bone. The wings are then returned to the cooking broth to be kept hot for final preparation. The liver is a real delicacy when poached and served on toast.	6–12 lbs. Whole fresh wings or fins. IMPORTANT: This fish is always better when 2 or 3 days old. A wing usually measures about 1 yd.	Curry, black butter, with noodles, fry, au gratin, fritters, various sauces when boiled. Liver on toast, in cream, à la Newburg
SMELTS*,† Season from September to May Fat	American, Eperlans in certain parts of New England and Canada. Surf in California and Oregon	Smelts are small fish found in salt or fresh waters. There are about 15 species. Most of them are excellent food fish. They are found along our Atlantic Coast from Virginia up to the Gulf of St. Lawrence. Often they are land-locked. Color is transparent greenish above, sides silvery; body and fins with some dark spots. Experts do not agree as to their origin, some claiming the word is a derivative of "smell it," due to the fact that when freshly caught they have an odor like freshly cut cucumbers. Others assert that the name came from the Anglo-Saxon "smelt," meaning smooth and shiny. In Scotland it is known as the sparling. The principal center	6–7 inches; run 12–14 lbs. Some have been found weighing 1 lb. and 1 foot in length Fresh, frozen, smoked, brined	Fry, bake, stuff, sauté, grill, casserole, loaf, pickle

* Fresh water.   † Salt water.

GUIDE TO THE PURCHASE AND PREPARATION OF FISH

NAME OF FISH SEASON TYPE: Fat or Lean	OTHER NAME (According to locality)	SPECIFICATIONS	SIZE and WEIGHT (average) MARKET UNIT	HOW TO COOK (Methods)
SMELTS*,† (Continued)		for Smelt fishing is Smeltania, on Lake Charlevoix, Michigan, which exists because the Michigan Fish and Game Commission made an error by placing Maine Smelts, commonly a salt-water fish, in Michigan waters as food for its newly stocked salmon. The salmon vanished but the Smelts have been multiplying so rapidly that the annual Michigan catch runs more than 1,000,000 lbs. The Surf Smelt is a fresh-water fish which attains a length of a foot and is found in considerable quantities on the Coasts of California and Oregon; a firm-fleshed and fat little fish of delicious flavor. Color is light olive with a silvery band along the lateral line.		
SNAPPERS† Summer and winter, but may be had all year at	Dog, also called Pargo Colorado, Flamingo, also called Lane, Gray, Mangrove in Florida, and Cabellerote or Pargo Prieto along the Gulf of Mexico and also known as Red-tailed. In Porto Rico it is known as Manchego or Raiado, Red on the American Coast	The Snapper is one of the largest and most important families among fish, comprising some 250 species. It inhabits the shores of the warmer seas. All species are valued as food. Color of the Dog Snapper is olive above, rosy or brick-red on sides, paler below, flushed so that the hue is coppery red. The sides are narrow with light cross bars; a line of small, round, bluish spots is below the eye. Flamingo is found on the Pacific Coast. It is a small species, and is a common food fish. It is the Pacific Coast representative of the Lane, found in Florida waters, which it somewhat resembles. Color is light olive above, the sides bright silvery; a large, round, black lateral blotch the size of	Dog reaches 2½ lbs.; Flamingo: 1 foot; Gray: 2–6 lbs.; Lane: ¾–4 lbs.; Pargo Colorado: 2½–3 lbs.; Red reaches 3–4 lbs., but as heavy as 25 lbs. Mutton, better known as Mutton fish, 4–5 lbs.; maximum:	Same as Mackerel and all fat fish

* Fresh water.   † Salt water.

GUIDE TO THE PURCHASE AND
PREPARATION OF FISH   [411

NAME OF FISH SEASON TYPE: Fat or Lean	OTHER NAME (According to locality)	SPECIFICATIONS	SIZE and WEIGHT (average) MARKET UNIT	HOW TO COOK (Methods
SNAPPERS† —(*Continued*)	everywhere	an eye, on lateral line below front of soft dorsal. Each scale has a faint, darker, grayish spot forming oblique streaks. The Gray is one of the most widely distributed, abundant, and best known of all the species, and is an important commercial fish. Color is very dark green above, middle part of each scale brassy black, the edge pearly white; below the lateral line the duskiness of the middle scale becomes brassy, and the lower, grayish. Blue stripe below eye in very young; top of head blackish olive. Those from deep water are redder. The Lane Snapper is found from Florida to Brazil. Its strongly marked coloration renders it easy of recognition. Color is rose, tinged with silver below; slight olive coloring but not dark above; a large, round, maroon blotch above the lateral line and below the front of soft dorsal. Series of deep golden yellow stripes on head and body. Pargo Colorado, found on the Pacific Coast, is dark olive above; head and lower parts of body bright red; scales on sides of head without dark spots. Pectoral and ventral reddish. The Red Snapper is found from New Jersey to Brazil. Its centre of abundance is in the Gulf of Mexico in deep water. Color is deep rose-red, paler on throat, bluish streaks along row of scales, becoming fainter and disappearing with age. Fins brick-red, dorsal bordered with orange, and a narrow blackish edge. Large, blackish blotch	25 lbs. Whole, pound, steaks, filets	

* Fresh water.   † Salt water.

GUIDE TO THE PURCHASE AND PREPARATION OF FISH [411]

NAME OF FISH SEASON TYPE: Fat or Lean	OTHER NAME (According to locality)	SPECIFICATIONS	SIZE and WEIGHT (average) MARKET UNIT	HOW TO COOK (Methods)
SNAPPERS† (Continued)		above lateral line and below front rays of soft dorsal in the young, usually disappearing with age. Mutton Snapper, generally called Muttonfish, is common in Florida. Color is olive-green above; many of the scales having pale blue spots forming irregular oblique streaks upward and backward; belly white, strongly tinged with brick-red; about 6 narrow, dusky vertical bars, a little broader than the interspaces and not well defined, between gill-opening and anal. Head bronze-olive, darker above.		
SUCKER* year lan	Common, Brook, White, June, Big-jawed, Blue-headed, Carp, Fine-scaled, Flannel-mouth, Gourd-seed, Hare-lip, Long-nosed, Missouri, Pea-lip, Spotted, Yellow	Everybody knows the Suckers, the clumsy dolt of every stream and pond. In all kinds of water it cruises languidly over the bottom, sucking mud and small bottom-living animals into its unshapely mouth. Color is brownish, mottled with darker color, but with a rosy appearance. There are about 60 species. In early spring they run up streams to spawn, at this time being gayer in color. The Brook Sucker is the commonest east of the Rockies. Its flesh is firm, flaky and sweet, though full of small bones. Illinois is called the "Sucker State" because its first settlers came up the river in the spring when the Suckers were running.	Maximum: 5 lbs.; Average: 2 lbs. Frozen, salted, smoked, canned	Bake, boil, broil, stew, chowder
SUNFISH* year, according to well as mate lan	Common, Blue, Blue-spotted, Copper-nosed, Green, Long-eared, McKay's	The Sunfish family comprises about 38 species, including some of our most important game fishes, notably the Black Basses. All have a flaky, sweet meat; oblong body; small mouth; jaws about equal; scales	1 lb. Fresh, whole, salted, frozen, smoked	Court-bouillon of wine or vinegar; bake, broil, pan-fry,

* Fresh water. † Salt water.

GUIDE TO THE PURCHASE AND [411]
PREPARATION OF FISH

NAME OF FISH SEASON TYPE: Fat or Lean	OTHER NAME (According to locality)	SPECIFICATIONS	SIZE and WEIGHT (average) MARKET UNIT	HOW TO COOK (Methods
SUNFISH* —(*Continued*)	Mud, Red-eared, Red-spotted, Round, Scarlet	moderate. A mighty good pan-fish. This fish has an orange-yellow belly, orange cheeks with wavy blue streaks, a greenish color, sides with vertical stripes of orange, and orange lower fins. It is found in abundance from Maine to the Great Lakes and south to Florida. Sometimes called Pumpkin-seed. Sun Bass and Sand Perch.		sauté, stew, loaf, aspic
STUR-GEON*,† All year, according to climate, except winter, when sold smoked or brined Fat	Common or Sea, Green, Lake, White, also known as the Columbia, Sacramento, Pacific or Oregon	This fish inhabits the salt and fresh waters of the northern regions, most of the species, numbering 20, being migratory. By far the most valuable part is the roe, from which Caviar is prepared. Color is olive gray, paler below. The Green Sturgeon is rarely found in fresh water. Its color is olive green, with olive stripes on the belly and on each side above the ventral plates. Lake Sturgeon is found in the Great Lakes and nearby larger rivers. Color is dark olive and reddish. On the Pacific Coast the White Sturgeon attains an enormous size. Its color is dark-grayish and olive-tinged; snout sharp in the young, becoming rather blunt and short in the adult. Sturgeon meat, a bit firmer than Halibut, and a better flavor than Swordfish, is very popular along both coasts. It is a supreme delicacy when smoked. It is richer than smoked salmon.	Common: 500 lbs.; maximum length: 8–10 ft.; Green: 35–150 lbs. Lake: average weight, 35–40 lbs. White: 900 lbs. maximum; average length: 10 ft.; average weight: 100 lbs. Fresh, smoked, brined, canned, pound	NOTE: A a rule, Sturgeon is not frie or grilled as the fish gets toug and string It is boile either in wine cou bouillon vinegar, and serve with sauc
SWORD-FISH† All year in South	Common, Espada, Broadbill	These fish are of great size with long, muscular bodies; upper jaw very much prolonged, forming a "sword," which is	Maximum weight: 700 or 800 lbs.;	Bake, boil, broil, pan-fry,

* Fresh water.　　† Salt water.

GUIDE TO THE PURCHASE AND PREPARATION OF FISH [411]

NAME OF FISH SEASON TYPE: Fat or Lean	OTHER NAME (According to locality)	SPECIFICATIONS	SIZE and WEIGHT (average) MARKET UNIT	HOW TO COOK (Methods)
WORD-ISH†— (Continued) tlantic; mmer and ll in orth tlantic at		flattened horizontally, and is half as long as the fish itself. No teeth in the adult; dorsal very long; no ventral fins. Abundant all over the world. Color is dusky purple above, almost black on top and the fins are dark. Like Tuna, it is all meat and no bone. The meat is flaky and oily. About ten years ago this fish was a drug on the fish markets, selling for a cent and a half a pound. To-day it is the morsel of epicures. It is a scaleless fish, travels slowly and migrates individually rather than in schools.	average weight: 200 lbs. Fresh, frozen, pound, steak	sauté, chowder, stew, scallopine or thin slices, brochette
ROUT*'† l year, cording climate lt	Blueback, also known as Oquassa, Brook, Speckled or Native, Colorado, Dolly Warden, Dublin Pound, Golden, Great Lakes, Green, Greenback, Jordan, Kamloop, Kern River, Lac de Marbre, Lake Tahoe, Long-headed, Mackinaw, Rainbow, Sea Trout, sometimes called Weakfish, Silver, Spotted, Steelhead,	The scales of the Trout are, in general, smaller than those of other Salmonidae. They are embedded in the skin to such a degree as to escape the notice of casual observers. Sea Trout, commonly known as Weakfish, or Gray Trout, or Speckled Trout, is found in Chesapeake Bay and the South. Speckled Sea Trout, also called Salmon Trout, is a delectable sea food. Brook Trout has a delicate flavor which is explained by the fact that they live in water that springs from the hills. Like all Trout, they are raised for market only in hatcheries and sold in two sizes—a third or a half pound each. Steelhead Trout is in season all the year-round, and is found on the Pacific Coast. This species lives in the sea and ascends rivers to spawn. The Brown Trout, which grows to an immense size, is a European importation and is hatched for the markets. Cutthroat Trout is named for	From ¾ lb. to 20 lbs. Whole, fresh, steak, filet, smoked	Bake, boil, broil, steam, pan-fry, sauté, braise

* Fresh water. † Salt water.

GUIDE TO THE PURCHASE AND PREPARATION OF FISH [411]

NAME OF FISH SEASON TYPE: Fat or Lean	OTHER NAME (According to locality)	SPECIFICATIONS	SIZE and WEIGHT (average) MARKET UNIT	HOW TO COOK (Methods)
TROUT*,†— (*Continued*)	Yellowfin	the deep red color under the lower jaw. Average 4 pounds. It is a Pacific Coast fish found as far East as the Rockies. Dolly Warden Trout is a red-spotted fish, common in many streams and hatcheries. In beauty it matches the Brook Trout. Its color is brownish. On its sides are round, red and orange spots, on its back are similar but smaller spots. This species is also known as the Bull, Oregon Charr, Western Charr or Red-Spotted Trout, according to locality. Lake Trout is found in most large lakes of the north. It averages 5 pounds, but 45- to 50-pound specimens have been caught. This gray, light-spotted swimmer is a delicious food fish. It is also known as Gray, Salmon, Laker and Namaycush Trout by the Indians.		
TUNA or TUNNY† All year, either fresh, frozen or canned Fat	Horse-Mackerel, Great Albacore, Great, Yellowfin, Bluefin, Striped, Bonitos	The Bluefin Tuna is the most numerous and famous of the mackerel tribe. The flesh is highly valued for canning purposes. On the Pacific Coast it is called Tuna. The British call it Tunny; in New England and Nova Scotia it is the Horse-Mackerel. Color is dark blue-gray, with grayish sides and dusky dorsal fins. The Great Albacores are distinguished from the Tunas by the excessive length of the pectoral fin. Otherwise they are practically the same as the Bluefin. It is also called the "Chicken of the Sea." It is a Pacific Coast fish. The Yellowfin, caught in the Gulf Stream off Florida, differs from the Bluefin in having a	30–800 lbs. or more. Great Albacore: 15–20 lbs. Yellowfin: 20–175 lbs. Allison: 20–200 lbs. Bonito: 3 feet; weight (average): 12 lbs., sometimes 15 lbs. Fresh, steak, canned	Bake, boil, broil, pie, stew, croquettes, patties, casserole, loaf, scallop in shell, soufflé, cream, pan-fry, salad

* Fresh water.　　† Salt water.

GUIDE TO THE PURCHASE AND PREPARATION OF FISH [411]

NAME OF FISH SEASON TYPE: Fat or Lean	OTHER NAME (According to locality)	SPECIFICATIONS	SIZE and WEIGHT (average) MARKET UNIT	HOW TO COOK (Methods)
TUNA or TUNNY†— (*Continued*)		long pectoral fin that reaches as far back as the second dorsal. It is also called the Allison Tuna. Its top side is dark metallic blue, then purple and lilac; a stripe of golden yellow marks the side, and the belly is white. The Pacific yellowfin is a warm-weather fish found in the late summer off California and Mexico. All Tuna and related fish vary in color and the flesh may be white, pink or darkish tan when canned.		
TURBOT† All year when frozen, but fresh season from January to March Fat	Halibut, Window Pane, Greenland	The Turbot is frequently called Halibut, although it is smaller and of much more delicate flavor. It has a body of almost square proportions. This fish inhabits the rocky shores. It is superior in flavor to fish which inhabit muddy shores, and has a firmer and more delicate flesh. It is a member of the flounder family and is found on the Atlantic Coast from Maine to the Carolinas. It is a near relative of the valuable European Turbot, known from antiquity, but which is unknown in our waters. The Greenland, also called Greenland Halibut and Little Halibut, is abundant off the Coast of Greenland and Newfoundland. Both the Window Pane and the Greenland are exceedingly palatable, the flesh being firm, white and flaky, much less dry and more delicate than that of the common halibut. Color is yellowish-brown.	1–2 lbs., but as heavy as 25 lbs. Whole, fresh, filets, steak, pound	Same as flounder. Large ones may be boiled, braised, stewed. When used as steak, broiled or pan-fried
WEAK-FISH† Summer	Squeteague Sea Trout, Speckled,	This fish belongs to the Croaker family of which there are about 150 species. It ranks high as a	1½–8 lbs. Whole, fresh,	Bake, boil, broil,

* Fresh water. † Salt water.

GUIDE TO THE PURCHASE AND PREPARATION OF FISH   [411]

NAME OF FISH SEASON TYPE: Fat or Lean	OTHER NAME (According to locality)	SPECIFICATIONS	SIZE and WEIGHT (average) MARKET UNIT	HOW TO COOK (Methods)
WEAK-FISH†— (*Continued*) and fall Lean	Spotted, from New Jersey down to Virginia	food fish, the flesh being rich and easily torn, hence the popular name Weakfish. It is abundant in New England waters with an annual commercial catch reaching more than 15,-000,000 lbs. Color is silvery darker above and marked with many small irregular blotches. The noise made by this fish and by most members of the Croaker or Drum family has been variously described as "drumming," "snoring," "moaning" and "thunder-pumping." It is supposed to be produced by movement of air in the air-bladder when the abdomen vibrates.	steak, pound	stuff, stew
WHALE† All year Medium fat		Whale meat is as dark red as that of a steer and free from any fishy flavor. The body of the Whale resembles that of a land animal. It is, in fact, a mammal. It breathes from the lungs, (this being the reason why it cannot remain more than 15 minutes under water) and feeds its young with milk. The flesh of this fish is nourishing and many fishermen attribute their good health to eating Whale meat.	Maximum length 50 yds. Fresh, pound, steak, filets. Soon to be brined and smoked	Boil, bake, stew, grill, brochettes, loaf, hamburger, pie
WHITE-BAIT*·† Winter Lean	Silversides, Spearing, Fish of the Kings, Lake Silverside, Skipjack. Blanchaille is the French culinary name of this little fish	There are some 70 species of Whitebait, all having a silvery band along the side, almost transparent. In some lakes Whitebait is exceedingly abundant. Late in the fall, even after ice has begun to form around the edges of the lake, these little fishes come in immense schools along the shores. They are caught in fine fishnets and often a motley crew of	3 inches maximum By the lb., a lb. counting approximately 500 fish	Usually fried after being rolled in seasoned flour or dipped in batter

* Fresh water.   † Salt water.

GUIDE TO THE PURCHASE AND PREPARATION OF FISH [411]

NAME OF FISH SEASON TYPE: Fat or Lean	OTHER NAME (According to locality)	SPECIFICATIONS	SIZE and WEIGHT (average) MARKET UNIT	HOW TO COOK (Methods)
WHITE-BAIT*,†— (*Continued*)		other sea life is in the haul, so they need to be carefully picked and washed. They are usually cooked whole and a few at a time. They are eaten whole—head, tail, eyes and insides.		
WHITE-FISH* All year, except in winter Fat	Humpback, Bowback, Highback, Shad of Lake Champlain, Round. Also known as Frostfish in the Adirondack lakes; Pilotfish in Lake Champlain; Chivey in Maine; Blackjack in Lake Michigan; Poisson Blanc in many parts of New England and Canada; White Salmon in certain parts of the Great Lakes	This delicious fish is caught mostly in the Great Lakes. It is one of the most important group of fresh-water fish of North America. Its flesh is sweet, flaky and white. It is a compressed, oblong fish with a small head, mouth, and blunt snout, the color being white, hence its name. The Round Whitefish is similar to the common species but has a rather broad back, a dark bluish color above, and a silvery blue below. This species is known under many names, according to locality. The Rock Mountain Whitefish, trout-like in habit, lives in the western mountain lakes and streams from the Rockies to the Pacific and from Utah to British Columbia.	1½–20 lbs.; average: 3 lbs.; length: about 1 foot Fresh, smoked, brined, pound, filet	Bake, plain or stuffed, boil, broil, stew, plank, gefulte, Kosher, cakes, fritters
WHITING† Summer and fall, but all year when frozen Lean	Cigarette fish, when caught in early summer; Merlan in many parts of New England and Canada; New England	A Whiting has but one triangular bone, which is broad at the head end, tapering to a point at the tail. This bone is easily removed for cooking. Its flesh is snow-white, sweet, flaky and delicate when strictly fresh. This fish is one of the few which lends itself to every form of preparation, but it does need plenty of butter or margarine.	¾ lb. up to 2 lbs. Fresh, frozen, whole by the lb., smoked, brined	Bake, boil, stuff, fry, broil, au gratin, shirr, meunière

* Fresh water.   † Salt water.

GUIDE TO THE PURCHASE AND PREPARATION OF FISH [411]

NAME OF FISH SEASON TYPE: Fat or Lean	OTHER NAME (According to locality)	SPECIFICATIONS	SIZE and WEIGHT (average) MARKET UNIT	HOW TO COOK (Methods)
WHITING† –(Continued)	Hake; California; Harvest-fish in Norfolk, Va.; California Pompano in California. Sand-fish or Deep-water	For broiling, this fish should not be placed on a wire, but in a pan. The flesh is so delicate it invariably breaks. Color is silvery gray above, with bluish and bronze reflections, without spots. The Whiting is native to the Atlantic Ocean and Gulf of Mexico, being found from Chesapeake Bay as far South as Brazil. It is closely related to the cod family, with which it is frequently found. Among the differing characteristics is the absence of a barb on the lower jaw.		

* Fresh water.   † Salt water.

GUIDE TO THE PURCHASE AND PREPARATION OF SHELLFISH [411]

NAME OF SHELLFISH SEASON TYPE: Fat or Lean	OTHER NAME (According to locality)	SPECIFICATIONS	SIZE and WEIGHT (average) MARKET UNIT	HOW TO COOK (Methods)
ABALONE† All year Lean	Black, Rough, Grand Ear Shell, Rainbow, Aurora	This mollusk is an important export article. The shells furnish high grade mother-of-pearl. The muscular foot makes delicious soups, chowders and entrées. It is found on the coasts of Southern California. It has a thin, elongated oval shell. The outer surface is of a uniformly dull brownish color, faintly ridged with spiral undulations, crossed by smaller and close-set rounded ridges. Each hole on the shell's surface is elevated into a tubercle and is water-proof.	7–8 inches Fresh, salted, dried, canned	Same methods as for Crab

* Fresh water.   † Salt water.

GUIDE TO THE PURCHASE AND PREPARATION OF SHELLFISH [411]

NAME OF SHELLFISH SEASON TYPE: Fat or Lean	OTHER NAME (According to locality)	SPECIFICATIONS	SIZE and WEIGHT (average) MARKET UNIT	HOW TO COOK (Methods)
CLAMS† All year Lean	Hard-Shell, Common, Quatog, Quahaug, or Quohog in New England; Bucards or Tourteaux in certain parts of Canada and New England; Outside, Little Neck, Cherrystone, Sand, Surf, Rosy Razor, Sword Razor, Soft Razor, Grand Rock, Dweller, Oregon, Morton or Trading, Giant Callista, Tivela or Thick-shelled, Ribbed Carpet, Netted Carpet, Soft-shell, Giant Washington	The Hard-shell clam is abundant from Cape Cod to Florida, also in New Brunswick. It is the "luxury" clam—firm-textured and sweet, and the chief commercial clam on our east coast. It measures 3½ to 4 inches on reaching mature age of five. Little Neck clams—the tiniest specimens of Hard-shell clams —are taken when about a year or two of age, and about 1½ inches in length. The Cherrystone, of the same species, measures 3 inches in length after 2 or 3 years. The Sand clam is an important food mollusk found all along the Pacific Coast. In San Francisco its demand is extremely great. Surf clams, sometimes called Jumping clams, are one of the largest bivalves on the Atlantic Coast. The California species look like the Little Neck, being thin-shelled and flattened; measures from 2 to 3 inches. There are several of this species, namely, the Solid Surf, Beaked Surf and the Mattock Surf. The Rosy Razor is a smooth, pinkish-white, flattened, straight tube clam. Its flesh is considered a delicacy along the coast of Southern California. In flavor it is unsurpassed. The Sword Razor is the common long Razor of the east coast. The foot is thick and strong, enabling this mollusk to disappear into the sand. Found chiefly from New England southward. The Soft Razor is less appreciated, perhaps on account of its	Different sizes Fresh, dozen, quart, canned, shucked, pickled	Half-shell, cocktails, steam, chowders, bouillon, fritters, patties, stew, pies, devil, scallop, rarebit, casseroles, clambakes, and almost all methods employed for oysters.

* Fresh water.　　† Salt water.

GUIDE TO THE PURCHASE AND PREPARATION OF SHELLFISH   [411]

NAME OF SHELLFISH SEASON TYPE: Fat or Lean	OTHER NAME (According to locality)	SPECIFICATIONS	SIZE and WEIGHT (average) MARKET UNIT	HOW TO COOK (Methods)
CLAMS†— (*Continued*)		high price and scarcity. It is found south of Cape Cod. The Giant Rock, also known as the Dweller, Oregon or Vancouver clam, is a large edible clam of the Northwest. It has the general form of the eastern Hard-shell species, and is found in the Aleutian Islands and Monterey Bay. The Morton or Trading clam is extensively used for chowders, the young onces serving as Little Necks or Cherrystones. Very popular on the Florida Coast. The Giant Callista is found from Cape Hatteras to Texas. It is shaped and painted like a rainbow—blue, lilac or gray on a pale ground. It is especially abundant on the beach of Western Florida and is extensively used for chowders and cream soup. The Spotted Callista is oval, with a shiny surface; fawn-colored with broken radiating bands of violet-brown. Extensively used for chowders only. The Tivela, Thick-shelled or Three-angled clam is one of the finest as well as one of the largest California species with the flavor of the Surf clam. The Ribbed Carpet has a thin, pod-like shell-oval, radially ribbed, hence its name; often marked with chevrons of darker shades. Found all along the West Coast, especially north of San Francisco. The Netted Carpet is distinguished by the very fine crisscrossing of sharply chiseled lines on its valves and is found on the Pacific Coast.		

* Fresh water.   † Salt water.

GUIDE TO THE PURCHASE AND PREPARATION OF SHELLFISH [411]

NAME OF SHELLFISH SEASON TYPE: Fat or Lean	OTHER NAME (According to locality)	SPECIFICATIONS	SIZE and WEIGHT (average) MARKET UNIT	HOW TO COOK (Methods)
CLAMS†— (*Continued*)		GENERAL: Clam shells, when tightly closed, indicate that the shellfish are alive. They must be thoroughly scrubbed and washed in several changes of cold water. To open, pour boiling water over them and let them stand for a few minutes. Or, place them in a pan in a moderate oven for a few minutes. The Soft-shell or Long-necked clams are thinner, flatter and less round than the Hard-shells. Two types are known to the markets: The Steamers, which average 2½ to 3 inches in length, and a larger size called "In Shells," about 4 inches in length, usually used for stuffed clam dishes. The Giant Washington is the largest of all the surf clams and is found in large quantities on the Pacific Coast. It is oblong, rounded at both ends and is a noble and estimable shellfish, which beats any other clam yet discovered for chowders, soups and pies. It has almost the consistency of the oyster as well as its flavor.		
CRABS† Hard-shell, the year 'round; Soft-shell, the year 'round in Louisiana, spring and summer elsewhere Lean	Hard-shell, Eastern Hard, Sweet Winter, Blue, Fiddler, King or Giant, Kampfer's or Dungeness, Soft-shell, Buffalo, Milk-fed, Oyster, Pea or Spider,	Most Hard-shell crabs are popularly known as Blue crabs. They form the basis of the crab meat industry, coming principally from Louisiana, Florida, Georgia, Maryland, Virginia, North Carolina, and particularly Chesapeake Bay. Those that migrate to fresh waters are called Sweet Water crabs. The Fiddler crabs are abundant in Tampa and Key West, Fla. They travel in large	By the dozen alive; by the lb. when canned or frozen; by the can when smoked or in oil	Boil, grill, bake, roast, au gratin, Newburg, casserole, soufflé, cakes, Maryland, devil, croustades, à la Dewey, imperial,

* Fresh water.   † Salt water.

GUIDE TO THE PURCHASE AND PREPARATION OF SHELLFISH　　　[411]

NAME OF SHELLFISH SEASON TYPE: Fat or Lean	OTHER NAME (According to locality)	SPECIFICATIONS	SIZE and WEIGHT (average) MARKET UNIT	HOW TO COOK (Methods)
CRABS†— (*Continued*)	Sand, Stone or Moro	schools, often numbering thousands. Soft-shell crabs are highly perishable and must be handled with care. In reality they are the Hard-shell or the Blue, caught while changing their shells. The King, Giant or Dungeness, found on the Pacific Coast, resembles the Hard-shell species, but is about four times as large. Oyster crabs are expensive and only Father Neptune himself would know how many there are to the pound. These pigmies are soft-shelled and come from Maryland and Virginia cape waters. This little crab is a "sponger" with no home of his own. He takes shelter with the oyster. The Stone or Moro is a native of the South Atlantic from Carolina to Florida and farther south. The claws are sold ice-packed, a pair costing 60 cents and up; a whole crab about 80 cents. The Hermit is known as the fighting crab. It is of the hard-shell type with its back denuded and concealed in a large empty shell which it drags along.		in pies, scallop, pancakes, Louisiana, curry, patty shells, fried, Meunière, ravigotte, croquettes, cutlets, loaf, mousse, aspic, chowder, bisque, cream soup
FROGS* and Land. May to end of August in fresh state. All year round for frozen,	Giant or Jug o'Rum; Green; Common spotted Leopard or Bull; Grenouilles in some parts of	Frog meat is generally snowy white. Often six pairs of legs will weigh a pound. The Northern Bull has grayish meat. The Grass frog, found in Vermont, is a small but delicate morsel. The frog is a vertebrate of the amphibian class.	4–6 pairs of legs to the pound Pair, dozen	Broil, sauté, bake, au gratin, in cream, curry, stew, Provençale Swedish method,

* Fresh water.　　† Salt water.

GUIDE TO THE PURCHASE AND PREPARATION OF SHELLFISH [411]

NAME OF SHELLFISH SEASON TYPE: Fat or Lean	OTHER NAME (According to locality)	SPECIFICATIONS	SIZE and WEIGHT (average) MARKET UNIT	HOW TO COOK (Methods)
FROGS†— (Continued) Canned or Cooked Lean	Louisiana, New England and Canada; Grass			omelet, poulette, fricassée, fry, chowder, cream soup
LOBSTER‡ Live all year Lean	Cardinal of the Sea, Homard in Louisiana, New England and Canada	Lobsters are graded in 3 sizes. The smallest are the "chicken," averaging 1 lb. each. Mediums are of two sizes, one called "quarters" which average 1¼ to 2 lbs. Oversize lobsters run 2½ to 4 lbs. The shells of freshly caught lobsters are brownish green. Those trapped on sandy bottoms have a tinge of red. Lobsters are all shallow water crustaceans.	See "Specifications" Whole, pound, canned, smoked, frozen	Bake, broil, boil, stew, cakes, rarebit, Ravigotte, shortcake, thermidor, stuff, à la Newburg, mousse, curried, à l'Améri-caine, pie, patty shells, bouilla-baisse, chowder, bisque, cream soup
MUSSELS* Spring and Summer Lean	Bouchots or Moules in certain parts of New England and Canada. Horse, Pleated Horse	An old Indian sea food greatly neglected until a decade ago, they are palatable, nutritious, inexpensive. They are found in great masses, closely crowded together, adhering to rocks, sand and to one another by the very tough byssus. Found in shallow sea water from New Brunswick to North Carolina. The shell, black on the outside and pearly inside, is oblong. HOW TO COOK AND PRE-PARE MUSSELS: Scrape with a knife, removing the seaweed which may adhere to them. Rinse in several changes of cold water, rejecting those which are open. Place in a large kettle with finely chopped	3 inches long Bushels, fresh, canned, pickled, smoked	Half-shell (raw), Marinière, chowder, stew, bordelaise, Parisienne, fritters, poulette, patties, bonne femme, cream, creole, stuff, devil, broil

* Fresh-water mussels are seldom eaten.
† Fresh water.   ‡ Salt water.

GUIDE TO THE PURCHASE AND PREPARATION OF SHELLFISH [411

NAME OF SHELLFISH SEASON TYPE: Fat or Lean	OTHER NAME (According to locality)	SPECIFICATIONS	SIZE and WEIGHT (average) MARKET UNIT	HOW T⦁ COOK (Method⦁
MUSSELS* —(Continued)		onions, a small bunch of tied-up parsley, thyme and bay leaves. Add some freshly crushed peppercorns and moisten with white wine, barely covering. Cover the kettle hermetically and set on a hot fire. A few minutes' cooking is sufficient to open the shells. Remove kettle from fire. Shell or not, according to recipe. The proper way to eat cooked mussels in the shell is by dipping an empty shell into one containing food—using it as a spoon. Each guest should have an extra plate on which to deposit the empty shells.		
OYSTERS‡ All year when shucked and canned. From September to May 15, when on the shell Lean.	Mattituck, Blue Point, Gardner Island, Oyster Bay, Peconic, Lynnhaven, Seawanhaka, Bay Salts, Seapure, Robbins Island and Greenport in Long Island; Cape Cod in New England; Chincoteague in Virginia; Chesapeake in Maryland; Coon in Florida; Cove and Virginia in Chesapeake Bay; Lurid on the	The oyster grows from a speck almost invisible to the eye to a succulent full-sized adult in from two to four years. Its age may be determined from the layers making up its shell—one layer for each year. As they appear in the market, these succulent bivalves vary in name as well as size, color, and flavor. The "beard," which certain oyster recipes require to be removed, is the gills. The "heart," so-called, is the adductor muscle. The Coon, or "Tree Oyster," is found in southern Florida. It is small and delicious. The Thorny oyster, with its irregular shell and spiny leaf-like scales, was admired and eaten by the early Greeks long before most shell families had been discovered. The number of oysters to a pint depends upon size. A gallon of small oysters numbers	Fresh, dozen, peck, bushel, barrel, quart minced, canned, smoked	On the h⦁ shell, pla⦁ or cockta⦁ Steam, chowders⦁ bouillon, soups, fritters, patties, stew, pies, devil, scallop, rarebit, casseroles⦁ stuff, clambake⦁

* Fresh-water mussels are seldom eaten.
† Fresh water.   ‡ Salt water.

GUIDE TO THE PURCHASE AND   [411]
PREPARATION OF SHELLFISH

NAME OF SHELLFISH SEASON TYPE: Fat or Lean	OTHER NAME (According to locality)	SPECIFICATIONS	SIZE and WEIGHT (average) MARKET UNIT	HOW TO COOK (Methods)
OYSTERS† (Continued)	Pacific Coast from Puget Sound to California; Hammer in China and Philippine Islands	240, medium-size, 200, and large 170. The oyster feeds on aquatic plants, and, during the spawning season, on its own eggs and fry. Those found on the Atlantic Coast are storage houses of iron, copper and manganese. They contain generous quantities of Vitamins A, B, C and D. However, strange as it may seem, the oyster, famous for its iodine content, which is supposed to aid goiter sufferers, has not as much iodine as the clam. All the oysters sold in our markets are farmed under Government supervision. Buying oysters by the barrel is most economical. But when the barrel comes in, have a few handfuls of corn meal ready to throw on top and wash it down with half a pail of cold water in which a handful of rock salt has been dissolved. This will have a remarkable result in removing that haggard look that an oyster gets after travel, because oysters obtain their food by filtering vast quantities of water for the minute organisms in it. An oyster may strain as much as 26 quarts an hour through its gills.		
SCALLOPS† year round en canned frozen. ing, fall l winter en fresh. an	Bay, Deep Sea or Giant, Quin, Petoncles or Pelerines in certain parts of New England and Canada.	The Beaming is the most common of the species found on the Atlantic Coast. Tons are dredged from the Jersey Banks annually, and from the New England shores down to Cape Hatteras. The Deep Sea variety is coarser in fiber but high in food value. They are found in deep cold waters. They are	Deep Sea: 2–3 inches. Bay: 1–2 inches Fresh, frozen, canned, brined	Cocktail, broil, fry, sauté, mince, stew, scramble, casserole, raw marinated,

* Fresh water.   † Salt water.

GUIDE TO THE PURCHASE AND   [411
PREPARATION OF SHELLFISH

NAME OF SHELLFISH SEASON TYPE: Fat or Lean	OTHER NAME (According to locality)	SPECIFICATIONS	SIZE and WEIGHT (average) MARKET UNIT	HOW T(COOK (Method
SCALLOPS† —(Continued)	Pilgrim, Beaming, Coquilles St. Jacques in French restaurants and large hotels	usually halved or quartered against the grain before cooking. The Bay is found in from 2 to 15 feet of sea water along the shores throughout the estuaries of Long Island Sound, N.Y., up to the Coast of Cape Cod, Nantucket and Martha's Vineyard. They mature in 2 years and reproduce by millions. They are the aristocrats of the species: unsurpassed for table use. In both the Deep Sea and Bay species only the great muscle, otherwise known as the eye or heart of the bivalve, is kept for table use. The rest of the soft part, which in an oyster would be the belly, is considered non-edible and is discarded. Like other tender fish and shellfish, the scallop does not tolerate high temperature or overcooking without becoming tough and dry.		brochette scallop, bake, devil, Newburg mornay, in shells, Coquilles St. Jacqu curry, Provença Meunière Louisiane
SEA URCHINS† Winter Lean	Aristotle's Lantern, Sea Eggs, Echinus, Sea-Chestnuts, Spiny Bristles, Orange Caviar of the Sea, Sea-hedge-hog, Oursins in certain parts of Louisiana, New England and Canada	When opened, sea urchins yield about $\frac{1}{4}$ cup each of orange-colored roe, which has a flavor that is a cross between an oyster, a mussel and a lobster. They are served like oysters: on the half-shell for the first course averaging six halves to a plate, the top of the shell being removed to expose the yellow roe. They are seasoned with lemon juice, Worcestershire, horseradish or catsup.	Bushel	Same as oysters
SHRIMPS*'† Spring and	Common, Grooved,	Closely allied to the crayfish and prawns; belong to the	Large: (Jumbo or	Boil, fry,

* Fresh water.   † Salt water.

GUIDE TO THE PURCHASE AND [411]
PREPARATION OF SHELLFISH

NAME OF SHELLFISH SEASON TYPE: Fat or Lean	OTHER NAME (According to locality)	SPECIFICATIONS	SIZE and WEIGHT (average) MARKET UNIT	HOW TO COOK (Methods)
SHRIMPS*·† (Continued) Summer. July first to October first Fresh Ice; All year and when canned. Lean	Sea Bob, Lake Shrimps of Lake Pont-Chartrain in Louisiana (fresh water); Bouquets and Crevettes in certain parts of Louisiana, New England and Canada; Jumbo	Carididae family. Of elongated form, tapering and arched as if hunchbacked, the whole structure is delicate, almost translucent, colors are such that the shrimp may escape observation, whether resting on a sandy bottom or swimming. The quick darting movements of these little shellfish betray them to one who looks attentively into a pool of water left by the tide. When alarmed, they bury themselves in the sand by a peculiar movement of the fanlike fin. Shrimps are found abundantly in America, off the Atlantic and Pacific Seaboards, wherever the bottom is sandy. Their natural color tint is greenish-gray, speckled with brown. Swarming in untold millions, they form a considerable part of the food of the flatfish and other shallow water species. Are used mainly for garnishing, salads, hors d'oeuvres and the like, but may be prepared in many delicious ways.	Bouquet) 2 inches. Medium: 1½ inches. Small: 1 inch Pound, fresh, dozen, bushel, canned, in brine	à la Newburg, curry, à la Creole, brochette, in pies, jellied, au gumbo, sour cream, divers wines, cold or hot, fritters, seafood cocktail, salad, garnishing

* Fresh water.   † Salt water.

DO dip the fish in salted milk, then in crumbs or fine corn meal, then you have that "fish fry," and see the difference.

DO keep frozen fish frozen until just before it is to be used, as it deteriorates rapidly after thawing. One may thaw it before cooking or let it thaw as it cooks, depending on preference. But, when cooking without thawing, a slightly longer time should be allowed. Room temperature is best if the fish is thawed before cooking—then it should be cooked immediately.

DO rub lemon juice over fish before broiling, baking or boiling it. This adds to the flavor, keeps the fish a good color and helps in preventing it from falling apart.

DO cover your fingers with salt when cleaning fish. You'll find them easier to handle.

DO add a little vinegar to the water when boiling fish. This will prevent fish from separating. Lemon juice will act in the same way.

DO poke a raw fish to make certain it is fresh. If the flesh springs back, all is well; if a dent remains, the fish is stale.

DO add a tablespoon of lemon juice, sherry wine or tarragon vinegar to the egg in which fish is dipped before frying.

DO shake a little salt into the fat in which fish is to be pan-fried, and the fish will have a better flavor.

DO ask your fish dealer not to cut off the top and bottom fins as is customary when buying fish. These are attached to tiny bones and, if left on, provide an easy means of removing these bones after the fish is cooked.

DO thoroughly dry fish for frying crisp; sprinkle both sides with plenty of seasoned flour and plunge it into boiling fat. Upon that depends the crispness and brownness.

DON'T leave fish, except salt fish, soaking in water; it extracts the flavor and makes the fish flabby.

DON'T skimp on the breading and don't skimp on the quality of fish when preparing fish cutlets, fish cakes or fish croquettes.

DON'T overcook smoked fish. It is already cooked, you know, and too much added heat destroys all the flavor.

BOUILLABAISSE MARSEILLAISE STYLE [412]

Author's Note. No wine or liquor enters into the concoction of this delightful chowder or rather stew, whatever it may be called, which was first prepared in Marseilles, France. The original recipe calls for 12 different kinds of fish, the list of which follows with its corresponding name in English between parentheses, and the name of the fish which may be substituted for those not available in any part of America.

RASCASSE (unknown in America). Sea Bass may be substituted.

SARD (unknown in America). Substitute Haddock or Codfish.

LANGOUSTE (Spiny Lobster).

GRONDIN (Red Gurnard).

GALIENTE (unknown in America) Substitute Grouper.

DORADE (Dory, also sometimes called John Dory).

BAUDROIE (Frog-fish, also sometimes called Sea-Devil).

CONGRE (Conger, Conger Eel).

TURBOT (Turbot, often erroneously called Halibut; Turbotin, a young Turbot).

MERLAM (Whiting).

FIELAN (unknown in America). Small eel may be used.

ROUQUIER (unknown in America). Eel may be used.

Assuming you have all the necessary fish or substitutes, which must be of firm flesh, the procedure is as follows:

Take altogether about 6 pounds of the above-mentioned fish or their substitutes in approximately equal amounts for each variety. Cut the large fish into pieces, leave the small ones whole. Place in a kettle a generous ½ cup of good olive oil and add to it 4 ounces (½ cup) of minced onion, 2 ounces (⅓ cup) chopped fine leeks (white part only), 2 medium-sized fresh tomatoes (pressed, peeled, and slightly crushed), 4 whole cloves of garlic (crushed), 1 teaspoon of finely chopped parsley, 1 generous pinch of saffron (drugstore), 1 bay leaf, 1 small sprig of sarriette (sweet savory, common marum savory, found in the field or drugstore), 1 pinch of the top of fresh fennel, salt and pepper to taste.

Place all the above ingredients in the kettle (with the exception of the whiting and red gurnard, which, being very tender, should be added when the bouillabaisse has been boiled from 8 to 10 minutes). Pour in sufficient cold water to cover the fish; season with salt and pepper to taste and let cook on a hot fire or flame for 12 to 15 minutes. *The bouillabaisse is ready*.

Have ready some slices of plain bread, not toasted or fried, but plain bread, on a hot deep platter, preferably round; pour the liquid over these slices and, on another platter, arrange the fish, surrounding the whole with pieces of langouste or spiny lobster. This recipe is the one used in Marseilles where the writer has been a Chef; is identical to that followed by Maître Escoffier; exactly the same as the one given by Maître Caillat and identical to the one given by Maurice Graillot, Chef of the Touring Club of France, and also to the formula of Urbain Dubois, onetime Chef to the former King of Prussia, who became the Kaiser.

> *Horace, had you tasted it,*
> *Far from speaking ill of it,*
> *You would have been better adorned*
> *And might have been on friendly terms*
> *With a chain of garlic instead of laurel.*
> *—Fabre*

Most bouillabaisse met in America is simply a pale reflection of the above, which, according to gourmets, is an immortal dish which may be imitated, but never equalled.

BAKED BLUEFISH CREOLE   [413]

Clean a 4–4½ pound bluefish. Rub with good cooking oil and season with mixed salt and pepper. Lay the fish in a generously buttered baking pan, add ½ cup of tomato juice and sprinkle 1 tablespoon of finely chopped onion over the fish. Bake in a moderate oven (350° F.) for

30 minutes, basting occasionally. Remove from the oven, pour 2½ cups of Creole Sauce (Nos. 1041–42) over the fish; sprinkle ¾ cup of buttered bread crumbs over the entire surface and brown under the flame of the broiling oven. Serve at once with a side dish of plain boiled potatoes.

It is suspected that one of the major reasons carp failed to become more popular among certain cooks lay in our disregard of sauces. Carp is a fish which can't be just thrown in a pan and fried. To achieve full perfection of flavor, it must be complemented with a savory sauce.

BAKED BREADED CARP   [414]

Wash and dry thoroughly one carp weighing 4 pounds; cut into 6 slices; dip slices in 1 cup of sifted dry bread crumbs, seasoned with 1 tablespoon of paprika, 1 teaspoon of salt, and a few grains of cayenne pepper, coating both sides. Heat 3 or 4 tablespoons of olive oil in a baking pan; put in the breaded pieces of carp, and bake in a moderate oven (350° F.) until tender or about 40 minutes, turning to brown both sides. Serve hot or cold. If served cold, serve a side dish of Tartare Sauce (Nos. 1128–29) and, if served hot, serve with a side dish of Egg Sauce (Nos. 1051–52).

Eating shad was an undercover job in seventeenth-century New England. Because it was considered a disgrace to eat shad, many colonists who caught them in New England rivers ate them secretly in their homes.

BAKED SHAD ROUENNAISE   [415]

Leave head and tail on one shad of about 4 pounds; clean and dry well, and stuff with the following stuffing:

Put through food chopper ½ cup of cooked, shelled shrimps, together with ½ cup of soft bread crumbs, 1 teaspoon each of chopped parsley, chives, onion and green pepper, ⅓ teaspoon of powdered tarragon leaves, salt, pepper, thyme and mace to taste. Sew up the opening. Place the fish in a baking pan, add 1 large bay leaf, 3 thin slices of onion, 4 sprigs of parsley, a small sprig of green celery leaves, 6 peppercorns; pour over 1 cup of dry white wine and add ¼ cup of butter. Cover the pan and bake in a moderate oven for 35 minutes. Uncover, and continue baking for 10 minutes longer, basting frequently with the liquid in the pan. Dress the fish on a platter, strain the liquid in the pan into a clean saucepan, bring to a boil, and let the liquid reduce to about ¼ cup. Add 1 cup of fish stock (No. 182), again bring to a boil and let boil up 2 or 3 times; remove from the fire and beat in, one at a time, 3 egg yolks, beating well after each addition. Taste for seasoning, and strain the sauce into a sauceboat, serving fish and sauce separately with a side dish of small potato balls rolled in butter, then in finely chopped parsley.

BAKED STUFFED CODFISH RHODE ISLAND STYLE [416]

Remove the head and tail, wash and dry a 4½-pound cod. Fry very gently without browning in 2 tablespoons of butter 2 stalks of celery and 1 medium-sized onion both finely chopped add 2 tablespoons each of finely chopped parsley and green celery leaves, and cook 3 or 4 minutes longer, stirring frequently. Now stir in ½ cup of scalded milk, alternately with 2 cups of bread crumbs, and season to taste with salt, pepper and thyme. Remove from the heat, cool slightly, and add 2 fresh eggs, slightly beaten and 2 dozen small, raw oysters. Stuff the fish, tie waxed paper around neck to hold stuffing, and sew up the opening. Place in a large baking pan, add 1 bay leaf, 4 thin slices of onion, 5 or 6 sprigs of parsley, and 2 whole cloves. Pour in ½ cup of fish stock, made as indicated for No. 182, and bake in a moderate oven (350° F.) for 1 hour, basting frequently with the liquid from the pan. Serve with Onion Cream sauce, made with part of the strained liquid from the pan and milk (No. 258) and a side dish of Potato Scallop (No. 1427).

BAKED SHAD ROE PLANTATION [417]
Also called "Charcutière"

Drop 2 pairs of large shad roe or 4 pairs of small shad roe into a white wine court-bouillon (No. 1037) and let simmer for 5 minutes. Drain and let cool. Separate the roes. Beat 1 large egg slightly and add ½ teaspoon of onion juice, ½ teaspoon of dry mustard, salt, white pepper and a dash of freshly grated nutmeg; brush roe with this mixture and press a cover of sausage meat onto the roe. Brush again with egg mixture; place in a shallow pan, add 1 bay leaf, 3 or 4 thin slices of onion, 1 blade of garlic, and 1 whole clove; pour over ½ cup of dry white wine, mixed with 1 tablespoon of tomato paste, and bake for 25–30 minutes in a moderate oven (350° F.) or until slightly browned, basting occasionally. Transfer the roes to a hot platter; strain the sauce into a clean saucepan; remove excess fat, bring to a boil, and stir in ½ cup of scalded heavy cream, mixing well. Taste for seasoning, then beat in 2 egg yolks, slightly beaten. Heat well, but do not boil, and pour over the roes. Garnish with parsley and lemon quarters and serve with a side dish of French fried potatoes.

Shad has two kinds of meat—white and dark meat. The white meat is on top, dark meat at bottom. In shad the bones are in dark meat. If cooked with dark meat exposed to fire, be it broiled on overhead gas broiler or underneath in pan, fried or baked, the thousands of bones will stick to the dark meat because it's cooked more and the top part, filets we call them, clean off the bones in a jiffy! So cook the dark meat five minutes more, or cover the white part of the shad with a buttered paper and your shad is perfectly cooked and not one single bone in it.

BAKED PLANKED SHAD SHERRY   [418]
NETHERLAND

Select a shad weighing 4 pounds; wash, scrape well to remove scales, working from tail toward the head. Wash the fish quickly; dry, split the underside; draw; do not cut the fins. Wash again carefully both inside and outside; rub the fish with sherry, then with mixed salt, pepper, powdered thyme and nutmeg to taste, and stuff lightly with the following stuffing:

Stuffing. Put through food chopper 1 cup of cooked Finnan Haddie, carefully skinned and boned. Add 2 cups of soft bread crumbs, 3 tablespoons of melted butter, ¼ cup each of finely chopped parsley and green celery leaves, 1½ teaspoons of grated onion, salt and pepper to taste, a dash each of nutmeg, thyme and mace, and enough dry white wine to make the stuffing pack readily.

Sew the opening loosely. Place on a generously oiled baking sheet, the sheet placed in a shallow pan large enough to catch the drippings, and bake in a moderate oven (375° F.), allowing 15 to 20 minutes per pound, and basting every 10 minutes with melted butter and Pique Seasoning in equal parts. Remove from oven; place baking sheet on an oblong plank, previously heated; garnish with small bouquets of cooked vegetables, such as buttered string beans, glazed small white onions, asparagus tips, the tips covered with Hollandaise sauce (No. 1062), small grilled mushroom caps, sautéed in butter and sprinkled with chopped chives, and any other desired cooked vegetables. Using a pastry bag, force all around the edge of the plank a narrow edge of Duchesse Potatoes (No. 1419—Variation), sprinkle with paprika and serve at once,

BRANDADE DE MORUE I   [419]
Codfish Scramble (Salt Cod Style)

Do not judge a Brandade de Morue by its recipe, or by any praises that may be written or sung, for it appears to be among the simplest of fish delicacies prepared by provincial French cooks and housewives. Yet it is made at the cost of infinite pains and devoted care, and today it ranks, with the more esoteric of bons vivants, as a chef-d'oeuvre of the Continental cuisine.

Though codfish is peculiarly exalted in the New England tradition.

it is commonplace and mildly despised in other sections of this land; but in Continental Europe both fresh and salt cod are valued for certain qualities of flavor that are not found in other fish. The illustrious Escoffier, creator of magic sauces and chef extraordinary to emperors, wrote an extensive monograph on the morue—codfish to us—and included three master recipes for brandade de morue. Now the person to whom an omelet is just so many broken eggs, and a primrose by the river's brim is just a yellow primrose, would be unlikely to regard a brandade de morue as anything more than a spot of creamed codfish on toast; but poets, novelists and dramatists of our day have celebrated brandade de morue in lyric measures and sounding prose, immortalizing French cooks and kitchens in its name, and you owe it to yourself and your friends to make at least one brandade, whether you ever liked codfish or not.

Most of the accepted authorities on the brandade recommend the dry salt cod, though Escoffier gave recipes for both salt and fresh.

A 2-pound piece of the salt fish is soaked, skin side up, in several changes of cold water for 24 hours, and then simmered very gently in water at the boiling point for 30 minutes. Drain it and remove all bones, then shred the fish from the skin. The French cook uses the familiar European mortar and pestle to reduce the fish meat to a smooth paste, but American cooks can do fairly well with a heavy bowl of crockery or wood, and a fork and wooden spoon. After every shred is beaten to a mere pulp, put the fish in a double boiler and keep it hot on the fire. A chafing dish is just the thing for a brandade, serving the purpose of a French bain-marie, but if you have neither, be satisfied with the double boiler.

Stirring the fish with a wooden spoon, beat into it the juice of half a lemon (about 1 tablespoon); then add 5 tablespoons of fine olive oil, slightly warmed, dropping it slowly from the spoon (as for mayonnaise), and never cease stirring till you have blended it smoothly with the fish. In the same manner, add 5 tablespoons of warm (not boiling) heavy cream, then a level tablespoon of very finely minced parsley, 1/4 teaspoon (scant) of white pepper and a dash of cayenne. This, as it stands, soft, smooth and creamy, is a typical brandade de morue ready to serve on triangles of crisp toast or with croutons of rich puff paste; but the exalted masters of the French cuisine would never let it pass without some extra touches of elegance and refinement. Escoffier suggested truffles, and probably would have added them in julienne or matchstick-like strips, glistening black on the golden cream mound with a border of crisp, curled parsley and fluted crescents of puff paste. His recipe for brandade de morue ménagère, or home style, is much like the foregoing one, with the addition of smooth mashed potatoes, which make the dish a little more bland, with the piquant tang of the morue a little less pronounced. He wrote in the grand manner of genius, addressing an audience of the elect and scorning trifles like weights and measures; so he recommended *"muscade et une pointe d'ail,"* meaning a mere pinch of freshly grated nutmeg, and of garlic only a speck, a touch. Garlic is hazardous in any delicate mixture, and there is quite enough of it if a split clove is rubbed once around the pan or bowl before the stirring begins.

BRANDADE DE MORUE II   [420]
Codfish Scramble (Fresh Cod Style)

For a brandade of fresh codfish, a boneless filet of fresh cod should be poached (simmered) in a white wine court-bouillon (No. 1037) for 25 or 30 minutes. The rest of the process is the same as that for the salt cod.

Brandade de Morue is not startling, not sensational, but there is about the carefully made dish an exquisite delicacy, a subtle piquancy, which stirs the critical gourmet to glowing enthusiasm; and even the satiated cocktail-and-snack addicts will admit that they have tasted something unusual and a little mystifying, which is very easy to prepare at home.

Virginia shares with New Orleans the distinction of being named in a Harlem vending song. Thus the clam man lifts his voice:

> *"In Virginny we goes clammin'—*
> *We goes clammin' ev'y night—*
> *An' de water lays dere still lak,*
> *Lawd, a mighty purty sight!*
>
> *Clams an' oysters fo' de takin',*
> *An we gits 'em ev'y one;*
> *Twell de sun comes up ashinin'*
> *An' our clammin' she am done.*
> *Ho! Clabmmmmmmms!*
> *Ho! Clabmmmmmmms!"*

Some songs die out as trade languishes, but others promptly arise to take their places. So long as there are curb markets in Harlem, and a spirited, joyous race to buy at them, the push-cart men of the section undoubtedly will continue to contribute to the unique street cries of America.

CANADIAN CLAM PIE   [421]

Cook ¼ pound of salt pork, cut into small cubes, together with 2 medium-sized onions, chopped, and 3 small carrots, cubed small, in a saucepan for about 7 or 8 minutes, stirring frequently, over a gentle flame. Stir in 1 cup of hot fish stock (No. 182), and continue cooking gently until carrot cubes are nearly done, then add 4 medium-sized potatoes, cubed small, 2 cups of clam juice, 1 small bouquet garni, composed of 1 bay leaf, 1 sprig of thyme and 7 or 8 sprigs of fresh parsley, tied together with white kitchen thread, and 1 whole clove. When potatoes are nearly done, stir in 2 dozen hard shell clams, cut into small pieces, and continue cooking gently for 10 minutes longer. Mix ⅓ cup of cold water and 2 tablespoons of flour until smooth, then add salt and pepper to taste. Gradually stir this into the pie, filling in the pan, and cook 5 minutes longer, stirring occasionally. Discard the bouquet garni, taste for seasoning, stir in ¾ cup of cooked or canned peas, well drained, and turn mixture into a casserole. Cover with your favorite biscuit dough recipe, cutting slits in several place for escape of steam, and bake in a hot oven (400° F.) until brown, or about 25 to 30 minutes. Serve at once.

CARP IN RED WINE AMERICAN STYLE [422]

Brown ⅛ pound of bacon cut into small pieces, in a large heavy kettle; stir in 2 tablespoons of flour previously kneaded with 1 generous tablespoon of butter, mixing well. Add an inch piece of scraped parsley root, 1 small piece of celery root, 7 or 8 peppercorns, gently bruised, 2 whole cloves, 1 large bay leaf and 3 slices of lemon. Sprinkle a 4-pound, cleaned carp with mixed salt and pepper to taste; place in the kettle; pour in 2 cups of hot water and 1 cup of fish stock (No. 182); bring slowly to a boil, immediately lower the flame and let simmer very, very gently for 15 minutes. Then stir in 2 cups of red wine and continue simmering until the flesh leaves the bones, or about 1 hour. Serve on a large, heated platter; strain the gravy through fine cheesecloth into a saucepan; heat to the boiling point, taste for seasoning, then stir in 1 cup of thinly sliced fresh mushrooms, previously cooked in a little butter and pour this gravy over the fish. Garnish with parsley and lemon quarters and serve at once, with a side dish of small potato balls, cooked in salted water and well drained.

CLAMS CASINO [423]

Purchase medium-sized cherrystone clams and have them opened on the half shell. Allow 6 or 8 to each portion. Arrange carefully picked clams on the half shell in a shallow baking pan which has been prepared with a layer of rock salt. Imbed the clams firmly in the rock salt, as this will steady them while cooking. Season with very little salt, a speck of cayenne pepper and paprika. To each clam add a tiny pinch of very finely chopped green pepper, a tiny pinch of very finely chopped red pimiento and a piece of sliced raw bacon, cut the same size as the clam.

Broil under moderate flame of the broiling oven until bacon is cooked. Bacon will cook first, so, when both sides are broiled, remove it to a warm dish while clams and peppers cook 5 to 6 minutes longer. Serve in the shells and garnish each clam with the small piece of grilled bacon, a tiny sprig of parsley and section of lemon, and a side dish of fresh brown bread and butterfinger sandwiches.

Clams contain more protein, carbohydrates and minerals than the oyster and you know how highly the oyster rates, dietetically speaking. It is believed that the clam, like the oyster, contains most of the essential vitamins, A, B, C, D and G. Clams are high in iron, copper, phosphorus, and calcium—and high in the American gourmet's regard.

CLAMS EPICURE [424]

This dish, appropriate for luncheon or after-theatre supper, is usually served in a chafing dish with Melba Toast (No. 214) on the side.

Cook 1 cup of peeled and sliced fresh mushroom caps in ¼ pound of sweet butter for 3 or 4 minutes, or until tender over a gentle flame, stirring frequently with a wooden spoon, then stir in 2 cups of scalded, sweet, rich cream, mixing well. Into this put 6 soft-shell crabs that have been shelled, cleaned, cut in two and sautéed in butter for 2 short minutes, over a bright flame. Add a dozen soft clams, that also have been carefully picked of any pieces of shell and sautéed in a little butter, then 2 generous tablespoons of good sherry wine. Mix all thoroughly, then put in the yolks of 2 eggs that have been slightly beaten with 1 tablespoon of sweet cream. Season to taste with salt, white pepper and a dash of nutmeg. Do not actually boil and do not stir after putting in the egg yolks. To give the necessary motion, shake the dish when taking it from the fire. Serve in a chafing dish with Melba Toast (No. 214) on the side.

> Happy as a clam, sez you—
> It surely gives me jitters,
> To think my happiness will end
> On a blue plate full of fritters.

CLAM FRITTERS [425]

For 6 servings, wash 3 dozen soft clams and remove the necks. Chop bellies into small pieces. Beat 4 eggs thoroughly. Sift ¾ cup of flour together with 1 tablespoon of baking powder and ½ teaspoon salt, mix in 1 tablespoon each of finely chopped parsley and chives, then add to beaten eggs. Should batter be too stiff, stir in a little milk. Combine with the chopped clams, shape into small cakes or drop from teaspoon (or tablespoon, if large fritters are desired) into hot deep fat. Serve with bacon, if desired, also a side dish of Tartare Sauce (Nos. 1128–29) and lemon quarters.

CLAM SOUFFLE CLUB STYLE [426]

Heat to the boiling point 1 cup of clam juice, previously strained through fine cheesecloth, together with 1 cup of undiluted evaporated milk, 1 large bay leaf, 4 thin slices of onion, 1 whole clove and 3 or 4 sprigs of parsley. Strain and keep hot. Heat ¼ cup of butter; stir in 3 tablespoons of flour, and when well blended, blend in the hot strained clam juice and milk mixture, stirring constantly, until mixture begins to bubble. Remove from the fire and beat in 4 egg yolks, beaten with 1 tablespoon of Pique Seasoning, beating briskly till thoroughly blended. Then stir in 1 cup of finely ground clams, previously carefully picked of any bits of shells, and necks removed and discarded. Cool. When quite cold, fold in 4 egg whites, stiffly beaten with a few grains each of salt, cayenne and nutmeg. Turn preparation into a generously buttered soufflé dish, then sprinkled with 2 tablespoons of finely minced chives, and bake in a hot oven (400° F.) for 25 to 30 minutes, or until soufflé is well popped and raised and top is delicately brown. Serve at once. You may bake this soufflé in individual ramekins or casseroles, if desired.

CODFISH BALLS MOTHER'S WAY [427]

Place ¾ pound of salt codfish in a bowl and rinse in cold water several times. Then, let stand in cold water, changing several times, for 25 to 30 minutes. Drain. Place the fish in a saucepan with 1 quart of cold water; cover; slowly, very slowly, bring to the boiling point and let simmer gently for 25 minutes. Drain well, and pick, shred or chop until fluffy; no small pieces should be overlooked. Add to the fish, 2 cups of hot, riced potatoes, seasoned highly with white pepper and a generous dash of nutmeg, 1½ tablespoons of grated onion, 1½ tablespoons of minced parsley, and mix lightly with a fork. Now add 1 well-beaten large egg, beaten with 1 additional egg yolk. Form into 2 balls; dip the top and bottom of each ball into flour; shake off excess of flour, and let the balls stand, apart from each other, for a good 20 minutes to form a crust. Fry the balls in a heavy skillet containing hot bacon or ham drippings or lard until brown on both sides. Serve at once garnished with parsley and lemon quarters. If desired, broiled bacon may be used for garnishing. For a Sunday breakfast, a poached egg added for each serving will not be amiss. For luncheon, cole slaw is very good with these fish balls.

CODFISH STEAK PORTUGUESE STYLE [428]

Heat 2 tablespoons of butter and 2 tablespoons of olive oil in a frying pan, stir in 3 tablespoons of grated onion and brown slightly, over a low flame. Add 2 cups of chopped, peeled, fresh tomatoes, 1 scant cup

of dry white wine, 1 whole clove of garlic, 1 bouquet garni composed of
1 bay leaf, 5 sprigs of fresh parsley and 1 small sprig of thyme, tied with
white kitchen thread, 1 medium-sized carrot, scraped, then sliced,
½ teaspoon of granulated sugar, and salt, black pepper, and nutmeg to
taste. Gradually bring this to a boil; let boil 3 or 4 minutes; lower the
flame and let simmer very gently for 15 minutes. Lay in 6 individual
slices of fresh codfish which have been rubbed with mixed salt and black
pepper, and poach gently until done, or about 15 minutes, over a very
low flame. Turn the codfish slices on to a hot platter; trim off neatly all
skin; let the sauce reduce until rather thick, then rub through a fine-
meshed wire sieve over the fish slices. Garnish with parsley and lemon
quarters and serve immediately. Any kind of white-fleshed fish slices or
steaks may be prepared in this manner. Serve with plain boiled potatoes
and thinly sliced cucumbers in sour cream.

COQUILLES SAINT JACQUES   [429]

The dish is one of the glories of French Cuisine and something which
almost every American visitor to Paris has sampled at some time or
another.

How to Cook Coquilles. Parboil a pint of large deep-sea scallops in
their own liquor; drain. Prepare 1 generous cup of Mornay Sauce (No.
1088) and place the scallops in it, adding ½ cup of finely sliced mushrooms cooked in butter and 1 teaspoon of finely chopped shallots. Let
stand a few minutes. Fill the shells with the mixture, sprinkle with fine,
buttered bread crumbs mixed with grated Swiss cheese in equal parts
and brown under the flame of the boiling oven. Arrange on individual
plates on paper doilies and garnish each with a sprig of curled fresh parsley
and a small quarter of lemon. Serve at once.

COQUILLES SARAH BERNHARDT   [430]

Proceed as indicated for Coquilles Saint Jacques (No. 429), substituting cooked fresh shrimps for scallops, and adding 2 tablespoons of
sherry wine to the Mornay Sauce (No. 1088).

COQUILLES ST. JACQUELINE   [431]

Proceed as indicated for Coquilles Saint Jacques (No. 429), substituting freshly cooked or canned crabmeat, carefully boned, for scallops,
and adding 2 tablespoons of Madeira wine to the Mornay Sauce (No.
1088).

CRABS BENEDICTINE   [432]

The story goes that the monks in some monastery of the Benedictine
order in France discovered in the course of their meditations and experi-

ments on refinements of the calm pleasures of the refectory, that crabs as well as chickens might be milk fed, and since that happy day full many a tender young crustacean has been torn from its seaweed bed, to be drowned luxuriously in rich custard or eggnog sauce as a prelude to immolation on the gridiron.

The ancient recipe of the brothers of the black cowl prescribes a bath of milk and eggs for the selected young soft-shell crabs that are to be treated in the Benedictine manner. The crabs are washed, but not dressed or killed, and then they are placed in a deep bowl and immersed in a rich mixture of beaten eggs and milk, and left to enjoy or lament their peculiar fate for at least three hours. If the bowl is full and the victim lively, a heavy cover should be provided to guard against a break for liberty.

After the ablution the crabs are drained, and dressed as usual; the pulpy substance is torn from the undersides of the shell points, and the apron stripped from the lower shell. Then they are dredged lightly in flour seasoned with salt and pepper, dipped in well-beaten eggs, covered with finely sifted bread crumbs, and fried to a golden brown in a kettle of hot oil or lard (360°–375° F.). Drain on absorbent paper and serve at once in a nest of crisp fried curled parsley (sprigs of clean parsley, dried, dipped into a light batter sprig by sprig, plunged into hot deep fat and removed at once) dotted here and there with small lemon or lime quarters.

This writer knows little enough of the physiology of crabs, but is satisfied by repeated experiences and demonstrations that they do imbibe enough of the egg and milk to retain an appreciable quantity in their tissues; and he has evolved some refinements in the honored tradition of the epicurean friars as follows:

CRABS EPICUREAN FRIARS STYLE [433]

Instead of using merely eggs and milk as indicated in Crabs Bénédictine (No. 432) a rich, unsweetened eggnog bath is prepared as follows:

One pint of French Cognac, ½ pint of Jamaica rum, ½ cup each of applejack (apple brandy) and peach brandy, 12 strictly fresh eggs, separated, 2 quarts of sweet milk, or equal parts of milk and thin cream or undiluted evaporated milk, 1 teaspoon of salt and freshly grated nutmeg. Beat yolks until light; gradually beat in the French brandy so as to cook egg yolks; then the combined other liquors. Now, gradually beat in the cold milk or combined milk and thin cream; lastly, fold in the stiffly beaten egg whites flavored to taste with nutmeg, salt and pepper.

Instead of rum, you may substitute sherry, Madeira or Marsala, using no other liquor—that is, use about 1 pint of either.

No large quantity of the eggnog is needed if the crabs are packed closely in a deep earthenware or enamelled or porcelain vessel. But do not use aluminum or copper utensils. Cover with a heavy plate and a weight.

During the usual cleaning operations, the crabs are handled gently, without pressure or squeezing, and dredged with seasoned flour as soon as possible, then well covered with beaten egg and fresh sifted crumbs of bread crusts. The frying basket and the kettle of good cooking oil complete the process to perfection, and a Bénédictine abbot could ask nothing better than a serving with crisp watercress and quartered lemons.

In these days of budgets and lightly equipped kitchens and kitchenettes, the deep kettle and the wire frying basket are not very familiar utensils; nor is olive oil bought in gallons by American families, unless they have learned that there is thrift and health in its use. Crabs, however, even for Bénédictine or Epicurean Friars fashion, may be cooked quite satisfactorily in the frying pan, without immersion, if they are sautéed carefully in plenty of butter, oil or fat. Turn and shuffle them about deftly with a spatula, to avoid burning and drying, and brown them as evenly as possible. Maître d'Hôtel Butter, Sauce Tartare and Sauce Ravigote (Nos. 1078, 1128, 1109, respectively) are the first thoughts for crabs, but for the delicate flavor of those fattened on egg and sherry or other wine or cordial or liqueur, a simple Maître d'Hôtel is the safest thing (No. 1078).

CRABS À LA MAYLIE   [434]
Also called Crabs à la Creole

In New Orleans' "Back o'town," near what is known as the New Basin, dug 101 years ago, is Maylie's Restaurant. An old wooden building houses a restaurant that was established sixty-five years ago by the father of the present proprietor, W. H. Maylie. There's a thirty-five foot wisteria tree growing right up from the center of the floor of a little hallway outside the dining room. The trunk rests in an earthy opening in the floor. It goes through the ceiling to the second floor, to the third, and through the roof, spreading out over galleries and back yard. Every day a bucket of wine-and-water is poured over the roots; just an old French ritual that has been carried out for nearly fifty-five years. To the world Maylie offers this perfect creation of culinary masterpiece:

Boil 1½ dozen fat crabs, adding cayenne, pepper and salt to taste; when tender, drain and clean them, remove claws and cut the crab into halves. Slice 1 medium-sized onion very thin and sauté it in a little lard. When beginning to brown, add 1 generous tablespoon of flour, and blend thoroughly until free from lumps. Now add ½ can of tomato paste to which has been added 1 cup or more of rich beef stock. Let this simmer very gently for 35 to 40 minutes. Heat 2 tablespoons of butter; stir in 1 large egg, slightly beaten, remove from the fire and beat vigorously until a creamy paste is formed, then combine with the first mixture; now add the prepared crab halves; season to taste with mixed salt and pepper; heat well, but do not allow to boil. Serve at once with a side dish of plain boiled, fluffy rice, cooked the Creole way—that is to say, with each grain separate, not too moist and briefly "ovened."

CRAB MEAT DEWEY [435]

Take 2 cans or an equivalent amount of fresh crab meat, bone thoroughly and set aside. In one frying pan place the crab meat, 2 chopped shallots and 2 wine glasses of dry white wine (about ½ pint). Simmer gently for 5 long minutes, stirring occasionally. In another pan blend ½ pound of sweet butter and 2 generous tablespoons of flour until very smooth and mixture begins to bubble, then add ½ pound of fresh mushrooms, peeled and finely sliced, using both caps and stems. Brown this delicately, stirring occasionally from the bottom of the pan, over a very gentle flame. Add mushroom mixture to the crab meat mixture, with 1 teaspoon of black truffles, chopped fine, and a generous ¼ cup of scalded heavy cream. Let this simmer very gently for 5 minutes. Turn mixture into a baking dish as evenly as possible. Then set in a very hot oven (450° F.) or under the flame of the broiling oven. Serve immediately. This may be prepared in individual casseroles or served on freshly made and buttered toast.

CRAB MEAT LOUISETTE [436]

Trim the crusts from thin slices of fresh white bread, then place 2 slices together with the corners overlapping to about the center of the slices. Press them down into muffin tins so that the corners stand up about a scant inch above the top of the tin. Using a pastry brush, brush lightly with melted anchovy butter (No. 979). Place in a moderate oven (350–375° F.) and bake for about 10 minutes, or until the buttercups are lightly brown. Remove from pans and fill with hot creamed crab meat made as follows: Prepare 1½ cups of Béchamel Sauce (No. 259); stir in 2 tablespoons of sherry wine, then 2 cups of carefully boned fresh or canned crab meat, mixed with ⅓ cup of chopped, well drained canned pimiento, and ¼ cup of blanched, shredded and toasted almonds. Serve as hot as possible with a side dish of cucumber cubes marinated in French salad dressing and dusted with paprika.

The Bénédictines of the fortunate original monastery seem to have indorsed only the fried fatted crabs, but other brothers of the order must have discovered in due course that the formula could be carried on, and adapted with great glory to broiled crabs, devilled crabs, and a particularly luscious dish of soft-shell crabs à la Newburg. For that last one, leave the milk-fed crabs whole, (see Crabs Bénédictine, No. 432) put them quickly into hot butter, then proceed with the familiar Newburg formula and you may astonish and delight your husband, your friends and your neighbors.

CRABS (SOFT-SHELL) NEWBURG   [437]

Bathe 2 dozen soft-shell crabs, previously washed in cold water and drained, in a milk bath as indicated for recipe No. 432. Meantime, prepare a Newburg sauce as indicated for No. 1095, and keep hot over hot water. There should be about 1½ to 1¾ cups of this sauce.

When ready to serve, drain the crabs, clean them in the usual way, handling them gently, without pressure or squeezing, by placing the crabs on their backs and cleaning by raising right and left flaps and removing the fins. Roll them whole in seasoned flour and fry in plenty of sweet butter until golden brown. Drain on absorbent paper, add to the Newburg sauce, and serve immediately with freshly made toast generously buttered and cut into finger lengths. A fine dish for an after-theatre supper when served in a chafing dish.

CRAB MEAT RAVIGOTE   [438]

Either canned or fresh cooked crab meat may be used. Pour ¼ cup of tarragon vinegar over 1 pound of carefully picked, flaked, boned crab meat and let marinate 15 minutes. Squeeze vinegar from crab meat and season to taste with mixed salt and white pepper. Add 2 tablespoons of finely chopped pimiento, 2 tablespoons of finely chopped chives and as much of finely chopped vinegar pickles. Then add ½ generous cup of home-made mayonnaise and toss lightly until thoroughly mixed. Serve in individual scallop shells or on crisp lettuce leaves, the mixture shaped dome-fashion; cover the entire surface with a light coating of mayonnaise forced through a pastry bag, and sprinkle all over with well-drained small capers. Serve as cold as possible, lightly dusted with paprika.

CREAMED CODFISH IN POTATO RING   [439]

Cover ½ pound of salt codfish with cold water and let stand at least 6 hours to freshen, changing water every hour. Drain, cover with cold water, and bring to boiling point. Drain again and flake. Melt 3 tablespoons of butter or margarine in a double boiler; blend in 2½ tablespoons of flour, and when just beginning to bubble, stir in gradually 2 cups of scalded sweet milk, stirring constantly, until mixture thickens. Now stir in 1½ teaspoons of grated onion, 1 teaspoon of finely chopped parsley and as much of finely chopped chives. Remove from the fire and beat in 1 or 2 egg yolks, one at a time, beating well after each addition.

Season to taste with mixed salt (very little of it) white pepper and a dash of nutmeg; stir in the flaked cod and 4 hard-cooked eggs, shelled and quartered. Arrange 4 cups of hot, smooth mashed potatoes around the edge of a hot platter by forcing the potatoes through a pastry bag, pour fish-egg mixture into the center, dust the potatoes with paprika and the fish-egg mixture with finely chopped parsley. Serve immediately.

CREAMED FINNAN HADDIE DELMONICO [440]

Put 1½ to 1¾ pounds of finnan haddie in a pan; cover with water, and bring to a boil. Let simmer 15 minutes or till tender and drain. Reserve the broth, and flake fish coarsely. Remove two thin center slices from 6 hard-cooked eggs and reserve for garnishing. Cut end portions of eggs into halves lengthwise. Make a cream sauce in the usual way, using the reserved broth and enough milk to make 3 cups, seasoning to taste with mixed salt, pepper and a dash of nutmeg; stir in the flaked fish and eggs, and heat well. Turn mixture into a buttered baking dish, sprinkle over ⅓ cup of grated cheese (any kind), and brown under the flame of the broiling oven until cheese bubbles and is nicely browned. Garnish with reserved egg slices sprinkled with paprika and serve at once.

DEVILED HERRING [441]

Clean, rinse inside and out 6 fresh herrings weighing a generous half pound each, and dry them well. Score or make little slits on the flesh on each side of each fish. This hastens the cooking and prevents the fish from curling. Sprinkle with mixed salt and black pepper—herring loves it—then brush with good cooking oil or melted butter or margarine, and spread the slits with 2 tablespoons of prepared mustard mixed with 1 teaspoon of Pique Seasoning and a few drops of Tabasco sauce. Preheat broiling oven 5 minutes, brush the rack with oil; arrange the fish on it and sprinkle them with 2 or 3 tablespoons of fine, dry, bread crumbs; sprinkle the crumbs with a little melted butter and broil about 5 minutes on each side, or until the flesh just begins to flake and the crumbs brown delicately, basting frequently with melted butter mixed with equal parts of Pique Seasoning. Serve on a hot platter garnished with parsley and lemon quarters. A side dish of Mustard Sauce (No. 1092) is usually served with this delicious and fine fish.

In the early fifteenth century, Arabians developed a fondness for fresh and smoked herring which were brought all the way from the North Sea to be sold in native bazaars.

EELS IN GREEN HERBS BRUSSELS STYLE   [442]
Anguilles au Vert Bruxelloise

Cut 2½–3 pounds of skinned, washed eels of approximately the same size (small or medium) and cook in ¼ generous cup of butter with 2 tablespoons each of finely chopped onion and green celery leaves for 5 minutes, over a bright flame, stirring frequently; moisten with enough dry white wine to generously cover; season to taste with salt and pepper, a tiny pinch each of thyme and ground cloves. Stir in ½ generous cup each of finely chopped sorrel leaves and watercress leaves; 1 tablespoon of minced parsley; 1 tablespoon of minced chervil; 3 tablespoons of finely chopped white nettle leaves; a small muslin bag containing ½ scant teaspoon of sage, summer savory and mint leaves, all finely chopped, the bag tied with kitchen thread; and cook, over a very bright flame, stirring frequently with a wooden spoon, for 12 to 15 minutes (too long cooking will break up the pieces of eel). Remove from the fire, and stir in 4 egg yolks, beaten with ½ cup of scalded sweet, heavy cream. Taste for seasoning and serve hot or cold. This formula is that of the famous Brasserie Universelle, Place de Broockère, Brussels.

To the tenant farmers of Kent and Sussex in England, eels were formerly known as "the gentlemen who paid the rent." A well-stocked marsh meant a sale for eels even if crops failed.

EEL STEW   [443]

Cut 2½–3 pounds of eels into 2-inch lengths; wash quickly in cold water and dry. Fry 1 large onion, chopped, 1 green pepper, chopped, and 1 clove of garlic chopped, in 4 tablespoons of butter or margarine, over a gentle flame until just beginning to take on color, stirring frequently; then gradually stir in 2 cups of fish stock (No. 182), and, when boiling, add the eel pieces—previously seasoned with mixed salt and pepper, 1 large bay leaf, a 2-inch piece of parsley root, 1 sprig of green celery tops, finely chopped with 1 tablespoon each of parsley and nettle— then cover and let simmer very gently for 30 minutes. Lift up the cover and stir in 1 cup of dry white wine, and bring to a boil. Let boil steadily for 3 or 4 minutes, or until the liquid in the stewpan is reduced to half. Arrange the pieces of eels upon a hot, deep platter. Remove the parsley root, the bay leaf and stir in ½ cup each of cooked peas, a dozen small potato balls and the same of carrot balls, cooked separately until tender in salted water, and well drained. Heat well; taste for seasoning, and pour liquid and vegetables over the eels. Dust with chopped parsley and serve at once.

SOLE (FLOUNDER)

Imported sole—real sole—is most difficult to get, except in the frozen state and imported from France or England. The European sole averages ¾ pound up to 2½ pounds in weight and is quickly frozen and shipped here with a leakproof casing of ice over its Quaker-like garb, then sold at fabulous prices.

Flounder, young flounder, when available is a good substitute, fresh or frozen. It may be prepared in all the hundreds of ways that the royal sole is. The fish filets sold under the name "sole" are usually those of flounder, or of some other white-fleshed fish. It is essential to stress this important fact for the sake of accuracy of quotation in general, for it must be emphasized that there is a great difference in flavor, texture, and flexibility between genuine sole and its various substitutes. However, as it is the common habit to call the flounder filet "a filet of sole," this writer deems it necessary to maintain the common usage of calling "filet of sole" a flounder filet prepared in the sole manner.

The winter flounder (*Pseudopleuronectes Americanus*) is a dextral fish, with color and eyes on the right side. It's a small-mouthed fish, and the scales are rough on the eyed side, but smooth to the touch on the blind, or white side. It is a year-round resident in these waters and is said to bury itself in the mud or move out into deep water during the colder winter months. Winter flounders reach weights of 4 to 5 pounds, but the average would run from about 1 pound to 2 pounds in weight.

The summer flounder, or fluke (*Paralichthys denatus*), is a sinistral or left-handed fish—in which respect it differs from the winter flounder. Although in general formation it resembles the winter flounder, it grows to greater weight and has a larger mouth which is equipped with plenty of sharp teeth. The largest fluke on record weighed 26 pounds.

In the following tasted and tested recipes, fresh flounder filets or whole fish or defrosted frozen filets may be used.

FILETS OF SOLE (FLOUNDER) AMANDINE   [444]

Sprinkle 6 individual filets of flounder with mixed salt and pepper; dust lightly with flour. Melt ¼ cup of butter in a large frying pan or baking pan, add the fish and sauté it until just beginning to get brown on one side; turn and brown the other side. It takes such a little time— 3 or 4 minutes. Meantime, put ¼ cup of sweet butter in another frying pan; stir in ¾ cup of blanched, slivered almonds, letting them brown slightly without salt. Arrange the fish filets on a large heated platter, squeeze lemon juice over all and top with the slightly browned almond slivers. Garnish with parsley and lemon quarters and serve at once, usually with a side dish of French fried, shoe string, or hot Saratoga potato chips (No. 1432).

FILETS OF SOLE (FLOUNDER) AMBASSADOR   [445] HOTEL

Arrange 6 filets of flounder in bottom of a generously buttered baking pan; dot each filet with a piece of butter the size of a large marble, creamed with finely chopped shallots and parsley in almost equal parts; squeeze over the juice of a large lemon, season with mixed salt, pepper and a dash of nutmeg, and barely cover with equal parts of fish stock (No. 182), and dry white wine; cover with a buttered paper and bake in a moderate oven (350° F.) for about 12 to 14 minutes. Remove from the oven; transfer the fish to a heated platter and keep hot. Place the liquid from baking pan in a saucepan, and let it reduce to about 1 generous half cup, over a bright flame. Then stir in 1½ cups of scalded sweet, heavy cream; bring to a boil, remove from the fire and strain through a fine-meshed wire sieve into a fresh saucepan. Now beat in 2 egg yolks, one at a time, beating briskly after each addition. Taste for seasoning. Arrange a nice fresh mushroom cap freshly grilled over each filet; pour the sauce over, entirely covering the fish and mushroom, place the platter under the flame of the broiling oven and glaze quickly. Serve at once.

FILETS OF SOLE (FLOUNDER) A   [446] L'AMERICAINE

Fold 6 filets of flounder in two, like a pocketbook, after seasoning to taste with mixed salt and pepper, and lay neatly in bottom of a buttered baking pan; barely cover the filets with dry white wine; cover the pan with a buttered paper, and "poach" gently in a moderate oven (325–350° F.) for about 15–20 minutes. Remove from the oven and keep hot. Cook ½ pound of small fresh peeled mushroom caps in butter over a low flame until done. Keep hot. Cook 2 medium fresh lobsters, cut into small pieces, in 2 tablespoons of olive oil and 4 tablespoons of butter until lobster pieces are done—that is, nicely red— shaking the pan frequently. When done, drain off the oil and butter, and pour over ¼ cup of good brandy and set on fire. When the flames are burned out, pour over 2 cups of the strained liquid in which the fish filets were poached, mixed with 4 tablespoons of tomato paste; add 1 large bay leaf, 4 sprigs of parsley, 4 thin slices of onion; cover and cook 15–20 minutes. Remove the meat from the lobster pieces, and add to the cooked mushrooms and strained liquid from the lobster; then reduce this liquid over a bright flame to about ½ its original volume. Now stir in 1½ cups of scalded heavy cream, taste for seasoning and dress the dish as follows: Arrange the fish filets in center of the hot platter, and pour over the combined mushrooms, lobster meat and cream sauce. Dust with a little paprika and glaze quickly under the flame of the broiling oven. Serve at once.

FILETS OF SOLE (FLOUNDER) BONNE FEMME   [447]

Carefully remove the skins from 6 neatly trimmed filets of flounders; sprinkle with mixed salt and white pepper, and lay the filets in a generously buttered baking pan. Sprinkle over 2 tablespoons of finely chopped fresh mushrooms and shallots in equal parts; barely cover the filets with equal parts of fish stock (No. 182) and dry white wine; place the pan over a bright flame and bring to a boil. Remove immediately, cover with a buttered paper and continue cooking in a moderate oven (325–350° F.) for about 3 or 4 minutes. Drain. Arrange the fish filets on a hot platter and, over each filet, place a nice fresh mushroom cap cooked in butter and well drained. Keep hot. Reduce the drained court-bouillon to half its volume over a bright flame, stirring occasionally. Strain through a fine-meshed wire sieve into a fresh saucepan, add 1 cup of White Wine Sauce (No. 1135); taste for seasoning and, when ready to serve, stir in 1 tablespoon of sweet butter. Pour over the fish, and serve at once, passing lemon quarters neatly arranged on a bed of crisp parsley separately.

FILETS OF SOLE (FLOUNDER) CARMEN   [448]

Soak 6 filets of flounders in half cold water and half cold milk for 2 hours. Drain and dry well. Fold each filet over in pocketbook fashion and place in a buttered baking pan. Sprinkle lightly with mixed salt and pepper, and poach in a white wine court-bouillon (No. 1037), to barely cover, for about 10 minutes. Prepare a rich cream sauce (No. 258) made with the strained white wine court-bouillon of the filets in the usual way, and thicken with 2 or 3 egg yolks. Taste for seasoning and keep hot. Fry or grill 6 nice thick slices of fresh tomatoes. Do likewise with 6 thick slices of large cucumber. Arrange the fish filets on a heated long platter, making a circle around the dish. Pour the hot sauce over the filets and garnish, over the sauce, with 1 or 2 thin slices of black truffle. Place a circle of fried tomato slices and cucumber in the center of the platter. Garnish with a few bouquets of green parsley and lemon quarters and serve at once.

FILETS OF SOLE (FLOUNDER) CHARLOTTE   [449]

Place 1 tablespoon of sweet butter in a saucepan with 1 tablespoon of grated onion (or shallots), ⅓ pound of peeled, chopped fresh mushrooms, and 3 tablespoons of finely chopped celery leaves. Cook 2 minutes, over a low flame, then stir in ¼ cup of fish stock, and continue cooking 2 or 3 minutes longer. Add 1 cup of fish stock (No. 182), and cook over a bright flame until liquid is reduced to half, stirring occasionally to prevent scorching. Strain through a fine-meshed wire sieve into a clean saucepan; add 1½ cups of scalded heavy cream with 1 large bay leaf and 1 whole clove, and bring to a boil. Let boil 1 minute, strain into a fresh saucepan; taste for seasoning, and keep hot. Poach 6 filets of flounder in enough white wine court-bouillon (No. 1037) to barely cover, cooking them 7 or 8 minutes over a gentle flame; drain; arrange the filets in a baking dish suitable for serving, and keep hot. To the hot strained sauce add 3 egg yolks, one at a time, beating well after each addition and adding with the last one 2 tablespoons of good sherry wine. Heat to the boiling point, but do not let boil; taste for seasoning, pour over the fish, sprinkle over all ½ cup of grated cheese (any kind desired) and brown under the flame of the broiling oven until cheese bubbles and top is nicely browned. Serve at once.

Provided they are both fresh, fish and milk (or any sea food and ice cream) may safely be eaten at the same meal. Spoiled sea food and stale milk are something else again—take them separately or together and you're in for trouble. It's a mystery how the strange notion got started that fish and milk in combination are dangerous—particularly in a country like the United States famous for its chowders, fish soups and fish stews.

FILETS OF SOLE (FLOUNDER) CONCARNEAU [450]

Lay 6 filets of flounder in a buttered baking pan; sprinkle with 2 or 3 tablespoons of lemon juice, then scatter over them ¾ pound of peeled, sliced fresh mushrooms (using both caps and stems). Dot here and there with ¼ cup of sweet butter and season to taste with mixed salt, pepper and nutmeg. Pour over 1½ cups of cold, sweet cream and bake in a moderate oven (325–350° F.) for 20 minutes. Remove from the oven, and arrange on a hot platter with the sauce and mushrooms, sprinkle with a little paprika, and brown slightly under the flame of the broiling oven. Serve at once.

FILETS OF SOLE (FLOUNDER) CORDON BLEU [451]

Cook 2 generous tablespoons of finely chopped shallots and 1 tablespoon of grated onion very gently in ¼ cup of sweet butter; stir in 1½ tablespoons of lemon juice with 1 cup of fish stock and sherry wine in equal parts, and heat to the boiling point. Lay 6 filets of flounder in bottom of a buttered baking dish suitable to be presented at table;

pour over them the first mixture and simmer very gently over a very low flame the dish, covered with a buttered paper, for about 15 minutes. Remove the buttered paper. Stir 2 slightly beaten egg yolks into a cup of sour cream, season to taste with salt and white pepper, and heat to the boiling point. Pour this over the fish; again heat to the boiling point, but do not allow to boil, and serve at once, right from the baking dish.

FILETS OF SOLE (FLOUNDER) JACQUELINE   [452]

Lay 6 filets of flounder in bottom of a generously buttered baking pan; season to taste with mixed salt and white pepper; then sprinkle with 1½ tablespoons of lemon juice. Pour over enough fish stock (No. 182) and Sauterne wine to barely cover; bring to the boiling point, cover with a buttered paper and poach gently for 12 minutes. Arrange the filets on a hot serving platter. Strain the liquid into a small saucepan and let reduce to a little less than half its original volume, then stir in 1 cup of scalded heavy sweet cream, to which has been added anchovy paste the size of a large pea; bring to a boil and let simmer very gently for 2 or 3 minutes. Meantime, arrange over each one of the fish filets 1 freshly poached egg yolk; cover with the sauce, sprinkle with ½ cup of grated American cheese, and brown under the flame of the broiling oven. Serve at once, passing lemon quarters on a bed of parsley.

FILETS OF SOLE (FLOUNDER) JEANINE   [453]

Lay 6 seasoned filets of flounders in bottom of a buttered baking pan; sprinkle over them 1 tablespoon of chopped shallots, 5 or 6 thinly sliced fresh mushrooms, 2 large fresh tomatoes, peeled and coarsely chopped, and pour over 1 generous cup of dry white wine, to which has been added 1 teaspoon of curry powder. Bake in a moderate oven (325° F.) 15-20 minutes. When done, arrange the fish filets in a hot platter and let the sauce reduce until it gets a little thick, rub through a fine-meshed wire sieve into a saucepan, and stir in 1 cup of scalded sweet cream. Heat to boiling point, taste for seasoning, and pour over the fish filets. Sprinkle top with ½ generous cup of fine bread crumbs and grated cheese in equal parts, and brown under the flame of the broiling oven. Serve at once with a side dish of lemon quarters on a bed of crisp parsley; also a side dish of tiny potato balls, parboiled in beef broth until tender, drained and rolled in butter, then in finely chopped chives.

In 1570 the Chinese passed a law compelling farmers who didn't meet their crop quota to maintain a fish pond to feed their family so that more vegetables could be sold in the cities.

FILETS OF SOLE (FLOUNDER) MARGUERY   [454]

Purchase 3 nice flounders of about 2 pounds each, have the fishman filet them or do this at home. Place the bones, skin and heads in a saucepan, add 1 pound of inexpensive fish, cleaned and cut into small pieces, with ⅓ cup of thinly sliced young carrots, 1 small leek finely chopped using the white part only, 4 sprigs of fresh parsley, 10 whole peppercorns, gently bruised, 6 thin slices of onion, 1 bouquet garni composed of 1 large bay leaf, 1 sprig of thyme and 1 whole clove, tied together with white kitchen thread, and pour over 1½ quarts of cold water. Bring this to a boil very slowly, let boil up 2 or 3 times, lower the flame and let simmer until fish stock is reduced to a pint, then strain through a fine cheesecloth into a fresh saucepan. Lay the filets in a buttered baking pan; pour over them 1 cup of the fish stock, season lightly with salt, cover with a buttered paper, and poach gently in a very moderate oven (300–325° F.), for about 20 minutes, or until fish is tender but not flaked. Carefully lift the filets out of baking pan and arrange them on a heated oven-proof platter suitable to be presented at table. Over each filet, arrange 2 cooked mussels (No. 490) and 2 cooked, large shrimps, shelled (the black vein removed). Keep hot.

Pour remaining cup of fish stock into the baking pan in which the fish filets were poached and simmer gently, scraping bottom and sides so as to recover the essence of the fish which may have adhered to the pan, and cook until mixture is reduced to about 4 tablespoons—no more. Strain this small quantity into top part of double boiler, and add 4 tablespoons of dry white wine and ¼ pound of sweet butter. Cook over hot water, stirring until butter is melted. (Be sure to have very little water in lower part of double boiler—just enough to create a gentle steam). Then add 5 egg yolks, which have been well beaten with 2 tablespoons of dry white wine and seasoned to taste with salt and pepper. Stir constantly until sauce thickens and is about the consistency of medium sauce. There should be about 1 cup of sauce. (If not enough, add a little hot fish stock or still better, hot sweet cream.) Pour this creamy, rich sauce over the fish fillets, mussels and shrimps (you may if desired, also add 2 small oysters, but this is not in the recipe); place under the flame of the broiling oven until nicely glazed or lightly browned and serve at once.

FILETS OF SOLE (FLOUNDER) MEUNIERE   [455]

Roll as many flounder filets as required in seasoned cream, then dip in flour and sauté in plenty of butter until just beginning to take on a light gold color on both sides. Arrange them on a hot platter; add more butter to the pan, with some finely chopped parsley or chervil and a dash of lemon juice and heat well. Pour sizzling hot over the filets and garnish with parsley and lemon quarters. Serve at once. A variation which is a bit unorthodox is to add a little anchovy paste to the hot butter before pouring it over the fish filets.

Fresh fish are mined in the middle of the Sahara Desert. The fish are caught by natives who dig into subterranean streams.

FILETS OF SOLE (FLOUNDER) MORNAY [456]

Lay 6 filets of flounder in bottom of a buttered baking pan with just enough fish stock (No. 182) to barely cover; cover with a buttered paper and poach in a moderate oven (325–350° F.) 15–20 minutes. Drain. Arrange filets crosswise on a hot platter, which will stand oven heat, and cover with Sauce Mornay (No. 1088), Place the dish in a moderate oven (350° F.) until top is golden brown. Serve at once with a side dish of lemon quarters arranged tastefully on a bed of parsley

FILETS OF SOLE (FLOUNDER) NADINE [457]

Poach as many filets of flounder as required in the usual way in white wine court-bouillon (No. 1037). Arrange side by side on a hot platter, and lay on each filet 2 or 3 thin slices of seeded orange. For each filet, heat 1 tablespoon of Anchovy butter (No. 979), and pour sizzling hot over the orange slices, sprinkle top with a little paprika and serve at once the dish garnished with parsley and lemon eighths.

FILETS OF SOLE (FLOUNDER) ST. MALO [458]

Clean, wipe with a damp cloth, and filet 3 nice flounders (the fishman will gladly do this for you). Season the filets (6 in all) with mixed salt and pepper to taste and lay side by side in a buttered baking pan, and pour over 1½ cups of fish stock (made from trimmings, bones and heads of flounders, with ¾ cup of dry white wine, as well as the liquor drained from 1 cup of parboiled oysters, 2 slices each of carrot and onion, 1 small bay leaf, tied with 4 sprigs of fresh parsley, a small sprig of green celery leaves, and a small sprig of thyme, all tied together with white kitchen thread). Cover with buttered paper and bake 15–20 minutes in a moderate oven (350°F.) Remove filets to a serving platter, and keep hot. Melt 3 tablespoons of sweet butter; stir in 2½ tablespoons of flour and cook until mixture just begins to bubble, stirring constantly, over a low flame; then pour on gradually, still stirring constantly, 1 cup of the strained fish stock from the pan in which fish filets were poached; bring to boiling point; then stir in ½ cup of scalded heavy cream. Taste for seasoning; strain the sauce through a fine-meshed wire sieve over

the fish filets; place 2 fresh oysters on each filet, sprinkle the entire surface with a ⅓ cup of grated cheese (any kind desired), and glaze quickly
under the flame of the broiling oven. Serve at once, with a side dish of
lemon quarters neatly arranged on a nest of green curled parsley.

FILETS OF SOLE (FLOUNDER) ST. RAPHAEL   [459]

Prepare 3 flounders as indicated for Filets of Sole (flounder) St.
Malo (No. 458). When the fish filets are done, arrange on a hot platter
and keep hot. Strain the fish stock from the pan into a small saucepan.
There should be only a cupful. If more, let reduce to that amount over
a bright flame. While still boiling stir in 1 cupful of Mornay Sauce
(No. 1088), to which have been added 3 tablespoons of finely chopped
well-drained capers; taste for seasoning, then pour over the fish filets.
Sprinkle with ⅓ cup of grated Parmesan cheese, and glaze quickly
under the flame of the broiling oven. Serve at once with a side dish of
lemon quarters arranged on a bed of parsley.

FILETS OF SOLE (FLOUNDER)   [460]
VALENCIENNES

Season 6 flounder filets to taste on both sides with mixed salt, pepper,
mace and thyme, and place them in a generously buttered baking pan,
preferably a copper pan, if available. Sprinkle lightly with a mixture of
finely chopped chives, shallots and grated onion in equal parts, using
about 1 generous tablespoon of each. Now arrange over each fish filet
4 scalloped medium-sized mushrooms, or enough to cover the length of
the filet. Add 1 scant cup of dry white wine, mixed with 2 tablespoons of
lemon juice, or enough to barely cover the fish filets. Cover and very
slowly—as slowly as possible—bring to a boil over a gentle flame. Immediately uncover and place the pan in a moderate oven (325° F.),
and bake, basting frequently with the wine in the pan, alternately
with melted sweet butter. When the cooking is complete, most of the
sauce should have been absorbed and the fish will have taken on a glossy
appearance. There is a very little sauce left to serve with the fish, but
this is quite sufficient with the filets, which melt like butter. Serve from
the baking dish with parsley and lemon quarters, and a side dish of
stewed cucumbers.

The best of frogs, from the eater's viewpoint, come from Florida,
Texas, the Middle West and Cuba, and are called under different names,
according to locality, such as "Swamp Pigeons," "Water-Chicken,"
"Jumping Jacks," etc.

The average portion of frog's legs is 3 pairs depending on size.

FROGS' LEGS FRICASSEE EN CASSOLETTES [461]

Wash quickly 3 dozen pairs of frog's legs, and sponge dry. Marinate them in dry white wine, barely to cover, with 1 large bay leaf, 12 sprigs of fresh parsley, 1 large clove of garlic, crushed; 2 whole cloves; 8 to 10 whole peppercorns, gently bruised; 1 sprig of thyme; 1 small onion, thinly sliced; 5 to 6 thin slices raw carrot; the juice of 1 large lemon (about 2½ tablespoons); 3 shallots, crushed; 2 sprigs of fennel tops; and a pinch of salt to taste. Let stand for 30 minutes, stirring occasionally. Now heat to the foaming point ⅓ cup of sweet butter, and add the dripping legs. Cook for 3 minutes, shaking the pan almost constantly. Remove the legs to a platter, and keep hot. To the heated butter add 1 generous tablespoon of flour, and cook to a golden brown, stirring constantly with a wooden spoon. Moisten gradually with the strained marinade, still stirring. The sauce must be of the consistency of thin cream. Taste for seasoning, then strain the sauce into 6 individual casseroles or ramekins; divide the frogs' legs among the casseroles, place the casseroles in a pan containing hot water, and let simmer for about 5 minutes, so that the meat from the frogs' legs soaks in the sauce. Just before serving, beat in a bowl 3 egg yolks with 2 tablespoons of tomato paste and a few grains each of salt and cayenne pepper and gradually stir into the casseroles. Place the casseroles on a baking sheet and glaze them under the flame of the broiling oven. Serve each casserole on a plate covered with a fancy paper doily, and garnished with a sprig of parsley and a quarter of lemon. A side dish of freshly made French fried potatoes is the usual accompaniment.

FROGS' LEGS FRY MY WAY [462]

Allow at least 6 small pairs of frogs' legs for each serving. Wash the legs rapidly in cold water, sponge dry, and place in a deep dish; then pour over them (for each dozen pairs) 2 tablespoons of good sherry wine. Let stand for 15 minutes; lift them from their bath, and season to taste with mixed salt and pepper, nutmeg, and thyme. Dip them in heavy fresh cream, then coat with seasoned flour. When ready to serve, and only then, fry them in butter which should be frothy, but not brown, for 4 or 5 minutes, the time depending on their size. Remove the legs to a hot platter, and keep hot. Heat the butter remaining in the frying pan to the foaming point, and add, for 6 servings, 2 tablespoons of chopped shallots and as much chopped parsley, and cook for a scant minute, stirring constantly. Then moisten gradually with 2 tablespoons of the sherry wine used for the bath, and 1 cup of heavy, scalded sweet cream, stirring constantly. Season to taste with salt and a few grains of cayenne pepper, and bring to a boil. Remove immediately from the fire, and beat in 2 egg yolks, one at a time, beating well after each addition. Arrange the fried legs on a hot platter, covered with a fancifully folded napkin; sprinkle over them a whole bunch of curled parsley fried in deep fat (380° F.), and garnish with grilled bacon slices and lemon quarters. Serve at once.

FROGS' LEGS GOURMET   [463]

For 6 persons, take 3 dozen pairs of frogs' legs and wash rapidly in slightly acidulated water, using either lemon juice or good tarragon vinegar. Sponge thoroughly, then bathe them for about 15 minutes in sufficient milk barely to cover, perfumed with 1 pony of good brandy for each cup of milk. Lift the legs dripping, and roll them in well-seasoned flour. When ready to serve, fry them in clarified butter to a golden color, until they are rather crisp. Arrange the legs in crown shape on a hot, round platter, and place in the center scallops prepared thus:

Scallops des Gourmets. Wash 1 generous cup of fresh scallops quickly in cold water, and drain. Place them in a mixing bowl and cover with dry white wine. Let stand 25–30 minutes, then cook in the wine used for marinating, adding 1 small bouquet garni (1 small bay leaf, 4 or 5 sprigs fresh parsley and 1 small sprig of thyme tied together with white kitchen thread), salt and pepper to taste, and a grating of nutmeg. Allow all this to simmer gently for 15 minutes. Drain, reserving the liquid, and cut the scallops in small pieces, keeping them hot. Now sauté ½ pound of sliced mushrooms in 3 tablespoons of butter for about 4–5 minutes, over a very low flame, stirring constantly with a wooden spoon, and add to the scallops. Heat the drained wine to the boiling point and add 2 teaspoons of anchovy butter (No. 979). Bring to a boil, taste for seasoning, beat in 2 slightly beaten egg yolks and mix with the scallops and mushrooms. Garnish the platter with triangles of bread fried in butter until brown and crisp on both sides, and small bouquets of fresh parsley or watercress. Serve at once.

FROGS' LEGS MORNAY   [464]

Allow 3 pairs of frogs' legs for each serving. Sauté the quickly washed and dried frogs' legs in 4 generous tablespoons of garlic butter (No. 986), until delicately brown on both sides. Place 3 pairs of separated legs in buttered individual earthenware casseroles, cover the legs with 2 tablespoons of thinly sliced mushrooms cooked in butter and well drained, then fill each casserole with Mornay Sauce (No. 1088), using about 1¼ to 1½ cups in all. Sprinkle over each casserole a little grated Parmesan cheese mixed with equal parts of grated Gruyère cheese or Swiss cheese and glaze under the flame of the broiling oven. Serve at once.

Nearly every people has a way of doing some dish better than any other people. In this country of many races there is rare opportunity to sample the food specialties of the world. Yet how many of you know gefuellte fish—that traditional Jewish dish, almost a must for the Friday night meal?

Some Jewish cooks include the flesh of whitefish, and yellow pike from Lake Superior—this is a matter of taste. In the following gefuellte fish, pike and whitefish are used.

GEFUELLTE FISH [465]

Filet 4 pounds of mixed fish such as pike and whitefish in equal amounts, removing all the meat from the skin and bones. Grind fish to a fine consistency, add 1 medium-sized onion, grated, and 1 medium-sized carrot, also grated, and mix all together. Add 2 large, raw eggs, slightly beaten with mixed salt and pepper to taste, mixing well. Put the bones in bottom of the kettle with 2 medium-sized onions, thinly sliced, and 2 thinly sliced medium-sized carrots. Shape ground fish mixture into small balls and lay over the onion-carrot bedding. Add enough cold water to cover the fish balls and additional seasoning of salt and pepper to taste. Gradually bring this to a boil; lower the flame, and let simmer very gently 2¼–2½ hours. Serve as an appetizer before the soup course with the sauce. This dish is also delicious when chilled in the refrigerator until the sauce has jellied. It is then served as a cold jellied appetizer or a first course.

For an entrée, serve a slice or two of fish ball on a lettuce leaf with a spoonful of its jelly. Pickles, olives and cooked carrots cut in decorative designs make fine garnishments. For a luncheon menu gefuellte fish may be served as a main dish—always cold, however—with vegetables.

GRILLED BLUEFISH [466]

Split a 4-pound bluefish from the back; clean; wash quickly in cold water; dry, and sprinkle with mixed salt and pepper to taste. Brush with oil or fat, and grill on both sides, first flesh side up, until brown, brushing frequently with melted butter. Served on a hot platter garnished with parsley and lemon quarters and with a side dish of French fried potatoes, a cucumber dish in sour cream, and a dessert and you have a regal meal.

Any kind of large fish or small fish may be grilled in this way.

GRILLED CODFISH CAPE COD STYLE [467]

Grill a large steak of fresh codfish in the usual manner; arrange on a hot platter and pour over it the following sauce:

Cape Cod Fish Sauce. To 2 cups of rich cream sauce, add 1 teaspoon of Worcestershire sauce, a tiny pinch of dry mustard, previously moistened with a little milk, 1 teaspoon each of parsley, grated onion and chives, all finely chopped. Heat well, but do not allow to boil. Remove from the fire, stir in 1 cup of picked, freshly cooked or canned crab meat. Let heat a few minutes before pouring over the grilled fish. Garnish with parsley and lemon quarters and serve. Any other kind of grilled fish or fish steak may be prepared in this fine way.

GRILLED LOBSTER GOURMET [467-A]

For 6 servings, take three live lobsters (one lobster for two), split lengthwise and crack the claws. Brush the lobster halves with fine olive oil or melted butter (even to the claws to keep the meat inside from drying out). Sprinkle with mixed salt, pepper and paprika, and broil over fairly hot, even heat, preferably charcoal or coal, until just rosy and soft, taking care neither to overbroil not underbroil, and broiling about 2 minutes less on the shell side than on the meat side. Baste frequently with the following basting sauce:

Basting Sauce for Shellfish. Mash ½ clove of garlic in a bowl, add 1 tablespoon each of finely minced parsley, onion and chives, 2 teaspoons of finely minced green celery leaves, and ¼ pound of sweet butter.

The remainder of this basting sauce is then mixed with the green from the heads of the lobsters, and served in a sauceboat at the table. The lobsters must positively be served very, very hot.

GRILLED SOFT-SHELL CRABS CREOLE STYLE [468]

The Creole recipe advises care in cleaning soft-shell crabs. They are quickly washed free of sand, but not blanched or scalded. The spongy, feathery substances under the side joints and the sand bag or pouch under the shells just between the eyes are removed. The "aprons" —the pointed pieces at the lower part of the shells—also are taken off. The crabs are washed again in cold water and dried on a towel. They are then ready to be broiled, fried or cooked in any one of several delicious manners.

Take, as far as possible, soft-shell crabs of approximately the same size. Clean as directed above, or have the fishman do it for you. Allow 3 crabs for each serving. Rub each crab with softened butter, then with mixed salt and pepper. Broil under moderate flame, having the crabs about 6 inches from the flame, until brown on both sides, basting frequently with melted butter. Serve at once with a side dish of Maître d'Hotel Butter (No. 1078) or Drawn Butter (No. 1050) to which may be added some finely chopped chives or Tartare Sauce (Nos. 1128–29).

HADDOCK DINNER BOSTON STYLE [469]

Ingredients are 4 pounds of haddock, or any other kind of firm-meated fish, as bass, pike, cod, lake trout, etc.; 2 pounds of potatoes, peeled and sliced thin; ¾ pound of onions, peeled, thinly sliced; 2 green peppers, parboiled, skinned and thinly sliced (seeds and white ribs discarded); 1 pound of bacon, cubed small; 1½ cups of condensed tomato soup or tomato purée; cold water; salt, pepper, cayenne to taste; a bouquet garni composed of 1 large bay leaf, tied with 10 sprigs of parsley and 1 sprig of thyme; and 1 dozen strictly fresh eggs.

Clean, wash, bone, but do not skin, then slice the fish into small pieces. Try out the bacon or salt pork, if preferred, and cook until crisp, over a gentle flame, then remove the cracklings and reserve. Drain off all bacon or pork fat except 4 or 5 tablespoons. On the bacon fat left in the kettle, arrange first a layer of fish, then a layer of potatoes, next a layer of onions, then a layer of green pepper, seasoning to taste with mixed salt, pepper, cayenne, and nutmeg, as you go along. Place the bouquet garni in center, and repeat with a layer of fish, and so on until all the ingredients are used and the kettle—a heavy one—is full to within 3 inches of the top. Now pour in enough cold water to fill the spaces, barely covering the mixture. Cover and cook over a brisk flame until boiling point is reached, then let simmer very slowly over a very low flame for about 30 minutes. Lift off the lid and very gently pour over the whole the condensed tomato soup or the tomato purée. Cover and let simmer gently 20–25 minutes longer. Then lift the lid again and slip in gently the dozen newly opened eggs. In a few minutes the eggs are poached with the full flavor of the fish, vegetables, and tomato flavors, and the stew is ready. Do not stir the mixture while cooking as gradually it will settle down a little and the top will be *soupy*. A fine dish indeed to be served right from the kettle, which, if decorative enough, may be brought right to the table, to the oh's and ah's of your guests.

HALIBUT STEAK MIRAMAR [470]

Take 6 fresh individual halibut steaks about a scant inch in thickness and weighing each about 7 or 8 ounces. Sponge with a damp cloth; season to taste with mixed salt, pepper and paprika; roll them in egg into which a little milk, seasoned with salt and pepper and 1 tablespoon of good olive oil has been beaten; then roll in grated Swiss cheese. Again roll in the beaten egg mixture, then in sieved dry bread crumbs. Heat plenty of butter with a whole clove of garlic; remove the garlic and pan-fry the fish steaks in the garlicky butter, over a gentle flame, turning the fish frequently, until nicely browned on both sides. Arrange on a hot platter, garnishing with 6 thick slices of fresh tomatoes rolled in seasoned olive oil and grilled in the usual way, a bouquet of fresh parsley and quartered lemon. Serve with Brown Butter Sauce (No. 1015) and freshly made Shoestring Potatoes (No. 1424).

HALIBUT STEAK ALSATIAN MANNER [471]

Wipe a 2-pound steak of fresh halibut or any other kind of white-meated large fish with a cloth dipped in tarragon vinegar, then season to taste with mixed salt, pepper, nutmeg, and thyme. Set aside. Melt in an earthenware casserole ⅓ cup of sweet butter; stir in 1 tablespoon of finely chopped shallots, mixed with 1 tablespoon each of finely chopped onion, parsley and chives, and cook for a minute or so, over a low flame. Lay the fish steak over this; add 1 bouquet garni composed of 1 bay leaf tied with 7 or 8 sprigs of parsley, 1 sprig of thyme and 1 small sprig of green celery leaves (tops), then pour over very slowly 1½ cups of dry white wine.

Bake, uncovered, in a hot oven (400° F.) for 15 minutes, basting frequently. Cover with a buttered paper, and continue baking 10 minutes longer. Arrange the fish steak on a hot platter. Strain the sauce through a fine-meshed wire sieve into a fresh saucepan. (there should be about 1 cup of sauce). Heat to the boiling point, remove from the fire and stir in ½ cup of Béchamel Sauce (No. 259), previously scalded. Taste for seasoning, and strain the sauce over the fish, covering it entirely. Sprinkle ½ cup of soft bread crumbs mixed with a little grated Swiss cheese over the entire surface and brown quickly under the flame of the broiling oven. Serve simply garnished with parsley and lemon quarters and a side dish of plain boiled potatoes.

Interesting Facts about Lobsters. The Roman gourmet, Apicius, is reputed to have set out promptly in search of African lobsters and shrimps when he heard that they were bigger than those in his city ponds. His epicurean journey has modern echoes in the seasonable jaunts of American inlanders to New England shores and New England sea food every summer. Like Apicius, they eat lobster and shrimp—and fish, in general, of course; but mainly they seek out that king of the sea, the lobster. Lobster eaters—and they are legion—stare suspiciously at the ten spidery legs. Some dig in. Ugh—green stuff! Do you know what that is? That green pastiness is the lobster's liver, to be spread on crusty bread and eaten with gratitude. The way to get the good from the lobster's body is to split it up the middle, eat out the liver, then pull off the legs one by one. Pull each between the teeth as you do with an artichoke petal. Sweet juice waiting, and at the end a nibble of meat. Discard the rest of the leg. The legs are off, the liver eaten, but still goodness is left. The shell holds melted butter and little shreds of meat and heaven knows what. Dip the bread into this nectareous gravy and mop it clean, every last drop.

To Boil a Lobster. Bring 3 quarts of water to boiling with 2½ table-spoons of salt. Lift the lobster by the back or tail and drop head first into the boiling water. Cover and count the cooking time after the water returns to boiling. Simmer the lobster 5 minutes for the first pound and allow 3 minutes cooking time for each additional pound. Lobster toughens and shrinks with overcooking. Boiled whole lobster may be served hot or cold with lemon butter sauce on the side for dunking.

To Remove Meat from the Body. Lay the lobster on its back. Cut through to the back side with a sharp, heavy knife from the head to the tail. With your hands, force the lobster open into two halves. Remove the intestinal vein which runs through the tail meat just under the back. All other parts of the lobster are edible.

Caution. Always purchase live lobster, which will be darkish when seen in market alive, and take on bright red color after cooking. Female is preferred because of roe—also called coral—and is distinguished from the male by broader tail, greater softness of 2 uppermost finlike ap-pendages near body. In buying cooked lobster, pay particular attention to the tail. Never buy lobster dead before cooking.

Lobster Is a Valuable Food. Because of its very high content of iodine, the lobster is a valuable preventive of thyroid disorders. It is also high in mineral content, and as a valuable source of calcium it is an effective safeguard against mineral deficiencies in diet.

LOBSTER A L'AMERICAINE   [472]

The first essential condition is that the lobster or lobsters should be alive. Sever and slightly crush the claws of a 2-pound live lobster with a view to withdrawing its meat after cooking; cut the tail into sections; split the carapace in two, lengthwise, and remove the "queen" (a little bag near the head containing some gravel). Put aside on a plate the intestines and the coral, which will be used in the finishing of the sauce, and season the pieces of lobster with mixed salt and pepper.

Put these pieces into a saucepan containing 3 tablespoons of olive oil and 2 tablespoons of sweet butter, both very hot, and fry them over a bright flame until the meat has stiffened well and the carapace is of a fine red color. Then remove all grease by tilting the saucepan on its side with its lid on; sprinkle the pieces of lobster with 1½ teaspoons of finely chopped shallots and 1 small clove of garlic crushed to a pulp; add ¾ cup of dry white wine, ¼ cup of Fish Fumet (No 1100), 4 table-spoons of burnt brandy, 1 tablespoon of melted meat-extract (commer-cial), 3 small, fresh, pressed, and chopped tomatoes (or failing fresh tomatoes, 2 tablespoons of tomato purée), a pinch of freshly minced parsley, and a few grains of cayenne. Cover the saucepan and set to cook in the oven for about 18–20 minutes. This done, transfer the pieces of lobster to a heated dish, preferably a silver platter; withdraw the meat from the section of the tails and the claws, and put them in a timbale; set upright thereon the 2 halves of the carapace and let them lie against each other. Keep the whole hot.

Now reduce the cooking sauce of the lobster to ⅓ pint; add the intestines and the chopped coral, together with a piece of butter the size of a walnut. Place over a gentle flame and bring to a boil, stirring frequently, then strain through a fine-meshed wire sieve into a fresh saucepan; heat it without letting it boil; remove from the fire and stir in, bit by bit, 5 tablespoons of sweet butter. Pour this unctuous sauce over the pieces of lobster, sprinkle with a little minced parsley, and serve at once.

LOBSTER BELLEVUE [473]
Aspic de Homard en Bellevue (Cold)

Select 8 one-pound lobsters boiled in the usual way, cooled off, and carefully taken out of the shells. Keep the tails whole, and trim so that they will stand up when placed on a platter. With the claw meat and the rest of the trimmings, prepare a salad. To this add ¼ cup of finely chopped celery for each cup of lobster meat, seasoning according to taste and mixing with freshly made mayonnaise. Be careful not to make the salad too soft and liquid. Then let it season and mellow in the refrigerator. In the meantime, cover the tails with aspic jelly several times so that they receive a coating about ⅛ inch thick. Drain all the liquid from the prepared, well-chilled salad, and mix in more mayonnaise with aspic jelly and whipped unsweetened cream.

Now pour the salad into a suitable mold, and let congeal in the refrigerator. Prepare a platter with a half-inch layer of aspic jelly, then transfer the salad to it, arranging it evenly and placing the 8 tails carefully on it. Surround with the same amount (8) of jellied molds of fresh macédoine (a mixture of cooked diced vegetables) and decorate the whole dish with 8 croutons of tomato aspic. Chop some aspic jelly which has been sprinkled very slightly with cold water to prevent sticking and simplify chopping, and turn into a pastry bag. Decorate the empty spaces with the piped-on jelly.

For the aspic proceed as follows:

Fish Aspic (Fish Jelly). Put 1 pound raw fish bones with 1 quart cold water, 1 cup dry white wine, 1 medium-sized onion, chopped, a few sprigs of tarragon herb and fresh parsley (about 5 of each), tied with 1 small bay leaf and 1 small sprig of thyme with white kitchen thread, ½ generous teaspoon of salt and 6 whole peppercorns, gently bruised. Gradually bring this to a boil; let boil 2 or 3 minutes, lower the flame and let boil very gently for 20 minutes, stirring occasionally. Beat 3 egg whites stiffly with 3 tablespoons of good white vinegar, and add to the unstrained fish stock, together with 2 tablespoons of granulated gelatine softened in a little cold water, and let come to a boil. Let boil gently until mixture is clear; strain through a fine muslin cloth into a shallow dish and let cool and jelly.

This jelly is very appropriate for any kind of cooked fish, shellfish or crustaceans.

LOBSTER BIARRITZ [474]
(Serves 2)

Split lengthwise a 2 pound live lobster. Put split lobster with claws attached on a double wire broiler, clamp handles together and broil under moderate flame, having split part exposed to the flame, for 10 minutes. Then pour 1 tablespoon of sweet heavy cream over each lobster half, letting it seep into the split shell. Dot with a few bits of anchovy butter and return to broiler for 8 or 10 minutes longer. Season lobster with mixed salt and paprika when it leaves the broiling oven. Transfer lobster halves to hot platter and serve with the following sauce:

Melt 3 tablespoons of sweet butter and heat until foaming; remove quickly from the fire and stir in 2 tablespoons of tomato paste, 1 teaspoon of Pique Seasoning, 1 tablespoon of chili sauce, ½ teaspoon of prepared mustard, ½ teaspoon of horseradish, and 1 tablespoon of sherry wine. Mix thoroughly; return to the fire and heat to the boiling point, but do not let boil. Remove from the fire again and stir in 1 teaspoon of lemon juice.

LOBSTER BOHEMIENNE [475]
(Serves 2)

Boil a 2 pound live lobster in salted boiling water in the usual way; cut it open lengthwise; remove the meat and cut it in neat, thin slices. Now replace this lobster meat in the shell, alternating with thin slices of foie gras and thin slices of black truffle. Lay the 2 halves thus prepared in a shallow buttered, earthenware baking dish and cover with the following sauce:

Sauce Bohemienne. To ¾ cup of Béchamel Sauce (No. 259), add 2 tablespoons of the best port wine you can get, mixed with 1 tablespoon of old fine champagne brandy. Mix thoroughly and heat to the boiling point, but do not let boil. The sauce should be rather thick. Spread the lobster halves with this sauce; sprinkle over a little grated Parmesan cheese, and thin half-moon-fashion cut slices of truffle. Place the baking dish in a very moderate oven (300° F.) to delicately brown and let the

cheese gently bubble. Serve at once with a side dish of Shoestring
Potatoes (No. 1424).

LOBSTER CARDINAL [476]
(Serves 2)

Boil a 2-pound live lobster in a white wine court-bouillon (No. 1037)
15 minutes, or until red all over. Split lengthwise; remove the meat from
the shell and cut it into neat, small pieces. Dry the shells carefully,
brush with melted butter and place in it a thin layer of Sauce Nantua
(No. 1094). Replace in the shells the lobster meat, previously heated in
a little butter (but not boiled, lest it toughen), and seasoned with a
little salt and pepper, mixed with a few grains of cayenne. Cover the
lobster meat with more of the Sauce Nantua; sprinkle with a little
grated cheese and brown quickly under the flame of the broiling oven
until cheese bubbles and is nicely colored. Serve at once garnished with
lemon quarters and bouquets of fresh curled parsley.

LOBSTER COURT-BOUILLON [477]
(Serves 2)

Prepare a 2-quart white wine or vinegar court-bouillon (No. 1037)
and let boil very gently for 20–25 minutes. Then put in 1 two-pound
lobster or 2 one-pound ones, and let boil for about 15–20 minutes, as
gently as possible, or until quite red and done. If to be eaten hot, split
lobster lengthwise and serve one half of the two-pound size to each
person with a side sauceboat of melted, clarified butter and a little of
the broth and vegetables on the side, garnished with quartered lemon
and parsley. If served cold, serve with mayonnaise.

LOBSTER CURRY RISOTTO CROWN [478]
(Serves 6)

Boil 3 one-and-one-half to 2-pound live lobsters in white wine court-
bouillon (No. 1037) for 15 minutes; then break off the shells and cut the
tails and claws in pieces, about the size of a walnut, and place them in
a saucepan containing 2 cups of Curry Sauce (No. 1047), to which has
been added 2 tablespoons of tomato paste. Keep hot over hot (not
boiling) water, lest the lobster toughen, while preparing a risotto (or
rizotto, as it is sometimes spelled) as indicated in recipe No. 1599.
Pack the hot risotto into a buttered or oiled ring mold, unmold upon a
hot, round platter, and fill center of the ring with the curried lobster.
Dust top of lobster with finely chopped parsley and serve at once.

LOBSTER FIGARO [479]
(Cold) (Serves 2)

Boil a 2-pound live lobster in white wine court-bouillon (No. 1037) until done. When cold, split lengthwise; remove the tail meat whole and trim lightly but neatly. Chop finely the meat from the claws; add the tail trimmings, a little flaked cooked or canned crab meat, 1 tablespoon of tomato paste, 1 teaspoon each of finely chopped chervil, chives and tarragon herb, and combine with 2 tablespoons of mayonnaise, mixing well. Fill the half-shells with this preparation; place the whole tail meat on top, decorate with mayonnaise forced through a pastry bag with a small fancy tube, and on top of the mayonnaise place thin strips of anchovy filets and red pimiento, and a few well-drained chopped capers. Serve very cold.

LOBSTER NEWBURG I [480]
With Raw Lobster (Serves 6)

Cut up 3 two-pound live lobsters and cook in ¼ cup of olive oil and ¼ cup of sweet butter (blended). When the pieces of lobster are stiffened and colored, drain off (by tilting the pan) all but about 2 tablespoons of the fat, then add ¼ cup of burnt brandy and 1 pint of sherry wine. Let this wine sauce reduce to a third of its original volume, then stir in 1 pint of sweet, heavy, scalded cream with 1 cup of fish broth (No. 182). Cover and cook over a gentle flame for about 12–15 minutes, shaking the pan frequently so as to keep the lobster constantly moist. Take out the pieces of lobster, remove the meat from them and keep in a covered timbale. Thicken the sauce with the reserved intestines and mashed coral of the lobsters and 2 tablespoons of butter. Bring to a quick boil; remove at once, stir in 2 slightly beaten egg yolks; season to taste with salt, pepper, paprika and a few grains of cayenne pepper, and strain the sauce through a fine-meshed wire sieve over the lobster meat in the timbale. Serve at once, the platter simply garnished with small triangles of bread fried in sweet butter and a few bouquets of fresh parsley.

LOBSTER· NEWBURG II [481]
With Cooked Lobster (Serves 6)

Cook 3 two-pound live lobsters in white wine court-bouillon in the usual way (No. 1037); split them lengthwise, remove the meat from the shell and cut in slices. Lay these slices in a saucepan containing 4 tablespoons of sweet butter and season highly with salt, pepper, paprika and a few grains of cayenne pepper. Heat the slices thoroughly, but do not allow to boil, lest the meat toughen. Beat 3 egg yolks slightly, then beat them into 1 pint of scalded sweet cream and ½ generous cup of warmed sherry or Madeira wine. Pour this into a saucepan and heat to the boiling point, stirring constantly from the bottom of the pan seasoning to taste as you stir. Turn this sauce over the lobster. Heat well and serve on freshly made toast, in timbales or in large or individual patty shells.

It was for Bonaparte that chef Bailly created the world-wide known recipe for *Lobster Thermidor*. When the dish was first presented to Napoleon, he inquired the name of the chef, who forthwith was called to see His Majesty the Emperor. When Napoleon asked for the name of the dish, the chef simply answered: "Lobster à la Napoléon." "Not at all," replied the Emperor. "We should call this indescribable creation of goodness Lobster Thermidor."

Author's Note. Thermidor used to be the eleventh month of the first French Republic, from July 19th to August 17th. And so the name "Thermidor" remained tagged to this lobster dish.

LOBSTER THERMIDOR [482]

Split from the middle, lengthwise, 3 live lobsters of 2 pounds each; clean, season to taste with mixed salt and pepper and broil very slowly under the flame of the broiling oven, basting frequently with melted sweet butter. Remove the meat from the shell and cut in small pieces, slantwise; pour in each of the six shells 1 tablespoon or two of rich cream sauce (No. 258), to which has been added a scant teaspoon of dry English mustard (more or less according to taste); refill the shells with the sliced lobster and cover with the same sauce and dust tops of the shells with a little paprika. Glaze quickly under the flame of the broiling oven. Arrange on a hot platter; garnish with fresh parsley or young crisp watercress and quartered lemons and serve with a side dish of thinly sliced cucumber salad in French dressing. If desired, stir into the sauce a little sherry wine—but this is optional, the original recipe not calling for such luxury.

Interesting Facts about Mackerel. The mackerel first appears in spring off Cape Hatteras, and later reaches the shores of the Middle and New England States and Canada, coming in from a southerly or southeasterly direction. It leaves the coast in the same way in fall and winter. It's a wandering fish, and its movements and the causes thereof are not fully understood.

Periods of scarcity alternate with season of abundance. Small mackerel are known among fishermen as "spikes," "blinkers," and "tinkers." Spikes are the smallest caught by the commercial fishermen, being 5 or 6 inches long and 5–7 months old or younger. Tinkers are under 9 inches in length and are supposed to be about 2 years old.

Blinkers are intermediate in size and age. Maturity is probably attained in the fourth year.

For the table, mackerel is at its best from the latter part of June until the end of August, although found throughout the year.

Spanish mackerel, found in Southern waters, is highly popular and more expensive than the common mackerel.

Salt mackerel must be freshened before cooking. Allow at least 24 hours. Put the fish in a large amount of cold water, meat side down. A good suggestion is to place it on a rack, a few inches from the bottom of the vessel, so that the salt may drop away from the fish. Change the water several times.

For broiling or frying, freshen the fish more than for boiling or cooking in any way with milk, as milk covers up some of the salty flavor. To hasten the freshening process, it may be helpful to cut out the bone of the fish or to make several gashes in the flesh.

Fresh and desalted mackerel, as well as Spanish mackerel, may be prepared like bluefish, herring, shad, etc.

MACKEREL BOILED DINNER   [483]

Split open a 3–3½-pound fresh mackerel; clean and carefully remove the back bone without separating the fish. Lay skin side up in a buttered shallow baking pan; cover with cold water; add 1 tablespoon of vinegar, 1 clove, 1 blade of garlic, 1 large bay leaf, 1 sprig of thyme, 6 sprigs of fresh parsley, 4 or 5 thin slices of onion, pepper and salt to taste. Gradually bring to the boiling point; lower the flame and let simmer gently for about 15 minutes. Carefully lift the fish onto a hot platter; remove the skin without spoiling the appearance of fish. Garnish with small potato balls boiled in salted water until tender, drained and rolled in parsley sauce (No. 1101) and serve an extra side dish of sauce with a dish of small cucumber cubes mixed with an equal amount of celery cubes and marinated in French dressing.

MACKEREL FRICASSÉE FISHERMAN   [484]

Clean and cut into 6 portions a 3½-pound fresh mackerel; wash quickly in cold water and cook in white wine court-bouillon (No. 1037) to barely cover, for about 15 minutes, over a low flame. Lift out the pieces of mackerel, drain well, remove the skin and arrange on a hot platter. Keep hot. Strain the court bouillon through a fine-meshed sieve into a fresh saucepan (there should be about a cupful; if not, add a little more white wine and hot water); bring to a boil; remove from the fire and beat in 2 egg yolks, alternately with ½ generous cup of sweet, heavy cream, previously scalded. Bring to a boil, remove from the fire and stir in ¾ cup of cooked, shelled fresh mussels. Taste for seasoning and pour this "stew" all over the pieces of mackerel. Garnish with parsley and lemon quarters and serve at once with a side dish of plain boiled potato balls rolled in melted butter, then in chopped parsley.

MACKEREL GRILL   [485]

Have a 3–3½-pound fresh mackerel split for broiling; brush with cooking oil or butter or margarine, then with mixed salt and pepper to taste. Lay it skin side down on a generously greased broiler and grill under moderate heat until well browned. Remove to hot platter; spread with Maître d'Hôtel Butter (No. 1078); garnish the platter with 6 thick slices of fresh tomatoes, seasoned to taste with salt and pepper, then broiled, 6 large fresh mushroom caps, also broiled, and 6 crisp slices of broiled bacon. Serve with a side dish of creamed potatoes, and garnish the platter with parsley and lemon quarters.

MARYLAND CRAB CAKES   [486]

This recipe is more than two hundred years old and is very popular throughout the South. For 6 persons, trim 6 slices of bread from their crusts; lay flat on a platter or tin, and pour over them ¾ cup of good olive oil. Let stand 1 hour; then pull the bread apart lightly with two forks. To the small bits of bread add 3 egg yolks, slightly beaten with a dash of dry mustard, ½ generous teaspoon of salt, a generous dash of paprika, 2 teaspoons of Worcestershire sauce, and blend thoroughly. Mix in 1 pound crab flakes and ½ pound of claw meat. Mix lightly with a fork. Now fold in 3 stiffly beaten egg whites and shape into about 18 cakes. Brown in butter or other fat in a hot skillet just brushed with fat. If carefully mixed, these crab cakes will be light and fluffy and of delicate flavor. Canned crab meat can, of course, be used.

The method of cooking mullet depends somewhat on the size of the fish. Small mullet may be broiled, but the larger fish are best baked. The baked fish, 3 pounds or over, are nicest stuffed. Have the fish dressed for baking at the market.

MULLET PLANTATION STYLE   [487]

Wash with cold water and wrap in waxed paper and keep it in the coldest part of the refrigerator until ready to cook. For a well-flavored stuffing, cut 3 slices of bacon into dice and fry with ¾ cup finely chopped celery and 3 tablespoons of chopped onions, until bacon is brown. Add 3 tablespoons of butter or margarine or bacon fat (in addition to the 3 slices) and then stir in 3 cups of finely cut stale bread. Season with salt, pepper to taste and ½ teaspoon of poultry seasoning. Moisten with hot water or still better, with fish stock, but keep the stuffing as dry as possible.

Stuff the fish and tie around with string. Cut four slits about 2 inches long, across the top and place 2 strips of bacon across the slits. Place the fish on a greased baking pan, pour ½ cup of water in bottom, add 1 large bay leaf, 4 thin slices of onion and 6 or 7 sprigs of fresh parsley, and bake about 45-50 minutes in a moderate oven (325-350° F.). Serve garnished with parsley and lemon quarters and a side dish of French fried potatoes.

MUSKELLUNGE [488]

The flesh of this mastado species of the pike family is delicate and divides easily, as in salmon, into large flakes as white as snow. Epicures consider it one of the best fish of the Middle West and West. It surpasses the black and striped bass. The quality of the flesh improves upon keeping, and is very much more juicy and of better flavor after a day or two on ice.

The various methods of preparation of pike, pickerel, shad, bluefish, herring, etc., may be adapted to this precious fish.

MUSSELS [489]

Palatable, nutritious and inexpensive, mussels are an ideal food. Although one of the best and most abundant sea foods, mussels have been much neglected in American cooking. Their nutritive value is even greater than that of oysters and clams, long recognized as valuable sources of minerals and protein. Mussels have the advantage of being in season part of the time oysters are out, and are in prime condition from December to July. They are marketed by the pound, averaging 15-20 to the pound, depending on size. They should be purchased in their shells. Be sure the shells are tightly closed or, if slightly opened, that they close readily to the touch. This shows that the mussels are alive, which is essential right up to cooking. Open shells with a knife or steam them open, after scrubbing the shells thoroughly. The water which clings produces enough moisture for the steaming process. This may be done in a regular steamer if you have one. If not, place in any covered kettle and steam in a slow oven or directly over a gentle flame until shells open. Mussels may be cooked in the same way as oysters and clams, but should never be overcooked or boiled. Steamed mussels may be served, the broth strained off and the mussels heaped on a platter. Allow a small bowl of melted butter and a cup of broth to each eater, who should remove the byssus, or beard, and eat the mussel like a steamed clam.

MUSSELS BONNE FEMME [490]

Wash 2 quarts of mussels carefully in several changes of cold water, scrape them, and remove the byssus or beard that is attached to the shell. Put in a large kettle and add 1 medium-sized onion; 4 shallots finely chopped; ⅓ cup of fresh mushrooms, peeled and cut in julienne fashion (matchsticks); ⅓ cup of celery stalks, scraped and also cut in julienne fashion; 1 bouquet garni composed of 1 large bay leaf, tied with 6 or 7 sprigs of fresh parsley and 1 sprig of thyme, using white kitchen thread; 1 clove of garlic, left whole, 2 cups of dry white wine; and freshly ground black pepper. Do not add salt as yet. Cover the kettle closely and let cook over a gentle flame for about 10 minutes, shaking the kettle every 2 minutes. By this time all the mussels should be opened. Lift out the mussels from the kettle, shells and all; turn into a heated deep platter and keep hot.

Reduce the broth to 1¾ cups over a brisk flame, first discarding the bouquet garni and the garlic; bring to a boil; remove from the fire and beat in 2 egg yolks, slightly beaten with ½ cup of sweet, heavy, scalded cream and 2 tablespoons of melted sweet butter. Return to the fire and cook 2 or 3 minutes, stirring constantly from bottom of pan; remove from the fire and taste for seasoning, adding salt as needed. Pour this sauce over the hot mussels and serve at once.

The proper way to eat mussels cooked in their own shells is by taking hold of the empty shell and using it as a spoon, dipping the other one in the sauce. Each guest should have an extra plate in which to deposit the empty shells. Serve with brown bread and butterfinger sandwiches.

MUSSELS BORDELAISE   [491]

Scrape and clean 3 quarts of mussels with the greatest care, washing them in several changes of cold water. Place the mussels in a large kettle without any water at all, adding 1 sprig of thyme, 1 large bay leaf, 2 medium-sized onions, finely chopped, and just a suspicion of garlic. Cover the kettle and cook over a low flame, shaking the kettle from time to time until the shells have all opened up.

For the sauce which is to be poured over the finished dish, melt 1 teaspoon of sweet butter for each dozen mussels and add slowly the liquor from the kettle, previously strained though fine doubled cheesecloth. This operation should be done with great care in order to avoid the sand, if any, which has settled on the bottom of the kettle. Now season to taste with mixed salt and pepper and the juice of a large lemon, and allow the sauce to come to a boil, after which beat in 2 egg yolks, adding them one at a time and beating well after each addition. Finally, remove the mussels from their shells; place them in a heated serving dish; cover with the sauce and sprinkle with finely chopped parsley.

The old tale that the Bideford Bridge, in London, is held together by the network spun by mussels has a grain of truth in a husk of fable. It is true that the town council, believing that the masses of mussels protect the foundations from being undermined by the tide, has forbidden the taking of mussels from this place. Mussel beds in various places act as barriers, protecting lowlands from inundation. An artificial jetty is soon loaded with mussels and filled with silt, which year by year increases its stability and efficiency as a breakwater.

MUSSELS GREEK MANNER [492]

Scrub and rinse in several cold waters 4 quarts of large fresh mussels; place in a heavy kettle without any liquid; place the kettle over a bright flame until mussels are all opened, discarding those which are not. Remove the mussels from their shells, reserving the shells.

Combine ½ cup of cooked rice, ½ cup of seedless or seeded raisins, plumped in boiling water or meat stock, drained and finely ground, ⅓ cup of fresh mushrooms, peeled, chopped and sautéed in a little butter for 2 minutes and well drained. Season with white pepper, a very little salt, and a generous pinch of paprika. Mix thoroughly. Fill one of the shells with this stuffing, another with one mussel and tie the two together in the middle with white kitchen thread. Repeat until all the mussels are thus prepared. Place the stuffed, tied mussels in enough water or fish stock and dry white wine in equal amounts to barely cover; add ½ cup of good olive oil; bring to a boil and let simmer very gently for 15 minutes. Skim off the mussels with a perforated ladle; reduce the broth to about 1 cup over a bright flame; strain through fine cheesecloth into a fresh saucepan; bring to a boil; stir in ¾ cup of scalded heavy sweet cream with 2 or 3 slices of seeded lemon; taste for seasoning and serve with, but not in the same dish as the hot mussels, which have been untied.

MUSSELS Ā LA HENRI PULLIG [493]

For six generous servings, select 6 dozen large, unopened fresh mussels. Clean, scrub, then place the mussels in a large saucepan, the bottom of which has been lined with 8 crushed shallots, 1 small clove of garlic, mashed, 2 whole cloves, a generous blade of mace, a pinch of tarragon herb, powdered, and 1 bouquet garni composed of 1 large bay leaf, 6 sprigs of fresh parsley, 2 sprigs of green celery leaves (tops) and 1 sprig of thyme, all tied up with white kitchen thread. Pour over 2½ cups of Moselle wine; cover the pan tightly and bring to a boil over a bright flame, shaking the pan every 2 or 3 minutes, until mussels are opened. Lift out the mussels with a perforated skimmer, returning to the pot any herbs which may be lifted out with them; when mussels are cold enough to handle, remove from their shells, discarding the shells, and placing the mussels on a hot platter. Allow the stock to stand a few minutes to let the sand and sediment, if any, to fall to the bottom, then strain through a coarse strainer, discarding the bouquet garni, and pressing gently to obtain all the pulp from the seasoning. Return the stock to the fire; bring to the boiling point, and let simmer gently while preparing the second part of this dish.

In another pan, melt ½ generous cup of sweet butter; blend in 4 rounded tablespoons of flour, working until smooth and stirring almost constantly with a wooden spoon, but do not allow to brown. Gradually pour over this the simmering mussel-wine stock, stirring constantly with a wire whisk, until the sauce is thick and smooth. Let it simmer gently, stirring frequently, for about 5 or 6 minutes. Remove from the fire, then beat in 5 or 6 yolks, diluted with a little cold milk, beating briskly while adding to prevent curdling. Season to taste with salt, pepper and a few grains of cayenne pepper; return to the fire and cook 2 or 3 minutes, over a gentle flame, stirring constantly from the bottom of the pan. This sauce should be so thick that the spoon will be heavily coated when dipped into it. Allow to cool to a little above lukewarm, stirring occasionally to prevent the formation of a film on top.

Now, take up the mussels one by one with a fork; dip each one into the sauce, seeing to it that each mussel is thoroughly coated with the thick sauce and placing them upon a slightly oiled large platter as you go along. When all the mussels have received their coating, let cool until this is firm when, on pressing with a finger, it doesn't stick. Rub a bowl with a cut clove of garlic, then beat in it 4 eggs with 4 tablespoons of olive oil; season with mixed salt, pepper and a very few grains of curry powder, and dip the cold, coated mussels into this one by one, then immediately roll them in fine, sieved bread crumbs. They should be thoroughly coated with crumbs. When ready to serve, place the mussels, a few at a time, in a wire basket and plunge immediately into hot, deep, clear fat, preferably oil, for a minute or so to delicately brown and crisp. Serve on a folded napkin arranged on a hot platter and strew over all a large bunch of fresh, curled parsley deep fried in the same fat. Serve at once with a side dish of Tomato Sauce (No. 1130).

MUSSELS MARINIÈRE [494]

Prepare 2 generous cups of white wine court-bouillon (No. 1037); strain through a fine-meshed wire sieve into a kettle and add 3 quarts of mussels, scrubbed clean. Cook over a bright flame until the mussels open, tnus adding their salty juice to the broth. Taste for seasoning, being careful about salt and generous with black pepper. Serve in heated soup plates as indicated for Mussels Bonne Femme (No. 490).

MUSSELS A LA NEWBURG [495]

Prepare 1¾ cups of Sauce Newburg (No. 1095) and keep hot. Cook 3 quarts of cleaned and scrubbed mussels in a white wine court-bouillon as indicated for Mussels Bonne Femme (No. 490), removing the mussels from the shells, which discard, and keeping the mussels hot. A few minutes before serving, add the hot mussels to the Newburg sauce; heat thoroughly and serve in individual heated patty shells, on toast, or in individual casseroles or ramekins.

MUSSELS A LA PROVENÇALE   [496]

"A la Provençale" means, of course, a spicy dish with oil and garlic. After scrubbing 3 quarts of mussels and rinsing them thoroughly in several changes of cold water, put them, dry, into a large saucepan on the fire, stirring them as they open. When all are open, remove one half of each shell. Into another saucepan, put ½ cup of good olive oil, with 2 tablespoons each of parsley, chives, mushrooms and truffles and a small clove of garlic, all chopped very fine. Gradually bring this to a boil, and when it boils, add 1 cup of dry white wine, 3 tablespoons fish stock, and 1 cup of the carefully strained mussel broth, and boil until mixture thickens, stirring frequently. Then season to taste with black pepper only, no salt at all, as yet; add the mussels and heat thoroughly. Just before serving add 2 teaspoons of lemon juice, a fresh grating of nutmeg, and salt as needed. Serve in hot, deep plates.

NEW ENGLAND KITCHEN CLAMBAKE   [497]
(Serves 4)

Ingredients for this recipe are 4–5 quarts of clams, 1½ pounds of fish filets (cod, flounder, halibut, or any other kind of white-fleshed fresh fish), 1½ pounds of pork sausage links, 8 medium ears fresh or canned corn on the cob, 8 medium-sized onions, 4 small white and 4 small sweet potatoes, and, if desired, 4 small (1-pound size) fresh lobsters or 4 hard-shell crabs, cleaned.

Parboil the onions about 20 minutes. Scrub clams to remove sand and place in the bottom of the kettle or, if you have an old-fashioned boiler, so much the better. Cut the fish filets into 4 portions and put individually into paper or muslin or cheesecloth bags, and place on top of clams; then sausage-links in bags; next, corn-on-the-cob and onions in bags on top of sausages; potatoes are last, and do not need to be in bags. Pour 2 cups of water into kettle and cover tightly. When potatoes are tender, all will be done—about 30–45 minutes. Paper bags should be removed before serving or by each guest as they are lifted from the "bake." The sausages flavor the vegetables nicely and the broth is delicious. But, remember, everything should be served piping hot.

OYSTERS   [498]

Why do people who wouldn't think of eating oysters in August buy them in quantity and eat them heartily in September? Simply because it is a custom sanctioned by tradition.

The four "R"-less months—May, June, July and August—must also be oysterless, tradition says. And why? Chiefly because oysters are supposed to spawn during these months, and spawning oysters should be preserved so that their millions of eggs will produce "spat" or fry." That, of course, is a good idea. But the taboo of oysters from May to August doesn't accomplish it. The oysters of the New England and New York beds do spawn during these months, and the oyster taboo is therefore useful in sustaining production in these beds during the period when consumption would be most destructive. But the oysters in the most productive beds in the world, those of Chesapeake Bay, don't spawn during the "R"-less months and are therefore not helped in the least by the traditional boycott. In Southern waters oysters may spawn at any season of the year. It can easily be seen, therefore, that this particular reason for the traditional taboo of oysters during the summer months is actually no reason at all. In fact, in some parts of the United States, oysters have long been eaten throughout the year, with no ill effects whatever. With the growth of the canning industry it is likely that we shall get further away from the old fad-tradition, until eventually the bivalve will be almost as popular in July as it is in October.

Today, oyster growing or culture is a highly specialized industry. Gone are the days of "free fishing," and now we have special oyster grants to private individuals for the purposes of seed production and maturing for market. For example, a young or "seed oyster" may be planted off Long Island Sound, where certain chemicals are added to the water to induce profuse breeding. Then, in a few months, the young oyster may be moved to Rhode Island or elsewhere, and finally, at the age of about three years, shifted to its permanent home, where it will stay until its plump maturity at about the age of five years.

The entire process and the equipment of oyster farming are most interesting. New appliances on the principle of the vacuum cleaner are now used to dislodge the oysters. In the early days of September the beds are "tonged" with long rake-like instruments lowered from small oyster boats, the jaws opened, closed and lifted aboard with their sea-food catch. In the later Fall, oysters in deeper water are similarly dredged.

How do you like your oysters—small, medium, or large? As they appear in the market, these succulent and healthy bivalves vary in name as well as in size, color and flavor. For example, around Long Island, large oysters are known as Mattitucks, medium-sized ones as Blue Points, and the small ones as Cape Cods. Or again, oysters taken near Gardiner's Island, Long Island, savor of salt, while the Oyster Bays are sweet, and those from the Gulf of Mexico have a coppery taste, as do those of the French Marennes.

On the Pacific Coast oyster culture differs greatly from that in the East, and follows the methods of the Japanese. There, cultivated beds are built on terraces of gravel with concrete walls, not unlike the "sets" of cement-coated tiles used by the French in producing their oysters. Western oysters are tiny, seldom larger than two inches at maturity, and most of these beds are utilized by canning factories.

So fond were the early Massachusetts settlers of the juicy bivalve, that "by 1775 the natural beds of Cape Cod were exhausted," and laws had to be passed preventing their further destruction. It was considered lucky to eat oysters on the first day that they appeared in markets, and several noted paintings feature these traditions, such as "The First Day of Oysters," painted in 1838, and "The Oyster Eater," painted in 1710.

OYSTERS BENEDICT [499]

Sauté 6 thin slices of boiled ham in its own fat and on both sides, until delicately browned. Keep hot. Drain 1 pint of oysters and sauté 1 minute in fat remaining in the pan. Remove at once. Split 3 English muffins and toast on cut side. If bread is used, toast on both sides. Arrange 1 slice of hot ham and 4 or 5 hot oysters on each split muffin; cover with Hollandaise sauce (No. 1062), and sprinkle the sauce with finely chopped chives and parsley mixed in equal parts. Serve at once.

OYSTERS CASINO [500]

Select large oysters for this recipe and have them opened on the deep shell. Allow 8 oysters to each portion. Arrange oysters on the deep shells in a shallow baking pan which has been prepared with a layer of rock salt (ice cream salt). Imbed the oysters firmly in the rock salt, as this will hold them steady while cooking. Season with very little salt, a speck of cayenne and paprika. To each oyster add a pinch of finely chopped pimiento and a piece of sliced bacon cut the same size as the oysters. Broil under moderate flame until cooked. Bacon will cook first, so when both sides are broiled, remove it to a warm dish while oysters and pimiento cook 7 or 8 minutes longer. Keep oysters moist by adding a bit of butter or oyster liquor while broiling. Serve in the shells and garnish each oyster with the small piece of broiled bacon and a tiny sprig of parsley.

OYSTER FRICASSEE BALTIMORE [501]

Delicately brown 4 tablespoons of butter and add 1 tablespoon of flour, a few grains of pepper, and ½ teaspoon of minced parsley. Mix well. Add 1 quart of well-drained oysters and stir until edges curl. Add 2 beaten egg yolks and stir constantly until egg is set. Serve at once on warm serving plates with a garnish of fried bread crumbs, parsley and lemon quarters.

OYSTER FRICASSEE BOSTON STYLE [502]

Proceed as indicated above (No. 501), using equal parts of oysters and deep sea scallops, quartered, and 4 egg yolks instead of 2. Serve in the same way.

OYSTER FRITTERS   [503]

For 6 generous servings select 3 dozen of freshly opened oysters and cut (do not chop) them in small pieces. Make a batter as follows: 1 cup of milk, 2 eggs, well beaten, 2 cups of sifted flour with 1½ teaspoons of baking powder, salt and pepper to taste, 1½ tablespoons each of finely chopped parsley, chives and grated onions, beating to a smooth batter. Then stir in the chopped oysters; drop by tablespoons into a pan containing ⅓ cup of good butter in the form of small patties or cakes and brown well on both sides. Serve at once with a side dish of Tartare Sauce (No. 1128), Tomato Sauce (No. 1130), or Maître d'Hôtel Butter (No. 1078), the platter garnished with parsley and lemon quarters.

OYSTER FRY   [504]

Important. None but perfectly fresh oysters can be flipped in corn meal and fried. Old oysters will not hold together, the natural juice of washed oysters will not be sufficient to hold the meal, and the fat in which oysters so treated are fried must be at just the right temperature and perfectly clean and sweet. Following this you'll enjoy the divine treat of "half dozen fry."

Select large oysters, freshly opened, and lay carefully on a colander to drain. Dry quickly and gently with a soft cloth, handling as little as possible. Sprinkle over the prepared oysters—a good half-dozen for each serving—½ cup of seasoned corn meal, having all the oysters well-coated. Have ready a frying pan, not too deep, with plenty of smoking-hot olive oil or sweet lard, to which a little butter may be added to help in making the oysters crisp and brown. Put in only enough oysters to cover the bottom without crowding. When brown on one side, turn over. Drain. Serve on a folded napkin or paper doily, garnished with 1 large head of fresh mushroom, peeled, dipped in oil and broiled, 1 thick slice of tomato dipped in French dressing and broiled, 1 thick slice of large onion, parboiled, drained, dipped in oil and broiled and 2 strips of bacon, freshly broiled, for each serving. Parsley and lemon quarters are passed on the side.

The first thing any true oyster fancier will observe is that oysters taste best when they are eaten with a little lemon juice, perhaps a few specks of horseradish, but definitely no tomato catsup sauce.

OYSTER AND MUSHROOM PIE   [505]

Cook 1 cup of fresh mushrooms, peeled and sliced (using both caps and stems), in 2 tablespoons of butter until partially tender. Stir in

3 tablespoons of flour, and when well blended, gradually stir in 1 cup of milk previously scalded with 1 bay leaf, 3 thin slices of onions, 3 sprigs of fresh parsley, 1 whole clove and a tiny blade of garlic, and then strained. Cook until mixture thickens, stirring constantly. Season with ½ teaspoon of salt, ⅓ teaspoon of celery salt, 1½ teaspoons of lemon juice, and a dash of freshly ground black pepper. Bring to a boil; remove from the fire and stir in 2 egg yolks, stirring briskly while pouring. Lastly add 1½ cups of oysters and their own liquor. Line bottom and sides of a casserole or deep dish with your favorite flaky pastry rolled ⅛-inch thick; brush with unbeaten egg white; line the bottom with 4 hard-cooked eggs, shelled and quartered; fill with oyster mixture after tasting for seasoning, and cover with pastry, making a few slashes to allow escape of steam; brush top with cold milk, and bake in a hot oven (425° F.) for 10 minutes. Reduce heat to moderate, and continue baking 10 minutes longer. Serve hot and cut in wedges.

NOTE. The addition of a dozen of very small white onions, previously cooked in boiling salted water and well drained, is a great improvement.

Get an oyster intoxicated and you can get him out of his shell more easily than a professional opener can! Experiments have shown that oysters immersed for 5 minutes in carbonated water become intoxicated by the carbon dioxide and then relax the muscle holding the shell closed. When oysters are in this state, a mere novice can shuck over 100 oysters in 20 minutes, which is fair going for a professional with sober oysters.

OYSTER PILOTE   [506]
A Supper Party Recipe

Allow half a dozen each for the ladies and a dozen for the men. Don't buy them too large or too small. Before anything else is done, 2 cups of Mornay Sauce (or more, according to number of guests) (No. 1088) should be made. Poach the oysters in their own liquor, but do not let them boil. Let them curl their beard (gills). Take the bottom shells of the oysters, clean them thoroughly and imbed them in a tray with coarse salt. Garnish each shell with a scant teaspoon of the following mixture: put through food chopper 3 large mushroom caps, previously peeled, 1 well-washed anchovy filet, 2 tablespoons each of chopped shallots, parsley and chives, and cook in 2 tablespoons of sweet butter. Season highly with cayenne pepper and a dash of nutmeg, and stir in 1 egg yolk. Lay in each shell one of the poached oysters, cover with Mornay Sauce; sprinkle over a little paprika and grated cheese, and let the oysters glaze under the flame of the broiling oven. Serve very hot, passing a dish of lemon quarters.

OYSTER STEW [507]
(*Serves 2*)

Pick over and remove any bits of shell from 1 dozen oysters. Put them in a pan with their own liquor, previously strained through fine cheesecloth, 2 tablespoons of butter, celery salt, pepper and paprika to taste, and cook until edges (gills) curl, stirring frequently. Pour over 2 cups of scalded milk, mixed with 1 cup of scalded cream. Serve immediately, each plate or bowl garnished with 1 tablespoon of sweet butter and a dash of paprika.

Oyster stew is a favorite American dish; it is one of the most informal and delightful foods to cook for two.

PANNED PORGIES [508]

Porgies are at their best when panned. This method of cookery brings out their sweet flavor and preserves the flaky quality of the meat.

Clean, or have the fishman clean for you, 2½ pounds of porgies. The size of the variety chosen determines whether 1 or 2 fish will provide a portion. Rinse the fish quickly in running water; wipe dry; dip into ¼ cup of corn meal or flour, mixed to taste with salt and pepper; lay apart from each other on waxed paper, and pan fry in ¼ cup of cooking oil, lard or other shortening until brown on both sides. Serve simply garnished with parsley and lemon quarters and a side dish of lemon butter sauce (No. 1070) for accent.

POACHED FINNAN HADDIE IN MILK [509]

Lay 2½ pounds of finnan haddie filets in cold water to cover; drain; place in a shallow baking dish; cover well with about 3 cups of milk; place over hot water; poach very gently for 15 minutes, or until the flesh just begins to flake. Arrange the filets upon a heated platter, after draining well. Dot freely with butter using about ¼ cup, and sprinkle generously with freshly ground black pepper. Serve with plain boiled potatoes, and garnish with parsley and lemon quarters.

POMPANO EN PAPILLOTES "LA LOUISIANE" [510]
(*Serves 2*)

Transcontinental travelers taking the Southern route either east or west stop off at New Orleans to sample this creation of Anatole, the chef of Antoine's Restaurant which, when served with a vintage sauterne, maketh the heart glad.

Take a 3-pound pompano, bone it or have this done by the fishman; remove the skin and poach in white wine court-bouillon to cover for

12 minutes. Drain, reserving the stock. Keep the pompano filets hot, while preparing the stuffing as follows:

Heat 2 tablespoons of sweet butter; stir in 1 tablespoon each of onions, mushrooms, green pepper, truffles, all finely chopped, ½ teaspoon each of shallots, parsley or chervil preferably, chives, green celery leaves, tarragon herb, and a thin blade of garlic, also finely chopped. Season with salt, pepper, thyme, mace and nutmeg and cook 5 minutes over a gentle flame, stirring almost constantly. Remove from the fire and stir in 2 tablespoons of good sherry wine and strained fish stock to make a stuffing of spreading consistency, rather on the moist side. Place half of the stuffing over a pompano filet; place the filet on a buttered waxed paper or patapar paper. Adjust another filet sandwich-style over the stuffing, bring the two edges of paper together and seal by folding the ends tight, allowing plenty of room around the fish filets. Repeat with the 2 remaining filets. Lay the 2 packages in a buttered shallow baking pan and place in a very hot oven (425–50° F.) for about 5 minutes. Serve at once, removing the paper only at table.

Pompano means "grape leaf" in Spanish. The filets of this southern waters fish may be prepared in all the recipes indicated for the so-called filets-of-sole, namely the flounder filets.

Great Yarmouth and Lowestoft on the North Sea have long been world-important centers of the herring trade. It was at Yarmouth that Nurse Pegotty told David Copperfield, in Dickens' book of that name, that she was "proud to call herself a Yarmouth bloater."

POTTED HERRING (FRESH)   [511-512]

Take perfectly fresh herrings and clean them well, but do not wash them; cut off the heads and fins, take out the bones and strew the fish over with mixed salt and black pepper to taste. Put a minced small onion in each and roll up tight, then pack them in jars and cover them with vinegar and water using 1 pint of good vinegar to 2 of water with ½ ounce of whole black pepper, gently bruised, 1 medium-sized bay leaf and 1 whole clove to this amount of liquid. Tie a sheet of paper over the jar and bake in a moderate oven (375° F.) for 1 hour. Take off the cover when the herrings are cold and pour a little cold vinegar over them. This makes a good supper, breakfast, or picnic dish and men especially like it with plain boiled potatoes or a potato salad.

POLISH HERRING STEW   [513]

Served very hot, this dish is unbelievably good!

Peel and cut in quarters 4 medium-sized potatoes and 1 medium-sized onion. Cover with cold water to cover, season to taste with salt and add 6 gently bruised peppercorns, 1 large bay leaf and 2 whole cloves. Cook until potatoes are half done, then place on top of the potatoes 3 fresh herrings which have been cut in half across, cleaned, and head and tails removed. Cover, and cook very gently until both fish and potatoes are done. Remove the fish carefully to a heated platter; add ½–¾ cup of scalded cream (or less if you prefer it less rich) to the stew and thicken with flour, but do not make it too thick. Cook a few seconds longer and pour the whole over the herrings. Serve as hot as possible.

Shad, mackerel, and all fish having the fat distributed throughout the entire body may also be prepared in this way. (See Fish Chart No. 411).

Of all the snappers, red snapper is by far the most important and best known, and there are more than 3 dozen of this species, which is related to the Sea Bass. (See Fish Chart No. 411). The various methods employed in the preparation of bass, herring, pickerel, pompano and whitefish may all be adapted to this delicate fish.

RED SNAPPER MIAMI STYLE [514]

Remove head and scales from a 6–8 pound red snapper; rinse; dry. Rub ⅓ cup of dry mustard into the fish inside and out. Place it in a long shallow baking pan and sprinkle with ¼ cup of flour mixed with 1 teaspoon of salt and ⅛ generous teaspoon of pepper; dot with ¼ pound of butter, then pour on 1 cup of fish stock mixed with 2 cups of dry white wine, and add 1 bouquet garni composed of 1 extra large bay leaf or 2 medium-sized ones, with 12 sprigs of fresh parsley, 2 sprigs of green celery leaves, 1 sprig of thyme, and 2 whole cloves, tied together with white kitchen thread, 1 medium-sized onion, thinly sliced, 1 medium-sized carrot, scraped then thinly sliced, and 1 small piece of white leek. Bake in a moderate oven (350–375° F.) for 45 minutes, or until the flesh just begins to flake, basting frequently with the pan liquid. Remove the yolks from 3 hard-cooked eggs; reserve the whites. Mash the yolks with ¼ cup of olive oil in a small saucepan; stir in ¼ cup of tarragon vinegar, and a pinch each of salt and pepper; then strain over this the fish broth from the pan; bring to a boil, stirring constantly, and let boil 2 or 3 minutes. Remove from the fire; stir in 4 dozen carefully picked medium-sized oysters.

Serve the fish on a heated long platter; garnish with rings of hard-cooked egg whites, lemon quarters and parsley, and pass oyster sauce in a sauceboat. A side dish of plain boiled small potato balls, rolled in melted butter, then in finely chopped parsley and chives mixed in equal parts, and another side dish of thinly sliced cucumber salad are the usual accompaniments for this fine fish.

RED SNAPPER VERA CRUZ STYLE [515]
Pargo Colorado al Vera Cruz

This kind of Mexican Bouillabaisse is very old and greatly relished in Florida. Ingredients are 6 individual slices of strictly fresh red snapper, 6 individual slices of red fish, ½ bottle of dry white wine, ½ medium-sized lemon, 6 large fresh tomatoes or ½ can of solid tomato pack, 3 medium-sized onions, 1 bouquet garni, 3 cloves of garlic, 2 large bay leaves, 3 sprigs of thyme, 10 sprigs of fresh parsley, 6 allspice, 2 tablespoons of olive oil, and salt, pepper, and cayenne to taste.

Important. If prepared in Pensacola, sea trout and black bass are substituted for red fish. If prepared in New England, codfish is used instead of red fish. If prepared in New Orleans, catfish is used instead of red fish.

Cut off head of fish and boil in 1½ quarts of water, so as to make fish stock with the usual ingredients; that is, a bouquet garni composed of 1 sprig of thyme and 2 whole cloves, 6 sprigs of fresh parsley, 2 sprigs of green celery leaves (tops), tied together with white kitchen thread. When reduced to 2 cups, take out the head and strain the stock through a fine-meshed wire sieve and set aside for use later on.

Take 6 slices of red snapper and 6 slices of red fish of equal size; rub well with mixed salt and black pepper to taste. Chop the 3 sprigs of thyme, sprigs of parsley, bay leaves and garlic. Grind the 6 allspice very fine, mix all these herbs and condiments together with the garlic and rub each slice of both fish until all are permeated by the mixture. Put 2 generous tablespoons of olive oil in a large, shallow pan so that the fish slices will not overlap one another; add the finely chopped onions to the hot oil, lay the fish slices in the pan and let them cook for about 10 minutes, turning once so that each side may partly cook. Remove the fish and place them on a perforated platter or drainer to drain, keeping them hot.

Now, pour the half bottle of dry wine into the pan and stir well over a gentle flame, then add the tomatoes (fresh or canned). If fresh tomatoes, slice them thinly after peeling. Let this mixture boil for 2 or 3 minutes, then add the half lemon cut in paper-thin slices and, if desired, 2 large green peppers, cut into very thin slices carefully seeded and white ribs removed. Pour in the fish stock made with the fish heads; season to taste with salt and pepper, and a dash of cayenne pepper, and let this boil gently until the liquid is reduced to half its original volume. Then lay the half-cooked fish, slice by slice and apart from one another, in the pan and let all boil steadily for 5 minutes.

In the meantime, chop a generous pinch of saffron very fine and add to it 2 or 3 tablespoons of the hot fish stock to dissolve the saffron well, then spread over the fish.

To Serve. Lay 1 slice of each fish on a slice of bread which has been fried on both sides in olive oil or butter till delicately browned; pour the sauce over and serve as hot as possible, dusted with equal parts of finely chopped parsley and chives.

SALMON COURT-BOUILLON, HOLLANDAISE [516] SAUCE

The quantity of "court-bouillon" or "short broth" is determined by the size of the piece of fish which it is to cover.

For a 2–2½ pound piece of salmon prepare 1 generous quart of white wine court-bouillon as indicated for No. 1037, having the broth cold. Lay the salmon (or any other kind of fish) in a pan; pour over the cold broth; bring very slowly to a boil; immediately lower the flame and let simmer, nay, let poach very gently for about 20–25 minutes, or until fish just begins to flake. The boiled salmon is then drained and dished on a napkin and served with a side dish of plain boiled potatoes and a sauceboat of Hollandaise Sauce (No. 1062), the dish simply garnished with parsley and lemon quarters. When served cold, the Hollandaise Sauce is replaced by a side dish of Mayonnaise.

SALMON MOUSSE HAVRAISE   [517]
(*Hot*)

Mousse means moss, or froth, or foam. We are familiar with delectable frozen desserts of whipped cream and egg flavored with strawberry, chocolate, or coffee, and announced as mousse; but of late years we have had scarcely more than a bowing acquaintance with those mousses of Virginia ham, chicken, and fish which appear as mere samples, for a moment's consideration, at formal dinners and in more pretentious table d'hôte restaurants.

In a more leisurely and contemplative age, when America's old families, of a stratum that escaped the social register, were grouped around midtown residential squares, mousses were of some importance as entrées, and as luncheon or supper dishes. It was the period in which huge soufflés were served at high tea on Sundays, and people discussed Brillat-Savarin's cheese fondue. Many of the family cooks of that day were Irishwomen, who seem to have been particularly capable and well trained, and presided in their kitchens with authority.

Poach a 2½ pound piece of fresh salmon in a white wine court-bouillon or short broth (No. 1037), as for Salmon Court-Bouillon, for about 30 minutes, counting 10–12 minutes per pound of fish. Drain; bone the fish carefully and remove all skin, then put the remaining meat through the food chopper, or still better, pound it to a pulp, adding while pounding, and little by little, 2 unbeaten egg whites. Place this paste in a mixing bowl, place the bowl over finely cracked ice and work it with a wooden spoon for 5 minutes, then rub through a fine-meshed wire sieve. Return it to the ice, cover and let stand for at least 30 minutes, stirring occasionally. Gradually beat in 1 cup of sweet, cold heavy cream, alternately with 2 more egg whites, this time stiffly beaten. Taste for seasoning. Turn into a generously buttered melon mold having a tight-fitting cover and place the mold in a pan containing hot water up to the brim of the mold; poach very gently in a moderate oven (350° F.) for 40–45 minutes, or until set and firm. Remove from the oven; let stand 5 minutes before unmolding and serve at once with a side dish of Mustard Sauce (No. 1092). A well-chilled, thinly sliced cucumber salad with sour cream dressing is the usual accompaniment for such a delicious dish.

For cold Salmon Mousse, simply add 1 tablespoonful of softened granulated gelatine for each 2 cups of liquid, mold and chill thoroughly before unmolding instead of poaching as for the hot Mousse.

SCALLOP EPICURE [518]

Wash 1 quart of bay scallops or sea scallops quickly in slightly salted water and drain. If sea scallops are used, they should be quartered. Place the scallops in a bowl; pour 1 quart of boiling water over them; add 2 tablespoons of tarragon vinegar and let stand 5 minutes. Drain well. Roll the scallops in 1 cup of fine cracker or bread crumbs, mixed with 1 teaspoon of salt and a generous dash of cayenne pepper. Dip in beaten egg (2 eggs) and again in crumbs. Place close together in a greased shallow baking pan; scatter over the top ¼ pound of bacon, cut into narrow strips, and bake in a very hot oven until the crumbs brown, or about 10–12 minutes. Serve with Tartare Sauce (No. 1128) and a side dish of Cole Slaw.

SCALLOP STEW [519]
(*Serves 2*)

Scald 1 cup of milk with 1 cup of thin cream, adding 1 piece of bay leaf, 2 sprigs of fresh parsley, 2 thin slices of onion, and a tablespoonful of coarsely chopped green celery leaves. Cover and let stand 5 minutes, then strain into a clean saucepan, and season to taste with celery salt and a few grains of cayenne. Again bring to a boil; lower the flame and let simmer gently (not boil) for 5 minutes longer, then add 2 tablespoons of sweet butter and 2 dozen bay scallops (if sea scallops are used, quarter them), and continue simmering for 12–15 minutes more. Place a piece of toast in each heated soup plate and pour the scallop stew over it. Dust top of each plate with finely chopped parsley (or chives in season).

SEA URCHINS [520]

Sea Urchins, those "green pin-cushions" of the ocean, are as delicious as caviar, or pâté de foie gras. The demand for sea urchins (see Fish Chart No. 411) is growing by leaps and bounds. New York markets alone consume more than 300,000 pounds, these coming from Maine every year. They are usually served as a first course, 3 or 4 to a plate, opened in halves and laid out like oysters, the top of the shell removed to expose the yellow roe, which is eaten with a tear of lemon, a dash of Worcestershire, a pinch of horseradish, and a dip of grated onion. Hot Melba toast, generously buttered, and dry white wine complete an appetizer of the first class. The edible sea urchin is greatly relished by the French, the Italians, the Spanish and the English. It is the ripe ovaries of the creature that are consumed, these being scooped out with a spoon and eaten either raw or cooked in an omelette.

SHAD ROE GRILL [521]

Wipe 3 shad roes with a damp cloth; sprinkle with mixed salt and pepper and a little lemon juice; place them on a generously greased broiler and broil 5 minutes, basting with a little melted butter and lemon juice in equal parts. Turn the roes and broil 5 minutes more on the other side. Serve split in two, on toast on a heated platter, and garnish each roe with 2 strips of grilled bacon, 1 thick slice of tomato, dipped in seasoned flour and pan-fried in butter, and 1 grilled large fresh mushroom cap. Garnish with parsley and lemon quarters. Pass a side dish of Maître d'Hôtel Butter (No. 1078).

The subject of the shad and its bones brings up a much-quoted jingle, *Poor Satan*, its author unknown. It goes as follows:
"When the Lord made shad, the devil was mad, for it seemed such a feast of delight, so to poison the scheme, he jumped in the stream, and stuck in the bones out of spite. When the strawberry red first illuminated its bed, the angels looked down and were glad. But the devil, 'tis said, fairly pounded his head, for he'd used all his bones on the shad."

SHAD ROE MEUNIERE [522]
(*Serves 2*)

Wipe a shad roe with a damp cloth; dust it with seasoned flour, and split in two crosswise. Fry the two pieces in clarified butter over moderate heat until nicely browned. Transfer to a hot platter or individual plate and sprinkle over it the juice of a small lemon or a half one if juicy. Melt 2 tablespoons of butter in the pan the roe was cooked in and just as it turns a rich golden brown pour it immediately over the roe. Sprinkle with finely chopped parsley and serve at once.

SHRIMP IN ASPIC   [523]

Bring 1 quart of water to a boil with 1 mashed clove of garlic, 1 medium-sized onion, thinly sliced, 6 peppercorns, gently bruised, 1 bouquet garni composed of 1 bay leaf, 6 or 7 sprigs of fresh parsley, 2 sprigs of green celery leaves, 1 sprig of thyme and 2 cloves, tied together with white kitchen thread, 1 scant teaspoon of salt and 1 small lemon thinly sliced. Let boil 2 or 3 minutes and add 1½ pounds of fresh shrimp which have been carefully washed. Cook 10–12 minutes, depending on size; drain and shell, carefully removing the vein which runs down the center of the back. Strain the stock into a fresh saucepan. Taste for seasoning and stir in 3 or 4 drops of Tabasco. There should be 2½ cups of stock. Bring slowly to the boiling point; remove from the fire and stir in 1 tablespoon plus 1 teaspoon of unflavored granulated gelatine, previously soaked in 3 tablespoons of cold water or fish stock for 5 minutes. When gelatine is dissolved, strain the hot broth through a fine cloth, into a fresh saucepan. Allow to cool to lukewarm. Arrange in a bowl a layer of the prepared shrimp; pour over a little of the lukewarm gelatine broth and let congeal. Then arrange carefully a layer of sliced black olives, a little more of the jelly, more shrimps, more jelly, a layer of finely chopped green pepper, some jelly, the remaining shrimp and remaining jelly. Set the bowl in the refrigerator to chill 3–4 hours or even overnight. When ready to serve, turn out on to a chilled round platter; garnish with quartered hard-cooked eggs, black olives, stuffed olives, gherkin fans, and tomato slices, the whole arranged tastefully over a bed of crisp watercress. Serve a side dish of mayonnaise to which have been added some chopped watercress leaves, chives and chopped capers.

Shrimp dishes have a special nutritional value, for shrimp, like other fish products, are rich in calcium, phosphorus, copper and sulphur, all of which are necessary body-building elements. They have a high percentage of all necessary digestible proteins as does any fish food. And in addition they contain vitamins A, B and D, natural protectives against Winter health trials, plus a high iodine content.

SHRIMP AND MUSHROOM A LA KING   [524]

Slice ½ pound of peeled fresh mushroom caps and stems and cook 4–5 minutes or until tender in 4 tablespoons of butter over a gentle flame, stirring frequently. Sprinkle over them 4 tablespoons of flour and stir until flour is thoroughly blended. Then stir in ¼ cup of rich chicken broth or stock (No. 301) mixed with 1¼ cups of thin cream, scalded, while stirring constantly. Place over hot water and cook until thickened, continuing to stir from bottom of the pan. Then stir in 2½ tablespoons of canned red pimientos, well drained, 2 tablespoons of finely chopped green pepper, and beat in 3 egg yolks, one at a time, beating well after each addition. Now season to taste with mixed salt, pepper and a few grains of cayenne pepper, and finally add 2½ cups of cooked, shelled fresh or canned shrimp, from which the black vein running down the back has been removed. Heat to near the boiling point but do not allow to boil and, when ready to serve, stir in 4 (more or less) tablespoons of good sherry wine. Serve on toast, in heated patty shells, or right from the plate, each portion dusted with a little paprika.

Lobster, scallops, oysters, prawns, etc., may also be prepared in this way.

SHRIMP—COQUILLE *(See recipe 430)*
SHRIMP Ā LA MARSEILLAISE [525]

Fry 1 clove of garlic, 2 medium-sized onions, 1 red pimiento, and 2 tablespoons of green pepper, all finely chopped, in 4 tablespoons of olive oil until just beginning to take on color, over a low flame, stirring occasionally. Have ready 2 cups of hot strained white wine court-bouillon (No. 1037); stir in 1 thread of saffron, then gradually combine with the garlic-onion mixture. Season to taste with salt, pepper and a tiny pinch each of mace and thyme. Finally stir in 1 pound of cooked, shelled (vein removed) large shrimp. Heat well. Grease an earthen-ware casserole generously; cover the bottom with 1 cup of cooked rice; over the rice arrange a layer of half of the shrimps and stock. Repeat with a second cup of cooked rice, then the remaining shrimp and stock mixture. Bake in a moderate oven (350° F.) for 30 minutes. Bring the casserole to the door of the open oven, quickly and carefully drop in, one at a time, 6 eggs; close the oven door and continue baking for about 5 or 6 minutes or until the eggs are poached. Serve right from the casserole with a side dish of thinly sliced cucumber with French dressing.

In selecting fresh shrimp be sure they are grayish green in color and have a fresh, clean, sea fragrance. The shell should fit the body closely. Shrinkage may be a sign of staleness.

SHRIMP PIE CHARLESTON STYLE [526]

Fry 1 medium-sized, chopped onion in 3 tablespoons of butter until just beginning to brown, then stir in 1 No. 2 can tomatoes, alternately with 4 thin slices of stale bread broken small, and 1 medium-sized chopped green pepper. Season to taste with salt, pepper and a dash each of nutmeg, thyme and mace; mix thoroughly and cook 3 minutes, stirring constantly. Now add 2 cups of cooked, shelled (vein removed) fresh shrimp (canned shrimp may also be used) and cook gently for 15 minutes longer over a low flame, stirring frequently. Lastly, add 3 hard-cooked eggs, coarsely chopped, and turn mixture into a casserole; sprinkle with ½ cup of toasted bread crumbs; dot with 2 tablespoons of butter and bake 15 minutes in a moderate oven (375° F.) or until well-browned. Serve immediately.

> *"Oh, lady, if you want somethin' sweet,*
> *Jes take a little piece of lobster and*
> *Mix 'em with tender, pure raw shrimp. . . . "*
> —*Negro Street Shrimp Vendor's Song*

SHRIMP PUFFS MAINE STYLE [527]

Sift 2 cups of bread flour, add 3 teaspoons of baking powder and ⅓ teaspoon of salt, a dash of grated nutmeg and one of thyme and sift again into a mixing bowl. Beat 1 large egg, combine with 1 cup of sweet milk, stir into the dry ingredients and beat until smooth. Now add ½ pound of freshly cooked, shelled (vein removed) shrimps. When ready to serve, drop mixture from a tablespoon into hot, clear, deep fat (360°–375° F.) and fry until delicately browned and well puffed. Serve at once with a side dish of Tartare Sauce (No. 1128), and another of French fried potatoes.

Lobster, prawns, crab meat, mussels, etc., may be prepared in the same manner.

SKATE WINGS AU BEURRE NOIR [528]
(Serves 4)

Wash and scrape 1 pair of skate wings, weighing about 4 pounds, carefully and thoroughly, or have the fishman do it for you, then cut each into 2 pieces. Place in a large saucepan, add boiling water to cover, and drain at once. Now cover with cold water and add 1 bouquet garni composed of 1 large bay leaf, 1 sprig of thyme, 7 or 8 sprigs of fresh parsley and 1 sprig of green celery leaves (tops), tied with white kitchen thread, also 1 medium-sized onion, sliced, a blade of garlic (optional, but it adds a fine flavor), 2 tablespoons of vinegar and 5 or 6 peppercorns, freshly bruised. Gradually bring to boiling point. Let boil 1 minute or two, lower the flame and simmer very gently for 20 minutes, or until fish appears to flake, skimming thoroughly. Drain, place in a towel and remove the skin from both sides and edges of the wings. Return to the cooking broth and keep hot. When just ready to serve melt and heat ⅓ cup of butter in a frying pan until foaming; immediately add 1 tablespoon of chopped parsley, 2 tablespoons of capers, a few grains of cayenne or tabasco sauce, and pour sizzling hot over the well-drained skate wings. Garnish with plain boiled potatoes, parsley and lemon quarters.

NOTE. Skate wings may also be cooked in a white wine court-bouillon, drained, skinned, then covered with curry sauce (No. 1045).

The skate is different from all other fish in that its small body is never eaten. The edible portions are the two circular sections, the wings attached to each side of the body. The body itself, which has an almost human face, is never shown in the markets. Another difference between the skate and other fish is that skates' flavor and texture improve if, after washing and cleaning, the wings are covered with cold water and allowed to soak for at least 24 hours, and of course stored in the refrigerator. Like sweetbreads, skate wings need preliminary preparation before being served, this consisting of boiling with herbs and condiments.

If not overcooked, the meat of skate wings may be used as crab meat or an extender of crabmeat. One skate wing weighs approximately 2 pounds and should yield about 2 cups of shredded meat, which may be served in a curry sauce or prepared by any of the methods applied to crab meat. (See Fish Chart No. 411.)

SMELT FRY CANADIAN STYLE   [529]

For six persons, clean at least 3 pounds of very small smelts; wipe dry; dredge with seasoned flour and place a few at a time in a wire frying basket and plunge the basket into hot, clear deep fat (375°–390° F.). Cook not even 1 minute, just until crisp and brown. Serve on a folded napkin placed on a hot dish; top with a bunch of fried parsley and garnish with 2 grilled strips of bacon, 1 grilled mushroom cap, and 1 thick slice of tomato, also grilled, per person. If desired, serve a side dish of Tartare Sauce (No. 1128).

For a mixed fry, use equal parts of smelts, shrimps, oysters and scallops all rolled in seasoned flour and deep fried.

Fish experts do not agree on the origin of the smelt's name. Some believe it a contraction of the words "smell it," due to the fact that fresh ones have an odor like freshly cut cucumbers. Others assert that the name came from the Anglo-Saxon *smelt* signifying smooth and shiny. In Scotland it is known as the sparling and its French name is *éperlan*. The famous food historian Beauvilliers said smelt smelled like violets. Hungarian food writers agreed with him, some of them likening the odor to syringa.

The true epicure cooks and eats his smelts "heads, guts, and feathers." The finicky may have theirs "gibbed," which means pulling out the entrails by the gills to which they are attached. A knife should never be used for this job. These little fish run 12–16 or even more to a pound, and half a dozen should be allowed for each serving.

SNAILS [530]

The snail is native to the mild regions around the Mediterranean Sea. North Africans, the people of Asia Minor, and of Southern Europe, all hold snails in high esteem as an article of diet, and have done so from the earliest times. In scattering to the Western Hemisphere these people have taken snails with them wherever they went; and these molluscan colonies have succeeded both in North and South America.

A great degree of intelligence is ascribed to the snail, including the homing instinct, which enables it to forage widely and return after each excursion to one "home" spot. Darwin reported that a pair of snails, one of which was feeble, were placed in a small garden where the food supply was scant. The stronger one set out alone, and found good pasture in the adjoining garden. The next day he returned and together the pair went over the wall, where plenty abounded. The slimy trail of snails is probably their means of returning after a night's foraging by the same route that led them forth. Their senses of sight, smell and hearing are well developed. Snails kept as pets wander about, curiously examining everything they come to with their sensitive tentacles and stalked eyes. The prominent rimmed jaw and the remarkably complex radula of twenty-one thousand teeth in serried ranks are freely exhibited in action by a hungry snail to which is presented a crisp leaf of lettuce or cabbage, its favorite diet.

In autumn the snail prepares to go into winter quarters. It burrows down among grass roots and leaf-mould until comfortably pocketed, with the mouth upward; then it makes a roof of dead leaves and other rubbish cemented with slime. Now the body is drawn into the well-hidden shell, and a thick limy stopper (the pot lid), called the epigram, is formed by the secretion of the foot gland. This has no single air hole, for it is porous, like plaster of Paris. Now the snail draws its body still further back, makes an inner, papery door, and "lies down to pleasant dreams." In Spring this period of hibernation ends, and a very hungry mollusk breaks through its doors and comes forth to feast on the young shoots of growing things. In June the pea-sized chalky-shelled eggs are laid in holes dug in the ground. The number of eggs varies—probably fifty is above the average. The young come out forty days afterward, eating for their first meal the egg shell that cramped their dusty growth.

The size of their snails was a matter of great pride to the Romans owning snail preserves, called "cochlearia." Meal and new wine fattened them for market. On this diet, the snails of Hirpinus reached such a size that a single shell held eighty-six penny pieces. Varro recommended that a ditch be dug around the snaileries to save the expense of a special slave to catch the runaways which scaled the walls. Pliny the Younger reproaches his friend Septicius Clarus for breaking a dinner engagement with him, at which the menu was to have been a lettuce, three snails and two eggs apiece, barley water, mead and snow, olives, beet roots, gourds and truffles, and going off somewhere else where he got oysters, scallops and sea urchins.

Snails are the accepted barometers of the common people. If they leave the herbage and take to the bare rocks, or if they climb trees you may expect rain. Dishonest dairymen manufacture "cream" out of skim milk by squeezing into it the clear mucus of snails. The consistency of the milk becomes creamy, and a little annatto (a yellowish-red dye obtained from the pulp enclosing the seeds of the annatto tree, used in coloring butter, cheese, cream and even varnish) gives the yellow color. This ancient practice is still in favor in parts of Germany and Austria.

SNAILS BOURGOGNE STYLE [531]
Escargots à la Bourguignonne

Place 6 dozen snails, using the large ones, in a wooden bucket with ½ cup of rock salt and 1 scant cup of vinegar; cover with a wooden board and let stand for 30 minutes, stirring every 5 minutes with a wooden stick and closing at once with the wooden board lest the snails escape Rinse under running cold water, stirring them constantly until there is no more foam or scum. Drain and at once plunge them into rapidly boiling water to which has been added ½ cup of clean wood ashes or, better still, 1½ teaspoons of baking soda, and let boil steadily for 10 minutes. Drain and, when cool enough to handle, remove the snails from their shells, reserving the shells.

The next step consists of cooking the shelled snails in white wine court-bouillon (No. 1037) to cover for 2 hours, over a very low flame, or until snails are tender, having the kettle partly covered.

Meantime, wash and scrub the snail shells carefully and thoroughly; drain and dry them in a very slow oven, leaving the door open and shaking the pan occasionally. Now prepare a special butter as follows:

Snail Butter. (This butter keeps several weeks in the refrigerator, and is delicious served over fish and meat steaks, grilled or pan-fried.) Place in a mixing bowl 1 pound of butter with 3 ounces of finely chopped shallots, 2 cloves of garlic mashed to a pulp, 1½ tablespoons of finely chopped parsley, salt, pepper and a dash each of nutmeg, thyme and mace, and cream until thoroughly blended and smooth.

Fill each shell with 1 snail, then fill up the shell with some of the snail butter, packing and spreading the butter as evenly as possible with the edges of the shell. Chill.

To Serve. Arrange the chilled, finished snails on a shallow baking pan or individual special snail plates and bake in a hot oven (425° F.) until butter melts and shells are very hot. Serve immediately.

Variation. Some gourmets, after having fitted the snail into its shell, first sprinkle with a little grated Swiss cheese before packing the snail butter.

SNAILS A LA PROVENÇALE [532]

Prepare and cook 3 dozen large snails as indicated for No. 531, remove the snails from their shells, reserve the shells and keep the snails hot. Wash and scrub the shells and dry them well.

Place in a saucepan 2 tablespoons of good olive oil and heat well; then stir in 1½ tablespoons each of parsley, fresh mushrooms, and green pepper, all very finely chopped, with 1 tablespoon of finely chopped shallots and 1 clove of garlic, mashed to a paste. Cook over a low flame for 5 minutes, stirring constantly, then sprinkle in 2 teaspoons of flour; mix well, then gradually add 1 cup of dry white wine. Season to taste with salt, pepper, nutmeg and a few grains of cayenne pepper, and when this stuffing has boiled 2 or 3 minutes, stir in, off the fire, 2 or 3 slightly beaten egg yolks, stirring briskly to prevent the egg yolks from curdling. Next, add the cooked snails and heat through. Fill each shell with one snail and some of the stuffing, filling the shell well, then cover with a thin layer of bread crumbs soaked in a little olive oil. Arrange the snails on a shallow pan and brown nicely in a hot oven (425° F.). Serve at once in the same manner as for Snails Bourgogne Style (No. 531).

STEAMED CLAMS [533]

Scrub 6 quarts of soft-shelled clams and wash under running cold water until sand has been removed. Place in large kettle with 1 cup of boiling water, bring to boiling point, cover and cook over low heat about 12–15 minutes or until shells open. Serve on a hot, deep platter and cover with a napkin. At the side of each plate have a small dish containing melted butter sauce, made by mixing ¾ cup of melted butter with 2 generous tablespoons of lemon juice or onion juice.

This amount of sauce will serve six. It should be warm, and each clam should be dipped into it before eating. White or brown bread and butterfinger sandwiches are the usual accompaniment.

SWORDFISH [534–5]

Like tuna, the swordfish is all meat and no bone. The meat is oily (see Fish Chart No. 411) yet delicate. It is the oldest known fish, yet least known as to habits. Twenty-three centuries ago the Greeks talked about this fish warrior of the sea. Today we still know nothing of its spawning habits or where it winters. Even less is known about those swordfish cousins, the blue and white marlins.

One of the many favorable features of this good food fish is the fact that it is boneless when it reaches the table, for the backbone—cut out in the market—is the only one it possesses. When cooked, its meat, which runs from light gray to cherry color, turns white and it has a close texture similar to that of the white meat of turkey. Its distinctive flavor is mild and delicious. It's a fish of great size, with long, naked body, upper jaw very much prolonged, forming a sword which is flattened horizontally.

The maximum size of the swordfish is 600 to 800 pounds. This species is rather abundant for so large a fish. Off the New England Coast, 3,000 to 6,000 of these fish are taken every year. Like the mackerel, the swordfish belongs to the category of rich food fish, and the various methods employed in the preparation of mackerel, bluefish, pompano, herring, etc., may be adapted to it. (See also Fish Chart No. 411.)

Because of its large size, the fish is sold in steak form. The best methods for cooking it are broiling, sautéing, or pan-frying, and baking as for halibut, cod, or any large fish steaks. Lemon is a *must* with this fish, so is cucumber and cucumber sauce.

TERRAPINS—TURTLES [536]

The diamondback terrapin can be grown in captivity "as easily as chickens," the only drawback being that it takes a terrapin 7 or 8 years to attain full growth. At Beaufort, North Carolina, is the Government terrapin farm, which liberates periodically large numbers of baby diamondbacks in the marshes of the South Atlantic and Gulf States.

Legend is that Chesapeake terrapins once ranged so abundantly from Cape Cod to Cape Hatteras that they were fed to slaves as a cheap food. Now about only 50,000 terrapins of the five recognized varieties are captured each year. The varieties are (1) the Chesapeake; (2) the Carolina; (3) the Florida; (4) the Louisiana; and (5) the Texas, the last-named supplying much of the trade.

As for the large sea turtles, they are mostly used to make turtle soup in large quantities, or sold as steak by specialty fishmen.

TERRAPIN—HOW TO PREPARE AND COOK [537]

In order to soften and dissolve the foreign matter attached to the flesh or the shell, plunge the turtle into a pan containing sufficient water to allow it to swim easily, renew the water several times, and allow the turtle to remain thus for about an hour. Then scrub thoroughly with a brush and immediately plunge into *unsalted* water boiling rapidly, until the skin of the head and feet becomes white and may be easily removed by rubbing with a dry, clean towel.

Cook the turtle in plain *unsalted* water or steam it. The time will vary according to size, although more than ¾ of an hour should not be necessary for an ordinary-sized turtle, the cooking point being determined when the feet are soft under pressure of the fingers. Any turtle of ordinary size requiring more than 45 minutes to cook is probably of inferior quality and should be set aside, as the meat, although acquiring tenderness through the long cooking process, is likely to be stringy and of poor quality.

After cooking, the turtle is set aside to cool, then the nails are pulled from the feet, the undershell is cut close to the upper shell and the flesh carefully removed, the feet separated from the body, cut in small pieces, and set aside. The upper shell is emptied and the gall bladder discarded (any small particle of the gall bladder remaining in the meat will impart a bitter flavor to the dish). The sand-bag, heart, and intestines are also discarded, as well as the white muscles of the inside.

The eggs are carefully removed and set aside with the feet and liver, and these are immediately sprinkled with salt and coarse black pepper, placed in a kettle with the turtle meat, a few slices of carrot and onion, a bay leaf and 2 whole slightly bruised cloves and covered with salted water. The covered kettle is set on the range for 20 minutes, to boil rapidly; then still covered, it is transferred to a moderately hot oven (350° F.), and the cooking process continued for another 20 or 25 minutes. If the turtle thus cooked is not to be used immediately, it is packed into earthenware or porcelain jars each holding approximately 2 pounds (meat and bones), tightly covered and kept in the refrigerator until wanted.

TERRAPIN BALTIMORE [538]
(*Serves 2*)

Add 1½–2 tablespoons of sherry wine to ¾ cup of white stock (No. 185), then 2 pounds of the prepared terrapin as indicated above (No. 537), the bones being cut in small pieces. Set over a very moderate flame and cook gently until the liquor or stock is reduced to half its original volume. Add the liver, cut in small pieces, 1½ tablespoons of butter; salt and coarse black pepper to taste; and lastly stir in 2 egg yolks, slightly beaten, stirring meanwhile. Do not cook any longer. Turn into a deep, hot, service platter and serve at once without any garnishing other than a side dish of freshly made dry toast.

As regards the wine to be used with this famous dish, our choice has always been champagne, and we have been upheld in that contention by one of the oldest clubs in the United States where the pleasures of the table have been elevated to a fine art. However, in the best of all Maryland clubs, nothing else is ever served with the great American dish but Madeira wine.

A 2-pound terrapin will serve 2. To serve 6 generously, use 4 terrapins, each of 2 pounds weight.

TERRAPIN MARYLAND   [539]
(Serves 2)

Proceed as indicated for Terrapin Baltimore above (No. 538), adding 1 tablespoon each of butter and flour kneaded together, ½ cup of scalded thick, sweet cream, 2 additional egg yolks, well beaten, and 1 generous teaspoon of strained lemon juice to ¾ cup of white stock. Then, just before serving, add 1½–2 tablespoons sherry wine; pour into a deep, hot, service platter and garnish with small triangles of bread fried in butter.

TROUT   [540]
Brook, Sea and Lake Trout

The brook trout you enjoy in hotel, restaurant or in your own home never knew freedom (unless you caught it yourself). He was born in captivity and reached maturity in an atmosphere of security experienced by no other fish sold for food. He is the product of commercial fish hatcheries. Commercial fish hatcheries exist to aid in stocking and re-stocking of privately owned streams. The hatchery, however, produces more fish than this outlet requires and the excess goes to the markets and thence to the tables of gourmets. This applies to brook trout only.

The delicate flavor of brook trout is explained by the fact that they live in water that springs from the hills and is freshened by the roots of trees, shrubs and ferns.

Sea trout, commonly known as weakfish, is a delectable sea food, plentiful at low cost during most of the year. Properly prepared, it compares favorably with many higher-priced fish. (See Fish Chart No. 411.)

Lake trout is a little oily and slightly fishy in flavor. To eliminate this taste, skin the fish just like an eel by cutting the skin all the way around, just behind the head, and pulling straight back with the aid of a clean, dry piece of cloth, which affords a non-slipping grip on the slimy skin. Small lake trout are the most desirable for cooking purposes. The big ones are apt to be a little tough, and strong in flavor. After skinning and cleaning—and, incidentally, the fish should be skinned first—cut into steaks, salt, roll in corn meal or flour, and fry in a skillet very slowly with a minimum of butter. A squeeze of lemon juice or a tart sauce adds to the flavor of the fish.

TROUT (BROOK) AMANDINE   [541]
(Serves 2)

Season two 12–16 ounce brook trout lightly with salt and pepper; dip in cold milk, then roll in flour and sauté over a gentle flame in 3 tablespoons of butter until brown on both sides. Place on a heated serving platter and keep hot. To the butter left in the pan, add 2 or 3 more tablespoons of sweet butter and heat to the foaming point. Then stir in 2 tablespoons of blanched shredded almonds and cook 1 minute, rocking the pan constantly over a medium flame. Pour over each fish 2 teaspoons of lemon juice and at once pour the boiling butter-almond mixture over the fish. Garnish simply with parsley and lemon quarters and serve with a side dish of small potato balls rolled in minced chives.

TROUT (LAKE) AMBASSADOR   [542]

Wipe a 3-pound lake trout with a damp cloth and skin as indicated under No. 541. Split open from the back; remove the backbone carefully and rub inside and out with sherry wine. Set aside. Cream ½ cup of sweet butter with 1 tablespoon each of parsley, chives, shallots, fresh mushrooms, all very finely chopped, 1 blade of garlic mashed to a paste, salt, pepper and ½ teaspoon of curry powder. Put half of this inside the fish and spread the remainder over the outer surface. Lay the fish in a generously buttered, shallow baking dish. Add 1 medium-sized onion studded with 2 whole cloves, 1 bouquet garni composed of 1 bay leaf, 1 sprig of thyme and 6 or 7 sprigs of fresh parsley, tied with white kitchen thread. Pour over equal parts of fish stock (No. 182) and dry white wine to barely cover the fish, and bake in a moderate oven (350–375° F.) for 30 minutes, basting frequently with the liquid in the pan. Transfer the fish to a heated serving platter; strain the liquid from the pan through a fine-meshed wire sieve into a saucepan; bring to a boil, let boil until stock is reduced to about ½ cup, then stir in 1 cup of sweet, heavy cream, previously scalded and mixed with 2 beaten egg yolks, stirring constantly from bottom of pan until mixture just begins to boil. Taste for seasoning and keep hot. Heat 3 tablespoons of brandy in a soup ladle; set aflame and distribute all over the fish, letting it burn until the alcohol is exhausted, pour the cream sauce over the fish, covering it completely; sprinkle 2 or 3 tablespoons of grated Swiss cheese over the entire surface and glaze quickly under the flame of the broiling oven. Serve at once with a side dish of freshly made Saratoga Chips (No. 1432) and another of thinly sliced cucumber with French dressing.

TROUT (BROOK) BOULEVARDIER,   [543]
HOLLANDAISE SUPREME

Clean and bone a dozen small brook trout, each weighing no more than 10 ounces; cut into filets and roll them. Put ⅓ cup of olive oil in a large, shallow frying pan and add the rolled trout filets, previously seasoned with mixed salt and black pepper; pour in 1 scant cup of fish stock (No. 182), 4 thin slices of onion, 4 sprigs of parsley and 1 sprig of thyme; cover with a buttered paper, and bake in a hot oven (400° F.) for about 10 minutes, basting several times during the baking process. Transfer to a heated platter, and pour over the following sauce:

Hollandaise Sauce Suprême. Clarify ½ pound of butter. Break the yolks of 2 eggs in top of double boiler, set over hot (not boiling) water, not allowing water to touch upper pan. Drip in the butter (as oil is dripped for mayonnaise), stirring constantly until thick. Stir in as slowly as possible the juice of 1 lemon and season to taste with salt and white pepper. Just before serving, stir in 12 shelled, veined cooked shrimp; ¼ cup peeled, thinly sliced, sautéed fresh mushrooms; 1 tablespoon finely minced black truffles; and a very little water from the pan in which filets were cooked. Blend thoroughly, pour over the fish, dust with paprika and garnish with lemon sections and parsley.

TROUT (BROOK) AU BLEU   [544]
Truite au Bleu

First make a court-bouillon for a dozen brook trout weighing ½–1 pound each (better less, than above, 1 pound). This will serve 6 gourmets.

Court-Bouillon (Short Broth). Put 3 quarts of water; 1 cup of tarragon vinegar; 2 teaspoons of salt; 15 whole peppercorns, gently bruised; 2 medium-sized carrots, scraped, then thinly sliced; 1 bouquet garni composed of 2 large bay leaves, 10 sprigs of fresh parsley, and 1 sprig of thyme tied with white kitchen thread, and 2 whole cloves; and 4 thin slices of onion. Gradually bring to a boil, and let boil gently 35–40 minutes.

For Truite au Bleu (Trout in Blue), the main idea is to have live trout, as the skin is viscous and cooking it in this way lends a particularly bluish color. Fifteen minutes before the trout are to be served, take them out of their fresh water; stun them by a blow on the head; empty and clean them quickly, then plunge into the boiling court-bouillon. At once lower the flame and simmer very gently for 10 minutes. Transfer to a hot platter on a fancifully folded napkin, garnishing with the vegetables from the court-bouillon, fresh parsley and lemon sections. Serve steamed potatoes and melted clarified sweet butter or Hollandaise Sauce (No. 1062) separately.

TROUT (BROOK) BOURGUIGNONNE   [545]

Clean 6 fresh brook trout weighing 12–16 ounces each. Wash quickly in cold water slightly acidulated with lemon juice or good vinegar; season on both sides with salt and black pepper, lay in a shallow pan and sprinkle over them 2 tablespoons of finely chopped shallots; add 1 bouquet garni composed of 1 bay leaf, 7 or 8 sprigs of fresh parsley, 1 sprig or top stem of fresh fennel, and 1 sprig of thyme, tied with white kitchen thread. Pour over all 2 cups of Burgundy red wine, previously brought to the scalding point; cover with a buttered paper and bake in a slow oven (300° F.) 15–20 minutes. Transfer the well-drained trout to a heated service platter; drain the wine from the pan through a fine strainer into a saucepan and let it reduce over a hot flame until there are about 1½ cups left. Remove from the fire; beat in 3 egg yolks, one at a time, beating well after each addition; return to the fire, bring to a boil, stirring constantly. Remove from the fire, taste for seasoning and let stand 1 minute. Squeeze 1 scant teaspoon of lemon juice over each fish, pour the wine sauce over, garnish with fresh parsley and lemon quarters and serve at once with a side dish of tiny cucumber cubes marinated in French dressing, drained, then tossed in a little mayonnaise, and dusted with paprika.

TROUT (BROOK) DELICES D'ANNECY AMANDINE [546]

Sauté 6 nice fresh brook trout (12–14 ounces each) in plenty of sweet butter for 5 minutes on each side. Arrange on heated service platter. To the butter left in the pan, add enough to make about ½ cup; heat to a sizzling foam; remove from the fire and stir in 1 tablespoon of lemon juice. Have ready ½ cup of blanched, shredded or halved almonds. Divide the almonds among the fish and pour the foaming butter over all. Place the platter under the flame of the broiling oven and heat until the almonds are lightly toasted.

This recipe may be used with almost any kind of small fish or fish filets or with soft-shell crabs. The fish or crabs may be broiled instead of being sautéed. The main point is to have the butter sizzling hot before pouring it over the almonds.

Omit the shredded almonds and you have Trout Meunière.

TROUT (LAKE) HOME STYLE [547]

Rinse one 3–3½ pound lake trout after cleaning in cold water; tie in a piece of cheesecloth; place in a long platter with 1 tablespoon of parsley, 1 tablespoon of green celery leaves and 1 tablespoon of onion, all finely chopped, scattered all over the fish. Put the platter and its contents in a large pan; barely cover with 3 cups of cold water and ¼ cup of vinegar; season with salt and pepper; add 1 large bay leaf tied with 1 sprig of thyme and 1 whole clove and bring slowly to a boil. Lower the heat and let simmer gently for about 20 minutes. Transfer the fish to a hot platter and remove the cheese cloth. Serve with the following sauce:

Sauce Bourgeoise. Melt 2 tablespoons of butter; blend in 1½ tablespoons of flour, and gradually stir in 1 cup of sweet cream, scalded with ½ cup of sweet milk; stir constantly until thickened. Season to taste with salt and pepper; stir in 1 tablespoon of chopped capers, 1 tablespoon of chopped dill pickle and beat in 2 egg yolks, one at a time, beating briskly after each addition. Pour this sauce over the hot fish and garnish with 3 hard-cooked, quartered eggs, parsley and lemon quarters.

Cooking Tuna. Cooking tuna is no problem at all. It is a member of the mackerel family, and what is good for one mackerel is good for another. Broiling is probably the first choice. For this, steaks from small tunas are best. If the steak is taken from a larger fish, it must be cut into slices or filets before cooking.

TUNA SOUFFLÉ [548]

Remove bones and skin from left-over cooked tuna (or use canned, drained tuna fish); separate into flakes; measure 2 cups and season with mixed salt, paprika, white pepper, 1 teaspoon each of finely chopped parsley and chives, 2 teaspoons of lemon juice and 1 teaspoon of onion juice. Set aside. Cook ½ cup of soft bread crumbs in ½ cup of rich, sweet milk for 3 minutes; remove from the heat and beat in 3 egg yolks, one at a time, beating well after each addition. Combine with the prepared tuna fish, blending well. Lastly, fold in 3 stiffly beaten egg whites; turn into a buttered soufflé dish and bake in a hot oven, no pan of water under (400–425° F.), for about 25 minutes or until soufflé is well puffed and firm on top. Serve at once with a side dish of Creole Sauce (No. 1041).

TUNA SCRAPPLE [549]

Mix 1 cup of yellow corn meal, 1 teaspoon of salt and 1 cup of cold water in top of double boiler; gradually stir in 3 cups of scalded fish stock (No. 182). Cook over hot water, stirring frequently for about 2 hours. Then stir in ¾ cup of finely shredded left-over cooked tuna or drained, canned tuna fish, and continue cooking for 25 minutes, stirring occasionally. Pour mixture into 2 greased small loaf pans and cover to prevent a crust from forming. When cold and firm, slice thin; dip in beaten egg, then in flour or in crumbs, and sauté in a skillet containing a little butter or margarine turning to brown both sides. Serve with a side dish of Egg Sauce (No. 1051). If preferred, broil the slices and serve hot with 2 strips of broiled bacon for each serving.

Any left-over cooked or canned fish may be prepared in this economical manner.

TUNA STEAK, LIME BUTTER   [550]

Cut a 2-pound piece of fresh tuna fish into 6 slices; season each slice to taste with mixed salt, pepper, nutmeg and thyme, place in pan in broiling oven; sprinkle with melted butter and broil on both sides until delicately brown and fish just begins to flake, basting frequently with a mixture of equal parts of melted butter, lime juice and hot fish stock. Serve at once with a side dish of melted butter flavored with a little lime juice and garnish with parsley and lemon quarters.

TUNA FISH TIMBALES   [551]

Put through food chopper (using the finest blade) 1¼–1½ pounds of fresh tuna fish, adding gradually ½ cup of sweet, heavy cream. Place in a mixing bowl and beat for 5 minutes, then season to taste with salt, pepper, 1 teaspoon each of grated onion, chopped parsley and chopped chives. Fold in 3 stiffly beaten egg whites; taste for seasoning, and turn into 6 buttered timbale molds; place these in a pan of hot (not boiling) water, and bake 25 minutes in a moderate oven (350° F.), or until firm. Let stand a few minutes, then unmold on a heated platter; garnish with parsley and lemon quarters and serve with a side dish of Madeira Mushroom Sauce (No. 1075).

TURTLE PIE GOURMET   [552]

From a 2½-pound turtle steak, cut off 1 pound and put through food chopper, using the finest blade. To this ground turtle meat, add 1 whole large or 2 small eggs, slightly beaten; salt and pepper to taste; 1 teaspoon of grated onion, and 1 teaspoon each of finely chopped parsley and chives. Moisten with enough sherry wine to make a rather soft mixture. Combine with enough fine cracker crumbs to permit of rolling this mixture into balls the size of a small walnut. Place these in a generously buttered baking dish. Pour over ½ cup of chicken broth 12 small parboiled whole white onions; 12 small mushroom caps, fresh or canned; salt and pepper to taste. Bake 20–25 minutes in a moderate oven (375° F.).

In a separate saucepan, place the remaining 1½ pounds of turtle steak, previously cut into small pieces, and cook until tender in enough chicken broth to cover (about 35 minutes). Combine the two, taste for seasoning, and turn mixture into a deep pastry-lined pie dish, adding at the same time 1 dozen tiny potato balls previously parboiled. Adjust the pastry top; make a few slashes for the escape of steam, and brush the top with cold milk. Bake in a moderate oven (375° F.) 25–30 minutes. Serve as hot as possible.

TURTLE STEAKS [553]

Rub as many turtle steaks as required with a damp cloth, then with mixed salt, pepper and powdered bay leaves mixed with thyme and powdered tarragon herbs. Now place the steaks in a shallow pan, pour over enough olive oil to barely cover and let stand 25–30 minutes, turning frequently. Place the steaks, dripping from the oil, under the flame of the broiling oven (about 6 inches from the flame) and broil very slowly, turning them now and then to ensure even browning on both sides. Serve on heated platter, each steak dotted with sweet butter kneaded with a little finely chopped chives, parsley and shallots, and garnish the platter with crisp watercress and small mounds of crisp shoestring potatoes (No. 1424).

Turtle steaks may be ordered thick for broiling or sliced wafer thin for egging and breading, to prepare as veal cutlet. When doing either, it adds a nice something at the very last to sprinkle the brown crusted thick or thin pieces of turtle with a few drops of sherry wine.

WHITEBAIT [554]

Whitebait or silversides belongs to the deep frying kettle. These silvery little fish are less than 2½ inches long when full grown. Common silverside is the spearing. It is the tidewater silversides that is called whitebait, a midget when compared to the spearing, which may stretch to 5 inches. This pigmy but royal race of the fish world count an average of 500 fish to the pound, and are served piping hot from the fat with brown bread and butterfinger sandwiches and a side dish of cole slaw.

WHITEBAIT FRY [555]

Place a pound of the thin silver "spears," as they are also known, in a wire basket; wash under running cold water and pick over carefully. (Remember these diminutive fish are caught in fine sieves and often a motley crew of other sealife is in the haul). Drain well and pat dry between towels, handling as little as possible, for whitebait are delicate as flowers. Do not remove the heads, tails and insides; place a few fish at a time in a wire basket; sprinkle over with seasoned flour, and shake the basket to remove excess of flour. Just when ready to serve, plunge the basket in hot, clear, deep fat (375°–390° F.) and cook a scant few seconds or until delicately crisp and brown. Drain; serve on a folded napkin, the platter simply garnished with parsley and lemon quarters.

Or dip first in a thin batter, then deep fry, but only a few at a time. The thin batter fries golden crisp without, and within the fish are of such delicate consistency they almost literally melt in the mouth.

WHITEFISH BOUILLABAISSE STYLE [556]
A Creation of the Author

Sauté 1 small carrot, thinly sliced; 1 clove of garlic, mashed to a paste; and ½ cup of thinly sliced onions, in ¼ cup of sweet butter for 5 or 6 minutes over a medium flame, rocking the pan frequently. Add 3 pounds of boiled, boned whitefish; 1 cup of tomatoes, chopped (or use canned tomatoes); 1 bouquet garni, composed of 1 large bay leaf, 1 sprig of thyme, 6 sprigs of fresh parsley, and 1 sprig of green celery top, tied with white kitchen thread; and gently pour over all 2 cups of fish stock (No. 182). Bring to a boil slowly and let boil 2 minutes; then lower the flame and let simmer gently for 10 minutes longer. Meantime, pick over carefully 1 cup of crab meat flakes, ½ cup of cooked shrimp, 1½ dozen fresh oysters, and add to the bouillabaisse, mixing well. Reheat, season to taste with mixed salt and pepper, and at the last moment stir a tiny pinch of powdered saffron into ¼ cup of sherry wine and add. Serve at once in deep soup plates with toasted French bread.

WHITEFISH FILETS, MUSTARD SAUCE [557]
AU GRATIN

Have skin and bones removed from a 5-pound whitefish or from two 2½-pound ones. Season the fish filets with mixed salt and pepper; lay them in bottom of a shallow baking dish; place a thin slice of lemon over each filet, and cover with equal parts of dry white wine and fish stock (No. 182). Cover with a buttered paper, and poach in a very moderate oven (300° F.) for about 10 minutes. Drain, then transfer the filets to heated, fireproof platter, first removing the lemon slices. Scatter 1 cup of cooked fresh mussels over the fish, then cover with mustard sauce (No. 1092). Sprinkle with ½ cup of grated cheese and buttered soft bread crumbs, these seasoned with a pinch of curry powder; sprinkle a little melted butter over all, and place the platter under the flame of the broiling oven to delicately brown and puff. Serve at once with lemon quarters arranged on a bed of crisp parsley.

WHITING FRY [558]

Wash quickly in cold water a dozen cleaned small whiting, weighing about 10 ounces each; drain; sprinkle inside and out with salt and pepper;

roll several times in ⅛ cup of flour mixed with an equal amount of corn meal. Heat 4 tablespoons of oil in a skillet and, when very hot but not smoking, arrange the fish in the pan and cover. Cook over moderate heat until brown (about 10 minutes), shaking the pan occasionally, and turn to brown the other side. Then cook more slowly until the flesh can be flaked with a fork. Arrange on a hot platter, garnishing with 6 thin slices of fresh tomato, rolled in seasoned flour and grilled, 6 grilled fresh mushroom caps, and 12 strips of bacon, also broiled or grilled. Parsley and lemon quarters are served with this dish.

Chapter Six

MEATS

BEEF—VEAL—LAMB—MUTTON—PORK—HAM

On Sunday a cut from a Sirloin,
On Monday cold ditto will do,
On Tuesday a hash, or Sausage and Mash,
On Wednesday a good Irish Stew;
Don't fill up your belly with buns, milk and jelly,
Have something with sustenance—do!
For troubles will fly, on a STEAK & KID PIE,
So have MEAT every day on your menu.

—Old London Song

MEATS
MAGIC MEAT COOKERY [559]

BEEF, LAMB, MUTTON, PORK AND VEAL ARE THE PRINCIPAL meats which the butcher handles. In cookery these meats are classified as: the dark or red meats, which include beef and mutton; and the white, embracing the remainder. When grilled, braised or sautéed, the succulent qualities of the dark meats must be retained. This is accomplished only when the meat has not been too recently slaughtered and the cooking process not overdone. The white meats, be they boiled, braised, sautéed, grilled, or roasted should be sufficiently cooked so that when carved the juice is not of reddish or pinkish color, otherwise the meat will not be well-digested by delicate stomachs.

QUALITY OF GOOD MEAT [560]

The quality of meat is dependent on the condition of the animal from which it is derived. The creature should be in perfect health and well-fed. Good beef is largely obtained from the cattle ranges of the West, but there is no reason why cattle shouldn't be raised to a greater extent in the East. Sheep for mutton are best raised where the climate is not too severe. Methods of slaughter, transportation, and preservation all affect the quality of meat. In meat, as purchased, we have bone, fat, and the flesh, consisting of the muscles of the animal with its connective tissue. The color of the meat should be clear and fairly bright, not purplish or dull. There should be little or no odor, and the meat should be firm and elastic to the touch. Beef should be a bright red and well-streaked with fat.

TOUGH AND TENDER MEAT [561]

To understand the difference between the tough and tender cuts, we must be familiar with the structure of the muscle. Each muscle consists of bundles of tubes held together by connective tissue. In tough meat, the muscle tubes are thicker and there is more connective tissue present. Exercise strengthens the muscle, and this accounts for the fact that the unexercised muscles of the young animal give us a softer meat. In the mature animal, the muscles most exercised furnish the tough meat, and the less used muscles the tender.

The tough cuts come from the neck and legs, the tender cuts from the middle of the back, the toughness increasing as the cuts approach the neck and the hind legs. The muscles of the abdomen are also tender, but they give a coarse-grained meat. The tender cuts from the ribs and loin are the most highly prized and therefore bring the highest price. These cuts are liked because of their tenderness, although the nutritive value of the tough meat is as high as, or possibly even higher than, that of the tender ones.

EXTRA EDIBLE PARTS USED IN COOKERY [562]

One vital essential of a well-balanced diet, simple or elaborate, is variety. Besides the different cuts and choice morsels of beef, there are delicious miscellaneous parts of the meat animals, as brains, hearts, kidneys, liver, lights, sweetbreads, tongue, tripe and sometimes also heads, tails, ears and feet, all of which may be prepared in many delicious ways, and which we will briefly describe here.

Beef Heart. The heart is sometimes eaten, but the meat is tough.

Beef Kidneys. Liver and kidneys are eaten more often than any other part of the viscera. If cooked too long, they become very hard and tough. To remove alkaline odor from beef kidneys, and in fact from any kidneys, including those of wild animals, first-parboil quickly in salted water; drain and sponge at once. If sliced for sautéeing, cook beef kidneys very rare, almost raw, in a little butter or margarine, which is then drained off and discarded. Cooked in this way, beef kidneys will never have the peculiar alkaline odor, which is their characteristic. When cooking beef kidneys whole, either baked, braised or roasted, the fat as well as the skin and nerves or ligaments should be removed.

Liver. Beef, calf, lamb, mutton, and pig liver as well as liver from wild animals and poultry varies greatly in price, but all can be appetizingly prepared. When properly prepared, liver has a rather delicate flavor and according to medical authorities possesses specific curative value for certain diseases.

Beef and calf liver do not require scalding, but lamb (or mutton) and pork liver *should* be scalded. Liver should be cooked at a moderate temperature just long enough to change the color, if its full flavor is to be appreciated. The various methods employed in the preparation of calf's liver may be adapted to any other kind of liver.

Lights. Furnish an economical dish or dishes, especially when mixed with other meats. Lights are not used very much in this country, although they are very nourishing.

Sweetbreads. Only lamb, mutton and calf sweetbreads are used in cookery, although beef sweetbreads may be used advantageously when mixed with other meats, as in stews.

Sweetbreads, always high-priced in cities, are too rarely found on the home table, and seem to be tacitly accepted as a delicacy peculiar to the rich and to the better hotel restaurants, where adroit chefs know precisely what to do with them. Many homemakers do not even know what a sweetbread is, or what sort of a beast it comes from.

Each animal possesses two kinds of sweetbreads: one found in the throat and the other in the body proper. The first are throat sweetbreads, actually the thymus glands of the neck, which in mammals shrink away to almost nothing as they attain maturity; they are of elongated shape, while the others, the heart sweetbreads, are of rounded contour. The latter are much sought after by the lovers of choice viands, while the former, being less expensive and finer as well as delicate, may be used for garnishing. Sweetbreads MUST be strictly fresh, otherwise they are unfit to eat. Soft gland tissue deteriorates and decomposes rapidly, the same being true of tripe, brains, livers and kidneys. Sweetbreads invariably require an operation before being used in cookery—blanching (see Sweetbreads, No. 835).

Tongue. Beef, veal, lamb or mutton and pork tongues may all be served fresh, salted or smoked, hot or cold.

Fresh tongue should be carefully washed before cooking; salted and smoked tongue should be soaked in fresh water overnight. Tongue, like heart, has received considerable exercise and thus developed connective tissue; for this reason, it is necessary to cook it by moist heat; simmering or cooking in water or other indicated liquid is the method used, preliminary to further preparation. First, wash the tongue thoroughly in warm water (smoked or pickled or salted tongues should be soaked overnight or for several hours before cooking). The heavy skin and roots (thick part of the tongue) are not removed until after cooking. Tongue may be boiled or steamed, braised, baked or roasted.

Tripe. Tripe, a part of the third stomach of the cow, when tender and well-cooked, is delicious and easy to digest, although somewhat fat. It contains about 16% fat and 13% albuminoids, rather more than most viscera. Tripe should always be cooked at a very low temperature and for a long period. When baked, its preparation is a matter of arduous labor and infinite pains—as, in fact, is all good cookery—but the results make it worth while. Tripe is always sold preblanched.

A great many people say they do not like tripe, but it may be because they have never eaten it properly cooked. Shakespeare must have enjoyed it, for he has Grumio ask Kate in *The Taming of the Shrew*, when he is tantalizing the hungry girl with descriptions of mouth-watering food, "How say you to a fat tripe finely broiled?" And Kate replies, "I like it well!"

> *Oh, help for the one whose lot is to plan*
> *The food to keep breath of life in man!*
> *Oh, mercy on her who must daily waver*
> *'Twixt budget, meals and the cook's disfavor!*
> *Oh, Science, whose blessings are widely strewn,*
> *Crash through with the housewife's longed-for boon*
> *And hasten the day when she'll serve, all sparsely,*
> *A vitamin pill, complete with parsley!*

GUIDE TO THE PURCHASE AND PREPARATION OF BEEF [563]

UTILITY BEEF CUT AND PART OF ANIMAL	CHARACTERISTICS	HOW TO COOK (Methods)
(FROM CHUCK) ARM STEAK	Rich in juices and well-flavored. Popular, economical and profitable. Requires long, slow cooking.	Braise, grill, Swiss, Spanish steaks
ARM POT ROAST	Juicy and flavorful. Largest wholesale cut in forequarter. Requires long, slow, steady cooking.	Same as above
BLADE POT ROAST	Same as above.	Same as above
BLADE STEAK	Same as Arm Steak.	Same as Arm Steak
NECK	Well flavored and juicy.	Stew, soup, stock
(FROM SHANK) HIND SHANK	Bony with varying amount of lean. Requires slow cooking.	Soup, stew, stock
(FROM BRISKET) FRESH AND CORNED BRISKET	Located just below the chuck. Juicy, well-flavored, mixed lean and fat. Used for corning, boned or not.	Boil, braise, barbecue, casserole, hash
(FROM PLATE) SHORT RIBS	Juicy, popular, and well-flavord. Fat and lean. Come from portion which lies right under ribs. Also called spareribs.	Rib crown, boil, stuff, barbecue, casserole, bone and roll stew, soups
(FROM FLANK) FLANK STEAK	One of the less tender cuts. Coarse in grain, but juicy. Only one in a side.	Stew, bake, braise, stuff, burgers
(FROM ROUND) ROUND STEAK	One of the less tender cuts but juicy. Requires long, slow cooking.	Bake, braise, stew, burgers, barbecue

GUIDE TO THE PURCHASE AND PREPARATION OF BEEF [563]

UTILITY BEEF CUT AND PART OF ANIMAL	CHARACTERISTICS	HOW TO COOK (Methods)
OP ROUND STEAK	Most tender cut of round. Popular, economical, and largest wholesale cut of hindquarter.	Broil, braise, bake, Swiss, Spanish steaks, steaks
OTTOM ROUND STEAK	Distinguished from top round by having two muscles and less tender cuts.	Same as above except broil
(FROM FIRST AND SECOND RIBS) IB ROAST, STANDING	Tender, juicy and well-flavored. From the Yoke.	Roast, corn, stew,
(FROM THIRD AND FOURTH RIBS) IB ROAST, STANDING	Tender, juicy and well-flavored, mixed lean and fat. From the Navel.	Same as above
(FROM FIFTH AND SIXTH RIBS) IB ROAST, STANDING	Very tender and juicy, with mixed fat and lean in equal parts, the fat streaked throughout the lean. From the Plate.	Same as above
(FROM SIRLOIN) LUB—DELMONICO and RLOIN STEAKS	Very tender and juicy. Streaked with clear fat in good proportions. Also from the sirloin are taken the pine bone steak and boneless sirloin.	Broil and sauté
(FROM TENDERLOIN) IATEAUBRIAND 'EAK	Very tender and juicy. Is a steak cut laterally from the thickest part of the tenderloin and of about 2½–3 inches in thickness.	Broil
(FROM TAIL SIDE OF TENDERLOIN) IGNONS (Filet)	Very tender and juicy.	Sauté, broil, pan-fry
(FROM ROUND) INUTE STEAK	Tender and juicy. Usually cut very thin.	Sauté, pan-fry, broil
(FROM SHORT LOIN) BONE STEAK	Very juicy and tender and streaked with fat, bone attached. Cut about 2–2½ inches in thickness.	Pan-broil, broil

BAKED SPANISH STEAK BARONESS [564]

Rub a 3-pound piece of bottom round steak with a damp cloth; cut into 6 slices and rub each slice with a mixture of salt, black pepper, a few grains of cayenne, clove, thyme and garlic salt, then brown on both sides in 4 tablespoons of olive oil over a hot fire. Transfer the meat to a generously oiled casserole, then add to any fat remaining in pan 1 large green pepper, coarsely chopped, seeds and white ribs carefully removed, 1 small bottle of well-drained small stuffed olives, 2 fresh tomatoes, peeled and quartered, 1 bouquet garni composed of 1 large bay leaf, 6 sprigs of fresh parsley, 1 sprig of thyme, 1 sprig of green celery leaves, all tied up with white kitchen thread; 2 whole cloves, 6 medium-sized fresh mushrooms, peeled, sliced, using stems and caps, enough beef stock or canned beef bouillon, or boiling water with added Pique Seasoning, to barely cover the whole; cover and bring to a quick boil; add to the meat in the casserole; place in a moderate oven (350° F.) and braise for about 1½ hours. Discard the bouquet garni, taste for seasoning, adding salt and pepper as needed, and stir in 3–4 tablespoons of sherry wine. Serve at once in the casserole with a side dish of plain boiled rice.

BARBECUED SHORT RIBS OF BEEF [565]

Heat 3 tablespoons of bacon drippings; stir in 1 small clove of garlic, finely chopped, then add 3 pounds of short ribs of beef, cut into individual portion size and brown thoroughly on all sides, stirring and turning frequently. Transfer the meat and drippings to a deep casserole having a cover, or to a Dutch oven, and add 3 medium-sized onions, thinly sliced. Now combine 1 cup of tomato catsup, ½ cup of vinegar, 1 teaspoon of curry powder, 1 tablespoon of paprika, a generous pinch of chili powder, 1 generous cup of beef stock (No. 301), salt to taste and ½ teaspoon of dried mustard and pour over the whole. Cover tightly and let bake or braise in a moderate oven (350° F.) 1½–1¾ hours, stirring once very carefully after 1 hour of cooking. Serve on a sizzling hot platter with its own gravy in a border of plain boiled rice.

BEEF BOURGUIGNONNE [566]

Put 1 tablespoon of lard and 1 cup of diced salt pork or bacon in a stew pan and cook gently over a low flame, stirring frequently, until cracklings become golden brown. Remove the cracklings and keep hot. Season 3 pounds of round of beef cut into small pieces, with mixed salt and pepper and brown on all sides in the fat remaining in the stew pan; add 18 tiny white onions, 6 small carrots cut into inch pieces, and continue to cook until onions and carrots just begin to take on color, Drain off all the fat, add 2 chopped shallots, 1 crushed clove of garlic, and 2 tablespoons of flour, and blend thoroughly. Now add 2 cups of red wine and 1 cup of beef stock (No. 301), which should cover the meat mixture; add 1 bouquet garni composed of 1 large bay leaf, 1 sprig of thyme, 6 sprigs of fresh parsley, 2 sprigs of green celery leaves (tops) tied together with white kitchen thread; bring gently to a boil; cover and let simmer gently for 2 hours, or until meat is tender. Meantime, cook ½ pound of small mushroom caps, peeled, stems separated and sliced, in 2 or 3 tablespoons of butter. Transfer the meat to a heated deep dish with the carrots and onions, add the pork cracklings and the mushrooms, and keep hot. If the stew has been cooked very gently, the sauce should be just right; but if it has been cooked fast or too quickly, it may be too thick. In such case, after skimming any fat from the surface, add a little hot beef stock; taste for seasoning, and strain over the meat. Sprinkle with chopped chervil or parsley and serve at once either with plain boiled potatoes or plain boiled noodles or macaroni.

The nutritious ingredients of Chop Suey or Chow Mein preparations found on our markets are low in calories and not particularly fattening, but essential vitamins are present in energy-building quantities. Pork, veal, mutton, ham and beef as well as chicken and even sea food may be prepared in chop suey fashion.

BEEF CHOP SUEY, PACIFIC COAST METHOD [567]

Heat 4 tablespoons of shortening; stir in ¾ cup of minced onions. cook 2 minutes, then add 1¾ pounds of round of beef, diced small or cut into narrow strips, and sear well over a bright flame. Then stir in 1½ cups of chopped celery stalks and ¾ cup of water or beef stock; cover and let boil steadily for 5 minutes, stirring occasionally. Meantime, moisten 1 tablespoon of cornstarch, salt and pepper to taste, with 1 tablespoon of Chinese Brown Sauce (commercial), 1 teaspoon of Chinese Soy Sauce and a little cold water and blend thoroughly and smoothly, then stir this into the meat mixture. Add ½ teaspoon of brown sugar and 1 cup of Chinese bean sprouts. Taste for seasoning; heat thoroughly, stirring constantly to prevent burning, and serve on a heated platter, heaped in mounds in center of the platter and surrounded with plain boiled rice.

Chow Mein is prepared in the same way, substituting Chinese Noodles for boiled rice.

Butchers of ancient Egypt sold meat and fowl only by the "manload." They refused to sell less than what would be a heavy burden for a grown slave to carry.

BEEF EN DAUBE [568]

Fry 6 strips of bacon or fat salt pork in their own fat until strips begin to brown but not until crisp. Remove the bacon, cut into inch pieces, and turn into a large earthenware casserole. Cut 3⅓–3⅔ pounds of round of beef into 2-inch pieces; roll in seasoned flour (about ¼ cup of flour with salt and pepper to taste), then add to the fat remaining in the skillet and brown on all sides, turning frequently. Transfer meat to the casserole with the bacon or salt pork cracklings, and to the fat left in the skillet add 1 cup of beef stock mixed with 1 cup of claret. Bring to a boil, then stir from bottom of skillet so as to remove and loosen any particles which may adhere, and turn all into the casserole. Add 1 dozen very small white onions, peeled; 1 dozen small carrots, thinly sliced or, still better, cut into tiny balls using a French vegetable cutter; 6 whole peppercorns, gently bruised; 4 whole cloves; 1 bouquet garni composed of 1 large or 2 small bay leaves, 8 sprigs of parsley and 1 sprig of thyme, tied with kitchen thread; and ½ cup of claret. Cover and bake in a slow oven (300° F.) for 3 hours without disturbing. Taste for seasoning, and serve from the casserole.

Goulash as it is made in our restaurants and cafeterias is as familiar to Americans as chop suey, and it is generally innocent of any contact with sauerkraut, and often free from any trace of sour cream, though both are vitally important ingredients of the national stew of Hungary.

Like all the stews of the nations, gulyas, or goulash is subject to variations without number, and it is not unusual to combine savory sausages in thick slices with the meat. Veal makes a delicious gulyas, and white wine is recommended especially in the seasoning of it, and beef is sometimes combined with diced beef or veal kidneys. Lamb or mutton is excellent, of course, and goat is also used—but that's quite another story; and it would involve a supplementary chapter on goats. Now the gulyas may be finished with a cup of rich sour cream, and be a perfect Hungarian rhapsody, but you are privileged to add other artistic touches, and a liqueur glass of kummel will be in order and provide a subtle note in the composition, and a further refinement comes from a wine glass of szamorodni, or other Tokay wine that is not too sweet. The sour cream goes in last of all, and then the gulyas is served at once, and usually with noodles, but sometimes with potatoes.

BEEF GOULASH HUNGARIAN STYLE [569]
Home Method

Heat 2½ tablespoons of lard; add 2 or 3 medium-sized onions, thinly sliced, and cook until brown. Skim out the onion and put it in the stew pot; then cut 2½ pounds of top round of beef into scant inch cubes. and brown them quickly in the onion-flavored lard. Turn the contents of the pan into the stew pot with the onions and season with salt, pepper to taste, 1 tablespoon of paprika, a blade of marjoram and 1 small clove of garlic, crushed to a pulp. Stir gently till seasonings are blended, then add enough boiling water to cover. Simmer for 30 minutes. Next, add 2½ pounds of well-washed sauerkraut and continue simmering for an hour, or until both meat and sauerkraut are tender; then thicken the sauce with 1 tablespoon of butter creamed with 1 tablespoon of flour; add 1 cup of sour cream; cook 7 or 8 minutes longer, adding 1 teaspoon of caraway seeds if desired. Serve very hot.

BEEF GOULASH TRANSYLVANIA STYLE [570]

Heat 3 tablespoons of butter; stir in 3 tablespoons of finely minced onions and cook until tender without deep browning, stirring frequently. Add 2½ pounds of round of beef cut into 1-inch cubes, there rolled in mixed salt and pepper, and 1 tablespoon of paprika; brown thoroughly. Sprinkle with 3 tablespoons of flour, mix well, and continue cooking for a few minutes, stirring constantly until flour is thoroughly blended with the other ingredients. Gradually pour in 1 quart of boiling beef stock, stirring while adding, and continue simmering gently for 1 hour, then add 1 bouquet garni, composed of 1 extra large bay leaf, tied up with 10 springs of parsley. Lastly add 1½ cups of potato cubes and a blade of marjoram, and continue cooking for 20–25 minutes longer or until potatoes are tender. Stir in 1 cup of scalded sour cream; taste for seasoning and, just before serving, add 2 tablespoons of tomato paste. Serve as hot as possible.

You may, in either the Hungarian or Transylvania Goulash, add the following dumplings;

Tarhonia or Hungarian Dumplings. Sift twice 1 pound (4 cups) of all-purpose flour and 1 teaspoon of salt. Make a well in centre; break 2 large whole eggs into this centre and combine well, adding a little cold water—as little as possible—so as to make a stiff paste. Knead 1 minute; then roll with the palm of the hands into balls the size of a large marble. If to be kept for future use, spread out and dry in the open. Tarhonya paste should be so stiff that it can be grated. In Hungary, special graters are used for making it into little grains of various sizes for poaching.

To cook these little dumplings, melt 2 tablespoons of bacon or ham drippings in a saucepan until hot and brown, stir in 2 cups of boiling hot stock, bring to a boil, add the small dumplings and let boil 4 or 5 minutes. These little dumplings are very delicious, and may be served with any kind of meat or chicken stew.

In the Middle Ages, Edward III of England induced the Flemish clothmakers to visit England and teach others their trade by offering them mutton and roast beef as a change from their herring diet.

BEEF LOAF MY WAY [571]

If you relish meat in meat loaf, with appropriate vegetable concomitants—and have courage to fly in the face of convention—try a meat and vegetable loaf, and forget the bread crumbs. Any kind of fresh ground meat may be used in this, my own method, and the result may be presented even at a formal luncheon or dinner. Whatever you do, do not mince the meat or vegetables, as the juices will run out, but coarsely grind or chop them.

Melt 3 tablespoons of fine beef suet in an iron pan and lightly brown in it 2 medium-sized onions, thinly sliced, then mince the onion slices finely with a sharp knife in the pan and add 2 peeled, large tomatoes or a No. 2 can of tomatoes, breaking up the pulp. Prepare 1 pound of fresh green string beans by cutting them lengthwise, then chopping them with a sharp knife on a cutting board but do not mince or crush them. Slice thinly 6 small stalks of fresh tender celery, including some of the tenderest leaves; peel ½ pound of fresh mushrooms and sauté both caps and stems in 3 tablespoons of butter 4–5 minutes over a low flame, stirring constantly, then chop the whole coarsely. Grate coarsely 2 tender carrots and finely mince enough parsley to make 2 tablespoons; peel and mash to a paste 1 small clove of garlic and chop enough chives to make 1 generous tablespoonful. Now add 3 pounds of ground lean beef.

Gather all the ingredients together in a mixing bowl and stir them up lightly with wooden salad spoon and fork, tossing them over and over till they are thoroughly mixed. Season with salt, freshly ground black pepper, a good pinch of thyme leaves (no powdered thyme, please), ½ teaspoon of dry mustard, ¼ cup of Pique Seasoning, ⅓ cup of Chinese soy sauce, and toss again. Set aside.

Separate yolks and whites of 2 large eggs; beat the yolks slightly with ½ cup of cold milk, then add to the mixture. Prepare a glass baking dish, or any suitable pan having a tight-fitting cover, by lining it on bottom and sides with very thin slices of bacon. Lastly, beat the egg whites until stiff but not dry, and fold them gently into the mixture.

The ideal set-up for the cooking of the loaf is a Dutch oven into which the baking dish, with its cover, will fit. Otherwise, cover the baking dish and place it in a pan of boiling water in a hot oven (400° F.), replenishing water as it boils away. Bake about 2 hours, reducing the heat to moderate (350° F.) after 20 minutes of baking. Meanwhile, prepare a roux (a roux is a mixture of flour and butter, or other fat, blended over a gentle flame until *slightly*, or *well*, browned, according to directions), and brown lightly. When you uncover the baking dish, you will discover that the loaf has shrunk away from the sides and is almost floating in a sea of rich, delicious sauce. Carefully drain off the sauce into a saucepan; skim off all but 2 tablespoons of the fat, and thicken with the roux. Then turn the loaf out onto a fireproof serving dish and peel off the strips of bacon or what there is left of it. Put the dish into a very hot oven (425–450° F.) or under the flame of the broiling oven and brown the surface quickly without drying it. The bacon will be dried off and crisped at the same time. Serve in the hot dish, garnishing the loaf with a glazing of the sauce and sprigs of water-cress. Pass the sauce, which will be abundant, in a very hot gravy boat.

BEEF A LA MODE [572]
Also called Beef Bourgeoise (Original Recipe)

The rump, ribs and legs are the most satisfactory cuts to obtain the best results. Beef à la Mode, also called Beef Bourgeoise, should be previously larded and marinated for at least 24 hours. With attention to these preliminaries a Beef à la Mode is a regal dish. It is delicious served cold, with a green salad.

Take a piece of the above indicated meat, weighing about 4½–5 pounds; insert in it through and through, 2 dozen long strips of fat larding pork previously marinated in a mixture of brandy and finely chopped fines herbes, such as parsley, chervil, chives, tarragon herb, and shallots, for about 30 minutes. Trim ends of pork off neatly, close to the meat. Rub the meat with salt, freshly grated nutmeg and ground peppercorns. Place it in a deep skillet with 3 tablespoons of bacon drippings and sear on all sides over a bright flame until thoroughly browned; drain off all the fat and add 2 medium-sized onions, thinly sliced, 2 medium-sized carrots, first scraped, then cut into inch pieces, with 3 calf's feet boned and blanched, then cover and let cook gently about 10 minutes. Sprinkle the meat with the brandy used for marinating the larding fat and 1 pony glass of fresh brandy; cover again and let simmer a few more minutes, then moisten with ⅕ bottle of good red wine, add 1 bouquet garni composed of 2 bay leaves, tied with 8 sprigs of fresh parsley, 2 sprigs of green celery leaves (tops), and 1 sprig of thyme, tied with white kitchen thread, 2 cloves of garlic, peeled but left whole, and 2 whole cloves, gently bruised; bring gently to boiling point; boil steadily for 1 minute; lower the flame and simmer very gently for about 4½ hours; when about half done, pour in ¼ cup of the best sherry wine obtainable. One hour before serving, remove the meat and calf's feet; place the meat in another casserole with 1 dozen each small carrot balls and small white onions, both previously parboiled then browned in a little butter and cut the calf's feet in small pieces and return to the vegetables; strain the sauce over and continue cooking until vegetables are done. (Some cooks add also a dozen small mushroom buttons, but this is optional.)

To Serve. Slice the meat against the grain, so the larding will show as small white spots in the meat; garnish with the onions, carrots (and mushrooms, if used) and the calf's feet meat; remove all grease that may appear on top of the sauce and pour a little of it lightly over the meat and vegetables. Serve remaining sauce in a hot gravy boat. In good bourgeoise cuisine, a side dish of small potato balls cooked in plain salted boiling water is also served on the side.

A very good law: On September 5, 1552, the English Government officially decreed that any butcher who sold meat at prices other than fixed by the Government would be imprisoned for life.

BEEF MIRONTON [573]

For this French preparation two distinct operations are necessary: The boiling of the meat, and the simmering of the meat into gravy.

Rub a 2¾-pound piece of lean round of beef with a damp cloth; then cut into inch squares and place in a stew pot with the following ingredients: 1 quart cold water, 1 teaspoon of salt, 6 whole peppercorns, freshly bruised, a bouquet garni, composed of 1 large bay leaf tied with 8 sprigs of fresh parsley, 2 sprigs of green celery tops and 1 sprig of thyme using white kitchen thread. Very slowly bring this to the boiling point, skimming off all the scum as it rises to the surface; cover and allow to simmer gently for 2 hours. Drain; remove the pieces of meat and reserve the stock, keeping it hot. Now, proceed as follows:

Heat 2 tablespoons of butter in a heavy skillet; blend in 2 tablespoons of flour until nicely browned, stirring constantly, over a gentle flame; slowly pour in 2 cups (generous) of the hot stock, stirring constantly until mixture boils, and let boil steadily for 3 or 4 minutes, then add 1½ cups of heated red wine and season with a little salt (the stock is already salted) and pepper to taste; then add ½ pound of small, very small yellow onions, thinly sliced, then the hot meat cubes. Now add a bouquet garni, composed of 1 small fresh bay leaf tied with 4 sprigs of parsley, 1 sprig of celery green (leaves), using white kitchen thread, and ¼ pound of small fresh mushrooms (or a small can of mushrooms, drained). Cover the skillet and let this simmer as gently as possible for 30 minutes to allow the meat to penetrate the full flavor of the sauce. Serve in a sizzling hot deep platter with a border of flaky rice, mashed potatoes, noodles or mashed turnips, or as is.

If desired, add to the sauce 1 or 2 tablespoons of washed capers and a tiny point of garlic. Some cooks add even some anchovy filets. If doing so, be careful about the salting. This delicious dish may also be made with left-over cooked beef, cut into small slices, added to the sauce, and simmered—not boiled, lest the meat get tough as rubber—

and a side dish of plain boiled small potato balls or plain cooked noodles
or macaroni.

BEEF AND KIDNEY PIE OLD SCOTCH STYLE   [574]

Sear quickly on both sides in a little hot fat $1\frac{1}{2}$ pounds of round
steak, cut into slices $\frac{1}{4}$-inch thick and 3 inches long. Wrap each slice
around a small strip of bacon and a stub of kidney, making a tight
roll, and securing with a toothpick. Combine $\frac{3}{4}$ teaspoon of salt, $\frac{1}{2}$
scant teaspoon of black pepper, $\frac{1}{8}$ teaspoon each of clove, thyme,
marjoram, allspice and cinnamon, all ground, and $\frac{1}{2}$ cup of bread flour,
and toss the meat rolls in this. Stand them on end, tightly packed,
in a deep dish pie; sprinkle the remaining spice-flour mixture over with
$2\frac{1}{2}$-3 tablespoons of grated onion. Gently and carefully pour $2\frac{1}{2}$ cups
of beef stock or condensed or concentrated canned beef bouillon over
the whole; add 1 small bay leaf. Cover and set the dish over a very
gentle flame or in a slow oven (300° F.) for 1 hour. Then pour in $\frac{1}{4}$ cup
of sherry wine; add 2 hard-cooked, sliced eggs; cover the dish with
your favorite flaky pastry; make a few slashes for escape of steam;
brush with a little beaten egg yolk, diluted with a very little milk,
being careful not to close the slashes, and bake in a moderate oven
(375° F.) 25-30 minutes, or until pastry is delicately browned. Serve
at once.

Lamb, pork, mutton, veal or poultry may be prepared in the same
way.

BEEF AND OYSTER PIE FLEMISH STYLE   [575]

Wipe a 2-pound piece of tender lean beef with a damp cloth; cut it
into 6 equal-sized pieces parts; roll them in mixed salt and pepper to
which has been added $\frac{1}{8}$ of a teaspoon each of thyme, sage, marjoram,
mace and clove, and sear in a little fat in a heavy skillet, turning constantly until well browned on all sides. Transfer the meat to a saucepan
and cover with the following mixed vegetables: 2 shallots, or onions finely
minced, $\frac{3}{4}$ cup each of cooked carrots, potatoes cut small, and $\frac{3}{4}$ cup
peas. Slice thinly $\frac{1}{4}$ cup of mushrooms, cook them in 2 tablespoons of
butter for 3 minutes, then add 1 dozen fat fresh oysters and cook until
the edges curl. Add these to the meat and vegetables and let simmer
(below boiling point) for 15 minutes. Turn all (liquid and solid) into a
deep dish pie or baking dish; sprinkle over 1 tablespoon each of chopped
parsley, chives and onions; cover with your favorite pie crust, slashing
the top to allow the steam to escape, and bake 25 minutes in a hot oven
(400° F.). Serve at once.

BEEFSTEAK CHEZ-SOI   [576]

This method of cooking a steak "Chez-Soi"—a French word meaning at home—is considered the most delicate of all. It may be a rump or a porterhouse steak, but whatever the kind, it is always prepared as follows:

Purchase as many individual steaks as required, or a large porterhouse or tenderloin, or even a chateaubriand steak, remembering that each individual portion should be at least 6 generous ounces. Then for each individual steak, melt 1 rounded tablespoon of butter and sauté meat on both sides until delicately colored and seared but not quite completely cooked; transfer the steak or steaks to a casserole slightly rubbed first with garlic to taste, then with butter, and add, for 6 individual steaks: 2 cups of raw potato cubes, 4 strips of bacon, chopped, 1 dozen very small silver onions, cooked in beef stock (or water) until tender and well drained, 1 small can of button mushrooms, well drained, all mixed together, and poured over the steaks. Add 1 small bay leaf, tied with 5 or 6 sprigs of fresh parsley, salt and pepper to taste, and pour over all ⅓ cup of beef stock and ¾ cup of dry white wine. Cover the casserole; bring to a boil; then cook, covered, over a very low flame for about 30 minutes. Serve in the casserole, dusted with finely minced parsley. A side dish of fresh French fried potatoes will not be amiss here.

During a meat shortage in Rome in A. D. 43, the Emperor Claudius ate mastodon steak cut out of Siberian icebergs in which the monsters had been frozen for centuries. A choice cut sold for $8 of our modern money per pound.

BEEFSTEAK ON HORSEBACK   [577]

Roll 6 individual steaks, cut in round shape, in mixed salt and pepper to taste. Sauté the steaks in 3 tablespoons of butter or other fat on both sides, until done to the desired point—that is, rare, medium or well-done. In another frying pan, fry 6 eggs in the usual way, over a very, very low flame, so the whites will remain pure whites. When the eggs are done, trim with a biscuit cutter, leaving a border of white about ½ inch wide attached to the yolk of each egg. Place each steak on a round piece of toast. Over the steak, arrange a round of cooked ham, cut very thin and heated in a little meat stock. Top the ham with the eggs; dust the yolks with a little paprika and the whites with very finely chopped parsley. Surround the base of the toast with shoestring potatoes (No. 1424) and serve at once, with a side dish of Spinach Mousse (No. 1469).

BEEF SOUFFLÉ FRENCH STYLE [578]

In a large mixing bowl, blend thoroughly 1 pound of twice ground lean bottom round of beef with ¾ pound twice ground beef kidney suet from which all skin has been carefully removed, 2 large fresh mushrooms, peeled and ground once, 1 teaspoon of salt, ¼ teaspoon of black pepper and a grating of nutmeg.

In another mixing bowl, cream thoroughly ¼ pound of butter, 3 unbeaten whole eggs, 1½ tablespoons of sherry wine, and ¼ cup of soft bread crumbs, and combine with the beef-kidney suet mixture, blending well. Then fold in 2 stiffly beaten egg whites. Turn into a generously buttered mold having a cover, and hollow in center (a tube mold). Set the mold in a pan containing hot water; cover lightly and loosely to allow the steam to escape, and bake for 1 hour in a moderate oven (350° F.). Remove from the oven; invert upon a heated serving platter; let stand a few minutes before lifting the mold so it will unmold easily. Pour around—not over—the soufflé a little Madeira wine sauce (No. 1076) or, still better, a Brown Sauce (No. 1018) to which has been added about ¼ cup of thinly sliced, cooked fresh mushrooms. Serve additional sauce on the side.

BEEF STEW [579]
Home Style with Parsley Dumplings

Cube 2 pounds of beef chuck, round or neck about 1-inch in size; roll the pieces in salted and peppered flour and brown in 3 tablespoons of fat, stirring frequently and shaking the skillet to prevent scorching. Transfer meat and fat to a stew pot; rinse the skillet with a little hot water and add enough more hot water to generously cover the meat. Bring to a boil and simmer gently over a low flame for 1½ hours. Then add 1 cup of canned tomatoes, 18 small white onions, peeled, 1½ cups of carrot, cubed small, 1 scant cup of string beans, diced, 1 large bay leaf tied with 8 sprigs of parsley, 1 sprig of thyme and 2 sprigs of green celery leaves (tops) tied with kitchen thread. Season to taste with salt and black pepper, and continue cooking very gently for about 35–40 minutes, or until vegetables are tender. Now add 1½ tablespoons of flour mixed with 1 tablespoon of Pique Seasoning, and add the Parsley Dumplings (No. 1628); cover and let steam 10–12 minutes. Turn out the flame and let steam 2 or 3 more minutes. Serve in a heated deep platter, surrounded with the dumplings and dusted with finely chopped parsley and a little paprika.

Perfect cooking, good food and the pleasures of the table depend on imponderables, individual taste, and no small amount of luck. The success of a meat dish lies not merely in the cut used nor in its manner of cooking in general, as much as in the care and attention to details given by the cook—as all professional chefs will tell you. They do not say, "Oh! it's only a stew—just stick it on the fire and let it go at that" —oh no! They give it even more thought, attention, seasoning and careful regard to temperature. They bear in mind that all the individual seasonings, as garlic, onion, different salts and Pique Seasoning, for instance, will have been lost in the slow, careful cooking, leaving their blended memory to flavor the dish.

BEEF STEW UNDER CRUST   [580]
A Home Method Meat Pie

Roll 2 pounds of beef round or shank or bottom round, cut into inch cubes in 3 tablespoons of seasoned flour, and sear in 3 tablespoons of bacon drippings until meat cubes are nicely browned on all sides, stirring frequently. Transfer to a stew pot; cover with hot water and add 1 whole clove of garlic (left whole), 1 bouquet garni, composed of 1 large bay leaf tied with 8 sprigs of fresh parsley, 2 sprigs of green celery leaves and 1 sprig of thyme, using white kitchen thread, 7 or 8 whole peppercorns gently bruised, 2 whole cloves, and a little salt. Bring slowly to a boil, lower the flame, and let simmer very gently, covered, 1¾–2 hours. Add 1 cup each of carrot cubes, potato cubes and ½ cup chopped onion with ½ cup of thinly sliced fresh mushrooms. Continue simmering 25–30 minutes, still covered, or until vegetables are tender. Taste for seasoning, and thicken with 1½ tablespoons of flour stirred to a soft paste with 2 tablespoons Pique Seasoning. Continue cooking gently for 5 or 6 minutes, stirring frequently. Turn the stew into a heated deep pie dish or pudding dish; discard the bouquet garni and garlic; taste for seasoning and cover with your favorite pie crust (Nos. 2066–2074); in the usual way. Bake 25–30 minutes in a moderate oven (350–375°F.), and serve as hot as possible.

BEEF A LA STROGONOFF   [581]

Cut 1½ pounds of beef filet into inch squares, and sprinkle freely with salt and pepper; place in a deep dish and let stand for 2 hours, in a cool place. When ready to serve, heat 1½ tablespoons of butter; blend in 1½ tablespoon of flour and cook to a smooth, brown paste over a low flame, stirring constantly, then stir in 1 pint of beef stock (No. 301) and cook, still stirring until mixture bubbles and is smooth. Strain through a fine-meshed wire sieve into a saucepan; bring to a boil; remove from the flame, then stir in 1 tablespoon of tomato paste, alternately with 3–4 tablespoons of scalded thick sour cream. Bring this gradually to a boil and let simmer while cooking the beef in 2 generous tablespoons of butter with 1 tablespoon of grated onion over a very bright flame until delicately browned. Taste the sauce for seasoning, add the meat to the sauce; let simmer gently 15–20 minutes and serve at once, the platter garnished with small triangles of bread fried in butter until crisp and brown, the meat sprinkled with finely minced parsley.

BOILED LARDED CHICAGO ROLL [582]

Have the butcher roll and the 4 pounds of boned beef roast (called Chicago roll), first spread with a good ½ pound of thinly sliced beef kidneys, skinned and membranes removed. When ready to cook, cut holes all over the roll, and stuff them with a mixture made of 2 tablespoons of chopped olives, ¼ pound of chopped lean raw ham, 2 tablespoons of chopped capers, and salt and pepper to taste, pressing this stuffing well into the holes. Heat 3 tablespoons of fat in a Dutch oven; add 1 clove of garlic, minced, then the beef roll and sear thoroughly on all sides. Now add ½ generous cup of sliced onions, 1 large green pepper, sliced and free from seeds and cores, 1 bouquet garni composed of 1large bay leaf, 8 sprigs of parsley, 2 sprigs of green celery leaves, 1 sprig of thyme and 2 whole cloves, tied together with white kitchen thread, also 2 cups of tomato juice. Bring to a boil; season lightly with salt and generously with pepper, then add 1 quart of boiling stock (or water). Simmer very gently for 2 hours; then add 2 large potatoes, pared and quartered, 1½ dozen black olives, pitted, 1½ tablespoons of minced parsley or chives, and 3 slices of lemon, and continue simmering for 30–35 minutes over a low flame or until potatoes are tender. Serve on a heated platter, pouring part of the broth over the meat, the remainder over 7-minute boiled cabbage served separately, the potatoes, olives and other vegetables being around the meat. A side dish of Horseradish Sauce is the usual condiment accompaniment for the beef.

BRAISED FILET OF BEEF WITH MADEIRA [583] SAUCE

Take 1 whole filet of beef, trimmed, skin and nerves removed, larded through and through with narrow sticks of larding pork (this is usually done by the butcher), and enough large slices of paper-thin fresh pork fat to cover the meat entirely, and attached with string. (This is also done by the butcher.)

Place the prepared beef filet in a generously-buttered braising kettle, add salt and pepper to taste, with 1 cup of minced, lean cooked ham, 2 whole cloves, ¼ teaspoon of thyme leaves, 1 blade of garlic, 4 thin slices of onion, 1 bouquet garni composed of 1 large bay leaf, tied with 7 or 8 sprigs of fresh parsley and 1 sprig of green celery leaves (top), and 1 generous cupful of rich beef stock. Cover and set the kettle in a moderate oven (350° F.), allowing for a 3½-pound filet of beef 30-35 minutes, if to be served rare, and 40-45 minutes for medium-rare. Turn the meat once or twice during the cooking process, or about every 10 minutes. Now, transfer the filet to a heated platter; slice the number of desired portions; replace in its shape and pour into the Madeira Sauce (No. 1076) the juice which runs from the meat. Stir, pour a little of the sauce over the entire surface of the filet, and serve the remainder in a sauceboat. Garnish the platter alternately with 6 small stuffed tomatoes, individual braised lettuce (No. 1350) and grilled mushroom caps, and arrange at each end of the platter a small mound of French Fried Onions (No. 1383).

According to sixteenth-century English cookery, "Olives" was a dish composed of thick slices of beef rolled with chopped onions and herbs, and stewed in brown sauce.

BRAISED HOT POT ENGLISH STYLE   [584]

Ingredients are ¾-pound round, cross rib or shoulder of beef, cut into 5 strips; ¾ pound lean veal, cut into 4 strips; ½ pound of lean lamb, cut into 4 strips; ½ pound of lean pork, cut into 3 strips; 4 medium-sized potatoes, pared, then quartered; 12 slices of bacon, cut into halves, crosswise; 4 small carrots, scraped, then quartered; 12 small white onions, peeled; 2 medium-sized turnips, pared and quartered; 6 medium-sized fresh mushrooms, peeled, caps whole and stems sliced.

Use several large cabbage leaves to cover the whole, and keep the meat from the lid and the moisture in.

For seasoning, you need 1 tablespoon of salt; 12 whole peppercorns, bruised; 1 teaspoon of paprika; 1 bouquet garni (bay leaf, parsley, celery green, tied together with white kitchen thread); ½ teaspoon each of marjoram, mace, thyme leaves and allspice; 3 whole cloves; 1 cup or more of beef stock (No. 301).

Wipe strips of meat, but do not remove the fat. Place 6 pieces of bacon in bottom of a braising kettle or Dutch oven and over this arrange a flat layer of meat, alternating the 4 kinds and placing over each the remaining 6 pieces of bacon. Over all this, spread the combined vegetables; sprinkling as you go along, with mixed salt and spices. Repeat until the meat, vegetables and seasonings are used, packing down so as to make a compact mass. Cover with cabbage leaves, which have been well washed, dried and trimmed of excess core, then, after pouring in very gently the beef stock (just enough to barely cover) or water, or canned beef bouillon if stock is not available, cover the kettle with the lid; set it in a moderate oven (350° F.), and forget it for 2½-3 hours. You may serve from the braising kettle or Dutch oven, or still better use a casserole attractive enough to be brought to table. When the hot pot, which is very popular in all England, is done, just enough delicious gravy will remain to pour over each serving.

Oxtail

An oxtail may be an awkward-looking piece of meat, but between its knobby joints are sweet shreds of meat, and in the joints is a gelatin protein which comes out during long, slow cooking. In the markets those frozen tails look like slender swords of some primitive tribe, borrowed perhaps from the Metropolitan Museum of Art. But, cut into pieces to braise, stew or pot or boil, oxtail offers a savory meat dish.

Have the butcher cut the tail or tails (1 tail serves 5 or 6, but plan to have some left-over, because when warmed over it tastes much, much better). He does it with a cleaver, leaving jagged edges. With patience, the tail can be disjointed at home. Here's how:

Lay a sharp knife across the tail and wiggle it along until you find the places where joint is fastened to joint by ligament and gristle. This cuts like soft cartilage, and the improved appearance of the pieces is sufficient to pay for perfecting the technique. Tails, cut or whole, should be very carefully and thoroughly washed, even brush-scrubbed.

BRAISED OXTAIL MODERNE   [585]

Washed 4 pounds of disjointed oxtails in several changes of cold water and dry well. Place the tail joints in a strong paper bag containing ¼ cup of flour, salt and pepper to taste, and shake well. Place the dredged tail joints in a pan. Cover with rapidly boiling water; gradually bring to a boil; let boil steadily for 25 minutes; drain, discarding the stock. Brown the oxtails in 3 tablespoons of fat with ½ cup of chopped onions, ½ cup of chopped celery stalks and 1 clove of garlic, left whole, over a bright flame for about 10 minutes, stirring constantly with a wooden spoon; discard the garlic; transfer the mixture to a stew pot; add 1 bouquet garni composed of 1 large bay leaf and 1 sprig of thyme tied together with white kitchen thread, 1 No. 2 can of tomatoes, 1 cup of small carrot balls, 1½ dozen very small white onions, salt and pepper to taste and 1 cup of red wine. Bring slowly to a boil, cover, transfer to a moderate oven (350° F.), and braise for 2 hours. One half hour before serving, add 1 small can of button mushrooms, with their liquid and continue cooking gently. Discard the bouquet garni and serve on a heated platter, the entire surface sprinkled generously with equal parts of mixed parsley and chives, chopped fine.

Among the ancient Druids of early Britain a bull's tail was especially prized. Eating it was supposed to add to their strength and wisdom.

BRISKET OF BEEF WITH SAUERKRAUT [586]
AND DUMPLING DINNER

Heat 3 tablespoons of shortening in a large pan and brown in it 1 medium-sized onion thinly sliced; then add two 3½-pound pieces of brisket of beef which have been rubbed with mixed salt and pepper to taste, and brown on all sides. Scatter 1½ quarts of sauerkraut all over the meat; cover with boiling water; add 2 bay leaves, 1 medium-sized carrot, thinly sliced, ¾ pound of fresh pork, 8 peppercorns, and a very little salt. Cover tightly, set the pan in a moderate oven (350–375° F.) and cook for 2 hours. Remove from the oven and bring to a boil; then add the following corn meal dumplings:

Corn Meal Dumplings. Add ½ teaspoon of salt to 1 cup of white corn meal and stir in 2 tablespoons of melted bacon drippings, with sufficient cold water to form a dough that will hold its shape. Mold the dough into small biscuit-size pieces and drop into the boiling sauerkraut. Cover tightly, and let simmer gently 15–20 minutes.

Serve the sauerkraut on a heated deep platter, the meat and pork sliced (enough to go around to start), and laid over the kraut, the dumplings around, and pour a little hot juice from the pan over the whole. Serve at once with a side dish of plain boiled potatoes.

A Club Steak may be 2–3 inches in thickness and when cooked, is usually cut slantwise. In turning meat, use 2 forks or spatulas. It saves time, temper, and spattering of fat.

BROILED CLUB STEAK [587]

Wipe a 3–3½ pound steak taken from a boned shell of beef between the first up to the thirteenth rib, cut to the desired thickness, with a damp cloth. Preheat the broiling oven; roll the steak in melted fat or good olive oil, salted and peppered to taste, and place under the flame; sear the meat first on one side, then on the other; continue turning and broiling until done according to taste, having the flame at least 6 inches from the meat. (The reason is that no matter how thick a steak may be, if broiled at lower temperature it will be attractively browned on the outside but not charred, and the interior will be uniformly done throughout; furthermore, there is less smoke in the kitchen, and the steak requires less watching.) When nearly done, place the steak in a shallow baking pan; pour over the drippings collected in the broiling oven pan; dot here and there with bits of butter creamed with an equal amount of chopped parsley or half parsley and half chives, and a few drops of lemon or onion juice, and finish in a moderately hot oven (350° F). to the desired point of doneness; transfer to a heated platter; pour over it the butter mingled with meat juices of the steak; season again with salt and pepper to taste, and serve at once, simply garnished with a generous bunch of watercress.

A side dish of French fried potatoes is the usual accompaniment for any kind of steak, independently of any other indicated garnish, such as mushroom caps, French fried onions, grilled thick tomato slices, etc.

BROILED MINUTE STEAK O'BRIEN [588]

Take as many minute steaks as required and broil slowly on each side until well seared. Transfer the steak or steaks to a shallow baking pan; dot with butter creamed with equal parts of finely chopped parsley and chives and a few drops of onion juice and finish cooking in a moderate oven (350° F.). Serve on a heated platter, pouring over the drippings from the pan, and garnish with O'Brien Potatoes and crisp watercress. Serve immediately.

BROILED PORTERHOUSE STEAK WITH [589] MARROW

Broil a porterhouse steak as indicated for Club Steak (No. 587). Just before serving, pour over the following sauce:

Melt 4 slices of marrow (beef) in a saucepan; add meat extract (commercial) the size of a walnut 1 teaspoon of minced parsley, 2 shallots, minced fine, 1 teaspoon of onion juice, creamed with 1 tablespoon of butter and a few drops of lemon juice. Serve simply garnished with crisp watercress.

BROILED PORTERHOUSE STEAK [590] MARCHAND DE VIN
(*Wine Dealer*)

Broil a 3–3½ pound porterhouse steak, cut from 1½–2 or more inches in thickness in the usual way, and to the desired point of doneness. When ready to serve, pour half of the following butter on top of the steak, and the remainder directly upon the sizzling platter.

Reduce to half volume over a hot flame, ½ cup of red wine in which ½ generous teaspoon of minced shallot is added with 2 freshly pounded whole peppercorns; then add meat extract (commercial), the size of a large pea, ½ teaspoon of minced parsley, and ½ generous teaspoon of lemon juice. Boil up once, then finish just before serving with ¼ cup of sweet butter. Boil up once more; taste for seasoning, and use immediately. This delicious butter, which may be served on any kind of grilled steak, keeps well in a refrigerator, so it may be prepared in ad-

vance and in quantity without fear of deterioration up to the point of
adding the butter.

Variations. Substitute Garlic Butter (No. 986) For Marchand de
Vin (Wine Dealer) Butter. Substitute Horseradish Butter (No. 988) for
Marchand de Vin Butter, or any kind of the Compounded Butters
(Nos. 978–1006).

BUBBLE AND SQUEAK   [591]

This popular English dish, which has gone by the name of "Bubble
and Squeak" for well over a century, was enjoyed as far back as the
XVIth century and in an old cookery book of that period we find a
recipe for "long wortes"—vegetables, but especially cabbage—and
"powdred beef"—meat salted or sprinkled with salt.

Following is the traditional recipe, as written by Dr. Kitchiner in
the *Cook's Oracle*, published in 1823, in London.

BUBBLE AND SQUEAK, OR FRIED BEEF   [592]
AND CABBAGE

When 'midst the frying Pan, in accents savage,
The Beef, so surly, quarrels with the Cabbage.

" . . . For this, as for a Hash, select those parts of the joint that
have been least done; it is generally made with slices of cold boiled
salted Beef, sprinkled with a little pepper, and just slightly browned
with a bit of Butter in a frying pan. If it is fried too much it will be hard.

" . . . Boil a Cabbage, squeeze it quite dry, and chop it small. Take
the Beef out of the frying-pan, and lay the cabbage in it. Sprinkle with
a little pepper and salt over it; keep the pan moving over the fire for a
few minutes; lay the cabbage in the middle of a dish, and the meat
round it."

As for the sauce given by Dr. Kitchiner, who recommends it as an
accompaniment to Bubble and Squeak—it goes by the delightful name
of "Wow Wow Sauce," the exact meaning of which nobody can trace.
Dr. Kitchiner had probably never heard of that expressive American
slang word, "a wow." This is how the sauce is made:

Wow Wow Sauce. Chop some parsley leaves very fine, quarter 2 or
3 pickled cucumbers or walnuts, divide them into small squares, and
set them by ready; put into a saucepan a bit of butter as big as an egg;
when it is melted, stir to it a tablespoon of fine flour and about ½ pint
of the broth in which the beef was boiled; add a tablespoon of vinegar,
the like quantity of mushroom catsup, or port wine, or both, and a
teaspoonful of prepared mustard; let it simmer together till it is as
thick as you wish it, put in the parsley and pickles to get warm, and
pour it over the beef, or rather send it up in a sauce-tureen.

CARBONADE OF BEEF FLAMANDE   [593]

This is one of the best known of all Belgian dishes, so well known, in fact, that we find the recipe in many French cook books. The word "carbonade" originally meant meat grilled over hot coals or embers, but in the course of time it has been misapplied and is now used for a method of slow stewing.

Cut 2¾ pounds of boned beef neck, top shoulder or thin flank or round into 2-inch lengths and about 1 inch thick. Season with mixed salt and pepper and brown in ⅓ generous cup of lard. Add ¼ pound of either salt pork or bacon, cut in small cubes, and brown over a very bright flame, shaking the pan and stirring the pieces at the same time with a wooden spoon. Take the beef and bacon cubes from the pan and keep hot. Drain off all but 2 tablespoons of the fat in the pan; blend in 2 tablespoons of flour and let brown nicely over a gentle flame. Now, add to this brown roux (French name of this butter or fat and flour mixture) 1 bottle of beer (the Belgian beers used in Brussels are the Lambic or the Faro, both dark beers) and bring to boiling point, stirring constantly. Let this simmer gently over a low flame while preparing the remaining ingredients. Heat 2 or 3 tablespoons of lard and brown in it ¾ pound of thinly sliced onions; add to the beer sauce with the beef and bacon or pork cracklings, 1 clove of garlic, 1 lump of sugar, 1 bouquet garni composed of 1 large bay leaf, 1 sprig of thyme and 6 or 7 sprigs of fresh parsley, all tied with white kitchen thread, salt and pepper to taste, and simmer very, very gently, covered, 2½–3 hours, adding more heated beer if necessary, as the meat should be well covered with the sauce. At the last moment add 1 scant tablespoon of tarragon vinegar. Serve at once with plain boiled potatoes.

It is usually regarded as rank heresy to hold that any distinctive dish of a country or a province can be prepared, eaten, or fully appreciated far from its native kitchens, but that cherished belief should be pinned into collections of antique fallacies. Imagination, ingenuity and a flair for things culinary can duplicate almost any one of the world's delicacies in any kitchenette, unless—and mark the exception well!—the essential ingredients have to be taken from a tin can or a sealed jar, pallid and savorless.

Chili con Carne is a piquant example of a successfully transplanted foreign viand, and its ingredients are obtainable in their highest excellence everywhere and at any season of the year.

For an *al fresco* luncheon on a torrid August afternoon, or a supper before a roaring log fire on February's most blustering night, prepare your chili con carne thus:

CHILI CON CARNE   [594]

For 6 servings, chop and melt ½ cup of beef suet in a frying pan; stir in 4 or 5 thinly sliced medium-sized onions and cook to a golden brown. Take out the onions, and to the fat remaining in the frying pan add 2½–3 pounds of tender lean round of beef, neatly cut, with a keen knife, into ½-inch cubes. Sear the meat cubes quickly, fiercely, to seal their juices, then take them up and keep hot. In a large stew pan combine the remaining fat, the onions and 6 fresh tomatoes, peeled and quartered, adding 1 cup of boiling water. As the mixture comes to the boiling point, rub 2 cloves of garlic on dry bread crusts, having at least 2 crusts per serving, and steep the crusts in the hot sauce for a few minutes. Then, and then only, add the seared, hot beef cubes and season with 1, 2, or 3 heaping tablespoons of chili powder, according to your natural tolerance of pungent condiments. Let stew gently for 30 minutes, then stir in 1 tablespoon of cider vinegar or red wine vinegar, 1 tablespoon of brown sugar, and salt the stew to taste. Do not let the meat disintegrate, but test it frequently and take the pan from the fire as soon as it is tender. Serve at once. This is real Mexican Chili Con Carne.

There are many and various modifications of Chili con Carne, and one of the most important and agreeable is in the use of green tomatoes in the summer and fall. As a matter of fact, the ideal Chili con Carne is made of green tomatoes, instead of ripe ones, for they give it a peculiar piquancy and charm. Use a full dozen of the early green ones and chop them rather finely, but later in the season, when they are larger and riper, scald, peel, and slice thinly.

Chili fortifies the Mexican heart and stomach against the shriveling heat of the desert, as curry braces the little brown Hindu for trial by fire; and when the Texas Northers sweep frost and sleet across the plains to the Gulf, the Mexican peon wraps himself in his serape and curls up over a fire of mesquite twigs, with a bowl of steaming Frijoles con Chili between his knees.

CHILI CON CARNE CON FRIJOLES   [595]
Home Style

The name of this recipe signifies chili pepper stew with meat and beans in it, the bean used being the plump red kidney bean or the more correct pinto bean. Remember, a good chili con carne should be a kind of a mushy stew, so do not add any other liquid unless absolutely necessary; should it be water, canned beef bouillon or stock, it should always be hot.

Cook 1 extra large Texas minced onion in 3 tablespoons of cooking oil or other fat over a low flame, till just beginning to brown, stirring constantly with a wooden spoon; stir in 1¾ pounds of freshly chopped (not ground) lean round of beef and continue cooking till mixture is well browned, stirring and shaking the pan almost constantly to prevent scorching. Now stir in 1 quart of canned tomatoes, 1 large green pepper, minced, 1 small can of red pimientos, drained and chopped, 1 No. 2 can of frijoles, pinto, or—lacking both—red kidney beans, 1 to 1½ or more tablespoons of real chili powder (according to taste), and season with ¼ teaspoon of powdered thyme, ½ teaspoon of dry mustard, ½ teaspoon (generous) celery seeds, and salt to taste. Cover and cook 25–30 minutes or until mixture is thickened down to a mushy consistency, stirring occasionally, and placing an asbestos pad under to prevent scorching. Serve hot with a side dish of plain, hot boiled rice.

CHINESE STEAK STRIPS, SOY BEAN SAUCE   [596]

Here is a dish for which the thrifty cook or the smart hostess will win praise from the family or guests.

Combine in a saucepan 2 cups of finely shredded cabbage, washed, then drained, ½ cup of fresh or canned chicken broth, and 4 tablespoons of peanut or cooking oil; cover and allow to simmer for 5 minutes. Meantime, in another pan, prepare the following: Heat 3 tablespoons of peanut or cooking oil (other fat may be substituted) and add 1 small clove of garlic, crushed to a paste; stir in ¼ cup of fresh or canned chicken broth, mixed with 2 teaspoons of soy bean sauce (commercial or home made), and season with ⅓ teaspoon of salt. Simmer gently for 3 minutes. Thicken with ½ teaspoon of cornstarch, moistened with 2 tablespoons of cold chicken broth, then mixed with 4 tablespoons of soy bean sauce. Continue to simmer gently while thoroughly searing a 2-pound sirloin steak, cut into strips about 1 inch wide and 2 inches long, in about 2 tablespoons of peanut oil. Drain the cabbage and arrange on a heated platter; stir the meat into the sauce and pour over the cabbage. Serve at once, with plain boiled rice.

CORNED BEEF   [597-A]

When Old King Cole and his Fiddlers Three held court and high carnival in the Café-Bar of the lamented Hotel Knickerbocker, where this writer was head chef with Jimmy Regan and the departed Malnatti, the richly furnished buffet in that oasis of the Rialto was immortalized not only by certain elixirs of the popular alchemists in attendance, but by baronial joints of a most excellent meat which was nothing more nor less than Yankee Corned Beef—yet it was of a distinction that fixed it in the memory of the discriminating as an ideal and a legend.

Many a good dinner appetite was sacrificed to that trencher of corned beef, to the mystification of hostesses and the chagrin of hosts.

Dropping in for a casual snifter, at what is known in these frivolous days as the Cocktail Hour, you looked furtively in the general direction of King Cole's own royal glance, and your hopes and expectations were gratified. Presently, without unbecoming haste, you ambled over to the goal of your desire and took up the sacrificial knife; and a mere gesture brought delicate, thin filets of the crimson meat in your hand, as if the tissue were that of milk-fed lamb or a poussin broiler. The flavor was that of—corned beef, but with a significant difference. It was corned beef entitled to rank with Southdown mutton, beechnut-fed razorback, or poularde de la Bresse. You ate and grew self-conscious. You affected an absent-minded air, toying with the sharp knife abstractedly; then you returned to King Cole's dais and ordered another of . . . the same. Such corned beef cheers without inebriating, yet those courtiers of King Cole went home babbling of green fields, to vow that they had taken little or nothing more than corned beef since leaving the office.

How did corned beef come to be? The word "corn" was synonymous back in the sixteenth century and prior thereto with the word "grain." What we call corn was not known in those days. About 1550 the manufacturers of gun-powders used the term "corned" to indicate that their product had been spread out and allowed to dry in single grains. Shortly thereafter they applied the term "corned" to the sprinkling of grains of salt on beef and other meats for the purpose of effecting a cure or preservation. In the years since the sixteenth century the original use of the word "corned" has been discontinued but it still stands to indicate the use of grains of salt in the curing of meat.

CORNED BEEF AND CABBAGE [597]
An Old-Fashioned Jiggs and Maggie Dinner

Soak a choice brisket of corned beef, about 4 pounds, in cold water for an hour. Drain; cover with fresh, cold water, gradually bring to a boil, and skim thoroughly. Simmer very, very gently for about 4 hours (do not let it actually boil lest the meat be tough). Peel 6 potatoes, 6 small white turnips, 6 small carrots, 6 small onions, and cut up a fine large cabbage to make 6 portions, removing the core. Thirty minutes before the beef is done, drop in the onions, carrots and turnips and cook until tender. In a separate pan, boil the potatoes, halved, in plain salted water, and in still another pan cook the cabbage only 15–18 minutes. When tender, lift the meat on to a large platter; rub over with butter, and slice thinly, allowing 2 slices for each portion, garnish the platter with the potatoes, carrots, turnips, onions and cabbage. Serve with freshly grated horseradish and mustard pickles.

Important. If the corned beef is to be eaten cold and enjoyed like Wesphalian ham, cold Southdown mutton, brook trout in aspic, or a terrine of pâté de foie gras, it should be cooked with devoted care, yet the cooking is of the simplest form.

Put it into cold water to cover, and bring to the simmering point very, very slowly, then hold it at that point without variation till it is cooked through and as tender as a quail. Even then, *do not lift the meat* from the pot or drain the water off, but set it away in a moderately cool place so that there will be no sharp changes of temperature, and allow it to cool in the cooking water. During the first heating and simmering, scum will rise to the surface of the water, and it should be skimmed off from time to time and kept clear.

CORNED BEEF AND FOWL SUCCOTASH [598]

This is the original Plymouth Succotash dinner which has been handed down through generations of Pilgrim descendants. It is the feature dish of every true Plymouth family on "Forefather's Day" each year.

Soak about 4 pounds of choice brisket of corned beef in cold water for an hour. Drain. Put it in a large kettle with a 4-pound cleaned, singed fowl and ½ pound of fat pork. Cover with cold water, season to taste with pepper, bring slowly to a boil, then simmer very, very gently for 4 hours, adding hot (not boiling) water as needed to keep meat covered. When both beef and fowl are tender, add 6 small turnips, quartered, 6 very small whole onions and 6 medium-sized potatoes, halved or quartered. Cook gently for 35 minutes longer. Remove meat and vegetables from the broth and stir in 1½ pounds of pea beans (navy beans) which have been cooked separately, then mashed to a pulp. Finally add 2½ quarts of cooked hulled corn. Each serving should include a portion of corned beef, chicken and vegetables. This makes several quarts and, according to the Old Pilgrim descendants, it is better each time it is reheated.

CORNED BEEF SOUFFLÉ [599]

Melt 2 tablespoons of butter or margarine; stir in 1 blade of garlic, ¼ cup each of finely chopped onion, parsley and chives, and cook until onion turns a little yellow, turning frequently, over a low flame, then stir in 1 tablespoon of lemon juice and 2 tablespoons of flour, blending well until smooth and thick; gradually stir in 1 cup of scalded milk; season to taste with salt and cayenne pepper and, when boiling and thick, remove from the fire, cool slightly, then beat in 3 slightly beaten egg yolks and return to the fire. Cook 1 minute longer; remove from the fire; let cool, then fold in 1 cup of shredded, cooked, left-over corned beef or canned corned beef, and lastly 3 egg whites stiffly beaten. Turn mixture into a buttered soufflé dish and bake 25 minutes in a hot oven (400–425° F.) (no water-bath, please). Serve at once with a side dish of Hollandaise, Tomato, or Mushroom Sauce (Nos. 1062, 1130, and 1090, respectively).

DOUBLE SIRLOIN STEAK LA PÉROUSE   [600]

Have the butcher cut a double-size sirloin steak about 3½ inches thick. Rub with mixed salt and pepper, then with melted butter, and broil in the usual way. Meanwhile, prepare the following:

Place in a small saucepan 1 tablespoon of wine vinegar, 1 teaspoon of shallots, minced fine, 1 tiny pinch of tarragon leaves, dry or fresh, ¾ cup of dry white wine, 1 sprig of fresh parsley, a small piece of bay leaf, with salt and freshly ground black pepper to taste, and bring to a quick boil. Cook until mixture is reduced to half its volume; then lower the flame and stir in ½ teaspoon of meat extract. Allow this to simmer gently for a few minutes; then add the drippings from the broiling pan. Bring to a boil; taste for seasoning; stir in 1 tablespoon of sweet butter and strain the sauce over the steak on a heated platter, the meat cut in portion-size pieces. Garnish with watercress and serve at once.

FILET OF BEEF CHIPOLATA   [601]

Have the butcher trim and tie compactly a whole filet of beef of about 2–2½ pounds. Place the meat in a generously buttered braising kettle; add ¼ cup of chopped, lean, leftover ham, ¼ cup each of chopped carrots and celery, stalks with leaves, 1 bouquet garni composed of 1 large bay leaf, tied with 6 or 7 sprigs of parsley and 1 sprig of thyme, using white kitchen thread, ½ clove of garlic, mashed to a pulp, and 1 medium-sized onion, thinly sliced. Sprinkle over the filet a mixture of ⅛ teaspoon each of cloves, mace, allspice and salt and pepper to taste. Pour over ½ generous cup of beef stock or canned consommé; cover hermetically and braise in a moderate oven (350–375° F.) for 30–35 minutes, turning the filet once during the cooking process. Transfer the filet of beef to a heated platter and keep hot while preparing the sauce as follows:

Strain the gravy from the kettle through a fine-meshed sieve into a saucepan; remove all the fat, add 1 teaspoon of butter, creamed with 2 teaspoons of flour, then cook, stirring constantly until mixture thickens and simmer gently for 15 minutes. Stir in ½ cup of Madeira Sauce (No. 1076) and keep hot. Slice as much filet as is likely to be needed; reshape in its natural form. Pour over a little of the sauce; garnish the platter with a dozen small pork sausages, cooked and well drained; garnish both ends of the platter with watercress and serve at once with the remainder of the sauce in a sauce-boat. Good accompaniments are Braised Lettuce or Braised Celery (Nos. 1350 and 1251, respectively) and small potato balls rolled in melted butter, then in finely chopped parsley or chives.

FILET OF BEEF GARIBALDI   [602]

Cut an entire beef filet weighing about 2 pounds into 6 equal parts and shape each part into plump round filets. Cut half as many slices of black truffles, rounds of ham, and thin rounds of beef marrow as there are filets. Blanch the marrow. Pound the lean trimmings of the filet of beef; add about 2 tablespoons of beef marrow, the yolk of 1 egg, a pinch of nutmeg, a seasoning of salt and pepper and rub mixture through a fine-meshed wire sieve. Spread a little of this paste on the pieces of filets, cover with a slice of marrow, add a little more of the paste, then the truffle, again a little paste, and lastly the rounds of lean ham, pressing all lightly but thoroughly together. Cover the surface with a thin layer of the remaining paste; brush over with egg white and sprinkle liberally with finely chopped black truffles. Arrange the filets thus prepared in a generously buttered baking pan, cover with a buttered paper and cook in a moderate oven (350-375° F.) for about 25 minutes; remove the paper and continue baking until filets are done, or about 10 minutes longer. Serve on a border of mashed potatoes, straining rich Tomato Sauce (No. 1130) over each filet and garnish with Rice Croquettes (Nos. 1594-95) and watercress.

In 1639, when Mynheer Bronchs bought from the Indians what is now the Bronx, New York, he paid $30 for it, half in money and half in preserved Dutch beef.

FILET OF BEEF AU MARSALA   [603]

Trim, then lard a 2-2½ pound filet of beef with narrow strips of pork fat back, using about a dozen of them (the butcher will do this for you on request). Heat ¼ cup of lard in a medium-sized braising kettle, roll the meat in it to coat on all sides with fat, season to taste with mixed salt, pepper and a dash each of nutmeg, thyme and mace. Cover and cook in a moderate oven (350-375° F.) about 25-30 minutes, turning the filet twice during the cooking process. Meanwhile, cook in 2 separate pans in 2 tablespoons of butter (a) 20 medium-sized peeled mushroom caps and (b) the thinly sliced mushroom stems, cooking each until tender and seasoning with salt and pepper. Drain and keep both hot. Combine the butter from the two pans and stir in 1½ tablespoons of chopped shallots. Cook 1 minute, then stir in 1 tablespoon of flour and blend well. Add, a little at a time, 1¼ cups of heated Marsala wine, stirring constantly until mixture just begins to boil. Remove from the fire; taste for seasoning, then stir in the mushroom caps and stems.

Transfer the filet to a heated platter; slice, re-shape; pour the sauce over it and garnish with watercress. Serve immediately.

Full details of the hundreds of methods of preparing and serving a filet mignon would fill a volume in itself. Space will not permit a complete list of names dedicated to the various preparations of this highly and justly appreciated piece of meat, including the innumerable garnishings which belong to it.

The filet mignon cut from the whole filet of the beef is generally served on a round of toast or of bread fried in butter, and the usual maximum weight for each serving portion is rarely above 6 ounces. Filet mignon may be grilled or sautéed. In either case it should be first seasoned with salt and pepper, then rolled in melted butter or good olive oil, before being placed under the flame, then turned once or twice to ensure uniform cooking throughout to the degree of "doneness" desired—rare, medium, or well-done. A grilled filet mignon may be served without any garnishing other than a sprig or two of crisp watercress and a handful of saratoga chip potatoes, shoestring potatoes or, still better, pommes soufflées (potato soufflé). When sautéed or pan-fried, one usually has single or several garnishings or prepared vegetables with it according to directions. The sauce, if any, is usually served separately after the meat has been slightly spooned or moistened with it. When sautéed, the skillet or frying pan in which the operation has been done should always be deglazed with either water, meat juice, wine, or a liquid corresponding to the sauce which should be served with it.

A Chateaubriand is a slice of beef cut laterally from the thickest part of the filet or tenderloin of beef; while Tournedos of beef are slices cut from the tail side of the filet or tenderloin, and should be 1½–2 inches thick per individual serving, a slice of fresh fat back pork being wrapped around each and tied with string.

A Chateaubriand of Beef (which has nothing in common with the brilliant father of the romantic movement in French literature) must be cut, at least 3 inches thick, and like filet mignon or tournedos of beef must be broiled or sautéed.

FILET MIGNON À LA RICHMOND   [604]

Cut a whole beef filet into 6 slices of even size; trim neatly, and season to taste with salt and pepper. Melt 3 tablespoons of butter in a sauté-pan; when hot, put in the 6 filets and sauté them on one side, then turn and cover the cooked sides with a mixture made with ½ pound of fresh mushrooms, finely ground and cooked in butter and a little lemon juice until soft. This type of purée of mushrooms should be smooth and thick. Arrange the mignons well apart in the sauté-pan; cover with a buttered paper and bake gently in a moderate oven for about 10 minutes. Transfer to a heated platter; top each mignon with a slice of black truffle; pour a little Madeira wine sauce over, also around the base of the dish; garnish with 6 grilled tomato slices, each slice topped with a poached egg yolk surrounded with a strip of anchovy filet, and in between the tomato slices a cooked mushroom cap. Serve with a side dish of Green Peas French Style (No. 1406), passing remaining sauce separately.

FILET MIGNON STÉFANIE [605]

First of all, prepare a Duxelles or stuffing as follows:

Mushroom Duxelles. Heat slightly 1 teaspoon of onion and 1 teaspoon of shallots, both finely chopped, together with 1 teaspoon of butter and the same of olive oil. Cook 1 minute over a bright flame, stirring constantly; then lower the flame and stir in ½ pound of fresh mushroom caps peeled, finely ground and well pressed in order to remove all water. Cook over a very low flame until all moisture has disappeared, then season with salt, pepper and a half teaspoon of chopped chervil of parsley.

Now sauté 6 filets mignons on both sides in ⅓ cup of butter for about 4 minutes. Remove from the fire, drain and cool. Cover each mignon with about ½ inch of mushroom duxelles, then wrap in flaky pie crust or, if preferred, in puff paste (No. 2076), bake 12–15 minutes in a moderate oven (375° F.), or until crust is golden brown. Before serving, cut a small hole in the middle of the top crust and, using a funnel, fill with Bearnaise Sauce (No. 1012).

As late as 1891, British butchers wrapped their meat in old newspaper. An ordinance passed that year required them to use clean wrapping paper.

GRILLED HAMBURGERS AND ONION RINGS [606]

Cut 6 thick slices of large Spanish onion, each slice a generous half inch in thickness, being careful not to separate the rings. Secure them with toothpicks pushed in sidewise. Lay the slices in a greased baking pan; pour over them 3 tablespoons of melted bacon drippings; season to taste with mixed salt and black pepper, cover closely and bake in a moderate oven (325–350° F.) until tender, or about 20–25 minutes Meanwhile, heat 2 tablespoons of butter; stir in 2 tablespoons of grated onion, 1 tablespoon of chopped parsley and ¾ cup of soft bread crumbs. Season to taste with salt and pepper and work into 1⅓ pounds of finely chopped, lean raw beef, mixing thoroughly. Beat 1 large egg and combine with the chopped meat mixture. Form into 6 flat cakes; wrap each with a slice of bacon, securing it with picks; place a cake on each onion slice in baking pan and brush over with melted bacon or ham drippings. Grill in broiling oven, having the pan about 6 inches from the flame.

broiling about 4 or 5 minutes on each side, and basting frequently with drippings from the pan. Serve on a heated platter, each burger surrounded with a wreath of crisp watercress.

Variation. Top each burger with a broiled mushroom cap or with a freshly poached egg, or with a grilled thick tomato slice.

Hamburgers can be fine food and varied food and since they are also cheap food, the wise cook will feel justified in allowing herself a few frills now and then so that her meat balls will have neither the taste nor the appearance of poverty. An extra dab of butter and a dash of Pique Seasoning and paprika slowly mingling with the pink juices of the grilled burger are all economies in the long run since they will preserve the family's taste for the burger.

And right here let me say that the family should never, never be taken in on the secrets of kitchen economy. People cannot be expected to enjoy codfish because they hear it's the cheapest fish in market, but, not being told anything, they'll like it if you have cooked it well, using butter or herbs or cream to advantage, as well as seasoning right to the point. All the same, the exemplary family does not exist that will cheerfully eat codfish and burgers and pigs' feet, and hearts indefinitely while there are salmon and ducks, oysters and steaks and chops. It is at this point that a cook can prove her ability. It is by doing her superlative best with plain dishes, and by spacing the luxuries, that the hard-pressed cook will get by.

HAMBURGER CELESTINE   [607]

Mix 2 pounds of chopped round of beef, 2 slightly beaten eggs and 2 tablespoons of grated onion. Season with salt, pepper, a few grains of curry powder, a pinch each of mace, thyme, clove and nutmeg to taste and shape into 6 balls, flattening them a little. Cut off the leaves of a white cabbage and put in a large kettle; cover with boiling water and let stand about 5 minutes or until the leaves are soft. Drain, then wrap each meat ball in a cabbage leaf and fasten with toothpick. Sauté in ⅛ cup of butter 5 or 6 minutes, or until thoroughly browned. Meantime, melt 3 tablespoons of butter in a large baking pan, add 4 thinly sliced large onions, and cook very slowly until onions are a golden brown, stirring frequently with a wooden spoon, then add the wrapped meat balls. Cover tightly and cook in a moderate oven (325° F.) for 1 hour, stirring occasionally; after the first ¼ hour add ½ cup of beef stock, fresh or canned, and baste frequently. Half an hour before ready to serve, add ¾ pound of peeled, fresh mushrooms, quartered if large, or halved if small. Taste for seasoning, and stir in 1 generous cup of scalded heavy sour cream. Serve at once. Do not keep over a heavy hot flame, lest the sour cream curdle.

The following dish is definitely masculine. It tickles the palate and warms the heart of every male—and, after all, that is important to every woman.

HAMBURGERS À LA CREOLE [608]

Prepare 6 individual hamburgers. Roll into balls, then flatten them slightly. Have ready 3–4 cups of Creole Sauce (No. 1041), sizzling hot; add the 6 prepared burgers; cover tightly and bake for 25–30 minutes in a moderate oven (375° F.), turning once during the cooking process. This will serve 6 the first time the dish is tried. The second time you serve "Hamburgers à la Creole" the above quantity will serve 2 persons nicely!

In 780 A. D., Italian physicians prescribed chopped beef fried with onions to cure colds and coughs. Thus was the now popular hamburger invented.

PEPPER CHUCK STEAK DINNER [609]

Brown on both sides in ¼ cup of hot lard 2 medium-thick cuts of beef chuck, each weighing about 1½ pounds. Place 1 steak in a baking pan having a cover, and cover with 3 green peppers, halved, seeded and cut in strips; season to taste with salt and pepper, then place the other steak on top of the pepper strips and cover with 3 green peppers prepared as before and mixed with equal parts of thinly sliced onions. Now combine 1 large can (No. 2) of tomato and 1 small can of tomato sauce, and pour over all again seasoning to taste with mixed salt and pepper. Lastly pour over ½ generous cup of beef stock and add 1 bouquet garni composed of 1 large bay leaf, tied with 2 sprigs of green celery leaves, 1 sprig of thyme and 8 sprigs of fresh parsley, all tied with white kitchen thread. Bring to a boil; cover, and bake in a moderate oven (350-375° F.) for at least 2 hours. Serve with mashed potatoes.

POT ROAST À LA ROMANE [610]
El Garofolato al Roma

Lard through and through two 3–3½-pound pieces of top round of beef with 1½ dozen narrow strips of fat back pork, previously rolled in finely chopped fines herbs, such as parsley, chervil, shallots, marjoram, fennel, and garlic. Tie compactly with white string and sear on all sides in ⅓ cup of olive oil (or butter, if preferred) until well browned. Heat in a stew pot a little of the oil or butter from the searing; stir in 3 cloves of garlic, 6 cloves and 1 pound of fresh tomatoes, peeled and quartered, and cook for 2 minutes, stirring frequently. Add the well-drained beef,

1 bouquet garni composed of 2 bay leaves, 10 sprigs of parsley, 1 sprig of thyme, and 3 sprigs of green celery leaves, tied with white kitchen string or thread. Season to taste with salt and freshly ground peppercorns, and pour over the whole 1–1½ cups of red wine. Cover; bring to a boil, and set at once into a moderate oven (350–375° F.) to cook gently for 2 hours. After 1 hour of cooking, add 2 cups of celery stalks, scraped and cut into inch pieces. Serve meat, sauce and celery all together in a heated deep dish.

ROAST BEEF WITH YORKSHIRE PUDDING [611]

According to old English cooks, a roast has to surmount six obstacles to be perfect. The meat must be choice. It must be well "hung," roasted at a good fire by a good cook in good temper. Finally the diner must have a good appetite.

There is no subject in cookery upon which there is more difference of opinion than that of meat when it comes to roasting. Among the meats, beef needs the most careful treatment, as generally tastes differ as to whether it should be done rare, medium, or well. To produce roast beef which will suit everyone is an art for which experience as well as a good recipe are necessary. This is especially true when the roast is small. More time per pound must be allowed for a small roast than for a large one. Formerly it was considered necessary to use small roasts in a home kitchen. Now, with the use of a thermometer, this is not necessary and a large roast may be used. Also, it was considered necessary to sear the roast at a high temperature in order to keep in the juices. Allow ½ pound of meat and bone per serving.

Roasting a Standing Beef Roast American Style. Wipe with a damp cloth 2, 3, or even 4 ribs of beef, trimmed for roasting by the butcher, then rub with mixed salt and pepper and dredge with flour. Place in an open roasting pan fat side up. If meat thermometer is used, make hole with a skewer through fat side and insert thermometer so that the bulb will be in the center of fleshy part of roast but not touching the bone. Roast according to either of the 2 methods given below. If meat thermometer is used, the final reading should be 140° F. for rare, 160° F. for medium and 170° F. for well done.

Method I—Searing Method, or English Method. Sear roast in a hot oven (500° F.) 20 to 30 minutes, or until meat is well browned on all sides. Reduce the heat to moderate (350° F.) for remainder of time. In estimating time per pound, include searing time. *Rare:* Allow 20 minutes per pound for roasts under 5 pounds and 18 minutes per pound for roasts over 5 pounds. *Medium:* Allow 25 minutes per pound for roasts under 5 pounds and 22 minutes per pound for roasts over 5 pounds. *Well Done:* Allow 35 minutes per pound for roasts under 5 pounds and 30 minutes per pound for roasts over 5 pounds.

Method II—Even Temperature Method, or American Method. Roast in moderately slow oven (325° F.). *Rare:* Allow 25 minutes per pound for roasts under 5 pounds and 21 minutes per pound for roasts over 5 pounds. *Medium:* Allow 35 minutes per pound for roasts under 5 pounds and 27 minutes per pound for roasts over 5 pounds. *Well done:* Allow 40 minutes per pound for roasts under 5 pounds and 33 minutes per pound for roasts over 5 pounds.

Basting. The main reason for basting is to render the meat tender, to prevent burning or charring, and also to return flavor to the meat. This is one of the major reasons why a coating of fat is always left on a roast, or, when a roast is lean, why fat is spread over it before roasting. On a piece of meat which is to be boiled, braised or broiled, on the other hand, the fat is usually partially or entirely removed. The basting for a roast is about every 15–20 minutes, depending on size of roast.

Pan Gravy—See Sauces.

Yorkshire Pudding. Sift 1 cup of bread flour with ⅓ teaspoon of salt in a mixing bowl. Make a well in center and gradually add 1 cup of cold milk to form a smooth heavy batter; then add 2 eggs, slightly beaten, and beat steadily for 2 minutes with rotary beater. A baking pan containing ¼–½ inch of the hot roast beef fat is the ideal and perfect pan for baking. Pour batter into the sizzling hot fat; place the baking pan in a hot oven (400° F.) and bake 20–25 minutes, decreasing the heat to moderate as the baking nears completion, and bake 5–8 minutes longer. Cut in squares and serve with a spoonful of the natural roast beef juice or "dish gravy" over the top. Hissing-hot iron muffins or gem pans or small cup-cake tins, generously greased, may be used instead of the large pan, the baking time then being reduced.

SALISBURY STEAK [612]
A Variation of the Hamburger Family

To 1¾ pounds of chopped lean, raw beef add 1 scant teaspoon of salt, ¼ teaspoon of pepper, 1 tablespoon of grated onion and enough cold thin cream or rich milk to moisten. Mix very lightly with a fork; divide mixture into 6 individual portions; coat lightly with fresh bread crumbs and broil as you would a hamburger steak, basting frequently with melted butter. A slice of finely chopped fat salt pork may be chopped with the beef to give additional flavor; or add chopped parsley and/or chives for yet another.

SAUERBRATEN BAVARIAN STYLE [613]
Sour Pot Roast

The best cut for a good sauerbraten is from the bottom round of a prime steer.

Prepare a marinade of half vinegar and half water, 8 whole cloves, gently bruised, 1 scraped parsley root, 1 teaspoon of whole peppercorns, 2 bay leaves tied with 2 sprigs of green celery leaves and 1 sprig of thyme, 2 juniper berries, crushed, 1 large onion, thinly sliced, 2 cloves of garlic mashed to a paste, and salt to taste. Put a 5–6-pound piece of bottom round or crossribs into an earthenware dish or crock; pour the marinade over and let stand, covered with a cloth, in a cool place for at least 4 days, turning the meat twice daily. When ready to cook, take the meat out of the marinade, place in a roasting pan and sear on all sides in a little lard or bacon drippings. Meantime, cook the marinade down to half its volume.

The meat being well seared, transfer it into a large kettle, add the reduced marinade, 1 small can of tomato puree, 1½ cups of beef stock, 1 tablespoon of brown sugar, 1 cup of red wine, 1 tablespoon of lemon juice, 2 or 3 strips of lemon peel, a few crumbled ginger snaps, and 1 tablespoon of Worcestershire or Pique Seasoning. Be sure that the meat is generously covered with the liquid; if not, add more beef stock. Cover, set the kettle in a moderate oven (375° F.), and cook gently 3½–4 hours, turning the meat once during the cooking process, or until meat is done but not falling to pieces. Transfer meat to a hot platter and keep hot while finishing up the gravy as follows:

Strain through a fine sieve into a fresh saucepan; taste for seasoning and bring to a boil. The gravy must have a piquant sour-sweet taste. Pour part of it over the meat first sliced for service, passing additional gravy separately with potato pancakes, noodles or spaghetti, but always with a side dish of the following potato balls:

Bavarian Potato Balls. Boil a dozen potatoes and, when done, mash them and let them cool. When cold, add 1 tablespoon of flour, 1 tablespoon of farina, 3 eggs, slightly beaten, salt to taste, a grating of nutmeg and a pinch of sugar. Mix thoroughly. Have some small cubes or, better still, crumbs of fried bread ready (about ½ cup) and add to the potato mixture. Shape into balls the size of a large walnut, and drop the balls, a few at a time, into rapidly boiling salted water. At once lower the heat and let simmer gently for 20 minutes. Skim out and serve hot.

Mid-European farmers of the eleventh century raised two kinds of beef cattle: "Noble's meat" for the men, and a soft, delicate grade for their ladies.

## SPICED POT ROAST DUTCH STYLE					[614]

Rub a 5-pound piece of top round of beef thoroughly with mixed salt and pepper and put in an earthen dish. Add 1 large onion, sliced thin, 3 large bay leaves, an inch piece of scraped horseradish, 1 medium-sized carrot, thinly sliced, 3 sprigs of green celery leaves (celery tops), tied with 1 sprig of thyme, also 1 teaspoon of peppercorns. Take equal parts of vinegar and water and pour over the meat, which should be entirely covered with the liquid. Let stand in this marinade for 24 hours. Next day, when ready to cook, drain the meat, put it in a roasting pan and sear well in a hot oven (400° F.). When well browned all over, add about 1½ cups of the strained, spiced marinade, cover the pan tightly and cook in a moderate oven (375° F.) for 3½ hours or until meat is tender, adding more of the liquid marinade if necessary. When cooked, remove the meat to a heated platter; slice what is likely to be needed and keep hot. Strain the liquid in the pan through a fine sieve into a saucepan; let reduce to half over a bright flame; stir in 1 cup of heavy sour cream; bring to a boil, taste for seasoning, then beat in 2 egg yolks, one at a time, beating well after each addition. Return to the fire, bring to a boil, stirring constantly from bottom of the pan, and pour half of this sour cream sauce over the sliced meat, serving the remainder separately with a dish of plain boiled cabbage quarters, cored, and another dish of plain boiled potatoes.

STUFFED BEEF SLICES [615]

Have the butcher cut 2½ pounds of round of beef into 6 slices about 1 inch thick, and then flatten them with his cleaver until they are not more than ½-inch in thickness. Trim neatly, rub each slice with mixed salt, pepper and thyme to taste. Set aside.

Pass through food chopper 1 medium-sized onion, 4 sprigs of parsley, stemmed, ½ small clove of garlic, 7 or 8 sprigs of chives, 1 tablespoon of green celery leaves, and 4 slices of bacon. To this, add the trimmings of the beef, finely chopped; season to taste with salt, pepper and a little thyme and clove. Divide this mixture among the 6 thin slices of beef; roll each slice up tightly, secure with kitchen thread, and arrange the rolls side by side in a shallow baking dish containing 2 tablespoons of chopped, cooked ham, ½ green pepper, seeded and finely chopped, 1 medium-sized onion, thinly sliced, and pour over all 1½–2 cups of red wine and beef stock mixed in equal parts. Cover tightly, set the dish in a moderate oven (375° F.), and bake for 2 hours without disturbing, except to turn the rolls after 1 hour of baking. Transfer the meat to a heated platter and keep hot. Strain the gravy from the dish through a fine sieve, rubbing through as much as possible of the pulp of the vegetable and the ham; bring to a boil and stir in 2 tablespoons of sherry wine. Taste for seasoning, and pour this sauce over the rolls. Garnish the platter with 6 nice fresh mushroom caps, broiled, 6 thick slices of tomatoes, broiled, and in between little bouquets of crisp watercress.

SWISS STEAK [616]

The original name of this recipe was "Schmor Braten." It is three centuries old.

Select a 3-pound piece of round steak, top round preferred about
2½ inches thick. Rub about ½ a cup of salted and peppered flour into
the meat on both sides. Heat to the smoking point 2 tablespoons of
drippings or lard; put the meat in it, and brown nicely on both sides.
Transfer to a stewpot; add 2 cups of boiling water, with 1 large onion,
thinly sliced, and season to taste with salt and black pepper. Now add
1 bouquet garni composed of 1 extra large or 2 small bay leaves, 8 sprigs
of fresh parsley, 1 sprig of thyme and 2 sprigs of green celery leaves all
tied together with white kitchen thread, 2 whole cloves, and a blade
of garlic. Let simmer very gently, covered, over a low flame for an hour.
Then stir in 1 cup of tomato purée, 1 teaspoonful of good prepared
mustard and 1½ tablespoons of tomato catsup, cover again and continue simmering for another hour, or until done, and the meat may be
cut with the fork. If there is not enough liquid, add more beef stock;
thicken, if needed, with a little flour; taste for seasoning and serve steak
and half of the gravy in a heated deep platter, the remainder of the
gravy separately with a side dish of plain boiled potatoes.

"Tied Meat" is a Chinese expression for "Teacher's Fee," going
back to the custom in ancient China of paying school teachers with
bundles of dried meat.

TOURNEDOS A LA BEARNAISE   [617]
Small Filets of Beef with Bearnaise

Take 6 slices of beef filet, just under 2 inches thick, and trim them
into rounds about 3½ inches in diameter. Carefully remove every
particle of fat and gristle and tie them with string, so that they will
retain their shape when cooked. Each tournedo should weigh about
3–3½ ounces. When ready to cook, sprinkle them with mixed salt and
pepper and sauté them in plenty of butter and oil (in equal parts) in a
frying pan, over a fairly quick flame. They should be somewhat underdone inside, so cook them 5–6 minutes on one side, then turn and cook
3 or 4 minutes on the other. If preferred a little more done, cook 1 minute longer on both sides. Dress each round of filet on a round of bread
cut slightly bigger than the tournedos and fried in clarified butter.
Serve on a heated platter, surrounding them with Potatoes Soufflées
(No. 1420); put a generous teaspoon of Bearnaise Sauce (No. 1012) on
top of each tournedo and pass additional sauce in a gravy boat.

VEAL   [618]

Silky little calves bunt fierce little heads in eagerness at their mother's
milky bags. May time is calf time in the cow country. Now tender,
sweet veal comes in greatest abundance to enhance the menu. To be

truly veal, calves should be entirely milk-fed. When a calf is old enough to eat grass and grain, its flesh takes on a reddish tinge and a different taste.

Americans have a fixed notion that veal is indigestible. In France it is regarded as the proper food for invalids. Cooked correctly, it is delicate and subtly flavored; but it requires skillful tricks in the handling. Veal doesn't respond to the same kind of cooking as mature beef. It has less fat, more connective tissue and is likely to be dry unless carefully treated. Veal's lack of fat necessitates the use of bacon or salt pork or fat-back pork for larding or laying on as strips over the top of the meat. One of the characteristics of veal, that makes it a joy to prepare, is its perfect tenderness, even in the least costly cuts. A shoulder of veal, for example, is inexpensive, yet can be roasted as easily as a choice leg or loin cut.

Veal presents a paradox. It comes from a young animal, but it is considered indigestible. Veal is the flesh of calves from three to twelve weeks old. Veal from milk-fed calves weighing about one hundred and twenty-five pounds, and from six to eight weeks old, is considered the most desirable. The best veal is fine-grained and velvety with a little creamy fat; the bones are soft, small and red in color.

VEAL—DO'S AND DON'TS

Don't try to broil veal chops or steaks. *Don't* cook a veal stew without first browning the meat to give added flavor. *Don't* cover up the delicate flavor of the veal with strong-flavored vegetables, use only the milder ones.

Do add extra fat to veal whether roast, stew or chop. Salt pork, fat pork back, butter and bacon fat are all very fine. *Do* cook veal thoroughly if you want the finest flavor. *Do* combine veal with such flavors as sausage, bacon, celery, spinach, spiced fruits, dill pickle and delicate vegetables, such as peas, asparagus, green limas, lettuce, and new potatoes. *Do* roast veal uncovered, whether it be a shoulder, a leg or a rack. It improves flavor and color. *Do* remember that fine flavor of soup stock made from veal shanks enhances sauces. *Do not* uncover veal when braising. It makes for loss of flavor.

The whiteness of veal is considered a sign of good quality. In Europe calves are killed much younger than is customary in this country, and they are fed on milk and white food, but no feeding will make every calf equally white fleshed. As immature meat keeps badly at all times, it is of importance that the calf should not be bruised in bringing it to market.

As with pork—"the gentleman who pays the rent," as the Irish saying goes—every part of the veal may be used in cookery, and delicious dishes may be made out of calf's head, as well as out of calf's feet.

GUIDE TO THE PURCHASE AND PREPARATION OF VEAL [619]

RETAIL VEAL CUT*	CHARACTERISTICS	HOW TO COOK (Methods)
ARM STEAK AND ARM ROAST	Both from shoulder. Often boned. Juicy and tender. Little fat. Both require slow, long, steady cooking in moist heat.	Stew, white stock, braise, pot roast
BLADE ROAST AND BLADE STEAK	Usually cut into thick chunks and boned. Juicy and tender but requires slow, steady cooking in moist heat. If roasted, frequent bastings are required.	Oven stew, braise, roast, pot roast, boil, loaf
BONELESS RUMP ROAST	From the leg. Each roast averages 4–4½ lbs. Similar to beef rump, with about ⅞ lean, juicy, tender meat. Requires frequent basting.	Braise, roast, pot roast, pot, loaf, Swiss steak
CROWN ROAST, RIB CHOP AND RIB ROAST	From the rib as in beef and lamb. Contains 7 ribs and "eye" muscle. Chops cut between ribs have no bone and are cooked like standing rib of beef. Juicy and tender. When roasted, baste frequently.	Braise, roast, stuff, loaf
HEEL OF ROUND	From the round; wedge-shaped. Economical boneless piece; juicy and tender. Sear before cooking to insure best flavor.	Braise, pot roast, stew, pot, Swiss steak
KIDNEY CHOP, LOIN CHOP, LOIN ROAST, SIRLOIN STEAK OR CUTLET	Kidney chop, with kidney, is taken from the rib end of the loin, with the shank wrapped around. Juicy and tender. Loin chop has a piece of tenderloin attached to it and is juicy and tender. The loin roast is from the loin, with backbone and kidney attached. Requires steady basting when roasted; self-basting when cooked in moist heat. The sirloin steak or cutlet is treated like beef.	Bake, braise, casserole, pot roast, Swiss steak, scallopini, pan fry, minute steak, pot, roast
POCKET ROAST	Also called "cushion roast." It is taken from the breast. A long, flat cut; savory, juicy and tender when cooked in moist heat and covered. Requires frequent basting when roasted after being seared.	Braise, stuff, oven-stew, pot roast, pot, roast

* Taken from the six wholesale cuts—round or leg, loin, breast, rib, shoulder and shank.

GUIDE TO THE PURCHASE AND PREPARATION OF VEAL   [619]

RETAIL VEAL CUT*	CHARACTERISTICS	HOW TO COOK (Methods)
RIBLETS	From the breast with flank and bone removed, and the breast separated by cutting between the rib ends. Juicy and tender when treated by slow cooking after being seared.	Casserole, bake, braise, stew, pot roast, Swiss steak
ROLLED SHOULDER	Always boned and rolled as for beef "Chicago Roll"; savory, tender and juicy when cooked in moist heat after being seared. When roasted, requires frequent basting. May be stuffed to stretch the meat.	Braise, roast, Swiss steak pot roast, casserole
ROUND ROAST	From the leg. Cut in any desired size. Same preparation as for round of beef. Requires thorough searing before being cooked in moist heat and covered to insure self-basting. Requires frequent basting when roasted. Cook in a slow oven.	Same as for round of beef
ROUND STEAK	From the leg. Similar to the oval shape of beef round. Juicy and tender when cooked slowly in moist heat.	Same as for round of beef
RUMP ROAST	From the leg. Always boned. Juicy and tender when cooked in moist heat after being thoroughly seared. When roasted, requires slow roasting and frequent basting.	Same as for rump of beef
SHANK	Very bony. Rich in gelatinous substance and appropriate for natural gelatine.	Soups, white stock, wine or other flavoring, jellied dishes

* Taken from the six wholesale cuts—round or leg, loin, breast, rib, shoulder and shank.

BLANQUETTE OF VEAL   [620]
French Veal Stew

Ingredients. 2½ pounds of veal from the breast, ribs, or leg, cut into rather small serving portions; 1 quart of cold water; 1 large onion halved, each half stuck with 1 clove; ¼ cup of thinly sliced carrots; 1 bouquet garni composed of 1 large bay leaf, 8 sprigs of fresh parsley, and 1 sprig of thyme, all tied together with white kitchen thread, 1 small stick of celery, coarsely chopped; salt and pepper to taste.

Place all ingredients in a stew pan; gradually bring to a boil, lower the heat and let simmer until the meat just begins to separate from the bones. Lift the meat out into a hot platter by means of a perforated ladle, and keep hot. Place 2 cups of the broth, strained, in a small saucepan; bring to a boil; thicken with 1½ tablespoons of butter which has been creamed with 1½ tablespoons of flour, and let boil 3 or 4 minutes. Remove from the fire, beat in 3 egg yolks, added one at a time, beating well after each addition; taste for seasoning; stir in 1 tablespoon of lemon juice, 1 scant teaspoon of chopped parsley and a grating of nutmeg. Bring to a boil; remove from the fire at once; add the meat and when well heated (without actually boiling) serve in a heated deep dish, sprinkling with finely chopped parsley. If desired, add when reheating meat, a dozen or so each of small mushroom caps and small white onions, previously cooked separately and well drained.

BLANQUETTE OF VEAL Ā LA WEIMAR [621]

Proceed as indicated above (No. 620) omitting the vegetables and adding, when the meat is half done, 1 teaspoon of grated lemon rind, and 2 or 3 small raw cucumbers, peeled, seeded and cut into cubes. When the meat is tender, thicken the sauce with about ½ cup of soft bread crumbs; bring to a boil; let boil 2 or 3 minutes and, when ready to serve, stir in a fresh grating of nutmeg and a fresh grinding of black pepper. Serve very hot in a deep heated platter.

BRAISED VEAL ROLL [622]

Bone, or have the butcher bone for you, 2½ pounds of breast of veal, chop coarsely, then pass through food chopper together with 4 ounces of fat bacon. Add 2 teaspoons of flour, 3 tablespoons of soft bread crumbs, 1 scant teaspoon of grated lemon rind, salt, pepper and nutmeg to taste, 2 hard-cooked eggs, chopped very fine, and enough milk, mixed with 1 large well-beaten egg, to make a rather stiff mixture. Shape into a roll, and sear on all sides in ¼ cup of butter, turning frequently. When well browned, turn into a baking pan. Add any remaining butter from the searing process, with 2 cups of beef stock or canned bouillon; 1 large bay leaf, 1 sprig of thyme, 6 or 7 sprigs of fresh parsley, 1 sprig of green celery leaves, and 2 whole cloves—all tied together with white kitchen thread; 6 whole peppercorns, freshly bruised; salt to taste; and lastly ¾ cup of sweet, heavy cream. Cover closely, and bake in a moderate oven for about 45 minutes, basting twice and turning the meat once during the cooking process. Transfer to a heated serving platter; strain the gravy from the pan into a saucepan; bring to a boil; Remove from the fire at once and stir in 3 tablespoons of tomato paste.

Taste for seasoning. Slice as much meat as is likely to be needed; re-shape the roll and strain the sauce over. Garnish simply with watercress and serve at once.

" . . . When we were very little," the Mock-Turtle went on at last, more calmly, though still sobbing a little now and then, "we went to school in the sea. The master was an old turtle—we used to call him Tortoise—"

" . . . Why did you call him Tortoise if he wasn't one?" Alice asked.

" . . . We called him Tortoise because he taught us," said the Mock-Turtle angrily; "really you are very dull!" (*Alice in Wonderland*)

And the tortoise has kept on teaching pathetic little calves' heads how best to impersonate a turtle, or even a terrapin, but never—or hardly ever—how to be just themselves; and there's nothing so very unusual about that, when all about us are bespectacled human tortoises frantically teaching hordes of little human mock turtles how to be anything and everything except plain, simple, honest calves' heads.

Though the very thought of imitations and make-believes is commonly repugnant, especially in relation to the things we eat, a census of the green-turtle addicts and the mock-turtle consumers would show the latter in an overwhelming majority. Mock-turtle soup is good soup, wholesome, filling and savory; green turtle soup is good, too, but it has always been dedicated to the higher caste epicures; and in these days there are not so very many gourmets who were reared and nurtured in the green turtle and Madeira and truffle tradition.

Many interesting things can be done with calves' heads; the butcher will clean and split them for you, and also take out the brains and tongues.

CALF'S HEAD   [623]
(*How to Cook*)

Put the head in cold water to generously cover, and blanch by bringing to a boil; at this point, take it off and plunge it again into cold water. Drain, then rub all over with a halved lemon, after which set it to cook in a small kettle, in boiling water to cover, with a generous cup of dry white wine, 1 small clove of garlic, sliced, 2 sliced medium-sized onions, 1 bouquet garni composed of 1 extra large bay leaf, 2 sprigs of green celery leaves (tops), 1 sprig of thyme, 8 sprigs of fresh parsley, all tied together with white kitchen thread, a dozen or so of whole peppercorns, 1 teaspoon of salt, and 2 whole cloves. Boil 2 hours, or until the meat is tender and will easily leave the bones but without breaking into shreds. Cut meat neatly from bones with a sharp knife. If brains and tongue are to be used, parboil the brains 10 minutes and cook the tongue separately till tender. The head, tongue and brains are now ready to be served à la Vinaigrette.

CALF'S HEAD A LA VINAIGRETTE [624]

For the generally familiar Calf's Head à la Vinaigrette, arrange the hot meat with the sliced tongue and brains on a warm platter, and dress with Sauce Vinaigrette (No. 1133).

CALF'S HEAD EN TORTUE [625]
Mock Turtle

To prepare this old favorite, cut the hot meat, tongue and brains into neat dice and heat very, very gently in a sauce made from 2 cups of the liquid in which the head was boiled, thickened with 1½ tablespoons of butter and as much of flour, slightly browned over a low flame; add 3 chopped hard-cooked eggs, seasoned to taste with salt and pepper, ¼ cup of either sherry or Madeira wine and 1 teaspoon each of finely chopped parsley and chives. Heat without boiling and serve at once.

CALF'S HEAD GRILL PROVENÇALE [626]

Take 6 portions (for individual service) of the hot calf's head (No. 623); sprinkle generously to taste with mixed salt, black pepper and a few grains of cayenne. Roll each piece in either olive oil or melted butter, then in fresh bread crumbs, and grill until crumbs are delicately and evenly browned. Also grill 6 fresh mushroom caps, 6 thick slices of ripe tomato, and 6 thick slices of onion skewered to hold their shape, and generously sprinkled with olive oil and paprika. Arrange on a heated serving platter, garnish with watercress and serve with a side dish of Poivrade Sauce (No. 1104) or Hot (warm) Ravigote Sauce (No. 1109).

CALIFORNIA VEAL ROLLS, OLIVE SAUCE [627]

Cut a 2-pound veal cutlet into 6 slices, each about 3 inches long and 2 inches wide. Trim neatly, then grind the trimmings with ¼ pound of bacon and 1 cup of soft bread crumbs. To this mixture, add 1 well-beaten egg, 1 tablespoon of grated onion, 1 tablespoon each of parsley, chives and green pepper, all finely chopped; season highly with mixed salt, pepper, poultry seasoning and 2 tablespoons of lemon juice. Spread each strip of veal with some of this stuffing and roll into cylinders. Fasten securely with kitchen thread or toothpicks, and brown on all sides in 3 tablespoons of butter or margarine. Lift out the rolls; add 1 tablespoon of flour to the butter in the pan, and stir till blended; then pour in gradually 1¼ cups of hot water, mixed with ¼ cup of Pique Seasoning stirring constantly, till mixture just begins to thicken. Arrange the browned rolls in a buttered, shallow baking dish and pour the sauce over; cover tightly and bake in a moderate oven (375° F.) for 35 minutes. Arrange the meat on a heated platter and stir into the sauce ½ cup of thinly sliced black olives. Heat well, and pour the sauce over the rolls, which have been freed from thread or toothpicks. Dust with chopped parsley and serve with plain boiled small potato balls.

COLYS [628]
Baked Veal with Tomatoes and Potatoes

Rub a 2½-pound piece of shoulder or neck of veal with a damp cloth, then with a cloth wrung out of a little vinegar, and dust with mixed salt and black pepper. Set aside. Cook 2 medium-sized onions, finely chopped with 1 clove of garlic, in 3 tablespoons of butter or margarine, till just beginning to color, then add 3 large fresh tomatoes, peeled and coarsely chopped, and cook for 10 minutes over low heat, stirring frequently. Turn this into a greased earthenware casserole, season to taste with ½ teaspoon of marjoram, ¼ teaspoon each of mace and thyme, a good pinch of powdered dried bay leaves and 1½ tablespoons of chopped parsley. Mix well, lay in the prepared meat, cover tightly, and bake in a moderate oven (375° F.) for 35-40 minutes, turning the meat once after 15–20 minutes of cooking. Add 2 cups of small potato cubes and 1 cup of beef bouillon; cover, and continue baking for 45 minutes longer. Arrange the meat on a heated platter, slice what is likely to be needed, reshape, arrange the potatoes and tomatoes around the meat, pouring gravy over it and dusting with chopped parsley.

Chinese visitors to this country are often amazed that meat comes to the table attached to the bone. This, they point out, marks the lazy cook who lets the diner do the work.

CUBED VEAL IN SOUR CREAM [629]

Brown 2½ pounds of veal cutlet, cubed small, in 3 tablespoons of butter, over a bright flame, stirring almost constantly with a wooden spoon. Turn both butter and meat into a greased casserole, the bottom and sides of which have been rubbed with a cut clove of garlic. Cover tightly and keep hot. Put 2 teaspoons of flour in top of double boiler; add 3 tablespoons of cold water and blend smoothly. Gradually stir in 1 cup of sour cream, which has been scalded with 1 small bay leaf, 3 or 4 thin slices of onion, 1 whole clove and 4 sprigs of fresh parsley, then strained. When thickened, season to taste with salt and white pepper and a dash of nutmeg; remove from hot water; stir in a generous ½ cup of finely chopped fresh, raw mushrooms and 1 tablespoon of grated onion; pour this over the veal; cover with a buttered paper and bake in a very moderate oven (300° F.) for about 30–35 minutes; remove the paper and continue baking 10–15 minutes longer, or until top is nicely browned and bubbles and blisters. Serve at once right from the casserole on freshly made toast.

It is not easy for a good hearty curry addict to comprehend an absolute distaste for curry, yet there are those who cannot tolerate even the smell of it—and the same is true of terrapin à la Maryland, corned beef and cabbage and bouillabaisse. Yet with curry definitely out of the picture, there is still hope for sweltering city dwellers, for our Spanish-American neighbors to the south regulate their thermal welfare with about fifty-seven varieties of pepper and little else, and most healthy men can eat pepper. It comes by way of natural sequence that we owe most of our knowledge of condiments to the peasant cookery of Europe and the Near East, Asia, and Africa, and it is not strange that some common flavors and aromas are a little difficult for unso-phisticated palates.

It is odd that we find such bland and delicate foods in the Greek, Turkish, Chinese and Japanese kitchens, when most of their next-door neighbors appear to subsist on fire and brimstone, as it were.

Curry seems to begin around Persia (Iran) and move southward with increasing heat and fury, and the Malays of the Archipelago may dump the pepper pot on a single dish, yet the people of China are contented with tidbits of soft ginger root in luscious sweet syrup.

Italians and Spaniards revel in flavor and richness, with little but the heat from oven and kettle to burn the tongue, but the Spanish settlers in the new world went in for warmth in a big way when they hit the equator, and the torrid cooking that now prevails as far north as Texas, New Mexico, and Arizona is the most sizzling rival of East Indian curry.

CURRIED VEAL BALLS NEW MEXICO STYLE   [630]

Grinding breaks down the tough tissues and obviates the need of the long, slow cooking ordinarily employed to tenderize the tough (or less tender) muscle tissues of meat. Some fat should be ground with most meats for, being largely lean, they may cook "dry" without the addition of fat.

Mix 1 pound of coarsely ground neck of veal, including a little fat, with 1 cup of soft bread crumbs which have been soaked in ⅔ cup of veal stock, 1 extra large or 2 small well-beaten eggs, salt and pepper to taste, ¼ cup of grated onion, 2 tablespoons of minced parsley, 1 table-spoon each of finely minced green celery leaves and chives. Form into 12 balls of equal size. Heat 3 tablespoons of bacon or ham drippings in a fireproof casserole; brown the balls in it a few at a time; remove to a hot platter, and to the fat remaining in the casserole (using a little more, if needed) add 2 tablespoons of grated onion, 1½ tablespoons of flour and 2 teaspoons—more or less, according to taste—of curry powder; when well blended, pour in gradually 1 cup of veal stock, stirring constantly until thickened and boiling, and replace the meat balls with ½ generous cup of seedless green grapes; simmer for about 20–25 minutes, placing an asbestos pad under the platter to prevent scorching. Serve on a heated platter or direct from the casserole. with plenty of hot, steamed rice.

ESCALOPES DE VEAU A L'OSEILLE   [631]
Escallop of Veal with Sorrel

There are innumerable ways of serving and dressing escalop of veal, and they can be laid on various vegetable purées other than sorrel, such as spinach, endive, potato, cabbage (red or green), lettuce, celery, peas, etc. They are simple to prepare and quickly cooked and are excellent when properly done.

Cut, or have the butcher cut, 6 nice individual veal cutlets just under ½ inch thick; beat 2 or 3 times with a mallet or other wooden beater, first sprinkling with mixed salt and pepper. Discard all skin and fat and trim the escallops to an oval shape. Each should weigh about 4 ounces. Dip them first in flour; then in slightly beaten egg yolk, seasoned to taste with salt and pepper; and finally in fine bread crumbs. Pat with a spatula or the blade of a knife to make sure that the crumbs adhere to the meat. Have ready ¼ cup of hot butter, and cook the escallops in it for 5 minutes on one side, then 5 minutes on the other, until of a nice, golden color. Arrange over a layer of hot purée of spinach (No. 1470), and garnish with little triangles of bread fried in butter until nicely browned on both sides.

GRENADINS OF VEAL PARISIENNE   [632]

With a rolling pin, pound mercilessly a 3½-pound piece of lean veal, taken from the leg or the pope's eye, seasoning to taste with salt and pepper mixed with a little powdered thyme and nutmeg as you pound, continuing the beating till the piece of meat is reduced to about an inch in thickness. Lard it through, crosswise, with about 18 narrow strips of pork fat-back, and trim neatly (the butcher will do all this for you on demand). Now cut the prepared veal into 6 equal sized pieces, and sear over a bright flame in ¼ generous cup of butter, till well browned on all sides. Transfer the pieces of meat, as browned, to an earthenware casserole; add ¼ cup each of coarsely chopped carrots, white parts of leeks, scraped celery stalks, and 1 bouquet garni composed of 1 extra large or 2 small bay leaves, tied with 1 sprig of thyme, 1 sprig of tarragon herb, and an inch piece of parsley root, scraped. Scatter over all 6 or 7 freshly crushed peppercorns, and 1 tablespoon of finely chopped shallots (or chives, if shallots are not available). Pour all over the surface 1½ cups of dry white wine; cover tightly, and braise in a moderate oven (375° F.) for 1 hour, turning the grenadins once after 30 minutes cooking.

Arrange the grenadins on a heated platter and keep hot. Strain the sauce left in the casserole into a saucepan, and let it reduce to almost nothing, over a bright flame, stirring occasionally. The ensuing result will be a glaze (name given to this operation in which the juices should be slightly calcinated). Then stir in 1 cup of good, rich veal stock (obtained by reducing 2 cups of veal stock to half over a bright flame), 2 tablespoons of sherry or Madeira wine, and again let this reduce to half, over a very bright flame. Taste for seasoning and, using a pastry brush, spread the glaze over the surface of the grenadins. Place the platter under the flame of the broiling oven and glaze quickly. Serve at once, garnished with small bouquets of crisp watercress, interspersed with 6 large fresh mushroom caps, nicely broiled.

Creamed sorrel or spinach is usually served with this delicious rich dish.

Beef, lamb and mutton may also be prepared in this manner.

HUNGARIAN VEAL STEW   [633]

Brown 6 medium-sized thinly sliced onions in ¼ cup of lard or other shortening; stir in 1 tablespoon of paprika and, when well blended, stir in 2½ pounds of lean veal from the leg, cubed small; season to taste with salt and pepper; add ½ cup of hot water, cover tightly, and cook over a very low heat till the meat is half done, or about 30 minutes, shaking the pan occasionally to prevent scorching. Then add 3 large, fresh tomatoes, peeled, seeded and coarsely chopped; 3 medium-sized thinly sliced green peppers, white seeds and ribs removed; and 1 cup of thinly sliced fresh mushrooms. Cover tightly and continue cooking for 30 minutes longer, or till the vegetables are done. Taste for seasoning and, when just ready to serve, stir in 1 cup of scalded heavy sour cream. Serve at once with a side dish of buttered noodles (No. 1560).

Pork, mutton, lamb, chicken, goose, duck or turkey may all be prepared in this same way.

JELLIED VEAL LOAF   [634]
(From Left-over)

Combine 1 grated onion, 1 finely minced stalk of celery and 1 cup of veal stock (No. 185) in a saucepan and boil 3 or 4 minutes. Strain through a fine-meshed sieve. Meantime, sprinkle 1 tablespoon of granulated, unflavored gelatin over ½ cup of cold veal stock, let stand 5 minutes, then add to the hot, strained stock and stir till gelatine is dissolved; remove from the fire, stir in 1 tablespoon of lemon juice and let cool to a little less than lukewarm; then add 2 cups of chopped, cooked, lean veal, 1 teaspoon each of finely chopped parsley, chervil and dill pickles, 1 tablespoon each of finely chopped green pepper and ¼ cup of finely chopped, well-drained red pimientos. Blend all thoroughly, then turn mixture into a well-oiled loaf mold. Chill several hours or, still better, overnight, and when ready to serve, unmold on a platter on a bed of crisp watercress; garnish with 3 hard-cooked eggs, quartered, and sprinkled with a little paprika; small dill pickles, cut fan-fashion; black olives; radish roses, etc.—all according to taste or fancy, so long as you use edible garnishing. A side dish of shredded lettuce and tomato salad will complete a hot day's luncheon.

MARINATED VEAL LOIN PORTUGUESE STYLE [635]

Take 5–6 pounds of boned loin; place in a deep dish and pour over it equal parts of dry white wine and white stock to barely cover; add 1 large clove of garlic, mashed, 1 large bay leaf, 8 thin slices of onion, ¼ teaspoon of thyme, 1 tablespoon of Worcestershire or similar sauce, 8 freshly crushed peppercorns, 7 or 8 sprigs of fresh parsley, and stir well. Cover with a cloth and let stand in a cool place overnight. Next day, drain and place the meat in a braising kettle with ½ cup of lard or other shortening and sear on all sides. When quite brown, drain off the fat and add half of the strained marinade; 18 small white onions; 18 small fresh mushrooms, caps peeled, stems sliced; 4 fresh large tomatoes, peeled and quartered; salt to taste and cover the pan. Braise in a moderate oven (350–375° F.) 2–2½ hours, turning the meat every half hour. Arrange the meat on a hot serving platter; carve enough for service and keep hot.

Take up the vegetables with a perforated ladle and arrange round the meat. Strain the sauce through a fine-meshed sieve and heat to the boiling point. When boiling, stir in 3 tablespoons of Madeira wine; remove from the fire; thicken, if needed, with a little flour, and pour half over the meat and vegetables, serving the remainder in a sauce boat.

OSSO BUCCO [636]
Italian Veal Stew

Saw (or have the butcher do it for you) 2½ pounds of knuckle of veal into 2-inch pieces in length (not chopped but sawed, as the marrow must remain inside the bone). Set aside. Chop together 3 small carrots and 2 small celery stalks, and cook in 2½ tablespoons of butter or olive oil over a medium flame until just beginning to brown, stirring almost constantly, add ¼ cup of chopped onions, and the prepared veal; season highly with salt and pepper and cook, stirring frequently, over a brisk flame, till meat and vegetables are well browned. Add 1 tablespoon of butter, creamed (kneaded) with 1 teaspoon of flour and continue cooking for 5 or 6 minutes longer. Now stir in 1 cup of tomato pulp, free from seeds and skin, alternately with ½ cup of dry white wine, and ½ cup of hot veal stock or white stock, more or less, to barely cover the meat; add also 2 small strips of lemon peel, 1 small bouquet garni composed of 1 small bay leaf, 4 sprigs of fresh parsley and 1 sprig of thyme, tied with white kitchen thread, and gradually bring to a boil; cover, and let simmer very, very gently 1¼–1½ hours, occasionally stirring very gently to prevent sticking. Transfer the meat to a hot platter; strain the sauce over it, first tasting for seasoning; dust with 1 teaspoon of grated lemon rind mixed with the same amount of finely chopped chervil or parsley and serve at once. Spaghetti is the usual accompaniment for this dish.

POTTED VEAL STEAK DUTCH STYLE [637]

Score 2½ pounds of veal from the leg, then pound into it the following seasoning: ½ teaspoon allspice, 2 tablespoons of flour, ½ teaspoon of powdered mustard, ½ teaspoon of salt, ½ teaspoon of paprika, ⅓ teaspoon of white pepper and ⅛ teaspoon of mace. Heat 3 tablespoons of fat and sear the meat in it. When well browned on both sides, pour over it 1¾ cups of boiling water, mixed with ¼ cup of Pique Seasoning. Cover and simmer very gently for 1 hour. Then add 18 very small peeled silver onions; 18 small mushrooms, caps peeled but left whole, stems thinly sliced; ½ clove of garlic; 18 very small carrot balls; and 1 cup of diced celery. Cover and continue cooking gently 25–30 minutes longer, or until vegetables are tender then stir in 1 cup of scalded sour cream and, when well heated, serve in a deep platter.

ROAST LOIN OF VEAL BEER GRAVY [638]
Flemish Method

Have the butcher lard a 5–6-pound piece of loin of veal, with long narrow strips of pork fat back, trim neatly and tie compactly with string. Heat 4 tablespoons of lard or other fat in a roasting pan; add the meat, and sear on all sides till almost black but not burned. Drain off all the fat and add 3 small carrots, quartered; 3 medium-sized onions, quartered, 1 bouquet garni composed of 1 small leek, split in two lengthwise and carefully washed, then tied with white kitchen thread with 1 large bay leaf, 1 large sprig of thyme, 10 sprigs of fresh parsley, 2 sprigs of green celery leaves and 2 whole cloves. Add also 1 small piece of garlic, salt and pepper to taste, and pour in 2 cups of dark beer. Roast in the usual way (see Time table for Roasting, No. 2187), basting frequently with the beer. When cooked to the desired degree of "doneness," place the meat on a heated serving platter; slice part or all, as needed, and keep hot. Strain the sauce through a fine sieve, pressing gently but thoroughly to extract all the vegetable pulp possible. Skim off all fat floating on the surface. Place the pan over the fire and bring to a boil; thicken with a very little flour, boil 3 or 4 minutes, and taste for seasoning. Pour part of this sauce over the sliced meat, serving the remainder separately. Baked potatoes and buttered string beans are appropriate vegetables.

SOUR VEAL STEW HOME STYLE [639]

Heat 4 tablespoons of fat in a heavy stew pot; stir in 1¾ pounds of boneless veal (cubed) and brown well on all sides, over a bright flame, stirring almost constantly; then stir in ½ cup of cider vinegar and ½ cup of boiling water or still better, ¼ cup each of boiling water and ¼ cup of Pique Seasoning; bring to a boil; add 1 cup of diced carrots, 12 small white onions, and ½ cup of freshly shelled peas, 1 bay leaf, tied with 1 sprig of thyme and 6 sprigs of fresh parsley, salt and pepper to taste and cover. Simmer gently 35–40 minutes. Serve with riced potatoes.

SWISS VEAL BALLS [640]

Put through food chopper 1¾ pounds of veal, together with ½ pound of raw, lean ham. Mix with 3 well-beaten eggs, 1 tablespoon each of finely chopped parsley, onion and chives, ⅛ teaspoon each of mace, marjoram, salt and white pepper with a few grains of cayenne and nutmeg, enough cooked rice or semolina to make mixture a little on the firm side, and shape into small round balls the size of a walnut. Cook these balls covered, in gently boiling veal stock for about 12 minutes. Drain, and transfer them in 1½ cups of rich Poulette Sauce (No. 1106). Serve surrounding a platter of buttered noodles, spinach or mashed potatoes.

VEAL BIRDS HUNGARIAN STYLE [641]

Cut 2 pounds of veal steak from the leg into 6 individual portions and flatten with rolling pin, seasoning to taste with mixed salt, pepper, paprika and thyme. Lay the meat on a wet table, while preparing the stuffing as follows: Combine 2 cups of soft bread crumbs with 1 tablespoon each of finely chopped parsley, onion, shallots and fresh mushrooms, and fry in ¼ cup of butter for 2 minutes, or until lightly browned, stirring constantly. Remove from the fire and mix in 1 tablespoon each of sweet-sour gherkins and olives, both finely chopped. Season with a little salt and pepper, and divide mixture among the 6 portions of veal. Roll up and tie with string. Brush over with butter, then roll in flour. Brown in 2 or 3 tablespoons of butter, then arrange in a casserole, first rubbed with a little garlic, then with butter. Pour over 1 cup of rich brown sauce (No. 1018) or, lacking that, ¾ cup of boiling water mixed with ¼ cup of Pique Seasoning. Cover and bake in a moderate oven (375° F.) for about 45 minutes, turning the birds once during the cooking process. Serve on a hot platter with a side dish of Viennese Noodles (No. 1568).

Because of its mild flavor, veal requires more seasoning than other meats. Slower cooking is also necessary.

VEAL BIRDS A LA ROSSINI [642]

This is said to have been one of the favorite dishes of the composer Rossini, who was also a great gourmet.

Prepare 6 individual veal pieces as indicated for Recipe No. 641 and set aside, while preparing the following stuffing: Chop 3 well-washed anchovy filets finely, and combine with 2 cups of soft bread crumbs, previously soaked in a little Madeira wine, then pressed gently and tossed so as to make them fluffy. Then mix in 2 tablespoons each of finely chopped shallots, parsley, onion, and green celery leaves, 1 tablespoon of finely chopped capers, ⅛ teaspoon each of sweet basil, marjoram and mace. Moisten with 3 well-beaten eggs. Divide the stuffing among the 6 veal birds, roll up securely and tie with string. Heat 3 tablespoons of olive oil and brown the rolls in it till well seared on all sides. Transfer a shallow, earthenware casserole; pour over 1 cup of Spanish Sauce (No. 1127), cover and bake very slowly for 1 hour in a moderate oven, turning the birds once during the cooking process. Meanwhile prepare the following garnish: Remove the pits from a dozen large black olives and replace with a piece of anchovy filet. Make a batter with flour and beaten egg, dip each olive into it, then fry in butter to a golden brown.

Have ready a dish of Spaghetti alla Campania (No. 1571). Heap the spaghetti on a hot platter, arrange the veal birds around, alternately, with the olives. Serve at once.

VEAL CHOPS EN PAPILLOTES [643]

Chop fine 2 medium-sized onions, and cook in 2 tablespoons of butter over a very low flame till they are transparent, stirring almost constantly; then stir in ½ pound of peeled, chopped fresh mushrooms, first twisted in a piece of cheesecloth to extract the moisture, 1 teaspoon of finely chopped parsley, a dash of powdered thyme and one of nutmeg. Season with salt and white pepper, blend well and cook over a low flame until mixture is almost dry; then stir in 1 tablespoon of sweet butter.

Take 6 individual veal chops. Cut a heart-shaped piece of paper to fit each chop, allowing a margin of 1½ inches all around for lapping. Oil the paper on both sides. Sauté the chops or cutlets in 4 tablespoons of butter until golden brown on both sides; season to taste with salt, paprika and a few grains of cayenne pepper. Now place a layer of the mushroom sauce, prepared as indicated above, on each paper; place a chop on it, cover with a little more of the sauce; fold the paper over and close the edges by rolling and twisting them, so that the steam and juices will not escape. Arrange in a buttered shallow baking dish and cook for 30 minutes in a slow oven (300–325° F.), or till the paper browns and swells up like a miniature balloon. Serve at once.

VEAL CHOPS PAPRIKA A LA HONGROISE   [644]
Hungarian Veal Chops Paprika

Try out 6 strips of bacon over a low flame until browned slightly on both sides, then remove to a hot platter and keep warm. Sauté 6 individual chops or cutlets to a nice golden brown in the bacon drippings left in the pan; pour over ½ cup of hot water, and simmer till the meat is quite tender (time depends on the thickness of the chops or cutlets), seasoning to taste with salt and with 1 tablespoon of paprika. By this time the water will have almost been entirely absorbed. Add 1½ cups of thick, scalded sour cream, stirring till the sauce thickens. Arrange the chops crown-fashion on a hot serving platter having a mound of freshly boiled rice in center. Lay the bacon slices over the rice; taste the sauce for seasoning, and pour half of it over the meat, serving the remainder separately.

VEAL CHOPS A LA ROSALIND   [645]

Season 6 veal chops (or cutlets) with mixed salt, black pepper and powdered thyme, and brown them in an earthenware casserole with ½ cup of sweet butter. When browned on both sides, remove the chops and keep them hot.

Stir into the butter remaining in the casserole 1 cup of sieved bread crumbs, and cook over a low flame until they are golden brown. Return the chops to the casserole, and moisten them with 1 cup of dry white wine and 1 cup of rich beef broth, seasoning to taste with salt and pepper. Add 1 clove of garlic, 1 medium-sized onion stuck with 2 whole cloves, and 1 bouquet garni composed of 1 large bay leaf, 3 or 4 sprigs of fresh parsley, 1 sprig of green celery leaves (top) and 2 tarragon leaves (lacking the fresh tarragon, use powdered), all tied together with white kitchen thread. Cover and slide the casserole into a moderate oven (330° F.) for 45 minutes. Then lift the cover, sprinkle the top with 2 tablespoons of finely minced shallots mixed with 2 tablespoons each of finely minced parsley and chives, and continue cooking, uncovered, for 15 minutes longer. Discard the bouquet garni, garlic, and onion, and skim off all the fat. Taste for seasoning, and serve at once with Creamed Spinach (No. 1466), creamy mashed potatoes, boiled rice or buttered noodles.

VEAL CUTLETS A LA D'AREMBERG   [646]

Cut 6 individual slices of veal taken from the top of the leg as indicated for Grenadins of Veal Parisienne (No. 632), but do not have them larded; arrange them in a shallow, earthen dish and cover with French dressing. Let stand for 1 hour, turning occasionally. Meanwhile, boil 2 lobsters, drain, remove the claws, which reserve for other use, cut the meat into ¼-inch slices, and drop them immediately into a little hot, melted butter. Place the intestines and coral from the shells as well as all trimmings of lobster meat in a small saucepan with 1 tablespoon of butter, 2 tablespoons of tomato paste, salt and pepper to taste, and heat to the boiling point but do not actually boil, lest the meat toughen; stir in 1 teaspoon of meat extract (commercial) and, when melted but not boiling, rub mixture through a fine-meshed sieve into a saucepan containing 1 cup of highly seasoned Béchamel Sauce (No. 259), and add the well-drained lobster slices. Keep hot, but do not allow to boil.

Heat the clarified butter in which the lobster slices were kept hot, add the 6 well-drained and dried marinated veal cutlets, and brown nicely on both sides over a bright flame. Drain; arrange the cutlets around the edges of a hot, round platter; taste the lobster mixture for seasoning, and pour it in the center. Sprinkle the lobster with a little minced parsley and chives in equal parts, and garnish the platter with small tufts of crisp green watercress.

VEAL CUTLETS CHASSEUR   [647]

Sauté 6 nice, individual cutlets or chops in plenty of clarified butter over a moderate flame until nicely browned on both sides. Transfer the cutlets to a casserole; pour over them 1½ cups of Hunter or Chasseur Sauce (No. 1066), cover and cook in a slow oven (300–325° F.) for 35 minutes. Serve right from the casserole with a side dish of buttered noodles.

VEAL CUTLET A LA SACHER [648]

This most delicious dish may be made with individual veal cutlets or with one large one cut a generous inch thick, which, in the opinion of gourmets, is the best as well as the original method of this Viennese super-dish.

Have the veal cut from top of the leg; it should be fully an inch in thickness and weigh about 2–2½ pounds. Pound it with a rolling pin with salt and freshly ground black pepper for a few seconds, so as to break down the tissues but do not flatten too much. Sauté 1 cup of thinly sliced onions preferably small ones in 3 tablespoons of butter over a low flame until lightly browned, adding more butter if necessary, because veal, being naturally lean, absorbs plenty of fat. Now, dredge the cutlet with flour. When onions are lightly browned, yet still underdone, bank them to one side of the pan, put cutlet in pan and brown on both sides; pour in 1 cup of heavy, scalded sour cream, and spoon the onions on top of the meat. Cover the pan and cook very, very gently, about 35–40 minutes, or till cutlet is tender, turning it once during the cooking, and again spooning the onions on to the top side of the meat. Serve with sliced carrots fried in plenty of butter until browned, and a side dish of Noodles Amandine (No. 1565).

VEAL CUTLETS SARAH BERNHARDT [649]

Purchase 6 nice, individual veal cutlets from the filet or the top of the leg, each cutlet weighing about 6 ounces, but not too thick, and beat them mercilessly with rolling pin to break down the tissues. Heat 6 tablespoons of sweet butter in a large, shallow frying pan or sauté pan. Season the cutlets on both side with mixed salt and pepper and fry them golden brown on both sides. Turn into a baking dish; pour over them the butter in the frying pan with 3 tablespoons of good Madeira wine, and scrape bottom and sides of the frying pan to loosen the gelatinous parts. Then slowly stir in 1½ cups of Béchamel Sauce, and continue stirring till mixture bubbles; pour over the cutlets, cover with a thin layer of grated Gruyere or Swiss cheese, and bake a few minutes, till the cheese begins to turn to a golden hue and bubbles. Serve at once.

VEAL CUTLETS SEVILLANA [650]

Fry golden brown on both sides 6 individual veal cutlets, each about 6 ounces in weight, in 4 tablespoons of olive oil (or butter, if preferred) and, when done, plac · in a baking dish and keep hot. In a separate frying pan sauté 6 thin slices of cooked lean ham, having them the same size as the veal cutlets, and, when nicely browned on both sides, arrange one slice over each cutlet. Peel, chop, then squeeze in a cloth, ⅓ pound of fresh mushrooms and sauté them in 2 tablespoons of butter together with 3 tablespoons of grated onion, and 2 tablespoons of finely chopped parsley or chives for 2 minutes, over a low flame. Scatter this over the ham slices; then pour over the whole, 2 cups of White Wine Sauce (No. 1135), to which has been added ½ cup of blanched, shredded and toasted almonds and a tiny pinch of powdered saffron. Bake in a moderate oven for 15 minutes, or until top just begins to brown. Serve at once in the same dish.

VEAL CUTLET SMITANA [651]

Pound, mercilessly, 6 individual veal cutlets, taken from the filet or the top of the leg, seasoning to taste with mixed salt, pepper and a little flour. Heat ⅓ cup of butter in a large baking dish; place the veal cutlets in it and cook till brown on both sides. Transfer them to a buttered, earthenware baking dish and pour over them 2 cups of highly seasoned Smitane Sauce (No. 1123). Sprinkle with a little grated Swiss cheese, and glaze quickly under the flame of the broiling oven. Serve with a side dish of Buttered Broccoli and another dish of Pommes Soufflées (potato ballons) (No. 1420).

VEAL AND HAM PIE A LA DICKENS [652]

The following delightful recipe for an old-fashioned English Veal and Ham Pie was found by this writer in an old family book. The recipe was preceded by this quotation from Dicken's *Cricket on the Hearth:* "You've got the basket with the Veal and Ham Pie and things, and the bottles of beer?"

The modern recipes for Veal and Ham Pie are not so elaborate and costly as the best of the old-English pies—nor are they so good. Here is the original rule:

Cut thin slices from a 2-pound piece of boned veal breast; season them with salt, pepper and a pinch of nutmeg to taste. Now, slice 2 blanched sweetbreads the same size as the veal breast slices and season these also. Lay a flaky pie crust in the bottom of a deep dish, and arrange on this alternate layers of veal, sweetbreads, hard-cooked eggs and fresh small oysters, then a layer of thinly sliced, peeled fresh mushroom caps, seasoning each layer to taste as you go along. Now top the entire surface with a layer of thin slices of ham. Pour over the mixture 2 cups (or as much as the dish will contain) of rich veal stock, slightly thickened with flour or, still better, with 1 or 2 egg yolks, slightly beaten and salted. Cover with a flaky crust; make a few holes on top for the escape of steam, and bake in a very slow oven (275–300° F.) for about

2 hours. Half an hour before serving, insert a funnel in the crust and pour in a cup of rich, sweet, scalded cream, seasoned to taste. Serve at once.

VEAL RAGOÛT (STEW) CREOLE, OVEN METHOD [653]

Cut 3 pounds of veal shoulder and ¼ pound of lean raw ham into individual portions. Heat 3 tablespoons of lard in an earthenware casserole and brown the meat in it with 1 large clove of garlic. This browning process should take about 15 minutes, over a bright flame. Sprinkle with 1 generous tablespoon of flour seasoned to taste with salt and pepper. Add 1 cup of hot water, and deglaze the bottom of the casserole by scraping it with a wooden spoon. Now add enough more hot water to cover the meat generously, and bring slowly to the boiling point. Lower the flame, cover the casserole, and simmer gently for about 40–45 minutes. Add 1 cup of small carrot balls; 1 cup of small potato balls; 1 stalk of celery, scraped and cut into small dice; 1 cup of small white turnip balls; and ½ cup of very small white onions, previously parboiled using both liquid and onions; 1 bouquet garni composed of 1 extra-large or 2 medium-sized bay leaves tied with 12 sprigs of fresh parsley, 2 sprigs of celery tops, 1 large sprig of thyme, and 2 whole cloves, using white kitchen thread. Taste for seasoning, adding salt and pepper as needed, cover the casserole, and bake in a very moderate oven (300–325° F.) for at least 1½ hours. When ready to serve, discard the bouquet garni, add 1 cup of drained canned peas, heat well and serve from the casserole.

VEAL RING SOUFFLE CELESTINE [654]

Heat ¼ cup of butter or lard, together with anchovy paste the size of a pea; blend in ⅓ cup of flour and, when smooth, stir in ½ cup of veal gravy, combined with ¾ cup of scalded milk, and ¼ cup of sherry wine, stirring constantly, over a low heat. Just when beginning to bubble, add 3 cups of chopped (not ground) cooked left-over veal, with 1 tablespoon each of finely chopped parsley, chives, onion and green pepper; season to taste with salt, pepper, nutmeg, and powdered thyme, and let boil 3 or 4 minutes, stirring constantly. Remove from the fire, stir in 3 egg yolks, mixed with 2 tablespoons of cold milk then well beaten. Lastly, fold in 3 stiffly beaten egg whites, salted and flavored with ½ teaspoon of finely grated lemon rind; turn into a generously buttered ring mold sprinkled with grated, dry bread crumbs. Bake in a moderate oven (325–350° F.) for 45–50 minutes or in a hot oven (425° F.) for 30–35 minutes, or until the soufflé is well risen, firm to the touch, and a golden brown. Turn out onto a heated, round platter and fill the center with creamed celery (No. 1257).

VEAL SCALOPINI AU MARSALA   [655]

Purchase 6 individual *escalopes* (or veal cutlets) taken from either the loin, the filet or the top of the leg, each *escalope* weighing about 5–6 ounces. Dip into clarified butter, then into finely grated dry Parmesan cheese (if Parmesan cheese seems too strong, substitute some other kind of cheese or use equal parts of Parmesan and other mild cheese). Heat ⅓–½ cup of clarified butter and sauté the prepared *escalopes* or cutlets until brown on both sides. In a separate pan, cook in 2 tablespoons of butter over a very low flame 1 generous cup of thinly sliced, peeled fresh mushroom caps, tossing and turning the mushrooms frequently. When *escalopes* are tender and well browned on both sides, season to taste with salt and black pepper; arrange them on a hot platter, having them overlap each other; add to the mushrooms 1 teaspoon of extract of beef (commercial) dissolved in 2 tablespoons of hot water with 1 tablespoon of sweet butter and 4 tablespoons of Marsala wine, or sherry wine. Bring to boiling point, but do not actually boil. Pour this mushroom-wine sauce over the hot *escalopes*. Serve immediately.

VITELLO (VEAL) AL MARSALA ROMANA   [656]

Take 2 pounds of lean veal from the leg, and with a very sharp knife cut and trim it into thin domino pieces, much as you would cut meat for Chinese dishes. Season ½ cup of flour to taste with white pepper and salt, adding ¼ teaspoon of dry mustard, ½ generous teaspoon of sugar, a light grating of nutmeg and a few grains of cayenne pepper. Dredge the veal wafers lightly with this, and toss them into ⅓–½ cup of bubbling butter or olive oil, in a frying pan or chafing dish. Stir gently with a wooden spoon or fork, and brown quickly on both sides, letting the edges get slightly crisp; then pour over them very slowly ½ cup of Marsala wine, Madeira or full-bodied sherry of good flavor. Taste for seasoning, adding salt and pepper if needed.

For luncheon they are served simply with crisp toast or croutons, garnished with crisp, green, young watercress; but for a heartier meal they are delicious with a rich Risotto (made as described in No. 1599), or even better when served on large, thick slices of polenta (No. 1541), or Italian cornmeal mush, delicately browned in butter or olive oil.

WIENER SCHNITZEL   [657]

As it was made at the Court of Austria for the Emperor Francis Joseph

All nations have their favorite tricks with veal, and Austrian cooks are deft and clever with their seasonings. Wiener Schnitzel is scarcely a novelty, unless the cook is determined to make it so, and then manual labor and mature judgment are involved. A delicious schnitzel (meaning "a little bit" in German) may be achieved if you beat your cutlet long and hard, then season and cook with care.

Have 6 individual veal cutlets, about ¾ of an inch thick, taken from the loin, the filet or the top of the leg. Lay each one, in its turn, on a board or block, rub it over lightly with mixed English mustard, a dash of Worcestershire sauce, and a sprinkling of grated Parmesan cheese; then pound it fiercely with the back of a cleaver, a heavy wooden potato masher or the dull edge of a heavy carving knife. Turn it over, season and pound again as before. The fiber will be broken down and the cutlet will expand under the punishment, which should not cease till the thickness has been reduced to three-eighths of an inch. With the final blows, beat in a sprinkling of black pepper and salt. Now, dip each cutlet first lightly in flour, then in beaten egg, and lastly in sifted bread or cracker crumbs. Sauté in a frying pan with plenty of butter or olive oil, turning each piece until it is well and evenly browned, and serve on a hot platter with a sprinkling of minced parsley.

The customary restaurant tomato sauce is a bit of an anticlimax, but a delicate bisque will outrage no sensibilities. So—

Cook 1 cup of tomato purée 15 minutes with a bay leaf, a small piece of celery stalk or green celery leaves finely chopped, 1 blade of garlic, 4 or 5 thin slices of onion, 1 whole clove, salt and pepper. Strain through a fine-meshed wire sieve, rubbing through as much vegetable pulp as possible; stir in a pinch of baking soda, then combine with a scant cup of hot, rich cream sauce and a half cup of thick, sweet, scalded cream. Serve in a sauce boat, sprinkling a teaspoon of minced chervil or parsley on the surface for color.

FACTS ABOUT LAMB [658]

Because of the lamb's reputation for purity—a reputation founded on fact—the meat is not excluded from the dietary of any religious sect or nationality.

Fewer lambs are condemned under Government inspection than any other class of meat animal.

Lamb should be marketed when carrying the "bloom," that is, when at top condition for the so-called "milk-fed" lambs, and when fat for those coming out of the feedlots.

The age of lamb is indicated principally by the appearance and texture of the flesh, which is lighter in color and of finer grain in the lamb than in the sheep, also by the bones, which are smaller and softer in the lamb.

Dressed lamb is "Spring Lamb" from June until December.

Early Spring Lamb is known as "Easter Lamb." It is used chiefly in connection with the religious ceremonies of Jewish and Greek portions of the population.

One of the desirable things about lamb is that it provides conveniently sized cuts. A leg, for example, or a shoulder of lamb makes a roast that is the right size for the average household, the same being true of the other wholesale cuts—loin, ribs, etc. It is wise to select the best grade in buying lamb.

The *legs* are about 30% of the carcass, and while they are used chiefly for roasting, boiling, or braising, delicious steaks may be cut from the thicker end and used for lamb steaks or cutlets.

The *loin*, which is about 20%, requires very little trimming, and makes its appearance, or rather appearances, usually in the fragmentary form of lamb chops.

What is known as *rib cut* contains nine ribs and constitutes about 15% of the entire carcass. On account of the rather high percentage of bone contained in it, the rib cut is the most expensive cut of lamb.

The *two chucks* (shoulders, shanks, breast and neck together) are about 35% of the total weight.

The *breast*, a delicate piece of meat, makes a delicious stew, or can be stuffed and roasted or grilled.

Together with the *shank*, the *breast* is often boned, rolled and roasted. The *shank* may be stewed. It also makes a delicious broth.

The two lamb *shoulders* are about 18% of the weight of the carcass. They are used to some extent as chops, also as roasts; in this latter instance they may be boned (stuffed or not), and rolled.

The *neck* alone may be prepared "en casserole" when cut into five or six pieces, the bone being sawed through.

The *brain, tongue, fries, heart* and *liver* also provide excellent dishes.

Lamb in the French Cuisine

In the French cuisine two kinds of lamb are used—*milk-fed* lamb, of which type the choicest is the Pauillac lamb; and *yearling* lamb, which is known as the *pré-salé*. The latter may be prepared by all methods and treatments used for full grown mutton.

The *baron* is composed of the two *legs* and the *saddle* of lamb combined.

Double implies two *legs* not separated. These pieces are roasted either on a spit or in the oven. "Poëlage," or cooking in a flat pan, is also applicable to them. Usually they are served whole, on large platters elaborately garnished. The accompanying sauce will be either clear or thickened lamb gravy, depending on the nature of the garnish.

Lamb rack is served whole, either roasted on a spit or in the oven, and elaborately garnished. *Rack of milk-fed lamb* may be roasted, but is best prepared "à la poële," that is, in a shallow-bottomed heavy pan, or broiled on the grill.

Medallons, also called *mignonettes*, are taken from yearling lamb. The average weight is 2½ to 3 ounces, and usually 2 are served as a portion. They are small morsels cut from the *rack* or *loin* and carefully boned and trimmed.

Noisettes are also called "English lamb chops." They are garnished in various ways like mutton chops. Most of the garnishes used for "Filets Mignons" of beef serve in the case of these cuts. The most popular ways of garnishing are: Bretonne, with mushrooms, Provençale, Reforme, Soubise, Villageoise, Villeroy, Paysanne, etc.

Lamb shoulder, aside from being prepared like *shoulder of mutton*, is prepared without being boned. Especially is this true of the *Milk-fed hothouse* lamb.

Filet and *mignon* of lamb is tenderloin of lamb, either boned or with the bones divided lengthwise. It is prepared in various ways—roasted, grilled or braised, sometimes with the *flank* attached, rolled and compactly tied with string.

Leg of lamb is a single leg of the carcass, and is prepared in the same manner as the *baron, double* and *loin*. It may also be braised with vegetables, or boiled.

Breast of lamb is chiefly used for making "*épigrammes*." ragoûts, etc.

Shoulder, neck and *breast* of lamb are used for "*Blanquette* of Lamb."

Quarter d'agneau or quarter of lamb consists of one *leg* and half of the *saddle* (*selle*) of lamb, and is treated the same as *baron* and *leg* of lamb.

Saddle (*selle*) of lamb is usually roasted on a spit or in the oven and is variously garnished.

Brochettes of lamb filets are tidbits of lamb served on skewers.

Lamb's head is prepared in the same ways as calf's head.

Lamb's feet may be prepared in many different ways, such as au Jus, à l'Italienne, fried, à la Camargo, à la Sainte Menehould, pickled, à la Robert, stuffed, à la Remoulade, à la Vinaigrette, etc. They are always boiled before the final preparation.

Lamb's brains may be fried, stewed, served in aspic, casserole, black butter, in patty shells, fritters, loaves, dumplings, au gratin, etc. Like *lamb's feet*, they are always blanched before being used in different preparations.

Lamb's *heart* and *lights* may be prepared en casserole, stuffed and braised, baked in loaves, pot-roasted, à la Bourgeoise, à la Creole, in "mock venison stew," in chop suey, stewed, grilled, etc.

Lamb's *tongue* may be prepared in the same ways as beef tongue, that is, smoked, brined, vinaigrette, braised, grilled, casserole, corned, à la Creole, etc.

> *I surely never hope to view*
> *A steak as luscious as a stew.*
> *The latter is the tasty goal*
> *Of elements in perfect whole,*
> *A mad assemblage of legumes*
> *Exuding warm ambrosial fumes,*
> *Each seasoning of proper length,*
> *Proving in Union there's strength,*
> *A steak is grander, it is true,*
> *Yet needs no special skill to brew.*
> *It is an art a stew to make,*
> *But anyone can broil a steak.*
>   —*Unknown Author* (1880)

GUIDE TO THE PURCHASE AND PREPARATION OF LAMB [659]

RETAIL LAMB CUT*	CHARACTERISTICS	HOW TO COOK (Methods)
BREAST— POCKET	From between ribs and shank. Best suited for moist heat after being thoroughly seared. Tender and juicy. If roasted, frequent bastings are required.	Bake, braise, pot roast, pot, stuff
BREAST— RIBLET	Same as for veal riblet.	Same as for veal riblet
BREAST— ROLLED	Juicy and tender with alternated layers of lean and fat. Requires slow cooking in moist heat after being thoroughly seared. If roasted, frequent bastings are required.	Bake, braise, casserole or Dutch oven, stuff, pot roast, roast
CHOPS— CROWN ROAST	From the rack (fore-saddle). Also called "Hotel Rack," with nine pairs of ribs. Split in center, lengthwise. Cut into rib chops not quite to the bottom. Shape and fasten into a crown. Usually stuffed. Juicy and tender. Cook at even temperature (325° F.) and baste frequently.	Roast, stuff
CHOPS— DOUBLE	From the rack with two chops in one, and only one rib bone attached. When cooked in covered casserole, requires moist heat.	Pan-broil, pan-fry, casserole
CHOPS— ENGLISH	From the loin and cut across in individual chops. Backbone removed, rolled around kidney and skewered into round shape. Requires slow, even cooking and frequent bastings, when broiled and pan-fried.	Broil, casserole, pan-fry
CHOPS— FRENCH	From the rack. Contains eye muscle. The meat is scraped from the end of the bone.	Broil, bake, pan-fry, casserole
CHOPS— KIDNEY	From the loin with the kidney cut with the chop. Served with paper cuffs.	Same as French chop
CHOPS— LOIN	From the loin with T-shaped bone. Require constant basting and slow cooking to render them juicy.	Broil, pan-fry, sauté
CHOPS— RIB	From the rack. Same as French chop, but omit scraping the meat from the end of the bone. Slow, steady cooking prevents escape of juice.	Same as loin and French chops
CHOPS— SHOULDER or SARATOGA	From shoulder. If cut from rib side, contains rib bone and portion of blade bone. If cut from arm side, contains small round bone and rib end. Usually boned and shaped. Require slow, steady cooking to retain juices.	Same as loin and French chops; also casserole

* Taken from the five wholesale lamb and mutton cuts: Loin, rack, shoulder, brea and shank.

GUIDE TO THE PURCHASE AND PREPARATION OF LAMB [659]

RETAIL LAMB CUT*	CHARACTERISTICS	HOW TO COOK (Methods)
CHOPS— SIRLOIN	From the sirloin; round. Juicy and tender. Requires slow, steady cooking.	Same as loin and shoulder chops
LEG— AMERICAN STYLE	The meat is carefully peeled back and the shank bone removed. The meat is then tucked back under the fell and skewered or sewed into place. Demands constant basting when roasted; self-basting when cooked in moist heat.	Braise, boil, roast, pot roast
LEG— FRENCH STYLE	The shank bone is "Frenched." It includes leg, shank, aitch and hip bones. Requires constant basting when roasted. Usually served medium done or rare. The blood which runs out when carved is used for gravy.	Same as American style leg
LEG— STEAK AND MINUTE STEAK	From top part of leg and treated as beef steak or beef minute steak.	Broil, pan-fry, sauté, Swiss steak method
LEG— SIRLOIN ROAST	From the top leg, with sirloin end removed, before leg is divided, boned, rolled and tied.	Braise, roast
LOIN ROAST	From the loin. Contains backbone and usually the kidney.	Same as sirloin roast
SHANK	From breast end. Requires slow cooking in moist heat. Well flavored and juicy.	Braise, pot roast, stew
SHOULDER— CUSHION	Boned, stuffed, skewered or sewed. Well flavored and juicy.	Braise, pot roast, stew
SHOULDER— MOCK DUCK	Made by removing blade and arm bones. Shank bones left in and shaped like a duck.	Roast
SHOULDER— NECK SLICES	Cut from neck with part of shoulder in round slices, neck vertebra in center. Juicy and well flavored.	Braise, stew, pot roast, pot, Swiss steak method
SHOULDER ROLL	Bone and roll similar to loin roast. Slow, steady cooking in moist heat. When roasted, requires frequent basting.	Same as loin roast
SHOULDER— SQUARE CUT	Square, flat piece with two faces corresponding to arm and blade chops directly behind neck, which is always removed.	Braise, casserole, roast, pot roast, stew

* Taken from the five wholesale lamb and mutton cuts: Loin, rack, shoulder, breast and shank.

LAMB HINTS [660]

Minted chops. Slit, or have the butcher slit lamb chops down to the bone, then skewer them together with fresh mint leaves between. (Before broiling of course.)

Curried Lamb Stew. Curry powder, used with discretion, will give an interesting flavor variation to any lamb stew.

Topping the Roast. Add peeled, quartered apples when you roast lamb or veal, spreading them over the surface. The apples add delicious flavor and give a soft topping to the roast.

Distinctive Flavor. Salt sprinkled with onion juice adds distinctive flavor to roast lamb.

A Fine Garnish. Mint or lime gelatine with seedless or seeded grapes added is good to serve with roast lamb, or lamb chops.

Proud of Itself. A loin lamb chop is as proud of itself as you are of having it if you dress it up with a slice of orange or grapefruit on top before broiling.

Bread Small Chops. Breading small chops or cutlets makes them appear larger. Dip them in beaten egg mixed with chopped parsley, chives or grated onion; roll in fine bread or cracker crumbs, and pan-fry slowly.

Neck of Lamb. This is inexpensive and nutritious. It can be made into such appetizing dishes as stews, pot pies, shortcake and scalloped dishes.

Remove Grease. If stew, potroast, potpie, or lamp soup appears greasy, stir (on surface) with an ice cube. This hardens the fat, which can then be removed. Reheat and serve.

French Lamp Chops. These are made by scraping the meat and fat from the bones of rib chops for a little distance from the end.

Relishes for Lamb. Among the relishes most acceptable with lamb and mutton are mint sauce, mint jelly, currant jelly, guava jelly, grape jelly, horseradish, spiced fruits and pickles, any kind of green salad, tomatoes and cucumbers, kumquats, etc.

The Fell. This is a thin, parchment-like covering on the outside of the lamb or mutton. It is neither necessary nor desirable to remove the fell from the leg before cooking. The leg will keep its shape better, be juicier and cook in less time if the fell is not removed. Also, there is no basis for the once-prevalent idea that the fell influences flavor. It is best to remove the fell from chops, because in the short time it takes to cook them this tough membrane would not become tender, as it does in roasting.

To Judge Lamb. It is fairly easy to differentiate between young lamb and yearling mutton just by its appearance. The flesh of lamb is light pink, contrasted to the darker, brownish tint which goes with mutton. Lamb fat is firm and white, with a pinkish, pearly sheen. The fat of mutton is harder, more solid and opaque.

Beauty in Lamb Stew. Decorate a lamb stew with swirls of mashed potato and brown under the flame of the broiling oven.

Lamb Trotters. Just another name for lamb shanks, a cut which all too frequently is used only for stew or ground meat because few cooks realize how delicious lamb shanks can be.

En Brochette. The term en brochette, noted on menu cards in restaurants and in cook books, means that the meat or fish or shellfish or other kind of food is skewered, then pan-fried or broiled.

Delicious Chops. Chops split and stuffed with deviled ham or liver paste before broiling are simply delicious.

Oriental Touch. Give lamb stew a delightful Oriental touch by adding a few canned water chestnuts, drained and sliced a few minutes before stewing. Heat thoroughly. These provide a pleasing crispness. Serve with dry fluffy rice to carry out the Oriental idea.

Meat for the Grinder. Inexpensive cuts of fine lamb which provide juicy, well-flavored meat for the grinder are breast, shoulder and shanks. Removal of fat is recommended for patties and meat loaves, and for the sake of variety a little lean pork, veal or beef may be put through the meat grinder twice with the lamb.

Croquettes. No one ever thinks of croquettes as being made from left-overs. With their golden brown exterior and creamy centers, they are always welcome. Ground, left-over lamb, beef, mutton, pork, ham or veal; mashed white or sweet potatoes or boiled rice, find a good use in the preparation of croquettes. Don't forget that the mixtures should be highly seasoned, then chilled before they are formed into balls, cones or cutlets, which must then be dipped in egg and crumbs before frying.

Barbecued Lamb. Cut cold roast lamb in thin slices and reheat in a sauce made by melting 2 tablespoons of butter, adding 3 tablespoons of grated onion, and cooking until just beginning to take on a little blond color, adding then 1 tablespoon of vinegar, $\frac{1}{4}$ cup of red currant jelly, $\frac{1}{2}$ teaspoon of French mustard, and salt and cayenne to taste.

Quality in Ground Meat. This depends upon the grade of meat, the cuts of the carcass used and the care taken in grinding and storing. Buying bargain hamburger meat—any kind—is doubtful economy. This is usually made from less desirable cuts and may be excessively fat, shrinking badly in cooking. Reputable dealers are careful to use perfectly fresh meats, have their grinders clean, and prepare meat only as ordered.

Ask for branded fresh meats for grinding and be assured of high quality. Cheaper cuts such as chuck, plate and flank of high-quality branded meat are superior in flavor and juiciness to the loin rib and round of low grade meat, a fact many cooks do not know. Whatever kind of meat you buy, keep it *cold* and keep it for the *shortest* possible time.

BARBECUED LEG OF LAMB [661]

Wipe a 6-pound leg of lamb with a cloth wrung out of vinegar, then rub into it a mixture of salt, pepper and dry mustard; brush with melted bacon drippings, dredge lightly with flour and place in an open roasting pan, together with 1 bouquet garni composed of 2 sprigs of green celery leaves, 10 sprigs of fresh parsley, 1 sprig of thyme, and 1 large bay leaf, tied together with white kitchen thread, 1 large onion, peeled and quartered, 2 quarters each studded with 1 whole clove; 1 whole kernel of garlic, 1 medium-sized carrot, scraped and sliced. Pour into the pan ½ cup of hot water and ½ cup of Pique Seasoning, place the pan in a hot oven (450° F.) and sear on all sides 25–30 minutes, turning repeatedly to brown the lamb well all over. Lower the heat to moderate (350° F.) and continue roasting, estimating roasting time at 18 minutes per pound for rare, 22–25 minutes for medium done and 30 minutes for well done. Baste frequently with the following mixture: 3 tablespoons of tomato catsup, 1 tablespoon of Worcestershire sauce, 1 tablespoon of chili sauce, 3 tablespoons of salad oil, 1 tablespoon of cider vinegar, 1 teaspoon of dry mustard, salt and pepper to taste; when exhausted, use the mixture from the pan and continue basting thoroughly, especially towards the end of the cooking process. Transfer meat to a hot platter; cut several slices and pour over a little barbecue sauce made as follows:

Strain the mixture in the pan without pressing. Let stand a few minutes to allow the fat to rise on the surface; skim thoroughly, then return the pan to the fire, bring to a boil, and thicken with flour to the desired consistency. Again strain the sauce, taste for seasoning, and serve.

Traditional barbecued lamb is usually cooked out of doors, but this recipe brings results as nearly the same as can be obtained in a kitchen.

To see a lamb first when looking out of a window on Easter Morning is considered a good omen—especially if its head is turned toward the house. (Old Legend of Poland.)

BARON OF LAMB BRABANÇONNE   [662]
A party dish serving 12–15

Note. For baron of lamb, see "Facts About Lamb" (No. 658).

Heat in a roasting pan large enough to accommodate a 10–12 pound baron of lamb ½ cup of bacon fat or lard, and add ½ cup each of carrots, onions, celery, leeks (white parts only), and raw ham, all finely chopped with salt and pepper to taste, 1 bouquet garni composed of 1 large bay leaf, 10 sprigs of fresh parsley, 1 sprig of thyme all tied together with white kitchen thread, 2 whole cloves, 1 clove of garlic, mashed to a pulp and a good pinch of mace. Brown this over a bright flame, then lay over these herbs and vegetable *brunoise* a 10–12 pound baron of lamb. Sear on all sides over a bright flame until quite brown, turning and basting the meat with the vegetables and fat from the pan. This should take about 30 minutes. Transfer the pan and its contents into a moderate oven (350° F.), add 1 cup of dry white wine and roast steadily, basting frequently with mixture from the pan, and allowing 18 minutes per pound of meat, which should be rather on the rare side when done. Transfer the lamb to a large heated serving platter; slice enough to go around and reshape in its natural form. Keep hot.

Strain the contents of the roasting pan through a fine wire sieve into a saucepan; let stand a few minutes to allow all the fat to rise to the surface, and skim very carefully. Place the saucepan over the fire and bring to a boil; taste for seasoning, stir in 2 tablespoons of tomato paste, and enough flour, moistened with a little cold water to give the sauce the good consistency of medium cream sauce. Remove from the fire; stir in 3 tablespoons of Crème de Menthe liqueur and 2 tablespoons of Curaçao liqueur. Heat to the boiling point, but do not actually boil. Serve this sauce in a sauce boat. Brush the roast with melted meat extract (commercial) and serve garnished with watercress and a dozen small individual tartlets filled with a purée of Brussels sprouts mixed with Hollandaise sauce (No. 1062), alternately with a dozen large fresh mushroom caps, broiled and brushed with melted butter; a side dish of small potato balls, cooked in beef stock, drained, rolled in butter, then in minced parsley is the usual accompaniment.

CROWN ROAST OF LAMB [663]

Crown roast of lamb is made from the loin and rib chops, requiring enough ribs to make the crown. This is definitely a party dish. The ribs are separated at the backbone, but left together, so, when serving, the knife goes down between each two ribs or chops, and the section is lifted out and served with some of the stuffing, which may vary, according to taste, but is usually a mixture of the chopped trimmings of the lamb and equal parts of pork sausage, highly flavored and seasoned with spices.

A crown roast of lamb is prepared by the butcher and usually weighs 8–10 pounds. When you order crown roast of lamb, have the butcher remove center of meat and chop it, then mix it with meat sausage. Also have him wrap pieces of salt pork around the end of each "Frenched" rib, to prevent charring during the roasting process.

To cook a crown roast of lamb, wipe it with a damp cloth, then rub the roast with mixed salt and pepper. Should the butcher omit to wrap the rib ends with salt pork, cover each one with a small white potato, or wrap it with several thicknesses of waxed paper to prevent burning. Place in the pan with the meat 1 bouquet garni composed of 1 large bay leaf tied with a dozen sprigs of fresh parsley, 2 or 3 sprigs of green celery leaves (tops), and 1 sprig of thyme, using white kitchen thread; 2 whole cloves; ¼ cup each of onions, carrots and celery, coarsely chopped. Sear over a bright flame, for 20 minutes, basting frequently

with the vegetables and the fat from the lamb. When well browned on
all sides, transfer to a moderate oven (350° F.), first pouring into the
pan 1 cup of boiling water and ¼ cup of Pique Seasoning. Roast basting
frequently, about 1½–1¾ hours, depending on weight of meat. A cup,
pressed down in center will keep the roast in nice shape. Serve with the
pan gravy, a side dish of Mint Sauce (Nos. 1086–87) and, usually,
buttered Brussels sprouts and pan-roasted potatoes.

NOTE. If desired, omit stuffing, place a cup in center to keep "crown"
in shape and, when ready to serve, fill center with creamed mushrooms
or creamed sweetbreads. Again, if desired, place small peeled and halved
potatoes in the pan when placing it in the oven, roasting them at the
same time as the roast. Be sure to baste them frequently.

DOLMAS   [664]

You may discover in some reputable cook books that, failing vine
leaves, perfectly acceptable dolmas can be made with cabbage leaves.
Such books say also that a little milk is just as good as ale or beer in a
Welsh Rabbit, and that Worcestershire sauce is a fair substitute for
sherry in any dish. Grapes are grapes and cabbages are grand with
corned beef, and cole slaw; but if you want to give the family cookbook
the benefit of the doubt, just try to roll your own dolmas in raw or
parboiled cabbage leaves—and don't tear up the book, for some of the
cake recipes may be pretty good.

There is a benign pleasure in rolling dolmas . . . real dolmas, and
wrapping them up, and when you do it you know exactly why grape
leaves were shaped as they are. obviously the Divine Artificer knew all
about dolmas when the grapevine was designed. There is a mild satisfaction about wrapping parcels for Christmas when you have precisely
the right paper and twine; and if you actually can roll a cigarette that
looks like one, you know how that feels, too. Well, a parboiled (blanched
is the more elegant term) vine leaf takes the dolma filling right into its
lap, and almost gets away from you as it rolls itself around it and tucks
in the loose edges.

Now, if you don't know anyone who owns a grapevine, for your
comfort you can buy little packets of fresh vine leaves in the Syrian,
Turkish or Greek markets around town. Select sound leaves of uniform
size, multiplying your number of guests by at least five, and put the
leaves into boiling water with a dash of vinegar or lemon juice. Boil
not more than ten minutes, or just long enough to make the leaves soft
and pliant, then drain them.

The filling may be as varied as that for ravioli, even meatless, if you
like, though minced lamb with a little beef suet is standard. Pignolias
or pine nuts, so lavishly and agreeably used in the Near East and on the
Pacific Coast by the Chinese cooks, are quite traditional, and should
not be left out; and a spoonful of sesame seeds may be added with good
effect. Uncooked rice usually forms about half of the mixture (it be-

comes soft during the cooking of the dolmas) but a refinement is in the use of rice cooked as for a real Italian Risotto (No. 1599) mixed with minced lamb and beef suet, pine nuts, minced onion, finely chopped parsley, a small pinch of thyme, salt and pepper. Some cooks add fine bread crumbs for a firm paste. Spread the leaves on a board and place a spoonful of the filling on each one, then roll them up and fold in the points and edges to make neat, symmetrical little cylinders, something like tamales. There is no tying or binding or skewering, but make a bed or nest of discarded vine leaves in the bottom of a kettle and arrange all the dolmas snugly in it. Put more leaves on top and weight them down with an inverted plate. Pour in boiling stock that is fairly free from fat, to cover, then simmer gently until the liquid is absorbed or evaporated.

The dolmas will hold their shape, and you let them cool in the kettle if you are using them as snacks, then chill them in the refrigerator; but if you serve them as a dinner or luncheon course, keep them hot and use a rich sauce of stock and tomato paste, or any desired sauce, such as Mushroom Sauce (No. 1090); Egg Sauce (Nos. 1051–52); Brown Sauce (No. 1017–18); Mustard Sauce (Nos. 1092–93); or even Hollandaise Sauce (No. 1062).

IRISH STEW [665]

Cut 2 pounds of lamb breast in 2 generous inch pieces, then dredge with seasoned flour, using about 1 teaspoon of salt, 3 tablespoons of flour and ⅛ teaspoon of pepper. Heat 3 or 4 tablespoons of fat (any desired kind) in a stew pot, add the meat and sear lightly; then add ⅓ cup of chopped onions and continue searing 3 or 4 minutes longer. Now add 10 whole peppercorns; 1 cup of diced turnip; 1 large stalk of celery, cut small; ½ cup of carrots, cut into ½-inch pieces; 3 medium-sized potatoes, quartered; 2 small fresh tomatoes, peeled and quartered; 1 cup of shredded cabbage and 5 cups of cold water. Cover, bring to a boil; reduce the heat and simmer gently for 1 hour and a half. Taste for seasoning, and serve in a hot, deep dish, dusting with finely chopped parsley.

> Resting on the butcher block
> As the cleavers fall and chop,
> You'll soon part from kindred ribs
> To hear the naughty butcher's fibs
> About your weight and quality,
> While hoping no good wife will see
> His helpful hand on the scale with thee.
> —Carl Francis Watts, "To a Lamb Chop" (1879)

LAMB CHOPS BERCY [666]

Sauté 2 "Frenched" lamb chops per person in butter over a medium flame until delicately browned on both sides, turning frequently. Transfer to a heated round platter, arranging the chops in crown shape; fill the center cavity with freshly made shoestring potatoes, and serve with a side dish of Bercy Butter (No. 982) and a dish of Sweet Peas French Manner (No. 1406).

Noisettes of Lamb may also be prepared in this manner.

LAMB CHOPS BONNE FEMME   [667]
Creole Manner

Sear 12 small lamb chops from which the rib bone has been somewhat shortened, in plenty of butter until brown on both sides; arrange them neatly in an earthenware buttered casserole, add 1½ cups of small raw potato cubes, ½ cup of small salt pork cubes, 1 cup of canned beans, season with salt and pepper, and pour over 2 cups of Creole Sauce (Nos. 1041–42). Cover and bake in a moderate oven 35–40 minutes. Serve right from the casserole.

LAMB CHOPS CLEMENTINE   [668]

Broil a dozen "Frenched" lamb chops in the usual way until delicately browned on both sides. Transfer to a heated round platter, placing each chop on a slice of cooked smoked tongue which has been dipped in melted extract of meat (commercial), and place in center of the platter a mound of freshly made Saratoga chips (No. 1432). Serve with a side dish of Brown Sauce (Nos. 1017–19).

LAMB CHOPS EN PAPILLOTES   [669]

Proceed as indicated for Veal Chops en Papillotes (No. 643), substituting 6 double lamb chops having their bone (rib bone) shortened somewhat, and serve as indicated.

LAMB CHOPS A LA PAYSANNE   [670]

Have the butcher cut the bones of 6 thick French chops rather short, and trim them carefully. Rub with mixed flour, salt and blackpepper, and brown quickly over a bright flame in 3 tablespoons of butter, or butter substitute, together with 6 peeled, large, fresh mushroom caps left whole, and 6 small white onions, which nave been parboiled in salted water for 15 minutes. Arrange the chops in a shallow earthenware casserole, place a mushroom on each chop, and the onions around them together with 6 pitted black olives and ¼ cup of small cubes of tried out salt pork. Pour in a generous ½ cup of broth made with the lamb chop trimmings, add 1 small bouquet garni composed of 1 small bay leaf, 5 sprigs of fresh parsley and 1 sprig of thyme tied with kitchen thread, and 1 clove of garlic. Cover closely and cook in a moderate oven (350° F.) for 25 minutes. Lift the lid, add 1 cup of shelled fresh peas which have been cooked in the usual way, but a trifle underdone, and continue cooking for another 10 minutes, still covered. Add 1 teaspoon of lemon juice, 2 tablespoons of sherry wine, and taste for seasoning. Discard the bouquet garni, and serve directly from the casserole.

John Sadler was a prominent maker of jugs in Liverpool, England, and in his employ was Richard Abbey, who designed the famous series of "Arms" jugs. One of these, the "Farmer's Arms," is a fine work of the potter's art. It shows a plump, contented farmer seated enjoying his mug of cider, at his feet the implements with which he works, the plough, harrow, flail, pruning shears; cattle, chickens, sheep, and a hive of bees close by. On the other side is the inscription:

> *Let the wealthy and great*
> *Roll in splendor and state*
> *I envy them not, I declare it.*
> *I eat my own lamb*
> *My own chickens and ham,*
> *I shear my own fleece and I wear it.*
> *I have lawns, I have Bowers*
> *I have fruits, I have Flowers,*
> *The Lark is my morning alarmer*
>   *So Jolly Boys now,*
> *Here's God speed the plough*
> *Long life and success to the Farmer.*

LAMB CHOPS SOUBISE [671]

Have 6 lamb chops cut 1 inch thick, season with mixed salt and pepper, dip in melted butter, place on broiler rack set about 2 inches below the flame, and sear quickly. Reduce the heat (or lower rack to about 4 inches from the flame) and continue broiling 15 minutes longer, turning once or twice. Arrange chops on top of 1½ cups of Soubise Sauce (No. 1125) and garnish the platter with small mounds of hot, well-seasoned vegetables as string beans, carrot dice, buttered peas, small potato balls, asparagus topped with Hollandaise (No. 1062), etc., according to individual fancy.

LAMB CURRY WITH BANANAS [672]
WEST INDIES STYLE
Using left-overs

Slice 1 medium-sized onion thinly, chop 1 small clove of garlic finely, and do likewise with 3 or 4 thin slices of green pepper. Cook in 3 tablespoons of good cooking oil or butter over a low flame, stirring frequently until onion is lightly colored, then blend in 2 tablespoons of flour. Now gradually pour in 2 cups of rich meat broth stirring constantly, and when beginning to thicken and bubble, stir in ½ cup of strained canned tomato pulp, or equivalent of peeled, seeded, chopped fresh tomatoes; then add 1 small carrot, scraped and thinly sliced, a 3-inch piece of celery stalk, finely chopped, 1 bouquet garni composed of 1 large bay leaf tied with 8 sprigs of fresh parsley and 1 sprig of thyme, 2 whole cloves and ⅛ teaspoon of ground mace. Cover closely and cook 20 minutes; then season to taste with salt and pepper and 1½ (more or less, according to taste) tablespoons of curry powder, which has been moistened with a little cold water. Bring to a boil, strain the sauce, pressing well, through a fine sieve into a saucepan; bring to a boil; add 2½–3 cups of cold, cooked lamb, cut in tiny cubes; remove from the fire, cover and let stand a few minutes to mellow and let the heat go through the meat cubes, but never allow reheated meat to boil, lest it get tough. Serve on a heated platter, surrounded with a rice border (No. 1593) and around this border arrange overlapping banana slices which have been sautéed in butter until delicately brown. A few grains of saffron added to the rice while cooking will enhance its flavor.

LAMB CUTLET CASSEROLE BIARRITZ [673]

Brown 6 individual lamb cutlets, taken from the leg, and weighing about 5 ounces each in 2 tablespoons of olive oil and 2 tablespoons of butter. When well browned, turn them into an earthenware casserole. In the fat left in the frying pan, cook ¼ cup of raw, lean chopped ham together with 1 medium-sized onion, also chopped, over a low flame, stirring frequently until mixture just begins to take on color. Then stir in 4 medium-sized tomatoes, peeled, and chopped, and season highly with salt and pepper, also ⅛ teaspoon each of nutmeg, mace, thyme and allspice. Cook over a gentle flame for 10 minutes, stirring occasionally. Pour this sauce over the cutlets in the casserole, cover tightly and bake in a moderate oven (375° F.) for 35 minutes. Serve from the casserole, first topping the cutlets with 6 small sausage patties which have been fried separately and well drained. Buttered noodles are the usual accompaniment to this casserole.

LAMB MIXED GRILL [674]

Broil 6 lamb chops prepared as indicated for Lamb Chops Soubise (No. 671) and cut to the same thickness; 12 slices of bacon; 6 lambs' kidneys, split, and 6 thick slices of ripe tomato. Arrange attractively on a heated serving platter around a mound of freshly cooked French fried potatoes, and pour over each item a little Maître d'Hôtel Butter (No. 1078). Dust with finely chopped parsley or chives. Serve as hot as possible.

LAMB AND PARSLEY PINWHEELS [675]

Have 2 breasts of lamb boned, reserving the bones and trimmings; spread out flat; cut off all excess fat and sprinkle meat with mixed salt, pepper, powdered thyme and nutmeg to taste. Wash and drain 1 large bunch of fresh parsley; remove stems and chop the parsley very fine together with 1 large green pepper, 2 sprigs of green celery leaves, and 1 cup of cold, cooked, lean ham. Cover the boned, flattened breasts of lamb with the seasoned parsley mixture; roll tightly and tie securely. Wrap the 2 rolls in cheesecloth and place them in a large kettle with the bones and trimmings; also 1 bouquet garni composed of 1 extra large bay leaf, 1 sprig of thyme, 2 small leeks, quartered and carefully washed, all tied with white kitchen thread; 1 medium sized carrot, scraped, cut into ½-inch pieces; 1 small stalk of celery, scraped and cut into small pieces after being halved lengthwise; 1 small white turnip, quartered, 2 medium-sized onions, peeled, quartered; 1 small clove of garlic, mashed to a pulp; 1 or 2 whole cloves; salt and black pepper to taste. Gradually bring to a boil; skim very carefully; lower the heat and simmer as gently as possible for 2½ hours, skimming frequently. Let the meat cool in the broth overnight. Remove the cheesecloth, wrap the rolls in waxed paper and chill thoroughly. When cold, slice and arrange on a cold platter having in the center 6 small tomatoes stuffed with chopped green pepper, cucumber, the pulp of the tomatoes and chopped celery, moistened with mayonnaise.

Rice, vermicelli, barley, chopped cooked noodles, macaroni or spaghetti may be added to the strained broth to make a delicious soup for the next meal.

LAMB POT PIE, CHEESE PIE CRUST [676]

Melt 3 tablespoons of bacon drippings in a stew pot; stir in 2½ pounds of breast of lamb, cut in 1-inch cubes, and sear well over a bright fire, stirring almost constantly, until well browned. Gradually add hot water to barely cover, with 1 bouquet garni composed of 1 extra large or 2 small bay leaves, 1 sprig of thyme, 2 sprigs of green celery leaves, 8 sprigs of fresh parsley, all tied with white kitchen thread, 2 whole cloves and 1 clove of garlic, mashed to a pulp. Bring slowly to a boil, cook 2 or 3 minutes, skim well, lower the flame and simmer gently for 1¼ hours. Lift out the meat with a perforated skimmer and carefully remove the bones. Strain the stock through a fine-meshed sieve into another stew pot, return the meat, and add 1 cup of peeled small silver onions, 1 cup of tiny raw carrot balls, 1 cup of small mushroom caps, ½ cup of celery scraped and cut into ⅓-inch pieces, 1 scant teaspoon of salt, ½ cup of tiny raw turnip balls, 8 whole peppercorns, gently bruised, and more hot water if necessary to barely cover the whole. Bring to a quick boil; lower the flame and simmer gently (covered) for 25–30 minutes, or until vegetables are tender. Using a perforated skimmer, transfer the meat and vegetables to a deep pie dish. Thicken the broth with a little flour moistened with a little cold water, taste for seasoning, and strain over the meat and vegetable mixture. Top the dish with Cheese Pie Crust (No. 2071), mark it with any desired perforated design to allow escape of steam during the baking process and seal the edges well around the pie dish. Bake in a hot oven (450° F.) for 10 minutes, brush with milk, and continue baking for 25 minutes longer in a moderate oven (350° F.). Serve as hot as possible.

If desired, add ½ cup of drained canned peas to the stew before covering with the pie crust.

LAMB STEW PARISIENNE   [677]

Sear 2¾ pounds of shoulder or breast of lamb cut into 2-inch pieces in ⅓ cup of lard until well browned on all sides, over a very bright flame, stirring and rocking the pan frequently; season with mixed salt and pepper, stir in 12 peeled, small onions and cook until onions are well browned. Drain off all the fat and transfer the mixture to a stew pot, preferably an earthenware casserole. Pour over 2 tablespoons of flour and blend well, then gradually stir in 3 cups of good meat stock, and add 1 bouquet garni composed of 1 large bay leaf, 1 sprig of thyme, 8 sprigs of fresh parsley, 2 sprigs of green celery leaves, all tied together with white kitchen thread, 1 whole clove of garlic, and 1 cup of tomato purée. Season to taste with salt and black pepper, bring to a boil, and lower the flame, then simmer very gently for 50 minutes, then add 12 small carrot balls, 12 small turnip balls, ⅓ pound of cleaned, green beans, cut into small lozenges, ⅓ pound of shelled green peas, 12 small raw potato balls, and 12 small fresh mushrooms, caps, peeled, stems thinly sliced, cover and continue simmering for 30 minutes longer. Discard the bouquet garni, taste for seasoning, adding more salt and pepper if needed, and serve in a heated deep platter, dusting with chopped parsley. NOTE. If desired, drop a dozen small dumplings into the simmering stew 10 to 12 or 15 minutes before serving (see "dumplings," No. 1617).

ROAST LEG OF LAMB VENISON   [678]
WEST COAST STYLE

Wipe a 6-pound leg of lamb (or mutton) with a damp cloth, then rub over with tarragon vinegar. Place in a crock, cover with buttermilk, add 2 cloves of garlic, mashed, 1 medium-sized onion, thinly sliced, 1 small carrot scraped, then thinly sliced, 12 whole peppercorns, freshly bruised, 3 whole cloves, 2 large bay leaves, 12 sprigs of fresh parsley, 3 sprigs of green celery leaves, 1 juniper berry, freshly crushed, ⅛ teaspoon each of ground mace, marjoram and allspice. Cover and keep in a cool place for 4 days, turning twice a day, and being sure the meat is constantly covered with buttermilk.

When ready to serve, drain the lamb; dry and rub all over with mixed salt and pepper. Place in a roasting pan and stud with 3 dozen whole cloves. Pour over ¼ cup of melted bacon or ham drippings, and ½ cup of dry white wine. Roast in a hot oven (450° F.) for 20 minutes, until well seared, turning frequently, lower the heat and continue roasting in a moderate oven (350° F.), allowing 18–20 minutes per pound of meat and basting frequently with 1 cup of the strained buttermilk alternately with the liquid in the roasting pan. Transfer the lamb to a heated serving platter, slice what is likely to be needed and keep hot. Strain the liquid in the pan into a saucepan. Let stand a few minutes and skim off all fat. Bring liquid to a boil, stir in 1 small glass of red currant jelly and 1 teaspoon of grated lemon rind. Thicken with a little flour moistened with a little cold water. Let boil up 3 or 4 times, strain part of this sauce over the sliced parts of the lamb, and serve the remainder separately with Pioneer Mush (No. 1540), and a green vegetable or green salad.

Remember that lamb should be served *hot* or *cold*—no lukewarm half-way mark will do. This applies to mutton, too.

ROAST LOIN OF LAMB WITH KIDNEYS [679]

Season a 3-pound piece of loin of lamb with mixed salt, pepper and powdered marjoram; split 3 lamb kidneys and arrange in a row along the inner side of the roasts, wrapping the flank around the kidneys. The butcher will do this on demand. Two and one half hours before serving dinner, place the roast, fat side up, on rack in open roasting pan, and add 1 bouquet garni composed of 1 large bay leaf, tied with white kitchen thread with 8 sprigs of fresh parsley, 4 fresh mint leaves, 2 sprigs of green celery leaves (tops), and 1 sprig of thyme. Pour 1 cup of meat stock into the pan and roast in hot oven (450° F.) for 15 minutes without basting; lower the heat to moderate, and continue roasting for ¾–1 hour, basting every 15 minutes with the liquid from the pan. Transfer the lamb to a hot platter and slice enough to go around once, reshaping the meat neatly and keep hot. Strain the liquid from the roasting pan into a saucepan. Let stand a few minutes, then skim off all fat. Bring the liquid in the saucepan to a boil and thicken, using 1 tablespoon of flour, moistened with cold water, for each 1½ cups of liquid, let boil 3 or 4 minutes, stirring occasionally, and stir in 1 small jar of mint jelly. Pour part of this sauce over the sliced meat and serve the remainder separately.

ROAST SADDLE OF LAMB OR MUTTON   [680] HOME STYLE

A roast saddle of lamb or mutton is a delightful cut to serve when the lamb is young, or alternatively, when the mutton is well mellowed.

Have the butcher prepare the saddle for roasting; rub it with mixed salt, pepper and a little powdered mint and dredge lightly with flour. Place in a roasting pan and pour over it ¼ cup of lard, bacon or ham drippings. Sear in a hot oven (450° F.) for 20 minutes, or until well browned on all sides; lower the heat to moderate (350° F.) and continue roasting, basting frequently with equal parts of melted butter and hot water, allowing 18–20 minutes to the pound. This particular cut of lamb should never be overcooked, but rather a little on the pink side. When saddle is cooked to the desired point, remove to a hot platter, cut enough to go around once, and reshape; strain the liquid in the pan through a fine sieve into a saucepan. There should be 2 cups; if not, add boiling water mixed with equal parts of Pique Seasoning. Bring to a boil, and stir in 1½ tablespoons of flour moistened with a little cold water, bring again to a boil and boil steadily for 3 or 4 minutes. Taste for seasoning and, just before serving, stir in 1 small jar of guava jelly and ½ teaspoon of grated lemon rind. Serve part of this sauce over the cut part of the saddle and the remainder separately. A saddle of lamb contains 12–16 chops, and 2 are served to each guest. This makes a delicious cold dish, when served with a green salad.

ROAST STUFFED BREAST OF LAMB   [681]

Buy a breast of lamb including the foreshank. Wipe with a damp cloth; cut off the foreshank and grind meat finely for the stuffing. Crack the bones of the breast so that it can be carved between the ribs, and make a pocket in the breast by cutting through the flesh close to the ribs. Sprinkle the inside of the pocket with mixed salt, pepper and a little grated lemon rind, and pile in lightly the hot forcemeat stuffing (see below) and sew in shape. Rub the outside with mixed salt, pepper and flour; lay the meat, ribs down, in a roasting pan, and sear in a very quick oven (450–480° F.) for 25 minutes, turning frequently. Now, the meat being well seared, lay 4 strips of bacon on top of it; then add 1 cup of meat stock, or 1 cup of hot water and ¼ cup of Pique Seasoning, 1 bouquet garni, composed of 1 large bay leaf tied with 2 sprigs of green celery leaves, 8 sprigs of fresh parsley, 1 sprig of thyme, all tied together with white kitchen thread. Also add 1 clove of garlic, mashed to a pulp, 1 whole clove and 1 medium-sized onion, thinly sliced. Roast in a moderately slow oven (300–325° F.) about 1½–1¾ hours, basting frequently. If there is more stuffing than can be placed in the breast, use it for stuffing onions to be baked and served with the meat. Serve with brown gravy.

To Make the Forcemeat Stuffing. Melt 2 tablespoons of butter or other shortening; stir in ¼ cup of chopped green celery leaves, 2 tablespoons of chopped onion, and 1 sliver of garlic, mashed. Cook 2 or 3 minutes, stirring to prevent burning. Now add the ground meat from the lamb foreshank and stir till the meat browns slightly. Then stir in 2 cups of fine, dry bread crumbs, ⅛ teaspoon of celery seeds, ½ teaspoon of poultry seasoning, 1 teaspoon of salt, and 5 peppercorns, crushed, 2 tablespoons of chopped parsley, and enough cold milk to make a somewhat moist stuffing.

SHISH KABAB   [682]
It's all in the way you mix 'em

Onions, okra and tomatoes—garlic, eggplant, lamb, crushed wheat and pine nuts—greens, chick-peas and olive oil—simple things, aren't they? Things as common to any cook as butter and bread. And, all too often, as monotonously mixed. But it's amazing what you can do with common things if you leaven them with imagination. And from Cape Cod to the Golden Gate, most cooks serve them in the same old stupid way. Just chow! But they weren't "just chow" there in Iran—the ex-Persia. They were Kulfa and Baba Ghanouge, Shish-kabab (or kabob), Bourghal, Baked Kibby, Halwa, Baklawa. Names to conjure with.

Names as old as the wanderings of man, sprung from that ancient soil where, so they say, the Garden of Eden lay. Back swings your heart to Sunday School memories as you bend over a steaming, savory plate filled with good things from the Near East. Shepherds herding their flocks in Old Testament times—goat-skin tents and water bags—lentils and dried figs—flickering fires of camel dung against a desert sunset—the pattering hooves of laden donkeys—veiled women, men in flowing robes and striped head-bands—the sense of dust and sunglare and moving mystery that lay over it all, to a dreaming ten-year-old.

Old! Old! Yet new as today when you dip your bread into the Shish Kabab that might have simmered over any shepherd's fire. Lamb stew, you'd call it today. And lamb stew it is—but something else, something more. For there's a taste to this, and all the other dishes, which no common stew or hot dogs ever had—a tang and fragrance—an essence that lingers on both palate and heart.

Perhaps it's the sesame seeds—they use them in almost everything. Or the rice that's soaked in butter before it's boiled. Or the white, sharp inner pulp and juice scraped from the bark of cherry and mulberry trees. Or the flavor of vine leaves, in which some of the meat dishes are wrapped—the dolmas of yore—vine leaves so young they are still furry on the underside.

Nothing exotic about any of these ingredients, nothing we might not procure easily for our own kitchens. The trick comes in putting them together, in using ordinary things extraordinarily, dramatizing the commonplace, extracting its full tang and flavor, tackling your daily chore as if it were an adventure instead of drudgery.

Amazing what a difference such an attitude makes in one's life—all the difference between high drama and deadly monotony!

Shish Kabab, or Kebab, or Kebob, is to the Near East people what corned beef is to Americans, Colcannon to the Irish, and Shalik to the Russians. The real fun of Shish Kabab is broiling it over a picnic fire.

With a picnic in prospect, skewer your lunch the night before and keep it in the refrigerator in waxed paper. Cut your cubes of lean lamb 2 inches thick and alternate them as you would string varicolored beads, with quarters of onion, whole mushrooms, quarters of fresh tomato, slices of thick fresh green or sweet red peppers—any or all of these. Allow a good 20 minutes for broiling the Shish Kabab; salt and pepper it while cooking, and turn often.

MUTTON   [683]

The herding of flocks was one of the earliest employments of mankind and the most ancient poetry was probably pastoral. The oldest representations we have of the poetic character of pastoral life are found in those books of the Old Testament which describe the shepherd life of the patriarchs.

Mutton is a meat of seasoned flavor for good eaters, meat for men who know that a mutton chop, properly conditioned, with its kidney in the center, is worthy of the employment of all the senses—eyes to see its crackling brown crust; nose to inhale the heavy, pungent fragrance; ears to hear the sizzle of the fat as it is taken from the grill; and taste buds to savor that rich and hearty flavor.

A "mutton flavor," which some consider objectionable, is chiefly due to the outside fat. This may or may not be removed before the mutton is cooked. The flavor may be rendered less noticeable by rubbing the meat with lemon juice before roasting or broiling by putting slices of lemon in the water in which the mutton is boiled, or by marinating, which renders the meat very tender.

BOILED LEG OF MUTTON, OYSTER   [684]
STUFFING, SCOTCH STYLE
Lamb may also be used

Have the butcher bone a 6–7-pound leg of mutton which has been hung for several weeks. About 2½ hours before serving, lay it flat on the kitchen table; rub with lemon, then generously with mixed salt and black pepper. Heat a dozen and a half plump fresh oysters in their own liquor until the edges curl. Chop them coarsely, and mix with ½ cup of soft bread crumbs previously soaked in sherry wine and slightly pressed or squeezed to remove excess liquid; 1 teaspoon each of grated onion, parsley and shallot, and, if desired, 1 tiny slice of garlic; also 2 sieved hard-cooked egg yolks. Moisten with the reserved oyster liquor mixed with the remaining sherry wine. Spread the stuffing over the mutton; roll and secure with white kitchen string. Meantime, make a quick stock with the mutton bones and trimmings. Lay the mutton in it and simmer very gently for 2½ hours. Serve on a hot platter, garnishing simply with watercress, gherkin fans and olives. Pour over the mutton a little Oyster Sauce made by adding 12 fresh oysters to 1½ cups of Cream Sauce (No. 258). Serve additional sauce separately with plain boiled potatoes and a green vegetable or salad.

BRAISED LEG OF MUTTON FRENCH STYLE [685]
As served to King Henry VIII of England

Bone a tender leg of well-hung mutton (except the knuckle), then roll and lard through and through with long narrow strips of fat-back pork, marinated in brandy and fines herbes, as follows: 1 teaspoon each of finely chopped parsley, chervil, shallots, basil, marjoram, tarragon and mint. Season with salt and plenty of freshly ground black pepper. Trim neatly any projecting lardoons, and tie the meat securely with kitchen string. Place in a braising kettle ½ cup each of chopped carrots, onions, celery, leeks, and lean raw ham. Also 1 clove of garlic, mashed to a pulp, 1 bouquet garni, composed of 1 extra large or 2 small bay leaves, 2 sprigs of thyme, 12 sprigs of fresh parsley, all tied with white kitchen thread then add 3 whole cloves, and pour over all ⅓ cup of lard. Cook 10 minutes over a very bright flame, stirring constantly with a wooden spoon and, when well-browned, lay in the meat and pour over it 1½–1¾ cups of rich mutton broth made with the bones and trimmings plus a few additional mutton bones and the usual vegetables. Season to taste with salt and 12 freshly bruised peppercorns, then pour in ½ cup of good brandy; cover closely, and cook in a moderate oven (325–350° F.) for 3–3¼ hours. Serve the meat upon a long hot platter, garnishing simply with crisp watercress. Serve the gravy separately, simply strained, the fat removed, but not thickened. Have a side dish of braised celery (No. 1251), and another of red currant jelly, guava jelly or grape jelly.

BRAISED LEG OF MUTTON PROVENÇALE   [686]

Have the butcher bone a leg of mutton as far as the knuckle and tie securely with string. Rub the mutton with brandy, then with mixed salt and black pepper to taste, and set aside. Place in a braising kettle ½ cup of olive oil or butter and, when hot, add ½ cup of each of chopped onions, carrots, turnip, celery, and ground lean veal with a bouquet garni composed of 1 large bay leaf, 12 sprigs of fresh parsley and 1 sprig of thyme all tied together with white kitchen thread, 10 peppercorns, and ½–¾ teaspoon of salt. Cook this for about 10 minutes over a very bright flame, stirring almost constantly, till well-browned, then lay the leg of mutton over this, add 2 cloves of garlic, mashed, and pour over all 2 cups of meat stock or stock made from the bones and trimmings. Cover and cook in a moderate oven (325–350° F.) for 2¾ hours, turning the meat twice during the cooking process. When ready to serve, pour into a ladle ½ cup of good brandy and set it aflame, then let it drop into the braising kettle. When the flame is extinguished, serve the meat on a heated platter; carve enough slices to go around once, and reshape the meat. Strain the gravy through a fine-meshed sieve, rubbing vigorously so as to obtain as much pulp as possible. Let stand a few minutes, then skim off all fat. Taste for seasoning, stir in 3 tablespoons of tomato paste, add ¾ cup of thinly sliced fresh mushrooms, which have been cooked in butter until tender, and well drained. Reheat, and pour part of this sauce over the carved portions. Serve the remainder in a sauce boat with a side dish of Mint Sauce (Nos. 1086–87) and another of braised olives.

CASSOULET A LA TOULOUSAINE   [687]

Soak 1 quart of dried lima beans overnight. Next morning, change the water and blanch them without any other ingredients, but salted water to barely cover. Drain, and return to a stew pot, add cold water to cover, with 2 finely chopped cloves of garlic, ⅓ pound of chopped fresh pork fat back, 1 large bay leaf tied with 12 sprigs of fresh parsley and 1 sprig of thyme and cook the beans until about half done.

Drain, reserving the broth for other use. Lay in the bottom of a generously greased large, earthenware casserole, 2 pounds of tender, mutton, sliced into 6 equal parts, 1 whole wing and 1 leg of a goose, also the neck of a duck, stuffed with pork sausage. Pour over all ½ cup of goose fat, season to taste with salt and black pepper, and sear till all are nicely browned, stirring almost constantly. Now add 1 pound of *saucisson de Toulouse*, or failing this, use the garlic sausage sold at any good delicatessen store. Add a bouquet garni composed of 1 large bay leaf, 10 sprigs of fresh parsley, and 1 sprig of thyme, all tied together with white kitchen thread, 2 whole cloves, 2 tablespoons of grated onion, and cover entirely with the half-cooked beans. Over the beans pour 3 tablespoons of finely chopped onions or shallots fried golden brown in goose fat with 2 cloves of garlic; also 2 tablespoons of chopped chives, moistened with 2 cups of hot, rich chicken broth, to which has been added 1 small can of tomato paste, reduced to half over a bright flame. Set the casserole in a slow oven (300° F.) to cook for 2 hours. Then sprinkle with ¾–1 cup of fresh bread crumbs, mixed with 3 tablespoons of finely chopped parsley and let this topping brown to a golden hue. Serve from the casserole at table, giving a little of each meat with a generous portion of the beans to each guest.

Among the first of many famous London clubs was the Kit Cat Club, which was organized by forty of Queen Anne's noblemen to do justice to Christopher Cat's tasty mutton pies.

CURRY OF MUTTON SINGAPORE [688]

Pound ¼ ounce of green ginger with 1 teaspoon of ghee (Hindu clarified butter) or use butter, season with a little salt and rub into a 2½-pound piece of lean mutton taken from the leg, then cut the meat into thin slices. Let stand for ½ hour, covered with a cloth. Meanwhile cook ½ pound of thinly sliced onions in 4 tablespoons of ghee or butter until lightly browned; stir in the meat, also 1 clove of garlic, finely chopped, ⅛ teaspoon of ground cloves, ⅛ teaspoon of cardamom seeds, salt and pepper to taste, and fry until meat is tender, taking care the onions do not burn. Now, stir in ¾ cup of scalded sweet cream mixed with ½ pound of blanched, finely ground almonds, and ¼ teaspoon of saffron, softened in a little cold milk. Cover closely, and let simmer very, very gently at least an hour. Serve in a deep dish with plenty of plain boiled, hot rice.

ENGLISH MUTTON CHOPS COUNTRY STYLE [689]

Remove excess fat from 6 mutton chops, each about 2 inches thick, and flatten somewhat. Mix in a soup plate 2 tablespoons of olive oil, 1 teaspoon of salt and ⅓ teaspoon of black pepper. Roll the chops in this mixture, broil on one side for 4 minutes, then lay aside to cool. Spread cooked, or rather, seared side. Prepare the following mixture: 3 egg yolks beaten with 3 or 4 tablespoons of sweet heavy cream, seasoned to taste with salt and freshly ground black pepper. Spread on the cooked, or rather, the seared side of each chop, then roll in fresh bread crumbs, mixed with an equal amount of grated Parmesan cheese; place in a buttered, shallow sauté pan; brush tops and sides with melted butter and bake in a hot oven (400–425° F.) for 15 minutes. Garnish with strips of grilled bacon and small mounds of freshly made French fried potatoes.

MUTTON CUTLETS A LA SOYER   [690]

Also called "Côtelettes à la Victime" (Victimized Cutlets), because two out of three were discarded. I do not recommend it to you on the score of economy, as it is the tip-top of extravagance; but present it as a curiosity, and shall relate the circumstance which caused its creation by a young French culinary chef.

Louis XVIII of France, at the palace of the Tuileries, a most intellectual monarch and gourmet, was completely paralyzed through a serious illness, and at the same time his digestive organs were much out of order; since he was a man of great corpulence and a great admirer of the festive board, much food was required to satisfy his royal appetite; and the difficulty which his physicians experienced was to supply this want of food in the smallest compass.

The head chef, on being consulted, begged a few hours for reflection before he could give an answer to so important a question, as nothing but mutton entirely deprived of fat was to compose His Majesty's meal. After profound study by the chef and his helpers, a voice was heard from the larder, which was a considerable distance from the kitchen, crying: "I have found it, I have found it."

It was a young man of the name of Alphonse Pottier, who, in saying so, made his appearance in the kitchen proper with three beautiful mutton cutlets, tastefully trimmed and tied together; he then, with a smaller skewer fastened them to a spit, and placed them, to the astonishment of all present, including the chef himself, close to the bars of the grate. Two of the cutlets soon got brown (observe, not a word was to be said until the trial was made), from brown they soon turned black; everyone gazed at each other in astonishment, whilst Alphonse Pottier, with quite a composed countenance, terminated his scientific experiment, took them off the spit, drew the skewer out, cut the string, threw the two burnt cutlets away, and merely served the middle one, which seems to have received all the nutriment of the other two.

It was served and greatly approved of by the physicians as well as by the gourmet potentate, who, in consequence of two being sacrificed for one, named it "Côtelette à la Victime," and often afterward used to partake of it when in the enjoyment of health.

Since then, this sort of cutlet is known by the name of "A La Soyer," one of the most illustrious chefs of all time, and author of the incomparable cook book *Modern Housewife or Ménagère*, published in London in 1849.

THE RECIPE. Cut three cutlets from the neck of mutton (not lamb), about half an inch thick, trim one very nicely, free from fat, leave the other two as cut off; put the trimmed one between the two, flatten them together, so that the fat of the outside ones meet over the middle one; tie them together thus and broil over a very strong fire, or close to the fire of the broiling oven of today, for ten minutes; remove it from the fire, cut the string and dish up the middle one only, on a very hot dish, with a little salt sprinkled over it.

MUTTON HOT POT LANCASHIRE STYLE [691]

Purchase a 2-pound piece of the best end of a boned neck of mutton and trim off the skin and the greater part of the fat. Grease a fireproof earthenware baking casserole; arrange a deep layer of thickly sliced potatoes in the bottom of the casserole, and over the potatoes arrange the mutton, which has been sliced into 6 individual cutlets of equal size and weight as far as possible, seasoning to taste with mixed salt, pepper, nutmeg, thyme and mace, having the cutlets slightly overlap each other. Place on each 2 thin slices of lamb kidney and 1 plump fresh oyster, using 3 kidneys and 6 oysters. Next, arrange another layer of sliced potatoes over the garnished cutlets; then pour into the dish 1 cup of hot mutton stock made with trimmings and mutton bones, or use water or, still better, ¾ cup of boiling water, mixed with ¼ cup of Pique Seasoning, season with salt and pepper, brush the top with melted butter; cover with a buttered paper and bake in a moderate oven (350° F.) for 1¼ hours; remove the paper and continue baking 20–25 minutes longer, or until top is delicately browned and crisp. When ready to serve, pour in a little more gravy or Pique Seasoning, and serve directly from the baking dish.

PORK [692]

A neighbor comes to the door with a large covered pan and with the hearty greeting: "We killed hogs on Friday and I want you to have some of our sausage. It is unusually good this Fall."

It is "hog-killin' time" in the country, and although these autumn weeks lack the high ardor of the Fall festival of former times, still they are sufficiently important to have a specific designation and destiny of their own. Never is hog-killing spoken of as slaughtering or butchering, and rarely is the meat mentioned as pork, except tenderloins, roasts and chops. And "hog-killin' time" has requirements both specialized and technical. The hog must be old enough and not too old; the day for the procedure must be cold yet not too cold, so that the slaughtered animal may cool off gradually, and never, never must the meat be allowed to freeze. The actual slaughter is performed by the farmer or by the hired men, away from the house and kitchen; the cutting and smoking take place in the shed and smoke-house; yet the housewife is busy also with the seasoning, curing, lard rendering and sausage making.

Headcheese, made from the head, is prized by many people, while pig's feet, pickled or fried in batter, are the choice of others.

Fattest of butcher's meats, so fat that it is practically self-basting, pork is unexcelled for roasting. It is sold both fresh and cured, that is, brined and smoked. It is also a valuable source of shortening, both fresh and cured, which is taken from the tremendous layer of fat that surrounds the whole creature and converted into lard, salt pork, fat back, bacon, etc.

Although quality variations in fresh pork are very slight, high grades are easily identified by the fine-grained, firm, not flabby flesh. The shoulder cuts, particularly, should be finely marbled with white fat. The skin should be smooth and free from wrinkles.

Three simple rules will help homemakers protect their families and guests from trichinosis:

(1) *Rule of Color.* Cook pork until it has lost its pinkish color. *Don't eat* pink pork.

(2) *Rule of Time.* Cook large thick cuts of pork at least 30 minutes to the pound.

(3) *Rule of Science.* Use a meat thermometer. Pork heated to a minimum of 137° F. is safe.

Pork is a tender-fibred meat, but it is notoriously indigestible if not thoroughly cooked, on account of the high percentage of fat present which may exceed 40%, or considerably more than the quantity of its nitrogenous material. The fat is composed chiefly of palmitic and oleic glycerides.

Like lamb and veal, pork should be cooked rather more slowly, also more thoroughly than beef.

Bacon is much more digestible than pork, while ham occupies an intermediate position.

Broiling of pork is seldom done, because broiling is likely to be done quickly (even though this is not the best procedure) and the pork chops are likely to be insufficiently cooked. Also, much of the rich flavor of pork lies in the fat, and broiled pork chops are apt to be dry and lacking in flavor.

Some Greek peasants still refuse to eat pork for fear of incurring the displeasure of Demeter, goddess of the corn-bearing earth, to whom the pig was sacred.

GUIDE TO THE PURCHASE AND PREPARATION OF PORK [693]

RETAIL PORK CUT*	CHARACTERISTICS	HOW TO COOK (Methods)
BUTT— BONELESS BOSTON	From the lower portion of shoulder. Includes foreleg down to a little above the knee joint—the arm, knuckle and shank bones being removed. Juicy, tender and well flavored.	Braise, bake, potroast, roast, pot
BUTT—BOSTON	Same as above but boned and rolled.	Same as above
BUTT—FRESH	Next to the loin. Contains aitch bone and part of foreleg bone. Juicy and tender.	Same as above
BUTT— BLADE STEAKS	Cut from Boston butt with small part of blade bone. Should be cooked very slowly in moist heat.	Braise, bake, potroast, stew
CHOPS—LOIN	From the loin. Contains both eye muscle and tenderloin, with T-shaped bone. Tender, well flavored and juicy. Better flavored when cooked in moist heat.	Bake, braise, potroast, Swiss steak method, pot
CHOPS—RIB	From the loin but with only one eye muscle. When cut thick there is a rib bone with every other chop, but no rib bone when cut thin. Juicy, well flavored and tender when cooked in moist heat.	Same as loin chops
FEET	Contains very little meat. Considerable bones and plenty of gelatinous substance. Requires initial boiling before preparing in any style.	Boil, bake, braise, broil, poulette, stew, jellied
HAM— CENTER CUT	From the ham, with a small round bone in center which should never be removed before cooking. This bone enhances the flavor of the meat.	Bake, boil, braise, casserole, roast
HAM— CENTER CUT STEAKS	From ham. Oval-shaped and with a small round bone in center which should never be removed before cooking, so as to enhance the meat flavor.	Same as center cut
HAM— FRESH, WHOLE	Ham with a heavy layer of fat under the rind. A good fresh ham should have grayish-white, lean meat.	Same as center cut
HAM—ROLLED	Ham, same as fresh whole ham, but boned, rolled and secured.	Same as center cut

* Taken from the seven wholesale cuts—butt, chops, feet, ham, loin, shoulder, and pare ribs.

GUIDE TO THE PURCHASE AND [693]
PREPARATION OF PORK

RETAIL PORK CUT*	CHARACTERISTICS	HOW TO COOK (Methods)
HAM—SHANK	From ham. Wedge-shaped, containing shank bone. Economical, tender, well flavored and juicy.	Same as center cut
LOIN—CENTER CUT	From the loin. Contains eye muscle, part of tenderloin, backbone and often ribs. Well flavored, juicy and tender.	Same as center cut
LOIN—END	From the loin with eye muscle, part of tenderloin with hip and backbone. Well flavored, juicy and tender, especially when cooked in moist heat. When roasted, requires frequent basting.	Bake, braise, potroast, roast
LOIN— SHOULDER END	From the loin with parts of blade bone, ribs and backbone. Well flavored, juicy and tender, especially when cooked in moist heat. If roasted, requires frequent basting and slow cooking. Cook at even temperature.	Same as end loin
LOIN—TENDERLOIN	From the loin. Often sold separately. It is a long, tapering, round, well flavored, tender and juicy muscle weighing ½–¾ lb.	Bake, braise, casserole, split lengthwise and bro
SHOULDER— ARM STEAKS	From the shoulder. Oval at one end and square at the other, with a small round bone in the center which should never be removed. Cook in moist heat, as slowly as possible.	Braise, potroast, pot, stew like Swiss steak
SHOULDER— CUSHION PICNIC	From shoulder. Usually boned. Square-shaped. Tender and juicy. Well flavored when cooked in moist heat. If roasted, requires frequent basting.	Same as arm steaks, plus roasting
SHOULDER—HOCK	From shoulder and wedge-shaped part of fore shank bone. Contains a good deal of gelatinous substance which renders it tender.	Boil, then bake, braise, pot
SHOULDER—PICNIC	From shoulder. Contains arm bone. May be boned and tied. Well flavored, tender and juicy. A miniature ham.	Same as fresh whole ham
SPARERIBS	Ends of ribs which have been removed from bacon strip. A little lean meat between the bones.	Boil, bake, braise, stuff, roast, barbecue

* Taken from the seven wholesale cuts—butt, chops, feet, ham, loin, shoulder, an spare ribs.

BAKED PORK CHOPS CHARCUTIERE   [694]

This highly delectable dish derives its name from the fact that the chefs in Paris prepare and cook their pork chops in this manner. It is an extremely popular luncheon dish, and very tasty.

Cook ¼ generous cup of chopped onions in a small saucepan with 2 tablespoons of lard till tender, without browning; then sprinkle with 1 teaspoon of flour, blending well with a wooden spoon over a gentle flame till mixture is of a golden color; gradually stir in 1 cup of meat stock, mixed with ½ cup of dry white wine, stirring constantly, over a medium flame. When mixture begins to thicken, season to taste with salt and freshly crushed black pepper; bring to a boil, then skim well. Lower the flame and let the sauce simmer very, very gently for 20 minutes. Meantime, cook 6 nice, thick pork chops (3 to a pound) "frenched" in 2 or 3 tablespoons of lard, over a brisk flame at first so as to sear on both sides; then over a gentle flame, until chops are tender, or about 20 minutes. Season to taste with salt and pepper; arrange on a hot dish; skim the sauce, taste for seasoning, then add 2 tablespoons of thinly sliced small gherkins and 1 teaspoon of prepared mustard. Pour over the chops, dust with chopped chervil or parsley and serve at once.

BAKED PORK CHOPS FLORENTINE   [695]

Dredge 6 shoulder pork chops with seasoned flour, and sear on both sides over a bright flame until well-browned. turning frequently; reduce the heat; cover the pan, and cook about 30 minutes, or until the chops are tender, turning them frequently. Now, arrange a layer of hot cooked spinach in a shallow, buttered baking dish, and lay the chops on it, side by side. Beat 3 egg yolks well, stir into 2 cups of medium-white sauce, and pour over the chops; sprinkle with grated cheese (any kind); place in a hot oven or under the flame of the broiling oven and brown until cheese bubbles. Serve right from the baking dish.

BAKED PORK CHOPS HAWAII   [696]

Heat 1½ tablespoons of lard in a heavy frying pan, and add 6 large loin pork chops (3 chops to a pound), seasoned with salt and pepper to taste, and brown thoroughly on both sides. Lay the chops, thus browned, in a greased casserole. Brown 6 slices of canned pineapple in the same fat and lay 1 slice on top of each chop. Pour 1 cup of pineapple juice over all, add 1 bouquet garni, composed of 1 bay leaf, 1 sprig of thyme, 8 sprigs of fresh parsley, and 2 sprigs of green celery leaves (tops) tied with white kitchen thread, 2 whole cloves, 2 tablespoons of grated onion, 1 thin slice of garlic, mashed, and baked in a slow oven (300–325° F.) for about 1¼–1½ hours. Cover the pan with a buttered paper if top browns too fast. Serve directly from the baking dish, first discarding the bouquet garni.

BAKED PORK CHOPS NORMANDE   [697]

Trim 6 thick loin pork chops neatly (about 3 to a pound) and season with mixed salt and pepper. Arrange in a buttered baking dish, side by side, and cover with thin slices of cored, pared apples, using about 3 large apples in all. Dust the apple slices with a teaspoon or two of sugar and ground cinnamon in equal parts, and dot here and there with 1 tablespoon of butter. Add 1 large bay leaf, 2 tablespoons of grated onion or shallots, if available, and 3 whole cloves. Pour over all ½ cup of hard cider and ½ cup of meat stock; failing this, substitute ½ cup of boiling water and 3 tablespoons of Pique Seasoning; cover hermetically and bake in a hot oven (400° F.) for about 1½ hours. Remove the cover, and continue baking 10–15 minutes longer, or till tops of apples are brown. Serve from the baking dish.

BAKED STUFFED DOUBLE LOIN CHOPS   [698]

Ask the butcher to make a pocket on each of 6 double loin pork chops. Dust them with mixed salt and pepper and set aside. Combine ¼ cup of bacon drippings, 2 scant cups of soft bread crumbs, 1 tablespoon each of chopped parsley, onion and green pepper, 1 blade of garlic, salt and pepper to taste, also ⅛ teaspoon each of nutmeg, thyme and mace, and ½ teaspoon of sage. Cook 4 or 5 minutes, stirring frequently. Spoon this stuffing in the pockets, being careful not to pack too tightly; arrange the chops in a buttered baking dish on a layer of thinly sliced onions (using 2 large ones), add 1 large bay leaf, tied with 8 sprigs of parsley and 1 sprig of thyme, 2 cloves, and pour over all ¾ cup of red wine and ½ cup of meat stock. Cover closely and bake in a moderate oven (350–375° F.) for 1½ hours. Serve right from the baking dish.

BARBECUED FRESH HAM VIRGINIA STYLE   [699]

Score a large fresh ham with a sharp knife. Mix 1 tablespoon of mustard seed, ½ teaspoon of celery seed, ½ teaspoon of peppercorns, gently bruised, 1 scant cup of brown sugar, 1 cup of wine vinegar, and 2 cups of meat stock, or 1½ cups of boiling water and ½ cup of Pique Seasoning, and let stand 30 minutes. Bring to a boil; cool, pour over the ham and let stand overnight, turning 2 or 3 times. After at least 12 hours, put the ham into a roasting pan, fat-side down; add the marinade, cover closely, and bake in a moderate oven for 4 hours. Strain the mixture from the pan and serve the roast hot or cold. The barbecue sauce or marinade may be used for something else. If pork is served hot, make a pan gravy in the usual way, using the marinade for liquid. Served cold, it is usually accompanied by green salad and applesauce.

Like the Chinese, the Greeks of 500 B. C. insisted that roast pork should be so tender that it could be cut with a small piece of blunt-edged wood.

BRAISED PORK CHOP DINNER CREOLE STYLE [700]

Wipe 6 nice, thick shoulder pork chops with a damp cloth; make a gash on the fat edges to prevent curling, season to taste with mixed salt and pepper and set aside. Rub an earthenware casserole first with garlic, then with pork fat, and lay in the pork chops. Cover with 1 cup of thinly sliced onions, 1 cup of thinly sliced green pepper, and pour over all 1 No. 2 can of tomatoes. Add 1 bouquet garni composed of 1 bay leaf, 8 sprigs of fresh parsley and 1 sprig of thyme, tied with white kitchen thread. Cover and braise in a moderate oven (375° F.) for 1½ hours without disturbing. Serve from the baking dish accompanied by baked apples.

CHOUCROUTE GARNI ALSATIAN STYLE [701]
Garnished Sauerkraut

For 6 persons, buy 3 pounds of uncooked sauerkraut. Put it into an earthware casserole with ½ teaspoon of caraway seeds and about 2 dozen peppercorns. Put in also a small calf's foot, 1 smoked pork shoulder, medium-sized carrot, and ¾ cup of dry white wine (Alsatian if possible). Now that already sounds as if it would taste pretty good, but don't forget the essential, which is a good tablespoon of goose fat. (If you have trouble getting goose fat, the easiest way out is to buy a small jar of Strasbourg pâté de foie gras (goose liver pâté) and scrape the fat from the top of that). Let this cook gently for an hour, then put in a chunk of bacon (about half a pound) and cook an hour longer. Half an hour before serving time, slip into the pot a few frankfurters, also 2 small cervelats and, when ready to serve, pile the sauerkraut on a platter, remove the calf's foot, and surround the platter with plain boiled potatoes. Slice the pork shoulder and use to cover the sauerkraut, alternately with slices of cervelat and make a necklace of the frankfurters. This dish is worthy of a first-class bottle of Rhine or Alsatian white wine, rather than the beer which German-American ritual prescribes. But whatever you do, don't omit the goose fat!

CORNED PORK SHOULDER DUTCH STYLE [702]

If the corning seems a trifle strong, freshen a little by soaking in cold water. Use the same cooking method as for corned beef or tongue. The fat left after trimming the cooked meat can be tried out and added to the dripping jar.

Select as lean a piece of mild corned pork shoulder as possible. Do not trim away the fat or any skin at this time. Place in a kettle with 2 quarts of cold water; bring slowly to a good rolling boil; drain. Again cover with cold water and bring slowly to a boil. Taste the liquid; if very salty, repeat the freshening process once more. Otherwise, the pork is ready to cook.

Add 1 medium-sized onion, sliced; 1 carrot, scraped and cut into small pieces; 1 stalk of celery, scraped, then cut into ½-inch pieces, 1 small turnip, peeled and quartered; 1 large leek, halved lengthwise, carefully washed, then folded in two or three and tied with 1 large bay leaf, 10 sprigs of fresh parsley, and 1 sprig of thyme, 2 whole cloves, 1 clove of garlic, left whole, no salt, but plenty of black pepper. Bring slowly to a rolling boil. Lower the heat and simmer very, very gently, half-covered with the lid, for 3 hours, or until the meat when tested with a fork, is tender. Turn out the heat; let stand for 50 minutes. Drain off the broth, reserving it for a lentil, split pea, or bean soup. Trim away some of the fat and any skin; score the fat in diamonds; rub with a mixture of ¼ cup or more of brown sugar, 1½ teaspoons or more of prepared mustard, moistened with a little of the broth, and stick with whole cloves (about 2 dozen). Place in a baking pan, and bake in a moderately hot oven (375° F.) for about 25–30 minutes, or until the meat is heated through and the outside slightly brown. Serve hot or cold.

Pigs "saw America first" when they toured with De Soto four hundred or so years ago! When the Spanish explorer arrived in Tampa he had six hundred soldiers and thirteen pigs, the latter reserved for the colony he planned to establish in Florida.

CROWN ROAST OF PORK [703]

Proceed as indicated for Crown Roast of Lamb (No 663), substituting a crown roast of pork of about 12–14 ribs. Stuff and roast as directed, and in addition to the pan gravy, serve a side dish of applesauce.

FRIED PIG'S KNUCKLES [704]

Have the butcher split 4 pig's knuckles each into 4 pieces; place in a deep saucepan; cover with 1 quart of boiling water, add 1 large onion, chopped, 2 bay leaves, tied with a 2-inch piece of parsley root, scraped, and 1 sprig of thyme, all tied together with white kitchen thread; then add 3 whole cloves and 1 small bulb of garlic, left whole. Bring to a boil, lower the heat and simmer very gently for 2 hours, or until tender, which may be seen by the meat falling from the bones. Remove from the broth; cool, separate the meat from the bones; dip the meat into flour, then into beaten egg and finally into fine bread crumbs. Fry golden brown in ⅓ cup of olive oil. Arrange a hot platter; sprinkle over ⅓ cup of melted butter, mixed with 2 tablespoons of lemon juice and serve at once.

HEAD CHEESE [705]
Tête Pressée or *Fromage de Cochon*

Have the butcher bone a pig's head. This is done exactly as for Calf's Head. Ask for the tongue and brains. Wash all in several cold waters, so as to remove all the blood. Set aside the brains; put the head and tongue in a large kettle; cover with equal parts of water and dry white wine, and add 1 large onion, peeled and quartered, each quarter stuck with a whole clove, 1 large bouquet garni composed of 2 large bay leaves, 15 sprigs of fresh parsley, 6 sprigs of green celery leaves tops, 2 or 3 sprigs of thyme, or lacking it, ⅓ teaspoon of thyme leaves in a small cheesecloth or flannel bag, also 3 or 4 sage leaves, all tied together with white kitchen thread. Salt to taste, and a dozen peppercorns, gently bruised. Bring to a boil, skim carefully, lower the heat and simmer very gently for at least 4 hours, or till a straw can penetrate the rind of the head. Carefully lift up the head and tongue (this last may cook sooner, so remove it as soon as tender); place on a large platter and, when luke-warm, remove all the rind. Cut the meat, including the tongue, into pieces, the size of a large walnut, and place in a large mixing bowl. Add the brains, previously parboiled in a little of the cooking broth. Toss mixture as you would a salad; season highly with cayenne, nutmeg and a little more sage. Now pack the mixture into a bread pan, or a large casserole either square oblong or round, and pour over it 8 tablespoons of the strained, lukewarm broth. Place a snugly fitting wooden board over the mold, put a weight over the board and cool. When cold, it will be jellied. Chill in refrigerator for at least 48 hours, then slice and serve with either a green salad or a potato salad, the platter garnished with olives, radishes, dill pickles, sliced tomato, quartered hard-cooked eggs, etc. If preferred, divide the meat mixture among several small molds or bowls, cover with melted lard, and, when the lard is cold, store in the refrigerator where it will keep for several weeks—even a month.

Mix a little love of adventure with the recipes on a page. That is the way that miracles are performed. This cookbook is a guide, not an oracle, and dishes are made, not born.

INTOXICATED LOIN OF PORK [706]

This amusing name comes from the fact that in the process of cooking, the red wine in which the pork is being cooked naturally reduces considerably and the pork is said to have drunk it and is therefore intoxicated.

Season a loin of pork to taste with mixed salt, pepper, nutmeg, sage, and marjoram, rubbing it well in on every side. Sear over a very bright fire in ¼ cup of lard until well-browned all over, with 3 or 4 cloves of garlic, chopped, and ¼ cup of chopped parsley. Transfer the pork to a shallow baking pan, pour over enough red wine to barely cover, add 1 bouquet garni composed of 1 large bay leaf, 1 sprig of thyme, 2 sprigs of green celery leaves, and an inch piece of horseradish root, tied with white kitchen thread. Season with a few grains of salt and bake in a moderate oven (375° F.) for about 40 minutes, turning the meat twice during the cooking process. By that time the wine will have reduced to almost nothing. Arrange the meat on a hot platter; add to the left-over wine 1½ cups of good beef stock, and gradually bring to a boil, scraping and stirring well, so as to loosen all the gelatinous particles of wine and meat from the roasting pan. Taste for seasoning; strain through a fine sieve, and reduce to half its original volume over a hot fire. Stir in 1 cup of Spanish Sauce (No. 1127), taste for seasoning, and serve separately from the meat.

JELLIED SOUR HEAD CHEESE RING [707]
COUNTRY STYLE

Place 3 pig's knuckles, 3 pig's feet, 1 pig's tongue and 1 pig's tail in a large saucepan; add 1 pound of fresh bacon rind, 3 large onions, quartered, each quarter stuck with 1 whole clove, 1 bouquet garni composed of 3 bay leaves tied with 12 sprigs of fresh parsley, 2 sprigs of green celery leaves, and 1 sprig of thyme, 2 tablespoons of salt and ½ teaspoon of freshly ground black pepper. Pour over all 3½ quarts of cold water; bring to a boil, skim carefully, and simmer very gently for 4 hours, or till meat is tender, and bones can be pulled out easily. Strain, saving the broth. Remove the meat from the bones and cut into small dice. Sprinkle 2 tablespoons of granulated gelatin over 1 cup of dry white wine; dissolve it in 2 cups of the hot strained broth and stir in ½ cup of tarragon vinegar. Cool. Place the meat in a 12-inch ring mold; pour the gelatin-broth mixture over it, stirring lightly with a fork as so to permit the semi-liquid gelatin blend throughout the mass. Cool and, when jellied, keep in refrigerator till needed. When ready to serve, unmold on a large round platter; place a nice bunch of green, crisp, young watercress in the center.

POKER HASH SOUTHERN STYLE [708]
Also called Mulligan Hash

Chop or cut fine, but do not grind, 2 small green peppers (freed from seeds and white ribs) 4 medium-sized onions and 3 large stalks of celery. Put all these in a stew pot; add 1 No. 2 can of tomatoes, and cook slowly 10–15 minutes, stirring frequently. Meantime, grind 2 pounds of lean, fresh pork and cook in 3 tablespoons of butter until just beginning to brown, stirring frequently. Blend thoroughly 1 package of cooked (medium cut) noodles with 1 cup of grated cheese; combine with the vegetables and ground pork; season highly with salt and pepper and turn mixture into a greased baking dish and bake in a moderate oven (350° F.) for about 30–35 minutes. Ten to fifteen minutes before it is done, cover with grated cheese and cracker meal in equal parts, and continue baking until brown. In some parts of the South they add ½ pound of fresh mushrooms, the stems chopped and cooked in a little butter separately from the caps, which are coarsely chopped after being peeled, then cooked in butter over a low flame and added, butter and all, to the mixture before baking.

There is a popular belief that the pig, because of its habit of rolling itself in the mire, imparts an unclean flavor to its flesh. This is a mistaken idea, because the pig doesn't follow this habit of its own accord, but resorts to it when clean water is not available.

PORK AND APPLE PIE [709]

Cut 2 pounds of lean pork from the neck into small cubes; dredge with seasoned flour and sear in 2 tablespoons of bacon drippings, till well browned, stirring frequently. Transfer the well-drained meat to an earthenware casserole, and ¼ cup of onions, chopped and cooked in a little butter till just beginning to take on color, ½ cup of cooked or canned peas, well drained, 1 tablespoon each of parsley and chives, finely chopped and well mixed, then season to taste with salt, pepper, nutmeg, sage and thyme. Add 1 large bay leaf and 2 whole cloves, and scatter over the whole 3 medium-sized apples, pared, cored and sliced. Pour in 1 cup of cream sauce (No. 258). Cover with your favorite pastry (Nos. 2065–2068), or with biscuit dough; slash with knife to let the steam escape and bake 25–30 minutes in a hot oven (400° F.), or till the crust is nicely browned. Serve hot.

PORK CHOW MEIN [710]

This Chinese dish may also be made with veal or chicken. Cut 2 pounds of lean, raw pork (about 4 cups) in small cubes, and brown

slightly in ⅓ cup of fat; add 2 cups of finely sliced small onions and cook
5 minutes longer, adding more fat as needed, and stirring almost constantly; then stir in 2 cups of hot water, season with salt and pepper;
cover and let simmer slowly for 40 minutes. Add 6 cups of finely shredded
celery, 2 cans of drained, sliced water chestnuts, 2 cans of well-drained
bamboo sprouts, 2 medium-sized green pepper, thinly shredded and freed
from white seeds and white ribs, and continue cooking 15 minutes
longer, stirring frequently. Mix ⅓ cup of cornstarch with 1½ tablespoons
of Chinese brown sauce (commercial), add to the meat and vegetable
mixture, and cook till slightly thickened, stirring almost constantly from
the bottom of the pan. Serve over plain boiled rice or Chinese noodles.
This will serve eight generously.

PORK SOUFFLÉ   [711]
Using Left-overs

Beat 3 egg yolks thoroughly; add 2 tablespoons of melted lard, bacon
fat or ham fat, 1 cup of milk mixed with 1½ cups of finely minced cooked
lean pork, 1 tablespoon each of finely chopped parsley and onion, and
beat thoroughly. Season to taste with salt, pepper, also a little sage and
thyme, and finally fold in 3 stiffly beaten egg whites. Turn into a greased
soufflé dish or 6 individual greased custard cups; place in a pan of hot
water and bake in a hot oven (400° F.) 20–30 minutes or until firm and
serve at once.

PORK STEW SOUTHERN STYLE   [712]
Using Left-overs

Brown 3 cups of cooked pork cut in scant inch cubes in 2 tablespoons
of bacon or ham drippings; stir in 2 cups of meat stock, or failing this,
1½ cups of boiling water mixed with ½ cup of Pique Seasoning, and
season with a dash each of cayenne pepper, mace, sage and thyme; bring
to a boil and simmer, covered, 15 minutes. Add 1½ cups of small white
onions, peeled and boiled and 1½ tablespoons of quick cooking tapioca
and bring to a brisk boil, stirring constantly. Taste for seasoning, adding
salt and pepper as needed, and transfer to a hot platter, placing hot sweet
potato biscuits around the edge. Serve with a green salad.

PORK AND SWEET POTATO PIE   [713]
Using Left-overs

Cook over a gentle flame ¼ cup of thinly sliced onions in 3 tablespoons of butter for 3 minutes, stirring frequently; blend in 2 tablespoons
of flour, and season to taste with a pinch each of sage, of thyme and of

nutmeg, also salt and pepper, and ¼ teaspoon of crumbled dried bay leaves. Gradually stir in 2 cups of scalded milk and cook, stirring constantly, until mixture thickens. Then slice 4 cooked sweet potatoes into the sauce, and add 2½ cups of cooked, diced pork. Turn mixture into a buttered casserole dish; scatter over ½ generous cup of cooked or canned drained peas, and cover with pastry, making a few slashes on top for escape of steam. Brush top with beaten egg yolk diluted with a little cold water, and bake in a very hot oven (425–450 ° F.) for 10 minutes; then reduce heat to moderate (350° F.), and continue baking 15–20 minutes longer. Serve at once.

PORK TENDERLOINS, SAUCE PIQUANTE   [714]

Split 2 pork tenderloins lengthwise and lay partially cooked young carrots (using about 4) on the lower halves; place the upper halves on top and sew or skewer in place. Lay 2 slices of bacon over the top; place the tenderloins on a rack in a roasting pan and add 1 small bouquet garni, composed of a small bay leaf, 6 sprigs of fresh parsley, and 1 sprig of thyme, all tied together with white kitchen thread, with 1 or 2 whole cloves, salt and pepper to taste, and roast in a very moderate oven (300–325° F.) until done, allowing 30 minutes per pound for cooking.   Meantime prepare 2 cups of Sauce Piquante (No. 1103) and, when the tenderloins are done, lay them in a large shallow saucepan and pour the sauce over them. Cook together 12–15 minutes, and serve the meat, sliced and reshaped, on a hot platter; pour the sauce over and serve, simply garnished with crisp watercress at both ends of the platter.

PORK TAMALE PIE   [715]
Mexican (This will easily serve 12)

Ingredients are 2 pounds of pork loin, cut into inch cubes, 1 medium-sized onion thinly sliced, ½ cup of diced celery, 1 large green pepper thinly sliced, 1 clove of garlic mashed to a pulp, 1 cup of thick tomato juice, 4 cups of hot water (or more), 2 teaspoons of chili powder (or more), 2 tablespoons of flour, 1 teaspoon of salt (about), 3 tablespoons of cold water, 1 cup of white or yellow corn meal, 1 cup of cold water, 3 cups of boiling water, 2 or 3 tablespoons of butter, 2 large eggs or 3 small ones, slightly beaten, 2 canned red pimientos, sliced, ½ cup of halved ripe or green olives.

Brown the cubed pork in its own fat in a heavy saucepan add the vegetables and hot water, and simmer to tenderness.   Meantime moisten the cornmeal with the cup of cold water, stir into the boiling, salted water in a double-boiler top, place over direct heat stir constantly, and when it boils hard, put over hot water and simmer gently for about 20 minutes.

Mix the chili powder, salt and flour in a cup, moisten with the 3 tablespoons of cold water and, when smooth, turn into the pork mixture, stirring until the sauce thickens slightly. Take the cornmeal from the heat; stir in the butter and beaten eggs; line a baking dish with part of the mixture; fill with the pork and gravy; sprinkle with the olives and pimientos; cover with the remaining hot cornmeal, and bake in a moderate oven (375° F.) until the sauce bubbles up through the cornmeal topping, or about 25–30 minutes. Serve very, very hot in the baking dish.

ROAST "FRENCHED" LOIN OF PORK DUTCH STYLE [716]

Have the rib ends of the pork loin "Frenched" at your butcher's. That is, have the meat scraped from the ends of the rib bones; season with mixed salt, pepper, a dash each of sage, mace, nutmeg and thyme, and place in a roasting pan with the unprotected rib ends down. Add 1 bouquet garni composed of 1 large bay leaf, 8 sprigs of fresh parsley, 2 sprigs of green celery leaves, 1 sprig of thyme, all tied with kitchen thread; 2 whole cloves, 1 clove of garlic, 1 medium-sized onion, thinly sliced, 1 small carrot, scraped, then sliced. Pour over all ½ cup each of dry white wine and meat stock; failing that, use ½ cup of boiling water mixed with 3 tablespoons of Pique Seasoning. Place the roasting pan in a hot oven (450° F.) and bake 15-20 minutes, or until nicely browned, then reduce heat to moderate (325–350° F.), and continue roasting, basting frequently with the liquid from the pan, allowing 25–30 minutes per pound. Transfer the roast to a hot platter; decorate the rib bones (ends) with paper frills and garnish the platter with 6 green peppers filled with picalilli or other spicy relish, 6 thick slices of unpeeled apples, pan fried in plenty of butter and dusted with a little paprika for color contrast, also crisp watercress. Make gravy from the drippings in the pan and serve with Boiled Cabbage in Mustard Sauce (Nos. 1092–93) and plain boiled potatoes.

ROAST FRESH HAM AMERICAN STYLE [717]

The rind should be left on a fresh ham, which will weigh, say, about 7–8 pounds. Wipe with a damp cloth; rub the meat well with mixed salt, pepper and flour, and place fat side up in an open roasting pan. Arrange thin slices of a large onion over the top, add 1 bouquet garni composed of 1 extra large or 2 medium-sized bay leaves, 15 sprigs of fresh parsley, 1 large sprig of thyme, 3 sprigs of green celery leaves (tops), all tied with white kitchen thread; 1 medium-sized carrot, scraped and sliced, 1 small white turnip, peeled and quartered, 1 small leek, halved, lengthwise, well-washed, folded in 2 or 3, and secured with thread, 1 clove of garlic, mashed, 2 whole cloves, 12 peppercorns, and 1 cup of meat stock or water. Roast for 25 minutes in a hot oven (450° F.); reduce the heat to moderate (325–350° F.), and continue roasting, allowing 30 minutes per pound and counting from the time the roast was placed in the oven, basting frequently with the liquid from the pan, adding more as it evaporates. When the ham is done—and it should be well done—remove from the oven; cut away the rind; score the fat diagonally with a sharp knife, forming small diamonds. Rub the meat with a mixture made of ½ cup of brown sugar and 1 teaspoon of prepared mustard, slightly moistened with pan liquid. If desired, stick the diamonds with whole cloves; return to a hot oven (450° F.) to brown about 12–15 minutes. Serve hot or cold. If served hot, make pan gravy with the liquid in the pan, and serve very hot with applesauce.

ROAST PORK FILET IN BLANKET   [718]

Wipe with a damp cloth 4 pounds of pork filet; rub with sherry wine, then with mixed salt, pepper and flour, dredging thoroughly. Place in a roasting pan, add 1 whole medium-sized onion, coarsely chopped, 1 bouquet garni composed of 1 bay leaf, 8 sprigs of fresh parsley, 1 sprig of green celery leaves (tops) and 1 small leek, quartered, lengthwise, well washed, and folded in two or three, the whole bouquet tied with white kitchen thread; also 2 whole cloves. Pour into the pan 1 cup of dry white wine. Roast in a steady, moderate oven (325° F.), allowing 30 minutes per pound of meat, basting frequently. When well done, cool, make a gravy from the pan drippings and keep hot.

When the meat is quite cold, brush the top and sides with 2 beaten egg yolks, mixed with a little sherry wine; cover with freshly made soft bread crumbs, moistened with a little of the cold pan gravy, then another layer of bread crumbs, gravy, again bread crumbs and gravy till a crust of about ½ inch is formed. Place the roast thus enrobed in a very hot oven (425° F.), to brown for 20 minutes, basting frequently with a little of the pan gravy. Serve on a heated serving platter, and pass the hot pan gravy on the side with buttered Brussels sprouts, baked potatoes and a green salad.

In the eighteenth century, Spanish mine owners in South America had a sure way to get the Indians to work for them. They tempted prospective workers with chocolate-coated cold roast pork.

ROAST SUCKLING PIG   [719]

The story is as old as the hills, and so, of course, is roast little suckling pig. As to which came first, the pig or the oyster, one cannot tell. Here however, is the story of the discovery of the art of roasting pig, said to have been obtained from an old Chinese manuscript. The art of roasting pig, according to this ancient document, was accidentally discovered in the following manner. The swineherd Ho-Ti, having gone out into the woods one morning, as his manner was, to collect mast for his hogs, left his cottage in care of his eldest son, Bo-Bo. A great lubberly boy who was fond of playing with fire, he let some sparks escape into a bundle of straw which, kindling quickly, spread the conflagration over every part of their poor mansion till it was reduced to ashes.

Together with the cottage, what was of much more importance, a fine litter of new farrowed pigs, no less than nine in number, perished. China pigs have been esteemed a luxury all over the East, from the remotest periods. Bo-Bo was in the utmost consternation, not so much for the sake of the cottage, which his father and he could easily rebuild, as for the loss of the pigs.

While he was thinking what he should say to his father, and wringing his hands, an odor assailed his nostrils unlike any scent which he had ever known. What could it proceed from? Not from the burnt cottage; he had smelt *that* before; indeed, this was by no means the first accident of the kind which had occurred through the negligence of this unlucky firebrand.

A premonitory moistening at the same time overflowed his lips. He knew not what to think. He stooped down to feel the pig lying at his feet, to see if there were any signs of life in it. He burnt his fingers and, to cool them, instinctively he applied them in his foolish fashion to his mouth. Some of the crumbs of the scorched skin had come away with his fingers, and for the first time in life (in the world's life, indeed, for before him no man had known it) he tasted—*CRACKLING!*

Again he felt and fumbled at the pig. It didn't burn him so much now; still he licked his fingers from a sort of habit. The truth at length broke into his slow understanding that it was the *pig* that smelt so, and the *pig* that tasted so delicious, and surrendering himself to the new-born pleasure, he fell to tearing up whole handfuls of the scorched skin with the flesh next to it, and was cramming it down his throat when his sire entered amid the smoking rafters. Finding how affairs stood, he began to rain blows upon the young rogue's shoulders. Bo-Bo heeded them no more than if they had been flies.

The pleasure which he experienced in his feast had rendered him quite callous to any inconveniences he might feel. Bo-Bo's scent being wonderfully sharpened since morning, he soon raked out another pig, and fairly rending it asunder, thrust the lesser half by main force into the fists of Ho-Ti, shouting, "Eat, eat; eat the burnt pig, Father; only taste."

In conclusion (for the manuscript here is a little tedious), both father and son sat down to the mess nor left off till they had dispatched all that remained of the litter.

ROAST SUCKLING PIG CREOLE STYLE I   [720]

In New Orleans the pig is always sold killed and cleaned by the butcher.

Wash the young piglet (4 or 5 weeks old) well, cleaning and scraping the ears and nostrils thoroughly. Wash again in several changes of cold water, inside and out, shaking the piglet vigorously, head downward. Then turn upwards and pour cold water over it. Wipe dry inside and out with a coarse towel and then rub well inside with blended salt, pepper, minced parsley, thyme and powdered bay leaves. Prepare an onion stuffing as follows:

Moisten 2½ cups of soft bread crumbs in dry white wine and squeeze thoroughly. Add 1 tablespoon each of finely chopped parsley, chives and chervil, 3 large onions, grated, ½ small clove of garlic, finely grated, salt and pepper to taste, with ¼ teaspoon each of thyme, mace, sage, nutmeg and marjoram. Next add ¼ cup of butter and 3 chopped hard cooked eggs. Remember that the piglet likes black pepper and sage, so you may be generous with these two ingredients. Cook this entire mixture, in ¼ cup of butter, over a gentle flame, stirring constantly with a wooden spoon for 5 minutes. Cool, then stuff the piglet and sew up the opening securely. Be careful not to stuff too full, but leave some space for swelling and expansion. Now, truss—the *forelegs forward* and the *hind feet forward* and close under the body, secured with kitchen string. Again wipe the little animal with a damp towel, then place a corn cob in its mouth to keep it open. Rub the piglet all over the outside with butter, dredging lightly with mixed salt and black pepper aplenty. Arrange the piglet in bottom of a roasting pan; add 2 bay leaves, tied with a 3-inch piece of grated parsley root, 2 sprigs of thyme and 5 or 6 fresh leaves of sage, 3 whole cloves, 1 medium-sized onion, chopped, 1 medium-sized carrot, scraped, chopped, 1 stalk of celery, scraped, chopped, 1 small white turnip, pared and quartered, and 1 small clove of garlic, left whole. Pour over all 2 cups of rich, cold white stock (No. 185). Roast in a steady moderate oven (325–350° F.), allowing 25–30 minutes per pound, and basting frequently with the drippings from the pan. After the pig has roasted for 1 hour, quickly brush it with butter and continue roasting. When done, transfer Master Piglet to a large hot, platter; surround him with a necklace of crisp, curley parsley; remove the corn cob from his mouth and place instead a nice, rosy apple. Serve very hot with pan gravy and applesauce.

Sweet potatoes are a nice vegetable to serve with roast suckling pig. Boil a half-dozen, then peel carefully and place them whole in the gravy pan about 15–20 minutes before serving the piglet. Let them soak in the gravy; brown nicely and serve either on a separate platter or as a garnish.

ROAST SUCKLING PIG KENTUCKY STYLE II [721

Prepare a suckling pig of about 6 weeks as indicated for No. 720 stuff with the same stuffing, except instead of soaking bread crumbs in dry white wine, soak them in milk. Roast in the same way, basting fre quently. Meanwhile, boil the pig's heart and, when nearly done, add the liver. Cover pig's ears with greased paper to prevent their burning. When the pig is done, put 1 cup of butter in a square of cheesecloth and rub skin gently until all butter is used and skin is crisp. Chop the heart and liver, mix with pan gravy and some of the liquid in which heart and liver were cooked; thicken with butter kneaded with flour and serve in a gravy dish. Serve the pig very hot and carve at the table.

Stuffed or not, big or little, pig roasted on a spit over coals is the making of an outdoor feast or picnic, recalling the joys of a Kentucky or a Mississippi smoked hog party. And barbecue sandwiches share its popularity for a quick snack. Cornbread in hoecakes, in cornsticks, or in pan, is required with jowl and its accompanying green vegetable.

SCRAPPLE [722

Benjamin Franklin, who certainly appears to have been very well-fed (judging from pictures of him known to every American), refers affec tionately to Philadelphia Scrapple in his writings. Whether or no Mrs. B. Franklin, being a *town wife*, made her own scrapple, we don' know, but the majority of our ancestors on the distaff side of Revolu tionary times had a strenuous week at hog-killing time, putting the hams and sides of bacon to cure, making sausages and scrapple.

What is scrapple? It's a pork and cornmeal mixture; about 30% lean pork, 20% pork fat, 10% cornmeal, both yellow and white, salt and white pepper, sage and plenty of marjoram. First the meat is finely ground, then combined with the cornmeal, to which the spices and salt and pepper as well as herbs are added. Next the water. Then the cooking at 200° F. for 7 hours while automatic paddles stir the mass. From the 1,000-pound cooking vats the grayish gruel goes to the filling machine which feeds it into enameled cans. Scrapple was originally a Philadelphia Dutch dish called *Pawnhaus* or *Panhaus*, a mixture of cornmeal and pork trimmings. Some cook thought to add marjoram, sage and plenty of black pepper, and scrapple was born. The scrapple season was once as definite as that of the oyster. It opened the first week of September it closed the middle of March. There was no way to keep scrapple from melting down in the summertime. A few years ago, canned scrapple was introduced, giving it year-round usefulness and making it available for shipment everywhere.

Cooking Scrapple. Canned scrapple is firmer than the bulk type which makes for easy cutting or slicing. Remove both ends of the can force the scrapple out ⅜-½ inch, then slice, and repeat. Coat the slice

with seasoned flour, fine cracker crumbs, sieved dry, bread crumbs or
cornmeal to give a heavier crust and to keep the sputtering fat at a
minimum. A little bacon fat may be added to the pan if the scrapple
seems dry. Never, never turn the scrapple slices more than once lest
they break into hash. Fry crisp, over a gentle flame; drain on absorbent
paper as it is removed from the frying pan. Then heat in the oven, for
scrapple must be served very, very hot. Arranged over spinach, mashed
potatoes, peas, turnips, noodles, macaroni, spaghetti, etc, this makes a
nourishing meal. Try it on slices of fried eggplant. Philadelphians want
the tomato catsup bottle handy for a scrapple luncheon, or even breakfast, while the Pennsylvania Dutch like scrapple with brown sugar syrup
or served with poached eggs. Toward the Pacific Coast, scrapple is
served over grilled slices of canned pineapple. New Yorkers like spiced
cinnamon applesauce with a thick slice of crusty scrapple.

SPARERIBS WITH APPLE STUFFING [723]

Cook ½ cup of chopped celery, stalk and leaves and ½ cup of finely
chopped onions in ¼ cup of bacon drippings, lard or butter for 4 to 5
minutes. Core and pare 4 tart apples and slice into the celery-onion mixture; sprinkle over them ⅓ cup of sugar, with salt, pepper, a dash of
cinnamon, and ¼ teaspoon each of sage, nutmeg and thyme. Cover and
cook very slowly until apples are tender, or about 15 minutes, shaking
and rocking the pan to prevent scorching. Now add 1 cup of dry bread
or cracker crumbs, 1 cup of shredded bran, ¼ cup of finely chopped
parsley, 2 tablespoons of finely chopped chives, and ½ cup of boiling
water to which has been added 2 tablespoons of Pique Seasoning. Have
ready 2 sections of fresh pork spareribs; spread the inside of one section
(previously salted and peppered) with the apple stuffing; cover with the
other section; sew or skewer sections together; lay in an open roasting
pan, add 1 large bay leaf, a 2-inch piece of scraped parsley root, 1 sprig
of thyme, ¼ cup each of chopped onions, carrots, and celery, 6 or 7
whole peppercorns and a dash of salt. Pour over all ½ cup of meat
stock and roast in a moderate oven (325–350° F.) for 1½ hours, basting
frequently with the drippings from the pan, turning the ribs after 1 hour
of roasting. Serve with pan gravy.

SPARERIBS CROWN ROAST [724]
NEW ENGLAND STYLE

Wipe with a damp cloth 2 sections, or strips, as sometimes they are
called, of pork spareribs with a damp cloth, each about 3 inches wide
and 6 inches long, the whole weighing about 3 pounds. Sew or skewer

the ends together. Place in a roasting pan and fill center with the following stuffing:

Cook slowly in 1½ tablespoons of bacon drippings 2 tablespoons of
chopped onion until just beginning to take on a light yellow hue, add 4
cups of soft bread crumbs, 2 cups of hot, mashed potatoes, salt and pepper to taste, 1 teaspoon of poultry dressing and cook for 10 minutes
stirring constantly. Remove from the fire and stir in 2 slightly beaten
eggs. Should mixture be a little on the dry side, add a little milk. Stuff
the center of the crown with this mixture; top with a layer, about ½ inch
thick, of pork sausage meat, seasoned to taste with salt, pepper and a
little sage, and pour in bottom of roasting pan ½ cup of water. Add a
bouquet garni composed of 1 bay leaf, 6 sprigs of fresh parsley, 1 sprig
of thyme, and 2 sprigs of green celery leaves (tops), tied with white
kitchen thread also 8 peppercorns, 3 tablespoons of chopped onion and
¼ cup of chopped carrot. Roast in a moderate oven (325–350° F.) for
1¼ hours, basting every 15 minutes with the drippings from the pan.
Transfer to a hot platter, and serve with pan gravy and applesauce.

HAM [725]

To the economical and resourceful cook, ham is one of the most
thrifty of all meat buys. In the first place, its smoked and cured condition
makes keeping and storing it less of a problem. A whole ham may be
purchased at the lowest price, then cut or sliced as desired, some to be
used at once but a considerable remainder to be laid away for later use.

Wrap this left-over portion in waxed or parchment paper, and lay
away in the lower part of the refrigerator. In a week or even longer it
may appear again as a new meat. The economy angle is very important
because the price per slice out of a whole ham is just about half the
price of the same cut, if sliced off separately by the butcher.

The average weight of a good smoked ham is around 10–12 pounds
with an 11-pounder an ideal size for any family. This may be left whole,
boned, rind removed, and tied for boiling or baking. Or the ham may
be cut in half after tying, making it suitable for a smaller family. Or
again, the ham may be cut into three portions—the choice center slice
reserved for frying, baking or broiling, the butt end for boiling, and
the shank for flavoring soups, sauerkraut, peas, greens, or for made of
minced dishes. Finally, the entire ham, rind and all, may be boiled or
baked whole in the grand manner.

To the last drop or ounce of fat, and to the last sliver of meat, ham
can be utilized. Grandmothers in all ages well knew the value of the
"hambone" and prized its succulent flavor when added to greens, to
soup or to dried beans as well as fresh vegetables. So, too, should her
modern daughters appreciate the flavor-giving qualities of even a simple
ham shank, or the bones, cracked open, as soup ingredients.

Much of the pleasure in eating ham dishes depends on the manner
and thickness of slicing it. Sliced 1 inch thick, we have a ham steak

ideal for oven braising, broiling or baking. This simple cooking method deserves wider use, for when a sauce of milk, fruit juice, cider or wine is added during the baking, we have a most delectable dish.

Like beefsteak, this ham-steak is excellent for service with mushrooms; with a border of grilled sweet potatoes or with nicely browned mashed potatoes, noodles or hot boiled rice. But sliced very thin, as thin as the proverbial "paper" or "wafer" thinness, we have ham in its epicurean form, delicate enough for the invalid's tray.

Ham is one meat equally suited to service at all meals—breakfast, lunch and dinner, as well as that late evening occasion, the supper party. Ham for breakfast is a popular choice with all men. Ham for lunch is equally acceptable. Ham for dinner often heads the cook's shopping list.

Some hams need to be boiled before roasting or baking. Others are partially cooked during the smoking and their cooking can be completed satisfactorily by roasting. Still others are entirely cooked and can be served cold without further treatment, or may be glazed and baked half an hour or so. Beside all of these types, we also have those which are known as Smithfield-type hams, which need to be soaked before being boiled.

Besides the smoked ham proper, which is fresh ham cured and smoked, and which is sold either with the skin on or skinned; whole, in half or in slice, there are numerous other pieces of smoked pork, such as the *loin*, which is the tenderloin with bones removed, cured and smoked; the *picnic ham*, which is the entire shoulder with shank on; the *Boston butt*, which is square, and cut right above the shoulder; the *Cala ham*, which is the smoked shoulder; the *Cala butt*, which is the entire shoulder with shank removed; the *cottage ham*, which is the boned Boston butt. This last should not be confused with pork tenderloin, which it resembles in shape. It may be boiled or baked like a large ham. Since it averages 3–4½ pounds in weight, it is a good choice for small families.

BAKED HAM GOURMET   [726]

Remove the wrapping from a 10–12-pound precooked ham, but do not remove the rind. Rewrap it in the glassine wrapper and place it on a rack in an open baking pan, fat side up. Roast it in a slow oven (300° F.) allowing 18 minutes to the pound and basting frequently with equal parts of hot water and butter. An hour before the ham is done, remove the wrapping and the rind, score the fat and stud it with whole cloves. Cover the ham with brown sugar (using about ¾ cup), and sprinkle over the sugar 3 tablespoons of fine brandy. Continue baking in a slow oven, basting frequently, from now on, with the syrup from a can of sweet pickled cherries. When done and ready to serve, garnish the ham with whole cherries stuck on with cloves, and serve garnished with Orange-Cherry Cups; for these, drain the juice from a No. 2 can of red cherries. Mix and bring to a boil ¾ cup of brown sugar, ¾ cup of granulated sugar, ½ cup of tarragon vinegar, ¼ cup of cherry juice and ¼ cup of sherry wine. Add an inch stick of cinnamon and 24 whole cloves, then add the drained cherries, and cook very gently for 18–20 minutes, stirring occasionally, or till the juice is syrupy. Cool and serve in orange peel cups. Small creamed onions and seven-minute cabbage are the usual accompaniments to this dish.

BARBECUED HAM SLICES BELMONT STYLE   [727]

Place in a small saucepan 2½ tablespoons of butter, ½ cup of tomato catsup, ½ cup of French dressing, 2 teaspoons of chili powder (more or less, according to taste), ⅓ cup of lemon juice, 1 tablespoon of prepared mustard, 1 teaspoon of Worcestershire sauce, 1 tablespoon of drained, then ground prepared horseradish, with salt to taste. Bring to a boil, let cook 2 minutes, then brush generously one side of 6 individual ham slices with the sauce; place, dripping, on broiler rack about 3 inches below a moderate flame, and broil 3 minutes; turn, brush the other sides with, sauce and continue broiling until done, which may be seen when ham takes on a deep brown color. Serve the ham over a layer of Risotto Milanaise (No. 1599).

BOILED HAM—PRELIMINARY   [728]
PREPARATION

A whole ham, other than a pre-cooked one, should be placed in a large vessel of water, thoroughly washed and scrubbed, then soaked overnight. Next day it is placed in fresh cold water without any seasoning, spices, condiments or vegetables, unless otherwise indicated, and slowly brought to a boil. The temperature is then lowered and the ham allowed to simmer very gently until done, allowing from 18–20 minutes to the pound. A whole ham is cooked when the pelvic bone can be easily removed or becomes loose and protrudes.

The slower the simmering the better the flavor will be. This slow cooking process has for its purpose the extracting of that eminently sapid part of the meat which is soluble in cold water. It is distinguished from the extractive part, which only renders its juice when subjected to the boiling process. If the water is allowed to boil too hard, the meat will shrink and become hard and tough. Ham may be boiled in other liquids such as cider, wine, meat stock, milk, buttermilk, etc. If the ham is all to be sliced cold, let it cool in the liquor or broth in which it was cooked. It is then ready to bake or roast. A good grade of sugar-cured ham need not be first boiled, but it should be soaked overnight, well washed, then placed in a covered roasting or braising pan, enough water or other indicated liquid added, the cover adjusted and the ham baked in a moderate oven (350–375° F.), allowing 30 minutes for each pound of meat.

When done, remove the ham from the oven and take off the rind, leaving about ¼ of an inch of fat over the entire surface. Cover with 1 generous teaspoon of dry mustard mixed with 1 tablespoon of prepared mustard, then pour over the ham a cup of fruit juice, such as orange, pineapple, or grapefruit, and return to the oven (uncovered) to brown, basting frequently with the liquid from the pan. This is the Old Plantation Method greatly used in the South.

BRAISED HAM IN RED WINE [729]
CALIFORNIA METHOD

Select a small ham neither too lean nor too fat. Scrub, then soak it overnight. Next day, place in a large kettle of cold water and cook as indicated for Recipe No. 728, "Boiled Ham—Preliminary Preparation." Take 1½ quarts of strong broth or failing this, use 1¼ quarts of boiling water and ⅓ cup of Pique Seasoning, and 1 bottle (a fifth) of red California wine, 1 tablespoon of brown sugar, 4 whole cloves and 6 very small onions. Bring these to a boil; let boil up three or four times, then strain over the ham (the rind removed) in the roasting pan. Bake in a moderate oven, basting frequently, at least every 15 minutes, for 45 minutes or until the ham is brown and glossy. Transfer ham to a hot platter. Strain the sauce remaining in the pan; add 1 teaspoon of lemon juice, and ½ generous cup of Madeira wine. Heat thoroughly without boiling and serve in a gravy boat. If desired, a very little browned flour may be added to thicken the sauce, but it is preferable not to thicken it.

Substitute sherry wine for Madeira wine, if preferred. Cider may be used instead of red wine.

BRAISED HAM IN RED WINE [730]
FRENCH STYLE

Have the butcher saw off the protruding bone of a 10–12-pound ham. Soak ham in clear water overnight after first scrubbing and rinsing it in several changes of water. Place in a large kettle containing enough rapidly boiling water to generously cover, adding 12 whole peppercorns, slightly bruised; let boil violently for 15 minutes, then reduce the heat and simmer gently, allowing 18–20 minutes per pound.

Let the ham cool in its own liquor or broth. One hour before serving, remove the rind carefully and trim off any superfluous fat evenly with a sharp thin-bladed knife, leaving about ½ scant inch of fat over the surface. Criss-cross the fat and place ham in a braising kettle. Pour over it a bottle (fifth) of good red wine, either burgundy or Bordeaux type. Do not add any seasoning, condiments, or vegetables, do not cover. Let cook gently, in a moderately hot oven (325° F.), turning often but not basting, till the meat takes on a dark reddish-brown color.

Meanwhile prepare the following gravy: Melt 3 tablespoons of ham fat; blend in 2½ tablespoons of flour; gradually and slowly, while stirring constantly, pour in 1 cup of the hot ham liquor, alternately with 1 cup of red wine. Stir till gravy thickens, then stir in ½ cup of the red wine from the baking pan. Boil gently a few minutes; strain through a fine-meshed sieve; taste for seasoning, adding salt and pepper as needed. Transfer to a heated platter; slice enough for service; reshape; pour over it part of the gravy, and serve the remainder separately, with buttered broccoli and plain boiled small potato balls, rolled in butter, then in finely chopped chervil or parsley.

COLD HAM PLATTER SUGGESTIONS   [731]

(1) Sliced ham, cole slaw, tomato slices and assorted pickles.

(2) Ham sandwiches, deviled eggs, potato chips and pickle fans.

(3) Cold ham, asparagus tips à la Vinaigrette, radishes and scallions.

(4) Cold ham cornucopias, chutney, jellied vegetable salad and olives.

(5) Jellied ham mousse, lettuce and tomato slices, mayonnaise dressing.

(6) Cold ham loaf slices, vegetable salad, pickle relish, radishes.

(7) Cold baked ham slices, cucumber salad, pickle relish, ripe olives.

(8) Cold baked rolls filled with corn relish, stuffed tomatoes, shredded cabbage.

(9) Potato salad with diced ham, tomato slices with mustard mayonnaise, olives.

(10) Sliced baked ham in red wine, cheese-stuffed eggs, cole slaw, green olives.

(11) Sliced ham and assorted sliced sausages, tossed green salad, hard-cooked egg slices on tomato slices, potato chips.

(12) Ham, chicken and swiss cheese club sandwiches, stuffed eggs, gherkin fans, red cabbage and apple slaw.

CREAMED HAM IN RICE BORDER   [732]

Prepare a rice border as indicated for Recipe No. 1593. In the meantime, melt 3 tablespoons of butter or margarine; blend in 2½ tablespoons of flour, and gradually add 1½ cups of scalded milk, stirring constantly until sauce is smooth and reaches boiling point; season with a few grains of nutmeg, salt and pepper to taste, and stir in 1¾ cups of cubed, cooked lean ham. Remove from the fire, stir in 2 egg yolks slightly beaten with 2 tablespoons of sherry wine, and heat to a boil, stirring constantly from the bottom of the pan. Unmold the rice border on a hot, round platter; fill center with creamed ham, dust with a little finely chopped parsley and serve immediately.

Variations: Substitute spinach noodles or spaghetti for rice. If desired, add 1 teaspoon of curry to the rice.

Two prepared hams were the usual fee charged by some New England schools in 1760 in exchange for a course in arithmetic.

FRUITED HAM STEAK PLATTER DINNER [733]

Broil a 1-inch center slice ham weighing about 2 generous pounds, in the usual way, for 5–6 minutes on each side, brushing it frequently with butter. Transfer to a hot, round platter and decorate with cloves which have been rolled in cooking oil, surround with half pineapple rings, fried in butter and topped with apricot halves, the hollows filled with minted applesauce. Garnish with bouquets of crisp watercress dipped in paprika and slightly shaken to remove the surplus. Serve at once with French fried potatoes and a Broccoli Soufflé (No. 1200).

GLAZED BAKED HAM [734]

The purpose of glazing is to add lustre, to give the ham the effect and the appetizing appearance of "glaze." Many are puzzled when seeing tempting glazed, shining ham or other meats or poultry in some restaurant or in a delicatessen window, and often wonder how this may be done. It is a very simple and rapid operation.

After having removed the rind from a boiled ham, and trimmed the fat neatly, so as to leave a thickness of about a scant half inch on the ham, proceed as follows:

Sprinkle granulated sugar or brown sugar evenly all over the surface of the prepared ham, and set the pan in a very hot oven (425–450° F.). The sugar will mingle and melt instantly with the fat, caramelizing at once and enrobing the ham with a golden dark-brown, appetizing coating of crackling morsels which will add extra flavor to that of the ham itself.

For added effect, criss-cross lines into the fat with a sharp knife, in the form of checkerboard, or lattice-work. Stick 1 whole clove into each lozenge of fat, sprinkle with sugar as indicated above, then glaze.

For greater piquancy, dilute 1 tablespoon of dry mustard (more or less, according to taste) with a little water, fruit juice, sherry or Madeira wine; brush the entire surface of the prepared ham fat with this mixture, then sprinkle with sugar as indicated above. Or brush the ham fat with slightly melted Anchovy Butter (No. 979) before sprinkling with the sugar. This will add a puzzling nutty, tangy flavor. Peanut butter may be substituted. Or you may brush the entire surface of the ham with honey, marmalade, or maple syrup and bake.

GLAZED HAM LOAF RAISIN SAUCE   [735]

Put through food chopper 1 pound of cooked lean ham, ½ pound of left-over cooked pork or, lacking pork, use an equal amount of cooked left-over carefully boned chicken meat. Place in a mixing bowl and add ¾ cup of milk, mixed with 1 large egg slightly beaten, mixing well. Next add ½ cup of bread crumbs, moistened with ½ cup of left-over gravy or, lacking it, ½ cup of cold water and 3 tablespoons of Pique Seasoning. Season highly with mixed salt and pepper, ⅛ teaspoon each of thyme, nutmeg, mace, marjoram, and sage. Mix thoroughly. Pack mixture in a 5 by 8-inch loaf pan, and bake 1½ hours in a moderate oven (375° F.), basting every 15 minutes with the following glaze: Put in a saucepan ¼ cup of cider vinegar, ¼ cup of water and ¾ cup of brown sugar. Boil together for 10 minutes. Transfer the loaf to a hot platter, garnish with watercress, and serve with Raisin Sauce (No. 1108).

HAM AND APPLE PIE   [736]
NEW ENGLAND STYLE

Cut 2 pounds of cooked ham into small pieces convenient for serving; pare and core 4 or 5 tart apples, and slice them not too thin. Arrange ⅓ of ham in a deep greased baking dish; cover with ⅓ of the apple slices, and sprinkle with a little brown sugar (amount of sugar depends on tartness of apples), mixed salt, pepper and cinnamon to taste; then dot with 1 tablespoon of butter or margarine. Repeat with another layer of ham, apple, brown sugar, seasonings and butter, continuing till ham and apple slices are all used, having a layer of apple on top. Now pour over all 2 tablespoons of lemon juice and ¼ cup of hard cider. Cook, covered, in a moderate oven until apples are almost tender (about 20 minutes); uncover and pour over, the following pancake batter:

Beat 1 large egg slightly; add ½ cup of cold, sweet milk, 2 tablespoons of melted shortening, and gradually stir in ¾ cup of sifted bread flour, beating briskly until smooth. Bake. uncovered, in a moderate oven

(325° F.) for about 25 minutes or until crust is nicely browned. Serve warm from the baking dish.

HAM BAKED IN RYE CRUST RUSSIAN STYLE   [737]

Scrub, soak overnight, then boil a 10-pound ham until tender as directed for Recipe No. 728; let stand until cool enough to remove the rind and any excess fat, then set aside while preparing the dough as follows:

Mix 4 pounds of rye flour with enough cold beef bouillon, carefully skimmed of all fat, to make a thick dough. Roll out to a scant half inch in thickness on a slightly floured board. Brush the dough with brandy or vodka, then sprinkle over it ½ cup of finely chopped fines herbes, such as parsley, chervil, chives, tarragon herb, shallots, onion, garlic, sage, and nutmeg, all well blended. Scatter over these 1 teaspoon of caraway seeds. Wrap the dough tightly around the ham, and bake in a moderate oven (325° F.) for 50 minutes, or until crust is thoroughly baked and brown. Break the crust and serve as an ordinary ham with Madeira Sauce (No. 1076) and Applesauce, this last mixed with a little drained horseradish.

HAM BUTT AND SAUERKRAUT DINNER   [738]

Sauerkraut is an age-old food and was not originated in Germany, as is commonly believed. It dates back to the building of the Great Wall of China, when the laborers ate it to combat deficiency diseases resulting from a diet consisting almost wholly of rice.

Wash 1 lean smoked pork butt (1¾–2½) pounds quickly in cold water; put in a stew pot with ⅓ cup of onions, sliced, 1 large bay leaf tied with 1 sprig of thyme and 8 sprigs of fresh parsley, also 1 tablespoon of sugar and 2 quarts of water. Bring slowly to a boil and boil steadily for 5 minutes; reduce the heat to very moderate, and continue boiling till tender or about 1½ hours, almost entirely covered with the lid. Remove from the fire and let stand, covered, for 5 minutes. In a second kettle or saucepan simmer 1½–1¾ pounds of sauerkraut with 1 medium-sized onion, thinly sliced, 2 tart apples, pared, cored and thinly sliced, 2 whole cloves, ⅓ teaspoon of caraway seeds, and 3 cups of the broth in which butt was boiled. Cook gently for about ¾ hour, then stir in 1 small raw potato, grated, a dozen whole peppercorns, with a very little salt, if needed, and boil gently till mixture is slightly thickened with the raw potato. Mound the well-drained sauerkraut in the center of a heated deep platter; drain the ham butt; slice crosswise neatly, using a very sharp knife; arrange the kraut, and border with fluffy, well-seasoned mashed white potatoes (or plain boiled potatoes, which may be cooked over the kraut for 30 minutes, or till tender). Serve with mustard and pickles.

HAM CASSEROLE BOURGEOISE   [739]

Arrange a thin layer of sliced potatoes in an earthenware casserole which has been rubbed with a piece of ham fat; cover with 6 individual portions of cooked ham and season with mixed salt, pepper and a dash each of sage, nutmeg, marjoram and thyme. Next arrange over the ham a layer of 3 sliced hard-cooked eggs mixed with ¾ cup of thinly sliced fresh mushrooms, using both stems and caps. Pour over all 1¼ cups of thick sour cream, and lastly add 1 large bay leaf and 1 or 2 whole cloves. Cover and bake in a moderate oven (350–375° F.) for 35 minutes. Uncover, sprinkle with ½ cup of bread crumbs mixed with an equal amount of grated cheese (any desired kind), and continue baking till crumbs are browned and cheese bubbling. Serve right from the casserole.

HAM HOT POT   [740]

Melt 3 tablespoons of butter; blend in 2½ tablespoons of flour, then gradually stir in 2 cups of meat stock or, failing that, 1½ cups of boiling water mixed with ½ cup of Pique Seasoning, stirring constantly. When smooth and well blended, stir in 1½ teaspoon of curry power, mixed with a little cold water, and mix thoroughly. Boil up once, remove from the fire and add 1¾ cups of cold, cooked, lean ham cubes, 1 can of small mushroom buttons, 6 large green olives, pitted, and 1 cup of freshly shelled peas. Season with salt and pepper, add 1 large bay leaf and cover. Cook in a moderately hot oven (375° F.), for 45 minutes. Remove from the oven, taste for seasoning and, when ready to serve, stir in 1 tablespoon of butter (added bit by bit) and 1 tablespoon of chopped parsley. Serve with plain boiled rice.

HAM MOUSSE I   [741]
(Hot)

This may be made with Virginia, Kentucky, or Vermont Ham. Remove all gristle from lean cooked ham. Chop sufficient to make two cups. Put through food chopper three times, then to ensure smoothness and fineness, rub through a fine-meshed sieve. This is usually done by pounding to a paste, in a mortar with a pestle but American kitchens rarely have mortars, so one must use the meat grinder. While rubbing through the sieve, add 2 egg yolks, slightly beaten with a small pinch of nutmeg, white pepper, a very few grains of cayenne, and a little salt. Now stir in 1 cup of heavy sweet cream, slightly beaten (heavy cream sauce may be used instead of sweet cream, but the flavor, the "finesse" of the finished product, will not be the same, and using cream sauce, omit the egg yolks), alternately with a pony of good dry sherry wine; then fold in very gently, 2 stiffly beaten egg whites, also seasoned with a very little salt.

Next, fill a buttered mold, soufflé dish, or baking dish suitable for table service. Set the dish in a pan containing hot, but not boiling water, and bake in a moderate oven (300–325° F.) until top is firm, or about 30–35 minutes. If baked in individual ramekins or casseroles, 20 minutes will suffice. When firm, slide the blade of a knife around the dish and unmold on a hot platter; garnish with watercress and serve with Hollandaise Sauce (No. 1062).

HAM MOUSSE II   [742]
(Cold)

The same basic formula, the same ingredients and the same directions are used for a cold ham mousse as indicated above (No. 741). This may be prepared ahead of time, even several days in advance, *except* that you omit one of the egg yolks and add 1 tablespoon of plain granulated gelatine which has been soaked 5 minutes in a very little cold water or ham broth.

For a formal occasion, a family dinner party, or a Sunday dinner, where appearance is of some importance, and also for piquancy in flavor, some sliced or fancifully cut green of leeks, minced nut meats with skin removed, chives, parsley leaves, or celery, fancifully cut hard-cooked egg white, black or green olives, etc., all cut in fancy shape with those French cutters, also cut truffles—almost anything that fancy, taste or imagination may suggest—may be added in the preliminary operation, that is, molding.

Cold mousse made out of any kind of edible, cooked food is most effective at table when there is clever double molding with aspic, or gelatine, to give a jacket of amber crystal jelly or colored aspic such as tomato for instance, and there may be decorations, also of the same ingredients as indicated above, cut in ornamental shapes, with the little fancy French vegetable cutters.

HAM AND RICE CASSEROLE   [743]

Wash 1 cup of rice and cook until tender, but rather on the underdone side as indicated for boiled rice No. 1582, using either of the three methods. Lay the rice in a buttered casserole, arrange over it 6 individual portion-sized slices of cold, cooked ham; sprinkle over 1 cup of thinly sliced fresh mushrooms; dot with 4 tablespoons of butter; season to taste with salt, pepper and a little nutmeg, and moisten with 1 scant cup of meat stock. Cover, and bake in a moderate oven (375° F.) for 35 minutes. Serve right from the casserole.

HAM STEAK BAKED IN MILK, COUNTRY [744] CLUB STYLE

Lay a 2½-pound slice of uncooked ham in a buttered baking dish, first spreading it on both sides with a little prepared mustard, then with 1 teaspoon of brown sugar (optional). Over this pour 1½ cups of medium sour cream, seasoned to taste with salt and white pepper; cover and bake 40 minutes, turning the ham once when half done. Transfer to a heated platter, thicken the cream with a little flour and pour over the ham. Serve with boiled greens, buttered carrots, and either freshly made baking powder biscuits or hot Kentucky corn bread.

Do you know that "left hams" are tenderer than "right hams"? There is a restaurant in Richmond, Virginia, which advertises that it serves only "left hams" and explains it thus: "A pig can use only his left leg to scratch himself. Therefore, the meat on the left ham is firmer, tenderer and not so fat; also there is less shrinkage in the cooking. Pigs rub themselves against the pen when the right side itches, but they scratch themselves with the left foot when the left side itches. It's the extra exercise that makes the left ham so much tenderer." Don't ask me why a pig can't scratch himself with his right leg!

HAM STEAKS CREOLE   [745]

Score a 3-pound piece of ham a full inch thick and place in a pan of cold water; bring gradually to a boil, and let boil 4 or 5 minutes; drain, discarding the water. Place the ham in an earthenware baking dish first rubbed with a cut clove of garlic, and add 3 green peppers, halved, seeded, and thinly sliced, 2 large onions, peeled, and thinly sliced, ⅓ pound of fresh mushrooms, peeled and sliced, using both stems and caps, 1½ dozen large green olives, pitted and sliced, 1 No. 2 can of tomatoes, 1 bouquet garni, composed of 1 large bay leaf, 1 sprig of fresh thyme, 10 sprigs of fresh parsley, and 1 sprig of green celery greens (top), all tied with kitchen thread, 2 whole cloves and 1 clove of garlic. Season generously with pepper, and lightly with salt, cover closely and bake

1½ hours in a moderate oven (350° F.). Taste for seasoning, stir in 2 tablespoons of butter, discard the bouquet garni, and serve right from the casserole. The ham is cut, steak-fashion, returned to the casserole and the casserole passed around. Wild rice cooked in milk (No. 1603) is the usual accompaniment of this one dish meal.

HAM SOUFFLÉ [746]

This is a good way to use a little left-over cooked ham. Mix 1 cup of ground lean, cooked ham with 1¼ cups of medium-white sauce, then stir in 3 well-beaten egg yolks, seasoned with ⅛ teaspoon each of white pepper, nutmeg, sage and thyme and ¼ teaspoon of salt, 1 tablespoon of grated onion, and 1 tablespoon of finely chopped parsley. Lastly fold in 3 stiffly beaten egg whites. Turn into a buttered soufflé dish, and bake in a hot oven (400° F.) for 20–25 minutes, or till soufflé is well puffed and slightly brown. Serve at once with or without a side dish of Egg Sauce (Nos. 1051–52).

HAM STEAK EPICURE [747]

Rub a 3-pound slice of ham with 1 tablespoon of brown sugar mixed with ⅛ teaspoon of ground cloves and ⅛ teaspoon of powdered sage. Place in a well greased baking dish which has first been rubbed with a cut clove of garlic: cover it with 6 slices of canned, drained pineapple, carefully-pour over ½ cup of beef broth or meat stock, mixed with ½ cup of red port wine; add 1 tablespoon of butter, creamed with ½ teaspoon of flour, 1 large bay leaf, tied with a 2-inch piece of scraped parsley root and 1 sprig of thyme and 2 cloves, 6 thin slices of onion, 8 peppercorns, and a dash—very little—of salt. Cover and bake in a moderate oven (375° F.) for 1 hour, turning the meat once during the baking process. Transfer the ham to a hot platter; strain the sauce through a fine sieve into a saucepan, and reduce it to about ½ cup, over a bright fire, then stir in 1 cup of scalded sour cream, boil up once and taste for seasoning. Pour part of the sauce over the ham, and serve the remainder separately, with small boiled potato balls rolled first in melted butter, then in finely chopped chives.

HAM STEAK GOURMET [748]
Mock Ham Venison Chasseur

Trim and wipe with a damp cloth 1 center slice of ham of about 3 pounds weight and a full inch thick. Place the steak in a shallow pan, add 2 tablespoons of chopped shallots, 1 teaspoon of chopped onion, 2 tablespoons of peeled, chopped fresh mushrooms, 1 blade of garlic, mashed, ⅛ teaspoon each of thyme, mace, marjoram, clove and nutmeg. Cover with milk, and let stand overnight in the refrigerator. Be sure that the meat is well covered with the milk. Next day, drain, wipe the ham, place in a buttered baking dish having a tight-fitting cover, add ½ cup of red port wine, with ½ teaspoon of grated lemon rind, 1 bay leaf, tied with 6 sprigs of fresh parsley and 1 sprig of thyme, using white kitchen thread, 1 whole clove, 1 small juniper berry, crushed, 12 black olives, stoned, 12 very small white onions, peeled and left whole, salt and pepper to taste, and pour over half of the unstrained marinade. Cover and bake 1¼ hours without disturbing, except to turn the meat after 35 minutes of cooking. Transfer the ham to a hot platter, slice it into 6 portions and reshape. Strain the sauce from the baking dish into a saucepan, bring to a boil; return the olives and onions to it, taste for seasoning, and pour over the ham. Garnish with watercress and thin slices of orange.

HAM STEAK MONTMORENCY   [749]

With a damp cloth wipe a 2¾–3-pound ham steak cut from center of ham. Rub with mixed salt and black pepper and brown quickly on both sides, under the flame of the broiling oven. Transfer to a casserole, add ½ cup of strained canned cherry juice, 2 thin slices of lemon, 1 bay leaf, 1 whole clove, 1 blade of garlic, 4 thin slices of a medium-sized onion, 2 tablespoons of finely chopped fresh mushrooms, salt and pepper to taste. Pour over all ½ cup of red wine, cover and bake in a moderate oven (350–375° F.) for 1¼ hours, turning the meat after 25–30 minutes of baking. Remove the ham to a heated platter; slice slantwise as you would a club beef steak, and reshape. Strain the gravy from the baking dish into a small saucepan; taste for seasoning, stir in 1 tablespoon of butter creamed with ½ teaspoon of flour and anchovy paste, the size of a pea. Bring to a boil, let boil up 2 or 3 times, and stir in ¾ cup of the drained canned cherries. Pour half of this sauce over the carved ham, and serve the remainder separately.

HAM STEAK MOSCOVITE   [750]

Have ready 1½ cups of hot Sauce Smitane (No. 1123), to which has been added 1 teaspoon of curry powder, previously moistened with a very little milk. Pan-fry 6 individual ham steaks each weighing about 6 ounces, turning frequently. Drain well, transfer to a shallow platter,

nd pour over them the hot sauce. Dust with finely chopped parsley
nd serve at once with a dish of plain boiled rice.

Apples, flavored with maple syrup, honey or molasses, and baked,
re good with roast ham.

IAM TENDERLOIN, PRUNE SAUCE   [751]

Simmer one 2–2½-pound smoked pork tenderloin (previously wiped
ith a damp cloth) with 2 quarts of cold water; 1 large onion, thinly
liced; 1 celery stalk, scraped, then cut into ½-inch pieces; 1 medium-
ized carrot, scraped, cut into small pieces, 1 white turnip, pared, quar-
ered, 1 pound of green cabbage, carefully washed and left whole, 1
mall leek, halved lengthwise and carefully washed; 1 bouquet garni
omposed of 1 large bay leaf, 8 sprigs of parsley, 1 sprig of green celery
reen, and 1 sprig of thyme, all tied with kitchen thread. Season lightly
ith salt and add 7 or 8 peppercorns. Allow 30–35 minutes to the pound,
ounting this from the time water boils, then is reduced to the simmering
oint. Take out the tenderloin and set aside the stock and vegetables
or soup. Slice the tenderloin into serving portions and keep hot while
aking the prune sauce as follows:

Combine 1 teaspoon of cornstarch, ⅓ cup of brown sugar, ¼ scant
easpoon of salt and 1 cup of prune juice in a small saucepan, and cook
ver a gentle flame, stirring constantly from the bottom of the pan until
ixture just begins to thicken. Remove from the fire, stir in 3 table-
poons of sherry wine and ⅔ cup of diced cooked prunes, pitted; return
o the fire and cook until the mixture is thick. Remove from the fire, stir
2 tablespoons of canned, drained, shredded pineapple, ½ generous tea-
poon of grated lemon rind, and taste for seasoning.

Serve part of the sauce over the sliced tenderloin and the remainder
eparately with a side dish of cooked spinach.

IZZA RUSTICA or ITALIAN HAM AND   [752]
AUSAGE PIE

Cut 1 pound of Italian ham and 1 pound of Italian sausage into small
ieces. Beat 6 eggs in a large bowl; stir in 2 pounds of ricotta cheese. This
ch, creamy, very delicate and fragrant cheese is made from the butter-
ilk of ewes. It is eaten either as ordinary pot cheese or like the French
ream cheese, with a little sugar. It is found in almost all Italian stores,
oth grocery and delicatessen). When smooth, stir in ¼ cup of grated
armesan cheese, ¼ teaspoon of ground cinnamon and 1 teaspoon of
inced parsley with salt and pepper to taste. Line a 9-inch pie plate with

pastry, turn in the filling; cover with a top crust; make several holes i
this with the tines of a fork; brush with cold milk, and bake in a very hc
oven (450° F.) for 5–6 minutes; reduce the heat to moderate (350° F
or even lower (300° F.), and continue baking 45 minutes longer, or unt
a nice golden brown. Serve hot or cold.

UPSIDE-DOWN HAM LOAF HOME STYLE   [75:
A popular old-fashioned plantation dish

Combine 2 cups of ground ham, 1½ pounds of ground fresh pork, an
2 slightly beaten eggs; also 2 tablespoons each of onion, parsley, gree
pepper and chives, all very finely chopped. Add 1 cup of milk, season t
taste with salt, pepper, thyme, mace and nutmeg and mix well Grea:
a large bread pan generously, and pour in ¾ cup of brown sugar, whic
has been mixed with 1 teaspoon of dry mustard and ¼ cup of cid
vinegar. Over this sugar mixture, press 6 slices of fresh or canned pin
apple, and fill cavity of each pineapple slice with a spoonful of red currar
jelly. Pack down the meat mixture over this, place 6–8 slices of bacc
over the top, and bake in a moderate oven (350–375° F.) for 1–1½ hour
covering the bacon with a greased paper if browning too fast. Lift o
the bacon, invert the pan over a long, hot platter; drain off all the bacc
fat carefully before removing the pan, also let stand a minute or s
before lifting the pan. Garnish with the bacon, some pickles, olives an
radish roses, and serve with a green salad. The loaf is so moist that
needs no gravy.

VIRGINIA HAM ROAST   [75·

Cover a Virginia ham with cold water and let soak overnight. Ne:
day, scrub with a stiff brush, rinse thoroughly, place the ham in a larg
long kettle and pour over boiling water to generously cover. Simm·
gently, allowing 18 minutes to the pound, adding also 1 large onio:
quartered, 1 small bunch of fresh parsley, 3 sprigs of green celery leave
15 peppercorns, 3 bay leaves, ½ scant teaspoon of thyme leaves, an
5 or 6 cloves. When cooked, let the ham cool in its own liquor until luk
warm; then place on a board and peel off the rind, using care not to te:
the fat.   Rub the fat with a good ½ cup of brown sugar, mixed with
cup of freshly grated bread crumbs. Stud the surface liberally with who
cloves. Place the ham in a large baking pan and pour around it 1 quart·
cider, or a pint of sherry wine, Madeira wine, or good Burgundy wine, ·
grape juice. Place in a hot oven (400° F.) and roast, basting frequentl
for about 25–30 minutes or until ham acquires an appetizing brown glaz
Thicken the gravy and serve separately with sweet potatoes either pla:
boiled, baked or baked in corn syrup.

Chapter Seven

VARIETY MEATS

Cradle rocking is no longer good practice but the hand that wields the ladle still rules the world. Through her ability to turn out nourishing, appetizing food, the homemaker satisfied not only the stomach but the senses as well. Food that is agreeable to the taste and that is tempting through its well-seasoned aroma has a definite reaction upon disposition and digestion. Both can be made more agreeable to live with by the homemaker who uses her seasonings and her ladle skillfully. A fragrant calf's brain in black butter, a grilled liver steak, a dish of ox-tongue sauce piquante, or a sweetbread in patty shells with mushrooms and a delightful cream sauce—all variety meats are bound to bring smiling faces to the table, for their aroma will advertise their deliciousness even before they are tasted.

GUIDE TO THE PURCHASE AND PREPARATION OF SUNDRY AND VARIETY MEATS [755]

NAME	CHARACTERISTICS	COOKING METHODS
BRAINS Calf, lamb, pork, beef	Very tender, soft in consistency, of delicate flavor, must be strictly fresh. Very perishable.	Precook to help make and keep firm. Then carefully wash and rinse in cold water. Then braise, bake, fry, in soufflé, fritters, custard, etc.
DRIED BEEF	Very tender, soft in consistency, fine, delicate flavor, combines well with starchy foods. Requires pre-soaking. Keeps well.	Soak, then cream, in fritters, bake with macaroni, noodles, etc., in casserole, chow mein, etc.
FEET Calf, sheep, pork	Very little meat, but rich flavor makes up for the small quantity. Very savory and tender meat. Requires long, slow cooking in salted water as initial preparation.	Precook to tenderize. Then pickle, in jelly, broil, stew, in casserole, devil, bake, etc.
HEARTS Calf, lamb, or mutton, beef, pork	Muscular organ which has had considerable exercise. Deserves to be better known and more used. Requires long, slow cooking. Beef heart has most waste. Sold by the pound. High percentage edible.	Bake, stew, in sour cream, braise, stuff, in casserole, loaf, pot roast, patties, etc.
KIDNEYS Calf, sheep, pork, beef	Considered great delicacy. High food value. Need a strong and long salt bath, particularly beef and mutton kidneys, to take away strong taste. Very popular. Veal kidneys are most expensive; lamb come next; beef and pork cost about the same.	Bake, in casserole, broil, stew, cream, en brochette, etc.
LIVERS Calf, sheep, pork, beef	Beef liver largest and least tender. All have same high food value, except that pork is highest in iron. Requires scalding and slow, short cooking.	Bake, stew, roast, terrapin, casserole, pan-fry, broil, en brochette, cream, curry, etc.
SAUSAGES I. Fresh pork	Made of selected fresh pork cuts chopped fine, highly seasoned, usually with thyme and sage. Links of different sizes; bulk pork sausage. Must be thoroughly done. Those labeled "pure pork," contain neither cereal nor filler. Marketed in a variety of ways: Pound boxes contains 16 links. Oblong patties without casings, 12 to a pound, etc.	Bake, boil, casserole, scrapple, with noodles, spaghetti, sauerkraut, in loaf, rolls, cobbler, cakes, etc.

GUIDE TO THE PURCHASE AND PREPARA-　[755]
TION OF SUNDRY AND VARIETY MEATS

NAME	CHARACTERISTICS	COOKING METHODS
SAUSAGES II. Smoked sausages	Made of selected cuts of beef or pork, or both, chopped fine and mixed with spices. Stuffed into casings, cooked, brined, and then subjected to hardwood smoke. Frankfurters, Bologna, Cooked Thuringer, Mettwurst, etc. Require reheating only, usually in water at simmering stage.	Frankfurters may be baked, boiled, roasted, served in casserole, with alimentary pastes, beans, sauerkraut, etc. The others may be served in the same ways or plain
III. Dry or "summer" sausages. Available all year	Made of pork and beef, or both, chopped, seasoned, cured, stuffed into casings. Some are then smoked and dried; other varieties dried without smoking. Two divisions of dry sausages: Salamis and cervelats. There are both hard and soft cervelats and salamis. Keep indefinitely in a cool place. Examples: Genoa salami, Gothaer cervelat, Goettinger cervelat, Pepperoni, Thuringer cervelat, Mortedella, Landgaeger, Lyon saucisson, etc.	Are ready to serve, sliced for sandwiches or added to various other dishes as a garnish. Used as appetizers, etc.
IV. Cooked specialties	Prepared meat products. Cooked, seasoned in variety of ways. Made from beef, pork, and veal, and tongue and liver. Examples: Minced ham, deviled ham, veal loaf, liver loaf, Braunschweiger, meat loaf, etc.	Ready to serve as a garnish, as appetizers, in sandwiches, etc.
SWEETBREADS Calf, beef, lamb	Considered a great delicacy. Tender. Thymus gland of calf, young steer and lambs. Thymus gland of calf divided into two parts: Heart and throat sweetbreads.	Precooked, then ready to be baked, broiled, en casserole, served in patty shells, creamed, or as fritters, etc.
TAILS Beef, sheep, pork, veal	Well-flavored. Considerable bone. Make tender by precooking. Juicy meat and very popular with gourmets.	Bake, broil, jelly, pickle, braise, in soup, casserole, stew, etc.
TONGUES Beef, calf, sheep, pork	Beef and calf tongues are both desirable. Pork and lamb tongues as well as mutton tongues are popular in Europe. Beef tongue usually sold fresh or smoked, corned or pickled. So are the tongues of other animals, which are also sold jellied and ready to serve.	Precooked until tender, skin removed, then may be baked, grilled, creamed, braised, sandwiches, etc.
TRIPE Beef	First and second stomachs of beef. A muscular inner lining. Smooth and honeycomb tripe; latter preferred in this country, former in Europe. May be purchased fresh, pickled, or canned. Fresh tripe is always cooked before selling, but needs further preparation. Cured tripe requires a shorter cooking time.	Precook to make tender, then may be fried, broiled, baked, stewed, creamed, etc.

BRAINS [756]

Brains, like any other organ from the inside of the animal, give more food value than the muscle meats. That is, brains are richer nutritionally than, say, a porterhouse steak. Brains are a good source of phosphorus and iron. They offer a good supply of vitamin B. Brains are easy to digest, quick to cook and cheap to buy. A calf's brain will weigh about half a pound; lamb's and pig's brains average about a quarter of a pound each. Beef brains weigh the most, three-quarters of a pound or over.

Beef, veal, lamb, mutton and pork brains may be prepared in many delicious ways. If well-cooked, they are very light and digestible. The initial preparation is obligatory and is of great importance as it will greatly influence their flavor as well as their digestibility. The various methods of preparation of lamb and mutton brains may be adapted to almost any kind of edible animal brains.

Because of their extremely perishable nature, brains should be rushed from the butcher's shop to the refrigerator if not indeed to the saucepan. Their texture is very delicate and some preliminary parboiling is necessary, regardless of how they are to be served; they are then trimmed of all membrane and either left whole, split or cut into dice, slices, etc., according to the recipe to be followed.

BRAINS AU BEURRE NOIR [757]
Brains in Black Butter

Cover brains (as many as desired, allowing 1 pair of brains per person) with cold water and let stand 1 hour. Remove skin and membrane and drop them into boiling water, slightly salted and acidulated. Simmer 15–20 minutes; drain and at once cover the brains with cold water and let stand till thoroughly cool. Pat dry with a towel and dip lightly in seasoned flour. Sauté in butter until nicely browned; remove to a hot platter. For each pair of brains, put 2 tablespoons of butter in the hot frying pan and, just as it turns brown, remove it from the fire and add 1½–2 tablespoons of vinegar or lemon juice, shaking the pan to mix well. Dust the brains with a little finely chopped parsley or chervil, and pour the sizzling hot butter over. Serve at once. If desired, sprinkle a half teaspoon of capers over the brains and pour the butter over it.

BRAINS A LA BOURGUIGNONNE [758]
Brain and Mushroom Stew in Red Wine

Parboil 4 pairs of brains in salted, slightly acidulated boiling water 18–20 minutes; drain, then rinse the brains in running cold water until cool, after which cut them into small pieces and set aside. Peel, and slice ⅓ pound of fresh mushrooms and sauté in 3 tablespoons of butter, over a low heat, stirring almost constantly until done. Drain and add to the brains. Turn into a serving casserole, pour over 2 cups of hot Red Wine Sauce (Nos. 1110–11) and let stand till mixture is well heated. Taste for seasoning, and serve in the casserole dusted with chopped parsley and a side dish of freshly buttered toast.

BRAIN FRITTERS [759]

Dice 3 pairs of brains which have been parboiled 18–20 minutes in salted, slightly acidulated boiling water and marinade them in French dressing for 30 minutes. Meantime, prepare a frying batter as follows:

Sift 1½ cups of bread flour with 2 teaspoons of baking powder and ¼ teaspoon of salt in a bowl; gradually add, while beating briskly and constantly, 1 whole egg and 1 egg yolk, slightly beaten with ⅔ cup or milk; season to taste with salt, white pepper and a few grains of nutmeg and, when smooth, add the well-drained brain cubes. Mix well and, when ready to serve, drop with a teaspoon into hot, deep fat (360°–370° F.) and fry until brown and crisp. Drain carefully, arrange on a bed of spinach and serve with Brown or Tomato Sauce (Nos. 1017–19 and 1130, respectively).

BRAINS AU GRATIN [760]

Cook 3 pairs of brains in salted, acidulated boiling water, drain, rinse in cold water and remove all membranes and tubes. Make a border of smooth mashed Potato Duchesse (No. 1419) forced through a pastry bag around 6 individual shells or shirred egg dishes; pour into each shell or dish 2 tablespoons of Tomato Sauce (No. 1130) to which has been added ½ cup of sliced cooked fresh or canned mushrooms. Over this arrange ½ cooked brain, sliced, and cover with Cheese Sauce (No. 1027). Top each with a medium-sized mushroom cap, which has been cooked in butter and brown quickly under the flame of the broiling oven. Serve at once.

BRAIN AND MUSHROOM DUMPLINGS [761]
OR TURN-OVERS

Roll pastry very thin; cut into six 4-inch squares and spread over each 2 or 3 tablespoons of cooked mushroom purée;—then, over the purée arrange 4 or 5 slices of brains, which have been cooked in salted, acidulated boiling water, rinsed, cooled and membranes and tubes removed, seasoning to taste with salt, pepper and nutmeg. Pour 1 or 2 more tablespoons of mushroom purée over the brain slices; fold over, sealing edges carefully; place the dumplings on a baking sheet; brush with

slightly beaten egg yolk, and bake in a very hot oven (450° F.) for about
15 minutes. Serve very hot.

BRAINS IN POPOVER CASES   [762]

Cover 3 pairs of brains (any kind, except beef) with cold water and let
stand 1 hour. Cook in salted, acidulated boiling water to cover, for about
18–20 minutes; drain, rinse in running cold water, dry and cut into small
cubes. Have ready 1½ cups of rich Cream Sauce (No. 258) to which
add ½ cup of thinly sliced, cooked fresh mushrooms, and season highly
with cayenne. Add the brain cubes, heat well, and use to fill 6 popovers,
bread cases, or patty shells. Dust with paprika mixed with a little
chopped parsley and serve as hot as possible.

BRAINS A LA POULETTE   [763]

Clean, wash and cook 3 pairs of brains in salted, acidulated boiling
water 18–20 minutes; rinse in running cold water and cut into cubes.
Set aside.

Heat 3 tablespoons of butter; blend in ¼ cup of grated onion without
browning; stir in 1½ tablespoons of flour and, when mixture bubbles,
gradually stir in 1¾ cups of rich beef bouillon or stock, stirring constantly, over a low flame, until mixture thickens; remove from the fire
and beat in 2 egg yolks, one at a time, beating well after each addition;
return to the fire; boil up once or twice. Again remove from the fire and
stir in the brain cubes with 2 tablespoons of lemon juice. Taste for
seasoning, adding salt and pepper as needed, with a grating of nutmeg.
When ready to serve, stir in 1 tablespoon of finely chopped parsley and
serve on toast, in patty shells, or in parboiled green peppers, onions,
tomatoes, etc.

GRILLED BRAINS   [764]

Clean, cook in salted, slightly acidulated boiling water 6 pair lamb's
or calf's brains 18–20 minutes, rinse under running cold water, remove
membranes and dry. When ready to serve, brush the cooked, cold brains
with melted, season to taste with mixed salt, pepper and nutmeg; place
on rack of broiling oven, about 3 inches below the flame, and broil,
turning frequently, until browned on both sides. Serve at once covered
with Maître d'Hôtel Butter (No. 1078).

DRIED BEEF OR CHIPPED BEEF—HINTS   [765]

If one buys from a reliable store, it is not necessary to purchase this
product packed in glass jars or tins; it can be purchased in bulk form.

High-grade dried beef in bulk is as delicious as the packaged meat and is much less expensive.

Good dried beef is prepared from the ham of the beef, which is divided into 3 parts. It is first treated with a mild pickling process followed with sugar curing, before it is smoked over hickory or maple wood. Dried beef prepared in this way is fine in texture, rich red in color and has a wonderful nut-like flavor.

Determine the saltiness. When preparing dried beef, one should determine its saltiness. Taste it and if there seems to be too much salt, pour boiling water over and drain it off *immediately;* if very heavily salted, let stand a minute or two, then drain. The dried beef is then ready to be converted into many dishes with varying sauces, eggs, vegetables, etc.

Tissue-thin slices of dried beef full of flavor and ready-cooked can be quickly whisked into those appetizing snacks that make informal entertaining so simple and so successful. Attractive sandwiches and canapés made from dried beef—or "chipped beef" as many prefer to call it—are tasty and colorful. Creamed dried beef on slices of crisp fried hominy, cornmeal mush, etc., is good for a light luncheon. Dried beef in well made cream sauce, usually served on toast, is equally tasty with waffles, rice, mashed potatoes, noodles, macaroni or spaghetti.

CREAMED DRIED BEEF   [766]
WITH POACHED EGGS

Cook 3 tablespoons of finely chopped onions, 2 tablespoons of finely chopped green pepper, and 1 blade of finely chopped garlic in 3 tablespoons of butter or lard for 3 minutes, stirring constantly. Pour boiling water over ¾ pound of dried beef, let stand 1 minute, drain, and toss in 3 tablespoons of flour. Add to onion mixture and blend well. Then stir, a little at a time, in 2½ cups of scalded milk, and cook stirring constantly, till mixture thickens; season to taste with salt, pepper, and a fresh grating of nutmeg. Remove from the fire, arrange on 6 pieces of toast, and top each portion with a freshly poached egg. Dust with paprika and garnish with parsley or watercress.

The Buccaneers were not originally pirates, but sailors who deserted their ships in the West Indies and dried the beef of stolen cattle into "buccan," which is prepared the same as the "biltong" of the South African Boers.

DRIED BEEF AMANDINE   [767]

Prepare 2 cups of Cream Sauce (No. 258) and keep hot. Blanch 1 cup of almonds, split and toast them, and stir into the Cream Sauce. Keep hot. Meantime, pour boiling water over 1 medium-sized jar of dried beef, drain, pressing gently, but thoroughly. Stir into the cream-almond sauce; heat to boiling point, and serve at once over freshly made toast which has been spread with Anchovy Butter (No. 979). Serve immediately, dusting with a little parsley and paprika.

DRIED BEEF AND EGG PIE [768]

Prepare pastry for a 1-crust pie (See No. 2104), and chill well. Pour boiling water over ⅓ pound of dried beef, toss and drain at once, then pat dry in a towel. Cook the beef in 3 tablespoons of butter until it curls, stir in 2½ tablespoons of flour, blending well, then gradually add 1½ cups of milk, which has been scalded with 1 large bay leaf, 4 thin slices of onions, 3 sprigs of parsley, 1 whole clove and 1 thin slice of garlic, and strained, stirring constantly, until mixture thickens; season to taste using very little salt but plenty of black pepper, a dash of nutmeg and a dash of mace. Arrange in baking dish in alternate layers with sliced hard-cooked eggs and ½–¾ cup of sliced stuffed olives; cover with thinly rolled pastry, make a few slashes on top for the escape of steam, and bake in a hot oven (425° F.), for 25–30 minutes, or till pie crust is nicely browned. Place a small funnel in one of the holes, pour in 2 tablespoons of sherry wine, let stand 5 minutes and serve at once.

DRIED BEEF AND NOODLE RING LUNCHEON [769]

Cook 3 cups of noodles until tender in boiling salted water with 2 bay leaves and 6 thin slices of onion. Beat 5 egg yolks until light, add ½ cup of scalded sweet cream (sour cream may be used, if desired), ¼ cup of melted butter, 2 tablespoons each of grated onion, green pepper and chopped parsley. Stir into the noodles, mixing thoroughly. Lastly fold in as gently as possible 5 stiffly beaten egg whites. Turn noodle mixture into a buttered ring mold, set the ring in a pan of hot water, and bake in a moderate oven (325–350° F.) for 45–50 minutes. Unmold on a hot, round platter and fill center of the ring with Creamed Dried Beef (No. 766), omitting the poached eggs.

DRIED BEEF SHORTCAKE CREOLE [770]

Have ready 2 cups of Creole Sauce (Nos. (1041–42) and keep hot. Pour rapidly boiling water over ⅓ pound of dried beef, stir and drain at once, drying well. Add to hot Creole Sauce, bring to a boil, and keep hot:

To 1 cup of sifted flour, add ⅓ teaspoon of salt and 1½ teaspoons of baking powder; sift into mixing bowl. Rub in 2 teaspoons of lard with finger tips and stir in ½ cup of light sour cream to which has been added a tiny pinch of baking soda, then mix with a fork. (If too dry, add a few teaspoons of cold milk, mixing until dough is soft enough to be handled easily.) Place on lightly floured board, roll into a smooth sheet about ¾ inch thick, and bake in a greased square pan for about 12 minutes in a moderate oven (375° F.) or 7 or 8 minutes in a very hot oven (425° F.). Split shortcake, spread lower piece with butter, then with half the Creole Sauce with dried beef; cover with the other half of shortcake and pour remaining sauce-beef mixture on top. Cut in squares for serving.

FEET [771]

Like brains and sweetbreads, edible animal feet always require an initial preparation which consists of long, slow boiling in salted water or other indicated liquid or broth. Calf's, sheep's, and pig's feet may be all prepared in the same way.

There may be little meat upon the feet, but the flavor makes up for the small quantity. Once the feet have been simmered to tenderness in water or other liquid, they are ready for further attention from the book.

BAKED PIG'S FEET GRANNY'S WAY [772]

Place 4 pig's feet and 4 pig's knuckles (which have been thoroughly washed and scraped) in a large kettle with cold water to cover; bring to a boil, drain, and again cover with fresh cold water. Bring to a boil, and let boil furiously for 2 minutes; lower the heat and skim carefully. Add 1 medium-sized onion, chopped; 1 medium-sized carrot, diced; 1 small green pepper, diced; 1 scant cup of scraped, then diced celery stalk; ½ teaspoon of peppercorns, ½ teaspoon of ground cloves; 2 large bay leaves, tied with 1 sprig of thyme, 2 sprigs of green celery leaves and 1 sprig of fennel, if available, all tied with kitchen thread. Bring again to a rolling boil, then simmer very gently for 2¾ hours, or till the meat is tender but not overdone. Arrange the drained pig's feet and knuckles in a large baking pan, scatter the drained vegetables (discarding the bouquet garni) over, and strain the broth through a fine sieve into a pan; thicken as needed, and pour over the feet and knuckles and vegetables in the baking dish.

Make a dozen small balls of fresh pork as follows: Grind 1 pound of lean pork with 2 tablespoons of chopped onion, ⅓ teaspoon of allspice and salt and pepper to taste. Brown them slightly in a little bacon drippings, then place around the baking pan, and bake in a moderate oven (325° F.) for about 45 minutes. Serve on a hot, deep platter dusted with chopped parsley. Pass dill pickles, pickled onions and mustard, as well as plenty of beer.

CALF'S FEET VINAIGRETTE   [773]

Scrub and wash thoroughly 3 calf's feet; place in a kettle, add cold water to barely cover, with 1 chopped onion, 1 chopped carrot, 1 chopped white turnip, 1 chopped small leek, 1 large bay leaf tied with 2 sprigs of green celery leaves, 12 sprigs of fresh parsley, and 2 whole cloves, all tied with kitchen thread; also ½ teaspoon of peppercorns, and ½–¾ teaspoon of salt. Bring to a boil, let boil up 2 or 3 times, lower heat to the simmering point and skim carefully, then simmer gently for 4 hours. Allow to cool in the broth overnight. Next day, remove the feet and reserve the broth for soup or as a foundation for sauce. Cut the meat from the feet into small pieces and arrange on a cold platter; garnish with hard-cooked quartered eggs, slices of tomato, gherkin fans, capers in little lettuce cups, black or green olives, and dust with chopped chervil or parsley. Serve with a side dish of lukewarm Vinaigrette Sauce (No. 1133). Some prefer to serve the cooked calf's feet lukewarm but this is a matter of taste.

DEVILED PIG'S FEET   [774]

Wipe 6 fresh pig's feet with a damp cloth; split lengthwise (the butcher will do this for you); place in a kettle with 2 quarts of hot water and season with 2 teaspoons of salt and 12 peppercorns, 1 large bay leaf tied with 2 sprigs of green celery leaves (celery tops), 12 sprigs of parsley and 1 sprig of thyme, all tied up with white kitchen thread. Bring slowly to a boil, let boil steadily for 5 minutes; lower the heat to the simmering point, and continue cooking 4–4½ hours, skimming thoroughly. When the meat is pierceable, they are cooked to the right point. Remove them from the broth and, when cool enough to handle, dip first in beaten egg diluted with a little milk, then in fine bread crumbs; repeat the egging and crumbing then place on a broiler rack and broil under a very moderate flame until brown on all sides. Serve with Deviled Sauce (No. 1049) and French fried potatoes.

MUTTON TROTTERS AU GRATIN,   [775]
MELBOURNE STYLE

Wash, scrub, wash again, rinse in running cold water, then split lengthwise 6 mutton feet, and wrap each two halves in a piece of cheesecloth. Place in a kettle of boiling water and boil for 4 hours, or until trotters are tender, skimming well. Unwrap the feet, arrange side by side in a greased baking dish; pour over 1 cup of Spanish Sauce (No. 1127), and 1 cup of dry white wine, add 1 whole clove of garlic, 1 small bouquet garni composed of 1 bay leaf, 1 sprig of thyme, 12 sprigs of chives, 8 sprigs of parsley and 1 sprig of green celery leaves, all tied together with white kitchen thread; add also 2 whole cloves, 10 peppercorns, and a little salt. Place over a medium flame and cook steadily until liquid is reduced to half. Remove from the fire, discard the bouquet garni, the garlic and the whole cloves, and sprinkle over ½ cup of bread crumbs, moistened with ⅓ cup of Cheese Sauce (No. 1027). Place the dish in a moderate oven and bake for 20 minutes or until the crumbs are brown, and top bubbles. Serve immediately in the baking dish with a side dish of applesauce mixed in equal parts with red currant jelly.

MUTTON TROTTERS RAVIGOTE [776]

Clean, scrub, and rinse in running cold water 6 mutton feet. Cook in boiling salted water slightly acidulated and with 4 added bay leaves for 4 hours, skimming carefully and replenishing the kettle as needed with rapidly boiling water. When tender, remove feet from the kettle and, when cool enough to handle, remove the large bones. Place the feet side by side in a shallow saucepan; cover with beef stock or, lacking stock, use boiling water to which an equal part of Pique Seasoning has been added, also 1 bouquet garni composed of 1 large bay leaf, 1 sprig of thyme and 6 sprigs of parsley, all tied together with white kitchen thread; season to taste with salt and pepper, add 1 whole clove of garlic, and boil steadily, over a gentle flame, till liquid is reduced to almost nothing. Discard the bouquet garni, the garlic and the clove; arrange the feet on a lukewarm platter, garnish with quartered hard-cooked eggs, gherkins, olives and watercress, and serve with a side dish of Ravigote Sauce (No. 1109) and freshly made Shoestring Potatoes (No. 1424).

PICKLED PIG'S FEET [777]

Cook a dozen feet in boiling, salted, acidulated water for 4 hours; drain well; place in a crock or jar with 12 medium-sized onions, thinly sliced, 2 small carrots, scraped, then thinly sliced, and 2 cloves of garlic, left whole. Combine in an enameled kettle 3 quarts of vinegar, 2 tablespoons of salt, 1 tablespoon of peppercorns, 6 large bay leaves, 6 whole cloves, ½ teaspoon each of marjoram, mace and nutmeg. Bring to a boil, let boil 5 minutes, then add 1½ quarts of the broth in which the feet were cooked. Pour this boiling hot over the feet in the crock; cover with a cloth, then with a board with a weight on it. Let stand at least 2 weeks in a cool, dry place before chilling and serving.

PIG'S FEET IN WHITE WINE JELLY [778]

Wash a dozen pig's feet and scrub thoroughly in several changes of cold water, the last with 1 teaspoon of soda added for each gallon of water. Drain well and pat dry in a towel. Place the feet in a large kettle;

cover with boiling water, add salt to taste and bring slowly to a boil.
Let boil briskly 3 or 4 minutes, lower the heat, and simmer gently for 2
hours, skimming well. Add 1 cup of scraped chopped celery, 1 cup of
scraped chopped carrots, ½ cup of chopped green pepper, 8 bay leaves,
1 teaspoon of thyme, 1 teaspoon of peppercorns, a 2-inch piece of parlsey
root, scraped. Bring again to a boil, and cook steadily for 20 minutes or
until the broth is reduced to less than half its original volume. Now add
2 cups of white wine vinegar and 2 cups of dry white wine, bring once
more to a boil, lower the heat and simmer very gently for 2 hours,
covered. Remove the feet from the broth; pick the meat from the bones
and set aside. Chill the broth; carefully remove the cake of fat which
forms on top. Now strain the broth through a fine cloth into a kettle,
add 2 slightly beaten egg whites and their crushed shells, bring to a boil,
and let boil 2 or 3 minutes; lower the heat and let simmer 20 minutes;
strain again through a fine muslin cloth wrung out of hot water into a
bowl. At this stage the broth should be very clear and gelatinous, with
the wine flavor predominating. If not, add more wine and a little granulated gelatine. Arrange the meat in a bowl, mold, or bread pan; pour over
the broth, cool, then chill until quite firm. Unmold and serve sliced.
Calf's or sheep's feet may be prepared in the same way.

PIG'S FEET ST. MENEHOULD [779]

Have your butcher split 6 pigs' or sheep's feet or calf's feet lengthwise.
Wash and rinse them carefully; tie each foot with white string; place in
a large kettle. Add 3 small carrots, scraped and cut into small pieces, 3
medium-sized onions, thinly sliced; 1 stalk of celery, scraped and cut into
small pieces; 1 bouquet garni, composed of 2 large bay leaves, 8 sprigs of
fresh parsley, 1 sprig of thyme, and 2 sprigs of green celery leaves (tops),
all tied together with white kitchen thread; also 12 peppercorns, 4 whole
cloves, with cold water to generously cover, and salt to taste. Bring to a
boil; let boil 3 or 4 minutes; lower the heat and simmer gently 3½–4
hours, skimming frequently and having the kettle covered. When the feet
are tender, let cool to lukewarm in the broth; then take them out and
bone them. Place the meat in a bread pan, place a weight over, and let
stand overnight. When ready to serve, dip each foot in beaten egg with
which has been mixed a little finely chopped shallot, parsley, chervil,
onion and tarragon herb; then roll in fine bread crumbs. Sprinkle melted
butter over and broil very gently until golden brown on all sides. Serve
as hot as possible with a sauceboat of Deviled Sauce (No. 1049).

FRANKFURTER SAUSAGES (HOT DOGS) [780]

According to the *National Provisioner*, a thoroughly reliable journal,
something like 4 billion hot dogs are eaten annually in the United

States. The average American does away with about 12 pounds of sausage a year. That means all kinds of sausage; all the kith and kin of the hot dog, and these are startingly numerous—somewhere around 2,000 different branches of the family. The annual ratio for consumption of the various branches goes something like this: Hot dogs, 30%; bologna, 17%; pork sausage, 15%; dry sausage (which covers a wide variety), 18%. The total sausage production in the United States before World War II amounted to approximately 200 million dollars.

Anyway, the first hot dog to bear the name is said to have appeared in 1883, the year of the wedding of the hot dog and the roll. The match was promoted by Anton Ludwig Feuchtwanger, a Bavarian sausage peddler in St. Louis. He had found that the white gloves he handed to his customers so they might seize the dogs were apt to vanish. With them went the profits. The Bavarian and his *gnaedige Frau* brooded over this; gave their nights and days to the problem and finally hit on the idea that started the hot dog on its triumphant march around the world. Why not, they suddenly thought, dress the hot dog's blushing nudity in a bun? The thing caught on and spread like a war rumor. The march was steady, and keeps going on bigger and bigger.

BARBECUED FRANKFURTERS WITH BACON   [781]

This popular sausage— the frankfurter—whether you call it a "hot dog," a "red hot" or "wiener," has made a place for itself in American history, especially when barbecued. First, the sauce:

Melt 2 tablespoons of butter in a saucepan; stir in 1 medium-sized onion, chopped fine, and cook until just beginning to brown; add a generous dash of black pepper, 1 tablespoon of sugar, 1 teaspoon of dry mustard, 1 teaspoon of paprika, ½ cup of tomato catsup, ¼ cup of cider vinegar, ¾ cup of cold water, 1½ tablespoons of Worcestershire sauce, ½ teaspoon of Tabasco sauce, 1 clove of garlic, finely chopped, 2 tablespoons each of finely minced parsley, chives and green pepper, and salt to taste. Bring to a boil; let boil 2 minutes; remove from the fire and keep hot.

With a sharp knife, cut 3-inch slits in a dozen frankfurters; place them in a shallow baking pan, slit side up. Pour sauce over them and bake in a moderate oven for 20 minutes, basting 2 or 3 times with the sauce in the pan. Serve on hot platter, each frankfurter covered with a slice of broiled bacon. Serve at once with potato salad, cool beer, plenty of mustard and brown bread.

FRANKFURTERS WITH CARAWAY CABBAGE   [782]

Cook 5 cups of finely shredded cabbage in a very little water (covered), adding a dash each of salt, pepper and sugar, for 8 or 9 minutes, stirring frequently. Drain and pour over ⅓ cup of melted butter, tossing all well together. Transfer to a heated serving platter; sprinkle with 1 teaspoon of caraway seeds mixed with 1 cup of tiny bread cubes fried in butter or other shortening, and surround with 12 frankfurters which have been cooked in a slightly greased frying pan. Serve at once, with mustard.

FRANKFURTER CROWN ROAST [783]
An unusual and very delicious and nourishing dish

Cut all the following raw vegetables in pieces, then run them through medium cutter of food chopper: 2 cups of raw well washed spinach tightly packed down, 2 cups of medium-sized raw carrots, scraped, 1 small green pepper, 2 sprigs of celery green (tops). Sauté in ½ cup of fat, stirring frequently until almost done; remove from the fire; add any juice remaining in food chopper, and mix in 2 well-beaten whole eggs, 1 cup of dry bread crumbs, ½ cup of boiling water to which has been added ¼ cup of Pique Seasoning with salt and pepper to taste, also a dash each of nutmeg, thyme, cloves, mace, and powdered bay leaf. Blend well. The stuffing should be moist but not wet. Turn it into a roasting pan, mold into a mound and arrange around it 18 frankfurters, standing up so as to resemble a crown roast of lamb or pork; skewer frankfurters with toothpicks or sew them with kitchen thread. Around the middle, place strips of bacon fastened on with toothpicks. Bake in a moderate oven (350° F.) for 25 minutes, or till done, lift on to hot serving platter with 2 pancake turners and serve with a tomato, mushroom, or barbecue sauce, the last made as follows:

Barbecue Sauce for Frankfurters. Cook 1 medium-sized onion and ½ cup of finely chopped celery leaves and stalks in 3 tablespoons of bacon fat over a medium flame until yellow, stirring frequently, then add and stir in, 2 tablespoons of brown sugar, 3 tablespoons of vinegar, 4 tablespoons of lemon juice, 1 cup of tomato catsup, 1 tablespoon of Worcestershire sauce, 1 teaspoon of prepared mustard and ⅓ cup of hot water, ¼ cup of very finely chopped dill pickles. Bring to a boil; lower the flame and let simmer 10 minutes. Serve hot. This sauce may be prepared in advance and stored in a glass jar, tightly sealed. It will keep for a month in the refrigerator. Heat to the boiling point before using over any kind of broiled or roasted meat or poultry.

FRANKFURTERS IN GOLDEN JACKETS [784]

Roll plain pastry out very thin. It should be quite soft. Brush with prepared mustard, then sprinkle with raw bacon mixed with a little chopped parsley, onion or chives. Cut in rectangles to fit the frankfurters; enclose them in the pastry, folding it evenly over them; seal the edges by wetting, then pinching the pastry firmly together. Lay on a greased baking sheet, make a few holes in each with the tines of a fork, and bake in a hot oven (400° F.) for about 12–15 minutes. Serve sizzling hot.

FRANKFURTER CASSEROLE CREOLE [785]

Prepare a quart of Creole Sauce (Nos. 1041–42) and keep hot. Wipe a dozen frankfurters with a damp cloth, and prick through and through with the tines of a fork. Put half the sauce in a greased casserole; lay in the frankfurters, and cover with remaining sauce. Sprinkle over the top ¾ cup of soft bread crumbs mixed with an equal amount of grated American cheese, and bake in a moderate oven (375° F.) till the crumbs are browned and the cheese bubbles. Serve at once in the casserole.

FRANKFURTER AND ONION CASSEROLE [786]

Rub the bottom of a large earthenware casserole with a cut clove of garlic, then grease well with bacon drippings. Lay a dozen frankfurters in the casserole, top with 2 large onions, thinly sliced; cover the onions with 1 cup of thinly sliced fresh mushrooms, using both stems and caps, and season to taste with salt, pepper and mixed thyme, mace and nutmeg. Add also a small bay leaf and 1 large green pepper, thinly sliced and freed, from seeds and white ribs. Pour over the whole 1 (No. 2) can of tomatoes; cover closely and bake in a moderate oven (375° F.) for 40 minutes. Serve right from the casserole.

Your butcher will tell you whether the frankfurters he sells are made of beef alone or are a mixture of beef and pork. Frankfurters are precooked and may be heated by immersing in hot water, bouillon or milk; by broiling, baking, grilling or pan-frying. Whatever the heating method, remember that high temperature causes them to split, and that pricking will cause them to lose some of their juices.

FRANKFURTER PLATTER DINNER [787]

Melt 3 tablespoons of butter or margarin in a heavy saucepan; add ¾ cup of thinly sliced onions and 1½ cups of sliced tart apples; cover and cook 4 minutes. Add 8 cups of finely shredded cabbage (red or green, or equal parts of each), mixing well from the bottom. Continue cooking (covered) for 10 minutes, stirring frequently. Lift the cover and stir in ¼ cup of cider vinegar, ¼ cup of chopped dill pickle, salt and pepper to taste. Replace cover and cook very slowly for 15–20 minutes longer. Meantime place 12 frankfurters in a greased large heavy saucepan, set over a low flame, and pan-broil until heated through and lightly browned on all sides, rolling them with a spatula to avoid pricking.

To serve, pile whipped potatoes in center of a heated platter; arrange the frankfurters at regular intervals around them; border with the hot cabbage mixture, and serve at once.

Cooked, hot sauerkraut may be substituted for the whipped potatoes, or unchopped spinach, buttered noodles, rice risotto, etc.

As man went, so went the sausage. In some form or another the sausage probably has been one of man's foods ever since primitive days. Scientists point out that when the caveman learned to cook his food he also learned instinctively to preserve part of the meat he had killed for a future meal, cleaning it of bone and gristle and stuffing it in a piece of skin. Thus the first sausage was probably invented. It acquired more and more refinement down through the ages until today it is even possible to get a hot dog neatly packed in a skin that has a "zipper."

HEARTS [788]

Very few cooks realize how very delicious heart can be when properly prepared, or how high it ranks in nutritive value. Hearts are less tender than kidneys or liver and must be cooked slowly. Although beef hearts are priced at a few cents less per pound than other hearts, the edible parts of each cost about the same. Beef heart has more waste. The edible portion of veal hearts, while still cheap, costs a few cents a pound more than the beef or pig's heart. Hearts are sold by the pound. They are often stuffed and baked, or can be used for braising, stewing, casserole dishes or meat loaves. If simmered very slowly in seasoned liquid for several hours, they may be sliced thin and served hot or cold. It is essential to remove the arteries, veins and fat before cooking.

The flavor of heart is a little like that of fresh tongue. However, despite the poets, tenderness is not the true nature of an animal heart, culinarily speaking, for it must work hard and exercise toughens it.

Small lamb hearts make nice individual servings. Calves' hearts yield 2, possibly 3, portions, being cut crosswise to form a ring of meat centered with stuffing. A beef heart weighing 4 or 5 pounds will serve 6 generously. The heart resembles tough muscle meat and consequently must be cooked slowly and long by moist heat.

Wash hearts thoroughly in plenty of hot water and discard any hard connective tissue.

BEEF HEART LOAF PARISIAN STYLE [789]

Wash carefully a 3-pound piece of beef heart. Be careful to remove all gristle and membrane, then put through food chopper with ½ pound of pork shoulder, cut from the fat end. Add 2 eggs, also 2 slices of crumbled bread, this moistened with as much sherry wine as the bread will absorb (about ⅓ cup), 1 teaspoon of sage, 1½ teaspoons of salt, ¼ teaspoon of freshly ground black pepper, ⅛ teaspoon each of nutmeg, thyme, mace and marjoram. Add also 1 tablespoon each of grated onion, finely chopped parsley and chives and green pepper. Blend all thoroughly; pack in a bread pan generously greased and rubbed with garlic, and bake in a moderate oven (325–350° F.) for 1½–1¾ hours. Unmold on a hot platter; garnish with watercress, pickle fans and olives. Serve sliced with a hot Brown Sauce (Nos. 1017–19).

BEEF HEART POTROAST   [790]

Wash heart and remove the veins and arteries, then soak for 1 hour in sour milk to increase tenderness. Drain, stuff with a well-seasoned bread stuffing, and sew up securely, taking care not to over fill the cavity; but leaving some room for expansion; rub with seasoned flour and sear thoroughly in ¼ cup of bacon drippings. Transfer to a stew pot, add a dozen very small white onions, peeled, 18 small fresh mushrooms, caps peeled, stems sliced; 18 small carrot balls; 1 cup of scraped, chopped celery, 1 bouquet garni, composed of 1 large bay leaf, 2 sprigs of green celery (tops), 1 sprig of thyme, all tied with kitchen thread; 2 whole cloves; 8 peppercorns, and a very little salt. Cover with cold water, bring to a boil, and simmer gently, covered, for about 3 hours, or till tender, adding, about 30 minutes before heart is done, 18 small potato balls and 18 small white turnip balls. Transfer heart to a heated platter, slice a portion, reshape, and surround the meat with the vegetables. Thicken part of the gravy with a little flour, and pour over all. If desired, add 2 or 3 large peeled, quartered fresh tomatoes under the potato balls.

Stuffing. 1 cup of dry bread crumbs, ½ cup chopped onions, 1 tablespoon of chopped parsley, finely chopped, 1 blade of garlic mashed, 3 tablespoons of chopped green peppers, 1 whole egg, and milk to moisten.

BEEF HEART STUFFED WITH RICE   [791]
AND RAISINS

Wash beef heart and remove veins and arteries, then season inside and out with mixed salt and pepper. Wash 1¼ cups of rice in several cold waters; cover with boiling salted water and boil 15 minutes, or until rice is about half done; drain. Add ½ cup of chopped onions; ¾ cup of seedless raisins, previously parboiled until plump then well drained; 1 teaspoon of poultry seasoning; 1 tablespoon of chopped parsley; salt and pepper to taste; and mix well with 1 egg. Fill the heart cavity lightly with part of the rice-raisin mixture; sew the edges together, and brown on all sides in ¼ cup of bacon or ham drippings. Transfer to a Dutch oven; add 1 No. 2½ can of tomatoes, 1 large bay leaf, 2 whole cloves, 1 dash of thyme, and ½ cup of boiling water mixed with ¼ cup of Pique Seasoning. Cover and simmer very gently for 3 hours. Add remaining rice mixture, cover again and continue cooking gently for 25–30 minutes longer. Transfer to a heated platter, slice and surround with part of the gravy.

LAMB HEARTS EN CASSEROLE [792]

Wash 6 lamb hearts and clean well; make an incision in the top of each. Soak 4 slices of bread and about 6–7 soda crackers in cold milk; when soft, drain, then add 2 medium-sized onions, chopped, 1 teaspoon of poultry seasoning, 1 tablespoon each of finely chopped parsley and chives, salt and pepper to taste and blend. Stuff hearts and sew up openings. Place a generously greased casserole; add any remaining stuffing, pour over 1 No. 2½ can of tomatoes, add 1 large green pepper, thinly sliced and freed from seeds and membranes, 1 bouquet garni composed of 1 large bay leaf, 8 sprigs of parsley, 2 sprigs of green celery leaves, all tied together with white kitchen thread, 2 cloves and 1 clove of garlic. Season to taste with salt and pepper; cover closely and bake in a moderate oven (375° F.) for 2½ hours. Serve from the casserole, first tasting for seasoning and discarding the bouquet garni.

VEAL HEART CHOP SUEY [793]

Carefully wash and remove excess of fat, veins and tough membranes from 3 veal hearts; soak in cold water for 1 hour; drain, then cut the hearts in quarters. Cover with boiling water, add ½ cup of Pique Seasoning, 1 medium-sized onion, studded, with 2 whole cloves, ¼ cup each of chopped celery and carrots, 10 peppercorns, 1 large bay leaf and ⅛ teaspoon of powdered thyme. Bring to a boil, skim carefully; add 1 clove of garlic, cover and simmer gently for 1½ hours or until the meat is tender. Drain, saving the stock, and cut the meat into thin, matchlike strips. Sprinkle with flour and brown in a heavy skillet in 3 tablespoons of drippings. Add 2 cups of the strained broth; 2 or 3 tablespoons of soy sauce; ⅓ pound of peeled, sliced mushrooms; 1 cup of thinly sliced onions and 1 cup of thinly sliced celery strips. Cover and simmer very gently for 20 minutes. Mix 1 teaspoon of cornstarch with ¼ cup of cold water, stir slowly into the mixture, let boil up 3 or 4 times, and serve with flaky boiled rice. Pass paper-thin slices of Bermuda onion to sprinkle over each portion and serve as hot as possible.

VEAL HEART STEW IN CLARET [794]
FRENCH STYLE
Coeur au Vin

Wash thoroughly 1 pound of veal heart, 1 pound of veal kidneys, and ½ pound calf's or beef liver. Remove fat and gristle from heart and kidneys, then cut all meat small. Dredge with seasoned flour and brown in ⅓ cup of lard or drippings in a stewpot, stirring almost constantly. Add 1 bouquet garni composed of 1 large bay leaf, 1 sprig of thyme, 2 sprigs of green celery leaves, 1 sprig of thyme, a dozen or so sprigs of chives, and 8 sprigs of fresh parsley, all tied with white kitchen thread. Add also 2 whole cloves, 1 clove of garlic, and cover with boiling water to which has been added ½ cup of Pique Seasoning. Bring to a boil, skim carefully; lower the heat and simmer, covered, for 3 hours by which time there should be only about ½ generous cup of liquid left, add 2 cups of Burgundy wine or Burgundy type red wine, 1 cup of sliced fresh mushrooms or 1 small can of small mushroom buttons, with salt and pepper to taste. Continue simmering for 20 minutes. Thicken if desired, with a little flour moistened with cold water, and serve in a heated deep platter, garnishing with canned peas, and dusting with finely chopped parsley. Small plain boiled potatoes are usually served with this dish.

KIDNEYS [795]

Man seems to have known instinctively many facts about nutrition which have taken centuries to prove scientifically. For instance, it was the custom to reserve for the chief and the young warriors the liver, the kidney and heart of a freshly killed animal, these being believed to contribute to both strength and courage.

Science has shown us that these organs play a most valuable part in nutrition. Liver has been studied meticulously and found not only to contribute essentials to daily nutrition, but also to be a specific remedy for pernicious anemia. Recent reports have shown that kidney apparently has specific influence upon blood pressure. A kidney extract has been and still is used to lower blood pressure and at the same time to play a part in reducing weight caused by retention of water in the tissues. More research work will, of course, be necessary before kidney extract will be used generally as a remedy for such conditions. In the meantime, however, it will be wise to use this organ in its natural form, not occasionally, but frequently. And nothing is more delicious than a good kidney dish, when properly prepared and seasoned.

Kidneys, which are rated highly by gourmets, also win praise for their food value. They are an unusually good source of riboflavin, one of the factors of the vitamin B complex which is apt to be lacking in the average diet; also of thiamine and niacin. They furnish the high-quality protein found in all meat and minerals, especially iron.

Kidney has a dual flavor and the trick of its cooking is to subdue the unpleasant taste to an artful blending with the pleasurable. Kidneys, be they from beef, sheep, pork or calf, provide delicious and economical, as well as nourishing and agreeable, dishes, but their apotheosis is achieved when they are sautéed. Kidneys of quadrupeds are all edible. They should always be plunged in rapidly boiling water and drained at once, at which time the thin filmy skin which protects them may be easily removed. The operation of scalding removes the *sui generis* flavor.

BEEF KIDNEY CHOP SUEY DINNER   [796]

Wash, scald and drain 3 beef kidneys. Split and remove skin, white centers and tubes; slice and soak in salted water for 15 minutes; drain, and parboil for 5 minutes. Drain again, then cook gently in ⅓ cup of drippings until well browned, stirring frequently with a wooden spoon. Dice 2 cups of onions; scrape 6 celery stalks, and cut in thin strips, matchlike fashion; add both to the kidneys, cover with 1½ cups of boiling water, to which has been added ½ cup of Pique Seasoning. Season to taste with salt and black pepper, cover and cook for 25 minutes, shaking the pan frequently, and adding more boiling water if needed. Stir in 3 tablespoons of Chinese soy sauce (commercial), and thicken, if needed, with a little flour moistened with a little cold water. Turn mixture into a rice border, and serve at once.

BEEF KIDNEY CREOLE   [797]

Trim fat, remove the skin and tubes from 2 beef kidneys, and soak in salted water for 25 minutes; drain, rinse in cold water, then parboil 3 or 4 minutes and drain well. Cut into ¾-inch slices; dredge with seasoned flour and set aside. Dice 4 slices of bacon and cook until just beginning to crisp, then add 2 tablespoons of good cooking oil and, when hot, the prepared kidney. Sauté 3 or 4 minutes over a low flame. Now add 1 cup of thinly sliced onions, 1 cup of thinly sliced green pepper and ½ cup of thinly sliced pitted green olives, and cook 5 minutes longer. Season to taste with salt and pepper and 1 large bay leaf, 1 sprig of thyme and 8 sprigs of parsley, all tied with kitchen thread; also 2 whole cloves and 1 clove of garlic, mashed. Pour in 1 No. 2 can of tomatoes, Mix well, cover, and simmer gently for 30 minutes. Serve in a hot deep platter dusting with minced parsley. Pass plain boiled rice separately.

CURRIED LAMB KIDNEYS   [798]

Split 12 lamb kidneys, remove the white part from center, and cover with boiling water. Let stand 15 minutes, drain, slice and set aside. Cook ¼ cup of grated onions in ¼ tablespoons of butter or lard, stir in 2 teaspoons (more or less) of curry powder and, when well blended, add 1 cup of beef stock and bring to a boil and simmer gently while cooking the kidneys.

Heat 3 tablespoons of butter, stir in the sliced kidneys, and cook, over a very bright flame, for 2 minutes, stirring constantly. Remove from the fire and drain off all fat, then add the curry sauce. Season to taste with salt, add 1 large bay leaf, 2 cloves, and 1 clove of garlic, and simmer gently for 20 minutes. Serve with flaky boiled rice.

DEVILED LAMB KIDNEYS ON TOAST   [799]
MONTE CARLO

Wash, drain, split open lengthwise but do not cut into halves, 16 lamb kidneys. Remove the white tubes and fat, then spread each kidney flat. Make a paste with ¾ cup of butter or margarine, ¾ cup of finely chopped parsley, ½ cup of grated onion, 1 grated clove of garlic, 2 tablespoons of Worcestershire sauce, ⅓ cup of sherry wine, 3 or 4 drops of Tabasco or cayenne pepper, salt to taste, and, if available, 2 tablespoons of finely chopped chives. Place 1 heaping tablespoon (about) of this deviled paste over each kidney; arrange on the broiler rack, place 3 inches from the flame, and broil until brown and tender or about 5–6 minutes if you like kidneys a little on the rare side, or 8 minutes if liked well done. Serve on freshly made toast, pouring the sauce from the broiler over the kidneys. Chutney should be served on the side with freshly made Shoestring Potatoes (No. 1424).

LAMB KIDNEYS EN BROCHETTE CHEZ SOI   [800]

Place in a saucepan 2 tablespoons of tarragon vinegar; add 1 tablespoon each of finely chopped chives, green olives, red pepper, capers and sweet pickle and heat thoroughly without boiling. Add this to 1½ cup of Brown Sauce (No. 1018), and simmer gently while preparing the kidneys. Wash quickly 6 lamb kidneys; split open and remove fat and membranes, then cut into quarters; sprinkle with mixed salt and pepper; dip in olive oil; arrange on 6 skewers with alternating squares of bacon and small fresh mushroom caps, peeled. Dip each skewerful in olive oil, then in cracker meal; broil until tender, under the flame of the broiling oven turning twice. Serve on strips of toast passing the sauce and Saratoga Potato Chips (No. 1432) separately.

LAMB KIDNEY STEW HOME STYLE   [801]

Wash 8 lamb kidneys; remove skin and split open, then remove the fat and membranes. Slice kidneys in ½ inch slices. Heat ¼ cup of butter; add the sliced kidneys, ¾ cup of peeled, sliced fresh mushrooms and 2 tablespoons of grated onion, and cook 5 minutes over a very hot fire, stirring constantly. Sprinkle with 2 tablespoons of flour and blend; gradually stir in 1¼ cups of good beef bouillon or, lacking it, 1 cup of boiling water to which has been added ¼ cup of Pique Seasoning, stirring constantly, until mixture boils and thickens. Season to taste with salt, pepper and a few grains of cayenne pepper, and let simmer very gently 12–15 minutes. Just before serving, stir in 2 tablespoons of good sherry wine and dust with finely chopped parsley or chives, or both. Freshly made toast is usually served with this dish. Pork or veal kidneys as well as beef kidneys may be prepared in this same way

LAMB KIDNEYS MONTAGNARDS [802]

Split 12 lamb kidneys lengthwise and remove fat, membranes and skin; soak in dry white wine for an hour, first washing the kidneys in several changes of cold water. Heat ¼ cup of sweet butter; stir in 1 tablespoon of finely chopped shallots (or onions if shallots are not available), 1 thin slice of garlic and 1 small carrot, scraped and thinly sliced, and cook until just beginning to brown, stirring frequently, over a gentle flame. Sprinkle with 2 tablespoons of flour and brown lightly, then pour in 1 cup of rich beef broth, or use ½ cup of boiling water and ¼ cup of Pique Seasoning and ¾ cup of red wine; season to taste with salt and pepper; add 1 small bay leaf, a pinch of thyme, and bring to a boil. Add drained kidney halves and simmer gently for 20 minutes, or till kidneys are tender. Serve on a hot platter, straining the sauce over them. Garnish with small triangles of toast fried in butter, and dust with parsley.

VEAL KIDNEYS ARDENNAISE [803]

Split, remove fat, membranes and skin from 8 veal kidneys, then cut into ½ inch-thick slices. Heat ⅓ cup of sweet butter in a saucepan, stir in 1 tablespoon each of finely chopped green pepper, mushrooms and shallots (or onion) and cook, over a low flame, till mixture just begins to take on color. Season the kidney with salt and pepper to taste and add to mixture in pan blending well. Continue cooking for 4 minutes longer, stirring frequently. Place 3 tablespoons of brandy in a soup ladle, set it aflame and let the flaming brandy drop over the kidney mixture, stirring meanwhile. When the flame dies out, add 1 cup of boiling veal stock (No. 185) and stir from the bottom of the pan. Cover and simmer gently for 10 minutes. Serve on freshly made toast and, after thickening the sauce a little, strain over the kidneys. Dust with mixed paprika and chopped parsley.

VEAL KIDNEYS BRABANÇONNE [804]

Split and wash in several changes of cold water 8 veal kidneys; remove fat, membranes and skin, and pour boiling water over. Drain at once and pat dry. Heat ⅓ cup of sweet butter in an earthenware casserole which has been rubbed with a cut clove of garlic; add seasoned kidney and cook, over a bright flame, till a nice brown, turning frequently. Now add ½ pound of chopped onions and, when they are slightly browned, sprinkle over them 1 tablespoon of flour and stir until well blended. Gradually pour in, while stirring constantly, 2 cups of good beer; add 1 bouquet garni, made of 1 large bay leaf, 8 sprigs of fresh parsley, 1 sprig of thyme, and 2 whole cloves, all tied together with white kitchen thread, and lastly stir in 1 tablespoon of brown sugar. Cover, and simmer as gently as possible until kidney is tender, about 20 minutes. Arrange kidneys on a hot platter, taste the sauce for seasoning, and rub it through a fine-meshed sieve into a saucepan; reheat and pour at once over the kidneys. Dust with finely chopped parsley and paprika, garnish with toast points, and serve with additional freshly made toast.

VEAL OR LAMB KIDNEYS CHASSEUR [805]

Remove the outer skin and fat from 6 veal kidneys or 12 lamb kidneys, and cut them into not too thin slices; season with mixed salt and freshly ground black pepper. Fry quickly in 4 tablespoons of butter until just beginning to brown slightly; sprinkle with 1 teaspoon each of finely chopped parsley or chervil, shallots, and, if desired, chives, and toss for 2 minutes over a hot flame, shaking and rocking the pan frequently; then sprinkle over the whole 1 generous teaspoon of flour. Sauté a few seconds, then moisten with ½ cup of good Madeira wine, ½ cup of dry white wine and ⅓ cup of beef bouillon or stock. Bring to a quick boil; lower the flame as far as possible, cover and simmer very gently 3–5 minutes; then add ¼ pound of fresh mushrooms, caps peeled, thinly sliced and cooked in a little butter until tender. Simmer 3 or 5 minutes longer, transfer to a hot platter, sprinkle with parsley and garnish with triangles of bread fried in butter.

VEAL OR LAMB KIDNEYS POLONAISE [806]

Remove the outer skin, split, then remove fat and membranes from 6 veal or 12 lamb kidneys, and slice not too thin. Pour salted water over and let stand 10 minutes. Drain well and dry between towels. Heat ⅓ cup of sweet butter, add sliced kidneys, and cook over a quick fire 4 or 5 minutes, stirring constantly and rocking the pan frequently. Then stir in ¼ cup of vinegar mixed with ¾ cup of boiling water and ¼ cup of Pique Seasoning. Simmer gently, covered, 10–15 minutes, stirring occasionally. Meantime, cook 1 cup of thinly sliced onions in 3 tablespoons of olive oil until browned, drain and add to the kidneys, and continue simmering 2 or 3 minutes, stirring once or twice. Mix 1 tablespoon of sugar, 1 tablespoon of flour and ⅓ cup of sherry wine, and add to the kidney mixture. Continue cooking until the sauce is slightly thickened; season to taste with salt, pepper and a grating of nutmeg and serve in a rice or potato border.

LIVER [807]

Liver is rich in protein and uncomplicated by excess fat. Liver is a real blood regenerator, containing the important mineral iron, with a trace of copper in the organic form most easily used by the body. Liver is rich in vitamins A and G; is a good source of vitamins B and C and even contains some vitamin D for good measure. Liver is the only meat containing glycogen, a body sugar, and an excellent energy food. There is no waste in liver, and it shrinks very little unless overcooked. One pound, sliced, will easily serve four.

Flavor in liver varies slightly. Calf's and sheep's liver is exceedingly mild, very tender. Pork liver has a stronger flavor and coarser structure and texture. Beef liver is darker, with good flavor. All liver, including furred game liver, is tender and may be prepared in approximately the same manner, but *slow* cooking is needed.

All kinds of liver, when ground or chopped, may be used in stuffings, loaves, hash, sandwich fillings, and similar combinations.

If liver is to be cooked in the piece, it should be washed thoroughly but never soaked in water. If roasted, strips of bacon or salt pork should be placed over the top, since in itself it contains little fat. If liver is to be braised in one piece peel off the outside membrane after first washing quickly.

When liver is to be ground, it may be covered with boiling water then simmered 3 or 4 minutes to facilitate grinding.

Important. Unless otherwise indicated, the following recipes may be prepared with beef, calf's, lamb, or pork liver.

BAKED LIVER AND ONIONS DELMONICO [808]

Peel and cut 2 large Bermuda onions into thin slices; arrange them flat in a generously greased baking dish. Melt 3 tablespoons of butter in ⅓ cup of hot water and pour over the onion; cover and bake in a moderate oven (350°F.), about 30 minutes, or until the onions can be pierced with a knife or the tines of a fork, turning them once with a spatula, and taking care to keep them in shape. Remove the skin and tubes from 6 slices of liver (any kind); dredge with seasoned flour; arrange over the onions, add 1 large bay leaf, 1 sprig of thyme and 8 sprigs of parsley, all tied up with kitchen thread; dot with butter (using about 2 tablespoons) and cover. Bake in a moderate oven (350° F.), about 25–30 minutes; uncover and continue baking until liver is brown. Serve from the baking dish with Delmonico Potatoes (No. 1416)

"Don't overcook" is the primary rule in liver cookery. High heat or long cooking toughens it. The flavor of pork or mature beef liver will be more delicate if braised with vegetables.

BRAISED LIVER HOME STYLE   [809]

Skewer or tie in shape then lard upper side of a 2¾ to 3-pound piece of beef, calf's, or pork liver, using about 12 narrow strips of pork fat back. Place in a deep baking kettle, add 3 small carrots, scraped and cut into inch pieces, 12 fresh mushroom caps, peeled and left whole, ½ cup of diced celery, ½ cup of white turnip cubes, a dozen small white onions, peeled, 2 of them studded with 1 clove, 1 bouquet garni composed of 1 large bay leaf, 1 sprig of thyme, and 8 sprigs of fresh parsley, all tied together with white kitchen thread, 8 whole peppercorns, a little salt, 1 clove of garlic, and 1½ cups of hot water, mixed with ½ cup of Pique Seasoning; cover closely, and bake in a moderate oven (350–375° F.) for 1¾ hours, turning the liver after 1 hour of cooking, and uncovering the last 20 minutes. Transfer the liver to a hot platter; discard the bouquet garni; drain out the vegetables and arrange them around the liver; strain the gravy through a fine-meshed sieve; remove all fat but 2 tablespoons, and bring the gravy to a boil; stir in a little flour moistened with cold water to thicken slightly; taste for seasoning, then add 3 tablespoons of Madeira wine and bring almost to boiling point. Pour half of the gravy over the liver, and serve the remainder in a sauceboat. Creamed lima beans and plain boiled potatoes, are good accompaniments.

When James Gordon Bennett was editor of the New York *Herald* he once summoned his London correspondent to meet him in Paris. The correspondent knew that his employer was a great lover of dogs. He also had a premonition that he was going to be discharged, but he was not without resources. After Bennett had kept him waiting for an hour he was finally admitted to the editor. Half a dozen French poodles began greeting him by licking his face and hands; Bennett's hostility melted like magic. He not only shook hands warmly with his employee but was solicitous of his health and gave him a substantial raise in salary. When the correspondent returned to his room he changed his clothes and removed from his pockets the choice cuts of liver which he had carefully secreted in them.

CHICKEN LIVER EN BROCHETTE   [810]

Wash 1½ dozen chicken livers in several changes of cold water, the last one with a little lemon juice in it. Drain and dry thoroughly. If the livers are large, cut them in halves with a sharp knife. Cut strips of bacon to make 18 one-inch squares. Peel 18 small mushroom caps, and half cook in butter. Arrange 3 chicken livers, alternately with bacon squares and mushroom caps, on each skewer; roll in melted butter highly seasoned with salt and black pepper, and place an inch apart on a baking sheet. Bake in a hot oven (400° F.) about 8 minutes, or until bacon is crisp, turning once or twice during the baking process. Serve on the skewers arranged on toast the size and width of the skewer, and pour a teaspoon or two of Mâitre d'Hôtel Butter over each portion. Serve with Saratoga Chips (No. 1432) and garnish with watercress.

Try rubbing a cut clove of garlic lightly over the toast before placing the skewers over them.

CHICKEN LIVER CURRY [811]

Wash 18 chicken livers thoroughly in cold water; dry, then cook them in ⅓ cup of butter, over low heat for about 5 or 6 minutes stirring frequently. Remove the livers and keep hot. Stir into the fat remaining in the pan ¼ cup of chopped onions and 1 cup of finely sliced fresh mushrooms. Cook 3 or 4 minutes and add to the livers. Have ready 1½ cups of highly seasoned Curry Sauce (No. 1045–46). Add the chicken livers, onions and mushrooms, reheat, and serve on a hot platter, garnished with small triangles of bread fried in butter and thick slices of apple, also fried in butter, until brown on both sides. Place a tuft of crisp watercress at each end of the platter and serve at once with a side dish of freshly made buttered toast.

CHICKEN LIVERS AND MUSHROOMS [812]
ON TOAST

Rinse 18 cleaned chicken livers in cold water and dry. Cut each liver in three pieces and sauté over a very low flame in ¼ cup of butter together with 1 tablespoon each of finely chopped green pepper, parsley, onion, shallots and mushrooms, for about 4 minutes, stirring frequently. Sprinkle with 1 tablespoon of flour, blend well, then moisten with ½ cup each of dry white wine and chicken stock. Add 1 small bay leaf, with 1 whole clove, 1 sprig of thyme and 8 sprigs of fresh parsley, all tied together with white kitchen thread; cover and let simmer very gently, for 15 minutes, stirring occasionally. Season to taste with salt, pepper and a grating of nutmeg, and serve at once on toast, each portion crossed with 2 strips of grilled bacon.

LIVER AND ANCHOVY MOLD BOURGEOISE [813]

Chop fine (do not grind) 1½ pounds of liver (preferably calf's liver) with 12 anchovy fillets, washed, drained and dried. Add ⅓ pound of fresh mushrooms, peeled, then chopped; ¼ pound of bacon, scalded, drained and chopped fine; 2 tablespoons each of onion, green pepper and 1 tablespoon of parsley all finely chopped. Moisten with 1 teaspoon of lemon juice, 2 eggs, and enough milk to make rather soft. Season to taste with salt, black pepper and ¼ teaspoon each of marjoram, mace, sage and thyme. Blend thoroughly and pack lightly into a buttered ring mold. Bake in a moderate oven (350–375° F.) for 10 minutes, then cover with a generous ½ cup of buttered crumbs, and continue baking 12 to 15 minutes longer. Unmold on a heated platter, and garnish the center with a mound of Risotto à la Milanese (No. 1599) and a sauceboat of Spanish Sauce (No. 1127).

LIVER CHOW MEIN HOME STYLE   [814]

Wash quickly a 2-pound piece of liver; dry, cut it into one-inch cubes, removing as much as possible of the skin tubes and membrane, and brown over a low flame in ¼ cup of cooking oil or bacon drippings, stirring constantly; then stir in 1 cup of celery, scraped and cut into inch pieces, each piece then cut into matchlike strips; as much of green pepper, cut the same way as the celery, and 1 No. 2 can of tomatoes, also 1 large bay leaf, a good pinch of thyme with salt and pepper to taste. Let all simmer gently for 30-35 minutes, over a low flame, stirring occasionally, then add 1 can of drained Chinese vegetables, and heat through; thicken with 2 tablespoons of flour, blended with 3 tablespoons of Chinese brown sauce (commercial) and 3 tablespoons of Chinese soy sauce (commercial), adding enough water to make mixture of pouring consistency. Serve as hot as possible over Chinese noodles (commercial).

LIVER CREOLE   [815]

Cut 1½ pounds of liver into 6 thin slices; remove the skin, veins and membranes, and wash quickly in cold water. Drain, dry well, roll in seasoned flour and sauté in a casserole in hot lard, bacon or ham drippings until well browned on all sides. Now stir in 1 cup of thinly sliced onions, the rings separated, 1 cup of thinly sliced green pepper, the white seeds and white ribs carefully removed, 1 cup of thinly sliced fresh mushrooms, 1 No. 2 can of tomatoes, ¼ cup of cooked, chopped lean ham, 1 clove of garlic, 1 bouquet garni composed of 1 large bay leaf, 2 sprigs of marjoram (if available, or lacking it, use dill), 1 sprig of thyme and 7 or 8 sprigs of fresh parsley, all tied with white kitchen thread. Salt to taste also 10 peppercorns, gently bruised, and pour over all ½ cup of dry white wine. Cover tightly, and bake in a moderate oven (350–375° F.) for an hour without disturbing. Discard the bouquet garni, taste for seasoning, and when ready to serve, stir in 3 tablespoons of good sherry wine.

LIVER DINNER COVENTRY STYLE   [816]
Also called in Coventry, England, "Liver Convent Style"

Sauté 12 slices of bacon until almost tender and place in a casserole. Over the bacon, arrange a layer of thinly sliced onions, and over the onions a layer of potatoes, thinly sliced after paring. Sprinkle over all 1 large green pepper, coarsely chopped, and absolutely free from white seeds and white ribs. Bury in center a bouquet garni composed of 2 sprigs of fennel, 1 large bay leaf, 1 sprig of thyme and 8 sprigs of fresh parsley, all tied together with white kitchen thread. Season to taste with salt and freshly ground black pepper. Set aside. Roll in seasoned flour 6 slices of liver, previously soaked in milk for 30 minutes, drained, patted dry, then rolled in seasoned flour, and cooked on both sides in a little lard until just beginning to brown. Add the liver to the casserole arranging the slices neatly side by side; pour over all 1 No. 2 can of tomatoes; top with 8 or 10 more slices of bacon; then adjust the lid tightly. Bake one hour in a moderate oven (375° F.) without disturbing. Serve right from the casserole after tasting for seasoning and discarding the bouquet garni.

LIVER FINES HERBES   [817]

Have 6 slices of liver, preferably calf's liver, cut ¼-inch thick. Wipe with a damp cloth, dip in milk, then roll in seasoned flour and cook in a sauté pan in 3 tablespoons of clarified butter, over a gentle flame, until nicely browned on both sides. Season with salt and pepper. Arrange liver on a hot serving platter and pour over it the following sauce: Heat in a clean frying pan 2 tablespoons of sweet butter; stir in 1 teaspoon each of chopped tarragon and parsley and the juice of half lemon. Blend well, then stir in 1 teaspoon of very finely chopped shallots, and as much of chervil, if available. Cook half a minute, and pour very hot over the liver. Garnish with 12 strips of broiled bacon, watercress and, if desired, small triangles of bread fried in butter.

LIVER LOAF FRENCH STYLE   [818]
A very fine imitation of the French Pâté de Foie Gras

For this delicious substitute for goose liver loaf, take 1½ pounds of calf's liver, remove the skin and tubes and cut in small pieces together with ¼ pound of pork loin. Cook in water barely to cover, with 1 large onion, chopped, 3 whole cloves, 1 large bay leaf, 4 sprigs of fresh parsley, and 1 sprig of thyme all tied with kitchen thread; salt and black pepper to taste. When the liver is quite tender, chop it, then run through food chopper, using the finest blade, and finally, rub through a fine-meshed sieve. Let the pork continue cooking until it, too, is perfectly tender, then remove and chop it into coarse pieces. Fry 8 chicken livers, previously cleaned, then quickly washed and dried, in 1 tablespoon of butter with 2 tablespoons of grated onion; discard the onions, and cut each liver into 4 pieces. Cream ¼ cup of sweet butter; gradually add the calf's liver paste, a tiny pinch of powdered thyme, 1 tablespoon of Worcestershire sauce, a few grains each of nutmeg, sage and mace, salt and pepper, and work to a smooth paste. Add the chicken livers and the pieces of pork, and mix well. Pack into small jars, the insides of which have been rubbed with butter, and seal. Keep in a cool dark, place and use as an appetizer, a sandwich spread, or serve with cold cuts. Keeps for months.

LIVER LOAF VIENNESE STYLE [819]

Wipe with a damp cloth 2 pounds of pork liver, cut into small pieces, then pass through food chopper three times together with 1 pound of fat pork, 1 medium-sized onion and 4 tablespoons of brandy. Place in a mixing bowl and add 2 tablespoons of flour, 2 eggs, slightly beaten, 2 teaspoons of salt, ¾ teaspoon of freshly ground black pepper, ½ teaspoon of cloves, ½ teaspoon of allspice, ½ teaspoon of sage, ¼ teaspoon of mixed mace and nutmeg. Moisten with 3 tablespoons of light cream (top of the bottle or undiluted evaporated milk). Rub mixture through a fine-meshed sieve. Pack in an ungreased loaf pan, which has been rubbed with a cut clove of garlic; place the pan in a pan of water, having the water up to the level of the meat mixture, and bake in a moderate oven (350–375° F.) 2½ to 3 hours, covering the loaf with a buttered paper if it browns too fast. There will be a brown crust on the top, but what you find underneath is simply delicious.

Wrapped in wax paper this will keep for several weeks in your refrigerator, and, spread on rye bread with a leaf of lettuce, makes a vitamin-rich sandwich.

LIVER SOUFFLÉ [820]

Heat 2 tablespoons of butter together with 1 strip of chopped bacon, over a low flame, and when bacon is just beginning to brown, lift-it out; add 1 tablespoon each of finely chopped onion, parsley and green pepper. and cook 1 minute, stirring almost constantly to blend. Sprinkle in 3 tablespoons of flour, and when blended, but not brown, stir in ¾ cup of rich milk, which has been scalded with 1 large bay leaf, 2 cloves and a blade of garlic, then strained. Stir constantly until mixture thickens. Scald ½ pound of liver; remove the skin and membrane, put through food chopper, then stir into the milk mixture. Boil up once, remove from the fire, let cool a little, then beat in 4 egg yolks, one at a time, beating well after each addition, and seasoning to taste with salt and white pep-

per with the last egg yolk. Now fold in 4 egg whites stiffly beaten with
¼ teaspoon of salt. Turn mixture into a generously buttered casserole,
and bake in a hot oven (425° F.) for about 20–25 minutes or until soufflé
is well puffed and nicely browned on top. Serve with tomato sauce
(No. 1130) to which has been added ½ cup of thinly sliced fresh mushrooms previously cooked in a little butter and well drained.

LIVER TERRAPIN IN CHAFING DISH [821]

Wipe with a damp cloth then remove the skin from a 1½-pound piece
of liver, preferably calf's liver; cut into half-inch pieces, removing tubes
and membrane if any; dredge the liver lightly in seasoned flour and sauté
in ¼ cup of butter in top of a chafing dish, over hot water, adding 1 teaspoon each of minced shallot, green pepper, grated onion, and chives and
stirring almost constantly. When liver is almost tender, pour in 1 generous cup of sweet cream, which has been scalded with 1 bay leaf, 1
whole clove, and 1 tiny blade of garlic, then strained, Let this cook 5
minutes, stirring occasionally, then add 2 finely chopped hard-cooked
egg whites, and 2 hard cooked egg yolks, rubbed through a fine sieve
and mixed to a paste with a little of the cream. Cook one minute, stirring
constantly; season to taste with salt and white pepper, and when ready
to serve (over small squares of freshly made toast) stir in a generous ¼
cup of good Madeira wine, that has been heated, but not boiled. Chicken
livers may be prepared in this same manner.

SAUSAGE [822]

Sausage may be bought in either the bulk form or in individual links
protected by transparent casings. These links may be large, medium, or
small—in this last case they are frequently spoken of as "baby sausages."

But whatever the size or style, the buyer should be sure the sausage
is pure pork, for not all sausage is choice pork and nothing else, but
may be composed of blended pork and cereal. So depend upon a well-
established brand for sausage quality and flavor.

Sausage quality and flavor are governed by choice meat, the right
proportion of fat to lean, and the character and blending of the spices.
In sausage containing too much fat, they are likely to be greasy, and
in sausage containing too many spices, the meat will be peppery and
coarse in flavor.

The gourmet's way of cooking sausage is to broil it after the manner
of broiled steak or chop. Prick each sausage with a fork, place on the
broiling rack about four inches below flame, and broil about 10 to
12 minutes, turning once.

The next best way is to pan-fry the sausage in a skillet on the top
burner. Have skillet hot, lay the pricked sausage in it and brown.

Reduce the heat, cover and pan-fry 6 to 10 minutes, depending on size and style of sausage.

Since sausage meat is solid protein plus fat, it requires the accompaniment of starch and green food to make a complete meal. Potatoes, rice noodles, macaroni, spaghetti and bread will supply the starch, and any green vegetables, particularly any members of the cabbage family or apples, cranberries or other tart fruits seem "naturals" with sausage meals. Apples are closely associated with sausage. Sliced apples may be fried in some of the fat taken from the pan as the sausage cooks, or they may be baked separately with only a small amount of sugar.

SAUSAGE—HINTS [823

Sausage patties are sure to please, when dipped in beaten egg, rolled in crushed corn flakes and fried. Applesauce on the side is the right accompaniment.

Small broiled sausages and scrambled eggs are popular for evening snacks. Vary the service with broiled pineapple rings or apricot or peach halves.

With breakfast sausage, sauté some prunes at the same time. Sausage does something to them and they to sausage.

Fried sausage meat will be less greasy and more tender when put on to cook in a cold frying pan and with no added fat.

Lay pork sausages loosely in a shallow pan and add boiling water barely to top of sausages. Place (uncovered) in a hot oven (400° F.) for 25–30 minutes, turning once or twice, to prevent sticking. You'll have plump, attractive sausages.

It is not necessary to prick link sausages if they are placed in a frying pan with 2 or 3 tablespoons of cold water, covered and cooked until water is evaporated. Then remove cover, increase heat and brown.

Try filling cored apples with sausage and baking them for breakfast or lunch.

Link sausages are cooked in much the same way as bacon, *slowly* with frequent turning. In this way, they are less likely to burst. The frequent turning insures even browning and even cooking throughout.

Parboil link sausage for a few minutes, drain and roll in flour before frying. This will keep the sausage from breaking or shrinking.

A good biscuit dough rolled out thin, sprinkled with a little grated onion, parsley and green pepper or chives, then wrapped around baked link sausages and baked again in a hot oven is delicious. Serve baked or fried apple slices with these rolls.

In buying sausages, it makes little difference whether you buy the one-pound boxes of links (sixteen to a pound, which serve 4); or little skinless patties (twelve to a pound, which serve 4); or the one-pound moisture-proof paper rolls to be cut off in slices for frying (serving 4) but be sure of one thing, *buy by brand.*

Pigs in hay—a paraphrase of "Chicken in the Rough"—popular on the West Coast are something new to serve when people drop in. Nicely browned pure pork link sausage in a bed of shoestring potatoes, served in individual wooden bowls. Fill them in the kitchen and bring them in. A tossed salad, a dessert, and you have a complete meal.

SAUSAGES IN BLANKETS FRENCH STYLE [824]

Pan broil 18 link sausages until well browned over a gentle flame, turning frequently to brown evenly. Sift 2 cups of flour once with 1 teaspoon of curry powder, add 2 teaspoons of baking powder and ½ teaspoon of salt, and sift again into mixing bowl. Cut in ¼ cup of butter or half butter and half lard; add ¼ cup of dry white wine gradually, stirring until soft dough is formed; turn out on slightly floured board and knead for a half minute, or enough to shape; roll out to ½-inch thickness and spread lightly with a mixture composed of 2 tablespoons each of grated onion, finely chopped parsley, mushrooms, green pepper, and chives, mixed with enough prepared mustard to have mixture of spreading consistency, like mayonnaise. Cut in 2½ inch squares; place half a pan-fried link sausage in center of each square; fold dough over sausage; pinch edges together and shape into roll, leaving ends open. Place seamside down on ungreased baking sheet, and bake in a hot oven (450° F.) for about 10 to 12 minutes. Fine with cocktails for buffet service or as snacks after the show.

SAUSAGE FRUIT GRILL [825]

Place 18 link sausages on broiler rack (first pricking each one with a fork) the rack adjusted to about 4 inches beneath a moderate flame, with 5 canned, drained peach halves, cup sides up; put a little butter, 1 teaspoon of lemon juice and a very few grains of powdered ginger in each peach cavity for added flavor, and broil on rack about four inches from broiler flame 10 to 12 minutes, turning once. Serve sausages heaped over a bed of freshly made shoestring potatoes (No. 1424), surrounded by the peaches; garnish with watercress and lemon quarters and serve at once.

SAUSAGE AND NOODLE DINNER [826]

Grill 18 link sausages as indicated for Sausage Link Fruit Grill above, No. 825). Cook 1 package of noodles, drain, then toss with 1 cup of grated American Cheese and ¼ cup of butter. Arrange on serving dish, place sausages on top and pour over all 1½ cups of tomato sauce (No. 130).

SAUSAGE LINKS A LA PROVENÇALE [827]

Parboil 18 link sausages 2 or 3 minutes; drain and roll in lightly seasoned flour mixed with a few grains of saffron, and sauté gently a few minutes, just to brown lightly all over. In another frying pan cook 1 large chopped onion in 3 tablespoons of olive oil, with 1 clove of garlic, mashed to a pulp. When onion begins to turn yellow, add the sausages with ¼ cup of capers and 2 anchovy filets, washed and finely chopped. Season lightly with salt and pepper, if needed. Turn into a baking dish, pour over 1½ to 1¾ cups of dry Rhine wine, add 1 bay leaf and bake in a moderate oven (375° F.), for about 20 minutes. Serve right from the baking dish with a side dish of plain boiled potatoes in their skins.

SAUSAGE LINKS SCALLOP [828]

Simmer 18 link sausages in beef broth for 10 minutes over a very, low flame. Cut 6 of them into small pieces; arrange a layer of sliced raw potatoes in a greased baking dish or casserole; sprinkle with a little flour, salt and pepper to taste, and add some of the sausage pieces. Repeat with another layer of raw, sliced potatoes flour and sausage, ending with a layer of whole sausages on top. Pour in 2 cups of milk; dot with 2 tablespoons of butter, and bake in a moderate oven (350° F.) for 1¼ to 1½ hours, covering with a greased paper if browning too fast. Serve right from the dish.

SAUSAGE MEAT CAKES WITH [829]
POACHED EGGS

Split 6 English muffins or baking powder biscuits and spread with a little prepared mustard, then with a little sausage meat, using ½ lb. in all; place under the flame of the broiling oven for 5 minutes. While broiling, poach 6 eggs in the usual way. Place an egg on each muffin; pour Mushroom Sauce (No. 1090) over and serve at once, garnished with French fried potatoes and watercress.

SAUSAGE MEAT "FRUMETS" ALSATIAN [830]
MANNER
A Variation of the "Sausage Links in Blanket French Way,"
No. 824

Mix and blend thoroughly the following ingredients: 1 pound of pork sausage meat, ¼ pound of lean beef, ground, 1 medium-sized green pepper, ground, 2 tablespoons of grated onion, 1 thin slice of garlic, 1 tablespoon each of shallots, parsley, and chives, all very finely chopped, ½ teaspoon of poultry seasoning, ¾ teaspoon of salt, ½ teaspoon each of thyme, mace, sage and nutmeg. Chill, then form mixture into small sausages about 2 inches long and the thickness of the thumb; have ready well chilled pie crust; roll out on a slightly floured board to a sheet ⅟₁₆ inch thick; cut in strips to fit the finger sausages (Called "Frumets"); roll the pastry strips around the meat rolls, sealing both ends; prick each one with the tines of a fork; place them, a good inch apart, on an ungreased baking sheet; brush with egg yolk, or melted meat glaze (commercial) and bake in a hot oven (425° F.) for 10 to 12 minutes. Serve hot as appetizers, snacks, or surrounding a dish of generously buttered spinach, cabbage or sauerkraut.

SAUSAGE MEAT PISCALLERIA [831] MARSEILLAISE

Partially pan fry 1⅓ pounds of pork meat sausage, crumbling it with a fork, and draining off all fat. Sift 1 cup of flour with 2½ teaspoons of baking powder, ¾ teaspoon of salt and 2 tablespoons of fine granulated sugar, over 1 cup of yellow corn meal, and mix thoroughly. Combine 1 large well-beaten egg with 1 cup of cold, sweet rich milk, and add to dry ingredients, mixing well, and adding at the same time 3 tablespoons of the sausage fat. Do not beat at all, merely mix well. Arrange half of the sausage meat in an ungreased baking pan. Pour the batter over, spreading as evenly as possible, arrange the remaining sausage meat on top, cover with ½ cup of buttered bread crumbs, and bake in a very hot oven (425° F.) for 40–45 minutes, covering with a greased paper if browning too fast. Serve with a side dish of Brown Sauce (No. 1018).

SAUSAGE MEAT AND ONION [832] SHORTCAKE CURRY

Cook 1 pound of sausage meat and 1 cup of thinly sliced onions in skillet in its own fat for about 20 minutes, stirring with a fork over a gentle flame; sprinkle in 3 tablespoons of flour, mixed with 2 teaspoons of curry powder; mix well, season to taste with salt, pepper and a dash of nutmeg, and when thoroughly blended add 2 cups of milk, which has been scalded with 1 bay leaf, 2 cloves, and 4 sprigs of parsley, then strained. Stir constantly, until thick. Split 12 hot baking powder biscuits and cover them with the mixture. Sprinkle over some finely chopped parsley and serve at once.

SAUSAGE MEAT PATTIES, CREAM GRAVY [833] CREOLE

Mix 1 pound of pork sausage meat with ½ pound of lean, ground meat, 1 teaspoon of salt, ¼ cup raw rice, 2 tablespoons of grated onion, 1 tablespoon each of finely chopped parsley, green pepper and chives in season, ⅛ teaspoon of pepper and a generous dash of marjoram. Shape mixture firmly into round patties, the size of a golf ball; flatten a little, and brown slowly but thoroughly in their own fat, turning them often, for 10 to 12 minutes. Add ¾ cup of boiling water mixed with ¼ cup of Pique Seasoning, and simmer very gently for 1¼ hours, or until liquid is almost all absorbed. Take out patties and keep hot. Add to the liquid left in the pan 3 tablespoons flour, blend smoothly; then stir in 2 cups of scalded milk and bring to a boil, stirring constantly; season to taste with salt, pepper, ⅛ teaspoon ground cloves and ¼ teaspoon ground cinnamon, and boil up once. Reheat the pattie in this cream gravy and serve very hot.

SAUSAGE MEAT RAMEKINS LUNCHEON   [834]

Butter 6 individual casseroles or ramekins with anchovy butter (No. 979). Fill each one ⅔ full of seasoned pork sausage meat, using 1 pound in all; make a cavity in each with a spoon and drop in a raw egg; sprinkle with salt, pepper and 2 teaspoons of grated cheese; dust the cheese with a little paprika, and bake in a moderate oven (350° F.) for about 15–18 minutes, or until eggs are set. Serve at once.

SWEETBREADS   [835]

Only calf's and lamb's sweetbreads are used in cookery, although beef sweetbreads may be used advantageously when mixed with other meats, especially in meat pies, meat patties, pasties, garnishings, etc.

Sweetbreads, always believed a bit costly, in cities, are too rarely found on the home table, and seem to be tacitly accepted as a delicacy peculiar to the rich and to the better hotel restaurants, where adroit chefs know precisely what to do with them. Many homemakers and cooks do not even know what a sweetbread is, nor what animal it comes from.

Each animal possesses two kinds of sweetbreads, one found in the throat and the other in the body proper. The first are throat sweetbreads, or the thymus glands of the neck, which in mammals shrink to almost nothing as they attain years of discretion, and are of elongated shape, while the others called heart sweetbreads, or belly sweetbreads, are of rounded contour. The latter are much sought-after by the lovers of choice viands, while the former, being less expensive, may be used for garnishing.

Many dealers try to substitute sweetbreads from young steers for those of veal, which are quite different both in quality and color, as are lamb sweetbreads. The veal and lamb sweetbreads are white and tender, while those of the steer are reddish and tough under pressure of the fingers.

Sweetbreads must be strictly *fresh*, otherwise they are unfit to eat. They should always come direct from the *abattoir*. Soft gland tissue deteriorates and decomposes rapidly and the same is true of tripe, brains, livers and kidneys.

Initial and First Obligatory Operation. When you buy sweetbreads, which always come in pairs, do not put them into the refrigerator to keep for the next day, but plunge them immediately into cold water to draw out the blood. Keep them in it an hour, changing the water several times, then put them into a pan of cold water using enough to cover, with a dash of salt, and the juice of half a lemon for each pair of sweetbreads. Bring to a boil slowly and simmer gently 15 minutes. This is called blanching and also disgorging. Return to the cold water to blanch them thoroughly; then carefully pick out the tubes and membranes without tearing the tissues. Place in refrigerator, but do not keep long before using, as sweetbreads easily absorb the flavor of any other foods with which they come in contact, so it is advisable to buy them to be used the same day, or at least within 24 hours.

BAKED LARDED SWEETBREADS CREOLE   [836]

The sweetbreads should be prepared as indicated at beginning of this chapter, and larded with thin, narrow, long strips of larding pork, rolled in mixed spices (sage, thyme, cloves, marjoram, salt and pepper to taste). Place 3 pairs of sweetbreads in a generously buttered earthenware dish, the bottom of which is covered with a thin coat of Creole Sauce (Nos. 1041–42). Cover with another layer of the same sauce and dot with butter. Cover with a buttered paper and set in a moderately hot oven (350° F.) for 25 minutes. Serve right from the baking dish.

BRAISED SWEETBREADS BONNE MAMAN   [837]

Cut 1 cup of vegetables—carrots, turnips, celery (white only), green pepper in match-like sticks—and strew in a generously buttered pan having a tightly fitting cover. Over the vegetables, arrange 3 pairs of sweetbreads previously prepared as indicated at beginning of this chapter, and sprinkle over them 2 tablespoons of finely chopped cooked ham. Add 1 bouquet garni, composed of 1 sprig of parsley, 1 bay leaf, and celery leaves all tied together with white kitchen thread, also 2 cloves, 8 peppercorns, bruised, a tiny pinch of thyme with salt and a few grains of cayenne pepper. Pour over 1¾ cups of veal stock. Place over the fire and bring to a boil. Cover tightly and set the pan in a moderate oven (350° F.) for 40 minutes. Transfer the sweetbreads to a hot platter and arrange the strained vegetables around them after removing the bouquet garni. Place the gravy in a pan and reduce a little over a hot fire. Correct the seasoning. Add 1 tablespoon of butter and pour over the sweetbreads. Dust with chopped parsley and serve garnished with small triangles of bread fried in butter.

BRAISED SWEETBREADS OLD STYLE   [838]

Prepare 3 pairs of sweetbreads as indicated at beginning of this chapter. Roll in beaten egg, then in breadcrumbs and place in a well-buttered baking dish having a tightly fitting cover. Pour over ½ cup of beef stock, add 1 bay leaf, 1 clove, 1 bouquet garni (composed of celery leaves and parsley tied together with white kitchen thread), a tiny pinch each of thyme, mace and allspice, salt and pepper to taste and lastly ½ cup of white wine. Cover and braise in a moderate oven for 35–40 minutes. Arrange sweetbreads on a hot platter. Strain the gravy. Add to it 1 tablespoon of kneaded butter, (equal parts of butter and flour, worked together). Cook 10 minutes and pour around the sweetbreads.

BREADED SAUTÉED LARDED   [839]
SWEETBREADS

Take 3 pairs of sweetbreads and prepare as indicated at beginning of this chapter. Split, then season to taste with salt and pepper; roll in beaten egg, then in breadcrumbs to which have been added a tiny pinch each of thyme, sage, clove and marjoram and fry in a skillet in 3 tablespoons of butter or bacon drippings until brown on both sides. Arrange on a hot platter, sprinkle with fried parsley, and serve with tomato sauce to which has been added 2 tablespoons of coarsely chopped hard-cooked egg.

BROCHETTE OF SWEETBREADS   [840]

Prepare two pairs sweetbreads as indicated at beginning of this chapter. Split, then cut each half into quarters. Thread on skewers, alternating slices of sweetbread, slices of salt pork, then sliced (or whole) mushrooms cooked in butter. Repeat till skewer is full. Dip in beaten egg, roll in cracker crumbs and broil under the flame of a slow broiling oven, sprinkling occasionally with melted butter. Serve very hot, each skewer placed on a slice of buttered toast spread with a tiny film of anchovy paste. Garnish with crisp young watercress. Serve with a Brown or Tomato Sauce (Nos. 1017–18, or No. 1130).

SWEETBREAD LOAF GASTRONOME   [841]

Line a buttered bread pan with rich pastry (No. 2104); brush the pastry with slightly beaten egg white, flavored with ½ teaspoon of curry powder, then cover the pastry (sides and bottom) with a coating of smoked turkey hash, not too moist, and flavored with a little Madeira wine, the coating to be about ¼ of an inch in thickness. Set aside.

Parboil for 15 minutes 1 pair of sweetbreads in equal parts of dry white wine and water, to which has been added 3 thin slices of onion,

2 whole cloves, 5 freshly bruised whole peppercorns, ½ teaspoon of salt, 8 thin slices of carrot, and 1 bouquet garni (composed of 1 large bay leaf, 6 sprigs of fresh parsley, 1 sprig of thyme, and 1 sprig of green celery leaves (tops), all tied with white kitchen thread). Drain, plunge in cold water and when cool enough to handle, remove all membranes and tubes carefully, then slice, and set aside.

Brown together in ¼ cup of butter ½ pound of cooked, lean ham, cut into small cubes, ½ cup of chopped green pepper, 1 cup of thinly sliced fresh mushrooms, using both caps and stems, stirring almost constantly; remove from the fire, stir in 2 drained, canned, chopped pimientos, 1 cup of Madeira wine sauce (No. 1076), and finally the prepared sweetbreads, with ½ cup of tiny bread cubes, previously fried in butter and well drained. Fill the prepared bread pan with this mixture, cover with pastry, slash top here and there with the tines of a fork and make a larger slash in center. Bake in a moderate oven (350° F.) about one hour, or until pastry top is delicately browned. Remove from the oven, pour in through the large slash; by means of a small funnel or a paper cornet, 2 tablespoons of Madeira wine, let stand about 10 minutes then unmold on a hot round platter. Garnish simply with a few bouquets of watercress and serve at once with additional Madeira sauce (No. 1076). This paté is also excellent served cold with a crisp green salad.

SWEETBREADS LYONNAISE [842]

Prepare 3 pairs of sweetbreads as indicated at the beginning of this chapter. Parboil ¼ lb. of fat salt pork (in one piece). Cut in narrow strips and lard the sweetbreads through and through with the strips. Place in a casserole, and barely cover with rich beef stock to which has been added 1 or 2 teaspoons of beef extract and add 1 bouquet garni (composed of 1 large bay leaf, 6 sprigs of fresh parsley, 1 sprig of thyme, and 1 sprig of green celery leaves (tops), tied with kitchen thread), 1 generous tablespoon of chives, chopped fine, 1 small clove of garlic, bruised, 2 whole cloves, 4 or 5 tarragon leaves, *no salt at all*, 8 whole peppercorns, gently bruised, scant ½ teaspoon of sage, scant ½ teaspoon of allspice, 2 tablespoons of finely chopped fresh mushrooms, and boil gently for 35 minutes. Lift out the sweetbreads and keep hot. Strain the broth in the casserole, and carefully remove all the fat. Return the broth to a hot fire and let it reduce almost entirely, then brush the sweetbreads all over with this remaining pure extract, or glaze of meat. Pour into the casserole 1 generous cupful of rich stock. Allow it to boil up, stirring from the bottom so as to loosen all the particles which may adhere. This in culinary language is called "deglazing." Add 2 or 3 tablespoons of white grape juice, made a little tart, by the addition of a few drops of lemon juice or vinegar. Bring to a boil and add 1 tablespoon of kneaded butter (equal parts of flour and butter, kneaded together). Cook 2 or 3 minutes to remove the raw flour flavor which is always present if not cooked a few minutes. Remove from fire and add gradually, one at a time, and beating vigorously after each addition, 3 egg yolks. Taste for seasoning and strain this rich sauce over the sweetbreads on a hot platter. Serve at once.

SWEETBREADS MELBA [843]

Note. The sauce for this delicious dish which used to be one of the favorites of the famous diva, is a creation of Mr. Julien, Maître d'Hôtel of the well-known restaurant Laperouse, in Paris, where the celebrated and inimitable diva, a *parfaite connaisseuse*, used to dine often. It may be prepared right at the table if desired, in a chafing dish.

Braise in the ordinary way 3 pairs of sweetbreads previously prepared as indicated at the beginning of this chapter. Transfer to a hot platter and have ready on the service table the following ingredients:

For each sweetbread—1 pat of butter, 1 teaspoon of prepared mustard, salt, pepper and lemon juice to taste, with 2 tablespoons of the strained gravy in which the sweetbreads have been braised. Melt the butter in a chafing dish, add the prepared mustard (English mustard may be used if a rather sharp sauce is desired) and stir until well blended. Add 2 or more tablespoons of strained gravy and season to taste with salt and coarsely ground pepper (pepper from the mill). Slice a sweetbread and add to the sauce. Serve with asparagus tips and purée of fresh mushrooms.

TONGUES [844]

"Go to the market place and bring me something good," said the mistress to the cook. "Yes, Madam," she replied and went to market, returning with a tongue. On another occasion, to test out her cook, the mistress said: "Go to the market place and bring me something bad."— "Yes, Madam," and again the cook went to the market place, and again returned with a tongue. "Why?" asked the mistress, "did you bring a tongue on both occasions?"—"A tongue, Madam," replied the cook, "may be the source of either good or evil. If it is good, there is nothing better. If it is bad, there is nothing worse."

A mild-cured smoked tongue appeals to those who consider fresh tongue rather insipid in flavor; soaked overnight in water, it loses its surface salt and becomes plump and desirable. Both the smoked and fresh tongues must be simmered very gently in water with vegetables as for a soup. Tongue may be served cold or hot. Calves' and lambs' tongues are available fresh, smoked and pickled and may be prepared in the same manner as beef or pigs tongues. Tongues, like heart, have received considerable exercise and thus developed connective tissue.

For this reason, it is necessary to cook tongues by moist heat, and simmering or cooking in water or other indicated liquid must be the preliminary preparation.

A tablespoon of vinegar added to tongue while boiling, makes it easier to peel the skin off. This should always be done while the tongue is still hot.

A little horseradish and lemon juice stirred into stiff mayonnaise makes a very good sauce to serve with tongue.

When preparing jellied tongue, add a bay leaf to the gelatin, and don't forget a little prepared mustard.

Fresh boiled tongue skinned, sliced, and arranged around a mound of creamed spinach, garnished with hard-cooked eggs and sautéed new potatoes is an acceptable dish, winter or summer.

BEEF TONGUE JARDINIERE [845]

Boil a fresh beef tongue 2 hours, skin and lay in a roaster on a layer of diced vegetables such as carrots, turnips, celery and potatoes, with peas, beans, small onions, and small tomatoes, as needed. Pour around the tongue some of the water in which it was boiled; cover and cook slowly until tender two hours or longer. Remove tongue and keep it hot, while taking out the vegetables with a skimmer. Thicken the gravy with browned flour. Place tongue on hot platter; arrange vegetables, around it, and pour over some of the gravy, serving the rest in a sauceboat.

BOILED BEEF TONGUE [846]

Cover a large beef tongue with about 2 quarts of water. Add ½ cup vinegar, 2 tablespoons sugar, a large clove of garlic (minced fine), 1 bay leaf and 1 teaspoon of cumin seed. Simmer until very tender. Allow to cool, then peel. Serve with any preferred sauce.

BOILED LAMB TONGUES PAYSANNE [847]

Wash 4 small lamb tongues, then place them in a saucepan; cover with boiling water and add 1 small bay leaf, 1 small onion, quartered, and 1½ teaspoons salt. Bring to a boil and in five minutes reduce the heat; cover and simmer about 2 hours or until tender, when the skin curls. Let cool about 30 minutes or longer in the stock.

Lift the tongues from the stock, reserving it for soup, such as minestrone, vegetable or split pea. Strip off the tongue skin using a knife if necessary; remove any small bones and fat. Serve with Raisin Sauce (No. 1108).

BRAISED FRESH BEEF TONGUE [848]

Cover a fresh beef tongue with boiling water and simmer for about 2 hours. Lift out tongue and trim off skin. Now place the tongue in a deep casserole and add ¼ cup chopped onion, ¼ cup chopped celery and ½ cup diced carrots. Then pour over all the following Pickle Sauce and bake, covered, in a moderate oven (350° F.) about 2 hours. Serve on a hot platter with sauce on the side also a dish of spinach en branch.

Pickle Sauce. Melt 3 tablespoons butter over moderate heat, and when brown blend in 3 tablespoons flour. Gradually add three cups of the water in which the tongue was cooked, and stir until boiling. Remove from the fire and add 1 teaspoon Worcestershire Sauce, salt and pepper to taste, and ½ cup of chopped sour pickle.

LAMB TONGUES IN ASPIC [849]

Remove lambs' tongues from jar and arrange in mold or loaf pan. Heat 1 can of concentrated beef bouillon, fresh or canned, ½ cup of tongue liquor from the jar, strained through a fine sieve and ¼ cup of tarragon vinegar to the boiling point, then stir in 1 tablespoon of gelatine previously soaked in ½ cup of cold water. Pour very gently over lambs' tongues in the mold or pan. Chill in refrigerator for at least 3 hours. When ready to serve, unmold on large, chilled platter; garnish with watercress, carrot sticks, quartered hard-cooked eggs, radish roses, pickles and black olives, and decorate the top of the aspic with mayonnaise forced through a pastry bag with a fancy tube.

SMOKED BEEF TONGUE IN ASPIC [850]

Remove skin from a 5-lb. freshly cooked smoked tongue; run skewers through tip of tongue and fleshy part, thus keeping the tongue in shape. When cool, remove skewers.

Imbed a round mold in ice; cover bottom with chicken aspic, and when firm, decorate with fancily cut slices of cooked, carrot, turnip, mushrooms, beets, and gherkins, also with parsley. Cover with more chicken aspic, adding it by spoon so as not to disarrange the garnishings. When thin layer of aspic is firm, put in the tongue, which has been sliced, then reshaped; or put the tongue in by layers, if preferred; gradually adding remaining aspic jelly, decorating as you go along with sliced olives, sliced gherkin, sliced radishes, etc., according to fancy. Chill at least 4 hours before unmolding on a cold platter: garnish with watercress, around the base of the aspic.

SMOKED BEEF TONGUE, CUMBERLAND SAUCE [851]

Let a smoked beef tongue soak in water for 24 hours. Boil from 2 to 3 hours, according to size, or until tender, in slightly salted water. Serve hot with Cumberland Sauce (No. 1044), and boiled rice to which has been added small, cooked dried currants.

SMOKED BEEF TONGUE, SAUCE PIQUANTE   [852]

Cover smoked beef tongue with cold water. Add a few sprigs of parsley, 1 medium sized onion, 1 bay leaf, a large piece of lemon rind, 3 whole cloves, and 10 peppercorns. Bring to boiling point and let boil for 5 minutes. Then simmer until tender, which will take about 4 hours. Lift tongue to cutting board, and when cool enough to handle, trim off thick skin and throat cords. Place tongue on large hot platter and pour Sauce Piquante (No. 1103), over it, serving additional Sauce in a sauceboat.

SWEET SOUR TONGUE   [853]

Place 1 medium-sized fresh beef tongue in a large saucepan; cover with water, and add 1 tablespoon salt. Simmer about 2 hours or until tender. Remove all hard parts and skin. While tongue is cooking make the following sauce: Fry 5 slices of chopped bacon, and 3 medium-sized chopped onions, in a heavy skillet for 10 minutes. Add 1 bay leaf, peel of 1 lemon and 3 peppercorns; fry 5 minutes longer. Now add the tongue stock strained (about 1 quart), 1 tablespoon vinegar, 1 tablespoon sugar, 2½ cups rolled gingersnap crumbs and 6 prunes, cooked and sieved; simmer for 15 minutes. Taste the sauce, making it sweet and sour. Strain; add ½ cup raisins, and ½ cup sliced blanched almonds. Slice the tongue; place in a saucepan, cover with the sauce, and reheat.

TONGUE MOUSSE   [854]

Soak 1 tablespoon gelatine in ¼ cup cold water for 5 minutes. Then add to ¾ cup boiling beef broth or bouillon, stirring until dissolved. Place in refrigerator until partially set. Then add 2 cups minced, cooked tongue, 1 teaspoon dry English mustard, 2 tablespoons grated onion, 2 tablespoons green pepper, minced, 2 tablespoons parsley, finely chopped, and 2 tablespoons lemon juice, stirring until thoroughly mixed. Fold in ½ cup whipped cream. Turn into small oblong mold, 3 inches deep. Chill, unmold, garnish with crisp salad greens and sliced tomatoes. Serve with Mustard Mayonnaise.

VEAL TONGUE HASH   [855]

Dice 2 cups of veal tongue and put it through grinder, using the medium blade. Combine in a bowl with 3 cups diced boiled potatoes, 1 small onion, minced, salt to taste, and a generous amount of pepper. Cover and chill. Heat 3 tablespoons drippings or bacon fat in a heavy skillet; add the tongue mixture; cover and heat through. Stir until well mixed. Then cook uncovered until brown underneath; turn with a broad spatula or pancake turner, and brown the other side. Transfer carefully to a heated platter and garnish with sprigs of parsley. Serve with white turnips and turnip tops.

TRIPE   [856]

Tripe, like certain alluring vices, is enjoyed by society's two extremes, the topmost and the lowermost strata, while the multitudinous middle classes of the world pass it by with genteel disdain and noses tilted to the sniffing angle. Patricians relished tripe in Babylon's gardens; plebeians always have welcomed it as something good and cheap; and always the peasant cook has taught the prince how to eat it.

The shrewd and calculated cooking methods of the masses and the peasantry have elevated many plain and homely comestibles from the earthen bowl of the thatched hut to the silver trencher of the castle hall, and tripe, scorned and rejected by the unknowing, has an honored place on the tables of epicures along with codfish, kidney stew, cabbage and good red herring.

In the great wide world there are probably as many persons who know the mediaeval city of Caen for its "Tripe à la Mode de Caen" as well as for all the Caen stone that has gone into Christendom's cathedrals.

Tripe has made Pharamond's restaurant famous in Paris, and it figures with bouillabaisse among the glories of Marseilles. Russia, Denmark, Poland, Italy, Greece, and the Balkan States have added chapters to the lore of tripe, yet there remains one simple humble dish which has not been exalted in culinary *belles lettres*—just tripe and onions stewed in milk—but it is worthy of a line in the index.

In the early days of World War I, this present writer was languishing in a small hotel in Le Havre which furnished quarters for several Army and Navy officers and their families, and one day the kindly and sociable innkeeper appeared in the dining room and announced with bold confidence that his chef had prepared a very special specialty, which was *Tripe and Onions in Cream*. And where there should have been plaudits and huzzas, there was ominous silence, with a wrinkling of noses and an arching of eyebrows; but one daring Navy man stood up and cried, "O boy!" or words of like import, and your writer took courage and joined him on the bridge, as it were. Special orders of chops and ham and eggs prevailed that day, and it's a matter of honest record that the gallant Navy hero and your servitor alone partook of tripe and onions, but did it as Falstaff might have done. "And, what is the matter with having this good stuff again tomorrow?" gasped the Navy man, leering at the disapproving multitude; and on the morrow the landlord dutifully and gratefully served two more portions of tripe and onions réchauffé (warmed-over). But so great is the power of popular opinion that tripe and onions appeared no more in that caravanserai.

A great many people say they do not like tripe, but it may be because they have never eaten it properly cooked. Shakespeare must have enjoyed it, for he has Grumio ask Kate in *The Taming of the Shrew*, when he is tantalizing the hungry girl with descriptions of mouth-watering food, "How say you to a fat tripe finely broiled?" And Kate replied, "I like it well."

The humble tripe—if culinary history be true—accredited a turning point toward victory during the darkest hours at Valley Forge.

Winter, and General Washington's soldiers were in rags, shoes had worn thin; misery came unrelentingly; food was ever lacking. Cooks made ends meet where there were nothing but ends, and they met just over the starvation line. Soldiers began to think of home. Why stay to starve and die at Valley Forge? Desertions were frequent. The story is that General Washington took matters into his own hands and called for the head chef of all the Revolutionary armed forces. He explained the seriousness of the hour. He demanded a great dish. The Chef protested: "There is nothing, my General, but scraps in the kitchens. There is only tripe—a few hundred pounds, the gift of a nearby butcher. And there are peppercorns, a gift from a Germantown patriot. All the rest is scraps and more scraps."

" . . . From nothing," said General Washington, "you must create a great dish." The chef experimented. The tripe was scrubbed, it was simmered tender. Additions went into the big kettles, all the odds and ends of the kitchens. The peppercorns were ground to add fire to the stew. The early darkness came. Great kettles sent up their heart-warming, belly-comforting fragrance to the miserable men. The call of the bugle, and men ate their fill of this fortifying dish. Men laughed again . . . they joked: " . . . Bring on the Red Coats!"

The general called for the chef: " . . . This dish is the stuff of heroes! What is its name?" "General, I have conceived it but not called it," the chef replied, "but pepper pot would be my humble suggestion, sir." "Call it Philadelphia Pepper Pot," said Washington, "in honor of your own home town."

"Pepper Pot . . . Pepper-y Pot, piping hot!" In Colonial days the pepper-pot vendor plodded Philadelphia's twisting streets and alleyways chanting the pepper-pot call:

> " . . . All hot! All hot!
> *Pepper Pot! Pepper Pot!*
> *Makes back strong*
> *Makes life long*
> *All hot! Pepper Pot!*

The vendor and her (or his) cart have gone but pepper pot lives on as one of America's favorite mid-winter soups. And no one can deny that pepper pot is hearty food. It is like pork, a dish for harsh days of winter, something to fortify against the cold. Pepper pot is a meal; it stands by you as chowder does, and as oyster stew doesn't.

GRILLED TRIPE [857]

Broiled tripe is perhaps the simplest way there is of serving tripe. Nevertheless, it is a favorite with a great many people.

Wash carefully 2 pounds of fresh tripe, and cook in salted boiling water to generously cover, together with 1 bouquet garni composed of 1 large bay leaf, tied with 3 sprigs of green celery leaves, 10 sprigs of fresh parsley and 1 sprig or two of thyme all tied together with white kitchen thread. Add also 10 peppercorns, gently bruised, and 1 clove of garlic. Simmer gently for 3½ hours, and let cool in its own liquor overnight. Drain, cut the tripe into serving pieces of about 3 by 5 inches; roll the pieces in melted, seasoned butter, then in fine bread crumbs and broil under a gentle flame until brown on both sides.

Just as soon as tripe is taken from the broiler spread it lightly with Maître d'Hôtel Butter (No. 1078), then sprinkle with finely minced chives and serve piping hot.

TRIPE A LA CATALANA [858]
Callos à la Catalana

Wash 3 pounds of fresh tripe and cook in salted boiling water, together with 1 bouquet garni composed of 3 sprigs of green celery leaves, with 2 bay leaves, 10 sprigs of fresh parsley and 1 sprig of thyme, all tied together with white kitchen thread, and 8 peppercorns, gently bruised, for 3½ hours, or until tripe is quite tender. Drain and cut in very fine strips. Heat ¼ cup of lard or butter, or olive oil in a large frying pan, and when hot, stir in ½ cup of chopped onions, 4 medium-sized fresh tomatoes, peeled and chopped, the tripe, 1 clove of garlic, minced fine, 1 bouquet garni composed of 1 bay leaf, 4 sprigs of fresh parsley and 2 sprigs of marjoram, or equivalent in powder form if fresh marjoram is not available, all tied together with kitchen thread, and season with salt, pepper and a generous dash of nutmeg. Cover the pan, as tightly as possible, and bake in a slow oven (275°–300° F.) for 30 minutes, shaking the pan once or twice during the baking process. Serve in a hot deep dish sprinkling with blended chopped parsley and finely chopped raw garlic. Serve with it potato chips or Saratoga chips (No. 1432).

TRIPE A LA CREOLE [859]

Prepare 1 quart of Creole Sauce (Nos. 1041–42) and keep hot. Wash 1 to 1½ pounds of fresh tripe; drain and simmer gently in salted boiling water until tender or about 3½ hours; drain well; cut in strips, add to Creole sauce and let simmer gently covered for one hour. Taste for seasoning, and serve at once.

TRIPE A LA LORRAINE   [860]

Cut 2 pounds of honeycomb tripe in long, narrow strips and sauté until tripe strips begin to take on color, in ¼ cup of lard to which has been added a small whole clove of garlic, peeled, stirring almost constantly with a wooden spoon. Sprinkle in 1 tablespoon of flour and 1½ tablespoons of finely chopped shallots and blend well, then pour on 2 cups of dry white wine, mixed with 3 tablespoons of brandy; season to taste with salt, pepper and a slight grating of nutmeg; add 1 large bay leaf. Turn into a baking dish and cover tightly. Seal the lid with a strip of muslin wrung out of cold water, then spread with a flour paste to prevent escape of steam, and bake in a moderate oven (325° F.) for 3½ hours without disturbing. Fifteen minutes before serving, open the dish and spread over the tripe ⅓ cup of grated Swiss cheese combined with ¼ cup of rich cream sauce (No. 258) flavored with 1 teaspoon of lemon juice. Continue cooking, uncovered, for 15 minutes and serve at once right from the baking dish.

TRIPE A LA MADRILENA also called   [861]
"MONDONGO" or "CALLOS MADRILENA"
A rather fiery dish

Wash carefully 1 pound of pre-cooked Spanish smoked sausage called Chorizo. Place 6 strips of bacon in a saucepan with ½ cup of olive oil, and ¼ cup of chopped onions and cook till onions are slightly browned, then stir in ½ cup of dry white wine, ½ cup of rich beef broth, to which has been added 4 tablespoons of tomato paste, 1 extra large bay leaf, 4 or 5 crushed peppercorns, 1 teaspoon of chili pepper (more or less according to taste), ½ teaspoon of chopped garlic, a generous pinch of thyme leaves, and salt to taste. Bring all this to a boil; add 2 pounds of honeycomb tripe, cut into inch squares and sausage pieces; cover tightly and cook over a low flame for 3 hours, opening the pot after 1½ hours of cooking to add ½ cup of dry white wine, previously heated. Thirty minutes before serving, add 1 cup of freshly shelled peas; cover again, and continue cooking. Serve right from the casserole with a side dish of Tortillas.

Note. Raw, lean ham may be substituted for Spanish sausage.

TRIPE MAITRE D'HOTEL   [862]

Cut 1½ pounds fresh tripe into 2-inch strips, and cook in a stew pan with a small bottle of drained capers, 1 cup good beef broth, 1 cup dry white wine, 2 thin slices of peeled and seeded lemon, a bouquet garni composed of 1 large bay leaf, 6 sprigs fresh parsley, 1 sprig green celery

top, 1 sprig thyme, and a sprig or two of marjoram, all tied together with
white kitchen thread. Allow the whole to stew until the tripe is tender.
Then strain off the liquid, keeping the tripe hot. Reduce the liquid to 1
generous cup, and season it with salt, pepper, and a dash of cayenne
pepper. Thicken with the yolks of 3 eggs, beaten with a dash of nutmeg.
Boil up once, stirring briskly; then put the tripe in the sauce, reheat
without boiling and serve on a hot platter, over freshly made toast.

TRIPE A LA MODE DE CAEN   [863]

Wash 3 pounds of fresh honeycomb tripe, in 2 or 3 changes of cold
water; drain, then cut it into strips about as long and as wide as a man's
thumb. Use preferably a large earthenware casserole or a bean pot; a
metal Dutch oven with a tight cover will serve however if your have no
earthen pot. Line the bottom of the casserole, pot, or Dutch oven with
3 or 4 slices of fat salt pork. Next, put in two diced carrots, 2 sliced
onions, also 2 leeks, and 2 stalks of celery minced rather finely with a
large green pepper. On this vegetable layer, arrange the strips of tripe,
and add 2 calves' feet cut into small pieces, using both meat and bones.
Season with 1 tablespoon of minced chervil or parsley, a generous pinch
each of thyme and marjoram, 1 blade of mace, 2 large bay leaves, 8 whole
peppercorns, freshly bruised, 2 whole cloves, 1 teaspoon salt, and a few
grains of cayenne: all this should nearly fill the pot. Now cover the mixture with equal parts of rich beef stock and white wine or cider.

Some will tell you that the next step is unnecessary, and advise you
to omit it, but this writer has tried it out laboriously and it is the magic
secret of the dish, developed through the ages in Norman kitchens.
Mix a very stiff plain dough of flour and water, and roll it quickly into a
thick rope as long as the circumference of your pot cover. Arrange it
carefully around the rim of the pot, moisten it with water, and fit the
cover upon it, pressing down firmly. If there are ventilating holes in the
cover, seal them with bits of the dough. Thus the pot is hermetically
sealed, and neither juices nor aroma may escape.

Let the oven be as slow as you can make it, and bake the dish overnight. Twelve hours will do a pretty good job, but in Normandy they
take as much as eighteen hours. When the seal is broken and the lid
lifted. Olympian vapors will assail your quivering nostrils, and you will
behold ambrosia richer than any ragout of green turtle or of terrapin.
A final step remains, and that is to add 6 finely minced shallots, lightly
cooked in butter, 1 cup of strained tomato paste, and 1 glass of brandy
or sherry. Serve in the casserole, or on a deep platter, and garnish with
puff paste croutons and parsley.

Some Continental authorities prefer cognac or apple brandy, but
that's a matter of choice; and there's little doubt that the bonne femme

of Caen town stews her tripe in Normandy cider and tops it off with eau-de-vie de Caen or Calvados, which is Normandy's applejack.

While France has long been considered the largest cider-producing country in the world, the State of New Jersey is a close contender for the honor. Cider which has been submitted to distillation becomes APPLEJACK, also known as Cider Brandy and frequently called "Jersey Lightning." If properly aged, it comes close to being as good as the best distilled liquors and ranks second to the French Calvados.

TRIPE AND ONIONS [864]

Wash 2½ pounds of fresh tripe in several waters, then parboil it 3 hours in water to cover, adding more water as needed, with 1 sliced carrot, 1 medium sized onion, sliced, 1 bouquet garni composed of 1 large bay leaf tied with 1 sprig of thyme, and 6 sprigs of fresh parsley tied with kitchen thread; salt to taste and 6 or 7 peppercorns, gently bruised. Then peel at least 18 small white onions and put them into the pot to boil with the tripe; add no more water, but let the liquid reduce by simmering till the pot is almost dry. Add then enough rich milk, thin cream, or undiluted evaporated milk to cover the tripe and onions and simmer until the onions can easily be pierced with a fork. The stew is at its best when unthickened with flour or starch, but if it seems too thin, you may stir in 2 beaten egg yolks. Just before serving, add 1 cup of rich, sweet cream, scalded. Taste for seasoning, and serve at once.

TRIPE, ONIONS AND OYSTERS A L'ANGLAISE [865]

Proceed as indicated for Tripe and Onions (No. 864) above, and just when ready to serve, stir in 12 to 18 small freshly opened oysters.

TRIPE STEW [866]

Fry 6 slices of bacon in a pan until brown; remove bacon and set aside. In the drippings remaining in the pan fry ¾ cup of minced green pepper and ½ cup of minced onions, until vegetables take on color, stirring frequently; drain off all fat carefully and transfer mixture to a stew pot; stir in 2 quarts of beef stock, and 1 bouquet garni composed of 1 large bay leaf, 2 sprigs of green celery tops, 8 sprigs of fresh parsley, and 1 sprig of thyme, all tied together with kitchen thread, 1 pound of precooked honeycomb tripe which has been washed and shredded; season to taste with salt, pepper and 1 clove of garlic, add 2 cloves, 1 cup of diced potatoes and 1 cup of freshly shelled green peas; cover and cook over a low flame until vegetables are tender, or about 35 minutes. Stir in 1 tablespoon of flour, creamed with 2 tablespoons of butter, alternately with ½ to ¾ cup of thick, sweet cream, scalded, and after tasting for seasoning, serve in a deep, heated platter, dusting with chopped parsley.

Chapter Eight

POULTRY

*. . . Birds, the free tenants of land, air and ocean
Their forms all symmetry, their motions grace;
In plumage, delicate and beautiful;
Thick without burthen, close as fishes' scales,
Or loose as full-blown poppies to the breeze. . . .*

—*The Pelican Island* (1860)

NO ANIMAL OR BIRD IS TODAY FURTHER REMOVED FROMS ITS original jungle existence than the ordinary, domestic chicken. The strange fact is that during the last fifteen or twenty years this easygoing fowl, has been the subject of many strange experiments that promise to take it even further from its former primitive state. At an experimental station conducted by the United States at Beltsville, Maryland, the spotlight of science has for several years been focussed on the poultry situation. And while we have not, as yet, found Nature's secret for making a black hen who eats *green* grass, lay brown eggs with *yellow* yolks, we have learned a great deal about the fowls who model for weathervanes. At Beltsville, for example, the age-old question of who shall get the white meat of the chicken has been all but eliminated. They raise a scientific chicken that is nearly *all* white meat! The turkey, too, came in for an overhauling. Rather than trying to raise huge forty pound gobblers like the old-fashioned turkey growers, scientists have concentrated on streamlining the turkey to smaller specifications to fit the average buyer's purse. They have finally produced a bird weighing between seven and fifteen pounds, mostly white meat, with more meat and less bone.

The technique of poultry raising has probably undergone the most sensational change of all! About fifteen years ago, before man could control vitamin D, chickens had to have plenty of sunshine to soak up an abundance of the lifegiving vitamin. When confined to their coops and shut off from the sun, they would die. But, when we conquered vitamin D and could feed it to chickens in cod liver oil and other products mixed with their food, it opened up a vast new streamlined way of producing eggs, called the battery method. No longer did a hen need barnyard freedom in order to lay regularly. Given plenty to eat, room to cackle, and a comfortable air-conditioned building, the hen produced eggs on a factory assembly line schedule. Under the battery system, each hen is confined in an individual wire cage. The cages are stacked one on top of another and the battery-enclosed birds lay their eggs in typical mass production style. In 1930, there were only a thousand such hens under the battery system. Today, more than forty million laying hens are contendedly producing, in separate wire cages. Their contentment can be measured by the fact that battery hens produce 15 per cent more eggs than their less civilized sisters who live on the range. This new system reached the height of efficiency recently when one big operator put in slanting floors under his hens. As they lay, the eggs roll off the floors onto a conveyor belt which carries them away for packing. Recently the chemical, Colchicine, was discovered to speed the growth of baby chicks, while still another scientific approach to better and speedier breeding of poultry has been artificial insemination. There is no telling where all these fantastic experiments will lead us, but the fact seems to be, as far as science is concerned, that a chicken makes a good guinea pig!

POULTRY PREPARATION　　　　　　　　　　　　　　[868]

If you have to clean, disjoint, and prepare a chicken, duck, capon, guinea hen, goose or turkey proceed as follows:

Drawing. Cut off the head, if not already done.

Remove pin-feathers by catching them between thumb and a paring knife. A strawberry huller is effective too.

Singe Bird. To remove hair, grasp bird firmly, neck in one hand, feet in the other and turn it from side to side over a flame.

Wash Skin. Scrub thoroughly in cold or tepid water, using soft brush or cloth. Rinse with cold water and dry.

Remove Tendons (sinews). Make a cut about 2 inches long at the side of shank just beyond the bone. Insert nut pick or hook into the opening and pull tendons out.

Remove Feet. Place bird on its back, grasp leg and hold the skin over the front leg joint taut. Cut across the front; forcing shank down to dislocate the joint. Cut through the skin at back of joint which releases the foot.

Remove Oil Sac. (On the back at the base of the tail.) Cut under the sac to the backbone and up toward the tail.

Remove the Neck. Cut neck skin down center of the back to shoulders. Free the neck from neck skin and cut off the neck at the shoulder and set aside.

Remove Gullet, Crop and Windpipe. Pull them away from skin and out as far as possible from opening into the carcass where the neck was removed. Cut off and discard.

Loosen Lungs and Heart. Insert fingers into the neck opening, moving fingers around the inside of cavity as far down as possible. The lungs, in two sections, are on each side of the backbone over the ribs; the heart is below the breastbone.

To Remove Entrails. (Including with the intestines, the edible organs: heart, liver and gizzard.) (A) Cut carefully through skin of abdomen along a straight line from the end of keel (breastbone) to within a half inch of the vent. (B) Insert forefinger into the opening and, after circling the intestines with the finger, lift them up. Cut a ¾ inch circle around the vent. (C) Holding the bird, in one hand, insert the other hand through the opening and locate the gizzard, near center of cavity. Remove entrails, heart, liver and gizzard—save them for gravy. The kidneys are in a hollow near the end of the backbone; remove them too.

Preparing the Giblets. (A) Cut away the heart, remove heart sac and blood vessels. Squeeze to remove any blood. (B) Lift the liver away from the intestines and hold in fingers, turning it to find the gall sac (a greenish brown or yellow sac holding the bile). Slip a knife under the gall sac and cut, taking any part of the liver stained by contact with it. Under no circumstances should this sac be allowed to break. If this should happen, however, any part of the bird on which it falls *must* be discarded. Do not try to wash it, its absolutely useless. (C) Remove the gizzard from its attachments. To clean gizzard, cut into one of the thick sides. Cut *to,* but not *into*, the inner sac. Pull gizzard away from the sac. Discard the sac. (D) Cut away any fat. Melt it over very low heat; strain, and save for cooking. (E) Wash the giblets quickly but thoroughly in cold water. Drain. (F) Simmer the giblets with the neck and the scraped (after scalding) feet in salted water to cover, until they are tender (about 1¼ to 1½ hours) and allow giblets, neck and feet to cool in the broth.

Washing inside of Carcass. Remove any remaining lung portions; rinse the cavity with cold water; drain thoroughly and dry.

Storing Chicken until ready to Cook. Store the prepared chicken in a shallow pan just below freezing unit in automatic refrigerator. Chicken or any kind of barnyard poultry can be frozen if desired. Whole birds keep better than disjointed birds.

To Disjoint and Cut Up a Drawn Carcass. (A) *Cut off the wings.* Grasp the wing, bend it back and away from the carcass; cut through taut skin, flesh and joint. Repeat for the second wing. (B) *Cut off the legs.* Hold leg away from body; cut skin from leg joint near the backbone to near the tail; sever the leg joint near the backbone; cut through the remaining skin. Divide the leg into thigh and drumstick. Repeat for the second leg. (C) *Separate back and breast.* Lay the carcass on one side; cut through the skin and flesh from abdominal opening through the ribs to the opening where the wings were removed; repeat on the other side. Hold the tail down firmly and grasp tip end of the breast, grasping it firmly. Lift the breast up and away from the back, pulling back until the shoulder joints break and the breast and back separate. Divide the breast and back into 2 or 3 portions each, as desired and according to size. (D) Total number of pieces 7 to 12 (not including the giblets).

To Divide Chicken into Serving Portions—Broilers—Squabs. (A) *Two Portions:* Split lengthwise, cutting from neck end to tail along one side of backbone, which should be discarded, splitting the breast along one side of the keel bone. (B) *Four Portions:* Divide each half, cut as described above by cutting crosswise into two portions—leg and breast pieces. *Fryers. Four Portions:* Cut into four portions as described for broilers above (3½ pound fryers or larger should be disjointed). *Roasters:* Usually roasted whole (4-pound roasters can be disjointed and fried as desired.) *Fowl (or Stewing Hen):* Fowl is one year old and over and has less tender flesh. It requires moist heat cookery. Can *never* be roasted. Fowl can be left whole or disjointed, or left whole, stuffed and boiled.

POULTRY—HINTS [869]

Before stuffing a bird wipe the inside with a damp cloth, then rub with salt and pepper or indicated seasonings.

When buying a chicken live weight, count on its losing 30 per cent or more of its weight between then and the time it is ready to cook. In other words, if the bird's live weight is two pounds, there will be a little under one and one-half pounds of it after dressing.

A small broiler weighing one and one-half pounds undrawn, (often called a squab broiler) will serve two, though not generously. A two-pound broiler split serves two, comfortably.

When roasting stewing or fricasseeing chicken season with salt and pepper, a clove of garlic and a tablespoon of rosemary.

When planning croquettes from left over, cooked poultry, make them well ahead and chill thoroughly. They handle better, fry better and taste better. A little mace in the mixture adds distinctive flavor. You know, a croquette is hash that has made the social register. Its seasoning determines how long it'll stay there. The sauce with which it is put together has something to do with its address.

Dressed poultry has had only feathers removed. *Drawn* poultry has had feathers, head, feet and entrails removed. Weight of waste is approximately 30 per cent of dressed weight or 35 per cent of live weight.

Soft flexible breastbone indicates chicken is young. Broad, well rounded breast with thighs well covered and fat well distributed gives more meat per pound. *Short-legged* stocky type, with well-rounded body is preferable to long-legged rangy type.

Milk-fed chickens are white-fleshed; *Corn-fed* are yellow-fleshed.

Dry-picked or *semi-scalded* poultry is preferable to *hard-scalded*. Well-dressed birds are free of pin feathers. Velvet-like skin marks fine quality. Skin should not be torn, or discolored.

If bird has not been well bled, skin will be reddened and blue clots of blood will show through neck skin. Such poultry doesn't keep well nor has it as good flavor.

As soon as poultry reaches the kitchen, WASH it thoroughly inside and out, wipe dry with soft paper and place in the refrigerator until cooking time.

A roasting chicken is done when the flesh is slightly shrunken away from the skin, the thick part of the breast and the thighs feels tender, and when the joints are not stiff if the legs are moved.

Well-scrubbed and split chicken feet are valuable in the stock pot. The poultry rack or carcass should not go into the stock pot until well picked over for the meat that can go into made entrées or main dishes. This applies to turkey, guinea hen, goose, duck, capon, chicken, and even game birds. This meat can be utilized for chicken salad, sandwiches, creaming, or in a loaf. Such a loaf is very much enhanced by the addition of hard-boiled eggs imbedded in the upper half. A section then appears in each slice.

French cooks cover their poultry with a paste of flour and water before roasting, taking it off just before the bird is done to finish browning. This keeps in the juices and flavor, and does away with wrinkles.

Add toasted, shredded, blanched almonds to creamed chicken or turkey or to chicken salad . . . In a chicken pie, small onions and mushrooms are indispensable: occasionally add a few whole, cooked cranberries, too.

Fowl for fricassée or for use in salad, aspic, galantine, loaf, or creamed dishes *should* be simmered with vegetables and herbs that the meat may be well flavored. The liquid in which it is simmered should be used in soup or in sauce, to which it gives a marvelous flavor.

GUIDE TO THE PURCHASE AND   [870]
PREPARATION OF POULTRY

GENERAL POINTERS ON POULTRY: DRESSED poultry has only the feathers removed. DRAWN poultry has the feathers, head, feet and entrails removed. Soft, flexible breastbone indicates chicken is young. Broad, well-rounded breast with thighs well covered and fat well-distributed, gives more meat per pound. Short-legged stocky type with well-rounded body is preferable to long-legged rangy type.

Milk-fed chickens are white-fleshed. Corn-fed are yellow-fleshed. Dry-picked or *semi-scalded* poultry is preferable to *hard-scalded*. Well-dressed birds are free of pin feathers. Velvet-like skin marks fine quality. Skin should not be torn, or discolored. Bleeding: If bird has not been well bled, skin will be reddened and blue clots of blood will show through neck skin. Such poultry doesn't keep well nor has it as good flavor. Frozen poultry is just as good as fresh. Best results for cooking poultry is to start operations at room temperature.

KIND OF POULTRY	CHARACTERISTICS	WEIGHT AND AGE	HOW TO COOK (Methods)
CAPON (*Chapon* in French)	Easily identified by the "capon pick," from which only part of the feathers have been removed. There is more flesh on the capon than on any other fowl. The fat is marbled and worked through the lean tissue rather than pocketed as in other fowl. The capon is a rooster gelded to improve the flesh and increase growth.	Minimum weight: 6 pounds Maximum: 8 pounds Age from 7 to 10 months	Bone, stuff, roast, boil (with sauce), fricassee, stew, braise, jelly, bake, smother, breast under bell, casserole, loaf, pie (crust or pot pie), curry, cream, scallop, mousse, à la King, chop suey, chow mein, soufflé
BOILER or FOWL	Is a mature chicken of any weight and should not be used for baking or roasting. After one year of age the feet are hard and the bones brittle. Cartilage at end of breastbone is stiff. Flavor excellent, but thick connective tissues require moist heat at low temperature and long, slow cooking. Bought live weight, the loss is 30% or more. A 5-pound fowl makes about one generous quart of coarsely cut meat. Boilers or fowl are also sold frozen, eviscerated as well as dressed. Once defrosted, they should be cooked immediately. A frozen package of fowl averages 2 pounds 8 ounces.	Dressed weight from 4 to 6 pounds Usually one year old or more	Boil, stew, fricassee, chicken à la King, curry, cream, chicken hash

GUIDE TO THE PURCHASE AND PREPARATION OF POULTRY [870]

KIND OF POULTRY	CHARACTERISTICS	WEIGHT AND AGE	HOW TO COOK (Methods)
BROILER	A young chicken sufficiently soft-meated to be cooked tender by broiling. If feet are dark and horny, the bird is old; if smooth, moist and yellow, it is young. If the neck is scrawny and full of tendons, the bird is tough. Usually sold dressed. Broilers, if loosely disjointed but not separated, will heat through faster, especially if rubbed with lemon juice. The backbone, neck and wing tips of broilers are always removed before broiling. Broilers are always cooked to order. A frozen broiler averages 1 pound.	From 2½ to 3½ pounds Age from 13 to 18 weeks	Fry, broil, fricassee, In cream or various sauces, à la Maryland, Southern, Tettrazini, casserole
FRYER	A young chicken sufficiently soft-meated to be cooked tender by frying. The practice of cutting a fryer in two before frying is not to be encouraged. In parts of the South the fryer is cut into component parts—drumsticks, thighs, breasts, wings, gizzard and liver—and fried together. For deep-fat frying, the bird should always be quartered, dipped in batter and fried at 350° F. Fryers are always cooked to order. A frozen fryer averages 2 pounds.	From 2½ to 3½ pounds Age from 13 to 18 weeks	Fry, roast, casserole, braise, bake, sauté, cold in aspic, breast with various sauces and garnishes, poach, bone and stuff or not, under pie crust or in pot pie, press, in wine, gumbo, Maryland
ROASTER	A chicken sufficiently softmeated to be cooked tender by roasting and which may be stuffed or not. If stuffed, do not pack hard as space is necessary for expansion. Fill neck opening, bring neck skin over onto back. Fill body cavity, and sew or lace opening. Bring leg ends together, then hang a loop around the ends and tail; draw string ends tightly and tie securely. Then grease and roast the bird. A stuffed bird may also be boiled or braised. After cleaning a roasting bird, rub the inside with a lemon, then with a little mixed salt and pepper. This whitens the bird and makes it deliciously tender. A frozen roaster averages 3 pounds.	Weight from 3½ to 4 pounds Age from 6 to 10 months	Roast, cream, on toast, barbecue, casserole, Maryland, Tettrazini

GUIDE TO THE PURCHASE AND [870]
PREPARATION OF POULTRY

KIND OF POULTRY	CHARACTERISTICS	WEIGHT AND AGE	HOW TO COOK (Methods)
SQUABS and PIGEONS	Squabs are available all year. They are young pigeons that have not been allowed to fly. Their sporting ancestry gives them their faintly gamy flavor. They are more plentiful and less costly during the summer months. Pigeons should be plump. They need long, slow cooking to make them tender.	Baby squab average ¾ pound. Jumbo squab from 1 to 1½ pounds Age: Baby, 2 months; Jumbo, 3 months	Broil when split, pot and stuff, casserole, on canapé, roast, on toast, stew, sauté in cream. Pie crust or pot pie
DUCK (Domestic) Season: Spring ducks from April 1st till end of November. Winter ducks from November till end of March. May be found all year at most markets	Almost all our ducks are the descendants of the imperial aviaries of Peking, China, eggs from which were originally imported into this country around 1872. The height of production comes in July. Ducklings are now frozen and packed in large quantities—12 to a box—for shipment to markets all over the world. The first 48 hours after the duck leaves the shell, it is left in the bottom tray of the incubator to keep dry and snug. Then it is moved to a hot shed for a 5-day period, then into a cold shed, slightly steam heated. At 8 weeks the young duck is pure white and ready for the markets. A mature duck should have a breast that is broad and pliable, with the flesh firm and free from bruises and with a fair amount of fat underneath the skin. The feet and bill should be yellow. The windpipe should yield when gently pressed with the fingers. Since ducks have more fat than other fowls, less fat is needed in the stuffing. Allow from ½ to ¾ pound of meat for each portion.	Weight from 5 to 6 pounds Age from 10 to 12 weeks. Duckling, 7 to 8 weeks Weight about 3½ to 4 pounds	Roast, bake, braise, salmis, curry, smother, pot, broil, fricassee, stew, Creole, plank, à la Presse, Cassoulet, pan, stuff, in aspic, bone, Bigarade, casserole, Pilaff
GOOSE (Domestic) Season: All year, but at its best during fall and winter	When buying goose select a plump bird with a good covering of fat because much of its weight will be lost in the fat that cooks out. Get a goose that has seen only one summer. The windpipes of young birds are soft and pliable, while hard and rigid on old ones. Older birds have coarser skin, are more yellow in color and the breastbone is harder. The legs of the goslings are too short to permit trussing like a turkey or chicken. Tie the trussing string around one leg and then the other, leaving about 2 inches of string between the legs. Bring the ends of the string under the back and tie it	Weight from 10 to 12 pounds Age from 8 to 10 months	Roast, stew, stuff, smoke, devil, pot, casserole, smother, broil (goslings only), breast with various sauces

GUIDE TO THE PURCHASE AND PREPARATION OF POULTRY [870]

KIND OF POULTRY	CHARACTERISTICS	WEIGHT AND AGE	HOW TO COOK (Methods)
GOOSE (*Continued*)	securely. When cooking a goose, figure 1 pound for each serving. Geese are sold fresh, frozen and smoked.		
GUINEA HEN also called "Pearl Hen," "Mitred Guinea Hen," "Horned Guinea Fowl," "*Poule de Numidie*," "Guinea Fowl," "*Poule d'Inde*," "*Pintade*"	The cleaning, cutting, trussing and cooking of a guinea hen is the same as for chicken. However, the breast should be covered with a thin sheet of fat larding pork to prevent drying. The bird should be plump, with light, semi-transparent fat, soft breastbone and tender flesh. They are best in fall and winter. The flavor is a little gamy, and when roasted, bread sauce as well as gravy should be served.	Weight from 2 to 3½ pounds Age: from 12 to 16 weeks	Same as a fryer or a small roaster
TURKEY Domestic, Wild, Smoked Fresh turkey is in season all the year round, but at its best in the fall	The turkey, which is domesticated in most parts of the world, is an original North American bird. Most of the early birds come in August and are from Delaware, Vermont and Maryland. To be in its prime, a bird should be young and have no blemishes. The breast should be broad and full, the breast bone straight and flexible. There should be a thin layer of fat discernible underneath the skin over the back, hips and breast. Turkeys not well fattened have a bluish look. Few, if any, pin feathers should be visible. Legs should be black. As a bird ages, the legs take on a gray or pinkish tinge. Soft, pliable feet and smooth, bright skin indicate a young bird. Both hen and tom turkeys are good. The hen has a wider, deeper breast. For serving allow ¾ to 1 pound of turkey (undrawn weight, head and feet on) for each person. Baby turkeys (from 8 to 10 pounds) are immature birds of the same development as fryers and broilers and are cooked the same way. Smoked turkeys are cured, then smoked and cooked at the same time. Quick-frozen turkeys are excellent eating. In this group you seldom find poor gobblers. Each one is a pampered bird, round and small; boned, cleaned and drawn before weighing. GENERAL: Poor fleshing is in many instances due to immature birds which have been dressed before they were ready for market. Excessive pin feathers are evidence of immature birds. Poor bleeding is another source of trouble.	Weight from 8 to 35 pounds. The small white turkey, a cross of white, Austrian and Scotch species, weighs from 6½ to 8 pounds dressed, and matures in 24 to 26 weeks	Roast, bake, braise, curry, casserole, stuff, turkey roll, devil, pie, soufflé, croquettes, in aspic with cranberry jelly, Amandine, fritters, Tettrazini, loaf in jelly or hot hash, à la King, scrapple, cream, smoked à la Pinesbridge, Mexican, mousse, Shortcake turnovers, chow mein, press, scallop

CAPON [871]

The saddest of legal blunders is that which tries to limit man's enjoyment of innocent pleasures. From the wise words of the philosopher we learn how it can be that rulers repeat this particular mistake over and over again. "We learn from history," says the savant, "that we learn nothing from history."

Most laws against pleasure have succeeded only in developing the victim's ingenuity, for he energetically applies himself to the business of finding devious ways in which to outwit the blue stockings. Thus it has come about that those laws which proscribed the pursuit of happiness have not always been unfruitful.

The Fannian Law was one of them. It was passed when Rome was at the height of its glory; at the apex of a civilization of which the keynote was luxury and extravagance. The Senators, chosen leaders of the people, sat with furrowed brows at their conference tables, and discussed with honest concern the ever-increasing excesses of the citizenry. Something had to be done. Romans of great wealth were expending unbelievably enormous sums on entertainment; and banquets where hundreds of gluttonous guests gorged themselves day after day on flamingo's tongues, shark's livers, and similar rare and costly delicacies, were commonplace. Extravagance ran riot, and the Senators knew that discontent was sure to follow on its heels. So the worried elders put their grave heads together, and composed the *Lex Fannia;* the stringent provisions of the law indicated the extent of their desperation.

The law established a maximum beyond which the cost of no feast could go; it restricted the number of guests who might be invited to dine, to three on ordinary days, and to five on gala occasions, and it specifically forbade the serving of any fowl except a hen at any such repast, with the further injunction that the hen could not be especially fattened.

It was the last provision, outrageous and obviously unjust, which caused the most grumbling. The citizens muttered angrily of reprisals at the next election, against the authors of this diabolical legal contrivance which would sacrifice the useful hen (unfattened, at that) and her innocent unlaid eggs on the gastronomic altar, and protect the indolent strutting rooster for a life of well-fed worthlessness. As ever free men will, when their intimate personal liberty is snatched from them, the Romans revolted. Hens destined for the table grew plump and sleek as if by happy coincidence. Chicken yards became hen heavens, where no clucking bird was permitted to scratch for food, lest she risk the loss of a fraction of an ounce of tender flesh.

In the meantime, a great deal of attention was being devoted to the problem of making the sacred rooster eatable within the law. Philosophers, farmers, perhaps even a renegade senator or two, studied the problem thoughtfully. But it was a skilled surgeon who found the way. With his expert knife he performed a trick which transformed the rooster into the eunuch of the barnyard. The bird grew plump of its own nature, without compelling its owner to disobey the law against fattening chickens. Its flavor was superior to that of the hen, its flesh more tender and yet more succulent. The new bird was a huge success, and took its place among the supreme delicacies of the table, a place of honor to which its right has not been challenged. Thus was the capon created—by man's unending revolt against injustice.

Not as large as the turkey, nor as small as the roasting chicken, the capon is a happy compromise between the two. The golden fat of this bird is marbled throughout the lean tissue, and the flesh is a pale delicate pink in color, firm yet meltingly soft, so that thin and succulent slices fall from the sharp knife that cuts it.

Carving the capon is simple enough. Its structure is identical with that of the turkey and the chicken, and the same procedure should be followed. Since the capon is more fleshy, however, it is possible to get a greater number of slices of white meat from its breast, pound for pound, than from those of either of the other birds.

The individual delicacy of the capon is frequently passed over too lightly in gastronomic literature, and instructions for its use too often comment briefly on the capon's resemblance to chicken, and recommend the same methods of preparation. There is at least one famous exception to this rule of general neglect, for Alexandre Dumas, gourmet author of the *Grand Dictionnaire de la Cuisine*, whose lyric tributes to fine viands are as honored in the history of literature as they are in the annals of gastronomy, created one formula for the preparation of capon which is worthy of this exquisitely flavored bird. The recipe was modernized by the chef at the Hotel du Pavillon, at Cannes, where it was among the most cherished and most famous specialties of the house.

A Norfolk capon is not a fowl but a red herring. Capon was used in Old English to designate a fish.

BRAISED STUFFED CAPON [872]

First prepare a stuffing by mixing together in a large bowl ½ pound calf's liver, and 1 cup cooked lean ham, both finely chopped, 2 cups bread which has been first soaked in milk, then squeezed in a clean cloth, 2 raw eggs, 1 medium sized onion finely chopped or grated, 1 tablespoon finely chopped parsley, a pinch of thyme, salt and pepper to taste.

Combine all ingredients, then put through food chopper to insure uniform blending, and use to stuff a capon which has previously been well washed. Sew up the opening, place the bird in a braising kettle, barely cover with cold water, and add a generous cup of sweet white wine. Set on a hot fire, bring to boiling point and allow to boil at a gallop for 15 minutes, then reduce the heat and simmer gently for 10 minutes longer. Now transfer the kettle with its contents to a moderate oven (350° F.) for 1 hour.

If preferred, substitute a fowl for the capon; although the meat may not be as tender or as juicy as that of the capon, it will still be delicious.

For the sauce, strain 3 cups of the capon broth through a fine sieve.

Place over a very hot flame and allow to reduce to half its volume; then add 1 tablespoon kneaded butter (equal parts of butter and flour). Boil, stirring constantly for 5 minutes; remove from the fire and beat in four egg yolks one by one, and finally, add half a cup of slivered, blanched almonds. Taste for seasoning. Pour half the sauce over the bird, and serve the remainder in a sauce boat. The bird should be carved at the table, and a generous helping of the stuffing served with each portion. A side dish of plain boiled rice and a bottle of your favorite domestic or imported red wine will complete a delicious feast.

BREAST OF CAPON DROUANT [873]

For 6 servings the boned breasts of 3 young capons are required. Pound them thoroughly with the flat side of a cleaver, then sauté in butter on both sides until pale golden brown. Drain, then lay the breasts flat on a board while preparing the following stuffing: Combine ¾ pound lean ground veal, 3 tablespoons sweet butter, 1 scant teaspoon each of finely minced shallots, onions, chervil, parsley, and tarragon leaves, 3 tablespoons finely ground fresh mushrooms, and ¾ cup fine soft bread crumbs, soaked in Madeira, then squeezed to remove excess moisture. Put this mixture twice through the food chopper, then cook it in 4 tablespoons of butter, for 5 minutes over a very gentle flame, stirring frequently. Spread the breasts with a layer of the stuffing, and roll them as you would a jelly roll; dip in beaten egg then in bread crumbs mixed with an equal amount of finely ground toasted pistachios. Fry in deep ham or bacon fat to a rich golden brown. Arrange on a hot platter, garnish with deep-fried, fresh green water cress, and serve with a sauce boat of Madeira Wine Sauce (No 1076).

CURRY OF CAPON A L'INDIENNE [874]
Curry of Capon Indian Style

Cut up a 5-pound capon as for fricassée, and brown the pieces well in butter. (Indians use *ghee*, which is a clarified butter.) Add 1 medium-sized onion, coarsely chopped, 1 crushed clove of garlic, and a medium-sized shredded green pepper, free from seeds and membrane. Sauté these with the capon for 15 minutes; then pour in 1½ cups good chicken broth, veal broth, or bouillon. Season with salt, black pepper, and a rounded tablespoon of fresh curry paste, or curry powder, if the latter is more convenient. Add 3 tomatoes, peeled, seeded, and sliced, or 2 cups tomato purée, 1 tablespoon finely minced parsley, a generous pinch of fresh thyme, and a cup of coconut water, which is the coconut liquid just as it comes from the shell. While the capon is simmering in this mixture, toast or sauté 1 cup blanched almonds until they are a rich brown in color, and add them to the sauce. Plump ⅓ cup seedless dried currants and the same amount of Sultana raisins in boiling water, drain them thoroughly, and add them also to the sauce. If currants are not obtainable, use ⅔ cup Sultana raisins. Let the whole simmer for another 1 minutes. Thicken the sauce with a little kneaded butter (equal parts of flour and butter kneaded together), let it come to a boil once or twice and serve with mounds of boiled rice, seasoned with saffron and garnished with strips of crisp bacon.

GALANTINE DE CAPON A LA REINE [875

Clean and singe a 5 to 6-pound capon, and bone it carefully, without cutting the skin. Stuff the cavity with alternated thin layers of strips of cooked ox tongue, strips of green peppers, cooked in butter and well drained, and Mousse of Capon (No. 876). Sprinkle each layer with a little coarsely chopped black truffle. When the cavity is full, roll the capon in a napkin which has been wrung out of cold water, and fasten the long roll thus obtained by tying it at both ends and in the middle with string which has been dipped in water. Place the roll in a large kettle, with cold chicken stock to cover, and boil steadily for 1½ hours. The bird should be completely covered with the boiling liquid throughout the cooking. Allow the capon to cool in the broth; then remove the napkin carefully, and transfer the roll to a chilled platter. Glaze with hot Demi-Glace Sauce flavored with Sherry (No. 1048).

For the final touch, brush another coating of Demi-Glace Sauce over the edge of the roll at top and bottom. Chill, and serve on a bed of crisp water cress, which may be sprinkled with paprika for its colorful effect. Slivers of toasted pistachio nuts may be stuck into the galantine to make it even more festive in appearance.

MOUSSE OF CAPON [876

Put the breasts of a large boiled capon through the finest disk of the food chopper with 2 unbeaten egg whites. Then rub the mixture through a fine meshed sieve or a hair sieve into a saucepan, and stir over cracked ice until thoroughly chilled. Add 1 cup heavy cream, and ½ cup rich sweet milk, whisking with a wire whisk until the mousse is fluffy and well blended. The longer the whisking, the fluffier the mousse will be. Season to taste with salt and white pepper and a tiny pinch of ground nutmeg and beat in 2 tablespoons good Sherry. Use about half of this mousse for the stuffing, and form the remainder into balls the size of a large walnut. Drop the balls into boiling chicken stock or bouillon, cover the pot, and cook for 5 or 6 minutes. or until the balls rise to the surface of the liquid.

ROAST CAPON ALEXANDRE DUMAS   [877]

Clean and singe a 5 or 6-pound capon. Turn back the head and the neck of the capon into the breast cavity, and sew up the neck skin, thus closing the opening. Rub the lower cavity with brandy and with salt and pepper, and stuff it with the capon's liver, coarsely chopped, 1 tablespoon kneaded butter (equal parts of butter and flour, kneaded together), and a small onion, peeled and stuck with a whole clove. Close this opening with a skewer, and brush the bird with melted sweet butter. Roast for 15 minutes in a hot oven (425° F.); then reduce the temperature to 350° F., and continue to roast for 1½ hours, basting frequently with the drippings in the pan, to which has been added 1 cup scalded heavy cream. When the bird is done, it will have a thick golden, crusty skin. Arrange on a hot platter, and serve with a sauce boat of the pan gravy *au natural*, which has been strained and allowed to come to a boil once or twice.

STUFFED CAPON WITH RAISINS   [878]

Clean and singe a 5 to 6-pound capon. Wipe the outside with a damp cloth and the inside with a dry cloth. Rub inside and out with a mixture of salt, pepper, and a soupçon of ginger, then set aside while preparing the following stuffing: Soak 3 cups white bread cubes in a sweet wine, preferably a Sauterne type, and squeeze gently to remove excess moisture. Peel off the thin skin of the capon liver, and chop the liver finely, with 2 tablespoons each of shallots, onions, parsley, and pistachio nuts, 1 scant teaspoon sage, ¼ teaspoon thyme, a generous pinch of ground cloves, salt and coarsely ground black pepper. Combine this mixture with the bread, and blend thoroughly. Moisten with ¼ cup heavy cream, and stuff the cavity of the bird with it. Truss carefully, and put the bird in an open roasting pan, with 1 cup good chicken bouillon. Roast for 20 minutes in a hot oven (425° F.); then reduce the heat to moderate (350° F.), and continue to roast for 1¼ hours longer, basting frequently.

In the meantime, cook together in a saucepan, stirring frequently, 1 tablespoon butter, 1 medium-sized onion, chopped, 1 medium-sized carrot, also chopped, 1 small blade of garlic crushed, a piece of parsnip the size of an egg, chopped, 2 whole cloves, and a bay leaf tied with 4 sprigs of parsley. After about 5 minutes the mixture will begin to take on color. Sprinkle over it 1 scant tablespoon flour, and blend well. Then add 1 cup chicken bouillon or chicken stock, and cook over a medium flame until the liquid is reduced to a scant ⅓ cup, stirring frequently. Rub the sauce through a fine strainer into another saucepan. Then blanch ¾ cup seedless raisins in hot water for a minute or two, add them to the sauce, and set it aside to keep warm. When the capon is done, place it on a hot platter. Skim the fat from the liquid in the pan, and add the liquid to the sauce. Adjust the seasoning, and just before serving, beat in 2 egg yolks, slightly beaten with 1 tablespoon Sherry. Garnish the capon with a necklace of crisp water cress, and serve it with the sauce on the side, and with another side dish of quince jelly.

Capons bridge the gap in size and weight between the roasting chicken and the turkey. Learn to recognize a capon when you see one. Beware of the "slip," an incompletely caponized male bird that is frequently sold as the genuine thing.

This has coarser meat, less fat and is in all ways inferior. A true capon will show large deposits of fat over its entire body and in the fat, remember, lies that delectable flavor. A capon's head "points"—and wattles are always shriveled. A capon will have spurs, but they are never sharp. In buying a capon with head removed, look for the scars. But scar evidence is not an absolute test, for a "slip" may result if the operation is not properly performed. Capons average 6 to 8 pounds each. A few weigh up to nine pounds and a very few down to five.

CHICKEN   [879]

Although chickens were tossed into the stew pots of antiquity and have been served up on the tables of almost every nation ever since, their use as the main course of the traditional Sunday dinner, or of some festive gathering, has never been so widespread as in our own country. A flavorsome chicken, prepared in any one of a number of delightful ways, has become an American symbol for a tasty kind of opulence common to all. How can we forget those Sunday dinners at Aunt Annie's when the clan—even down to the second cousins who were within buggy-drive of the old farmhouse—gathered to be regaled with sumptuous fare of which the *piece de resistance* was almost certain to be chicken? There are almost more ways to prepare a chicken for the table than there are tables to serve it on, including such diversified methods as the oil-simmered chickens of the Phoenicians, the mud-baked chickens of our American Indians, and the galantines of capon of the French; yet we Americans have taken the chicken under our own wing and have made of it a series of regional dishes whose fame and aroma have spread, the length and the breadth of our land.

Chicken prepared in any one of the good American styles is expressive of our own national character, perhaps almost as much so as our native art and literature; for in such dishes you will find a certain simplicity and a rugged honesty, plus a disdain for the frivolous, that loses none of the essential goodness of the chicken. To list just a few of the regional names for the different ways in which the bird is prepared, we have chicken Maryland, Virginia fried, Vermont potpie, New Jersey barbecue, New Amsterdam Dutch potpie, and—to go political in a good old-fashioned American way—chicken Mark Hanna.

Like all nations, however, that respect their palates, we have borrowed a flock of chicken recipes from France, the land where culture and good food were born simultaneously and have since become the true gourmet's favorite twins. Many famous Frenchmen have lent their names to distinctive methods of preparing chicken. King Henry IV was one of these. That wise old royal bird also knew how best to placate his disgruntled peasants, for he promised them a chicken in every pot—a promise which, incidentally, seems to have gone the way of most campaign promises.

Since the advent of that sublime artist of fork and ladle, the Gallic chef, chicken has been elevated from the rough-hewn log cabin to the banquet halls of the nobility. Indeed, the chicken has practically turned into a swan which can grace every table where good eating is the rule. Fricasseed, creamed, curried, truffled à la Perigueux, or à la Grimod de la Reyniere (when stuffed with liver, truffles, mushrooms, chives and beef marrow), the lowly chicken becomes a veritable bird of paradise to the gourmet palate. And don't overlook chicken à la Campine, partly cooked in olive oil over a slow flame with shallots, mushrooms, parsley, and four spices, and then wrapped in oiled paper to finish cooking. And there is chicken à la Vapeur, which is guaranteed to drive away the most persistent vapours. For it, you fill a young hen with truffles and mushrooms, and then cook her, first in champagne and later in white wine. After such a dish you will undoubtedly be in a position to understand more comprehensively Brillat-Savarin's famous gustatory cry, "If Adam and Eve ruined themselves for an apple, what would they have done for a truffled fowl?"

If, by chance, you have a barnyard of your own and your appetite is eager for chicken, be patient. Poultry, as a rule, ought not to be cooked until six or eight hours after it has been killed, although it should be picked and drawn, then thoroughly chilled, as soon as possible. Again, the fat from a heavy roasting chicken should *not* be allowed to accumulate in the roasting pan. Drain most of it off, leaving just enough for basting. Removal of the surplus abdominal fat inside the cavity is also advisable before roasting. This bit of care will not only better preserve the true flavor of the fowl, but it will also make the bird more digestible.

The age of a chicken is an important consideration. Do not attempt to roast or broil an old chicken, for the result will be disastrous to both palate and temper. A one-year old is about right for roasting, and only spring chickens should be broiled. It is not necessary, however, to place the older birds in an Old Hens' Home, for they can be made tender and delicious by braising, and they will present the same appearance as when roasted. They are also delectable when boiled, either stuffed or not.

One more word of caution in case you don't have your own barnyard. The surest way to determine whether your future chicken dinner is young enough is to try the skin under the leg and the wing. If it is easily broken, the bird is young. Also press the lower tip of the breastbone to see whether it is flexible. When young, a chicken is bright of eye, thick of body, and fat of breast. Now, after determining these luscious qualities, whet both your knife and your appetite in hungry anticipation.

In general, one need be concerned only with four types of chicken, depending to a great extent on their age. First pullets—fat, young hens —and capons for roasting; then roasting chickens, used for both roasting and frying; spring chickens, for broiling; and lastly those tiny delights, squab chickens, which are grilled or served in individual *cocottes*.

Although the gourmets among the various state legislatures may have to settle the issue concerning which of our states devised the most famous and delectable fashion for preparing chicken, we cast our vote for chicken Maryland. This delicacy, which so delighted the Colonial palate and has since been spread so lavishly upon our own tables, was created by the lordly Calverts on St. Clement's Island, whence the bird, under its new, tempting guise flew through the Colonies as the favorite dish of Lord Baltimore.

Until well into the ninetienth century the Siamese served the liver and drumsticks of a chicken only to the head of a family. A father could share a drumstick with his son, but never a chicken liver.

ARROZ CON POLLA CASTILLANE [880]
Chicken with Rice

There are good simple folk who don't like mutton, and high-bred aristocrats who scorn truffled pheasant, but take the teeming population of the great round world as a whole, and if there is unanimity of opinion on any one thing under the sun, it is on the eternal goodness of chicken— old or young, roasted, broiled, fried or boiled.

The name of arroz con polla is more or less familiar to Americans, but they pass it on the menu of the Spanish restaurant and select something that sounds more exotic and thrilling than chicken with rice, yet there is nothing more thrilling in the Spanish or Mexican cuisine than *arroz con polla*, if your Spanish or Mexican chef is an artist, and not a scullion. The term "polla" however, is too often a mere euphemism, for many a cackling *gallina* (chicken), too ancient to lay eggs has renewed her youth in the frying pan and gone to glory as a "polla"— which should in all honesty be a chick of kindergarten age and melting tenderness; yet the process of making arroz con polla is in the realm of white magic, and may renew even the pristine freshness of youth.

Spaniards use excellent olive oil with prodigality, and Mexicans too often use lard. When you make your first arroz con polla be extravagant and get olive oil as fine as you would use for a salad. An Andalusian cook uses an earthen cazuela (earthenware casserole), right on the fire, but the family frying pan will do very well. Garlic is traditional, but you will find a half-dozen minced shallots and a couple of sliced onions fried brown in the oil, a little more delicate in a very delicate dish.

Heat ¼ cup of olive oil to the smoking point, stir in 6 chopped shallots, and when slightly browned, add ¼ cup of finely chopped onions. Cook till onion begins to take on the hue of daffodils, then lift it out and replace with 2 nice, plump young roasting chickens, each weighing about 3 pounds, disjointed, then dredged with flour. Cook until each piece is delicately browned, turning often to prevent burning or scorching; then slice 6 medium-sized fresh tomatoes into the pan, over the chicken and add 2 cupfuls of chicken broth, sizzling hot. Now put in a large bay leaf, 2 whole cloves, 1 or 2 tablespoons of minced parsley, and a quarter of a teaspoon of powdered Spanish saffron, and let the chicken simmer gently, closely covered.

Next, wash 1 pound of good rice in several waters, and drain it well. If your chicken is really a "polla" or fowl, put the rice in the pan at once; but if it is of doubtful age, try it with a fork, and add the rice when you think that the bird should cook about 30 minutes more. Incidentally, a good Spanish cook insists on Valencia rice; and get it at a Spanish shop if you can, but failing that, use the best sound head rice that's available.

With the arroz (rice) simmering gently with the polla (chicken), shred a large sweet green pepper and a large sweet red pepper into a pan. If red peppers are not obtainable, use a can of sweet Spanish peppers, or pimiento, well drained, but it will be for appearance more than for flavor.

When rice and chicken are both done, pour into the pan 1 scant sherry glass of good sherry or Madeira, and this should be considered seriously. You are using several pungent and piquant flavors, and if either the saffron or the wine should assert itself too definitely, the subtle effect is lost. All the flavors of herbs or condiments, must suggest themselves in the finished composition with the elegance of Castillian manners, yet none be permitted to dominate—and that is why Spanish Arroz con Polla is superior to Mexican Arroz con Polla, for the latter is usually allowed to reek of fiery chili pepper and garlic, and one might as well leave out such subtle graces as saffron and good wine.

The advantage in using a fine brown earthen cazuela (casserole) is that it looks so well on the table, but you can arrange the chicken and rice effectively on a great, hot platter. Individual taste comes into the matter of garnishings. Some nicely browned mushrooms, over which a little sherry has been poured, make a spectacular border around the golden chicken and rice, and ravishing color effects can be carried out in watercress which may be dipped in paprika and very gently shaken of the excess, or parsley with some slender strips of bright red peppers.

BRUNSWICK STEW MARYLAND   [881]

Cut 1 fat tender chicken into frying pieces, and cook golden brown in bacon drippings well flavored with onion. Pour off the fat, and, having the chicken in a deep container, pour over it 3 cups boiling water, and add salt to taste, with 1 bay leaf, 2 cups tomatoes, 1½ cups green lima beans, 1½ cups sweet corn, ½ cup okra cut fine, and ½ cup sherry with

1 teaspoon Worcestershire sauce. Simmer gently from 1½ to 2 hours. Serve in deep plates with crisp corn sticks.

BRUNSWICK STEW OF OLD DIXIE [882]

Note. After all is said and done, squirrel meat must have a big part in the pot.

Brunswick stew, luscious prelude to plantation barbecues and all major festivals of the Southland's spacious hospitality, is a hazardous subject for a writer, and may provoke a fortnight's newspaper controversy; yet the reasonably orthodox formula will have its defenders, for it all depends on the circumscribed tradition of States or counties and even of parishes.

This writer was gently ridiculed in the uplands of Mississippi for mentioning chicken in relation to Brunswick stew, though the historic recipes of Georgia and the Carolinas call for it as an essential ingredient. But chicken, say the Mississippians, is a feeble substitute for squirrel meat, which is as necessary as corn and tomatoes and okra—and there you are again, for okra is not even mentioned in some of the recipes that are engrossed on parchment in the archives of two or three Atlantic States.

Squirrels, however, are extremely prominent in the fauna of Mississippi, and literally drop from the trees like ripe apples wherever there are men and boys and guns. There the cook and homemaker may buy dressed squirrels in quantity from street peddlers any day in the week.

Because Brunswick stew in Mississippi is imperishable among happy memories, let us assume that squirrel is the word and start with a brace of plump gray ones. Cut them up in joints and saddles, as for frying, dredge them with seasoned flour, and brown nicely in bacon fat with 6 onions thinly sliced. Put meat and onions in a large iron stew pot, or an earthenware casserole, as done in Mississippi for almost any kind of stew; now add 3 cups of boiling water, 6 tomatoes, peeled and sliced, 3 red peppers, sliced, and a generous pinch of thyme leaves (not the powdered kind) also a little salt and 1 large bay leaf tied with 8 sprigs of fresh parsley, and let simmer for an hour. Then put in 1 quart of fresh lima beans, the kernels neatly cut from 6 ears of green corn, 1 quart of sliced okra pods, 1 tablespoon of chopped parsley and 1 of Worcestershire sauce, and let simmer till meat and vegetables are done. The consistency should be that of rich soup, but sometimes the broth is thickened slightly with a roux (flour and butter or fat browned together) or some fine bread crumbs.

At a barbecue in one of the Gulf States the stew is ladled out of a cauldron half the size of the Great Tun of Heidelberg, and after two or three bowls of it you proceed to the mass attack on whole quarters of beef, whole calves and pigs, turkeys and geese, all roasted in pits of smoking embers. Between the courses light hors d'oeuvres are passed around, consisting of more squirrels, broiled chickens, partridge, quail and pigeons—and a few roasted 'possums. At last, when you languish, gasping and groaning on the greensward, watermelons, cantaloupes, rich cakes, and pastries and ices are served, and something like euthanasia is attained.

In New York it must usually be chicken instead of squirrel, and the season may force you to use canned vegetables; but if the canned corn is of the finest, tenderest sort, all will be well; and the stew is a glorious success at little dinners on winter evenings.

Try as many variations as you please and use even beef, veal or pork along with the chicken, and you will still have Brunswick stew, for they are all included in authentic recipes from every section of Dixie. Also you may add diced potatoes, rice or noodles; and hearty folks of the Old Dominion put a glass of good sherry or Madeira into their stews to give an agreeable tang. In Louisiana they may tell you, in good faith, that you are already so close to gumbo, that a little gumbo filé powder will do no harm; and it does give a rich consistency to a stew without seriously altering the flavor.

GUMBO FILE POWDER. Gumbo is quite another story, but lest we forget, you really ought to get a jar of the filé powder at one of the few New York shops that keep it.

Dried sassafras leaves are pulverized to make the rich green flour, but the flavor is bland and delicate. If you add it to any mixture that is still on the fire you will have a sorry mess or a ropy glue; but stir it in *after* the kettle is taken off the range and the result will be perfect and delightful.

For your first Brunswick stew, stick to fundamentals, using chicken or squirrel, and know the dish in its essential lusciousness of tender meat and fresh vegetables. Afterwards you may experiment with variations and settle on a formula of your own. Any gracious lady or experienced mammy from the South will tell you it's all wrong, but you'll never find two Southerners who can agree on Brunswick stew, fried chicken or spoon bread.

The Leg of Chicken for Mother. She was a mother who always ate the neck of the chicken. The family grew to think it was her favorite piece and saved it for her at reunions and church suppers.

This went on for years until one Christmas the mother helped herself to a leg of chicken with thigh attached and the family passed away from shock.

MORAL. Cook more than one chicken.

BURNT CHICKEN PRINCESS [883]

Wash three 2-pound broilers inside and out with warm water and soda (½ teaspoon soda to each quart water), rinse well with cold running water, and singe. Sponge the broilers dry; rub with butter seasoned with salt and freshly ground black pepper, and roast in the usual way after placing in each cavity 1 small white onion stuck with a whole clove, 2 thin carrot slices, 1 small piece celery stalk, 2 sprigs parsley, a bit of bay leaf, and a tiny sprig of thyme.

When the chickens are done, remove from the oven, and split in two from the back. Discard the herbs in the cavity, and bring the chickens to the table on a very hot platter, which must be *kept* hot. In the top part of the chafing dish pan, which should not be over water, heat ¾ pound best sweet butter; add 1 teaspoon each finely chopped tarragon, chives, shallots, parsley, chervil, sweet summer savory, and celery tops. Let these cook for 2 or 3 minutes; then add ¾ pound fresh mushrooms, using both caps and stems, peeled and thinly sliced, and cook 5 or 6 minutes longer, stirring gently but thoroughly.

Now place in a soup ladle 2 tablespoons each of fine rum, gin, and yellow Chartreuse. Dip a lump of sugar into the rum; light the rum, and add it to the liqueur mixture in the ladle, which will burn. Pour the flaming mixture on the contents of the chafing dish pan until the liqueur is completely burned. Then pour this sauce over the chicken, and serve at once.

Francis Bacon was an epicure as well as a literary figure. An early experimenter with refrigeration, he is supposed to have died from a chill caught while stuffing a fowl with snow.

CHICKEN BREAST SAUTÉ CHASSEUR [884]

Lift the breasts from 3 nice, plump chickens, each weighing about 3 pounds, leaving the wing bone on (the butcher will do this for you); remove the surrounding meat from the wing bone and the skin from the breast; season the chicken with mixed salt and pepper. Heat 6 tablespoons of sweet butter in a sauté pan and place the breasts in it as soon as the butter foams. Cover the pan and cook the chicken over a brisk flame, for about 18–20 minutes, shaking and rocking the pan occasionally. Ten minutes before the breasts are cooked, add 18 fresh mushrooms, peeled and sliced. Remove the chicken and mushroom from the pan, and add to the butter remaining in it 1 tablespoon of finely chopped shallots, sauté and add to the chicken and mushrooms. Drain the butter from the pan; stir in ½ cup of dry white wine and reduce almost dry, scraping and stirring frequently to remove any gelatinous matter which may adhere to the pan; then stir in 1 cup of Brown Sauce (No 1018); boil up once, remove from the fire and stir in 2 tablespoons of sweet butter adding it bit by bit. Return the chicken breasts to the pan; roll them nicely in the sauce; then transfer to a hot platter, add the mushrooms and shallots to the sauce and pour the sauce over the chicken breasts.

Sprinkle with 1 teaspoon of finely chopped parsley or chervil and finely chopped tarragon. Serve at once.

Chicken stuffed with veal was a seventeenth century Dutch specialty. One of the most famous inns in Holland, The Wurfbain Tavern, attracted epicures from all over Europe and charged 1 florin for a whole stuffed chicken.

CHICKEN CACCIOTORA [885]

Cut 2 nice, plump chickens, each weighing about 2 to 2½ pounds into pieces for serving; season with salt and pepper and dredge lightly with flour. Heat ½ cup of good olive oil to the smoking point, add the chicken and brown thoroughly on all sides. Then add 8 small white onions, 2 small green peppers, drained and 2 slices finely chopped canned red pimientos, 1 large clove of garlic finely chopped, and 2 cups of canned tomatoes; season to taste with salt and pepper, add 1 large bay leaf tied with 6 fresh sprigs of parsley and 1 small sprig of thyme; cover and simmer very gently for 1¼ to 1½ hours; then add 2 cups of peeled, thinly sliced mushrooms and continue simmering 25 minutes longer. If you have some good beef extract on hand (commercial), stir in 1 teaspoonful just before serving as this will enrich the sauce. Serve as hot as possible. Generously buttered spaghetti or spaghetti seasoned with tomato paste is the usual accompaniment of this dish.

CHICKEN CASSEROLE HENRIETTA [886]

Cook two cleaned, singed, trussed chickens each weighing 2½ pounds in a shallow pan in ½ cup of butter over a gentle flame until golden brown on all sides, turning frequently. When nicely browned turn the chickens into a buttered casserole; add 1 cup of dry white wine, ½ cup of heavy sweet cream, and ½ cup of veal stock. Cook over a brisk flame, uncovered, until the liquid in the pan is reduced to half, then add 1 bay leaf tied with 6 sprigs of fresh parsley and 1 sprig of thyme, 8 freshly crushed peppercorns, salt to taste, 1 blade of garlic, and 3 tablespoons of chopped onions. Cover tightly and cook in a moderate oven (375° F.) for 25–30 minutes, turning the chickens once. Transfer to a hot platter; strain the sauce into a saucepan, bring to a boil, and add ½ cup of scalded sweet cream. Boil up once; remove from the fire and stir in 2 egg yolks, one at a time, beating well after each addition. Taste for seasoning, and pour half of the sauce over the chicken, serving the remainder separately. Garnish the platter with 6 endives, cooked in butter, 6 cups of fresh mushrooms cooked in butter, and 6 small potato croquettes, browned in deep fat. Arrange a small bunch of watercress at each end of the platter and serve at once.

CHICKEN CASSEROLE METROPOLE [887]
Recipe of the Hotel Metropole, London, England

Cut up two 3 pound roasting chickens as for fricassée; roll in mixed salt, pepper, powdered majoram and powdered thyme to taste, and brown on all sides in ½ cup of good salad oil, preferably olive oil, over a bright flame, stirring frequently with a wooden spoon. Transfer the chicken to a well-oiled earthenware baking dish; pour over enough scalded thin cream to barely cover, and bake in a moderate oven (375° F.) until the chicken is tender and the cream almost evaporated.

Meanwhile cook ⅓ cup of minced onions until tender but not browned, in the oil left in the pan, stirring frequently with a wooden spoon; then stir in 1 tablespoon of curry powder, sifted with 2 table-spoons of flour, until thoroughly blended. Gradually add 2 cups of thin cream or evaporated milk, scalded with 1 large bay leaf, 1 whole clove of garlic, 1 sprig of fennel top, or an equal amount of powdered fennel, and 1 whole clove, and bring to a boil, stirring frequently; simmer gently for 5 minutes; remove from the fire and stir in, one at a time, 2 egg yolks, stirring briskly after each addition. Season to taste with salt bring to the boiling point; pour over the chicken and glaze under the flame of the broiling oven. Serve right in the casserole or in individual heated cassolettes.

The wedding feasts of the Bedouin tribes of Palestine usually include a dish which consists, from its appearance, of only a roasted camel. But inside the camel are two roasted sheep; inside the sheep are several roasted, stuffed chickens; roasted guinea hens stuffed with fish, and inside the fish are fried eggs.

CHICKEN CASSEROLE NEWLYWED [888]
(Left-over)

Cover the bottom of a generously buttered earthenware casserole, with ½ cup of hot buttered bread crumbs; add 1½ to 1¾ cups of chopped, cooked chicken, mixed with 1½ cups of sliced cooked fresh mushrooms, using stems and caps, season to taste with salt, pepper and a dash each of nutmeg, thyme and marjoram, then pour over ¾ cup of scalded heavy cream, mixed with ½ cup of hot chicken bouillon, or stock made from the bones and strained; top with ½ cup of buttered bread crumbs, and bake in a moderate oven (350° F.) for 20 minutes, or until crumbs are nicely browned. Serve in the casserole.

CHICKEN CELESTINE [889]

Just before World War I, there existed in Lyon, France, a restaurant called Café du Cercle. The cuisine was elegant, with all foods of the best, and nothing too good. To a little guest room of the café, every evening around seven, came the select gourmets—all of illustrious name, full of inspiration and of merriment. Their humor was as fine as their palate, and their discourse had the flavor of the morsels which they enjoyed. Rousselot, their chef—a genius for sauces—prepared frequently for them the famous chicken dish which he named "Célestine," after his wife.

For 6 gourmets take 3 young broilers—preferably plump. Cut these into serving portions. Heat ⅓ cup finest butter in a casserole, spreading the butter evenly. Add the chicken and brown on all sides over a bright flame, so that the juices of the meat are sealed in, and no steam is given off. When the chicken is golden brown, add ½ pound small mushrooms and 2 large peeled tomatoes which have been diced and seeded; continue cooking for 10 minutes, stirring gently meanwhile. Now add 1 cup dry white wine, 2 tablespoons meat jelly, and 2 tablespoons good brandy. Mix well; bring to the boiling point; and season with salt and pepper to taste, together with a few grains of cayenne pepper. Cover, and simmer very gently for 10 minutes. Transfer the chicken to a hot platter; then remove all fat from the sauce remaining in the casserole, and add 2 teaspoons finely minced parsley, 2 teaspoons finely minced chives, and a tiny piece of mashed garlic. Let this sauce reduce to nearly half over a bright flame and pour immediately over the chicken. Serve at once, with a garnish of small triangles of bread fried in butter.

CHICKEN AUX CHAMPEAUX [890]

A specialty created in Paris in 1800 by M. Champeaux, a restaurateur

Clean and wash a young 4-pound hen; rub it with a little powdered juniper berry, then with good brandy. Grind the liver and the gizzard with 3 ounces raw lean ham, 1 slice bread, soaked in milk and squeezed out, and 1 tablespoon each of chopped parsley, chives, and fresh mushrooms. Season to taste with salt, pepper, and a pinch of thyme; then stir in 2 well-beaten egg yolks. Blend thoroughly by putting the whole through the food chopper again and add 2 stiffly beaten egg whites. Stuff the chicken with this mixture, sew up the openings, and place the bird in a large soup kettle with 1 gallon cold water, a 2-pound piece of lean shin of beef and salt to taste. Bring to a boil, and skim carefully; then add 2 leeks tied together with 1 stalk of celery, 3 young carrots, a strip of parsnip, 1 large onion, stuck with a whole clove, and 10 peppercorns, gently bruised. Cover and simmer gently for 3½ hours. Arrange the hen on a bed of crisp watercress on a hot platter, and flank it on either side with the beef. Serve piping hot.

In the sixteenth century, guests at French banquets tossed dice to decide who would get the drumsticks of the fowls served.

CHICKEN CINTRA [891]

Cut a plump tender chicken, weight about 4½ pounds, into 6 pieces as for a fricassée. Brown these in butter with a whole shallot and a whole clove of garlic, both peeled.

Add ½ cup light Cintra Port, or Port of comparable quality, ½ cup dry white wine, a liqueur glass of brandy, and a liqueur glass of Cherry Brandy; when the mixture boils, light it with a match, shaking the pan until the flame dies. Allow the sauce to simmer down to about half. When the chicken is cooked, transfer it to a serving platter and keep hot. Complete the sauce with a cup of double cream and 2 egg yolks, cooking until it thickens, but taking care not to boil it, and stirring constantly and briskly. Strain, pour over the chicken, and serve very hot.

CHICKEN CLOISTER STYLE [892]
Poulet du Cloître

Cut a young chicken in pieces, and cook it in butter in a casserole. When golden brown in color, add salt, pepper, a few small onions, and a few pinches of spice. Cover tightly, and cook over a very slow fire for an hour or an hour and a quarter. Now add ½ pint cream and ½ pound mushrooms which have been previously sliced and sautéed in butter. Stir gently, and cook 15 minutes longer.

Heat some thin slices of cooked ham in butter; then add 2 tablespoons of Madeira, or possibly Sherry. Remove the ham, and pour any remaining liquid into the casserole. Beat two egg yolks in a bowl with some of the sauce. Place the slices of ham on a serving platter, and arrange chicken on these. Complete the thickening of the sauce with the egg yolks, and pour over the chicken. Serve very hot.

During Napoleon's campaigns, his chef, uncertain as to when dinner would be served, roasted a fresh chicken every twenty minutes.

CHICKEN A LA CREOLE [893]

Prepare 4 cups of Creole Sauce (No. 1041) and add to it 1 large clove of garlic and 1 cup of dry white wine. Let simmer very gently while preparing the chicken as follows: Cut into quarters 3 small broilers, each weighing about 2 pounds, wipe with a damp cloth, season to taste with mixed salt and pepper, and sauté in ⅓ cup of sweet butter over a bright flame, until golden brown on all sides, turning frequently. When quite brown, drain the chicken and add to the Creole Sauce. Cover, set the kettle or stew pot in a moderate oven (375° F.), and cook for 40–45 minutes without disturbing. Turn the sauce, which should be slightly reduced into a hot deep platter, arrange chicken over it, and serve at once with plain boiled rice.

CHICKEN EXCELSIOR [894]
Poularde Excelsior

It is the creation of a lady cordon bleu, Madame Martineau, head of the Duc de Luynes; it is called "excelsior," meaning "still higher," "ever upward," and is a well-deserved name for this dish.

To give the pullet a snow-white skin, scrub it with soap suds; rinse carefully, then encase in a pork bladder and boil as you would a fowl. The aim of this method is to keep within the bladder the quintessence of the flavor of the bird. No loss of flavor is possible. Accepted with delight by the most sophisticated gourmets, it is recommended as a good food for convalescents or persons with delicate stomachs.

Why the use of the bladder? Because the bladder, carefully cleaned, forms, during the boiling process, a most perfect meat jelly which mingles with that of the fowl. A fowl thus cooked, served cold, and surrounded with the clarified jelly, is one of the most succulent and flavorful dishes that one gourmet may offer another.

CHICKEN FRITTERS GRAND'MERE [895]
(Left-over)

Sift together 1 cup of flour, 1½ teaspoons of salt, ¼ teaspoon of paprika and a pinch of powdered marjoram. Beat 2 egg yolks until thick, then beat in ⅓ cup of cold milk, to which has been added 2 tablespoons of sherry wine, and stir into the flour mixture, beating until smooth. Now stir in 1 cup of chopped, cooked chicken and 1 cup of drained, cooked or canned peas, mixing well; finally fold in 2 stiffly beaten egg whites, and when ready to serve, drop from the tip of a tablespoon into a little hot fat, in a frying pan to brown on all sides, or drop into hot, deep fat, (350°–375° F.) if desired. Drain on absorbent paper, and serve on a hot platter covered with a folded napkin. The fritters should be piled high, and garnished with crisp watercress.

CHICKEN IN HALF MOURNING [896]
Poularde en Petit Deuil

Cleaned and trussed, the pullet is started by covering its breast with a layer of thin, seeded lemon slices, these in turn being covered with a thin sheet of fat pork. Now the bird is cooked in a braising kettle until two-thirds done. After it has cooled, and the lemon and the fat pork have been removed, the breast is pierced through and through with narrow strips of truffles rolled in finely minced *fines herbes*, forming fancy designs. The chicken again is covered with slices of fat pork, and the cooking continued until done. Serve with the gravy from the pan.

CHICKEN A LA MARYLAND [897]

For 6 servings, choose 2 milk-fed chickens of about 2 pounds each. Quarter them, and remove necks and backbones. Clean thoroughly, wash and dry, then season with salt and pepper. Dip each piece in milk, roll in flour, and cook in an inch of melted lard in a hot pan until golden brown turning frequently. Transfer them to another pan, cover, and place in a moderate oven (375° F.) until they are thoroughly steamed through. Meanwhile, sprinkle the necks and the backbones lightly with seasoned flour, and brown them in the pan in which the chicken was cooked. Add enough scalded rich milk to the fat in the pan to make a medium-thick cream sauce, which is then enriched with 2 well-beaten egg yolks. Pour this sauce on to a hot platter, and arrange the chicken on it. Garnish with corn fritters (No. 1271), strips of broiled bacon, and small potato croquettes.

CHICKEN MOUSSE [898]

Beat 3 egg yolks, and gradually add 1½ cups cold milk, beating steadily. Place over hot water, (double boiler) and cook, stirring constantly until the mixture coats the spoon. Soak 1½ tablespoons gelatin in ¼ cup cold water for 10 minutes, add ½ cup hot chicken broth and stir until gelatin is dissolved. Add 1½ cups of cooked ground chicken and mix well, stirring, meanwhile, from the bottom of the pan. Do not actually boil, lest the mixture curdle. Season with salt, pepper, and a dash of paprika. Cool, and when cold, fold in 1 cup heavy cream which has been lightly whipped. Turn mixture into a well-buttered ring mold, and let it stand in the refrigerator overnight.

CHICKEN AND MUSHROOM PIE [899]

Clean, singe, wash quickly and dry a 3½-pound chicken; cut into eighths—2 wings, 2 thighs, 2 backs and 2 breast pieces—and rub with mixed salt and pepper. Heat ⅓ cup of butter, add the chicken, and cook over a gentle flame until very lightly browned, for about 10 minutes, stirring almost constantly. Cover with hot chicken stock and simmer very slowly, (covered) for about 40 minutes, or till chicken is tender. Thicken with a little flour moistened with cold water. Garnish the bottom of a deep dish with 6 thin slices of fried lean ham; then add the chicken and 6 hard-cooked egg yolks, halved. Pour a little of the sauce over, then add a layer of peeled, coarsely chopped raw fresh mushrooms, using about ¾ of a pound; sprinkle the mushrooms with 1 tablespoon of chopped parsley mixed with as much each of grated onion, shallots, chives and green pepper; strain the chicken sauce over all; cover with your favorite pie crust; brush the surface with milk; make a few slashes for the escape of steam, and bake in a moderate oven (375°–400° F.) for about 25–30 minutes. Remove from the oven, and, using a small funnel, pour in 3 tablespoons of good Madeira wine. Let stand a minute or so, to allow the wine to blend, and serve immediately.

CHICKEN IN THE POT [900]
La Petite Marmite of France

Who doesn't love the simple homely dishes with their appetizing aromas pervading the house, such as, for instance, a Chicken in the Pot of historic fame? This dish is still made—especially in the southern part of France—when the kettle exhales for several hours its exquisite fragrance of *pot au feu* while the vegetables hesitatingly and lightly waltz about around a nice piece of beef round and a plump fowl, cleaned, singed, stuffed with meat sausage, soaked bread, chopped parsley, onions, garlic, spices and condiments and a bouquet garni, all well blended and discreetly (oh very discreetly) moistened with a few drops of brandy. With pleasurable anticipation of the treat ahead, the fowl is filled with care and tenderness, then, with skilled hands placed, along with the round of beef or a two-pound piece of boneless ham tenderloin in the singing kettle where both will cook, slowly and gently, and deliciously perfume the entire house, the while escaping steam attunes its voice to the song of the fire.

In the midst of all the pots and pans which bubble and emit enticing odors, the big squat kettle is queen of the kitchen.

Lifting the cover to peep once in a while at the process of cooking, one sees all the ingredients bubbling at the surface; the carrots, the leeks, the turnip, the bouquet garni and even the clove of garlic perform a somewhat indolent and rythmic dance around the fowl which, lying upon its side like a grounded boat, displays to the interested its light ambered colored breast and its steaming carcass.

At the psychological moment the fowl is lifted out with tender care and dressed, as a queen, on a bed of strictly fresh curled parsley as green as the fields of Erin.

Coarse salt, prepared mustard and sweet pickles placed in small dishes are the only accompaniments of this regal dish which, before being carved, is admired and savored by the hungry guests.

This is the famous *Chicken in the Pot*. It is an antique dish. Its name is as famous as is that of George Washington. Henry IV, of France promised a chicken in the pot of every family in his kingdom, a promise which made every peasant's mouth water in anticipation, as he kindled the fire and prepared the kettle to receive the fowl. But alas the fowl remained in the egg, and the poor peasants never knew the fragrance of chicken in the pot, save in imagination.

With how many wonderful and diverse sauces has this visionary fowl been dished up since the time of Henry IV, of France! Many cooks of many nations have promised it but the kettle is still a widow, waiting vainly for the one who will not come. The official list of all the cooks of state in the nations of the world would be too cumbersome and distressing to recall, the list of those who have let the stew burn and spent enough on butter alone to ruin the governmental household.

Louis Phillipe of France, made a slight change; he substituted "Chicken with Rice" "La Poule au Riz," the "Arroz con Polo of Spain" for the Chicken in the Pot of his crafty ancestor, and gave it in some measure. During the reign of this noble scion of the House of Orléans, the bourgeois and privileged Frenchmen fed themselves on it somewhat greedily, until the Revolution of 1848 cleared the tables. As for the King himself, he ate the dish at home and managed in such a way as to have always some left for the next day, under the economic pretense that rice was better when warmed over.

Not being officially qualified, I cannot make any promise, but for all who have tasted, in imagination only, the Chicken in the Pot as prepared by the drudges in the state and national kitchens, I do wish from the bottom of my heart a real Chicken in the Pot.

However, if Henry IV, of France, and many others after him *didn't* give us the promised chicken in the pot, here is a recipe for one which I beseech all my readers to try.

Ingredients. 3½ quarts of cold water, 1 large onion, quartered, 2 medium-sized carrots, scraped, then quartered, 1 large white turnip, peeled, and quartered, 2 leeks, halved, carefully washed in several changes of cold water, then folded in three and tied up with 1 large bay leaf, 12 sprigs of fresh parsley, 1 sprig of thyme, 1 clove of garlic, peeled and left whole, 3 whole cloves, slightly bruised, 12 peppercorns, gently crushed, a pound head of green cabbage, quartered and soaked in hot water, drained, then cooled in cold water, 1 piece of parsnip the size of an egg, scraped and left whole, two 3½-pound or larger plump chickens, a 2½-pound piece of bottom round of beef, or brisket of beef, and finally 2 pounds of beef bones.

Stuffing for the Chickens. Cook the gizzards and hearts of the chickens together with a few spices in water to cover until tender. Drain, and put through food chopper together with ¼ pound of ham scraps from cooked lean ham. Mix with 1 cup of bread, soaked in a little milk, and squeezed of the excess moisture, 1 tablespoon of chopped parsley, 2 tablespoons of finely chopped fresh mushroom trimmings, ¼ cup of finely chopped green celery leaves (tops), 1 tiny slice of garlic, 1 medium-sized onion, grated, salt and pepper to taste, with a dash each of powdered thyme, mace, sage and nutmeg. Mix well, then blend with 2 well-beaten eggs. Fill the cavities of the chickens with this stuffing and sew openings solidly and securely, then truss the birds.

Place the meat, bones and stuffed chickens in a large soup kettle; add the water; bring slowly to a boil, and skim carefully, then lower the flame, and let simmer gently for 1½ hours, skimming occasionally. Now add all remaining ingredients in the order named; bring to a boil, lower the flame as much as possible, and simmer covered for 2 hours longer.

The bouillon in which the wholesome flavor of all these garden vegetables and condiments mingles with the flavor of the meat and fowl is a delight.

Transfer the chickens to a hot platter, with the meat which should be sliced and reshaped; arrange the vegetables around and pour a little of the bouillon over the whole. Serve with pickle fans, pickled onions, grated fresh horseradish mixed with sour cream, prepared mustard, sliced fresh tomatoes with vinaigrette sauce, and any other pickles and relishes you may desire.

CHICKEN RISOTTO PIEMONTAISE [901]

As the Western World boils its potatoes, so China boils its rice, solemnly and monotonously, day after day; and only the blasé Chinese who has taken on the ways of the effete foreign devils, knows or cares anything about bread. Rice from morning to night, from the cradle to the grave, is the lot of the Chinese; and familiarity has not bred contempt. An aged horse munches its hay with the relish of a colt; and the venerable Chinese sage bends over his rice bowl with quiet gratification, just as did the illustrious Confucius 2500 years ago.

It is the impatient and temperamental European who has refused to accept rice merely as bulk or roughage; and from Gibraltar to the Golden Horn the people have a thousand ways of transforming the wholesome grain into rich delicacies and confections. The pilaffs of the Near East are a succulent tribe; *arroz* figures in a hundred delectable dishes of the Iberian peninsula; and *risotto* is as essentially Italian as spaghetti and *polenta*.

Risotto in its purity and simplicity represents merely an admirable method of cooking rice; but in the hands of talented chefs and caterers it has come to mean something more formidable and complicated, something usually found among the entrées on the menu.

If you would find *risotto* in its pristine innocence, follow this authentic recipe; wash a pound of rice in many waters, rubbing the grains between the hands as the Chinese do, then drain it in a colander. Into an iron skillet put olive oil—if you have been initiated otherwise use butter; and when the oil or the butter is hot, put in the rice. Do not fry it, but let it heat up slowly, and stir it lightly, gently, but constantly with a wooden spoon or fork. Presently the white rice begins to show a yellow tinge, and as it absorbs the oil or butter you must add more to keep it moist. Little by little the grains take on a peculiar gloss; they begin to glisten like jewels. Don't let them scorch; but stir them about until each grain is a separate gilded oval, the color of ripe field corn. Then it is time to set about the completion of the *risotto*.

You will have prepared a quart of rich soup stock in which is steeped a crust of dry bread rubbed with garlic, and you will have added to the strained stock some minced onions or shallots, well browned in oil or butter. If you have started with oil, keep on using oil, and it must be *olive* oil; but if butter is your taste, keep on with butter. Pour the hot stock slowly onto the rice, which will drink it up thirstily. You will be amazed to see how swiftly the liquid is absorbed. Keep pouring till the whole is well moistened; each grain separate, and covered by the stock; then season accordingly to your taste. A tin of Italian tomato paste may be mixed with the stock, and a half-cup of grated Parmesan cheese stirred in; a small pinch of sweet basil is a novel touch. Lastly, transfer the *risotto* to a casserole, or leave it in the skillet if you prefer and put it in a moderate oven (350° F.) for half an hour, while preparing the chicken as indicated below, removing the rice when it is soft but still firm, with the grains separate and distinct. If you can obtain saffron, stir in a few pinches with respectful care.

This rice dish forms the bed on which the chicken will eventually repose.

For the chicken cut 2 or 3 tender birds into pieces for serving, preferably using broilers, each broiler serving two. Chill. Roll the pieces in flour seasoned to taste with salt and pepper. Fry in very hot olive oil until golden brown; drain off all the fat, and arrange the chicken around the risotto. Serve an abundance of grated cheese, preferably Parmesan; but if the tang and the taste of this delicious cheese are not to your liking, use equal parts of Parmesan and Swiss cheese; and offer your guests a rich tomato sauce, for the thirsty rice will have absorbed most of the stock.

CHICKEN SALAD TUXEDO PARK [902]

Combine 2 cups water, 3 tablespoons good wine or tarragon vinegar, 2 tablespoons granulated sugar, 1 teaspoon salt, 2 teaspoons prepared mustard, and ¼ cup olive oil in a saucepan. Heat to the boiling point, then remove from the fire. Soften 3 tablespoons gelatine in a generous ¼ cup cold water, add to the hot mixture, and stir until dissolved. Now beat 3 whole eggs and add to the mixture, beating until thoroughly blended. Cool. Add a few drops Tabasco sauce, 3 tablespoons tomato catsup, and 1 cup mayonnaise, and beat until well blended. Pour sufficient dressing into a mold, round or oblong, to cover the bottom. Arrange ½ cup sliced radishes mixed with ¼ cup cucumber cubes in the bottom of the mold in any desired design, and place in the refrigerator until firm enough to hold the design in place. Combine 4 cups cubed cooked chicken, 1 cup finely chopped celery, 2 cups sliced ripe olives, ¼ cup capers, and blend thoroughly, but lightly with the remaining dressing. Pour into the decorated mold and place in the refrigerator. When the mixture is firm, unmold on a salad platter and garnish with whole ripe olives, lettuce, and tomato wedges. (Or alternate with rings of chopped dark colored meat aspic jelly.) This recipe will easily serve 12.

CHICKEN SAUTÉ BOURGUIGNONNE [903]

Cut 2 chickens, each weighing 2½ lbs. in 4 pieces each, and brown in ¼ cup of clarified butter; season to taste with salt and pepper, and when golden brown on both sides remove the chicken from the pan, and keep hot. Add 1 tablespoon of chopped shallots to the butter left in the pan, brown lightly, then stir in 1 tablespoon of flour, blending well. Return the chicken to the pan, add 1 bouquet garni composed of 1 large bay leaf, 8 sprigs of fresh parsley, and 1 large or 2 small sprigs of thyme, all tied together with white kitchen thread, and cook very gently, stirring frequently, for 35 to 40 minutes. Meanwhile, cook 1 dozen very small white onions in half a pint of chicken broth, just long enough to blanch them; drain, and cook in 1 tablespoon of butter; then add the stock in which the onions were parboiled, 1 cup of salt pork, cubed small after being first parboiled in water, ½ pound of thinly sliced mushrooms, also cooked in a little butter and drained. Season to taste with salt and black pepper, stir in the chicken, add ¾ cup of red wine, discard the bouquet garni, and let simmer 5 or 6 minutes to heat through. Serve at once.

CHICKEN SAUTÉ JAMBALAYA NEW ORLEANS [904]

Clean, singe, wash and cut two chickens each weighing 2½ pounds in serving pieces as for stew; season to taste with salt and pepper, and brown nicely, over a gentle flame in ⅓ cup of butter, turning the pieces frequently. When well colored, lift out the chicken and keep hot. Lightly brown 2 tablespoons of chopped onion, in the remaining butter in the pan; stir in 2 cups of well washed, drained, rice, adding more butter if needed so that each grain will be moistened by the butter, then stir in a tiny pinch of saffron, mixing well. Add 1 bouquet garni composed of 1 bay leaf, 8 sprigs of fresh parsley and 1 sprig of thyme, all tied together with white kitchen thread, and cook for 5 minutes, stirring occasionally; then arrange the chicken over the rice; gently pour over all 1½ quarts of chicken broth; bring to a fast boil; stir and cover tightly. Set the pan in a moderate oven (375°–400° F.) and bake for about 25 to 30 minutes, or until the rice has absorbed all the stock or liquid. Discard the bouquet garni and arrange the rice on a heated platter, with the chicken on top. Dusted with minced parsley. Serve immediately.

"Don't count your chickens before they're hatched" is supposed to have originated with seventeenth-century Baltic farmers. They never counted their fowl, believing it unlucky to do so.

CHICKEN SAUTÉED WITH MUSHROOMS AND OLIVES [905]

Wash, and soak 1 cup of dried mushrooms in warm water for 30 minutes, or until plump. Then dry. Disjoint two 3-pound chickens, roll in seasoned flour, and fry in ⅓ cup of butter over a medium flame until golden brown, turning frequently. When nicely browned, add 1 large bay leaf, 2 whole cloves, an inch piece of scraped parsley root and a pinch each of thyme, nutmeg and powdered ginger. Stir in 1¼ cups of scalded cream, 12 pitted black olives and the coarsely chopped mushrooms. Cover tightly and bake in a moderate oven (350°–375°F.) for 1½ hours without disturbing. Serve from the casserole.

CHICKEN SOUFFLE, SOUTHERN STYLE [906]

Combine 2 cups finely chopped cooked chicken with 2 cups cream sauce (No. 258), salt, pepper, and nutmeg to taste. Add 1 tablespoon each of minced parsley and grated onion or onion juice, and mix well. Stir in 3 slightly beaten egg yolks, and fold in the stiffly beaten whites of 3 eggs. In the meantime, cook 3 chicken livers in a little butter, without browning. Split the livers, and put one-half in each of 6 individual unbaked pie crust shells. Fill the shells with the soufflé mixture, and arrange them on a baking sheet. Bake 20 to 25 minutes in a hot oven (400° F.), until the crust is golden brown and the soufflés well puffed. Serve at once, on individual plates garnished with watercress.

Egyptian restaurant keepers of 500 B. C. featured a table d'hôte dinner of cereal, wild fowl and onions.

CHICKEN AND SWEET POTATOES EN CASSEROLE [907]
(Left-over)

Have ready 3 cups of diced cooked chicken, 4 cups of sliced cooked sweet potatoes (boiled or baked), 2 cups of well-seasoned chicken gravy and 6 thin slices of bacon.

Arrange chicken and potatoes in alternate layers in a buttered earthenware or glass casserole, seasoning each layer with mixed salt, pepper and nutmeg to taste. Pour the hot chicken gravy over the top; letting it drip down the chicken-potato mixture; and lay the raw bacon slices over all. Bake in a moderate oven (375° F.) for 30 to 35 minutes, and serve at once.

CHICKEN TARTAR STYLE [908]
Poularde à la Tartare

This method implies a split young pullet, trussed, rubbed with mixed salt, pepper, and condiments, dipped in the best of olive oil then in soft bread crumbs, and broiled as you would an ordinary broiler. A side dish of Remoulade Sauce is *de rigueur*. Remoulade is made of mayonnaise highly seasoned with mustard, chopped gherkins, capers, parsley, chervil, and tarragon.

CHICKEN TETTRAZINI [909]

Select 2 young plump chickens, each weighing about 2½ pounds; have them cut in 8 pieces; cover with boiling water and simmer until tender, adding just a little salt to the water to season. Cool the birds in the broth, then shred the chicken meat fine and put the skin and bones back into the broth; cover, bring to the boiling point and simmer for 45 minutes; remove cover from the pan and let the broth boil furiously for 10 to 15 minutes, or till reduced to about 2 cups.

Meanwhile, thinly slice 1 pound of peeled fresh mushrooms, and sauté them in 3 or 4 tablespoons of butter until tender and lightly browned, stirring frequently. Break one pound of Italian spaghetti into small pieces and cook in a large amount of boiling salted water until tender, or about 15 minutes.

Make a rich cream sauce as follows: Melt 3 tablespoons of sweet butter; blend in 3 tablespoons of flour, and gradually stir in the hot, strained reduced chicken broth, stirring constantly until perfectly smooth and absolutely free from lumps; let it boil up 3 or 4 times, then stir in 1½ to 1¾ cups of scalded heavy sweet cream, and ⅓ cup of dry sherry wine. Divide the sauce into two parts; add the shredded chicken to one, the cooked, well-drained spaghetti and mushrooms to the other and season both to taste with salt and pepper. Put the prepared spaghetti half into a baking dish, making a cavity in the center and banking it around the side of the dish. Pour the chicken half in the center; sprinkle with grated Parmesan, using about ½ generous cup (or a mixture of grated Swiss and Parmesan cheese, if preferred), over the top and bake in a moderate oven until lightly browned, about 10 to 12 minutes; serve right from the baking dish.

COLD CHICKEN LOAF MY WAY [910]
Pâté Froid de Volaille, Ma Façon

Bone very carefully a plump young 5-pound fowl, (or the butcher will do it for you). The whole skin should be removed. Lay the fowl flat on a wet board and spread it on the inside with part of the following stuffing: put through a food chopper, using the finest blade, ½ pound lean raw veal, ¼ pound raw ham, ½ pound lean raw pork, and ¼ pound peeled fresh mushrooms. Blend with ½ cup heavy cream, and season with ½ teaspoon salt, ¼ teaspoon pepper, a few grains cayenne, and nutmeg to taste, plus generous pinches of thyme, clove, and allspice. Wet enough bread with milk to yield a full pressed down cup, when squeezed in a dry towel, add this to the stuffing with 2 tablespoons grated onion and 1 cup dry cracker crumbs. Put the mixture again through the food chopper to ensure smoothness and thorough blending. Divide this stuffing into three parts, and use one part to stuff the fowl. Reshape the bird in its natural form, and lard through and through with about ¼ pound fat back pork cut into long narrow strips and rolled in *fines herbes* (parsley, chives, tarragon, and the like), finely minced. Do not tie the bird, but roll it up as you would a jelly roll.

Now line a large oval mold with rich pastry about ⅛ inch thick (puff paste may be used, if desired); and spread the paste on bottom and sides, with the second part of the meat stuffing, pressing down well with a spatula. Place the reshaped fowl in the center and spread the remaining third of the stuffing on top. Set in a moderate oven (350° to 375° F.), for 2½ hours. If the top browns too fast, cover with a buttered paper. When done, remove from the oven, and let stand 15 minutes to set. Unmold on a baking sheet, brush all over with egg yolk mixed with a little cold milk, and return to a hot oven (425° F.) to crisp and brown the crust. Let cool thoroughly before serving. Slice at the table and serve with a bowl of green salad. This *paté* or loaf in crust keeps well in the refrigerator.

COQ A LA BOURGUIGNONNE [911]

Collect the blood of 2 fat young roosters in a bowl in which you have previously mixed ¼ cup good brandy and 2 tablespoons tarragon vinegar, stirring gently so that the blood will not curdle. Clean and disjoint the roosters, and season them to taste with salt, allspice, and freshly ground black pepper and set aside for a few hours. Meanwhile, brown 8 ounces salt pork, cut in fingerstrips and 24 whole, small, peeled white onions in a flat-bottomed pan large enough to hold the 2 birds. Add the chicken and sear to a light brown, turning frequently. Remove the fat from the pan, pour in 3 tablespoons brandy, and flame until the liquor burns out. Now add 1¾ bottles good red Burgundy, 1 large lump of sugar, and a *bouquet garni* of 2 sprigs green celery tops, 1 of thyme (wild thyme is better), 6 or 7 of fresh parsley, 2 of rosemary, and 1 large bay leaf, all tied together; and then drop in 2 mashed cloves of garlic and 12 small, whole, fresh mushrooms, peeled and stemmed. Cover, and simmer gently for 1 hour. About 15 minutes before serving, arrange the chicken on a very hot serving dish, with the onions, the salt pork, and the mushrooms. Discard the *bouquet garni*. Strain the sauce through a fine sieve; pressing lightly; then gradually add 2 tablespoons sweet butter, and taste for seasoning. Just before serving, pour the blood mixture into this sauce, stirring very slowly from the bottom of the saucepan with a small wire wisk. To prevent curdling, do not boil. Garnish with bread triangles browned in butter and drained, also small bunches of curled parsley.

King Henry IV of France raised and cooked his own chickens. In 1008, he wrote a small cookbook of recipes giving directions for the preparation of chicken dishes.

COQUELET AU CORTON   [912]
Little Rooster in Corton Wine

Wash one 3½-pound roasting chicken quickly in cold water and dry at once, then cut up as for fricassée. Roll the pieces in seasoned flour and sauté in sweet butter over a bright flame until well-browned all over, turning the chicken frequently. Remove from the frying pan and, in the fat remaining in it, cook 12 small fresh mushroom peeled caps, 6 small peeled white onions, and ⅛ of a pound of salt pork, cut into tiny cubes, for about 5 minutes, stirring frequently. Place the chicken on top and slowly pour over 1½ cups of Burgundy Corton Wine, add a small bouquet garni composed of 1 small bay leaf tied with 4 sprigs of parsley and 1 small sprig of thyme, all tied with kitchen thread, season to taste with salt and pepper, cover and simmer very gently, over a low flame, shaking the pan occasionally, for about 40 minutes. Remove the chicken to a hot platter and keep hot. To the sauce and vegetables remaining in the pan, add 2 tablespoons of flour kneaded with 2 tablespoons of sweet butter and ¾ cup of rich chicken stock; taste for seasoning, discard the bouquet garni and bring to a boil. Simmer for 5 minutes, stirring well, and pour over the chicken. Garnish with a dozen small triangles of bread fried in butter and crisp, green watercress.

Vincenzo Cervio, official carver to Cardinal Farnese in the late 1500's, couldn't cook, but he could carve a roast so exquisitely that he was held in high esteem throughout Italy.

CREAMED CHICKEN RAGOUT (STEW)　　　[913]
WITH ALMONDS (CREOLE)

Wash and dry two 3-pound chickens cut for frying; roll in ⅓ cup of flour, mixed with 1 teaspoon of salt, ⅛ teaspoon of white pepper, ¼ teaspoon of freshly grated nutmeg, and ⅛ teaspoon of mace. Heat ⅓ cup of butter or margarin in a large stewpot or casserole having a cover, and brown the chicken in it on all sides, turning the pieces frequently. Gradually stir in ¾ cup of boiling water, mixed with ¼ cup of Pique Seasoning, add 1 bouquet garni composed of 1 large bay leaf, 8 sprigs of fresh parsley and 1 sprig of thyme, all tied together with white kitchen thread, 1 blade of garlic and ⅓ cup of chopped onions. Cover and simmer gently for about 45 minutes, or until chicken is tender. Measure the casserole liquid and add enough boiling water (about 1½ cups) to make 2 generous cups. Blend ½ cup of cold, sweet cream, with 3 tablespoons of flour, and gradually stir into the ragout. Now add 1 cup of well drained canned mushroom buttons and cook 15 minutes longer. Taste for seasoning, discard the bouquet garni, and stir in ⅓ cup of blanched, shredded and toasted almonds. Serve at once over plain boiled rice.

CURRY OF CHICKEN NAPAL MANNER　　　[914]

Cut a 3½ to 4-pound chicken into neat joints, as for fricassée; wipe each piece with a damp cloth; place in a stewpot; barely cover with cold water, and add ¼ pound of thinly sliced onions, ⅛ of a teaspoon of coriander seeds, 1 inch stick of green ginger, salt and black pepper to taste, and ½ pound of Kabool or Indian corn, previously well washed. Cover and cook very gently until the chicken is almost tender. Covered. Lift out the chicken and keep hot.

Mix ⅛ of a teaspoon each of ground cinnamon and ground cloves, with 2 or 3 teaspoons of curry powder; moisten to a paste with a little cold stock or cold water, and add this paste bit by bit to the stock in the stewpot. Bring to a boil, lower the flame and simmer very gently for 15–20 minutes, stirring occasionally.

Meanwhile heat ⅓ cup of *ghee* or butter; stir in the chicken, and fry until golden brown, turning and lifting the pieces of chicken frequently. Drain well and add to the curry sauce. Cover closely and simmer gently for about 15 minutes, to mellow. Serve hot with plain boiled rice.

GRANNY LEE'S LITTLE CHICKEN PIES　　　[915]
An Old Timer from the Old South

Note. This recipe was given to the writer by an old lady 35 years ago, who said that she used it for nearly 60 years, and that she got it from a lady who used it for 40 years, so you can readily see that it is pretty old, but it is truly a delicious recipe.

Cut a young fowl weighing about 4 pounds into joints and cover with cold water. Then add 1 large bay leaf, 1 medium-sized onion, stuck with 3 whole cloves, 1 stalk of celery, cut into inch pieces, a 2-inch piece of parsley root, scraped and halved, and ½ clove of garlic. Season with little salt but plenty of pepper. Bring to a boil, skim carefully, lower the flame and simmer very gently until chicken is tender, but not until the meat leaves the bones. Have ready 6 individual deep dish pie dishes lined with flaky pie crust (See Nos. 2066 and 2104), and in each lay a piece of light and a piece of dark meat, having the meat boned; add 1 teaspoon of very finely minced parboiled salt pork, a few thin slices of raw potato, 3 very tiny parboiled silver onions, 1 teaspoon each of cooked or canned peas, carrot cubes, and canned corn, cream style; sprinkle ½ teaspoon each of finely chopped parsley and chives into each pie. Thicken 2 cups of chicken broth, previously strained, with butter kneaded with flour in equal parts; season to taste with salt; fill each pie with the gravy; cover with pie crust; make a few slits for the escape of steam, and bake in a hot oven (400° F.) until the crusts are golden brown. Serve immediately.

HODGE PODGE CHICKEN FARMER STYLE [916]

Brown the pieces of a 4½ to 5-pound chicken on all sides in ¾ cup of lard in a Dutch oven, over a bright flame, turning frequently until browned on all sides, but not scorched nor burned; remove the chicken to a hot platter and keep hot. Pour off all but ¼ cup of the fat; in this sauté lightly 1 large onion, chopped, 2 green peppers, chopped, and 1 cup of sliced mushrooms. Stir in 1 No. 2 can of tomatoes, 1 cup of diced celery stalks, and 3 small diced carrots; season to taste with salt and pepper, add 1 bouquet garni composed of 1 large bay leaf, 1 sprig of thyme and 10 sprigs of fresh parsley, all tied together with white kitchen thread, cover and cook gently for 20 minutes. Put in the chicken; cover, and continue simmering 1½ hours, or until tender; add then 1 cup of canned kernel corn, 1 cup of canned green peas, and 1 cup of cooked rice. Simmer again for 15 minutes and serve in a heated deep platter, sprinkling with chopped parsley.

JELLIED CHICKEN LOAF [917]
ARMENONVILLE STYLE
Galantine de Volaille Armenonville

Clean, singe, and split a 4½-pound plump fowl down the back. Remove all the bones and tendons; then spread the fowl on a buttered towel which has been wrung out in cold water. Remove the legs and wings and cut the meat of these parts into small cubes. Reserve all bones and trimmings for later use. Combine 1 pound fresh pork, ½ pound lean veal and ¼ pound very lean salt pork and put through a food chopper, using the finest blade. To this mixture add ¼ pound fresh ham and ¼ pound smoked beef tongue, both cubed very small, the cubed meat from the legs and the wings of the fowl the flesh of a small boned broiler, cubed small, 1 scant teaspoon salt, ¼ teaspoon freshly ground pepper, ½ teaspoon each of thyme, cloves, allspice, and marjoram, a pinch each of sage and nutmeg, and 2 tablespoons each of chopped truffles and pistachio nuts. Blend well, then moisten with 1 tablespoon good brandy and enough heavy cream to bind mixture together. Heap the stuffing on the boned fowl, and fold the bird in the wet, buttered towel. Tie both ends with kitchen string, and tie at intervals of two inches in order to keep the chicken in shape.

Set the galantine aside. Place the bones, trimmings, and 3 pounds beef bones in a large soup kettle, add 2 carrots, 2 medium sized onions, 2 small leeks, 1 white turnip, 1 small parsnip, 2 stalks celery, all chopped, 1 large *bouquet garni* composed of the tops of the 2 celery stalks, 12 sprigs parsley, 2 large bay leaves, and 2 sprigs thyme all tied together with white kitchen thread, 1 very small piece garlic (optional), 12 whole peppercorns gently bruised, and 4 whole cloves. Place the galantine over this mixture. Fill the kettle with cold water to a full inch above the galantine, which should be kept constantly covered with water. Bring the mixture to a boil, as you would a *pot-au-feu*, skimming off all scum as it foms. Then reduce the flame, cover the pot, and simmer gently for 4½ hours without disturbing—except that after 2 hours of simmering, turn thre galantine over so as to cook it evenly.

Remove the kettle from the fire. Let the galantine cool in its own liquid. Then remove all the strings, also the towel. When the galantine is well cooled, put it in the refrigerator until wanted. Strain the stock remaining in the kettle; then return it to the fire, and allow to reduce to half its volume. Pour the stock into shallow pans to congeal and form a jelly. When ready to serve, either chop the jelly or cut it into squares, lozenges, cubes, or into fancy shapes with fancy cutters, and surround the galantine with it.

Note. Not all cold chicken dishes need be as elaborate as the above, and a light, chilled mousse more easily and quickly prepared might be more acceptable as a warm-weather specialty. It would bring to the palate the cooling delicacy of such smooth concoctions as the large family of meat, fowl, and fish mousses offers. Bear in mind that it is always possible to substitute fish or shrimp, lobster or crab, with the proper seasonings, for the chicken or the meat in a mousse recipe.

MINCED CHICKEN BELMONT STYLE   [918]
Eminée of Chicken Belmont

First, cook a plump 3-pound chicken in sufficient chicken stock barely to cover, with 1 stalk celery, 1 young carrot, thinly sliced, 1 small onion stuck with a whole clove, a *bouquet garni*, 6 bruised peppercorns, and salt to taste. When the chicken is tender, remove it from the broth, and slice the breasts crosswise into thin sections. Prepare rice pilaf Belmont as follows: Melt ⅓ cup sweet butter in a saucepan, and add 1 generous tablespoon minced shallots and 1 cup polished rice, well rinsed. Stir for a minute or so, and strain over this mixture 3 cups of the stock in which the chicken was cooked. Season to taste with salt and white pepper, mix well, and set the saucepan in a hot oven (400° F.) for 20 minutes. In the meantime prepare a velvet sauce. For this melt 2 tablespoons butter in a saucepan, blend in 2 tablespoons flour, and cook for 2 minutes, stirring constantly from the bottom of the pan. Gradually beat in 2 cups strained stock mixed with 1 cup scalded heavy cream, and simmer for 18 or 20 minutes, stirring frequently. Then, off the fire, add 3 egg yolks, one at a time, beating well after each addition. Season with salt and pepper, and keep hot, but do not allow sauce to boil again. Pour ½ cup good dry white wine into a small saucepan containing 1 tablespoon lemon juice, a piece the size of a small walnut of meat glaze butter (1 part sweet butter and 2 parts meat glaze or meat jelly, kneaded together), and ½ pound minced fresh mushrooms. Cook for about 10 minutes, and season to taste with salt and white pepper; then strain, and set the mushrooms aside to keep hot. Let the liquid in the pan reduce to about 3 generous tablespoons. To serve the dish, spread the rice on the bottom of an oven-proof dish. Combine the minced chicken, the mushrooms, and the velvet sauce, and arrange over the rice. Glaze by brushing the top with 3 tablespoons of the sauce reserved for this purpose, adding to it a well-beaten egg yolk, and 2 tablespoons whipped cream. Place under the broiler flame for a minute, and serve immediately.

OVEN COOKED BROILERS SOUTHERN STYLE   [919]

Allow 1 broiler weighing 2 pounds for two servings. Wipe 3 broilers with a damp cloth, then rub well with salt and pepper to taste. Divide each broiler in two, lengthwise; roll each half in good oil or melted butter; place in a dripping pan and sprinkle each half with 1 generous teaspoon of chopped onions. Bake in a hot oven (400–425° F.) for 25–30 minutes or until tender, turning once and basting with fat from the dripping pan. Serve on a hot platter, crown fashion, having a mound of freshly made Shoe String or Match Stick Potatoes (No. 1424) in center. Garnish with watercress and pour the butter from the dripping pan over the chicken.

POACHED CHICKEN SAUCE IVOIRE   [920]

Clean, singe, wash quickly in cold water and dry a 4½- to 5-pound chicken. Fill the cavity with a small apple, 3 slices of onion and a thin slice of lemon, after rubbing inside and out with salt and pepper. Truss; place the bird in a large kettle, and add 3 young carrots, scraped, and cut into 1 inch cubes, 2 medium-sized onions, halved, the cleaned neck and giblets of the bird, 1 small white turnip, peeled and quartered, also 3 leeks, trimmed, halved, carefully washed, then folded in three or four and tied with 1 large bay leaf, 12 sprigs of fresh parsley, 2 sprigs of thyme and 3 sprigs of green celery leaves (tops), all tied together with white kitchen thread. Season with 2 teaspoons of salt and 12 peppercorns, then add 4 quarts of cold water. Bring to a boil, skimming carefully; lower the flame and simmer very gently for 1¼ to 1½ hours, or until the bird is tender but not overcooked. Remove the chicken and keep hot, while preparing the sauce:

Sauce Ivoire. Heat 6 tablespoons of sweet butter; blend in 3 tablespoons of flour, stirring constantly until mixture bubbles, but do not allow to brown. Gradually add 1 quart of strained chicken broth, carefully freed of all fat, still stirring constantly, until mixture thickens, over a low flame. Simmer for 10 minutes with frequent stirring. Strain this sauce through a fine-meshed wire sieve into a shallow pan, and reduce it to half, over a bright flame. Remove from the fire and add 1 cup of scalded heavy cream, again stirring constantly. Return to the fire and bring to a boil; remove again to one side and beat in, one at a time, 3 egg yolks, one at a time, beating briskly after each addition. Return to the fire and bring just to a boil. Strain through a fine sieve into a heated sauceboat and serve with the hot chicken, which has been garnished with watercress. The carving for this supreme dish is always done at the table.

ROAST SPRING CHICKEN EN CASSEROLE,   [921]
ENGLISH STYLE
(*Serves 2*)

Select a nice broiler weighing 2 to 2½ pounds. Clean, singe, wash quickly, dry, then rub with mixed salt and pepper. Heat in an earthenware casserole 3 tablespoons of butter; add ½ cup of boiling water; place the trussed chicken on its side (as the legs take longest to cook) in the casserole, and cook, uncovered, in a moderate oven (350°–375° F.) about 40 to 45 minutes, basting and turning the chicken until both sides are golden brown. It is done when the juice from the chicken, after a fork is inserted, shows no red color. Should the liquid in the casserole reduce too fast, add a little more. Serve plain with its own gravy from the casserole, which if desired may be thickened with a little flour after tasting for seasoning.

SPRING CHICKEN SAUTE AU CHABLIS [922]
HOLLYWOOD STYLE

Cut 3 two-pound spring chickens (broilers) in two lengthwise, with mixed salt and pepper; to taste. Place in a pan containing ½ cup of sweet butter and cook very slowly for about 20 minutes, or until done, turning frequently. Arrange the chicken on a heated serving platter and keep hot. To the butter left in the pan, add 2 tablespoons of finely chopped onion, and 1 teaspoon of finely minced shallot, and cook till just beginning to take on a yellowish hue, then add 6 large mushroom caps, peeled, and sliced, and 1 avocado pear sliced. Cook a few minutes, stirring well, then slowly add ½ cup of Chablis wine and 4 medium-sized peeled tomatoes, quartered. Cook very gently for 10 to 15 minutes, stir in 2 tablespoons of sweet butter, adding it bit by bit, also 1 tablespoon of chopped parsley. Mix well, pour over the chicken, and serve at once.

TIMBALE OF CHICKEN GASTRONOME [923]

Butter the inside of a large charlotte mold; line the bottom and sides with rich, flaky pastry, or puff paste, if preferred. (Place the mold on a 9-inch pie plate for easier handling.) Cover the pastry lining with a buttered paper; then in order to hold the crust in shape, fill the mold up to the brim with equal parts of bran and flour mixed together. Top with a cover of the same pastry exactly as you would for an ordinary pie. Brush the top with a little milk or with egg yolk and milk, and bake in a moderate oven (350°–375° F.) for about 40 minutes, or until the top crust becomes a delicate brown. (Put buttered paper under top cover.)

Meanwhile, place in a small pan 1 cup chopped fresh ham, 6 fresh mushrooms, chopped fine, 1 *bouquet garni*, and ½ cup good Madeira wine. Cook this mixture over a gentle flame for about 25 minutes, stirring occasionally. In another saucepan heat 1 cup rich tomato sauce No. 1130 with 1 tablespoon meat extract (Commercial). Strain the Madeira mixture into the hot tomato sauce; season to taste with salt, pepper, and a few grains of cayenne. Boil up once, then remove saucepan and stir in 1 tablespoon sweet butter. To this sauce add a dozen small chicken dumplings, 3 dozen canned button mushrooms, 1 dozen slices of truffle cooked in butter and well drained, 1 dozen stuffed olives, and 3 sweetbreads, parboiled, then cubed.

To make the chicken dumplings, combine, blending thoroughly, ⅔ pound ground raw chicken meat, ⅓ teaspoon sage, ⅓ pound lean ground pork, 1 cup bread soaked in milk, then squeezed dry and loosened by shaking between the fingers, 1 whole egg and 1 egg yolk, ¼ teaspoon salt, pepper and grated nutmeg to taste. Put this mixture through the food chopper, using the finest blade; shape into small balls, and drop into briskly boiling stock. Allow to boil constantly from 25 to 30 minutes, and drain. Remove top crust of timbale, empty filling, and unmold bottom over hot platter. Have ready ½ lb. warm, drained macaroni cut into ½ in. pieces, blended with ½ cup equal parts grated Gruyère and Parmesan. Fill timbale with layers of macaroni, dumplings and sauce. Replace top crust and serve immediately so that dish is hot.

DUCKS   [924]

According to those human beings who do not despise the gifts of bounteous Providence; those to whom eating assumes a classical and solemn ritual, and whom we call "gourmets, connoisseurs and sometimes classical gourmands"; those who know that there is a moment when reason says to appetite " . . . non procedes amplius . . . " (you shall go no further), the Long Island duck is one of the most esteemed, the "ne plus ultra" of succulence in our domestic duckdom. According to them, beside this élite of ducks, the northern duck would be an amiable brag, except for its illustrious liver, that pure diamond of the culinary art. The Southern duck seems to have taken the wise resolution to retire to the earthenware dish to be potted or pastied, and transformed into delicious and incomparable pies and salmis.

Long Island duck possesses fine flesh and delicate fat. It is, according to the opinion of true connoisseurs, a duck of noble origin, a direct descendant of the wild duck, of which it has kept parts of its beautiful feathers, and more or less of its original wild flavor, notwithstanding its almost scientific raising. Perhaps on one day of starvation it let itself be seduced by the charms of the manger and the attraction of the grain in it and was then and there conquered by civilization . . . and pots.

A little bulky and heavy, its staggering walk makes one believe that it does not belong to the water-wagon. Like a good farmer it seems to be happy with its lot. It balances and drags itself along like a good bourgeois and walks on the right side to go to the left—an inveterate jaywalker. Chicks, chicken and even turkeys and guinea-fowl of the farm-yard seldom find anything to glean after madam duck has passed, so keen is her sight.

LIKED BY EVERYONE   [925]

Almost everyone—rich and poor alike—enjoys duck, with its rich luscious flavor, and it seems strange that, with the exception of the roast, cook books seem to ignore its great possibilities in the realm of the kitchen. We write of chicken, turkey and game birds, but the flavorful duck has almost been consigned to oblivion.

ITS ORIGIN   [926]

Duck was much appreciated in antiquity by Greeks and Romans alike. In Athens it was sprinkled with wine of Chio, while in Rome it was perfumed with the white truffles of Libya. Most certainly neither knew of the luscious croquettes, delicious salmis, timbales, soufflés, and mousses, of our modern day. Neither did they know of the savory and incomparable aiguilettes of duck with orange; of "Duck à la Bearnaise" (in which white wine mingles its bouquet with that of spices and onions), or of "Duck à l'Italienne" (when the duck is cooked in Chianti wine and olive oil, with a little garlic of course). Did they know how to prepare "Duck en Chausson" delicious, boned, stuffed and very, very slowly cooked in Clos Vougeot wine—that father of the red Burgundy— made from grapes originally planted by Cistercian Monks, almost a thousand years ago? This inimitable wine remained in the possession of the Order until confiscated during the 1789 French Revolution. A massive, yet velvety wine of a quite unforgettable flavor and "bouquet," grown from a particular grape on a particular soil, with a particular exposure in a particular climate, and between a particular latitude and longitude. It is claimed to be the wine before which an entire regiment was ordered to present arms.

Would they had known the "Potted Duck à la Creole," so deliciously prepared by our Creoles of Louisiana. For this dish an old guard duck is required. It is larded through and through with thin strips of larding pork rolled in a scented mixture of finely chopped chives, parsley, shallots, garlic, basil, nutmeg and what not, then slowly simmered for several hours in white wine and water, plus a pony glass of brandy, until it is in jelly. It is served cold. They most surely wouldn't have fared for 300 years on cabbage!

MORE DELICIOUS METHODS   [927]

Many other delicious methods of preparation may be adapted to this fine palmiped. It may be "Braised in White Wine" after being wrapped up delicately in a very thin slice of pork fat—this is also one of the favorite Creole preparations. "Duck Aux Navets," duck with turnips, a favorite Parisian dish, a stew-like compound to the gravy of which when ready to be served, a streak of good tarragon vinegar is added. "Canard à la Paillard," a duck stuffed with parts of its own liver, then roasted and constantly basted in a bath of red wine, to which is added the remaining parts of the liver, parboiled, then crushed with a fork. More prosaic may be the "Duck à la Bourgeoise," a delicious home-like dish of which the writer partook at a Virginia farm. The duck is stuffed with quartered apples, seedless raisins and quartered oranges, then roasted with almost continual basting until tender. It is then served on a hot platter covered by a purée of peas, rich in protein, sugar, and starch, dried vegetable, to which parts of the pan gravy has been added with an abundance of small cubes of fried salt pork. Giblet Sauce.

and Frosted Apple Sauce made of 2 cups of sweetened apple sauce, one cup of drained, crushed pineapple and a scant teaspoon of preserved ginger, rolled very fine, the whole thoroughly mixed and set in the tray of the refrigerator overnight should be served with this dish.

BRAISED BABY DUCKS COUNTRY STYLE [928]

Have two 5-pound ducklings cleaned, singed, and washed quickly in cold water. When cleaning, do not make too large an opening. Fill with a stuffing made of equal parts of bread crumbs soaked in cider—then squeezed gently from excess of liquid—and apple sauce, highly seasoned with pepper and nutmeg. With a needle and white kitchen string, sew the opening together, but not tightly. Place the birds in a braising kettle; rub with salt and pepper, and add 1 green pepper, coarsely chopped, 1 small carrot, scraped and chopped, 2 medium-sized onions, peeled and halved, two halves being studded with 1 clove, a bouquet garni composed of 1 large bay leaf, tied with 8 sprigs of fresh parsley, 2 sprigs of green celery (tops), and 1 sprig of thyme, all tied together with white kitchen thread, 1 blade of garlic (thinly sliced), also 8 peppercorns. Pour over all 1 cup of cider, cover tightly and braise in a moderate oven (375° F.) for one hour, turning the birds twice during the cooking process. Transfer the ducks to a large, hot platter. Straining both liquid and solid from the braising kettle and skim off all the fat rising to the top. Measure. There should be 1 scant cup of liquid, absolutely free of any duck fat. Bring to a boil, add ½ cup of chicken stock, and reduce this to half, so that there is only ¾ cup of liquid remaining in the pan. Thicken with 1 teaspoon of flour creamed with 1 teaspoon of butter, boil up once or twice, then stir in 3 tablespoons of red currant jelly mixed with 3 tablespoons of red port wine. Serve in a sauceboat with the ducklings, accompanied by mashed turnips and a green vegetable.

BRAISED DUCKLINGS WITH CHESTNUTS [929]

Take two 4½-pound ducklings, clean, singe and wash quickly in running cold water and sponge dry with a towel inside and out. Rub inside and outside with Calvados or applejack, then with mixed salt and pepper, and set aside while preparing the chestnut stuffing as follows: Boil 1½ pounds of chestnuts until tender, remove the skins, and chop the nuts. Chop 1 large onion and cook in chicken stock to cover until tender. Add to the chestnuts together with 1 tablespoon of chopped parsley, 1 tablespoon of chopped green pepper, salt and pepper to taste, and blend with 2 slightly beaten eggs, and 1 tablespoon of grated raw onion. Stuff the ducks with the mixture, sew up the openings, and set aside. Heat, in a braising kettle, ¼ cup of butter or margarin; stir in ¼ cup of chopped carrots, ¼ cup of chopped onions, ¼ cup of chopped green celery leaves, and ¼ cup of chopped white parts of well-washed leeks, with 1 bouquet garni, composed of 2 bay leaves, 8 sprigs of fresh parsley and 1 sprig of thyme, all tied together with white kitchen thread, also 1 or 2 cloves, 10 peppercorns, and 1 teaspoon of salt. Cook gently, and when slightly browned, add the prepared ducks, cover and cook, stir gently over a medium flame, for 15 minutes, turning the birds twice. Remove from the fire and add 1 cup of chicken stock and ½ cup of dry white wine. Cover tightly, and braise in a moderate oven (375° F.), for 40 minutes, turning the birds once. Remove the cover and continue baking for 20 minutes longer.

Meantime, heat 1 cup of Sauce Espagnole (Spanish Sauce, No. 1127) with ¼ cup of port wine and 1 tablespoon of red currant jelly; season to taste with salt and pepper, and keep hot. Remove the ducks from the kettle, take out the strings, and arrange on a hot platter. Strain the gravy in the kettle through a fine sieve into a saucepan. Let stand a few minutes, and skim thoroughly, discarding all fat from the surface. Place the saucepan over a bright flame and let mixture reduce to about ¾ cup. Add this to the Spanish-port-currant sauce, bring to a boil, taste for seasoning and serve in a sauceboat. Pass glazed turnips and Brussels sprouts if desired.

BREASTS OF DUCKLINGS MARQUISE [930]

Roast 3 small ducklings in the usual way until tender. Remove the birds from the roasting pan, slice the breasts neatly and carefully and keep them hot in enough hot chicken stock to cover. With the carcasses of the birds you may prepare a salmi of duck, or a stew, hash or creamed duck.

Strain the gravy in the pan into a saucepan without pressing and let it stand until all the fat rises to the surface, then skim thoroughly. Stir into the roasting pan 3 tablespoons of cognac, set aflame and scrape and stir so as to remove all the gelatinous particles which may adhere to the pan, then stir in the strained gravy. Bring to a boil, let boil up 2 or 3 times, then strain into a saucepan. Bring again to a boil, and boil until there is no more than ½ cup of gravy remaining. Now stir in 4 tablespoons of port wine, 1 tablespoon of guava jelly, and ¾ cup of Sauce Espagnole (No. 1127). Boil up 2 or 3 times, taste for seasoning, and strain through a fine muslin cloth. Let simmer gently while arranging the duckling breasts on a hot platter. Pour half the sauce over the breasts, garnish the platter with 6 potato puffs, 6 broiled, peeled fresh mushroom caps, and 6 small pork sausages, pan-fried until well-browned, and in between these garnishes, arrange tufts of crisp watercress. Serve at once, passing the remainder of the sauce and a dish of guava jelly separately.

In sixteenth-century England, sailors ate cold duck meat as a charm against drowning while young girls believed eating it would help to make them beautiful.

BROILED DUCKLING   [931]

Split and remove breastbones from 3 ducklings, each weighing about 2½ to 3 pounds; wipe with a damp cloth, then rub with mixed salt and pepper and melted butter. Place on broiler rack, which should be well greased and broil 10 minutes on each side. Remove from the broiler rack, place in a greased baking dish; brush generously with butter and bake in a moderate oven (350° F.) until nicely browned, brushing frequently with melted butter. Arrange on a hot platter on pieces of toast and garnish with crisp watercress and at each end of the platter a nice mound of shoestring potatoes. Serve with applesauce, Maître d'Hôtel Butter (No. 1078) and red currant jelly.

CANARD AU SANG   [932]
Duck in Its Own Blood

I have no apostolic vocation, but had I been a missionary, it would have been most certainly my irresistible duty to convert the culinary *barbarians*, the vandals, who under the pretense of enjoying a roast duck, begin to completely bleed this contented bird.

Never bleed a duck. Choose another method of killing it for your feast; after it has been bled and its blood saved, roast it "au naturel" —plain, that is—with no stuffing at all, to the desired point, about 25 minutes, or according to size, so that when pricked with a fork, ruby-like pearls of blood will ooze from its surface. Serve it then as follows:

Slice the breast in thin filets, and arrange the slices on a hot platter. Keep hot. With great care, collect all the blood which may run out and add to what ever you have saved previously. Crush the raw liver in it, using a fork in order to obtain a kind of paste. To this paste add rapidly a few drops of lemon juice, very little, just the juice from a slice of lemon. This will prevent the blood from curdling. Dust generously with freshly crushed peppercorns. Add a little salt and a few grains of nutmeg.

Moisten this mixture with a small glass of good dry Zinfandel, and heat in a double boiler. Do not worry if you see the sauce changing color. Stir very gently, until it is a soft, unctuous brown cream. Roll each piece of hot filet of duck in the sauce, and methodically, slowly, eat this summum of epicurean art, simple, but how good. A culinary epic which (after roasting) you may prepare right on your dining table, using a chafing dish.

There is a Swiss saying: "A duck is a strange bird—for one too much and for two not enough." While in Canada they say: "A duck is a fool of a bird, as it is too much for one and not quite enough for two."

DUCKLING CHIPOLATA MENAGERE   [933]

Clean, wash quickly in cold water, and singe a 5½ to 6-pound duck and truss the legs and wings securely close to the body. Rub with mixed salt and black pepper inside and out; place in a roasting pan, and add 1 small carrot, scraped, 1 medium-sized onion, peeled and halved, each half studded with a whole clove, 1 bouquet garni, composed of 1 large bay leaf tied with 1 sprig of thyme, 8 sprigs of fresh parsley and 2 sprigs of green celery leaves, all tied together with white kitchen thread, and sear in a very hot oven (450° F.) for about 20 minutes, or until nicely browned all over, turning the bird frequently. Parboil ¼ pound of salt pork for 10 minutes, drain and cut into small cubes and set aside. Put a dozen very small white onions in the fat remaining in the pan and cook until light brown all over, rocking and shaking the pan frequently, but do not prick the onions, then stir in ¾ cup of small carrot cubes and cook till they too are brown. Remove the onions and carrots and add to the pork cracklings, keeping them hot. Into the remaining fat stir 1 scant table-spoon of flour and 1 small clove of garlic, peeled and crushed to a pulp. Blend till flour begins to bubble and brown, stirring frequently, then moisten with 1 cup of good chicken stock, ½ cup dry white wine and 2 medium-sized fresh tomatoes, peeled and coarsely chopped. Cook over a low flame, stirring frequently until mixture is smooth and thickened. Season to taste with salt and pepper, place the seared duck in a braising kettle, pour the sauce and the pork-cracklings-onion and carrot mixture over it, add a fresh bay leaf tied with 2 sprigs of green celery leaves, 1 sprig of thyme and 8 sprigs of fresh parsley, 1 dozen small chestnuts, cooked in boiling salted water until tender, then peeled, ½ pound of small fresh mushroom caps, peeled, then cooked till almost tender in a little pork fat or lard. Set the kettle in a moderate oven (375° F.), and bake 35–40 minutes longer, or until duck is tender, but not falling from the bones. Transfer the duck to a hot platter, carve and arrange in center of the platter, placing the drained vegetables and a dozen small pork sausages, broiled and drained around the duck. Strain part of the sauce over the duck and vegetables, first tasting for seasoning. Serve the remainder in a sauceboat. Pass apple sauce separately.

DUCKLING MONTMORENCY   [934]

Roast a cleaned, washed, 5½ to 6-pound duckling in the usual way, until tender. Transfer the bird to a hot platter and drain all the fat from the roasting pan, strain all remaining juices through a fine-meshed wire sieve into a saucepan. Set aflame 3 tablespoons of brandy and let it drop into the pan alternately with ⅓ cup of port wine. Boil up 2 or 3 times, and strain again into a saucepan. Let this boil up once, and add 1 cup of canned black pitted cherries. Thicken the sauce with a little flour creamed with an equal amount of sweet butter; boil up once or twice, and pour over the carved duck. Garnish simply with watercress and serve at once with chilled applesauce.

DUCK WITH OLIVES   [935]

Brown a 5½ to 6 pound duckling, previously cleaned, washed and trussed, in 4 tablespoons of butter; remove from the saucepan and drain out the butter, then swirl the pan with 1 cup of dry white wine. Add 1½ cups of good chicken stock, and scrape bottom and sides of pan until mixture boils. Strain through a fine sieve, over the seared duck placed in a braising kettle, add 1 bouquet garni composed of 1 large bay leaf, 2 sprigs of green celery leaves, 8 sprigs of fresh parsley and 1 sprig of thyme, all tied together with white kitchen thread; season to taste with salt and black pepper and cover closely. Set the kettle in a moderate oven (375° F.), and bake for about 45 minutes, time depending on age of the bird. When the duck is tender, strain the sauce through a fine-meshed wire sieve into a saucepan. Let stand until the fat rises to the surface. Skim carefully, bring to a boil and let boil until only 1⅓ cups of sauce are left. Taste for seasoning, and add ½ pound of green pitted olives. Carve the duckling, reshape, pour half of the sauce over the bird, arrange the olives around it, and pass the remainder of the sauce in a sauceboat. Serve with chilled applesauce.

DUCK AND RICE DINNER DAKOTA STYLE   [936]

Clean, wash quickly, rub inside and out with lemon, then mixed salt and pepper a 5 to 6-lb. duckling. Place inside 1 small onion, a 2-inch stick of celery, and 1 tablespoon of marjoram. Truss and sew. Place the prepared bird in a kettle, cover with boiling water; add 1 bouquet garni composed of 1 large bay leaf, 3 sprigs of fresh parsley and 1 sprig of thyme, all tied together with white kitchen thread, also 1 or 2 cloves, and gradually bring to a boil. Boil gently and steadily until tender but firm and skin unbroken. Then, and only then, season to taste with salt and pepper just before removing from the kettle. There should be about 1½ quarts of broth. Place the duck on a baking pan; brush with melted butter and brown in a moderate oven (350° F.). Strain the broth and set half of it aside for gravy to serve on rice. In a heavy kettle melt 3 tablespoons of butter; add 1 cup of well-washed and well-drained rice, also 1 tablespoon of chopped parsley, and fry the rice over a low flame until golden brown, stirring almost constantly. Now stir in enough broth to cover the rice well, set over a very low heat and cover tightly. Let cook for about 15–20 minutes, then add about 2 more cups of broth, but do not stir at any time after adding the broth. Let cook until all broth is absorbed by the rice and each grain is fluffy and a separate unit.

To make gravy, brown 3 tablespoons of flour in 4 tablespoons of butter, blending well. Then gradually stir in enough boiling broth to made a gravy of the consistency of cream. Transfer the duck to a heated platter; carve, and garnish all around with the fluffy rice. Serve the gravy separately, also applesauce mixed with a little drained, prepared horseradish.

ROAST DUCK A L'ORANGE [937]

Clean, wash quickly, dry, rub inside and out with lemon juice, then with mixed salt and black pepper. Place a small peeled orange inside and truss and sew up a 5½ to 6-pound duckling. Rub the skin with bacon drippings, and roast in a hot oven (500° F.) for 15 minutes, turning the bird frequently until well seared; decrease heat to moderate (350–375° F.) and continue roasting for about 50 minutes, or until duck is tender.

Meanwhile, cook the thinly sliced peel of 1 orange in water to cover for 10 minutes; drain, discarding the water; chop the peel and simmer with 1 cup of dry white wine and the cleaned, finely chopped duck giblets for 30 minutes. Brown 2 tablespoons of flour in 2 tablespoons of butter or margarin; add the giblet sauce, the giblets, and the (chopped) orange from the cavity. When thoroughly blended and boiling, rub mixture through a fine-meshed wire sieve into a saucepan; taste for seasoning and serve with the hot duckling which has been carved, and with segments of two more oranges, peeled and absolutely free from all white pith.

> There are three tame ducks in our back yard,
> Dabbling in mud and trying hard
> To get their share, and maybe more,
> Of the overflowing barnyard store,
> Satisfied with the task they're at,
> Of eating and sleeping and getting fat.
> —Kenneth Kaufman.

GOOSE [938]

The stupidity of this bird is more proverbial than real. If any one doubts this, let him try to stalk one when it is feeding, or listen to the tales the farmers tell of its provoking vigilance and cleverness. The goose's recognition of spring is just one example of its astuteness. The first thunder is one sign to the goose of the change in season; strayed robins another; there is a ruddier tone in the pale sunlight; dryness in roads and fields gets drier under gusty winds and begins to turn into something forgotten about for many months: actually dust again! Not until he has received full proof do light sleepers hear the goose on its early spring mission—honking in the barnyard, announcing with funeral pomp the end of the winter; announcing, for better or worse, one more spring. The goose is no fool. He has assembled all the meteorological data, sifted the reddening light through the prism of his eye on to his pituitary, and circled the yard. It's spring!

Why do wild geese migrate? The answer is lost in the antiquities of the ice age. Ornithologists believe that the prehistoric urge to migrate was implanted during those centuries when the ice invaded the feeding grounds of the birds, and they were forced to new haunts further South. Innate love of home urged them back again as the ice retreated.

Geese, domestic or wild, sometimes live to a great age, sometimes even to 35 years.

It is impossible to tell at a glance whether a bird is a goose or a gander. One is no bigger than the other, and they are marked the same.

Goose is the traditional holiday bird; it has a certain fitness which goes with the season of benevolence. No food can be more golden brown, more filled with good juices, more tender under the onslaught of the fork, more crustily delicious. It has a Dickensian touch, remindful of Tiny Tim and *The Christmas Carol* and the olden days when a good dinner was needed for a happy season.

The goose is identified with old Viking ideas as an outstanding Christmas delicacy, but tired old geese have no place in the roasting pan. You will want one of last spring's babies, plump but not portly, its windpipe pliable to the touch, its feet soft, its flesh firm. If a goose is to make a good appearance at table, it must be carefully drawn and prepared. Pull out the pin feathers and singe off the hairs and down quickly over a flame; then cut off the head, feet and the oil sack on top of the tail. To give the neck a trim finish, first make a cut in the skin at the back of the neck and carefully remove the crop. Then pull the skin down and cut the neck off short, saving it for making stock for the giblet gravy. Finish drawing the bird from a lengthwise cut made under the tail. Wash the bird carefully both inside and out with cold water, and dry at once. Do not soak in water under any circumstance.

Don't "pack" the stuffing. (Wild rice makes a delicious stuffing for both goose and duck.) Fill both neck and body cavity with stuffing, *but do not pack*. Draw the skin of the neck back and fasten neatly with kitchen string. Sew up the opening in the tail. Tie the legs close to the body and fasten the wings with kitchen string that crosses at the *back* where the marks will not show.

Start roasting the bird, breast down, on the rack of a shallow pan, with the indicated liquid and vegetables; baste frequently. Basting is absolutely indispensable for any kind of roasting, because this returns the drippings and juices to the meat or bird. Drain the fat from a roasting goose or duck constantly as it accumulates in the pan, leaving in it only the liquid juices. As it melts in any quantity, the pan should be taken from the oven, the fat drained off, butter spread on the Crisp brown skin, and the bird put back in the oven to finish roasting, frequently basting.

Young geese are called "green geese" and their marks of identification are soft, pliable bills and soft feet. Once the presence of many pin feathers was considered sure evidence that a goose was a youngster. But modern dressing methods now produce a clean-plucked bird, be it young or old.

When roasting a goose, puncture the skin around the wings and legs with the sharp tines of a fork to release excess fat. This fat may later be clarified and used for cooking, or adding to cooked vegetables. Geese for roasting, the most popular method of preparation, are in market from November to January and weigh from 8 to 16 pounds.

What to use for stuffing a goose depends on individual taste, but the traditional one of apples and prunes seems to hold first place over all newcomers. For those who enjoy something sturdier, a combination of ground beef, pork and veal in equal parts mixed with breadcrumbs and seasonings makes an excellent stuffing; it is sometimes used in addition to the apple or prune stuffing, one part of the cavity being filled with the meat stuffing, the other with fruit.

In addition to being generous benefactors of humanity, geese are very intelligent, cunning, keen, agile, vigilant and courageous. They make better watchdogs than dogs and all hunters agree that it's impossible to fool a goose. A goose may waddle on land, but so does man. A goose hisses, but so do theater goers; a goose cackles, but so do politicians. They never do the goose step. The ancient Egyptians and Anglo-Saxons wooed the goose, and the Declaration of Independence was written with a goose quill.

In 1272 when Edward I fixed the price of fowl in England a goose sold for fivepence, a hen for three halfpence and a capon for twopence.

BOILED GOOSE OYSTER STUFFING   [939]
BECHAMEL

Clean, wash quickly, dry, rub inside and out with mixed salt and pepper and a good dash of powdered marjoram, and fill the inside of a goose with 2 dozen small, carefully picked, fresh oysters. Truss and sew up the opening carefully; place the bird in a soup kettle, cover with cold water, and add 1 bouquet garni composed of 1 large bay leaf, 2 sprigs of fresh celery green (tops), 1 sprig of thyme, and 8 sprigs of parsley, all tied together with white kitchen thread, 8 peppercorns, 1½ teaspoons of salt, 2 whole cloves, 1 medium-sized onion, 1 small carrot, cut in small pieces, 1 small piece of white turnip, and 1 large leek, cut in two lengthwise, carefully washed, drained and folded in three or four, then tied with kitchen thread. Gradually bring to a boil; skim carefully, cover tightly, and simmer steadily and gently for about 2 hours, or till the goose is tender. Transfer the bird to a hot platter, remove the string and carve, then reshape in its natural form. Drain the platter well as some stock may remain in the bird. Have ready 1 cup of Béchamel sauce (No. 259) hot and highly seasoned, stir in ½ cup of sweet, heavy cream, then beat in 2 egg yolks, adding one at a time and beating well after each addition. When ready to serve, pour half the sauce over the carved bird, and to the other half, add 1 dozen small, carefully cleaned fresh oysters, heat without actually boiling, and serve separately, first tasting for seasoning.

Strain the stock, let it cool, remove the cake of fat floating on top, and use the fat for cooking and the stock as a soup.

GOOSE GIBLETS FARMER STYLE   [940]
Abatis d'Oie, Fermière

Wings, feet, neck, liver and gizzard of a goose are included in the French term for giblets, "abatis." Scald all these in boiling water and carefully scrape the feet. Drain, place in a stew pot with 4 tablespoons of butter and sear over a bright flame for 12 to 15 minutes, stirring constantly. Add 1 bouquet garni, composed of 1 large bay leaf, 2 sprigs of fresh celery green (tops), 8 sprigs of fresh parsley, 1 sprig of thyme, 12 sprigs of chives and, if available, 1 small sprig of sweet basil, all tied together with white kitchen thread. Add also 1 small clove of garlic, 2 whole cloves, ¼ pound of fresh, peeled, coarsely chopped mushrooms, and continue cooking 4 or 5 minutes longer, stirring almost constantly. Lower the heat, pour over enough hot chicken stock or chicken bouillon to cover, season to taste with salt and pepper; bring to a boil, and skim carefully. Cover and let simmer gently for 25 minutes, then add 1 scant teaspoon of flour moistened with a little cold bouillon or stock, and 4 small white turnips pared and quartered. Continue cooking gently for about 20 minutes or until turnips are tender. Taste for seasoning, transfer to a heated deep dish and dust with chopped parsley. Serve with apples stewed with a little stick cinnamon.

In England giblets cooked in this manner are also served in pie form. The hot stew is poured into a deep dish, covered with a flaky pie crust, brushed with beaten egg yolk, diluted with a little cold milk, and baked 20–25 minutes in a medium oven (350–375° F).

JELLIED GOOSE HOME STYLE   [941]

Clean, wash, singe and rinse again in cold water a young gosling of about 10 to 12 pounds. Using the tines of a kitchen fork, prick through the skin under the wings and legs, but not on the breasts; place in the cavity 1 pared, cored small apple, the core filled with chopped onion and parsley mixed together; sew up the opening and truss. Place the bird in a soup kettle, cover with boiling water, add 1 bouquet garni, composed of 1 large bay leaf, 12 sprigs of chives, 1 sprig of thyme and a 2-inch piece of scraped parsley root, all tied together with white kitchen thread. Add also 2 medium-sized onions, quartered, ½ cup of chopped celery, green and stalk, 1 clove of garlic, 2 small carrots, scraped and quartered, ¼ cup of lemon juice, salt to taste and 8 peppercorns, freshly crushed. Bring to a boil, skim, and let boil gently for 15 minutes, skimming frequently; cover and simmer as slowly as possible for about 2½ hours, skimming occasionally. Remove the bird. Cool, skin carefully and slice first the breast then the legs, and the remaining meat, all in thin slices. Strain the broth through a fine muslin cloth into a saucepan. Set aside to cool. Then remove the cake of fat from the top. Place over the fire, add 2 slightly beaten egg whites and their crushed shells, gradually bring to a boil, stirring constantly, and when boiling stop stirring and let boil gently for 8 to 10 minutes, over a gentle flame. Then stir in 1 cup of cold dry white wine in which 4 tablespoons of granulated gelatine has been softened, and when melted, strain again through a wet jelly bag or fine muslin, into a shallow container. Pour a thin layer of the gelatine mixture into a bread pan or mold, and decorate tastefully with sprigs of chives arranged like a sheaf of grass, a few small designs cut from hard-cooked egg whites, olives, truffles, etc., with small fancy French vegetable cutters; when solid, arrange over these a layer of sliced goose (smoked goose may also be substituted for fresh goose or you may use both, if desired). Pour in more of the gelatine mixture and repeat the layers until all ingredients are used or the mold is full. Chill in refrigerator for at least 5 or 6 hours, or, better still, overnight. When ready to serve, unmold carefully on to a chilled platter and garnish with coarsely chopped gelatine and watercress. Serve at once.

ROAST GOOSE CELERY STUFFING [942]

Celery Stuffing. Combine 4½ cups of soft bread crumbs with ⅔ cup of dry white wine (milk may be substituted) and ¼ cup of melted butter, ¼ cup of grated onion, 1 cup of finely ground green celery leaves, 2 tablespoons of minced parsley, 1 tablespoon of finely minced green pepper, and season to taste with salt (about 1 teaspoon) ¼ teaspoon of black pepper and ⅛ teaspoon each of sage, mace, nutmeg, thyme and marjoram. Mix well and use to stuff a 10 to 12-pound goose, which has been cleaned, washed, singed, rubbed inside and out with lemon, then with salt and pepper. Sew up the opening, truss and place in a roasting pan. Set in a very hot oven (450° F.) to sear on all sides for 15 minutes, or place in a very moderate oven (300° F.), and do not sear. But in either case add ¼ cup each of coarsely chopped carrots, celery, turnip, leeks; 1 bouquet garni composed of 1 large bay leaf, 1 sprig of thyme and 12 sprigs of fresh chives all tied together with white kitchen thread. Pour into the pan over the vegetables 1½ cups of cold chicken stock or bouillon, and roast steadily allowing 20 to 25 minutes per pound. Serve with pan gravy, giblet gravy or Cream Gravy (Nos. 1060, 1061, and 1038) respectively; also apples stewed in syrup or apple sauce. Buttered Brussels sprouts and mashed turnips are also suitable accompaniments.

ROAST GOOSE MILANAISE   [943]

Make a stuffing of 2 cups of cooked macaroni moistened with tomato sauce then mixed with 1 cup of peeled, sliced fresh mushrooms, sautéed in butter until tender, and ¼ pound of finely chopped lean, raw beef, the whole highly seasoned. Use to fill a 10 to 12-pound goose, which has been cleaned, washed, dried, and rubbed inside and out with mixed salt and pepper; truss, and roast as directed for Roast Goose Celery Stuffing (No. 942) and serve with Sauce Espagnole (No. 1127)

ROAST GOOSE PRUNE STUFFING   [944]
(FRENCH STYLE)

The recipe takes two days to prepare, but it is really delicious.

Clean 1 plump goose weighing about 10 to 12 pounds, wash inside and out, dry; then rub inside and out first with lemon, then with salt and pepper. Set aside while preparing a prune stuffing as follows:

Soak 1 pound of sound large prunes for 6 hours in cold water; drain; place in a saucepan together with 1 small lemon, thinly sliced; cover with half water and half red wine and cook the prunes until tender. In a separate saucepan, cook until tender ½ to ¾ pound of lean, fresh pork, finely chopped, with ¼ cup of grated onion, 12 green olives also finely chopped, and ¼ cup of butter. Season to taste with salt, black pepper and a dash each of nutmeg, marjoram, thyme and mace. When lukewarm blend in 2 well-beaten eggs. When cold, stuff the cooled prunes with the mixture and keep in refrigerator for 24 hours. Next day, 2 hours before roasting, stuff the goose with the stuffed prunes, sew up the opening, and truss. Brush the bird with melted butter, and wrap in oiled paper, tie with kitchen string, and roast in a moderate oven, allowing 25 minutes per pound. Serve with Hot Mushroom Sauce (No. 1090) mashed white turnips, and buttered kale. A side dish of stewed apples will not be amiss.

When you have plenty of geese and want to preserve them, smoke them as follows:

SMOKED GOOSE HOME STYLE [945]

Split the goose or geese down the back, clean, wash, dry, and rub in, for each bird, ¼ of an oz. of saltpeter, mixed with 2 ounces of common salt (rock salt) and 1 ounce of granulated sugar. Place in an earthenware crock covered with a cheesecloth in a cool place, for 12 days in summer and 14 days in winter. Rub each day with a fresh mixture of saltpeter, salt and sugar, then roll in sawdust and smoke in the usual way in a smoke house. Fine for hors d'oeuvres or a platter of cold cuts.

> *Those consecrated geese in orders*
> *That to the capital were warders*
> *And being then upon patrol*
> *With noise alone beat off the Gaul.*
> *—The Geese of Troy*

GUINEA HEN [946]

The cries of most of the barnyard flock are easily imitated: "Gobble-gobble, cluck-cluck, and cock-a-doodle-do," we know very well. But there's one fowl often found on the farm whose natural cry is not so easily imitated—and therein lies one of the reasons why many farms maintain a small flock of guineas. For the shrill shriek and harsh cry— "ptrack-ptrack," or "buckwheat, buckwheat"—is sufficiently inimitable to serve a certain purpose. Few are the hawks or other poultry yard marauders who will brave the pugnacious disposition of these guards of the poultry flock. They set up a terrible cry when any stranger —man or animal—comes around, and are regarded as good burglar alarms.

Although originally descended from a wild species found on the coast of Africa (hence the name "guinea"), this fowl has long been domesticated, having been introduced to this country by the early settlers. The "wild" instinct is strong in this bird, however, as evidenced by the fact that in England where a few flocks are left to shift for themselves, they soon revert to their own nature and provide excellent hunting as game birds.

The guinea hen, sometimes called "Pearl Hen," is, it is said, the replica of the pheasant. This is *culinary insult* to this bird. Its flesh is endowed with a perfectly individual and distinct flavor.

With her agile and gracious gait, her fine feathers, with symmetrical and coquettish dots, similar to precious pearls, the guinea hen is an ornamental bird. The park claims her for her beauty; the table demands her for her fine flesh. She is certainly a bird of distinction, but her raucous shriek is only tolerated in the barnyards as the warning of a watchdog.

BREAST OF GUINEA HEN ADELINA PATTI   [947]
(Serves 2)

Select a young, medium-sized bird; clean it as for a roasting chicken; wipe with a damp cloth. Place in the opening a peeled, small orange, 2 slices of onion, and truss. Roast in a moderately hot oven (375° F.) for about 30–35 minutes, basting frequently with a mixture of port wine and butter in equal parts. Remove the breasts and cut in two, leaving part of wing on each piece of breast. Brown ⅓ cup of bread crumbs in a little butter, pat this over the breasts, and brown them in 3 tablespoons of sweet butter on both sides, over a very low flame, turning frequently. Serve on toast, garnished with watercress and a few lozenges of fried hominy, having on each lozenge a small fresh mushroom cap sautéed in butter and dipped in finely chopped chervil. Serve as hot as possible with Bread Sauce (No. 1014) and Bar-le-Duc Jelly mixed with a little drained prepared horseradish.

BREAST OF GUINEA HEN CONNOISSEUR   [948]
(Serves 2)

Roast a young, plump, cleaned, washed and trussed guinea hen in the usual way (without basting) in a hot oven for about 25 to 30 minutes; remove the breast, reserving the carcass and legs for another dish, such as a salmi, stew, and so forth. Remove the skin from the breast, and rub with butter mixed with a little finely chopped parsley, chives, tarragon, shallots, grated onion, in about equal parts, spreading this mixture over the breasts. Wrap both in a piece of buttered brown paper, and place in a small saucepan, large enough to hold them both. Pour over ½ cup of chicken broth, cover tightly and bake in a hot oven 20 to 25 minutes, or till the broth is almost evaporated. Remove from the casserole, discard the paper, and arrange the breasts over a layer of chestnut purée mixed with equal parts of purée of chicken (cooked, then rubbed through a fine sieve with a little sweet cream). Garnish the platter with toast points, watercress and thick grilled tomato slices dusted with chopped chives. Serve at once with bread sauce (No. 1014), and red currant jelly diluted with a little port wine, then heated over a low flame.

BREAST OF GUINEA HEN CREOLE   [949]
(Serves 2)

Clean a plump, young guinea hen, wash quickly in cold water and sponge dry. Split the bird down the back; season with salt and pepper, and sprinkle with melted butter. Broil like a chicken. When done and nicely browned, remove the breasts carefully, leaving part of the wing. Arrange each breast on a piece of toast first covered with a thin slice of broiled Virginia ham, and surround the toast with Creole Sauce (No. 1041). Serve with Broiled Sweet Potato slices.

BREAST OF GUINEA HEN AU GENIEVRE [950]
(Serves 2)

Remove the breasts from a young, plump guinea hen previously cleaned, washed quickly in lukewarm water, and dried. Season with mixed salt and black pepper, then dredge with flour. Heat ⅓ cup of clarified butter, add the breasts of guinea hen and cook about 14–15 minutes, over a gentle flame, turning frequently. Transfer each breast to a piece of bread, cut the shape of the breast, then fry in butter, and keep hot. Swill the pan with ½ cup of chicken broth and let it boil down to almost nothing. Then pour in ¼ cup of good gin, set aflame, let it burn out, and stir in ⅓ cup of rich chicken broth, ⅛ of a teaspoon of powdered juniper berry and again let this reduce to half over a low flame, stirring occasionally. Lastly stir in 2 tablespoons of sweet butter; taste for seasoning, and pour over the breasts. Garnish simply with crisp watercress and a few small triangles of bread fried in butter and serve immediately, each breast sprinkled with fried bread crumbs and a tiny pinch of powdered juniper berry.

GRILLED BABY GUINEA HEN A LA DIABLE [951]
Deviled Grilled Baby Guinea Hen (Serves 2)

Grill a cleaned, split young guinea hen as you would a small chicken until nicely browned on both sides, basting frequently with melted butter. Arrange a hot platter on toast and serve with Deviled Sauce and red currant jelly. For Deviled Sauce, see No. 1049.

GUINEA HEN A LA CASTILLANE [952]

Prepare a large guinea hen as for roasting. Rub with butter, then with seasoned flour; place in a baking pan, add ½ cup of chicken broth, 2 or 3 thin slices of onion, 3 sprigs of parsley and 1 bay leaf, and roast until half done, or about 20 minutes, basting frequently, then add 1 cup of hot chicken broth; reduce the heat and continue roasting 15 to 20 minutes longer, in a slow oven, basting frequently.

Remove the bird from the oven; pour off the broth, into a pan, disjoint the bird, and keep hot. Melt 4 tablespoons of olive oil or butter in a large saucepan; stir in 2 large onions, thinly sliced, then coarsely chopped, 2 large green peppers, halved, seeds and pith removed, then thinly sliced, and cook 5 minutes, stirring almost constantly. Sprinkle in 1 tablespoon of flour, mix well, then stir in 1 cup of peeled, sliced fresh mushrooms, 1 cup of cooked strained tomatoes, and 1½ cups of the broth from the roasting pan. Cook, covered, for about 20 minutes, and when thickened and the vegetables are tender, season to taste with salt, pepper and a pinch of juniper berry powder. When ready to serve, stir in 1 cup of scalded sweet cream, taste for seasoning, heat to a boil, then add the guinea hen. Heat through and serve in a hot, deep dish or casserole, dusting with finely chopped parsley.

ROAST GUINEA HENS HOME STYLE [953]

One guinea hen will serve 2 or 3, so for 6 take 2 guinea hens each weighing about 2½ pounds; clean, wipe with a damp cloth, and fill each cavity with a small apple pared, cored and quartered, a bit of bay leaf, 2 sprigs of parsley, and 1 clove. Sew up the openings and roast as you would ordinary small chicken, basting frequently with melted butter mixed with a little hot chicken broth or water. Roast about 35 minutes, and make pan gravy as for a roast chicken. Serve with the pan gravy and red currant jelly mixed with equal parts of applesauce.

PIGEONS [954]

There are perhaps but few gourmets who can remember the wild pigeon. Any one who never saw the large flocks which appeared in the forests when the acorns began to drop in the fall might think that we in describing those flocks were over-drawing the picture. And this is but natural considering the fact that there is not a single specimen of this most interesting bird now to be found on the whole earth. The wild pigeon is extinct. A number of years ago there was a standing offer of one thousand dollars to any one who would locate a flock. As far as we know the prize was never claimed.

After it was realized that the wild pigeon was entirely lost to the world, various theories were advanced to account for its strange disappearance. One was that the birds had attempted a mass migration to some other countries and had perished in the ocean. The theory advanced of late years is that they fell victim to hunters. If this is the case, it must be that in some places pigeons were more popular as game birds than they were in this part of their native haunts, the East. It was only after the disappearance of wild pigeons that farmers started to raise pigeons or squabs.

NEW ORLEANS PIGEON PIE [955]

Line a deep casserole with rich pastry dough, and brush bottom and sides with slightly beaten egg white. Allow to dry in order to prevent a soggy crust. Parboil 3 large squabs until tender, but not too well done, in water in which has been added a bouquet garni composed of 1 large bay leaf, 8 sprigs of fresh parsley, 1 sprig of thyme and 3 sprigs of green celery leaves, all tied together with white kitchen thread. Add 2 whole cloves, 8 peppercorns, gently bruised, 1 mashed clove of garlic, and a very little salt as yet. Add water to barely cover the birds. When tender, drain and reserve the stock for the base of a soup or a sauce. Dry the squabs, then sauté them in butter until they are well browned on all sides. Drain and split them. Place in each half, 1 generous tablespoon of mushroom purée, mixed with a little onion and a slight grating of lemon peel. Season highly with a few drops of Worcestershire sauce, or, better still, a few drops of kitchen bouquet. Close the two halves, arrange the birds over the crust in the casserole. Blend 3 tablespoons of flour with an equal amount of butter, and stir slowly into 1½ cups of the pigeon stock, mixed with ¼ cup of Madeira wine. Season to taste with salt, pepper, and a few drops of onion juice, and heat, stirring constantly, until the mixture is slightly thickened. Pour the sauce over the squabs, add 12 glazed small white onions and 24 canned, drained button mushrooms; sprinkle ½ cup of buttered bread crumbs on top and place in a hot oven (450° F.) for 12 to 15 minutes; reduce the heat to moderate (350° F.) and bake 8 to 10 minutes longer, or until the crumbs and the edges of the top are nicely browned. Serve from the casserole as hot as possible.

LES PIGEONS DU GENERAL PERSHING [956]
Squabs General Pershing Style

Bone 6 little baby squabs; place the bones in a saucepan, and cover with cold water. Add 2 young carrots and 1 medium-sized onion, both chopped, 1 bouquet garni composed of 1 bay leaf, 2 sprigs of green celery leaves (tops), 8 sprigs of fresh parsley and 1 sprig of thyme, all tied together with white kitchen thread, 5 or 6 peppercorns, slightly bruised, 1 shallot, crushed, and very little salt. Simmer gently, covered for 2 hours in order to make a very concentrated broth. Put ½ pound of boiled, cold, lean ham through the food chopper. Soak in cold milk 6 slices of decrusted bread, squeeze dry; toss, and add to the ham mixture. Cook the squab livers in a little butter till golden brown; chop these fine and add to the first mixture with 1½ cups of coarsely chopped raw asparagus tips, 1 tablespoon of grated onion, and 3 tablespoons of the best Madeira wine. Blend all thoroughly, adding more of the wine if too dry. Stuff the boned birds to a full plumpness; reshape them, and sew up. It is best to prepare the birds the day before using, and allow them to stand in the refrigerator to mellow.

When ready to cook them, melt 6 tablespoons of butter in a roasting pan large enough to accommodate all 6 birds. Brush the breasts with part of the melted butter, and arrange the pigeons in the remainder of it. Brown them on all sides over a hot flame, turning frequently; pour the concentrated broth over them; cover and bake in a moderate oven (350–375° F.) for 30 to 35 minutes. When done, drain off the gravy, and skim off all the fat; Over a bright flame reduce the sauce to a glaze—that is, until the pan is almost dry. To this glaze, add ½ cup of rich chicken broth, to which 1 scant teaspoon of meat glaze (meat extract) has been added; taste for seasoning, adding the necessary salt and pepper, pour this sauce over the birds. Garnish with 6 individual bunches of asparagus tips (6 tips in each bunch), cooked and very hot; turn the bunches in the sauce to coat them with it, and after removing the binding strings, serve simply garnished with a small bunch of watercress at both ends of the platter.

PIGEON POT PIE COUNTRY STYLE [957]

Have 3 jumbo squabs cut in halves after being cleaned, quickly washed in lukewarm water, dried and singed. Take ¾ pound of lean, raw beef from the rump and cut into 6 individual thin slices. Dredge the pigeon halves and brown in ⅓ cup of butter on all sides. Do likewise with the 6 thin slices of beef. Now arrange the birds in a deep pie dish; place over each half, ½ hard-cooked egg, and in between, the six thin slices of beef. In a separate saucepan cook over a low flame 1½ table-spoons of finely chopped onion, together with the same quantity of green pepper and leek (white part only); moisten with 1½ to 1¾ cups of good chicken stock, add 1 bouquet garni composed of 1 large bay leaf, 2 sprigs of green celery leaves (tops), 1 sprig of thyme and 7 or 8 sprigs of parsley all tied together with white kitchen thread; 2 whole cloves, 1 whole clove of garlic, 1 teaspoon of Worcestershire sauce, 8 pepper-corns, and 1 teaspoon of salt. Pour this over the pigeons. Cover with a rich, flaky pie crust; make a few slashes on top for the escape of steam, brush with cold milk, and bake in a moderate oven for 35 to 40 minutes. Serve right from the pot.

POTTED STUFFED SQUABS WITH [958]
CHESTNUTS

Clean and singe 6 baby squabs; dredge with seasoned flour and brown them over a low flame on all sides in ⅓ cup of butter, turning them frequently. Press 1 pound of cooked chestnuts through a sieve; stir in 2 tablespoons of butter and 3 tablespoons of sweet thick cream, and season to taste with salt, pepper and a teaspoon of Worcestershire sauce. Stuff the seared birds with this, sew up the openings, and place in a heavy iron stew pot with 1 stalk of celery, scraped and chopped, 1 large onion, chopped, ¼ cup of scraped young carrots, scraped and thinly sliced, 1 can of button mushrooms with their liquid, 1½ cups of hot chicken stock, 1 large bay leaf, a 2-inch piece of parsley root, scraped, 8 peppercorns and 1 teaspoon of salt, and cover tightly. Cook in a moderate oven (375° F.) for 1 hour without disturbing. When ready to serve, taste for seasoning, and stir in 1 can of drained peas. Serve in a deep platter, dusting with chopped parsley.

SQUABS MOSCOVITE [959]

Split 6 small baby squabs, previously cleaned, washed and singed, brown them on both sides in ⅓ cup of sweet butter. Cover and simmer gently for 10 minutes, turning the birds once. Arrange on a hot platter, season with salt and pepper, and keep hot. To the butter left in the pan add 1½ teaspoons of chopped shallots, 2 ripe tomatoes, peeled, and chopped, and simmer for 3 or 4 minutes, stirring frequently; season with salt and pepper, a pinch of powdered thyme and 1 teaspoon each of finely chopped parsley and chives. When thoroughly blended, add 1 cup of scalded sour cream, stirring constantly. Taste for seasoning and pour over the squabs on a hot platter. Garnish with watercress and serve at once.

SQUABS WITH OLIVES [960]

Clean, wash quickly, dry, then singe 6 small squabs, and brown on all sides in ⅓ cup of butter. Turn the birds into an earthenware casserole, and, to the butter left in the skillet, add ½ scant cup of Madeira wine, 1 piece of bay leaf, 1 tiny slice of garlic, and cook 2 minutes. Stir in 1 cup of rich chicken stock, boil up once or twice and add to the casserole with 12 peeled fresh mushrooms caps and 18 small pitted green olives. Season to taste with salt and pepper, cover, and bake in a moderate oven (375° F.) for 35 to 40 minutes, turning the birds once. Taste for seasoning, and serve right from the casserole with freshly cooked peas French Style.

SQUABS ON TOAST [961]

Roast 6 cleaned, washed and singed baby squabs as you would spring chicken until tender and nicely browned. Serve on buttered toast, simply garnished with watercress and pass red currant jelly, freshly made French fried potatoes, and stewed peas.

TURKEY [962]

The turkey among its own flock is both fierce and quarrelsome, but among other birds of the farmyard is usually both weak and cowardly.

The domestic cock will often keep a flock of turkeys at a distance and they will rarely attack him except in a united body, when the cock is crushed rather by the superior weight of his antagonists than by their prowess. The female is less ferocious in her disposition than the male, and when leading forth her young, to which she is very affectionate, to collect their food, gives them, if attacked, but slight protection, warning them of their danger rather than offering her personal protection.

There is a beautiful legend still believed among the Indians, who still use a turkey wing for fanning their fires. The reason for this is explained in the following tradition which is part of Indian lore.

Many years ago, long before Christopher Columbus was born, the fires of the world were nearly extinguished. This happened just at the beginning of the winter season. The birds were troubled because they knew that men would need heat to keep them warm through the winter.

A bird council was held and it was decided that the birds which could fly highest should soar into the air and see if they could find a spark of fire anywhere. The efforts of the eagle, lark and raven were of no avail. The honor was left to the little brown sparrow which found a spark of fire in the hollow of an old stump in the heart of the deep forest.

The birds flocked about the stump and tried to decide who should pick the spark out. But all their efforts were in vain. To their dismay they saw the spark growing smaller and fainter. The wild turkey then volunteered to keep the tiny spark alive by fanning it with its large wings. The heat became greater and greater until the feathers were singed off the turkey's head.

If one looks carefully one can still see the lumps on the head of a turkey—lumps which look like blisters.

Legend has it that all turkeys since that time have bald heads and wear blisters as a memento of their brave ancestor. The faithful turkey lost its head feathers but it gave fire back to the world. So, in its honor, and as a memorial to its faithfulness, the Indians use turkey wings to make their fires burn.

Today we order our holiday turkey over the telephone. Not so our ancestors. They took a firing piece from the wall, went into the forests and presently returned home with their bird in the bag, so to speak. But that was in the days when wild turkeys were plentiful. The bird still exists but in comparatively small numbers.

TURKEY—HINTS　　　　　　　　　　　　　　　　　[963]

We need to know something about the selection of this king of birds. A good bird will have layers of yellow fat under the skin which should be creamy in shade and comparatively free from pin feathers.

The breastbone and joints should be flexible. The tendons should be removed from the legs when the bird is prepared for cooking. Birds sold in city markets are generally already drawn and singed. Singeing, if necessary, may be done by turning the bird over a flame.

The cavities, which should have a clean fresh odor, should be washed under running cold water and the outside, as well as the inside, thoroughly washed. Pieces of the red spongy lungs which remain in the cavity should be removed, as well as the oil sac above the tail.

After draining, drying, and sprinkling the inside with salt and pepper, the bird is ready to be stuffed and roasted. The time for roasting depends upon size and age. Larger birds are a good choice, as they furnish more meat per pound and take a shorter time per pound to cook. Choose one of any preferred size, depending on the size of the family or number of guests.

As a rule a ten-pound turkey, weighed after cleaning, serves twelve people. For a party of twenty, two ten-pound turkeys are preferable to one twenty-pound bird; to obtain variety each turkey may be filled with a different stuffing.

Steam wild rice until almost done. Tie it in a cheesecloth bag and put it into the roasting pan to finish cooking along with the bird. Simply delicious and labor-saving. . . . And, if in doubt as to when the bird is done, test it by grasping the end bone and moving the leg. When it is done the drumstick— (thigh joint) breaks or moves easily.

Don't discard the turkey carcass, the scraps of skin or fragments of dressing until you have first extracted their goodness for the soup kettle.

BAKED TURKEY ROLL [964]
(Left-over)

Turn 1½ to 2 cups of minced roast turkey into a bowl; season with 2 teaspoons of minced onion and moisten slightly with 2 tablespoons (more or less) of turkey gravy or Pique Seasoning; taste, adding any seasonings that seem desirable.

Measure 2 cups of sifted flour, add 4 teaspoons of baking powder, ½ teaspoon of salt, and ⅛ teaspoon each of mace, nutmeg and thyme, then sift together into a mixing bowl; cut in thoroughly ⅓ cup of shortening; add ¾ cup (about) of cold milk to make a soft dough. Turn out onto a floured board, and knead a few minutes, then roll out ½-inch or less in thickness. Spread with turkey filling almost to the edges; roll as for jelly roll, moistening the edges to make them adhere. Place in a lightly greased baking pan, and bake in a very hot oven (425° F.) until brown, or about 20 minutes. Serve on a hot platter with Brown Sauce (No. 1019) to which you may add a few cooked, sliced fresh mushrooms. Serve with cranberry sauce.

CURRY OF TURKEY WITH WILD RICE [965]

Pick meat from bones of turkey, scraping away as much stuffing as possible; disjoint the carcass, and barely cover with cold water mixed with ¼ cup of Pique Seasoning for every pint of water; add salt, pepper, bay leaf, parsley celery tops, onion, clove, etc. as if making a broth. Cover and simmer covered for 1 hour or longer. There should be 3 cups of broth.

Cook 2 medium-sized thinly sliced onions, in ¼ cup of drippings for 3 minutes, over a very low heat, stirring occasionally; blend in 3 table-spoons of flour, mixed with 2½ to 3 tablespoons of curry powder (more or less, according to taste), and when well blended, gradually add the hot strained broth, stirring constantly, until mixture is thickened. Season to taste with salt, pepper and a dash of nutmeg, then stir in 2½ to 3 cups of turkey scraps. Simmer gently for 15–20 minutes, and just before serving, if desired, stir in 1 teaspoon of cider vinegar. Have ready boiled 2 cups of wild rice. Press it into a greased ring mold, unmold and fill center with the curried turkey. Dust with chopped parsley and Serve at once.

ROAST TURKEY [966]

Singe, clean, dry, rub inside and out with mixed salt and pepper, and stuff the bird with your favorite stuffing (See Stuffings No. 1634) taking care not to pack stuffing in too solidly. Close openings by sewing with heavy kitchen thread. Truss the bird by folding skin over back and holding in place by folding wings back. Tie the legs and wings to body with heavy white kitchen string. Rub lightly with butter or bacon drippings and sprinkle with mixed salt and pepper. Place the bird breast side up in a large baking pan; lay 2 slices of salt pork (optional) over the breast and start the roasting in a very hot oven (450° F.) for 15 to 20 minutes, to sear the bird thoroughly, thus closing the pores. Reduce the heat to moderate (350° F.) and add 1 large onion, chopped, 1 stalk of celery, scraped and chopped, 2 medium-sized carrots, scraped and chopped, 1 bouquet garni composed of 2 bay leaves, 12 sprigs of parsley, 3 sprigs of green celery leaves (tops), and 2 sprigs of thyme, all tied together with white kitchen thread, 2 whole cloves, and pour over 2 cups of boiling water mixed with ½ cup of Pique Seasoning. Roast steadily, allowing 20 to 25 minutes per pound and basting frequently with the drippings and liquid from the pan, turning the breast down 30 minutes before it is done. Serve with cream gravy (No. 1038), or Giblet Gravy (No. 1060). Mashed or baked sweet or white potatoes, Brussels sprouts or Chestnut Purée, or any kind of cooked, buttered greens go well with roast turkey. Don't fail to serve too, hot or cold Cranberry sauce.

TURKEY ASPIC SUPPER [967]
(Serves 12 to 14. For less, reduce accordingly)

At buffet suppers the hostess like to offer guests a choice of hot and cold main dishes. Popular hot dishes include turkey or chicken a la king, patties, turkey scalloped with oysters, etc., and among the cold dishes turkey aspic, made as follows:

Place in a large saucepan 1½ cups of cold water, ½ cup of Pique Seasoning, 3 tablespoons of cider vinegar, 2 tablespoons of sugar, ½ teaspoon of salt, 2 teaspoons of prepared mustard and ¼ cup of butter or margarin. Blend thoroughly and heat to boiling point. Meantime, sprinkle 3 tablespoons of granulated gelatin over 4 tablespoons of cold water and let stand 5 minutes, then add to the first (boiling) mixture, stirring until quite dissolved. Beat 4 eggs as for an omelet in a large bowl; gradually beat into them the hot gelatin mixture, beating with rotary beater till thoroughly blended. Let cool, to a little under the lukewarm stage, then stir in 1 cup of mayonnaise, which has been blended with ¼ cup of tomato catsup and a few drops of tabasco sauce.

Cover the bottom of a mold (10½ × 7½ × 2 inches) with the cool gelatin mixture. Chill for 5 minutes. Arrange 1 cut pimiento in a fancy design, on the gelatin; chill until firm. Now, combine 4 cups of flaked, cooked, cold turkey meat, 1 cup of finely chopped celery, 1 cup of thinly sliced ripe olives, ½ cup of finely chopped green pepper, and ½ cup of cooked, coarsely chopped, cooled fresh mushrooms and mix with the remaining gelatin. Pack gently into the mold as evenly as possible. Chill until very firm, or about 5 hours. To serve, unmold upon a large chilled platter and garnish with wedges of peeled tomatoes, pieces of stuffed celery, whole ripe olives, quarters of hard-cooked eggs, and decorate here and there with daubs of mayonnaise forced through a pastry bag with a rose tube.

When Cortes met Montezuma, the Spanish Conquistador was served mole, a dish still in vogue in Mexico. Chocolate, pumpkin seeds, chili and 16 kinds of herbs and spices are in the recipe for the sauce which goes with the turkey, or pork which is the main ingredient.

TURKEY CHOW MEIN [968]
(Left-over cooked turkey)

Make a rich broth of 1½ cups of boiling water and ½ cup of Pique Seasoning. Cut into neat shreds enough cold, cooked turkey to make 3½ to 4 cups (using both dark and white meat). Heat 3 tablespoons of peanut oil in a heavy saucepan and stir in 1½ tablespoons of soy sauce (commercial), then add the shredded turkey and cook till light brown, stirring constantly. Remove to a hot platter and keep hot. Add 1 tablespoon more of peanut oil to the pan and stir in 2 cups of thinly sliced onions, 1 cup of small celery sticks cut the size of a match and cook over a gentle flame until just beginning to brown, stirring frequently. In a separate frying pan cook ¾ cup of fresh, peeled, sliced mushrooms until tender. Drain and combine with the well-drained onion-celery mixture. Then add the turkey mixture. Moisten 2 tablespoons of cornstarch smoothly with cold water and stir into 1 cup of boiling water, cooking until mixture thickens, then add 2 tablespoons of Chinese brown sauce (commercial) season to taste with salt and pepper, and add the turkey; onion mixture. Heat through and serve on a hot platter which is covered with crisp fried noodles, and sprinkle with ½ cup of blanched, shredded toasted almonds. Serve at once with soy sauce.

Sophocles was the first Greek to mention the turkey. Two of these birds were exhibited in Athens, when they were regarded as a great curiosity.

TURKEY FRITTERS [969]

Beat 2 egg yolks and add 2 cups of cold, cooked, chopped (not ground) turkey; season to taste with salt, pepper, nutmeg and a few grains of cayenne pepper. Mix in ¼ cup of flour sifted with 1 teaspoon of baking powder, then fold in 2 stiffly beaten egg whites. The batter should be of the thickness of whipped cream. Drop by generous teaspoonfuls into hot, deep, clear fat, and cook until fritters are delicately browned, stirring with a wooden spoon, and cooking only a few at a time. Drain on unglazed paper, and keep hot until all the fritters are cooked. Serve generously garnished with fried green parsley.

Any kind of cooked poultry, meat, vegetables, etc. may be prepared similarly.

TURKEY AND OYSTER FRITTERS [970]

Proceed as indicated for Turkey Fritters (No. 969), popping in each fritter a small, raw, plump oyster.

TURKEY GALANTINE A LA PADEREWSKI [971]
(Cold)

Have your butcher bone a plump, young turkey weighing about 10 to 12 pounds. Spread the bird on a wet board, and cover with the following forcemeat: Put through food chopper ½ pound each of lean raw veal, lean raw ham, lean raw pork, raw calf's liver and pork sausage meat, together with ½ cup of chopped onions, ½ cup of chopped green pepper, ¼ cup each of chopped parsley, chives and chervil, if available, ¼ teaspoon each of mace, nutmeg, cloves, thyme, marjoram and all-spice, 2 cups of soft bread crumbs, moistened with ½ cup of Madeira wine, 2 generous teaspoons of salt, and ½ teaspoon of freshly ground black pepper. Mix all this well in a mixing bowl. Heat ¾ cup of butter in a large, shallow pan, and stir in the stuffing. Cook over a low flame, stirring constantly, until mixture leaves the sides and bottom of the pan. Remove from the fire, and when cool enough to handle rub through a fine-meshed wire sieve into a mixing bowl, and add 5 slightly beaten egg yolks, mixed with 1 cup (more or less) of sweet, heavy cream, or enough to make a forcemeat neither too stiff nor too soft.

Spread this forcemeat over the boned turkey; roll out as for jelly roll, folding the ends inside so as to keep the stuffing in place, and tie first at both ends, then every two inches around and every two inches length-wise, like a large sausage. Wrap the roll in wet cheesecloth and tie at both ends. Place in a large kettle, cover generously with boiling stock made from the bones and trimmings of the bird; bring slowly to a boil, and simmer as gently as possible for 5 hours, replenishing the kettle with boiling stock, or with stock made with boiling water and Pique Seasoning in the proportion of ½ cup of Pique Seasoning to each pint of boiling water. Cool in the stock overnight.

Meanwhile, prepare a Madeira Aspic as follows:

Combine 1 cup of cold clear, chicken consommé, a dash of salt and ½ cup of dry white wine in a large mixing bowl, and sprinkle 6 table-spoons of gelatin on top. Let stand 5 minutes, then stir into 3 cups of hot, clear consommé alternately with 2½ cups of heated Madeira wine. Turn mixture into a saucepan, add 3 slightly beaten egg whites and their crushed shells, and place over a medium flame. Stir constantly until mixture just begins to boil, then stop stirring and let simmer gently for 10 to 15 minutes. Strain through a wet jelly bag into a bowl, and let cool to lukewarm. Remove the string, then the cloth from the turkey roll, and place into a long, narrow bread pan approximately the same size as the roll itself. Pour a little of the Madeira gelatin over it and let set. Over this decorate fancifully according to taste with small cuts of truffles, black olives, green pepper, leeks, hard-cooked egg whites, tarragon leaves, parsley leaves, chives sprigs, etc. and pour in more Madeira wine gelatin, until the mold is full and the turkey roll is entirely covered. Cool, then chill overnight. To serve, unmold on a chilled long platter, decorate and garnish with small tomatoes, stuffed with whatever cold mixture you may desire, quartered hard-cooked eggs, fancy cuts of red beets, etc. and surround the base of the roll with the remaining gelatin which should be as clear as crystal and coarsely chopped. An attractive dish for a buffet, or summer party luncheon or supper. This dish is usually served with a green salad tossed in French dressing just before serving.

The turkey was held in such esteem in Mexico in the time of Monte-zuma that life-size models were fashioned in pure gold as tribute to the bird.

TURKEY GRILL CHATELAINE [972]

Clean, wash quickly and split a 6 to 7 pound turkey, then wash again thoroughly and let stand in a shallow dish, covered with sherry wine for 24 hours. Next day drain, dry, rub the bird with highly seasoned melted butter or seasoned olive oil; place on the broiler, skin side down; brown lightly on both sides, then transfer to a shallow baking pan; brush with a little melted butter and bake in a moderate oven (325–350° F.) basting frequently with melted butter, for about 30 minutes, turning the bird twice during the cooking process. When done, remove from the oven and season to taste. Transfer to a hot platter; garnish with 6 small pan-broiled pork sausages, 6 little tomatoes, stuffed with creamed new peas, 12 slices of broiled bacon, and 6 grilled large fresh mushroom caps, brushed with anchovy butter (No. 979). Serve at once with the following sauce:

Sauce Chatelaine. Place in a small saucepan ¾ cup of dry white wine, 3 chopped shallots, 2 tablespoons chopped fresh mushrooms or trimmings of fresh mushrooms, and reduce this to almost nothing, over a gentle flame. Then stir in ¼ cup of the drippings from the pan in which the bird was baked, and ¾ of heavy, sweet cream, scalded with 1 small bay leaf, 3 slices of onion, and 4 sprigs of parsley, then drained. Bring to a boil; taste for seasoning, and strain through a fine sieve into a sauceboat.

TURKEY AND OYSTER SCALLOP [973]

Have ready 3 cups of rich cream sauce (No. 258). Arrange a pint of cleaned fresh oysters in a generously-buttered baking dish; sprinkle over them ¼ cup of small cubes of bread, and pour over 1 cup of the hot sauce. Over the sauce arrange a layer of ¾ cup of cooked, diced turkey meat, repeat with bread cubes and sauce. Again add a layer of 1 cup of cleaned oysters, bread cubes and all the remaining sauce. Sprinkle top with ½ cup of buttered bread crumbs mixed with an equal amount of grated cheese, and bake in a very moderate oven (300–325° F.) until nicely browned and piping hot. Serve at once in the baking dish.

TURKEY PIE HOME STYLE [974]

Have ready pastry crust for a two-crust pie. Line a rather deep pie tin with pastry; brush the bottom and sides with egg, well-beaten with a little milk. Mix 4 cups of diced, carefully boned and skinned cooked turkey ¼ pound of boiled ham, cut into thin strips, 2 tablespoons of toasted bread crumbs, ½ cup of cooked, sliced mushrooms, 2 hard-cooked eggs, sliced, 12 tiny white onions, parboiled and well drained, and season to taste with salt, pepper and nutmeg, also 1 teaspoon each of finely chopped parsley, green pepper and chives. Toss well and mix in ½ to ⅔ cup of medium cream sauce (No. 259). Turn mixture into the prepared pie tin, cover with the top crust slashed in the center for the escape of steam; brush with cold milk; place in a very hot oven (450° F.) to set the crust for 15 minutes; reduce the heat to moderate (325° F.) and continue baking for 35 minutes longer, or until top is golden brown. Serve at once.

TURKEY SOUFFLÉ [975]

Blend 2 tablespoons of butter and 2 tablespoons of flour in a saucepan without browning; gradually stir in 1 cup of scalded milk, mixed with ½ cup of turkey stock made from bones and trimmings, and stir until mixture boils and thickens. Season to taste with salt, pepper, nutmeg and thyme, then stir in ½ cup of dry bread crumbs and ½ teaspoon of grated lemon rind, alternately with 1 cup of finely minced cooked turkey. Blend thoroughly, then beat in 3 egg yolks, added one at a time, beating well after each addition, adding with the last yolk 3 tablespoons of sherry wine. Lastly fold in 3 stiffly beaten egg whites, and turn mixture into a buttered soufflé dish. Bake in a hot oven (400° F.) for 25 to 30 minutes or until soufflé is puffed up and well-browned on top.

TURKEY TETRAZZINI STYLE [976–7]

Make a cream sauce of 2 tablespoons of butter, 3 tablespoons of flour, 1 cup of sweet, heavy cream, which has been scalded with 2 or 3 thin slices of onion, 3 sprigs of parsley, a bit of bay leaf and 1 whole clove and strained, season to taste with salt, pepper and a dash of nutmeg. When mixture is smooth and boiling, stir in 1 cup of cold, cooked turkey, cut in thin strips, ½ cup of cooked, drained and chopped spaghetti and ½ cup of sautéed, sliced fresh mushrooms. Mix well, turn mixture into a baking dish or 6 individual baking dishes, sprinkle with buttered crumbs mixed with ⅓ cup of grated Parmesan cheese, and bake in a moderate oven (375° F.) until crumbs are brown. Serve at once bubbling.

Chapter Nine

COMPOUND BUTTERS, SAUCES AND GRAVIES

. . . One can learn to cook, and one can be taught to roast, but a good sauce-maker is a genius born, not made.

—Brillat-Savarin

COMPOUNDED (CREAMED) BUTTERS [978]

THE ADAGE "GOOD DIGESTION WAITS ON APPETITE AND health on both," holds today. Of course, we mean an appetite that is normal—one that is satisfied with wholesome edibles. When a child rushes into the house in the afternoon with "Please, mother, may I have a slice of bread and butter?" he is simply asking for enough energy to continue play. Butter is an excellent food for all of us. We have learned not to waste it. But, in eastern Tibet all that glitters is not gold—it's butter. In this mysterious land of the Si Fan, fresh milk is never used. Tibetans believe this substance is unhealthy, so all that is produced is immediately churned into butter for which the Mongols have an insatiable appetite.

Butter, in Tibet, is begged, borrowed, bartered and burned. It is molded into altar offerings, consumed in lamps, eaten and worn. Pressed into hard little bricks it becomes the medium of exchange, the natural currency of the country. Housewives keep receptacles of it hanging in the kitchen for years, its aging rancidity being highly prized.

Both men and women smear themselves with the greasy substance during the winter months until they figuratively reek and shine with it. Their tea, a kind of strained soup, is invariably "boiled" and "buttered." In Si Fan is located the historic Kounboum Lamasery where 4,000 yellow-mitered lamas continually venerate the precepts of Buddhism. The great monastery surmounts the bluff of a precipitous cliff to which devout pilgrims from the remotest part of Tartary journey once a year to honor the *Feast of Flowers*, the most curious spectacle to be found anywhere in the world. On this occasion the interior of the lamasery is a veritable museum, where statues of people, animals, landscapes and flowers are all made of fresh butter. The most accomplished monk-artists of Kounboum are engaged daily for three months in these butter works, keeping their hands continually in icy water, so that the heat of the fingers doesn't disfigure their reproductions. As their labors take place in mid-winter, the operators suffer terribly from the cold. The work is assigned to different *artists*, each an expert in his line.

Paintings and sculptures in famous lamaseries throughout Tibet serve as models. The flowers and designs in bas-relief, of colossal proportions, represent every phase of Buddhistic history. The features of disciples are invested with wonderful expression and the attitude is natural. The *Feast of Flowers* reflects a dazzling brilliancy at night, being extravagantly illuminated, but all these masterpieces serve as an exhibit for only a single evening. By dawn the collection of sculptured butter is thrown down the ravine where hungry crows await their feast.

Butter, one of the oldest of foods, was used more than two thousand years before the Christian era. It is mentioned throughout the Bible. It was used in early times as an ointment for the skin, and sold in medicine shops, and when fresh has been used as a salve for burns and sore eyes. Today, we do not waste butter as do the Tibetans. There is no substitute for butter in important food elements, notwithstanding

549

statements to the contrary. Butter should on no account be dispensed with in an economy diet.

Compounded (creamed) butters in cookery, especially in hors d'oeuvre making, are the finishing touch to a food, be it a soup, a fish, a piece of meat, a sauce or a vegetable, as is powder and makeup to the face of a beautiful woman. They may be prepared in advance and stored in a closed jar, in the refrigerator for use when necessary. They may be used for spreading bread for a child's afternoon snack; for spreading sandwiches, and so forth. The complete list of compounded (creamed) butters would be too lengthy to be given here, so I will simply describe those most used in present day cookery in America.

ANCHOVY BUTTER [979]

Pound or cream 2 tablespoons of sweet butter with anchovy paste the size of a hazelnut (more or less, according to taste).

ALMOND BUTTER I [980]

Grind 6 blanched almonds using the finest blade, and cream with 2 tablespoons of salt butter.

ALMOND BUTTER II [981]

Grind or pound 6 sweet blanched almonds, adding a few drops of egg white to prevent their oiling and cream with 1 generous tablespoon of salt butter.

BERCY BUTTER [982]

Reduce to half volume a scant cup of white wine to which has been added a scant ½ teaspoon of finely chopped parsley. Let cool, then cream thoroughly with ⅓ cup of salt butter.

CAVIAR BUTTER [983]

Pound finely 1 tablespoon of black caviar. Place in a fine cloth and twist to remove the oily liquid and briny water; then cream with 2 tablespoons of sweet butter and chill.

CHIVRY BUTTER [984]

Mix together a scant ½ teaspoon each of finely chopped parsley, chervil, tarragon, chives and shallots, and cream with 2 tablespoons of salt butter. Chill.

CRAYFISH BUTTER [985]

Pound 1 tablespoon of meat trimmings of crayfish in a mortar, together with the same amount of salt butter. Chill.

GARLIC BUTTER [986]

Blanch in a very little water 1 clove of garlic. Drain, dry, then cream or pound with 1 tablespoon of salt butter. Chill.

GREEN BUTTER [987]

Butter creamed with sufficient green vegetable coloring to obtain the desired hue. Chill.

HORSERADISH BUTTER [988]

Pound or grind 1 teaspoon of freshly grated horseradish, then cream with 1 tablespoon of salt butter. Chill.

Natives of those parts of Africa where the shea tree grows, don't need cows. They prepare butter from the sap of the tree which is said to be richer than cow's milk.

KNEADED BUTTER [989]

This butter is seldom used for decorating or garnishing hors d'oeuvres. It is usually employed for the quick blending and thickening of soups, stews, gravies, sauces, and so forth, whenever needed. It consists of creaming 1 tablespoon of butter with approximately 2 teaspoons of flour, using more or less flour, according to directions. Chill or use immediately.

HERRING BUTTER [990]

Cream together a walnut-size portion of herring paste with 2 table spoons of sweet butter. Chill.

LOBSTER BUTTER [991]

Pound or grind several times, the equivalent of a tablespoon of lobster trimmings such as coral, milky meat, roe, and so forth, with 2 tablespoons of salt butter. Chill.

MUSTARD BUTTER [992]

Cream 1 tablespoon of sweet butter with 1 scant teaspoon of prepared mustard. Chill thoroughly before using.

MARCHAND DE VIN BUTTER [993]
Wine Dealer Butter

Reduce to one-half its volume over a hot flame, 1 cup of red wine to which 1 small, finely chopped shallot has been added; add 2 freshly crushed whole black peppercorns, meat extract the size of a hazelnut, ½ teaspoon of finely chopped parsley, and 3 or 4 drops of lemon juice. Cool, then cream thoroughly with ¼ cup of salt butter. Chill.

PAPRIKA BUTTER I [994]

Cream 2 tablespoons of sweet butter with 1 scant tablespoon of paprika. Chill.

PAPRIKA BUTTER II [995]

Cook together 1 tablespoon of butter, 1 teaspoon of paprika and ½ teaspoon of grated onion. Strain through a fine-meshed sieve, and when cold, cream with 1 generous tablespoon of butter. Chill.

ROE BUTTER [996]

Poach over a very gentle flame in enough butter to cover, 1 tablespoon of soft or hard fish roe (any kind). Drain, add ¼ teaspoon of lemon juice to the roe, mash and cool. When cold, cream the mashed roe with an equal amount of salt butter and 1 scant teaspoon of prepared mustard. Blend well. Chill.

RUSSIAN CINNAMON BUTTER [997]

Cream 2 tablespoons of butter with ½ teaspoon (more or less, according to taste) of ground cinnamon. Chill

RUSSIAN NUTMEG BUTTER [998]

Cream 2 tablespoons of salt butter; add a generous grating of nutmeg, ¼ teaspoon of lemon juice, a dash of white pepper and 1 teaspoon of finely chopped chives. Blend thoroughly. Chill.

SMOKED SALMON BUTTER [999]

Cream 2 tablespoons of sweet butter with 1 teaspoon (more or less, according to taste) of smoked salmon paste.
Variations. Almost all smoked fish may be used in this manner.

SHALLOT BUTTER [1000]

Pound (or grind several times) 1 shallot, previously blanched in a little butter. Strain, cool, then cream with the strained butter and enough salt butter to make a tablespoon. Chill.

SHRIMP BUTTER [1001]

Pound (or grind several times, using the finest blade) 6 large cooked, shelled fresh shrimps, then cream with 2 tablespoons of salt butter. Chill.

TARRAGON BUTTER [1002]

Pound, then rub through a fine-meshed sieve enough tarragon leaves (fresh or dried) to make 1 teaspoon, cream with 2 tablespoons of salt butter, blending thoroughly. Then rub through a fine-meshed sieve. Chill.

The young guacharo of South America (also called the oil bird) is simply a mass of fat and is used for butter and illuminating oil.

TOMATO BUTTER I [1003]

Cream 1 tablespoon of tomato paste (commercial) with 2 tablespoons of salt butter, a pinch of granulated sugar, a dash of salt and a few grains of cayenne pepper. Blend thoroughly. Chill.

TOMATO BUTTER II [1004]

To tomato pulp, reduced to the consistency of heavy cream and strained through a fine-meshed sieve, add double its weight of butter and cream thoroughly. Chill.

TRUFFLE BUTTER [1005]

Pound (or grind several times, using the finest blade) 1 whole cooked black truffle (cooked in a little butter, over a very gentle flame); rub through a fine-meshed sieve, add treble the amount of salt butter. Rub through a fine-meshed sieve and chill.

VEGETABLE BUTTER [1006]

Make from any desired vegetable finely ground, then rubbed through a fine-meshed sieve. The vegetable used is first cooked, strained, ground and sieved, then creamed with an equal amount of salt butter. Again the mixture is rubbed through a fine-meshed sieve and when smooth, chilled in a glass container. This butter is seldom used for hors d'oeuvre but rather for thickening soups.

The butter mentioned in the Bible was not like the modern variety, but something that could be drunk. As it didn't keep, it was boiled over a slow fire and clarified with a handful of meal.

SAUCES [1007]

At every meal, just before the dishes are brought to the table, there is always a "last touch." Perhaps it's a bit of flavor added to the sauce, perhaps it's a deft tossing together of the salad, or a sprinkling of color. Often these ministrations are inspired strokes of genius that turn mediocrities into masterpieces. They are like the secrets of a smartly groomed woman. Her basic costume naturally is faultless, but it is the faint dab of perfume that touches off or dramatizes the whole ensemble.

Take the matter of seasoning, for instance. Today, cooks have been so often criticized for high seasoning that seasoning is becoming a lost art. Or maybe you'd prefer to be a Spartan. You may remember that the Spartans compelled all citizens to eat the same food, in order to banish luxury. One of their dishes was black broth, highly regarded by the older men. The tyrant Dionysius, a guest, called it insipid. "I do not wonder," said the chef, "for the seasoning is lacking." "What seasoning?" asked Dionysius. "Running, sweating, fatigue, hunger and thirst," replied the other, "with these ingredients we season our food."

The Greeks certainly had a word for it when they described their idea of seasoning. Essentially they were absolutely right. But in lieu of these five "ingredients," let's turn to pepper, salt, mustard, onions, garlic, and so forth. Actually, well-seasoned food is preferred by a majority of persons, provided it is prepared by someone who knows what and how to season and flavor and does not cook just by guesswork. Know your spices, your sauces, and your dressings and know what they will do. This means that you must be familiar with the reaction of thirty or forty or more spices and herbs. They are a wonder brush with which to paint your flavor pictures.

Spices, sauces, dressings, and other stimulants are used in culinary combinations of food not merely to impart their *own* flavor but to excite our taste organs to a keener perception of the flavor of the soups, fish, meats, poultry, games, and salads in which they are present. It is not alone the biting quality of pepper that is valued for itself; nor is wine used in sauces merely for the purpose of making the wine taste stand out. The art of making memorable culinary combinations lies in producing a happy blending in which the elementary flavors are all lost and indistinquishable in a new union created by their combined effect on the palate. Certain seasonings lift up certain foods, but in using them the cook must be careful not to overseason—rather to obtain a delicious blend which will bring out the flavor of the predominant ingredient in the dish, and add an elusive aroma so subtle that even the epicure hesitates to name it.

Many new cookbooks scarcely mention sauces. *Quel dommage!* since it is from the sauce that gourmets for centuries have derived the ultimate in satisfaction. A perfect sauce is always a triumph. A touch of this, a sprinkle of that, plus a dash of imagination, and the most prosaic food is "saucily served."

The preparation of foods so that the most is made of natural flavors and textures—that's *good cooking*. The enhancement of natural flavors and textures, generally in sauce form—that's *fine cooking*. The ambrosia, about which the Greeks rhapsodized as the food of their gods, was probably only a clever way with garlic. Anybody who knows even a nickel's worth about seasoning must agree that a discreet use of garlic may very well result in something that tastes as fine as ambrosia sounds. When it comes to sauce seasoning, and in fact all food seasonings, most cooks are either too cautious or too venturesome. The caution school sticks closely to salt and pepper, and not very much of either, only occasionally risking some cookbook's directions for "one-eighth teaspoon onion juice." On the other hand, there are those amateur cooks, who fancying themselves as saucemakers and tossers together of exotic stews and such, have discovered what herbs, spices, and so on can do for a sauce, and they proceed to lose their heads completely splashing those virile seasonings in almost everything. A professional chef would not permit exponents of either school to do his cooking. But, on the whole, there would be more chance of making a respectable cook out of the garlic or onion addicts, herb-tossers, and spice-dispensers than in placing any hope on the timid soul who is afraid to risk a seasoning the recipe doesn't call for. In experimenting, the venturesome cook shows that his heart, even if not always his palate, is in the right place, and with a little judicious criticism, he can probably be toned down to becoming a very fine flavorer and seasoner.

"A sauce should be smooth, light without being glossy to the eye and decided as to taste." This was learned by the writer from the great Escoffier, in reference to thickened sauces. There is no effort too great for a fine cook to make when it comes to the preparation of a fine sauce.

The trouble with giving advice about sauce-making is that every inexperienced cook is likely to have his or her own difficulty. Your own sauce weakness may be in getting a perfect delicate seasoning; somebody else may fall down on consistency, while still another is always having his or her sauces curdle. How is even the best-intentioned adviser going to supply the wisdom that will cover all these emergencies? It is, however, safe to lay down a few basic rules as to what to do, and what not to do, in order to turn out a fine sauce.

Sauces are very—and yet not very—difficult to prepare. There has unfortunately been little or no education in the matter of sauces and no disposition to explore the mysteries of them. That is the aim of this chapter.

WHAT IS A GOOD SAUCE? [1008]

Escoffier would not have stopped with thyme in praising herbs. "Use pick-ups to pep up your food," the great master was wont to advise this writer when the latter was learning the art of sauce-making. A "pick-up" is anything that literally "picks up" a dish and carries it to the heights of the extraordinary. That dash of paprika atop a pale sauce, the pinch of herb, the snip of chives on the potatoes—these things are pick-ups—the stimulants of any dish and of any sauce. Their number, though large, has been built up within the limitations of two characteristics: decided flavor and distinction of color.

It's the pick-ups with their use of herbs that make the French cuisine and its sauces the delight of gourmets. In the Middle Ages, sauce-making was considered so important that the *saucier*, or Master of the Sauces, was retained by rich gourmets as well as by royal personages, and was always present at banquets and notable functions. Old engravings show this master of sauces working at elaborately equipped side tables, with a corps of young assistants to aid him.

But sauces, as such, have their origins in the most simple cooking practice. In the beginning, they were merely broths of meats, or fowls, or game simmered long hours in capacious soup pots. The beef, the bones, and the remnants of chicken and veal which the cook daily dropped into the soup stock pot were condensed, after slow and long simmering, into the rich essences which make up both soup and sauces worth eating.

French sauces developed along two different lines, giving us the three chief—and highly different—sauces: brown and white, each with its myriad family connections, and butter sauce, from which, alone, hundreds upon hundreds of variations have resulted. These have become so specific that their making is now not only an art, but a science.

An infiltration into France of both Italian and Spanish chefs, about the time that the making of sauces was well under way, brought such innovations as the use of smoked ham, sausage, tomato paste used lavishly, and the addition of wines to sauces. The use of these higher seasonings, beaten eggs, and many other fascinating changes resulted in the sauces which the French have given the world of gourmets and gourmands, and which are familiar to us as sauces individually named.

To have an idea of what used to go into classic sauces, here is a short story:

The Prince of Soubise one day intended to give a feast which was to finish with a supper, and he asked that the menu be shown to him. To his *levée* came the chef with a beautifully ornamented document, and the first item which caught the eye of the prince was "fifty hams."

"Chef!" he exclaimed, "you must be out of your senses. Fifty hams! Do you want to feed all my regiment?"

"No, Your Highness, only one will appear on the table; but the others are not the less necessary for my concentrated sauces, my *blonds* (stocks), my trimmings, my . . . ."

"Chef, you are cheating me, and I cannot let this item pass."

"Ah, my lord," said the artist, scarcely able to retain his rage, "you do not know our resources. Give the order and I will put these fifty hams that annoy you in a glass phial not much larger than my thumb."

What reply could be made to so positive an assertion? The prince smiled, nodded assent, and so the item was passed. . . .

"When is a sauce *not* just broth, bouillon, or essence?" is a cooking conundrum which can be answered by the reply which this writer made to an inquisitive listener during one of his practical demonstrations, "When it is thickened." It is the thickening which makes sauce out of soup; otherwise it is a *jus*, the natural liquid extracted from the flesh of meat, fish or game. Here the French creative imagination went way beyond its cooking competitors, because it gave us *roux*—the specific scientific method of blending flour, fat, and liquid into a sauce with body and texture.

Indeed, he who would become a good sauce-maker must understand the importance of what we might call the "ritual of the *roux*"; that is, (*he must know*) how to make a *roux* with all the precision required in making up a baby's feeding formula, how long to cook it, and at exactly what point to remove it from the fire.

In general, this blending of flour, or whatever thickening agent is used, with butter—no substitute will make a real sauce any more than a silk hat will make a gentleman—with the broth of fish, meat, poultry or game, must take place (note this well) over *low* heat in a very *slow* tempo, with *constant* stirring. Long, slow, even cooking or simmering, or *smiling* —is necessary to sauce success.

A good sauce must possess the following characteristics: (1) a glossy, colorful appearance; (2) a bouquet as in wine, subtle, well blended; (3) a smooth, velvety texture, with fluidity of body; and (4) complete absence of any sight or taste of fat. Thus, the perfect sauce must be appetizing and inviting in its look; it must seem vaguely in motion even after it has been poured over the food for which it has been prepared. Never, by any chance, must it seem cold, or set, or solid, greasy, lumpy, pasty!

A good sauce requires precision; it requires patience, time, and watching. It demands smelling and tasting by its blender which may be why French chefs (almost all of whom are males) seem to excel as modern sauce-makers.

Despite all arguments to the contrary, men, in general, seem to have a keener sense of smell than women (though it is admitted that men are greatly inferior in some of the other human qualities!); they have a true gustatory tongue for flavor—one of the reasons that men exclusively are engaged in wine, tea, and coffee tasting. They make, therefore, the best chefs. They know taste, and taste's the thing in sauce-making, for obviously, unless a sauce tastes good, why bother to eat it? Indeed, why bother to make it at all?

Make your own sauces by your own magic; your brown, golden yellow, or creamy white sauces; for it is only by making them yourself that you will appreciate their goodness.

Learn to use herbs in them, the herbs that add gusto to flavor. Taste, and smell, and stir; then eat, with savoring tongue, and look on yourself as a miracle worker.

However, for many a sauce, it is on the stocks (see No. 178), that French cooks chiefly rely. For it is in the kettle of stock that the French keep the secrets of some of their indescribable sauces. And it is those sauces that famous chefs use to impart exquisite flavor to foods.

They have used them for centuries. In Paris, during the reign of Louis XI, the corporation of sauciers ran the same risks as those of today in cooking and seasoning too much or too little, or in committing gustatory crimes of *lèse-sauc majesté* against discriminating palates that commended or censured certain combinations of flavors. But today, as yesterday, the proper sauce, properly prepared, is, as Rabelais remarked about the finished brown *sauce Robert*, "tant salubre et nécessaire." Or, to put it in the Dickensian words of Sam Weller, "It's the seasoning as does it."

Sauce, finished sauce, sauce which has received the last touch, tones up a pallid platter of almost anything.

> *Kin and friend and goodly neighbor,*
> *In our fold you'll find true zest;*
> *Table spread with food of flavor,*
> *Cool, refreshing! Pause and rest,*
> *Health and joys of happy-living;*
> *Everyday a well-done task.*
> *Noonday, evening—early morning*
> *"be at home is all we ask."*
> *—Abbe Delille.*

AIOLI SAUCE [1009]
(*Cold*)

Mash 2 or 3 (more if a sharper taste is desired) cloves of garlic, then pound very smooth with 2 egg yolks and 7 or 8 (or more) tablespoons of olive oil, added drop by drop at first, increasing gradually to a thin stream as soon as the sauce begins to thicken, stirring constantly as for mayonnaise. When half of the oil has been incorporated, alternate with a scant teaspoon of tarragon vinegar or lemon juice and a few drops of ice-cold water. Season to taste with salt and pepper, stressing a little on the black pepper. Should the mixture curdle, start over again with another egg yolk, using the curdled part in the same way suggested for fallen mayonnaise.

In certain parts of Provence, France, where this sauce originated, a little sieved pulp of cold baked potato is sometimes added to give it more body, and lemon juice is used instead of ice-cold water. The writer mentions this method as purely indicative. (This heavily loaded garlic sauce is appropriate for any kind of cooked fish.)

BARBECUE SAUCE [1010]
See "Frankfurter Crown Roast" (No. 783).

BASTING SAUCE FOR SHELLFISH [1011]
See "Grilled Lobster Gourmet" (No. 467 (a))

BEARNAISE SAUCE [1012]
(*Cold*)

Reduce to ½ volume, over a hot flame, 1 cup of dry white wine, mixed with 1 scant tablespoon of tarragon vinegar, 1 tablespoon of finely chopped shallots, 2 sprigs of parsley and 1 sprig of tarragon all coarsely chopped, a tiny pinch of chervil, 3 or 4 peppercorns, bruised, no salt, at all. Let cool, strain through a fine sieve into a saucepan, and beat in 3 egg yolks, added one at a time, beating well after each addition, alternately with as much butter melted to luke warm as the sauce will hold, or until it is the consistency of cream cheese. Appropriate for any kind of meat cooked in any style, fish and fish filets, and so forth.

Variations. Add 1 or 2 tablespoons of tomato paste with the butter or substitute lobster, shrimp, anchovy, herring or smoked salmon butter for the plain butter (see Compounded Butters).

BECHAMEL SAUCE [1013]

Follow the directions given at Soups (No, 259.).

BREAD SAUCE [1014]
(*Hot*)

To 1½ cups of good game stock if the sauce is for game, or meat stock, if the sauce is intended for meat or poultry, add 2 tablespoons of very lean cooked ham, chopped, and 2 small shallots, chopped fine. Let this simmer very gently for 15 minutes. Meanwhile, fry in 2 tablespoons of butter ½ generous cup of bread crumbs (more if the sauce is desired thick) until lightly browned. Drain and add to the stock with 1 teaspoon of finely minced parsley and ½ teaspoon of lemon juice. Appropriate for game, boiled meat and poultry.

BROWN BUTTER SAUCE [1015]

Let ½ cup of butter bubble and foam in a small saucepan until it becomes a very light brown. Remove from the fire, add 2 tablespoons each of lemon juice, chopped parsley and chopped chives, or serve without parsley and chives after seasoning to taste with salt and a few grains of pepper. Serve at once. Appropriate for grilled fish filets, any kind of grilled meat, cauliflower, asparagus, broccoli, cabbage, and so forth.

BROWN FLOUR [1016]
For thickening gravies, sauces and soups

Spread 2 cups of flour upon a large tin plate or baking sheet; place in a moderate oven and stir frequently until flour is of the desired shade.

Salt to taste and store in a covered jar. This will keep indefinitely and is very handy, saving loss of time in browning when needed.

BROWN SAUCE I   [1017]
(*Short Method*)

Melt 2 tablespoons of butter or other fat in a small saucepan; blend in 1 tablespoon of chopped onion, 1 tablespoon of chopped carrot, 1 tablespoon of chopped celery leaves, a dash of thyme leaves, 1 bay leaf tied with 4 sprigs of fresh parsley, and cook over a low heat for about 5 minutes, or until vegetables are beginning to brown, stirring frequently. Sprinkle in 2 tablespoons of flour, blending well, then add 1 cup of meat stock, or failing this, ½ cup of boiling water and ½ cup of Pique Seasoning, stirring constantly until mixture boils and thickens. Let boil gently for 4 or 5 minutes, taste for seasoning, then strain through a fine sieve.

BROWN SAUCE II FRENCH STYLE   [1018]

This sauce is generally used for and as a foundation sauce, and should be always on hand in a well ordered kitchen, to be added to certain other sauces, gravies, stews, and to enhance left-over dishes.

Have the butcher cut 2 pounds of beef bones into small pieces; wash them very quickly, drain, place in a shallow baking pan, place the pan in a hot oven (400° F.) and let brown until dark colored, stirring frequently. Transfer them to a stew or soup kettle, cover with 2 quarts of boiling water and simmer very gently and steadily until wanted.

Place in another stew pot or soup kettle ½ cup of beef or veal fat; stir in ½ cup each of chopped onions, carrots, celery and cook until vegetables are golden brown, stirring frequently; sprinkle in 2 tablespoons of flour and continue cooking till mixture is a deep brown, stirring occasionally. Now add the strained stock made from the browned bones, stirring constantly, 1 bouquet garni composed of 3 bay leaves, 1 sprig of thyme, 12 sprigs of parsley and 2 small leeks cleaned and all tied together with white kitchen thread, 1 teaspoon of peppercorns, very little salt, also 1 small clove of garlic, and bring to a boil. Skim, lower the heat and let simmer constantly for 3 or 4 hours, adding to the stock pot all the trimmings, bones and left-overs which cannot be used otherwise, with boiling water to constantly maintain at least 3 quarts of brown foundation sauce. The entire stock pot contents should be renewed once a month.

BROWN SAUCE III AMERICAN STYLE   [1019]

Cook 1½ tablespoons of chopped onions in 3 tablespoons of butter or margarin until slightly browned, stirring constantly; sprinkle in 3 tablespoons of flour (you may use Brown Flour No. 1016) instead of white flour; season to taste with salt and pepper, and gradually stir in 1½ cups of Brown Sauce or Stock II (Nos. 1017–18) French Style. Bring to the boiling point, let boil 3 or 4 minutes, lower the heat and simmer gently for 10 to 15 minutes. Strain through a fine sieve into a sauceboat and serve at once.

BROWN TOMATO SAUCE [1020]

To 1½ cups of Brown Sauce (either No. 1017–18 or No. 1019) add 2 tablespoons of tomato paste, heat well, taste for seasoning, and serve at once. Appropriate for veal cutlets, made-over dark meats, spaghetti, macaroni or noodles.

CAMBRIDGE SAUCE [1021]
(*Cold*)

Pound together 4 hard-cooked egg yolks, 2 anchovy filets, sponged dry, 2 small leaves of tarragon, finely chopped (dry leaves may be used), ½ generous teaspoon of finely chopped chives, moistened with ½ teaspoon of prepared mustard, then mixed with ¼ cup of olive oil and 2 teaspoons of tarragon vinegar. Beat briskly until mixture is reduced to a paste; season to taste with a few grains of cayenne pepper, but no salt, and when ready to serve, add ½ teaspoon of finely chopped parsley or chives. This sauce does not keep well and should be made just before serving. Appropriate for cold ham, cold tongue, or any cold dark meat.

CAPE COD FISH SAUCE [1022]

See No. 467, "Grilled Codfish Cape Cod Style."

CAPER-HOLLANDAISE SAUCE [1023]

To a cup of Hollandaise Sauce (No. 1063) add 3 tablespoons of parboiled, drained and dried capers, and 1 teaspoon of finely chopped chervil or parsley. Appropriate for any kind of boiled white-fleshed fish, asparagus, broccoli, cauliflower, boiled onions, and so forth.

CASANOVA SAUCE [1024]
(*Cold*)

To 1 cup of mayonnaise, add 1 large truffle, ground, 1 teaspoon of finely chopped shallots, the finely chopped white of a hard-cooked egg and 2 hard-cooked egg yolks, rubbed through a fine sieve. Taste for seasoning, and serve very cold. This sauce keeps 2 weeks in a good refrigerator. Suitable for any kind of cold cuts, game, and cold fish.

CHAMBERTIN SAUCE [1025]

Place 1¾ cups of red wine court-bouillon (using Chambertin burgundy wine instead of ordinary red wine) in a saucepan, and reduce to half volume, over a bright flame, with 1 generous pinch of freshly ground black pepper and 1 teaspoon of lemon juice. While still boiling, stir in 1 tablespoon of kneaded Butter (No. 989) and simmer very gently for 5 minutes. When ready to serve, stir in 1 generous teaspoon of sweet butter, taste for seasoning and pour over the fish filets. Appropriate for poached or broiled fish filets.

CELERY SAUCE [1026]

Cook ¾ cup of finely chopped celery until tender in enough meat stock to generously cover. Drain, pressing hard to extract all the liquid from the celery. Make ½ cup of cream sauce using this liquid instead of milk and having the cream sauce rather on the thick side. When ready to serve, stir in ¾ cup of scalded, heavy sour cream and season to taste with salt, white pepper and a generous grating of nutmeg. Appropriate for any kind of boiled fish.

CHEESE SAUCE [1027]

To 1 cup of medium white or cream sauce (No. 258 & 259 respectively) stir in ⅓ cup of grated cheese (any kind) until cheese is melted.

Variations: I. Stir in 2 tablespoons of finely chopped raw green pepper, or finely chopped, drained canned red pimiento.
II. Stir in 2 tablespoons of tomato paste.
III. Stir in 2 tablespoons of drained prepared horseradish.
IV. Stir in 1 tablespoon of prepared mustard.

CHERRY SAUCE HOME STYLE [1028]

Reduce to half, 1 cup of good port wine, to which has been added 1 whole clove, a generous pinch of freshly grated nutmeg, one of allspice one of thyme leaves, and ¼ teaspoon of grated orange rind. Stir in ½ cup of hot brown sauce (No. 1017, 1018, 1019) and ¼ cup of red currant jelly, then, finally, ½ cup of chopped black canned cherries. Taste for seasoning, and when ready to serve, stir in the juice of half an orange and

1 tablespoon of sweet butter. Serve very hot. Suitable for roasted domestic or wild duck, venison game, hare and wild boar.

CIDER SAUCE [1029]

Melt 3 tablespoons of butter; stir in 3 tablespoons of flour, and brown lightly, stirring constantly. Pour over 1 cup of ham stock (liquid in which ham or tongue has been boiled), gradually, stirring constantly, until boiling and thickened. Let boil gently for 5 minutes, stirring occasionally, then gradually pour in ¾ cup of scalded cider and cook, stirring constantly for 15 minutes. Strain through a fine sieve, taste for seasoning, and simmer gently for 10 minutes before serving. Appropriate for almost any kind of smoked meat as ham, tongue, leg of lamb and even smoked turkey or other birds.

CLARIFIED BUTTER [1030]

This butter is almost constantly used in French cuisine to add to sauces, soups and the like. It may be prepared several days in advance and kept in the refrigerator until wanted.

Place the required, or desired, amount of butter in top of a double boiler, over hot water and allow the butter to melt by itself, without stirring. The clear butter will rise on the surface, oil-like, while the impurities, whey, milk, and so forth, will remain in the bottom. Very gently and slowly, pour the clear butter into a container, leaving the residue behind and, when butter is cold, store in the refrigerator.

COCKTAIL SAUCE I [1031]

Combine and mix well, ¾ cup of chili sauce, 2 tablespoons of drained, prepared horseradish, 2 teaspoons of lemon juice, salt and pepper to taste, also a few grains of cayenne, mixed with ½ generous teaspoon of Worcestershire sauce. Chill thoroughly before using. Keeps weeks in a good refrigerator. Appropriate for almost any kind of cooked or uncooked sea food.

COCKTAIL SAUCE II [1032]

Combine and mix thoroughly, 1 cup of tomato catsup, ¼ cup of chili sauce, 1½ tablespoons of lemon juice, 1 generous teaspoon of cider vinegar, ¼ cup of freshly grated horseradish, a few drops of Tabasco sauce, 1 tablespoon of prepared mustard, salt and black pepper to taste, 2 teaspoons of crushed celery seeds, and ½ scant teaspoon of anchovy paste. Chill and shake well before serving in individual small cocktail sauce glasses into which each guest "dunks" small pieces of sea foods, cooked or raw, lobster oysters, clams, and the like. Especially suitable for "dunking" for cold sea food parties at the beach, at clambakes, and so forth.

COCKTAIL SAUCE III   [1033]

Combine and mix well the following ingredients: ½ cup of tomato catsup, 2 tablespoons of chili sauce, 1 tablespoon of drained prepared horseradish, 1 tablespoon of Worcestershire sauce, 2 tablespoons of lemon juice, a few drops of Tabasco sauce, ½ cup of mayonnaise, salt and pepper to taste, 1 teaspoon of curry powder, and ¼ cup of heavy sweet cream, whipped stiff, with a little crushed celery seed. Chill thoroughly before using. Especially appropriate for shellfish and crustaceans.

COCOANUT MILK   [1034]
Used in making a real curry sauce

Heat 1 quart of milk, add the meat of a grated fresh cocoanut and allow mixture to cool for 2 hours, covered. Strain before using.

COURT BOUILLON I RED WINE   [1035]
Short Broth for Fish

Combine the following ingredients in a fish kettle, add the fish and cook until it is tender: 2 quarts of cold water, ¾ cup of red wine, salt to taste, 2 small carrots, scraped and sliced, 2 small onions, peeled then sliced thin, 1 bouquet garni composed of 1 large bay leaf, 8 sprigs of fresh parsley, 1 sprig of thyme and 2 whole cloves all tied together with white kitchen thread, ½ teaspoon of peppercorns, slightly bruised. Bring to a boil, let simmer gently for a few minutes; again bring to a boil; add the fish; lower the heat and simmer or "poach" gently until fish is done. Appropriate to cook almost any kind of trout, eel, pike, pickerel, and so forth.

COURT BOUILLON II VINEGAR   [1036]
Short Broth for Fish

Proceed as indicated for Court-Bouillon I (Red Wine, No. 1035) substituting vinegar for red wine.

COURT BOUILLON III WHITE WINE   [1037]
Short Broth for Fish

Proceed as indicated for Court-Bouillon I (Red Wine, No. 1035), substituting dry white wine for red wine.

CREAM GRAVY COUNTRY STYLE [1038]

To the butter and juices in the frying pan in which chicken has been fried, add 1½ cups or sweet, scalded heavy cream; let this boil steadily for 2 or 3 minutes, taste for seasoning, and, if desired, thicken with a little flour in the usual way. Reheat the chicken in it and serve at once. Appropriate for Fried Chicken or other birds.

CREAM SAUCE [1039]

See "SOUPS" (No. 258)

CURRANT JELLY GRAVY [1040]

To each cup of brown gravy (No. 1019) add ¼ cup of red currant jelly. Pour over meat, heat through without letting boil. Serve at once. Appropriate for any kind of cold roasted meat left-over.

CREOLE SAUCE I NEW ORLEANS STYLE [1041]

Heat ⅓ cup of butter or margarin; stir in 1 cup of thinly sliced onions, 2 thinly sliced green peppers, previously parboiled and skinned, white seeds and pith removed; cook about 5 minutes, over a gentle heat, stirring frequently. Cover, and simmer 5 minutes longer, shaking the pan occasionally. Then add 1 No. 2 can of tomatoes, liquid and solid, with 12 stoned, sliced green olives, 1 cup of fresh mushrooms, peeled, thinly sliced, using both stems and caps, 1 bouquet garni composed of 1 large bay leaf, tied with kitchen thread with 12 sprigs of fresh parsley and 1 sprig of thyme, 2 whole cloves, a slice or two of garlic, salt and pepper to taste, and cook, covered for about 25 minutes, over a gentle heat, stirring occasionally. Discard the bouquet garni, taste for seasoning and serve as hot as possible either separately or over the food, according to directions in the recipe. Very good as an omelet filling. Appropriate for almost any kind of cooked meat, left-over meats, fish, poultry, game, alimentary pastes, rice, eggs, and even vegetables.

CREOLE SAUCE WEST INDIES STYLE II [1042]

Same uses as Creole Sauce (No. 1041).

Cover 2 thinly sliced green pepper and 1 extra large, thinly sliced onion with cold water; bring to a boil, let boil 5 minutes, then simmer gently for 5 minutes longer. Meanwhile saute in 2 tablespoons of butter, ½ cup of peeled, thinly sliced fresh mushrooms also 12 black olives, pitted and sliced, for 3 or 4 minutes. Strain the green pepper and onions and stir into the mushrooms, together with 1 pound of peeled, sliced, fresh ripe tomatoes. Add 1 large bay leaf, a good pinch of thyme, a dash of sage, one of nutmeg, and ½ cup of good chicken stock. Season to taste with salt and pepper; cover and simmer gently for 25–30 minutes, stirring frequently.

CUMBERLAND SAUCE I   [1043]
(*Cold*)

Melt 3 tablespoons of red currant jelly. Cool, then add 1 tablespoon of red or white wine, 2 tablespoons of orange juice, 1 scant teaspoon of prepared mild mustard, 1 scant teaspoon of paprika, ½ teaspoon of ground ginger, and 1½ tablespoons each of shredded lemon and orange peel. (The orange and lemon peel should first be covered with cold water, brought to a rapid boil, drained, then cooled before being added to the mixture. Serve very cold. Appropriate for any kind of cold cooked ham, duck, game, tongue, and so forth.

CUMBERLAND SAUCE II   [1044]
(*Hot*)

After the meat or bird is done, remove it from the pan. To the juice in the pan add 2 tablespoons of flour, blend well and let simmer gently to a nice light brown. Stir in ¼ cup of good red port wine, 1 tablespoon each of orange and lemon rind, cut julienne-fashion, like match sticks, and 3 tablespoons of red currant jelly, mixed with a little prepared mustard. Bring to a boil, and at once strain through a fine sieve. Skim out the orange and lemon; wash quickly under running hot water, and return to the sauce. Serve hot. Appropriate for goose, duck, guinea hen, game birds, ham, tongue, and almost any kind of smoked meat.

CURRY SAUCE I INDIA STYLE   [1045]

Heat in a saucepan 3 tablespoons of olive oil, and stir in 1 rounded (more or less, according to taste) tablespoon of curry powder, and 1 finely chopped clove of garlic; then add 2 good-sized grated—not chopped—Spanish onions with their juice, and allow the mixture to reduce over a gentle flame until nearly dry. Put through the food chopper 8 cleaned, washed chicken livers, and stir into the curry mixture, alternately with 3 cups of rich beef stock, mixed with 1½ cups of tomato purée. Season with ½ teaspoon of Worcestershire sauce, 2 tablespoons of Bengal chutney, ½ cup of freshly grated coconut with its milk, and bring the mixture to a boil, stirring occasionally. Reduce the heat and let simmer gently for ¾ of an hour, or until mixture is reduced to half, stirring occasionally, then season to taste with salt, a dash of cayenne and the juice of a small lemon or lime. Appropriate for any kind of cooked fish or shellfish, meats, poultry, game, and rice as well as certain vegetables, like tomatoes.

CURRY SAUCE II HOME STYLE [1046]

(Same uses as for Curry Sauce I.)
To 1 cup of Cream Sauce (No. 258), add 2 teaspoons of curry powder, mixed with ¼ teaspoon of grated or ground ginger, mix thoroughly, and boil a few minutes. Season highly to taste with a little onion juice and paprika.

CURRY SAUCE III HOME STYLE [1047]

To 1 cup of Brown Sauce (No. 1019), add 2 teaspoons of curry powder mixed with ¼ teaspoon of ground ginger; season highly with a little cayenne pepper.

DEMI-GLACE SAUCE SHORT STYLE [1048]

If the meat or fowl, or game, for which this sauce is intended has been braised or roasted, strain the gravy or juice and remove all fat very carefully. Place the gravy or juice in a saucepan, and for each cup, add 1 cup of Spanish sauce (No. 1127), ⅓ cup of dry white wine and 4 table-spoons of tomato purée. Bring to a boil; let boil over a bright heat until reduced to half, correct the seasoning and add whatever kind of sauce is indicated in the recipe, with as much as indicated of meat extract (commercial).

DEVILED SAUCE [1049]
Sauce Diable

Place in a small saucepan, 1 shallot, minced very fine, and 1 table-spoon of vinegar. Allow this to reduce to half, over a hot fire. Then add, 1 scant cup of good meat stock, 2 tablespoons of tomato paste, 1 whole clove, head removed, and cook for 10 long minutes. Meanwhile, mix on a plate or saucer, 1 tablespoon (scant) of flour, as much butter, and a few grains of cayenne pepper to taste, and add to the sauce. Heat well without letting boil, stirring occasionally.

DRAWN BUTTER SAUCE [1050]

Melt 3 tablespoons of butter and blend in 3 tablespoons of flour; season to taste with salt and pepper, and gradually add 1½ cups of fish or vegetable stock, stirring constantly. Let boil gently for 5 minutes, then add bit by bit 3 tablespoons of butter, still stirring gently, alternately with 1 teaspoon of strained lemon juice. Appropriate for any kind of boiled, broiled or baked fish and vegetable.

EGG SAUCE I FRENCH STYLE   [1051]

To 1 cup of Drawn Butter (No. 1050), add 2 hard-cooked eggs, chopped, and 1 teaspoon of finely chopped parslcy. Appropriate for any kind of boiled fish.

EGG SAUCE II AMERICAN STYLE   [1052]

Same use as Egg Sauce No. 1051.
To 1 cup of White or Cream Sauce (No. 258 and 259, respectively), add 2 hard-cooked, chopped eggs.

EPICURE COCKTAIL SAUCE   [1053]

See "Melon Ball Cocktail Epicure" under Hors d'Oeuvres (No. 68).

FISH ASPIC   [1054]

See Lobster Bellevue (No. 473).

FISHERMAN'S FISH COCKTAIL   [105 5]

See Raw Fish Cocktail (No. 72).

FRYING BATTER I FOR FRITTERS   [1056]

Mix, in order given, in a bowl, 1 cup of all-purpose flour, sifted with 1/4 teaspoon of salt and a few grains of white pepper. Combine 2 well-beaten eggs with 2/3 cup of cold milk, and gradually stir into the flour mixture until smooth. Finally stir in 1 tablespoon of olive oil, or good cooking oil. Appropriate for any kind of food to be batter coated and fried.

FRYING BATTER II FOR FRITTERS   [1057]

Same uses as for No. 1056.
Proceed as indicated above, separating the eggs, and folding the stiffly beaten egg whites into the thoroughly blended mixture just before using.

FRYING BATTER III [1058]

Same uses as for No. 1056.
See Fritto Misto No. 57

FRYING BATTER IV FRENCH STYLE [1059]

Same uses as No. 1056.
Blend 4 tablespoons of flour and 2 egg yolks, and enough beer to make a smooth batter which will coat the back of a spoon. Then add 2 teaspoons of olive oil. (Olive oil renders the batter more crisp than the usual melted butter). When thoroughly blended, stir in 2 stiffly beaten egg whites, folding them in gently but thoroughly. Season to taste with salt, pepper and a few grains of cayenne.

GIBLET GRAVY I OLD-FASHIONED STYLE [1060]

When putting the chicken, duck, goose, or turkey in to roast, put the neck, heart, liver and gizzard (called giblets) into a saucepan with 1 pint of water; add 1 small bay leaf tied with 6 sprigs of parsley and 1 sprig of thyme, salt, pepper to taste, and simmer until the giblets are quite tender; drain, reserving the broth, and chop the heart and gizzard, mash the liver, and discard the neck; return chopped mixture to the broth in which it was cooked, and let simmer very gently. When turkey or chicken or duck, and so forth is done, pour off liquid in roasting pan in which the bird has been roasted; skim from that liquid 4 tablespoons of fat; return to the pan and brown with 4 tablespoons of flour, stirring constantly; gradually add the strained giblet stock, stirring constantly, until thickened; season to taste with salt and pepper, then add the chopped giblets. Simmer gently for 5 minutes and serve hot in a sauceboat. Appropriate for roasted poultry of any kind.

GIBLET GRAVY II MODERN STYLE [1061]

Same use as No. 1060.
Clean the giblets, wash, then cut in small pieces; cover with 2 cups of boiling water, or still better, 1 cup of boiling water and 1 cup of Pique Seasoning, add 1 small carrot, chopped, 1 small onion, chopped, 1 bay leaf, 1 whole clove, a very little salt, (if any) and 3 peppercorns, crushed. Cook until giblets are tender, adding more liquid as it evaporates. Then proceed as indicated for Giblet Gravy I.

HOLLANDAISE SAUCE I [1062]

That aristocrat of sauces—Hollandaise—is an aim and ambition of every cook. To be able to make this smooth, velvety, stimulating sauce perfectly, is the crowning glory of his or her success as a culinary artist. Even the simplest and humblest of vegetables takes on a proud company air when served with Hollandaise. It is one of the easiest sauces to make if the proper recipe is followed. Too often, however, it is made unsuccessfully, although more pains than are necessary are taken in its production. Many recipes for Hollandaise sauce call for washing the butter. Contrary to general opinion this has no effect on the texture of the sauce. These directions originally were put into American recipes for this essentially French sauce—notwithstanding its Hollandish name—in the interest of flavor. Unsalted butter is commonly used in French cuisine and produces a sauce with a delicate bland flavor. In this country, however, a little salt in the sauce is generally liked. Why take salt out and then put it back? Appropriate for fish, Shellfish, Poultry, Eggs, Asparagus, Artichoke, Cauliflower, and so forth.

The Recipe. Divide ½ cup of butter (sweet or salt) into three parts. Put the first part in top of double boiler with 2 egg yolks and 1 teaspoon of vinegar or lemon juice, and stir with a wire whisk until the butter is melted. Add the second part of the butter, and, as the mixture thickens, the third part. When the butter has melted, and the whole is well mixed, add gradually ⅓ cup of boiling water, continuing to whisk constantly. Cook in the double boiler, over *hot*, not *boiling* water for a minute or two longer. Then, and only then, season to taste with salt and white pepper.

Should the mixture curdle, beat in another 2 tablespoons of boiling water or, better still, 2 tablespoons of heavy sweet cream.

You may prefer a simplified version of Hollandaise such as the following recipe.

HOLLANDAISE (MOCK) SAUCE II   [1063]

Same uses as Hollandaise No. 1062.

Melt 2 tablespoons of butter; blend well with 2 tablespoons of flour, then moisten gradually with ¾ cup of scalded rich milk, and season to taste with salt and white pepper, stirring constantly, until mixture just begins to boil; remove from the fire, and stir in 3 egg yolks, adding one at a time and beating well after each addition, alternately with ½ cup of sweet or salt butter, added also bit by bit. Lastly, stir in 1 tablespoon of strained lemon juice or mild vinegar.

HOLLANDAISE SAUCE SUPRÊME III   [1064]

Same uses as for Hollandaise Nos. 1062 and 1063.
See "Trout Boulevardier" (No. 543) under Fish and Shellfish.

HORSERADISH CREAM COCKTAIL SAUCE [1065]

See Mussel Cocktail (No. 69).
Appropriate for almost any kind of shellfish or crustaceans.

HUNTER SAUCE [1066]
Sauce Chasseur

Sauté in 2 tablespoons of butter, ¼ lb. fresh mushrooms, peeled and sliced, using both caps and stems, with 1 tablespoon of shallot, minced fine, for 3 minutes, stirring constantly but gently, using a wooden spoon. Pour in 1 cup of good white wine, stir, and allow to reduce to half volume. Then add ½ cup of good tomato sauce (No. 1130) and ½ cup of Spanish sauce (No. 1127). Bring slowly to a boil, and let simmer for 5 minutes. Just before serving, add 2 scant tablespoons of butter, 1 teaspoon of chervil, minced fine, and 2 leaves of fresh tarragon, also chopped fine. Suitable for any kind of meat, poultry or furred game.

JARDINIERE SAUCE [1067]

To 1 cup of Brown Sauce (No. 1017) add ⅓ cup of cooked, mixed vegetables, cubed very small, and 1 teaspoon each of finely chopped parsley, chives and chervil. Serve very hot. Appropriate for any kind of boiled fresh or smoked meats.

LAGUIPIERE SAUCE BOURGEOISE STYLE [1068]
(Short Cut)

Place on a hot fire a saucepan containing 2 cups of White Wine Court-Bouillon (No. 1037) and reduce to half volume. This being done, add commercial meat extract the size of a walnut, stirring until melted; thicken with a little flour mixed with a little butter; taste for seasoning, let boil 2 or 3 minutes and serve immediately. This is a fine sauce for almost any kind of boiled fish.

LAPEROUSE SAUCE [1069]

Put into a small saucepan 1 tablespoon of red wine vinegar, 2 teaspoons of finely chopped shallots, 1 cup of dry white wine, 2 whole peppercorns, crushed, a very small piece of bay leaf and 2 or 3 sprigs of fresh parsley. Bring to a boil and let boil over a bright flame until reduced to half, then stir in 2 tablespoons of good commercial meat extract; let simmer for 15 minutes before straining through a fine sieve into a saucepan. Taste for seasoning and pour the sauce over a freshly grilled steak, and dust with finely chopped chervil or parsley and serve at once. Especially suitable for grilled club, sirloin or porterhouse steaks.

LEMON BUTTER SAUCE AMERICAN STYLE   [1070]

Brown ½ cup of butter; add 3 tablespoons of lemon juice and ½ teaspoon of Worcestershire sauce. Sprinkle the steak with finely chopped parsley, chives or chervil and pour the hot butter over the steak. Serve immediately. Appropriate for any kind of broiled steak.

LOBSTER SAUCE   [1071]

To 1 cup of Hollandaise sauce (No. 1062), add ⅓ cup of cooked lobster meat cut into small cubes. Appropriate for boiled or grilled fish.

LOUISE SAUCE   [1072]

This sauce enhances the rather bland flavor of any kind of cooked pork.

Heat 2 tablespoons of butter; stir in 2 tablespoons of finely chopped onion, and cook until onion takes on color; then sprinkle in 1 tablespoon of flour; blend thoroughly, stirring constantly, then add 1 cup of rich beef stock obtained by reducing (over a hot flame) 2 cups of already rich beef bouillon to 1 cup. Boil up once; and, just when ready to serve, stir in 2 tablespoons of prepared mustard (more or less, according to taste). Taste for seasoning, and serve very hot.

LYONNAISE SAUCE   [1073]

Cook 3 medium-sized, finely chopped onions very slowly, until light yellow, in 3 tablespoons of butter; gradually stir in ½ cup of dry white wine, mixed with ½ cup of good vinegar, and let this reduce to ⅔ its original volume over a bright flame. Stir in 1 cup of thinly sliced well-drained small onion rings, previously cooked in butter until tender, but not browned. Taste for seasoning and serve very hot. Especially appropriate for pork cooked in any style.

MADEIRA WINE ASPIC COATING JELLY   [1074]

See Turkey Galantine à la Paderewski (No. 971).

MADEIRA MUSHROOM SAUCE   [1075]

To each cup of Madeira Wine Sauce, Home Style (No. 1076), add ⅓ cup of thinly sliced, peeled fresh mushrooms, cooked in a little butter and well drained.

MADEIRA WINE SAUCE HOME STYLE [1076]

Heat 1½ cups of rich brown sauce (No. 1018) to the boiling point. Should the sauce be thin, let reduce to one cup, over a bright flame, stirring frequently, and for each cup of brown sauce, add ¼ cup of good Madeira wine Do not boil after the wine is added. Appropriate for almost any kind of braised, roasted, or baked meat or fowl. Especially fine for smoked meat.

MALTAISE SAUCE [1077]
(Warm)

To each cup of Hollandaise sauce (No. 1062) or Mock Hollandaise sauce (No. 1063), add, just when ready to serve, the juice of a small blood orange, strained, and 1 teaspoon of grated rind of the orange. Serve warm over the very hot vegetable. Especially suitable for asparagus, artichoke, broccoli, cauliflower and so forth.

MAÎTRE D'HÔTEL BUTTER [1078]

This French butter, erroneously called by certain amateur cooks "Parsley Butter," is appropriate for any kind of pan-fried, grilled or baked meat, fish, poultry, game and vegetables. It may be prepared in advance and kept in the refrigerator until wanted.

Work ½ cup of butter with a wooden spoon until light and fluffy; then work in 2 teaspoons each of lemon juice and finely chopped parsley or chervil, seasoning to taste with salt and white pepper as you work.

Variation. The addition of a little prepared mustard is greatly recommended by professional chefs.

MARCHAND DE VIN SAUCE [1079]
BOURGEOISE STYLE
Wine Dealer Sauce

Put into a saucepan 2 cups of good red wine, the best you can get, with 1 tablespoon of finely chopped shallots, 1 teaspoon of finely chopped chives, 1 small bouquet garni composed of a piece of bay leaf tied with 4 or 5 sprigs of fresh parsley, a small sprig of thyme and 2 whole cloves. Add also a tiny pinch of allspice, 5 or 6 whole peppercorns, gently bruised, and a generous slice of garlic, crushed. Place over a hot flame and bring to a boil, then boil steadily until liquid is reduced to half, stirring occasionally. Add ¾ cup of rich brown sauce (No. 1018), meat extract (commercial) the size of a small walnut, and let simmer for 15 to 20 minutes, over a gentle flame, stirring occasionally, and frequently skimming off any fat rising to the surface of the sauce. Strain through a fine muslin cloth or fine-meshed wire sieve into a saucepan; taste for seasoning, and when ready to serve stir in, ⅓ cup of poached beef marrow, cut into small cubes and well drained, also 1 scant teaspoon of finely chopped chervil or parsley. Serve sizzling hot. Appropriate for pan-fried steaks, broiled large steaks, filet of beef, filet mignon, and large roasted pieces of beef.

MARGUERY SAUCE HOME METHOD   [1080]

Over a hot fire reduce to 3 tablespoons 1 cup of White Wine Court-Bouillon, (No. 1037) or Short Broth, in which the fish filets have been poached. Strain through a fine sieve. There should not be more than 3 tablespoons of broth. Place in top of double boiler, add 2 generous tablespoons of the strained court-bouillon and ¼ pound of sweet butter. Cook over hot water, stirring until butter is blended, having the water just warm enough to create a gentle steam. Then beat in 4 egg yolks, adding one at a time, and beating well after each addition, until the sauce thickens, and is about the consistency of medium cream sauce. Taste for seasoning, and pour over the cooked fish filets, these being arranged side by side in a fireproof baking dish and garnished with 12 small poached oysters, 12 cooked fresh shrimps, and sprinkled with finely chopped chervil or parsley. Place the dish in a hot oven (400° F.) until glazed and lightly browned. Serve at once. Appropriate for poached or baked fish filets, as sole, flounder, filets.
Note. Instead of oysters you may substitute, as the original recipe calls for, 12 cooked mussels.

MARINADES   [1081]

The word *marinate* comes from an old Spanish word meaning "to pickle" and it is the acid of the marinade that does the work, adding new flavor; softening tough fibers; increasing their natural sapidity through the action of penetration; lifting ordinary foods out of the commonplace and, in most cases, ensuring their preservation. There are several kinds of marinades such as:

MARINADE I—LIGHT MARINADE   [1082]

A light marinade commonly used for small fish, meats, game, poultry, vegetables, and so forth which is also called "Instantaneous Marinade." It may be plain and consist only of lemon juice or vinegar, mixed with a little oil, and a few spices and seasonings.

Ingredients for a Light Marinade.

1 small lemon, sliced thin	2 small bay leaves
1 small raw carrot, sliced thin	2 or 3 whole cloves, slightly bruised
1 tablespoon of vinegar	2 or 3 sprigs of parsley
1 tablespoon of oil	8 to 10 peppercorns, crushed
1 sprig of thyme or thyme leaves	Salt to taste

All the above ingredients are placed in a flat-bottomed dish, preferably an earthenware one, then the meat, fish, bird, game or vegetables is placed in it, gently stirred once in a while and turned often. The food should always be completely subjected to the marinade, lest the action of the air decompose the exposed part, so add more ingredients accordingly. Keep in a cool place and let marinate for an hour or so.

MARINADE II—ORDINARY MARINADE   [1083]

This kind of marinade may be hot or cold, according to indications, but it is more often made hot and for the same kind of meat, fish or game as indicated for Marinade I, above. The ingredients are almost the same as for Light Marinade, and are prepared in the same way, except that they are heated up, nearly cooked, then poured over the food to be marinated.

MARINADE III—HEAVY MARINADE   [1084]

This type of marinade is intended for large pieces of meat or game, seldom for fish. It may be used hot or cold according to indications in the recipe. Included in it are additional aromatic herbs, such as rosemary, sarriette, sweet basil, salt mace and sage. The directions are the same as for Marinade I—Light Marinade and Marinade II—Ordinary Marinade, except that the proportions are larger,(according to the size of the piece of meat) and if the meat is to remain several days in the marinade, the vinegar is less in proportion to the other liquids; if of short duration the vinegar is equal or thereabouts. Keep in a cool place, covered with cheesecloth.

MEUNIERE BUTTER   [1085]

This butter is always prepared when ready to serve and cannot be reheated. The amount depends on the surface of food to be covered, so here the cook must use good judgment.

Melt, for say 4 fish filets, $\frac{1}{3}$ cup of butter and heat until foamy and brown; while still very hot, stir in 1 teaspoon of lemon juice and pour at once over the fish which has been sprinkled with finely chopped chervil or parsley. Serve immediately. Special for brains, fish filets, eggs, sweetbreads, and certain vegetables.

MINT SAUCE I   [1086]
(Original Recipe)

Simmer very gently 1 cup of hot water with ¼ cup of finely chopped fresh mint leaves until mixture is reduced to half its original volume. Remove from the fire and strain through a fine muslin cloth placed over a strainer, into a saucepan or a bowl; stir in ¼ cup of boiling water and ¼ cup of strained lemon juice, 2 tablespoons of sugar and ½ teaspoon of salt. Chill thoroughly, then add ¼ cup of freshly chopped mint leaves. Blend well and serve cold or lukewarm. Appropriate for lamb and mutton cooked in any style.

MINT SAUCE II AMERICAN STYLE   [1087]
Same use as Mint Sauce No. I

Simmer ½ cup of cider vinegar with 1 cup of water and ⅓ cup of finely chopped fresh mint leaves until reduced to half its original volume. Strain into a bowl through a wet cloth placed over a strainer, add ½ cup of cold water mixed with ¼ cup of strained lemon juice, 2 tablespoons of sugar and a few grains of salt with cayenne pepper to taste. Serve cold or lukewarm.

MORNAY SAUCE   [1088]

Appropriate for almost any kind of fish, shellfish, crustaceans, eggs, asparagus, artichoke bottoms, broccoli, cauliflower, and so forth.

To each cup of Cream Sauce (No. 258) or Hot Béchamel Sauce (No. 259) add ¾ scant cup of dry white wine and let this reduce to ⅓ its volume over a bright flame, stirring frequently. Then stir in 2 tablespoons of your favorite grated cheese or equal parts of two different kinds. When ready to use, blend in 1 tablespoon of sweet butter and taste for seasoning. *Home Style.* Simply add ⅓ cup of grated cheese to each cup of cream sauce and stir until the cheese is melted. It is merely a cheese sauce.

When using Mornay Sauce (1088) to top a dish to be made au gratin, it is usually, in the French cuisine, considered improved if a tablespoon or two of whipped cream is folded into each half cup of Mornay Sauce before spreading over top of fish or other main ingredient. The top then takes on an even golden brown glaze.

CAUTION. This sauce cannot be boiled when it is made, lest it curdle, so, if for any reason it has to stand, keep it over hot, never boiling, water. This applies to any sauce containing eggs.

MOUSSELINE SAUCE [1089]
(*Warm*)

To each cup of Hollandaise Sauce (No. 1062) add, when ready to serve, 1/4 generous cup of whipped cream, and serve at once. Appropriate for boiled fish, eggs, asparagus, broccoli, artichoke, cauliflower, cardamon, celery, and so forth.

Note. This sauce like many butter sauces cannot be served very hot, but the food to which it accompanies should be very hot.

MUSHROOM SAUCE HOME STYLE [1090]

Reduce to 2/3 its original volume 1 cup of mushroom stock (No. 1091). Add 2/3 cup of Brown Sauce (No. 1018) and simmer very gently for 5 minutes. Strain through a fine sieve, into a saucepan; season to taste with salt and pepper, and when ready to serve, stir in 1/3 cup of canned, drained button mushrooms or 1/3 cup of peeled, thinly sliced fresh mushrooms cooked in a little butter until tender, then well drained.

Note. A couple of tablespoons of sherry or madeira wine added to this sauce will not be amiss. Appropriate for poultry, any kind of roasted meat and game, eggs, and especially smoked meat.

MUSHROOM STOCK [1091]
Very useful to flavor soups, sauces and gravies

Quickly wash, drain and dry 2 cups of mushroom trimmings, including the peelings, stems, or parts too tough to be used otherwise. Put through food chopper, and place in a saucepan together with 1 small bouquet garni composed of 1 small bay leaf, 5 sprigs of fresh parsley, 1 small sprig of thyme and 1 whole clove, all tied together with kitchen thread, 2 cups of cold beef stock 4 thin slices of onion, and 1 thin slice of garlic. Do not season as yet. Gradually bring to a boil, and boil steadily until liquid is reduced to half its original volume. Strain through a fine-meshed sieve into a hot, sterilized jar, and when cold, seal and store in refrigerator until needed, or use at once. This stock, which should never be salted nor peppered will keep several weeks in a good refrigerator and affords an opportunity of using all the left-overs and trimmings of fresh mushrooms.

MUSTARD SAUCE I [1092]

Important. If this sauce is not served at once, keep over hot water, but do not boil, lest it curdle. This applies to any sauce to which mustard or eggs are added.

To each cup of Drawn Butter Sauce (No. 1050), add, just before serving, 1 tablespoon of prepared mustard and blend thoroughly. Serve at once.

MUSTARD SAUCE II [1093]

To each cup of Hot Cream sauce, (No. 258), add, just before serving 1 tablespoon of prepared mustard. Mix well, heat thoroughly, but do not allow to boil. Serve at once or keep hot over hot water.

NANTUA SAUCE [1094]

To each cup of Hot Béchamel Sauce (No. 259) add ¼ cup of scalded heavy cream; blend well, then strain through a fine sieve. When ready to serve, taste for seasoning and stir in 2 tablespoons of Crayfish Butter (No. 985) and 2 tablespoons of finely chopped, cooked crayfish. Appropriate for any kind of fish, crustacean, or shellfish cooked in any style.

French under-cooks assigned to the tearful job of grating fresh horseradish for the sauces are afterwards excused from the kitchen for 24 hours to finish their weeping.

NEWBURG SAUCE [1095]

Newburg dishes, such as fish, lobster, shrimp, crayfish or crabmeat, are merely reheats—all heated up in a Newburg sauce. This popular sauce is 100 per cent French, although its name is American. The French chef of the old Delmonico's in New York was the one who originally conceived this culinary creation. The name of the town up on the Hudson River had no connection whatsoever with this sauce. Delmonico's wanted to honor one of its best cash customers, by the name of Wenburg, and named this sauce in his honor. Mr. Wenburg accepted only on condition that the three letters of the first syllable of his name be reversed—hence Newburg.

The original recipe was first intended for lobster, but like many others, this sauce may be used for almost any kind of reheated food, including fish, meats, eggs, game, and vegetables.

Here is the original recipe as prepared by its creator, French Chef Pascal of the Old Delmonico's.

Cut a live lobster into small pieces and sauté it in 2 generous tablespoons of sweet butter. Remove the lobster to a hot platter and keep hot. To the butter and lobster juices remaining in the pan, add 2 tablespoons of sherry wine, and scrape and stir at the same time, from bottom and sides of the frying pan, so as to remove all the gelatinous particles which may adhere (the French culinary term for this procedure is called "deglacé"). Then, slowly, stir in 1 cup of hot, sweet, heavy cream, blending thoroughly. Let this simmer very gently for 15 minutes; strain through a fine sieve into a saucepan; return to a gentle flame, and allow the sauce to reduce to half its original volume, stirring occasionally; then stir in ½ cup of hot Béchamel sauce (No. 259). Boil up once or twice, taste for seasoning and stir in the cooked lobster coral, then, when thoroughly blended, the lobster pieces (or any other kind of cooked fish, meat, eggs and so forth) alternately with 4 tablespoons of Hollandaise sauce (No. 1062). Serve at once, as this sauce cannot wait, and does not keep long. For a dish supreme, add 1 generous tablespoon of finely chopped black truffles.

OLIVE SAUCE I [1096]

Stone 2 dozen small green olives; cover with fish stock (No. 182) or with fish stock made from fish trimmings in the usual way, and cook 5 minutes. Drain and add the olives to 1 generous cup of Drawn Butter Sauce No. 1050). Heat well and when ready to serve, stir in 1 tablespoon of finely chopped parsley. Especially appropriate for boiled fish and fish filets.

OLIVE SAUCE II [1097]

Same uses as Olive Sauce No I (No. 1096).
To each cup of Hot Cream Sauce (No 258) or hot Béchamel Sauce (No. 259) add ⅓ cup of finely chopped ripe olives, 1 tablespoon of finely chopped parsley and ¼ teaspoon of finely chopped tarragon. Mix well and serve hot.

OYSTER COCKTAIL SAUCE [1098]

See Pickled Oyster Cocktail (No. 71).
The ancient Greeks considered the onion an object of worship, and its oil was used in anointing the heads of the religious. At festivals, onion plants were placed in the temples to prevent evil spirits from disturbing the worshippers. It was also used in the halls and fields where dances and games were held in honor of the gods.
In the home, an onion was hung over the front door during an epidemic so that no sickness could enter.

ONION SAUCE [1099]

Mince enough onions to make 1½ cups; place in a saucepan, and pour over enough sweet milk to cover; season to taste with salt, pepper and a generous grating of nutmeg, and add 1 small bay leaf and 1 whole clove. Cook onions until tender; drain thoroughly, pressing gently, then chop them again and combine with 1 cup of cream sauce, made as indicated for recipe No. 258, but using the milk in which onions were cooked instead of plain milk. Bring to a quick boil, and simmer gently for 5 minutes, or until sauce is of the consistency of heavy cream. Taste for seasoning and serve at once. Appropriate for rabbit, fowl, tripe, boiled lamb or mutton, game, grilled steak, this sauce is usually poured over the food sizzling hot.

PARISIAN FISH FUMET [1100]

An indispensable mixture to enhance fish soups, fish sauces and any kind of fish preparations; easy to prepare, it keeps well in a good refrigerator.

For 1 pint of fish fumet (fish essence), place in a saucepan the trimmings, heads, and bones of about 1 lb. of fish; add 1 tablespoon of chopped onion, 6 sprigs of fresh parsley, 1 whole clove, 1 small bay leaf, a generous pinch of thyme leaves and one of freshly ground black pepper. Do not add any salt at all. Pour over 2 cups of dry white wine and 2 cups of fish stock (No. 182), or use cold water, if preferred or if fish stock is not available. Bring slowly to a boil; reduce the heat, and allow fumet to simmer very gently, to "smile," covered, until mixture is reduced to half its original volume. Strain through a fine-meshed wire sieve, pressing gently but thoroughly; season to taste with salt; pour into hot, sterilized jar; seal, and when cold, store in refrigerator until wanted.

PARSLEY SAUCE [1101]

To 1 cup of hot Béchamel Sauce (No. 259) or Cream Sauce (No. 258) add and blend thoroughly an infusion of 3 tablespoons of parsley leaves, strained; taste for seasoning, and just when ready to serve, stir in 2 tablespoons of finely chopped parsley and a few drops of lemon juice. For the parsley infusion, proceed as if making tea. Especially appropriate for almost any kind of fish cooked in any style.

PICKLED SAUCE [1102]

See "Braised Fresh Beef Tongue" (No. 848).

PIQUANTE SAUCE FRENCH STYLE [1103]

Place in a small saucepan 1 scant cup of dry white wine, ¼ cup of wine vinegar and 1 generous tablespoon of finely chopped shallots; let this reduce to half its original volume, over a bright flame; then stir in ¾ cup of Spanish sauce (No. 1127), and again let this reduce to a scant cupful; season with salt and pepper to taste, then stir in, off the fire, 2 tablespoons of thinly sliced small French gherkins (cornichons), 1 teaspoon each of finely chopped parsley and chervil, and a good ¼ teaspoon of finely chopped tarragon. Serve on the side or use over reheated leftover cooked meat. This sauce needs plenty of freshly ground black pepper. Appropriate for pork cooked in any style, also smoked meats and game. Also used for reheated left-over meat as lamb, beef, mutton, veal, and boiled beef, corned beef, and so forth.

POIVRADE SAUCE FRENCH STYLE [1104]

Heat 2 generous tablespoons of olive oil; add 2 tablespoons of finely chopped raw carrots, 3 tablespoons of chopped onions, 1½ tablespoons each of celery and leeks, both finely chopped, add 1 bouquet garni composed of 1 piece of bay leaf, 1 small sprig of thyme and 6 sprigs of fresh parsley, all tied together with white kitchen thread, and finally ⅓ cup of chopped, cooked, left-over ham or meat trimmings. Cook over a medium flame until delicately browned, stirring frequently, almost constantly. Drain off all the oil, then add 1 tablespoon of vinegar and ½ cup of dry white wine. Bring to a boil, and let boil steadily, until the liquid is completely evaporated, stirring frequently, but do not burn or scorch. Now stir into this dry mixture 1 cup of Spanish Sauce (No. 1127) and gradually bring to a boil. Let boil steadily for a minute or two, stirring constantly, then stir in ½ scant cup of the marinade used for the meat (strained). Cover, let simmer very gently for about 35 to 40 minutes or until the mixture is reduced to half. Strain into a saucepan, place over hot water, and add 6 whole peppercorns, freshly and coarsely ground. Then strain through a fine sieve, and serve as hot as possible. Appropriate for any kind of dark meat and marinated furred game.

PORT WINE ASPIC COATING JELLY [1105]

Proceed as indicated for recipe for Sherry Aspic Coating Jelly (No. 82), substituting Port Wine for Sherry Wine.

POULETTE SAUCE [1106]

This slightly tart cream sauce may be used with almost any kind of fish, eggs, meat, game, poultry or vegetable. The liquid used to moisten the blended butter and flour mixture should always correspond to the kind of food for which this sauce is intended. For instance, if for fish, use equal parts of fish stock and milk; if for poultry, use equal parts of poultry stock and milk, and so on, but never pure milk alone.

Blend in a small saucepan, until mixture begins to bubble, but do not permit to color, 2 tablespoons each of butter and flour, stirring constantly; gradually stir in 1 cup each of blended scalded milk and stock, stirring constantly, till mixture thickens. Continue cooking for 10 minutes longer, over a low flame, stirring occasionally. Remove from the fire and add 3 egg yolks, one at a time, stirring well after each addition and from the bottom of the pan. Return to the fire, cook 5 minutes longer, stirring constantly; again remove from the fire and stir in 2 tablespoons of strained lemon juice. Strain through a fine-meshed sieve into a saucepan. Taste for seasoning, and just before using, stir in 2 teaspoons of finely chopped parsley.

PRUNE SAUCE [1107]

See Ham Tenderloin, Prune Sauce (No. 751).
Appropriate for any kind of smoked meat.

RAISIN SAUCE or SAUCE Ā LA ROMAINE [1108]

Blend 1 tablespoon of butter with 1¾ tablespoons of flour over a low flame, until mixture bubbles and takes on a light brown color, stirring almost constantly. Gradually stir in ¾ cup of rich beef stock (stock made rich by reducing 1½ cups of stock over a bright flame to half its original volume). After mixture reaches boiling point, boil steadily, but gently, for 5 minutes, stirring frequently. Meantime, reduce 4 tablespoons of vinegar to half, together with 1 bit of bay leaf, tied with 4 sprigs of fresh parsley, 1 whole clove, 1 sprig of tarragon and 1 bit of thyme, and 4 or 5 peppercorns, freshly and coarsely crushed. When there are only 2 tablespoons of the vinegar left in the pan, stir in 1 tablespoon of tomato paste. Add this to the first mixture, mix well and simmer for 10 to 12 minutes, skim well; strain through a fine sieve into a saucepan, taste for seasoning, then add ⅓ cup of seedless raisins, washed, plumped in boiling water and well drained. Just before serving, stir in ¼ of a teaspoon of sugar. This is the original recipe created in Italy, hence its name "Sauce Romaine." Appropriate for almost any kind of smoked meat and game.

RAVIGOTE SAUCE [1109]
(*Lukewarm*)

The French word "Ravigote" is really well applied to this admirable sauce, the meaning of which is "to recover one's appetite, when applied to food." Especially appropriate for any kind of reheated food, as meat, fish, eggs, shellfish, poultry, and so forth.

Chop 2 shallots very fine; place in a small saucepan with 1 tablespoon of white wine vinegar, and let this reduce to half over a bright flame, stirring constantly; then stir in 1 tablespoon of tomato paste, previously diluted in 1 cup of good meat stock, bouillon or consommé. For fish, use fish stock (No. 182). Let all simmer gently for 10 minutes, then thicken with 1 scant teaspoon of flour, which has been moistened with a little cold meat stock or water, simmer 5 minutes longer, stirring occasionally; season to taste with salt and generously with black pepper. Remove from the fire; cool to lukewarm, then stir in 1 tablespoon each of finely minced parsley, chervil, capers, and ½ teaspoon each of finely minced tarragon and chives, then, lastly 1 teaspoon of prepared mustard. Blend well and serve lukewarm.

RED WINE SAUCE HOME STYLE I   [1110]

Brown in 2 tablespoons of butter 2 tablespoons each of chopped carrot, celery and onion, stirring frequently; add 1 small piece of bay leaf, a tiny pinch of thyme and stir in 1½ cups of red wine, and ½ generous cup of fish or meat stock, depending on the kind of food for which the sauce is intended; also a tiny slice of garlic. Cook over a bright flame until liquid is reduced to half. Then add 1 more cup of fish or meat stock, and let simmer 15 to 20 minutes. Strain through a fine cloth into a saucepan, and stir in 2 teaspoons of butter, creamed with 1 teaspoon of flour, and anchovy paste the size of a little pea. Boil up once, taste for seasoning and just before serving stir in 1 teaspoon of sweet butter. Appropriate for almost any kind of fresh or smoked meat, baked, roasted, and so forth, as well as for fish.

RED WINE SAUCE DAGOURET METHOD II   [1111]

Blend in a small saucepan 3 tablespoons of red currant jelly, together with 1 cup of stock made from the trimmings of lamb and mutton, in the usual manner also ¾ cup of red wine, 1 scant teaspoon of sugar and ¼ cup of Tomato Sauce (No. 1130), 1 bouquet garni composed of 1 large bay leaf tied with white kitchen thread with 1 sprig of thyme and 6 sprigs of fresh parsley. Place over a bright flame and reduce the liquid to half its original volume, stirring occasionally. Strain through a fine-meshed sieve into a saucepan, thicken with 1 teaspoon of butter creamed with 1 teaspoon of flour, and simmer gently for 5 minutes. Taste for seasoning, and when ready to serve, stir in 2 teaspoons of strained lemon juice and 1 teaspoon of finely chopped chervil or parsley. Appropriate for venison and especially well-seasoned (aged) mutton.

REMICK SAUCE   [1112]

(See Crabmeat Remick No. 51.)
This sauce, which is a variation of Mayonnaise, was originally intended for crab meat, but may also be used with almost any kind of

cooked meat, fish, game, poultry and game as well as cooked vegetables. Very appropriate for Hors d'Oeuvres.

ROCHELAISE SAUCE [1113]

To 1 cup of Egg Sauce (No. 1051 or No. 1052), add, when ready to serve, 6 small oysters, parboiled in their own liquor till edges curl, then halved; also 1 tablespoon of Anchovy Butter (No. 979), with 1 teaspoon each of chopped parsley and chives. Appropriate for any kind of boiled white-fleshed fish.

ROUX [1114]

This is not a sauce, but a mixture of butter and flour used as the foundation of sauces, soups, and so forth. Combine equal parts of butter and flour and stir constantly over a very low heat until almost dried up, when the mixture becomes the desired brown color, either light or dark brown. Nothing could sound simpler than this process, but in reality many cooks go wrong in this initial step. Perhaps it is the very simplicity of the operation that leads them to believe that the roux will automatically be a success, but no roux can be trusted to take care of itself.

Without a well made "roux" no sauce is well made. It must be allowed to cook very slowly over the lowest possible fire until the heat has penetrated evenly and achieved a perfect blending and drying of the flour with the butter.

In the highly seasoned dark or brown sauce a *brown roux* is used for binding, and the mixture is cooked so slowly, that a nutty flavor is the result, a flavor similar to that of baked bread just at the beginning of the baking, when the bread begins to set and take on color. For the more delicate sauces, a pale roux is required, which the French call *Roux Blond*. The same combination of flour and butter is cooked just as slowly as for *Dark Roux*, but only until it is of a blond hue. Either roux keeps perfectly when stored in a tightly closed tin container in a cool, dry place.

SAUCE BERCY [1115]
(*Hot*)

Place in a saucepan 3 finely chopped shallots and 1 cup of Velouté for Fish Home Style (No. 1131), and let this reduce to half its original volume over a bright flame. Then stir in 3 tablespoons of Parisian Fish Fumet (No 1100) and boil gently for 2 or 3 minutes, stirring frequently. Remove from the fire, stir in 2 tablespoons of butter, alternately with 1 generous tablespoon of lemon juice. Season to taste with salt, pepper and a dash of cayenne pepper, and when ready to serve, stir in 1 generous teaspoon of finely chopped chervil or parsley. Appropriate for grilled fish and fish filets, this sauce should not be confused with Bercy Butter (No. 982) which is used for grilled meat, especially steaks.

SAUCE BOHEMIENNE [1116]
Bohemian Sauce

See Lobster Bohémienne (No. 475).
Very appropriate for crustaceans and shellfish in any style.

SAUCE BOURGEOISE [1117]

See Trout (Lake) Home Style (No. 547).
Appropriate for fish filets, small fine-textured flat fish and fish steaks.

SAUCE CHATELAINE [1118]

See Turkey Grill Chatelaine (No. 972).
Appropriate for poultry and wild birds cooked in any style.

SAUCE IVOIRE [1119]
Ivory Sauce

See Poached Chicken à l'Ivoire (No. 920).
Appropriate for eggs, fish, veal, poultry and wild birds cooked in any style.

SAUCE PROVENÇALE HOME STYLE [1120]

Heat 1 scant half cup of olive oil to the smoking point; stir in $1\frac{1}{2}$ teaspoons of finely chopped shallots, 1 tablespoon of peeled, cnopped fresh mushrooms, 1 clove of garlic, crushed, and 1 teaspoon of finely chopped parsley, and cook for about 3 to 5 minutes, over a low heat, stirring almost constantly, until mixture is soft, but not brown. Combine a small can of tomato paste with double the amount of stock (the kind depending on kind of food with which this sauce is to be used), and add to the shallot-mushroom mixture, stirring from the bottom of the pan until mixture boils, at once lower the flame and simmer very gently for 15 minutes, stirring occasionally, and keeping the sauce covered. Season to taste with salt and a generous dash of freshly crushed black pepper. Serve separately, or pour over the indicated food.

Also called "Fondue de Tomates" (Stewed Tomatoes) this sauce is especially suitable for frog's legs, baked fish, left-over made-up meats and venison.

SAUCE PIEMONTESE [1121]

There is a charming story about the origin of this sauce: An old chemist and sorcerer, named Cico, lived in an ancient house on the outskirts of Milan during the thirteenth century. He was also a lover of good foods. After a long and adventurous life Cico decided to devote his last years to the discovery of something that would bring happiness to all mankind. After trying many strange concoctions and recipes, he finally perfected a dish, seasoned with the most exquisite sauce, made as follows:

Cook very slowly and stir almost constantly 3 medium-sized onions, finely chopped, until they begin to take on a blond hue; moisten with ½ cup of dry white wine, to which has been added ⅓ cup of good vinegar, and let this reduce to about ⅓ of a cup, over a bright flame, stirring occasionally; then add 1 cup of thinly sliced onion rings, previously cooked in a little butter or oil until tender, but not browned, and perfectly drained, and 6 cooked chicken livers, chopped. Season to taste with salt and pepper, and when ready to serve, stir in ¼ cup of heated tomato paste to which has been added 1 small clove of finely chopped garlic.

SHERRY ASPIC COATING JELLY [1122]

See Hors d'Oeuvres (No. 82).
Appropriate for coating any kind of food dressed in aspic.

SMITANE SAUCE RUSSIAN STYLE [1123]

Sauté in 1 generous tablespoon of butter 1½ tablespoons of grated onion until soft but not colored, stirring constantly; moisten with ½ cup of dry white wine, and let this evaporate completely. Then stir in 1¼ cups of heavy sour cream, stirring constantly. Bring to a boil, strain through a fine-meshed sieve and season to taste with salt and pepper. Appropriate for almost any kind of food.

SNAIL BUTTER [1124]

See "Snails Bourguignonne" (No. 531).

SOUBISE SAUCE [1125]

A recipe for this very fine sauce, published in *Memoires of Madame de Maintenon*, is quite different from that of today. The following is the method used by Monsieur Etienne, Esquire of Cuisine of Mme. Bagration, who was Princess and Lady in Waiting to Mme. de Maintenon. Appropriate for any kind of boiled fish or meat.

Blanch 1 lb. of minced onions in just enough slightly salted water to cover. Drain thoroughly. Smother the onions in ¼ cup of butter, cover and cook over a very gentle flame, shaking and rocking the pan frequently to prevent scorching, until onions are almost tender. Transfer onions and butter to a saucepan having a tight fitting lid; pour over them 1½ cups of Béchamel Sauce (No. 259), season to taste with salt, white pepper, a tiny dash of nutmeg, and ½ teaspoon of sugar. Cover the pan and bake in a moderate oven (350–375° F.) for about 25 minutes, or till onions are in a mush and mixture is of the consistency of heavy cream. Rub through a fine-meshed wire sieve into a saucepan, stir in ½ cup of heavy, sweet, scalded cream, taste for seasoning, and when ready to serve, stir in 2 tablespoons of sweet butter. Serve very hot.

SOUR CREAM HORSERADISH SAUCE   [1126]
(Cold)

Blend 1 cup of chilled sour cream, ¼ cup of drained, chilled, prepared horseradish and 1 teaspoon each of finely minced parsley, shallot, chives and onions; season to taste with salt and pepper and serve well chilled. If a tart flavor is desired, stir in 1 teaspoon of lemon juice. Appropriate for hot or cold fish, meat or poultry.

SPANISH SAUCE   [1127]
Sauce Espagnole

Because this sauce is very often used in cookery it is important to read the recipe carefully before starting it, and it is suggested that some be kept on hand, as it may be used for fish, eggs, meats, poultry, game and vegetables. In fact it is really the brown sauce universally used where good cooking is appreciated. It may seem elaborate, difficult, and costly, but it is not. If one wants to enjoy good cooking, healthful cooking, the best ingredients are essential. The following is a short cut.

Melt, in a saucepan large enough to hold 2 quarts, 3 tablespoons of clarified butter or margarine, which has been slowly melted over hot water. (Slow melting allows the particles of solid matter, such as whey, and so forth to fall to the bottom of the pan.) Stir in 3 generous tablespoons of flour, and cook slowly over a very low heat, stirring almost constantly, till thoroughly blended. If the recipe calls for a dark blending —a dark roux—let brown to the right color; if the recipe calls for a light brown, as for Béchamel sauce, for instance, do not overcook. For Sauce Espagnole the browning should be a deep brown. Cooking slowly will give a nutty flavor; cooking too fast will impart a bitter taste to the sauce. The roux being done, moisten gradually with Brown Stock (No. 179), stirring constantly and using about 1¾ quarts. Let this boil gently and steadily for almost 50 minutes, stirring frequently. Then skim off all the fat, and strain through a fine sieve or cloth into a pan and continue to simmer gently.

Meantime, in another saucepan, cook ¾ pound of lean veal or pork, cubed small, until brown on all sides, together with ¼ cup each of carrot, onion, celery and leeks, all carefully washed and chopped fine, 1 bouquet garni composed of 1 large bay leaf, 8 sprigs of fresh parsley and 1 sprig of thyme, all tied together with white kitchen thread, 1 whole clove. When well browned, gradually pour over the hot brown stock, and stir constantly until mixture boils. Let simmer gently for 1 hour, taste for seasoning, and strain through a fine sieve into hot, quart jars. Close tightly and when cold, store in refrigerator until wanted. This will keep weeks, and whenever a brown sauce is needed it is ready to use at once or to combine with another sauce.

TARTARE SAUCE I   [1128]
(*Original Recipe*)

Suitable for fried fish, when cold, and for hot fish, when hot. May also be used with almost any kind of cold cuts.

Pound 2 hard-cooked egg yolks to a paste, season to taste with salt and pepper and gradually add 1 cup of olive oil, as for making mayonnaise, alternately with 1 generous teaspoon of vinegar. When mixture is thick like mayonnaise stir in 1 teaspoon each of finely chopped chives, parsley, onions, shallots, capers with 1 tablespoon of finely chopped gherkins, and 1 of finely chopped olives.

For a short cut, use a cup of ready made mayonnaise and stir in the finely chopped ingredients.

TARTARE SAUCE II AMERICAN STYLE   [1129]
(*Hot*)

To ½ cup of hot Cream Sauce (No. 258), add ⅔ cup of mayonnaise, and mix well. Then stir in the following well-chopped ingredients: 1 teaspoon each of shallots, capers, sweet pickles, chives, black olives and parsley. Season to taste with salt and pepper and serve really hot. Appropriate for fried, boiled or steamed fish.

TOMATO SAUCE   [1130]

Heat 3 tablespoons of olive oil, butter or lard in a saucepan; add 1 small clove of garlic and 1 large onion, both finely chopped, ½ large green pepper, ½ small carrot, also chopped, and cook for 3 or 4 minutes, over a medium heat, stirring almost constantly, or until mixture takes on a light brown color. Then stir in 1 quart of canned tomatoes or the equivalent in fresh tomatoes, peeled and seeded, 1 bouquet garni composed of 1 large bay leaf, tied together with 2 small sprigs of green celery leaves (tops), 8 sprigs of fresh parsley and 1 small sprig of thyme using white kitchen thread; season lightly with salt and pepper and bring to a brisk boil. Lower the flame and simmer slowly for 35 to 40 minutes, over a low heat, stirring occasionally, or till mixture thickens. Strain through a fine-meshed sieve or cloth, pressing gently to obtain all the liquid possible. Stir in ½ teaspoon of sugar and serve; or turn into jar and when cold, store, sealed, in refrigerator until needed. Suitable for use in compounded sauces, or as is for any kind of fish, meat, game, or vegetable, cooked in almost any style.

There are several formulas, but the following is the most used:

VELOUTÉ SAUCE OR STOCK HOME STYLE [1131]

This is another foundation sauce, like the Spanish sauce, which is used in compounded sauces, or as is. Like brown or tomato sauce, it may be prepared far in advance and stored in refrigerator until wanted. Proceed as for Spanish Sauce (No. 1127) but do not brown the roux (No. 1114).

The liquid used for moistening should be either chicken, veal or fish stock. The cooking process is the same as for Spanish Sauce (No. 1127), but the liquid is different; for Chicken Velouté use Chicken Stock (No. 238 or 301); for Veal Velouté use Veal Stock (No. 185), and for Fish Velouté, use Fish Stock (No. 182).

VENISON SAUCE   [1132]

Put in a saucepan about 1 pound of scraps of raw venison meat or trimmings (if used for mock venison, use raw trimmings of mutton or lamb), 1 quart of cold water, 2 whole cloves, ½ teaspoon of powdered mace, 1 scant teaspoon of nutmeg, a generous dash of cayenne and salt to taste, also 1 bouquet garni composed of 1 large bay leaf tied with 8 sprigs of fresh parsley, 2 small sprigs of green celery leaves and 1 sprig of thyme using white kitchen thread, and, if available, a generous pinch of juniper berry powder. Bring to a boil very slowly, stirring occasionally, then let simmer very gently until liquid is reduced to half its original volume (that is, there should be 2 cups of liquid left in the saucepan), skimming carefully. Strain this through a very fine-meshed wire sieve, pressing gently, into a saucepan. Stir in 3 tablespoons of red currant jelly, 1 cup of hot red wine and 2 tablespoons of meat extract (commercial). Taste for seasoning and thicken, if needed, with a little Roux (No. 1114). Let boil gently 2 minutes and serve. Or store in refrigerator in a glass jar, sealed, until needed. Keeps weeks in refrigerator. Appropriate for seasoned lamb or mutton, or for furred game, such as game steak.

The expression "Watered Stock" is believed to have originated with Dan Drew, old-time Wall Street operator who got his start as a cattle dealer after the Civil War. According to the story, Drew, who sold his cattle by the pound, did so immediately after they drank a quantity of water.

VINAIGRETTE   [1133]
(*Warm*)

Place in a mixing bowl ½ cup of French Dressing (No. 1755), 1 tablespoon of grated onion, 1 generous teaspoon each of finely chopped chives, parsley, chervil, shallots, capers and cucumber pickles. Place in top of a double boiler and warm mixture over hot (not boiling) water; then, just before serving, stir in 1 rounded tablespoon of chopped hard-cooked egg white and season to taste with salt and plenty of pepper.

When cooled and chilled this sauce may be used for any kind of left-over cooked meat, fish and game, as well as certain vegetables as asparagus, artichoke, broccoli, cauliflower and green salads. Appropriate for calf's head, left-over cold meat, fish or game, vegetables, and so forth.

WHITE SAUCE   [1134]

This is a misnomer, and should never be used in cooking. The flour lost in making this spurious sauce could be used for something better.

Proceed as indicated for No. 258, Basic Standard Recipes for Cream Soup, omiting the egg yolk. This sauce belongs to the compounded sauces when egg yolks are added and may be prepared far in advance, like Béchamel Sauce, then kept in sealed jars in the refrigerator.

WHITE WINE SAUCE   [1135]
(*Short Cut*)

Blend 1 tablespoon of butter with one of flour, or take 1 tablespoon of White Roux (No. 1114); gradually stir in 1 cup of strained White Wine Court Bouillon (No. 1037). Let this boil gently for 5 minutes, stirring occasionally to prevent scorching, and when ready to serve, stir in 2 egg yolks, adding one at a time and stirring well after each addition; season to taste with salt and pepper. Place over a gentle flame for a minute, or until mixture reaches the boiling point, and just before serving, stir in 1 tablespoon of sweet butter and ½ teaspoon of strained lemon juice. Appropriate for fish cooked in any style, but especially for fish filets, fine-textured fish, boiled or poached, and small flat fish sautéed in butter. Also used on boiled poultry.

WINE DEALER SAUCE   [1136]
See Sauce Marchand de Vin (No. 1079).

WOW WOW SAUCE   [1137]
See Bubble and Squeak (No. 592).

Chapter Ten

VEGETABLES

*When God on earth was making the primal
Paradise, a garden, say the Scriptures, was
fashioned to suffice. And man these years
remembers, and every spring recants one
step toward his Eden with every seed he
plants.*

—*Chateaubriand*

VEGETABLES [1138]

I T IS A GREAT MISTAKE TO TAKE FOR GRANTED EVERYDAY DISHES and to expect them somehow or other to look out for themselves while we lavish our tender care and skill on the foods which we consider superior. It is that sort of attitude which is responsible for all the bad hashes, the sodden codfish balls, and the sloppy corned beef and cabbage. If the cooks who make these homey dishes only said to themselves, "Now here is an opportunity for me to turn out something perfectly magnificent," there would be some very different hashes and codfish balls and corned beef set before us.

Vegetables especially we treat as if we do not care whether they survive or perish. As a matter of fact, Americans love vegetables, but there are times when you would never know it, so brutally are the poor things often handled. Who of us has not been offered those depressing string beans cooked for hours to a purplish-gray color and a purplish-gray taste, or to the bright and startling bicarbonate of soda green? Who of us, for that matter, is entirely guiltless of having cooked them that way at one time or another ourselves? And that in a land where tender string beans flourish in the fields from Connecticut to California and from Maine to Florida.

Cabbage, turnips, string beans, spinach, carrots, all known as ordinary vegetables, certainly do not become any less ordinary from the preparation they commonly receive. We are terrible snobs about our vegetables, for let them cost less than fifteen cents a pound and all they get from most of us is a potful of water and complete neglect, while it is a hopelessly careless cook who doesn't do her or his best by asparagus, which costs real money.

The recklessness with which some of us cast our vegetables into water, stems, I daresay, from the old-fashioned theory about teaching a boy to swim by throwing him into water over his head. If he comes out alive he is made of the right stuff, and, moreover, he will have learned how to swim; if he goes under he couldn't have been much of a sport, anyway. And so it is with string beans, cabbage, turnips, parsnips —if they survive the ordeal by water, to which they are sometimes subjected, they must have been pretty good to start with, and if they turn out water-logged and soggy there is no great harm done, since beans and cabbage and so on, are cheap.

Learn a few basic rules about vegetable cookery; treat the humblest vegetable with respect and even affection, and do your cooking with the resolve to make the best of them all.

ARTICHOKES [1139]

I love asparagus, but I regard with equal favor the artichoke with its soft leaves and tender heart—exquisite leaves which one dips into a vinaigrette, beautiful heart which the butter goldens.

In the opinion of many lovers of good things, the artichoke may be considered one of the most delicate, and most refined of the vegetable kingdom, and it may be prepared in many delicious and delicate ways. In an omelet, a tender artichoke bottom, diced small, adds incomparable relish; cold, with a plain French dressing, gently flavored with a hazelnut-size portion of prepared mustard, it is both a salad and a meal.

Oblong pieces of cut raw artichoke cut ¼ inch thick; dipped in flour, or a mellow batter, then French fried in deep fat, are a delight. *A la Favorite* artichokes are stripped of their leaves, and the hearts are well-trimmed; next they are rubbed with lemon juice to prevent them from getting black, then cooked in water in which a cup of flour and the juice of two medium-sized lemons have been blended—underdone of course; then they are stuffed with fresh string beans in cream, covered with a well-made sauce Mornay, sprinkled with grated Swiss cheese and finally glazed under the flame of the broiling oven, or in a hot oven. A revelation! One relishes artichoke *à la Provençale*. Neatly trimmed of their outside leaves, with about an inch cut from the top, they are tied, soaked upside down in cold salted water, drained, then cooked until tender and served with a hot French dressing profusely garlicqued.

The artichoke is an inexpensive vegetable. Its place of origin is Africa, where legend says that it was a favorite dish with Anthony and Cleopatra. It grows almost everywhere in the temperate regions and belongs to the thistle family. It contains tannin and mucilaginous materials, but nothing of true nutrient value, although, according to Professor Moleschott, it holds 17.75 per cent of organic matter, is easily digested, is among the few vegetables which diabetic patients are allowed to eat with impunity. Its chemical composition (edible portion) is as follows according to Bulletin 28, Department of Agriculture, Washington, D. C.: Water, 78.5%; Protein, 2.6%; Fat, 0.2%; Carbohydrates, 16.7%; Mineral Salts, 1.0%; Fuel value (calories) per pound, 365, and Vitamin content, B and C.

In Southern Europe, when the harvest is abundant, artichokes are preserved in this way: The leaves are removed and the bottom carefully cleared of its choke, after which the bottoms are dried on a special wooden screen, under the sun's rays. These yellowed, shrunken, dried artichoke bottoms are then stored in bags for winter use. Cooked in boiling water, they rehydrate, expand and soften, recapturing their natural and original flavor under the penetrating action of the heat. After draining, they are ready for any final delicate preparation.

The artichoke flower is oddly shaped, purple-violet in color. It looks something like the enormous tuft of an imaginary military shako, and nothing is more picturesque than an artichoke field in bloom, when the spring has velveted the pale, long, thin and finely-notched leaves and hoisted all these tufts. Soon the artichoke will be ready for the vinaigrette; the sour cream and horseradish beaten together into cream cheese and minced chives sauce, or a chiffonade or Russian dressing; or it may be rolled in a smoking omelet, or stuffed with a savory dressing.

Artichokes are by no means new to the soil of the United States, for as far back as 1605, Champlain, the French explorer, tells of seeing them in Indian gardens at Cape Cod.

ARTICHOKES (GLOBE) A LA CALABRESE [1140]

Cut off the stems of 6 globe artichokes and also the tips of the leaves and the very top leaves; then strike on the kitchen table to open the center. Fill each leaf with the following stuffing: Combine 1⅓ cups of soft bread crumbs, ¾ cup of grated Parmesan cheese, 2 teaspoons each of finely chopped parsley, chives, green pepper and onion; season to taste with salt pepper and nutmeg and secure the artichokes with kitchen string. Arrange close together in a kettle just large enough to hold them; pour over all ⅓ cup of olive oil, then 1 cup of cold water. Cover tightly and bring to a boil; at once lower the flame and simmer very gently for one hour, adding more hot water as needed. Serve as hot as possible with the strained sauce to which may be added a little butter, chopped parsley and chives or green pepper or both.

ARTICHOKES (GLOBE) KNICKERBOCKER [1141]

Trim 6 nice globe artichokes, soak in lukewarm water a few minutes and shake, then cook until tender in a well-seasoned consommé or white stock. Drain by placing them upside-down in a colander, squeezing gently to remove all moisture. Dip the artichoke in melted butter, then roll it in equal parts of grated Gruyère cheese and Parmesan cheese, seasoned with salt and pepper. Glaze the artichoke quickly under the flame of the broiling oven, in a fireproof platter. Serve at once, pouring over them the following sauce: Sauté a finely chopped hard-cooked egg in a little butter, and when mixture foams, stir in a piece of anchovy paste the size of a hazelnut, which has been kneaded with 1 teaspoon each of minced parsley and minced chives.

ARTICHOKES (GLOBE) MOTHER'S WAY [1142]

Parboil 6 medium-sized globe artichokes in boiling salted water to cover for 5 minutes. Drain. Cool slightly; remove the "choke" of fuzzy part from the center, and set aside. Heat ¼ cup of butter with a peeled whole clove of garlic; when butter is hot, discard the garlic, and stir into the butter ¼ lb. of peeled, chopped fresh mushrooms, ¼ lb. of finely chopped cooked lean ham, 1 tablespoon of grated onion, and 1 teaspoon of chopped parsley. Cook this for about 5 minutes, stirring constantly, then season to taste with salt, pepper and a dash of nutmeg. Stuff the cavity of the prepared artichokes with the mixture; wrap each artichoke with a thin sheet of larding pork, securing with kitchen thread; arrange close together in a heavy saucepan just large enough to hold them and having a tight-fitting lid; pour over 1 cup of dry white wine, mixed with ½ cup of tomato sauce and the juice of half a lemon (about 1 tablespoon),

6 peppercorns, gently crushed, a good pinch of nutmeg and salt to taste; cover tightly and cook in a moderate oven (325–350° F.) for 35 to 40 minutes. Transfer the artichokes to a heated platter after removing what may be left of the salt pork fat; skim off all the fat; strain the sauce through a very fine cloth or sieve into a saucepan; reduce it to about 1 cupful; taste for seasoning and serve in a sauce boat.

When ancient Greece and Rome were at the height of their glory, the artichoke was a favorite food. It suddenly disappeared, only to be "discovered" once again in 1473 by a wealthy merchant of Venice.

ARTICHOKES (GLOBE) A LA NINON [1143]

Shape 24 (4 apiece) raw hearts of globe artichokes into little cork forms with a knife; arrange them in a shallow baking dish, generously buttered, and bake in a very moderate oven (300° F.) until tender. Arrange them on a layer of hot mushroom purée, well seasoned and buttered; sprinkle a little grated Swiss cheese mixed with buttered bread crumbs over all and brown quickly under the flame of the broiling oven. Serve as a side dish or as an appetizer.

BOILED (GLOBE) ARTICHOKES, DIVERS [1144] SAUCES

Wash 6 nice, plump, green globe artichokes (one per person) under running cold water; remove tough outer leaves and trim stems neatly, close to the artichokes. Have ready in a kettle about 3 inches of boiling water, seasoned with salt, sugar and a few grains of black pepper; place artichokes stem-end down in the water; cover tightly with the lid, and cook over a low flame for about 25 to 30 minutes, depending on size, or until an outer leaf can easily, be pulled from the stem. Drain upside down and serve hot or cold. If cold, serve with a French vinaigrette or remoulade dressing, mustard mayonnaise, or any preferred spiced cold sauce. If served hot, serve with one of the following sauces: Hollandaise (No. 1062), Mousseline, (No. 1089), Maître d'Hôtel Butter, (No. 1078), or Parsley Sauce (No. 1101).

Note. Artichokes (Globe) should be served either ice-cold or piping hot.

ARTICHOKES (JERUSALEM) or AMERICAN [1145] ARTICHOKE

At the beginning of the sixteenth century, food shortage and blight caused some European countries to import the Jerusalem artichoke from Chile, a proof that this tuber originally came from America. In 1611 a French missionary discovered that the Indians of La Nouvelle France (Canada) used it along with the ginseng.

Nobody seems to know why the Jerusalem artichoke is so named, for actually it is a perennial sunflower with tuberous roots. The name is neither descriptive or true. The first word, "Jerusalem," has for many years been explained as an English corruption of the Italian word "girasole," meaning "sunflower"; but the English name of "Jerusalem" was used before there was any evidence that girasole meant sunflower.

At any rate, the Jerusalem artichoke neither tastes nor looks like the green or globe artichoke—it is not related to it botanically or otherwise. In shape, it resembles an irregular potato. "Knotty potato" would have been a better name for it—certainly more descriptive.

Its sweet, nutty flavor may be derived from its three main components: *dextrose*, which is found principally in corn; *sucrose*, found in cane and beets; and *levulose*, sweetest and most soluble of all sugars (quite dominant also in the artichoke). Delicious, economical and nourishing dishes may be made from this tuber after it has been scrubbed, rinsed, and peeled.

In France it is prepared in many ways: hot, it is fried, baked, mashed, creamed, or adapted to any of the recipes for the white potato, including a delicious cream soup similar to the pumpkin soup of fame. Cold, it is used in salads.

BOILED JERUSALEM ARTICHOKES [1146]

For 6 servings, scrub 1½ pounds of Jerusalem artichokes well and soak in slightly salted cold water for 30 minutes; drain, rinse in several cold waters, and cook in salted cold water for 25 to 30 minutes, or until tender, time depending on size. Peel. They are now ready to be prepared in almost any form applied to the white potato.

CREAMED JERUSALEM ARTICHOKES [1147]
AU GRATIN

Cook 1½ pounds of Jerusalem artichoke as indicated for No. 1146. Peel, cube, and mix with 2 cups of cream sauce (No. 258). Turn into a baking dish, sprinkle over the top ½ cup of soft bread crumbs, mixed with ¼ cup of grated cheese (any kind desired) and bake in a hot oven (400° F.) for 15 minutes, or until nicely brown and piping hot. Serve at once from the baking dish.

If desired, stir ½ cup of grated cheese into 1½ cups of cream sauce, instead of using pure cream sauce.

FRENCH FRIED JERUSALEM ARTICHOKES [1148]

Cook 1½ pounds of Jerusalem artichokes as indicated for Boiled Jerusalem Artichokes (No. 1146) until tender. Cool. Peel, cut like regular French fried potatoes and fry in the same manner.

JERUSALEM ARTICHOKE A LA LYONNAISE [1149]

Boil 1 pound of Jerusalem artichokes as indicated for recipe No. 1146. Cool and slice to about ⅛-inch in thickness. Peel and slice 1 pound of onions; parboil (blanch) them in a little salted water; drain well. Sauté the Jerusalem artichoke slices in butter in a frying pan. Sauté the sliced onions in another frying pan in butter. When both are delicately browned, combine them and continue cooking until well browned, stirring constantly, season with salt and a little pepper, then stir in 3 tablespoons of finely chopped chives. Serve at once.

MASHED JERUSALEM ARTICHOKES [1150]

Prepare and cook 1½ pounds of Jerusalem artichokes as indicated for Boiled Jerusalem Artichokes (No. 1146). Drain, cool slightly; peel, and put through ricer; season to taste with salt, pepper and a little lemon juice, then beat in 3 or 4 tablespoons of butter until fluffy. Pile on a hot dish and serve at once.

Important. *If Jerusalem artichokes are not peeled as soon as cold enough to handle, much of the flesh comes off with the skin.*

MUSHROOM AND JERUSALEM [1151] ARTICHOKES PANCAKES

Wash and scrub 1 pound of Jerusalem artichokes and soak in slightly salted water for 30 minutes. Drain, dry, pare thinly, then grate them on a coarse grater. Drain off ¼ cup of artichoke liquid, and stir in 3 tablespoons of sweet heavy cream, and 1 medium-sized onion, grated; season to taste with salt and pepper, and stir in ½ teaspoon of Worcestershire sauce. Now add ¼ cup of flour, sifted, with 2 teaspoons of baking powder, mixing well, alternately with 2 well-beaten eggs. Mix thoroughly, and finally stir in ½ pound of peeled, fresh mushrooms, finely chopped, blending thoroughly. When ready to serve, drop by tablespoons on a hot greased griddle or a buttered, individual frying pan, and cook as ordinary pancakes, turning to brown on both sides.

ASPARAGUS [1152]

Asparagus time: time for the homemaker to prepare her vinaigrette, mixing the clear vinegar with the golden fluid of virgin oil; her immaculate white sauces, those soft velvety white sauces which add more nutriment to this forerunner of the hot days; sauces which she may enhance with African capers; or golden liquid butter flavored with a few drops of onion or lemon juice. That is what the asparagus, that slightly diuretic vegetable which owes this property to a substance called "asparagin," loves and assimilates so well.

From the oddly swollen ground springs forth, and all at once, a green and fragile stalk. It's the asparagus, elegant shoot with a slightly bent, violet head. With each ray of the sun this head ascends and grows. One cuts it, it shoots out again, one keeps on cutting it, it always shoots out anew. It's a stalk of greediness for life.

Its origin is Italian, as the tomato is Spanish, the eggplant Sicilian, the bean Greek, the pea Egyptian, the potato Peruvian, the truffle French, the artichoke African, and the okra American, and on the volcanic slopes of Mount Vesuvius and Mount Etna, asparagus is kissed by the sun rays of beautiful Italy. It is agreeable and *magnifique*, but the asparagus of Catania, Sicily, is considered by connoisseurs, as the prime of the asparagus species.

Asparagus is grown in almost every part of the United States but most connoisseurs prefer the green variety to the giant asparagus of California.

What kind of sauce best suits this delicious vegetable? Some claim that for luncheon oil and vinegar, or French dressing, or vinaigrette are best, while others prefer the cream sauces; others demand hot sauces such as Hollandaise or Mousseline for dinner service. For the green, fragile, bended head, oil and vinegar in one form or another, seems in favor in the opinion of most gourmets; while for the big, corpulent, melting variety, an unctuous cream sauce which may be punctuated with green capers seems to be the classic, though many others prefer a rich, foamy sauce.

The famous gourmet d'Aigrefeuille, satisfied himself with simply dusting his asparagus with salt. " . . . There is no need for sauce . . . " he used to say. " . . . to swallow asparagus, if one wants its full delicate flavor. It passes; it has passed; it is a fondant . . . ."

It is to the French Marquis de Cussy, that illustrious gastronome and author that we owe "Asparagus au Gratin." He used to say that with a wineglass of old Alicante, a dish of "Asparagus au Gratin" was the most sublime dish.

We all know or should know that asparagus is the best friend of new peas and what an appetizing and delicate flavor is born from their sweet wedding in cookery, especially when one adds to this gastronomic duo a finely shredded, tender heart of lettuce, and a tiny sprig of tarragon.

And "Asparagus Tips Omelet," delicious and renowned, that omelet without a rival which the royal cook, Louis XV, of France, invented and prepared with his own hands, for the pink-mouthed "La Du Barry." It was France which paid for the butter, the eggs, and the asparagus too—and very dearly at that.

ASPARAGUS TIP OMELET [1153]

If you wish a perfect omelet, blanch the asparagus tips first. Add a tender diced artichoke heart and sauté both gently in butter but do not brown. Nothing else, no parsley, chervil or chives.

The asparagus and artichoke singing in the butter, make a harmonious duet, to which no other voice should be added unless it be that of a truffle cut in thin blades, but then this would be a dream rather than an omelet.

The Flemish serve asparagus with quartered hard-cooked eggs and plain melted butter with a profusion of chopped parsley; the Italians sprinkle it first with grated Parmesan cheese, then with melted butter, and just before serving, glaze this delectable dish under the flame of the broiling oven; the Polish sprinkle it with sieved yolk of hard-cooked eggs mixed with finely chopped parsley and when ready to serve, cover the whole with freshly made fine breadcrumbs toasted to a light golden color in butter; the Germans serve it with brown sauce; the French like it "au gratin" and à la vinaigrette; the Spanish with a highly seasoned sauce into which both garlic and onion enter; while the British and Americans—more prosaic and practical—prefer the Hollandaise, or the Mousseline sauces, or sometimes the delicious Maltaise sauce; everyone to his liking—there is no accounting for taste.

I have often served asparagus with Bearnaise sauce, slightly flavored with tomato.

When served cold, asparagus, in addition to vinaigrette or French dressing, loves mayonnaise, especially when it is blended with an equal part of whipped cream. A fine dish for a summer luncheon. However, according to gourmets and connoisseurs, asparagus patty, when combined with button mushrooms and diced, cooked sweetbreads is the apogee of its gastronomic preparation and a bottle of Chablis, or Montrachet will never be amiss with such a regal dish.

Green asparagus contains more bitter and resinous principles than the white.

The chemical composition of an edible portion of fresh asparagus is as follows: Water, 94.0%; Protein, 1.8%; Fat, 0.2%; Carbohydrates, 3.3%; Ash or Mineral Salts, 0.7%; Fuel value, (calories) 1.05%, and Vitamins B and C.

ASPARAGUS AMANDINE RUSSIAN STYLE   [1154]

Drain 1 can of asparagus tips; arrange neatly in a generously buttered shallow baking dish; barely cover with 1 cup of Smitane Sauce (No. 1123) and sprinkle the sauce generously with ground blanched almonds (about ¾ to 1 cup); then equally generously with buttered bread crumbs, and brown the crumbs under the flame of the broiling oven. Serve at once from the baking dish.

ASPARAGUS BUCA LAPI   [1155]
Italian asparagus dressed on hot plates with butter and cheese

Cook a nice bunch of fresh asparagus in the usual way in boiling salted water until tender, or about 18 to 20 minutes. Divide it among six hot plates; sprinkle the tips generously with melted clarified butter, then sprinkle equally generously with grated Parmesan cheese. Serve at once.

ASPARAGUS CUSTARD COUNTRY CLUB   [1156]
STYLE

Mix 1 can of condensed asparagus soup with 1¼ cups of rich milk, and add 1 tablespoon of grated onion, a tiny slice of garlic and a grating of nutmeg. Beat in 6 egg yolks, seasoned to taste with salt and white pepper. Divide among 6 buttered custard cups; drop into each cup 6 or 7 small cubes of bread (croutons), fried in butter, and bake in a moderate oven (325 °F.) until set or for about 45 minutes. Serve hot after unmolding on to a hot platter spread with generously buttered spinach en branch or mashed potatoes, or boiled rice also generously buttered.

ASPARAGUS FRANCONVILLE   [1157]
(Serves 6)

Asparagus should always be handled tied as a bouquet. Keep in a cool place—but not too cold, with their feet in water. For cooking, they should be stood upright in a double boiler, after being tied loosely in groups of 6 to 8. Handle as little as possible. When buying asparagus, decline budded tips or dry stalks for they will not regain their flavor, no matter how much you wet them. And don't forget that the discarded ends of good stalks may be cooked in slightly salted water, then pressed through a sieve, to form the basis of cream of asparagus soup.

Arrange 2 bunches of fresh cooked asparagus on 6 individual hot plates, with 2 hot, hard-cooked egg quarters on each plate. After serving, present 1 whole nutmeg with a small grater to each guest, so that each may season the food according to his or her taste. Pass a side dish of drawn butter sauce. Each guest ceremoniously crushes his hard-cooked egg quarters and mixes them with the butter sauce.

ASPARAGUS AU GRATIN AMERICAN   [1158]
STYLE I

Wash 2 pounds of asparagus thoroughly and cut into inch pieces. Cook tougher portions in a small amount of slightly salted water until almost tender. Add remaining pieces; continue cooking 5 or 8 minutes and drain. Make a cream sauce, using ½ cup of water in which asparagus was cooked, with 1 cup of milk, 2 tablespoons of butter and 2 tablespoons of flour, in the usual way; then, when the sauce has thickened, stir in ¾ cup of grated American cheese, and stir until cheese is melted. Now combine the sauce and well-drained asparagus stirring very gently. Pour into a buttered baking dish; sprinkle over the entire surface 1 scant cup of soft bread crumbs, and sprinkle with 1½ tablespoons of melted butter, then with a little paprika. Place the dish under the flame of the broiling oven until crumbs are delicately browned and serve immediately.

ASPARAGUS AU GRATIN FRENCH STYLE II   [1159]

Arrange little bundles (individual) of cooked asparagus tips, (fresh or canned) on thin slices of freshly made toast, in an au gratin dish and pour over each well-seasoned Béchamel Sauce (No. 259). Sprinkle over each bundle some graded cheese mixed with buttered crumbs; cover stalks with buttered brown paper and place in a hot oven (400° F.) to melt the cheese. Serve at once.

ASPARAGUS AND OLIVES AU GRATIN   [1160]

Cut 1 bunch of freshly cooked or canned asparagus tips into 1-inch pieces. Have ready 1½ cups of very hot Cheese Sauce (No. 1027) and stir in ½ cup of sliced, stuffed olives. Combine the sauce and asparagus very gently and pour into a buttered baking dish, as evenly as possible. Arrange over it a layer of sliced hard-cooked eggs, and top the eggs with ½ cup of buttered bread crumbs mixed with ⅓ cup of grated American cheese. Bake in a moderate oven (350° F.) for 20 minutes or until the crumbs and cheese are browned and bubbling. Serve at once in the baking dish.

ASPARAGUS PIE FRENCH STYLE   [1161]

Bring to the scalding point 2 cups of sweet cream with 1 large bay leaf, 4 sprigs of fresh parsley, 4 thin slices of onion, a tiny pinch of thyme leaves, a sprig of marjoram and 6 freshly whole peppercorns. Do not salt. Let simmer gently for 15 minutes.

Meanwhile, heat 1 tablespoon of butter, stir in 3 tablespoons of chopped lean ham or veal and cook 2 minutes, stirring constantly; gradually stir in the strained hot cream, still stirring constantly until mixture begins to boil; lower the flame and let simmer *very, very* gently, over the lowest flame possible, uncovered, for 30 minutes, stirring occasionally to prevent scorching.

Have ready a 9-inch pre-baked pastry shell. Line the bottom of it with a row of cooked or canned asparagus tips, having all the points turned toward the center. Pour a thin layer of the sauce, just enough to barely cover; arrange another asparagus row, this time having the points toward the edge of the pie shell, and pour the remaining sauce, to which has been added and thoroughly blanded, ½ cup of grated

Gruyere cheese or Swiss cheese; spread over the top ¾ cup of sieved, buttered bread crumbs and brown quickly under the flame of the broiling oven. Serve very hot.

ASPARAGUS A LA POMPADOUR [1162]

Allow 6 or 8 small asparagus stalks or 4 large ones for each serving. Cut the stalks off at the tender part, and cook them in slightly salted boiling water, (keeping the tips above the surface) for 15 or 20 minutes, or until they are tender. Drain them, and place in a napkin to keep hot while preparing the following sauce (for 4 servings). Melt ¼ pound sweet butter in a chafing dish over hot water. Add a generous pinch of mace, salt to taste, and a few grains of cayenne pepper. Stir in alternately 1 scant teaspoon flour and 3 egg yolks beaten carefully with 1 tablespoon sherry. Stir over hot water until the sauce begins to thicken; then spoon it over the asparagus, and finish with a grating of nutmeg.

ASPARAGUS SOUFFLE AMERICAN STYLE [1163]

Trim a bunch of asparagus, removing all the tough ends and leaving about 3½ to 4 inches of tips. Boil in salted water for 15 minutes; drain and arrange carefully in a generously buttered baking dish. Melt ⅓ cup of butter; blend in 3 tablespoons of flour, and when quite smooth, without browning, stir in 1 cup of milk, scalded with 4 thin slices of onion, a bit of bay leaf, and 1 whole clove, and drained, stirring constantly, until mixture thickens and boils; remove from the fire and cool slightly, then add the well-beaten yolks of 3 eggs, seasoned with a little salt, a little white pepper and a dash each of paprika and nutmeg. Fold in 3 tablespoons of grated Parmesan cheese, alternately with the stiffly beaten whites of 3 eggs. Pour over the asparagus and bake in a moderate oven (350–375° F.) for about 35 to 40 minutes or until well puffed, brown and firm. Serve at once.

CREAMED ASPARAGUS IN TOAST RINGS [1164]

Prepare 1½ cups of Cream Sauce (No. 258), and keep hot. Heat 1 can of asparagus tips (in the can) until very hot; drain. Prepare 6 rings of bread; brush lightly with melted Anchovy Butter (No. 979) and toast to a golden brown. Slip asparagus tips through the toasted bread rings, and pour cream sauce over each. Serve immediately, the sauce dusted with a little paprika.

FRENCH FRIED ASPARAGUS [1165]

Cook 2 bunches of asparagus (canned asparagus may be used), and drain. Separate the stalks, and roll each in sieved bread crumbs seasoned with pepper and salt, then dip in a mixture consisting of 1 egg beaten with 3 tablespoons milk, a dash of salt, pepper, and cayenne or paprika, and again roll the stalks in crumbs. Fry in deep fat (370° F.) about 2 minutes, or until the asparagus rises to the top of the fat and is delicately browned. Drain. Serve with or without egg or cheese, or Hollandaise Sauce (No. 1062), or Cream Sauce (No. 258), or any sauce except butter. Or use as a garnish for steak or chops.

BEANS [1166]

Beans have been cultivated in the Americas since prehistoric times. Lima beans have been discovered in burial mounds in Peru, and early explorers found beans being cultivated by the Indians, from Canada to South America. In 1605, in a letter concerning the Indians in the Kennebec region, Champlain noted: " . . . with corn they put in each hill three or four Brazilian beans which are of different colors. When they grow up they interlace with the corn, which reaches to the height of from 5 to 6 feet; and they keep the ground very free from weeds . . . "

This habit of planting beans with corn was practised by Indians everywhere and is still sometimes done. The first French explorers in Canada took beans home with them for cultivation in France; consequently beans in England were originally known as "French beans." Captain John Smith in 1614 found beans grown by Indians in New England, and when the Pilgrims landed on November 19, 1620, Miles Standish dug up corn and "a bag of beans" from a pit.

The records of bean cultivation in ancient history all seem to refer to field beans rather than pole beans. The culture of the latter was not common until the sixteenth century. Dwarf beans are also a fairly recent mutation, and the first mention of dwarf snap beans was not until 1542.

Small seeded or *Sieva beans* were grown in the Carolinas as early as 1700. Large seeded beans were first introduced into North America by Captain John Harris of the U.S. Navy who brought some seeds back from Lima, Peru, in 1824 and planted them on his farm at Chester, New York. These seeds from Lima were the forebears of our modern Lima bean. The botanical name *Phaseolus*, according to a writer in 1865, is derived from the resemblance between the shape of the pods and a special form of ship supposed to have originated at Phaselis, a town of Pamphylia.

Garbanzos or *Chick-peas*, are the fruit of a pea-like plant, probably the "pulse"; roundish, flattened on two sides, wrinkled when dry, and with a projection of the summit, both ripe and unripe. In Mediterranean countries it forms the basis of the Olla Podrida of Spain and Mexico and is well known and liked in California, Mexico, and Spanish-American countries generally, where it is eaten in many ways—boiled, roasted, in soups, also coated with sugar or syrup as a confection.

There are a number of varieties: white, black and red, white being the best. The *garbanzo* is a leguminous plant of the vetch tribe. It contains over 6 per cent of fat and is the leading protein food mentioned in the above countries. In India, it is called "Gram."

Colorado Pinto is a bean as sacred to the West as the codfish to Boston. When the Spaniards first overran the country, they found the dappled pink bean a staple food of the Indians. Pinto they named it, the Spanish word meaning paint. Pinto was the bean that helped build Western railroads and clear the settlers' land. A "stick-to-the-ribs" bean, and today we know why. In the pinto bean, nature has hidden an abundant supply of the B-1 vitamin. There are other vitamins, too, as well as important body-regulating minerals.

The soybean, called "Food of the Ancients," and "The Little Honorable Plant," known throughout the Orient, has a useful history dating back five milleniums.

In the year 2838 B. C., Emperor Shen-Nung, father of Chinese agriculture, listed some 300 medicinal properties to be found in the soybean. Soybeans furnished Orientals the proteins lacking in a diet of rice; they contain twelve times the fat of ordinary beans but have little sugar and *no starch*. Their protein content equals the protein of meat, eggs and milk . . . the finest there is. It builds tissue, restores energy, yet doesn't put on fat.

The broad bean is one of the aristocratic vegetables of English gardens. It is one of the most ancient beans (except the soybean) of Europe, Asia and Africa, dating back to unknown periods, some say to the Bronze Age; also known as the Fava bean.

BEANS—HINTS [1167]

One of the most satisfactory food extenders is soybean meal. Frankfurters as purchased today are largely reinforced by soy meal. It is very digestible.

Sprouted soybeans should be kept refrigerated like fresh meat. For long storage, they may be blanched in boiling water for from 2 to 3 minutes, then either frozen or dried. Remember that vitamin C is developed as the bean sprouts.

Dried soybeans, (even after soaking overnight), require long, slow cooking to make them tender, unless they can be cooked in a pressure cooker. Under 5 pounds pressure they will cook in about 20 minutes. Otherwise, give them from 4 to 6 hours cooking.

A touch of curry powder added to canned baked beans is a good idea; use a level teaspoon to 2 cups of beans.

Maple syrup may be substituted for molasses to sweeten baked beans.

A few onion rings and some thin strips of salt pork placed on top of beans as they are baking add goodness and flavor; and how about baked beans with a layer of melted cheese in the middle? Or corn meal waffles with crisp bacon in the batter to serve with baked beans?

Hot baked beans served in ramekins, with hot rolls, relishes and a fruit dessert, make a satisfying lunch or supper any day in the year.

Soak kidney beans in hot water and you shorten the cooking time. If you have soft rain water so much the better because hard water tends to toughen the beans so that they never seem done.

To improve the flavor of home-baked beans, stir in very gently when half cooked, some finely chopped green pepper and grated onion . . . and remember, one pound of dry beans has twice as many calories and nearly twice as much protein as one pound of beefsteak.

If tired of baked beans as such, mash them; season with onion, catsup and an herb or two, make into croquettes, dip in egg and crumbs and fry in deep fat. Also, try serving baked beans in green peppers, in tomatoes, large onions or in bread cases.

If you have neglected to soak either navy or lima beans over night, pour boiling water over them after washing them, and let stand covered for about an hour before cooking.

Dry beans stored in a can with a close-fitting cover or in a tightly closed bag are safe from dirt, insects, and mice.

The ancients used "beans" medicinally. Bruised and boiled with garlic, they were taken to cure coughs.

ARIZONA BAKED FRIJOLE BEANS PIMAN   [1168]

Out in the great open spaces of the Southwest, *frijole* beans have been popular for hundreds of years. But of all the bean dishes that have been set before them, cowboys at their chuck-wagon meals on the range, cattle barons in their luxurious ranch houses and section hands playing plaintive guitars in railroad cabooses have most loudly sung the praises of *frijoles* piman.

Take 2 pounds of pink, or pinto beans; wash, soak over night, drain, and place in a kettle in cold water to cover, with 1 large onion, quartered, 1 large bay leaf, 1 teaspoon of salt, and 1 clove of garlic, and cook until beans are tender. Place 2 finely chopped, medium-sized onions in a casserole; add 3 tablespoons of strained honey; drain the water carefully from the beans, and place them in the casserole over the honey. Season with celery salt, a few grains of cayenne pepper and 3 tablespoons of finely chopped chives. Rub the lid of the casserole gently but thoroughly with garlic; cover the casserole, place in a medium oven (350° F.) and bake until beans are almost but not quite dry, or about 30 minutes. Serve right from the casserole.

BAKED CHICK-PEAS   [1169]
Garbanzos

Pick over, well and wash carefully 4 cups of dried chick-peas, another name for *garbanzos* or Mexican beans; place in a saucepan with 6 cups of lukewarm water and let stand, covered, for 2 hours. Add ¾ pound of salt pork, cut into 6 pieces, 1 medium-sized onion, chopped, 1 large bay leaf tied with 8 sprigs of parsley and 1 sprig of thyme, 2 whole cloves, 1 small clove of garlic, peeled and left whole, ½ generous teaspoon of salt, and 8 peppercorns. Cover; bring slowly to a boil; lower the flame, and simmer for 2 hours, or until beans are tender and liquid is almost gone. Stir in 1 tablespoon of prepared mustard, ¼ cup of dark corn syrup; turn into a greased baking dish, and bake in a moderate oven (250° F.) until brown on top, or about 45 to 50 minutes. Serve from the baking dish.

Few people know that the jewelers' "carat" owes its origin to a lowly bean the fruit of an exotic tree which is native of southern Abyssinia, on the east coast of Africa. This tree is known as the "kuara" or sun tree. When in blossom its fruit and flowers are a beautiful coral red color. The fruit, a large red bean called "carat," has a little black spot on the side and hangs from the branch in a spherical pod of a pithy and fibrous substance as tough and hard as the bark of the tree. As the beans are always uniform in size and weight, the natives employed them many years ago as their standard for weighing gold. The use and popularity of the fruit spread over the length and breadth of Africa, being readily accepted by both white and black traders, and by money changers. In time the practice passed from the dark continent to India where the shrewd native goldsmiths, who were without a standard, early adopted the carat as a medium and likewise applied it to the grading of all precious stones. The expression of the diamond and gold standards in terms of carats eventually grew into universal usage and continues today.

BLACK-EYED PEAS POT LIKKER VIRGINIA STYLE [1170]

Pick over sound black-eyed peas, and wash enough to make 2 cups. Soak overnight in 1½ quarts of cold, soft water, or soak in lukewarm water for at least 6 hours. Put on to cook in the same water, to save vitamins and minerals, and add a 1-pound piece of bacon, or a pork shoulder, or a 1-pound piece of salt pork. Add 1 large bay leaf tied with 1 sprig of thyme, and 8 sprigs of parsley, 2 whole cloves, 1 clove of garlic, left whole, 10 peppercorns, and ½ teaspoon of salt, 1 medium-sized onion, quartered, and simmer, covered, till peas are tender, or about 2 hours. Add hot water as needed as the peas absorb a great deal of water, and a Southern Pot Likker should never be dry since the rich, flavored liquor is soaked up with corn pone.

For corn pone as made in Virginia: mix 1 cup of white corn meal with ½ teaspoon of salt and enough cold water to make a dough as wet as can be shaped into biscuit-size cakes. Bake on a greased baking sheet in a hot oven (450° F.) for 15 minutes and serve very, very hot. Better make up a second batch as the pones disappear very fast.

BOSTON BAKED BEANS [1171]

Pick over 1 quart of navy or pea beans and wash; then soak over-night in cold water. In the morning, drain and cover with fresh water. Cook slowly, simmering the beans from 10 to 15 minutes; drain, then rinse the beans in cold water.

Scald and scrape ¾ pound of fat bacon or salt pork; cut it in thin slices; pour the beans into a bean pot, and place a layer of pork every half-inch, using the beans to bury the pork slices. Mix 1 tablespoon (scant) of salt, 3 tablespoons of sugar, ½ teaspoon of dry mustard, ⅓ cup of molasses and 1 cup of boiling water, and pour over the beans, adding enough additional boiling water to cover the beans. Cover the bean pot and bake steadily for 6 hours in a slow oven (250° F.). Uncover during the last half hour of baking to brown the top. Add boiling water as needed.

BOSTON BAKED BEAN CROQUETTES [1172]

Mash 2 cups of baked beans with a fork, then rub through a fine sieve; work in to the bean purée 1 medium-sized onion, grated, 1 tea-spoon of salt and ¼ teaspoon of black pepper. Shape into croquettes. Beat an egg with 2 tablespoons of water or meat stock; dip the cro-quettes, first in cracker crumbs, then in egg mixture, being careful to cover the entire surface, then again in cracker crumbs. Fry in deep hot fat (360–370° F.) until delicately browned, or about one minute. Drain on absorbent paper and serve with tomato catsup.

BRETON BAKED BEANS [1173]

Soak 1½ cups of pea or navy beans overnight in cold water; next morning, drain and place in a kettle with 1 bouquet garni composed of 1 large bay leaf, 2 sprigs of green celery leaves, 10 sprigs of fresh parsley, and 1 sprig of thyme, all tied together with white kitchen thread, 1 medium-sized onion, stuck with 2 whole cloves, salt and pepper to taste. Bring to a boil; lower the flame, and simmer gently for about 2½ hours or until soft but not mushy. Turn the beans into a greased baking dish; discard the bouquet garni and mash the onion. Bury in the beans ½ cup of pork cracklings and stir in 6 sieved canned red pimientos, 1 cup of strained tomato pulp, ⅓ cup of finely chopped green pepper, 2 tablespoons of grated onion, and ⅓ cup of sweet butter. Taste for seasoning, mix well, then bake in a very, slow oven (275° F. maximum) until beans have nearly absorbed the liquid. Serve immediately. If desired, stir in 1 tablespoon of sugar before baking.

CREAMED (FRESH) LIMA BEANS FRENCH STYLE [1174]

Shell the beans; wash them very quickly in cold water; drain, and cook uncovered in enough slightly salted boiling water to cover, for 20 to 35 minutes, depending on size of beans, or until just tender. Drain well. Season to taste with salt and pepper and a dash of freshly ground nutmeg. Scald ½ cup of heavy cream with 1 bay leaf, 3 thin slices of onions, 1 clove and 2 sprigs of parsley, and when very hot strain over the beans, and stir in ¼ cup of sweet butter. Serve dusted with finely minced parsley.

DEVILED LIMA BEANS [1175]

Melt ¼ cup of butter in a saucepan; stir in ½ cup of grated onions, ¼ cup of finely chopped green pepper and ¼ cup of drained, chopped canned red pimientos; cook till the onion is lightly browned; add 2 teaspoons of prepared mustard, a few grains of garlic powder, 1 cup of tomato sauce (freshly made or canned) and a 3-ounce can of deviled ham. Mix well and thicken slightly with a little flour, if needed. Cook for about 10 minutes, stirring frequently; then add 2 cups of canned, drained lima beans, alternately with ½ cup of grated cheese (optional) and season to taste with salt and pepper. Cook a few minutes to heat the lima beans through and melt the cheese. Serve dusted with finely chopped parsley or chives.

FRENCH LIMA BEANS [1176]

Wash, rinse, and soak overnight in cold water to cover, 2 cups of dried lima beans, first picking them over very carefully. Next day, drain off whatever water is left; place beans in a kettle, cover with boiling water, season to taste with salt and pepper, add 1 bouquet garni composed of 1 large bay leaf, 8 sprigs of fresh parsley, 3 sprigs of green celery leaves, 2 sprigs of fresh marjoran, and 1 sprig of thyme, all tied together with white kitchen thread, 2 whole cloves, 1 clove of garlic, peeled and left whole, 2 small onions, each studded with a whole clove, and a ham bone. Cover; bring to a boil, lower the flame and simmer gently for 2 to 2½ hours, or till beans are soft, but not mashed. The water should be almost evaporated. Drain, place in a serving platter, and discard the bouquet garni and the garlic as well as the ham bone. Taste for seasoning, then toss in 1 tablespoon each of finely chopped chervil or parsley and

1 of chives, alternately with 3 tablespoons of thick sweet cream scalded with 3 tablespoons of sweet butter. Serve at once.

HOPPING JOHN OF THE CAROLINAS [1177]

Many lands as well as many sections of America have special "lucky" foods and pastries which are served on New Year's Day. In Holland, for example, when a Dutch lad goes a-courting on New Year's Day, he takes his sweetheart a pastry made in the shape of her initials. In Scotland, "Hogmanay" dumplings are customarily served on New Year's Day, etc. Among the lucky recipes served in various sections of the United States on New Year's Day, is this pea (bean) dish from the Carolinas. It is an old Southern custom to serve it on New Year's Day at the noon dinner, a ten cent piece being added to the big bowl of peas just before it is brought to the table. The person finding the dime in his or her plate will have good luck all year. The recipe is called "Hopping John." Whence the name came nobody exactly knows, but it is very popular in the South.

Wash and pick over one pound of black-eyed peas (called black-eyed beans almost everywhere else except in the Old South). Cover with 2 inches of cold water, add ¾ pound of cubed, parboiled salt pork, ½ teaspoon of salt (more or less according to saltiness of pork), 1 large bay leaf and 1 medium-sized onion, sliced, as well as 8 peppercorns, freshly ground. Cook till the beans are tender, adding more boiling water to keep the peas quite moist. While the peas are cooking, wash 1 cup of rice and shake very slowly into 2½ quarts of salted, rapidly boiling water. When the rice is tender, drain in a colander, and rinse under the hot water faucet. Season to taste with salt and white pepper. When ready to serve, the rice and pea-beans are served separately. A mound of rice is first placed on each plate, the peas poured over it, and a dish of stewed canned tomatoes is served separately.

ITALIAN BAKED BEANS [1178]

Pick over and wash 2 cups of navy beans, then soak overnight in cold water to cover. Turn both the beans and the water in which they have soaked into a saucepan, adding more water if needed, to barely cover the beans with 1 large bay leaf, 2 medium-sized onions, grated, 1 clove of garlic, grated, 2 tablespoons of finely chopped parsley, 1 teaspoon of finely chopped dill, and salt and pepper to taste. Boil till beans are tender but not soft, or about 1½ hours. Cook 2 cups of strained tomato pulp with ½ cup of olive oil slowly in a saucepan, stir in 3 small chopped, pickles, ½ cup of chopped green olives, and 1 cup of chopped celery and cook together till tender, then pour over the beans. Turn mixture into a casserole or bean pot; cover and bake in a slow oven (275° F.) about two hours. Remove from the oven; cover the top with half cup of grated cheese; return to the oven and bake until cheese browns. Serve at once.

LIMA BEANS AND BACON CASSEROLE [1179]

Pick over, then soak 1 pound of small dried lima beans overnight in cold water to cover. Drain, cover with fresh water and add 2 small onions, quartered, 1 bouquet garni composed of 1 large bay leaf, 2 sprigs of green celery leaves, 8 sprigs of fresh parsley, and 1 sprig of thyme, all tied together with white kitchen thread, 1 small clove of garlic, left whole, salt and 8 peppercorns, gently bruised. Bring to a boil; lower the flame and simmer gently for 50 to 55 minutes, or until beans are tender. Meanwhile peel and chop ½ cup of onions, and mix with 1 cup of finely chopped, scraped celery stalk, and cook in ¼ cup of bacon fat or ham fat until vegetables are tender, or about 25 minutes. Drain the beans, but save the water. Discard the garlic and the bouquet garni, and mix with the celery-onion mixture; taste for seasoning, and turn into a greased baking dish. Heat 2 tablespoons of butter or margarin, blend in 2 tablespoons of flour without browning, then, when mixture bubbles, stir in 1½ cups of the water, strained from the beans, stirring constantly. Cook until thickened, pour over the beans; arrange strips of bacon close together over the top, and bake in a moderate oven (350° F.), for about 40 minutes, or till the beans are tender and the bacon crisp, covering the bacon with a buttered paper if browning and crisping too fast.

Note. ¼ to ½ cup of tomato catsup may be added to the sauce before pouring over the beans.

RED KIDNEY BEANS CASSEROLE BERCY [1180]

Melt ⅓ cup of butter; stir in 6 thinly sliced small white onions, 1 green pepper, finely chopped and freed from seeds and white ribs, and cook over a gentle flame for 5 minutes, stirring occasionally, then add 1 clove of garlic, chopped fine. Have ready 2¾ to 3 cups of red kidney beans cooked until tender, but not mashed. Add the onion-green pepper mixture and season highly with salt, pepper and a few grains of cayenne.

Lay ⅓ of the beans in a greased baking dish, preferably an earthenware one. Over them arrange a layer of 6 frankfurters, previously slightly browned; then add a layer of beans, another layer of about a dozen of pork sausage links, still another layer of beans, and top with a layer of lean, thinly sliced cooked ham, the slices cut into individual portions. Pour over all 2 cups of red wine, brought to the boiling point, with 1 large bay leaf and 2 whole cloves, strained, then mixed with 3 tablespoons of tomato paste. Place the dish in a moderate oven (350° F.), and bake 30–35 minutes. Serve right from the baking dish.

Note. If preferred, instead of lean ham, use a layer of bacon strips or blanched salt pork slices.

SPROUTED SOYBEAN CURRY [1181]

Chop finely 1 medium-sized onion, 1 medium sized peeled apple and 3 stalks of scraped celery, and brown lightly in 3 tablespoons of butter; stir in 1½ cups of beef stock, or lacking this, 1 cup of boiling water and ½ cup of Pique Seasoning. Mix 2 tablespoons of flour, 2 teaspoons of curry powder and salt and pepper to taste moisten with a little cold water, then add to the first mixture. Now stir in ½ cup of seedless raisins, previously plumped in boiling water, then drained and dried, and lastly, add 3 cups of sprouted soybeans which have been steamed or boiled for 10 to 15 minutes. Allow all to simmer gently for 30 to 40 minutes and serve as hot as possible.

The Chinese have been eating sprouted soybeans for fifty centuries. One reason for their popularity is that they require little fuel to cook, in a land where fuel is scarce.

SPROUTED SOYBEANS CREOLE [1182]

Wash and steam for 12 to 15 minutes 3 cups of sprouted soybeans which have been previously cooked and cooled. Have ready 3 cups of Creole Sauce (No. 1041-42). Add the beans; season to taste with mixed salt and pepper; simmer for 5 minutes and serve as a side vegetable dish with any kind of cooked meat or poultry.

Soy milk is greatly used in Chinese cookery, and you can make 1 quart of soy milk with 1 cup of dry soybeans. The soy milk doesn't look or taste like cow's milk, but it is recommended as a healthful food when used in cooking soybeans.

SOY MILK HOME STYLE [1183]

Wash 1 cup of dry soybeans and soak overnight in cold water to cover; drain but do not discard the water. Put the beans through a food chopper, using fine blade. Measure liquid drained from beans, and add enough cold water to make 6 cups; stir in the ground beans; bring to a boil; reduce the heat and simmer, uncovered, for 15 minutes. Strain through a fine-meshed sieve or cheesecloth and when cold, store in refrigerator until needed.

The soy pulp which remains when the milk is strained from the ground beans is called soy mash. Use this soy mash as an extender in meat loaves or to thicken soups and gravies. The milk may be used in a white or cream sauce, made as follows: Melt 2 tablespoons of butter or other fat; blend in 2 tablespoons of flour; add salt and pepper to taste, then gradually stir in 1 cup of soy milk, previously scalded, stirring constantly until mixture thickens.

BEETS   [1184]

Of the goosefoot family, the name beet comes from the fact that when the seed pods swell they look like the Greek letter béta β.

The modern beet, as such, was not apparently known in ancient times. There is a story that when the Greeks paid homage to Apollo they served him beet roots on a silver platter, but the first recorded specific reference to beets is in the third century in Rome. They were mentioned in 1390 in some old French and English cooking recipes.

Beets are natives of Europe and North Africa, and were originally found near the sea in southern Europe and around the coasts of the Mediterranean as far east as the Caspian Sea and Persia.

The beet is not only rich in nutrients but has a decidedly beneficial effect on the stomach and kidneys. While it has a high water content, it owes its food value to the carbohydrates it contains. In beets will be found fair amounts of the important vitamins A, B, C, and G. But by no means should we forget the leafy green tops in considering the food value of the beet, for these contain generous amounts of vitamins and minerals and add greatly to its importance as a health sustaining vegetable. Of course this applies only if the tops are cooked quickly, in a very little liquid, and not with soda.

BEETS—HINTS   [1185]

In preparing beets remember that the pigments which give the color are soluble in liquid. To help beets hold their color, cook them in their skins and with two inches of the stem retained, in water to cover. Cook them covered.

Sliced cooked beets in seasoned sour cream are good with any fish. They must be very cold . . . and dressed just before serving.

Hard water may cause the beet color to fade, but you can save it by putting a little acid in the water. Use vinegar or cream of tartar. Or bring back the red after the beets are cooked by serving them with a sauce containing vinegar.

When the beets are cooked tender, drain off the water, and slip off the skins, roots and stems with your fingers.

Good beets should be free from blemish. Those that are rough or ridged, or that have deep cracks are always wasteful. Do not purchase beets without at least 4 inches of attached stems.

Harvard beets are so called because they are a specialty of the Yale Club.

As soon as beets are cooked, plunge them into cold water for several minutes before skinning.

Cold beets—either pickled or plain boiled—make good ingredients for salads. Dice or slice them, and combine with sliced hard-cooked eggs. The red color makes a good contrast to the salad greens and other chopped vegetables. But be sure to wait until just before serving to mix the beets with other ingredients. If the beets stand long, they will transfer their red color to anything that touches them. Beets and grated cheese are another good combination.

When you feature beets on the menu, it won't matter whether the meal is planned for looks or taste—they hit the jackpot either way. For hors d'oeuvres, combine diced beets chopped, hard-cooked eggs, chopped celery and onions and serve on crackers.

Flavor beets with meat drippings or melted butter or margarin; add salt and pepper to taste just before serving as hot as possible. For a little "lift," add chopped chives, onions, parsley, scallions, or green pepper. And also a little spiced vinegar or a squeeze or two of lemon or onion juice to the fat, and serve hot.

BEETS IN ORANGE SAUCE   [1186]

Combine 3 tablespoons of grated orange rind, 2 tablespoons of lemon juice, ⅓ teaspoon of salt, a dash each of black pepper and nutmeg, and stir in 1 scant tablespoon of flour. Blend until smooth, adding 1 tablespoon of sherry wine. Cook in top of double boiler, over hot water, stirring frequently until thickened. Let simmer gently for 10 minutes, stirring occasionally, and when ready to use, add ⅓ cup of butter and stir until melted. Finally add 3½ cups of cooked, sliced beets; heat through, and serve in a hot vegetable dish dusting with finely chopped parsley.

BEETS IN SPICY SAUCE   [1187]

Heat in top of double boiler 4 tablespoons of butter with ⅓ teaspoon of dry mustard, 3 tablespoons of tarragon vinegar, ½ teaspoon of sugar, a dash of mace, 2 tablespoons of grated onion, 1 tablespoon of finely chopped parsley, and 2 teaspoons of Worcestershire sauce. Bring to a boil, stirring frequently, and stir in 3½ to 4 cups of cooked beets cubed very small. Toss together and when well heated, serve in a heated vegetable dish sprinkling with chopped parsley or chives.

Napoleon was so fond of beets that he often drank a glass of warm beet soup as a "pick-me-up" at noon. He is also said to have originated a beet pie.

BOILED BEETS   [1188]

Cut off tops about two inches above beets, scrub and rinse well; place in a saucepan; cover with salted boiling water and cook gently till tender allowing 30 to 35 minutes for small young beets and at least 2 hours for winter beets. Drain, rinse in cold water, rub off the skins and cut off roots. They are then ready to serve hot or cold with various sauces.

Beet tops from young beets may, and should, be cooked and prepared like spinach, buttered, or in croquettes. They may also be served raw in salads, especially with raw, young spinach mixed with thinly sliced raw radishes.

BUTTERED BEETS [1189]

Slice or dice 4 cups of cooked young beets. Heat ¼ to ⅓ cup of sweet butter stir in the beet slices or dice and sprinkle over (optional, but this adds a fine flavor) 1 teaspoon of sugar. Sauté the beets, until thoroughly coated with the butter, and serve dusted with finely chopped parsley.

Variation. Add to the butter 1 teaspoon of prepared mustard, 1 teaspoon of sugar and 1 tablespoon of lemon juice, heat well and add the diced or sliced beets.

MASHED BEETS [1190]

Cook the beets (about 3 bunches) in the usual way until tender. They are done when the skins can be slipped from them easily with the fingers. Drain, and cool slightly; remove the skins with the fingers; trim the roots, and mash or force the beets through a sieve or ricer into a saucepan. Add 3 generous tablespoons of butter; season to taste with salt, pepper and a little sugar, and stir in 1½ tablespoons of lemon juice. Mix well, and heat thoroughly. Serve in a heated platter, dusting with a little chopped parsley or chives.

SAVORY WHOLE BEETS [1191]

Drain the juice from 1 large can of whole small beets into a saucepan. To each cup add 3 tablespoons of brown sugar, 1 teaspoon of grated onion, 2 tablespoons of tarragon vinegar, salt to taste, 2 teaspoons of mixed whole spices tied in a small muslin bag, and 3 tablespoons of sweet butter. Bring to boiling point; add the beets, and simmer gently for 15 minutes. Drain. Roll the beets in ⅓ cup of melted butter, then in equal parts of finely chopped chives and parsley. Serve hot and at once.

BROCCOLI [1192]

Broccoli, of the mustard family, which includes the cabbage, was known to the Romans at the time of Pliny, but references to this vegetable group it with cauliflower. The first notice of broccoli, as such, was made in 1724 by an English writer who called it "Sprout Colliflower," or "Italian Asparagus."

In 1729 another English gardener reported that there were several kinds that he had been growing in London for two years: " . . . that with small, whitish-yellow flowers like the cauliflower; another like the common sprouts and flowers of a colewart; a third with purple flowers; all of which come mixed together . . . " The seeds of the plant that he described came from Italy, and all the types now grown originated there since it has been extensively cultivated in that country for many years. It has been grown also in America for a number of years. Thomas Jefferson mentions that it was available in Washington markets, but it has become popular only within recent years. In fact, it probably holds a record for the short time required to gain wide acceptance by the public and importance as a commercial crop.

Broccoli Rabe, which is the broccoli plant that has not headed up, is cooked and served the same as the larger plant. The type of broccoli now generally grown is often called "Sprouting Broccoli," "Branching Broccoli," "Asparagus Broccoli," or "Calabrese Broccoli," which was the original Italian name for it.

BROCCOLI—HINTS [1193]

Cook broccoli like cabbage, that is, uncovered, and lay two slices of bread in the water. This will prevent odor.

Broccoli is best if cooked quickly. Cut off the heavy stalks, cube them and cook with the top sections or flowerets. This plan saves time.

If the stalk of the broccoli is thick and you feel certain it will not cook in the same length of time as the bud, split it lengthwise up to where the bud begins. It will cook much more quickly.

Don't buy broccoli that has the buds open. It is no good. And do not get water on the buds when you are keeping them before cooking as this makes them open.

Broccoli may pall, but dressed with a butter sauce literally bestrewn with silvered browned almonds, it ranks high as a vegetable. Cauliflower responds to the same treatment.

Broccoli looks more like cauliflower than other members of the cabbage family but because of its greeness it ranks as an excellent source of vitamin A—which the white cauliflower is not. Broccoli is also a good source of vitamin C, but not as good as Brussels sprouts, collards, kale, kohlrabi and cabbage. It is listed as a fair source of vitamin B and a good source of vitamin G.

After the well-known fact that asparagus should be cooked standing up, comes the reminder that broccoli should be handled the same way. When broccoli is cooked "on its feet," there is less breakage of the tender top buds, and they are not cooked to pieces.

Like other members of the cabbage family, broccoli retains its color and flavor through cooking just to pierceability in rapidly boiling salted water. Overcooking causes change in color, taste and texture. The use of soda is *most objectionable* because it destroys certain vitamins, ruins flavor, gives an unnatural green color and breaks down cellulose. Fresh broccoli has leaves and soft stems that make good greens for a second meal; the coarse stalk ends may be peeled and cubed, cooked and served mixed with cream sauce, cheese sauce served au gratin, and so forth. The amount of waste or lack of it depends largely upon the utilization of all edible parts.

BOILED BROCCOLI [1194]

Remove large leaves and tough portions of stems; wash and soak in lukewarm salted water about 30 minutes; drain and tie securely into bunches with kitchen string. Cook, tightly covered, in a small amount of water or uncovered, in a large amount of boiling salted water 15 to 25 minutes or until tender; drain, remove strings and dress with butter, lemon butter, browned crumbs, Hollandaise, cream sauce, brown butter, and so forth. If eaten cold, serve a French dressing, a Vinaigrette, a sour cream dressing, or a remoulade sauce. (See Salad Dressings and Sauces.)

BROCCOLI AMANDINE [1195]

Cook 2 bunches of broccoli as directed for recipe No. 1194; drain and season with salt and freshly ground black pepper. Dress over a hot platter and squeeze a little lemon juice over it. Sauté ⅓ cup of blanched, shredded almonds in ¼ cup of sweet butter until lightly browned, adding 1 clove of garlic, finely chopped, to the butter. Pour butter over broccoli at the same time sprinkling the almonds over all. Serve at once.

BROCCOLI A LA DROUANT [1196]

Arrange a layer of cooked broccoli in branches in a generously buttered earthenware casserole; cover with a layer of cooked, diced chicken, and repeat until the casserole is nearly full. Pour over all 2 cups of hot Béchamel Sauce (No. 259), to which has been added 4 tablespoons of sherry. Sprinkle with ½ cup of grated Swiss cheese, and brown under the flame of the broiling oven until mixture bubbles and top is delicately browned. Serve at once, in the casserole.

BROCCOLI ITALIAN STYLE [1197]

Wash very quickly under the cold water faucet 2 bunches of broccoli; drain and soak them in salted cold water for 30 minutes. Drain and rinse again under the running cold water faucet; remove the large leaves and tough portions of stems and scrape gently the more tender parts, as you would fresh asparagus. Cut off the clusters or heads and set aside; cut the stems in inch pieces. First cook the stems for 10 minutes in boiling salted water, slightly acidulated, with 1 tablespoon of lemon juice to each pint of water, then add the clusters or heads and continue cooking 10 minutes longer. Drain thoroughly and transfer to a hot platter. Heat ½ cup of pure olive oil over a bright flame, with 3 tablespoons of lemon juice, a small clove of garlic, mashed to a pulp, salt and pepper to taste. Pour over the broccoli, dust with chopped parsley or chives and serve at once.

BROCCOLI ALLA MILANESE [1198]

Clean and wash quickly 2 bunches of broccoli in the usual way as indicated for recipe No. 1194; drain well and place in a baking dish. Sprinkle with grated Parmesan cheese (about 1 cup), and bake in a hot oven (425–450° F.) or place under the flame of the broiling oven until cheese melts. Serve two fried eggs over each portion of broccoli.

BROCCOLI DIVERS SAUCES [1199]

Boil broccoli as directed for recipe No. 1194; drain well; transfer to a hot platter, dust with chopped parsley, and serve with one of the following sauces: Mustard Butter (No. 992); Anchovy Butter (No. 979); Barbecue Sauce (No. 1010); Béchamel Sauce (No. 259); Caper Sauce (No. 1023) Hollandaise sauce (No. 1062) Mousseline Sauce (No. 1089) Smitane Sauce (No. 1123) and so forth.

BROCCOLI SOUFFLE RESTAURATEUR [1200]

Melt ⅓ cup of butter; blend in ¼ cup of flour, stirring constantly until mixture is smooth; gradually stir in ½ cup of sweet heavy cream, scalded, and mixed with ½ cup of rich chicken bouillon, or lacking it, ⅓ cup of boiling water and 3 tablespoons of Pique Seasoning, stirring constantly until mixture thickens. Remove from the fire and add 3 stiffly beaten egg yolks beaten with 1 teaspoon each of grated onion, finely minced parsley, Worcestershire sauce and finely chopped chives. Season to taste with salt, pepper and a good dash of nutmeg, and stir in 1½ cups of cooked, chopped broccoli and ⅓ cup of grated American cheese. Lastly fold in 4 stiffly beaten egg whites, seasoned to taste with salt and black pepper. Turn mixture into a buttered soufflé dish, and bake in a hot oven (400–425° F.) for 25 minutes. Serve at once.

CREAMED BROCCOLI AU GRATIN [1201]

Separate 2 bunches of washed and carefully picked over broccoli into flowerets; wash them again in slightly salted water, trim the stems if necessary, and place, tops up, in a saucepan containing 3 quarts of boiling salted water, and boil steadily until stems are· pierceable, or about 12 minutes. Meantime, have ready 2 cups of Cream Sauce (No. 258), to which has been added 1 tablespoon each of grated onion and finely chopped green pepper. Drain the broccoli in a colander; place in a heated serving dish; pour the sauce over it; dust with ½ cup of buttered bread crumbs, and brown quickly under the flame of the broiling oven. Serve from the baking dish.

BRUSSELS SPROUTS [1202]

Because the season for Brussels sprouts is rather brief, they never reach really low prices, but during the winter season the markets are very well provisioned, as the Brussels sprout is a winter vegetable par excellence.

Records indicate that Belgian markets sold Brussels sprouts around 1213. They were grown in America in 1806, and to build up the market for the miniature cabbages, a New York produce merchant interested the circus midget "Tom Thumb" in the new vegetable, and for a time the sprouts were called "Tom Thumb Cabbages." Being a cool weather vegetable, the miniature cabbages mature in the fall and seem to taste better after a touch of frost.

Dainty in appearance, each tiny ball is as good as it looks. It's flavor, however, is often spoiled by overcooking. Seven or eight minutes should be the limit.

There are two good ways of preparing sprouts. Use plenty of boiling salted water, drop them in and cook without covering, or use just enough water to barely cover the bottom of the pan and cook them tightly covered. It is advisable to soak the sprouts in lukewarm salted water for a few moments after they have been cleaned. Nutmeg enhances them; so does grated sharp cheese. A quart basket of brussels sprouts will make 5 to 6 servings. When of good quality these attractive little green balls are firm, compact, of fresh bright appearance and good green color. When puffy-looking, they are edible, but the quality and flavor are poor. Those that are wilted or have yellowed leaves are usually old or stale.

BOILED BRUSSELS SPROUTS [1203]

Trim the ends slightly; remove any yellow or imperfect leaves and wash well 1 quart of fresh, green Brussels sprouts. Be sure to examine for insects. Let stand 10 minutes in a bowl of lukewarm salted water. Place them in a saucepan; pour over 1 quart of boiling salted water; cover and boil steadily until pierceable but not soft, or about 10 minutes. Drain well. Turn them into a heated vegetable platter, and top with ¼ cup of butter. Or serve with Maître d'Hôtel Butter, Brown Butter, and so forth.

BRUSSELS SPROUTS WITH CHESTNUTS   [1204]

Cook 1 quart of Brussels sprouts as indicated for (No. 1203). Meanwhile cover ½ pound of large, sound chestnuts with boiling water and boil for 15 minutes, or until soft; drain, peel off both the outer shell and the thin brown inside skin. Cut the chestnuts in quarters. Drain the cooked sprouts well; add the chestnuts, ¼ cup of butter, salt and black pepper to taste, a dash of freshly ground nutmeg and a generous ¾ cup of Cream Sauce (No. 258). Let stand in a double boiler or over a very low heat for 5 minutes, then serve very hot.

BRUSSELS SPROUTS CHEZ NOUS   [1205]

Heat in a frying pan 3 tablespoons of butter; into this put 1 medium-sized onion finely sliced in rings and fry until rings begin to turn yellow, stirring frequently, over a gentle flame; then add a scant ⅓ cup of highly seasoned chicken bouillon, and 4 cups (1 quart) of cooked Brussels sprouts seasoned to taste with salt white pepper and a few grains of cayenne pepper. Cook, stirring almost constantly, until the liquid is absorbed and the sprouts are tender but whole, not crushed. Serve sizzling hot sprinkled with equal parts of chopped parsley and chopped chives.

BRUSSELS SPROUTS CRUMB SAUCE   [1206]

Cook 1 quart of cleaned Brussels sprouts as directed for recipe No. 1203, and drain well. Put 4 slices of bacon, cut in 1-inch pieces in a saucepan; fry till crisp over a very, low flame, stirring frequently; stir in 4 slices of bread which have been cut into tiny cubes, stirring till the cubes are delicately browned. Add 3 tablespoons of tarragon vinegar, and 1 cup of rich sweet cream. Boil up once, taste for seasoning, and pour over the drained cooked sprouts tossing well; sprinkle with chopped parsley and paprika.

BRUSSELS SPROUTS AU GRATIN   [1207]

Cook 1 quart of Brussels sprouts, which have been trimmed and cleaned, with 2 tablespoons of coarsely chopped onion, 1 large bay leaf, and 4 sprigs of parsley, in 2 quarts of boiling water; season with salt and pepper, and boil 10 to 12 minutes, or till the sprouts are tender. Meanwhile prepare 2 cups of Cream sauce (No. 258). Stir in a good dash of nutmeg, and ½ cup of grated cheese. Drain the sprouts well, add them to the cream sauce; sprinkle with ½ cup of buttered crumbs mixed with ⅓ cup of grated cheese, and brown in a hot oven (400–425° F.). Serve bubbling hot.

BRUSSELS SPROUTS GOURMET   [1208]

Cook 1 quart of cleaned and trimmed green Brussels sprouts in chicken stock instead of boiling water for 10 minutes; drain well. Have ready 2 cups of Béchamel sauce (No. 259) to which add ½ cup of small seedless grapes, which have been washed in cold water; then stir in the drained, cooked sprouts. Turn into a casserole or baking dish, sprinkle with ½ cup of buttered crumbs, and brown quickly under the flame of the broiling oven.

FRENCH FRIED BRUSSELS SPROUTS   [1209]

Cook 1 quart of Brussels sprouts as directed for recipe No. 1203 and drain well. When ready to serve, roll them in well-seasoned flour (pepper, salt and nutmeg to taste) then roll in beaten egg diluted with a little milk, and once again in fine bread crumbs, and fry in hot, deep, clear fat 360–375° F. Drain, and serve heaped on a hot platter covered with a folded napkin. Fine with venison, goose, duck, guinea hen and pork.

CABBAGE   [1210]

This good peasant, honored in the rustic marmit, is certainly the most popular and the most healthful of the vegetable kingdom. For three centuries, Rome knew no other medicament than the cabbage, and did not feel the worse. Cabbage is indigenous to Europe, but today its robust odor perfumes almost all the kettles in the world. Numerous and colorful is its family: green, white, yellow, violet, red, curled, round headed, fringed cabbages, Milan or Savoy cabbage, sea kale, rape-colewort, palm cabbage, collard, kohlrabi, broccoli, cauliflower, Brussels sprouts, and many others.

Stout drumhead cabbages of the farm, as solid and heavy as cheese, make a first line of defense along the front of the stall of the greengrocer, and are ready for the corned beef platter or the salad bowl of creamy multicolored cole slaw. Cabbage, the old warrior, is ever on hand for a gastronomic emergency. The Romans and Greeks used this budget vegetable as moderns do the "prairie oyster" and the Turkish bath, to pull their world back together the morning after the night before. In Egypt cabbage was considered to be an antidote for overindulgence in wine. Athaneus, gossip and epicure, once wrote: "The Egyptians . . . are the only people among whom it is a custom at their feasts to eat boiled cabbage before all the rest of the foods." And if we quote Eulubus: "Wife, quick, some cabbage boil of virtues, that I may rid me of this seedy feeling." Apicius, the epicure of ancient Rome, ranked cabbage with the tongues of flamingoes as a rare dish. Cato really thought that cabbage could cure almost everything, and said that Rome, because it possessed plenty of them, could expel all physicians. But Peter the Great of Russia forbade his army, navy, and other officials to eat cabbage or cabbage soup lest they become "cabbage heads."

CABBAGE—HINTS [1211]

Cabbage should never be overcooked, 8 to 10 minutes being ideal. It should be like spaghetti, that is "al dente" cracking under the teeth, and only a small amount of water should be used, since cabbage, like green peas, loses much of its vitamin content not only in long continued cooking, but when drowned in too much fluid.

Buying cabbage calls for a certain amount of careful inspection to secure quality. The best heads of mature cabbage are firm, with leaves crisp, unwithered and free from damage. Those with a white appearance on the outer leaves are overripe and likely to be tasteless and tough, while immature heads wilt badly and should be avoided.

The art of cooking cabbage, so as to retain its palatability and food value, lies in quick cooking. Brief cooking not only gives delicate flavor, texture and color, but conserves the valuable minerals in this popular and ancient vegetable.

Celery or Chinese cabbage looks like a cross between romaine and Swiss chard but appears among the cabbages in the seed catalogues. In our markets we see more of the "pet-sai" variety, having heads 14 to 16 inches long, than the short-headed Wong Bok type. The vegetable tastes like cabbage and yet is faintly bitter. Its leaves are very tender and crisp and the heads are usually blanched before being marketed. Celery cabbage may be used in any way suited to cabbage: in salad, with French, cooked or cream dressing, in mayonnaise, and so forth. It may also be cooked like the green cabbage, that is, boiled, baked, scalloped, fried, in cole slaw, and so forth.

Cabbage used for salad is much more tender if shredded fine and put into ice water for at least 30 minutes, then drained, dried and wrapped in waxed paper until ready to use.

To neutralize the odor of cabbage, cauliflower, broccoli or Brussels sprouts while cooking, place 2 or 3 slices of stale bread on top of the vegetables. Discard the bread when the vegetables is done. Or use broken bits of stale bread in a small cheesecloth bag. The bread also helps to keep cauliflower and cabbage white.

Cabbage may not have the most aristocratic reputation; but creamed with ham or sausages it is something to think about.

Remember that one pound of cabbage yields about 3½ cups of shredded raw or 2½ cups of cooked cabbage. And that 2 pounds of the crisp young green will easily serve 5 to 6.

A dish of cabbage and celery au gratin made with a rich cheese sauce, with fine crumbs on top and chopped blanched almonds, or Brazil nuts sprinkled over all, is worthy of any cook.

Braise sweet sour cabbage, in a skillet, keeping the cover on most of the time.

To retain color in red cabbage and beets, add a tablespoonful of vinegar to each pint of cooking water.

CABBAGE A LA BRETONNE [1212]

Cut 1 medium-sized new cabbage head into eighths, remove the core, and cook in 2 cups of beef stock in a tightly covered pan for about 10 to 12 minutes, or until cabbage is pierceable, keeping the sections of cabbage intact. Beat 2 eggs until light with salt, pepper and nutmeg to taste, then add 1 cup of sweet cream and beat thoroughly. Bring ¼ cup of olive oil, ¼ cup of tarragon vinegar and 1 tablespoon of sugar to a boil in top of double boiler, stirring over direct flame. Gradually stir in the egg-cream mixture, and when just beginning to bubble, return to hot water and cook until quite thickened, stirring almost constantly. Drain the cabbage well, place in the sauce. Cover and let stand 5 minutes without further cooking. Serve in a hot deep platter, preferably with fresh or smoked tongue or ham.

GERMAN RED CABBAGE [1213]

This is a rather long recipe, but not too complicated, and although it takes some time to prepare it is well worth while.

Strip a large head of red cabbage of its outer leaves and cut it in two. Cut away the hard center stalk, or core, then shred it or cut it into fine strips. Cover with boiling water and cook quickly for ten minutes, draining well immediately. Now heat ½ pound of lard or pork fat in an earthenware casserole. Add the cooked shredded cabbage and pour over it ½ cup of hot meat broth (or hot water mixed with a couple of tablespoons of Pique Seasoning). Add 1 large bay leaf tied together with a 2-inch piece of parsley root, previously scraped and halved lengthwise, and a large sprig of thyme, 10 peppercorns and salt to taste; cover closely and simmer gently for one hour, after which add 1 cup of red wine and 2 tablespoons (more or less, according to strength) of vinegar.

Next, add 4 pared, cored green apples, sliced; cover again and cook gently until apples are tender, or about 20 to 35 minutes. Then stir in 1 teaspoon of flour mixed with 1 teaspoon of sugar, moisten with a little water, and, if desired, ½ to 1 teaspoon of caraway seeds. Simmer 10 minutes longer and serve, preferably with goose, duck, hare, roast pork or ham, pork chops or fried sausage.

HOT BUTTERED CABBAGE [1214]

Hot buttered cabbage has a distinctive flavor with a certain crispness of texture when properly cooked, and is a lovely delicate green in color. Soggy, watery cabbage, grayish in color and mushy as to texture, either has been cooked too long, or in too much water, or both. Getting the most in food value and flavor from cabbage depends a great deal on its preparation for cooking.

When shredding cabbage for cooking, avoid cutting too finely. Finely shredded cabbage is best for salads, but wider shreds, about $\frac{3}{8}$ or $\frac{1}{2}$ inch across, are better for cooking. Remove the coarser, thicker part of the leaves; but avoid shredding too close to the core if you would keep cooking time and loss of food values at a minimum. Add very little water, and have it boiling briskly. Cook the cabbage only until it is barely tender. It should still retain a little of its original crispness, enough so that it sits up instead of lying down in a soggy mass. About 6 to 8 minutes' cooking should be long enough for fresh cabbage. Serve on a hot platter, dotting the cabbage with $\frac{1}{4}$ cup of butter, and season with salt and black pepper.

HUNGARIAN CABBAGE [1215]

Discard the outer leaves from 1 large green cabbage and shred coarsely. There should be 2 to $2\frac{1}{2}$ quarts of shreds. Cook in a large amount of boiling salted water, uncovered, 5 to 7 minutes, or until tender. Drain thoroughly and stir in 1 generous cup of heavy sour cream, scalded and seasoned to taste with salt, freshly ground black pepper, and a dash of nutmeg. When ready to serve, stir in 2 or 3 tablespoons of butter and 1 teaspoon of caraway seeds.

HUNGARIAN STUFFED CABBAGE [1216]

Remove the core from 1 large head of green cabbage and set aside. Place the cabbage in a closely covered kettle with about 1 cup of cold water and cook until cabbage leaves just begin to soften. Grate together $2\frac{1}{2}$ lbs. of raw potatoes and 1 medium-sized onion, season to taste with mixed salt, pepper and nutmeg, and add $\frac{1}{4}$ lb. of cooked rice and 4 tablespoons of butter. Blend thoroughly. Place 2 generous tablespoons of this potato mixture on each large leaf of cabbage; fold the leaf envelope style, then secure with kitchen thread. Line a shallow generously buttered earthenware casserole with 2 medium-sized, thinly sliced onions, the left-over cabbage leaves, coarsely chopped, and the finely chopped cabbage core; sprinkle over these a little mixed salt, pepper and paprika, add 1 large bay leaf, 2 whole cloves, 1 whole clove of garlic, and $1\frac{1}{2}$ tablespoons of finely-chopped parsley. Arrange the cabbage rolls over this bed of cabbage; pour in enough rich chicken broth to prevent sticking (about $\frac{1}{2}$ to $\frac{3}{4}$ cup). Cover tightly, and bake in a moderate oven (350–375° F.) for 35 to 40 minutes, or until rolls are quite tender. Uncover, add 1 scant cup of scalded sour cream, taste for seasoning, and serve from the casserole.

IRISH COLCANNON [1217]

Cook 1 medium-sized head of cabbage until tender in as little water as possible—just enough to prevent burning; drain. Boil 8 medium-sized potatoes, and mash them together with the cabbage, as you would mash potatoes; season with pepper and salt to taste, and beat in ¼ to ⅓ cup of good butter, alternately with 2 tablespoons of grated onions. Serve on a heated platter, make a depression in the center and place in it a large lump of sweet butter.

KOLDOLMA [1218]
(Original Recipe)

Remove twelve nice outer leaves from a large head of cabbage and scald them. Chop enough of the center to make 1 cup of finely chopped raw cabbage. Save the rest for some other dish, such as coleslaw or other kind of salad. Mix the finely chopped cabbage with 2 cups of ground, raw lamb or mutton, and 1 small onion, grated; season to taste with ¼ teaspoon of nutmeg, 2 teaspoons of salt, and ¼ teaspoon of freshly ground black pepper; then mix in 2 well-beaten eggs and ½ cup of soft bread crumbs, soaked in olive oil, and gently squeezed. Take a portion of the mixture the size of an egg; shape in a roll, croquette-fashion; place each roll on a cabbage leaf; roll up and place, folded side down, in a baking dish; pour in ½ cup of olive oil (butter or other shortening if oil is not liked), and as much of molasses, and bake in a moderate oven (350° F.) for about 50 minutes, turning the koldolma twice during the cooking.

Note. This is a traditional Swedish dish, borrowed from the Russians, who in turn got it from the Turks, whence its name "Koldolma," meaning "Cabbage Cloaks."

POLISH *BIGOS* [1219]

Methods of preparing Polish Bigos are so numerous it would take a book to encompass all of them. Perhaps the best known is that made with sauerkraut and sausage. However, a simpler—and equally delicious —form of bigos is the summer variety in which fresh cabbage is used. This is one of the most delectable and satisfying of cabbage dishes. It is fine with roast pork, goose, duck, hare, venison, and sausages.

Shred 1 large head of cabbage; wash quickly in cold water, drain and dry well. Sprinkle a little salt over the shredded cabbage and allow it to stand until slightly wilted. Cut ¼ pound of lean raw pork, cut into small cubes and brown in its own fat; stir in 1 tablespoon of lard, and mix well. Then add ¼ cup of scraped and small celery, ¼ cup of chopped green pepper, free from white seeds and ribs, adding more fat if needed, and brown slightly. Turn mixture into a stew pot; stir in the cabbage, also 3 medium size green apples, pared, cored, and sliced, 1 small tin of tomato paste, 1 No. 2 can of Italian tomatoes, pulp and juice, 1 large bay leaf, 3 whole cloves, 1 thin slice of garlic, mashed, and salt and pepper to taste. Mix well, cover and cook over a very gentle flame or in a slow oven (275–300° F.) for 1½ hours.

This is even better when warmed over in a frying pan the next day.

RED CABBAGE AND CHESTNUTS [1220]
CASSEROLE

Shred or cut 1 large head of red cabbage as finely as possible. Melt 3 tablespoons of butter in an enamel or earthen casserole; stir in the cabbage, ⅓ cup of cider vinegar, ⅓ cup of hot water or meat stock, or equal parts of water and Pique Seasoning, 6 whole cloves and 2 small bay leaves. Season to taste with salt and freshly ground crushed black pepper, bring to a boil, cover and simmer very gently for one hour, stirring occasionally. Meantime, cook ½ pound of chestnuts in water for 15 to 20 minutes, peel and cut them in quarters; add to the cabbage, and continue simmering for 15 minutes longer. Taste for seasoning, and serve at once with pork, ham, hare or rabbit, goose duck, or fried sausage.

SAVOY CABBAGE FRENCH STYLE [1221]

Clean and cut up 1 medium-sized head of Savoy cabbage; cover with boiling water, add a little salt, and cook for ten minutes. Drain well, then chop very finely. Chop 3 strips of bacon very small and put in a saucepan; add 2 tablespoons of grated onion, 1 teaspoon of grated shallots and 1 tablespoon of finely-chopped chives, and brown carefully over a gentle flame, stirring frequently. Now stir in the chopped hot cabbage, season to taste with salt, pepper and a generous dash of nutmeg, add ½ cup of sweet scalded cream, or just enough to hold the cabbage together and not show an excess of liquid. Heat through and serve at once. Especially good with pork, duck, goose, venison and sausages.

STEAMED CABBAGE AU GRATIN [1222]
AMANDINE

Steamed cabbage will require 10 minutes' cooking when shredded, or slightly longer when quartered.

Wash and quarter a 3½ to 4-pound cabbage and steam or cook it in boiling salted water for about 15 minutes. Do not overcook it. Drain, chop, and mix with 1 cup shredded blanched toasted almonds. Pour over this mixture 2 cups hot rich cheese sauce (No. 1027); sprinkle ¾ cup buttered bread crumbs over all and bake in a hot oven (400° F.) just long enough to brown the crumbs.

STUFFED CABBAGE [1223]

Parboil a 2 pound firm green cabbage; turn upside down in a colander and drain thoroughly, then gently unfold the leaves, but without separating them from the stem, as a rose would unfold.

Prepare a dressing of milk-soaked stale bread, squeezed dry after soaking, left-over meat, poultry or liver, and a small onion, passing all through a food chopper. Season highly with thyme, ground cloves, finely chopped parsley and a touch of garlic (optional), all blended and moistened with 2 or 3 slightly beaten egg yolks. There should be 1½ to 2 cups of stuffing. Using a spatula, carefully spread this dressing on the cabbage leaves, being careful to do it evenly. Now bring the leaves back into their (more or less) original positions and tie securely.

Place the cabbage in a generously buttered baking dish containing a can (No. 2) of tomatoes thickened with a light roux. Stick with two or three cloves and bake in a moderate oven, (350° F.) about 45 minutes, basting occasionally.

Just before serving add a generous tablespoon of good sherry to the sauce, and sprinkle with a tablespoon or two of capers. Serve right from the baking dish.

STUFFED CABBAGE, MADRAS [1224]

Boil a large head of cabbage from which the core has been removed, until the leaves are pliable and tender. Stuff with the following mixture:

Fry slowly over a low flame, 1 medium-sized onion and a large clove of garlic until just beginning to color, stirring frequently. Add ¾ pound of ground, lean beef, and ¼ pound of lean veal, and continue cooking 3 or 4 minutes longer, stirring constantly. Now add ¾ cup of cooked rice and blend thoroughly. Season to taste with salt, pepper and a dash of powdered thyme. Remove from the fire, mix in 2 slightly beaten eggs, with 1 tablespoon each of parsley and chives, finely chopped.

Remove the leaves from the cabbage and select 6 nice, large ones. Divide the stuffing among these 6 and roll tight; secure with kitchen thread, and arrange the rolls, side by side in a buttered baking pan. Sprinkle over each 1 teaspoon of grated onion, then 1 No. 2 can of tomatoes over the rolls. Bake about 25 minutes in a moderate oven (350° F.), then cover the pan with a buttered paper, and continue baking for 15 minutes longer. Remove the paper; transfer the rolls to a hot platter; taste the sauce for seasoning, and pour over the rolls.

I wonder if the Cabbage knows
He is less lovely than the Rose;
Or does he squat in smug content,
A source of noble nourishment;
Or if he pities for her sins
The Rose who has no vitamins;
Or if one thing his green heart knows—
That self-same fire that warms the Rose?
—Unknown Author.

CARDOON [1225]

The cardoon is a thistle-like plant resembling the artichoke, but generally taller. Some varieties attain a height of eight to ten feet, with pale green leaves, often 3 feet long, covered with a silvery down. It is grown for the fleshy leaf midribs of the young plant which are cut into short lengths and cooked in boiling salted water until just tender. Keep the vegetable well covered with water to avoid its tendency to blacken. After draining, free from strings, (if any remain), and serve with a butter sauce, or a rich cream sauce (No. 258), seasoning to taste with salt, pepper and a dash of nutmeg. The Italians prefer to bread the cooked pieces and sauté them in olive oil; the oil is then drained off and a thick tomato sauce flavored with dill, fennel and plenty of garlic added. Cardoons may be dipped in a batter, then fried in deep fat. Also they may be used in salads, stews, soups and casserole combinations.

Cardoons may also be prepared according to all the different methods applied to celery, *but* in all cases they must be blanched before the final cooking, in order to remove the skins and slime.

BOILED CARDOONS, DIVERS SAUCES [1226]

Strip the stalks of a 2-pound bunch of cleaned, washed, and dried cardoons from the prickles and cut the white stalks into 2½ to 3-inch lengths. Place in a saucepan; cover with salted boiling water and boil gently for 15 minutes; drain well; rub off the skins with a cloth; return cardoons to the saucepan; cover with cold water, slightly seasoned with salt, and boil gently until tender. Drain and serve hot with parsley butter, Maître d'Hôtel butter. brown butter, cream sauce, Hollandaise sauce, Mousseline sauce, egg sauce, cheese sauce, smitane sauce, Béchamel sauce, etc. (See Sauces.)

Cardoons may be used in salads in the same way as celery, but should always be previously blanched.

CARROTS [1227]

Carrots are native to Europe and the adjoining portions of Asia. They were introduced from there into North and South America and

China; and today they are grown throughout a large portion of the world.

It is believed that they were cultivated in early times but probably were not used generally as a food. Pliny says: "They cultivate a plant in Syria like the wild carrot, and of the same properties, which is eaten cooked or raw and is of great service as a stomachic . . . "

References to carrots are frequent in records: In China, from the Thirteenth Century on, in Japan in 1712, in India in 1826, in Arabia in 1775, in Europe by nearly all the writers and herbalists since 1536, in Virginia in 1609, in Brazil in 1647, etc.

Carrots are rich in vitamins A, B, and C, also in precious minerals, but we cannot say that they are the leading vegetable in this respect. Nature has distributed these elements over a wide range of vegetables and for this reason it is wise to serve a combination of vegetables. Generally speaking, the deeper the color of the carrot, the better the source of vitamin A.

CARROTS—HINTS [1228]

Scrub carrots with a small brush and boil them. When tender, rinse in cold water when the skins may be rubbed off easily, no scraping being necessary.

Soak carrot strips in ice water with a few slices of onion for a half hour or so to keep them crisp.

Carrots retain more vitamin C when they are steamed for 20 minutes than when boiled for 15.

When serving whole carrots, give them a touch of realism by inserting a sprig of parsley or chervil in the stem end. For variety, roll carrots in finely chopped mint leaves instead of crumbs and serve with roast lamb or mutton. Add a teaspoon of sugar when cooking carrots, tomatoes or peas to bring out the flavor of the vegetables.

Season young cooked carrots with butter, salt, pepper and a touch of nutmeg, then force through a ricer in a golden pile in a hot vegetable dish, and surround the base with smooth, light, creamy mashed potatoes forced through a pastry bag with a rose tube, and dust the potato circle with finely chopped parsley, chervil, chives or green pepper.

Aniseed added to buttered carrots add exotic flavor to a delicate dish.

Vegetables such as carrots and beets retain their natural sweetness if not overcooked.

Grated raw carrot in potato salad is as good as it is attractive. Also nourishing is grated raw carrot in meat loaf and coleslaw.

Slice carrots lengthwise rather than crosswise. The reason. There is less loss of food value when they are cut this way.

A little grated nutmeg is good on candied carrots . . . Nuts added to creamed carrots or plain buttered carrots give new flavor, crunchiness and more nutrition . . . The carrot is more sinned against than sinning. Those obese monstrosities which need table carving should never be boiled and served as is . . . Eat all the raw carrots you can and you will get all the carotene (from which vitamin A is produced in the liver) you need. Whether the juice squeezed from raw carrot or that from steamed carrot gives the most carotene nobody knows as yet.

Carrots are good when smooth, firm and bright in color, with tops green and unwilted. Beware of deep cracks in carrots, for that is usually a sign of poor quality.

Try grating carrots before cooking, and season with salt, pepper and butter. These *riced* carrots have a mild flavor and will most likely find favor with those who object to the usual taste of carrots.

BAKED CARROTS FRENCH STYLE   [1229]

A simple but elaborate-looking vegetable combination to serve with cold roast beef or pot roast (Boeuf à la Mode).

Bake together (using equal parts) whole tender carrots, medium-sized onions, each stuck with a whole clove, and peeled medium-sized potatoes. Cover them with melted butter, add a clove of garlic, season to taste with salt and pepper, and bake for about an hour in a moderate oven or until they are brown and the potatoes crisp.

Baking whole carrots this way, or alone, gives them almost a caramel taste, much more pronounced than the flavor that carrots usually have when they are cut up or mashed and boiled in so much water that most of the taste is lost. Even plain boiled whole carrots taste better than when they are cut up. Always cook carrots whole when they are not too enormous. The *very* large ones should be cut in quarters.

CAROTTES A LA CYRANO   [1230]

Scrape a dozen young carrots, and cook them in slightly salted water until tender. Cut in lengthwise halves; dip the halves in slightly warmed honey, and arrange them in layers in a generously buttered baking dish. Salt to taste, and sprinkle generously with grated Swiss or Gruyere. Bake in a hot oven (400° F.) for 10 minutes. Serve hot.

CAROTTES FLAMANDES   [1231]
Flemish Carrots (Serves 6)

Only new carrots should be used. Blanch 1 generous pound carrots for 5 minutes; then run them under cold water and rub off the thin skins with a clean cloth. Cut the green parts from the tip and a little piece from the root. Place the carrots in a buttered casserole and add ¼ cup butter, a pinch of salt, and 1 scant teaspoon granulated sugar. Cover and bring to a boil, then reduce the heat and continue cooking for 25 minutes or so, taking care to shake the casserole every 5 minutes in order to obtain equal cooking and prevent scorching. Test for tenderness by pressing a carrot with the fingers. When it feels just right, not too soft or mushy, add the following mixture: 3 egg yolks, beaten into ¼ cup rich, heavy sweet cream, 2 tablespoons slightly melted butter, and 1 tablespoon finely minced fresh parsley. Stir gently, and serve at once.

CAROTTES VICHY [1232]

Take 1 generous pound very young cleaned carrots, and place in a casserole with ½ cup butter, 1 scant teaspoon sugar, and a few grains salt. Cover closely and bake in a very moderate oven (325° F.). Let cook slowly for 10 to 12 minutes. Shake occasionally since carrots scorch very easily. Serve dusted with finely chopped parsley.

CARROT CUSTARD CUPS [1233]

Mash 3 cups cooked carrots; add salt and pepper to taste with 2 tablespoons finely minced onion, and ⅓ cup top milk. Stir in 3 slightly beaten eggs; pour into individual greased custard cups; set in a pan containing ½-inch hot water; bake in a moderate oven (350° F.) about 30 minutes, or until a silver knife inserted in center comes out clean. Turn out and serve with well seasoned Cream Sauce (No. 258), to which a spoonful of chopped raw green pepper or parsley has been added.

CARROT FRITTERS [1234]

Sift 1¾ cups flour, add 3 teaspoons baking powder and ½ teaspoon salt and sift again. Combine 1 slightly beaten egg, 1 cup of milk and 1 tablespoon melted shortening; pour into the flour mixture and stir just until smooth. Add 2 cups of chopped, cooked carrots and 1 teaspoon grated onion. Drop by tablespoons into hot, deep fat (375–400° F.) and fry 3 to 5 minutes, or until well browned on all sides, turning the fritters as they rise to the surface. Drain on absorbent paper. Serve with Egg Sauce (No. 1051–52).

CARROT JUICE [1235]

Wash and scrape two bunches of young carrots. Grate on a fine grater, put in saucepan, add 2 cups of water and cook slowly until tender, stirring frequently. Strain and press all juice through sieve. Put in a glass jar, seal and chill in refrigerator.

CARROT SOUFFLE [1236]

Melt 3 tablespoons of butter in a saucepan, add 3 tablespoons of flour, ¼ teaspoon each of salt and pepper, then gradually 1 cup of milk and bring to a boil, stirring constantly. Let boil over a low flame for three minutes still stirring. Add 1 pint mashed cooked carrots, and the yolks of 3 eggs beaten until thick, then fold in whites of 3 eggs beaten to a stiff froth, turn into a buttered baking dish and top with buttered crumbs. Bake in a moderate oven (350° F.) for 25 minutes.

GLAZED CARROTS [1237]

Wash but do not peel or scrape one bunch of young carrots. Cook whole, or halved crosswise, until pierceable in just enough salted boiling water to cover in a closely covered saucepan. Drain, reserving the liquid to make a soup or a hot drink. Peel or rub off the skins from the carrots if necessary. Add 2 tablespoons of butter and ⅓ cup of corn or cane syrup to the drained carrots in saucepan; cook without a cover over a medium flame until the carrots have a glazed appearance, which will take about 20 minutes. Turn occasionally. Serve hot.

SHOESTRING CARROTS [1238]

Wash and scrape firm young carrots, and cut them into shoestring strips. For 6 persons, 3 generous cups will suffice. Place in a heavy saucepan with 4 tablespoons butter, 1 teaspoon minced chervil, ½ teaspoon aniseed, 1 teaspoon grated onion, 1 small bay leaf, a small sprig of thyme, and salt and pepper to taste. Cover the pan, and steam over a low flame for 10 minutes, shaking the pan frequently to keep the carrots from sticking. Add 1 scant teaspoon sugar, honey, or corn syrup, and a generous tablespoon butter; blend gently with a wooden spoon, cover, and simmer 5 minutes longer.

CAULIFLOWER [1239]

Early historians placed cauliflower and broccoli in one botanical variety, and it was not until 1724 that broccoli was mentioned separately. It is believed that the Romans knew them both, in which case they have been in cultivation for a considerable period of time, but little is known of the history of the cauliflower. It is, however, of the cabbage family, which is a big one and cauliflower is the queen of it.

Cauliflower appears on the market in greatest abundance in the late summer or early fall and is shipped from different sections of the country all winter. Fine quality in cauliflower is indicated by a white or creamy-white, clean, heavy, firm, compact curd or flower head. The jacket or outer leaves which protect the head should be fresh, firm and green. A compact, clean curd means a minimum of waste and such a head is easily prepared for cooking. The size of the head has nothing to do with maturity. Large and small heads may be equally mature.

"Riciness" is the term used to describe the granular appearance when the flowerets of cauliflower have begun to grow. It is not objectionable if not too far advanced. Yellow leaves may indicate staleness or age, but are not important if the curd is otherwise of good quality. Avoid spotted, speckled or bruised curd and the presence of plant lice. Examine the head closely. Often the thick growth of green leaves hides the shallowness of the curds. The odor should be sharp but sweet and clean.

In order to preserve both color and flavor during cooking, care must be taken to boil the cauliflower only until it is tender. This may be accomplished in one of two ways; either by cooking it closely covered, in a small amount of water, or uncovered in plenty of boiling salted water. The green leaves, if tender, may be cooked with the cauliflower, chopped and served with a butter, cream or cheese sauce around the cauliflower, as it is done in Finland. The Finns also add a piece or two of lemon peel to the water to keep the cauliflower white; a little sugar will do the same thing.

CAULIFLOWER COUNTRY STYLE [1240]

Melt 4 tablespoons of butter in a heavy saucepan; add 1 medium-sized cauliflower which has been separated into flowerets, washed and well-drained, 3 medium-sized fresh tomatoes, peeled and sliced, 1 large green pepper, parboiled, halved, skinned and thinly sliced and free from any white seeds and white ribs, and 1 large onion, peeled and thinly sliced; cover, and cook gently for about 25 to 30 minutes, or until the flowerets are pierceable, stirring frequently. Season to taste with mixed salt, white pepper and nutmeg, then pour over 3 eggs, slightly beaten. Continue to cook gently over a low flame until the eggs are set. Serve directly from the pan.

CAULIFLOWER CUSTARD [1241]

Boil 1 medium-sized, trimmed, washed cauliflower in boiling salted water for 10 minutes after breaking it apart. Drain and chop fine. Blend thoroughly 2 slightly-beaten eggs, $\frac{1}{2}$ teaspoon salt, white pepper to taste and 1 cup of thin cream or undiluted evaporated milk, with 1 or 2 teaspoons of curry powder (optional). Pour into buttered custard cups, set in a pan of hot water, and bake in a moderate oven (350° F.) for 25 to 30 minutes, or until set. Unmold and garnish with bacon curls, watercress and crisp potato chips.

CAULIFLOWER RING MOLD SOUFFLÉ [1242]
AMANDINE

Select a nice, medium-sized cauliflower, separate the flowerets, wash thoroughly in slightly salted lukewarm water and let stand 5 minutes, stirring often. Drain and place the flowerets in a saucepan with 5 or 6 cups of boiling salted water, 2 or 3 teaspoons of lemon juice and a generous pinch of white pepper. Cook, uncovered, for 15 minutes, or until pierceable. Drain and rice into a mixing bowl. Add to this pureé 4 egg yolks, one at a time, beating well after each addition; then fold in 4 egg whites stiffly beaten with a few grains of salt and nutmeg; stir in very gently 2 tablespoons of lukewarm butter. Turn into a large buttered ring mold, sprinkled with ¼ cup of blanched, peeled, ground and toasted almonds, and bake in a hot oven (400° F.) for 20 to 25 minutes, or until soufflé is well puffed and firm and delicately browned on top. Unmold on a hot, round platter and fill center with creamed eggs, dusted with paprika, creamed fish, shellfish, oysters, shrimps, scallops, and so forth, for a Lenten dish, or with creamed chicken or meat for other days; dust the top of the meat or chicken with mixed, finely chopped parsley and chives and serve as hot as possible.

CAULIFLOWER A LA ROMANE [1243]

Remove leaves and any discolorations from a large, sound cauliflower; cook in boiling salted water until tender; drain and break into flowerets. Arrange the flowerets in a shallow, buttered, bread-crumb-lined baking dish; sprinkle generously with grated Parmesan cheese using about 2 ozs. Beat 2 teaspoons of flour with 2 egg yolks, then stir in ¾ cup of cold milk, and season to taste with salt and pepper. Pour this over the cauliflower; top with pieces of butter and bake in a moderate oven (350–375° F.) for 25 to 30 minutes. Serve right from the baking dish.

CURRIED CAULIFLOWER HOME STYLE [1244]

Boil a well-washed large head of cauliflower in slightly salted water and let stand 5 minutes. Drain, then divide into 6 equal portions and lay the cut sides down upon a hot serving dish. Pour over them 1¼ cups of Curry Sauce, (No. 1045–1046–1047) dust with finely chopped parsley, and, over the parsley, with paprika. Serve immediately.

FRENCH FRIED CAULIFLOWER [1245]

Remove leaves and trim thick stalks from a medium-sized, sound cauliflower which has been thoroughly washed. Separate flowerets by gently inserting a knife between sections of head and cutting apart. Cook flowerets in boiling salted water, (uncovered) until tender, or about 10 to 12 minutes, depending on size of flowerets. Drain and cool. Sift 1 scant cup of bread flour once, add 2 teaspoons of baking powder, ½ teaspoon of salt and a few grains of nutmeg and resift into a mixing bowl. Add 1 large egg, well-beaten with about ¾ cup of cold milk, and mix until smooth and absolutely free from lumps. Season cauliflower with a little lemon juice, also salt and pepper to taste, and when ready to serve, dip in batter and fry in deep, hot, clear fat until golden brown. Drain on absorbent paper and serve on a hot platter, on a paper doily or a folded napkin.

LEMON BUTTER CAULIFLOWER [1246]

Wash 1 large or two small heads of sound cauliflower in slightly salted lukewarm water, after separating the flowerets. Drain, rinse quickly in cold water and cook in slightly salted water to cover until tender, or about 15 to 20 minutes. Drain, cover and keep hot. Heat ¼ cup of butter over a gentle flame; stir in ⅓ cup of lemon juice, mixing well, add 3 tablespoons of washed capers, and pour over the cauliflower in a hot vegetable dish. Dust generously with equal parts of finely chopped parsley and chives.

SMOTHERED CAULIFLOWER AU GRATIN [1247]

Cook a well-washed large head of cauliflower (do not break it up) in salted water until tender. Drain well. Place in a baking dish head up; pour over it 2 cups of thickened stewed tomatoes mixed with 1 medium-sized grated onion. Sprinkle over all ¾ cup (about) of sieved bread crumbs mixed with ½ cup of grated American cheese, and bake in a moderate oven (375° F.) until golden brown and cheese and crumbs bubble. Serve at once.

CELERY [1248]

Celery, which belongs to the parsley family, has grown wild and been used as a medicine for hundreds of years. The wild plant is a native of marshy places in European regions, and extends from Sweden to Algeria, Egypt, and Ethiopia, and eastward to the Caucasus. It was not until 1623 in France that any attempt was made to develop a cultivated variety. The wild celery was called "smallage," and it was an herb eaten to purify the blood.

The first commercial production of celery in America was started by some Dutch gardeners in Kalamazoo, Michigan in 1874. They offered it for sale to passengers who went through Kalamazoo on the train, and later the train boys and express messengers on the Michigan Central Railroad sold celery to the passengers and to people along their routes. It was from this small beginning that celery production has now brought the crop to be the second most important salad crop in America. It is now grown in almost every State.

CELERY—HINTS [1249]

The utility rating of celery is a clear 100 per cent, for every part of this all-year vegetable can be eaten.

To crisp celery, take apart, wash thoroughly, and stand in the refrigerator for a few hours in a pitcher or cold water to which 1 teaspoonful of salt has been added. Lemon juice will help to keep it white.

Stew all the celery leaves and tops, strain the "juice" and store it in the refrigerator for future use. Use it instead of water or milk for sauces, gravies, soups and stews and for moistening left-overs when reheating them.

Instead of cooking for the "juice," dry celery tops thoroughly and then reduce to powder by rubbing through a sieve. This is a convenient way to add the flavor of celery to fish, meat, vegetables, soups, sauces, stews, and so forth.

Celery cut into pieces and boiled with potatoes or carrots is flavorful as well as healthful, also it is one way of using bits of celery which otherwise might be wasted.

To complement meat or fish, try creamed celery and toasted slivered almonds. Call this *Celery Amandine*.

Celery root, also known as celeriac and celery knobs, has the celery flavor intensified. It combines well with mashed white potatoes and the two vegetables may be cooked together, with a little more time allowed for the root. Sliced or diced and cooked for 10 minutes in boiling salted water or meat stock, it is delicious with butter, cream or Hollandaise sauce. The French like to cook the sliced root in bouillon and serve it with a cream sauce highly flavored with chervil. Or they make a purée and add some thick Béchamel sauce (No. 259) and a little grated Gruyère cheese; or just some meat juices and seasoning.

Celery doesn't lose its flavor through cooking although it does undergo a change in texture.

BOILED CELERY KNOB HOLLANDAISE [1250]
Celeriac

Trim the tops from 2 large celery knobs; wash well; peel each one and cut into wedge-shaped slices of medium size and thickness. Place in a saucepan; add boiling water to barely cover with 1 teaspoon of salt, 1 large bay leaf and 1 small clove of garlic, left whole. Cover and boil steadily until pierceable—about 15 minutes. Do not over-cook, lest the vegetable fall apart. Drain well and transfer to a heated vegetable dish; cover with 1½ cups of Hollandaise sauce (No. 1062); dust with finely chopped chives and serve at once.

Celery received its name from the Greek word for parlsey—*selinon*.

BRAISED CELERY HOME STYLE [1251]

Trim off outer stalks and leaves of a large bunch of celery. Split the stalks lengthwise, and scrape carefully, then cut into inch lengths, dropping them into cold water as cut. Drain; place in a stewpan, cover with cold water; bring to a boil, let boil up once or twice and drain well. Cook 2 tablespoons of minced onion in 3 tablespoons of butter until soft, or about 3 or 4 minutes; arrange the drained celery on top; barely cover with a rich beef stock; cover the pan and bake in a hot oven (400° F.) for 25 minutes, or till celery is tender; season to taste with salt and pepper, and add 1 teaspoon of beef extract (commercial) adding more beef stock if needed to cover celery. Cover with a buttered paper and continue baking for 15 to 20 minutes longer. Serve on a heated platter, dusting with chopped parsley.

CELERY CUSTARD CUPS [1252]

Cook 2½ cups of cleaned, scraped celery stalks cut into ½-inch lengths with ⅔ cup of chopped onions in 2½ cups of rich milk until tender, or about 25 minutes; season to taste with salt, pepper and nutmeg, and remove from the fire. Cool slightly, then beat in 4 egg yolks, one at a time, beating well after each addition, alternately with 3 slightly beaten egg whites. Turn mixture into 6 buttered custard cups, adding to each cup half a teaspoon of butter, and place the cups onto a baking sheet. Bake in a slow oven (300–325° F.) for about 40 minutes or until a knife inserted in them comes out clean. Serve at once as a vegetable or as a main supper dish.

An interesting way of using up the less desirable stalks of celery is to make fritters out of them. These fritters are good served with pork chops, or any white meat such as veal and even poultry.

CURRIED CELERY FRITTERS [1253]

Sift 1 cup of flour, 1 teaspoon of baking powder, ½ teaspoon of salt, and 2 teaspoons of curry powder into a mixing bowl. Combine 1 well beaten egg with ¾ cup of cold milk, and mix thoroughly, beating with rotary beater, and drop all at once into the flour mixture. Blend well to make a smooth batter; add 1½ cups of finely chopped celery stalk, previously carefully scraped, and when ready to serve, drop by tea or tablespoons into deep, hot, clear fat, and fry golden brown. Drain on absorbent paper, and serve on a folded napkin placed on a heated platter.

Variations. Carrots (raw or cooked), cooked peas, raw or cooked cauliflower flowerets and cooked or canned corn may be similarly prepared.

CELERY AU GRATIN GASTRONOME   [1254]

Clean, scrape, cut in two, lengthwise, then crosswise into 2-inch pieces, 4 or 5 nice celery stalks. Wash quickly, drain, then blanch in boiling water for 5 minutes; drain well and rinse under running cold water. Place in a saucepan with a half lemon, peeled and seeded, 1 small bouquet garni composed of 1 bay leaf, 4 or 5 sprigs of fresh parsley and 1 sprig of thyme all tied together with white kitchen thread; cover with beef bouillon and cook very gently for about 35 to 40 minutes, covered, stirring frequently with a wooden spoon. Drain the liquid into a saucepan, and keep the celery hot. There should be about 1½ cups of bouillon; if not, add enough to make up this amount, then reduce to about a half cup, over a very bright flame. Stir in 1 cup of scalded sweet cream, taste for seasoning, and add 3 tablespoons of sherry. Keep hot over hot water.

Arrange ⅓ of the celery in a generously buttered casserole, pour over ⅓ of the sauce, and over the sauce sprinkle 2 or 3 tablespoons of grated Swiss cheese. Repeat with celery, sauce and cheese until all ingredients are used. Top with ½ generous cup of buttered bread crumbs and grated cheese in equal parts, and brown in a quick oven (425–450° F.). Serve at once. Especially good with feathered game, capon, guinea hen and turkey.

Celery knob (celeriac) may be prepared in the same way, as also may carrots, leeks, parsnips, and turnips.

CELERY KNOB BOURGEOISE   [1255]
Celeriac

During most of the year this relative of celery can be obtained by those appreciating the agreeable flavor of the root.

Wash and peel 2 celery knobs; cut in small slices and simmer until tender in 2 cups of water or, better still, in meat stock until tender. Drain. Place in a saucepan and keep hot. Heat 4 tablespoons of butter in a saucepan; stir in 3 tablespoons of minced onion and 2 tablespoons of minced green pepper; cook gently until beginning to soften. Add the cooked celery knob, mixing with a fork and taking care not to break it. When very hot, add 2 tablespoons of minced parsley and 1 tablespoon of chopped chives and season to taste with salt and pepper. Serve at once.

In the seventeenth century a sect of Chinese Buddhists in Pahang, Malay, ate nothing but celery and drank only rain water.

CREAMED CELERY AND CHESTNUTS   [1256]

Cut enough celery stalks into small dice to make 2½ cups; place in a saucepan with 3 cups of slightly salted boiling water. Cover and boil steadily until celery is tender, or about 15 to 20 minutes; drain, reserving the liquid. Blend 4 tablespoons of butter with 3 tablespoons of flour in top of double boiler, and stir in ¾ cup of celery liquid, with ¾ cup of thin cream or undiluted evaporated milk. place over a low flame and cook, stirring constantly, till mixture thickens and is smooth. Add the drained celery and 1 cup of cooked, peeled, quartered chestnuts; return to hot water; taste for seasoning, and heat through. Serve in a heated vegetable dish with a sprinkling of paprika and minced celery. To prepare the chestnuts see Brussels Sprouts with Chestnuts. (No. 1204). Celery Knob, or celeriac, may be prepared in the same way.

Important. Low temperature and high humidity, such as the grocer's icebox or home refrigerator provide are very important in preserving the quality of fresh celery. When the homemaker buys celery she should place it in the moist chamber of the refrigerator without removing the wrapping.

CREAMED CELERY KNOB [1257]
Celeriac

Clean, wash and peel 2 large celery knobs; cut in slices and cook as indicated for Boiled Celery Knob (No. 1250) until tender. Have ready 2 cups of Cream Sauce (No. 258) or, if preferred, 2 cups of scalded sour cream to which has been added 2 or 3 egg yolks. Drain well and add the celery to the sauce, heat through, and serve hot, dusted with a little nutmeg.

MASHED CELERY KNOB [1258]
Celeriac

Wash and pare 2 large celery knobs (celeriac) carefully, then slice and cook in 1 quart of boiling water, to which has been added 1 teaspoon of lemon juice or vinegar to keep the vegetable white, also a little salt. Boil until pierceable or about 15 minutes; drain well, reserving the liquid for soup stock. Force the drained knob through a ricer, or mash it smoothly; season to taste with salt and white pepper, a generous dash of nutmeg, and 3 or 4 tablespoons of butter or margarin and beat until light. Serve in a heated vegetable dish.

If preferred spread the mashed celery knob in a generously buttered shallow baking dish, brush the top with melted butter, then brown quickly under the flame of the broiling oven. Or force the purée through a pastry bag with a large tube onto a buttered baking sheet; brush lightly with beaten egg yolk, and bake in a moderate oven until golden brown. Or, again, beat 3 egg yolks into the purée and use the mixture as a border into which to place creamed fish, meat, poultry, mushrooms, and so forth.

STEWED CELERY [1259]

Wash and scrape the stalks from 2 large bunches of sound celery carefully, then rinse in cold water. Drain and cut crosswise into thin slices or lengthwise, into about inch lengths. Cook until tender, in slightly salted water to barely cover. Drain, turn into a saucepan, add ¾ cup of scalded heavy cream, season to taste with salt, pepper and a dash of nutmeg, stir in 3 tablespoons of butter; cover and simmer for 15 minutes. Serve dusted with chopped parsley.

CHARD [1260]

Chard, or Swiss chard, belongs to the goosefoot family, and apparently was the so-called beet of the ancients and of the Middle Ages. Aristotle mentioned a red chard in 350 B. C.; Roman writers made frequent references to this vegetable; it is found in Chinese writings as early as the seventh century; and in Europe all the old herbalists noted it. Red, yellow and white chard were all known in ancient times.

The wild form is found in the Canary Islands, along the coast of the Mediterranean as far as the Caspian Sea and Persia, and also along the sea coasts of England.

Chard is a close relative of the beet, and the variety in color and leaf formation of this vegetable explains why it has numerous popular names, such as "silver beet," "leaf beet," "kale beet," "Swiss beet," "Spinach beet," "Asparagus beet," and so forth. There's also a variety called "rhubarb chard," which has ribs of the same tone of red as rhubarb and is highly recommended as an excellent variety.

An attractive dish consists of a platter with the stalks in the center, surrounded by a ring of the chopped green chard. Rhubarb chard with its red stalks served in this manner provides a festive and unusual looking as well as a delicious vegetable.

Swiss chard is often called the "cut and come again" vegetable because it permits continuous cropping. It contains vitamins B, C, and D. The leaves, when the size of spinach, can be used as spinach. Some people prefer to allow the leaves to grow until very large, when the leafy portion is cooked as greens and the thick, fleshy stalks or midribs are prepared like asparagus, cardoons and celery stalks.

Important. Be sure to use unsalted water to keep the chard from turning a dark color. Season just before serving.

Although the preference is largely a matter of taste, it is well to keep in mind that light green chard leaves are milder than the deep green chard. However, to introduce chard into your menu successfully, care must be taken to pick only that which appears crisp tender and fresh, with fleshy stalks and wholly free from insect injury. Wilted or rubbery stalks will prove tough, coarse and stringy, and chard with yellowed leaves is too old to be satisfactory.

BOILED CHARD GREENS SOUTHERN STYLE   [1261]

Trim roots and carefully pick over the greens from 2 pounds of bunched chard greens and wash well in several changes of cold water. Cook in very little water or in its own moisture until tender, or about 15–20 minutes. Drain, chop or not as desired, season to taste with salt and pepper as well as a dash each of nutmeg and cloves, and toss in ¼ cup of butter. Sprinkle with coarse buttered crumbs sprinkled with 1 tablespoon of lemon juice or vinegar, and serve as hot as possible. The stalks or midribs will provide a vegetable for another meal. Cut them into two-inch lengths; cook in plain water until pierceable, or about 25 to 30 minutes, and drain well; season to taste with salt and plenty of black pepper and serve as hot as possible with melted butter, parsley butter, cream or white sauce, Hollandaise or Smitane or sour cream sauce. (See Sauces.)

CHARD CROQUETTES PARISIAN STYLE   [1262]

Clean, remove roots and midribs, and pick over the greens from 2 pounds of chard. Cook the greens until tender in their own moisture, exactly as you would spinach or about 15–20 minutes. Do not add any water at all. Drain; then put through food chopper with ¾ cup of grated cheese and ½ teaspoon of grated lemon rind, salt, pepper, nutmeg and cloves to taste. Beat in 5 eggs, one at a time, beating well after each addition and adding with the last egg, 1 cup (more or less) of bread crumbs and ½ cup of peeled, ground fresh mushrooms. Shape into croquettes, dip in beaten egg, then in sieved bread crumbs, again in beaten egg and in crumbs, and chill. When ready to serve, place a few croquettes at a time in a frying basket and plunge the basket into hot, deep clear fat. (375–390° F.) Fry until nicely browned; drain and serve with meat, fish, poultry or game.

CHARD RING WITH MUSHROOMS   [1263]

Cook 2 pounds of cleaned chard greens in their own moisture for 15 to 20 minutes; drain well, then put through food chopper, and stir in 1½ cups of cream sauce (No. 258), or enough to make a mixture not too firm. Turn into a buttered ring mold; set the mold in a pan of hot, but not boiling water, and bake 35 to 40 minutes in a moderate oven (350–375° F.) or until firm. Unmold on to a heated round platter and fill center with creamed mushrooms.

Variation. Fill center with creamed carrots, creamed fish, such as crab meat, lobster, shrimps, cod or other cooked fish, creamed onions, and so forth.

CHARD SOUFFLE [1264]

Prepare 1½ cups of White Sauce (No. 258) and keep hot. Have ready 1⅓ cups of cooked, ground or finely chopped green chard leaves. Add 1 cup of the white sauce to the chard and mix well. Turn into a generously buttered soufflé dish, and to the remaining white sauce, add ½ teaspoon of Worcestershire sauce, then beat in 4 egg yolks, adding one at a time and beating well after each addition, and adding with the last yolk, 1 tablespoon each of finely chopped parsley and grated onion. Season to taste with salt, pepper and a dash of nutmeg, and fold in 4 stiffly beaten egg whites. Pour over the greens in the soufflé dish, and bake in a moderate oven (375° F.) for 35 to 40 minutes, or until soufflé is well puffed, set and brown. Serve at once.

CHARD SWISS STYLE [1265]

Pour ¼ cup of cold milk over 2 slices of bread, broken into small pieces in a mixing bowl; let stand until absorbed. Soak ⅓ cup of cleaned, dried mushrooms 5 minutes in a little warm water; squeeze dry, then chop fine. Add the mushrooms to the bread with 2 leeks, chopped very fine after being first carefully washed in several changes of cold water, also 3 tablespoons of finely chopped parsley or chives, ½ cup of finely chopped green celery leaves, ½ clove of garlic, mashed to a pulp, 4 cups of cooked, chopped chard greens, and ⅓ cup of grated Swiss cheese or equal parts of grated Swiss and Parmesan cheese, if a sharp flavor is desired; season to taste with salt, pepper and nutmeg and mix in 4 large unbeaten eggs, adding one at a time, and mixing well after each addition. Butter a baking dish generously, pour in 2 tablespoons of olive oil, spreading well over the bottom of the dish, turn mixture in, and top with ½ cup of fine bread crumbs mixed with 1 tablespoon of olive oil. Bake in a moderate oven (350° F.) for about 30 minutes, or until firm and nicely browned. Serve from the baking dish.

Spinach or any other greens, may be prepared in the same manner.

CORN [1266]

Botanists have failed to clear up the mystery of corn's origin, merely guessing that it was a wild weed possibly in Peru; but our red Indians laid claim to it for this continent, and cherished a legend of the corn spirit that came to earth trailing robes and plumes of emerald and was slain by a red hero, but sprang to life again as the giver of food for all the tribes of a hero race.

> *. . . Till at length a small green feather*
> *From the earth shot slowly upward,*
> *Then another and another,*
> *And before the summer ended*
> *Stood the maize in all its beauty*
> *With its shining robes about it,*
> *And its long, soft, yellow tresses;*
> *And in rapture Hiawatha*
> *Cried aloud, "It is Mondamin!*
> *Yes, the friend of man, Mondamin!*

Maize, as it is pretty generally called in Europe, has traveled to many countries in flinty kernels and fine ground meal, but the green corn remains peculiarly American, even in these days when fruits are flashed around the globe from garden to market at lightning speed.

Corn, according to the dictionary, is an Anglo-Saxon word that means grain, a small seed of a cereal grass such as rye, wheat, and so forth, or, collectively, the seeds of any cereal grass used as food. When corn is mentioned in the Bible it probably means wheat, for at that time the word was used in its original meaning and did not refer to the Indian cereal whose real name is maize.

Maize was the first grain seen by Columbus when he landed in Cuba. We are told that it may have come to the United States from the West Indies or Northern or Central Mexico. At any rate it was not until after Columbus discovered the new continent that corn, as such, was known in Europe.

Naturally, there are many American-Indian legends told of the origin of the Indian corn. One says that the first kernel was brought by a blackbird, but there is another, not so practical but much more beautiful and appropriate for our holidays. According to legend the story is something like this: Once upon a time there was an Indian youth who went to the woods to fast in honor of his approaching manhood. He built himself a hut and wandered about it praying that the Great Spirit might acknowledge him by sending him a gift for his people who were in great need. Finally, after several days of absolute fasting, he was too weak to walk further and so lay on the ground looking at the sky. On the third day of this idleness a spirit appeared before him, adorned with flowing green plumes. The young spirit youth commanded the Indian to rise and wrestle with him if he wished to attain his heart's desire. After the exercise he was exhausted and before he revived, the spirit left. This was repeated for four days, and then the spirit said that he would return once more, on which occasion the youth would overcome him, after which he was to strip off the green clothes and bury them in the ground. The mound over the clothes was to be tended and kept free from weeds. If this were done, so said the spirit, the young Indian would get his desire.

The lad did as he was told and one day a plant grew up from the spot where the green plumes had been buried.

Here is another story: In the spring of 1621, a friendly Indian told the Pilgrims of Plymouth to use the herring as a fertilizer. Governor Bradford's diary recorded they were advised " . . . that unless they got fish and set with it, it would come to nothing and that they would have fish enough come up for the brook by which they began to build . . . " Strangely, herring have never failed to return to the town brook from that year to this date. So every year six Plymouth children reenact a Pilgrim scene by dropping five grains of corn and a herring in a corn patch behind the seventeenth-century Sergeant William Harloy house. As they drop the grains one by one, they chant a 300-year old bit of verse:

> . . . *One for the Blackbird,*
> *One for the Crow,*
> *One for the Cutworm*
> *And two to let it grow* . . .

Corn, the American Indian believed, was the gift of the Great Spirit. And all primitive races from the beginning of time have linked the staple grain with the symbols of worship. According to an ancient tradition, maize consented to bring its gifts to the fertile earth on condition that man should treat them with respect.

CORN—HINTS   [1267]

Adding salt to the boiling water or milk in which sweet corn is cooked tends to toughen the kernels. A little sugar may be added to the liquid.

Corn should not be husked until time to cook it, and it should be boiled not more than five to six minutes. Over-cooking toughens the kernels and takes away their sweetness.

If the kernels are not tender and sweet, they may be grated and used for corn pudding, for fritters, for frying or for soup or chowder. Left-over cooked corn on the cob may be combined with sweet or white potatoes for frying; it may also be used as a stuffing for tomatoes, green peppers, onions, squash, etc.

In buying sweet corn, it is well to remember that corn loses its natural sweetness almost immediately after gathering, so avoid wilted, yellowed husks. Do not buy corn that *has been husked;* the husk helps to preserve the flavor and prevents the kernels from becoming dry and hard. Look for husks that are dark green and fresh looking: kernels should not only be plump and well filled, but also soft and full of milk. Most early sweet corn has creamy white kernels, but later in the season a yellow golden bantam corn is more abundant.

Waterless method of cooking corn. Wet the tender inner husks and place them in the bottom and along the sides of a heavy kettle of the Dutch oven type. Place the ears of corn on this and cover it with several layers of husks. Cover the kettle tightly and set over about one-half of full flame on gas; "low" or "medium" on electricity. When cover gets hot, reduce heat to lowest point and cook 12 to 15 minutes longer, or until corn is tender. Just before it is taken out, the top layer of husks may be removed, salt and butter added, the cover replaced, and heat turned off—allowing 5 minutes or so for the butter to melt and be absorbed by the corn.

Green Corn may also be roasted in the husk in a moderate oven (350–375° F.) in about 35 to 40 minutes.

Cut a few kernels from the cob, add a beaten egg or two; season well, not forgetting a little sugar, then sauté but don't brown it.

Scraps of left-over chicken, veal, lamb, and so forth, combined with cooked corn, eggs and milk as in corn custard make an attractive way of using up two left-over foods.

Corn soufflé is a glorified corn pudding with grated cheese. Remember the pepper. Corn needs plenty. For "squaw-corn," cut corn from the cob, mix with green pepper, lightly sautéed, dice bacon, salt and pepper and fry the whole thing together. Let's pay homage to corn. The story of corn is the story of America. Corn is sugar and starch. Corn is bacon and eggs; corn is oil. When slush is underfoot and the wind knife-edged and you come home wet, weary and incredibly hungry, corn meal may be the hearty basis of a satisfying supper. Corn meal and thick dark molasses, early American sweethearts, meet again in a fruited pudding served with shaved maple sugar.

To Keep Corn Fresh, leave in the husk, put in a shallow pan of water with the tassel ends up and place in refrigerator. The corn will absorb just enough moisture so that it will be as fresh several days after cutting as if used the day it was gathered.

Fresh or canned corn is a valuable addition to the diet, supplying both vitamins A and B. Yellow corn is a good source of both these vitamins.

Broiled Corn Picnic Fashion is a delightful way to cook fresh corn. To prepare it, lay ears wrapped in their own husks on a grate over hot coals or on the rack of your broiling oven. Of course, prepared in this way it lacks something of the woodsy flavor acquired from outdoor cooking but it is tasty nevertheless.

Serve hot corn on the cob with attractive pimiento butter balls, made in advance and stored in your refrigerator. This is done by creaming 4 tablespoons of pimento purée with ½ cup of butter and shaping in balls.

CANNED CORN ON THE COB   [1268]

You may use 2 quart jars if you prefer not to break the long cobs. Carefully remove husks and silk, and boil the corn for 5 to 6 minutes. Pack the cobs in sterilized jars, and fill the jars with cooking water, to which 1 teaspoon salt for each quart has been added. Close the jars, and cook for 70 minutes at 10 pounds pressure in a pressure cooker, or for

3 hours in a water bath. Seal immediately after removing from the canning vessel.

CANNED CORN CREAM STYLE [1269]

Scrape sound, fresh ears of corn; and to each quart of grains and pulp, add 2 cups boiling water and 1 teaspoon salt. Boil together for 5 minutes, and pack into sterilized jars. Close the jars, and cook for 1½ hours in a pressure cooker at 10 pounds pressure or for 3 hours in a hot water bath. Seal at once.

CORN CUSTARD PIE [1270]

Melt 2 tablespoons of butter in a saucepan over a low flame; stir in 1 tablespoon of grated onion, cook for a minute, then add 1 tablespoon of flour, and, when blended, gradually stir in ¾ cup of scalded milk, previously scalded with 1 bay leaf, 2 whole cloves, a clove of garlic, and 3 sprigs of fresh parsley, then strained. Stir until smooth and thickened; remove from the fire; season with salt, pepper, nutmeg to taste, 1 teaspoon of Worcestershire sauce and a few grains of clove. Combine the sauce with 2½ cups of canned yellow corn, gradually add 3 slightly beaten egg yolks, then fold in the stiffly beaten whites of three eggs. Turn into a buttered baking dish; cover the top evenly with tiny bread cubes rolled in melted butter, and bake in a moderate oven (350° F.) until firm in center, and bread cubes are nicely browned. Serve hot with any kind of roast meat, or as the main course of a light supper.

CORN FRITTERS MARYLAND [1271]

Blend 1 generous cup corn (fresh green or crushed canned), 2 whole eggs, with salt and white pepper to taste. Stir in 1 teaspoon baking powder and flour to make a heavy batter. Drop spoons of the batter into ½ inch of hot lard in a shallow frying pan. Fry golden brown, but cook only a few at a time lest they stick together.

CORN O'BRIEN [1272]

Sauté 2 cups of corn freshly scraped from the cob in 1⅓ cup of butter, together with 1 cup of finely chopped green pepper and ½ cup of finely chopped, well drained canned pimiento, cooking until the corn is nicely browned. Serve as a side dish with meat or fish or poultry, dusting with chopped parsley or chives.

CORN OYSTERS [1273]

Slit the kernels of 8 ears of fresh corn and scrape it. Combine with 3 well-beaten egg yolks, ½ teaspoon of salt, ¼ teaspoon of white pepper, and ¼ cup of sifted flour. Fold in 3 stiffly beaten egg whites seasoned with a small pinch of salt, and when ready to serve, drop by tablespoons, the size of an oyster, onto a well greased griddle or skillet. Cook on both sides until well browned. Serve at once.

CORN PUDDING [1274]

Prepare 1½ cups of Cream Sauce (No. 258); stir in 2 cups of freshly grated corn mixed with 2 well-beaten eggs, and season to taste with salt, pepper and a dash of nutmeg; turn into a buttered casserole and set in a pan of hot, but not boiling water. Bake in a moderate oven (325--350° F.) until set, or about 35 to 40 minutes.

CORN SCALLOP SOUTHERN STYLE [1275]

Mix 1¼ cups of corn meal, 1½ teaspoons salt and 3 tablespoons of brown sugar in a mixing bowl. Combine ¾ cup of rich scalded milk and 3 tablespoons of butter, and stir very slowly into the corn meal. Add 1 well-beaten egg, alternately with 4 cups of corn cut from the cob, season to taste with salt and white pepper, and turn into a generously buttered baking dish. Bake in a moderate oven (325° F.) until set, stirring frequently the first 20 minutes to prevent the corn meal from settling. Serve with broiled bacon or ham.

CORN SOUFFLE [1276]

Prepare 1 cup of Cheese Sauce (No. 1027); stir in 1 cup of canned corn cream style, which has been rubbed through a sieve. Reheat, remove from the fire, add 4 slightly beaten egg yolks, stirring briskly, and season to taste with salt, and a few grains of cayenne pepper. Lastly fold in 4 stiffly beaten egg whites, turn into a buttered soufflé dish, and bake in a hot oven (400–425° F.) 20 to 25 minutes, or until soufflé is puffed and delicately browned. Serve at once.

CORN SQUAW [1277]

Cut 12 slices of bacon into small pieces and cook over a very gentle flame until brown but not crisp. Pour off all but 4 tablespoons of the drippings, and to these, add ½ cup of grated onion, or, if preferred, use grated green pepper instead of the onion. Cook slowly for 5 minutes; add 3 cups of fresh corn cut from cob, season to taste with salt and pepper and heat thoroughly. Serve with the bacon pieces on top.

An old Oregon game law permits fish to be caught using single kernels of corn as bait but makes it a misdemeanor to feed fish on canned corn.

CURRIED CORN PUFFS [1278]

Combine 1 cup of mashed sweet or white potatoes with 2 well-beaten eggs and beat briskly until thoroughly blended. Sift ½ cup of flour, measure, return to sifter and add 1 teaspoon of baking powder, ¾ teaspoon of salt, 2 teaspoons (more or less, according to taste) of curry powder, a good dash each of pepper and nutmeg and sift over the potato-egg mixture. Blend well, adding while blending 1 cup of cooked fresh corn mixed with 1 tablespoon each of grated onion, minced parsley and chives. When ready to serve, drop by tablespoonfuls into hot, deep, clear fat and fry (375–385° F.) till nicely browned turning with a fork. Drain on absorbent paper. Delicious with roast meat or poultry.

GREEN CORN CAKE PUFFS [1279]

Cut the grains from 6 or 7 ears of raw green corn. Combine ½ cup of thin cream or undiluted evaporated milk and 3 well-beaten egg yolks, beaten with ½ teaspoon of salt and a fresh grating of nutmeg; and fold in the stiffly beaten whites of 3 eggs, alternately with the corn. Drop by tablespoons onto a well-buttered griddle or individual frying pan, brown on both sides, and serve in stacks of 4 or 5, like pancakes, on a hot platter and cut into wedges. Serve as a vegetable or for breakfast with honey, maple or any preferred syrup.
(**Note.** No, the flour has not been forgotten. It is the lack of it that makes these puffs so tender and delicious as well as light.)

OLD-FASHIONED CORN ON THE COB [1280]

Remove husks and silk of as many ears of corn as needed. Wet the tender inner husks, and arrange several layers of them in the bottom and along the sides of a heavy aluminum pot. Place the thoroughly washed ears of corn on the wet husks, covering the ears with several layers of the latter. Put the cover on, and set the pot over a medium heat. When the cover gets uncomfortably hot to the touch (the heating time depends on the quantity of corn and the size of the pot), reduce the heat to the very lowest point and cook 10 to 15 minutes longer, or until the corn is tender. Just before the corn is taken out, the top layer of husks may be removed, salt and butter added, the cover replaced, and the heat turned off. Allow 5 minutes or so for the butter to melt and be absorbed by the corn.

ROAST CORN [1281]

Husk as many ears of corn as desired, counting at least 2 ears per serving; remove the silk; brush generously with butter; arrange prepared corn on a wire broiler, or under the flame of the broiling oven, and roast, turning often and basting frequently with melted butter.

To cook in husks, open husks so as to remove the silk; brush with melted butter or drippings, then tie the husks back around top; arrange the ears on a wire broiler and place over coals, turning frequently, or under the flame of the broiling oven if done at home.

CROSNES [1282]

Crosnes are a vegetable coming from France and Belgium, seldom seen in the United States, but sometimes found in markets. These queer little tubers look like short strings of fat beads as knotty as Jerusalem artichokes (French Topinambours) but more graceful with their curves. They taste something like Jerusalem artichokes, but with a flavor twice as delicate. A pound will serve about four, and the usual way to prepare them is to brush and scrub the tubers very thoroughly, then boil about 12 minutes or till tender, and serve with a butter, cream, mushroom, or tomato sauce. They are very good in salads, when boiled in salted water, peeled and sliced, tasting then like celery knob or celeriac. It is a crisp and succulent vegetable, and after they have been washed and scrubbed, they may be eaten raw.

CUCUMBERS [1283]

Cucumbers date back probably 3000 years. They are mentioned in the Old Testament as an article of food the lack of which the Israelites lamented in the wilderness. The Roman Emperor Tiberius grew cucumbers and had a supply for his table every day of the year. They are definitely identified in Chinese writings by the fifth century. Charlemagne had cucumbers planted on his estates. Columbus discovered cucumbers growing in Haiti in 1494, and the early French explorers in the United States found cucumbers grown by the Indians both in the North around what is now Montreal and also in Florida. The English colonists started planting them in 1600. Botanical books from the sixteenth century on, mention their culture.

The cucumber plant is a trailing vine producing fruit which is the edible part of the plant. At first the plant grows erect; then it falls over and begins to run or "vine." The stems are hairy and angular and the leaves quite large. The stems produce many tendrils, enabling the vines to climb over any bushes, or obstacles in their path. The cucumbers are borne on the first node of each fruiting branch. The green fruit is usually covered with white or black spines or prickles.

Occasionally a plain glass tube will turn up, and the collector or finder is more or less baffled to explain the use for which it was originally made. The tube, or cylinder, will resemble a glass lamp chimney with parallel sides. It is possible that it is an English cucumber glass, a device used to make cucumbers grow straight.

These cucumber glasses were invented by George Stephenson of locomotive fame; and Samuel Smiles, in his biography of the great engineer, said many years ago, "He took much pride also in his growth of cucumbers. He raised them very large and fine, but he could not make them grow straight. Place them as he would, notwithstanding all his propping of them and humoring them by modifying the application of heat and the admission of light for the purpose of effecting his object, they would still insist on growing crooked, in their own way. At last he had a number of glass cylinders made at Newcastle, for the purpose of an experiment; into these he inserted the growing cucumbers and then succeeded in growing them perfectly straight."

Carrying one of the new products into his house one day, and exhibiting it to a party of visitors, he told them of the expedient he had adopted, and added gleefully, "I think I have bothered them noo!" Soon these glass cylinders were being used by many gardeners in England.

CUCUMBERS—HINTS [1284]

Sliced cucumbers, as crisp as ice can make them, give that refreshing touch when you pine for something cool.

Peel and score them deeply lengthwise with a fork before slicing to give them that finished French look. Keep them in ice water for about 20 minutes, then drain and dry at the last moment before serving, and pour over them French dressing, curried French dressing, onion French dressing, chive French dressing, sour cream dressing or plain thick sour cream.

If you have never tried cooking cucumbers you'll have a pleasant experience if you serve them with Hollandaise Sauce (No. 1062), cheese or rich Cream Sauce (No. 258), to which a few finely chopped chives and a little chopped chervil have been added.

Maybe a cucumber now and then isn't essential to the diet. Its food value is small; it couldn't be otherwise, being from 90 to 95 per cent water. But don't forget it contains vitamin C in goodly amount and some of both vitamins A and B. What's more, it is a versatile food. It gives a cool, crisp quality to the green salad. It has an extra special affinity for tomatoes, lettuce, green peppers and radishes in salads, either formed or tossed. Cucumbers combine exceedingly well with pineapple and cabbage and marshmallow. But it rates first importance in the pickle crock or jar.

For a light luncheon or supper, stuffed cucumber provides an ideal light-but-filling entrée.

In a cool, secluded garden spot, properly shielded by taller and more dominating plants, the cucumber, eaten right off the vine, is discovered to be very cool indeed. Take a knife with you to the garden, select your cucumber, peel and eat it then and there. There are few more refreshing experiences in life. Pick a hot, sultry day and try it.

Cucumber has a great affinity for fish. Pliny tells us about drawing the great tunny from the sea and how the emperor had it served to his imperial guests and favorites with cucumbers grown under mica and thought it the rarest of luxuries.

Wilt it with salt, drain and dress with vinegar, sugar and seasoning; or have cucumber in sour cream—the natural concomitant for fish, but good any time. . . . Try it sliced or diced hot with sour cream. . . . Chopped nasturtium leaves are good on sliced cucumber . . .

When selecting cucumbers, choose those which are crisp and firm to the touch. Those which have a withered appearance are likely to be old and pithy. Their ripeness and size vary greatly with the strain.

For pickling purposes, cucumbers from 2 to 3 inches long are generally used, but the most desirable are those of only 1 to 2 inches long—or of one to two days' growth. The small, prickly ones are known here as "gherkins," but a true gherkin is really a West Indian or a French product.

When the cucumber was brought to England from France and the Netherlands in 1538, it was regarded as a curiosity.

BAKED STUFFED CUCUMBERS   [1285]

Select 4 medium-sized cucumbers. Cut in half lengthwise; remove the seeds and place in cold water for 15 minutes. Parboil about 4 minutes in a small amount of water.

Combine ½ cup of chopped left-over cooked meat with a cream sauce made with 1 tablespoon of butter, 1 tablespoon of flour and 1 cup of milk. Add 1 or 2 chopped hard-cooked eggs, 1 teaspoon each of finely chopped parsley, chives and grated onion, and ½ cup of tiny celery cubes. Salt lightly, add a few grains of nutmeg and pepper; and fill the cucumbers. Top with buttered crumbs, and bake about 20 minutes in a moderate oven (375° F.). Serve as hot as possible. A side dish of stewed fresh tomatoes is a nice accompaniment.

BOILED CUCUMBER PARISIAN MANNER   [1286]

Peel or not as preferred and slice in inch thick pieces 3 large sound cucumbers. Cook in salted boiling water until tender. Drain well and serve with melted butter, Cream or White Sauce (No. 258) or Béchamel Sauce (No. 259), or Cheese Sauce (No. 1027).

Note. When cold, serve as a relish with French dressing to which has been added some coarsely chopped hard-cooked egg.

BROILED CUCUMBERS   [1287]

Choose large, sound cucumbers, peel and slice; dip the slices in beaten egg seasoned to taste with salt, pepper and thyme; roll in cracker crumbs or bread crumbs, and lay the slices in a generously oiled, shallow pan.

Dot each slice with a little fat, place the pan under the flame of the broiling oven and cook until brown on both sides.

CREAMED CUCUMBER SLICES [1288]

Peel 4 medium-sized fresh cucumbers and slice into thin rings. Place the slices in a saucepan, cover with boiling salted water, and cook for 15 minutes, or until slices are tender. Drain, reserving the liquid as a base for soup. Whip with a fork, then drain again. There should be no water left. Scald ½ scant cup of heavy cream with a bit of bay leaf, 2 sprigs of parsley, 1 sprig of thyme and 1 clove of garlic, peeled and left whole, and strain over the cucumber slices after tasting for seasoning and adding salt and pepper as needed; stir with the tines of a fork to mix well, adding while stirring 1½ tablespoons of butter. Dust with paprika and serve hot.

CUCUMBER COTTAGE CHEESE ASPIC [1289]

Peel, quarter and remove the seeds from 3 large cucumbers; grate and strain. Soften 1 tablespoon of unflavored gelatine in the cucumber juice then dissolve over hot water. Season with 1 teaspoon of salt, white pepper to taste, 2 tablespoons of grated onion, and ½ teaspoon of paprika. Mix thoroughly, and let cool to lukewarm. Then stir in the grated cucumber; and when cold, fold in 1½ cups of drained, sieved cottage cheese, mixing well. Turn into a wet melon mold; chill for 2 to 3 hours in refrigerator. When ready to serve, unmold onto a cold platter, over a bed of crisp, green watercress. Serve very cold.

Cucumber peel has been found to be very efficacious in ridding houses of roaches. It should be scattered around the kitchen in the evening, particularly in the corners of the room. The insects soon discover the peel which acts as poison.

CUCUMBER FRITTERS [1290]

Peel, cut in ½-inch slices and sprinkle with salt, 3 large cucumbers; let them stand 25 minutes. Drain thoroughly, and when ready to serve, dip in batter, and fry a few slices at a time, in hot, deep fat (375° F.), until delicately browned and crisp. Drain on absorbent paper, arrange on a folded napkin placed on a hot platter, and sprinkle with fried parsley. Serve immediately.

CUCUMBERS AU GRATIN [1291]

Blend 2½ tablespoons of bacon or ham drippings with 2½ tablespoons of flour, and when bubbling, stir in 1¼ cups of scalded milk which has been scalded with a small bay leaf, 1 clove, 2 thin slices of onion, and 3 sprigs of parsley, then drained. Stir constantly over direct medium flame until sauce boils and thickens. Add 1 bouillon cube, season to taste with mixed salt, pepper, thyme, and nutmeg; stir in 1 tablespoon of grated onion, and let boil up once. Remove from the fire and add gradually 1 cup of grated sharp cheese stirring until cheese is melted.

Arrange in a generously buttered or greased earthenware casserole, alternate layers of sliced cucumber (peeled or not as preferred, but if not peeled be sure to wash them thoroughly), and cheese sauce. Top with ½ cup of buttered bread crumbs, cover, and bake for 30 minutes in a moderate oven (350–375° F.). Uncover, and continue baking until top is delicately browned. Serve hot in the casserole.

CUCUMBER IN SOUR CREAM [1292]

Most summer menus need added crispness—in raw vegetables, salads and breads. And that crispness is not only for the good of your teeth— but also for the eye and taste appeal lacking in an all-soft menu.

Combine ½ teaspoon of salt, 1 teaspoon of sugar and a good pinch of cayenne pepper; mix well and add 1 tablespoon of lemon juice and 2 tablespoons of vinegar, then stir in 1 cup of sour cream. Pour the sauce over sliced cucumbers (about 3 medium-sized cucumbers). Chill and serve as a salad, an appetizer or relish or as an accompaniment to cooked fish.

SAUTEED CUCUMBERS [1293]

Cut 3 large cucumbers (peeled or unpeeled) lengthwise into ¼-inch slices; dip in beaten egg, then in seasoned flour, and sauté in a little olive or other cooking oil or fat for about 15 minutes, or until delicately browned. Serve as a vegetable.

SCALLOPED CUCUMBERS CASSEROLE [1294]

Wash and score 4 large cucumbers with the tines of a fork; do not peel. Cut them into half-inch cubes, removing the seeds. Arrange a layer of the cubes in a generously buttered earthenware casserole, season to taste with mixed celery salt, pepper and nutmeg and sprinkle with 1½ teaspoons of grated onion, mixed with 1 teaspoon of lemon juice and 1 tablespoon of water. Now scatter over ½ cup of soft bread crumbs, and dot with 1 tablespoon of butter. Repeat layers until the casserole is full, having bread crumbs on the top. Cover, and bake in a moderate oven (350–375° F.) for 40 minutes. Uncover, and bake 15 minutes longer, or until the top is nicely browned. Serve right from the casserole and as hot as possible.

Once regarded with suspicion, due to an ancient erroneous belief that it was poisonous, the cucumber in the last 15 years has increased in popularity until it is now one of the twenty most important vegetable crops in the United States. While its food value is small, being largely water, it does contain a quantity of vitamin C, and "as cool as a cucumber" is a remark that is literally true. A thermometer inserted into a growing cucumber showed a temperature of 78° F., while the ground temperature was 98° F. A cucumber is 90 per cent water.

EGGPLANT [1295]

Eggplant (Solanum melongena) is called by a variety of names, such as guinea squash, mad apple, and so forth and the French word "Aubergine." It is a close relative of the potato and its name undoubtedly comes from the fact that there is a small white kind that looks very much like a chicken egg.

Its exact history is unknown, but its growth in India and China has been recorded for at least 1500 years. Probably India is the original habitat and it still grows wild there. It was known in Europe in ancient times but was first introduced to Europe when trade routes with the Orient were opened up. The kind of eggplant originally grown there was the small, egg-shaped, white, yellow, and brown type which are grown today only for decoration or as curiosities. The modern fruit may be oval, round, long, or pear-shaped; the skin is smooth and shiny. The stem and leaves are often covered with spines. A good-sized fruit is about from 6 to 9 inches in diameter, and a plant will bear from 3 to 8 fruit.

All through the Near East, the eggplant is a blessing to Turkish, Greek, Armenian, Rumanian and Bulgarian cooks, no matter what the temperature, and we Westerners might well take a leaf from the eggplant section of their cookbooks.

The ancients believed eggplant to be poisonous and the wits dubbed it "mala insana" or mad apple. From this erroneous notion, came the custom of soaking eggplant for hours in salt water. In India it is served with sugar and wine.

EGGPLANT—HINTS [1296]

Select eggplant by its weight; the heavier the better. Be sure the outside skin is intact or it will impair the flavor.

It is not necessary to salt and soak slices of eggplant before cooking. Many people do it in the belief that it draws out a bitter substance and makes the eggplant more palatable. However, it also draws out some of the nutritive value and flavor.

The high water content in eggplant makes this vegetable a good balance for concentrated foods, having a heavy starch or protein content. Eggplant is a good source of vitamin G and B-1.

The most popular method of preparing eggplant is to slice it, dip in egg, then in cracker or bread crumbs and fry in hot, deep, clear fat, crisp and golden brown. The secret lies in having the fat just the right temperature, 325–350° F. and in draining the slices thoroughly on brown paper.

Eggplant is a favorite in Turkey, and they have a special dish which is called "Eggplant Iman Baildi" which has a story. The name Iman Baildi is Turkish and means "the Iman (Mohammedan Priest) fainted." Once upon a time there lived in Istanbul an elderly Iman who was notorious throughout the city for his avarice and his *gourmandise*. One day, to the surprise of all who knew him, he announced his approaching marriage to the daughter of a wealthy oil merchant, but the surprise was considerably lessened when it became known that the lady was famed for her skill as a cook and also that she was to bring as her dowry twelve jars of the finest olive oil. Now, to appreciate the point of the tale, one must visualize twelve huge oriental oil jars, each large enough to conceal a full-grown man, as in the story of Ali Baba.

A few days after the wedding, the bride served her husband with the dish famous in Turkey "Eggplant à l'Armenienne," which requires a great deal of olive oil. The Iman was delighted with it and commanded her to prepare it every day for the evening meal. All went well for twelve days, but at supper on the thirteenth day the dish of eggplant was lacking. The Iman, furious, demanded why his orders had been neglected. "Dear husband," was the respectful reply, " . . . you will have to purchase me some more oil, as I have used all that I brought with me from my father." The shock, alike financial and gastronomic, was too much for the elderly Iman who straightway fainted.

BAKED CRABMEAT STUFFED EGGPLANT [1297]

Boil 1 large eggplant in boiling salted water 15 minutes. Dry and cut in half, removing pulp. Sauté 1 small minced onion, 1 tablespoon minced green pepper, ½ clove minced garlic, ½ teaspoon minced parsley, and ½ cup fresh corn, grated from the cob in a small amount of bacon fat over a low flame 15 minutes. Combine ½ lb. crabmeat, the chopped eggplant pulp, and vegetable mixture, adding 1 beaten egg and blending well. Stuff eggplant shells, top with ¼ cup grated cheese and bread-crumbs, if desired. Bake in a moderate oven (350–375° F.) for about 35 minutes.

EGGPLANT ARMENIAN STYLE [1298]

Melt 1 tablespoon of vegetable fat in a heavy pan. Add 1 pound stewing lamb, cut in small pieces and 2 medium-sized onions, if desired, and brown lightly. Turn into a buttered casserole. Sprinkle with salt and pepper to taste. Pour ½ cup of water into pan, bring to a boil and pour over the meat in the casserole. Sprinkle with 2 tablespoons of flour. Add a layer of tomatoes (3 tomatoes thinly sliced) and ¼ pound of cheese, also thinly sliced. Sprinkle with another 2 tablespoons of flour, and salt and pepper to taste. Add 2 cups eggplant, cut in finger strips. Pour ½ cup evaporated milk over the whole. Cover and bake in a moderate oven (350–375° F.) for 45 minutes, or until vegetables are tender. Remove cover, sprinkle with 1 cup fine bread crumbs, dot with 2 tablespoons butter and allow to brown about 10 minutes.

EGGPLANT CASSEROLE [1299]

Wash 1 medium-sized heavy eggplant; cut off the stem and peel; slice crosswise into slices ¼-inch thick.

Heat 2 tablespoons of oil or vegetable fat in a heavy skillet; place as many slices as will fit easily in the hot fat; brown on one side then turn and brown on the other. Remove to a heated dish. Add 2 more table-spoons of fat and brown the remaining eggplant.

In fat remaining in skillet fry two small onions, peeled and sliced thin, 1 small green pepper, sliced thin, and 1 small clove garlic minced.

Arrange a layer of the eggplant slices in a shallow baking dish; cover with the onions and peppers; add remaining eggplant; cover with 1 large ripe tomato which has been peeled and sliced. Sprinkle with ½ teaspoon salt, ⅛ teaspoon pepper, and 1 tablespoon minced parsley. Cover; place in a moderate oven (350–375° F.) and let bake 15 minutes when the liquid should begin to bubble.

Sprinkle ½ cup buttered crumbs over the tomatoes; return to the oven and bake uncovered until the crumbs are brown. Serve in the baking dish.

EGGPLANT FRIED IN BATTER [1300]

Cut a peeled eggplant into ¼-inch thick slices, sprinkle with salt and press between two plates for several hours. Drain carefully and season to taste with salt and pepper. Dip the slices in flour, egg and bread crumbs and fry in hot deep fat. If desired, the eggplant may be dipped in a well-seasoned batter instead of the egg and crumbs and fried in the same way.

Frying Batter. Mix and sift 1 cup previously sifted flour, ½ teaspoon salt and a few grains of pepper, and add gradually ⅔ cup milk which has been previously blended with 2 beaten eggs.

EGGPLANT AU GRATIN [1301]

Cut the eggplant into half-inch dice, and sauté in bacon fat or butter until slightly brown Make a thick sauce of strained tomato and rich beef, veal, or chicken stock thickened with a roux of butter and flour. Put a layer of the diced eggplant into a buttered baking dish, and spread first a little sauce over it, then a thin layer of grated Cheddar cheese. Continue these layers until the dish is filled. Cover the top with coarse buttered crumbs and a sprinkling of grated cheese, and bake in a fairly hot oven (425° F.) until the crust is richly browned.

EGGPLANT A LA ROMAINE [1302]
Eggplant Roman Style

Peel eggplant, cut in oblong shape and slice in ½-inch slices. Dip slices in beaten egg, then in soft grated bread crumbs. Fry in deep fat and drain. On top of each slice, place a thin slice of American cheese and a few dashes of Pique Seasoning and cover with another slice of fried eggplant, sandwich-fashion. Place in a moderate oven until cheese is melted. Serve with Tomato Sauce (No. 1130).

EGGPLANT SOUFFLE [1303]

Cook 2 large eggplants in 2 quarts slightly salted boiling water for 15 minutes, or until tender. Remove the skins and mash the pulp; then add 2 tablespoons butter, 3 egg yolks, slightly beaten, ½ cup rich milk or thin cream, salt, pepper, and grated nutmeg to taste. Soak ½ cup soft bread crumbs in a little milk, then squeeze the crumbs in a dry cloth to remove the moisture. Add the crumbs to the eggplant, together with ½ cup cold cooked tongue. Cut into very small dice. Fold in 4 stiffly beaten egg whites, and turn into a generously buttered soufflé dish. Sprinkle with 2 tablespoons blanched, toasted, finely chopped almonds mixed with the same amount of toasted bread crumbs and a little melted butter, and bake for 30 minutes in a hot oven (400° F.). Serve immediately in the baking dish.

EGGPLANT AND TOMATO EN BROCHETTE [1304]

Cut small eggplants and green tomatoes into half-inch slices. Dredge the slices with seasoned flour mixed with a little minced parsley, then thread the slices of tomato and eggplant alternately on metal skewers, *en brochette*, and grill them in a pan under the flame of a broiling oven, basting them liberally with melted butter. Or pan broil them in plenty of butter, turning the skewers constantly. Serve on toast, garnished with rashers of crisp bacon.

FRENCH FRIED EGGPLANT [1305]

Pare 1 medium-sized eggplant and cut into finger lengths. Soak in salted water for 1 hour. Drain and dry thoroughly. Sprinkle with salt and pepper to taste and dredge with flour. Dip in slightly beaten egg, which has been diluted with 2 tablespoons water, and roll in fine breadcrumbs. Fry in deep hot fat until golden brown. Drain on soft paper.

GRILLED EGGPLANT STEAK LUNCHEON   [1306]

Mix 3 tablespoons olive oil, 1 teaspoon salt, 6 ground peppercorns and 1 teaspoon lemon juice. Peel 1 young medium-sized eggplant, cut in ¼-inch slices, brush slices on both sides with olive oil mixture, arrange in double broiler, and broil about 3 minutes on each side. Brush quickly with melted butter and serve.

Variations. Add 1 tablespoon of hot Tomato Sauce (No. 1130) to each slice and top with a few capers. (This goes well with meat, especially mutton.) Or, place 1 poached egg on each slice of eggplant, mask with 1 tablespoon of onion-flavored White Sauce (No. 258), and sprinkle with paprika.

GREEN PEPPERS   [1307]

The pepper (capsicum frutescens) of the nightshade family, appears to be native to tropical America. It was cultivated in Mexico and Peru long before the arrival of Columbus and formed one of the favorite dishes of the Aztecs. It was also used as a spice by the Indians. Columbus took green peppers back to Europe on his first voyage and a record dated 1493 refers to such green peppers as being more pungent than the previously known black pepper obtained from the Caucasus. A writer in 1550 mentions the pepper obtained from America as being of two kinds: " . . . the one yellow, the other red, both, however, grow in like manner. When green, it is as large as the haws that grow on hawthorns. It is a small shrub, about half a fathom high and has small leaves; it is full of peppers which burn the mouth . . . "

In the following century peppers were used for a variety of purposes, including dyeing. Medicinally they were used both externally and internally for numerous ailments with results which history does not reveal.

The cultivation of green peppers spread rapidly throughout southern Europe, especially Spain, Greece, France, Hungary and Turkey. In Hungary and Turkey very pungent varieties were developed for the manufacture of paprika, which after being manufactured turns very mild.

Also commonly called "Bell Peppers," the sweet peppers come in three colors: green, yellow and red, with the green ranking as the people's choice. All three, however, vary little in flavor.

Green peppers are a good source of vitamin A and second only to red peppers as a source of vitamin C. Their flavor blends with practically all food materials and their color adds an attractive touch to almost any dish.

In buying them, select peppers that are mature, well-shaped, thick-fleshed, firm and fresh in appearance. The color should be bright, and the pepper should yield slightly to pressure. Blemishes on the skin are not serious unless they pierce the flesh. Peppers should be used soon after they are bought, or kept in refrigerator.

Green peppers make interesting cases for holding hot creamed foods or crisp salads. The peppers will stand up better if they are halved lengthwise. Discard seeds and white ribs and simmer five minutes in water to cover for the hot foods. Serve as is, but well washed and chilled for the salad containers. These filled pepper cases make serving easier for party fare.

FRENCH FRIED GREEN PEPPER RINGS [1308]

Cut a slice from tops of as many green peppers as required and scoop out the seeds and white ribs. Slice peppers in rings about a scant ¼-inch thick; sprinkle with salt and pepper and a little flour and fry in plenty of butter until tender and crisp. Good for garnishing almost any kind of fish, meat and poultry.

Variations. Parboil green peppers 5 minutes in boiling water to cover. Let stand 2 or 3 minutes, then drain and peel, slice thin, drop in a good frying batter and fry like French fried onions (No. 1383). Drain and serve as a garnish or as a side dish.

SMOTHERED GREEN PEPPERS LYONNAISE [1309]

The skins may or may not be removed from the peppers, as preferred. Cut off the stems and remove the seeds carefully; also discard the white ribs or membranes, using 5 green peppers. Slice into rings ½ inch wide. Peel and slice one large onion thinly, then cut the rings in two crosswise. Heat ⅓ cup of bacon drippings in a saucepan, add the mixed pepper rings and onion slices; sprinkle with salt; cover, and cook very slowly until just pierceable, turning frequently, or for about 12 to 15 minutes. Uncover and brown slightly before serving as a garnish with fish or meat or as a side dish.

Variations. Dip the green pepper and onion slices in frying batter and fry in deep fat like French fried onions (No. 1383).

STUFFED GREEN PEPPER VARIATIONS [1310]

Green peppers are very useful when the question arises as how to use up left-overs; almost any combination of filling may be used for the stuffing.

STUFFED GREEN PEPPERS—HINTS [1310a]

Cut off the tops of, say, 6 green peppers or, if large, cut them in two lengthwise, having a half for each serving; remove the seeds and inner ribs; drop in boiling water, remove from fire, let stand 5 or 6 minutes, then drain well. Fill with any desired stuffing or filling, of which there follow a few suggestions.

Mexican Style. After parboiling the pepper or pepper halves, remove the outer skin; fill with cottage cheese, seasoned with salt and pepper; place peppers, first rolled in flour in a baking dish; pour in 2 tablespoons of good olive oil, heated to the smoking point, then add 1 cup of hot tomato sauce, and bake in a moderate oven until tender, or about 20 minutes; separate 3 eggs, the whites stiffly beaten, the yolks slightly beaten and seasoned with salt and pepper to taste; then pour over both white and yolks, well mixed, and bake 15 to 20 minutes longer.

Crab Meat Stuffing. To 1 cup of hot, rich cream sauce (No. 258), add ⅓ cup of grated cheese, stir until cheese is melted, then stir in 1 cup of cooked or canned crab meat, 1 tablespoon of onion juice and 2 teaspoons each of chopped chives and celery leaves. Heat well and fill the prepared peppers. Cover with buttered crumbs, and bake in a hot oven for 10 minutes, or till crumbs are well browned. Serve very hot.

Meat Stuffing. Add 1 cup of cooked, chopped meat to 1 cup of cream sauce (No. 258) with 1 teaspoon (more or less) of curry powder, season with salt and pepper, stir in 3 tablespoons of soft bread crumbs. Fill the peppers, top with buttered crumbs and cheese in equal parts, and brown quickly in a hot oven or under the flame of the broiling oven. Serve at once.

Poultry Stuffing. To 1 cup of strained brown gravy (No. 1017), add ¼ cup of thinly sliced fresh mushrooms, cooked in a little butter, 1 cup of finely chopped cooked poultry (any kind), season highly with salt and pepper, and fill prepared peppers. Top with buttered crumbs and brown quickly in a hot oven. Serve at once.

GREENS [1311]

Grandmother had the courage of her convictions and not the least of these was the firm belief that "greens" were food good for the family. So when the long trek across the plain began, there were several little bags of seeds tucked away in the drawer of the highboy packed near the middle of the covered wagon. Although in grandmother's time vitamins were unheard of, there is no doubt that her firm belief in the virtues of "green stuff" had much to do with the fact that she was able to raise ten children to robust maturity.

Land was cleared and a small cabin erected on the edge of the forest. Grandmother gave the men folks no peace until her garden patch was cleared too and the rich soil made ready for her precious seeds.

Meanwhile she used to go "a-greening" and brought home some greens which today very few cooks know about, such as:

Fiddlehead Ferns. Originated in France and today, of all those grown in this country, the finest come from Maine. Fiddleheads are ferns, and the sturdy stems curving about the delicate fronds look like the end of a fiddle—hence its name. In flavor fiddleheads resemble somewhat a combination of asparagus, broccoli and artichokes. Grandmother used to boil them and serve them with pork or bacon fat, but today they are served in large restaurants creamed, with Hollandaise sauce, or on toast with butter. Cold, in salad, a French dressing or vinaigrette is best.

There is a beautiful legend about the fern, which goes as follows: fern means a feather, and the ferns are sacred to the Archangel Gabriel because, stepping aside to let Adam and Eve pass the eastern gate of Eden, down into the wilderness where they should earn their bread by the sweat of their brows, he brushed his wings against a boulder and a feather dropped. It took root and grew into a fern. It was still Gabriel, according to the legend, who was captain of the guard at that eastern port of Eden; near where the Tree of Life grew; it was he who took special loving interest in mankind's first parent; he it was who prophesied the coming of the Messiah, and years later dictated the Koran to Mohammed. The mystic fern seed, the dustlike asexual spore of ferns formerly thought to be seeds, are always in the shoes of elfin maids who sleep in abandoned birds' nests after nesting time or before the eggs. And that's the reason the Old Herb Gatherer tells the Archangel Gabriel to pass and let the men gather the ferns for food.

Ostrich Fern. The ostrich fern grows in clumps on land that is very wet or overflowed with water in early spring. These clumps will as a rule, be close together and very noticeable as one walks over them. The inner side of the stalk of the ostrich fern has a groove. The clumps will contain from nine or ten to twenty or more heads that emerge as the growth pressure inside the clump pushes them up. Each clump will as a rule, produce heads for 3 or 4 weeks. The heads should be picked while the brown sheath is on. Soak them for an hour in cold water, then rinse under running cold water.

BUTTERED OSTRICH FERNS NEW ENGLAND STYLE [1312]

To cook for the table the following recipe is popular in New England:
Clean off any brown sheaths that may be on them, rinse in several changes of cold water; put into furiously boiling salted water (or steam them) and cook over a low heat until a sharp fork will pierce them, not too easily. Drain and serve hot with melted sweet butter or French dressing, or Vinaigrette. A most delicious salad is made by cooling the greens, then serving them with sliced hard-cooked eggs, or with peeled, quartered tomatoes with a French dressing.

CANNED OSTRICH or FIDDLEHEAD FERN [1313]

Wash the greens carefully and blanch quickly in boiling water. Pack jars full, fill with hot water, add 1 teaspoon of salt and process 25 minutes in hot water baths, then tighten cover.

Local game wardens, forest fire wardens, woodsmen, hunters and fishermen in the various States can probably tell civilians who are unacquainted with the wild greens where they are to be found in the individual communities.

Other edible ferns are *cinnamon fern* and the *bracken fern* also called "interrupted" and "turkeyfoot."

BUTTERED CINNAMON FERN [1314]

Wash ferns carefully, soak them in cold water for at least 30 minutes, then rub them with a cloth to remove the fuzz. If this fuzzy down refuses to disentangle itself readily from the curled ends, the ends are thrown away and only the stalks eaten. Break up the stalks into 2-inch pieces after first scraping carefully; then boil in salted water till tender, and serve with butter, cream sauce, or mustard sauce, if a piquant sauce is desired.

The brackens grow on higher land than either ostrich or cinnamon ferns and instead of coming up in clumps like the other two, they come up in a single green stalk covered with a delicate silvery bloom which must be removed before cooking. They usually appear a week or two after the cinnamon and ostrich ferns. They are picked when from four to eight inches tall. They are prepared for cooking by removing the bent leafy ends and the tough bases. The gray bloom is then rubbed from the stalks which are cut or broken into 2-inch lengths, and boiled until tender in salted water with 2 or 3 slices of lemon. They are served hot with butter or a cream sauce or cold in salad form. Along the eastern seacoast one may find the goose neck green which has the reputation of being very delicious. It used to be a favorite dish of the late Theodore Roosevelt, when boiled in meat stock, drained and served with a rich cream sauce flavored with a tablespoon of prepared mustard.

Other greens which grandmother used to collect in the field and cook for the "boys" were nettles, wild rhubarb, wild asparagus, bullrushes, manna, fireweeds, wild mustard greens, wild collards, wild chicory, spice grass, and so forth, never forgetting the dandelion greens, which held a high place in the menus of the old farm family, and rightly so, because the green or even white inner leaf of dandelion is just full of lime, iron and the whole packet of food minerals. It has been found that the craving for green stuff, so common in the Spring, is the natural consequence of lime-starvation imposed by the average winter diet.

An old recipe for dandelions serves them much like a hot slaw, combined with bacon, vinegar or lemon juice and eggs. It is a good dish and worth adding to our more sophisticated meals. Dandelion soup, like fern soup, is another old favorite in New England and down in the Old South.

WILTED DANDELION GREENS [1315]

Wash 3 good quarts of dandelion greens thoroughly after first cleaning them well, cutting off the root end and discarding the damaged leaves; drain and chop coarsely. Heat in a frying pan ⅓ cup of bacon drippings, ⅓ cup of mild vinegar and season to taste with salt and black pepper. You may also add 1 clove of garlic, but this is optional. Add the drained greens and cover tightly. Cook over a low flame until the greens are wilted. Serve hot on toast. If desired, brown some bread crumbs in bacon fat and strew them over the dandelion greens.

DANDELION GREENS FARMER'S STYLE [1316]

Wash 3 pounds of carefully picked dandelion greens very carefully and drain. Put through food chopper. Heat ⅓ cup of lard or bacon drippings, add the greens and cook until almost tender, then add 5 or 6 sliced cooked potatoes, and pour over all ½ cup of mild cider vinegar and 1 teaspoon of sugar. Mix well and when thoroughly heated, season with salt and black pepper and 2 or 3 tablespoons of grated onion. Serve on a heated platter topped with six freshly poached eggs with a dozen slices of bacon grilled until crisp.

KALE [1317]

Kale, or Borecole, as it is sometimes called—that hardy green vegetable which improves in frosty weather—deserves the attention of the cook interested in adding an appetizing and low-priced vegetable to the winter menu. Kale, which is really a member of the cabbage family, may be likened to a cabbage plant that produces no head. The leaves spread out from the stem of a dark green to bronze shade and are closely curled. It is one of the most important potherbs grown in the home garden and for commercial sale. While extensively grown in the North in the fall and early spring, most of the winter kale comes from the South.

While kale has been cultivated in Europe from the most ancient times, it first became known in America in the seventeenth century. Many types are known, but they all probably belong to the same species. Some kale is grown as an ornament, being variously curled and of a beautiful color. However, the varieties grown in the United States belong to two groups: the Scotch and the Siberian. The foliage of the former is grayish-green in color, much curled and crumpled, while the Siberian kale is of a bluish-green color and curled though not quite so much as the Scotch.

Kale is an important source of calcium as well as vitamin A and ribo-flavin, and all three of the B vitamins, vitamin C and vitamin D, also phosphorous and iron. One-half cup of cooked kale yields ten times the vitamin A that one sweet potato does, and three times the amount contributed by one-half cup of cooked spinach.

Cooking kale, is a very simple process. The leaves are stripped from the heavy stems, well washed then cooked just like spinach, except that kale takes a few minutes longer. It should never be over-cooked, just till tender, and always over a low flame. With plenty of butter and a generous sprinkling of nutmeg, kale is a delicious vegetable dish. In buying, it is well to remember that kale of good quality has a fresh appearance. Plants with wilted or yellow leaves should be avoided, unless they can be trimmed without too much waste.

BUTTERED KALE   [1318]

Wash 1½ pounds of kale in several waters. Trim off heavy stalks. Place in a large kettle with ¾ cup water. Cover and cook quickly for 15 minutes or until tender. Drain. Cut with scissors. Add 2 tablespoons butter, ½ teaspoon salt and ⅛ teaspoon pepper. Serve with sections of lemon.

KALE AND BACON   [1319]

Cook ¼ pound scored piece of bacon or salt pork very slowly in a saucepan in 1 quart of cold water for about 1½ hours or until pierceable. Add 1 pound washed and trimmed kale; cover, and cook until both the bacon and kale are done but not soft, which will take about 20 to 30 minutes.

Skim the kale from the saucepan liquor; chop fine and keep hot. Cut the bacon into neat pieces; keep hot. Heat 1 teaspoon bacon drippings in a saucepan; add 1 onion, minced fine and cook about 5 minutes; add the cut bacon and chopped kale; reheat thoroughly. Serve in a heated vegetable dish; the kale liquor, may if desired, be served in a sauceboat.

KALE IN THE CREOLE STYLE   [1320]

Strip the kale leaves from the stems from 3 pounds of kale. Wash the leaves well. Drain and set aside.

Important. Like spinach or any green vegetable, kale should never be soaked for a long time.

Place a left-over ham bone in a soup kettle, add 1 bouquet garni composed of 1 large bay leaf, 2 green sprigs of celery tops, 8 sprigs of fresh parsley, 1 sprig of thyme, all tied together with white kitchen thread; 1 large onion, left whole and studded with 2 whole cloves, 1 medium-sized carrot, scraped, quartered, 1 small white turnip, peeled, then quartered, 3 cups of cold water, 7 or 8 whole peppercorns, gently bruised, a little salt to taste, and bring slowly to the boiling point. Lower the flame and simmer gently for about 1 hour. Strain the ham stock into a saucepan; add the prepared kale; cover; cook over a low flame until kale is tender but not broken nor mushy about 20 minutes. Taste for seasoning, and serve both kale and liquid in a rather deep vegetable dish. The liquid is considered an asset, as it is used to "dunk" freshly made corn bread.

KALE AND FRANKFURTER DINNER   [1321]

Trim and wash 1 pound of kale. If young, all of it may be used; if old, be sure to trim off the lower stems if very thick. Place kale in kettle with very little additional water and 1 teaspoon salt and boil until tender. Drain and chop fine with a knife or put through chopped. Dice 4 slices bacon into a large heavy skillet and add 1 large onion chopped fine. The bacon will supply the necessary fat. Then add 6 medium pared and thinly-sliced potatoes, with salt to taste and fry until well done. While this mixture is frying, chop the sliced potatoes with a spatula as for hashed brown.

When potatoes are tender and lightly browned, add the chopped kale. Now mix potatoes and kale thoroughly together and fry the whole mixture until lightly browned. The moisture of the kale will cause the mixture to steam and it will not begin to brown until most of the moisture is cooked out. Do not cook too dry as this dish should be served fairly moist. Serve with 1 dozen grilled frankfurters.

KALE RING   [1322]

Cook 1 pound of washed kale in boiling salted water until tender; drain well and force through a colander. Steam 1 tablespoon minced onion in 2 tablespoons of butter or melted drippings for about 3 minutes; add the sieved, cooked kale; remove from the heat; stir in 4 tablespoons milk, 1 egg, slightly beaten and a pinch of cayenne. Taste for seasoning, adding salt if necessary. Press into a greased ring mold; set in a pan of hot water and bake in a moderately slow oven (325° F.) until firm about 20 minutes. Unmold onto a heated platter and fill the center with 2 cups of creamed carrots and peas or mushrooms or chipped beef, or any other preferred filling.

SCALLOPED KALE [1323]

Combine 1½ pounds of cooked and chopped kale, with 2 diced hard-cooked eggs, and add enough gravy, stock or cream sauce to moisten. Arrange alternate layers of the kale-egg-sauce mixture and grated cheese (½ cup in all) in 6 greased individual baking dishes, sprinkle ¼ cup buttered crumbs over the top ₍nd bake in a hot oven (400° F.) for 10 minutes.

SMOTHERED KALE [1324]

Trim 1 pound of fresh kale and discard any wilted leaves. Separate the bunches into leaves and wash several times in lukewarm water until free of sand or soil. Drain; strip the leaves from the stems, using all the tender stems. Cut these into 2-inch pieces. Heat 2 to 4 tablespoons of bacon drippings or oil in a good sized heavy saucepan. Add the prepared kale stems; cover and cook 5 minutes. Now put in the kale leaves and mix with the bacon drippings or oil; add salt and pepper to taste and 2 tablespoons of hot water, if desired. Cover and cook slowly until pierceable or about 15 minutes, stirring from the bottom once or twice to prevent the greens from sticking. Taste for seasoning and correct if necessary. Transfer (without draining) to a heated vegetable dish, and garnish with lemon slices, if desired. Serve with hot corn bread.

Variations. Add 1 clove of garlic to the bacon drippings or oil. Another suggestion is to sprinkle bits of crisp bacon over the kale when served.

STEAMED KALE [1325]

Wash 1 pound of kale in several waters and separate leaves from tough stems; drain and place in top of steamer. Bury 2 cloves of garlic (halved) in the kale. Season with ½ teaspoon salt, and a dash each of pepper and marjoram, and pour 1 tablespoon of tarragon vinegar over all. Cover and steam 30 minutes, or until just tender. Combine ¼ cup of oil and 1 tablespoon of tarragon vinegar and pour over kale before serving.

KOHLRABI [1326]

Kohlrabi, stepchild of the vegetable garden, can go to town as brilliantly as a Cinderella. Caught in tender youth, this vegetable goes to table bursting with flavory virtue. Kohlrabi is one of the brassica family, a sister to cabbage, to broccoli, to cauliflower. But it looks like a turnip and tastes turnipy, too, but is much more delicate in grain. Unlike the turnip, the root thickens above ground and the stems grow up around the bulged tuber. A dual-purpose vegetable, as both root and tender young leaves may be eaten as one dish or the leaves cooked separately as greens. Kohlrabi is an educated and refined turnip though it has a cabbage-like flavor. The knob, just above the root ends, appears to be slung in a network of vinelike stems that shoot up to make leaves. It is a very beautiful apple-green color and very clean looking.

Buy only small ones, as the vegetable becomes tough and fibrous as it matures. Wash it well, trim off the root end and the vinelike stems and peel, then cut into slices or dice. Cook in a generous amount of water as you would cauliflower. Drain and dress with butter, cream sauce, egg sauce, et cetera. The pared kohlrabi, boiled till tender, scooped out and styled with a sausage filling, is a famous dish from the Old South.

FRENCH FRIED KOHLRABI [1327]

Cut the leaves from 5 or 6 medium sized kohlrabi; drain, pare and cut as you would cut potatoes to French fry. Place in a saucepan, cover with a large amount of boiling salted water and cook about 25 to 30 minutes, or until tender. Drain. Cool. When ready to serve, place a few at a time in a frying basket and plunge the basket into hot, deep, clear fat. Cook until nicely browned, drain on absorbent paper and serve like French fried potatoes.

KOHLRABI BROWN PARSLEY BUTTER [1328]

Prepare 5 or 6 medium sized kohlrabi as indicated for French Fried Kohlrabi (No. 1327), cutting into slices instead of in French fried style, and boil as indicated until tender. Drain, and sauté in plenty of butter until brown on both sides. Serve dusted with plenty of chopped parsley.

KOHLRABI COUNTRY STYLE [1328a]

Trim off the tops and stems of two bunches of kohlrabi; wash, drain, pare by inserting a knife under the tough fiber at the base and stripping off the skin. Cut the peeled kohlrabi into eighths, or into thick slices, and cook in plenty (about 6 cups) of boiling salted water until tender, or about 18 to 20 minutes; drain. Blend 2 tablespoons of butter and 2 teaspoons of flour in a small saucepan; stir in $\frac{1}{2}$ cup of thick sour cream, scalded, and cook 2 or 3 minutes, stirring frequently; add the drained kohlrabi; let heat a minute or so over a low flame, or keep over hot water if not ready to serve at once. Serve in a heated vegetable dish and sprinkle generously with chopped chives. Good with almost any fish or meat.

KOHLRABI IN CREAM [1328b]

Prepare and cook 2 bunches of kohlrabi as indicated for Kohlrabi Country Style, (No. 1328a) and when tender drain and add 1 cup of cream sauce into which has been stirred 1 tablespoon each of finely chopped parsley and onion, cooked in butter and well drained. Taste for seasoning, and serve as a side dish with any cooked fish or meat.

KOHLRABI AU GRATIN [1329]

Cook 2 bunches of kohlrabi as indicated for Kohlrabi Country Style (No. 1328a) and cut into small cubes or dice. To 1 cup of white sauce (No. 1134), add ⅓ cup of grated American cheese; stir in the drained, cubed kohlrabi, and turn into a baking dish. Sprinkle with ½ cup of buttered bread crumbs, mixed with ¼ cup of grated cheese, and brown quickly in a hot oven (425° F.). Serve as a side dish with boiled meat such as beef, ham, pork, and so forth.

KOHLRABI HOLLANDAISE SAUCE [1330]

Cook 2 bunches of pared, sliced kohlrabi as indicated for Kohlrabi Country Style (No. 1328a) until tender. Drain, and serve sprinkled with parsley, finely chopped, then covered with 1 cup of Hollandaise. (No. 1063-65).

LEEKS [1331]

March 1 is St. David's Day. On this date all good Welshmen wear leeks in their hats. According to the legend, St. David was the uncle of King Arthur, the semi-legendary King of the Britons who captured the imagination of the people by his prowess against the invading Anglo-Saxons. Some historians maintain that Arthur is a purely legendary figure. It is, however, probable that, in the long struggle of the British race against absolute extermination by ruthless invaders, some valiant chief would have arisen as the center and leader of defense. As related, Arthur was the son of Uther Pendragon, King of Britain. In his childhood he was long held in concealment, and was suddenly presented to the people as their king; he proved wise and valiant, gathered a great company of trusty knights, whom—to avoid all question of precedence— he feasted at a "round table" in his palace. With his Queen Guinevere, he maintained a magnificent court at Caerlon-upon-Usk, on the southern border of Wales (in the district where it is historically certain the Britons longest held out), and probably made many a meal on such roots as the leek. He is supposed to have lived with a contented mind to the age of 146 years. We are not told whether his consumption of leeks had anything to do with either his serenity or his long life.

Sometimes called "the asparagus of the poor" by the French leeks lend themselves to most asparagus recipes.

The leek is, actually, an elegant first cousin to the onion. Even Nero, more ill-famed for his cruelties than beloved for his human trait, was a lover of leek soup. Swank Vichyssoise is descended from Roman *porrophagus* for *porrum* was the leek of ancient Rome. From this come the "porrée" of France in the Middle Ages, and finally, the present name "poireau."

When Cadwallen, the king and Welsh leader, was about to meet Edwin, King of Northumbria, he ordered his men to wear a leek in their helmets to enable him to distinguish them from the enemy soldiers. The result was victory for the Welsh and the choice of the leek as the nation's emblem.

Leeks are individual in that their leaves are flat, while all the rest of the onion clan have *tubular* leaves, and that is one of the main reasons that leeks should always be washed very carefully, as the sand has a tendency to locate between the flat leaves and may spoil an otherwise well prepared dish.

BOILED LEEKS WITH DIVERS SAUCES [1332]

Remove root ends and any green tops from leeks leaving about 2 or 3 inches above the white portion, and split them, lengthwise. Then wash them in several changes of water, spreading the leaves gently so as to dislodge the sand. Drain, tie the leeks in small bunches with kitchen thread, and cook in plenty of salted boiling water about 20 minutes more or less, depending on size of leeks. Drain; arrange on a folded napkin on a heated dish and serve with any one of the following sauces: Maître d'Hôtel Butter, Parsley Butter, Cream Sauce, White Sauce, Hollandaise Sauce, Mousseline Sauce, Egg sauce, and so forth.

BRAISED LEEKS BOURGEOISE [1333]

Remove the green parts from a dozen large white leeks and split the white parts after removing the root ends. Wash very carefully without separating the leaves, and blanch 2 or 3 minutes in 1 cup of boiling water mixed with ⅓ cup of Pique Seasoning. Drain, reserving the liquid. Melt 2 tablespoons of butter; stir in 1½ tablespoon of flour and, when beginning to brown, gradually stir in the hot leek liquid used for blanching, stirring constantly until mixture boils and thickens. Simmer gently for 5 minutes, and meanwhile arrange the drained leeks in a generously buttered baking dish, preferably an earthenware one; sprinkle over, scattering well, 1 teaspoon of finely chopped shallots; then add the hot brown sauce; season lightly with salt and black pepper; cover with a buttered paper, and cook in a slow oven (300–325° F.) for 1 hour. Fifteen minutes before serving, discard the paper, and add bit by bit, 1 tablespoon of sweet butter, creamed with 1 teaspoon of finely minced parsley and 1 teaspoon of lemon juice. Keep hot and serve right from the casserole.

CREAMED LEEKS AU GRATIN   [1334]

Cook a dozen large leeks until tender as indicated for Boiled Leeks with Divers Sauces (No. 1332). Drain, pressing very gently, but thoroughly, and cut the leeks into inch lengths. Arrange them in a buttered baking dish, pour over 1 generous cup of cream sauce (No. 258), or, if preferred, 1 cup of sweet, heavy cream, which has been scalded with 1 small bay leaf, 1 clove, a blade of garlic, 3 thin slices of onion and 3 sprigs of fresh parsley then strained. Sprinkle over the top ½ cup of soft bread crumbs, mixed with ⅓ cup of grated cheese, and brown quickly in a hot oven (400° F.). When bubbling and nicely browned, serve from the baking dish.

Variations. If desired, top with half bread crumbs and half blanched, shredded almonds.

LEEKS WITH LEMON BUTTER ON TOAST   [1335]
WITH POACHED EGGS

Cook until tender 2 dozen small leeks from which the green part as well as the root ends has been removed, in boiling salted water. Drain well, arrange on individual pieces of toast, spread with a little anchovy butter (No. 979). Brush each piece of toast with melted butter, top with a freshly poached egg, dust with paprika, and serve at once.

LENTILS   [1336]

Ever since Esaü sold his birthright for a mess of pottage, lentils have been known as the food of the strong and the poor. And, like so many foods that belong to the poor, lentils give health and strength. The black bread of the European peasant, the garlic of the rice growers in China, the cabbage soup of the common people in Russia, cannot claim sturdier value. Yet, to many in this country, lentils are an unknown food.

In commerce two kinds of lentils, the French and the Egyptian, are important. French lentils vary in color from yellow grey to dark brown; Egyptian lentils are reddish. The lentil plant grows to about 16 inches in height and has many long branches. The broad oblong pods are about one-half inch long, and each contains two seeds. The red lentil is widely grown in Mexico and in our own United States. It was from the ancestors of these same lentils that Jacob, of old, prepared the red pottage, for which Esaü sold his birthright.

The lentil belongs to a food classification called legumes. These are seeds. As they mature their water content decreases, and they contain a concentrated amount of protein, carbohydrate and fats. Like navy and kidney beans and indeed the whole bean family, the dried peas and lima beans, frijoles and pinto beans, lentils and cow peas are a rich source of thiamin, a part of which, however, is lost in the usual cooking process. Lentils, like all the other legumes, supply significant amounts of riboflavin.

The preliminary cooking is the same for all of the legumes. Wash well and soak in water to cover, over night, or at least 6 hours. Then add more water and cook very slowly until tender. If in a hurry, soak the washed, picked lentils in boiling water for one hour, then cook according to directions in the recipe.

BOILED LENTILS [1337]

Pick over 1 pound of dried lentils and wash. Place in a saucepan with cold water to cover. Let soak covered until softened, which will be about 6 hours. When ready to cook the lentils, do not drain them but add 2½ cups of boiling water with ½ cup of Pique Seasoning, salt to taste and 1 bay leaf. Cover and simmer until tender but not broken. There should be very little liquid left; if necessary, cook a little longer to evaporate it.

CASSOLETTES OF LENTILS [1338]
A L'AUVERGNATE

Pick over, wash, then soak overnight 1 pound (2 cups) of lentils. Next day, drain, place in a saucepan, cover with cold water and add 1 bouquet garni composed of 1 large bay leaf, tied with 6 sprigs of fresh parsley, 1 sprig of thyme, and 1 sprig of green celery leaves using white kitchen thread, also 1 medium-sized onion, peeled, left whole and studded with 2 whole cloves, 1 small clove of garlic, peeled and left whole, 1 teaspoon salt and 8 or 10 whole peppercorns, gently bruised. Bring to a boil, cover, and simmer for one hour, or until lentils are tender. If there is much liquid left, drain off a little. Stir in 1 tablespoon of lemon juice, taste for seasoning, adding more salt if necessary, and divide the lentils and liquid equally among 6 individual casseroles. Top each with 2 small strips of fresh pork fat or bacon and bake in a gentle oven (350° F.) for about 15 minutes, or until pork or bacon is browned. Serve hot. Appropriate with pork sausages, or frankfurters.

LENTIL AND CHEESE LOAF [1339]

Put ¼ pound American cheese and 2 cups canned or cooked dried lentils through food chopper. Add 1 cup bread crumbs, 1 teaspoon grated onion, and salt and pepper to taste, and moisten with a little melted butter or milk if the mixture seems dry. Form into a roll and bake in a moderate oven (350° F.) for 45 minutes, basting occasionally with melted butter and water. Serve with a well seasoned Tomato Sauce (No. 1130).

LENTIL CROQUETTES [1340]

Soak ½ cup dried lentils and ¼ cup dried lima beans overnight in cold water to cover. Drain, add 1½ quarts water, ½ cup grated onion, 1 stalk celery, finely chopped, 3 slices carrot, and 1 sprig of parsley, finely minced. Cook covered, until lentils are soft, drain and rub through a sieve. To the pulp, add ½ cup stale bread crumbs, 1 egg, slightly beaten with salt and pepper to taste. Melt 1 tablespoon butter, add 1 tablespoon flour, then, gradually, ⅓ cup hot cream and ⅔ cup milk. Combine mixtures and cool. Stir until thick and smooth. Shape, roll in bread crumbs, fry in deep hot fat (390° F.) and drain on absorbent paper. As more croquettes are fried, more fat will have to be added and slightly reheated.

LENTILS A LA DAUPHINOISE [1341]

Marinate 3 diced tomatoes in French Dressing (No. 1755) for 3 hours in refrigerator. Soak 1 cup lentils until soft. Drain and cook, covered in 1 quart of boiling water with 1 teaspoon of salt for about 30 minutes or until they are just tender. Wash 1 cup rice and cook in 2 quarts boiling water with 1 teaspoon salt for 20 minutes or until just soft. Drain lentils and rice and combine. Keep hot. Sauté 8 slices bacon, drain on absorbent paper and chop. Sauté 3 minced onions in remaining bacon fat, drain and add with the bacon to rice and lentils. Serve at once with the cold marinated tomatoes, using the French dressing as sauce.

LENTILS WITH FRANKFURTERS [1342]

Pick over 2 cups of large lentils, cover with cold water and let soak overnight. Drain, then cover with boiling water, add 1 teaspoon salt and 1 small onion and cook until tender about 50 minutes. Drain, saving the water for soup. Mix the lentils with 1 cup of cooked rice, 2 cups of canned tomatoes, 2 tablespoons of bacon or sausage drippings, 2 tablespoons of chopped parsley and 2 tablespoons of prepared mustard. If necessary, add more salt, having the lentils well seasoned. Pour into a fairly shallow casserole, cover and bake for 35 minutes.

Meanwhile, broil as many large tender frankfurters as needed, then arrange them over the top of the casserole.

LENTILS, HUNGARIAN STYLE [1343]

Wash and pick over ½ pound of lentils. Cover with cold water and soak overnight. Drain, again cover with cold water and simmer until tender. Sauté 1 minced onion in 2 tablespoons bacon fat and blend in 2 tablespoons flour. Add ¼ cup cold water, 1 tablespoon sugar, 1 teaspoon salt and 2 tablespoons vinegar and blend well. Cook 2 minutes or until smooth and thickened and pour over lentils. Serve very hot on small squares of hot toast.

LENTILS, MECKLENBURG STYLE [1344]

Clean 1 cup lentils and soak several hours, or overnight, in 1 quart water. Cover, and cook in same water seasoned to taste with salt and pepper until lentils are tender, but still hold their shape. Fry 1 cup diced salt pork until crisp and light brown. Add 2 minced onions, and 1 stalk diced celery, and cook three minutes. Sprinkle with 1 tablespoon flour and stir until well mixed. Add ¼ cup vinegar, ¼ cup water and lentils, heat and serve with game or fowl, or as a luncheon dish.

LENTIL PIE [1345]

Wash and pick over ½ pound of lentils and soak several hours in cold water to cover. Drain, again cover with cold water and simmer for 20 minutes. Add 4 tomatoes, peeled and sliced, salt and pepper to taste and simmer until tender. Sauté 2 small sliced onions in 2 tablespoons butter or vegetable shortening in a saucepan; add the lentils with ½ cup grated cheese, and ½ cup bread crumbs. Pour into a 9-inch greased pie plate. Top with ½ cup bread crumbs and dot with 1 tablespoon of butter. Brown under the flame of the broiling oven for five minutes. Serve with a mixed green salad.

LENTIL PUREE [1346]

Pick over 2 cups of lentils and wash in several cold waters. Drain, again cover with cold water and soak several hours. Drain, add fresh water and simmer with a ham bone, 1 sliced leek, and a few grains of thyme until tender. Drain and press through a sieve. Add 2 tablespoons butter, enough hot milk to develop the consistency of mashed potatoes, 1 teaspoon chopped parsley, salt and pepper to taste, and serve in a hot dish.

LENTIL RAMEKINS [1347]

Pick over 2 cups of modern-processed lentils and soak in boiling water for one hour. Add 1 teaspoon minced onion, 1 teaspoon chopped parsley and 2 tablespoons drippings, with salt and pepper to taste. Cover, bring to a boil and simmer for 1 hour, or until tender. Add 1 tablespoon vinegar or lemon juice. Pour into individual ramekins, adding enough water from the lentils to moisten. Top with 2 pieces of bacon and brown under the flame of the broiling oven.

LENTIL AND WALNUT LOAF [1348]

Pick over 2 cups of lentils and wash in several cold waters. Cover with cold water and soak several hours. Drain, cover again with cold water, and simmer until tender. Drain once more and put through food grinder with 1 cup walnut meats and 1 large onion. Add 1 cup tomato sauce or canned tomatoes, 1 teaspoon sage, salt and pepper to taste, 1 beaten egg and ⅓ cup salad oil. Mix well. Turn into a loaf pan and bake about 45 minutes in a moderate oven (350–375° F.).

LETTUCE [1349]

Lettuce (of the composite or sunflower family) has been cultivated for so many years that no one knows when and where its beginning was. It was served at the royal tables of the Persian (Iran) kings about 550 B. C. It was used as a salad by the Greeks and Romans, and Chaucer makes an allusion to it in 1340. Numerous varieties have been grown in Europe and in this country for many years. Today it is the standard salad crop and vegetable dish for gourmets.

Types and Varieties. There are three types of lettuce. Head lettuce (comprising butterhead and crisphead) leaf lettuce, and cos or romaine, then two more types may also be found in greengrocers: the iceberg and the celtuce or China lettuce.

Butterhead has smooth, soft-textured, finely veined leaves, the inside leaves being light yellow.

Crisphead has brittle, crisp, coarsely veined leaves and a white center. It is often erroneously called iceberg lettuce.

Iceberg lettuce is a variety of this type, not a type itself, and is exceedingly good.

Leaf Lettuce. This type of lettuce has large, loose, frilled leaves which spread in growth. The leaves grow in bunches, and the inner ones do not overlap to form a definite head. There are many green outside leaves and just a few white ones in the center.

Cos or Romaine. This type of lettuce grows upright with large, smooth, erect, crisp, oblong leaves having broad midribs. The outside leaves are dark green, while the inside of the head may blanch somewhat.

Until the fifth century, lettuce was called "lactuca," taking the name from the Latin word for milk. If you have ever cut lettuce in the garden you know that it has a milky juice which forms a gummy coating on your hands. For years this "lactuca" or lettuce was considered too delicate a food for any but royal folk.

With lettuce in market the year around, it is hard to believe that less than thirty years ago cabbage was the only salad plant available during the fall, winter and spring and that by April it had begun to lose its fresh taste. Folks became so hungry for fresh vegetables they searched the fields for tender greens and longed for new onions and radishes. Wilted lettuce was indeed a treat.

In Europe lettuce is grown for salad and for use as a cooked vegetable as a matter of course. The heads may be offered braised (cooked in short stock in a tightly covered pan) stuffed and baked, or creamed, and so forth.

BRAISED LETTUCE [1350]

Select small solid hearts of lettuce, having at least one per person. Scald them with boiling veal stock or water. Drain and cool; then press the sides of the lettuce together gently and lay them in a baking dish, sides down. Dot generously with butter, and pour in sufficient veal stock, enriched with 1 teaspoon of beef extract (commercial), to barely cover. Bake in a moderate oven (375° F.), basting frequently, until the lettuce has absorbed most of the liquid. Serve in a vegetable dish dusting with minced chervil, if available, failing that, use parsley.

The Greek philosopher Aristoxenus called lettuce "the green cakes that the Earth has prepared." He assisted in the preparation by moistening the lettuce plants in his garden with sweet wine of Chios.

CREAMED LETTUCE [1351]

Wash 4 or 5 heads of sound lettuce; trim off the root ends and remove any discolored leaves; drain, and separate the leaves. Drop into a saucepan containing about ⅓ cup water and boil 10 to 12 minutes, or till tender, turning the lettuce with a pancake turner several times. Drain, reserving the stock or juice. Rub the lettuce through a fine sieve into a saucepan; scald about 1 cup of sweet, heavy cream with 1 bay leaf, 1 clove, 3 thin slices of onion and 4 sprigs of parsley; strain over 2 well beaten egg yolks, beating well, then combine with the lettuce, mixing well. Season to taste with salt, pepper and a dash of nutmeg; heat well and serve at once in a heated vegetable dish garnished with sliced hard-cooked eggs.

LETTUCE ROYALE [1352]

Remove the outside green leaves of 6 very small, young heads of lettuce. Blanch the lettuce in chicken stock, and drain thoroughly, pressing a little to extract as much liquid as possible. Place on a dry towel, and gently unfold the leaves as far as the heart, which is removed carefully without separating the leaves. Mash with a fork 6 duck or 8 chicken livers, carefully removing all nerves and skin. Combine liver purée with 3 tablespoons of cooked ground ham, 3 large peeled and ground fresh mushrooms, using both stems and caps, 2 finely chopped shallots. a thin slice of garlic, finely chopped, 1 generous tablespoon of good olive oil, and salt and pepper to taste. Put this mixture into a small saucepan, add ½ cup of chicken consommé, and cook until the whole boils, stirring frequently. Then turn the mixture into a hair sieve, and rub through. The result should be a fragrant paste the consistency of cream cheese. Brush each leaf with this paste, starting at the center and raising each leaf as you go along. Tie up each lettuce bundle with white kitchen thread and place all close together in a small baking dish or pan. Pour over each bundle enough tomato juice barely to cover. Cover the pan and bake the lettuce in a hot oven (400° F.), basting occasionally, for about 30 minutes. Transfer the lettuce to a hot platter, remove the thread, and spoon a little of the gravy from the baking dish over each portion. Any remaining gravy may be used as the base of either a soup or a sauce.

SMOTHERED LETTUCE [1353]

Wash 4 heads of fresh, sound young lettuce; trim off the root ends and remove any discolored leaves; cut the heads into lengthwise quarters; heat ¼ cup of olive oil in a wide shallow saucepan, but do not let the oil scorch; drop in a slice of garlic; simmer a few seconds, just enough to flavor the oil, then discard the garlic and very gently drop the prepared lettuce into the oil; scatter over all 2 tablespoons of grated onion, and pour over ⅓ cup of rich beef stock, sprinkle with salt, pepper and ½ teaspoon of sugar. Cover closely and simmer gently for 30 minutes. Remove the cover; sprinkle with 1½ tablespoons of lemon juice; turn the lettuce so that the bottom quarters are on top and simmer for 6 to 7 minutes longer, or till tender, adding a little more juice if too dry. Serve in a heated, deep platter pouring the juice from the pan over the lettuce after first tasting for seasoning; and dust the top with chopped parsley or chives.

STEWED LETTUCE A LA ROMAINE [1354]

Clean 4 or 5 heads of lettuce carefully by soaking them in water with a tablespoon of lemon juice or vinegar added for each quart, placing the lettuce head down for about 25 to 30 minutes. Drain well; trim off the root ends close to the leaves, and discard any discolored leaves. Cut each lettuce into lengthwise quarters, and again drain well. Heat ⅓ cup of sweet butter in a shallow, broad saucepan, with 2 tablespoons of good olive oil; add 1 whole clove of garlic, peeled and left whole, 1 large bay leaf, 2 whole cloves, 1 medium-sized onion, thinly sliced and 1 medium-sized green pepper, thinly sliced. Lay the lettuce quarters over this; cook over a very gentle flame until lettuce begins to soften, or about 10 minutes; then pour in ¾ cup of rich chicken broth; turn the lettuce with a pancake turner; sprinkle with mixed salt, black pepper and nutmeg to taste, and continue cooking, covered, for 10 minutes longer. Now stir in very gently 1 No. 2 can of tomatoes. Cover and cook gently for 20 minutes. Taste for seasoning and serve directly from the baking pan.

STUFFED LETTUCE A LA DAME SIMONE [1355]

Blanch 6 rounded young heads of lettuce by allowing them just to feel the heat of the boiling salted blanching water; then drain thoroughly. Pound together, or put twice through a food chopper the following ingredients: 1 cup of cooked chicken or breast of capon; ½ cup of cooked lean ham, 4 extra large fresh mushrooms, peeled (caps only); 1 teaspoon each of chopped parsley and chives, and 2 slices of bread, trimmed and soaked in heavy sweet cream. Add 3 egg yolks, salt and pepper to taste, and a pinch each of dried, crushed tarragon leaves, sweet basil, thyme, and ground nutmeg. Stand the blanched lettuce heads up on their stem ends, and one at a time, unfold gently, pushing leaf by leaf apart, without tearing. Carefully remove the lettuce hearts and in their stead place portions of this stuffing. With a light hand press the leaves together again, and tie with white kitchen thread.

Now slice thinly ½ pound of lean veal, and garnish the bottom of a casserole with the pieces. Place over each slice a thin, narrow strip of fat larding pork and a few slices of onion. Cover the casserole, and heat it very slowly on the top grate or compartment of the oven, or over a very low flame. When the mixture is just beginning to scorch at the bottom of the casserole, sprinkle it with 1 tablespoon of flour, and stir, using a wooden spoon, till mixture is the color of a russet pear. Then moisten with 1 cup of Sauce Espagnole (Spanish Sauce No. 1127) and mix well. When boiling, lay in the stuffed lettuce heads, and add more sauce using only enough barely to cover. Place the lid tightly over the casserole, and set it in a moderate oven (350–375° F.) for 40 minutes without disturbing. Then very carefully, using a pancake turner, lift out the lettuce heads one by one; remove the thread, and place the lettuce on a heated platter for service, or use as a garnish for a baked ham. Strain the pan gravy, which should be smooth and of the consistency of thin cream, through a fine-meshed sieve over each head and serve at once.

MUSHROOMS [1356]

Although it is only within recent years that the mushroom has come to any great popularity in this country, it has a history that fades into the distances of time. Hippocrates, about 400 B. C., mentioned that mushrooms were eaten in great quantities, and were even, on occasion, exported from Greece as a part of its vast commerce. But Greece first learned of the mushroom from Egypt, where the Pharaohs regarded it as almost a divine food, a magic food that appeared mysteriously overnight—a belief that is still widely accepted today. The Greeks paid no less homage to the plant, for they called it *broma theon*—food of the gods. Later, in Rome, the poets Horace and Ovid sang sweetly of these fragile growths, destined only for the tables of the wealthy. They were strictly a seasonal plant then, and rare even in season, so that the common man was fortunate if he so much as saw one. Julius Caesar, indeed, thought the common man so unworthy of the mushroom that he passed severe laws limiting its sale.

In Europe, however, the little man made mushrooms—in season— a part of his daily diet, which would indicate that the growths were plentiful and cheap. Fortunately for their economic status, the wealthy and the nobility developed an inordinate taste for the more delicate species of the plant—truffles and cèpes and morels. The exquisite taste of these was not so important to their peasant gatherers as their value. But they were known and prized and eaten savoringly by the élite. In America, however, there is no record of any kind of mushroom before colonial times, although it is probable that they were here to greet the coming of man.

The history of mushroom cultivation is almost as vague as that of the plant itself. The Greek philosopher Theophrastus, whose time was about 300 B. C., in his writings made a reference—no more—to the cultivation of mushrooms. But the art of breeding the plant seems to have had no considerable success until the seventeenth century, when the French, under Louis XIV, discovered that the caves and abandoned quarries near Paris made ideal mushroom beds.

Eventually the new art leaped the Channel to England, where it was carried on in greenhouses rather than in caves, but it was not until fifty years ago that the cultivation of mushrooms was attempted on any great scale in America. Even here it was not particularly successful until new methods of germinating the mushroom spores were discovered, about twenty-five years back. The extreme difficulty of growing mushrooms can be better understood when one realizes that although a single good-sized mushroom will contain 10 billion spores, or seeds, less than a single one of that number, on an average, will succeed in growing if left to nature. The mushroom, indeed, was known at one time as the plant whose seeds would not grow. The success of the new methods of cultivation is apparent in the increase in mushroom sales, which have leaped from a negligible amount to an annual total of about 40 billion pounds, of which approximately one-half is grown in one area alone, Chester County, Pa.

But this tremendous metamorphosis of the mushroom into an industry has still not stopped the gathering of mushrooms in the fields. Those who in their youth gathered mushrooms, still swear that no cultivated mushroom can compete in flavor with the wild one—perhaps because the former may lack that uncivilized taste that civilization so often craves. Or perhaps there is another sort of tang in the wild mushroom— a tang which this story, for the truth of which the writer vouches, may demonstrate.

There was a young botanist in a small university town of France, a carefree, happy fellow who was a great lover of mushrooms. He became enamoured of the young wife of a rather elderly minor public official who, in his line of duty, was required to travel about the country a good part of his time. The young wife naturally grew lonesome during his absences; and purely—I assure you—in the spirit of friendliness and pity, the botanist attempted to console her—not always, at first, to her liking. But in her loneliness she began to listen more eagerly to his words, warm words of love.

And when spring came, at the end of the winter of alternating loneliness and happiness, she found she could not resist the invitation of the botanist to stroll with him one day through the near-by wood in quest of plants for his studies. They started early in the morning, so that their day might be long as well as pleasant, and after a short hour's walk, reached a young forest of elm and ash, bordered on the nearest side by a meadow. In the wood, since there was no one to see, and since there were numerous small brooks, he found it necessary to aid her across them. She protested lightly, and then less. The waters tinkled rhythmically over the rocks and through the tufts of grass bordering the streams, while the birds above sang ardently their eternal songs of Spring.

All was going well for the young botanist. They had just crossed another stream—this time on only one pair of feet—when before them they found the meadow that they seemed to have left so far behind. And on its very edge were growing the mushrooms that he loved—and that she loved, too.

He was a good botanist; he delighted in studying each plant he came across. So the two sat down to pick mushrooms, she perhaps a little disappointedly, he torn between the touch of her and his craving for mushrooms.

They filled his herb case, and then, arm in arm, fingers interlaced, they turned to the nearest inn. It was noon now, and their hunger was for food. There, at the secluded little table, they were served brook trout, and wine, and an omelette flavored with the mushrooms they had just picked. In their secluded little nook, they bent their heads together, whispering words that they alone could speak to one another.

But even as they murmured thus, the botanist noticed his companion turn pale and fall back in her chair. He was immediately alarmed; but almost at that moment he, too, felt extremely ill. "The mushrooms!" he thought at once. But he could not believe that he, a botanist, almost a connoisseur of mushrooms, had mistaken the bad for the good. Shortly, however, he was too ill to think about anything.

A doctor was called, and he promptly gave the two an emetic. Before the afternoon was over, they had recovered sufficiently to return to town. The botanist was both ardent and apologetic, but the young woman left him with a curt good-by.

It was a final good-by as the young man knew, but his pride as a botanist was hurt more than his pride as a lover. The next day he returned to the woodland spot, and inspecting the place carefully, found near by an extremely poisonous plant called the "calf's foot." The wind had carried the toxic pollen of this plant onto the mushrooms.

There are, of course, poisonous varieties of mushrooms as well as edible kinds; but the two, after one learns their differences, are easily distinguished, as a group of Siberian tribesmen, on the peninsula of Kamchatka, is well aware. These men—I swear it—discard the edible mushrooms and make a drink out of a poisonous fungus called *Amanita muscaria*, known locally as the *mukhomor*. Some of the men don't even bother to make the drink; they simply chew the *mukhomor* fresh or dried.

The edible mushroom, fortunately, produces no such memorable effects; it is, on the contrary, an excellent food. Both poisonous and edible varieties are parasites; *fungi*, the Romans called them, and *fungi* they are today. If you are going mushroom picking, learn beforehand which kinds are, and which are not, edible.

It is a wise policy, however, to take along an illustrated book on mushrooms which clearly pictures both good and bad varieties. As soon as you have learned the difference between them, pick to your heart's content, and fear not.

With cultivated mushrooms, of course, there is not a particle of danger. There is simply no opportunity for poisonous varieties to be mixed with the edible, since cultivated mushrooms are grown indoors and are handled literally with surgical cleanliness.

If you are living within a reasonable distance of a mushroom grower, you may have fresh mushrooms in and out of season. But mushrooms are hard to ship, and if there is not a grower near by, do not hestitate to use canned or dried mushrooms. Canned mushrooms which reach you in three packs: *buttons*—small and select, *sliced*—larger growths, and *stems and pieces*—broken plants, frequently have more flavor than the fresh mushrooms sold in market. Mushrooms are generally canned within two or three hours after they are picked, and are cooked in the can, whereas fresh mushrooms may be many hours twixt picking and table. Dried mushrooms, since they are not cooked, require preparation much like the fresh.

Do not think that mushrooms require long cooking. They are so tender that sautéing for five or six minutes in butter is sufficient. Cooked even for so short a time, however, white mushrooms will slightly darken. But they can be kept light in color by steaming them in milk and butter in the top of a double boiler for perhaps fifteen to twenty minutes.

CREAMED MUSHROOMS [1357]

Wash 5 or 6 dozen mushrooms quickly in cold water, and drain thoroughly. Do not peel or remove the stems. Sauté the mushrooms in plenty of butter over a very gentle fire. Season to taste with salt, pepper, and a generous tablespoon of *fines herbes*. Then drench with thick sweet cream, and, if possible, with some roasted partridge juice, and, finally add a few drops of lemon juice.

CURRIED RICE WITH MUSHROOMS EN CASSEROLE [1358]

Peel, stem and slice 1 pound of fresh mushrooms. Do likewise with 5 medium-sized fresh tomatoes. Heat ¼ cup of butter or margarin in an earthenware casserole with 1 clove of garlic, peeled and left whole; discard the garlic, add the sliced mushrooms, and cook, over a medium flame, until mushrooms are nearly tender, stirring frequently; season to taste with salt and pepper, then stir in 2½ cups of cooked rice mixed with 3 tablespoons of butter, ¾ tablespoon of curry powder, a grating of nutmeg and ¼ cup of finely chopped onion (raw). Spread mixture evenly over the sliced tomatoes; dot with 2 tablespoons of butter and cover the entire surface with 1 cup of mixed soft bread crumbs and grated cheese in equal parts. Bake in a moderate oven (350° F.) for 40 minutes, covering top with a buttered paper if browning too fast. Serve hot from the casserole.

DEVILED MUSHROOMS AU GRATIN EN CASSEROLES [1359]

Peel 1½ pounds of fresh mushrooms and put through food chopper, using coarse blade with 1 large green pepper, cut into shreds after white seeds and ribs have been removed. Place mixture into a mixing bowl, season to taste with salt, pepper, ⅓ teaspoon of chili powder, 2 tablespoons of unstrained lemon juice, 3 hard-cooked egg yolks, mashed or sieved, 3 egg yolks, slightly beaten, 2 tablespoons of melted butter and enough thin cream to make creamy paste. Press mixture in bottom and sides of six previously buttered individual casseroles, and drop an egg in center; sprinkle tops with mixed fine bread crumbs and grated American cheese in equal parts and bake in a moderate oven (325–350° F.) for 20 minutes, or until crumbs are brown and cheese oozes. Serve hot.

GRILLED FRESH MUSHROOM CAPS [1360]

Peel 1½ dozen large fresh mushrooms, remove the stems and roll the caps in salted and peppered cooking oil; place the caps in an oiled shallow baking dish, pour over them 3 tablespoons of the remaining oil; season with mixed salt, pepper, a dash of cayenne and nutmeg; place the baking dish under the flame of the broiling oven, 3 inches from the flame and broil 6 or 8 minutes. Remove from the broiler and sprinkle over the mushrooms 3 tablespoons of melted butter mixed with equal parts of chopped chives. Serve hot from the baking dish.

MUSHROOM AND ONION SHORTCAKE [1361]

Prepare one recipe of baking powder biscuit dough, roll out and press into a deep buttered 9-inch pie tin or shallow cake pan of similar size and set aside. Heat 3 tablespoons of butter or margarine in a saucepan or frying pan; stir in 1 large thinly sliced onion, and 1¼ cups of thinly sliced, peeled (not washed) fresh mushrooms, using both caps and stems, and cook over a very low flame, stirring almost constantly for 6 or 7 minutes, having onion and mushrooms both a little underdone; season to taste with salt, pepper, paprika, a dash each of thyme, powdered bay leaves and mace, and spread as evenly as possible over the biscuit dough, previously brushed with melted butter. Then pour over 2 slightly beaten eggs or 3 egg yolks, previously blended with ¾ cup of sour cream, spreading well. Bake in a moderate oven (350° F.) for about 30 minutes, or until custard is firm on top. Serve as hot as possible, as you would a pie.

MUSHROOMS A L'ANDALOUSE [1362]

Wash, peel, and stem 1 pound mushrooms. Braise—that is, cook half-way—stems and caps in ⅓ cup good butter. Sauté ¾ pound diced, cooked Virginia ham in pure olive oil; then combine mushrooms and ham, and cook together for 5 minutes, shaking the pan occasionally in order to blend the mixture thoroughly. Pour in ½ cup sherry mixed with 2 tablespoons rich port and season to taste with salt, coarsely ground black pepper, and a dash of ground nutmeg. Add 2 tablespoons chopped pimiento and 1 generous tablespoon finely minced parsley. Cover the pan tightly, and place in a very slow oven (275° F.) for 40 minutes, shaking and rocking the pan occasionally to ensure thorough blending of the ingredients. Just before serving (on freshly made dry toast) add 1 generous teaspoon meat glaze or rich meat extract and a few drops lemon juice.

MUSHROOMS AND BACON AU SHERRY [1363]
ON TOAST

Peel 1½ pounds of fresh mushrooms, separate the stems from the caps, peel the caps and scrape the stems, discarding the tough ends of the stems. Chop the stems coarsely; leave the caps whole. Butter a baking dish generously and put in the mushroom caps, flat sides up, and sprinkle over them the chopped stems, previously mixed with 1 tablespoon each of finely chopped chervil or parsley, grated onion, chopped chives and chopped green pepper. Season to taste with salt (very little), freshly ground black pepper, a grating of nutmeg and a little thyme. Combine

1 cup of boiling water with 1½ teaspoons of Pique Seasoning and 1 tablespoon of lemon juice and pour very gently over the mushrooms. Cover the dish and bake in a moderate oven (350° F.) for about 25 to 30 minutes. Cook 12 slices of bacon, preferably Canadian style bacon, under the flame of the broiling oven until crisp, but not overdone, and toast 6 slices of bread on both sides. Butter the toast with anchovy butter (No. 979), and heap the mushrooms on the buttered side; garnish each portion with 2 slices of bacon. To the sauce remaining in the baking dish, add 3 to 4 tablespoons of good sherry wine, heat to the boiling point, but do not actually boil, and distribute the sauce among the six portions. Serve as hot as possible, garnishing the platter with crisp, green watercress.

MUSHROOMS A LA DON GASPER [1364]

Peel and cut 1½ pounds of fresh mushrooms in halves after first removing the stems, (which reserve for other use) and sauté them over a very gentle flame in equal parts of butter and olive oil, using about ½ cup in all, rocking and shaking the pan frequently. When half done, or after about 5 minutes cooking, season with salt and freshly ground black pepper (this is very important as the pepper is part of the undescribable flavor of this dish) and ½ generous teaspoon of finely chopped tarragon. When almost done, stir in about 1½ cups sweet, heavy cream together with 1½ to 2 tablespoons of sweet butter, added bit by bit. Cover, let simmer very gently, just "smile" for 5 minutes, or until sauce is a little thick. Stir in 1 scant teaspoon of lemon juice, and serve on freshly made toast cut quite thick then fried in butter, or, if preferred, in individual vol-au-vent, or patty shells. Serve simply garnished with crisp watercress.

MUSHROOMS A LA POULETTE [1365]

Knead together 2 tablespoons butter and 2 tablespoons flour, and stir over a low flame until light brown. Add 2 cups rich beef or chicken stock, stirring constantly until the mixture is smooth. Simmer gently for 20 minutes, skimming off all scum as it rises to the surface. Remove the pan from the fire; then add 3 egg yolks, one at a time, stirring briskly after each addition. Return to the fire, bring to the boiling point, stirring vigorously from the bottom of the pan to prevent the eggs curdling. Remove from the fire once again, add the juice of a lemon, season to taste with salt and white pepper, and strain through a fine sieve. Add 1 tablespoon sweet butter and 1 teaspoon finely minced parsley. Wash quickly ¾ pound mushrooms, and slice both stems and caps coarsely. Sauté them for 5 minutes in ¼ cup butter, over a low flame, then drain well and add to the sauce, which has been kept warm over hot water. Bring the mixture to a boil, stirring briskly with a wooden spoon. Serve at once, on toast, in patty shells, in scooped out par-boiled green peppers or in freshly baked popover shells.

MUSHROOM SOUFFLE [1366]

Wash, peel, and put through the food chopper, using the finest blade, 1½ pounds fresh mushrooms. Simmer them in ¼ cup butter for 10 minutes; remove from the fire, and combine with 6 egg yolks, beaten until light. Over a low flame blend ¼ cup flour and 1½ cups cream or undiluted evaporated milk. Cook in the top of a double boiler until thick, add the mushrooms; season to taste with salt, pepper, and a pinch of ground nutmeg, and cook, stirring briskly from the bottom of the pan, until the mixture coats the spoon. Remove from the fire, cool slightly, and fold in 6 egg whites beaten until stiff. Pour into a generously buttered soufflé dish; set in a pan of hot water; and bake in a moderate oven (350° F.) for 30 minutes. If preferred, bake the mixture in 6 individual soufflé dishes. If the soufflé is to be served as an entrée, it should be accompanied by brown bread and butter finger sandwiches. As a vegetable, it is especially delicious served with creamed chicken or turkey.

MUSHROOMS SAINT GERMAIN [1367]

Select one pound of medium-sized fresh mushrooms, peel and halve them lengthwise, leaving the stems on, but neatly trimmed. Sauté them in ⅓ cup of butter until nicely browned and tender; sprinkle with 2 tablespoons of lemon juice, season to taste with salt, pepper and a pinch of nutmeg, then stir in ⅓ cup of meat jelly and simmer for 5 minutes, stirring occasionally. When ready to serve, gradually add 3 egg yolks, slightly beaten, stirring constantly, and serve at once on toast freshly fried in butter and dust with finely chopped parsley.

MUSHROOMS SOUS CLOCHE [1368]
Mushrooms under Bell

For mushrooms under a bell, select 6 or 7 large fresh mushrooms for each guest. Put 1 generous teaspoon butter in the center of an au gratin or shirred egg dish, and place atop the butter a slice of freshly made toast—soaked in sherry or madeira, if you wish. If the mushrooms are fresh and white, they need not be peeled; dip them in cold water and wipe them dry, or wipe them with a wet cloth. Trim the stems. Bank the mushrooms on the toast, season to taste with salt and pepper, and pour around the toast 4 or 5 tablespoons heavy sweet cream. Cover each dish with a glass bell cover, and set in a moderate oven (350° F.) for 30 minutes. After the first 15 minutes of cooking, add a little more cream to each dish, tilting the bell covers as little as possible in order to avoid loss of steam. If the toast was not soaked in wine, a tablespoon of sherry or madeira may be added just before serving as a luncheon dish or entrée.

MUSHROOMS STEWED IN RED WINE ON TOAST   [1369]

Remove stems from 2 pounds of fresh mushrooms and set aside for other use. Peel the caps and halve them crosswise. Heat in a saucepan 1 tablespoon of lard and 3 tablespoons of butter with 1 whole clove of garlic, peeled and left whole; when fat is hot, discard the garlic and stir in 2 tablespoons of finely chopped onions, 2 tablespoons of finely chopped green pepper and 1 tablespoon of finely chopped shallots and cook for one minute, stirring constantly, then stir in 1½ teaspoons of flour and blend thoroughly until mixture just begins to bubble. Now gradually add ¼ cups of good red wine, stirring constantly until mixture begins to boil. Boil 3 or 4 minutes, stirring occasionally, season with salt, black pepper, a fresh grating of nutmeg, 2 tablespoons of finely minced chives, and add the prepared mushroom caps. Mix well, cover, and simmer gently for 25 minutes, stirring occasionally. Serve on freshly made dry toast.

MUSHROOMS ON TOAST CANADIAN MANNER   [1370]

Wash and peel 1 pound of medium sized fresh mushrooms; cut off the stems, scrape and chop coarsely. Butter a shallow baking dish; put in the mushroom caps and sprinkle the chopped stems over them. Season to taste with mixed salt and pepper, then sprinkle over the surface 4 tablespoons of minced parsley, 1 generous tablespoon of lemon juice and ⅓ teaspoon of grated lemon rind. Pour in ¾ cup of hot water mixed with ¼ cup of Pique Seasoning, cover the dish and bake in a moderate oven (350–375° F.) for 25 minutes. Meanwhile, cook a dozen thin slices of Canadian bacon and toast 6 slices of bread. Rub the toast with a little garlic, then brush with melted butter. Keep hot. When mushrooms are tender, remove the cover and stir in 3 tablespoons of good sherry wine. Serve mushrooms heaped on the toast, garnish with the hot bacon slices and pour over all the sauce in the dish.

> *Oddly fashioned, quaintly dyed,*
> *In the woods the mushrooms hide;*
> *Rich and meaty, full of flavor,*
> *Made for man's delicious savor.*
> *—The Maid and the Mushroom.*

OKRA [1371]

Southern cooks revere that green mucilaginous vegetable, the okra. Northern cooks are inclined to pass it by with a curious glance, underestimating its cunning power as a thickener. Southern cooks, and this includes the Creoles of Louisiana, use okra in soups, casserole dishes and other mixtures, usually with tomato and onion. The plant was first cultivated in tropical Africa, where large quantities are still produced. The species of okra are numerous That in general use, both in the East and West Indies and in the United States as an article of food, is the Hibiscus Esculentus. Its name in the West Indies is "gobo." There it is an important ingredient of Pepper Pot, erroneously called Philadelphia Pepper Pot. Because okra has long been associated with the Creole gumbos, the pods are sometimes called "gumbo." Okra is a body-building and regulating food; it contains lime or calcium to build teeth and bone; cellulose or roughage to regulate digestion; starches to give heat and energy; vitamin B, which builds appetite, helps growth and prevents beri-beri.

Charlestonians have great reverence for okra soup with corn sticks. Their devotion to the subject may have something to do with the freshness of the vegetable as it is peddled through the street. "Okariee— okariee! They fresh an' they fine, Yes, Mam'."

The okra pod (edible part of the plant) is rich green in color, deeply ridged and about four inches long. Its fuzzy exterior is somewhat like that of the peach, and the fuzz disappears in cooking.

FRENCH FRIED OKRA CREOLE [1372]

Select small tender pods. Wash in cold water and drain. Cover with salted boiling water and cook until tender, about 10–12 minutes, after having cut the stem from each pod. Drain and season to taste with salt and pepper; dip in beaten egg, then in fine cracker crumbs, and fry in deep, hot, clear fat until brown. Drain and serve on a folded napkin as an accompaniment to steak.

OKRA CREOLE [1373]

Brown 1 large chopped onion and 1 large green pepper (cut into strips and free from seeds and white ribs) in 3 tablespoons of drippings or lard for 2 or 3 minutes, stirring constantly, over a gentle flame; add 1 No. 2½ can of tomatoes; season with salt, pepper and 1 tablespoon (more or less, according to taste) of chili powder; bring to a boil, then stir in 1 cup of rice, washed and well drained. Add 1 bay leaf, 2 cloves and 1 slice of garlic; cover and simmer gently for 15 minutes, then add 1 pound of okra, washed, cleaned, trimmed and sliced about ⅓ inch thick, also ½ cup of boiling water mixed with ⅓ cup of Pique Seasoning. Cover and simmer gently for 25 to 30 minutes, stirring occasionally. Ten minutes before serving add 1 tablespoon of sugar and 1 tablespoon of cider vinegar. Good with roast pork, roast veal and roast turkey.

OKRA FRITTERS I   [1374]
(Slices only)

Wash in cold water, trim and cut into ¼-inch slices 1 pound of okra. Dip in beaten egg mixed with a little milk and seasoned with salt, pepper and a dash of nutmeg, and when ready to serve, fry in hot, deep, clear fat (375° F.) until delicately browned. Drain on absorbent paper and serve on a folded napkin on a hot platter as a vegetable or use as a garnish for broiled fish, meat or poultry.

OKRA FRITTERS II   [1375]
(Whole Small Okra Pods)

Wash 1 pound of okra, drain, cut off the stem end and the tip of each pod, and parboil in salted boiling water, or better still, in boiling water mixed with ¼ cup of Pique Seasoning for each cup of boiling water, for 5 or 6 minutes; drain well, wiping each pod separately on a dry towel; roll in corn meal seasoned to taste with salt, pepper and nutmeg, and fry in plenty of bacon drippings, or in deep fat, until delicately browned. Drain well and serve as a vegetable.

OKRA AU GRATIN   [1376]

Wash 1 pound of fresh sound okra carefully to remove any sand, and cut off end stems and tips; place the pods in an enamel saucepan containing 2 cups of slightly salted boiling water; stir with a wooden spoon until every pod has been immersed in the boiling salted water. Drain and at once add 2 more cups of boiling water salted to taste, and boil steadily until pods can be pierced with a knife but are not broken, for about 15 minutes. Okra cooks quickly.

Drain well, reserving the liquid for soup if desired. Arrange the soft pods in a buttered shallow baking dish; pour over them 1½ cups of hot cream sauce (No. 258); wait a minute or so to allow sauce to reach bottom of dish; top with ½ cup of buttered crumbs, and bake in a moderate oven until crumbs are brown. Serve in the baking dish, as a vegetable. Especially good with Southern fried chicken, roast turkey, roast pork or veal.

ONIONS   [1377]

Onions (lily family) have been grown and used as a food since the beginning of recorded history. One story traces the origin of the onion back to the Garden of Eden, relating that when Satan stepped out of the Garden of Eden after the fall of man, onion sprang up from the spot where he placed his right foot and garlic from the place his left foot touched.

Onions, radishes, and garlic were consumed in quantity by the laborers who built the Great Pyramid in Egypt. Among the complaints which the Israelites made to Moses was one about food. " . . . We remember the fish, which we did eat in Egypt freely; the cucumbers, and the melons, and the leeks, and the onions, and the garlic . . . "

Pliny said that the Romans used onions to cure the sting of serpents and other reptiles, that they made poultices of onions and barley meal for those who had watery eyes because onions clear the sight by the tears they draw, and that onion juice was given to those who suddenly became speechless.

Great would be the loss were the onion removed from the world's food stock. From the earliest times of which there are any authentic records it has been highly esteemed. In desert regions it was also used as a preventive of thirst by travelers and soldiers on the march. The original home of the plant was probably southern Asia or the borders of the Mediterranean. Egyptians cultivated the onion at the dawn of history. The high regard in which it was held by the ancients is supported by modern food scientists, who point out that it supplies bulk, some minerals and, when eaten raw, vitamins B and C. Robert Louis Stevenson wrote of the onion as "the poetic soul of the capacious salad bowl," and Sidney Smith, in his rhymed "Receipt for Salad," directed:

> *Let onion's atoms lurk within the bowl,*
> *And, half suspected, animate the whole . . .*

Hamburger is pepped up when fried with a few onion rings. Onion soup in the French Style is food for gourmets. Onion sauce, fried, baked, buttered and creamed onions and onions au gratin are other culinary treats.

Nothing so reconciles us to a life of scarcity as an onion at hand. How right Dean Swift when he rhymed:

> *. . . This is every cook's opinion,*
> *No savory dish without an onion,*
> *But lest your kissing should be spoil'd,*
> *Your onions must be thoroughly boiled . . .*

It is odd that scientists have just got around to discovering what grandma knew forty or fifty years ago—that onions are good for you. Scientists have found in the onion a "mysterious bacteria-destroying substance" which operates in different fashion from other recently discovered substances. This may have been a mystery to grandma, too, but sufficient for her was the knowledge that steak smothered with fried onions was better for her men folks than a visit to the doctor. And perhaps even you will be willing occasionally to place an onion sandwich, made with Boston Brown Bread, plenty of butter and salt and a thick slice of sweet Spanish onion, even above kissing.

ONION HINTS [1378]

The flavor of onions in casserole dishes (fish, meat or poultry) is universally popular. However, it is improved if the chopped onions are browned in butter or oil before they are added. And be sure to chop them fine.

Extract juice from onion by cutting small pieces from blossom end and scraping pulp with a spoon; or grate.

Never take liberties with an onion. It will get back at you. Peel them under running cold water, unless prepared to shed tears. Or cover them with hot water, let them stand a minute or so; then that thin skin, so hard to remove, can be peeled off as if by magic.

Of the small onions the white is the mildest in flavor (also the most expensive).

In selecting onions, choose those that are well shaped, with dry skins, and avoid those that have began to sprout. Rub your hands thoroughly with salt or vinegar after peeling onions to remove any unpleasant odor. Then wash with soap and water. To remove the odor of onions from a frying pan, boil in the pan for 3 minutes a mixture of three cups of water and 3 tablespoons of vinegar. Drain, wash in hot, soapy water and rinse in boiling water. Wipe very dry.

Thinly sliced onion added to any kind of beans when cooking gives them a different and excellent flavor. Bermuda onions stuffed with highly seasoned fish, meat, poultry or game, or a vegetable mixture accompanied by a green salad, a hot bread and a fruit is an ideal meal.

Charles Dickens in his *Christmas Carol* reminded us of his fondness for onions when he wrote: " . . . There were ruddy, brown-girthed Spanish onions, shining in the fatness of their growth like Spanish friars . . . " We would not be so bold as to say that George B. Shaw likes onions, but in *Candida* he announces, " . . . Maria is ready for you in the kitchen, Mrs. Morrell, the onions have come."

A good way to preserve cut onions for future use is to put them in a glass jar, screw the top on tight, and place them in the refrigerator. They will keep perfectly for a long time, and the odor will not penetrate other food in the refrigerator.

Or, slice partly used onions, and toast the slices to a golden brown in the oven. Store in a tightly-covered jar in refrigerator for soup, stew or sauce flavoring.

Onions glazed in butter and honey are flavorful and delicious.

BAKED LIVER—STUFFED ONIONS [1379]

Pan-fry or grill 1 pound of liver, taking care not to overcook it. Cut it into small pieces, then grind with 2 stalks of celery (carefully washed and scraped), 1 tablespoon each of finely chopped parsley, green pepper, chives and pimiento. Season with salt, pepper, a little thyme and nutmeg, and stir in 3 tablespoons of butter or bacon drippings—enough to make a mixture which can be handled easily. Have ready 6 large onions, parboiled and with the centers scooped out. Chop these finely and add to the liver mixture, mixing well. Stuff the onion cups with the liver mixture; top with bread crumbs and dot with butter or margarin. Bake in a moderate oven (350° F.) until the onions are tender, about 30 to 35 minutes. Serve as hot as possible, each onion placed on a bed of generously buttered cooked spinach.

BAKED ONION RINGS [1380]
(*For hamburgers or garnish*)

Cut ½-inch thick slices of large mild onions, lay the slices in a baking dish or pan, sprinkle with mixed salt and pepper, dot with butter or margarin, allowing 1 teaspoon for each slice; add 2 or 3 tablespoons of hot water. Cover and bake in a moderate oven (350° F.) for about 30 minutes or until tender. Serve a hamburger cake on each onion ring.

One of Cleopatra's favorite desserts was candied melon with stuffed onions which she ate with a golden single-pronged fork.

BAKED STUFFED ONIONS TEXAS WAY [1381]

Scoop out 6 large onions and brush the insides generously with butter then season with salt and freshly ground pepper mixed with a tiny pinch of cayenne. Don't be niggardly with the pepper; turn the handle of the mill rapidly twice into each scooped-out onion. Fill the cavities with equal parts of chicken liver and cooked ham that have been chopped fine and seasoned with a generous pinch of thyme and a soupçon of nutmeg. Place the fully packed onions in a flat, generously buttered earthenware baking dish, and brush melted butter over their tops and sides. Set, tightly covered, in a very slow oven, so that they may cook, slowly, barely simmering. The cooking will take about an hour, the time depending on the size of the onions.

When ready to serve, enrich the smoking sauce which has exuded from the onions, with a little sherry and a few grains of nutmeg. Also, if desired, press whole cloves into each onion before baking.

CURRIED ONION CHEESE PIE [1382]

Roll enough soda crackers to make 1½ cups of sieved crumbs (about 3 dozen crackers), and combine with ½ cup of melted butter, or equal parts of butter and lard, seasoned to taste with salt and a few grains of curry powder; press mixture evenly into a buttered, deep, 9-inch round pie plate. Set aside.

Fry 3 cups of thinly sliced onions until lightly browned in 3 table-spoons of butter or margarin, stirring almost constantly; and when cooled to lukewarm, spread in bottom of cracker crumb crust, and again set aside.

Scald 1½ cups of rich milk or equal parts of rich milk and undiluted evaporated milk or thin cream; remove from the fire and beat in 3 eggs, slightly beaten, and seasoned with 1 scant teaspoon of salt, and 1½ teaspoons of curry powder, blended in a little cold milk; add ½ cup of grated cheese (any kind); return to the fire and cook until cheese is melted, stirring constantly from bottom of the pan. Pour this sauce over the onions, toss gently, but thoroughly; sprinkle top with ½ cup of buttered crumbs and grated cheese in equal parts, and bake 30 minutes in a very moderate oven (300–325° F.), or until a silver knife blade inserted in center comes out clean. Serve at once.

FRENCH FRIED ONIONS [1383]

Peel and cut 6 large Spanish or Bermuda onions into ¼-inch thick slices, and soak in milk for 30 minutes. Drain, and roll in seasoned flour, then in beaten egg, and again in flour. Keep the smaller rings and odd pieces for a soup or sauce. Shortly before serving time, place the prepared rings in a wire frying basket; shake gently to remove excess flour and immerse in deep hot fat (380° F.). Allow the rings to remain in the fat until they are delicately browned, shaking the basket gently to prevent their sticking to one another. Drain then turn the golden crackling rings into a paper-lined pan and keep hot. Do not fry more until the fat again reaches the right temperature; also be sure not to fry too many rings at once.

Note. Onions and beefsteak make good companions—they are natural partners, and, when served together, enhance each other. But most of us like variety, even in our favorite combinations.

Epicures who have tasted the fruit of the Durian tree in the East Indies say that it tastes like a combination of onions and ice cream.

ONION CHEESE CUSTARD PIE [1384]

Slice thinly 3 or 4 large onions; fry in ⅓ cup of butter or margarin until the slices just begin to take on a light yellowish color, stirring almost constantly, over a gentle flame. Drain off all the butter or margarin; turn the onions into a buttered baking dish, and pour over them 2½ cups of soft boiled custard, mixed with ⅓ cup each of grated Swiss and Parmesan cheese, and highly seasoned with salt, a few grains of cayenne pepper, and nutmeg to taste. Bake in a moderate oven (325° F.)

until the custard is set and delicately browned, turned to the color of ripe wheat. Serve cut in wedges as an ordinary pie, and as hot as possible.

ONION CROQUETTES [1385]

Appropriate for service with almost any kind of meat, especially reheated meat, as a side dish or a garnish.

Cook 8 or 9 medium-sized onions until tender, in boiling, salted water; drain and chop them fine. Make 1 cup of white sauce with 2 tablespoons of butter, 2 tablespoons of flour and 1 cup of scalded sweet milk; stir in the chopped onions, season with paprika, nutmeg and white pepper to taste, and add ½ cup of fine dry bread crumbs, sieved. Spread the mixture out to cool. When quite cold, shape into croquettes; roll in beaten egg mixed with a very little cold milk, then in fine, dry breadcrumbs. When ready to serve, place a few croquettes at a time in a frying basket, plunge the basket into hot, deep fat, (375° F.) and fry golden brown. Drain and serve at once.

Like the cultivated onion, the wild onion belongs to the lily family. The nodding wild onion is very common on banks and hillsides from New York to South Carolina, west to Minnesota, South Dakota and New Mexico. The bulb of this species is very strong, but if parboiled is very good to eat.

ONIONS A LA BORDELAISE [1386]

Select 6 Bermuda onions, large and flat, and scoop out the centers. Fill the cavity of each onion with a rich stuffing made with 1 pound of chicken liver, ¼ pound of fresh mushrooms, 1 large truffle, and ½ cup cooked lean ham, all put together through the food chopper several times to insure smoothness and perfect blending. Season this mixture highly with salt, pepper, nutmeg, and a tiny piece of garlic, and moisten with a little heavy sweet cream. On top of each onion, place a cover of pork fat back ⅛ inch thick, sprinkling this with a little powdered thyme. Place the onions side by side in a casserole, then line with 1 cup rich Lyonnaise Sauce (No. 1073). Set the casserole in a slow oven (275° F.) and cover. Let cook exceedingly slowly, scarcely with a quivering, until the onions are tender, or about 1 hour, the time depending on the size of the onions. When ready to serve, add a pony glass of the best brandy and a grating of nutmeg on top. Serve in the casserole.

ONIONS AU GRATIN [1387]

Peel about 18 small white onions; cook in boiling salted water until just tender, or pierceable with the tines of a fork. Drain, reserving the liquid for the base of a soup, and arrange the onions in a generously buttered casserole. Cover with 1½ cups of Cream Sauce (No. 258); top with a generous ½ cup of buttered crumbs; sprinkle the crumbs with a scant ½ cup of grated cheese, and bake in a slow oven (300–325° F.) for about 25–30 minutes or until well-browned. Serve at once from the casserole.

ONIONS AND PEPPER RAGOUT [1388]

Fry 2 large chopped onions, with 3 green peppers, also chopped, in ¼ cup of bacon or ham drippings, 5 to 6 minutes over a gentle flame, stirring almost constantly; then stir in 2 cups of tomatoes, fresh or canned, ⅓ cup of good beef stock, 1 large bay leaf tied with 8 sprigs of fresh parsley and 1 sprig of thyme, and season to taste with salt, pepper, and a little nutmeg. Bring gradually to a boil, and simmer very gently over a low flame, for about 20 minutes, stirring occasionally with a wooden spoon. Now bring to a boil, drop in your favorite dumplings by tablespoons on top, cover and cook for about 15 minutes. Serve right from the casserole.

ONIONS A LA REINE [1389]

Take as many large Spanish onions as required. Stick each with 2 or 3 whole cloves from which the heads have been removed. Let the onions cook slowly in water perfumed with thyme, slightly salted, having just enough water barely to cover. When the water is reduced to almost nothing, add, for each onion, 1 pony glass of the best madeira, which the onions will readily absorb. Serve with a rich Cream Sauce (No. 258) with African capers.

ONION SOUFFLE FRENCH METHOD [1390]

Peel 6 medium-sized onions, cut in quarters, and boil until very soft, changing the water once. Turn the onions into a sieve, and drain well, saving the water. Now chop the cooked onions very fine, and drain again. Season with ½ teaspoon salt, ¼ teaspoon white pepper, a few grains nutmeg, and, if desired, a pinch of cayenne. Allow to stand. Make a cream sauce of 4 tablespoons butter, 4 tablespoons flour, and ⅓ cup heavy cream and ⅓ cup of the water in which the onions were cooked. Prepare the sauce as usual by cooking in the top of a double boiler until it is quite thick, stirring constantly. Then add the onion pulp and 3 egg yolks, slightly beaten. Mix well, and fold in 3 egg whites, stiffly beaten. Turn the mixture into a fairly deep buttered soufflé dish, and bake for 25 to 30 minutes in a moderately slow oven (325° F.). Serve at once with or without a rich Tomato Sauce (No. 1130).

PARSNIPS [1391]

Parsnip, that pale root, which you might think would tax the talent of a professional chef, is one of the finest tubers we have. All evidence seems to indicate that the cultivated parsnip was known to the ancient Greeks and Romans. The Romans were supposed to have served parsnips boiled with a sauce made with mead or honey wine; and the Emperor Tiberius liked parsnips so much that every year he had them brought from France and Germany, where the climate enabled them to be grown to perfection. The plant grows wild in parts of Europe and the United States and in South America around Buenos Aires. The cultivated varieties were brought here from France and England by the early colonists and were generally grown by 1630.

Parsnips " . . . are not sweet 'til bit by frosts," according to an old gardening book. Frost changes the starch in the parsnip root to sugar, and greatly improves the taste. An old English cook book warns that "Parsnips eaten too old, and in great quantities, cause delirium and insanity, on which account they have been called fool's parsnips." However, you probably won't suffer if you take a chance.

BOILED PARSNIP [1392]

Wash and scrape—do not peel—parsnips. If large, cut in halves. Cook uncovered in a large amount of boiling salted water 30 to 35 minutes, or until tender; drain, slice, dice, cut like French fried potatoes, or mash, but always remove the woody core. Then dress with melted butter, lemon butter, cream sauce, Béchamel sauce, or French fry, and so forth. Two pounds of parsnips will serve six easily.

CREAMED PARSNIP AU GRATIN [1393]

Slice or dice 2 pounds of boiled parsnips as indicated for recipe No. 1392. Have ready 1½ cups of cream sauce (No. 258), add the hot sliced or diced parsnips, heat through, and pour the cream sauce over them, mixing well. Sprinkle with ½ cup of buttered crumbs and ⅓ cup of grated cheese, mixed together and bake in a moderate oven (350–375° F.) until brown. Serve from the baking dish.

GLAZED PARSNIP SLICES I [1394]

Heat to a boil in a frying pan 1 cup of molasses; drop in slices of cold cooked parsnips and let them simmer till they brown and glaze. Serve hot as a substitute for candied sweet potatoes.

GLAZED PARSNIP SLICES II [1395]

Arrange 6 medium-sized, cooked and halved parsnips from which the woody core has been removed, in a shallow baking dish. Prepare a mixture as follows: Combine 2½ to 3 tablespoons of butter, ¼ cup of brown sugar and ½ cup of sweet cider or, if preferred, plain water, pineapple juice, or any kind of canned fruit juice, and pour over the parsnip halves. Bake in a hot oven (400–425° F.) until nicely browned. Serve with turkey, chicken, roast pork, or veal.

PARSNIP or SARATOGA PARSNIP CHIPS   [1396]

Scrape a dozen medium-sized parsnips; discard stem ends and tips; cut in very thin lengthwise slices, discarding the woody core and dropping the slices in ice-cold water as you go along. Let stand in ice-cold water for at least 30 minutes. Drain and dry with a cloth. Fry, a few at a time, in hot, deep, clear fat (390–395° F.) until delicately browned. Skim off with perforated ladle, drain well and serve hot or cold.

PARSNIP FRITTERS   [1397]

Cook 6 or 7 medium-sized parsnips as directed for Boiled Parsnips (No. 1392) and cool. When ready to serve, rub through ricer or mash; beat in 1 egg and 1 egg yolk, 1 tablespoon each of finely chopped onion, parsley or chives and green pepper. Season to taste with salt, pepper, nutmeg and thyme, then beat in gradually, ¼ to ⅓ cup of flour, beating till smooth. Drop by teaspoons or tablespoons into hot, shallow fat, and cook, turning to brown both sides. Serve very hot.

PARSNIP PIE FARMER STYLE   [1398]

Boil 8 medium-sized parsnips as directed for Boiled Parsnips (No. 1392) until tender, quarter and remove the woody core. In a separate saucepan cook 3 medium sized potatoes, cubed, in salted boiling water until tender. Mix ½ cup of well-drained cooked or canned peas with ½ cup of cooked or canned drained string beans cut in small lozenges. Cook separately ⅓ cup of diced salt pork. Arrange layers of parsnips, potatoes and half of the pork cubes, repeat, then arrange layers of mixed peas and string beans, seasoning to taste with salt, pepper, nutmeg and thyme. Pour very gently over all 1½ cups of cream sauce (No. 258) to which has been added 1 tablespoon each of finely chopped green pepper, parsley and onion. Cover top with small baking powder biscuits cut with small doughnut cutter; brush the biscuits with cold milk, and bake in a hot oven (400° F.) for about 20 minutes, or till biscuits are nicely browned. Serve right from the baking dish.

PARSNIP PUFFS   [1399]

Cook together in salted boiling water until tender 1½ pounds of scraped, halved, cored parsnips and 2 or 3 medium-sized potatoes, also cut into small pieces. Drain and season to taste with salt, pepper and ¼ teaspoon of dry mustard. Mash and form into small cakes; roll in flour and fry in shallow fat until crisp and brown on both sides; drain and serve as a vegetable or as a garnish.

Variation. Add ⅓ cup of finely chopped nutmeats or almonds to the mixture, beat in 2 slightly beaten eggs, and fry as indicated.

PEAS [1400]

Peas are among the most popular of all vegetables. Dishes too numerous to mention are proudly served in a setting of delectable green peas. And few vegetables are available fresh throughout so long a season; few are so adaptable, so delicious in flavor.

But peas are no new sprouts of vegetables; modern science can claim no credit in their development. Their pedigree is long, romantic, historic—possibly even prehistoric, for some authorities assert that they were eaten in the Stone Age. Certain it is that the people of ancient Egypt ate them, for they have been found in a tomb near the remains of Thebes. And peas long dried were uncovered among the ruins of once great Troy, where they had remained buried in pottery jars for some thirty-four centuries.

Theophrastus, the Greek who is called the father of botany, and who died in 287 B. C., referred frequently to peas as a common vegetable of his land. They were mentioned, too, a short time before the birth of Christ by the Roman poet Virgil. Much later, in the Middle Ages, the writings of the time indicated that peas were grown as one of the chief guards against famine, and that they were given a major part in the rations, home and abroad, of medieval armies and navies.

In the England of that time, peas were so generally in use that the terms "pottage" and "porridge" came to be practically synonymous with peas, and nursery rhymes revolved about them—"Pease porridge hot, pease porridge cold." The people of the Middle Ages, unlike the ancients who used dried ripe peas alone as food, cooked the green pods whole, dipped them in sauce, picked out the peas, and then threw away the empty pods.

It was the French who first popularized the eating of shelled green peas, and at first they themselves regarded purely as a fad such treatment of this vegetable. The writings and the memoirs of the times of many a Louis of France are replete with commentaries on the heights of folly to which the taste for green peas had led all the court. Madame de Maintenon, in a letter dated May 10, 1696, remarks: "The subject of peas continues to absorb all others. The anxiety to eat them, the pleasure of having eaten them, and the desire to eat them again are the three great matters which have been discussed for four days past by our Princes. Some ladies, even after having supped, too, returning to their homes . . . will again eat peas before going to bed. It is both a fashion and a madness."

Because of this royal fondness for the delicate taste of these *petits pois*, green peas gained fame as a French vegetable *de luxe*. But the *petits pois* are a small, wrinkled, very sweet variety of peas, and the English preferred a different type. They developed a larger pea, smooth and unwrinkled, which they brought with them to colonial America.

But large or small, wrinkled or smooth, peas have a definite appeal, not only for the eater, but for the cook. Purely aside from their qualities of taste, they present a bright, refreshing color contrast for the darker foods.

When you're shopping for peas, look for pods that are a bright green, fresh looking, and somewhat velvety to the touch. The pods of immature peas are usually flat and of a dark green, while those of old peas are often yellowish. The pods should be filled two-thirds or more with fairly well developed peas.

Green peas, quickly cooked, retain their natural color without the aid of a "fixing" agent like baking soda. Parisian cooks retain the beautiful green hue of peas by cooking them in Vichy water or in a similar liquid instead of in plain water, or in meat or chicken stock. Put the peas in a heavy saucepan with a tight-fitting cover, and cook over a low flame. So little liquid should be used in their cooking that there will be very little left when the peas are done.

BAYOU CREAMED GREEN PEAS [1401]

Cook 2½ cups of shelled green peas quickly in a little boiling salted water until tender, together with 6 sprigs of parsley tied up with 1 large bay leaf and 1 large leaf or 2 small ones of fresh mint, 1 whole clove and ⅛ teaspoon of pepper. Drain off the water, discard the bay leaf bouquet, and stir in 2 tablespoons of butter and ½ cup of scalded heavy cream. Bring to a boil and serve at once dusted with chopped parsley.

CREAMED PEA PODS [1402]

Wash 2 pounds of pea pods, snap off the stem ends and peel them from the thin skin; cut into small squares; wash in cold water; drain, then cook in cold water to cover, slightly salted, until tender. Drain well. Have ready ½ generous cup of cream sauce very hot, stir in the drained pea pods, season to taste with salt and pepper, and serve dusted with chopped chives or parsley.

Note. You may cook the peas proper separately from the pea pods, until tender, combine them and stir in ¾ to 1 cup of hot, cream sauce.

Because of the unavoidable lapse of time between picking and cooking, market peas lack the sweetness and the tenderness of those rushed from garden to sauce pan. By selecting the freshest market offerings early in the morning, however, before they have wilted, and by cooking them well—though not to a mush—you can be sure of enjoying the full flavor of a dish such as the following one.

GREEN PEAS NICOISE [1403]
Petits Pois à la Niçoise

Combine 2½ cups of fresh, shelled green peas, all, as far as possible, the same size, 2 cups of tiny potato balls—hazelnut size—1 bouquet garni made of 4 sprigs of fresh parsley, 4 sprigs of chervil, 1 tiny sprig of summer savory, and 1 tiny sprig of thyme, all tied together with white kitchen thread, salt, pepper and a fresh grating of nutmeg in a saucepan. Pour over ½ to ¾ cup of tomato juice; cover very tightly, and cook over a gentle flame for 35–40 minutes, shaking the pan occasionally. Remove the cover, discard the bouquet garni and stir in bit by bit 3 tablespoons of sweet butter kneaded with 1 tablespoon of flour. Shake the pan meanwhile to mix thoroughly. Serve immediately.

MASHED PEA PODS IN CREAM [1404]

Wash 4 or 5 pounds of pea pods; snap off the stem ends and peel the pods. Cook in enough chicken stock or better still in veal stock until tender. Drain off any excess stock, and rub pods through a fine-meshed wire sieve into a saucepan. Season to taste with salt, pepper and nutmeg, stir in 2 tablespoons of butter mixed with ½ cup, or more or less, of scalded cream, to make a purée of the consistency of mashed potatoes. Serve as a vegetable sprinkling with ½ generous cup of tiny bread cubes (croutons) fried in butter and well drained.

PETITS POIS BONNE FEMME [1405]
Green Peas Good Woman Style

Fry a dozen very small white onions and ¼ pound of lean salt pork cut into small dice, parboiled 2 or 3 minutes, then well drained over a low heat. Stir frequently until onions are tender and pork cubes are crackling; drain off excess fat, leaving about 1 generous tablespoon, and sprinkle over the onions and cracklings 1 teaspoon of flour; stir one minute, then moisten with 1 cup of chicken stock, and bring to a boil. Simmer till onions are perfectly tender but not mashed. Put 1 quart of freshly shelled green peas into this sauce, add 3 or 4 sprigs of fresh parsley; season with salt (if needed) and a good dash of white pepper. Boil very gently until peas are tender. Serve in a hot vegetable dish.

PETITS POIS A LA FRANÇAISE [1406]
Green Peas in the French Style

Heat in a saucepan 2 tablespoons of butter; stir in 2 quarts of fresh green peas, shelled, ½ head of Boston lettuce, finely shredded, 4 or 5 small white onions, thinly sliced, 4 or 5 sprigs of fresh parsley, 1 teaspoon of sugar, ⅓ teaspoon of salt and ⅛ teaspoon of finely ground black pepper; then stir in ¼ cup of hot water, or better still, chicken stock; cover and cook very gently, over a low heat, for about 45 minutes to one hour, shaking and rocking the pan frequently. Cream 1 tablespoon of butter and 1 teaspoon of flour, add this bit by bit to the peas, cook 5 minutes longer, taste for seasoning, and serve as a vegetable.

PEAS IN ONION CUPS [1407]

Parboil 6 large onions for 20 minutes and remove the centers leaving the root ends intact. Place prepared onions in a buttered baking dish, and bake in a moderate oven (350° F.) until delicately browned, brushing them occasionally with melted butter. Transfer to a hot platter, and fill them with creamed, buttered or minted peas. Use the onion centers for another dish. Serve onions dusted with finely chopped parsley or chopped fresh mint. Serve very hot.

SPLIT PEA PURÉE [1408]

Put 1 cup of washed and picked quick-cooking split peas into 2½ cups of boiling water and boil gently for 25 minutes; rub through a sieve, season to taste with salt and white pepper and a dash of nutmeg, and stir in 2 tablespoons of sweet butter. The purée should have the consistency of mashed potatoes. It may be kept for several days in the refrigerator if desired. Serve as a vegetable dish or with cooked link pork sausage or baked pork chops.

SPLIT PEA SAUSAGE [1409]
(A Lenten dish)

Mix together the following ingredients: 1 cup of split pea purée (No. 1408) ½ cup of dried, fine bread crumbs, 2 tablespoons of heavy sweet cream or thick cream sauce, salt and pepper to taste, ½ teaspoon of powdered sage, 1 egg, 2 teaspoons of well beaten Worcestershire sauce, and 1 tablespoon of grated onion mixed with ½ small clove of garlic, mashed to a pulp. Shape in form of small sausages; roll in fine bread crumbs and fry in bacon drippings until brown. Serve with fried apple or pineapple rings, and cucumber relish.

PETITS POIS A L'ÉTUVÉE (FERMIÈRE) [1410]
Stewed Green Peas French Style

This recipe for green peas, though one of the best, is really a simple one; but the directions must be followed exactly to achieve the full effect.

Shell 3 pounds or more of fresh green peas to obtain a full quart of peas. Place the peas in a saucepan having a tight-fitting lid together with a small head of lettuce finely shredded, ½ cup of thinly sliced onions, the rings separated, ½ cup of finely chopped green pepper, and ½ cup of chopped lean, cooked ham. Add also 1 bouquet garni composed of 1 large bay leaf, 6 sprigs of fresh parsley, and 1 sprig of green celery leaves, tied together with kitchen thread, 1 or 2 whole cloves, and ⅓ cup of sweet butter melted into ½ cup of chicken stock. Season to taste with salt, pepper and 1 teaspoon of honey. Cover tightly and bake in a moderate oven (350–375° F.) for about 30 minutes. Then shake the pan, close the oven and continue braising for 30 minutes longer. Remove from the oven and stir in slowly ¼ cup of scalded heavy sweet cream. Taste for seasoning and serve as a side dish or a main dish, if the peas are topped with cooked link pork sausages.

POTATOES   [1411]

From the plunder of Peru came the first potato. But no priest or pirate of the conquest ever guessed that the tuber he trod underfoot on the upland Peruvian plain would spread to every corner of the temperate zone and be worth more than all the mines of Potosi. No dream of Inca gold, not the very Temple of the Sun itself, would buy one year's potato crop today.

We owe the first mention of the potato to Pedro de Cieza de Leon who, in 1538, the year after the conquest, left newly settled Cartagena, crossed the steaming Isthmus of Panama, and scrambled up the face of the Andes. There he discovered the potato, which, instead of being cooked by heat, was cured by frost and then dried. This *chunu* was, and still is, the staple food of those Indians who live above the zone where corn can be grown. Vast quantities of *chunu* were stored for the Indian army, for tribute to the Great Inca, and against famine. Potato culture was highly developed; guano from the sea islands fertilized this vegetable, an elaborate irrigation system was maintained, and many different varieties were grown.

For years after the conquest, a motley mixture of priests, pirates and soldiers traveled homeward across the blood-soaked Isthmus. Forty thousand carriers of Inca loot perished there. On one of those trips, probably between 1580 and 1585, someone carried the first potato to Europe. From Spain it went to Italy, and by 1588 it reached the hands of Charles l'Ecluse, keeper of the botanical garden of Vienna. Neither Sir Walter Raleigh nor Sir Francis Drake brought the potato from Virginia to Ireland, for it did not grow in Virginia in their time. The Raleigh legend is pure myth, but the romantic Irish have always clung fondly to it. The Germans insist that Drake is the man, and today his statue stands in Offenberg, with an inscription reading:

Sir Francis Drake
Introducer of the Potato into
Europe in the year of Our Lord
1580

The Raleigh and Drake *canards*, still widely current, were based partly upon the groundnut and partly upon the sweet potato.

The potato, like all new foods, was slow to overcome the prejudices of the people, in spite of the most exalted attention. Scientists not only wrote it up, but improved it. Marie Antoinette wore its blossoms in her hair. Scotch divines thundered against it, because it was not mentioned in the Bible and yet was the forbidden fruit, so they said, that caused Adam's fall. English apprentices, save for once a week, had it banned from their diet. Frederick the Great planted potatoes in the Lustgarten, and his grandson threatened to cut off the noses of all who would not plant them. There was even a Potato War in Germany.

Through all this fanfare, the potato gradually came into its birthright because poor people of Northern Europe found that if there wasn't much else to eat, potatoes would keep body and soul together. And nowhere was poverty so bitter and the potato so welcome as in Ireland. The Irish lavished pet names upon the lowly tuber. Priests and altar boys marched up and down their fields drenching the crop with holy water. They little dreamed that failure of the crop would one day decimate their country.

In 1719 a group of Irish Presbyterians founded the town of London-derry, New Hampshire, and started potato growing in the United States. This was more than 130 years after Drake and Raleigh were supposed to have carried the potato from Virginia to Europe. But, as an occasionally imported food, potatoes were known in New England long before that. Coming perhaps from Bermuda, potatoes appeared on a dinner menu of Harvard College in 1708.

The Rev. Chauncey E. Goodrich of Utica, New York, imported from the Andes the seeds of several varieties of potato. From this fresh stock, after a few cross-pollinations, he produced a variety in 1853 that he called the *Garnet Chili*, from which was later derived the *Early Rose*, a variety still widely grown today.

The potato didn't sweep to victory unimpeded. Along the eastern slopes of the Rocky Mountains grows a wild relative of the potato, the buffalo bur. Upon this a certain beetle innocently nibbled. As the potato crept westward during the Civil War, the range of the cultivated potato and this wild one overlapped, and the insect turned to the lusher feeding of the cultivated plant, soon becoming a number one pest. Spreading eastward, it reached the Mississippi by 1868 and the Atlantic coast by 1874. All Europe quickly set quarantines against American potatoes, and the beetle didn't reach Europe until the first World War when it was accidentally introduced near Bordeaux, France, and is now actively fought by the French.

An earlier potato blight greatly influenced the course of history. Until 1844 Ireland had reasonably good crops. She needed them, for by that time the potato was the chief food of her peasants. A crop failure came in 1846, diminishing the supply and infecting the seed. The Irish tried every conceivable thing that hunger and terror could suggest but still the crops failed and nearly a million peasants died of starvation. The young and progressive fled to America; more than a million and a half came to New York within the next few years and as the blight spread to Germany and Poland fresh waves of potato pilgrims fled here. Thus the potato forever links the Incas with the sturdy immigrants who have played so large a part in the development of America.

POTATOES—HINTS [1412]

If pricked with a fork before cooking, baked potatoes will be mealy, as the steam will escape more easily.

New potatoes should be put into boiling salted water. They should be prepared just in time for cooking, by scraping, not peeling. They require about 20 minutes more or less to boil, depending on size.

To ensure success in mashing potatoes, dry them thoroughly after boiling and draining, by placing the pan over a gentle flame.

When ricing potatoes, do not overfill the potato ricer.

To cook potatoes in their skins or, as some say, "in their jackets," it is necessary to cover them completely with cold salted water after scrubbing them (old potatoes only), and to keep the pan covered throughout the process.

Try adding a few caraway seeds or a few drops of onion juice, or a dot of anchovy paste the size of a peanut mixed with a little butter, to a baked stuffed potato.

When peeling potatoes, and in fact all roots and tubers, peel thinly, the best and most nourishing parts lie near the skin, the centers being usually more aqueous and stringy.

A scant teaspoon of baking powder added to mashed potatoes insures their lightness and fluffiness.

When two tablespoons of milk and one teaspoon of butter are added to a potato of medium size, the mixture resembles the imaginary "perfect food," furnishing those elements essential to health.

When adding cream or milk to mashed potatoes, scald first, to insure smooth, fluffy mashed potatoes. Potatoes mashed and beaten with an electric beater are white and fluffy but they do take extra milk.

Add a pinch of nutmeg to creamed potatoes.

When purchasing potatoes, look for clean, firm, smooth ones, free of cuts, spots and green ends. Avoid those with unsightly scabs and knobs.

The potato has been the innocent victim of a widespread impression that it is exceptionally fattening. Weight-conscious people have come to look with suspicion on it simply because it is listed among the starchy foods. Actually 78 per cent of this sturdy tuber is water—only 11 to 20 per cent being starch. One medium sized potato totals 100 calories. But so does each of the following; 1 large apple, 1 large orange, 1 medium baking powder biscuit, 1½ tablespoons of French salad dressing . . . and so forth.

Save the water in which potatoes have been boiled and use in place of part of the milk in muffins, pancakes and bread.

To prevent unpleasant color changes and keep potatoes white, it is recommended to (a) keep pared or cut potatoes under water until put on to cook; (b) use cooking utensils free of chips or exposed iron; (c) add scalded milk immediately upon removing the potatoes from the stove, because experience has proved that potatoes mashed with milk as soon as they are cooked retain their good color.

Grated raw potatoes added to hamburger and meat loaf make the meat go farther, keep it moist and prevent it from falling apart when cut.

Sweet potatoes and apples will not turn black if placed in salt water immediately after peeling.

The halved rinds, left over from the morning orange juice, filled with mashed sweet potatoes and baked, are very attractive.

Potato cakes made from left over mashed potatoes should be rolled in bread crumbs or dry flour to prevent their sticking to the frying pan or skillet when fried. This also helps to brown them nicely.

To avoid watery mashed potatoes, mash them over low heat, stirring meanwhile to prevent scorching. Do not add milk or cream or cream sauce until all excess water has been evaporated.

A little water added to the pan used for baking potatoes is approved by professional chefs. Some prefer to rub a little butter or oil over the individual potato.

Never French fry potatoes until just before serving. If allowed to stand they will surely be soft and soggy.

Add 3 or 4 slices of American cheese, cut into tiny pieces, to hot potatoes when mashing, to give them a new and different flavor.

Grated coconut makes a delicious topping for mashed sweet potatoes.

BAKED POTATO SOUBISE [1413]

Scrub and oil 6 large sized baking potatoes and bake until tender. Meanwhile, prepare the following sauce:

Cook 2 cups of finely chopped onion until tender in a little salted beef bouillon. Drain thoroughly, squeezing very gently to remove excess moisture, then blend with 1 cup of rich cream sauce. Keep hot. Cut a slice from the top of each potato and scoop out contents with a spoon. Mash with a little hot milk, salt, white pepper and a dash of nutmeg, with 2 tablespoons of butter. Beat until light and fluffy, adding while beating, 2 egg yolks, slightly beaten, a little at a time. Refill the potato shells, heaping them up high, dome-fashion, and with a spoon scoop out a little of the potato in the center, replacing it with the creamed onions. Sprinkle the surface with grated cheese and brown under the flame of the broiling oven. Serve at once.

BAVARIAN POTATO BALLS [1414]

See Sauerbraten (No. 613)

CREAMED POTATOES OLD FASHIONED [1415] STYLE or POTATOES IN HASTE

Slice 6 medium-sized cooked, peeled potatoes. Place in top of double boiler; cover with rich, scalded milk; cover and cook over hot water until milk is very hot. Then stir in 1½ tablespoons of butter, previously creamed with 1 teaspoon of flour; season to taste with salt and white pepper, and cook over hot water, covered, for about 20 minutes, shaking the pan occasionally. Turn into a hot platter, taste for seasoning, and dust with 1 teaspoon each of finely chopped chives and finely chopped parsley.

DELMONICO POTATOES [1416]

Melt 3 tablespoons of butter; blend in 2 tablespoons of flour, season to taste with salt and white pepper, then add gradually 1 cup of hot milk, stirring constantly, till creamy, boiling and thick. Have ready ½ cup of grated cheese (any kind desired), 3 hard-cooked eggs, coarsely chopped or thinly sliced then blended with 1 quart of sliced, cold, cooked potatoes. Arrange in a generously buttered baking dish in alternate layers. Top with ½ cup of buttered crumbs and bake until well browned in a moderate oven (350° F.). Serve right from the baking dish.

When Canada was first settled, potatoes sent to England were "dainties" for the Queen, according to Parkinson, a seventeenth-century historian. But in 1629 he wrote, " . . . by reason of their great increase they are so commonly here with us at London that even the most vulgar begin to despise them . . . "

FRENCH POTATO FRITTO MISTO [1417]

Fritto misto, the mixed fry of all Italy and of Italians wherever they may be, comes to the table in infinite variety, limited only by human imagination. It may be a one-plate banquet for the vegetarian, a spectacular platter of richness and delicacy for the gourmet, or a glorified fish fry for the sea food lover, but always it comes smoking and sizzling from the deep frying kettle and always shrouded in mystery.

Although prepared in about the same way, the French potato fritto mix differs a little in the fact that the mysterious morsels are wrapped in mashed potatoes instead of being rolled in a batter, then fried.

Pick up the left-overs of cold meat, chicken, veal, beef, pork, lamb, tongue, sausage and mince them separately, making a composite hot dish of as many varieties of balls as you have ingredients, and mix each ingredient in a rich cream or a rather firm Béchamel sauce No. 259, then proceed as follows:

Boil 4 medium-sized potatoes in their skins in salted water just until tender. Drain and peel, then rice them. Add 2 egg yolks, one at a time, beating briskly after each addition, alternately with ¼ to ⅓ cup of scalded milk in which 1 large bay leaf, 2 sprigs of parsley and 2 thin slices of onion have been steeped and then removed. Season to taste with salt, pepper, nutmeg and a teaspoon of curry powder, mixing well, then beat in ½ cup of grated Gruyère cheese. Spread mixture on a cold platter to cool, and when cold, take a portion the size of a large walnut and wrap in it a small amount of creamed meat, poultry, game, vegetables, fish, or a whole shrimp or an oyster, shaping into a ball. Roll the balls in seasoned flour, then in egg beaten with a little milk, then finally in bread crumbs. When ready to serve, place a few balls at a time in a frying basket, plunge into clear, hot, deep fat (375–390° F.) and brown. Drain on absorbent paper and serve on a folded napkin placed on a hot platter; garnish with parsley or watercress and serve sizzling hot.

HASHED BROWN POTATOES [1418]

Potato cookery would fill a book because the potato is the most versatile vegetable in the world. One good rule is to cook potatoes, old and new, in their jackets whenever possible. This method saves flavor, food value (especially the mineral salts which lie close to the skin), and time. Another good rule is to give the potatoes a quick start over high heat, and keep them cooking at a high, even temperature.

If potatoes are to be boiled in their jackets, they should be washed, then put on the stove in *cold, salted water* (never in hot water). Cook them only until a fork will pierce them easily; drain promptly and thoroughly, lest they absorb moisture and get soggy; and shake them in the saucepan over the fire for a minute or so, until the skins burst. Then peel while the potatoes are hot. Let them cool, chill them thoroughly, then chop very fine.

Season the cold potatoes with salt and pepper, tossing well. Heat plenty of bacon drippings in a light frying-pan—not a skillet. When the drippings are sizzling hot, put the potatoes in so that they almost swim in the fat. Watch the fat disappear almost instantly. Add more if necessary. Lower the flame and let the potatoes brown on the bottom. The browning is indicated by puffs of steam rising here and there from the mass. Fold the mixture like an omelette; allow it to brown for a minute or two longer, then slide it on to a hot platter.

The important point to remember is that there should be plenty of smoking hot bacon drippings in the pan before you put in the potatoes to brown. The potatoes will absorb all the fat needed, no more, no less. They should be kept moist with fat, for they will never absorb more than they absolutely require.

MASHED POTATOES and VARIATIONS [1419]

To make mashed potatoes fluffy, creamy and white, select firm potatoes. If using large potatoes, quarter or halve them. To cut them smaller results in loss of vitamins and often in watery potatoes. Cook in salted water; drain and dry over a low flame to evaporate the moisture. Mash or rice. As some potatoes absorb more liquid than others, the scalded milk should be added gradually, beating while adding. A little cream improves the flavor. Season to taste with salt and white pepper. Serve very hot.

Variation. For Duchesse Potatoes, add 3 egg yolks, one at a time, to freshly mashed hot potatoes. Beat well after each addition. Then add a little hot cream, and season to taste with salt and white pepper. Pile in small mounds on a lightly greased baking sheet, and brown delicately in a hot oven (400° F.).

POMMES SOUFFLÉES [1420]
Potato Balloons

Using a sharp knife slice crisp peeled potatoes about ⅛ inch thick. They must be uniform in size and thickness, and must be trimmed to the shape of a flattened football. Put the slices in ice water; then drain, and dry on a linen cloth. In the meantime, heat a kettle of cooking oil to just below the boiling point. Drop in the iced and dried slices and cook 3 minutes, then lift them out into a colander for 5 minutes to drain and cool. Reheat the oil until it smokes and boils, while the slices are cooling. Place the cooled slices, a few at a time, in a frying basket; lower them quickly into the very hot oil. Lift them out again before they have a chance to burn, and drain on absorbent paper. Serve crisp and hot. The extreme heat will have caused instant expansion, but the brown skins will not crack.

POTATO AND CARROT FRITTERS [1421]

Peel and cube, or cut small, 5 medium-sized potatoes, and cook until tender in boiling salted water. Peel and slice thinly 5 carrots, and cook separately in boiling salted water until tender. Drain both, reserving ½ cup of liquid from each. Mash potatoes and carrots together until smooth, adding, while mashing, 1½ cups of flour, sifted with 1 teaspoon of salt, a dash of cayenne pepper and ⅛ teaspoon of nutmeg, alternately with the cup of reserved vegetable stock. Mix well; then stir in ½ cup of thin cream or undiluted evaporated milk. Return to the fire and continue cooking, over a low flame, stirring constantly, for about 5 minutes. Drop by tablespoon into shallow hot fat, and cook quickly, turning to brown both sides.

POTATO CHEESE BALLS [1422]

Prepare 2 cups of hot mashed potatoes; beat in ½ cup of grated Parmesan cheese and ¼ cup of scalded thin cream or undiluted evaporated milk; season to taste with salt, white pepper, nutmeg and a dash of cayenne, mixing well. While still hot, shape into small balls, the size of a walnut; roll these in mixed fine bread crumbs and grated Parmesan cheese, using equal parts of each, and when ready to serve place a few balls in a frying basket and plunge into hot, clear, deep fat (375–390° F.) to brown. Drain on absorbent paper and serve hot.

POTATO CHEESE NESTS [1423]

Cook in their skins until tender, 6 medium sized potatoes; peel and rice them while hot; beat in briskly one at a time, 2 egg yolks, alternately with ⅓ cup (about) of cream cheese sauce, or enough to make a soft, yet not too liquid mixture. Using a pastry bag with a large plain tube, form with the mixture 6 circles of three layers each to imitate a brioche; brush the circles with beaten egg yolk diluted with a little cold milk; place them on a greased baking sheet in a moderate oven (350–375° F.) and bake until golden brown. Fill while hot, with the selected mixture, and serve hot. Appropriate for filling with a creamed mixture of fish, meat, ham, poultry, vegetables or game.

POTATO MATCH STICKS or SHOE STRINGS [1424]
Pommes de Terre Allumettes

Cut potatoes in thin strips the size and length of a wooden match. Fry in deep fat until lightly browned. Being smaller than French fried potatoes, they cook in much less time.

POTATO PANCAKES HOME STYLE [1425]

Scald, then cool ½ cup of thin cream or undiluted evaporated milk; pour over ½ cup of sieved bread crumbs and let stand overnight to absorb the liquid. Next day, add 2 teaspoons of grated onion, 2 cups of left over mashed potatoes mixed with 2 egg yolks, and season to taste with salt, pepper, a fresh grating of nutmeg and a tiny pinch of powdered thyme. Mix thoroughly. When ready to serve, butter 2 or 3 individual frying pans with bacon or ham drippings and, when the fat is smoking hot, drop a generous tablespoon of the potato mixture in it, flattening immediately with a spatula to fill bottoms of pans completely. Cook over a very gentle flame until the under side is well browned; turn with a spatula or toss the pancakes and brown the other side. Serve as hot as possible as a garnish or side dish with pot roast, pork chops, hamburger steak or any other kind of steak.

Note. Raw grated potatoes may be used instead of mashed potatoes, but they should be well drained.

POTATO SCALLOP AND VARIATIONS [1426]

Peel and slice thinly, or cube small 6 large potatoes; cover with boiling water and boil for 3 minutes. Drain and arrange in layers in a buttered baking dish, sprinkling each layer with salt and pepper, 1 teaspoon of flour, a few dots of butter and about 3 or 4 tablespoons of fresh bread crumbs over each layer. Repeat till all the potatoes are used. Very thin slices of onion may also be added, over each layer, if liked. Pour slowly over the whole enough scalded milk to cover the potatoes, and bake in a moderate oven (350° F.) for 40 to 45 minutes or until top is golden brown and the potatoes tender. Serve at once.

Variations. Sauté an equal amount of peeled, thinly sliced fresh or canned mushrooms and potatoes and proceed as indicated above using a layer of potatoes, then one of mushrooms. Sliced carrots and strips of green pepper make a colorful and savory addition. Grated cheese may be sprinkled over each layer, thus giving potato au gratin, home style. Chipped beef, first scalded and drained, then frizzled a minute or two in melted butter and placed over the potato layers makes a savory luncheon or supper dish. Diced ham or bacon may be used in the same way.

POTATO SCALLOP VILLAGE STYLE [1427]

Heat 2 tablespoons of butter or other fat; blend in 4 tablespoons of flour, stirring well until mixture is smooth and begins to bubble; gradually stir in 1 cup of thin cream, top of the bottle milk, or undiluted evaporated milk and cook, stirring constantly until mixture thickens. Season to taste with salt, white pepper and a fresh grating of nutmeg, then stir in ⅓ cup of grated cheese (any kind desired). Keep over hot water. Arrange in a buttered baking dish a layer of cooked, small-cubed potatoes, cover with a layer of cooked or canned, drained green peas, then a layer of thinly sliced onions, previously cooked in butter, repeat layers, sprinkling over each 3 or 4 tablespoons of soft coarse bread crumbs and part of the sauce. Top with ½ cup of buttered bread crumbs, sprinkle with 2 tablespoons of melted butter and brown in a moderate oven (350–375° F.). Serve right from the baking dish.

POTATO SOUFFLE AMANDINE [1428]

Beat 4 egg yolks until fluffy and light, seasoning while beating with salt, white pepper, a dash of powdered thyme and cayenne, and a generous grating of nutmeg. Then beat in 1½ tablespoons of lemon juice and 1 teaspoon of grated lemon rind, alternately with ½ generous cup of potato boiled, peeled and riced. Fold in 4 stiffly beaten egg whites, with a pinch of salt, to which has been added ¼ cup of blanched, skinned, shredded, then toasted almonds. Bake in a hot oven (400° F.) for 20 to 25 minutes, or until potato mixture is well puffed and serve at once.
Note. If desired, divide mixture among 6 individual buttered custard or soufflé dishes and bake 15 minutes in a hot oven (400° F.).

POTATO AND SPINACH CROQUETTES [1429]

Boil 4 medium sized potatoes in their skins in salted water, drain, peel and rice them. Beat in 2 egg yolks, one at a time, (beating briskly after each addition to prevent the egg yolks from cooking) alternately with ¼ scant cup (more or less) of rich milk scalded with 1 large bay leaf, removing the bay leaf before adding the milk; season to taste with salt, white pepper, a dash each of cayenne and nutmeg and spread on a platter to cool. Take portions the size of an egg and wrap around walnut sized portions of cooked, well drained and ground spinach, seasoned to taste with salt, pepper and nutmeg. Shape into oblongs and chill. When ready to serve, roll croquettes into egg beaten with a little cold milk, then in sieved bread crumbs, again in egg, then again in crumbs. Place, a few at a time, in a frying basket, plunge into clear, hot deep fat (385° F.) and fry golden brown; drain and serve on a folded napkin placed on a hot platter or use as a garnish.

POTATO SPIRALS [1430]

Pare 4 or 5 long potatoes; cut them in spiral fashion, lengthwise, dropping the spirals at once in ice-cold water. For about 25 to 30 minutes; drain and pat dry between towels. When ready to serve, place a few at a time in a frying basket; plunge in clear, hot deep fat (375°–390° F.) to brown and crisp; drain on absorbent paper and serve hot as a vegetable or use as a garnish.

POTATO AND WALNUT CROQUETTES [1431]

Combine 1 cup of soft bread crumbs and 1 cup of blanched, skinned and ground walnuts in upper part of double boiler; stir in 1 cup of scalded milk and mix thoroughly. Cook over hot water until mixture thickens, stirring constantly from bottom of pan. Remove from hot water and beat in 2 egg yolks, one at a time, beating briskly after each addition, alternately with 2 cups of hot mashed potatoes, seasoning to taste with salt, white pepper and a dash of nutmeg. Spread mixture on a platter to cool. When cold, take portions the size of an egg and shape in oblongs, cones, balls, and so forth. Dip each in egg beaten with a little cold milk and seasoned with salt and white pepper, then in fine bread crumbs; again in beaten egg and again in bread crumbs. Place a few at a time, in a frying basket and plunge into clear, hot deep fat (375°–390° F.) to brown. Drain on absorbent paper and serve hot.

SARATOGA or POTATO CHIPS [1432]
Pommes de Terre Copeaux

These may be made in large quantities as they retain their crispness for months if kept in a cool, dry place, in a tin container. The following will serve 15 easily.

Pare 15 large potatoes and slice as thin as possible with vegetable slicer, letting the chips fall into a pail containing ice cold water as you slice. Soak for at least an hour, changing the water twice. Drain; dry thoroughly between towels, and fry in deep, clear hot fat, (380° F.) until pale gold in color, cooking only a few at a time to prevent them from sticking together; stir almost constantly while frying. Lift out with a perforated ladle; drain on absorbent paper; sprinkle at once with salt and serve or store. To reheat, simply place the necessary amount onto a baking sheet and heat in a moderate oven (350–375° F.).

Who but historians know that Saratoga chips were invented by a Saratoga tavern keeper named Crumbs who had five Indian wives?

BAKED SWEET POTATOES [1433]

Select medium sized sweet potatoes; scrub with a vegetable brush, rinse, dry, and rub with fat; place on rack and bake in a hot oven (400° F.) about 35 to 45 minutes, or until soft. When done, remove from the oven, cut in halves lengthwise and scrape potatoes into a warm bowl, reserving the skins. Mash potatoes with butter and add enough cream to moisten; season to taste with salt and, if desired, 1 or 2 tablespoons of sherry wine; beat till light and fluffy; refill shells and bake in a hot oven (425° F.) until tops are brown. Serve at once.

CANDIED SWEET POTATOES [1434]

Wash, then cook six medium sized sweet potatoes in boiling salted water to cover. Drain, peel, cut in halves, lengthwise, arrange in layers in a generously buttered baking dish, sprinkling each layer with brown sugar, using ¾ cup in all; pour over all ½ cup of melted butter and sprinkle with a little salt. Bake in a slow oven (300–325° F.) for about 1½ to 1¾ hours.

FRENCH FRIED SWEET POTATOES [1435]

Pare 6 large sweet potatoes, cut in lengthwise strips as for French fried potatoes, and dry thoroughly between towels. Divide into three portions. When ready to fry, place one lot in frying basket, plunge the basket in hot, deep fat, (375–390° F.) and cook 5 to 6 minutes; drain on absorbent paper and keep hot. Repeat with the remaining two lots, and when ready to serve, complete the frying, cooking until potatoes are crisp and brown or about 1½ to 2 minutes. Drain on absorbent paper, sprinkle with salt and serve at once.

GRILLED SWEET POTATOES [1436]

Cook medium-sized sweet potatoes in boiling water for 20 minutes, or until tender. Cool, peel, and cut in halves lengthwise. Brush with melted butter, and grill under the flame of a broiling oven until browned on both sides. Sprinkle with salt and serve hot.

MASHED SWEET POTATOES IN ORANGE [1437] SHELLS
Patates Douces dans Coquille d'Oranges

Peel, then boil sweet potatoes in slightly salted water until tender. Mash smoothly, stirring in 2 egg yolks, slightly beaten during the process. To 3 cups of the mixture, add ⅓ cup orange juice, salt, pepper, and a pinch of powdered nutmeg, and 3 tablespoons butter (the butter being added bit by bit). Turn the mixture into a pastry bag with a large fancy tube, and fill 6 half orange skins which have been brushed with butter, and seasoned with a little mixed salt and pepper. Sprinkle a little granulated sugar on top of each orange, place on a baking sheet, and bake in a moderate oven (350° F.) for 15 to 20 minutes, or until the tops are nicely browned. Serve very hot.

SWEET POTATO AND BANANA FLUFF [1438]

Boil 5 medium-sized sweet potatoes until tender; peel, rice, then add 2 medium-sized mashed bananas, season to taste with salt, and a very little pepper, a dash each of mace, and nutmeg. Add ¼ cup of hot milk (or enough to moisten), with 2 egg yolks, and beat until fluffy and light. Fold in 1 large egg white, and pile lightly in a greased baking dish.

Bake in a very hot oven (475–500° F.) for about 10 minutes, or until lightly browned. Serve hot with any main dish.

SWEET POTATO CUSTARD CREOLE [1439]
(*Individual serving*)

Beat 2 large eggs as for an omelet; gradually add ¼ cup of sugar and continue beating till sugar is thoroughly dissolved, adding with the last portion of sugar, ½ teaspoon of salt mixed with ¼ teaspoon of powdered nutmeg. Then stir in 1¾ cups of cold, rich sweet milk, with 2 well beaten egg yolks and 1 teaspoon each of grated lemon and orange rind, mixing thoroughly. Now, shred into the mixture enough raw sweet potatoes (shredded at the last moment only lest they turn dark) to make 2½ cups, and, finally, 1½ tablespoons of lukewarm butter.

Pour into 6 buttered individual custard cups or individual cassolettes, place in a pan of hot (not boiling) water, and bake in a moderate oven (325–350° F.) for about 25 to 30 minutes or until custard is set. Serve hot.

Appropriate for service with roast, stuffed turkey.

Note. This same mixture may be poured into an unbaked pie shell and baked in a moderate oven (350° F.) for about 45 to 50 minutes. Cool and serve as a desert.

SWEET POTATOES ALLUMETTES CREOLE [1440]

Make a syrup with 1 cup each of water and sugar, and add 2 cups of sweet potatoes, cut into match-like strips. Cook until strips are lightly browned, stirring gently with the tines of a kitchen fork; drain off part of the syrup; stir in ½ cup of scalded heavy cream seasoned to taste with a little salt and simmer gently until light-colored. If too watery, drain off excess.

SWEET POTATOES IMPERIAL [1441]
(*Chafing Dish*)

Peel and cut 5 medium sized sweet potatoes crosswise into ½-inch slices. Melt ¼ cup of butter in a frying pan; add the potatoes and sauté over medium flame until light brown, turning frequently. Melt 2 tablespoons of sweet butter in a chafing dish, add the browned potato slices; sprinkle with ½ cup of sugar and stir lightly over a low flame. When butter is melted, add ½ cup of good rum, tip chafing dish to ignite the rum, and baste potatoes with this syrup and flaming rum. Serve as soon as possible.

SWEET POTATOES ROYAL   [1442]
(Chafing Dish)

Combine 2 cups of hot mashed sweet potatoes and 2 cups of hot, mashed chestnuts, fresh cooked or canned. Heat ½ cup of sweet butter, stir in the potato-chestnut mixture and when heated through pour in ⅓ cup of rum mixed with the same amount of brandy. Set aflame at the table, and serve while flaming.

SWEET POTATO ROLLS   [1443]

These are a rich, golden color and most unusual. Mash well through a colander 2 cups boiled yams. While still hot, beat in 3 tablespoons butter. Cool to lukewarm, add 1 teaspoon salt, 1 well-beaten egg, 3 tablespoons sugar, and 1 yeast cake (½ ounce) softened in a cup of lukewarm water. Sift and add 2 cups of flour (or enough to make a soft dough). Knead until smooth. Cover, and let rise in a warm place until it has doubled in bulk. Knead down, put into well greased muffin pans, let rise until again doubled in bulk and bake in a moderate oven. Brush lightly with butter just before removing from oven. (This may also be used as an icebox dough.)

WHIPPED SWEET POTATOES FLORIDA   [1444]

Cut off tops of 8 oranges and remove pulp and juice with a sharp knife and spoon. Whip 4 cups of boiled or baked sweet potatoes with 2 teaspoons of salt, 2 tablespoons of melted butter and unstrained orange juice to moisten to the desired consistency. Fill orange shells and top each orange with a marshmallow. Brown in a moderate oven (350° F.) until heated through and marshmallow is melted and begins to brown. Serve at once.

In colonial days, boiled sweet potatoes were seasoned with lemons, dates, mace, nutmeg, cinnamon and pepper and served with sugar frosting.

PUMPKIN   [1445]

To the lover of nature the end of October weather usually brings awareness of the pause before autumn succumbs to winter. To the student of folklore it may mean reflections on the ancient Druidic custom of lighting bonfires on English hills and sacrificing to the moon god for protection against witches and spirits of the dead, both of which haunted the earth on the night that later Christian eras knew as All Hallows Eve. To the country dweller it may mean thoughts of harvest and Halloween, as they are symbolized in the pumpkins that glow warmly from the lintels of white houses. To the boys of America it may mean jack-o'-lanterns and an excuse to lift gates from their hinges. But to the general public, which likes its pumpkin pie, these are all subsidiary interests. The primary fact is that Halloween is here to mark the traditional opening of the pumpkin season.

When the early settlers reached The New World, they discovered pumpkins and squashes. They learned about these foods from the Indians, and they soon became a staple part of pioneer diet; and because the variety of foods was limited, many ingenious ways of preparing these new vegetables were devised.

Valuable food elements are present in pumpkins. Aside from carbohydrates they contain minerals and vitamins.

Many centuries ago a Chinese cook with the heart of a poet wrote down this recipe: "Cut the pumpkin into slices and let stand in the juice of golden limes. Beat to a sea foam the whites of 2 eggs and make into a paste with the yellow of one rice flower of cinnamon. Dip each slice of pumpkin into the paste and fry in sesame oil to the color of gold. Sprinkle with powdered Li-chee nuts and sugared ginger and eat while smoking hot."

Perhaps Marco Polo, first European to find his way to the Court of Cathay, tasted pumpkin cooked in this manner in the thirteenth century, while in America the Indians were planting pumpkins in the midst of their corn.

But though pumpkin pie may be the Number One pumpkin dish in the hearts of Americans, it is by no means the only one. Here as in other countries, pumpkin has always been used in many of the same ways as the Winter Squash from which is made a pie almost exactly like the pumpkin in taste.

BAKED HAMBURGER STUFFED PUMPKIN [1446] COUNTRY STYLE

Select a well-shaped sound pumpkin not too large; remove top and scoop out the seeds and threads attached to them very carefully. (Don't discard the seeds, dry them and toast and salt them like almonds.) Combine 1½ pounds of finely chopped—not ground—lean beef with 4 thin slices of bacon, finely chopped, 4 medium sized potatoes, peeled and diced small, 3 small carrots, scraped, parboiled and diced small, 1 large green pepper chopped, and 2 medium-sized onions chopped, 1 clove of garlic, mashed to a pulp. Season to taste with salt, pepper, sage, nutmeg and thyme. Stuff prepared pumpkin with this mixture; add ½ cup of cold water mixed with ⅓ cup of Pique Seasoning; replace the top; place in a shallow baking pan and bake in a moderate oven (350° F.) for 3½ to 4 hours, adding a little boiling water blended with an equal amount of Seasoning if mixture seems dry. Serve on a large round platter slicing in wedges right through both pumpkin shell and stuffing.

BAKED WHOLE PUMPKIN [1447]

Cut top from a washed, plump, sound pumpkin, leaving stem on for a handle; remove seeds carefully; replace top and put pumpkin on shallow baking pan. Bake in a moderate oven (350° F.) about 1½ to 1¾ hours or until tender. When cool, pumpkin skin can be removed and pulp used in any recipe requiring cooked pumpkin.
Note. Whole Hubbard squash may be cooked the same way, when mashed squash is desired.

BOILED PUMPKIN [1448]

Wash a plump, sound pumpkin and cut in pieces, remove seeds carefully then peel. Cut into 2-inch cubes and cook in a small amount of water until tender or about 45 to 55 minutes. Rub through a fine-meshed wire sieve to make a smooth purée and discard the stringy portion. Then use as directed in any recipe, calling for mashed pumpkin.
Note. Whole Hubbard squash may be cooked in the same way.

BROWNED PUMPKIN [1449]

To 4 cups of boiled or baked pumpkin purée (Nos. 1447 and 1448) (Baked Whole Pumpkin and Boiled Pumpkin), add salt, pepper and nutmeg to taste; turn into a generously buttered earthenware casserole; dot with 2 tablespoons of butter or margarin; sprinkle with 2 teaspoons of granulated sugar, and brown lightly under the flame of the broiling oven, or in a very hot oven (425–450° F.). Serve in the same dish as a vegetable.

DEEP FRIED PUMPKIN BLOSSOMS [1450]

Remove stems and buds, wash and let dry on a towel. Do not try to dry, lest you crush them. A full basket of blossoms will be needed for 6 servings. Make an ordinary batter of 2 well beaten eggs, 4 or 5 tablespoons of flour, salt, pepper and 1 teaspoon of finely chopped parsley. Dip one (if large) or 2 (if small) blossoms into the batter and fry in hot, deep, clear fat (375–398° F.) until brown. Drain on absorbent paper and use as a garnish for any kind of meat, poultry or game.

As a breakfast dish, serve with butter and syrup, honey or maple syrup, and add a little sugar and cinnamon to the batter.

Gather a large basket of pumpkin blossoms when you are picking them for cooking because they cook down quite a little. Pumpkin blossoms may be picked until late Summer.

BAKED FLUFFY PUMPKIN IN ITS OWN SHELL [1451]

Slice the top from a washed, plump sound pumpkin and scoop out the seeds. Clean thoroughly. Sprinkle inside of pumpkin with any desired spices; then place in a moderate oven (350° F.) and bake 1 to 1½ hours, or until tender, testing often to guard against over-cooking. Carefully scoop out the meat and place in a bowl, keeping pumpkin shell intact. Season with salt, white pepper and abundant butter, and beat to a cream. Return fluffy purée to the shell; dot generously with butter, and return to oven to reheat. Serve piping hot.

SALSIFY [1452]

A long, and sometimes spindly white carrot which goes by the name of salsify, or oyster plant, or vegetable oyster, or, as in England, "John-go-to-bed-at-noon" because its light purplish-red flowers close at mid-day. The plant is a native of southern Europe, but it came to America early. Salsify is a tall plant, often reaching four feet in height at maturity. The white part of the stalk and the leafy heart of the young top leaves, if well blanched, make an excellent salad or cooked, buttered green. But it is the long tapering roots which are put to most frequent use. The roots are covered with a yellowish-gray skin, but the flesh is white and holds a milky white juice. Cooked, the flavor is scarcely discernible from that of the oyster, hence the name. To keep scraped salsify from discoloring upon exposure to the air, drop it into cold water made slightly acid with lemon juice or mild vinegar. A little lemon juice or vinegar added to the cooking water also aids in preserving the natural appearance of the vegetable without injuring its flavor.

BOILED SALSIFY WITH DIVERS SAUCES [1453]

Trim the tops from a bunch of salsify; wash, scrubbing with a brush; scrape and drop each root as scraped into a bowl of cold water containing 1 tablespoon of vinegar or lemon juice. Slice ⅓-inch thick or cut into small dice. Drain; place in a saucepan; add salted boiling water to cover, with 1 tablespoon of vinegar or lemon juice; bring to a boil, cover, and cook until tender, or about 15 to 20 minutes. Drain, reserving liquid for soup. The salsify is now ready to be mashed, scalloped, creamed, and so forth, or served with butter, parsley butter, Maître d'Hôtel butter, cream sauce, egg sauce, Béchamel sauce, Hollandaise, or Mousseline sauce, or any preferred smooth and thick sauce, which may be found under "Sauces."

SALSIFY FRITTERS SURPRISE [1454]

Beat 1 large egg; gradually add 1½ cups of boiled and mashed salsify (No. 1453), salt and pepper to taste, 1 teaspoon of mixed mustard or Worcestershire sauce and stir in ¼ cup of bread flour mixed smoothly with ½ cup of sweet milk. Beat well and spread on platter to cool. When quite cold, shape into small balls. In each place a small shrimp, cooked and shelled, a piece of cooked lobster, of cooked fish or a small oyster. Roll the balls in sieved bread crumbs, then in egg beaten with a little water or milk then again in crumbs. Fry in hot, deep, clear fat (390° F.), until nicely browned.

The mixture may also be made into croquettes, cutlets, or flat cakes and sautéed in a small amount of butter or margarine.

SALSIFY PUFFS [1455]

To 2 cups of cooked, mashed salsify, add 1 stiffly beaten egg white, highly seasoned with salt and a few grains of cayenne pepper. Force mixture through a pastry bag, (using a large plain tube) on to a greased baking sheet; bake in a hot oven (400° F.) a few minutes, or until puffed and delicately browned. Serve hot as a vegetable or use as a garnish.

SALSIFY SCALLOP [1456]

Pour 2 cups of cream sauce (No. 258) over 4 cups of cooked salsify previously cut into inch pieces, and mix with 2 tablespoons each of parsley, green celery leaves, green pepper and onion all finely chopped. Place in a buttered baking dish; sprinkle with ½ cup of buttered bread crumbs, and bake 15 to 20 minutes, or until brown, in a moderate oven (350–375° F.). Serve from the baking dish.

SAUERKRAUT [1457]

Sauerkraut is an age-old food and did not originate in Germany, as is commonly believed. It dates back to the building of the Great Wall of China, when the laborers ate it to combat deficiency diseases resulting from a diet consisting almost altogether of rice.

Originally the Tartars introduced the acid cabbage from the Orient into eastern Europe, and from there kraut went to Germany, Alsace-Lorraine, and France. Crisp kraut is a delightful accompaniment to spareribs, sausages, wieners, ham or pork.

Salt draws out the cabbage juice, which contains sugar. This the bacteria ferments, and lactic acid forms, producing that faint tangy flavor and distinctive texture that stimulates the appetite and makes kraut so well liked the world around.

While admittedly widely used during warm weather, it takes a nip in the air to stir thoughts about sauerkraut. Few food products lend themselves to such delightful and diversified utilization.

Of equal importance is its health value: it is rich in vitamins A, B and C and in phosphorous, calcium and iron—all vital to good health. Added to these factors is the presence of generous quantities of lactic acid so valuable in cleansing the intestinal tract of toxic-forming bacteria. Properly cooked, sauerkraut loses virtually none of its health properties and is considered on a par with the raw product. Raw or cooked it has a favored place in the menu, either when consumed as a side dish or in soups in stuffings, or in combination with various cuts of meat and vegetables. Sauerkraut juice makes an excellent cocktail. Just ice a glass of it or mix with an equal quantity of tomato juice, add a little salt, paprika and cracked ice and shake.

SAUERKRAUT ARMENONVILLE [1458]

Prick 12 frankfurters with the tines of a fork; place in a saucepan, and pour over them 1 cup of Chablis wine. Simmer very gently for 20 minutes over a low flame. Meanwhile melt ¼ cup of bacon drippings in a heavy skillet; stir in 2 medium-sized thinly sliced onions and cook, covered, over a low flame, until just beginning to brown, shaking the pan frequently. Then stir in 2½ to 3 pounds of sauerkraut. (Do not drain off the juice.) Cook 10 minutes, stirring frequently so as to loosen the sauerkraut a little. Now stir in 1 large, raw, grated potato with 1 teaspoon of caraway seeds, mixing thoroughly. Arrange half the mixture in a greased earthenware casserole; lay the frankfurters over this, and pour in the Chablis wine; scatter in 7 or 8 freshly bruised peppercorns; add a bouquet garni composed of 1 large bay leaf, 8 sprigs of fresh parsley and 1 sprig of thyme, all tied together with white thread, and top with the remainder of the kraut and kraut juice. Lay a dozen strips of bacon on top. Cover with a buttered paper, adjust the lid tightly, and cook in a moderate oven (350–357° F.) for 45 to 50 minutes without disturbing. When ready to serve, taste for salt; discard the bouquet garni; arrange the kraut on a round, hot platter, dome-fashion, place the frankfurters over the kraut and in between the frankfurters lay the bacon strips. Serve with plain boiled potatoes and of course, cold beer.

SAUERKRAUT HUNGARIAN STYLE [1459]

Combine 1 pound of fresh pork, ¾ pound of beef and ¼ pound of salt pork, first cut into pieces then ground, in a mixing bowl; soak 3 slices of bread in 1 cup of milk; add to the meat with 2 medium-sized onions, chopped fine. Season to taste with salt, a dash of cayenne pepper and nutmeg, then work in 2 well-beaten eggs. Mix 4 pounds of kraut with 1 teaspoon of caraway seeds, ½ teaspoon of crushed bay leaves and 8 whole cloves, and divide into 4 parts. Form the meat mixture into 12 flat cakes. Now place in a kettle a layer of kraut, then one of meat cakes; repeat until all are used, having the top layer kraut. Add 1 pint of rich beef broth, or, lacking it, 1½ cups of boiling water and ½ cup of Pique Seasoning; cover tightly and bake in a moderate oven (325–350° F.) for 2 hours, adding more hot stock or boiling water mixed with equal parts of Pique Seasoning, if necessary. Serve with mashed potatoes and rye bread.

SAUERKRAUT WITH RAISINS [1460]

Heat ½ cup of bacon drippings in a saucepan; stir in 2½ to 3 pounds of sauerkraut, home-made or canned, gently squeezed, but not necessarily dry, add 1 teaspoon of celery seed, ½ cup of chopped onions, cooked in a little fat until slightly browned, ½ clove of garlic, mashed to a pulp, ½ cup of boiling water mixed with ½ cup of Pique Seasoning and cook for 35–40 minutes, over a gentle flame, stirring frequently to separate the kraut. Heat through, then stir in 3 tablespoons of grated raw potato, 8 freshly crushed peppercorns, and ¾ cup of seedless raisins previously plumped in boiling water and drained. Cover and continue cooking 10 minutes longer. Serve hot with pork roast, pork chops, broiled ham steak, roast ham and even roast stuffed turkey.

SAUERKRAUT IN SOUR CREAM [1461]

Cook 3 pounds of sauerkraut in a pan together with 1 cup of boiling water mixed with ½ cup of Pique Seasoning for 30 minutes, stirring frequently to separate the kraut, and when almost dry, stir in ½ cup of chopped onions, cooked in a little fat until slightly brown, also 1⅓ cups of thick sour cream, scalded with 1 large bay leaf and 4 sprigs of parsley, then drained. Heat through, and serve as a vegetable with roast pork, roast turkey, baked pork chops and baked ham.
Note. The addition of 2 tart apples, pared and cored, then sliced is a great improvement.

SHEPHERD'S SAUERKRAUT [1462]

Drain well 1 quart of sauerkraut and arrange loosely in a generously greased casserole. Chop and stir in 4 slices of bacon with ½ cup of thinly sliced small onions. Slice 8 frankfurters and cook a few minutes in 2 tablespoons of fat, then add to the kraut and mix well. Cook, covered, for 30 minutes, stirring frequently, adding after 15 minutes of cooking 6 freshly crushed peppercorns, ½ teaspoon of caraway seeds, and a little hot water, if too dry. Remove cover, top the casserole with 2 cups of well-seasoned hot, mashed potatoes mixed with 2 tablespoons of finely chopped chives or green onion tops, and bake (uncovered) in a moderate oven (375° F.), until delicately browned and crusty. Serve at once as a main dish.

SAUERKRAUT WOODSMAN'S STYLE   [1463]

Place 1½ pounds of canned sauerkraut in a saucepan with 1½ cups of boiling water and ½ cup of Pique Seasoning, 2 medium-sized tart apples, pared, cored and sliced thin, ¼ cup of minced onions, ¼ teaspoon of black pepper, and a very little salt. Cook very slowly for about 40 minutes, stirring occasionally, then stir in 2 tablespoons of grated raw potatoes, and place on top 6 small, individual pork sausage meat cakes. Cover and cook 25 minutes longer. Serve from the casserole with plain boiled potatoes.

SPINACH

It's a strange fact, but after all these years of basking in the limelight as the body builder de luxe, spinach, our favorite muscle building vegetable is now fighting not only for its good reputation, but for its very existence as a food! Recently a nutritional chemist from Columbia University issued a statement that spinach was not only a highly overrated food, but was, in fact, potentially harmful! He pointed out that spinach contains a large amount of oxalic acid which destroys any calcium value contained in the green. According to this chemist, the oxalic acid in certain spinach (maybe he meant sorrel), sometimes actually robs the human body of its own store of calcium. As he tells it, the presence of oxalic acid in spinach definitely puts that vegetable on the black list. Naturally, doctors, who have advocated this iron building food for so many years, have a word or two to say by the way of refutation. They argue that it is not the truth, as this vegetable has enjoyed prestige as a body builder for more than twenty centuries.

Traced from its early origin in Persia, it has remained a favorite from the time of king Nebuchadnezzar, of Babylon, down to the present. Twelfth-century Spaniards called it . . . "the prince of vegetables." A fourteenth-century cook book used by King Richard II of England carried a recipe for "spinoches." Even the famous Boswell's *Life of Johnson* carried a reference to the green grass. And finally, in the twentieth century, admiring Frenchmen named a famous race horse *Epinard* which means spinach in English. In America, ever since Colonial Days when spinach was imported from France, it has remained a favorite of diet-conscious mothers. It was said to contain roughage for the stomach, hence the French call it "the balai de l'estomac," or the "stomach broom."

SPINACH—HINTS [1464]

Pick over all spinach very carefully. Cut off the roots and put leaves and stems in a large pan of warm water . . . swish it up and down several times and let it stand for 2 or 3 minutes; then lift out. This is very important. The grit and sand are at the bottom of the pan and if the water is merely poured off the sand remains. Repeat the process a second time and finish off in a pan of cold water. Lift it up, then put it into the cooker, or pan just as it is, that is without adding any water or other liquid.

Mint in Spinach. A little mint plus a dash of nutmeg adds interesting flavor to creamed spinach.

Fluffy Mashed Potato with spinach, is an attractive dish. Put alternate mounds around meat, fish or fowl.

Other Flavorings for Spinach. A teaspoon or two of lemon juice added to cooked spinach when served as a left-over adds greatly to its flavor; so does a little vinegar and sugar which gives a pleasant sweet-sour tang. Try a little horseradish in green, leafy vegetables. Save ham or bacon fat to season them with—this includes spinach, of course. Mix or use pork cracklings, especially with spinach.

BOILED SPINACH WITH WHIPPED SOUR CREAM [1465]

Wash 2 pounds of fresh spinach as indicated in Hints (No. 1464) and cook them in their own moisture, until tender, seasoning with about 1 teaspoon of salt. Whip ¾ cup of sour cream, season with salt, pepper and a generous grating of nutmeg, and toss into the well-drained spinach. Transfer to a hot platter; garnish with sliced hard-cooked eggs and small triangles of bread fried in butter and drained.

CREAMED SPINACH WITH CHIVES [1466]

Wash 2 pounds of fresh spinach thoroughly (No. 1464) and cook covered until tender in the water that clings to the spinach. Meanwhile cook ¼ cup of chopped onions in 2 tablespoons of butter 3 or 4 minutes, but do not brown. Add drained chopped spinach, then stir in ½ cup of scalded thin cream and season to taste with salt, pepper and nutmeg. Serve at once garnished with a ring of fried tiny bread croutons, sprinkling the top with chopped chives.

SPINACH ENTREE DUBROVNIK [1467]

Melt 2 tablespoons of butter, add ½ tablespoon of flour and blend till smooth; then stir in gradually 1 cup of scalded milk. Cool slightly, then beat in 4 egg yolks, adding one at a time and beating well after each addition, then stir in 2 cups of cooked, finely ground spinach, and season to taste with salt, white pepper, and a dash of nutmeg. Whip the 4 egg whites until stiff with ¼ teaspoon of salt and fold into the spinach mixture, gently, but thoroughly. Have ready a long, shallow baking pan, the bottom covered with an ample and strong single sheet of buttered paper. Cover the paper with bread crumbs and small bits of butter; pour in the spinach mixture, very gently and slowly; smooth evenly with a knife or spatula, and bake in a hot oven (400–425° F.) for 15 minutes. Remove from the oven and cover with ¼ pound of finely chopped lean cooked ham. Pour over all 1 cup of sour cream which is at room temperature, and spread evenly. Roll this combination into two folds with the aid of the buttered paper, and roll it off on to a hot, long serving platter. Pour another full cup of sour cream down the length of the flat roll, leaving a border of green spinach on each side. Sprinkle the cream with freshly grated Parmesan cheese and serve at once.

SPINACH AU GRATIN JEANETTE　　　　　　[1468]
Gratin d'Epinards Jeanette

Carefully wash 2 pounds of fresh spinach, having the final rinsing water tepid in temperature. Blanch the leaves, rinse them under running cold water, and pat dry in a towel, setting them aside in a cool place. Peel ½ pound of fresh mushrooms, and put them through food chopper, then cook over a gentle flame for 4 minutes in 3 tablespoons of melted butter, without browning. Drain off the butter and mix the mushrooms with 1 cup of Béchamel sauce (No. 259). Season to taste with salt, pepper and a grating of nutmeg. Arrange a layer of spinach in a generously buttered baking dish or soufflé dish, cover with ⅓ the mushroom mixture, and repeat in alternating layers until the dish is full. Pour over the top ¾ cup of Béchamel sauce flavored with 2 tablespoons of blended grated Gruyère cheese and American cheese; top with buttered crumbs and set the dish in a pan containing hot water. Bake in a very moderate oven (325° F.) for about 50–55 minutes or until the top is brown and bubbly, and serve at once in the baking dish.

SPINACH MOUSSE　　　　　　　　　　　　[1469]

Combine 2 cups of cooked, ground, well drained spinach, 2 well beaten eggs and 1 cup of sweet heavy cream; season to taste with salt, white pepper and nutmeg; rub through a fine-meshed wire sieve, and pack in a buttered ring mold. Set this in a pan of hot water, and bake in a moderate oven, (350° F.) until firm, or about 30 minutes. Remove from the oven and let stand a few minutes to set, then unmold on to a round, hot platter and fill center with creamed fish, shellfish, chicken or mushrooms. Serve hot.

SPINACH PURÉE SAINT MANDÉ   [1470]

Wash carefully and discard stems from enough fresh spinach to make 2 well packed cups, or about 2½ pounds of raw spinach. Put spinach through food chopper twice, then rub through a fine-meshed wire sieve. Have ready ½ to ¾ cup of piping hot Smitane sauce (No. 1123), stir in the raw spinach, turn mixture into top of double boiler, season to taste with salt, white pepper and a dash of nutmeg, and cook, covered, for about 25–30 minutes. Taste for seasoning and serve as a vegetable or as a base for poached or fried eggs, or small fried pork sausages. By this method no vitamins are wasted by throwing part of the water away.

SPINACH SHORTCAKE WITH HAM—MY   [1471]
STYLE

Cook 2 cups of spinach as indicated for Spinach Purée Saint Mandé (No. 1470) and stir in ¾ cup of cooked lean ham; cut into tiny dice. Heat through.

Put 2 cups of white, water-ground corn meal in a bowl, mix in ½ teaspoon of salt, then stir in about 2½ cups of boiling water or enough to make a stiff dough. Cool slightly. Beat 2 eggs and mix with 2 cups of cold milk; stir this into the corn meal dough to make a batter the consistency of thin cream. Heat 2 tablespoons of butter or lard in a large, shallow pan until almost smoking. Pour the batter into the hot fat and bake in a hot oven (425° F.) about 25 minutes, or until well browned. Cut into 6 squares, then cut each square in two, lengthwise; pour a little of the spinach-ham mixture over one slice; place the other on top, then top with more of the spinach mixture. Place shortcakes on to a baking sheet; sprinkle 1 tablespoon of grated cheese over each one; dust with paprika and brown under the flame of the broiling oven until cheese bubbles and brown. Serve at once.

SPINACH SOUFFLÉ AMANDINE   [1472]
Soufflé d'Epinards au Lait d'Amandes

First prepare a cup of almond milk as follows: Blanch ¼ cup of almonds, drain, skin, then put through food chopper, using the finest blade. To the resulting paste, add 1 cup of rich milk, or half milk and half cream; bring to a boil, stirring often; reduce the heat and simmer gently for 12 to 15 minutes. Strain through a fine cloth and keep hot.

Melt 2 tablespoons of butter and stir in 2 tablespoons of flour, blending well without browning; season to taste with salt and pepper and nutmeg. Very slowly, stir in the almond milk, to which has been added ½ teaspoon of Worcestershire sauce, stirring constantly, over a low flame, until mixture thickens and boils; remove from the fire and stir in 2 cups of cooked, ground, then sieved spinach, blending well. Cool slightly, then beat in 3 egg yolks, adding one at a time and beating well after each addition. Finally fold in 3 stiffly beaten egg whites, beaten with a few grains of salt. Turn into a buttered soufflé dish and bake in a moderate oven (350–375° F.) for 35 to 40 minutes, or until soufflé is well puffed and delicately browned on top. Serve immediately.

For plain spinach soufflé, substitute plain cold milk for almond milk and bake in a quick oven (400–425° F.) for 20 to 25 minutes, or until puffed and brown. Serve at once.

SPINACH TARTS [1473]

Prepare 1 cup of medium white sauce (No. 258); add ¼ cup of any preferred grated cheese and season to taste with salt, pepper and a pinch of rosemary. Then stir in 1½ cups of cooked, ground spinach, 1 tablespoon of lemon juice and 2 teaspoons of grated onion. Stir until well blended. Have ready 6 freshly baked individual pastry shells; fill with the spinach mixture; sprinkle the top of each with 2 teaspoons of grated cheese mixed with 1 tablespoon of fine bread crumbs, dust with paprika and brown quickly under the flame of the broiling oven. Serve with fish as a variation of plain buttered spinach.

SPINACH TIMBALES [1474]

Drain well 4 cups of cooked spinach, chop fine and stir in ⅓ cup of butter, adding it bit by bit; season highly with salt and pepper and 1 teaspoon of Worcestershire sauce. Press into buttered individual molds; set in a pan of hot water and steam until ready to serve. Unmold on a hot platter and serve with creamed fish, meat, poultry or vegetable, or as a side dish.

STUFFED SPINACH ROLL [1475]

Beat 4 egg yolks until light; stir in 1 generous teaspoon of melted sweet butter, mixed with anchovy paste the size of a pea then add 3 cups of finely chopped cooked spinach, alternately with ⅓ cup of bread softened in ¼ cup of cold milk. Season to taste with salt, pepper, nutmeg and cloves, then stir in 1 tablespoon of grated cheese and 2 tablespoons each of chopped parsley and grated onion. Lastly, fold in the 4 egg whites, stiffly beaten with ¼ teaspoon of salt. Spread mixture in a 10 × 14-inch pan, lined with well buttered heavy paper, and bake in a moderate oven (375° F.) until firm, or about 12 to 15 minutes. Remove at once from the oven; cut off the hard edges; spread at once with filling, and roll as for jelly roll. Cut into 1½ inch slices and serve with egg sauce (No. 1051–52). The filling must be ready when the roll comes from the oven.

Filling. Chop fine 4 large fresh peeled mushrooms, using both stems and caps, and cook with ½ pound of hamburger in 3 tablespoons of drippings; add 1 tablespoon of grated onion, and 1 tablespoon of chopped chives, season highly with salt pepper and nutmeg.

STRING BEANS [1476]

The varieties of our common garden or bush bean have their origin in *Phaseolus vulgaris,* which is supposed to be a native of the East Indies, though there are none of the species found wild that in any way resembles the varieties under cultivation. The earliest notice that we have of the string bean or wax bean is that given by Pliny, who calls them *Phaseoli,* and says the pod is to be eaten with the seed. According to Diodorus Siculus, the Egyptians were the first to cultivate it and to make it an article of common diet, yet they conceived religious notions concerning it which made them at length refrain from eating the seeds. Their priests dared not either touch it or look at it. Pythagoras, who was educated among the Egyptians, derived from them their veneration for the bean itself, and forbade his disciples to eat it, but permitted them to eat the pod or shell. He taught that it was created at the same time and of the same elements as man; that it was animated and had a soul, which, like a human soul, suffered the vicissitudes of transmigration. Aristotle explains the prohibition of Pythagoras symbolically. He says, that since beans were the ordinary means of voting on public matters, the white bean meaning an affirmative, and the black a negative, Pythagoras meant to forbid his disciples to meddle with political government.

The Roman priests affirmed that the bean blossom contained infernal letters, referring to the dark stains on the wings, and it is probable that all the superstitions on the subject sprang from the fruit.

STRING BEANS—HINTS [1477]

Strictly fresh, young and very finely cut beans will cook in 12 to 15 minutes, using only enough salted boiling water to cover. For extra flavor, sprinkle a small amount of grated onion, chopped chives and chopped parsley over beans during last few minutes of cooking.

Do not drain, but serve string beans with pot liquor and butter as sauce. With canned string beans, pour the beans with their liquid into a saucepan, sprinkle with salt and pepper, add a piece of butter, and heat. One can of beans will serve 4 or 5. For the epicurean touch, add a fresh grating of nutmeg. And, if you like garlic, try cooking a clove of it with fresh string beans. Removing it before serving.

Squeeze a little lemon juice over string beans. Also try adding a few fresh mint leaves to fresh string beans when cooking. Slice or "French" beans very thin. A little vinegar and sweetened cream or evaporated milk added to string beans gives a sweet-sour flavor that is liked by many.

Cook mature string beans with bacon or salt pork, sometimes adding onion and potatoes to the pot. Try string or wax beans with mustard sauce, egg sauce, tomato or brown sauce, or after cooking, bake them under a blanket of cheese sauce and crumbs.

Cook string beans, be they green or yellow, with the same care and forethought that a meat or fish dish receives, and the lowly garden bean will repay you with added flavor. And, very important: Drop the cut beans into slightly salted, rapidly boiling water, a few at a time so that the water will continue to boil. Do not use any more water than necessary to barely cover them. Vitamins are water soluble.

For added flavor boil one or two strips of bacon or pork with the beans. It's the foundation for a good sauce.

The use of some liquid other than salted water for the cooking of string beans varies the flavor advantageously. Try cooking cleaned, stringed beans in boiling water flavored with Pique Seasoning, using ¼ cup to each cup of boiling water.

BOILED STRING BEANS MAGIC [1478]

Wash 1½ pounds of fresh string beans or wax beans in clear water; drain well; remove the ends and any strings attached, and cut in halves or in lengthwise strips. Place in a saucepan 1¼ cups of boiling water, stir in ½ cup of Pique Seasoning, bring to a rolling boil, and add the beans, and 1 medium-sized onion thinly sliced. Bring again to a quick boil, covered, and cook gently for 12 to 15 minutes. Pour almost all the liquid from the beans into a jar to be used later for a soup or a sauce foundation, and add to the beans, ¼ cup of butter and 2 tablespoons of finely chopped parsley; toss all together.

FRENCHED STRING BEANS [1479]

Wash 1 pound of fresh string beans or wax beans in clear water; drain, remove the ends and any strings attached, cut into halves lengthwise and if very long, into halves crosswise; place in a casserole, add 1 cup of strong beef broth, ½ cup of small onions, thinly sliced, 1 bouquet garni composed of 1 bay leaf, 1 sprig of thyme and 7 or 8 sprigs of fresh parsley, all tied together with white kitchen thread, also salt and pepper to taste; cover and bring to a rolling boil; lower the heat and simmer gently for about 15 minutes or till beans are tender. Drain off almost all the liquid, which reserve for later use, and add bit by bit 2 tablespoons of butter creamed with 2 teaspoons each of finely chopped parsley and chives. Toss well and serve as a side dish.

OLD-FASHIONED STRING BEANS [1480]

Wash 1 pound of string or wax beans; drain well, cut off both ends sparingly; cut the beans into narrow strips diagonally. Dice 4 slices of bacon and try out in a saucepan until fat is rendered, but not until bacon is crisp. Stir in the prepared beans; season to taste with salt, pepper, a dash each of thyme and nutmeg, and stir in ½ cup of finely shredded lettuce, top this with 2 or 3 outside lettuce leaves, tucking them in at the sides to keep in the steam. Cover tightly, and cook over a gentle flame until beans are just tender or about 13 minutes. Discard the lettuce leaves used for topping; taste for seasoning, and serve hot.

STRING BEANS A L'ARMENIENNE [1481]

Heat 3 tablespoons of olive oil or butter in a skillet, stir in 3 medium-sized finely chopped onions, and 1 cup of chopped lamb or mutton. Stir until mixture is nicely browned over a low heat; then add 1 pound of Frenched string beans; and ¼ cup of beef bouillon; cover tightly, and cook over a gentle flame until beans are tender, or about 15 minutes, shaking the pan occasionally. Open the skillet and cover the beans with 6 thick slices of fresh peeled tomatoes. Cover tightly and simmer 12 to 15 minutes longer, rocking the pan frequently, but very gently. Season to taste with salt, pepper, and a dash each of nutmeg and clove; serve as a vegetable.

Alexander the Great paused long enough while conquering the world to bring the first string beans to Greece from India, as well as the first onion from Egypt.

STRING BEANS CREOLE [1482]

Prepare 1 quart of very hot Creole Sauce (1041–42). Stir in 1 No. 2 can of string beans; simmer gently for 10 to 15 minutes, taste for seasoning and serve hot, dusting with chopped parsley.

STRING BEANS AU GRATIN [1483]

Have ready 1½ cups of Cream Sauce (No. 258). Stir in ⅓ cup of grated cheese, and when cheese is melted, stir in 1 pound of cooked string or wax beans or a drained No. 2 can of string or wax beans. Taste for seasoning, turn mixture into a buttered casserole and sprinkle ½ cup of soft generously buttered crumbs mixed with ¼ cup of grated cheese. Bake in a moderate oven (350–375° F.) until top is nicely browned. Serve from the baking dish.

STRING BEANS A LA LYONNAISE   [1484]

Melt ¼ cup of butter in a frying pan; add 4 tablespoons of minced onions and brown lightly over a gentle flame, stirring frequently. Now stir in ¾ pound of drained cooked or canned string or wax beans with 1 generous tablespoon of minced parsley. Season to taste with salt, pepper and a dash each of cloves and nutmeg; cover and simmer very gently for 12 to 15 minutes, rocking and shaking the pan occasionally to prevent scorching. Serve at once. If desired, simmer 1 large onion, slice into thin rings, and smother separately in ¼ cup of butter, then combine with the browned onions and string beans.

SQUASH   [1485]

The history of squash is of particular interest to us because it is one of the few vegetables that has its origin in America. The squash and pumpkin grown today were common food crops of the Indian not only when the first explorers landed in this country but, according to archaeological research, for many centuries previous. Pieces of rind and seeds have been discovered in the ruins of cliff dwellings which belong to a period dating back to 1500 to 2000 B. C. Seeds have been found in ancient tombs and burial bowls, and the flower is the Hopi Indian emblem of fertility. The very name "squash" has its derivation in an Indian word.

The first explorers found the Indians growing squash in such widely scattered places as Florida, New England, Virginia, the St. Lawrence Valley, the Southwest, the Dakotas, Central America and Peru. An early Dutch writer about 1650 wrote: "The natives have another species of this vegetable peculiar to themselves, called by our people *quasiens* (squash), a name derived from the aborigines, as the plant was not known to us before our intercourse with them. It is a delightful fruit, as pleasant to the eye on account of its fine variety of colors, as to the mouth for its agreeable taste. They do not wait for it to ripen before making use of the fruit, but only until it has attained a certain size. They gather the squashes, and immediately place them on the fire without any further trouble . . . "

Allusions to the various members of this family of squash, pumpkins and gourds, run all through the writings of the earliest explorers and colonists. Only the two generally grown types of squash interest us— summer squash and winter squash. There are numerous divisions of the two main types. The summer or bush squash has several varieties: Early Yellow Prolific, Giant Summer Straightneck, Early Bush Scallop, Patty

Pan, or Cymling, Cocozelle, or Italian Vegetable Marrow, English Vegetable Marrow, and so forth.

Winter or Vine Squash. This type bears large fruit with a richer, heartier—and some people think—better flavor than the bushy type or summer squash. It includes the Hubbard, Golden, Delicious, Boston Marrow, Buttercup, Table Queen, and is also called Des Moines or Little Acorn, Vegetable Spaghetti, and so forth.

The white flat squash streaked with green and yellow bring back to us the Indian legend of the squash seed. Again and again travelers from the Southwest had told the Indians of old New York about a certain plant which yielded a flat disk-like vegetable of rare sweetness when baked. The story goes that on a hot day in the lands of the Senecas, an old Indian dreamed out loud of his wish to possess the seeds of that flat squash for his people. Yellow birds in the oak branches heard the wish and determined to make the dream come true. They flew West until they reached the squash fields, but the broad flat seeds were too big for their beaks. So the birds held a council and determined to ask the wild ducks from the swamp lands with their broad bills to help in the plan. The ducks, remembering their feasts of corn as they winged their way each spring and fall over the lands of the Senecas, gave assistance, and guided by the yellow birds, each carried a squash seed in his mouth from the Southwest into the East. Even today, as the Senecas listen to the yellow birds, they call them by a name which means *bringers of squash seeds*, in memory of the feasts of sweet baked squash first enjoyed by their forefathers long moons ago. White men, too, love these flat squashes because of their sweetness and because of variety of ways in which they may be prepared as main dishes, appetizers and desserts.

SQUASH—HINTS [1486]

Peel summer squash, slice it thin, bake it with butter or margarin, a little milk or thin cream and a few dribbles of honey or maple syrup or fill the hollow with maple syrup. Squash seeds may be toasted and served at the cocktail hour.

Young summer squash is usually cooked without peeling. Select those with rinds free from dark spots or bruises.

A simple savory luncheon dish is made by boiling whole acorn squash about 15 minutes, peeling, then cutting in halves, stuffing the cavities with sausage meat and baking until tender.

The half-bud brilliant orange flowers of the zucchini squash are seen frequently in Italian markets when they are sold for sautéeing. Don't be astonished when they burst into bloom in the skillet. Use them in omelets or any egg dish. Squash blossoms dipped in batter and fried crisp in deep hot fat are food for epicures. Early in the season, the small tender zucchini vines and leaves are sold as greens.

Winter squash is satisfactory as soon as it has developed a ripe color, although it will improve in flavor, texture and keeping quality if allowed to ripen on the vine.

The most common method of cooking summer squash of any type is to cut it into pieces and either steam or cook in a very small amount of water. A double boiler may be used. It may be served in the pieces or mashed with plenty of butter, as squash, like spinach, is what the French call a "butter assassin."

Squash combines well with potato. Mash equal quantities of these two vegetables and add a little cream, salt, pepper and marjoram. Whip until light and fluffy.

When buying winter squash, select one that is heavy for its size and free from blemishes. The rind should be firm and smooth. Winter squash with a soft rind is usually immature and its flesh may be thin and watery when cooked. Summer squash is best when young. Choose those which are fresh looking and heavy for their size. Be sure the rind is soft and free from marks and bruises. The skin should be easy to puncture. A medium-sized squash weighs about one pound and will serve two.

ACORN SQUASH RINGS WITH APPLE SAUCE　　[1487]

Wash 3 acorn squash, dry, and cut each crosswise into 4 slices. Place in skillet; add a scant ½ cup of water, 1 large bay leaf and 4 thin slices of onion; cover and steam about 20 minutes, or until tender. Let the water evaporate then brown squash quickly on both sides in a little butter or margarin. Season with salt, pepper and a dash of marjoram, and serve with a tablespoonful of apple sauce in each ring.

BAKED ACORN SQUASH NEW ENGLAND　　[1488] METHOD

Wash dry and cut in halves 3 acorn squash weighing about a pound each; remove seeds and membranes, and place the halves, cut sides up, in a shallow baking dish; pour about an inch of hot water around them, season lightly with mixed salt and pepper, and bake in a moderate oven (375° F.) until beginning to tender or about 35 to 40 minutes, renewing water as it boils away. Meanwhile, simmer (blanch) ¼ pound of mild-cured salt pork a few minutes in water; drain, and set in the oven until pork begins to take on color, turning frequently, then drain off the fat. Take the squash from the oven; brush the flesh with some of the salt pork fat, and sprinkle generously with black pepper. Dice the pork very small, place a tablespoon of the dice in each half squash; return to the oven and bake until the squash is very tender, renewing water as necessary. Serve at once on a heated platter dusting with finely chopped parsley.

GLAZED CROOKED NECK SQUASH　　　　[1489]

Wash, dry and cut into one-inch slices 3 yellow or green squash. Sprinkle with brown sugar and dot with salt butter. Place in a shallow dish, and bake in a moderate oven (350° F.) 20 minutes, or until nicely glazed, basting frequently with the syrup in the pan. Serve with ham, pork or smoked tongue.

SQUASH FRITTERS I [1490]

Drop small cubes of pre-cooked squash into a fritter-batter and cook in hot deep fat (375° F.) until nicely browned. Drain on absorbent paper and serve piping hot with roast pork, roast veal or roast turkey.

SQUASH FRITTERS II [1491]

Cut well washed and dried summer squash into round slices about an inch thick, dip in well seasoned flour (salt, pepper and a dash of nutmeg and clove) then roll in egg beaten with a little cold milk, then in sieved dry bread crumbs, and fry in hot, deep, clear fat (375° F.). Serve as a garnish for turkey, roast pork, ham, veal or tongue.

SQUASH PATTIES I [1492]

Drain thoroughly 1½ to 1¾ cups of cooked summer or winter squash; season to taste with mixed salt and pepper, also a dash of marjoram and clove. Shape into patties, roll in seasoned flour, then in egg beaten with a little milk, then in crumbs. Repeat and fry in hot bacon drippings until brown on both sides. Serve with baked pork chops or any kind of smoked meat.

SQUASH PATTIES II [1493]

Grate 1 pound of unpeeled and washed zucchini squash, and combine with 1 well beaten egg, 1½ tablespoon of grated onion, 1 tablespoon of finely chopped parsley or green pepper or both. Season with salt, pepper, a dash of nutmeg, and ½ tablespoon of grated Parmesan cheese. Moisten ½ cup of soft bread crumbs with 3 tablespoons of thin cream or undiluted evaporated milk, and add to squash mixture, mixing well. Shape into 12 individual patties, roll first in seasoned flour, then in beaten egg, and finally in sieved bread or cracker crumbs. Fry in hot bacon or ham drippings until nicely browned on both sides. Serve with pork chops, or any kind of cooked smoked meat or fowl.

SQUASH SOUFFLÉ SOUTHERN STYLE [1494]

Brown 1 large thinly sliced onion lightly in butter or cooking oil in a heavy skillet over a low heat, stirring almost constantly; then stir in 2 pounds of small green summer squash, washed, dried, and cubed small.

and cook until tender, or about 10 minutes, stirring frequently with a wooden spoon; drain off all the juice carefully. Combine 6 lightly beaten eggs, with ½ cup of finely chopped (not grated) American cheese, 1 tablespoon each of finely chopped parsley and green pepper; and stir into the squash-onion mixture; season to taste with salt, pepper and a grating of nutmeg; turn into a greased, paper-lined casserole or mold; place in a pan of hot water, and bake in a moderate oven (375–400° F.) until firm or about 20 minutes. Unmold on a hot platter and remove the paper.

WHIPPED HUBBARD SQUASH [1495]

Wash, dry, peel and cut into 2-inch pieces enough Hubbard squash to make a full quart (4 cups); place the pieces in a colander over a pan of slightly salted boiling water, cover tightly and steam until tender or about 20 minutes; drain well, then mash and season to taste with salt, pepper and 1 teaspoon of sugar. Beat in 1 tablespoon of heavy cream, heated with 2 tablespoons of butter, and whip to a cream over a very low flame. Transfer carefully to a heated vegetable dish and sprinkle a little finely chopped parsley over all. Serve plain at once, or make 6 nests in the fluffy squash; drop into each a freshly poached egg, and serve as an entrée.

SUCCOTASH [1496]

This dish is a combination of corn, freshly cut from the cob, with freshly cooked lima beans, and dressed with butter or a little cream, according to family custom. Given the general idea, our forebears adapted this dish to their needs and the materials at hand, and the recipe, as handed down from mother to daughter, varied in certain respects. Succotash is not the same dish in every section of the country, although corn and shell beans do always have a place in it. "Miskuto-tash," or "Sukqutahhash," known today as succotash, and believed to be the first truly American dish, originated around 1620, when the American Indians taught the Pilgrim mothers how to make it, has different versions according to localities.

MAINE SUCCOTASH [1497]

This is made with fresh corn scored from the cob, with small pieces of salt pork and a little fresh, sweet cream. The lima beans are cooked separately, added to the corn-pork mixture and simmered 5 minutes or until heated and well blended. More cream and butter are added just before serving, and the dish is seasoned with salt (very little on account of the salt pork) and plenty of pepper

MASSACHUSETTS SUCCOTASH [1498]

There are two versions. The "original" Indian recipe, which the squaws prepared for their braves, was made in huge quantities and in a large black iron kettle or kettles hanging in their open fireplaces. They used to freeze the mixture and chop off a little as needed for their families during the winter.

NEW ENGLAND SUCCOTASH [1499]

This is made with shell beans, not with lima beans. The corn used is the yellow kind, not the white variety, and salt pork.

CONNECTICUT SUCCOTASH [1500]

This is or was made with "cranberry beans"—never lima beans—and cooked with a few slices of salt pork till thoroughly done. After the ears of corn are cooked, the kernels are scraped, added to the "cranberry beans" with a few small pieces of the cob to "cook the sweetness out"; then, when ready to serve, these pieces of cob are removed and the mixture is slightly salted, then well peppered before serving.

PENNSYLVANIA DUTCH SUCCOTASH [1501]

This is more a vegetable stew than a succotash, and is very, very delicious. Into it go green peppers, potatoes, tomatoes, brown sugar, corn and limas.

PACIFIC COAST CHINESE SUCCOTASH [1502]

This is made like the New England succotash, but is high y flavored with soya sauce or Chinese brown sauce (commercial).

SOUTHERN SUCCOTASH [1503]

This contains onions, okra and tomatoes, besides the limas and corn, with a generous sprinkling of grated nutmeg to boot.

PLYMOUTH (MASS.) SUCCOTASH [1504]

This is not a side dish of corn and lime beans cooked together. It is a far more important dish. It has a historical background and is served at all celebrations on Forefather's Day, December 21st. During the Winter, some people have it once a week, like the famous French

Pot-au-Feu, or pot-on-the-fire soup. Here is the original recipe as found in the Library of Plymouth:

OLD PLYMOUTH SUCCOTASH [1505]

This recipe will serve twenty persons generously. For less, reduce the amount of ingredients accordingly. But as this famous dish keeps well— for more than a whole week—it is wise to make plenty of it and see it disappear fast.

Soak 1½ pounds of pea beans or navy beans, after washing them in several changes of cold water, overnight. Next day, drain thoroughly; place in a kettle, cover generously with cold water, add 3 medium-sized onions, peeled, quartered, a bouquet garni composed of 1 extra large bay leaf tied with a 2-inch piece of parsley root, scraped, and 12 fresh sprigs of parsley, all tied together with white kitchen thread, season with salt lightly; bring to a rolling boil; lower the flame and let simmer very, very slowly until almost tender. Keep hot without draining, but discard the bouquet garni. The simmering time depends on the age of the beans as well as the quality. Dried pea or navy beans are fine after one year of drying.

Meanwhile, clean, wash, truss a 5-pound fowl after placing a peeled onion in the cavity; wash quickly in cold water a 4-pound piece of corn beef rump, and a 1-pound piece of fat salt pork of equal parts of fat and lean; place these in a large kettle; cover generously with cold water; bring to a boil, add 3 bay leaves, a small bunch of fresh parsley and 2 sprigs of thyme, all tied together with kitchen string. Gradually bring to a boil, and let simmer gently, till the meats and fowl are tender, skimming frequently. As the chicken will be tender before the corned beef, remove it first, then the salt pork, and lastly the corned beef. Reserve the broth for soup or as a foundation for a sauce.

While the meats and fowl are cooking, cut 1 small yellow turnip (rutabaga) into small cubes; cut 5 medium-sized potatoes into thin slices; cover with cold water and cook till tender. In another saucepan or kettle cook 3 quarts of hulled corn. (Some of the oldest families use hominy instead of corn; in this case, use 3 large cans of hominy instead of the freshly hulled corn); cook in enough water to cover until tender.

Remove most of the fat from the broth. Take 1½ gallons of the broth, bring to a boil; then add the cooked mashed pea beans (mashed by rubbing through a fine sieve to remove the skins of the beans) and the mashed turnip-potato mixture. Cut the fowl, corned beef and salt pork into serving portions, and add to the bean-turnip-potato mixture, mixing and heating well. Season to taste with salt and black pepper, remembering that the salt pork is already salty; put on the lid; heat through but do not allow to boil. Serve at once.

SUCCOTASH [1506]

Cook 2 cups of fresh lima beans in a small amount of boiling salted water till tender, but not broken; add 3 cups of fresh corn kernels and cook 6 to 8 minutes longer. Drain well; stir in 1 teaspoon of salt and a pinch of pepper, ¼ cup of butter and ¾ cup of light, scalded cream or undiluted evaporated milk. Serve immediately.

SUCCOTASH AU GRATIN [1507]

Turn succotash, prepared as indicated for recipe No. 1506, into a buttered baking dish, and top with 1 scant cup of buttered bread crumbs. Brown quickly in a hot oven and serve at once.

SUCCOTASH SOUFFLE [1508]

Simmer 4 medium-sized thinly sliced onions, in 3 tablespoons of butter in a saucepan, and mix with 2 No. 2 cans of succotash. Season to taste with salt and pepper. Cut ½ pound of bacon into inch pieces and fry. Drain off the fat, and add the bacon to the succotash mixture. Sauté 12 small fresh mushroom caps in a little of the bacon fat and when done, drain and add these also, with 4 egg yolks. Blend all thoroughly, then fold in the stiffly beaten egg whites with ¼ teaspoon of salt. Turn into a buttered soufflé dish and bake in a hot oven (400–425° F.) for 25 to 30 minutes, or until soufflé is well puffed and delicately browned. Serve at once.

TOMATOES [1509]

Upon an unpretentious old frame house in Newport, Rhode Island, the Historical Society of that community has placed an equally plain marker, with the legend: "CORNE HOUSE; HOME OF THE ARTIST, MICHELE FELICE CORNE, WHO INTRODUCED THE TOMATO INTO THIS COUNTRY."

Tomatoes seem to have originated in Central or South America. The name itself comes from an Aztec word *Zitomate*. The plant was grown by Indians in Mexico and Peru long before the time of Columbus. It was taken from Peru to Italy, where it met with favor. There it was called "golden apple" (pomidor), "love apple," and many other names, but by 1695 the name "tomato" had come into general use.

The first written mention of tomatoes in the United States was made by Thomas Jefferson in 1781, but they were not grown commonly for use even then. Some time later, the secretary of the Connecticut Board of Agriculture wrote: "We raised our first tomatoes about 1832 as a curiosity, but made no use of them, though we had heard that the French ate them. By about 1835 culinary use had become more general, although many people still considered them poisonous. . . . "

TOMATOES—HINTS [1510]

To ripen: Put solid tomatoes together in brown paper bag; leave for three or four days where it is dark but not damp. Result: Quicker ripening, but still solid tomatoes. Do not place green tomatoes in the hot sun, as this softens them.

Canned tomatoes combined with bread crumbs and cheese make a good scalloped dish, suitable for luncheon. . . . Sliced tomatoes slightly spread with honey and more than a sprinkle of freshly ground black pepper are delicious. . . . Broiled green tomatoes are good with all types of hash. . . . Baked tomatoes are not "surprises" any more except when stuffed with tomato pulp, and fine chopped pecans with fresh basil added for flavor. . . . Green tomatoes, sliced thick, seasoned and sautéed, are perfect with steak or chops. Dust with sugar before frying.

To peel tomatoes easily, drop them into boiling water for just a minute or so, then into cold water. Using a small sharp knife, remove the skins, then chill the tomatoes.

Add a slice of lemon to tomatoes when stewing, remove it before serving.

It may sound odd, but the juice of canned *tomatoes* contains MORE vitamin C than can be had from canned *tomato juice*.

Both ripe and green tomatoes form the background of many delicious homemade relishes, marmalades and pickles.

Try serving a bowl of grated cheese with stewed tomatoes.

Acid foods such as tomatoes are best stored in porcelain enameled utensils, since this ware is acid resistant.

When buying tomatoes, select those that are mature yet firm; not overripe, fairly well formed, plump, smooth, of good red color and free from blemish. Tomatoes which are rough or irregular in shape, may not be attractive to serve in salad or as stuffed tomatoes, but will be good in tomato juice cocktail or combined in a casserole with other vegetables or with meat. Puffy or watery fruit is wasteful and usually of poor flavor.

Try stuffing tomatoes with succotash. Scoop out the pulp, replace with succotash that has been made with a little cream; season well with salt and pepper; dot with butter or margarin and bake until the tomatoes are tender but not unduly soft.

BAKED CURRIED TOMATOES ENGLISH STYLE [1511]

Scald 6 or 7 tomatoes; peel, then place the tomatoes in a buttered deep baking dish. Combine 1 cup of tomato sauce, 1 teaspoon of curry powder, 1 tablespoon of red currant jelly, salt, pepper and nutmeg to taste, and cook slowly for about 5 minutes, or until mixture boils, stirring occasionally. Pour the sauce over the tomatoes; sprinkle with grated cheese (any kind desired) and 1 tablespoon of melted butter. Bake in a hot oven (400° F.) for 15 to 20 minutes or until cheese is melted and bubbling and tomatoes soft. Serve at once right from the baking dish.

Fresh tomato juice in earthen jugs was sold in Holland for medicinal purposes in the 1860's. A jug containing a little more than a quart cost about one dollar.

DEVILED TOMATOES MIDDLEWEST STYLE [1512]

Make a dressing of 1 tablespoon of butter and 1 tablespoon of cider vinegar rubbed smooth with the yolk of one hard-cooked egg; add a little sugar, salt, pepper and a dash of dry mustard. Beat until smooth then heat to boiling point in a small saucepan. Remove from the fire and pour slowly over a large well beaten egg, beating until smooth. Keep hot over hot water while broiling 6 thick slices of fresh, ripe tomatoes. Arrange these on a hot platter, and pour the dressing over them. Serve at once as a vegetable with roast poultry, including turkey.

FRENCH TOMATO FRITTERS [1513]

Rub 2 cups of canned tomatoes through a colander, add 1 scant teaspoon of salt, a good dash of pepper, 1 tablespoon of sugar and 1 tablespoon of grated onion and bring to a slow simmer. In another pan blend ¼ cup of butter and ¼ cup of cornstarch over a gentle flame, then stir in the tomato mixture. Boil for a minute or two or until quite thick, stirring almost constantly. Remove from the fire and stir in 2 well-beaten egg yolks. Pour into a shallow buttered pan or pie plate and let stand until cold. When ready to cook, cut into circles with a small biscuit cutter, dip these in bread crumbs, then in beaten egg white to which 1 tablespoon of cold water has been added, then in fine crumbs again. Place a few at a time in a frying basket, and brown in hot, deep, clear fat (399° F.). Drain on absorbent paper and serve immediately as a side dish or as a garnish for pork, lamb or veal chops and hamburgers.

GRILLED TOMATO SLICES AND VARIATIONS [1514]

Cut firm tomatoes in half-inch thick slices, sprinkle with salt and pepper, then with fine crumbs and lay on an oiled broiler. Dot with butter and broil until nicely browned on both sides. Dust with chopped parsley and serve piping hot.

Variations. (1) Roll in bread crumbs mixed with grated onion, sage, thyme, salt and pepper. (2) Roll in bread crumbs mixed with grated onion, a little curry powder, and salt and pepper. (3) Roll in bread crumbs mixed with grated cheese and bread crumbs in equal parts with salt and pepper to taste. (4) Roll in bread crumbs seasoned with a little powdered ginger, sugar and grated lemon rind, with salt and pepper to taste.

NAPOLITAN PIZZA   [1515]
Tomato Pie Napolitan Style

The true pizza pie is made with bread dough; but a pastry crust is often substituted.

Prepare dough or pasty for six 5-inch pies. Roll out or flatten the dough to about ⅛ of an inch in thickness and use to line 6 greased individual pie plates, pressing the dough or pastry neatly into the form, and trimming it at the edge. Dot with butter, place in a hot oven (400-425° F.) for 2 minutes and set aside. Combine 3 red, ripe tomatoes, peeled and coarsely chopped, 4 tablespoons of finely chopped anchovy filets, ¼ pound of Italian salami, coarsely chopped, 3 tablespoons of green olives, coarsely chopped, 1 large onion, finely chopped, 1 clove of garlic (more or less, according to taste), very finely chopped or mashed to a pulp, 1 tablespoon each of finely chopped celery and parsley, and ¼ pound of Italian cheese or any other preferred cheese, cubed very small. Divide the well blended ingredients among the six individual shells; place in a medium oven (375° F.) and bake 15 to 20 minutes, or until filling is cooked and crust nicely browned. Serve hot as a main dish for luncheon or supper.

SCALLOPED TOMATOES WITH ONIONS   [1516]

Peel and slice thinly enough white onions to make 2 cups by measure. Melt 4 tablespoons of butter or margarin in a saucepan, stir in the onions, sprinkle with 1 tablespoon of sugar and 1 teaspoon of salt and cover. Cook gently over a low flame for 14 to 15 minutes, shaking and rocking the pan frequently. Do not brown. Arrange the onions in a baking dish, add 2½ cups of canned tomatoes mixed with ½ cup of soft bread crumbs, and mix well with the onions. Season with a good pinch of pepper; sprinkle over all ½ cup of buttered crumbs, or equal parts of crumbs and grated American cheese; bake in a moderate oven (350-375° F.) about 20 minutes or until brown. Serve as a side dish with any kind of meat or fish.

STEWED TOMATOES [1517]

Season 4 cups of canned tomatoes to taste with salt, pepper and 2 teaspoons of sugar; stir in 2 medium-sized onions, very thinly sliced; cover and cook 15 minutes over a very low flame, stirring once or twice. Remove the cover, and if very juicy, boil rapidly about 5 minutes. Remove from the fire, taste for seasoning, and, just before serving, stir in ¼ cup of butter added bit by bit, and dust with chopped parsley. Serve as a side dish with fish, meat or poultry.

STUFFED TOMATOES AND VARIATIONS [1518]

Initial Preparation. Select medium-sized tomatoes of uniform size; scald and peel. Scoop out pulp, leaving just a thin shell, and stuff with whatever is available, such as fish, shellfish, corn, scrambled eggs, peas, creamed meat or poultry. If possible, add at least part of the scooped out pulp to the stuffing.

Here are a few suggestions for stuffings.

Cut canned, or freshly cooked shrimps in 2 or 3 pieces; add a little cream, cheese or curry sauce; top with buttered bread or cracker crumbs and bake until top is brown.

Creole Rice. Cook minced onion in a little butter, add cooked rice, tomato pulp and seasonings, top with buttered crumbs and bake until top is brown.

Chopped Meat with Curry. Use any left-over cooked meat or cold cuts; bind with a little sauce made with meat stock or milk, seasoned to taste with curry powder and a little grated onion. Top with buttered crumbs and brown.

Broccoli. Dip cooked broccoli tips or ends in melted butter. Top with buttered crumbs and brown.

Vegetable Jardiniere. Chop left-over cooked vegetables as cucumber, onion, green pepper, peas, cauliflower, and so forth; mix with a little cream sauce or cheese sauce; top with buttered crumbs and brown.

Corn and Green Pepper. Use left-over corn cut from cob, mix with cooked chopped green pepper, season with salt, pepper and onion, top with buttered crumbs and brown.

STUFFED TOMATOES WITH CHEESE CUSTARD [1519]
(*A Lenten dish*)

Pour boiling water over 6 firm, large, ripe tomatoes; plunge into cold water, peel and scoop out the pulp. Turn tomatoes upside down to drain, then brush insides with melted anchovy butter.

Scald 3 cups of rich milk with 4 thin slices of onion, 1 large bay leaf, 4 sprigs of parsley and 1 sprig of marjoram; strain. Gradually stir in ¾ cup of grated American cheese or any other kind of desired cheese, beating briskly after each addition; season to taste with salt, pepper and 1 teaspoon of Worcestershire sauce, and boil up once, stirring constantly. Remove from the fire and beat in 3 egg yolks adding one at a time and beating briskly after each addition. Cool to lukewarm, then fold in 2 stiffly beaten egg whites. Place the empty, drained tomato shells in individual custard cups; fill with the cheese custard; dot each top with a bit of butter; place cups thus filled in a pan containing hot water and bake in a moderate oven (325–350° F.) 25 to 30 minutes, or until custard is set. Unmold onto hot, individual plates and serve hot, simply garnished with a few sprigs of watercress. Serve as a separate course.

TOMATO CHEESE PIE [1520]

Prepare a baking powder biscuit dough. Cook together 2 cups of canned tomatoes, 2 medium sized onions, grated, and 1 green pepper, scalded, peeled, and finely chopped, for 15 minutes over a low flame, stirring frequently; season with salt, pepper and 1 tablespoon each of chopped parsley and chives, also 1 teaspoon of Worcestershire sauce. Stir in 1 cup of chopped or finely cubed American cheese, and stir until the cheese is melted. Turn mixture into a baking dish; roll out the biscuit dough to a scant ¼ inch thickness and cut into biscuits with a two-inch floured biscuit cutter. Arrange biscuits side by side on tomato mixture in the casserole; brush over with egg yolk beaten with a little cold water or milk, and bake in a hot oven (425° F.) for 20 to 25 minutes or until biscuits are nicely browned. Serve at once, either as a side dish, or as a main dish for a light luncheon or supper.

TOMATO CHEESE SOUFFLE [1521]

Never plan a soufflé for a dinner that may be delayed, as this must be served hot from the oven. Do not place the soufflé in an outer pan of hot water unless the recipe specifically calls for this procedure. This applies to any soufflé, including dessert ones. The water method produces a soft soufflé, and in some instances the outside should be crusty.

Melt 2 tablespoons of butter; blend in 3 tablespoons of flour, and cook until mixture is frothy and bubbling, but do not brown, Gradually stir in ¾ cup of milk which has been scalded with 1 bay leaf, 1 clove, 4 sprigs of parsley, 4 thin slices of onion, and a tiny pinch of powdered dill. Drain, then add ½ cup of tomato juice, or ½ cup of good canned or freshly made tomato soup, stirring constantly. Add while stirring 1¼ cup of any preferred grated cheese; season to taste with salt and pepper, and remove from the fire. Beat 4 egg yolks lightly, add ¼ to ⅓ teaspoon of dry mustard or curry powder, and beat again till well blended; gradually stir egg yolk mixture into the cheese sauce beating briskly and constantly after each addition. Lastly fold in the 4 stiffly beaten egg whites, seasoned with ⅓ teaspoon of salt. Bake in a hot oven (400° F.) for 20 to 25 minutes or until soufflé is well puffed up and nicely browned on top. Serve immediately.

TOMATO JELLY AND EGG LUNCHEON   [1522]

Slice tops from 6 green peppers and take out the seeds and white ribs. Place in each pepper 1 soft-cooked boiled egg, or a chilled poached egg; fill up the peppers with tomato jelly made as follows:

Combine in a saucepan 2 cups of canned or peeled, chopped fresh tomatoes, 1 bay leaf, ½ cup of finely chopped green celery leaves, a dash each of salt and cayenne pepper, 1 whole clove, a thin slice of garlic, and 3 sprigs of fresh parsley. Bring gradually to a boil, and simmer very gently for 15 minutes, stirring occasionally. Meanwhile, soak 1 tablespoon of gelatin in 4 tablespoons of dry white wine or sherry wine for 5 minutes, and stir into the simmering tomato mixture. Now add 2 slightly beaten egg whites and their shells and bring to a quick boil, stirring frequently. Lower the flame and simmer gently for 10 minutes, then strain through a wet jelly bag or muslin cloth, into a saucepan. Taste for seasoning; and, when beginning to set, spoon the jelly a little at a time over the eggs in the peppers. When set and peppers are full, chill and serve on a chilled platter, garnishing with watercress, gherkin fans, radish roses, black and green olives, and mayonnaise.

TOMATO TORTE PIEMONTESE   [1523]

Have ready a half recipe for rich, flaky pie crust. Cut 5 or 6 tomatoes in thick slices without peeling. Sprinkle with salt and pepper and dredge in corn meal. Fry in plenty of butter, turning with cake turner to brown on both sides, and fry slowly so that the slices will be well-cooked. Sprinkle a few grains of sugar on each slice after frying. Line a layer cake tin with rich pastry dough; fill with the tomato slices, sprinkle with melted butter and bake in a hot oven (450° F.) for 10 minutes; lower the heat to moderate and continue baking for 15 minutes longer. Serve at once.

TURNIP (WHITE)   [1524]

The turnip (*Brassica rapa*) has been in cultivation for hundreds of years. It grows wild in Europe from the Baltic Sea to the Caucasus. In 42 A. D., a writer stated that this vegetable was eaten by both men and animals. Pliny mentioned five different kinds of turnips and said that one root weighed 40 pounds. This great weight, however, has often being equalled and exceeded in modern times; in California in 1850 there is a record of a root of 100 pounds weight.

Turnips are mentioned frequently in the writings of herbalists in Europe and England. In England this vegetable was used in armorial bearings to represent a kind-dispositioned person who relieved the poor. The cultivation of turnips in this country dates back to the seventeenth century, and in 1612 the first settlers in Virginia suffered from scurvy until they were able to get relief from the turnip crop they cultivated.

Rutabaga, more commonly called "yellow turnip," "Swedish turnip," or "Lapland turnip" was first introduced into England toward the end of the seventeenth century and into America in 1806. Its name implies an origin either in Sweden itself or in some part of northern Europe.

Turnip greens, popular particularly in the South, have a well deserved reputation. They furnish minerals in generous quantities and offer a ready source of vitamins, chiefly A and C. If we fail to use these leaves, we overlook prime deposits of calcium, phosphorus and iron. In this respect turnip greens are as valuable as milk, and almost as well utilized. A single serving will supply one-third the entire adult daily minimum requirement of calcium.

BOILED TURNIPS [1525]

Both white and yellow turnips are prepared in the same manner. Scrub, pare and cut in large pieces for mashing, or dice if to be served with a sauce, fried, scalloped, and so forth. Cook uncovered in a large amount of boiling salted water. Young turnips or rutabagas will cook in 15 to 25 minutes. Old ones may need to be boiled an hour or more. Drain, mash if desired, and season like mashed potatoes; in the South a little sugar is added for extra flavor.

COTTON PICKER'S DELIGHT [1526]

When the cotton fields of Alabama have turned to snow white; when the cooks have rolled up their sleeves and banjos have been tuned up for an evening of old Dixie melodies, then an old Southern meal, appropriately nicknamed "Cotton Picker's Delight," supplies a culinary harmony of its own. Turnip and mustard greens, white meat and golden brown corn bread make a simple but thoroughly satisfactory banquet. Here is the way it is prepared:

Wash 2 bunches of turnip greens, 1 bunch of mustard greens and 4 white turnips pared, and coarsely chopped, in several waters. Drain thoroughly. Put ½ to ¾ pound piece of white meat (pork is called white meat) in stew pan, cover with slightly salted cold water and boil until tender, approximately 40 to 45 minutes, adding more boiling water as it evaporates, then add the prepared greens and chopped turnips and cook on a slow fire for 40 to 45 minutes. Drain and serve with corn bread to mop up the pot liquor of the greens.

COTTON PICKER'S MASHED FLUFFY TURNIPS [1527]

To 3 cups of cooked, mashed turnips, seasoned to taste, add 3 beaten egg yolks, then fold in 3 stiffly beaten egg whites. Bake 15 to 20 minutes in a hot oven (400° F.) or until lightly browned. For a crusty surface, sprinkle with a little light brown sugar before baking.

GLAZED TURNIPS [1528]

Peel and cube small 2 bunches of young white or yellow turnips and cook in boiling salted water until tender. Drain. Melt 3 tablespoons of butter, add turnips, and cook a few minutes, stirring frequently, then sprinkle with a little sugar and continue cooking, over a gentle flame, again sprinkle with sugar and keep on cooking and sprinkling with sugar until turnips are delicately glazed. Serve as a side dish or as a garnish for roast pork, pork chops or veal cooked in any style.

The king of Bithynia while on a winter campaign against the Scythians far from the sea expressed a longing for a dish of Aphy, a small fish. His chef cut a turnip into the exact shape of the fish, fried it in oil, and sprinkled it with black poppy seeds. The king was not only deceived, but delighted and praised the "fish" highly to his guests.

HUNGARIAN TURNIPS [1529]

Wash 7 or 8 medium-sized white or yellow turnips, peel and quarter. place in a saucepan, add ¼ teaspoon of caraway seeds, and cover with boiling salted water. Cook uncovered until tender, or about 15 to 20 minutes; drain well and turn into a generously buttered casserole; pour over ½ cup of scalded sour cream seasoned with salt, a few grains each of cayenne and powdered sweet basil, and 1 teaspoon of grated lemon rind. Sprinkle lightly with ⅓ cup of buttered bread crumbs, and bake 10 to 12 minutes in a hot oven (400° F.). Serve directly from the casserole as a side dish.

Appropriate with roast pork, pork chops, roast duck, wild or domestic, and almost any kind of feathered wild bird.

TURNIP CUSTARD [1530]

Beat 3 eggs slightly; stir in 1½ cups of grated raw turnip, white or yellow, alternately with 3 cups of scalded sweet milk, seasoned to taste with salt, pepper and nutmeg. Beat very briskly until foamy. Stir in 1 teaspoon each of grated onion, finely chopped parsley and green pepper, and finally 3 tablespoons of melted butter. Turn into a buttered baking dish, dust with ½ teaspoon of granulated sugar and bake in a moderate oven (325° F.) for about 40 to 45 minutes, or until set. Serve at once from the baking dish.

TURNIP A LA PARISIENNE   [1531]
(A Lenten dish)

Add 3 hard cooked sieved egg yolks, to 2 cups of white sauce (No. 258) and cook over hot water till smooth, then stir in anchovy paste the size of a large pea and finally 3 cups of cooked, diced turnips (white or yellow); heat thoroughly and serve at once as a side dish, or as a main dish when topped with 6 poached eggs.

TURNIP SOUFFLES FRENCH STYLE   [1532]
(Individual)

Cook 1 pound of pared turnips, cut in small pieces, in boiling salted water till tender; drain well, then rub through a ricer. Set aside. Heat ¼ cup of butter; blend in 3 tablespoons of flour, and when bubbling, but without browning, stir in ½ cup of heavy sweet cream, which has been scalded with 1 small bay leaf, 3 sprigs of parsley, 1 whole clove, ⅛ teaspoon of grated nutmeg. Strain before using and add alternately with the turnip purée. Cook, stirring constantly, until mixture thickens. Remove from the fire, season to taste with salt and white pepper, then beat in 4 egg yolks, adding one at a time and beating well after each addition. Let cool a little, then fold in 4 stiffly beaten egg whites. Turn mixture into 6 buttered individual soufflé dishes, and bake 18 to 20 minutes in a moderate oven (375° F.) or until tops are nicely browned and well puffed. Serve at once. Good with roast turkey.

YELLOW TURNIPS EN CASSEROLE   [1533]

Cook in boiling salted water 4 cups of pared, diced yellow turnips; drain, saving ¾ cup of the turnip stock, which add to ¾ cup of evaporated milk. Melt 2 tablespoons of butter, stir in 1 cup of coarse dry bread crumbs, and then stir in, off the fire, ½ cup of grated American cheese. Gradually add the turnip stock-milk mixture, stirring constantly until mixture boils and thickens. Add the turnip dice, mix well, turn into a baking dish, sprinkle with ½ cup of buttered bread crumbs, and brown in a moderate oven (375° F.) for 15–20 minutes, or till top is nicely browned. Serve at once from the baking dish, with roast pork, roast veal, roast turkey or duck.

Chapter Eleven

CEREALS, ALIMENTARY PASTES AND RICE

I see the dark-skinned women kneel beside their footworn sills to grind their grain beneath flat stones; I see today's great mills; tall shafts of light across the land that nations may be fed—and flour becomes a sacrament, my loaves, much more than bread. . . .

—Grace N. Crowell, "Cereals."

CEREALS

To many cooks the word "cereal" is just another word for "breakfast." But while the many popular forms of different cereal grains make delicious, hot, tasty and highly nourishing breakfast dishes, the whole class of cereals has many additional uses, even to being employed as ingredients in fancy cooking as well as plain, ordinary, every day cooking.

Natural grains—oats, corn, rice, barley and rye—are food staples the world over. In breads, they are "the staff of life"; when rolled and milled, they form the basis of the familiar porridge of childhood. Some, like rice, form the staple starch food of millions of people, to whom the sight of a rice paddy is far more familiar than an acreage of potatoes or wheat.

But it is mainly in America that these long-familiar and wholesome grains have been developed into new shapes, forms and textures by the aid of highly mechanical skill in production. The wheat grain is scientifically puffed, the corn kernel is flaked, the rice grain is crisped, and bran, once discarded, takes its place as a true cereal food. Some of these cereals are also shaped into small wafers, biscuits or cakes, to make them more appetizing. They also make an excellent base for such dishes as creamed dried beef, creamed fish, chicken, eggs, and so forth.

Corn meal is an old-time staple, which should be brought back to favor. Whether yellow or white in tint, whether preferred stone-ground or water-ground, corn meal was intimately connected with our pioneer days. Like many another native American food, corn meal was demonstrated to the first settlers by the Indians, and after them was called "Injun Meal." Both North and South were familiar with it, and excelled in specialties made from it.

Grandmother's stanch standby, *hominy*, too, has become modernized: It is now sold in convenient tins or packages instead of growing in our own back yards. Furthermore, hominy is no longer reserved for breakfast alone. It appears with meat, poultry and game as well as with vegetables. It even goes into muffins.

Hominy is a product of corn. The whole kernels are soaked in lye to remove the husks, and are then cooked until tender. Because hominy is mild yet distinctive in flavor, it combines most successfully with other foods. It may substitute for rice as a ring, and be served filled with any kind of creamed or curried food. Hominy is also ideal for use in a stuffing.

Macaroni, spaghetti, noodles, gnocchi, raviolis, lazagnes, polenta, semolina, and similar "pastas" or "pastes" have had such an important place in the food history of the world that nations compete for the honor of their invention. While we associate these forms of cereals with Italy, the evidence seems to show that the honor belongs to the Orient, probably to China. Yet, these "pastes" are made with hard wheat, known as durum or semolina, used entirely or in part, but no rice flour at all is used in their making. The shape into which the paste is molded decides what name it is to be given. There are more than fifty shapes including that of fish, animals, crescents, flowers, shells, crowns and letters, beside the most used spaghetti of various thicknesses and the tubular macaroni. Some of these are colored with egg yolks, spinach, beef juices, and so forth.

Noodles differ from the other pastes in that they may be made from bread flour and that eggs are used to provide the moisture. They are cut in flat strips in various widths.

Although good the year round and appropriate at practically any time, these pastes as well as the cereals mentioned above seem to have an added appeal during cold weather.

CORN MEAL BALLS, CHILI SAUCE   [1535]

To 3 cups of freshly cooked, still warm corn meal mush (No. 1540), add 2 slightly beaten egg yolks, and beat well. Cool, form into flat cakes with a cube of American cheese in the middle of each, and cover cheese well with the mush. Pan fry in plenty of butter or butter substitute until nicely browned on both sides. Arrange on a heated serving platter, and pour over the following hot sauce:

Chili Sauce. Fry 1 medium-sized chopped onion, with 1 chopped green pepper and ½ clove of finely chopped garlic in 2 tablespoons of cooking oil over a low flame till onion just begins to color. Stir frequently; then add 1 can of tomato, 1 bit of bay leaf, a pinch of thyme, 1 scant teaspoon of sugar, 2 tablespoons of finely chopped green celery leaves, salt and 1 teaspoon (more or less) of chili powder. Cook over a low flame until as thick as a light boiled custard; then rub through a fine sieve, pressing well. Reheat, pour over the corn meal balls or cakes, and serve immediately.

CORN MEAL SOUFFLE DINNER COUNTRY   [1536] STYLE

Cook ½ cup of either white or yellow corn meal in 2½ cups of milk in a double boiler, stirring until smooth. Beat 5 egg yolks until thick, with ½ teaspoon of salt, a fresh grating of nutmeg, a dash of mace and ⅛ teaspoon of white pepper, and gradually stir into the mush, beating briskly. Cool to lukewarm, then fold in 4 stiffly beaten egg whites. Turn into a buttered oblong casserole, and press through the mush, lengthwise and crosswise, 1 pound of link pork sausage, which have been parboiled one minute and drained. Dot with 1½ tablespoons of butter and bake in a moderate oven for 25 minutes. Make six depressions in the top of the soufflé between the sausages, with a tablespoon; drop an egg in each; return to the oven, and bake 8 to 10 minutes, or till eggs are set. Serve immediately.

CORN MEAL FRITTERS SOUTHERN STYLE [1537]

Bring 1 cup of creamy milk to a boil; remove from the fire and sprinkle in ¼ cup of corn meal, stirring rapidly, until smooth and free from lumps. Season with 1 scant teaspoon of salt, a few grains of cayenne pepper and a fresh grating of nutmeg. Stir in 2 eggs, which have been well beaten with 1½ teaspoons of sugar, 1 teaspoon of baking powder and mix till smooth. Return to the fire and continue cooking over a gentle flame, stirring constantly from bottom of the pan, until mixture begins to thicken. Drop by spoons on to a hot greased griddle and bake, turning to brown both sides. Serve as a garnish, a side dish or a main dish. If used as a main dish, serve with Egg Sauce (No. 1051), Mushroom Sauce (No. 1000) or Tomato (No. 1130) or Brown sauce (No. 1017–19) respectively.

These fritters are a food for epicures when served with brown or soft maple sirup or sugar. If desired, add a few seedless raisins.

CORN MEAL RING LUNCHEON [1538]

Stick 5 or 6 whole cloves (heads removed) in 1 medium-sized onion. Place in a saucepan; add 2 cups of milk and 1 cup of cold water with a little salt and bring to a brisk boil. Sprinkle in gradually ¾ cup of corn meal and cook for 20 minutes, stirring constantly, or at least frequently. Remove from the fire and beat till thoroughly blended with the onion, which should by now be reduced to a pulp. Season to taste with mixed salt, pepper and nutmeg. Beat in 3 slightly beaten eggs. Turn into a generously buttered ring mold and bake for 20 minutes in a moderate oven (350° F.). Remove from the oven and let stand 5 minutes before unmolding on a round, hot platter. Fill center with creamed fish, mushrooms, crab meat, lobster meat or shrimp meat. Dust with mixed chopped parsley and paprika, and serve at once.

Don't continually serve the same cereal in the same style. Provide appetizing variation.

OLD-FASHIONED CORN MEAL PUDDING [1539]
(*A main dish*)

Combine ⅓ cup of white or yellow corn meal with 1 tablespoon of butter; then pour over 2 cups of creamy scalded milk, stirring constantly. Cook over hot water until of the consistency of smooth mush. Then add ½ cup of grated sharp American cheese, 1 teaspoon of salt and a few grains of cayenne pepper. Mix well. Remove from the fire and add 3 egg yolks, one at a time, beating well after each addition to prevent curdling.

Cool and when quite cold, fold in 3 stiffly beaten egg whites; turn into an ungreased baking dish, and bake in a moderate oven (350° F.) about 25 minutes. Serve as a main dish with egg sauce, tomato sauce, mushroom sauce, or brown sauce (which see at Sauces).

PIONEER MUSH [1540]

Add ¾ teaspoon salt to 1 quart of briskly boiling water; gradually sprinkle in ¾ cup of home-ground corn meal, stirring constantly. Boil 15 minutes, stirring frequently from bottom of pan to prevent lumping and scorching. Continue cooking for 45 minutes over hot water (double boiler). Serve with scraped maple sugar and cream or with honey, corn sirup or maple sirup. The addition of ⅛ to ½ cup of seeded or seedless raisins is a great improvement.

Left-over cereal can be used in puddings or muffins, or as thickening for soups, gravies or stews, as dressing for poultry, fish or meats, on griddle cakes, or combined with meat, cheese or vegetables in scalloped dishes.

POLENTA A LA PIEMONTESE [1541]

Bring 6 cups of water to a rapid boil; stir in 1 teaspoon of salt; then sprinkle in gradually 2 cups of yellow corn meal, and cook, stirring constantly till thick. Cover and cook over hot water for 20 minutes longer. Turn into a mold or shallow pan, let stand until firm, then cut in slices. Arrange these slices on a very hot platter and pour Sauce Piemontese over them.

Sauce Piemontese. Heat ¼ cup of olive oil or good salad oil to the smoking point; stir in 1½ teaspoons of paprika, a good pinch of pepper and a few grains of cayenne. Mix well; then stir in ½ clove of garlic, mashed to a pulp, and 1 scant teaspoon of salt. In this hot mixture cook ¼ cup of minced onion, 2 cups of whole pack tomatoes, and 1 small can of tomato purée, mixed with ½ cup of hot water, into which 1 tablespoon of Pique Seasoning may be stirred till thoroughly blended. Cook over a low flame for 15 minutes, and pour immediately over the polenta slices. Serve at once.

POLENTA ROMANA [1542]
(*As made by this writer for Caruso at the Hotel Knickerbocker*)

Ingredients. 2 gallons of water, 4 tablespoons of salt and 2 pounds of corn meal of special coarse quality.

The pan used to prepare the *Polenta* is usually made of solid copper with a handle, by which it hangs from a chain with hook, suspended in the fireplace. A special wooden stick, bent at one end, is used for stirring. When the water is boiling furiously, sprinkle in very slowly, first the salt, then the cornmeal. Stir constantly to avoid lumping. Cook from one and a half to two hours on a very low fire. In Italy it is cooked on a wood fire, but in this country Italians use any container and the gas stove. The flavor, however, does not seem quite the same.

What is served as a side dish for the Polenta Romana, is called "uccelletti scappati," the meaning of which is found in a popular story. An Italian housewife was expecting guests for dinner and birds were to be served. These, alas, were stolen and eaten by the family cat. To remedy the situation the good lady bought some veal, stuffed it and prepared it in such a way as to look and taste like birds.

Uccelletti Scappati. Select a piece of veal from the shank, cut it in three-inch slices and flatten them with a rolling pin.

Prepare a stuffing of chopped parsley, Italian "prosciutto" (ham) chicken meat, parmesan cheese, finely chopped garlic, pepper and salt.

Bind all these ingredients with two raw, beaten eggs to form a firm stuffing. Spread a portion on each well-beaten and seasoned slice of veal; roll up, and place in twos on a long wooden skewer, having a small piece of prosciutto and possibly a fresh sage leaf at each end and also between the two rolls.

Heat in a frying pan a piece of butter, a little olive oil if liked, and a piece of garlic. Fry the rolls quickly until golden brown, then more slowly for about ten minutes.

Just before removing from the fire add a tablespoon of minced parsley, and stir in ½ cup of good dry white wine.

CREAMED HOMINY COUNTRY STYLE   [1543]

Combine 1 quart of cold, rich, creamy milk or, still better, equal parts of milk and thin cream or undiluted evaporated milk with 3 well beaten eggs. Stir in 1¼ cup of granulated hominy, 1¼ to 1½ teaspoons of salt (or to taste), 3 tablespoons of grated onion, ¼ cup each of finely chopped green pepper, green celery leaves, and chives. Mix well. Turn into a greased casserole; place in a pan containing hot water, and bake in a moderate oven (350° F.) for 1 to 1¼ hours and stir occasionally during the first part of cooking.

HOMINY BURGER SQUARES   [1544]

Sprinkle 1 cup of hominy grits into 3½ cups of rapidly boiling salted water in the upper part of a double boiler. Place over direct heat, and cook, until thick, stirring constantly. Now place over hot water; cover, and continue cooking for one hour. Stir in ¾ pound of cooked chopped lean meat (any kind) with 1 cup of drained peas, lima beans, or canned beans, mixing thoroughly. Turn into a shallow pan; cool; chill until firm. Cut in squares; dip in beaten egg; roll in crumbs, and brown in a small amount of fat in a heavy skillet. Serve with tomato or mushroom sauce.

HOMINY AND BURGER CROQUETTES LUNCHEON [1545]

Combine 2 cups of cooked hominy grits, 2 cups of ground cooked meat, fish, poultry, or game, 2 tablespoons each of finely chopped onions, parsley and green pepper, 1 well beaten egg, 2 tablespoons of Pique Seasoning, salt, pepper to taste. Shape into croquettes; dip in beaten egg, roll in fine bread crumbs; dip again in egg and again in crumbs. Chill. When ready to serve, fry in hot, deep, clear fat (390° F.) until golden brown. Serve with tomato sauce, brown sauce, mushroom sauce or egg sauce.

HOMINY AND CHEESE TIMBALES RUSSIAN STYLE [1546]

Combine 2 cups of drained canned hominy, ⅔ cup of grated Gruyère cheese, 2 whole eggs and 1 egg yolk, beaten with ⅔ teaspoon salt, a dash of black pepper and 1 teaspoon of paprika, 2 teaspoons each of chopped green pepper, red pimiento and chopped parsley, and stir in 1 cup of scalded creamy milk, mixing thoroughly. Pour into 6 generously buttered ramekins; set these in a pan of hot water and bake 30 minutes in a moderate oven (300–325° F.). Serve hot with Smitane sauce, rich tomato sauce, mushroom sauce or piquant sauce (Nos. 1123 and 1130 and 1090 and 1103 respectively.)

HOMINY WITH SHERRY [1547]

For six servings, open a tall can (No. 2) of hominy, and heat it in its own juice or liquor. Drain; add 1 cup of heavy cream, scalded with 3 or 4 tablespoons of sherry wine, salt and pepper to taste and ¼ cup of finely minced parsley or chives, if available, or both in equal parts. Re-heat over hot water and serve at once.

SAMP [1548]

The cookery of eastern Long Island has several characteristics which are definitely its own. Although just 102 miles from New York, the exploring epicure steps into a world of distinctive cookery, with three centuries of tradition behind it. Samp, Amagansett Salt Codfish, Montauk Blackberry Duff and similar culinary delicacies sound like New England. They are and yet they aren't, a paradox which has an historical explanation.

In 1657, East Hampton, now a famed summer resort, was united with Connecticut colonies, though it was on Long Island. A few years prior to that, in 1640, the first settlers had found whales stranded on the beach, and whaling soon became such an industry that a little later in 1672, an East Hampton man, James Loper, was invited to Nantucket to teach the art to the inhabitants. As East Hampton grew, its cooking, in the New England tradition, grew with it and gradually adapted refinements of its own.

There was the old standby, samp, for example. Coastwise skippers used to swear they could tell when they were nearing East Hampton by its appetizing aroma. Samp for Sunday had become an old Long Island custom. Most of the day was spent at church and Sunday school and no unnecessary work was to be done on Sundays. A native now in his sixties, tells how samp was prepared when he was a boy: "We took dry seasoned field corn, put it in a hollowed oak log and pounded it with an iron bolt flattened at the end. This cracked the kernels; then we winnowed it. A quart of samp (nowadays you might ask for big hominy at the store) was put to soak Saturday night, together with a handful of white beans and a two-pound piece of salt pork, streak o' fat and streak o' lean. On Sunday morning it was put on the stove, and by the time church was over the samp was done. (**Note.** Fifty years ago it was morning up to 8 a.m., after that, it was forenoon.) Then we had a few boiled potatoes, and topped off with pie, baked in large quantities every Saturday. Monday, being washday, we had whatever was left over from Sunday."

BOILED MACARONI [1549]

Macaroni is made from semolina, milled from durum wheat, that specialized hard winter grain, grown mostly in Minnesota and the Dakotas, which contains practically all the vitamin and mineral elements present in durum wheat itself. According to the legend, Gio Cico was chef in an Italian prince's palace and was always in search for novelties for the prince's table.

One day he presented a dish made from a paste brought by Marco Polo from far away China. His Majesty enjoyed it so much that he exclaimed "Cari!" (meaning "dear"). He took a second helping, then enthusiastically he exclaimed "ma Caroni." ("O but how very dear.") And so what made the prince exclaim "ma Caroni" became "macaroni" for all the world.

To cook, drop broken macaroni into a saucepan containing rapidly boiling salted water to cover generously and boil steadily for 15 minutes, or until tender. Drain. Your macaroni is then ready to eat plain or use, according to recipe directions.

MACARONI ALL' AGLIO   [1550]
Macaroni with Garlic

This recipe is for adventurers with stout hearts and stomachs. It is called macaroni *all' aglio*, and that means garlic in the ascendant. One boils the macaroni—in any form, for no one will have a chance to think about such details. Then fry 25 plump kernels of garlic in olive oil with minced basil and parsley.

When the twenty-five garlic kernels are fried golden brown and soft, mash them to a smooth paste with a fork. If the oil has been absorbed in the paste, add ½ cup more, then enough tomato paste to make sufficient sauce for the dish of macaroni. In this instance, even grated Parmesan cheese is omitted, which is significant. When the sauce is ready, place the boiled macaroni on a hot platter, mix the sauce into it thoroughly and serve.

Macaroni all' aglio is said to be a swift and sure cure for the common cold and garlic is known to be highly nourishing and an appetizer and tonic.

MACARONI ALLA CREMA   [1551]
Creamed Macaroni

Boil macaroni in the usual way, or as indicated on the package. The Italian cooks keep their macaroni, in fact all the alimentary pastes, underdone, i.e. "al dente" meaning cracking under the teeth. Drain thoroughly, transfer to a heated, deep platter, and drench it with melted butter, tossing well. Then pour over 2 cups of cream sauce (No. 258), after dredging the macaroni with a liberal amount of freshly grated cheese. For special occasions substitute scalded, thick, sweet cream for the cream sauce. Blend thoroughly and serve with grated Parmesan cheese in a separate dish or turn into a casserole, cover with buttered crumbs and brown in the oven. This is a fattening dish, but it is also a dish de luxe.

MACARONI AND CHEESE CUSTARD   [1552]

Cook 1 cup of uncooked macaroni (broken small) according to directions on package or until tender. Slice thinly 1 medium-sized onion, 1 medium-sized green pepper, and ½ cup of peeled, fresh mushrooms, and cook them in ⅓ cup of butter or margarin till soft but not brown, over a gentle flame, stirring constantly. Pour 1½ cups of scalded milk over 1 cup of soft bread crumbs, and stir into the onion-green pepper mixture, mixing well. Next work in 4 well-beaten eggs, stirring and mixing very thoroughly. Season to taste with salt, pepper and a little nutmeg, and pour over the cooked well drained macaroni. Set the dish in a pan of hot water and bake in a moderate oven (325° F.) for 25 to 30 minutes, or till custard is firm and set. Serve at once.

MACARONI ALLA TITA RUFFO [1553]
Macaroni with mushrooms and chicken livers

Cook ½ pound of macaroni in salted boiling water keeping it slightly underdone. Drain. Keep hot. Cover 6 nice chicken livers with cold water; bring to the boiling point, and drain at once. Add more fresh cold water to barely cover, bring to a boil, and simmer 10 minutes. Drain and chop.

Peel and slice ¼ pound of fresh mushrooms, and sauté over a low flame, in 2 tablespoons of butter for 4 to 5 minutes, stirring occasionally. Have ready 2 cups of Béchamel Sauce (No. 259). Combine the chopped, cooked macaroni, chicken livers, and cooked mushrooms with the hot Béchamel Sauce. Taste for seasoning. Heat well, and serve at once with grated Parmesan cheese.

MACARONI AU GRATIN [1554]

Cook ½ pound of macaroni in a large amount of salted water about 12 to 15 minutes, or until tender. (The time of cooking macaroni, and in fact any kind of paste, cannot be exactly defined, since it varies with the age, and quality of the paste.) Drain and cut macaroni into one-inch pieces. Add ½ cup of minced, well-drained, canned red pimiento, 2 tablespoons of grated onion, 2 tablespoons of finely minced parsley (or chives in season), 1 pint of scalded creamy milk, or hot, thin white or cream sauce, salt, pepper and nutmeg to taste and ¼ cup of butter, added bit by bit. Mix thoroughly. Turn into a buttered baking dish, sprinkle the top with buttered crumbs, or equal parts of crumbs and grated cheese. Bake in a moderate oven (325–350° F.) 30 to 35 minutes. Serve at once.

MACARONI PIE [1555]

Cook ½ package of macaroni in boiling salted water until tender, about 12 to 15 minutes. Drain well and keep hot. Chop finely ½ cup of green pepper and slice thinly ½ cup of peeled fresh mushrooms, using both caps and stems; cook in 3 tablespoons of butter or margarin over a low flame until delicately colored, stirring frequently. Add 1 tablespoon of flour, and blend well. Then stir in 2 cups of boiling water, combined with 3 tablespoons of Pique Seasoning and 1 teaspoon of Worcestershire sauce, and cook until mixture just begins to thicken. Season to taste with mixed salt, pepper, thyme and nutmeg, add 2 tablespoons of grated onion and 1 tablespoon of lemon juice. Bring to a boil, remove from the fire and stir in 2 cups of cooked meat (any kind), cubed small, the chopped macaroni, and ½ cup of well drained cooked or canned peas. Turn into a deep pie dish; cover with pastry; make a few holes on top to allow escape of steam, brush with milk and bake in a hot oven (325° F.) for 10 minutes; lower the heat, and continue baking 20 minutes longer. Serve at once. If desired, use cheese pastry instead of plain crust.

MACARONI SOUFFLE RING [1556]

Cook ¼ pound of macaroni until tender (about 15 minutes) in rapidly boiling salted water containing 1 large bay leaf, 4 or 5 thin slices of onion, 4 or 5 sprigs of parsley and 2 whole cloves. Drain, discard the bay leaf, and so forth and chop macaroni very fine. Set aside. Peel and slice thinly ¼ pound of fresh mushrooms, using both stems and caps and cook in 2 tablespoons of butter or margarin for 2 or 3 minutes, over a low flame, stirring frequently. Add to macaroni, then mix in 1 tablespoon each of very finely chopped parsley, chives, green pepper and onion. Now sprinkle over all 2½ to 3 tablespoons of flour, blending well. Gradually stir in 1 cup of scalded sweet milk, to which has been added ⅓ teaspoon of grated lemon rind, and stir until mixture just begins to thicken. Remove from the fire, stir in briskly 3 egg yolks, adding one at a time, beating briskly after each addition and adding with the last yolk, ¼ pound of any preferred grated cheese. Taste for seasoning, then fold in the macaroni, and 3 stiffly beaten egg whites. Turn into a buttered ring mold; dot with 2 tablespoons of sweet butter, set the mold in a pan of hot water and bake in a moderate oven (375–400° F.) for 45–50 minutes. Loosen with a spatula unmold on a round, hot platter and fill center with any creamed food, such as fish, meat, mushrooms, sweetbreads, chicken, and so forth. If ring is unfilled, serve with tomato sauce.

BOILED NOODLES [1557]

Drop 1 pound package of noodles or ¾ pound of homemade noodles into a saucepan containing rapidly boiling salted water, using at least 2½ quarts of water, and boil steadily until tender, or about 15 minutes, stirring occasionally with a long-handled fork or wooden spoon, so as to separate each noodle ribbon. Drain. The noodles are now ready to be prepared in many ways, or maybe served plain, stirring in plenty of butter and cheese, and seasoning to taste with a little pepper and nutmeg.

DEVILED CREAMED NOODLES AU GRATIN [1558]

Cook 2 tablespoons of minced onions in 3 tablespoons of butter or margarin until just onion begins to brown; sprinkle in 2½ to 3 tablespoons of flour, and blend well. Gradually stir in 3 cups of scalded milk, and cook, stirring constantly, until thickened. Add a small can of deviled ham or potted meat; season to taste with salt and pepper if necessary, 1 teaspoon of Worcestershire sauce, ½ teaspoon of dry mustard and a few drops of Tabasco sauce. Pour this sauce over ½ pound of noodles, cooked in the usual way and well drained, and toss to thoroughly blend and mix. Turn noodles into a buttered baking dish, sprinkle with ½ cup of bread crumbs and grated cheese in equal parts, sprinkle with melted butter, and bake in a moderate oven (350° F.) for 20 to 25 minutes or until crumbs and cheese are browned. Serve at once.

EGG NOODLE RING CLUB STYLE [1559]

Boil 1 package of egg noodles or its equivalent of homemade egg noodles for 10 to 12 minutes in 3½ quarts of rapidly boiling salted water. Drain well. Beat 5 egg yolks thoroughly and stir into the hot, drained noodles, then mix in ½ cup of hot Béchamel Sauce. (No. 259.) When slightly cooled, fold in 5 stiffly beaten egg whites. Pack in a buttered ring mold; press down well and bake 30 minutes in a moderate oven, unmold on a heated platter, and fill center with creamed shrimps, curried fish, chicken or eggs. Dust with a little paprika and serve at once.

FRENCH BUTTERED NOODLES [1560]

Cook 2 cups of broken homemade egg noodles (No. 1563) in boiling salted water to generously cover, until tender, or about 12 to 15 minutes. Drain thoroughly but do not make the mistake that so many do, of rinsing the noodles. (This applies also to macaroni, spaghetti or any other kind of pastes, unless indicated.) Cream ⅓ to ½ cup of sweet butter, and beat in 3 egg yolks, one at a time, creaming well after each addition, then beat with rotary beater until mixture is of the consistency of mayonnaise. Place noodles in top of double boiler or over a bainmarie; let the water in the bottom part of the double boiler steam, but not actually boil; gradually add the well-creamed butter-egg yolk mass and mix thoroughly with a wooden spoon. Now fold in ½ to ⅔ cup of freshly grated Swiss or Gruyère cheese. Sprinkle ⅓ cup of grated cheese in a hot serving dish, spread the noodle mixture over, and sprinkle with another ⅓ cup of cheese. Serve immediately.

FRIED EGG NOODLES [1561]

Boil 1 package of noodles or its equivalent of homemade noodles in the usual way until tender, and drain thoroughly. Melt ⅓ cup of butter or margarin in a frying pan; stir in the noodles, then pour over them 3 eggs beaten with 3 tablespoons of cold milk or thin cream. Fry to a delicate brown, stirring almost constantly, over a low flame. Serve at once.

FRIED EGG NOODLES, CHINESE STYLE [1562]
Ju-Mein

Boil in salted water 2 cups of broken, fine egg noodles until tender, or about 12 to 15 minutes, exact time depending on freshness of noodles, drain and rinse under cold water faucet. Spread out on a platter and chill thoroughly in refrigerator. When ready to serve, heat 1 quart of cooking oil or fat in a heavy, deep, 10-inch frying pan to 380–390° F. or until it will brown a cube of bread in 30 seconds. Drop in ⅛ of the cold, cooked noodles, separating them with the tines of a fork, if necessary. Cook until golden brown. Skim out with a perforated skimmer, drain on absorbent paper and keep hot while frying the remaining noodles.

HOMEMADE EGG NOODLES [1563]

Break 2 eggs into a cup; add 2 half shells of ice cold water and 1 teaspoon of salt; mix lightly. Sift 1½ cups of bread flour into a mixing bowl; make a hollow in the center; pour the egg-water mixture into this, and with the handle of a knife stir in one direction until dough is so stiff that stirring is difficult. Then add ½ cup (more or less) of sifted bread flour if needed. Turn the dough on to a floured board and knead until smooth and elastic; then roll out as thin as possible, turning and lifting the dough to prevent its sticking to the board. Now lift the dough very carefully, flour the board lightly and let the dough stand half an hour to dry. If a noodle cutter is available, run it evenly across the dough and shake noodle lengths apart. If no cutter is at hand, cut the dough into two portions and roll each up like a jelly roll; slice thin or wide as desired, shaking the slices apart. Let the noodles dry a few minutes before boiling in the usual way, that is, in rapidly boiling salted water for 12 to 15 minutes.

HOMEMADE GREEN NOODLES [1564]

Mash 3 cups of boiled potatoes with a fork, then rub through a sieve. Add 2 whole fresh eggs, a little parsley, 2 or 3 tablespoons of grated onion or 5 or 6 chopped scallions, with salt to taste. Mix thoroughly and divide into six parts. Make a noodle dough as indicated in recipe No. 1563. Divide this also into six parts, and roll into rounds. Put a portion of the potato mixture on one half of each round, turn the other half over, and moisten and pinch the edges firmly together. Drop the noodles into rapidly boiling salted water and cook for 12 to 15 minutes. Drain, pour brown butter over them, and serve on a heated platter.

NOODLES AMANDINE [1565]

Blanch ½ cup of almonds; skin, cut into thin slivers and sauté in butter or margarin until crisp and golden brown. Meanwhile, peel, and slice thin ½ pound of fresh mushrooms, using both stems and caps, and cook in 1¾ to 2 tablespoons of butter or margarin over a gentle flame for 4 or 5 minutes, stirring frequently; then add 2 tablespoons of grated onion, or finely minced shallots, if available. Combine the almonds and mushroom mixture and gradually stir in 2 generous cups of rich cream sauce (No. 258), adding a little more cream, if needed. Cook 1 package of noodles or its equivalent of homemade noodles (No 1563) and drain. Toss the noodles in the sauce; turn into a deep, heated platter, and sprinkle with ¾ cup of grated Swiss cheese. Serve at once.

NOODLE RING AND SAUSAGE CREOLE [1566]

Make an Egg Noodle Ring Style (No. 1559). Unmold on a heated, round platter; fill center with 4 cups of Creole Sauce (No. 1041–42) and top the sauce with 6 individual sausage cakes.

SOUTHERN CORN MEAL NOODLES [1567]

Scald 2 cups of corn meal with sufficient boiling salted water to make a smooth, moderately stiff mush, then stir in gradually 1 cup of bread flour, sifted with 1 tablespoon of baking powder and ¾ teaspoon of salt, mixing well. Beat in 1 large, well-beaten egg, with 1 rounded tablespoon of butter, lard or margarin. Roll out as thinly as possible, as for ordinary noodles, and cut as indicated for No. 1563 Homemade Egg Noodles. Cook as ordinary noodles.

VIENNESE NOODLES [1568]

Cook 1 package of noodles or its equivalent of homemade egg noodles (No. 1563) until tender; drain well and combine with ¾ cup of cooked, ground lean ham, mixed with 1 pint of scalded, seasoned heavy sour cream. Turn into a buttered earthenware casserole; cover with ½ pound of sieved cottage cheese, and bake in a slow oven (300–325° F.) for 20 minutes. Serve as a main dish.

COOKING SPAGHETTI [1569]

One of the most delectable of wheat foods, the nutritious pasta of Italy, that comes to us most often as macaroni, spaghetti and vermicelli, may be served in any or every course of a dinner from soup to savory, as garnish, vegetable, entrée, dessert, or even a piquant and truly British savory in ramekins.

The best spaghetti (whose definition is little cords, while vermicelli means "little worms") is made, as already stated, from the glutinous semolina meal, ground from the hard durum wheat of southern Europe and of this continent, and, oddly enough, some of our Italian immigrants never ate it before coming to this country, but regarded it as a luxury of the rich, and had to content themselves with the sustaining ration of *polenta*, which is corn meal.

Between the simplest and the most elaborate sauces there is a vast host of comparatively insipid, uninspiring forms; and it is a sorry reflection on our easy acceptance of things put before us that most of the ready-made preparations are merely palatable blendings of tomato paste and cheese, calculated neither to offend nor unduly excite the unsophisticated taste of the multitude.

Spaghetti sauce should be made with the utmost care. It may be either mildly or highly seasoned, but it *must* contain tomatoes and onions as well as meat. Garlic is almost always present, too, and does a good deal for the flavor of the sauce. Grated Parmesan cheese is the orthodox topping and mixing for spaghetti and sauce.

Drop spaghetti into rapidly boiling previously salted water, and cook 10 to 12 minutes, or until tender, but not mushy. If the long sticks of spaghetti are used, place the ends in the boiling water first and coil them around the pan as they soften. Long spaghetti is much to be preferred, especially if it is being prepared for a party occasion. An eight-ounce package is sufficient for six portions. Always drain cooked spaghetti thoroughly.

SPAGHETTI ALLA BOLOGNESE [1570]
(Serves 12 generously)

Cut ½ pound of beef tenderloin into very small dice; peel and chop ½ pound of mushrooms, using both caps and stems. Melt 1 tablespoon of butter in a saucepan, add 1 onion finely chopped and cook gently till brown. Add the diced meat and fry gently, then add the mushrooms, a clove of mashed garlic, 1 glass of sherry wine, 1 tablespoon of tomato purée and two cups of brown sauce (No. 1017), with salt and pepper to taste. Let all cook together over low heat for 25 to 30 minutes. Taste for seasoning and just before serving stir in ¼ cup of sweet butter. Pour over the spaghetti and serve plenty of grated Parmesan cheese separately.

SPAGHETTI A LA CAMPANIA [1571]

Fry 1 medium sized onion light brown in 2 tablespoons of butter blended with 2 tablespoons of olive oil; stir in 5 fresh tomatoes, peeled, and coarsely chopped, 6 finely minced anchovy filets, previously well washed and dried, 1 tablespoon of finely chopped parsley, ⅛ teaspoon of powdered basil, ⅛ teaspoon each of powdered thyme and nutmeg, and 1 clove of garlic, mashed to a pulp; season to taste with very little salt and generously with black pepper, and lastly add ½ generous cup of rich beef broth. Bring to a boil, lower the heat and simmer gently for 25 minutes. Just before serving, stir in 3 tablespoons of grated Parmesan cheese, pour over the cooked, well drained spaghetti, and pass grated Parmesan cheese, to be sprinkled on each helping.

SPAGHETTI ALLA CARUSO [1572]
(*Original recipe as prepared by this writer*)

Tomato paste is precious, invaluable. Buy some good Italian tomato paste if you would honor a party of chosen guests with an authentic dish of spaghetti, but buy also 3 pounds of good lean beef, a veal knuckle, a slice of ham, some fat bacon and leeks, celery, carrots, parsley, chervil . . . and, of course, plenty of garlic. Thrifty Italians grow sweet basil in their gardens, on their kitchen window sills; and you should get some of the fresh herb if you possibly can; otherwise, use a pinch of dried basil.

Fry 4 slices of diced bacon and ¼ pound of lean ham in an iron skillet, then chop them and put them into a large stew pot. Dredge the beef lightly with powdered sugar, and sear it fiercely in the hot bacon fat, turning it over and over till it is nearly black and all crusty and glistening. Put it in the stew pot with the chopped ham and bacon, the well washed, split veal knuckle, 1 whole bunch of well cleaned and washed leeks, 3 stalks of celery, scraped and chopped, 2 carrots, scraped and chopped, 1 tablespoon each of parsley and chervil, also finely chopped, 2 large bay leaves, tied with 2 sprigs of thyme, 2 cloves of garlic, sliced thinly; but, if you have conscientious scruples, you may substitute six shallots. Season with a tablespoon of salt, one of black pepper, 4 whole cloves, and either the fresh or dry sweet basil, then pour in boiling water to cover; bring to a boil, and simmer 3 or 4 hours, or until the fiber of the meat is broken down and all its essence is in the sauce. Strain through a colander, pressing through all the soft pulp and leaving behind only the lumps and shreds. Add 1 cup of the tomato paste and ½ cup of Marsala, sherry, or Madeira wine.

Now, take one medium truffle from a tin, wash and brush it, slice it thinly, and cut the slices into julienne strips. Peel ½ pound of fresh mushrooms, chop the stems and slice the caps thinly in transverse sections. Add all these to the sauce and simmer very gently, while the spaghetti is boiling.

Using a large kettle of salted boiling water, put in 2 packages of whole length spaghetti, without breaking. Twelve to 18 minutes is the time depending on the hardness of the paste. Italians—and Caruso was one—when I prepared this dish of dishes in the kitchen of the 9th floor, at the old Knickerbocker Hotel, prefer it not too tender, not too soft; just *al dente*, that is, a little crackling, a little chewy; but some Americans like it as soft as boiled rice. While it boils, grate your cheese, rubbing the granite-like block of Parmesan furiously on a fine grater till you have a mountain of light and feathery flakes. The dry and tasteless grated Parmesan that comes in bottles or cartons is an insult to spaghetti and to cheese. Incidentally, if Parmesan is a bit too much for you, in bouquet and tang, you may grate a little Swiss, Gruyère or old Cheddar along with it.

When done, drain the spaghetti, then pile it on a huge platter and pour the golden bronze sauce over it with luxurious abandon; be sure to make a small mountain of the cheese in the middle, and have an extra dish of cheese on the table. How does one eat it? Well, an Italian can turn the trick with elegance, by catching up the strands on a fork and twirling them into a neat bolus in the bowl of a soup spoon. Try it.

SPAGHETTI ALLA FIORENTINA [1573]

Put 3 tablespoons of olive oil and 4 tablespoons of sweet butter in an earthenware casserole; add 3 cloves of garlic mashed to a pulp and 12 anchovy filets, washed then dried and shredded in thin slices. Fry 2 or 3 minutes, stirring constantly with a wooden spoon, then pour in 1 No. 2 can of Italian tomatoes, liquid and solid; add a bouquet garni composed of 2 bay leaves, 8 sprigs of fresh parsley, 1 sprig of thyme and 1 sprig of fennel or basil, all tied together with white kitchen thread, and cook gently for 15 minutes, stirring occasionally. Meantime parboil and drain 12 chicken livers. Chop them, stir into ½ cup of tomato juice, and add to the pot. Cover and simmer gently for 25 minutes. Discard the bouquet garni; taste the sauce for salt and pepper, and pour sizzling hot over a platter of boiled spaghetti. Sprinkle with grated Parmesan cheese and serve with additional cheese.

SPAGHETTI WITH MEAT BALLS HOME STYLE [1574]

Cook ½ pound of spaghetti in rapidly boiling salted water until tender. Meantime, combine 1 pound of hamburger, ⅓ cup of soft bread crumbs, 2 tablespoons of Pique Seasoning and black pepper to taste. Add 1 tablespoon each of grated onion, chopped parsley and chopped green pepper, and blend thoroughly by putting mixture through food chopper. Form very lightly into 12 small balls, and brown on all sides in 2 or 3 tablespoons of bacon dripping. Drain well and keep hot. Heat 1 No. 2 can of tomatoes, add 1 bay leaf, 1 sprig of thyme, and when boiling, strain through a fine-meshed sieve into a small saucepan. Add the meat balls, let come to a boil, and turn into a depression made in the cooked, well-drained spaghetti. Sprinkle generously with grated Parmesan and American cheese, mixed in equal parts. Serve at once with additional grated cheese.

GNOCCHI—LASAGNE—RAVIOLI [1575]

Gnocchi is made from a basis of corn meal mush or from a potato and flour mixture. If you call the first "Corn Meal Mush," there is no element of interest. If you label it *Gnocchi*, those who know this dish will have their appetites aroused, and the others will taste it with curiosity and expectation of pleasure. *Gnocchi*, as the name indicates, is an Italian specialty, and while it is generally served with cheese or cheese sauce, it is also frequently offered with a highly seasoned tomato sauce or any rich sauce similar to that used for spaghetti.

Lasagne is a paste made into a wide, flat ribbon-like type of spaghetti, usually broken into pieces and cooked in boiling salted water.

Ravioli is of two kinds: the meat-filled and the cheese-filled. To produce them the baker rolls his dough thin, to spread over a board with oval depressions, one hundred to a big square. Carefully the dough is pressed into the small ovals. Now the filling is added: another sheet of dough is laid over all this and pressed down with the rolling pin. Upside down the baker turns the load of a hundred little bumps of filling cased between two sheets of thinly rolled dough. Then, with a cutting wheel he "hemstitches" the dough lengthwise, then crosswise to shape these delicious pin-cushions called ravioli.

GNOCCHI ALLA ROMANA [1576]
(Unfilled)

Sift ½ cup of corn meal gradually into 2 cups of rapidly boiling salted water, and stir constantly over direct heat until mush thickens and boils. Gradually add 1 cup of scalded milk, stirring briskly, and cook over hot water for 30 minutes. Pour into a wet square pan to a depth of ½-inch, and chill until firm. Cut into diamond-shaped pieces; arrange alternately with ½ cup of grated Parmesan cheese in a buttered or oiled baking dish, seasoning each layer with salt and pepper; pour over some milk or tomato sauce; cover and bake in a moderate oven (375–400° F.) for 30 to 35 minutes; uncover and continue baking until lightly browned. Serve at once.

HOMEMADE GNOCCHI PIEMONTESE STYLE [1577]

Boil 1 pound of pared potatoes until tender and, while still hot, rub through a ricer. Add ¾ cup of flour, 1 whole egg and 1 egg yolk, and season to taste with salt and pepper. Blend thoroughly; shape into small balls the size of a walnut; flatten out in the shape of cylinders and poach in boiling salted water, chicken stock, milk or tomato bouillon for about 10 minutes. Drain and serve with tomato, brown or mushroom sauce, as well as grated Parmesan cheese.

HOMEMADE RAVIOLI NAPOLI STYLE [1578]

Sift 1½ cups of bread flour once; add ½ teaspoon of salt and resift. Combine with one large egg and enough warm water to moisten, to make a stiff dough. Knead until smooth; cover and let stand while preparing the filling. For this combine ¼ cup of soft bread crumbs, ½ cup of well drained, cooked and chopped spinach, 1 slightly beaten egg, and ¼ cup of raw, finely ground beef, mixing thoroughly Moisten with a little meat stock and season to taste with salt and pepper. Roll the dough out as thin as paper. Cut in strips 2½ to 3 inches wide. Drop scant teaspoonfuls of the filling on half strips about 2 inches apart. Lay a second strip of paste over the filled lower part; wet, then press edges together and cut apart.

Cook 18 to 20 minutes in highly seasoned chicken or meat stock or fish stock, if filling is fish. Sift out the ravioli with a perforated skimmer, draining well; arrange on a heated platter, and sprinkle generously with grated cheese.

Note. Almost any available left-over cooked fish, fowl, meat, or game may be used in the filling. Serve at once with rich spicy tomato sauce.

HOMEMADE TAGLIATELLI [1579]

Either buy or make about 1½ pounds of Italian tagliatelli. To make, use 1 whole egg to every ½ cup of flour with a pinch of salt. Make the dough quite stiff, roll out and cut into very, very fine strips. For a good sauce which goes well with these kinds of Italian pastes, proceed as follows: Heat 1 scant half-cup of fine Italian olive oil; drop one kernel of garlic into it and let cook till nicely browned. Discard the garlic. To the oil remaining in the saucepan, add 1 No. 2 can of Italian tomato paste and stir till dissolved and creamy; then stir in 1½ pounds of finely chopped or ground lean raw pork, and cook gently for 15 minutes, stirring frequently. In a separate saucepan combine 1 No. 2 can of Italian tomatoes, or its equivalent of fresh tomatoes, peeled, and coarsley chopped, 1 large bay leaf, 1 sprig of fennel, one of sweet basil, 3 or 4 sprigs of fresh parsley all finely chopped, with a pinch each of thyme and mace; bring to a boil, discard the bay leaf, and add tomato to the first mixture. Simmer covered, very gently for 45 minutes, stirring frequently. Season to taste with salt and black pepper. Meantime drop the *tagliatelli* in rapidly boiling salted water and cook about 10 minutes, or till tender. Drain thoroughly and arrange on a hot platter, between layers of sweet red pepper and grated Parmesan cheese. Pour the hot sauce over, sprinkle with grated Parmesan cheese and serve at once with additional grated Parmesan cheese.

LASAGNA AL' RICOTTA CHEESE [1580]

La Riccota Romana is another cheese made from the buttermilk of ewes. It is rich and creamy, very delicate and fragrant. It is eaten either as ordinary cream cheese, or, like the French cream cheese, with a little sugar or with fresh berries. In some parts of the Province of Rome, this cheese is eaten with powdered cinnamon or powdered coffee. Spread on thin strips of Italian bread, the Italians have it for breakfast with their café au lait. It makes an excellent sweet when cut in strips, dipped in flour, then in beaten egg yolk, and fried, then sprinkled with sugar. This cheese is found in almost every first-class Italian grocery or delicatessen store.

If you cannot find it, substitute pot cheese, but the results will not be the same.

Melt ¼ cup of butter or heat same amount of good olive oil in a saucepan; stir in 1 medium-sized onion and ¼ cup of hot water or still better, hot water to which has been added 1 teaspoon of Pique Seasoning, and cook until onion is soft, and liquid has completely evaporated. Stir in 3 tablespoons of olive oil, or good salad or cooking oil and cook, stirring constantly, till onions are golden brown. Add a 6-ounce can of Italian tomato paste, diluted with an equal amount of hot water, salt and black pepper to taste, 1 small clove of garlic, mashed to a pulp, and 1 scant tablespoon of sugar. Let this simmer gently while cooking the lasagna (wide, flat ribbon-like spaghetti). For this break ½ pound of lasagna into small pieces, drop into rapidly boiling salted water and cook for 18 to 20 minutes, or just until soft and no raw starchy taste remains. Wash in a colander under running hot water, and drain well.

Add 3 tablespoons of the water in which the lasagna was cooked to ½ pound of Riccotta cheese, and mix thoroughly. Have ready a generous ¾ cup of freshly grated Parmesan cheese, then proceed as follows:

Place a layer of the hot lasagna in a square or oblong earthenware baking dish. Then add a layer of the tomato sauce, a layer of the Riccotta cheese and a layer of grated Parmesan cheese; repeat till all the ingredients have been used, having the top layer Parmesan cheese. Place the dish under the flame of the broiling oven until top just begins to bubble and takes on a rich brown color. Serve at once with grated Parmesan cheese.

RICE [1581]

There are many varieties of rice produced in the United States. They are all, however, of three general types: long grain, medium grain, and short grain; with several grades of each type. The standards for these types are based principally on the color, cleanliness and wholesomeness of the kernels.

Rice is ideally suited for the basic energy dish of the lighter meals of the day. To this good foundation, add left-over meat, fish, eggs or vegetables, thus making more costly foods go farther.

Rice constitutes the staple food of a majority of the world's inhabitants and is much used in America. Rice is chiefly grown in Louisiana, Texas and South Carolina. In Oriental countries, it is the grain upon which life depends. More rice is planted, harvested and eaten each year than any other grain. Today, most of our supply of rice comes from Louisiana, Texas, Arkansas and California, where it was introduced over 200 years ago. Enough is raised in this part of the country to supply our own needs and to export some for the use of other countries.

We have as well a native wild rice, which is, however, different from the transplanted product. It is darker in color and has an individual flavor which makes it particularly suitable with game and poultry. Comparatively small quantities are grown in the United States, and for this reason wild rice is far more expensive than the staple rice we use every day.

There is also a rice called "converted rice" and again, "natural brown rice." This last cooks tender in 15 minutes, having the fluffy character and speckly dark look of wild crop. It has something, too, of the wild's smoky sweetness but nothing of its excessive price. This kind of rice is partly cooked, then dehydrated, but it still needs a quick rinse under running cold water.

HOW TO COOK RICE [1582]

Although it should be an easy matter to cook rice properly, not everyone seems to produce quite the right result. There are several "good" methods, all, according to their authors, the best. However, rice cooked by anyone of the following methods will give dry fluffy rice with each kernel distinct.

CHINESE STYLE [1583]

Wash rice until the water runs clear. Put 1 cup of washed rice in a large heavy pan; add 2 cups of cold water and 1 scant teaspoon of salt.

Cover, bring to a boil; reduce the heat to very low. Do not stir. When rice has cooked for 40 to 45 minutes, test a few grains by rubbing them between fingers. When done, cook uncovered for a minute or so to eliminate the steam.

DOUBLE-BOILER STYLE [1584]

Wash rice until the water runs clear. Put 1 cup of well washed rice, 2 cups of cold water and 1 scant teaspoon of salt in top of double boiler. Cover; bring to a boil over direct heat. Do not stir. When boiling, put top of double boiler over *not more* than 1½ inches of gently bubbling water in bottom part of double boiler. Cook over low heat. When rice has cooked 40 to 45 minutes over water (replenishing with hot water as needed) without being stirred or uncovered, it will be tender, dry and fluffy. Do not drain or rinse.

BOILING METHOD [1585]

Wash rice until the water runs clear. Add 1 cup of washed rice slowly to 2 quarts of rapidly boiling well salted water, while stirring gently with a kitchen fork. Reduce the heat. When rice grains are tender, (after 18 to 20 minutes of cooking) and have no hard center when pressed between thumb and first finger, drain through colander. Pour hot running water through rice in colander till water runs clear, making sure that all rice grains are thoroughly rinsed and separated. Place colander of rinsed rice in saucepan containing hot water; cover with cloth, or put cloth covered rice in a warm oven for a short time to dry a little.

RICE COOKED IN HARD WATER [1586]

This is never as white as that cooked in soft water. One teaspoon of lemon juice, one-half teaspoon of cream of tartar, or one tablespoon of vinegar may be used in hard water to insure a snowy-white color in cooked rice.

REHEATED RICE [1587]

Left-over rice may be added to boiling salted water, milk, or any kind of meat or fish or poultry stock, cooked for 5 minutes, then drained and allowed to dry out and fluff, or left-over rice may be reheated in the oven by adding a little water, milk, or stock to the pan, covering and heating until the grains are thoroughly hot through.

BROWN RICE OR WILD RICE   [1588]

This may be cooked the same as white rice, but the time required for cooking is at least twice as long. Either may be soaked an hour in tepid water to soften the bran coats and shorten the cooking period.

Together with other Romans, Pompey used a cure-all made of 2 walnuts, 2 dried figs, 20 pounds of rice and some salt all pounded together.

CREOLE RICE   [1589]
Martinique

Cook 1 thinly sliced extra large onion, and 3 green peppers, thinly shredded and white seeds removed, in 4 tablespoons of butter for 5 or 6 minutes, over a gentle flame, stirring almost constantly. Gradually stir in 1 cup of rice, which has been washed until the water runs clear, then well drained, and cook, stirring constantly, until rice begins to turn a little yellowish; add ¼ pound of fresh mushrooms, peeled and sliced, using both stems and caps, 1 cup of canned tomatoes, or the equivalent of fresh tomatoes, peeled and chopped, ½ to ⅔ cup of olives, pitted and sliced, 1 teaspoon of salt, ¼ teaspoon of freshly ground black pepper, 1 bouquet garni composed of 2 small bay leaves, 1 sprig of thyme, 8 sprigs of parsley and 2 sprigs of green celery tops, all tied together with white kitchen thread, 2 whole cloves and 1 clove of garlic, mashed to a pulp. Mix well. Now stir in 2 cups of boiling water to which has been added ¼ cup of Pique Seasoning. Cover and simmer gently for 45 minutes, in a moderate oven (325–350° F.) without stirring. Serve directly from the casserole after discarding the bouquet garni and tasting for seasoning.

CURRY OF RICE HOME STYLE   [1590]

Wash 1 cup of rice until the water runs clear, then drain. Cook 1½ tablespoons of finely chopped onions, 2 tablespoons of finely chopped green pepper, ½ kernel of garlic, mashed to a pulp, and 2 tablespoons of finely chopped parsley in 4 tablespoons of butter or margarin for 2 minutes, stirring constantly; stir in the rice and cook over a very bright flame for 5 minutes, stirring constantly. Remove the pan from the fire and add 1 bouquet garni composed of 1 large bay leaf, 1 sprig of thyme, 2 whole cloves and 1 sprig of dill (if not available in the fresh state, use about ⅛ teaspoon of powdered dill) all tied together with white kitchen thread; season to taste with pepper only, then stir in 2½ cups of meat stock, or still better, 2 cups of boiling water and ½ cup of Pique Seasoning, to which has been added 1½ or 2 tablespoons of curry powder (more or less, according to taste). Cover the saucepan or casserole and bring to a boil. Let boil steadily, without stirring, for 10 minutes; lower the flame and cook very slowly for 35 to 40 minutes. Curry of rice is appropriate for service with any kind of meat, fish, poultry and game, including left-overs.

MEXICAN BURGER RICE [1591]

Wash 1 cup of rice until water runs clear; wash ⅔ cup of raisins in hot water, drain, then chop coarsely. Heat 3 tablespoons of good cooking oil or butter in a frying pan; stir in the washed rice and fry to a light brown, over a gentle flame, stirring constantly to prevent burning. In another frying pan, heat 3 tablespoons of oil or butter, and stir in 1 pound of hamburger, 1 medium-sized onion, finely chopped, 1 kernel of garlic, mashed to a pulp, with 1 tablespoon of chili powder which has been dissolved in ¼ cup of cold water (more or less, according to taste), and continue cooking for 10 minutes, stirring occasionally. Season to taste with salt, stir in 1 cup of canned tomato pulp and cook 5 minutes longer, stirring once or twice; then mix in the rice and raisins. Turn mixture into a greased baking dish; pour over 1¼ cups of hot water mixed with ¼ cup of Pique Seasoning; lay 4 strips of bacon over the top, and bake for 45 minutes, in a moderate oven (350° F.). Should bacon get too brown, cover the dish during the last part of the cooking. Serve directly from the baking dish.

An Arab when asked by an arrogant Englishman why he didn't eat his rice with a spoon instead of his fingers, said: "My fingers have never entered any mouth but mine; can you say that of your spoon?"

NEAR EAST BOILED RICE [1592]

Soak 1 cup of rice overnight in salted cold water, and next morning wash it until the water runs clear. Drain, place in a casserole, just cover with cold water and boil until the rice kernels will crush easily between thumb and forefinger. Remove from the fire; turn into a colander rinse with hot water and shake lightly to separate the grains. Drain well; turn into a heated fire-proof serving dish; cover with a cloth and heat in a slow oven (275–300° F.) just before serving pour over it ½ cup of melted sweet butter. Again set in a slow oven until the rice absorbs the butter; sprinkle with paprika and serve at once as a side dish or a substitute for potatoes. Fine with fish.

RICE BORDER FRENCH STYLE [1593]

Wash 1 cup of rice in cold water until water runs clear, then drain. Place in a saucepan; add 3 cups of White Stock (No. 185), and cook for

30 to 35 minutes, then stir in 2 tablespoons of sweet butter, and continue cooking for 15 to 20 minutes longer. Beat 3 egg yolks with 3 tablespoons of sweet cream and 1 teaspoon of salt, and stir into the rice. Rub a border mold (ring mold) with butter; pack the rice firmly into it; let stand 5 minutes in a warm (not hot) place and invert onto a hot, round platter. Fill the center with any creamed meat, fish, sweetbreads, kidneys, fish, shellfish or vegetable.

RICE CROQUETTES I (FRENCH STYLE)   [1594]

Steam 2 cups of cooked rice in a double boiler, if necessary, adding a little hot sweet cream to soften it. Then add 2 well-beaten egg yolks, alternately with 2 tablespoons of sweet butter, and season to taste with salt and cayenne pepper, 1½ tablespoons each of finely chopped parsley and onion. Blend thoroughly and heat to boiling point. Remove from hot water. Spread on a cold, flat platter; take portions the size of a large egg and shape into croquettes, cones, cylinders, and so forth; Dip in seasoned fine bread crumbs, then in beaten egg and again in crumbs. Chill. When ready to serve, place a few at a time in the frying wire basket and plunge into hot, deep fat (300° F.), cooking them until delicately browned all over. Drain on absorbent paper. Serve as a side dish. For Lenten season serve with Egg sauce (Nos. 1051–52).

RICE CROQUETTES II (AMERICAN STYLE)   [1595]

Mix 2 cups of cold (or hot) boiled rice with 1 tablespoon of finely minced parsley, 1 tablespoon of grated onion, and 1 cup of thick white sauce (No. 258), highly seasoned with salt and white pepper. Chill, shape as croquette, or in any desired shape; roll in bread crumbs, then in beaten egg and again in crumbs. Fry in hot, deep fat (390° F.) to a golden brown; drain on absorbent paper. Serve with any main dish instead of potatoes or as an entrée with cheese sauce, brown sauce or tomato sauce.

Half a cup of chopped nut meats may be substituted for the same amount of rice if desired.

RICE NESTS I (FRENCH STYLE)   [1596]

Prepare rice as for Rice Croquettes I (No. 1594–95), shape into 6 individual nests, and fry in hot, deep fat until delicately browned; drain and serve hot with a spoonful of red currant jelly or other red jelly, or mint jelly in each nest. Serve as an accompaniment to roast lamb, roast pork or roast chicken, duck or turkey.

RICE NESTS II (FRENCH STYLE) [1597]
Croustades or Cases or Baskets

Wash 1 cup of rice until water runs clear, and cook in rich chicken stock (No. 185) until tender. Drain and cool. When quite cold, mix with 1 cup of Béchamel sauce (No. 259); spread on a shallow pan to a depth of about two inches, cover with oiled paper and place a weight on top to make the mixture compact when cold. To form the nests, cut rice mixture into circles or oblong pieces of equal size and carefully hollow out the center of each to form a case. Dip each case in sieved bread crumbs, then in beaten egg mixed with a little cold water and slightly beaten to make it spread evenly. Roll again in sieved bread crumbs and chill for several hours before using. Fry in deep hot fat, like croquettes to a golden brown, and serve hot filled with any kind of rich creamed food. Use as an entrée or as a hot dish for luncheon, or serve cold, garnished with relishes, jelly, preserves, chutney, etc.

If preferred roll the fried nests in buttered crumbs and brown in a hot oven instead of frying.

In some parts of the Malay Peninsula, tag is played with a monkey "It" and the whole village competing. The winner gets the monkey and enough rice for a complete family dinner.

RICE VALENTIENNE [1598]

Wash 1 cup of rice until the water runs clear, then drain. Heat ½ cup of sweet butter or good olive oil in a shallow, heavy pan; stir in 2 tablespoons of grated onion and 2 tablespoons of ground raw, lean ham and cook slowly without browning, and stirring constantly, for 2 minutes. Stir in the rice and cook over a gentle flame, stirring constantly, until rice just begins to take on a yellowish color; then stir in 3 whole fresh tomatoes, peeled, seeded and coarsely chopped, 3 cups of rich, chicken broth, salt, and pepper to taste, 1 bouquet garni, composed of 1 large bay leaf, 8 sprigs of fresh parsley, 1 sprig of thyme and 2 sprigs of green celery leaves, all tied together with white kitchen thread, also 2 whole cloves, heads removed, 1 blade of garlic, and 1 blade of mace. Cover and cook in a moderate oven (350° F.) for 25 to 30 minutes, or until rice is tender. Discard the bouquet garni, and serve on a heated, deep platter as a accompaniment to braised veal, roast chicken, roast turkey, roast guinea hen or any kind of wild bird, venison, etc.

As the Western World boils its potatoes, so China boils its rice, solemnly and monotonously, day after day, and only the blasé Chinese who has taken on the ways of the effete foreign devils knows or cares anything about bread. Rice from morning to night, from the cradle to the grave, is the lot of the Chinese, and familiarity has not bred contempt. An aged horse munches its hay with the relish of a colt, and the venerable Chinese sage bends over his rice bowl with quiet gratification just as the illustrious Confucius did two thousand five hundred and some years ago.

It is the impatient and temperamental European who has refused to accept rice merely as bulk, roughage, or hay, and from Gibraltar to the Golden Horn the people have a thousand ways of transforming the grain into rich delicacies and confections. The pipau of the Near East is succulent, *arroz* (rice) figures in a hundred delectable dishes of the Iberian peninsula, in Havana, Mexico, and South American Republics, and *risotto* is as essentially Italian as spaghetti and *polenta*.

Risotto represents merely an admirable method of cooking rice, but in the hands of talented chefs, caterers and cordons bleus, it has come to mean something more complicated, usually found among the entrées on the menu.

If you would know *risotto* in its pristine innocence, wash 1 pound of rice in many waters, rubbing the grains between the hands as the Chinese do. Then proceed as follows:

RISOTTO ALLA MILANAISE [1599]
(*Serves 10*)

Wash and drain one pound of rice. Place in an iron skillet into which, if you have been initiated, pour ½ to ¾ cup of good olive oil, otherwise use butter; when it is hot, put in the rice. *Do not* fry it, but let it heat up slowly, and stir it lightly, gently, but constantly, with a wooden spoon or fork. Presently the white rice will begin to show a yellow tinge, and as it absorbs the oil or butter you must add more to keep it moist. Little by little, the grains take on a peculiar gloss; they begin to glisten like jewels. Do not let them scorch, but stir them about until each grain is a separate gilded oval, the color of ripe field corn. Then it is time to set about the completion of the risotto.

Have ready 1 quart of rich hot soup stock in which is steeped a large *chapon* of dry bread rubbed with garlic; add to the strained stock 2 tablespoons of minced onion or shallots, browned in butter or olive oil. Pour this hot stock slowly over the rice it; will drink it up thirstily. Keep pouring till the rice is well moistened, every grain covered by the stock, then season according to your own taste.

A tin of Italian tomato paste may be mixed with the stock and half a cup of grated Parmesan cheese stirred in; a small pinch of sweet basil is a novel touch. Some Italian and Spanish cooks use saffron pinch by pinch, but always with respectful care.

Transfer the risotto to a casserole, and put into a moderate oven (325–350° F.) for half an hour, removing it when the rice is soft, yet still firm, with the grains separate and distinct. Serve an abundance of grated cheese with it, and offer your guests a rich tomato sauce, for the thirsty rice will have absorbed most of the stock. The variations are limitless. It is excellent garnished with sliced *cervelat* or salami sausage, and some crisp, green watercress.

SAFFRON RICE AMERICAN STYLE [1600]

Wash 1 cup of rice until water runs clear, and slowly pour it into several quarts of briskly boiling salted water, adding the rice so slowly that the water will not cease to bubble. Cook for 20 minutes; then strain through a colander, and rinse under hot water. Put the pan in a warm oven or over boiling water to dry, and fluff the grains so that each is separate from the others. Just before serving, season to taste with salt and white pepper, then sprinkle with a generous pinch of saffron (more if desired) and ¼ cup of slightly melted butter mixed with 2 tablespoons each of finely chopped parsley and chives. Toss well together and serve at once.

WILD RICE [1601]

Wild rice, for many years a staple food of the Indians in the neighborhood of lakes and rivers in Minnesota, Wisconsin, Michigan and southern Canada, and a favorite of the wild duck, is gaining in popularity as a delicacy for the dinner table. It is now marketed, processed and shipped to all sections of the country. It is winning popular favor, while once only gourmets sought it.

Wild rice, known botanically as *Zizania aquatica*, is native of the United States. It is found in fresh water and brackish swamps from New England to Texas and North Dakota, with its center of abundance in Wisconsin and Minnesota. It grows in nearly every State east of the Rocky Mountains. It has no fewer than sixty popular names, and the fact that the greater number of them are Indian shows its close association with the red man. In Connecticut wild rice is known as *blackbird oats;* in Texas as *duck rice;* in Louisiana and Wisconsin, as *Frenchman's fool oats;* in Delaware and Pennsylvania as *Indian oats, Indian rice, marsh rice;* in North Carolina as *wild oats,* and so forth. Moreover wild rice bears eleven Japanese and Chinese names. It grows in both Japan and China.

The plant is the *folle avoine* of the French voyageurs and the *menomin* of the Northwest Indians. Indeed, it gave its name to one tribe—the Menominee—which means literally, wild rice men, a title derived from their use of wild rice. Formerly the tribe lived in the northern part of Wisconsin and adjacent territory of Michigan, chiefly along the Menominee River. It is now on a reservation near Green Bay, Wisconsin. There is a city and county of Menominee in Michigan, and also Menomonie, a city in Dunn county, Wisconsin. Wild rice has also given its name to lakes and other physical features.

The Indians harvested wild rice in a rather primitive, but nevertheless effective, way. While one squaw paddled her canoe among the rice beds, another, with a stick in each hand, bent the stalks over with one hand and with the other struck them, thus knocking the grain into the canoe. The rice was taken ashore and dried in the sun or over a fire, after which it was placed in a hole in the ground lined with the skin of an animal. It was threshed by a simple but effective method, trampling with the feet or beating with sticks. It was then winnowed in birchbark trays and stored for winter use in boxes or bags of skin or cloth.

Wild rice reaches its greatest size in the Southeastern States, where it may grow twelve feet high with a stalk two inches in diameter. It may grow not higher than three or four feet in its Northern range. On the whole, it prefers deep, rich, mucky soil. It reaches its greatest development at the hands of a truly gifted cook.

Wild rice has a legend. Until 1928 the Indian held traditional right to the harvest. Only the residents of the wild-rice areas and a few city sportsmen knew how tasty it was when served with wild duck and venison. It was the redman who discovered wild rice as a food. The story told me by the Ojibaways of Minnesota is perhaps one of the most authentic of early tribal legends.

The ghost of famine was a persistent winter visitor to their tribe. Daily they prayed the Great Creator to provide them a food that would give a reliable harvest. After many moons the spirit heard and the medicine man had a mysterious visitation. It was revealed that the lakes and streams were rich with grains waiting to be garnered for winter keeping. "Look to the seeds of sharp hulls," the spirit directed, "and beneath the husk find the sweet food."

Explicit directions were given for the harvesting; how to hull and parch the grains. Warning came too, that no man should touch the plants before the ripening. Solemn ritual was made of the harvest. The wrath of the Great Spirit, it was believed, would strike to death the brave who dared to touch a rice grain before maturity. When the day came tobacco was strewn on the water so that the Great Spirit could smoke in peace and would answer the prayer of the medicine man that his people should not suffer. Then the wild rice grains were shaken into slim canoes and the harvest was on.

Almost all the recipes adapted to white rice may be applied to wild rice.

WILD RICE WITH CHICKEN LIVERS [1602]

Wash 1 cup of wild rice in cold water till the water runs clear, then let it soak in cold water for 30 minutes. Meantime, wash, clean and mince 18 chicken livers. Heat ½ cup of butter or margarin and stir in 1½ cups of chopped onion, cooking over a low heat until nicely browned, stirring frequently; stir in the chicken livers and cook 3 or 4 minutes more. Now, stir in the well drained wild rice, and cook 5 minutes longer, stirring frequently. Add 3 cups of boiling water, with ½ cup of Pique Seasoning. Bring to a boil; transfer to a casserole, season to taste with salt, pepper and nutmeg, and add 1 bouquet garni composed of 1 large bay leaf, 8 sprigs of fresh parsley, 1 sprig of thyme and 2 sprigs of green celery leaves (tops), all tied together with white kitchen thread. Cover and simmer gently for 40 to 50 minutes, stirring frequently, or place an asbestos pad under the casserole and simmer gently without stirring. Taste for seasoning and serve directly from the casserole.

Note. Any other kind of liver, such as turkey, duck, or goose liver may be prepared in this delicious, economical and easy way.

WILD RICE IN MILK [1603]

Wash 1 cup of rice carefully in cold water; cover with boiling water and let stand 30 minutes. Drain, and repeat this process four times, using fresh boiling water each time, and adding the last time 2½ teaspoons of salt. Drain, cover with 1 quart of milk, or equal parts of scalded milk and thin cream; add also 1 bay leaf, 4 thin slices of onion, an inch piece of stick cinnamon, and pepper to taste. Cook 35 minutes, over a low flame, stirring frequently. There should be almost no milk left. Stir in ¼ cup of sweet butter and serve as a vegetable with cooked poultry or game.

At the time of the rice harvest, the Balinese arrange elaborate pyramids of fruit and flowers which they offer to their gods to show their gratitude.

Chapter Twelve

FRIED BREADS, DUMPLINGS AND STUFFINGS

Ever since the wandering shepherd tribes of biblical times discovered the food value of "balls of sweetened dough cooked in oil," doughnuts have been known for the strength and energy they have furnished the peoples of many nations. A recipe for making doughnuts is given in De Re Rustica, a work of the Roman Cato, written in the second century B. C.

DOUGHNUTS [1604]

WITH SO MUCH NOISY HISTORY IN THE MAKING NOWADAYS, it is a genuine relief to come upon some quiet history that has already been made—even if only by a press agent. The National Doughnut Dunking Association has always credited the invention of its pet provender to a Maine sea captain named Hanson Gregory. It was Gregory who, according to the story, objecting to the soggy center in his mother's fried cakes, is said to have remarked, "Why don't you cut a hole in the middle where it doesn't cook?" That was in 1847.

But now a Cape Cod historian places the great event earlier by a good two hundred years. It seems that one day back in the seventeenth century a Nauset Indian playfully shot an arrow through a fried cake his squaw was making. The squaw, frightened, dropped the perforated patty in a kettle of boiling grease—and the result was a doughnut.

Another legend suggests that the modern doughnut was given us by the Dutch of early colonial times. The good Dutch housewives or "frouws" were in the habit of making "vet cookies" or "olykoecks" (fried cakes), and serving them with their fine cheeses and good Dutch bitters and schnapps. When the persecuted Pilgrims left England, they fled to Holland, where they spent considerable time before embarking to seek religious freedom in the New World. It is quite reasonable to suppose that during their stay in Holland, they learned to enjoy and also to make the kind of cake, which the Hollander to this day *still* makes and calls "oly-koecks."

DOUGHNUTS—HINTS

There are two kinds of doughnuts: those made with baking powder, and those made by the longer raised method using compressed yeast. Both are cooked in deep, neutral, clear fat held at between 370 and 380° F. And there are several do's and don'ts to be observed:

They should be turned frequently during frying, as it has been proved that doughnuts turned frequently crack less. After frying, lay on unglazed paper to absorb excess fat. Cool and shake in powdered sugar.

Dough should be as soft as can be handled. . . . Turn out only small portions on board at a time. . . . Pat or roll out to only ¼-inch in thickness. . . . Flour the cutter frequently to prevent sticking.

Test the fat which should be 370° F. to start. . . . Fry only a few at a time and turn frequently.

If the batter or dough is rich and sweet the fat will soak in more easily, unless plenty of egg yolk is used. If there is not enough baking powder or yeast, they may be doughy. If the sugar content equals the shortening and the egg is high in proportion to the liquid, the consistency will be cake-like and sweet. Dipping doughnuts or fried breads or cakes in boiling water as they are removed from the frying pan will remove excess of fat and make the crust soft.

A few whole cloves added to a kettle of fat when frying doughnuts gives a pleasing flavor; so does a small stick of cinnamon.

To sugar doughnuts, shake them in a paper sack with sugar. . . . Doughnuts are a dessert in the Cape Cod manner when split horizontally and spread with cranberry sauce and cream cheese in equal parts. Combine and stir thoroughly before spreading.

ALSATIAN COQUILLAGE DOUGHNUTS   [1605]

Note. First of all you must have a funnel, an ordinary little funnel, if possible with a handle, to pour the batter through into the hot deep fat in such a way that it makes a snail-like crisp fritter or doughnut, which when dusted with vanilla confectioner's sugar, or other flavored sugar, is usually served during fall and winter with afternoon coffee.

Mix 2 well beaten eggs with 1 pint of rich, creamy, cold milk and strain through a fine sieve to remove the foam. Set aside, while sifting 3 cups (about) of pastry flour once, then once more with 2 teaspoons of baking powder and ½ teaspoon of salt. Gradually stir in the egg-milk mixture, beating briskly while adding. The batter should be of the consistency of pancake batter. If too thin, add a little more sifted flour. When the batter is perfectly smooth, beat in 1 scant teaspoon of vanilla, lemon, pineapple or other desired flavoring. In some parts of Alsace, the flavoring is 2 or 3 tablespoons of good kirsch liqueur, rum, brandy or calvados. Pour the batter into a wide mouthed pitcher, then, through the funnel, into hot, deep fat (375° F.), starting to pour at the side of the frying pan, and giving a light twist to the funnel so as to make a snake-like coquillage, the size of an ordinary small doughnut. Fry to a delicate brown, turning the shell or doughnut with a long pronged fork to brown the other side. Drain on unglazed paper or kitchen towel, transfer to a hot platter covered with a folded napkin, dust with confectioners sugar, cover with another napkin, and serve at once, with cinnamon jelly, currant jelly or Bar-le-Duc jelly.

BUCKWHEAT DOUGHNUTS   [1606]

Follow recipe for Buckwheat Cakes batter (No. 1659) or your own favorite buckwheat batter using yeast. Take a cup of the batter and add a beaten egg, ¼ cup sugar, ¼ teaspoon soda, 1 cup white flour, ½ teaspoon salt and 1 teaspoon baking powder.

If more flour is necessary to make a stiff dough, add more with additional baking powder in the proportion of a teaspoon of baking powder to a cup of flour. The dough should be of a good consistency to roll.

Form into round balls and pat out. Let them rise until they start to puff up a little, then fry in deep fat heated to 370° F. When they rise to the top of the fat, turn them to brown evenly.

CALAS [1607]

Celebrated in song and story. In olden days vendors sold these delicious rice cakes in the Vieux Carré of old New Orleans. On Sundays after church service, the family took a trip to this unique and charming spot to hear singing and to carry supplies of Calas home for breakfast.

Cook ½ cup of rice until very soft. Drain, mash and cool to lukewarm. Add ½ yeast cake, softened in ½ cup lukewarm water, beat and let rise overnight. In the morning add 3 eggs well beaten, ¼ cup sugar, ⅛ teaspoon nutmeg, ½ teaspoon salt and ¼ cup sifted flour. Beat again and let rise about 20 minutes in a warm place. Drop by tablespoons into hot deep fat, 360° F., and fry golden brown. Drain on absorbent paper and serve hot. Makes 20 calas.

CRULLERS [1608]

Crumble 1 compressed yeast cake into a bowl; add slowly 1 cup scalded milk, cooled to lukewarm, stirring until yeast is dissolved. Stir in 1 teaspoon salt, ¼ cup sugar, 2 tablespoons melted shortening and 1 well beaten egg, with 2 cups of flour and beat until smooth. Add another 2 cups of flour, and after mixing well, stir in a further 2 tablespoons of melted shortening and blend thoroughly. Knead on a floured board until smooth, place dough in a greased bowl, cover, set in a warm place and let rise until doubled in bulk. Roll out on a floured board, to ½-inch in thickness. Cut in five by one-inch strips and again let rise until double in bulk. Fry in deep hot fat (365° F.) 2 or 3 minutes or until light brown. Drain on soft paper and roll in powdered sugar. Makes about 24 crullers.

CRUMPETS [1609]

Combine in a large mixing bowl 1 teaspoon granulated sugar, ½ teaspoon salt, 3 tablespoons melted butter, and 2 cups rich, scalded milk. Stir well; and when cooled to lukewarm, crumble in ½ yeast cake, and mix thoroughly. Gradually beat in 3 cups sifted bread flour; and when smooth, cover with a light towel. Set in a warm place to rise for 2½ hours. Cut down dough for half a minute, and fill half full buttered muffin rings or patty pans with it. Let the dough rise again to double its bulk, and bake in a hot oven (450° F.) for 10 to 12 minutes. Serve the crumpets split, with plenty of good butter.

DOUGHNUTS [1610]

Mix and sift together three times 2 cups warmed, rolled brown sugar, 4 cups pastry flour, 3 teaspoons baking powder, ½ teaspoon ground cinnamon, and ½ teaspoon salt. Add 2 whole eggs and 1 egg yolk which have been beaten until light, with 1 cup cold sweet rich milk, and ¼ cup melted butter. Mix carefully. The dough should be soft enough to handle, but too much mixing will make it very tough. Turn on to a lightly floured board, roll out a little at a time, and cut with a floured doughnut cutter. Fry in hot deep fat (370 to 375° F.).

FILLED DOUGHNUTS [1611]

Roll yeast doughnut dough very thin as in recipe for Raised Doughnuts (No. 1616). Cut into small rounds. Place a little jam, marmalade, jelly or preserve on ½ of the rounds. Brush the edges with ice water. Press the other rounds over the filling, pinching edges together. Let rise until light. Fry in hot deep fat. Drain on unglazed paper.

GINGERBREAD DOUGHNUTS [1612]

Cream ½ cup butter or vegetable shortening with ¼ cup granulated sugar. Add 1 beaten egg. Measure and sift 2½ cups flour, 1¾ teaspoons soda, 1 teaspoon cinnamon, 1¼ teaspoons ginger, ½ teaspoon cloves, and ¾ teaspoon salt. Combine ½ cup molasses and ¼ cup hot water. Add the dry ingredients alternately with the liquid to the creamed mixture a little at a time, beating until smooth after each addition. Roll and cut into doughnut forms and fry in hot cooking oil or fat. Makes about 2 dozen doughnuts.

GREFFELS [1613]

Scald 1 cup of sweet milk, cool to lukewarm, then combine with 2 large eggs, well beaten with a good pinch of salt, and blended with ½ cup of sugar and ¼ cup of melted sweet butter. When thoroughly mixed, stir in 1 yeast cake, which has been crumbled in ¼ cup of lukewarm water, and add gradually 4 cups of cake flour, sifted once, mixed with 1 scant teaspoon of salt and sifted again (1 teaspoon of powdered cinnamon may also be added to the flour before the second sifting). Use only enough flour to make a soft dough. Cover and let rise until doubled in bulk, then roll out on a slightly floured board; cut in 2 to 2½ inch squares, let rise again till very light, and fry in deep, hot, clear fat. Drain on absorbent paper and serve hot, dusted with confectioner's sugar.

LEMON DOUGHNUTS [1614]

Mix 1 cup sugar with 2 tablespoons thick sour cream. Add 3 beaten eggs, ½ teaspoon lemon extract and 1 cup rich sour milk. Mix and sift 4 cups sifted flour, 1 teaspoon baking powder, ½ teaspoon soda, ½ teaspoon salt and ½ teaspoon nutmeg. Combine with sugar mixture. Add flour to make a dough that is just stiff enough to handle without sticking. Turn out on a floured board, roll and cut out. Fry in hot deep fat (365° F.). Drain on unglazed paper and when cold, roll in powdered sugar.

POLISH BOW KNOTS [1615]
Chruszczik

Beat together 3 egg yolks and 1 egg white. Add 3 tablespoons melted butter, 3 tablespoons sugar, 2 tablespoons cream, and ¼ teaspoon baking powder. To this gradually add 1 pound of flour. When well mixed, turn on to a floured board, knead, then roll out very thin. Cut into narrow oblong pieces. Cut a gash in the center, insert one end and fold the other over to resemble a knot. Fry in deep hot fat (365° F.) for few seconds. Do not brown. Take out, drain, and sprinkle with powdered sugar.

RAISED DOUGHNUTS [1616]
Fasnachts

Scald and cool 1 cup milk; when lukewarm, add ¼ yeast cake dissolved in ¼ cup lukewarm water, 1 teaspoon salt and flour to make stiff batter; let rise over night. In the morning, add ⅓ cup melted vegetable shortening, 2 well beaten eggs, 1 cup light brown sugar, and enough more flour to make a stiff dough (not more than 4½ cups in all); also add 1 teaspoon nutmeg. Let rise again, and if too soft to handle, add a little more flour. Cut into strips, roll under hands into long, thin pencil like strips and tie. Place on a floured board, let rise one hour, turn and let rise again. Fry in deep hot fat (365° F.) and drain on brown paper. Cool and roll in granulated sugar.

DUMPLINGS [1617]

The world's best culinary art has its roots in the cookery of peasants who evolved marvels in their tireless efforts to make plain food savory, to avoid waste, to secure nourishment. And one universal habit of cooks has been to wrap up choice morsels in leaves, dough, or puff paste, to be popped into hungry mouths without loss of juices, flavor, or aroma. But there are dumplings and dumplings. And here I mean boiled dumplings, those best of all "extenders." A little meat stew or fricassée of chicken, or a chowder, or soup, will go a long way if served with dumplings. Serve them too with pot roasts or casserole dishes. Serve them as an entrée, as a main dish for a light luncheon, drenched with butter and rolled in grated cheese. Chicken fricassée will stand a lot of very good dumplings: and that adds up. Serve much well made gravy. Dumplings should be neither soggy or dry, nor yet short processed to save time.

Dumplings are always popular, and rightly so, for what is better than well-made chicken and dumplings, or a savory combination of boiled pork, sauerkraut and dumplings? At their best, steamed or boiled, dumplings are light and fluffy in texture, moist on the outside, of course, but dry and flaky within. As a rule they are made from a flour or dough mixture but there are exceptions—potato dumplings for example, or those in which bread crumbs or cereals replace the flour.

BOHEMIAN POTATO DUMPLINGS [1618]

Peel and cut into small pieces 4 medium-sized potatoes; cook them until tender in cold water to barely cover, with a little salt. Put through ricer, then mash to a pulp and cool. Add 2 tablespoons of farina, 1 scant teaspoon of salt, ⅛ teaspoon of white pepper, also a dash of nutmeg, and beat in 1 large egg, mixing thoroughly. Work in enough flour (about 1 cup) to make a medium-stiff dough and blend well. Roll on a lightly floured board into 1½-inch cylinder, and cut in 1½-inch lengths. When ready to serve, drop into a large amount of gently boiling meat stock and cook, uncovered, for about 20 minutes, turning the dumplings in the stock, when half done.

BREAD CRUMB DUMPLINGS [1619]

Put 1½ cups of bread crumbs in a mixing bowl; blend in 1 tablespoon of flour, ¼ teaspoon of salt and a few grains each of white pepper and nutmeg. Combine 1 scant cup of cold milk and 1 well beaten egg; gradually add this to the bread crumb mixture, mixing well. Drop by teaspoonfuls into rapidly boiling soup or stew. Cover tightly, and cook steadily for about 10 to 12 minutes without uncovering. Appropriate for soup, stew or fricassée.

CRACKER DUMPLINGS [1620]

Combine 20 soda crackers, finely rolled, then sieved, 1 teaspoon of baking powder 1 teaspoon of salt, ¼ scant teaspoon of pepper and a dash each of thyme and nutmeg, then stir in 3 tablespoons of melted shortening. Beat 2 egg yolks with ⅓ cup of cold milk, and add to the first ingredients. Fold in gently the 2 stiffly beaten egg whites. Drop by tablespoons on top of boiling stew or soup (for soup use teaspoons);

cover tightly and cook 12 to 15 minutes without removing cover. Appropriate for soup, stew or fricassée.

EGG-ALMOND DUMPLINGS [1621]

Sift 2 cups of bread flour once, return to sifter, add 2 teaspoons of baking powder and ½ teaspoon of salt and sift into a mixing bowl. Add cold sweet milk to a lightly beaten whole egg mixed with 1½ tablespoons of blanched and ground almonds to make 1 cup, and gradually work into the flour mixture, beating briskly until smooth. Drop by teaspoons into boiling soup, stew or fricassée; cover tightly and cook 12 to 15 minutes. Appropriate for clear soup, stew or fricassée.

FLUFFY DUMPLINGS [1622]

Sift 1 cup of pastry or cake flour once, return to sifter, add 1 teaspoon of baking powder and ¼ teaspoon of salt and sift again; cut in 2 teaspoons of shortening, mixing to consistency of corn meal. Combine 1 well beaten egg yolk and ¼ cup of cold milk; add to the flour mixture and mix quickly until smooth but *do not beat*. Grease top part of a steamer; place over rapidly boiling water or stock, or boiling water and Pique Seasoning, to make a fine meat broth, and drop batter by teaspoons (or tablespoons, if large dumplings are desired) into steamer. Cover closely, and steam 12 to 15 minutes. Serve sizzling hot.

FRIED CROUTON DUMPLINGS [1623]

Cube 3 or 4 slices of stale bread very small, then fry in hot drippings until nicely browned. Drain and cool. Beat 3 eggs as for an omelet; add ¼ cup of cold milk, with 2 tablespoons of clarified butter, and beat thoroughly. Sift 1½ cups of bread flour, ¾ teaspoon of salt, ⅓ teaspoon each of nutmeg, thyme, mace and powdered bay leaf into a mixing bowl containing the bread cubes and mix well; then add the egg-milk mixture, stirring thoroughly. Let stand 30 minutes to mellow. Form into balls the size of a small walnut and drop into rapidly boiling meat, chicken or vegetable stock or rapidly boiling water flavored with Pique Seasoning. Cover closely and boil gently for 12 to 15 minutes. Appropriate for any kind of fish, meat or vegetable soup, clear or thick; stew, chicken fricassée, noodles, macaroni, spaghetti, vegetable stew, and so forth.

FRIED FARINA DUMPLINGS [1624]

Sprinkle ¾ cup of farina, into 2 cups of hot milk, stirring briskly to prevent lumping; season to taste with salt, a small dash each of nutmeg and mace, and cook until mixture just begins to thicken, stirring constantly, over a gentle heat. Remove from the fire and add 2 slightly beaten eggs, a little at a time, beating briskly after each addition. Set aside until cool enough to handle, or until needed. Take portions about the size of a small walnut, form into small balls, roll in sieved bread crumbs, then in beaten egg diluted with a little cold milk, and again in sieved crumbs. Brown on all sides in plenty of butter or margarin over a medium heat, rolling and shaking the pan frequently. Drain on absorbent paper and serve either as a side dish, or as a main dish, on a hot platter first covered with a layer of grated cheese, the dumplings themselves also sprinkled with grated cheese. Pass tomato sauce separately.

HAM DUMPLINGS [1625]

Sift-together into a bowl ¾ cup of flour, 1 teaspoon of baking powder, ¼ teaspoon of salt, ½ teaspoon each of thyme, mace and sage; add 1 scant cup of finely ground, cooked ham, free from fat; moisten with ¼ cup (more or less) of cold milk, or enough to make a dough not-too-stiff; Form into small balls, then roll in flour, and drop into boiling stock (any kind); cover closely and cook gently for about 12 minutes. Appropriate for soup, chowder, stew or fricassée.

LIVER DUMPLINGS MODERNE [1626]

Slice ¾ pound of liver (beef, calves, lamb or pork) and let stand in hot stock or, failing this, in boiling water and equal parts of Pique Seasoning to cover generously, for 10 minutes; then grind with ½ medium-sized onion and 1 strip of raw bacon. Soften 3 slices of bread with the liquid used for the liver and squeeze out as much moisture as possible. Combine the squeezed bread with 2 well-beaten eggs, season with 1½ teaspoons of salt, ¼ teaspoon of black pepper, ⅛ teaspoon each of thyme and nutmeg, and 1 tablespoon of finely chopped chives, and add to liver mixture. Sift ¼ cup of flour with ½ teaspoon of baking powder. Sprinkle over the mixture and blend thoroughly. Drop by teaspoons into 2 cups of boiling water mixed with 1 cup of Pique Seasoning. Cover tightly and simmer for 10 to 12 minutes. May be served as a main dish with fried onions or sauerkraut. Appropriate for soup, stew, fricassée chowder, macaroni, noodles, spaghetti, and so forth.

MEAT DUMPLINGS [1627]

Mix thoroughly in the order given: ⅔ pound of lean, ground beef, veal, lamb or pork, 1 teaspoon of salt, ¼ teaspoon of pepper, 1 teaspoon of sage, ⅛ teaspoon each of thyme, mace, nutmeg and allspice, 1 cup of bread soaked in cold water and gently squeezed, 1 large egg, well beaten, and 1 teaspoon each of grated onion and finely chopped parsley. Form into balls the size of a small walnut, and drop slowly into boiling soup, stew, and so forth. Cover and simmer very slowly for 35 to 40 minutes. Appropriate for soup, chowder, stew and fricassée.

PARSLEY DUMPLINGS [1628]

Sift 2 cups of bread flour once, return to sifter, add 4 teaspoons of baking powder, 1 scant teaspoon of salt, and ⅛ teaspoon each of thyme, nutmeg, sage and cloves and sift again over ¼ cup of finely chopped parsley. Mix well, then cut in 1 generous tablespoon of shortening and moisten with ½ cup of boiling water, combined with ½ cup of Pique Seasoning or enough to moisten ingredients. Drop by teaspoons on top of soup, stew or fricassée; cover and steam for about 12 minutes, keeping closely covered. Appropriate for soup, chowders, stews, fricassée and so forth.

RIVVLES or LITHUANIAN DUMPLINGS [1629]

Sift 1 cup of flour in a bowl; make a hollow in center, and break in a whole unbeaten egg; sprinkle with about ⅓ teaspoon of salt and a few grains of pepper and nutmeg. Then, with the fingers, work the flour into the egg until the whole is a crumbly mass of pieces not larger than an uncooked navy bean, adding more flour, if necessary. They are ready to drop into the boiling soup mixture, ten minutes before serving, then cooked covered, or maybe spread thinly on a tray or board to dry for a couple of days, before storing for future use. Appropriate for soup or chowders.

Note. These dumplings may be prepared far in advance and stored in a closed tin for future use.

SALMON DUMPLINGS [1630]

Flake any kind of cold, cooked, carefully boned and skinned fish to make about a half pound, or 1½ cups. If using canned fish, drain carefully. Melt 1 tablespoon of butter over a low flame; stir in, blending well, 2 tablespoons of flour, and when bubbling, but not brown, gradually add ⅓ cup of scalded sweet milk, stirring constantly, until mixture boils and thickens; lower the heat and simmer very gently over an asbestos pad, if available, or over hot water, for 5 minutes, stirring occasionally. Season to taste with salt, pepper, and a dash each of nutmeg, clove, and thyme. Cool slightly, then beat in 2 egg yolks, adding one at a time and beating well after each addition. With the last yolk, stir in 1½ table-spoons of good sherry wine, then add the flaked fish, alternately with 4 tablespoons of sieved dry cracker crumbs. Shape into 6 large dumplings or 12 small ones, and drop into salted boiling fish stock. Cook until dumplings rise to the surface, drain and serve at once.

Note. Almost any kind of cooked or canned fish may be used for these dumplings which are appropriate to garnish any fish platter, fish soup or a chowder. May be served as a course with Cream sauce or Hollandaise (Nos. 258 and 1062, respectively).

TOMATO JUICE DUMPLINGS [1631]

Sift once 2 cups of cake flour. Return to sifter and add 2 tablespoons of baking powder and ½ teaspoon of salt with a few grains each of nutmeg, thyme and sage, and sift again into a bowl. Stir in 1 teaspoon each of finely chopped dry parsley, grated onion, green pepper, and chives. Gradually pour over ¾ cup of tomato juice, stirring constantly until mixture is well blended and adding more flour if batter is too soft. Drop by teaspoonfuls into boiling soup, stew, fricassée, macaroni, and so forth. Cover tightly and boil gently for 12 to 15 minutes. Serve hot. Appropriate for soup, stews, fricassée, macaroni, noodles, spaghetti or to be served as a main dish with grated cheese and egg sauce.

WATERCRESS DUMPLINGS [1632]

Sift together 2 cups of bread flour, 4 teaspoons of baking powder, ¾ teaspoon of salt, ¼ teaspoon each of curry powder, thyme and sage. Stir in ½ cup of finely chopped, cleaned and picked watercress leaves, then cut in 1 tablespoon of bacon drippings. Moisten with 1 scant cup of cold broth, or ½ cup of cold water and ½ cup of Pique Seasoning to make a drop batter. Drop by teaspoonfuls into the boiling soup; cover closely and steam for 12 minutes without uncovering. Appropriate for any kind of soup, especially cream soup.

YORKSHIRE PUDDING [1633]

See Roast Beef With Yorkshire Pudding (No. 611).

STUFFING [1634]

When the gala feast days coincide with soaring meat prices, the result is apt to be a moaning cook instead of a groaning board—unless the cook is skillful at making a three-pound chicken look and taste like a prize turkey with spicily seasoned stuffing, of course. Fowl isn't the only meat that can be stretched and improved by a substantial stuffing. The cheaper cuts of beef, breast of veal or lamb and cuts of pork may be supplemented in the same way. Besides making a small amount of meat go further, a properly made stuffing adds flavor.

There lies the secret of stuffings. They are toothsome successes *only* if the seasoning is wisely done. With one simple bread stuffing as a working basis, infinite variety can be developed by changing the seasonings to complement the various kinds of meat.

"Stuff, truss and roast." These words of direction in regard to the preparation of poultry and meats are likely to be heard often, especially during the holidays. For *stuffing*, sometimes erroneously called "*dressing*," is needed to upholster the inner cavities of turkey, duck, or goose, so that the fowl will be kept pleasingly extended in its natural shape. Moreover, this inner padding also serves as a slow distributor of its own spicy flavors back into the flesh or meat, while at the same time absorbing juices and fats as they exude and trickle downward during roasting or baking.

ALMOND SAUSAGE STUFFING [1635]
(For a 12 to 15-pound turkey)

Sauté until well browned, stirring to break apart, over a gentle heat, 1 pound of pork sausage, add 8 cups of dry bread crumbs, not too tightly packed, stirring to blend thoroughly and let the crumbs absorb the excess fat from the pork. Rinse the pan with 1 cup of rich beef broth or failing this, add ½ cup of boiling water and ½ cup of Pique Seasoning. Add 2 cups of finely chopped green celery leaves (tops), 1 cup of chopped onion, 2 cups of blanched, shredded and toasted almonds, 1 cup of peeled, thinly sliced fresh mushrooms, ¼ cup each of finely chopped parsley, chives and green pepper, 1 tablespoon of salt, ¼ teaspoon of black pepper, a few grains of cayenne, ¼ teaspoon each of mace, sage, thyme, nutmeg and marjoram. Mix thoroughly, then add 4 well-beaten eggs, mixed with ½ cup of thin cream or undiluted evaporated milk. Beat well, then toss lightly to loosen.

BURGER TURKEY STUFFING [1636]
(For a 10–12-pound turkey)

Combine 2 pounds of lean beef, finely ground with 2 cups of soft bread crumbs, ½ cup of finely chopped green celery leaves (tops), ½ cup of grated onion, ¼ cup each of parsley and chives, finely chopped,

4 strips of raw bacon, finely chopped, 3 well beaten eggs, ¼ cup of grated raw carrot, and ½ cup of finely chopped peeled fresh mushrooms. Season to taste with salt and pepper, a few grains each of cayenne, thyme, marjoram, mace and sage and 1 large bay leaf, powdered. Return mixture to food chopper to ensure fineness and thorough blending. Do not cook. Stuff cavity of the bird, truss and sew.

This stuffing may be used to stuff cabbage leaves, tomatoes, green peppers, large onions, eggplant and in fact any so-called vegetable-pocket, i.e. vegetables which may be stuffed. Or the mixture may be baked as a loaf, or in greased deep muffin pans, or, again, line muffin pans with it and fill centers with onion, rice, mushroom, potato, or any other favorite stuffing.

CELERY STUFFING [1637]
(For a 4-pound chicken)

Cook ⅓ cup of finely chopped celery, 2 tablespoons of finely chopped onion, and 1 tablespoon of finely chopped green pepper in 4 tablespoons of butter or margarin for 5 minutes over a medium flame, stirring frequently; then stir in 1½ cups of soft bread crumbs, ½ cup of undiluted evaporated milk or thin cream, and season to taste with ½ teaspoon of salt and ⅛ teaspoon each of mace, pepper, thyme, sage, and nutmeg. Mix well, and cool before using.

CHESTNUT STUFFING [1638]
(For a 10–12-pound turkey)

Cover 1 pound of chestnut with boiling beef stock, or, failing this, with equal parts of boiling water and Pique Seasoning, and cook for 15 minutes, or until tender; drain, remove shells and inner brown skin with sharp pointed knife, then slice. Brown ⅓ cup of onions in ½ cup of bacon drippings over a gentle heat until just beginning to take on a light brown color, stirring frequently; then add 3 tablespoons each of finely chopped parsley, chives and green pepper, and season with 2 teaspoons of salt, 1 teaspoon of sage, ¼ teaspoon of pepper, ⅛ teaspoon each of thyme, mace, nutmeg and marjoram. Remove from the fire, stir in 6 lightly packed cups of soft bread crumbs, and the sliced chestnuts. Mix thoroughly and cool before using.

CORN BREAD STUFFING [1639]
(For a 10–12-pound turkey, 2 capons, or 3 chickens)

Cook 1 cup of chopped onions in ½ generous cup of butter or margarin for 5 minutes, or until just beginning to take on color, stirring frequently. Remove from the fire and add: 6 cups of crumbled, cold corn bread, ¼ teaspoon each of finely chopped parsley, green pepper and green onion tops; season highly with 2 teaspoons of salt, ¼ teaspoon of black pepper, 1 teaspoon of sage, 1 small clove of garlic, mashed to a pulp, ½ teaspoon each of thyme and mace. Then moisten with sufficient cold milk to make a somewhat moist stuffing.

CRANBERRY STUFFING [1640]
(For a 10–12-pound turkey)

Cook ½ cup of chopped celery leaves, 2 tablespoons each of parsley, green pepper and spinach, all finely chopped in ½ cup of butter or margarin for 5 minutes, over a low heat, stirring constantly. Then stir in 1 quart of bread crumbs, ½ cup of sugar and 3 cups of chopped raw cranberries, and blend well. Remove from the fire and season to taste with salt and pepper, also 2 teaspoons of onion juice and ½ teaspoon each of marjoram, sage, thyme and mace. Mix well, then blend in 5 well beaten eggs.

EPICURE STUFFING [1641]
(For a 4½ to 5-pound fish)

Chop (in equal parts) the flesh from carefully boned pike, carp and eel so as to obtain 1½ cups of raw fish flesh. To this add 1 whole well beaten egg, 2 large fresh mushrooms, peeled and chopped, 1 tablespoon of chopped black truffle, 1 generous teaspoon each of parsley, chervil, chives, shallots and 1 teaspoon of grated onion; ¾ cup of soft bread crumbs, soaked in fresh milk and gently squeezed, 1 generous tablespoon of melted butter, salt and white pepper to taste, with a dash each of thyme, nutmeg and sage. Mix thoroughly. Melt 2 tablespoons of butter and cook the stuffing in it, over a gentle heat, for about 5 minutes stirring to prevent scorching. Fill a cleaned, dried, opened fish; sew up the opening with kitchen thread and cook according to directions.
Note. This may also be used to stuff cabbage leaves, green peppers, large onions, tomatoes, and so forth. Or, use for croquettes or cutlets.

GIBLET STUFFING [1642]
For a goose, duck or a fowl

Simmer giblets in boiling salted water seasoned with a few celery tops, 1 chopped onion, 1 bay leaf, a dash each of thyme, rosemary and marjoram and a few peppercorns and when done (about 1 hour) strain and save broth for gravy and basting. Brown 1 medium-sized onion in 3 tablespoons of butter; stir in 3 cups of sieved, dry bread crumbs, and season with 1 teaspoon of salt, pepper to taste. Remove from the fire, mix in 2 coarsely cut apples, pared and cored, and the strained, chopped giblets. Moisten the mixture with a little of the giblet broth.

If using the prepared stuffing which comes in a package be sure that it is fresh. The same rule applies to packaged seasonings.

HAM AND ONION STUFFING [1643]

Heat ¼ cup of bacon drippings; stir in ¾ cup of finely chopped onion and cook over a low heat, stirring frequently until onion is transparent; then add 2 cups of soft bread crumbs, 1 cup of finely chopped cooked lean ham, and cook 2 or 3 minutes longer, still stirring frequently; season to taste with salt and pepper, a dash each of thyme, sage and cloves, and 2 tablespoons of finely chopped parsley. Moisten with ¼ cup of hot stock, or 2 tablespoons of boiling water and 2 tablespoons of Pique Seasoning. Cool before using. Appropriate for pork chops, meat loaves, fish loaves or small roast birds.

HAM-WALNUT BRANDIED STUFFING [1644]
For a 10–12-pound turkey, or a large capon, and 3 chickens

Soak ½ loaf of day-old white bread in milk 15 minutes, then squeeze dry and toss lightly to render it light and fluffy. Brown ½ cup of finely chopped onions in ¼ cup of bacon or ham drippings until onion just begins to take on color; remove from the fire, stir in 2 tablespoons each of chopped parsley and chives, 2 chopped hard-cooked eggs, ¾ pound of cold, cooked lean ham, chopped, and 1 cup of black walnuts and mix well while seasoning to taste with salt and pepper, and a generous dash each of thyme, nutmeg and cloves. Mix thoroughly, adding at the same time a good ¼ cup of brandy. Cool before using.

MINT STUFFING [1645]

Combine ⅓ cup of chopped fresh mint leaves, 1½ cups of soft bread crumbs, 1 teaspoon of salt, ½ teaspoon of grated lemon rind, ¼ teaspoon of black pepper, a dash each of thyme, nutmeg and mace. Beat 1 large egg, and add with ⅓ cup of melted shortening and enough hot water to moisten the crumbs. Appropriate for stuffing a boned leg of lamb, a shoulder of lamb or thick lamb chops, or a crown roast of lamb, if sausage meat is added.

OLIVE STUFFING CALIFORNIA STYLE [1646]
For a 10 to 12-pound turkey or a large capon, 2 or 3 geese, 4 ducks, or 4 roasting chickens

Melt ½ cup of butter, stir in ½ cup of chopped onion, ½ cup of finely chopped celery leaves, and a thin slice of garlic, mashed to a pulp, cook for 5 minutes, stirring frequently, and remove from the fire. Add ¼ cup of finely chopped parsley, ⅓ cup of finely chopped lean, cooked ham, 2 tablespoons of finely chopped green pepper, and 1 cup of coarsely chopped green stuffed olives. Season to taste with 1 teaspoon of salt, ½ teaspoon of black pepper, ½ teaspoon of sage, ¼ teaspoon each of marjoram and cloves, and a dash of nutmeg. Moisten 6 cups of soft bread crumbs with white wine, as much as the crumbs will absorb, then squeeze very gently, to remove the excess of liquid, but leaving enough to make a moist stuffing.

ONION STUFFING ENGLISH STYLE [1647]
For a roasting chicken, a veal cushion, a shoulder of lamb, and so forth

Cook 3 finely chopped large onions over a low heat, stirring frequently, until transparent; stir in ¼ cup of bacon drippings, 2 cups of soft bread crumbs, 1 teaspoon of salt, 1 teaspoon of sage, ¼ teaspoon each of thyme, cloves and mace and 2 tablespoons of finely chopped parsley. Mix well, and cool before using. Should the stuffing seem too dry, moisten with 2 or 3 tablespoons of hot water.

OYSTER STUFFING NEW ENGLAND STYLE [1648]
Sufficient to stuff a 5-pound chicken. For a 10–12-pound turkey, double the recipe; for a 16 to 18-pound turkey use three times the amount of ingredients. If you decide to use two stuffings for the turkey— one for the crop cavity and one for the body cavity, remember that the crop cavity holds about as much stuffing as the body. If the turkey is stuffed the day before roasting, make sure stuffing is cold before using. Then fill and truss the bird and keep in the refrigerator.

Melt ½ cup of butter or margarin in a large skillet or pan; stir in 1 large onion, finely chopped, ¾ cup of finely chopped green celery leaves (tops), 1 tablespoon each of finely chopped parsley and green pepper; season to taste with ¾ teaspoon of salt, ¼ teaspoon of black pepper, ½ teaspoon of sage, ¼ teaspoon each of thyme, mace and clove, cook 3 or 4 minutes, over a low heat, stirring almost constantly. Add then 1½ quarts of soft bread crumbs; mix thoroughly, and last of all add 1 pint of drained, chopped oysters.

PADEREWSKI'S STUFFING OR FORCEMEAT   [1649]

See Turkey Galantine à la Paderewski (No. 971).

PECAN STUFFING   [1649a]
(*Southern Method*)

INGREDIENTS	FOR 5-lb. ROASTING CHICKEN OR HALF A TURKEY or A CAPON	FOR A 10-12 POUND TURKEY
Butter or margarin—cup................	½	¾
Onions, chopped—cup.................	¼	½
Celery leaves and stalks, chopped—cup...	½	1
Parsley, minced—tablespoons............	2	¼ cup
Thyme—teaspoon......................	1	1¾
Sage—teaspoon........................	½	1
Clove—teaspoon.......................	¼	½
Salt—teaspoon.........................	¾	1½
Black pepper—teaspoon.................	¼	¾
Celery seeds—teaspoon.................	½	¾
Nutmeg—teaspoon.....................	¼	½
Soft stale bread crumbs—quarts.........	1½ to 2	3 to 3½
Pecan meats, chopped—cup.............	½	1

Melt butter in a Dutch oven; add onion, celery and seasonings; cook 3 minutes, stirring constantly, over low heat; add bread crumbs and pecans and mix well.

PRUNE AND APPLE STUFFING   [1650]

Chop 3 slices of bacon and cook over a very low flame until almost crisp. Stir in ½ cup of finely chopped onions and cook 2 minutes, stirring constantly. Mix in 2 cups of soft bread crumbs, 3 cups of pared, cored, chopped apples, and ½ pound of cooked, drained, pitted prunes chopped. Season with 1 generous teaspoon of salt, ⅓ teaspoon of freshly crushed peppercorns, ⅛ teaspoon each of thyme, mace, sage, and nutmeg. Should stuffing seem too dry, moisten with a little of the juice of prunes. Cool before using. Appropriate for pork and veal roast, goose or duck also for meat loaf.

SAGE STUFFING I ENGLISH STYLE   [1651]

Chop coarsely 2 pounds of onions; parboil 5 minutes in boiling salted water; strain well. Melt ¼ cup of butter; stir in the onions, and cook gently, over a low heat, for 15 minutes, stirring frequently and being careful not to brown them too much; add 1½ cups of soft bread crumbs, season to taste with salt and pepper and stir in 2 teaspoons of sage. Mix well; cool before using. Appropriate for roast chicken or boiled mutton, goose, duck or capon.

SAGE STUFFING II FRENCH STYLE [1652]

Chop coarsely 2 pounds of onions, parboil 5 minutes in boiling salted water, then add a dozen fresh or dried sage leaves, and let stand 5 minutes. Strain and drain thoroughly. Rub mixture through a fine-meshed sieve, and cook the resulting purée in ½ cup of sweet butter without browning, stirring constantly, over a low flame. Remove from the fire and cool to lukewarm, then beat in 3 egg yolks, adding one at a time, and beating well after each addition, then stir in the chopped cooked liver of the bird. Season highly with salt, pepper, thyme, mace and nutmeg, adding also a few grains of cayenne pepper. Appropriate for goose, duck and wild birds.

STUFFED PRUNE STUFFING [1653]
FRENCH STYLE

See. No. 944, Roast Goose Prune Stuffing (French Style).

WILD RICE AND SAUSAGE STUFFING [1654]

Cook 1 cup of well-washed wild rice in boiling salted water until tender. Rinse with boiling water and drain thoroughly. Mix with 1 tablespoon each of finely chopped parsley and green pepper, 1½ tablespoons of grated onion, 1 teaspoon of poultry seasoning, a generous dash of pepper and salt to taste. Sauté ½ pound of pork sausage over a low flame, breaking it up in small pieces with the tines of a fork; mix sausage with rice mixture, and stir in 2 tablespoons each of the sausage drippings and good sherry wine. Cool well before using. Will stuff 6 pigeons. Especially appropriate for stuffing squabs and pigeons.

PANCAKES AND GRIDDLE CAKES [1655]

It was Benjamin Franklin who, with his usual discernment, observed that some folks think it will never be good times until houses are tiled with pancakes. The thought probably came to him after a Shrove Tuesday. As fit "as a pancake for Shrove Tuesday," Shakespeare had previously written reminiscently and prophetically.

Food historians have to go a long way back in exploring the origin of pancakes, the winning of pancake popularity, and, in particular, the pleasant association of pancakes with Shrove Tuesday. One conscientious investigator is of the opinion that pancakes came into being in the very early days because with the approach of abstinence from meat in Lent it became customary to use up all the drippings and lard in the making of pancakes ere Lent actually appeared. The Vicar of Wakefield's parishioners religiously ate pancakes at Shrovetide. There were others who, perhaps, thought more of food than ritual.

John Taylor, the English "Water Poet," called attention in the first part of the eighteenth century to the Pancake Bell scheduled to be sounded from the churches at 11 o'clock on Shrove Tuesday morning. Taylor didn't think much of Shrove Tuesday, or, at least, of the festal observances which had grown up around the day, and he noted with distaste that sextons of the "knavish" variety were willing to ring the bell before nine. A long jingle, sung in Northamptonshire began:

> *Pancakes and fritters,*
> *Says the bells of St. Peter's.*

In Dorsetshire and Wiltshire hungry children used to chant:

> *I'm come a-shaving*
> *For a piece of pancake;*
> *Or a piece of bacon,*
> *Or a little truckle cheese*
> *Of your own making.*
> *If you give me a little I ask you no more;*
> *If you don't give me nothing I'll rattle your door.*

Sometimes the rimes featured doughnuts—the "doughty doughnut," as Washington Irving termed it. But the pancake easily had pre-eminence. Thomas Tusser, the sixteenth-century poet, indicated the way in his "Five Hundred Points of Good Husbandry United to as Many of Good Wiferie," when he advised:

> *Fritters and pancakes enough see you make.*

All of which brings one back to Franklin's comment.

A curious pancake story about Napoleon illustrates how simple and human he could sometimes be. Napoleon announced to his first wife that he would pay her a visit at Malmaison, on the occasion of the Chandeleur, which is Candlemas for the French.

Josephine, as superstitious as he—what Creole is not?—was hurrying to prepare the crêpes, which are pancakes in French. And, as soon as Napoleon arrived, she led him to the kitchen. He was very gay. "Let me," he begged, "I am going to toss them myself, every one of them!"

"Listen!" she warned him, laughingly, "You run the risk of failing with one of them. And spoiled crêpes spell misfortune."—Napoleon smiled, took the handle of the pan, made the circle of batter float up, then caught it again intact. Josephine clapped her hands.

"One—two—three!"

"That's enough, stop!" begged Josephine. "You'll end by missing."

"Four," counted the Emperor, as he succeeded with one more crêpe.

"Enough!" repeated Josephine. Too late. the fifth crêpe slipped down by the side of the frying pan, and spread itself out on the flagstones. One would have believed that Napoléon would forget the incident. But he didn't! When the Russians were burning Moscow beneath his eyes, Marshal Ney heard him sigh: "There, it's my fifth crêpe which avenges itself."

The proper place for a pancake fifty odd years ago was on the breakfast table. Times change. The pancake of today is just as likely to appear at luncheon or supper as at breakfast.

PANCAKES—HINTS [1656]

Don't turn a pancake after it has been cooked on both sides. The excuse some cooks give for this trick is always the same. They "want to be sure it is thoroughly done."

Don't stand waiting, turner in hand, until the last air bubble has broken and expelled all the cake's precious airiness, leaving it as porous and tough as a sponge.

Don't lift an edge of the pancake to peek under and check the browning progress. Needless to say, such cakes turn out a flop.

Don't try to improve on ready-prepared pancake mix by additions of your own. Follow mixing directions to the dot.

To make very tender hot cakes for breakfast prepare the recipe the night before, omitting baking powder, and in the morning add the required amount of baking powder and fry.

If you like thick, hearty pancakes, use less liquid.

In baking griddle cakes rub the hot griddle frequently with salt tied firmly in a piece of cloth. The griddle will then be freed of bits of extra batter and the cakes will be less likely to stick.

To prepare a new aluminum griddle for use, first wash well in warm water and soap suds and remove any labels. On a gas range the griddle is hot enough when a small piece of paper placed on it will brown. Lower the heat and start baking. With an electric stove preheat the griddle four minutes, then lower the heat and start baking. Cakes often stick if the griddle is too hot. Wash the griddle in hot soapy water after using and wipe perfectly dry before storing.

Try grating or shredding a large peeled, cored apple and add to pancake batter as an aid to both flavor and digestion.

To canned peach juice, or other fruit juice left over from canning, add sugar to taste and boil down to the consistency of medium syrup. It is delicious on either pancakes or French toast.

Add 1 cup of drained canned crushed pineapple to a rather thick pancake batter; serve with butter and brown sugar.

Use left-over pancake batter for cutlets or croquettes. Or thin the batter with milk, and use for dipping bread to make French toast. . . . That late corn might be cooked, cut from the cob, added to griddle cake batter and baked on a griddle. . . . A teaspoon of molasses added to pancake batter will make the cakes brown nicely. . . . If using pancakes as a dessert course at luncheon or supper stir in a little grated orange rind for new flavor.

ALMOND PANCAKES [1657]
Pannequets aux Amandes

To French Fried Pancakes (No. 1665), add 1 tablespoon softened butter, also a dozen blanched almonds and 2 or 3 bitter almonds, pounded or put through food chopper (using the finest knife) with 2 teaspoons powdered sugar. Cook as French Fried Pancakes, or cook the pancakes in individual frying pans as indicated for French Pancakes (crêpes à la Française) (No. 1666) using either method. Serve very hot, sprinkled with powdered sugar.

BREAD PANCAKES [1658]

Tear apart with two forks enough fresh white bread to make 4 cups; place in a mixing bowl and pour over it 1 quart of scalded milk. Let stand until cool, or about 10 minutes. Beat 4 egg yolks, and stir gradually into the mixture. Sift lightly over the mixture and mix thoroughly 1¾ cups of flour, 2 teaspoons baking powder and 1 scant teaspoon salt. When thoroughly blended, stir in ¾ cup of melted butter, and fold in the 4 stiffly beaten egg whites, beaten with a few grains of salt. Bake in small individual buttered frying pan or on a hot griddle, and, when brown on both sides, serve with syrup, honey, jelly, marmalade or preserves.

BUCKWHEAT CAKES [1659]
(As made 75 years ago on a farm in Kalamazoo, Michigan)

It takes more than a list of ingredients to make good buckwheat cakes. It takes equal parts of imagination, experience and that indescribable quality similar to instinct in animals, or so a 90-year-old grandmother told me in the kitchen of her century-old farm.

To start the pancakes, take three parts buckwheat flour, one part wheat flour and one-half part yellow corn meal; stir them into enough sweet or sour milk to make a moderately stiff batter. Dissolve one compressed yeast cake in a cup of lukewarm water and add to the batter, stirring thoroughly. Set in a warm place to rise over night. With sour milk the batter can be used for breakfast the next morning; with sweet milk they will not be good until the milk sours.

To complete the pancakes, take out what batter you think you will need and mix with it a cup of milk to which has been added a half teaspoonful of soda and the same of salt. The pancake batter will improve as it gets older. Do not put salt in the kept-over stock batter and never put sugar in it. Also, never pour any mixed batter back into the kept-over batter as the soda tends to turn it pink and also changes the flavor.

Variations. From time to time, broken-up bread in milk may be added before setting aside for the day. Do not however use sweet bread or cake. A little rye flour, oatmeal or whole wheat flour may be added occasionally to vary the flavor. These are the things in which only experience can properly guide you. Each night when you want buckwheat cakes for breakfast (or in the morning if you want them for supper) bring in your kept-over batter and add milk, buckwheat and wheat flour and corn meal as stated above and mix to quite a stiff batter. No more yeast will be needed, as the mixture makes its own yeast if enough batter is saved each time.

BUTTERMILK GRIDDLE CAKES [1660]

Sift together 3 cups of bread flour, 1 teaspoon of baking powder, 1½ teaspoons of baking soda, 1½ scant teaspoons of salt and 1 tablespoon of fine granulated sugar. Combine 2 well beaten eggs with 2½ cups of buttermilk, then stir in ¼ cup of melted butter or any other preferred shortening, and gradually add to the flour mixture, beating and stirring until smooth. Drop by tablespoons onto a hot, ungreased griddle, or into individual greased frying pan, and cook until puffed, full of bubbles and cooked on the edges; turn, and cook on the other side. Serve as hot as possible.

CURRIED CLAM GRIDDLE CAKES [1661]
(*Makes about 24 cakes*)

Chop finely 24 large, shucked clams, saving all the juice. Sift twice 4 cups of bread flour, 2 tablespoons of baking powder, 1½ teaspoons of salt, ½ scant teaspoon of pepper and 1 tablespoon of curry powder. Beat 2 eggs lightly, mix with 1 cup of milk, then with the chopped clams, alternately with the clam juice, previously strained through a fine muslin cloth, and stir into the flour mixture, adding more milk if necessary to make a thin batter. Bake as any griddle cakes. Serve hot with a mixture of 1 cup of tomato catsup, and 3 tablespoons of lemon juice.

DUTCH NANIES [1662]

The words "Dutch Nanies" come from the name Dutch Banana Pancakes. "Nanies" is a corruption of the word bananas.

Beat 4 large eggs thoroughly with a dash of freshly grated nutmeg; sift ½ cup of flour and ½ teaspoon of salt, and add alternately with ½ cup of chilled sweet milk, a little at a time, beating briskly until the batter is smooth. Spread 2 tablespoons of sweet butter over the bottom and sides of an unheated ten-inch frying pan; pour the batter into the frying pan and set in a hot oven (400° F.) to bake for 20 to 25 minutes, reducing the heat gradually to moderate (350° F.). The pancake should puff up at the sides and be crisp and brown. Sprinkle with powdered sugar and lemon juice, then with sliced bananas, roll up like an omelet. Serve at once.

ELDER BLOSSOM PANCAKES [1663]

Put 2 cups of prepared pancake mix in a bowl; gradually add 1 cup of rich, cold milk, beating and stirring constantly. When smooth, beat in 1 tablespoon of melted sweet butter.

Wash in ice water and pick from the stems 1 cup of fresh elder blossoms. Drain well, and dry. Add to the pancake batter and bake in individual frying pan in the usual way. Serve with honey, maple syrup or crushed fresh raspberries or strawberries.

FLEMISH PANCAKES [1664]

Mix and sift together 1½ cups of flour and ½ teaspoon of salt. Beat 2 large eggs; combine with 1½ cups (about) of sour milk, and gradually stir into the flour mixture, beating briskly after each addition to make a smooth batter of pancake consistency. Let stand for 1½ hours, then stir in ¼ cup of melted butter, alternately with 1 scant teaspoon of soda which has been dissolved in a little hot water. Beat briskly for a minute. Cook in individual greased frying pan, using hot lard in preference to any other shortening, for the greasing. Pile the pancakes one on another, with a thick layer of crushed sweetened ripe fruit between. Sprinkle with powdered sugar and serve as hot as possible.

FRENCH FRIED PANCAKES [1665]

Beat together until smooth 5 tablespoons of pastry flour, 2 tablespoons of granulated sugar, 1 whole egg, 3 egg yolks, and ⅛ teaspoon of any preferred flavoring extract. Gradually add enough cold milk to make a batter heavy enough to coat the bowl of a spoon.

Drop 3 tablespoons of this batter into a large, light frying pan, brushed with melted butter, tilting the pan so that the batter completely covers the bottom. Cook, browning on both sides, as for ordinary pancakes. Turn the pancake on to a hot large round platter; sprinkle with 1 generous teaspoon of kirsch, rum, brandy, or other preferred liqueur; then spread over this a thick layer of jam, jelly, marmalade or preserve. Roll up sausage-like; cut into slanting inch-wide pieces; roll in slightly beaten egg, then in sieved macaroons, ladyfingers, cookies or cake crumbs. Place a few at a time in a frying basket, and when ready to serve, plunge quickly into hot, deep fat (375° 390° F.) for a minute, or until crisp and brown. Drain on absorbent paper; arrange on a hot platter on a folded napkin, or paper doily, sprinkle with powdered sugar, and serve with liqueur hard sauce (See Dessert Sauces No. 1993.)

FRENCH PANCAKES [1666]
Crêpes à la Française

There are two kinds of French pancakes, those made with yeast, and those made without leavening of any kind.

One associates French Crêpes with the more exclusive eating establishments rather than with the average American kitchen, especially when he thinks of Crêpes Suzette as a de luxe dessert whereas in reality these pancakes are very economical. Combine 6 eggs, 4 tablespoons of flour, 2 teaspoons of cold water, or better still, brandy, rum, applejack or any preferred liqueur, and a few grains of salt.

Mix thoroughly to the consistency of cream. When ready to serve, put into a small, individual, light frying pan ½ scant teaspoon of butter; spread it all over the bottom of the pan, and pour in 1 tablespoon of the batter or enough to just cover the bottom of the pan. Shake the pan deftly so as to spread the batter evenly and cook for about a minute, over medium heat, then turn the pancake and cook the other side. If you are skillful you can toss it. When nicely browned fold or roll each pancake. If folding, fold first in half, then in quarters and keep hot while repeating the performance till all the batter is used.

Pancakes or "crêpes" may be filled with jam, jelly, or marmalade, or simply sprinkled with powdered sugar. They may also be set aflame, using brandy and sugar, in the usual way. Makes 16 pancakes.

NETHERLAND CHICKEN PANCAKES [1667]

Using the coarse blade, put 2 cups of boned, cooked chicken through food chopper. Using the finest blade, put through food chopper ½ cup of peeled chopped, fresh mushrooms. Cook the mushrooms in 1 tablespoon of butter for a minute or two, or until they just begin to take on color, stirring constantly, then stir in ½ cup of sifted flour, mixed with the ground chicken, also 3 tablespoons of melted butter. Blend well. Gradually add 2 cups of hot chicken stock, highly seasoned with salt, pepper a few grains each of cayenne pepper, thyme, nutmeg, cloves, mace and allspice, 2 teaspoons of onion juice and 1 clove of garlic, mashed. Cook gently until mixture begins to thicken, stirring constantly.

Have ready a dozen baked French pancakes (No. 1666); fill each pancake with part of the mixture; roll up carefully, tucking in the ends;

dip each pancake in seasoned beaten egg, then roll in fine bread crumbs; arrange close together in a generously buttered baking dish, and bake in a moderate oven (350° F.), basting frequently with melted butter, until crisp and well-browned. Serve immediately.

PEACH GRIDDLE CAKES [1668]

Sift together 2½ cups bread flour, ½ teaspoon salt, 1 tablespoon granulated sugar, and 1 teaspoon baking soda. Add very slowly 1½ cups sour milk, and 1 whole egg and 1 yolk, beaten together. Beat briskly until smooth; then add 1 tablespoon melted shortening, 1 cup fresh or canned peaches, very finely sliced or chopped, and beat the mixture again. Bake the cakes on a hot generously greased griddle. Serve very hot, accompanied by a hot peach syrup made with the juice from a can of peaches, ½ cup brown sugar, or less, as needed, a dash of salt, and a few drops vanilla extract, all brought to a boil and simmered for a few minutes. Or, if preferred serve with plain cream.

RICE PANCAKES [1669]

Sift 2 cups of flour once; measure, return to sifter; add 1 tablespoon of baking powder, 2 tablespoons sugar and ¾ teaspoon salt, and resift. Beat 2 eggs, stir into 1½ cups of cold sweet milk, and add gradually to the flour mixture, stirring constantly, adding with the last portion 1 cup of cold, cooked rice and ¼ cup of melted butter. Drop from a tablespoon on to a hot, greased griddle, browning on both sides. Serve with maple, corn or any desired syrup, honey or crushed berries in season.

SCOTCH MUTTON PANCAKES [1670]

Combine 2 cups of cold oatmeal with 2 cups of cold cooked ground left over mutton (or lamb) and beat in 3 eggs, one at a time, beating well after each addition and seasoning to taste with salt, pepper and a dash each of nutmeg and thyme. Blend well and cook as ordinary pancakes.

These cakes make a delicious breakfast dish when served with hot fruit sauce. For luncheon, serve with Tomato, Cheese or Egg Sauce (No. 1130, No. 1027 or No. 1051).

SOURDOUGH PANCAKES [1671]
(*Makes 18*)

Take 1 cup sourdough (see below), stir in 1 cup flour and let stand overnight. Add 1 cup water and 1 egg. Beat thoroughly. Sift in another cup of flour, combined with ½ teaspoon salt, 1 tablespoon granulated sugar, and 1 teaspoon soda. Beat with a spoon or small wire whip until smooth. Add 1 tablespoon bacon drippings, or melted fresh bacon fat, and fry on a hot griddle. The batter should be about the consistency of heavy cream.

To make Sourdough. Mix 1 cup flour and 1 cup water and then let stand 2 or 3 days in a warm place until fermented. (Or a little unused pancake batter may be allowed to sour, or bread sponge can be used, but should be quite sour.) A sponge, which ferments the fastest of all, can be purchased at a bakery, and if water is added after each making, the original start of sourdough can be drawn upon continuously.

SOY FLOUR GRIDDLE CAKES [1672]

Sift together 1 cup of bread flour, 1 cup of soy flour, 2½ tablespoons of sugar, ½ teaspoon of salt and 4 teaspoons of baking powder. Make a hollow in center and add 2 eggs beaten as for an omelet, combined with 2 cups of cold milk and ¼ cup of melted butter or margarin. Beat mixture thoroughly, until smooth and free from lumps. Bake as any griddle cakes

WAFFLES [1673]

The waffle is generally regarded as a southern invention because it is most often served in tearooms as an accompaniment to fried chicken. Actually the first waffle dates from the time of the Crusades. One October day in the year 1204, Sir Giles Wimple returned from Jerusalem to his country place in Cornwall. It was a Friday and his good lady Ermintrude was in the midst of baking cakes when he arrived; but she dropped everything to greet him.

"And now sitte downe and tell me all about ye pilgrimage," said lady Ermintrude after she had bussed him on both cheeks. "Didst bagge any Saracens, pardee?"

Sir Giles who was attired in full suit of chain armor, sat down heavily on the settle by the stove. "Ye feete are damme near kyllynge me!" he sighed. "Wel, to beginne with—" And for the next half-hour he regaled his good lady with an account of his journey to Jerusalem.

"I hadde a hunche thou wolde be back today," said Lady Ermintrude when he had finished. " . . . and did thy favorite oaten cake y-bake."

"Hot dogge!" exclaimed Sir Giles, slapping his mailed thigh. "Fain wolde I eate it now."

Lady Ermintrude glanced into the oven. "I wist not," she began, puzzled. Then she uttered a cry of dismay.

"Giles! Methinks 'tis on ye settle."

Sir Giles clanked hastily to his feet.

There on the settle lay a disk of delicately browned pastry. But it was smashed as flat as a pancake. In fact, it might have been a pancake except that its surface was covered with rows of little indentations—the imprint of Sir Giles' chain armor. At sight of it, lady Ermintrude flew into high dudgeon. "'Tis ruined!" she cried.

"Fetch me a firkin of Devon butter, and I will eate ye whole damme thynge," he declared.

Spreading the butter over the still warm cake, he began devouring it with unaffected enjoyment. Meanwhile, Lady Ermintrude, observing how the pattern on the cake caught and held the melted butter, was tempted to taste it herself. "Pardon ye ermintrusion," she said finally, sitting down beside her husband. "Methinks I will trye just a smydgyn."

It proved delectable beyond her expectation, largely because of the little indentations that kept the butter from running away. So every Friday thereafter it became Sir Giles' duty to put on his suit of chain armor and sit on the oaten cakes his good lady baked. Her fame spread throughout the land, and the cakes were called "waffles" because it is a word that is easy to pronounce when one's mouth is full.

WAFFLES—HINTS [1674]

There are two kinds of waffles: (1) "raised" waffles made from a yeast mixture, and (2) a batter leavened by the use of baking powder or soda. Since the latter are more commonly used, we will consider them only, here.

There are two ways of achieving delightful crispness in waffles: The first is to use *no sugar at all* because a batter with sugar fails to remain crisp for any length of time after baking. The second is *not to overload* the waffle baker because obviously the thinner the waffle is, the crisper it will be when baked. Thick waffles with soft bready centers never become really crisp throughout, although the crust will become crisp and brown with prolonged baking.

Eat your ham and waffles together by sprinkling each waffle with finely chopped ham before baking.

Serve creamed shrimp, crab or tuna fish on hot waffles. Delicious for Sunday night supper.

Honey, a little cream, a dash of cinnamon; heat together and serve. . . . Cider sauce is something a little different to serve with pancakes and waffles. Boil 1 cup of sugar and ½ cup of cider 4 or 5 minutes. Serve either warm or cold. Or substitute a sweet white wine, if desired, as Sauterne, for example.

Top dessert waffles with cream cheese mixed with cherry or blackberry jam. Be generous with both cheese and jam. No need for butter; the cheese is rich enough.

Have the waffle iron hot, the batter reasonably thin, be generous with butter . . . and to temper a waffle iron, clean the grids well with steel wool or a wire brush; wash well, heat the iron to baking temperature, then brush the grids with unsalted cooking oil or sweet butter.

If waffles bake unevenly, perhaps more batter is needed. Do not discard left-over batter. Store it in a tightly-covered jar in the refrigerator for subsequent use.

For a change, add a teaspoon of cinnamon and ¼ teaspoon cloves to your regular waffle recipe.

Waffles should brown *as soon as* they are poured into the iron, so see that the iron is very hot.

What's Wrong and Why. Heavy waffles may be caused by: (a) Too little baking powder. (b) Too much flour—batter should be thin enough to pour easily. (c) Opening lid before waffles are baked will cause them to fall and be heavy.

Dry waffles may be due to (a) too little oil or shortening; (b) wrong kind of flour used—pastry or cake flour makes the most tender waffles; (c) corn meal, if used in waffles, should be pre-cooked, that is, have boiling water poured over it to prevent that dry, mealy taste.

Waffles stick to the iron because of: (a) too much sugar; (b) too little oil or shortening; (c) iron not sufficiently greased (if the kind which requires greasing); (d) iron not sufficiently hot; (e) added material such as nuts, cheese, chopped meat, chopped fish or shellfish, fruits, etc., in too large pieces.

APPLE WAFFLES [1675]

Chop ½ cup of peeled, cored raw apples; add 2 tablespoons of orange juice and a generous dash of nutmeg. Let stand 15 minutes. Add to Basic Waffle recipe (No. 1676). Heat waffle iron 6 to 8 minutes; pour on batter and bake 2 or 3 minutes. Serve with butter and syrup.

BASIC WAFFLE RECIPE [1676]
(Makes 6 waffles of 4 sections each)

Sift 2 cups of pastry or cake flour once; return to sifter, add 2 teaspoons of combination-type baking powder, or 4 teaspoons of tartrate or phosphate baking powder, and ¼ to ⅓ teaspoon of salt, and sift again. Beat 2 egg yolks until light, add to 1¼ cups of cold milk and 6 tablespoons of melted shortening, and stir into flour mixture, beating until smooth and free from lumps. Beat 2 egg whites until stiff and fold gently into batter. Pour batter into a pitcher, this being the simplest method to use for pouring onto hot waffle iron. Be sure that the iron is the proper temperature before waffle batter is poured. This is a simple matter with those having automatic timers. For irons not so equipped, a good test is to heat the iron until smoking hot, then sprinkle in a teaspoonful of cold water. When it stops steaming, the iron is sufficiently cool to use. If the water does not steam the iron is *not* hot enough. With non-electric irons, heat both sides of the iron. Grease (except with aluminum) and reverse so that the fat is evenly distributed. Open the iron and pour batter in center of each section until iron is two-thirds full. Close lid quickly and bake

1 to 1½ minutes, then reverse iron and bake 2 to 2½ minutes longer, depending on heat used.

If using an electric iron equipped with automatic timer, it is merely necessary to "set the timer." When the cooking or baking is completed, a green light shows that it is time to open the iron and take out the perfectly baked waffle. All guesswork is eliminated. Waffles should be put onto a very hot plate and served at once.

Important. Before making the next waffle, the lid should be closed to allow the iron to reheat to the proper temperature. With non-electric irons, which require greasing each time, the waffle mixture should contain less shortening than with irons which require no greasing. Before using an iron for the first time read the directions carefully. It is well to use a little extra shortening for the first waffle mixture when using a new iron.

BACON WAFFLES   [1677]

To Basic Waffle Recipe (No. 1676), add 3 strips of bacon cut very fine. Bake. Serve with maple or other preferred syrup.

BLUEBERRY WAFFLES   [1678]

To Basic Waffle Recipe (No. 1676) add 1 cup of picked, washed, dried sound blueberries. Bake and serve with honey or any preferred syrup.

BUTTERMILK CORNMEAL WAFFLES   [1679]

Cook 1 cup of corn meal in 1½ cups of salted water and 1½ tablespoons of shortening for ten minutes, stirring constantly. The mixture should be absolutely free from lumps. Cool, then beat in 2 well-beaten egg yolks. Now stir in 1 cup of pastry or cake flour, sifted once, then resifted with ¾ teaspoon of soda and 1 teaspoon of sugar, alternately with ½ cup of sweet milk. Fold in the 2 egg whites, stiffly beaten, alternately with enough buttermilk to make a pour batter. Bake. Serve with heated currant jelly.

Note. This batter is improved by standing a short time before baking.

CHEESE WAFFLES   [1680]

To Basic Waffle Recipe (No. 1676) add ¾ cup of grated cheese and bake. Serve topped with a piece of fried ham, a poached egg, or 2 or 3 strips of grilled bacon.

CHICKEN WAFFLES [1681]

To Basic Waffle Recipe, (No. 1676), add ¾ cup of finely ground, cooked chicken, turkey or any kind of cooked poultry. Bake. Serve with mushroom sauce, tomato sauce, or egg sauce.

CHOCOLATE WAFFLES [1682]

To Basic Waffle Recipe (No. 1676), add, mixing well, 3 tablespoons of ground unsweetened chocolate. Bake. Serve with whipped cream or honey.

CODFISH WAFFLES [1683]

To Basic Waffle Recipe (No. 1676) add ½ cup of cooked, flaked codfish (or substitute other fish if desired) and ½ teaspoon or more of prepared mustard. Bake. Serve topped with scrambled eggs.

GINGERBREAD WAFFLES PARISIAN STYLE [1684]

Mix and sift twice 2½ cups of pastry or cake flour, 1½ teaspoons of soda, 1 teaspoon of cinnamon, 1 teaspoon of ground ginger, ½ teaspoon of cloves and ½ teaspoon of salt. Combine ½ cup of melted butter, margain, or lard, 1¼ cups of dark molasses and 1 well beaten whole egg, and beat with rotary beater until thoroughly blended and add to the dry mixture alternately with ¾ cup of cold strong black coffee. Bake. Serve hot with drained, shredded pineapple.

MEAT WAFFLES [1685]

To Basic Waffle Recipe (No. 1676) add ¾ cup of finely chopped, cold, cooked meat (any kind). Bake. Serve with Curry Sauce (No. 1045) or Cheese Sauce (No. 1027) or Currant Jelly Gravy (No. 1040).

OATMEAL WAFFLES SCOTCH STYLE [1686]

Combine 2 cups of thin cream, coffee cream, or undiluted evaporated milk with 2 tablespoons of white vinegar, mixing thoroughly, and stir in 2 cups of quick cooking whole grain oats, let stand overnight in a cool place, but not in refrigerator. Next day beat in 2 egg yolks, one at a time, beating well after each addition, alternately add 6 tablespoons of melted butter or margarin. Then stir in ⅓ cup of cake flour, sifted with ½ generous teaspoon of salt and a very few grains of white pepper and 2½ teaspoons of baking powder mixed with ½ teaspoon of baking soda.

Fold in 2 stiffly beaten egg whites. Bake in the usual way (No. 1676) and serve topped with a poached egg and 2 strips of bacon.

RAISIN WAFFLES [1687]

To Basic Waffle Recipe (No. 1676) add ¾ cup of seedless raisins, previously plumped in boiling water, and dried, and 1 scant teaspoon of grated lemon rind. Bake. Serve with Butterscotch Sauce (No. 1969).

Variations. Substitute ¾ cup of finely chopped dried figs for raisins.

RICE WAFFLES [1688]

To Basic Waffle Recipe (No. 1676) add ¾ cup of firm cooked, rice. Bake. Serve with creamed chicken, chicken à la King, or chicken hash.

Variation. Add with the rice 2 teaspoons of curry powder moistened with a little cold milk.

BERRY WAFFLES [1689]

To Basic Waffle Recipe (No. 1676) add 1 tablespoon of sugar and 1 extra tablespoon of shortening, preferably butter. Bake. Serve with crushed fresh strawberries, raspberries or any other kind of berries.

SWEET POTATO WAFFLES [1690]

To 1 cup of mashed, cooked sweet potatoes, add ¼ cup of sugar, ½ cup of melted butter or margarin or other shortening and 1 cup of milk. Beat until smooth, then stir in 2 well beaten egg yolks. Mix thoroughly. Add 1 cup of pastry flour, sifted twice with 3 teaspoons of baking powder and ½ teaspoon of salt, and lastly fold in 2 stiffly beaten egg whites. Bake. Serve with chocolate, blueberry or eggnog sauce. (Nos. 1998, 1967 and 1974, respectively.)

Chapter Thirteen

SALADS, DRESSINGS AND SANDWICHES

SALADS, SALAD BOWLS, FRUIT SALADS, SALAD DRESSINGS, SANDWICHES, SANDWICH FILLINGS

Food never should be prepared in a dim light. Turn the brights on your salad, and see how it looks before your guest does.

—Oscar of the Waldorf.

SALADS

T HE TYPE OF SALAD SERVED DEPENDS UPON THE PART IT IS TO play in the meal, for "salad" is a term that has come to be loosely used. Salad may be served as a first course; immediately before the dessert, or as a part of the main course. In any of these instances it should be the green, leafy or Continental type, served with French dressing. It may be in itself a main dish at luncheon or supper, especially in spring and summer; in which case it should contain solid, nourishing ingredients, such as fish, chicken, shrimp, lobster, meat, or hearty vegetable.

Since appearance and texture are very important to the success of the salad, the ingredients must be fresh and of high quality. They must be handled quickly. Wilted vegetables do not appeal to the appetite, and the contents of the salad plate or bowl must be both in taste and appearance.

Among the absolutely necessary requirements of a good salad are: (1) freshness; (2) crispness; (3) appetizing flavor combinations; (4) color combinations; (5) appropriateness of dressing to the salad; and (6) perhaps more important than anything else, coldness.

The little extra care and time it takes to make a salad look like a picture is well worth while and pays in the end.

SALAD MAKING—HINTS

Young tender cucumbers give a cool enticing look if used unpeeled and fluted. Draw the prongs of a fork deeply lengthwise down the cucumber to make parallel grooves, then slice. Older cucumbers may also be fluted, but should be peeled first.

Brighten up the edges of lettuce leaves, or pineapple rings, by dipping them in paprika. Pineapple looks tempting, too, when the edge is rolled in finely chopped parsley, chives, or nut meats.

Ripe olives add zest to salad dressing. They are especially good with banana and orange salads. A tart French dressing should be used for the base.

Use the fruit juices from salad fruits or fruit cocktail, to thin mayonnaise and to mix with French dressing.

Raw cranberries chopped and mixed with chopped apples make an attractive and flavorable garnish for fowl, meat or fish salads.

Grated walnuts are a pleasant surprise, either in the dressing or sprinkled on the salad.

Candied fruit peels add a festive touch to fruit salads.

Radish roses are easily and quickly made by cutting through the skin of red radishes to form petals. They make a decorative garnish, especially for vegetable salads.

Good toppings for fruit salads are chopped peanuts, raisins, shredded coconut, chopped candied fruit peels or shredded cherries.

A soupçon of Tabasco sauce or horseradish tones up a plain French dressing.

When dressing salad greens with oil and vinegar, first season with salt and pepper, add oil, then vinegar. If vinegar is added before oil, the greens become wet, and the oil doesn't cling to them, but settles to the bottom.

Vegetable salads are colorful, with almost pencil thin rings of red or green peppers. Wash peppers, remove seeds and slice very thinly crosswise.

Canned fruits for fruit salads are enriched with the aid of cubes or slices of fully ripe bananas.

Crisp young carrots cut into slivers dress up the plainest salad

Add some bits of crisp bacon to a green salad or a few anchovies or flaked sardines. Not too many, just enough to flavor.

The dark and often bruised and homely outside leaves of lettuce may be cooked with other greens. Do not throw them away.

Shake a few drops of onion juice into your French dressing; a faint suspicion of garlic, or a little paprika atop mayonnaise; and shake a little coconut on dessert salads.

Two small salads on one plate are being featured in many restaurants; one is of meat, fish or fowl, the other of fruit or a fruited gelatine salad.

A bit of Roquefort cheese crumbled into French dressing adds a sophisticated flavor. It's especially good with fruit salads.

Ripe olives chopped or sliced incorporated in the salad or used whole as garnish, do much to establish a reputation as a good salad-maker.

To improve the flavor and texture of chicken used in salads, let the cooked chicken stand at least an hour or so in the broth. Then cut into small cubes. Do not mince or chop it. Thin the salad dressing with a little chicken stock.

To sour cream for salad dressings, add a little lemon juice or vinegar to sweet cream.

A fruit gelatin sliced or cut into glistening cubes, gives that cool, colorful effect to a salad that is always enticing.

The tender inside leaves of raw spinach add an interesting flavor to other salad greens. They may also be served alone with a French dressing.

Substitute orange juice for vinegar in mint sauce and serve with fruit salad.

Escarole is a flat bunch of wide, curly-edged green leaves with a yellow center. It is a sandy vegetable, so needs soaking for at least half an hour. It is in great favor as a salad, and needs a good French dressing.

To assure crispness of celery, place in a pan of water with a few slices of lemon for an hour or two.

Lettuce can be decroated by filling a small bowl with water and sprinkling paprika on top. Revolve a head of lettuce in it; the leaves will be fringed with red.

Save all liquid from mustard pickles and add it to salad dressing in place of fresh vinegar and mustard. When making meat sandwiches this liquid may be mixed with the meat.

To flavor a fish salad, add a tablespoon or more of grated horseradish and chopped pimientos.

For salad purposes, tomatoes that average four or five to the pound are the most economical.

Even the tiniest hint of garlic will do much toward improving a green salad, or try rubbing the salad bowl with garlic instead of adding it to the salad.

Accent crisp light greens with dark parsley or watercress for color contrast.

When a few drops of onion juice are needed for flavoring, sprinkle a little salt on a slice of onion, then scrape the salted surface with a knife or spoon to obtain the juice.

ASPARAGUS   [1693]
(Jellied)

Dissolve 1 package of lemon gelatine in a cup of boiling water. Squeeze the juice of 2 tomatoes and the liquid from the asparagus into a cup and fill up with cold water and 2 teaspoons of vinegar. Add to the gelatine with the minced solid tomato and chop the asparagus tips into it. Place in individual molds and when firm turn onto nests of lettuce. Cover with a thin mayonnaise dressing, and garnish with red or green pepper rings and chopped celery.

ASPARAGUS AND STUFFED GREEN OLIVES   [1694]

Cut large olives in halves lengthwise and remove the pits. Moisten a cake of cream cheese with an equal amount of thick mayonnaise, shape into small balls the size of an ordinary walnut and roll in finely chopped nut meats. Place a cheese ball between the halves of olives and press together slightly. Arrange in nests of finely shredded crisp lettuce and place 6 asparagus tips on the inside of the nest. Serve with French dressing.

ASPARAGUS, SPINACH AND   [1695]
HARD-COOKED EGGS

Marinate one bunch of cooked asparagus and chill thoroughly. Arrange in small bouquet-like designs on a round platter covered with cold cooked spinach in branch. Decorate with quartered hard-cooked eggs. Serve with French dressing.

BEET RING AND COLE SLAW MARINETTE   [1696]

To 1 cup of diced cucumbers, add 1½ cups of diced cooked beets and arrange in a previously wet ring mold. Soak 1½ tablespoons of gelatin in ¼ cup of cold mushroom stock, then add 1¾ cups of hot, highly seasoned mushroom stock, the juice of 1 medium-sized lemon, and 1 teaspoon of grated lemon rind. Stir over hot water till thoroughly dissolved, then pour over the beets and cucumbers. Chill till firm. Unmold on crisp shredded romaine salad mixed with equal parts of watercress also shredded. If desired, fill center with seasoned coleslaw or any other kind of salad.

BEET, CELERY AND APPLE MOLDS [1697]
(*Individual*)

Dice 1 cup of celery. Add 1 cup peeled, cored, diced apples and the same amount of cooked, peeled and diced cold beets. Dissolve 1 package of lemon-flavored gelatine in 1 cup of warm beet water, add 3 tablespoons of wine vinegar, ¾ cup of cold orange juice and season to taste with salt and pepper. Mix thoroughly and chill. When beginning to set, fold in the celery, apples and beets, 1 tablespoon of minced chives, 1 tablespoon of minced parsley, and 1 tablespoon of grated onion. Turn the mixture into individual wet molds, and chill till firm. Unmold on crisp lettuce and serve with Mustard Mayonnaise dressing.

CABBAGE, CARROT AND APPLE [1698]

Marinate in French dressing for an hour 2 cups of finely shredded green cabbage, 1 cup of diced tart apple, and 1 cup of carrot cut julienne. Drain well. Arrange on a nest of finely shredded iceberg lettuce; cover with mayonnaise forced through a pastry-bag with a tube and sprinkle with very finely chopped walnut meats mixed with a little paprika and very finely chopped parsley.

CABBAGE AND PINEAPPLE [1699]
(*Molded*)

Combine 3 cups of finely shredded green cabbage, 1 teaspoon of finely chopped onion, ½ cup of pecan meats and 3 slices of diced pineapple, with ½ cup of finely chopped pimiento. Blend with thin mayonnaise. Press into a wet mold and chill. When ready to serve, unmold on a round platter over crisp watercress. Garnish with strips of mayonnaise forced through a pastry-bag with a tube, and sprinkle with finely chopped capers.

CABBAGE BOWL [1700]

Select a fine head of white cabbage. Trim neatly and soak in ice water for an hour. Carefully turn back the outer leaves, fasten with whole cloves or toothpicks. Cut out the inner part of the cabbage with a sharp knife and shred fine as for cole slaw. Wrap the cabbage shell in a damp cloth, and place in refrigerator to chill thoroughly. Fill with dressed vegetable salad mixed with either mayonnaise of French dressing, using the shredded cabbage, cooked string beans, peas, carrots and whatever other vegetables are available. Serve on a cold platter on a layer of shredded red cabbage mixed with chopped pimientos and chopped green pepper.

CAESAR SALAD   [1701]

Prepare 2 cups of fried croûtons (No. 203) in garlic-flavored olive oil. Place in wooden salad bowl rubbed with garlic, 2 medium-sized heads crisp chilled romain, leaves separated and broken. Sprinkle over it ¼ teaspoon dry mustard, black pepper, ½ teaspoon salt, 4 ozs. grated Parmesan or crumbled blue cheese. Add 6 tablespoons pure olive oil and juice of 2 medium-sized lemons. Break 2 raw eggs over salad, toss and mix gently, until all trace of eggs has disappeared and the leaves have absorbed all liquid. Taste for seasoning. Just before serving, add the fried croûtons, mixing and tossing salad again, being careful croûtons do not become soggy. Make at table just before serving.

COLE SLAW   [1702]

Soak crisp, finely shredded white cabbage in ice water to which a little lemon juice has been added. Drain and chill. Marinate with French dressing for an hour, then add 1 cup of finely chopped celery, 1 cup of finely sliced cucumber and 1 medium-sized onion chopped very fine. Toss well together and chill. When ready to serve, add ½ cup of French dressing. Mix thoroughly and arrange on a round platter on a bed of crisp lettuce or watercress.

CUCUMBER (*Plain*)   [1703]

Remove and discard thick slices from both ends of a well-chilled cucumber, pare and slice thinly over a bowl, sprinkling well with salt. Place a heavy weight over it and let the cucumber stand in this salt marinade for at least 2 hours. When ready to serve, pour off water, placing a saucer over the bowl and pressing well so as to extract all the liquid possible. Arrange on a round platter on a bed of crisp, green lettuce. Serve with French dressing No. (1756).

Cucumber prepared in this way will never be indigestible.

CUCUMBER BASKETS [1704]

Select 3 large heavy well-chilled cucumbers of the same size; pare them and shape into baskets. Fill with any left-over cooked vegetables, such as peas, string beans, carrots, small diced potatoes, beets, and so forth, mixed with washed capers and finely chopped sweet and sour gherkins marinated in French dressing (No. 1756). Arrange on a bed of finely shredded lettuce sprinkled with finely chopped hard-cooked eggs. Serve with additional French dressing.

CUCUMBER CREAM CHEESE SLICES [1705]

Cut 2 large cucumbers in half crosswise. Peel and remove the seeds. Sprinkle the insides with mixed salt and white pepper to which a few grains of nutmeg may be added. Combine $1\frac{1}{2}$ packages of cream cheese with 1 tablespoon of onion juice, 2 tablespoons green pepper, minced very fine, 2 tablespoons of ground nutmeats, 1 tablespoon of pimiento, minced fine, 1 tablespoon of sweet-sour gherkins minced fine, salt, pepper and a few grains of Cayenne pepper. Mix thoroughly, then add 2 teaspoons Worcestershire sauce. Now fill the hollow parts of cucumbers, packing solid, and chill for at least 2 hours. To serve, slice $\frac{1}{4}$-inch thick, place 3 or 4 slices in crisp lettuce cup, garnish with ripe olives and a few capers, and decorate with a dot of mayonnaise forced through a pastry bag with a small fancy tube. Just before serving, dust with finely minced parsley, and a little paprika.

CUCUMBER HORSESHOE [1706]

Pare a long straight, well-chilled cucumber of the so-called telegraph species, cut in two lengthwise, remove the seeds and soft parts and slice lengthwise as thinly as possible. Arrange horseshoe fashion on a bed of crisp young watercress. Sprinkle with finely chopped hard-cooked eggs. Serve with Cream (Mayonnaise) dressing (No. 1785).

CUCUMBER POLONAISE [1707]

Arrange on a bed of finely shredded lettuce a small bouquet of equal parts of the following cooked vegetables marinated in French dressing (No. 1756): diced potatoes, string beans, carrots and white turnips; sliced beets, sliced hard-cooked eggs, navy beans and cauliflower. Place in center of larger bouquet of fine sliced cucumber marinated in thin mayonnaise. Sprinkle with finely chopped parsley. Serve very cold with additional mayonnaise and thin slices of buttered brown bread.

CUCUMBER, TOMATO AND LETTUCE [1708]

Arrange peeled, sliced and well-chilled tomatoes on a bed of finely shredded lettuce. Place on each slice, ½-inch cucumber cubes, first paring and chilling the cucumber and removing the seeds. Serve with French dressing.

LEEKS FRENCH METHOD [1709]

Select 1 dozen (or a bunch of) large leeks. Cut off the roots close to the stem, then cut out the green parts, reserving them for the soup. Wash in several waters. Tie them 3 or 4 together as you would asparagus. Cook in salted boiling water for 25 minutes or till tender (depending on size). Lift out carefully and drain thoroughly. Chill and arrange on a cold long platter on a napkin. Sprinkle with 2 hard-cooked eggs, coarsely chopped and mixed with 1 tablespoon each of minced chives and parsley. Serve ice cold with French dressing (No. 1756). They may also be served hot, with the same kind of dressing.

POTATO SALAD [1710]
(Hot)

Wash five or six medium-sized potatoes and cook in their skins in cold salted water until tender, taking care that the water just covers the potatoes so they will be mellow. Cool, peel and cut in very thin slices. Cover the bottom of a baking dish with sliced potatoes, season to taste with salt, pepper and a little paprika. Sprinkle with finely chopped celery leaves, parsley, chopped onion, tarragon leaves in the order given and pour over all ½ cup of French dressing (No. 1756). Cover with another layer of potatoes and seasoning ingredients. Set on the fire and bring slowly to boiling point. Serve with additional French dressing.

POTATO SALAD CARUSO [1711]

Arrange in a round bowl a layer of potatoes (cooked) cut the size of a silver quarter with a round cutter, sprinkle with finely chopped chervil; next a layer of cooked celery root, cut like potatoes; sprinkle with a few finely chopped capers, then a layer of artichoke bottoms cut like the potatoes, and sprinkle with finely chopped celery. Repeat until the bowl is full. (All ingredients should be first blended with thin mayonnaise.) Unmold on a bed of crisp, young watercress; decorate the edge with asparagus tips, pointing outward. Surround the base of the potato with stiff mayonnaise mixed with a little tomato purée forced through a pastry bag with a fancy tube. Finally, sprinkle over the yolk of a hard-cooked egg pressed through a fine sieve.

POTATO SALAD ESCOFFIER   [1712]

Toss in a large salad bowl carefully—so that they won't be broken—a julienne of cooked new potatoes, with French dressing and arrange loosely on a cold platter covered with crisp watercress. Surround the base of the potatoes with a ring of cooked string beans cut julienne and marinated in French dressing. Then another ring of finely sliced beets with French dressing. Decorate with mayonnaise forced through a pastry bag with a tube between each ring of vegetable, and sprinkle with finely chopped pistachio nuts.

POTATO SALAD RACHEL   [1713]

Arrange the following on a cold platter covered with crisp lettuce, using in equal parts of each: bouquet of julienne of celery; julienne of truffles; julienne of artichoke bottoms; julienne of cooked new potatoes; and small green asparagus tips. Decorate with a ribbon of stiff mayonnaise forced through a pastry bag with a small fancy tube, and between the bouquets of vegetables have a large dot of the same mayonnaise topped with a blanched almond.

TOMATOES A LA GREQUE   [1714]

Scald, peel and cut in sections 4 tomatoes of uniform size. Marinate each separately with French dressing and chill thoroughly. Pare and cut a large tart apple in 8 lengthwise, then cut sections in thin slices, crosswise. Parboil a large green pepper in boiling salted water for about 5 minutes. Cut in halves, remove the seeds and slice julienne style (strips). Wash, scrape and cut a small stalk of celery, julienne style. Arrange all the ingredients on a cold, round platter covered with finely shredded lettuce; decorate with slices of hard-cooked eggs and small designs from mayonnaise forced through a pastry bag and tube. Sprinkle paprika over the mayonnaise, and finely chopped parsley and chives over the rest of the ingredients. Serve green-colored mayonnaise (No. 1793) separately.

TOMATO BASKET BEATRICE   [1715]

Select medium-sized, ripe firm tomatoes of uniform size. Cut a thin slice from stem ends and scoop pulp out carefully. Rub the insides with salt and pepper and fill with mayonnaise mixed with a little paprika and small cubes of chicken. Smooth the tops, and cover with narrow criss-cross strips of pimiento. Form a handle of a strip of tomato and stick a small sprig of curled parsley on each side. Serve on individual plates, garnishing with shredded lettuce and green pepper.

TOMATO BASKET EMILY [1716]

Prepare tomatoes as indicated for recipe "Tomato Basket Beatrice" (No. 1715). Brush the cavities with slightly melted anchovy butter and fill the tomatoes with vegetable salad. Garnish with thin slices of smoked salmon rolled in rosettes, and thin slices of sweet-sour gherkins. Form a handle with a strip of green pepper. Arrange on individual plates on mixed crisp watercress and shredded celery. Garnish with a thin slice of lemon topped with a stuffed rolled anchovy filet.

TOMATO PORCUPINE [1717]

Scald, peel, and chill tomatoes of equal size, then stick with narrow strips of celery and green pepper at regular intervals allowing 12 altogether for each tomato. Force stiff mayonnaise through a pastry bag with a fancy tube, and use to make fancy designs between the sticks, entirely covering the red of the tomato. Sprinkle paprika mixed with very finely chopped chervil or parsley over the mayonnaise. Arrange on a round, cold platter or on individual plates on crisp green lettuce, placing under each tomato a round of freshly made toast spread with anchovy paste, cream cheese, Roquefort or any other preferred cheese.

TOMATO ROBERT [1718]

Cut 3 small, ripe firm tomatoes of uniform size in halves. Scoop the pulp slightly from the insides. Have ready 6 hard-cooked eggs, cut a slice from the small end of each, so that they may stand upright. Decorate the bottom of a large, round cold platter with 1 generous cup of green mayonnaise forced through a pastry bag with a small fancy tube. Press the hard-cooked egg, flat end down in a circle around the edge and into the mayonnaise. Top each egg with a half tomato, round side up, to form a mushroom. Garnish with 1 dozen small red radish roses. Dust the top of each tomato (which has been brushed with melted butter) with cinnamon and arrange a large bunch of crisp, green watercress in center of platter.

TOMATO (JELLIED) SURPRISE [1719]
(*Molded*)

Soak one package of gelatin in a cup of cold water for 10 minutes. Strain a 2 quart can of tomatoes. Heat the tomato liquid, add the softened gelatin, season with salt, white pepper and 1 tablespoon of granulated sugar. Pour a thin layer of this liquid into a wet mold, and when almost at the setting point, add a layer of chopped celery, another of jelly, next a layer of peas (cooked), one more of jelly, another of stuffed olives, and lastly the remainder of the jelly. Chill, unmold on a nest of very finely shredded lettuce or crisp young watercress and serve with boiled salad dressing.

WATERCRESS [1720]

Watercress, sometimes called "peppercress," belongs to a group of vegetables of which lettuce is the chief type. The leaves and stems are eaten raw. Watercress contains iron, which helps build teeth and bones, a good amount of roughage to regulate digestion; vitamin A, which gives strength, aids growth, prevents some eye diseases and builds resistance; vitamin B, which builds appetite, helps growth and prevents beri-beri; and vitamin C, in abundance, which builds health and prevents scurvy; and a trace of vitamin D, which makes strong bones and prevents rickets.

When fresh, watercress is bright green. If too many of the leaves are yellow, the watercress is probably old and of disagreeable flavor. The large-leafed variety is as well-flavored as the small-leafed, although a little stronger.

To clean watercress, untie, throw into cold water and soak for a good half hour when all the sand will have settled on the bottom. Lift out, put into a salad bag or salad basket; shake free from water and put on ice.

APPLE AND CREAM CHEESE BALLS [1721]

Wipe and pare extra large apples; shape with a ball cutter into balls the size of a small walnut and dip immediately into French dressing. Chill thoroughly. Meanwhile mash a cream cheese and add 1 teaspoon, each, of chopped pimiento and Worcestershire sauce, with a few grains of salt. Shape into balls the size of the apple balls. Arrange on a nest of finely shredded lettuce and sprinkle with paprika, leaving a space in the center for mayonnaise mixed with whipped cream in equal parts, then forced through a pastry bag, using a fancy tube.

APPLE, DATES AND ALMONDS [1722]

Peel and dice five medium-sized tart apples and add to them $\frac{1}{4}$ cup of coarsely chopped almonds and $\frac{1}{2}$ cup of stoned, chopped dates. Moisten with thin mayonnaise to which has been added half a teaspoon of finely chopped lemon peel and a tablespoon of prepared horseradish. Arrange on a platter covered with crisp lettuce nests and surround each portion with stiff mayonnaise forced through a pastry bag with tube. Garnish with thin slices of pickled beet on which place a well washed caper.

APPLE GELATIN ROSITA   [1723]
(Molded)

Peel, halve and core several large red apples and drop them immediately into boiling sugar sirup with cinnamon drops added to color the apples red. Cook until tender. Meanwhile dissolve 1 package of lemon gelatin in two cups of hot water. Let cool and when beginning to set pour a little into individual molds, and sprinkle on each a tablespoon of seeded red currants; add a halved apple, fill up with gelatin and chill. Dress on a cold, round platter on a bed of field salad sprinkled generously with finely chopped hard-cooked eggs and walnuts. Top with Suzette's Dressing (No. 1816) forced through a pastry bag using a small fancy tube.

APRICOT JELLY   [1724]
(Molded)

Soften 1½ tablespoons of lemon gelatin in a little cold water and add ¼ cup of heated French dressing. Stir well and keep hot. Meanwhile combine one can of apricots, well-drained and halved, ½ cup of coarsely chopped orange and lemon peels, ½ cup of coarsely chopped walnut meats, 2 tablespoons of coarsely chopped pimiento and 2 tablespoons of green pepper finely chopped. Toss, then add the gelatin mixture. Stir and cool. Turn into a wet mold and chill. Unmold onto a round cold platter on a bed of finely shredded red cabbage interspersed with slices of pineapple. Serve with Whipped Cream Jelly Dressing (No. 1818).

APRICOT ORANGE CHEESE ROSETTE   [1725]

Thoroughly drain a can of apricots. Fill cavities with Roquefort cheese mixed with finely minced chives. Arrange 3 apricot halves on individual cold plates, on a bed of finely shredded red cabbage marinated with French dressing, (No. 1756). Between two of the apricot halves place a section of orange; and on top of each apricot place a rosette of creamed Roquefort cheese with 3 smaller rosettes around each base.

Rosettes are made by softening any kind of cheese with a little undiluted evaporated milk, cream or even plain milk and forced through a pastry bag with a small fancy tube.

AVOCADO, DATE AND ORANGE   [1726]

Peel 3 medium-sized avocados and cube small. Place in a bowl and add 1 teaspoon of thinly sliced onion. Over this strew 1 cup of pitted and coarsely chopped dates, and sprinkle with 1 tablespoon of chives, minced; then add 1 cup of peeled, sectioned orange, also cubed. Season to taste with salt and pepper and pour over ¾ cup of French dressing (No. 1756). Toss well and serve on individual plates in lettuce cups, dusting with a little paprika.

AVOCADO, EGG AND ROQUEFORT   [1727]
CHEESE-BOWL

Peel 2 medium-sized avocados and cube small. Place in a bowl and sprinkle with a little lime juice. Add 3 sliced hard-cooked eggs, with ½ cup of French dressing (No. 1756) to which a generous teaspoon of prepared mustard has been added, and toss. Now rub a salad bowl with a little garlic. Line the bottom and sides with crisp, green lettuce and turn the avocado mixture into it. Crumble 2 tablespoons of Roquefort cheese over all, dust with 1 tablespoon of minced chives and serve at once. Just before serving, toss again to mix the cheese and chives with the fruit and eggs.

AVOCADO, GRAPEFRUIT AND MINT   [1728]

Peel 3 medium-sized avocados, cut in half lengthwise, remove the seed. Have ready 1 large grapefruit, sectioned, with membranes removed. Arrange grapefruit sections in cavities of avocados, sprinkle with fresh minced mint and arrange on individual plates in watercress nests. Serve with French Dressing (No. 1756).

BANANA BALLS IN BASKET   [1729]

Scoop out six large oranges of even size, leaving a handle to form a basket. Make sufficient small banana balls with a vegetable cutter to fill the baskets. Dip ⅓ of the balls in beaten egg and roll in paprika, ⅓ in very finely chopped parsley and the remaining third in very finely chopped nuts. Spread the bottom of each orange basket lightly with mayonnaise and drop in 2 or 3 balls of each flavor. Arrange the baskets on a large, cold round platter or on individual plates, garnishing with very finely shredded lettuce. Serve with boiled fruit dressing.

BANANA, DATE AND WALNUT   [1730]

Peel 5 bananas, scoop out small balls with a vegetable cutter and dip rapidly into lemon juice. Drain and roll in very finely chopped blanched almonds until heavily coated. Arrange on a cold round platter in nests of finely shredded green crisp lettuce. Remove the stones from 1½ dozen large dates, stuff with pineapple and place 3 dates on the edge of each nest. Surround the base of each nest with mayonnaise forced through a pastry bag with a small fancy tube, and sprinkle the mayonnaise with coarsely chopped walnut meats. Serve with mayonnaise dressing to which has been added 2 tablespoons of tomato paste.

BANANA, ORANGE AND CANTELOUPE   [1731]

Arrange a bed of lettuce on a salad platter, over this place sliced bananas, marinated in French dressing (No. 1756). Cover the bananas, in turn, with sections of orange. In the center set a nest of watercress, filled with small balls scooped from a ripe cantaloupe. Dot the base of the nest with mayonnaise and whipped cream, blended in equal parts, and flavored with lemon juice, forcing this through a pastry bag, using a small fancy tube. Between the dots of mayonnaise place half walnuts peeled and dipped in oil.

Serve with additional whipped cream, lemon flavored mayonnaise.

CHERRY DELMONICO   [1732]

Drain thoroughly a can of large red sweet cherries. Remove the pits and replace with small blanched roasted almonds.

Arrange nests of crisp watercress on individual chilled plates. Line each nest with mayonnaise and fill with the stuffed cherries, each rolled in cream cheese softened with cream or undiluted evaporated milk, having the finished balls the size of a large walnut. Use three balls in each nest and dust with a few grains of paprika blended with cinnamon.

CHERRY AND PINEAPPLE WHEEL   [1733]

Arrange finely shredded lettuce or romaine on chilled, individual plates. Place over a pineapple slice cut into 6 sections; between each 2 sections arrange a large pitted cherry filled with Roquefort cheese, creamed smooth with a little minced chives. In the center place a date pitted and filled with a piece of walnut. Surround the edge of the lettuce with mustard mayonnaise forced through a pastry bag using a small fancy tube; dust with a little cinnamon mixed with paprika.

CANTALOUPE NELLIE MELBA   [1734]

Peel and dice as many ripe cantaloupes as required. Wash and drain one pint of raspberries for each two cantaloupes. Combine the two fruits and add one banana diced. Toss the fruit rapidly and gently with French dressing (No. 1756) made with raspberry vinegar instead of vinegar.

Arrange on slices of crisp lettuce placing a ring of canned pineapple on each slice. Serve very cold.

CRANBERRY, GRAPES AND CELERY RING MOLD [1735]

Soften 2 tablespoons of granulated gelatin in a little cold water. Cook 1 quart of cranberries in 3 cups of water until soft, then strain into gelatin; stir and cool until almost at the setting point, then add 1 cup of halved seedless grapes and ½ cup of diced celery. Pour into a wet ring mold and chill. Unmold on a cold round platter on a bed of finely shredded romaine and fill the center with boiled cream Russian dressing. Garnish with slices of hard-cooked eggs topped with thin slices of large sweet gherkins.

GRAPES, DATES AND NUTS [1736]

Wash and thoroughly dry 3 cups of small seedless white grapes. Add 1 cup of coarsely chopped walnut meats and ¾ cup of pitted chopped dates. Combine with thin mayonnaise and arrange on individual lettuce leaves. Cover with stiffly whipped cream to which has been added 2 tablespoons of tomato paste and a few drops of Worcestershire sauce, forced through a pastry bag, using a fancy tube. Top each salad with a nut-stuffed date.

GRAPE MARIA [1737]

Wash and thoroughly dry 2 cups of white seedless grapes and combine with equal parts of diced pineapple and celery. Moisten with a thin mayonnaise and mold in individual portions by means of demi-tasse cup. Unmold on a bed of undressed, finely shredded white cabbage sprinkled generously with finely chopped pickled beets and chopped parsley to give color contrast. Cover with thick mayonnaise to which has been added a teaspoon of prepared mustard and 1 teaspoon of tomato paste, forced through a pastry bag with tube, and sprinkle with paprika.

GRAPEFRUIT ASPIC ANNETTE [1738]

Soak 2 tablespoons of granulated gelatin in ½ cup cold grapefruit juice and dissolve in 2 cups of grapefruit juice that has been heated to boiling point. Decorate the bottom of an oiled large straight mold (or individual ones) with sections of grapefruit from which all the white membranes have been carefully, removed; cut each section in two crosswise. Pour in gently enough of the cooled gelatin mixture barely to cover the grapefruit. Chill and arrange another layer of the grapefruit sections. Repeat with the gelatin mixture barely to cover; let set and cover with a thin layer (about 1 inch) of peeled, cored, cubed apples. Cover with more gelatin and let set, then fill entirely with grapefruit sections. Pour in gelatin mixture to completely fill the mold and place in refrigerator to set. Unmold on a large chilled round platter on a bed of crisp young watercress, dipped in French dressing (No. 1756), and thoroughly shake. Decorate with small designs of mayonnaise forced through a pastry bag, using a small fancy tube. Serve at once.

GRAPEFRUIT, CHERRY AND CELERY [1739]

Shred one large head of chilled, cleaned lettuce as fine as possible, and combine with ½ cup of diced celery, ¾ cup of well-drained canned red cherries and 1 generous cup of grapefruit sections, and mix with ½ cup of French dressing (No. 1756). Arrange lightly on crisp romaine and serve with cheese straws.

GRAPEFRUIT MINT RING [1740]

Soften 2 tablespoons of lemon-flavored gelatin in 4 tablespoons of cold water. Add 3 cups of strained grapefruit juice heated to the boiling point (*do not boil*), 3 tablespoons of granulated sugar and 6 tablespoons of syrup from minted cherries. Stir till gelatin begins to thicken, then add 12 whole mint cherries, 12 grapes, and 12 small strawberries, hulled. Turn mixture into an oiled ring mold. Chill for 3 hours. Unmold on a large, round, chilled platter covered with crisp watercress and fill center with the following: A large honeydew melon, peeled, halved and cut into small balls, using a small French ball cutter. Do likewise with 2 large ripe pears, and also with 2 large bananas, dropping the fruit in lemon juice as soon as scooped into balls. Drain well and moisten with French dressing.

GRAPEFRUIT RAINBOW [1741]

This attractive and delicious salad may be prepared the day before using as it keeps well in a refrigerator for several days. It does require meticulous care to make, but the reward is worth while.

Three distinct operations are involved in its making and when the directions are strictly followed the effect is a delight both to the eye and to the palate.

Select small thin-skinned grapefruit of equal size (one grapefruit makes 4 portions). Make an opening at the end of each large enough to permit the entrance of a teaspoon. Carefully scoop out the inside.

Rinse the grapefruit shells under running cold water, turn upside down and drain thoroughly. Strain the pulp through a fine cloth, pressing a little to obtain as much juice as possible. Measure juice, and for each 1¼ cups, take 1 tablespoon granulated gelatin.

Soften this in grapefruit juice using 2 tablespoons of juice to the tablespoon of gelatin. Heat, *but do not boil* remaining juice and add 2 tablespoons of tarragon vinegar for each measure. Pour over the softened gelatin, and stir until dissolved. Divide into three equal portions, each in a separate container, and place these in a pan containing tepid water. Tint one portion red with vegetable coloring ,tint the second green, and leave the third portion clear. Place the prepared fruit shells in a pan containing crushed ice. Pour into each a tablespoon or two of the red mixture; let this just set, then pour in the same amount of the green, when this, also, has set add a portion of the clear mixture. Repeat the layers, in the same order until the shells are full to the top. Keep in refrigerator till needed, then cut each grapefruit in quarters with a sharp knife.

Arrange on a cold, round salad platter, crown-like, on a bed of very crisp finely shaved lettuce sprinkled with finely chopped red and green Maraschino cherries, and finely chopped blanched almonds.

With a pastry bag, using a fancy tube, place designs with blended mayonnaise and whipped cream. Pile cut up fruits in season in the center.

ORANGE, BANANA AND PECAN   [1742]

Cut 2 bananas (peeled) in quarters lengthwise and again crosswise and roll in finely chopped pecan meats. Peel 3 oranges, slice, and with an apple corer remove the center core. Place a cube of banana on center of each slice or orange. Arrange on individual plates on a bed of crisp shredded white cabbage, marinated in French dressing (No. 1756), squeezed, then tossed loose. Sprinkle over all a few chopped pecans, mixed with minced parsley. Serve with French dressing (No. 1756).

ORANGE CREAM CHEESE RING   [1743]

Peel, quarter, and remove seeds and membranes from 2 large oranges, then slice each section crosswise. Marinate in French dressing (No. 1756) for 30 minutes, in refrigerator. Soften 1 tablespoon granulated gelatin in ½ cup of cold orange juice and dissolve in ½ cup of orange juice heated to the boiling point, adding a small pinch of salt. Stir well and blend in 2 packages of cream cheese, seasoned to taste with a few grains of white pepper and ½ teaspoon of Worcestershire sauce, 2 tablespoons each of minced green pepper and parsley, and ½ teaspoon of grated onion, beating with a wooden spoon till mixture is smooth. Turn into an oiled ring mold, packing solid, and chill in refrigerator for 3 hours. Unmold on a cold round platter on a bed of crisp lettuce and fill center with well-drained orange slices. Dust a little paprika over the cheese and minced chives over the orange salad.

ORANGE RING JELLY [1744]
(Molded)

Soften 2 tablespoons of gelatin in 2 tablespoons of cold water, add 1 cup of boiling water sweetened with 1 tablespoon of granulated sugar; stir until gelatin is dissolved then add 1 cup of strained orange juice and 1 tablespoon of strained lemon juice. Blend thoroughly and pour into a wet border mold. Chill. Marinate 3 cups of orange sections with French dressing (No. 1756). Drain well and use to fill center of the jelly when unmolded on a cold round platter on a bed of crisp young watercress. Cover the top of the jelly ring with whipped cream to which has been added ½ teaspoon of French mustard and a generous tablespoon of tomato paste, forced through a pastry bag using a fancy tube.

PEACH (SPICED) AND CREAM CHEESE [1745]

Arrange on a cold round platter a bed of crisp lettuce and in center place a large cream cheese mashed, then mixed with a little fresh cream, 1 tablespoon of chopped pimiento and a scant teaspoon of prepared mustard. Cover the cheese with stiff mayonnaise forced through a pastry bag with fancy tube, and surround with halved spiced peaches.

PEACH, GRAPE AND GINGER ALE MOLD [1746]

Dissolve 1 package of orange-flavored gelatin in 1 cup of boiling water, add 1 cup of ginger ale, 1 tablespoon of lemon juice and ½ teaspoon of grated orange rind. Pour a little of the mixture into a lightly oiled ring mold. Arrange fresh sliced peaches in bottom of mold and place in refrigerator to set. Add a layer of grapes (seedless) and more of the gelatin mixture, allowing this to set after each addition and alternating the layers of peaches and gelatine, and grapes and gelatine, till the mold is full. Chill thoroughly. Unmold on a large round cold platter on a bed of crisp lettuce. Fill center with fresh strawberries washed and hulled, and serve with Cream Mayonnaise Dressing (No. 1785).

PEAR CACTUS [1747]

Stew ½ dozen Bartlett pears or use canned ones. Strain the juice from the pears and place on the fire with a small bag of mixed spices hanging in the liquid. Simmer for fifteen minutes and add the pears to soak for a few minutes. Drain carefully and stick each pear with shelled peanuts until covered with the nut "spines." Arrange on very finely shredded lettuce or young watercress and serve with a dish of the juice and another of mayonnaise.

PEAR FRENCH STYLE [1748]

Wipe, pare and cut in eighths, lengthwise, as many fresh pears as required, removing the seeds and coarse part of the center. Arrange on crisp green lettuce and garnish with ribbons of pimiento, green pepper and celery. Just before serving, pour over all a generous tablespoon of French Dressing (No. 1756).

PEAR NINA LANCLOS [1749]

Peel, cut in two lengthwise and core 6 large fresh pears. Scoop out a little of the pulp and place in the cavities 2 or 3 small fresh strawberries dipped in French Dressing (No. 1756) and well drained. Cover the berries with cream cheese seasoned to taste with salt and black pepper, spreading the cheese rather thickly all over the cut surface. Adjust another halved pear, also filled with berries, and press sandwich-like. Dip the pears thus formed in raspberry syrup to which has been added a tablespoon of lime juice, and carefully spread over one side finely chopped pistachio nuts, and on the other side parsley, minced fine and mixed with paprika. Arrange the pears standing in a circle of cream cheese moistened with a little French Dressing (No. 1756), and forced through a pastry-bag using a small fancy tube. With the handle of a knife make 3 holes in the cheese circle and fill each with a Bar-le-duc jam.

Serve with a side dish of whipped cream flavored with lemon juice and colored with saffron to the desired hue.

PINEAPPLE COLLETTE [1750]

Marinate 6 slices of canned pineapple in French Dressing (No. 1756) for 30 minutes. Drain and spread one side with cream cheese softened with whipped or plain thick cream. Halve and seed Malaga grapes and lay cut side down on cheese and pineapple, taking care to cover completely the cheese with the grapes. Arrange on individual plates on a bed of very finely shredded lettuce mixed with equal parts of red cabbage and a slice of pineapple. Garnish center of pineapple with a pompon of mayonnaise forced through a pastry bag with a small fancy tube; top with a red Maraschino cherry. Serve with a dish of mayonnaise dressing mixed with finely chopped walnuts.

PINEAPPLE GLORIA   [1751]

Arrange thin slices of fresh pineapple on a round platter covered with finely shredded French endive, and pile in the centre chopped peanuts equal in amount to a julienne of white celery (shredded) moistened with French Dressing (No. 1756), well drained. Garnish the pineapple circle with sections of peeled and seeded orange and grapefruit and place in the middle a few seedless grapes. Pass a dish of red mayonnaise (Nos. 1798–99) separately.

PINEAPPLE GOLDEN GLOW   [1752]

Dissolve 1 package of lemon-flavored gelatin in 1½ cups of boiling water to which has been added a small piece of cinnamon and ½ cup of canned pineapple juice. Stir in 1 scant teaspoon of salt, a few grains of cayenne and cool until partially stiffened; then add 1½ cups of strained crushed pineapple mixed with 1 cup of freshly grated carrot. Turn mixture into individual molds (or one large one) or a ring mold, either being generously oiled, and chill for 3 hours. Serve on crisp lettuce with boiled dressing.

POMEGRANATE WEST COAST   [1753]

Toss together 2 cups of diced white celery, 2 cups of peeled, cored and diced apples, 1 cupful of cooked whole cranberries and a few grains of salt. Moisten with thin mayonnaise. Arrange in the center of a round platter on crisp shredded romaine, cover with stiffly whipped cream, to which has been added a little prepared mustard. Using a fancy tube, force this through a pastry bag and garnish with pomegranate seeds.

PRUNE LOAF   [1754]
(Molded)

Force through a sieve ½ pound of large, cooked, stoned prunes. Soak a package of lemon gelatin in ½ cup of cold water for 5 minutes and dissolve with 1¼ cups of hot water. (Heated prune juice may be used, or any other kind of fruit juice.) Cool slightly, add the strained prunes, 1 cup of seedless raisins previously plumped in hot water and halved, ½ cup of finely chopped celery and ½ cup of finely chopped green pepper, and stir well. Pour into a wet loaf pan and chill. Slice on individual salad plates on a bed of crisp watercress mixed with very finely shredded lettuce and cover with stiff mayonnaise which has been forced through a pastry bag by using a fancy tube. Sprinkle lightly with hard-cooked egg yolks forced through a sieve and dust with paprika.

FRENCH DRESSING [1755]

French dressing is a *temporary emulsion*. If you pour oil and water together, they will not mix, but if you shake them violently, little drops of oil can be seen throughout the liquid. That is exactly what happens in making French dressing, and the finer these droplets, the less likely will be a separation. This is the reason French dressing should be shaken in a jar or bottle for a small quantity, and mixed in an electric mixer when a large quantity is required. French dressing will be less likely to separate if the ingredients are cold when combined. It is also well to have the mixing bowl surrounded by ice during the mixing or beating.

French dressing is called a temporary emulsion because it contains no substance which keeps the drops of oil suspended in the liquid, as in mayonnaise.

French dressing is very elastic. There may be many variations and the wise cook will always have this basic dressing as well as mayonnaise on hand. At least one quart of each may be prepared in advance, as these two dressings keep well for at least two weeks.

HOW TO MAKE REAL FRENCH DRESSING [1756]
(*One Quart*)

3 cups of oil
1 cup vinegar

1½ tablespoons of salt
½ teaspoon white pepper

Mix all the ingredients in a bottle and shake violently.
This is real French dressing, but there are some variations:

FRENCH DRESSING VARIATIONS [1757]

BAR-LE-DUC DRESSING [1758]

Using lemon juice instead of vinegar, prepare French Dressing as indicated for (No. 1756) and add two tablespoons of Bar-le-Duc jam.

BRESLIN DRESSING [1759]

To French dressing add one tablespoon of finely chopped pistachio nuts and ½ tablespoon of finely chopped black truffles.

CALIFORNIA DRESSING [1760]

Prepare French Dressing (No. 1756), using grapefruit juice instead of vinegar.

CHIFFONADE DRESSING [1761]

To a cup of French dressing, add 3 finely chopped hard-cooked eggs, 1 tablespoon of grated onion, 1 tablespoon of finely chopped parsley (chervil is much better), 2 tablespoons of finely chopped pickled beets and 1 teaspoon of finely chopped green olives. Mix thoroughly.

CHUTNEY DRESSING [1762]

To a cup of French dressing, add, just before using, half a cup of Indian chutney. Stir well.

CREAM DRESSING I [1763]

Follow recipe No. 1756, using lemon juice instead of vinegar and, just before serving, add 4 tablespoons of heavy cream. Stir thoroughly.

CREAM DRESSING (FOAMY) II [1764]

Follow recipe No. 1756, adding one well beaten egg white instead of heavy cream.

CREAM CHEESE DRESSING [1765]

To ½ cup of French dressing add 1½ ounces of cream cheese and mix to a thick semi-liquid paste. Add another ½ cup of French dressing and beat thoroughly.

CLUB DRESSING [1766]

Prepare a French dressing with the following ingredients: ½ teaspoon salt (very scant), a small pinch of white pepper, 2 tablespoons of brandy, 2 tablespoons of tarragon vinegar and 6 tablespoons of olive oil. Combine and mix thoroughly.

CURRANT JELLY DRESSING [1767]

Follow recipe for Bar-le-Duc (No. 1758), using currant jelly instead of Bar-le-Duc jam.

CUCUMBER DRESSING [1768]

This dressing is excellent with a fish salad. To 1 cup of French dressing add ½ cup of grated cucumber, and 1 teaspoon prepared mustard. Mix well and serve very cold.

CURRY DRESSING [1769

Mix ¾ of a teaspoon of salt with ¼ teaspoon of curry powder moisten with 2 tablespoons of French dressing, mixing thoroughly Finish by beating in ¾ cup of French dressing.

EGG-CHEESE DRESSING [1770

To 1 cup of French dressing add 1 teaspoon sugar, also a few drop onion juice and stir well; then add 1 hard-cooked egg chopped fine 4 tablespoons chopped American cheese, 1 tablespoon each choppe parsley and chives, 1 tablespoon each of chopped green pepper and re pimiento. Stir well.

HONEY DRESSING [1771

To 1 cup of French dressing add 1 tablespoon of strained honey 1 tablespoon each of chopped parsley and chives and 1 teaspoon o drained prepared horseradish.

MINT DRESSING [1772

This dressing is excellent with a meat salad, especially lamb. T ¾ cup of French dressing add 1 tablespoon of fresh mint leaves finel shredded with scissors, also a scant teaspoon of finely chopped shallot Mix well.

ROQUEFORT CHEESE DRESSING [1773

To a cup of French dressing add 1½ ounces of Roquefort chees crumbled with a fork. Mix thoroughly before using.

VINAIGRETTE DRESSING [1774

To 1 cup of French dressing add a scant teaspoon each of finel chopped and mixed green olives, capers, chives, parsley, gherkins and finely chopped hard-cooked egg. Serve very cold.

WALDENSTEIN DRESSING [1775

To 1 cup of French dressing add 1 hard-cooked egg yolk force through a fine sieve, 1 scant teaspoon of finely chopped chives, 1 scan teaspoon of finely chopped onion, the same amount of finely choppe parsley and 2 filets of anchovy well washed and dried and finely dice Stir well and chill. An excellent dressing for vegetable salad.

WILMOT DRESSING [1776]

To 1 cup of French dressing, made with raspberry vinegar instead of ordinary vinegar, add 1 scant teaspoon of finely chopped chives, and one teaspoon of finely chopped shallots. Shake well before serving and when ready, add one generous tablespoon of finely chopped walnut or other nut meats.

MAYONNAISE [1777]

Mayonnaise is an *emulsion* consisting of: *oil, egg yolk, vinegar, condiments* and *spices. Nothing else.*

Unlike French dressing, it is a *stable emulsion.* This is formed when the tiny drops of oil are held in solution. Since oil and water will not mix, it is necessary to keep these drops of oil separated by adding a substance which is dissolved in one solution but not in the other, and which will form a covering for the drop of oil. Egg yolk is such a substance. Gelatin, condensed milk or a cooked starch paste will have the same effect.

Egg yolks are as a rule used in mayonnaise, because they form a heavier emulsion and produce a deeper yellow color. Whole eggs give a thinner dressing, while egg whites give a dressing which is entirely unlike mayonnaise. Only fresh eggs should be used in making mayonnaise. Frozen eggs may be used, but eggs which are the least bit stale will not form a stable mayonnaise. A certain amount of salt is necessary for flavor, but an excessive amount may break the solution. Sugar helps to hold the emulsion. Some cooks add a small amount of hot stock to the mayonnaise at the very end of the beating, which is said to keep the dressing from separating.

Mayonnaise may be called "temperamental" because it will behave contrary to rule at most inopportune times. In order to prevent these embarrassing moments, we should thoroughly understand what mayonnaise is and treat it accordingly.

CARE OF MAYONNAISE [1778]

The care of mayonnaise is very important. It should be stored at a temperature of 60° to 75° F. and kept covered. Glass or earthenware crocks are suitable containers. If the container is not tightly covered the contents should be protected by a damp cloth to prevent the surface from turning dark.

If mayonnaise is frozen it will separate on thawing, or if it is exposed to too much heat, the same thing will happen. Sudden changes of temperature will cause separation: mayonnaise which has been kept in a refrigerator often separates when it is brought into a warm room or placed on a hot plate. The most practical solution is to keep it in a

cool place of even temperature or in a refrigerator with properly regu-
lated temperature.

FIRST AID TO MAYONNAISE [1779]

If egg yolks separate into tiny lumps instead of forming a smooth
paste with the oil, the emulsion may be restored in either of two ways:
(1) Beat additional egg yolks, then beat in the curdled mixture gradually
and proceed as in the first place until it becomes a smooth paste; (2) Use
1 tablespoon of water or vinegar in place of the egg and beat the curdled
mixture into the water or vinegar. If a film of oil forms on top of mayonnaise do not stir it in, because doing so will cause the entire mass to
separate. Instead, remove the layer of oil and use the remaining dressing.

The flavor of any salad dressing is improved if allowed to stand at
least a few hours after making. Experiments have proved that a temperature of 70° is best for mixing mayonnaise. One safeguard against
failure is to have the oil at that temperature before starting the dressing
and the egg *strictly fresh*. Ingredients should be weighed or measured
accurately, and the process should not be hurried, for best results.

MAYONNAISE DRESSING [1780]

½ teaspoon prepared mustard
½ teaspoon granulated sugar (optional)
Few grains of cayenne pepper
(white pepper may be substituted)

1 egg yolk (strictly fresh)
1 tablespoon vinegar
1 tablespoon of strained lemon
  juice
Few grains of salt
Enough oil for mixture to hold
  its shape.

Sift the first four ingredients into a bowl, add the egg yolk, mix
thoroughly, then pour in the vinegar while stirring constantly. Add
teaspoons of oil at a time while beating thoroughly and constantly.
When very thick add the lemon juice and remainder of oil rapidly. The
whole process should take about *10 minutes* to obtain a mayonnaise stiff
enough to hold its shape. If dressing is to be kept for subsequent use,
double or treble the recipe.

MAYONNAISE WITH CONDENSED MILK [1781]

1　cup condensed milk
2　egg yolks
⅛　teaspoon salt

⅛ teaspoon dry mustard
⅓ cup vinegar
⅔ cup of oil

Beat the egg yolks, add the condensed milk and seasonings, then the
oil and vinegar alternately.

MAYONNAISE WITH COOKED BASE [1782]

2½ tablespoons flour
⅛ teaspoon salt
1 teaspoon dry mustard
1 tablespoon oil

1 cup boiling water
2 egg yolks
1 cup oil
⅛ teaspoon white pepper

1 tablespoon strained lemon juice

Mix the dry ingredients and add 1 tablespoon of oil to make a paste. Add the strained lemon juice and boiling water and cook in top of double boiler stirring constantly until mixture thickens. Cool, add the well beaten egg yolks and remaining oil gradually, beating constantly.

MAYONNAISE WITH GELATINE [1783]

1 tablespoon gelatin
3 tablespoons cold water
1 teaspoon dry mustard
1 teaspoon salt

⅛ teaspoon white pepper
2 egg yolks
1 tablespoon strained lemon juice
1 pint oil (2 cups)

Soak the gelatin in the cold water for 5 minutes, then dissolve over boiling water. Mix the mustard, salt, pepper and egg yolks, then add 1 teaspoon of strained lemon juice and dissolved gelatin. Cool, add the oil gradually, beating constantly. As the mixture thickens, add the remaining lemon juice.

Mayonnaise variations include the following recipes:

ALMOND MAYONNAISE DRESSING [1784]

To one cup of mayonnaise (No. 1780), add ½ cup of finely chopped blanched sweet almonds. Stir thoroughly.

CREAM MAYONNAISE DRESSING [1785]

To 1 cup of mayonnaise (No. 1780), add 3 tablespoons of stiffly whipped heavy cream. This should be made on the day required as it does not keep well.

CHUTNEY DRESSING [1786]

To 1 cup of mayonnaise (No 1780), add 2 tablespoons of English chutney. Mix thoroughly.

CAPER DRESSING [1787]

To 1 cup of mayonnaise (No. 1780), add a scant half cup of finely chopped, well-washed capers. Mix thoroughly.

CAVIAR DRESSING [1788]

To 1 cup of mayonnaise (No. 1780), add generous tablespoon of caviar. Blend well and carefully.

CAVIAR HORSERADISH DRESSING [1789]

To 1 cup of mayonnaise (No. 1780), add 1 tablespoon caviar and one tablespoon of well-drained prepared horseradish.

CUMBERLAND DRESSING [1790]

To 1 cup of mayonnaise (No. 1780), add 1 generous tablespoon of well-beaten currant jelly and 1 teaspoon of grated lemon peel. Mix thoroughly.

CRANBERRY DRESSING [1791]

To 1 cup of mayonnaise (No. 1780), add 2 tablespoons of well-beaten cranberry jelly and 1 teaspoon of grated orange peel. Mix thoroughly.

EGG DRESSING [1792]

To 1 cup of mayonnaise (No. 1780), add one chopped hard-cooked egg and 1 tablespoon of very finely chopped onion. Mix well.

GREEN DRESSING [1793]

Color 1 cup of mayonnaise (No. 1780) with juices expressed from watercress and parsley, using twice as much parsley as watercress. To obtain the coloring, break the greens in pieces, pound in a mortar until thoroughly macerated, then squeeze through cheese cloth. This method of coloring is much preferable to the use of artificial coloring as it contains all the mineral salts of the greens. If desired add 2 tablespoons of well-washed capers.

HORSERADISH DRESSING [1794]

To 1 cup of mayonnaise (No. 1780), add three tablespoons of prepared horseradish and mix thoroughly. An excellent dressing for cold meat, especially beef.

OLIVE DRESSING [1795]

To 1 cup of mayonnaise (No. 1780), add 1 generous tablespoon of finely chopped black olives, 1 teaspoon of finely chopped green olives and 1 generous tablespoon of finely chopped boiled cranberries. Mix thoroughly. You may add just before serving, a scant teaspoon of finely chopped parsley.

OLGA'S DRESSING [1796]

To 1 cup of mayonnaise (No. 1780) add 2 well-washed, well-sponged and finely chopped filets of anchovy and 1 teaspoon of finely chopped chives. Mix thoroughly.

PIQUANTE DRESSING [1797]

To 1 cup of mayonnaise (No. 1780), add 1 teaspoon each of finely chopped green olives, pickles (sour), capers (well washed), chervil, onion and chives, then add a scant teaspoon of prepared mustard. Mix thoroughly.

RED DRESSING I [1798]

To 1 cup of mayonnaise (No. 1780), add one tablespoon of strained beet juice and 2 tablespoons of finely chopped red beets. Mix thoroughly and chill.

RED DRESSING II [1799]

To 1 cup of mayonnaise (No. 1780), add 1 tablespoon or more of pounded lobster coral rubbed through a fine sieve. Mix thoroughly.

RUSSIAN DRESSING I [1800]

To 1 cup of mayonnaise (No. 1780), add 1 tablespoon of Chili sauce, 1 generous tablespoon of finely chopped India relish and a pinch of granulated sugar. Mix thoroughly.

RUSSIAN DRESSING II [1801]

To 1 cup of mayonnaise (No. 1780), add 1 tablespoon of Chili sauce, 1 tablespoon of finely chopped celery (white part only), 1 tablespoon of finely chopped red pimiento, 1 tablespoon of finely chopped green pepper, and 1 teasponful of finely chopped parsley. Mix thoroughly.

RUSSIAN DRESSING III [1802]

To 1 cup of mayonnaise (No. 1780), add 1 tablespoon of chili sauce, 1 tablespoon of grated onion, 1 tablespoon of finely minced sour pickles, a small pinch of granulated sugar, 1 tablespoon of finely chopped red pimiento and a tablespoon of finely chopped green olives. Mix thoroughly.

ROQUEFORT CHEESE DRESSING [1803]

To 1 cup of mayonnaise (No. 1780), add 2 tablespoons of crumbled Roquefort cheese, a few drops of Worcestershire sauce, 1 tablespoon of French dressing and 1 tablespoon of finely chopped chives. Mix gently but thoroughly.

SOUR CREAM DRESSING [1804]

To ½ cup of mayonnaise (No. 1780), add ½ cup of thick sour cream, 1 teaspoon of prepared mustard (scant), 1 teaspoon of finely chopped olives and a scant ½ teaspoon of granulated sugar. Mix thoroughly.

THOUSAND ISLAND DRESSING I [1805]

To ½ cup of mayonnaise (No. 1780), add 1 tablespoon of chili sauce, 1 tablespoon of finely chopped celery, 1 tablespoon of finely chopped red pimiento, 1 tablespoon of finely chopped green pepper, 1 tablespoon of coarsely chopped hard-cooked egg. Fold in ½ cup of stiffly beaten heavy sweet cream gently but thoroughly.

THOUSAND ISLAND DRESSING II [1806]
Especially suitable for fruit salad.

To 1 cup of mayonnaise (No. 1780), add 1 tablespoon of finely chopped seedless raisins previously rolled in flour, 1 tablespoon each of red and green Maraschino cherries, 1 teaspoon of finely chopped angelica, 1 tablespoon of finely chopped pineapple. Finally fold in a cup of stiffly beaten heavy cream, unsweetened, but colored with a little grenadine.

VICTORY DRESSING [1807]

To ½ cup of mayonnaise (No. 1780), add the same ingredients indicated for recipe No. 1806, also ½ cup of shredded coconut and a tablespoon of finely chopped blanched almonds. Finally, fold in a cup of stiffly beaten, unsweetened, heavy cream flavored with Crème de Menthe or Maraschino. Suitable for fruit cup and fruit salad.

BOILED DRESSING [1808]

Boiled dressing is prepared like a custard mixture, usually in a double boiler. It is a very inexpensive dressing and is sometimes used with mayonnaise, as in potato salad, cold meat salad or fish salad, or diluted with whipped cream for fruit salad.

Blend in the upper part of a double boiler, 1 scant teaspoon of salt, 1 teaspoon of dry mustard, 1½ tablespoons of granulated sugar, a few grains of cayenne pepper and 2 tablespoons of sifted flour. Add 1 whole egg previously beaten, 1½ tablespoons of melted butter, with ¾ cup of milk. After mixing well, pour in gradually ¼ cup of tarragon vinegar. Place over hot water and cook until thickened, stirring constantly. Strain and cool.

BOILED CARLTON DRESSING [1809]

Reduce to half on a hot fire ½ cup of rich chicken stock. Add ½ cup of tarragon vinegar, 5 slightly beaten egg yolks, 2 tablespoons of prepared mustard, salt, pepper and a few grains of Cayenne pepper. Cook in a double boiler, stirring constantly until mixture thickens. Strain, add ½ cup of heavy cream and 2 tablespoons of clarified butter. Cool.

BOILED SOUR CREAM DRESSING [1810]

Mix thoroughly ½ tablespoon of salt, ½ tablespoon of dry mustard, 2 teaspoons of powdered sugar and 1 tablespoon of sifted flour. Add 3 slightly beaten egg yolks, 4 tablespoons of melted and clarified butter, ¾ cup of milk and ½ cup of lime juice. Cook in double boiler, stirring constantly, until mixture thickens. Strain, add ½ cup of heavy sour cream and beat thoroughly. Cool.

BOILED WALTHAM DRESSING [1811]

To 1 cup of heavy sour cream, add 1 whole slightly beaten egg, ¼ cup of tarragon vinegar, 2 scant teaspoons salt, 2 scant teaspoons of powdered sugar, and 1 teaspoon of prepared mustard, with a few grains of Cayenne pepper. Cook in a double boiler until the mixture thickens, stirring constantly. Remove from the fire. Cool and stir in 2 generous tablespoons of finely chopped hickory nuts.

MISCELLANEOUS DRESSINGS

HOT CUCUMBER DRESSING [1812]

Place in a saucepan 3 tablespoons salad oil, 1 tablespoon granulated sugar, 1 teaspoon prepared mustard and ¾ cup of tarragon vinegar. Mix well and bring slowly to a boil, stirring frequently. Then add 2 hard-cooked eggs, coarsely minced, and 1 tablespoon of minced chives. Mix well and while still hot pour over chilled, sliced or diced raw cucumbers. Sprinkle with minced parsley and paprika. Serve over sliced cucumber. Cool. Chill and serve.

INDIAN DRESSING   [1813]

Press yolks of 2 hard-cooked eggs through a fine sieve and add a pinch of salt, 1 teaspoon of powdered sugar, a dash of paprika, a few grains of Cayenne pepper, a few grains of white pepper, 1 tablespoon of strained lemon juice, 2 tablespoons of tarragon vinegar and a generous half cup of good olive oil. Shake well and add 1 tablespoon each of finely chopped red pimiento, green pepper and pickled beets, 1 scant teaspoon of finely chopped parsley and a generous tablespoon of finely chopped walnut meats. Stir well and chill.

MUSTARD DRESSING   [1814]

Blend thoroughly 1 can sweetened condensed milk, 1 teaspoon salt, ½ cup vinegar, 1 tablespoon each finely minced chives and parsley, a few grains Cayenne pepper and 1 generous tablespoon dry mustard. Chill, An excellent dressing for coleslaw, which will keep well in refrigerator.

POT CHEESE DRESSING   [1815]

Press a generous ½ cup of pot cheese through a sieve and moisten with a scant tablespoon of undiluted evaporated milk. Season with 1 scant teaspoon salt and a few grains of pepper. Add 1 beaten egg yolk with 1 tablespoon of sugar, then 3 tablespoons vinegar. Beat well and stir in gradually ¼ cup of undiluted evaporated milk. Beat till smooth. Serve on fruit salad.

SUZETTE'S DRESSING   [1816]

Cream a package of cream cheese, work into it gradually ½ cup of currant jelly, alternating with the juice of a medium-sized lemon. Beat with egg beater till smooth and thoroughly blended, seasoning to taste with salt and a few grains of pepper. Fold in 1 cup of whipped cream with 2 tablespoons of chopped, blanched pistachio nuts. Delicious with fruit salads, especially jellied and molded ones.

SWEET SOUR DRESSING   [1817]

Combine and mix well the following ingredients in the order given: ½ cup sugar, ½ cup tarragon vinegar, 2 tablespoons salad oil, 1 tablespoon each minced onion, chives, celery, green pepper, pimiento and parsley. Add 1 teaspoon salt, 1/4 teaspoon pepper, 1 teaspoon prepared mustard, 1 teaspoon paprika and 1/2 generous teaspoon Worcestershire sauce. Finally add a small lump of ice and beat till mixture thickens. An exceptionally good dressing for fish salads.

WHIPPED CREAM JELLY DRESSING [1818]

To each cup of whipped cream, add, just before serving, 1/2 cup of tart red jelly such as currant, cranberry, raspberry or strawberry.

ORIGIN OF SANDWICHES [1819]

Doubtless the Greeks, Romans and Babylonians enjoyed a wedge of meat between two slabs of bread, but it was the fourth Earl of Sandwich who made the English people sandwich minded. Actually, however, the sandwich was the invention of the great Jewish teacher, Rabbi Hillel, the prince who lived between 70 B. C. and 70 A. D.

The Jewish people during the Passover feast ritual still follow Hillel's custom of eating sandwiches made of two pieces of matzoh (unleavened bread) containing mohror (bitter herbs) and haroseth (chopped nuts and apple, to resemble the mortar of the Egyptians) as a reminder of Hebrew suffering before the Deliverance from Egypt.

All this is to prove that sandwiches are as old as bread and cheese. Since they are intended to assuage the pangs of hunger, they should not be made paper-thin and practically tasteless. Sandwiches are not canapés, and canapés are not sandwiches, although the same spreads may be used for both.

SANDWICHES—HINTS [1820]

Traditionally, day-old bread is supposed to be used in sandwich making because it is easier to cut, but even fresh bread may be cut easily into thick or thin slices if you have a sharp knife and cut the bread horizontally with a sawing motion. The slicing of bread should be done ahead of time. Then comes the spread or spreads which may be plain butter, creamed butter (*see* Compounded Creamed Butters) or one of the spreads indicated for canapés. These spreads should be soft enough to be spread thinly and evenly with a knife blade, or a wooden or bone spatula.

In placing meat or other filling on the spread, be sure all four corners of the bread are covered. This means a proper distribution of the filling in the sandwich, so that the guest biting near the edge will find something besides bread. The spread or meat, or fish, or whatever be the filling, may in turn be topped with crisp lettuce, cabbage (red or green), watercress, coleslaw, or other greens. These greens as well as the filling should not protrude over the sides of the bread, but should be neatly trimmed. The bread may be decrusted or not, as desired.

To lift completed sandwiches from the board to the plate, always use a sandwich knife or spatula and the tips of fingers. Never pick up the sandwich from the board with your hand and do not slide it from the board onto a sandwich plate, which, by the way should be hot, for hot sandwiches and cold for cold sandwiches. Do not place a sandwich on a damp or wet plate. Sandwiches prepared in advance should be kept in a cool place, covered with a damp towel. Never prepare salad or fruit or any very moist sandwiches in advance, lest they become soggy and unfit to be served.

There are innumerable sandwiches, some of which may be served hot, some cold—on plain bread, fancy bread, on toast or between sliced roll; open-faced, double or triple decked. The pinwheel and the loaf or layer sandwich may be prepared in advance and sliced to order.

Under no circumstances use too stale a bread, unless specially requested. When toast is used for sandwiches, butter it as soon as it is done. This preserves the moisture and keeps it from drying too quickly.

SANDWICH GARNISHINGS [1821]

The difference which garnishings make to a dish, is unbelievable until actually seen. Like dress accessories, they should be chosen with taste and with a sure sense of their appropriateness. The shape, color and edible texture of these accessories should always be suited to the dish on which they are used, and should harmonize with the decorative scheme of that dish.

There are so many simple, attractive inexpensive garnishings that their complete listing would require many pages. Here are a few suggestions:

Apples. Cubed, sliced, in rings, rolled in paprika, minced parsley, chives or curry powder.

Cheese. Cubed, sliced, rolled into small balls, then in paprika, parsley, curry powder, saffron, nuts or chives.

Dill Pickles. Cubed, sliced, cut in fan shape or sticks; or added to cups filled with cottage cheese or mayonnaise.

Green Pepper. In cups, sliced in rings, chopped.

Hard-Cooked Eggs. Chopped, sliced, quartered, halved or sieved, then mixed with minced parsley, chives, chopped dill, or capers.

Horseradish. Plain or mixed with prepared mustard or dressing, fresh and shredded, in small balls, mixed with cottage cheese, and so forth.

Lemon. Sliced thin, dipped in paprika, minced parsley, chives; or cut in half, scooped, then filled with dressing.

Lettuce. Shredded, crisp leaves in cups, then filled with dressing.

Mint. Especially for lamb sandwiches; fresh mint leaves, mint jelly cubes, and so forth, or mint jelly chopped.

Olives. Black, green, ripe or stuffed, pitted, filled with cottage cheese or horseradish.

Parsley. Must be crisp and fresh; minced, sprig or bunches.

Pimiento. Sliced, chopped, minced or diced.

Radishes. Sliced, dressed with mayonnaise, or hollowed out and filled with horseradish, mayonnaise or cheese. Shaped as radish roses.

Relishes. Tomato and onion; pickled beets, spiced string beans, curried tomato relish, chow-chow, pickled cucumbers and onion slices, cabbage, relish, coleslaw (red or green), pickled cauliflower.

Tomatoes. Ripe or green, sliced, quartered, halved then filled with almost anything edible, as chopped nuts, cream cheese with nuts, or olives.

Watercress. Must be crisp and green, using either sprigs or a generous bunch.

The use of these must be left to the innate taste, talent or imagination of the sandwich maker.

CHEESE SANDWICHES

COTTAGE CHEESE AND MARMALADE SANDWICH [1822]

Unless otherwise indicated, these recipes serve 1

Use brown bread. Spread one slice generously with well-drained cottage cheese, seasoned to taste with salt, pepper and onion juice. Top with lettuce. Spread another slice of brown bread with any kind of marmalade (orange, pineapple, strawberry, and so forth) and adjust over the first slice. Cut from corner to corner, once, then from corner to corner once again. Garnish with a small slice of tomato topped with a slice of hard-cooked egg, this again topped with a slice of olive.

COTTAGE CHEESE AND RAISIN SANDWICH [1823]

To a scant ¼ cup of well-drained, then sieved cottage cheese, add 2 rolled saltines or Graham Crackers, 1 scant tablespoon mayonnaise and 1 scant ¼ cup of seedless raisins, chopped very fine or ground. Blend thoroughly and spread between two slices of bread or split long roll. Cover with crisp lettuce and garnish or spread mixture between the two slices of roll. Garnish with a little jelly (any kind) placed upon a crisp lettuce leaf.

CREAM CHEESE AND ALMOND SANDWICHES [1824]

This spread keeps well in icebox or refrigerator and may be made in advance. Keep covered with a buttered paper.

1 lb. cream cheese	¼ cup celery leaves, ground
¼ cup pickle relish	Salt, pepper and paprika to taste
½ cup ground blanched almonds	A dash of Worcestershire sauce

Blend all ingredients, and to ensure smoothness, put through food chopper. Serve between thin slices of whole wheat, raisin, nut or any kind of fruit bread. Cut diagonally.

CREAM CHEESE AND APRICOT SANDWICH   [1825]

Blend equal parts of cream cheese and apricot pulp made by pressing through a sieve stewed or canned apricots which have been thoroughly drained. Add mayonnaise to taste, and spread between thin buttered slices of bread topped with crisp lettuce. Nuts may be added if desired. Cut diagonally, and top each part with a slice of hard-cooked egg, this again, topped with a caper. Garnish with a scant tablespoon of dressed cole slaw.

CREAM CHEESE AND JELLY SANDWICH   [1826]

Spread well-creamed cream cheese on 1 slice of any kind of sandwich bread and spread any preferred jelly on the other slice. Press together and cut from corner to corner twice, so as to make 4 small triangular sandwiches. Garnish with shredded pineapple, place on a crisp lettuce leaf.

CREAM CHEESE AND PINEAPPLE SANDWICH   [1827]

Combine and blend thoroughly equal parts of creamed cream cheese and well-drained, canned shredded pineapple. Spread between two slices of any preferred bread. Cut from corner to corner twice, so as to make 4 small triangular sandwiches. Garnish each small sandwich top with a thin slice of stuffed olive.

SWISS CHEESE AND COLESLAW SANDWICH   [1828]

Spread coleslaw evenly between two slices of any preferred bread and top with thin slices of Swiss cheese. Cut diagonally. Garnish with 1 olive and 1 radish.

SWISS CHEESE AND HAM SANDWICH [1829]

Arrange on 1 slice of bread spread with mustard or mustard butter (Compounded Creamed Butters), thin slices of Swiss cheese. Cover with crisp lettuce, then with a thin slice of cold cooked ham. Top with a second slice of bread, also spread with mustard or mustard butter. Cut from corner to corner so as to make 4 small triangular sandwiches or cut diagonally. Garnish with a little horseradish placed upon a small leaf of lettuce.

SWISS CHEESE AND LIVERWURST [1830] SANDWICH

Proceed as indicated for the Swiss Cheese and Ham (No. 1829), substituting liverwurst for ham.

SWISS CHEESE AND SALAMI SANDWICH [1831]

Proceed as indicated for recipe Swiss Cheese and Ham (No. 1829), substituting salami for ham. Salami may be mashed or left whole.

CLUB OR THREE-DECKER SANDWICHES [1832]

Club or Three-Decker Sandwiches are made of three slices of bread which may be plain, toasted, buttered, or spread with a creamed (compounded) butter, and served cold or hot. They may be cut in halves from corner to corner (that is, diagonally), in thirds, or quarters.

First the lower layer is filled with a spread or a filling, topped with another slice of bread or toast, filled with a spread or a filling, and finally topped with a plain or toasted slice of bread, gently pressed together with the tips of the fingers and the sandwich knife, then cut as indicated above. When cut in thirds or quarters, they may be held together with toothpicks. In any case hot club or three-decker sandwiches should be served on a hot plate. Either hot or cold club or three-decker sandwiches—in fact any kind of sandwich—should be daintily garnished before serving.

The following recipes, ideas and suggestions for Club or Three-Decker Sandwiches are sufficiently clear to eliminate further details and explanations; they are not rigid rules but are sufficiently elastic to allow for all the changes which circumstances may require. Above all, they are concise, practical and economical, and to eliminate loss of time, they are all numbered and classified alphabetically. The main ingredient for each layer is printed in capital letters so that at a glance the cook will find immediately what he or she is looking for.

Crusts may be removed from the bread if the sandwiches are to be served for tea, but these club and three-decker sandwiches are almost a meal and many people prefer to have the crusts left on. Mayonnaise may be substituted for butter as a spread for the bread.

APRICOT-HAM ON TOAST　　　　　　　　[1833]

Lower Layer. Cooked, sieved APRICOTS topped with lettuce.
Second Layer. Cold cooked HAM topped with lettuce and mayonnaise.

ALMOND-PINEAPPLE ON BREAD　　　　　[1834]

Lower Layer. ALMOND BUTTER, lettuce.
Second Layer. PINEAPPLE slice, lettuce spread with mayonnaise.

ALMOND-MARMALADE ON TOAST　　　　　[1835]

Lower Layer. ALMOND BUTTER and MARMALADE, lettuce.
Second Layer. SLICED ORANGES and lettuce.

AMERICAN CHEESE-HAM AND TOMATO　　[1836] ON TOAST

Lower Layer. AMERICAN CHEESE and lettuce with mayonnaise.
Second Layer. GRILLED HAM topped with TOMATO SLICES and lettuce.

APPLE-PEANUT BUTTER FILLING AND　　[1837] PINEAPPLE SLICE ON TOAST

Lower Layer. SLICED APPLE-PEANUT BUTTER FILLING and shredded lettuce.
Second Layer. PINEAPPLE SLICE and shredded lettuce.

BACON-ORANGE MARMALADE AND　　　　[1838] BANANA ON RYE

Lower Layer. BROILED BACON topped with lettuce.
Second Layer. Rye bread spread with ORANGE MARMALADE, then with SLICED BANANA topped with lettuce.

BACON-CHICKEN AND ANCHOVIES　　　　[1839] ON TOAST

Lower Layer. BROILED BACON topped with lettuce.
Second Layer. SLICED CHICKEN topped with ANCHOVY filets, then with SLICED TOMATOES and lettuce.

BACON-CHICKEN-GREEN PEPPER AND TOMATO ON TOAST [1840]

Lower Layer. BROILED BACON topped with SLICED CHICKEN, then with lettuce.
Second Layer. GREEN PEPPER SLICES and SLICED TOMATOES.

BACON-GREEN PEPPER AND TOMATO ON TOAST [1841]

Lower Layer. BROILED BACON topped with GREEN PEPPER slices.
Second Layer. Coleslaw and SLICED TOMATO.

BACON-CHICKEN LIVERS AND TOMATO ON TOAST [1842]

Lower Layer. BROILED BACON topped with BROILED CHICKEN LIVERS.
Second Layer. SLICED TOMATOES topped with watercress.

BACON-ONION AND TOMATO ON RYE [1843]

Lower Layer. BROILED BACON topped with thinly sliced raw ONION topped with lettuce.
Second Layer. SLICED TOMATOES topped with watercress.

CAVIAR-ONION AND TOMATO ON TOAST [1844]

Lower Layer. CAVIAR topped with SLICED ONIONS.
Second Layer. TOMATO SLICES topped with watercress.

CHICKEN-NUT MEATS AND JELLY-LETTUCE ON PUMPERNICKEL [1845]

Lower Layer. SLICED CHICKEN topped with NUT MEATS mixed with a little mayonnaise.
Second Layer. JELLY (any kind) mixed with chopped lettuce.

CHICKEN-BACON AND TONGUE-TOMATO ON WHOLE WHEAT [1846]

Lower Layer. SLICED CHICKEN topped with BROILED BACON.
Second Layer. SLICED TONGUE, TOMATO SLICES and lettuce leaves.

CHICKEN SALAD AND HAM-TONGUE ON   [1847]
PUMPERNICKEL

Lower Layer. CHICKEN SALAD and lettuce leaves.
Second Layer. Thin slice of HAM topped with thin slices of cold
cooked tongue.

CRAB MEAT MAYONNAISE-TOMATO AND   [1848]
EGG SALAD-CRESS ON TOAST

Lower Layer. CRAB MEAT dressed with mayonnaise, then topped
with TOMATO SLICES.
Second Layer. EGG SALAD topped with WATERCRESS.

CRAB MEAT-RAW SPINACH AND EGG   [1849]
SALAD-LETTUCE ON WHITE

Lower Layer. CRAB MEAT MAYONNAISE and chopped RAW
SPINACH.
Second Layer. EGG SALAD (mayonnaise) topped with lettuce leaves.

HOT SANDWICHES
(Unless otherwise indicated, these recipes serve 1)

BACON AND TOMATO SANDWICH   [1850]

Broil 3 slices of bacon and put between slices of toast with crisp
lettuce and sliced tomato, the latter raw or broiled with the bacon.

BROILED TOMATO SANDWICH   [1851]

Wash a ripe tomato, slice thin, season to taste with salt and pepper
and dip in oil or bacon fat. Broil on both sides and put between slices of
buttered toast, previously topped with crisp lettuce.

CAPE COD SANDWICH   [1852]

Top a slice of hot buttered toast with a generous layer of creamed
flaked crabmeat, not too moist. Over this place a slice of American
cheese and set in the broiling oven until the cheese is melted.

Cover with a second piece of toast and serve immediately, cut in
quarters and garnish with a piece of dill pickle.

CORNED BEEF SANDWICH   [1853]

Place a slice of bread on a hot plate; cover with a slice of hot corned beef; spread with prepared horseradish. Serve with hot horseradish sauce, a boiled potato and a slice of dill pickle.

CREAMED TUNA SANDWICH   [1854]

Put a slice of hot toast on a hot plate. Spread with anchovy paste, and heap with creamed tuna fish. Top with lettuce, then with another piece of toast, also spread with anchovy paste. Garnish the halved sandwich with a slice of broiled tomato.

Any kind of left-over cooked fish may be prepared this way.

DENVER SANDWICH   [1855]
(*Serves 6*)

Mix 1 pound chopped—not ground—raw ham, 2 well beaten raw eggs and 1 teaspoon onion juice; season to taste with salt and pepper. Heat 1 generous tablespoon of bacon fat in a frying pan. Pour the mixture in and cook over a low flame for 5 minutes, stirring occasionally. Spread on buttered toast, cover with more toast and serve immediately, garnished with coleslaw.

FRIED EGG SANDWICH   [1856]

Place a fried egg between 2 pieces of buttered toast (the egg fried on both sides, the yolk broken and spread). Serve garnished with a slice of dill pickle placed on a leaf of lettuce.

FRIED HAM SANDWICH   [1857]

The ham may be fried in advance and kept hot over hot water, but it will be better if served hot and fresh from the frying pan. Fry a thin slice of ham in the usual way, and place between two slices of toast spread with prepared mustard. Have a crisp leaf of lettuce under and over the ham. Garnish with a scoop of mashed potatoes and 1 piece of dill pickle.

HAM AND SWISS CHEESE SANDWICH   [1858]

On one slice of buttered bread place a slice of freshly broiled ham, then a slice of Swiss Cheese seasoned with mustard; another slice of ham, then the second slice of buttered bread, butter side down. Toast slowly on both sides. Cut through diagonally, and garnish with a slice of seasoned broiled tomato, (placing this on top of the sandwich) also a stalk of crisp celery and a radish or radish rose.

HAMBURGER SANDWICH   [1859]

Place 1 or 2 steak patties on a slice of bread, or toast, or between halves of a split roll. Spread either meat or bread with prepared mustard. Cover with brown gravy and garnish with a few French fried potatoes and 1 mound of buttered peas.

LAMB SANDWICH   [1860]

Place a slice of bread on a hot plate; spread with mustard butter, and cover with a slice of hot lamb. Garnish with a sprig of fresh mint, and serve with creamed cabbage.

PORK SANDWICH   [1861]

Place a slice of bread on a hot plate; spread with mustard butter, and cover with a slice of hot pork; Garnish with a thick ring of apple fried in butter on both sides, placing in center of the apple ring a large black olive, rolled in olive oil.

Serve with this a scoop of mashed potatoes sprinkled with minced parsley, also a mound of any preferred green vegetable.

SALMON CLUB SANDWICH   [1862]

Drain canned salmon; remove skin and bones carefully, leaving salmon in large whole flakes. For each serving, arrange crisp lettuce, then salmon flakes slightly heated over boiling water, on one slice of hot buttered toast. Top with 2 slices broiled bacon, and 1 slice of broiled tomato. Repeat the process after covering with a second piece of toast, seasoning each layer to taste with salt and pepper. Top the sandwich with a slice of cucumber, seasoned to taste and garnish with scallions, radishes and dill pickle. Serve at once.

STEAK AND EGGPLANT SANDWICH   [1863]

The steak may be broiled, fried or panned. Serve plain on a slice of bread. On another slice place a thick round of fried eggplant, and surround with Spanish sauce. Garnish with a scoop of mashed potato sprinkled with tiny fried croutons or fried breadcrumbs.

TONGUE SANDWICH [1864]

Heat slices of cooked tongue in meat or chicken broth, or in brown gravy. Place 2 or 3 slices on a plain slice of bread; cover with a thick layer of spinach, and cover with hot egg sauce. Serve with a scoop of mashed potatoes and a slice of dill pickle.

TURKEY SANDWICH [1865]

Place a slice of unbuttered bread on a hot plate; cover with a thin slice of hot turkey meat. Cover with gravy made from turkey stock. Serve mashed potatoes and string beans on the side.

WESTERN SANDWICH [1866]

Beat an egg slightly and add 1 tablespoon chopped cooked chicken and 1 tablespoon chopped pimiento. Fry in a small frying pan on both sides and serve on toast spread with horseradish butter. Garnish with a slice of broiled tomato placed upon a crisp lettuce leaf, also 1 large black olive, the stone removed, and the cavity filled with cream cheese blended with chopped walnut meats.

SANDWICH FILLINGS [1867]

Gone are the days when food was cooled by hanging in the well. Gone, too, are the days when milk cans flanked the brook's edge. Correct temperatures, accurate measuring and the right proportions mean perfect results. Today good judgment is needed to build a well-balanced meal; a good palate is necessary to season the foods to perfect taste, and a good cookbook will supply the necessary inspiration and information for infinite variety in the menu, especially in sandwich-making. Cooks sometimes think that the spices and seasonings called for in a recipe can be omitted and still get good results. They think that the lack of an eighth of a teaspoon of pepper and of other spices "won't make any difference" in the finished product. There could be no greater mistake. It is just as fatal as omitting some other basic ingredient. The sandwich may *look* all right without these little seasonings, but it will not have the essential perfection of tastiness.

Certain seasonings "lift" certain foods; in using them however, the cook must be careful not to over-season, but to obtain a delicious blend which will bring out the flavor of the predominant ingredient in the dish—even in a sandwich—and also add that elusive aroma so subtle that even the epicure hesitates to name it. Food properly seasoned is an art in itself, so season your sandwiches as you would your other dishes.

There are dozens of spices which American cooks seldom use because they do not know how to taste for them when preparing foods. But wonders can be worked with them by a cook who has the imagination to try them and who also knows how to taste.

SANDWICH FILLING—HINTS [1868]

All hot sandwich fillings may be served on hot waffles or freshly made toast.

The kind of bread is indicated for every filling but plain bread, nut bread, fruit bread, rye bread, or any other kind of bread may be substituted.

All the following fillings may be used for canapés, or appetizers, when garnished appropriately.

Sandwiches, with the following fillings, may be left open, closed, halved or quartered from corner to corner.

The garnishing is left to the imagination of the maker.

Closed sandwiches, be they halved through the middle, or triangular, or quartered, must be reinforced with either lettuce or watercress or shredded red or green cabbage before being covered.

1 cup of filling will suffice for 7 full-sized sandwiches.

Spread bread or toast used for these fillings with either plain butter or one of the Seasoned and Compounded (Creamed) Butters for Sandwiches, (No. 978 to 1006).

ANCHOVY AND PARMESAN CHEESE FILLING [1869]
(Serve on toast)

To 10 tablespoons of freshly grated Parmesan cheese, add 1 tablespoon of anchovy paste (or more, if desired sharp). Beat well with a little mayonnaise, and spread between slices of freshly made toast.

AMERICAN CHEESE AND NUT FILLING [1870]
(Serve on rye bread)

To 10 tablespoons grated fresh American cheese, add ¼ cup coarsely chopped nut meats and moisten with a little mayonnaise.

APPLE AND PEANUT BUTTER FILLING [1871]
(Serve on whole wheat bread)

To 10 tablespoons of pared, cored, finely chopped eating apple, add quickly 1 teaspoon of lemon juice, and mix with softened peanut butter, (using about 4 tablespoons) mixed with a little mayonnaise.

AVOCADO FILLING [1872]
(Serve on rye bread)

Put 1 cup of avocado pulp through ricer. Add 2 teaspoons lemon juice, ½ teaspoon onion juice and 1 scant teaspoon salt. Stir until smooth.

CRAB MEAT FILLING [1873]
(Serve either on toast or any bread)

Lobster, shrimp, tuna fish and salmon, as well as chicken, veal or pork may be similarly prepared.

Mix all the ingredients, after boning whenever necessary, as well as flaking well. Add ½ cup finely minced celery, 1½ tablespoons grated onion, and ½ scant cup mayonnaise. Blend well. Keep in refrigerator until wanted.

CARROT FILLING [1874]
(Serve on graham bread. Makes 1½ cups)

To 1 cup grated raw carrots, add 5 tablespoons mayonnaise, 1 scant teaspoon salt, a few grains of pepper, ½ cup broken nut meats, 1 tablespoon lemon juice and a few drops of Worcestershire sauce. Blend well. Store in icebox until wanted.

CHICKEN FILLING I [1875]
(Serve on toast. Makes 1¼ cups)

Put ½ cup cold cooked chicken, 3 olives, ½ green pepper, 2 hard-cooked eggs through food chopper, add 1½ teaspoons chili sauce, 3 tablespoons mayonnaise or more to moisten and a few drops of Worcestershire sauce. Mix well. Store until wanted.

CHICKEN FILLING II [1876]
(Serve on buttered graham bread. Makes 1½ cups)

Chop very fine enough cold cooked chicken to obtain 1 cup. Do not grind. Combine with ½ cup of finely chopped nut meats, and enough well seasoned mayonnaise to which has been added 1 tablespoon of prepared mustard. Store in refrigerator until wanted.

COTTAGE CHEESE FILLING [1877]
(Serve on any desired bread. Makes 1½ cups)

Sift 1 cup cottage cheese; add 2 tablespoons each of minced chives, grated onion and minced parsley, and 2 tablespoons minced green olives. Season to taste with salt and white pepper. Store in icebox. Does not keep very long.

CREAMED HAMBURGER FILLING [1878]
(Serve hot on toast, spread with peanut butter. Makes 1 cup)

Cook 1 tablespoon minced onion in 1 tablespoon of fat, then add ½ pound hamburger steak, chopped coarsely, season with salt and pepper and 1½ tablespoon minced parsley. Cook 10 minutes, stirring well, then add enough thick white sauce to moisten. Keeps well.

DRIED BEEF AND AMERICAN CHEESE [1879] FILLING
(Serve on white bread. Makes 1 cup)

Blend ½ cup of ground dried beef and ½ cup ground American cheese, moisten with a little catsup and a few grains of dry mustard. Keeps very long.

EGG MAYONNAISE FILLING [1880]
(Serve on graham bread. Makes 1 cup)

Finely chop the whites of 6 hard-cooked eggs. Press the hard-cooked yolks through potato ricer. Mix yolks and whites, season to taste with salt and paprika and moisten with mayonnaise or cream salad dressing. Keeps 1 week.

FIG AND DATE FILLING [1881]
(Serve on thin slices of nut bread)

Put enough dried figs and dates through food chopper to make 1 cup of each kind. Add cold water, to barely cover and cook to a paste stirring constantly. Add 1 teaspoon lemon juice. Cool. Keeps several weeks.

FISH ROE MAYONNAISE FILLING [1882]
(Serve on peanut buttered toast)

Grain about 2½ to 3 tablespoons of any kind of cooked or smoked fish roe, moisten with mayonnaise and add 1 teaspoon of grated onion. Does not keep.

FLUFFY PEANUT BUTTER FILLING   [1883]
(Serve on raisin bread)

Combine ¾ cup peanut butter, ¼ cup lemon juice, 2 tablespoons sugar, salt to taste and evaporated milk to make of spreading consistency. Whip until very light and fluffy. Keeps 1 week.

GINGER AND DATE FILLING   [1884]
(Serve on graham bread spread with peanut butter)

Mix ½ cup finely chopped dates, ½ cup chopped (not ground) walnuts and generous ¼ cup of chopped preserved ginger. Moisten with a little lemon juice or ginger syrup. Blend thoroughly. Keeps 2 or 3 weeks.

HAM AND MAYONNAISE FILLING   [1885]
(Serve on white or Boston baked brown bread)

Blend 1¼ cups ground ham, 6 tablespoons mayonnaise, 3 tablespoons finely chopped chutney, 1½ tablespoons chutney syrup. Mix well. Keeps weeks.

HONEY NUT FILLING   [1886]
(Serve on buttered whole wheat bread)

Combine and mix thoroughly ½ cup each of strained honey and chopped nut meats. Keeps indefinitely.

LIVER AND EGG FILLING   [1887]
(Serve on any kind of bread)

Brown ½ pound beef liver in butter for 3 minutes. Remove the skin and tubes, cut meat into small pieces and grind, adding the fat from the pan, also 1 tablespoon grated onion, 1 tablespoon minced parsley, 1 tablespoon minced green pepper, a few drops of Tabasco sauce, ½ teaspoon Worcestershire sauce, salt and pepper to taste and 2 hard-cooked eggs. Moisten with 2 tablespoons of mayonnaise, and blend thoroughly. Store in a small jar in the refrigerator until needed. Keeps 1 or 2 weeks.

PEACH AND NUT MEATS FILLING   [1888]
(Serve on buttered white bread)

Combine one cup of fresh or canned peach pulp, ½ cup of ground nut meats, and ½ cup of ground chicken, add 1 teaspoon ground cinnamon and season to taste with salt and pepper. Keeps 1 week.

ROQUEFORT CHEESE AND CAMEMBERT [1889] AND HAM FILLING
(Serve on pumpernickel or Boston baked brown bread)

Cream together ½ cup each of camembert and Roquefort cheese, with ½ cup of ground walnut meats. Add 1 teaspoon each of Worcestershire sauce and tomato catsup, and season with salt, pepper and a few grains of curry powder. Blend thoroughly. Put in a jar, and keep in refrigerator until needed. Keeps months.

SPICY HAM FILLING *(Serve on any kind of bread)* [1890]

Combine 1 cup ground cooked ham, ⅓ cup finely chopped or ground pickle, ⅓ cup ground ripe olives, 1 tablespoon each of finely minced parsley, onion and red pimiento, 2 teaspoons brown sugar, ½ teaspoon dry mustard and salt and pepper to taste. Moisten with mayonnaise. Put in a jar, and keep in refrigerator until needed. Keeps 2 weeks.

TEXAS FILLING *(Serve on white bread or buns)* [1891]

Put through food chopper fragments of left-over meat; there should be 2½ cups. Add 2 tablespoons grated onion. Combine with ½ cup of tomato juice, season highly with salt, a pinch of cayenne pepper and 1 teaspoon of chili powder. Cook until mixture is thoroughly blended and reaches the boiling point, stirring constantly. Cool or serve hot.

TONGUE AND HORSERADISH FILLING [1892]
(Serve on any preferred bread)

To 1 cup of ground cooked tongue, add 3 tablespoons prepared drained horseradish, 3 tablespoons chili sauce, 2 tablespoons minced green pepper, 2 tablespoons minced onion and ½ cup chopped ripe olives. Season with 1 tablespoon Worcestershire sauce, salt and pepper to taste and moisten with mayonnaise. Pack in a jar, and keep in refrigerator until wanted. Keeps 2 weeks.

WELSH RAREBIT *(Serves 6)* [1892A]

Shred 1 pound of sharp American cheese and melt it with ½ cup beer over direct heat, stirring constantly until cheese is melted. Add 1 tsp. salt, mustard, paprika and Worcestershire sauce and ¼ tsp. white pepper. Slightly beat 2 eggs and add to mixture. Stir rapidly over direct heat for one minute until thick and creamy. Serve on toast.
NOTE: For Golden Buck add freshly poached egg on top of each serving.

Chapter Fourteen

DESSERT AND DESSERT SAUCES

Hospitality is a precious human privilege. Was it not Emerson who wrote his wife from distant lands that if an Englishman were to visit her, she must build a fire in the guest room and give him bread and wine at bedtime, for should an Englishman get cold, he said, it would chill his own bones, and should an Englishman go hungry, he himself would be hungry all his life, so great had been the hospitality of the English toward him.

DESSERTS

T HE DESSERT SHOULD BE DRAMATIC. IT SHOULD HAVE GLAMOUR. Unless it creates a little stir of interest at its appearance, there is no object in having this final course. A dinner can perfectly well end after the salad—no one is really hungry by the time dessert is reached anyway.

But dessert does give the finishing touch to a good meal, so make it interesting and attractive, colorful and flavorful.

ALMOND FRITTERS [1894]
(Hot)

Beat 2 egg yolks and 2 tablespoons of sugar together until creamy, then stir in 1/4 cup of blanched, peeled and ground almonds, 1/2 teaspoon of vanilla extract, a few grains of salt, 2 tablespoons of pastry flour (more or less) and beat well. Lastly stir in very gently 2 stiffly beaten egg whites. When ready to serve, drop by teaspoons into clear, clean, hot, deep fat and fry until of a pale brown color. Drain and serve on a folded napkin on a hot platter.

ALMOND SOUFFLE [1895]
Serves 8 generously (Hot)

Mix thoroughly then sift, 2 cups powdered sugar, 1 cup flour, and 1/4 teaspoon salt. Gradually stir in 2 cups fresh milk, mixed with 3/4 teaspoon (more or less, depending upon the strength of flavor desired) of almond flavoring. Strain through a fine sieve (to eliminate any lumps) and bring the mixture to the boiling point, stirring constantly. Remove from the fire and stir in the slightly beaten yolks of 6 eggs. Now, fold in 8 egg whites, beaten until stiff, but not dry. Butter a large soufflé dish gen‧erously, then sprinkle with powdered sugar. (This is for the purpose of allowing the soufflé to swell more easily, thus making it soft and very spongy.) Pour in the mixture as evenly as possible. Decorate the top with thin slices of blanched toasted almonds (cold); sprinkle a good layer of powdered sugar over all; set in a pan of hot (not boiling) water and bake in a moderate oven (375° F.) from 20 to 25 minutes, or until the soufflé is almost double its original size and delicately browned.

Important. Do not open the oven door while the soufflé is baking. Serve at once. A soufflé cannot wait—it will fall almost immediately. No sauce of any kind should be served with an almond soufflé. But with a fruit soufflé, serve a dish of crushed fruit, if desired.

APPLE DUFF NEW ENGLAND STYLE   [1896]
(*Hot*)

Peel and core 2 pounds of cooking apples, then cut in eighths, and place in a large saucepan. Combine ¾ cup of dry, hard cider, 1½ table-spoon of quick cooking tapioca and 1 cup of sugar; stir until sugar is dissolved, then pour over the apples. Bring quickly to a boil; lower the flame, and continue simmering very gently for 10 to 12 minutes, then transfer to a large baking dish. Set aside. Beat 2 egg yolks well with a few grains of salt and 6 tablespoons of sugar, and set aside. Beat 2 egg whites with a few grains of salt until foamy, add ¼ teaspoon of cream of tartar, and beat until stiff but not dry. Fold the egg yolk mixture into the stiffly beaten egg whites and flavor with ½ teaspoon of vanilla extract, then gradually fold in lightly, but thoroughly, 6 tablespoons of sifted bread flour, and lastly ¼ teaspoon of almond extract. Pour this batter over the apples and bake in a moderate oven (325° F.) for about 35 to 40 minutes, or until delicately browned.

APRICOT TRIFLE   [1897]
(*Cold*)

Drain 1 can of apricots and boil the syrup, with 1 tablespoon of sugar, gently for 30 minutes. Cut a stale sponge cake into ½-inch slices, and stamp out rounds a little larger than a half apricot. Place these on a flat dish, pour the hot syrup carefully over them, and let them soak for 30 minutes. Using a narrow spatula, transfer the sponge cake discs to the dish in which they will be served, usually a glass dish, and top each with a half (pitted) apricot. Strain the remaining syrup through a fine sieve; add 1 tablespoon of lemon juice, and pour over the apricots. Stick 1½ tablespoons of blanched, shredded almonds in the apricots, and pile 1 cup of stiff, whipped cream, in center of the dish, forcing this through a pastry bag using a fancy tube. For a plain dish, day-old bread may replace the sponge cake, and a good custard may be substituted for the cream.

BAKED APPLES BELMONT   [1898]
(*Cold*)

Core and wipe 6 large baking apples with a damp cloth. Remove a strip of peel from stem end. Fill cavities with ¾ cup of sliced dates; place in skillet, pour over them 1 cup of maple syrup mixed with ¾ cup of water and ¼ teaspoon of salt. Cover and simmer very gently over a low flame, until apples are tender. Sprinkle peeled surface with a little granulated sugar; place under flame of broiling oven until apples are glazed, or about 5 minutes. Cool before serving.

BANANA BLANC MANGE   [1899]
(Cold)

Mix and stir until smooth ½ cup of cold milk and ½ cup of sifted cake flour. Scald 3½ cups of rich milk, stir in ⅓ cup of sugar and when dissolved stir in the milk-flour mixture. Bring gradually to a boil, lower the flame and simmer gently for 6 or 7 minutes, stirring constantly from the bottom of the pan. Cool, and when quite cold, beat in 3 egg yolks, one at a time, beating well after each addition; return to a low flame and cook gently, stirring constantly, until mixture boils. Remove from the fire, stir in 2 large, ripe, peeled bananas, rubbed through a fine-meshed sieve, and 1 teaspoon of vanilla extract. Turn into a wet mold, cool, then chill thoroughly in the refrigerator; unmold and serve with a cold custard sauce to which has been added a little melted red currant jelly.

BANANA TRIFLE   [1900]
(Cold)

Peel and rub 6 medium-sized ripe bananas through a fine-meshed sieve, with 1 cup of lemon jelly (marmalade), 2 tablespoons of apricot jam and ½ cup of curaçao or maraschino liqueur. Soak 1 tablespoon of granulated gelatin in a tablespoon of cold water, dissolve over hot water, cool to lukewarm and mix thoroughly with the banana mixture. Add a few drops of red vegetable coloring to obtain a light pinkish hue and brighten the color, and pour into a deep glass dish. Blanch and toast, then chop 1½ tablespoons of almonds and cool. When ready to serve, whip 1 pint of sweet, heavy cream stiff with ¼ teaspoon salt; sweeten with 3 tablespoons of powdered sugar, and flavor with (optional) 1 tablespoon of the liqueur already used. Pile lightly on top of the banana mixture, which should be very cold, sprinkle the almonds over the entire surface of the whipped cream; and surround the serving dish with macaroons.

BLACKBERRY DUFF   [1901]
(Hot)

Combine 2 cups of flour, 2 teaspoons baking powder and ½ teaspoon of salt; sift into a mixing bowl. Stir in 1 generous cup of milk mixed with 2 well beaten eggs. Sprinkle 1 cup of sugar over 2 cups of cleaned, washed, and drained blackberries. Let stand 30 minutes and stir into the flour mixture, mixing well. Turn into top of double boiler, cover and cook over boiling water for 2 hours, replenishing the lower pan with boiling water as it evaporates. Serve with Eggnog Sauce (No. 1974).

BLUEBERRY FLUMMERY [1902]
(Cold)

Mix 3 tablespoons cornstarch, ¼ teaspoon salt, and ½ cup granulated sugar in a saucepan. Combine 2 cups blueberry juice with the grated rind and strained juice of 1 lemon, and stir this mixture into that of the cornstarch, blending thoroughly until smooth. Place the saucepan over a gentle flame, and cook, stirring constantly, until thick. Pour immediately into wet individual molds or a large mold, and chill. Unmold on a chilled platter, and serve with whipped cream, or heavy sweet cream, and cookies. If a ring mold is used, the center may be filled with chilled blueberries, and topped with whipped cream.

BLUEBERRY SOUFFLE [1903]
With Egg Whites Only (Hot)

Press 2 cups washed and thoroughly dried blueberries through a fine strainer. Sprinkle over the juice thus extracted 1 teaspoon lime or lemon juice. Boil 1 cup granulated sugar with 3 tablespoons water until the mixture spins a thread (280° F.); then stir in the blueberry juice, and blend well. Remove from the fire, and set aside to cool. Beat 7 egg whites until stiff, and add 4 or 5 drops almond extract and ½ teaspoon grated lemon rind, beating continuously. Fold into the cold blueberry mixture, and turn into a generously buttered soufflé dish. Bake in a hot oven (400° F.) for 20 minutes. At the end of this time, sprinkle over the soufflé ¼ scant cup blanched, toasted, and shredded almonds. Close the oven door carefully, and bake 5 minutes longer. Serve at once.

BOSTON CINNAMON CREAM [1904]
(Cold)

Scald 1 cup of rich milk; add 2 tablespoons of sugar and stir until dissolved, flavor with ¾ teaspoon of vanilla and strain over 2 egg whites beaten with 1 egg yolk, stirring briskly meanwhile with a wire whisk. Return to top of double boiler and add 1 tablespoon of granulated gelatin, previously soaked in 2 tablespoons of cold water, also 2 cups of sweet heavy cream. Stir constantly over hot water, until mixture thickens. Place 3 tablespoons of crumbled stale Boston bread in a bowl, add ¼ teaspoon salt, and ⅓ teaspoon of ground cinnamon and mix well. Slowly, by driplets, pour the custard mixture over the brown bread mixture, blend thoroughly then stir frequently until mixture is cold.

Turn into a wet melon mold (or individual molds) and chill for 2 hours in refrigerator. Unmold on a cold glass dish, and decorate with rosettes of whipped cream forced through a pastry bag with a small rose tube.

CABINET PUDDING   [1905]
(Cold)

Prepare a mold as indicated for Charlotte Royal (No. 1907). Scald 1 cup of rich milk with 2 tablespoons of sugar. Cool slightly, then add 4 slightly beaten egg yolks, with a scant ¼ teaspoon salt; cook over hot water until mixture thickens, stirring constantly from bottom of pan, but do not actually boil. Dissolve 1 tablespoon of granulated gelatin in 2 tablespoons of cold water, and stir into the custard. Remove from hot water, cool to lukewarm, then stir in ⅓ cup of heavy sweet cream, and flavor with 1 scant teaspoon of any preferred flavoring extract. Stir in 1 teaspoon each of finely chopped angelica, candied apricot, candied pineapple, candied red and green cherries, candied pears, candied citron, and ⅓ cup of diced firm sponge cake, lady fingers or macaroons. Turn mixture into a mold, brushed with red currant or some other jelly. Chill in refrigerator for at least 2 hours. Unmold on a chilled silver or crystal platter, and garnish or decorate with tufts of plain whipped cream.

CALIFORNIA PRUNE WHIP CRUNCH   [1906]
(Cold)

Cook ½ pound of dried prunes; drain and rub the prunes through a fine sieve. To the pulp, add 2 tablespoons of brandy and whip until thoroughly blended, adding while whipping, ½ cup of crushed dry macaroons. Beat 4 egg whites until stiff with ½ teaspoon of salt, fold in 1 teaspoon of unstrained lemon juice, ½ teaspoon of grated lemon rind and ½ peeled and ground walnuts. Pour into a buttered baking dish (or individual baking dishes), set in a pan of hot water and bake in a moderate oven (350° F.) for 20 minutes, with individual dishes use the same temperature but bake only 12 to 15 minutes. Cool, then chill in refrigerator. Serve with a soft custard sauce.

CHARLOTTE ROYAL   [1907]
(Cold)

Combine ¼ cup sugar, a pinch of salt, 2 egg yolks, grated rind and juice of 1 small lemon, and ½ cup of muscatel in an enamel saucepan. Place over low heat and cook slowly, stirring constantly with a wire whisk until the mixture thickens. Beat for a few minutes until frothy, then remove from the heat. Beat the egg whites very stiff, and gradually add the hot mixture, beating constantly. Line one large or six individual dessert dishes with split lady fingers (18 for the large dish or 3 for each individual) standing on end around the sides. Pour in the fluffy mixture and chill. Serve topped with whipped cream.

CHERRIES IMPERIAL [1908]

Sprinkle ¼ cup of granulated sugar over 1½ cups of pitted sweet red cherries in a bowl; cover, let stand for an hour, in a cold place. Drain off the juice into a cup and fill up the cup with brandy, rum or kirsch. Empty one package of cherry gelatin, into a bowl; add 1 cup of sparkling cider, or if a richer dessert is desired, use dry champagne, either cider or champagne being heated to the boiling point, and stir until gelatin is dissolved. Then add the cherry juice, brandy, rum or kirsch mixture with 1 tablespoon of strained lemon juice. Cover bottoms of six individual wet molds with a little of the mixture and place in refrigerator just until set.

Fill the drained pitted cherries with blanched, toasted, cooled almonds, shaping them to look whole. Distribute the stuffed cherries among the six molds; cover with gelatin and chill thoroughly keeping remaining gelatin slightly warm meanwhile. Cut 1 large peeled ripe banana, into thirds crosswise and then into thirds lengthwise. Arrange in the molds; cover with remaining gelatin and chill for at least 3 hours. Unmolding on chilled individual dessert plates and serve with whipped cream.

CHOCOLATE OMELETTE [1909]
(*Hot*)

A chocolate omelette is not easy to make but the results justify the labor. Mix 1 ounce of melted chocolate, 4 tablespoons rich, heavy cream, and 3 tablespoons powdered sugar with 6 beaten eggs, as in a rum omelette, but omit the ice water. Cook the omelette; sugar the top well; then carry it to table on a tray, together with a wine glass of rum and another wine glass of Crème de Cacao topped with a half inch of heavy cream. Pour the rum over the omelette and burn it until the fire flashes out; then let the cordial and the cream flow smoothly over the smoldering volcano.

CHOCOLATE SOUFFLÉ FRENCH STYLE [1910]
(*Hot*)

Heat ½ cup of milk to boiling point: moisten ½ cup of flour with another ½ cup of milk, pour the hot milk over, stirring constantly; return to the fire and cook over hot water (double boiler) until thickened.

Remove from the fire and beat until perfectly smooth. Add four unbeaten egg yolks, one at a time, beating them in very thoroughly. Add also, ¼ cup of sugar and 2 squares of melted chocolate. Beat 4 egg whites stiff, adding ¼ cup sugar while beating. Combine the two mixtures lightly.

Spread a baking dish generously with creamed, (not melted) butter, then sprinkle with a heavy coating of granulated sugar. Pour in the soufflé mixture; set in a pan of hot water and bake 25 minutes in a moderate oven (375° F).

COFFEE CREAM   [1911]
(*Cold*)

Beat 3 egg yolks until light; pour over them gradually 1 cup of milk scalded with a few grains of salt, and cook over hot water (double boiler), beating briskly with a wire whisk, until thick. Add 5 tablespoons of powdered sugar, and stir until sugar is dissolved. Soak 1 tablespoon of gelatin in 1½ tablespoons of cold, strong coffee, and add to the custard, stirring until well blended. Fold in 1 cup of heavy cream, whipped with a few grains of salt, and flavored with 1 teaspoon of coffee extract or coffee essence. Turn into a wet mold and chill for at least 2 hours. Unmold on a cold platter, and decorate with plain whipped cream forced through a pastry bag using a small rose tube.

COTTAGE CHEESE MOLD BELGIUM STYLE   [1912]
Crème Fromage au Café (*Cold*)

Soften 1 envelope of unflavored gelatin in ¼ cup of cold strong black coffee, then stir in 1 cup of strong black hot coffee with 3 tablespoons of rum, and 3 tablespoons of sugar. Stir until gelatin and sugar are thoroughly dissolved, cool to lukewarm, then stir in 1¼ cups of cottage or cream cheese, sieved and beaten with 2 egg yolks, and beat thoroughly with rotary beater. When well blended, fold in 3 egg whites, stiffly beaten with ¼ teaspoon of salt. Turn into a wet mold and chill for at least 2½ to 3 hours. Unmold on a chilled glass platter, and garnish with sliced peaches, freshly crushed raspberries, strawberries, dewberries, or pitted sweet cherries.

CREME AMANDINE   [1913]
(*Cold*)

Blanch 2 ounces of almonds, chop coarsely and toast in a slow oven until lightly browned, stirring frequently. Sprinkle 1 tablespoon of granulated gelatin over 3 tablespoons of cold water, let stand five minutes, then dissolve over boiling water. Whip 1 cup of heavy sweet cream with ¼ teaspoon of salt, then fold in the dissolved gelatin. Flavor with a few drops of almond extract, then beat in 2½ tablespoons of sugar, alternately with the toasted (cold) almonds. Turn into a wet mold and chill for about 2 hours.

CREME AUX MARRONS [1914
(Cold)

Shell, parboil and skin 1 pound of chestnuts, then cook until tender with 1 pint of milk, the thinly-cut rind of a medium-sized lemon, and ½ teaspoon salt. Dissolve 8 tablespoons of sugar in 1 cup of milk; sprinkle over it 1 tablespoon of granulated gelatin, let stand a few minutes, then place the pan over a gentle flame and stir until the gelatin is dissolved without actually boiling. Cool slightly, then beat in 4 egg yolks, one at a time, beating well after each addition. Return to the fire and cook until mixture thickens, stirring constantly. Cool and when cold, stir in the chestnuts which have been rubbed through a fine-meshed sieve, alternately with ¼ cup of maraschino liqueur, and a few drops of red vegetable coloring, until a pale pink color is obtained. Now fold in gently but thoroughly 1 cup of sweet heavy cream. Pour into a decorated melon mold (small pieces of fancifully cut angelica, green and red maraschino cherries, candied pineapple, citron, apricots and pears), and set in refrigerator for at least 2 hours before serving. Unmold on a chilled silver or crystal platter and decorate the base with plain whipped cream forced through a pastry bag, using a small fancy rose tube.

CRÊPES [1915
Pancakes

According to a cook book which appeared in 1674, compiled by "L. S. R.," Jean Reboux is credited with creating *crêpes suzette* which were served with afternoon tea to Louis XV and fellow huntsmen in the Forest of Fontainebleau by order of Princess (Suzette) de Carignan who was infatuated with the king.

Crêpes Suzette are glorified pancakes, so thin and delicate that they take the place of honor as the dessert course at any meal. The batter for these *crêpes* is rich and thin and requires a good beating before being cooked. It takes time to make these delicious morsels but they're worth every minute you spend.

CRÊPES HELENA [1916
(Hot)

Created in honor of Princess Helena of Montenegro, who married, in 1896, King Victor Emmanuel III.

Batter. 1 cup, plus 2 tablespoons of sifted pastry flour, 6 tablespoons of sugar, ½ teaspoon salt, 10 whole eggs, 1½ cups of heavy sweet cream mixed with 1½ cups of fresh milk, ⅓ cup of whipped cream, 6 dry macaroons—crushed—2 tablespoons of orgeat syrup.

Combine sifted flour, sugar and salt, in a mixing bowl. Add the whole eggs, one at a time, beating well after each addition. Then beat briskly, until smooth and of the thickness of medium cream. Strain through a sieve into another bowl, then fold in the whipped cream. Cover with cheesecloth, and keep in a cool place at least 2 hours before cooking the crêpes. Then add macaroons and orgeat syrup.

Sauce. Knead together ¾ cup of sweet butter, 5 tablespoons of sugar and the grated rind of a small orange, being careful not to add any white part, which may give a bitter taste.

Serving. Melt in blazer of a chafing dish 1 teaspoon of the sweet butter mixture and when this begins to foam, pour in 2 tablespoons of the batter. Cook the crêpe about 1 minute, tilting the pan almost constantly. Turn and cook on the other side; then pour over each crêpe thus cooked, 1 pony glass each of fine champagne and Grand Marnier Cordon Rouge. Set aflame and turn the crêpe twice. Remove to a hot platter; dust with powdered sugar; fold in half, then in quarters. Keep hot. Repeat till batter and butter are both exhausted.

Now melt ¾ cup sweet butter in top pan of chafing dish and add 4 tablespoons of sugar. When thoroughly blended, pour in 2 teaspoons each of curaçao, cointreau and brandy, mixed with ½ teaspoon of grated lemon peel. Set aflame, put a few crêpes into this sauce, turn twice carefully, serving those ready at once. Repeat till all the crêpes have received their burning bath and are generously sauced.

CRÊPES LISETTE MERINGUÉES [1917]
(*Hot*)

Proceed as indicated for Crêpes Suzette (No. 1919). Have ready a meringue flavored with Kirsch, and sweetened to taste. As soon as the crêpes are ready, place them on a silver or porcelain platter capable of withstanding the flame of the broiler. Fill a pastry bag with the meringue; decorate each crêpe with the meringue, and slide the platter under the flame of the broiling oven to gild the top as delicately as possible.

CRÊPES NANTAISES [1918]
(*Hot*)

For 6 servings, sift into a mixing bowl 2 cups of pastry flour with ¼ teaspoon salt and 1 teaspoon of powdered sugar, then add, one at a time, 6 eggs, beating well after each addition and adding with the last egg 1 tablespoon of rum. Gradually stir in 1¾ cups of rich milk or half cream and half milk, or use undiluted evaporated milk, scalded with 1 teaspoon (scant) of grated lemon rind, then cooled, and mixed with 1 generous tablespoon of blanched, halved, toasted, then ground almonds.

Heat an individual frying pan, and rub with a piece of sweet butter; pour in 1 tablespoon of the batter, tilting the pan so as to distribute the batter all over the bottom of the pan, and cook 1 minute. Turn the crêpe or toss it, and cook the other side also until brown, or about 1 minute. Slide the crêpe onto a hot platter, spread with sieved apricot marmalade; roll up; trim the edges neatly and cut in half right in the middle. Keep hot. When all are cooked have ready a frying batter made as follows:

Sift into a mixing bowl 1½ cups of flour, 2 teaspoons baking powder, and ⅛ teaspoon salt. Gradually add 1 whole egg and 1 egg yolk, well beaten, and mix with ⅔ (scant) cup of rich cold milk and 1 tablespoon of good rum. Mix until smooth. When ready to serve, roll the half-crêpes in this batter, and fry in plenty of butter a few at a time, until golden brown and deliciously crackling and *croustillantes*.

Note. These crêpes usually made at Easter are often served with crushed raspberries or strawberries. They may be served also with jams or jellies.

CRÊPES SUZETTE   [1919]
Makes 16 (Hot)

The Batter. Combine in a mixing bowl 6 whole eggs, 4 tablespoons flour, 2 tablespoons cold water and a generous pinch of salt. Beat vigorously until the mixture takes on the consistency of light cream or thick olive oil. Next put into an individual frying pan a piece of sweet butter the size of a small pecan. When the butter begins to bubble pour in enough of the batter (about 1 tablespoonful) to cover the bottom of the pan with a thin layer. Shake the pan deftly to spread the batter evenly, and cook for about one minute, then turn and cook the other side. If you are skillful you can toss it by raising the pan from the fire and, making a shaking movement forward, then one backward; return the crêpe to the frying pan. *Advice:* The first time, do this over the sink.

When the crêpe is nicely browned, fold it in half, then again in quarters, using a fork, and keep warm until the other 15 crêpes are cooked in the same manner.

Sauce. The sauce should be prepared in advance as follows: Take 2 tablespoons of sugar, flavored with a dozen drops of good vanilla extract (the recipe calls for vanilla sugar, which is made by placing a large vanilla bean in a covered bowl of sugar and letting it stand several weeks before using). Now take two thin pieces of the yellow outside rind of a lemon, and the same amount of the rind of an orange; the pieces should each be about the size of a quarter, and absolutely free from any of the white under layers. Cut all into thin strips, add to the sugar and store for a day or two in a tightly stoppered jar.

The Finale. Take ½ pound of sweet butter and place it in a thin silver-plated pan made for the purpose (the top pan of a chafing dish will do nicely). When the butter bubbles, pour into it a mixture of two ponies each of maraschino, curaçao and kirschwasser. These will catch fire. When the flames die down, add the flavored sugar. Now put a few of the folded crêpes into the hot sauce, and turn them carefully, adding while turning 2 more ponies each of curaçao and kirschwasser, and the fire will start again. Serve immediately on very hot plates from the flaming pan, spooning a good teaspoon of the flaming liquid over each serving. The liqueurs may be varied, according to the taste of the guests.

CUSTARDS—HINTS [1920]

Custard is composed of ingredients which are absolutely needed in our daily diet and surely no more delightful way of consuming milk and eggs can be found than in the form of custard of which there are many varieties.

Custard may be sweetened or not. As a dessert, it can be prepared with fruits or nuts and may be served plain or with a sauce. Moreover it can be served hot or chilled as desired.

A curdled custard is a failure; a thin custard a disappointment; at a point between the two is a perfect custard, smoothly thickened, creamy and delicate. True custards are thickened by eggs alone; that is why they seem difficult to make. The temperature at which eggs coagulate is almost unbelievably low, and since we are accustomed to watching food bubble as it cooks, custard trouble is apt to occur occasionally.

Common causes of custard failure are cooking too long or cooking at too high temperature. The custard should be set in a pan of hot water and baked in a moderate oven (325–350° F.) only until it is set or until a silver knife inserted in it comes out clean.

If boiled custard shows signs of curdling, remove from heat at once and cool quickly by placing the pan in ice water to stop further cooking. To improve the texture, pour the custard into a jar, close securely and shake well.

When making custard pies, always heat the milk to boiling point before combining with the eggs. If this rule is followed, the undercrust will be crisp.

If preferred use only the yolks of eggs when making custards. The whites do not improve the custard and can be utilized for other purposes. This does not apply when making custards for invalids and those who need nourishment.

If a baked custard is to be served in the cup and you wish the top to be a rich brown, beat the eggs well instead of just lightly. This forms a foam that rises to the surface of the cup after the custard is poured in and this foam browns beautifully during the baking. The same rule applies to a custard pie.

Try sprinkling a few dry cake, cookie or macaroon crumbs over custard before baking to give a crisp, crusty surface . . . also to tone up the bland flavor, drop left-over fruit, candied cherries, nuts or jelly into the bottom of the cup before pouring the custard in.

If a custard is to be unmolded, the eggs must be only lightly beaten. In this instance the browning is unimportant. The texture will be smoother and firmer than when a volume of air is whipped into the eggs.

In baked custards: 1 *egg* to 1 cup of milk or 4 eggs to a quart will produce a very delicate custard, rather slow in setting, and not capable of being unmolded unless chilled thoroughly.

One and a half eggs to 1 cup of milk, or 6 eggs to a quart will produce a firm, creamy custard, which sets in a shorter time and unmolds well when cold, but not necessarily chilled.

Two eggs to 1 cup of milk or 8 eggs to a quart, gives the traditional rich French custard with smooth, mellow flavor and satisfying body.

Baked custards are used for desserts and many variations can be made. A spoonful of jelly or a little maple, caramel, or other sugar syrup in the bottom of the custard cup before the custard preparation is poured in, makes a pretty dish when unmolded after baking.

BAKED CUSTARD   [1921]

Scald 1 quart of rich milk. If custards are to be unmolded beat the eggs slightly and add ¼ cup of sugar and a scant ¼ teaspoon of salt. Add milk slowly, mixing until sugar is dissolved. Add 1 teaspoon of vanilla, or ½ teaspoon each of vanilla and almond, or vanilla and lemon, etc., depending on taste; turn mixture into custard cups; place in pan of hot, not boiling, water, and bake in a moderate oven (325-350° F.) 25 to 30 minutes or until set. Run a sharp knife blade into the custard and if it comes out clean, the custard is baked. *Do not mind* if it seems a little shaky; as custards become firm on cooling. When perfectly cold, insert a knife down one side of the cup or mold, or baking dish, turn the custard on a slant, and it will loosen like jelly. Invert on to a cold serving platter, and garnish as desired.

Soft custards or *boiled custards* are a slightly different problem. They *must* be cooked over simmering water, or over the lowest heat given by an electric unit. They *must* be stirred constantly during the cooking and watched for signs of thickening. The time required varies from 6 to 8 minutes for 2 cups of soft custard, and usually a metal spoon is used for stirring. The type of custard desired determines the proportions of eggs to milk.

In soft or boiled custards: 1 *egg* to 1 cup of milk will not give any noticeable thickening, nor smoothness; 2 *eggs* to 1 cup of milk will give considerable thickening, and will have a certain gentle pull on the metal spoon as the mixture is stirred. 4 *eggs yolks* to 1 cup of milk will give a beautifully colored, nicely thickened, soft or boiled custard.

Soft or boiled custards are used for sauces, also for numerous hot or cold desserts, including frozen desserts.

SOFT CUSTARD [1922]

Scald 2 cups of rich milk. Combine 4 slightly beaten eggs, with 2 tablespoons of sugar and a dash of salt, and stir into the milk. Cook over gently simmering water, stirring constantly with a metal spoon, until custard just begins to thicken. At this time, the liquid will begin to exert a slight drag and to show faint traces in the wake of the spoon, which will be coated with the custard. Remove from heat, stir in ½ teaspoon of vanilla or equal parts of vanilla and almond extract, and turn into a dish to cool, stirring occasionally during the cooling.

ENGLISH PLUM PUDDING [1923]
Serves about 10 persons generously (Hot)

Mix ½ pound of sugar, ½ pound of finely chopped suet, ½ pound of Sultana raisins, cleaned, ½ pound of seedless raisins, ½ pound of currants, washed and dried, ¼ pound of shredded mixed candied peel, ¼ pound of bread flour, ¼ pound of soft breadcrumbs, 2 ounces of blanched, shredded almonds, the grated rinds and juice of 1 medium-sized lemon and 4 eggs, slightly beaten. Season with ½ teaspoon of salt, ¼ teaspoon each of grated nutmeg and ground cinnamon, a generous dash of clove and add 1 cup of cold, sweet, creamy milk, alternately with ½ cup of French brandy. Turn the mixture into 2 well-buttered molds; cover each mold with a buttered piece of muslin, adjust the covers tight, and steam steadily, but gently, for 4½ to 5 hours, replenishing the pan with boiling water as it evaporates. Unmold upon a heated platter and serve as hot as possible with your favorite hard sauce. Lemon Hard sauce is suggested (No. 2003) or Brandy Sauce (No. 1994).

FIGS IMPERATRICE [1924]
(Hot)

Separate 1 pound of large, plump California dried, yet moist, figs, place in a steamer, over very little boiling water, until well plumped. Remove from fire and when cold enough to handle, open up each fig without actually separating, and stuff with finely chopped blanched, toasted almonds, mixed just enough with honey to blend rather dry. Place the stuffed figs in a shallow baking dish, pour over them 1 cup of port wine; heat thoroughly without boiling, basting the figs occasionally with the wine. Serve hot with whipped cream sweetened to taste and flavored with a few drops of almond extract, and with any preferred cookies.

FLOATING ISLAND MY STYLE   [1925]
Oeufs à la Neige

Put 1½ cups of sweet, rich milk, 3 lumps of sugar, and 1 scant teaspoon of vanilla, or a vanilla bean, if available, in a shallow saucepan. Bring to a boil, stirring well to melt the sugar. Beat 6 egg whites to a very stiff froth with a few grains of salt, and test the stiffness by placing an egg on it. If the egg doesn't sink, the whites are sufficiently beaten. Now gradually add ¾ cup of powdered sugar to the whites, beating steadily. Take up a little of this meringue in a tea or dessert spoon, and with a knife smooth it and give it the shape of an egg. Drop one at a time in the boiling milk, and after 1½ minutes or so turn each meringue "egg" carefully with a fork, so as to cook the upper side. Leave them in for exactly 2 minutes more—not longer, or they will collapse. Remove from the milk with a perforated spoon, and drain either in a large sieve or on a dry cloth.

Strain the milk through a fine-meshed sieve. Beat the 6 egg yolks and gradually add the warm milk to them. Return to the fire and stir till the mixture just begins to thicken. When quite cold, put the custard in a shallow crystal dish and arrange the whites on top. They will float on the surface, hence the English name "floating island."

FLUFFY ALMOND CREAM PUDDING   [1926]
(Hot)

Blanch, and shred finely (do not chop, nor grind) 2 ounces of almonds; dry them in a mild oven (250° F.) but do not brown. Combine 2 ounces of previously sifted pastry flour and ¼ teaspoon of salt, and resift into a mixing bowl. Make a hollow in center and pour in ½ cup, less 1 tablespoon, of cold, rich milk; stir gradually, starting from the center until flour is all moistened, then beat vigorously until batter is smooth and free from lumps.

Put ½ cup of milk into a saucepan with ¼ cup of butter, and when boiling, stir in ½ cup of sugar with the batter and cook over a gentle flame, stirring constantly until thick. Cool slightly, then beat in 4 egg yolks, one at a time, beating vigorously after each addition, adding the almonds with the last egg yolk. Fold in 4 stiffly beaten egg whites. Turn mixture into a buttered baking dish or 6 individual buttered custard cups. Set in a pan containing hot water to about half the depth of the dish and bake in a moderate oven (350° F.) for 1¼ hours if in one large dish, or 45 minutes for the individual ones. Serve hot with Sabayon Sauce (No. 1987).

FRAMBOISE A LA NINA [1927]
(*Cold*)

Combine and beat together 1 glass of raspberry and one of red currant jelly until thoroughly blended; fold in 2 stiffly beaten egg whites sweetened with ½ cup of powdered sugar, flavored with ¼ teaspoon of almond extract, then mixed with 1 pint of fresh, hulled raspberries, which have been previously soaked in 3 or 4 tablespoons of sherry wine and well drained. Chill for at least 2 hours. Serve in chilled sherbet glasses with cookies.

GELATIN [1928]

Gelatin has become a practical necessity in every kitchen, but few cooks take full advantage of its possibilities as a versatile, nourishing, economical and interesting food. Automatic refrigeration has added considerably to the convenience and usefulness of gelatin which, of course, helps the speed with which numerous desserts may be chilled, and also makes molded desserts simpler, surer, and completely independent of weather. Gelatin is obtained by extraction from the white connective tissue in the skins, and from the bones of food animals, principally from beef and veal.

In early days, cooks made their own gelatin by boiling calves' feet for hours then straining the broth through a muslin cloth, not once but several times, and finally clearing it with the whites of several eggs. Today they purchase it in convenient small packages already cleared and accurately measured for exact results in the kitchen.

Two Types of Gelatin. There are two types of gelatin, plain, unsweetened, unflavored granulated gelatin and sweetened gelatin dessert powders, which carry fruit flavors and contain 10 to 12 per cent gelatin, just enough to congeal a pint of liquid. The remainder of the powder contains the sugar, flavoring and coloring. A plain granulated beef bone gelatin is usually preferred for soups and for use in aspic, fresh fruits, coffee, wine, liqueurs, tomatoes, and left-over canned fruit juice. Lime or lemon gelatin is popular with meats and fish as a garnish or jellying agent.

Gelatin is used to stiffen many desserts other than simple clear jellies. Merely beating the jelly after it has begun to stiffen produces a different type of dessert which in culinary parlance is called "a whip." Sometimes beaten egg whites or whipped cream are folded into the thickened jelly and we have a sponge, or a Spanish or Bavarian cream. Sometimes milk instead of water or wine and both egg yolks and whites are used for these desserts. There is no clear distinction among them when it comes to their titles.

Definition of Jelly Desserts. Jellies may be described as solutions of gelatin in a liquid; their clear, brilliant transparency is one of their chief recommendations. However, jellies of this class do not comprise the whole list, for in addition there are the opaque nourishing milk and egg jellies, also those made of fruits. Calf's foot jelly which is stiffened by the gelatin extracted from the feet by boiling, has the advantage of being perfectly pure, but is no more nourishing than the jelly made from bought gelatin. When nourishing jelly is required, it is better made from good veal stock. For ordinary garnishing and masking purposes, jelly made from manufactured gelatin is more frequently employed than that made from meat. A plain lemon jelly answers admirably for coating the molds for creams; and, variously colored and flavored, it forms the basis of many other jellies. Pleasing effects may be produced by filling the projecting divisions of a mold with colored jelly and the body of the mold with jelly that differs either in color or character. Of course, the colors must be blended artistically and tastefully; bright-colored creams, like strawberry, should be very simply decorated, while the creamy-white of the almond or the delicate green of the pistachio nut, imbedded in the amber-hued jelly with which the mold is lined, contrast favorably with chocolate.

Clearing the Jelly. The agent employed for this purpose is albumen, of which substance the white of egg is largely composed. The shells and lightly-beaten egg whites are added to the water, wine, and so forth, when cold, the whole being continuously beaten while coming to the boil. At a temperature of 160° F., the albumen coagulates, and as the hardened particles or scum rise to the surface, they entangle and carry with them all the insoluble substances with which they come in contact; this forms the scum and the filtering medium, through which the jelly must be afterwards passed and repassed until clear. The jelly should always be allowed to simmer for a short time after it reaches boiling point, but it must on no account be whipped, stirred, or otherwise disturbed. A little lemon juice, lime, or any other acid assists in the coagulation of the albumen.

Definition of Cream Desserts. The term "cream" is used in culinary parlance to describe compounds of cream and fruit, fruit-purée or custards, variously flavored, stiffened with gelatin, and more or less elaborately decorated. For this purpose, heavy cream is required, that is, cream skimmed from milk that has stood for 24 hours instead of 12, or been well drained from the milk after being separated. Cream is more quickly whipped to a stiff froth when cold, and the air introduced by whipping should be as cold as possible. The whipping should not be continued one moment after the proper degree of stiffness is obtained; great care is needed in this respect in warm weather, when the cream, if over-whipped, is apt to turn rather quickly to butter.

The gelatin added to cream desserts is always first softened in a little cold water, and should be added at a definite temperature, for if too hot it may cause the cream to lose some of its lightness; if too cold, it sets in small hard lumps instead of being intimately mixed with the whole; and, after the gelatine is added, the cream preparation should be stirred until just on the point of setting, more particularly when it contains fruit, almonds, pistachios, nuts, and so forth, which would otherwise sink to the bottom of the mold or dish. On the other hand, if the mixture is allowed to become too cold, it does not take the shape of the mold. Hot weather has quite a wilting effect on these delicacies. Of course there is no season for gelatin desserts, and in summer, a quivering mold of jellied fruit, a sponge, a whip, a cream or a Bavarian cream type of dessert makes a particularly attractive finale for a meal.

Unmolding Gelatin Desserts and Others. It is much better to dip the mold or molds once into hot water than 3 or 4 times into lukewarm water. One sharp "down and up" jerk will instantly detach the cream, or jelly from the mold. The point of a knife should be used to loosen it at the edge. The molded dessert is then gently inverted and shaken over a chilled dish when the jelly or cream should slip free from the mold.

Desserts of this description are usually garnished with a macedoine of fruit, crushed berries, whipped cream, chopped or molded jelly, as cubes, fancy designs, and so forth. When chopping jelly for garnishing, the coarser the better for the effect, for large pieces reflect the light, whereas finely chopped jelly has a slightly opaque appearance.

GINGER CREAM   [1929]
(*Cold*)

Beat 3 egg yolks until light and fluffy with a scant ¼ teaspoon salt. Pour over them slowly ½ cup of milk, scalded with 2 tablespoons of sugar, stirring while pouring. Set aside to cool. Soften 1 tablespoon of granulated gelatin in 1 tablespoon of cold water and dissolve over a very low flame or over hot water, together with 2 tablespoons of ginger syrup and 2 ounces of preserved ginger cut into tiny cubes. Combine with the custard, and let cool. Fold in 1 cup of sweet, heavy cream, whipped with a few grains of salt and 3 drops of almond extract. Turn into a wet melon mold, and chill in refrigerator for at least 2 hours. Unmold on a chilled crystal platter; garnish with little tufts of plain whipped cream forced through a pastry bag using a fancy tube, dotting the mold all over, and press onto each tuft a tiny piece of blanched, toasted almond.

GOLD CREAM   [1930]
(*Cold*)

Soak 1 tablespoon, plus 1 teaspoon of granulated gelatin in ½ cup of cold milk for 5 minutes. Scald 2 cups of milk together with the thinly-cut peel of 1 lemon and 8 tablespoons of granulated sugar, then let boil up once or twice and stir in the gelatin mixture. When dissolved, cool to lukewarm, then stir in the juice of the lemon. Now beat in 6 egg yolks, one at a time beating briskly after each addition and adding with the last yolk ¼ teaspoon of salt. Return to the fire and cook, stirring constantly, until mixture thickens. Remove from the fire, cool, stirring occasionally, and when almost cold turn into a wet mold and chill in refrigerator for at least 2 hours. Unmold on to a chilled glass platter; pour a thin layer of Melba Sauce (No. 1980), around the mold and serve at once.

GOOSEBERRY TRIFLE [1931]
(Cold)

Clean, removing stem and blossom ends and wash and drain well 2 pounds of green gooseberries. Place the fruit in a saucepan, add 12 tablespoons of granulated sugar, and 4 tablespoons of water, and cook over a gentle flame, stirring frequently to prevent scorching, until the fruit is tender, then press through a fine sieve. Divide 3 individual sponge cakes into 3 or 4 slices, crosswise, place them in a deep glass dish, cover with the gooseberry pulp, pour over all 1 cup of lukewarm soft custard, and chill. At serving time cover with sweetened flavored whipped cream putting this on through a pastry bag, and covering the entire surface with the cream, making any kind of fancy designs desired, then sprinkle with blanched, shredded toasted almonds.

GRAPE SPONGE [1932]
(Cold)

Soften 1 tablespoon of unflavored gelatin in 3 tablespoons of cold grape juice, stir in ¼ cup of sugar, ¼ teaspoon of salt and 1 cup of hot (not boiled) grape juice and stir until gelatin and sugar are thoroughly dissolved, then add 1 tablespoon of lemon juice. Cool until beginning to thicken. Place the bowl in a pan of ice and water and beat with a rotary beater until fluffy and thick. Fold in 2 stiffly beaten egg whites, beaten with a pinch of salt, turn into a wet mold and chill until firm. Unmold and serve with custard sauce.

GUAVA SOUFFLÉ HAVANAISE [1933]
(Hot)

Melt 1½ tablespoons of butter; blend in 1½ tablespoons of flour, sifted with ¼ teaspoon of salt, stirring constantly until mixture just begins to bubble, but does not brown. Gradually stir in 1 cup of rich milk plus 3 tablespoons of sweet thick cream, scalded together, stirring constantly over a gentle flame until smooth and just beginning to thicken. Remove from the fire, and beat in, one at a time, 3 egg yolks, beating briskly after each addition, and from the bottom of the pan.

Cool and when quite cold, stir in 1 cup of stewed guavas, which have been rubbed through a fine-meshed sieve and sweetened with ⅓ to ½ cup of sugar, depending on sweetness of the fruit, alternately with 1 tablespoon of Benedictine or Cointreau liqueur. Lastly, fold in 3 stiffly beaten egg whites and turn into a baking dish, first buttered then sprinkled with 2 tablespoons of finely chopped pistachio nuts. Sprinkle top with 1 generous teaspoon of very finely chopped pistachio nuts, and bake in a hot oven (400° F.) for 25 minutes, or until soufflé is well puffed and slightly browned. Serve at once.

HONEY SOUFFLE   [1934]
(Hot)

Beat 4 egg yolks and 1 tablespoon Kirsch until thick and lemon-colored. Add gradually 1 cup granulated sugar sifted with 1 tablespoon pastry flour, ¼ generous teaspoon salt, and a good grating of nutmeg beating the whole until very light. Beat together ½ cup of clarified butter and strained honey, and add a little at a time, still beating briskly after each addition. Lastly, fold in 4 stiffly beaten egg whites. Turn into a large buttered soufflé dish having it not more than ⅔ full, to allow room for rising. Sprinkle with 1 teaspoon ground pistachio nuts, and set the dish in a pan of hot (not boiling) water. Bake 35 to 40 minutes in a moderate oven (375° F.). Serve at once with Raspberry Sauce with Cherry Brandy (No. 1985).

HONEY SPONGE LEMON PUDDING   [1935]
(Cold)

Cream 1½ tablespoons of butter until light; gradually work in ¾ cup of strained honey and when thoroughly blended, beat in 2½ tablespoons of bread flour, and ¼ teaspoon salt, alternately with 3 slightly beaten egg yolks. Beat again for about a half minute, adding while beating 3 generous tablespoons of lemon juice, mixed with the grated rind of a small lemon, alternately with 1¼ cups of cold buttermilk. When thoroughly blended, fold in 3 stiffly beaten egg whites, beaten with 2 or 3 drops of lemon extract. Pour into 6 custard cups; place these in a pan of hot water, and bake in a moderate oven (325-350° F.) until delicately browned and custard is set. Cool well before serving.

JELLIED BANANAS EN CHARTREUSE   [1936]
(Cold)

Peel and slice thinly 5 or 6 medium sized bananas which should be quite ripe, but not too soft.

Line a charlotte mold with a thin coating of lemon jelly (No. 1937) and let it set. Arrange overlapping banana slices around the mold and let them set before pouring in another layer of semi-liquid jelly; again let set, and place more banana slices similarly on it, proceeding in this way until jelly and fruit are all used and the mold filled. There should be about a pint of jelly in all.

Be sure to have the layers of banana slices and the spaces of lemon jelly between them uniform. Chill in refrigerator for at least 2½ hours. Unmold on a chilled crystal platter, and garnish with 1 cup of coarsely chopped Port Wine Jelly (No. 1957). Serve with plain whipped cream and petits fours or cookies.

Oranges, tangerines, peaches, apples, plums, and so forth may be prepared in the same manner.

LEMON JELLY   [1937]
(*Cold*)

Put 2½ cups of cold water, the finely pared rind of 4 medium-sized lemons, ½ cup of strained lemon juice, ¾ cup of sugar and ⅛ teaspoon salt into a saucepan. Stir until sugar is dissolved, then add the whites and shells of 2 eggs and 1½ tablespoons of gelatin, previously softened in 3 tablespoons of cold water; bring mixture very gently almost to the boiling point, stirring and beating at the same time; lower the flame and simmer very gently for 10 minutes. Strain through a muslin cloth into a fresh saucepan, stir in 1 cup of pale sherry wine, heat well, but do not boil. Turn jelly into a wet mold, and when cold chill in the refrigerator for at least 2½ hours before unmolding upon a layer of sponge cake, cut the shape of the mold, and cover the cake with plain whipped cream, spooned on with a tablespoon to imitate rocks. Dust the whipped cream with coarsely chopped blanched almonds, shredded, toasted and cooled.

Note. When this jelly is intended to line or garnish molds, an extra ½ tablespoon of gelatin should be added, especially in hot weather. Orange or grapefruit may be substituted for the lemon.

LOST BREAD   [1938]
Pain Perdu (Hot)

Cut 6 medium thick slices of bread; and remove the crust. Moisten them with a little milk, previously scalded with 1 tablespoon of sugar and a generous teaspoon of vanilla; then chill. Do not over-moisten the bread or it will break. Dip slice in beaten egg yolk coating them evenly on both sides, and fry golden brown in hot, clarified butter. Drain on a cloth, and serve on a dish, on a folded napkin, after having first sprinkled them generously with confectioners or powdered sugar.

MAMA SUZY TURNER'S MOLDED PUDDING   [1939]
(*Cold*)

Soak 1 tablespoon of granulated gelatin in 1 pint of cold milk for 10 minutes. Stir together over a gentle flame until dissolved, adding also 8 tablespoons of fine granulated sugar. Cool slightly, then beat in 6 egg yolks, one at a time, beating well after each addition, and adding with the last yolk ¼ teaspoon of salt, and 1 cup of sweet, heavy cream, previously scalded and slightly cooled. Place over a gentle flame and cook, stirring constantly, until mixture thickens, but do not boil. Let cool thoroughly then stir in 2 tablespoons of coarsely chopped glacé cherries, 1 tablespoon of finely chopped citron, 1 tablespoon of finely chopped candied apricots, 1 tablespoon of finely chopped candied pineapple, and ½ teaspoon each of almond and vanilla extract. Turn into a large melon mold, previously lined with currant jelly, and chill in refrigerator for at least 3 hours. Unmold onto a chilled crystal platter, and decorate tastefully with whipped cream (unsweetened and unflavored) forced through a fancy tube using a small rose tube, dusting the whipped cream lightly with very finely chopped or ground pistachio nut meats.

MELON A L'ORIENTALE   [1940]
(*Cold*)

Pare a cantaloupe neatly and slice the meat horizontally as you would an orange. Carefully remove the seeds and surrounding tissue; then sprinkle each slice with powdered rock candy (obtainable at a drugstore) then with 1 generous teaspoon Kirsch or rum. Reconstruct the melon in its original shape, and place it in a round covered melon mold, sealing the rim with a strip of cloth spread with butter to prevent the penetration of salt water. Pack for 2 hours in a freezer pail, using a mixture of 3 parts cracked ice and 1 part rock salt.

MERINGUES—HINTS   [1941]

In making meringues, there are a few points to be observed:
Whites of eggs that are several days old rather than strictly fresh will whip more readily. A watery egg white whips to a greater volume than a thick white.
Have eggs cold before separating to insure a clean division of white and yolk.
Allow egg whites to stand, covered, until they reach room tempera-

ture before whipping. Unlike cream, egg whites whip better with the chill taken off.

Although the addition of water increases the volume of meringue it also increases the tendency toward leaking shortly after baking.

The most satisfactory proportion of sugar is 2 tablespoons for each egg white for a soft meringue and 3 or 4 tablespoons for the firm type.

Do not add sugar until egg whites have reached the stiff foam stage, then add 1 tablespoon at a time. Honey may be used in place of sugar and in the same proportion, but it requires more beating.

Other flavoring, salt, lemon juice or extract should be added before beating. Allow a pinch of salt and ¼ teaspoon of desired or required extract, or 1 scant teaspoon of lemon juice or grated lemon rind for each egg white.

For beating, use a bowl with round bottom and slightly sloping sides and either a rotary beater or wire whisk.

Baking time and temperature vary from a very slow oven for a firm meringue (250° to 275° F.) for 30 to 50 minutes, depending on size and thickness—to a high temperature (500° F.) and 4 minutes baking time as for baked Alaska. For general purposes a temperature of 350° F. to 400° F. is recommended.

When adding a soft meringue over a pudding or pie filling, first spread a small amount around the edge, leaving no space between meringue and edge of dish, to prevent wateriness. "Spoon" on the remainder and spread with broad irregular strokes to meet meringue at the edge.

Butter the knife or dip it into cold water before cutting a soft meringue.

Whipped cream was used in Rome as early as the ninth century. It was served with grapes and was very expensive because the secret of making it was closely guarded by the chefs.

MILK DUMPLINGS   [1942]
(*Hot*)

Combine thoroughly and smoothly 1 quart of milk, 1 cup sugar, 3½ tablespoons of corn starch, 8 egg yolks and ¾ teaspoons of vanilla. Turn into a saucepan, place on a slow fire and stir continuously till the mixture thickens. Pour into a dish or pan about 2 inches deep, and when cold cut into almond-shaped dumplings; pile in a buttered fireproof dish, dot with a few pats of butter and brown in a moderate oven (300-325 F.).

MOCHA SPONGE   [1943]
(*Cold*)

Soften 1 tablespoon gelatin in ¼ cup cold water. Add ¾ cup granulated sugar and a pinch of salt, and stir; then pour in 1½ cups very strong black coffee, which should be as hot as possible, though not actually boiling. Stir until the gelatin is entirely dissolved, adding meanwhile, 2 tablespoons strained lemon juice. Cool until nearly set, then beat with a rotary egg beater. When the mixture has become very stiff, fold in 2 stiffly beaten egg whites, a little at a time, beating until the mixture holds its shape. Turn into a fancy mold that has been rinsed in cold water, and set in the refrigerator for several hours. To serve, unmold onto a cold platter—preferably a glass one—and decorate with tufts of sweetened, flavored whipped cream, surrounding the base with a circle of the cream forced through a pastry bag using a fancy tube. The cream may be left plain or flavored with maple syrup, molasses, flavoring extract, or any desired liqueur. For additional flavor and crunchiness, stir into the stiff gelatine mixture ½ cup each chopped, toasted, cooled, blanched almonds and toasted, cooled long threads of coconut.

ORANGE CUSTARD [1944]
(*Cold*)

Place 8 tablespoons of sugar, the very thinly-pared rind and juice of 4 oranges a few grains of salt, and 3 cups of cold water in a saucepan, stir until sugar is dissolved, bring to a boil; remove from the fire, cover and let stand to infuse for 1½ hours, then strain through a fine cloth into another saucepan. Bring almost to boiling point; remove from the fire, and stir in briskly 4 eggs, slightly beaten with ¼ teaspoon salt; continue cooking, over a gentle flame until mixture thickens. Cool. Fill 6 chilled glasses with the custard and chill. When ready to serve, whip ¾ scant cup of sweet, heavy cream until quite stiff and, using a teaspoon dipped in cold water, pile the whipped cream high in the glasses, and strew over all a little finely chopped candied orange peel.

PEACH DUFF [1945]

Proceed as indicated for Apple Duff (No. 1896) substituting peaches for apples.

PEACHES POACHED IN WHITE WINE [1946]
(*Cold*)

Combine ½ cup of sugar and ½ cup of hot water in a saucepan, stir until sugar is dissolved, then heat to boiling point, and boil steadily for 3 minutes. Peel small ripe peaches and leave them whole. Drop them into the hot syrup, and let stand 2 or 3 minutes; then lift carefully with a skimmer into a serving dish. It is best to put 2 or 3 peaches at a time into the syrup, so that they will be covered with it. When the required number of peaches have been heated—they are not really more than heated in the syrup—add 1 cup of dry white wine to the remaining syrup and pour it all over the peaches and chill. If desired the syrup may be colored with a few drops of red vegetable coloring.

PEARS CONDE   [1947]
(*Cold*)

Wash ½ cup of rice; drain thoroughly, place in a saucepan with 2 cups of cold water, cover, set over a low flame, and bring slowly to a boil. Boil steadily for about 10 minutes. Drain well. Turn the partially cooked rice into a double boiler containing 2 cups of hot milk, ½ cup sugar, and ¼ teaspoon salt. Cook without stirring until tender, but not mushy, or about 35 to 40 minutes. Beat the yolks of 3 eggs until foamy, and stir into the rice mixture with ½ teaspoon of vanilla and 1 tablespoon of butter. Press the hot rice gently into a deep vegetable dish, then unmold on a hot platter. Place on it 6 halved pears, peeled and cored, then poached in a sugar syrup and well drained. Pour hot Melba Sauce (No. 1980) over all and serve at once.

If desired, decorate with maraschino cherries (red or green), tiny sticks of angelica, or fancy small designs of candied fruits.

PEACHES ANNABELLE   [1948]
(*Cold*)

Halve 3 large, ripe fresh peaches and peel carefully. Cook until tender in a medium sugar syrup, drain well, and cool. Fill the hollows with apricot purée, and arrange each half, hollow side down, on a round of cold rice pudding; cover each peach with a meringue made with 2 stiffly beaten egg whites, beaten with a few grains of salt, flavored with a little curaçao liqueur, and tinted with a few drops of red vegetable coloring. Bake in a slow oven (300–325° F.) until the meringue is nicely browned. Cool and serve, surrounded by freshly crushed ripe raspberries.

PINEAPPLE CHARLOTTE MONTE CARLO   [1949]
(*Cold*)

Line the bottom of an oval charlotte mold with Wine Jelly (No. 1122) and when set, decorate with fancifully-cut pieces of canned pineapple, using about 2 slices; then add 2 more slices of pineapple cut into small cubes, "setting" the pineapple with a little of the wine jelly, having this coating of jelly and pineapple about ½ inch in thickness. Place in refrigerator to set, then line the sides of the mold with either fingers of sponge cake or ladyfingers, halved lengthwise. Soak 1 tablespoon of gelatin in 4 tablespoons of cold milk, which has been sweetened with 2 tablespoons of powdered sugar and 1 tablespoon of pineapple sirup. Whip 1 cup of sweet, heavy cream with ¼ teaspoon of salt; fold in ½ cup of drained canned pineapple cubes, and the gelatin mixture. Pour this gently into the prepared mold, and chill in refrigerator for at least 2 hours. Unmold onto a chilled glass platter, and pour around a small glass of red currant jelly, previously melted to the point of running easily, and sprinkle over the jelly 3 tablespoons of blanched, coarsely chopped, then toasted almonds.

PLUM DUFF   [1950]
(Hot)

Proceed as indicated for Apple Duff (No. 1896), substituting plums for apples.

POT DE CREME AU CHOCOLAT   [1951]
(Cold)

Break 6 ounces of sweet chocolate into a saucepan, add ¼ cup of water; place over a very low flame and stir until chocolate is thoroughly melted. Remove from the fire and stir in 1 teaspoon of vanilla extract, then beat in 3 whole, unbeaten eggs, one at a time, beating vigorously after each addition. Cool, then fold in 3 egg whites stiffly beaten with ⅛ teaspoon of salt. Pour into 6 individual glass dishes; chill well, and when ready to serve, decorate with whipped cream sweetened to taste with sugar and flavored with a few drops of almond extract, then forced through a pastry bag with a small rose tube. Sprinkle the cream with finely chopped pistachio nut meats.

PUDDINGS   [1952]

Puddings—subtle blends of flavor, defying analysis; spicy, fragrant mixtures, or mild, delicate ones! Topped with just the right sauce, they become epicurean desserts. And they allow for almost unlimited ingenuity and originality as well as economy on the part of the cook. For generations, puddings have been closely associated with the three major mid-winter holidays: Thanksgiving, Christmas and New Year's. From the very beginning of American history, sweets have played a large part in our cooking. The aristocrats of colonial Virginia vied with each other in collecting and serving intricate desserts—Duke of Gloucester pudding, Queen Charlotte pudding, Princess cake, and many others reflected royalist tastes among loyal Virginia cooks.

The Christmas and holiday season will be here before we know it, and wise indeed is the hostess who not only does her shopping early, but her Christmas baking as well. With every moment occupied in selecting gifts, decorating the house, or entertaining, there is little spare time for real holiday baking unless we follow the oft-quoted advice, *Do it now*.

While we do not go in for rich plum puddings for everyday fare, most of us at this time of year make a ceremony of the preparation of our Christmas puddings. Perhaps we will double or triple the recipe in order to have a few homemade gifts for fortunate friends. In this case, we may even like to steam the gift puddings in gaily decorated bowls, in stainless steel and copper, perhaps, which have been brought together to produce utensils that defy time, heat, or stain, and which will find many a use after the pudding has long since been enjoyed. After bowls or casseroles have been filled with the pudding batter, they must be covered tightly with waxed paper, which can be held in place with rubber bands or vegetable parchment strips. After all, the basic materials cost but little. True, considerable work is entailed, but the finished product guarantees many servings and perhaps even several gift packages—and if it isn't all eaten at Christmas dinner (and it generally isn't), it will always keep for that birthday or anniversary, or other very special occasion in the future.

The recipes then, for Christmas puddings, vary from the simplest steamed pudding, well spiced, and rich with suet for which raisins must supply the only fruit, to those which are so rich with figs, dates, candied pineapple, cherries, fruit peels, nuts, and currants, as well as raisins, that they seem to be held together merely by the batter. That batter may be made with flour or grated bread crumbs, thinned with molasses, coffee, fruit juice, wine, or jelly, and bound with beaten eggs. The mold into which the batter is poured should be well buttered. The time for steaming depends largely on the size of the mold. Overcooking is not a detriment to steamed puddings so that if the molds vary in size, one need be concerned only with the longer period the large molds demand.

The flavor of the pudding ripens with time, so make your Christmas puddings early. They need only be reheated for serving. Then, of course, there must be the preparation of the sauce without which holiday puddings would never have attained fame. Perhaps your choice will be that mixture of creamed butter and white or brown sugar which is known as Hard Sauce (No. 1992). Instead you may prefer one of the soft sauces in which the pudding will almost float as the guests help themselves. Sauces are generally flavored with good rum, brandy, or wine, even if the pudding itself comes to the table blazing in rum or brandy as all good Christmas puddings should. For English Plum Pudding, see No. 1923.

RED CURRANT FRITTERS [1953]
(*Hot*)

Combine and mix well 3 egg yolks and 2 tablespoons of flour sifted with ⅛ teaspoon of salt; stir in 3 tablespoons of cold boiled rice, a generous grating of nutmeg, 2 (or more) tablespoons of sugar, 4 table-spoons of fresh red currants, stemmed, then rapidly washed and dried, and lastly 2 stiffly beaten egg whites; drop preparation by teaspoon into clear, hot (370° F.), deep fat and fry until golden brown. Drain and serve on a folded napkin or paper doily placed on a hot platter.

RICE PUDDING MERINGUE TOPPED OLD FASHIONED STYLE [1954]
(*Hot or Cold*)

Boil ¾ cup of rice, previously rinsed in several cold waters and well drained, with 3 cups of cold water for 5 minutes; reduce the heat and continue cooking until tender or about 25 minutes; drain off whatever water is left. Beat 4 egg yolks, add ¾ cup of sugar, ½ teaspoon salt and ½ teaspoon of vanilla extract. Stir in one quart of scalded milk, and cook, stirring constantly, until thickened like a custard. Add the rice; turn into a buttered baking dish, and top with a meringue made by beating the 4 egg whites until stiff with a few grains of salt, then folding in 4 tablespoons of sugar and flavoring with ¼ teaspoon of vanilla. Brown in a very moderate oven (325° F.) for about 12 to 15 minutes. Serve hot or cold, with cream or crushed fruits.

Variations. (1) Spread the pudding with a thin layer of jam, jelly or preserves before topping with the meringue. (2) Stir into the mixture before baking ¾ cup of parboiled seedless raising left whole or coarsely chopped. (3) Stir into the mixture before baking ¾ cup of blanched, coarsely chopped almonds or other nut meats. (4) Stir into the mixture before baking ½ cup of canned, shredded and thoroughly drained pineapple. (5) Use molasses instead of sugar. If you do, stir ½ teaspoon of baking soda into the milk. (6) Spread bottom of the baking dish with caramel before pouring in the rice mixture. (7) For a mocha rice pudding, use equal parts of milk and strong coffee instead of plain milk.

RUM OMELETTE AFLAME [1955]

Break 6 eggs into a bowl, add 2 tablespoons of powdered sugar and ¼ teaspoon salt and beat thoroughly while adding 3 tablespoons of rum. Cook in a hot buttered pan, lifting the edges of the omelet after it has partially formed so that the liquid part can run down to the bottom of the pan. When omelet is formed and bottom is lightly browned fold it in half with a spatula. Turn onto a hot plate and sprinkle liberally with powdered sugar; add a small glass of rum and ignite. Baste omelette with flaming rum until sugar is browned.

SABAYON   [1956]
Zabaglioni (Hot or Cold)

Allow the yolk of one egg per person plus one extra for every 3 yolks used; 1 generous teaspoon of powdered sugar, and 1 generous tablespoon of good Marsala wine for each egg yolk and a tiny pinch of salt for all.

Put all above ingredients in top of double boiler and stir, off the fire, till thoroughly blended. Place the pan over hot (not boiling) water and beat the mixture steadily and always in the same direction with a rotary beater, occasionally scraping bottom and edges of the pan. As the mixture becomes thick and fluffy remove from hot water but continue beating to prevent curdling as the egg yolks keep on cooking. Serve hot or cold.

For an extra touch, as it is done in certain parts of Italy, stir in 1 tablespoon of whipped cream for each serving. If served hot, pour into glass cups as it comes from the fire; if served cold, place a ponpon of whipped cream (optional, but very decorative) forced through a pastry bag using a small fancy tube. Some put a dash of nutmeg on top of either hot or cold sabayon or zabaglioni.

Variations. Use rum, brandy, whiskey, Madeira wine, sherry, vodka, and so forth, instead of Marsala wine.

SHERRY WINE JELLY   [1957]
(Cold)

Soften 2 tablespoons of gelatin in ¼ cup of cold water and dissolve in 1¾ cups of boiling water. Stir in 1 cup of sugar, 1 cup of good sherry wine and 3 tablespoons of lemon juice. When almost cold, pour into a mold lined with red currant jelly, which should be stiffened in refrigerator. Chill in refrigerator for at least 2 hours; unmold on a chilled glass platter, and decorate with tufts of unsweetened whipped cream, each tuft studded with a tiny piece of angelica.

Variation. For Madeira Wine Jelly or Port Wine Jelly proceed as indicated for Sherry Wine Jelly, substituting ½ cup of good Madeira or Port wine for ½ cup of sherry. Chill and serve as directed.

SOUTHERN RICE MOLD   [1958]
(Cold)

Simmer ¼ pound of washed Carolina rice, with 1 quart of rich milk, 7 tablespoons of sugar and the thinly-pared rind of ½ lemon until rice is perfectly tender and the milk almost absorbed. Discard the lemon rind, pour the rice into a wet mold, and when well chilled, turn out on to a cold platter and serve with jam, stewed fruit or custard sauce.

STEAMED APPLE PUDDING [1959]
(Hot)

Cream together ¼ cup of butter and ½ cup granulated sugar until smooth and thoroughly blended; add 1 large slightly beaten egg, and beat until well blended, then stir in ¼ cup of rich, cold milk. Set aside.

Sift 1½ cups of cake flour, measure, return to sifter and add ¼ teaspoon of allspice and ½ teaspoon of salt and sift into a mixing bowl. Stir into this the first mixture, blend thoroughly, then add 2 cups of coarsely chopped peeled, cored apples. Turn into a greased pudding mold, cover with a buttered paper, adjust the cover, and steam steadily for 2 hours, replenishing the pan with boiling water as it evaporates. Serve hot with a foamy sauce, whipped cream, eggnog sauce or any other preferred sauce.

STEAMED MINCEMEAT PLUM PUDDING [1960]
(Hot)

Beat 2 large eggs as for an omelet; gradually add 1¾ cups of brown sugar, and continue beating until mixture is light. Beat in 1 cup of mincemeat, alternately with 2 cups of washed, dried, seedless raisins, 1 cup of shredded dried figs, ¼ cup of finely chopped candied orange peel, 1 cup of blanched, shredded and slightly toasted almonds, 3 tablespoons of finely chopped candied citron, also the juice of ½ orange, and mix thoroughly. Set aside to mellow for at least one hour, covered with a clean cloth. About 3 hours before serving, mix and sift 2 cups of already once sifted cake flour, 1 teaspoon of baking powder, ½ teaspoon of powdered cinnamon, ⅓ teaspoon of nutmeg, ½ teaspoon of salt and a dash of mace. Combine thoroughly with the first mixture, adding, while blending ½ cup of good sherry wine. Turn batter into a generously buttered large mold (about 2 quarts), cover with a cloth wrung in hot water and dusted with flour, adjust the cover of the mold, and steam for 2¾ to 3 hours in constantly boiling water, adding more boiling water as it evaporates. Sever hot with hard sauce.
Note. This pudding may be set aflame at table in the usual manner if desired.

SURREY PLUM PUDDING [1961]
(Hot)

Rinse and drain 1½ cups currants and 1 cup raisins, and combine with 2 cups prunes, 1½ cups candied citron, ¾ cup candied orange peel and 1 cup candied cherries all cut small; also 1 cup broken English walnut meats, and ¼ cup prune juice mixed with ¼ cup apricot juice. Allow this mixture to stand while sifting and mixing 3¾ cups bread flour, 1 teaspoon baking soda, 1 teaspoon salt, 1 tablespoon ground cinnamon, and 1 teaspoon each of cloves, nutmeg, and ginger.

Mince very finely 1½ cups beef kidney suet, discarding all skin and fiber. Work into it 1½ cups granulated sugar, then add 4 well beaten eggs, one at a time, beating the mixture thoroughly after each addition. Now mix in 1 teaspoon vanilla stirred into ¼ cup good brandy, next 2 cups soft bread crumbs, and the previously sifted dry ingredients, and finally the fruit mixture. Mix the whole well to insure even distribution and blending.

Divide the puddings among three large well buttered bowls or molds and cover tightly. Wrap each in an individual cloth wrung out in hot water and dusted with flour. Cook steadily for 3 hours, in boiling water to cover completely, replenishing the water as needed. Unwrap the bowls, and let the puddings cool, then store in a cool, dry place. Reheat by steaming for 45 minutes or more in boiling water; unmold, drench with good rum or brandy; ignite, and bring into the dining room flaming. Since this recipe is for three puddings, one may be served at Thanksgiving, one at Christmas, and one at New Year's.

TRIFLE [1962]

One should really have a trifle bowl, but an ample salad dish, low, broad and gracefully rounded, will serve very well. From the pastry cook one must get ladyfingers, and sponge cake, and two dozen macaroons, and three dozen ratafias. Now, ratafia may mean something to eat or something to drink, but in this instance it means the little button macaroons usually found in French or Italian pastry shops. There must be plenty of fine jam or jelly, a big box of assorted glacé fruits, a pint of heavy cream, eggs, lemons, and powdered sugar. And in the cellar there must be sherry and brandy and malaga or port, or perhaps Madeira.

Line the bowl with uniform slices of sponge cake, and make an ornamental border of halved ladyfingers. Within that border, arrange another of macaroons and ratafias, spaced carefully with some attention to design; then pour slowly over all a half-pint of good sherry or Madeira and let it stand till the cake has absorbed it. Make a rich boiled custard of 6 egg yolks with sugar and scalded milk, and the grated zest (rind) of half a lemon; and when it is cool, add a teaspoon of vanilla extract and a glass of brandy, and pour it over the cake and macaroons. On the custard, as it is partially absorbed by the cake, spread one cup of jam, which should be apricot, quince or peach, but may be strawberry or raspberry. The clear topaz brilliance and the flavor of the apricot are most effective in both appearance and taste.

The pyramid within the bowl is completed with a carefully arranged pinnacle of well sweetened whipped cream, and the trifle is done, except for the garnishing. Crisp, bright angelica may be cut in fancy little forms with French vegetable cutters, or with a knife, to give flashes of emerald to contrast with the ruby of candied cherries. All around the border, among the ladyfingers and macaroons, should be slender blanched almonds, and some jewels of cubed apricot jelly, glacéd Malaga grapes, and a few more candied cherries.

This, however plain or elaborate you may care to make it, will be a typical British trifle, but there are scores of recipes and you can always make up your own. Fine cordials may enter into the flavoring, and color schemes may be glowing or softly subdued. Fresh strawberries may take the place of jam, and be drenched with kirsch; and in the season of ripe peaches, the very thinly sliced fresh fruit should be piled on the custard, and flavored with a jigger (2 ounces, or 4 tablespoons, or ¼ cup) of *noyau* cordial, and a dash of fine peach brandy.

TRIFLE SUZETTE   [1963]
(Cold)

Place a layer sponge cake on a round crystal dish and force 3 egg whites stiffly beaten with a pinch of salt through a pastry bag using a fancy tube (preferably a rose tube) to form a raised edge or border. Return the cake to a slow oven (250–275° F.) and bake until the meringue hardens, but do not allow it to acquire too much color. Remove from the oven, and when quite cold, place a layer of ratafia macaroons, stale and freshly crushed, on the top of the sponge cake but not on top of the meringue; and pour over this ½ cup of good sherry wine, taking care not to touch the meringue border. Let it soak for at least an hour. Just before serving, whip 1 cup of heavy cream, unsweetened and unflavored and force it all over the top through a pastry bag using a rose tube. Garnish with tiny candied cherry roses (cherries cut into four petals without being separated, then slightly flattened), small cuts of crystallized pineapple, small cuts of crystallized apricots, and small sticks of angelica, and dust over all a light film of ground pistachio nut meats. Serve immediately.

WATERMELON SUPREME   [1964]
(Cold)

Cut at least 6 cups of small cubes from the ripe flesh of a large watermelon. Crush 1 pint ripe raspberries with ⅓ cup sugar and ¼ cup Bénédictine. Mix well; then stir in 1 tablespoon very finely chopped fresh mint leaves. Pour over the watermelon cubes in a dessert bowl, and chill at least 1 hour. When ready to serve, surround the edge of the bowl with orange sections, halved, dipped in a little brandy, and well drained, the sections being arranged as a scalloped edge. Serve also a side dish of plain whipped cream.

ALMOND CHOCOLATE SAUCE   [1965]

Cut up 3 squares (3 ounces) of unsweetened chocolate in a small saucepan; add ½ cup of cold water, and melt chocolate over a very gentle flame, stirring constantly. Then stir in ¼ cup of granulated sugar and ¼ teaspoon of salt, and cook, still over a gentle flame, stirring constantly until mixture is slightly thickened. Now stir in 2 tablespoons of sweet butter, alternately with ⅓ cup of blanched, shredded and toasted almonds and ¾ teaspoon of almond and vanilla extracts in equal parts. Serve lukewarm. Suitable for any kind of pudding as well as frozen desserts.

ALMOND CREAM SAUCE   [1966]
(*Hot*)

Blanch 1 ounce sweet almonds and 6 bitter almonds. Pound them in a mortar, or put twice through a food chopper, using the finest blade, adding alternately a little unbeaten egg white (to keep the almonds from souring), 4 ounces granulated sugar, and 1 tablespoon orange flower water. Place in a saucepan, add ½ cup heavy cream mixed with 2 well beaten egg yolks, and beat with a whisk over a very low flame, or over hot water, until the mixture is smooth, thick, and frothy. Serve as hot as possible. Suitable for any hot pudding.

BLUEBERRY SAUCE   [1967]
(*Cold*)

Crush 1 pint of well-washed blueberries with ¼ cup of powdered sugar and a scant ¼ teaspoon of salt. Stir in 4 or 5 drops of almond extract and chill thoroughly before serving. Appropriate for any kind of hot or cold dessert as well as frozen desserts.

BRANDY GINGER SAUCE   [1968]
(*Hot*)

Put 1 scant teaspoon of ground ginger, 4 tablespoons of sugar, 2 or 3 strips of lemon rind, and 1 cup of water in a saucepan, and stir until sugar is thoroughly dissolved and mixture well blended. Place on the fire, bring to a boil; lower the flame, and simmer gently for 15 minutes, stirring occasionally. Strain through a fine cloth into another saucepan; return to the fire, heat well, but do not actually boil, then stir in 1 table-

spoon of strained lemon juice, mixed with 3 tablespoons of good brandy.
Serve hot. Appropriate for almost any hot pudding.

BUTTERSCOTCH SAUCE [1969]
(Warm)

Combine 1 cup brown sugar, ⅓ cup melted butter, and ⅓ cup heavy
cream. Boil 5 minutes without stirring; then beat until the sauce is
foamy, or for about 30 seconds.

CHERRY BRANDY RASPBERRY SAUCE [1970]

Press through a fine sieve 1 pint fresh or frozen raspberries, and
combine the sieved berries with ½ pint sugar syrup. The resulting sauce
should be of a rich, creamy consistency. Complete it with a flavoring
of 2 tablespoons Cherry brandy.

Note. Cherries, strawberries, gooseberries, white and red currants,
oranges, and other fruits may be prepared in the same manner. Flavor
the cherry and the strawberry sauces with a good kirsch; the orange,
with Curaçao. Or combine strawberries and raspberries in equal amounts,
or oranges and sieved apricot jam or marmalade.

CHOP SUEY DESSERT SAUCE [1971]

Combine equal parts of chopped dates, figs, and walnuts with sugar
syrup to moisten thoroughly. Tint the mixture a rich red with vegetable
coloring, and store it in jars in the refrigerator where it will keep for
weeks.

CLOTTED ALMOND BRANDY SAUCE [1972]
(Cold)

Blanch and grind 10 bitter almonds, then rub through a fine-meshed
sieve into a cold bowl. Cream 4 ounces of butter until light, gradually
add 2 ounces of sugar, alternately with the almond paste and ⅓ cup of
good French brandy, and continue creaming until the sauce has the
appearance of clotted cream. Chill thoroughly, and just before serving,
cream again for a minute to restore the clotted appearance. Appropriate
for Christmas puddings, fruit puddings, cottage puddings, fruit char-
lottes, betties, and similar puddings, hot or cold.

COFFEE SAUCE [1973]
(Cold)

Pour 1½ cups of boiling water over 8 tablespoons of freshly ground
coffee, cover and let infuse until quite clear, then strain through a fine

cloth into top of a double boiler. Stir in 5 well-beaten egg yolks, previously beaten with 6 tablespoons of sugar and ¼ teaspoon of salt; add also 1 teaspoon of unflavored gelatin previously softened in 1 tablespoon of cold water. Cook over hot water, beating with rotary beater until mixture has the consistency of thick cream. Strain through a fine sieve and chill. Appropriate for frozen desserts.

EGGNOG SAUCE   [1974]

Scald 1 pint light cream, and stir into it, first, ½ cup sugar, then gradually, 4 egg yolks previously beaten with a few grains of salt, and ½ teaspoon vanilla. Cook over hot water, stirring constantly until slightly thickened but do not boil. Flavor with 2 tablespoons rum, and serve warm.

Note. Eggnog sauce, or, as the French call it, *Sabayon*, is also made with such dessert wines as Madeira, Xérès, Marsala, Asti, sherry, and champagne. When one of these wines is used, the vanilla is omitted.

FLUFFY RUM SAUCE   [1975]
Sauce au Rum Mousseuse (Uncooked)

Beat 4 chilled egg yolks for 5 minutes or until of the consistency of mayonnaise; gradually beat in ¼ cup of fine granulated sugar alternately with 2 tablespoons of good rum. Then fold in the 4 egg whites stiffly beaten with ⅓ teaspoon of salt and a tiny pinch of powdered ginger. Serve as cold as possible. Suitable for any hot or cold pudding as well as frozen desserts.

FOAMY BANANA SAUCE   [1976]
(Hot)

Blend ¼ cup of sweet butter with 1 tablespoon of flour over a low flame; do not allow them to brown. Gradually stir in ½ cup of fine granulated sugar, dissolved in 1 cup of rich milk, with a few grains of salt, stirring constantly from bottom of saucepan until mixture begins to thicken. Remove from the fire and beat in 1 egg yolk. Return ot the fire and cook 2 or 3 minutes over a very gentle flame, stirring constantly from the bottom of the pan. Put a small, ripe banana through a fine sieve and add to 1 cup of scalded heavy cream. Stir this gradually into the sauce, beating constantly. Appropriate for fruit, rice, noodles, cottage and plum pudding.

FRENCH CHOCOLATE SAUCE   [1977]
(*Hot*)

Combine ½ cup cold water and 1½ ounces chocolate cut small; cook over a low flame until the mixture is smooth, stirring almost constantly. Blend ½ cup granulated sugar, 1 tablespoon cornstarch, and a few grains of salt and add to the chocolate; then stir in slowly 1½ cups hot water, and cook until the mixture is smooth, stirring constantly from the bottom of the pan. Add ¼ teaspoon each of almond and vanilla extracts.

HONEY CINNAMON SAUCE   [1978]
(*Warm*)

Heat 1 cup of honey in top of double boiler, stir in ¼ cup of butter and ½ teaspoon of cinnamon, mixed with a generous dash of salt. Mix well. Appropriate for pancakes and waffles.

HONEY NUT SAUCE   [1979]
(*Hot*)

Heat ½ cup of liquid honey to the boiling point, but do not actually boil; stir in ½ cup of broken, peeled nut meats or blanched almonds, and serve immediately. Appropriate for any kind of hot pudding.

MELBA SAUCE   [1980]
(*Cold*)

Combine ½ cup currant jelly with 1 cup crushed raspberries and bring to the boiling point. Mix 1 teaspoon cornstarch with a pinch of salt, add ½ cup sugar, and stir the whole into the fruit mixture. Cook over a low flame, stirring constantly, until the sauce is thick and clear. Strain, and cool, chilling before serving.

MOCHA SAUCE   [1981]

Into a small saucepan, add ½ cup of sugar, 2 tablespoons of flour and ¼ teaspoon of salt; blend well, then stir in gradually and slowly 1 cup of cold, strong coffee. Cook over a low flame until mixture thickens, stirring constantly. Then boil briskly for 2 or 3 minutes. Remove from the fire; cool to lukewarm, and fold in 1 large egg white, stiffly beaten, alternately with 2 tablespoons of rum. Serve as cold as possible. Appropriate for cold or hot pudding or dessert.

OLD-FASHIONED PLUM SAUCE   [1982]

Stone enough plums to fill 2 cups with the fruit, and cook over a bright flame with ½ cup water and ½ scant cup granulated sugar, stirring frequently over a bright flame until the plums are mushy. Then rub through a fine sieve, and stir in 1 generous tablespoon rum. Serve as hot as possible on any steamed pudding.

ORANGE CUSTARD SAUCE   [1983]

Beat 4 egg yolks until fluffy and lemon-colored, adding gradually 1 tablespoon of flour. When thoroughly blended, beat in 1 cup of cream with ¼ teaspoon of salt and a dash of ginger. Place over hot water and cook until thickened, or until mixture coats the back of the spoon, stirring almost constantly. Remove from hot water; stir in 1 teaspoon of grated orange rind, ⅓ teaspoon of grated lemon rind, and a few drops of orange extract. Cool; chill. At serving time stir in 2 teaspoons of Curaçao liqueur, if desired. Appropriate for any hot or cold pudding or frozen dessert.

ORANGE FLUFF SAUCE   [1984]
(Cold)

Beat 1 egg white until stiff but not dry, with ¼ teaspoon of salt. Gradually add ⅓ cup of powdered sugar beating constantly, also the juice and grated rind of ½ orange and 1 teaspoon of lemon or lime juice, with a few drops of orange extract. Chill well before serving. Appropriate for any hot or cold pudding or frozen dessert.

RASPBERRY SAUCE   [1985]
(Cold)

Pick over 1 pint of fresh raspberries; wash by placing into a colander and letting cold water run gently over them, shaking the colander frequently; drain, then crush. Add ¼ cup of granulated sugar and ¼ cup of water and mix well. Bring to the boiling point; simmer gently for 5 minutes; press through a fine sieve; then flavor with a few drops of almond, vanilla, orange or lemon extract. Chill before serving. Appropriate for any hot or cold pudding as well as frozen desserts.

RUM MOCHA SAUCE   [1986]

Into 1½ cups of very strong coffee, beat in 3 egg yolks, one at a time, beating well after each addition, adding with the last one a few grains of salt. Cook over hot water, stirring constantly until mixture thickens. Remove from the fire, cool, stirring occasionally to prevent a film forming on the top, and when ready to serve, stir in ½ cup of heavy cream, whipped with a few grains of salt and 2 generous tablespoons of good rum. Appropriate for almost any frozen dessert.

SABAYON SAUCE   [1987]

Beat until almost white 6 egg yolks with 1 generous tablespoon sugar, a tiny pinch of salt, and a few drops of vanilla; then gradually beat in ¼ cup sherry, alternating with 1 scant cup granulated sugar and 2 tablespoons cold water. Place over tepid water and beat steadily until thick. Add just a pinch of nutmeg and serve immediately.

SAUCE CREME DE NEIGE   [1988]
(*Cold*)

Cream ½ cup of sweet butter with 1⅓ cups of fine granulated sugar or confectioner's sugar until fluffy and lemon-colored, stirring in, while creaming 1 tablespoon of strained lemon juice and 1 tablespoon of Anise liqueur. Fold in 2 egg whites stiffly beaten with ¼ teaspoon of salt, alternately with ½ cup of strained applesauce, and ¼ cup of whipped heavy cream. Serve cold over hot pudding or other hot dessert. Appropriate for any hot pudding or other hot dessert.

SAUCE MONTMORENCY   [1989]

Whip 1 cup of heavy cream, with a few grains of salt and 4 tablespoons of confectioner's sugar; fold in 3 tablespoons of maraschino liqueur alternately with ¾ cup of coarsely chopped fresh or canned cherries.

STRAWBERRY SAUCE I   [1990]
(*Cold*)

Wash, stem, then wash again enough fresh strawberries to make a full cup of juice when strained. Stir into this 2 tablespoons of brown sugar and 1 teaspoon of flour which has been moistened with a little strawberry juice. Turn into a saucepan, and cook over a gentle flame stirring constantly for 5 minutes, or until clear and slightly thickened. Remove from the heat and add in ¼ teaspoon of almond extract mixed with ⅓ teaspoon of vanilla extract. Cool, then chill thoroughly. Appropriate for any hot or cold or frozen dessert.

STRAWBERRY SAUCE II   [1991]
(*Cold*)

Put 4 tablespoons of butter in a small saucepan and cook over a low flame with ¾ cup of sugar until sugar is thoroughly melted and blended. Remove from the fire, cool slightly; then stir in 1 stiffly beaten egg white, beaten with a few grains of salt, alternately with ½ generous cup of crushed fresh strawberries, and 1 teaspoon of kirsch liqueur or maraschino liqueur. Serve well chilled. Appropriate for cold and frozen desserts.

HARD SAUCES   [1992]

Traditional—though not invariable—companion for many hot desserts is a hard sauce, a proper supplement for puddings, dumplings, and fruit betties. The sauce, which itself is chilled, melts over the warm dessert in a slow trickle, and mingles its delicate flavor with the more robust one of its foundation.

A hard sauce is really an uncooked sauce made of butter and sugar with whatever flavoring is desired. The butter is first creamed, then the sugar is added gradually in the proportion of three parts sugar to one of butter. The longer the beating, the creamier the sauce.

An attractive form of service is to roll portions about the size of a large walnut between two wet, grooved paddles, these balls having the shape, though not the color, of butter balls. The sauce, of course, must be chilled firm before rolling.

ALMOND KIRSCH HARD SAUCE   [1993]

Cream ½ cup butter, then gradually beat in 1½ cups of granulated sugar, adding while beating 1 tablespoon of kirsch, and 3 tablespoons ground almonds.

BRANDY HARD SAUCE   [1994]

Cream ½ cup butter, then gradually beat in 1½ cups of granulated sugar, and 2 tablespoons of good brandy (or more if desired.)

BROWN SUGAR HARD SAUCE   [1995]

Cream ½ cup butter; then gradually beat in 1½ cups of brown sugar.

BUTTERSCOTCH HARD SAUCE   [1996]

Cream ½ cup butter; gradually beat in 1½ cups of dark brown sugar, creaming and beating thoroughly. Add 1 well-beaten egg yolk and 4 tablespoons of cream, flavored with 1 teaspoon vanilla. Beat well.

CHERRY HARD SAUCE   [1997]

Cream ½ cup butter; gradually beat in 1½ cups granulated sugar alternately with 2 tablespoons cherry juice and ½ cup of canned, chopped, unsweetened well drained cherries.

CHOCOLATE HARD SAUCE   [1998]

Cream ½ cup butter; then gradually beat in 1½ cups of granulated sugar, alternately with 3 tablespoons of grated, unsweetened chocolate.

CHRISTMAS HARD SAUCE   [1999]

Cream ½ cup butter; gradually beat in 1½ cups of granulated sugar, alternately with 2 tablespoons of Cointreau liqueur. Roll into small balls, stick a small stick of angelica on each ball with a few cinnamon drop candies to simulate holly berries.

COCONUT HARD SAUCE   [2000]

Cream ½ cup butter; gradually beat in 1½ cups of granulated sugar, alternately with ½ cup toasted, cooled, chopped coconut and a pinch of nutmeg.

DATE HARD SAUCE   [2001]

Cream ½ cup butter; gradually beat in 1½ cups of granulated sugar, alternately with ⅓ cup of pitted, chopped dates and a pinch of nutmeg.

FRENCH HARD SAUCE   [2002]

Cream ½ cup butter; gradually beat in 1½ cups of granulated sugar alternately with 1 tablespoon benedictine, mixed with 1 tablespoon of Chartreuse and 1 teaspoon brandy, the three liqueurs beaten with 1 egg yolk, and a pinch of nutmeg.

LEMON HARD SAUCE [2003]

Cream ½ cup butter; gradually beat in 1½ cups of granulated sugar alternately with 3 tablespoons of lemon juice added very slowly, beating constantly until very light, and a pinch of grated nutmeg.

MELBA HARD SAUCE [2004]

Cream ½ cup butter; gradually beat in 1½ cups of granulated sugar alternately with 3 tablespoons of raspberry jam, mixed with ½ teaspoon lemon juice and ¼ scant teaspoon grated nutmeg.

MOCHA HARD SAUCE [2005]

Cream ½ cup butter; gradually beat in 1½ cups of dark brown sugar with ⅓ cup of very strong black coffee added very slowly and a generous pinch of nutmeg.

Chapter Fifteen

CAKES AND COOKIES

"Animated Specialties" were the specialty of eighteenth century French chefs. They made huge pies and cakes which, upon being cut, released birds, frogs, and butterflies. Some of the larger cakes, more fantastic, concealed dwarfs under the crust. The dwarfs jumped out and entertained the delighted guests.

Cookies, cakes, flapjacks, crullers, pancakes, and so forth, were the major part of the good old New England diet, and little need be said about the ruggedness of the people nourished on such provender. They pioneered across the plains to build the West, and lived out of the cookie and cruller jars between battles, living dangerously—and living well.

CAKES [2006]

CAKES, LIKE PIES AND PASTRIES, HAVE A VALUABLE PLACE IN the dietary for, when eaten in moderation, they are wholesome and nutritious, supplying the body with important food constituents.

Cake in some form has been known since earliest times. The use of sweetened dough is referred to in ancient writings. In England as elsewhere, nearly every religious occasion was celebrated with a cake of one sort or another, and to this day there is something serious about an English cake which our own more frivolous sweets lack. "Black as the Devil, heavy as sin, sweet as young love," is the way an Englishman has described the ceremonial cakes of his country; solid, romantic, and frequently good, but with quite a different kind of goodness from our own more casual sort.

The recipes from which English cakes are still made have been altered surprisingly little. To this day there are cakes thrown from the tower of Biddenden Church in Kent on the Eve of the Epiphany; cakes which bear the image of the two sisters who gave money to build the church, back in the twelfth century. Both the custom and the recipe for the cakes go back to the reign of Henry I.

Hot cross buns were originally ecclesiastical consecrated cakes, which later on came to be eaten on Good Friday. Our own Sally Lunns were first Good Friday buns, but only in the eighteenth century did they appear at tea tables under name of Miss Sally Lunn of Bath, who sent them out, hot and buttered, for parties of the Bath gentry.

The ancient prototype of our Mother's Day is Mothering Sunday, known in the Church of England as Refreshment Sunday, or the Fourth Sunday in Lent. For the celebration of this event a cake was especially indicated and sons and daughters (especially those who lived away from home) went "a-mothering" with the gift of a cake, which was eaten while the family was reunited in worship.

Later on, the day became an occasion to honor the mother of the family, and to this day in parts of rural England, sons and daughters bring a Mothering Day, or simnel cake, to their mothers.

Plum cake, of course, was eaten at Christmas. The spices and fruit indicated the gifts of the Wise Men to the Christ Child. Mince pies were for the same festival, and were until the seventeenth century baked in oval crusts to represent the manger, although after the Reformation the custom was looked upon with disfavor by the Protestants.

Richmond "Maids of Honour," which may still be bought in all the bake shops of the little town of Richmond on the Thames, got their names because the maids of honour of Queen Elizabeth, whose palace was at Richmond, were inordinately fond of them. Banbury tarts were sold in the town of that name long before the old lady ever dreamed of getting on a grey horse, and are still made there from what purports to be the same recipe.

And our own Bride's Cake is merely a descendant of the Honey

Cake, which was so important a part of every marriage that the word honeymoon derives from it.

All these cakes, made in England today, go back into distant centuries of English history.

COMMON CAUSES AND REMEDIES IN CAKE BAKING FAILURES   [2007]

LAYER CAKES, POUND CAKES, and so forth.

(A) DEFECT: *Cakes Sink in Center*

CAUSE	REMEDY
1. Insufficient moisture.	1. Increase liquid to proper absorption.
2. Inferior shortening.	2. Use special hydrogenated shortening for best results.
3. Improper mixing.	3. Follow accurately the mixing speed and time specified in recipe being used.
4. Improper oven temperature.	4. For best results, use oven temperature of 350° F.—never over 375° F.
5. Inferior flour.	5. Use only high quality cake flour for best results.
6. Under-baking.	6. Do not disturb cakes until batter has "set," or until baked in center.

(B) DEFECT: *Cakes Expand, Then Fall during Baking*

1. Too much moisture.	1. Due to climatic conditions, flour will sometimes pick up moisture in storage, thus altering the moisture content of the formula. If batter is already mixed, add more flour.
2. Inferior flour.	2. Use high quality cake flour.
3. Poor emulsification.	3. Use special hydrogenated cake shortening, or half shortening and half butter.
4. Too much baking powder.	4. Reduce amount.
5. Over-creaming.	5. Reduce speed and creaming time of shortening.

CAUSE	REMEDY
6. Too low oven temperature.	6. Regulate oven temperature before placing cakes in oven.

(C) DEFECT: *Cakes Shrink or Pull from Sides of Pan*

1. Too much liquid.	1. Balance formula. If batter is already mixed, add more flour.
2. Poor emulsification.	2. Check quality of shortening. Use high grade hydrogenated shortening, or half shortening and half butter.
3. Wrong temperature of ingredients when mixed.	3. All ingredients, especially the eggs, liquid and shortening should be between 70 and 80° F. when mixed.
4. Unbalanced formula.	4. Check, measure and weigh all ingredients, as the case may be, carefully. Do not use guess work in this very important step.
5. Over-baking.	5. Bake only enough to set the cake.
6. Not enough batter in pans.	6. Increase amount of batter.
7. Oven too cold or too hot.	7. Regulate oven at 350° F. before placing cakes in it.
8. Improper cooling.	8. Remove cakes from pans as soon as possible and cool on special cake racks, free from drafts.
9. Inferior flour.	9. Use high grade cake flour.
10. Mix too plain and "bready."	10. Increase proportion of eggs, sugar and shortening.
11. Over-mixing.	11. Cut down speed and time of mixing.
12. Too much leavening.	12. Reduce baking powder.

(D) DEFECT: *Poor Volume*

1. Oven too hot.	1. Regulate oven at 350° F. while mixture is being prepared.
2. Insufficient leavening.	2. Increase amount of leavening agent.

CAUSE	REMEDY
3. Excess leavening.	3. Cut down amount of leavening agent.
4. Under-mixing.	4. Use speed and full time given in the recipe especially in last stage.
5. Mix too plain and "bready."	5. Increase amount of eggs and shortening.
6. Weak or watery eggs.	6. Be sure eggs are fresh, if using shell eggs.
7. Improper measuring.	7. Check weights of ingredients carefully.
8. Poor emulsification.	8. Check shortening. Use only special hydrogenated shortening.
9. Excess moisture.	9. Reduce amount of liquid.
10. Not sufficient moisture.	10. Increase amount of liquid.
11. Improper mixing temperature.	11. Batter should be 70 to 80° F., and not over 80° F.

(E) DEFECT: *Coarse Grain*

CAUSE	REMEDY
1. Over-mixing.	1. Check formula and use correct mixing speed and time.
2. Cold oven.	2. Regulate oven at 350° F.
3. Too much leavening.	3. Reduce amount of leavening agent, especially at high altitudes.
4. Unbalanced formula.	4. Measure and weigh all ingredients carefully.
5. Insufficient moisture.	5. Increase liquid.
6. Under-mixing.	6. Give correct speed and full mixing time.
7. Too much sugar.	7. Reduce amount.
8. Poor shortening.	8. Use special hydrogenated shortening.
9. Too high speed on mixer.	9. Use slower speeds in early stages.
10. Too much shortening or egg yolk.	10. Reduce amounts accordingly.
11. Wrong type of flour.	11. Use high grade cake flour.
12. Batter stands too long before baking.	12. Batter should be baked as soon after mixing as possible.

(F) DEFECT: *White Cakes Off-Color*

CAUSE	REMEDY
1. Off-color shortening.	1. Use best quality shortening.
2. Poor flour.	2. Use high quality cake flour.
3. Poor baking powder.	3. Use best grade.
4. Poor egg whites.	4. Check for quality and freshness.
5. Wrong mixing temperature.	5. Best mixing temperature is between 70 and 80° F.
6. Not enough acidity.	6. Add cream of tartar or phosphate.
7. Insufficient mixing.	7. Increase speed and mixing time.

(G) DEFECT: *White Cakes Bake Out Yellow*

1. Too much soda.	1. Cut down on soda or use a little cream of tartar or phosphate.
2. Excess invert sugar.	2. Cut down on amount.
3. Poor shortening.	3. Use special hydrogenated shortening.
4. Poor egg whites.	4. Check for freshness.
5. Poor cake flour.	5. Use high grade cake flour.

(H) DEFECT: *Whole Egg Cakes Have Greenish Tint*

1. Too much soda.	1. Reduce amount.
2. Frozen eggs too old.	2. Use fresh frozen eggs as soon as thawed.
3. Mixing temperature too low.	3. Use temperature between 70 and 80° F.

(I) DEFECT: *Soggy Streaks in Cakes*

1. Excess moisture.	1. Cut down on liquid.
2. Excess leavening.	2. Use less baking powder.
3. Excess acid in mixture.	3. Cut down on sour milk, phosphate, cream of tartar, and so forth.
4. Insufficient mixture of dry ingredients.	4. Sift together all dry ingredients, one or more times.
5. Excessive top oven heat.	5. Bake in uniform oven.
6. Poor flour.	6. Use high grade cake flour.

CAUSE	REMEDY
7. Improper cooling.	7. Do not ice cakes until cooled.
8. Cakes knocked in oven.	8. Handle cakes carefully during baking, do not jar.
9. Under-baked.	9. Bake until cakes are well set.

(J) DEFECT: *Cakes Crack in Baking*

1. Batter too stiff.	1. Add more liquid.
2. Over-mixing.	2. Cut mixing speed and time.
3. Oven too hot.	3. Lower heat and regulate to 350° F.
4. Uneven oven heat.	4. Regulate oven to uniform heat before baking.
5. Excessive acid or soda.	5. Cut down on amount.
6. Mixture too poor and "bready."	6. Use more shortening and sugar.

(K) DEFECT: *Crust Too Thick*

1. Too much sugar.	1. Reduce amount.
2. Oven too hot.	2. Reduce temperature.
3. Too long in oven.	3. Bake shorter time at higher temperature.
4. Weak flour.	4. Use best grade cake flour.

(L) DEFECT: *Crust Peels and Flakes Off*

1. Too much steam in oven.	1. Open oven damper slightly.
2. Oven too cool.	2. Raise temperature accordingly and regulate.
3. Weak eggs.	3. Check for freshness and quality.
4. Weak flour.	4. Use best grade cake flour.
5. Poor formula.	5. Check for proper balance.

(M) DEFECT: *Cakes Peak Up in Center or on Side*

1. Mixture too lean.	1. Add more shortening and sugar.
2. Not enough leavening.	2. Add more baking powder.
3. Insufficient moisture.	3. Add more liquid.
4. Over-mixing.	4. Cut mixing speed and time.
5. Flour too hard.	5. Use best cake flour.
6. Too much flour.	6. Add more liquid.
7. Oven too hot.	7. Reduce temperature accordingly.

(N) DEFECT: *Cakes Are Tough*

CAUSE	REMEDY
1. Poor flour.	1. Use high grade cake flour.
2. Over-mixing.	2. Cut down on speed and mixing time.
3. Over-baking.	3. Cut baking time.
4. Mixture too plain and "bready."	4. Increase shortening and sugar.
5. Excess egg whites.	5. Cut down on amount accordingly.
6. Oven too cool.	6. Raise temperature accordingly.
7. Eggs not beaten enough.	7. Beat eggs to proper volume, especially in sponge cakes.
8. Insufficient richness.	8. Add more shortening and sugar.

(O) DEFECT: *Cakes Too Tender to Handle*

CAUSE	REMEDY
1. Excess sugar.	1. Reduce amount accordingly.
2. Excess shortening.	2. Reduce amount accordingly.
3. Excess leavening.	3. Reduce amount accordingly.
4. Under-mixing.	4. Increase mixing time.
5. Over-mixing.	5. Cut speed and mixing time.
6. Poor flour.	6. Use good grade cake flour.
7. Not enough eggs.	7. Increase amount accordingly.

(P) DEFECT: *Cakes Dry Out Too Rapidly*

CAUSE	REMEDY
1. Climatic conditions.	1. Use invert sugar.
2. Insufficient shortening.	2. Increase amount accordingly.
3. Insufficient sugar.	3. Increase amount accordingly.
4. Poor shortening.	4. Use hydrogenated cake shortening.
5. Too few eggs.	5. Increase amount accordingly.
6. Too much leavening.	6. Reduce amount accordingly.
7. Oven too cool.	7. Raise temperature accordingly.
8. Over-baked.	8. Bake only until cakes are set.
9. Insufficient moisture.	9. Increase amount of liquid or egg accordingly.

(Q) DEFECT: *Cakes Mold Quickly*

CAUSE	REMEDY
1. Bad storage.	1. Store in dry, well ventilated room.

CAUSE	REMEDY
2. Contamination.	2. Check storage room for sources of contamination.
3. Improper cooling.	3. Do not pack or store until cool.

(R) DEFECT: *Uneven texture*

1. Poor shortening.	1. Use hydrogenated cake shortening.
2. Under-mixing.	2. Follow mixing instructions in formula.
3. Over-mixing.	3. Use low speed in first stages of mixing.
4. Too much liquid.	4. Reduce amount accordingly.
5. Insufficient sugar.	5. Increase amount accordingly.
6. Wrong oven conditions.	6. Check for temperature, drafts, and so forth.
7. Mixing speed too high.	7. Use low speeds.
8. Mixing temperature too warm or too cold.	8. Mix between 70 and 80° F.

(S) DEFECT: *Dark Spots On Bottom Of Cakes*

1. Undissolved sugar.	1. Use fine granulated sugar.

ANGEL FOOD AND SUNSHINE CAKES

(A) DEFECT: *Cakes Shrink from Sides and Bottom of Pans*

1. Oven too hot.	1. Regulate ovens to temperature stated in recipe.
2. Air pockets between cakes and pans.	2. Gently knock pans to work mixture down before placing in oven.
3. Flour too hard.	3. Use best quality cake flour.
4. Grease in pans.	4. Wash in hot water and rinse in cool water just before using.

(B) DEFECT: *Spots and Thick Crust on Top of Cakes*

1. Baked too long.	1. Bake until set only.
2. Poor flour.	2. Use high grade cake flour.
3. Undissolved sugar.	3. Use fine granulated sugar.
4. Temperature too slow.	4. Increase temperature.

(C) DEFECT: *Cakes Fall When In or Out of Oven*

CAUSE	REMEDY
1. Oven too hot.	1. Reduce temperature accordingly.
2. Egg whites whipped too much.	2. Reduce whipping time. Do not whip whites dry.
3. Egg whites whipped at wrong temperature.	3. Whip at temperature between 70 and 80° F.
4. Pans contain too much moisture.	4. Turn pans upside down and drain off excess water just before using.
5. Too much liquid.	5. Do not add water to mixture.
6. Improperly cooled.	6. Invert cakes in pans on rack to cool.

(D) DEFECT: *Cakes Stick In Pans And Cannot Be Removed*

1. Pans too dry.	1. Rinse pans in cool water and drain just before filling with mixture.
2. Soiled pans.	2. Keep pans and other utensils thoroughly clean.

(E) DEFECT: *Dark Cakes*

1. Poor acidity.	1. Use pure cream of tartar.
2. Old or weak eggs.	2. Check eggs for freshness and quality.
3. Soiled mixing utensils.	3. Utensils must be thoroughly clean and free from grease.
4. Unbleached flour.	4. Use best quality cake flour.

Important. *Careless measuring usually means failure. Failure, in turn, means waste. Waste means loss of money, time, and energy, and—worst of all—discouragement.*

ANGEL FOOD CAKE   [2008]

Measurement. Correct procedure of measuring and mixing is extremely important for this cake. The flour must be sifted once before measuring (to be certain that measurement is accurate) then three times after measuring (to incorporate air).

Flour. Cake flour gives a more tender, fluffy, fine grained cake and therefore should always be used. Sugar should be measured and sifted.

Preparation of Eggs. The separating and beating of the egg whites requires special attention. It has been found that eggs separate more easily when cold, but the whites beat up with more volume when at room temperature; so in preparing eggs for the angel food cake, separate them when first taken from refrigerator. In separating be sure to get the small tough portion attached close to the yolks as this portion also beats up and holds air. Then allow the whites to stand at room temperature while measuring other ingredients.

Beating Egg Whites. There is a stage in beating the whites when they reach the highest point of their leavening power and it is important to stop beating at just this moment. That stage is when they are stiff enough to stand alone and hold their shape but still have a moist, shiny appearance.

Any type of beater may be used: rotary, flat whisk, globe whisk, or electric mixer.

Cream of Tartar (or other acid). Cream of tartar or other acid, as lemon juice, is an essential ingredient of angel cake. Without it the cake is cream colored rather than white, and during the last few minutes of baking the cake has a tendency to shrink, giving a volume which is not greater after baking than before. The action is not to leaven but rather to strengthen the cell walls of the egg white so they will retain their maximum size.

Salt. Salt is a necessary ingredient to improve flavor.

Flavoring. The flavoring depends largely upon individual preferences —whether one likes almond, lemon or vanilla. The general requirement is that it should be delicate. Frequently flavors are blended; mix almond and vanilla for instance, or vanilla with a few drops of lemon extract.

Sugar and Flour (Mixing). In combining the sugar and flour with the beaten whites, a gentle folding motion is used. Fold only until the sugar and flour are well blended with the egg whites. If they are not sufficiently mixed, the cake will be coarse. If overmixed the cake will be heavy.

Baking Temperature. A low baking temperature is desirable to give a tender cake. Bake at 300° F. for about one hour for best results.

The following is the recipe for a standard angel food cake:

Ingredients. 1 cup of cake flour; 1¼ cups of fine granulated sugar; 1 cup of egg whites (8 to 10); 1 teaspoon of cream of tartar; ⅓ teaspoon of salt; 1 teaspoon of flavoring extract.

Directions. Light oven, set the temperature at 300° F., assemble utensils and ingredients. Sift flour, measure and sift 3 times with ¼ cup of sugar. The remainder of the sugar should be sifted twice.

Beat the egg whites in a large bowl using a rotary beater; or they may be beaten on a platter using a wire whisk. When frothy, add the salt and cream of tartar, and continue beating until they stand in peaks but still retain a moist shiny appearance.

With Electric Beater. If using an electric beater, beat the egg whites at high speed to a froth, then add the salt and cream of tartar, and continue beating at high speed till the whites have the appearance described above. From then on it is best to fold in the ingredients by hand.

Fold in the sugar, about 2 tablespoons at a time and add flavoring. Now, fold in the flour, sifting a small amount at a time over the egg whites, folding only as long as dry flour can be seen. Follow this procedure with the electric mixer at low speed, if experienced in using it; however, if at all doubtful it is best to fold in the sugar and flour by hand to avoid overmixing.

When all the flour has been gently folded in and the mixture is smooth, with no large portions of egg white not folded in, pile lightly into an *ungreased* angel cake pan, spread evenly and place in the preheated oven (300° F.). It will take about 1 hour to bake. When done the crust will retain no imprint when lightly pressed with the finger and will be of a delicate brown. Invert pan and let stand until cake is cold, about 1 hour. The cake should then fall out easily.

APPLE RAISIN CAKE   [2009]

Soak ½ cup of seedless raisins in boiling water for 5 minutes; drain but do not dry. Mix 2 cups of prepared biscuit flour and 3 tablespoons of fine granulated sugar, then add 1 large egg, well beaten, mixed with ½ cup of sweet milk and 3 tablespoons of coffee cream or undiluted evaporated milk, and stir in the flour, mixed with the raisins, stirring just until all flour is moistened. Line a baking pan (6 × 10 × 1½ inches) with buttered waxed paper, letting the paper extend slightly above sides of the pan; spread batter in pan as evenly as possible; arrange 4 or 5 tart apples, cored and sliced neatly over the top of batter, each slice overlapping another as in tarts, and in thickly packed rows. Top the apple with streusel made as follows:

Streusel. Cream ¼ cup of butter or margarin with ¾ cup of brown sugar and 1½ teaspoons of ground cinnamon.

Bake in a hot oven (425° F.) about 25 minutes, let cool 5 minutes, then carefully pull off waxed paper. Serve warm with cream, or cold, plain.

APRICOT UPSIDE-DOWN CAKES   [2010]

Soak ½ pound of dried apricots in warm water for 3 or 4 hours, and cook in water to cover until soft. Sift once 2 cups of flour, add 1 tablespoon of baking powder and ½ teaspoon of salt, and sift together into a mixing bowl; then cut in ¼ cup of melted butter alternately with ¾ cup of milk, to which have been added 2 well-beaten eggs and mix just enough to blend. Place in large generously buttered muffin pans, the following mixture; ½ teaspoon of butter, ½ teaspoon of water, and 1 tablespoon of brown sugar, well mixed; on top of this, spread 1 tablespoon of apricots. Half fill with batter, and bake in a moderate oven (350° F.) for about 20 minutes. Allow cakes to remain in pan for a few moments, then turn on sheet of waxed paper, and when cold, serve.

BLUEBERRY CAKE [2011]

Sift together 2 cups flour, ½ cup sugar, ½ teaspoon baking soda, and ¼ teaspoon salt. Combine ¼ cup sour cream and ¾ cup sweet milk, and add to the dry ingredients, beating until smooth. Fold in 1 cup washed and dried blueberries, handling them lightly to avoid crushing. Bake in a greased shallow baking tin, and cut into squares to serve either hot or cold.

The first wedding cakes were made by brides to show their skill in cooking. Then one day, a French chef showed them how to make "classic" or "professional" cakes. Pretty soon they were all doing it, and so the wedding cake became one of the baker's wares.

BRIDE'S CAKE [2012]

Ingredients. 3¾ cups of sifted cake flour; ½ teaspoon salt; 1½ teaspoons double-action baking powder; 1¾ cups of butter; 2 cups of fine granulated sugar; 1¾ cups of unbeaten egg whites (about 12); ½ teaspoon of vanilla; ¼ teaspoon almond extract.

Directions. Sift flour once, measure, add salt and baking powder, and sift together three times. Cream butter until light and fluffy; gradually add sugar and continue creaming till thoroughly blended and very light. Now fold in unbeaten egg whites, ¼ cup at a time, beating briskly about 3 minutes after each addition, adding with the last portion, the mixed flavoring extracts and flour. Then beat for 1 minute. Turn batter into 10-inch tube pan lined on the sides and bottom with buttered paper. Bake in a slow oven (275° F.) for 1 hour; then increase heat to 300° F. and bake 50 minutes longer or until done. Insert wedding favors if desired, into small slits cut in the baked cake, wrapping each favor in waxed paper. When cool, spread with ornamental butter icing and trim with silver dragées or fancy colored candies. Serve on a silver tray or platter surrounded with delicate sprays of fern, cosmos, or bridal wreath. Attach special bridal favors (wedding bells and similar ornaments) to white ribbons and place with sprays of flowers on top of cake.

Ornamental Butter Icing. Cream 4 tablespoons of sweet butter till light and fluffy. Gradually beat in confectioner's sugar, using about 5 cups in all, previously sifted with ¼ teaspoon of salt, blending well after each addition. Add to keep the icing creamy, 2 unbeaten egg whites alternately with 2 tablespoons (more or less) of sweet cream flavored with 1 teaspoon of vanilla mixed with ¼ teaspoon of lemon extract. Beat till very smooth and of right consistency for spreading, then spread smoothly on top and sides of cake. With remaining icing make borders, festoons, and rosettes for decoration, using fancy pastry tube. Decorate with silver dragées. This makes enough icing to cover a 10-inch tube cake and to use for decorating.

CHEESE CAKE [2013]

Line a well greased 10-inch spring form with a mixture of 10 ounces crumbled zwieback, 5 tablespoons melted butter, ¼ teaspoon cinnamon, and 1¾ teaspoons sugar all thoroughly blended. Pat the mixture ¼ inch thick on the bottom of the pan, sprinkle it lightly on the sides, and reserve a little for the top of the cake. Then stir for 15 minutes the following mixture: 2 pounds pot cheese, finely sifted, 8 egg yolks, ⅔ cup sugar, 2 teaspoons salt, and 2½ teaspoons vanilla; then blend in ½ cup heavy cream. Beat the whites of 8 eggs until stiff with a further ⅔ cup of sugar, and fold them gently into the cheese mixture. Add ⅓ cup melted butter. Pour this filling into the crumb-lined form, and sprinkle the top of the cake with the mixture set aside for the purpose. Bake 40 to 50 minutes at 400° F.

CHOCOLATE CAKE [2014]
(Moist) (Yeast Method)

Cream 1 cup of butter until light, gradually adding 2 cups of granulated sugar. Then work in 3 well beaten egg yolks, a little at a time, creaming and beating after each addition. Add 3 squares of melted unsweetened chocolate alternately with 1 cup of rich, cold milk, which has been mixed with ½ cake of dry yeast dissolved in ¼ cup of lukewarm water. Blend thoroughly. Sift 2¼ cups of cake flour and ½ teaspoon of salt 4 times and gradually add to the first mixture. Mix well then fold in 3 stiffly beaten egg whites; cover the bowl; place in the refrigerator overnight. In the morning stir in ½ teaspoons of baking soda, dissolved in 3 tablespoons of hot water, and 1½ teaspoons of vanilla or 1 teaspoon of vanilla and ½ teaspoon of almond extract. Blend thoroughly. Turn batter into two buttered cake pans (9 × 9 × 3 inches) and bake in a moderate oven (350° F.) for 40 to 45 minutes, or until firm. Cool, then cover with chocolate frosting.

Let them eat cake—but have it real cake and not a spurious imitation. It is better to eat a corn muffin than a poor cake.

CHOCOLATE CREAM ROLL [2015]

Do you remember that childish jingle?

> First's the worst, second's the same,
> Last's the best of all the game.

In almost every family, dessert is the big game of the dinner—and that is why many home cooks plan the meal backward and put their freshest, most inspired thought on the dessert. When they want to be very, very popular with the family they produce for their delectation a chocolate cream roll made as follows:

Sift 6 tablespoons of cake flour once; measure, add 6 tablespoons of cocoa, ½ teaspoon of baking powder and ¼ scant teaspoon of salt, and sift together three times. Beat 4 egg whites until stiff; fold in gradually ¾ cup of sugar; then 4 egg yolks, beaten until thick and lemon-colored, and flavored with 1 teaspoon of vanilla. Lastly, fold in the flour mixture a little at a time, blending well after each addition. Turn batter into a 15 × 10-inch pan which has been buttered and lined with greased paper to within ½ inch of edge. Bake in a hot oven (400° F.) 12 to 13 minutes. Quickly cut and trim off crisp edges of cake; invert on a damp cloth to cool; remove paper, and when cold spread with whipped cream. Roll as for jelly roll and serve well chilled.

COFFEE CUSTARD CAKE   [2016]

Mix together and sift 1½ cups of cake flour, 1 teaspoon of baking powder, and ½ teaspoon of salt. Beat 3 eggs slightly, then add little by little, 2 tablespoons of extra strong black coffee, beating briskly after each addition till light and fluffy. Now gradually beat in 1 cup of sugar and continue beating well for a few seconds; gradually beat in the flour mixture, a small amount at a time, adding with the last of it ½ teaspoon of vanilla. Bake in 2 buttered and floured 8-inch pans in a moderate oven (350° F.) for 20 minutes. Turn out and cool on cake racks. When quite cold, split each layer and spread with coffee custard filling. Beat 2 eggs slightly in top of a double boiler, add ¾ cup of sugar, sifted with 2 tablespoons of flour, and mixed smoothly with 1 cup of strong coffee combined with 1 cup of rich, creamy cold milk and ½ teaspoon of salt. Cook over hot water until mixture just begins to thicken, or about 5 minutes, stirring constantly, then add ½ teaspoon of vanilla and 3 tablespoons of sweet butter, stirring till well blended. Cool and spread between layers of cake. Let stand an hour or two before serving; dust each portion with confectioner's sugar.

DOBOS CAKE   [2017]

Beat 6 egg yolks until very creamy and light; gradually add 1¼ cups of sugar, beating well after each addition and adding with the last portion, 1 tablespoon of lemon juice. Mix and sift ¾ cup of pastry flour, ¼ cup of cornstarch or potato flour, and ½ teaspoon of salt; add half of it to the egg yolk mixture, stirring gently till blended and adding, while blending, another tablespoon of lemon juice. Now, fold in 6 stiffly beaten egg whites alternately with remaining flour mixture, a little at a time, stirring as gently as possible. Butter and line an 8-inch spring mold with waxed paper. Turn in a few tablespoons of batter at a time, spreading evenly over bottom of mold, and bake in a hot oven (450° F.) 5 to 6 minutes or till very lightly browned. Remove cake to cake rack and repeat baking process until batter is entirely used. The usual result is 8 layers, though if very thin, 12 layers can be made. When cool put 1 layer aside, spread the following filling between and on top of remaining seven layers, pressing the layers firmly, but gently together, then chill.

Chocolate Filling for Dobos Cake. Melt 4 squares of unsweetened grated chocolate over hot water, and when quite liquid, stir in gradually and very little at a time, 4 egg yolks, slightly beaten with 1/2 cup of heavy cream and sweetened with 2/3 cup of fine granulated sugar, stirring briskly after each addition; cook over hot water 5 or 6 minutes, stirring constantly until thick and smooth. Cool thoroughly. Cream 1 1/4 cups of sweet butter with 2 or 3 drops of coffee extract until light, soft and fluffy and add to the chocolate mixture a tablespoon at a time, beating and stirring at the same time after each addition until blended and of spreading consistency.

Icing the Dobos Cake. Melt 3/4 cup of powdered sugar over very low heat until of a light caramel color, stirring constantly; then pour quickly onto remaining cake layer, spreading evenly and working very rapidly. As soon as sugar begins to set, mark it with the dull edge of a small spatula. Place this layer on top of the cake, pressing down as firmly as possible, yet very gently. Spread remaining chocolate filling on sides of cake and if desired dust very lightly with chopped nut (almond) meats. Cool, and keep in a cool, dry place (in refrigerator) for at least 24 hours before slicing. This type of cake will keep a week in a good refrigerator.

FROZEN FRUIT CAKE [2018]

Mix and sift 2 cups of cake flour, 1/2 teaspoon of baking soda, 2 teaspoons of baking powder, 1 teaspoon of cinnamon, 1/2 teaspoon allspice, 1/4 teaspoon of mace, and 1/4 teaspoon of cloves into a mixing bowl, and combine, mixing thoroughly with 3/4 cup of seedless raisins, 3/4 cup of currants, and 1/2 cup of citron, all the fruits finely chopped. Cream 1/2 cup of butter until soft, light and very smooth; gradually add 3/4 cup of brown sugar, blended with 1/4 cup of white sugar, alternately with 2 well-beaten fresh eggs to which 1/2 teaspoon of lemon extract has been added. Now stir in, beating at the same time 1/4 cup of dark molasses; and gradually work in the flour-fruit mixture, alternately with 1/2 cup of milk.

Pour cake batter into greased standard cans for keeping or even for mailing, filling them only half full to allow for rising, and covering top of each can with 3 thicknesses of waxed papper. Pour 4 quarts of hot water into pressure cooker; place cans on the rack, lock the cover on cooker, and steam with petcock wide open for 20 to 30 minutes depending on size of cakes, then close petcock and cook for one hour at 15 pounds pressure. Make the cake or cakes at least 3 days before packing. Pour boiled icing in on top of cakes after cooling and before putting on can lids, to help protect against mold.

FROZEN HONEY FRUIT CAKE   [2019]

Sift 4½ cups of cake flour, 1 teaspoon baking powder, 1 teaspoon of baking soda, ½ teaspoon of salt, 1 teaspoon of allspice, and 1 teaspoon of ginger into a mixing bowl, and combine, mixing well, with 1 cup of seedless raisins and ½ cup of finely cut dates.

Cream ½ cup of butter or shortening until soft, light and smooth; gradually add ½ cup of granulated sugar, creaming and beating well, then add 2 well-beaten eggs, and when well blended 1 cup of dark, strained honey. Now, gradually add flour-fruit mixture and 1 cup of cold, rich milk, and follow the same directions as given for processing in pressure cooker as for Frozen Fruit Cake (No. 2018).

GOURMET HONEY CAKE   [2020]

Cream ½ pound butter with 1 cup strained honey. To this add 4 well-beaten eggs, then 1 tablespoon lemon juice with 1 teaspoon grated lemon peel. Sift in 3 scant cups flour with 2 teaspoons baking powder and ½ teaspoon salt. Blend smoothly but do not overmix. Add 1 cup cut citron and ¾ cup chopped nuts. Turn into a large loaf pan lined with greased brown paper, and bake in a moderate oven about 1 hour.

HOW TO WHIP THIN CREAM AND/OR   [2021]
EVAPORATED MILK

Pour quantity of thin cream or undiluted evaporated milk called for in recipe into top part of double boiler or sauce pan. Heat with the lid off over boiling water until very hot (not boiling), just to the scalding point. Add to the hot milk granulated gelatin which has been softened in cold water. For this see "Table of Proportions" (No.2022). Stir until gelatin is dissolved. Pour into a bowl and chill, then beat until stiff with rotary beater. (Having both beater and bowl ice-cold helps to whip the cream or milk more rapidly.)

Important. Do not remove the film of milk solids that forms on top of the hot milk. It will whip up just like the rest of the milk. If using a cooking thermometer, heat to about 150° F. and chill to about 45° F.

TABLE OF PROPORTIONS OF MILK, GELATINE AND WATER TO WHIP MILK [2022]

MILK or THIN CREAM	GELATINE	WATER
½ cup...	¼ teaspoon	1 teaspoon
¾ cup...	½ teaspoon	2 teaspoon
1 cup...	½ teaspoon	2 teaspoon
1½ cups..	¾ teaspoon	1 tablespoon

HOW TO COLOR WHIPPED THIN CREAM, EVAPORATED MILK OR CREAM [2023]

Whipped thin cream, evaporated milk or cream may be tinted with vegetable liquid or paste coloring. Fold liquid coloring, a few drops at a time, into the whipped mixture until the desired shade is reached. Mix a small bit of paste coloring with a few drops of cold milk and add gradually to the whipped mixture. This is attractive when decorating pastries, pies, cakes, fruit salads, fruit cocktails, and so forth.

ICE CREAM CAKE [2024]

Cream ½ cup of butter or other shortening with 2 cups of sugar; sift together 3 cups of pastry flour, 2 teaspoons of baking powder and ½ teaspoon of salt and add to sugar mixture alternately with 1 cup of sweet, cold milk, beginning and ending with the flour mixture. Mix to a smooth batter. Flavor with 1 teaspoon of vanilla mixed with ½ teaspoon of almond extract, and lastly, fold in 4 egg whites stiffly beaten with ¼ teaspoon of salt. Bake in a large greased loaf pan or in 3 layer cake pans. Put layers together with any preferred filling; dust the loaf cake with confectioner's sugar.

> *My mother keeps in two big books*
> *The secrets of the things she cooks.*
> *If I could ever learn to bake,*
> *I'd send my brother Bill a cake.*
> *But mother says it's hard to learn*
> *How to bake cakes that never burn.*
> *—"Lullaby" of Mother Goose.*

'LECTION OR HARTFORD CAKE [2025]

According to a classic recipe engrossed in a family cook book, 3 pounds of brown sugar and 3 pounds of butter were creamed together and blended smoothly with a quart of lukewarm rich, creamy milk 2 cakes of yeast and 5 pounds of flour. This mixture was set to rise from noon till tea time, when it was enriched with 12 beaten eggs and spiced with nutmeg, mace, clove and cinnamon and a tablespoon of salt.

It was allowed to rise again overnight, and in the morning the grated rind and juice of 2 lemons were added with ½ pound of thinly sliced, then chopped citron, 2 pounds of raisins, seeded and chopped, 1 pound of dried currants, 2 tablespoons of baking soda, 1 cup of good sherry and 1 of good French brandy, Medford rum or rye whisky, and 1 tablespoonful of rose or orange flower water. When it was well mixed and kneaded, it was shaped in loaves and baked 1½ hours in bread pans, then cooled and iced or decorated according to the fancy of the hostess.

It is a delicious, hearty and filling cake, and from Maine to Connecticut it was nearly always spoken of as Hartford 'Lection Cake, and is so set down in the cook books. Hartford in the early years, and later, was often a scene of lively storm and stress, in colonial and national policies, and it is likely that the Dutch and English traditions were drawn upon when the women devised sustaining and appropriate rations for the defenders of hearth and State, who seem to have been forever holding conventions, conferences and mass meetings to shape the destinies of six States and a continent.

MARASCHINO CHERRY CAKE   [2026]

Cream ½ cup of butter or other shortening; gradually add 1¼ cups of sugar, and cream together, adding with the last of the sugar, 2 tablespoons of sifted flour. Sift 2 cups plus 3 tablespoons of cake flour with 1 tablespoon of baking powder and ⅓ teaspoon of salt, over ½ cup of broken nut meats (any desired kind); mix well and add to the creamed butter and sugar mixture alternately with ¾ cup of rich sweet milk; blend in 16 quartered maraschino cherries, with ¼ cup of cherry juice. Lastly fold in 4 stiffly beaten egg whites, with ¼ teaspoon of salt and 3 drops of almond extract. Pour into a well greased and floured cake pan, and bake in a moderate oven (350° F.) for 50 minutes. Cool thoroughly before slicing.

MARBLE LOAF CAKE   [2027]

Cream ⅓ cup of butter or margarin with a wooden spoon; gradually blend in 1 cup of fine granulated sugar, and beat until smooth, light and fluffy. Then, add one at a time 2 unbeaten eggs, beating for one minute after each addition, with a wooden spoon or rotary beater.

Melt 2 squares of unsweetened chocolate over hot water. Sift once 1¾ cups of pastry flour; return to sifter, add 2 teaspoons of baking powder and ½ teaspoon of salt and resift twice, into a mixing bowl. Make a hole in center, and pour in ½ cup of very cold, rich milk, then the creamed butter-egg-sugar mixture, and mix well, beginning from the center and bringing the flour mixture into the liquid mixture.

Divide this batter into two equal parts. Add the melted, smooth chocolate and ½ teaspoon each of almond and vanilla extracts to one part of the batter, and stir into the other part ½ teaspoon of lemon extract, or ¼ teaspoon of pineapple extract and ¼ teaspoon of lemon extract. Put the two batters into a buttered loaf pan by tablespoonfuls, alternating white and chocolate batter. Bake in a moderate oven (350°F.), for about 50 minutes, or until cake leaves sides of pan and is firm to the touch. Turn out on to a cake rack, and when cool, ice with uncooked white icing made from 1 egg white, 1 teaspoon of sweet cream, and enough sifted confectioner's sugar to make a thick, spreading icing.

Note. The marbled effect of this delicious and unusual cake is obtained by filling the buttered loaf pan with alternating tablespoons of light and dark batter. There's no *pattern* to follow.

MOCHA SPONGE [2028]

Pour ¼ cup cold water over 1 tablespoon sparkling gelatin. Let stand 5 minutes to soften. Add ¾ cup granulated sugar and a pinch of salt, and stir, then pour in 1½ cups very strong black coffee, as hot as possible, without being actually boiling. Stir until the gelatine and sugar are entirely dissolved, adding, meanwhile, 2 tablespoons strained lemon juice. Cool until nearly set; then beat with a rotary egg beater. When quite stiff, fold in 2 stiffly beaten egg whites, a little at a time continuing to beat until the mixture holds its shape. Turn into a fancy mold previously rinsed in cold water, and chill in the refrigerator for several hours. To serve, unmold on a cold glass platter and decorate with tufts of sweetened and flavored whipped cream, surrounding the base with a circle of the cream forced through a pastry bag, using a fancy tube. This cream may be left plain or flavored with maple syrup, molasses, flavoring extract, or any desired liqueur. For additional flavor and crunchiness, stir into the stiff gelatine mixture ½ cup each chopped, toasted, cooled, blanched almonds and toasted, cooled long threads of coconut.

OLD-FASHIONED MICHIGAN [2029]
APPLESAUCE CAKE

Melt ¼ cup of butter in skillet; stir in 2 cups of soft bread crumbs and toss together over a very low flame, until golden brown. Let cool and when cold, stir in 2 cups of applesauce, previously mixed with 3 well-beaten egg yolks, sweetened with 2 tablespoons of sugar. Mix thoroughly, then fold in 3 stiffly beaten egg whites, beaten with ¼ teaspoon of salt and, when stiff, sweetened with 2 tablespoons of sugar.

Finally, stir in ⅓ cup of chopped nut meats, turn into a 9-inch deep pie plate, generously buttered, then dusted with fine bread crumbs and bake 1 to 1¼ hours in a moderate oven (350° F.). Serve cold with whipped or plain cream.

"PETTICOAT TAILS" [2030]

Small cakes which have been made for generations from a handed-down recipe from Arkansas.

Sift together several times 5 cups of pastry flour and 1 cup of finely powdered or confectioner's sugar and ¾ teaspoon of salt. Cut and knead into this 2 cups of butter. Shape the dough into small rolls and chill overnight. Slice thin and bake in a moderate oven (350° F.) a few minutes, or until delicately browned. Serve hot or cold with tea or coffee or with a fruit dessert.

A cake may be ruined by any of the following: Too much, or not enough liquid; too much, or not enough sugar; too much, or not enough flour; damp, or wrong type of flour; too much, not enough or wrong type of shortening; too hot or too cold an oven; too thick, too thin or too rich a batter; too much, or insufficient beating; too much, or not enough creaming or mixing; over- or under-baking; overcrowded or tilted oven; uneven distribution of heat; slamming oven door.

PIONEER SALT PORK RAISIN CAKE [2031]
NEW ENGLAND STYLE

Cut the rind from ¼ pound of fat salt pork; put the coarsely chopped pork fat through food chopper, using the finest knife, with 1 cup of seeded or seedless raisin. Place mixture in a saucepan, add ½ cup of boiling water or hard cider and stir over a gentle flame until boiling. Boil for 2 minutes, remove from the fire and stir in ½ cup of dark brown sugar and ½ cup of dark molasses, or ¾ cup of molasses without the brown sugar. Mix thoroughly, then stir in very briskly, 1 well-beaten large egg yolk, alternately with 1¾ cups of bread flour, mixed and sifted with ¼ teaspoons of baking soda, 2 teaspoons of baking powder, 1 teaspoon of powdered cinnamon and ½ teaspoon each of ground allspice, nutmeg and salt. Stir and beat to a smooth batter, and pour into a generously greased loaf cake pan.

Bake in a moderate oven (350° F.) for 1 hour, or until well risen and firm to the touch. Turn out onto a cake rack, and when cool, ice with uncooked white icing made from the egg white, 1 teaspoon of cream (sweet) and confectioner's sugar to make a thick icing.

REFRIGERATOR CHEESE CAKE [2032]

This is another gelatin favorite; very popular dessert because it requires no baking and no last minute attention.

Sprinkle 2 tablespoons granulated gelatin into $\frac{1}{4}$ cup of cold water, and let stand 5 minutes. Place 2 slightly beaten egg yolks, in the top of a double boiler; add a scant teaspoon salt and $\frac{1}{2}$ cup rich milk scalded and slightly cooled; cook until the mixture thickens, stirring almost constantly. Remove from the hot water, and add $\frac{1}{2}$ cup each granulated and brown sugar. Beat until the sugar is dissolved, adding while beating 2 tablespoons lemon juice, 2 tablespoons orange juice, and the grated rind of 1 lemon. Return to the hot water and again bring to boiling point, stirring frequently. Remove from the hot water, and add the softened gelatin, stirring until it is entirely dissolved.

Cool until beginning to set; then beat in 1 pound dry cottage cheese (strained then squeezed in cheesecloth), mixed with 1 teaspoon vanilla and $\frac{1}{2}$ teaspoon almond extract. If vanilla flavor alone is desired, omit the almond extract and use 2 teaspoons vanilla. Beat well until the mixture is thoroughly blended; then fold in 2 stiffly beaten egg whites alternately with 1 cup heavy cream, whipped until stiff. Butter generously the bottom and sides of a large spring form and sprinkle thickly with crumbled zwieback mixed with equal parts of crumbled stale cake, macaroons, or vanilla wafers. Pour in the cheese mixture as evenly as possible, and sprinkle over it a little of the zwieback-cake crumbs. Chill in the refrigerator overnight, or at least 5 or 6 hours before using.

SPICE CAKE [2033]

Cream $\frac{1}{2}$ cup of butter or other shortening with $1\frac{3}{4}$ cups of brown sugar. Add 3 well-beaten egg yolks and blend thoroughly. Add $\frac{3}{4}$ cup of thin cream or undiluted evaporated milk alternately with 2 cups of pastry flour sifted with 1 tablespoon of baking powder, $\frac{1}{3}$ teaspoon of salt, 1 teaspoon of cinnamon, 1 teaspoon of cloves, 1 teaspoon of nutmeg, and fold in the 3 egg whites stiffly beaten with $\frac{1}{4}$ teaspoon of salt and flavored with 1 teaspoon of vanilla. Lastly stir in 1 cup of plumped, dried, seedless raisins, previously rolled in a little flour to prevent their sinking to the bottom of the pan. Bake in layers in a moderate oven (350° F.) about 20 minutes or till cake shrinks from sides of pan. Put together with Caramel filling and chocolate icing.

When baking, use an alarm clock to remind you that a cake, bread, pie, or other dish is done. Just set the alarm to ring at the time the product should be ready to take out of the oven.

SPICED CHOCOLATE FRUIT CAKE CREOLE [2034]

Sift 5 cups of cake flour once, measure, add 1 tablespoon of baking powder, $\frac{1}{4}$ teaspoon of soda, $\frac{3}{4}$ teaspoon of salt, 3 teaspoon grounds cinnamon, 1 teaspoon each of allspice and mace, and $\frac{1}{2}$ teaspoon each of nutmeg and ground ginger, and sift together three times. Place in a mixing bowl 3 pounds of finely chopped seedless raisins, 3 pounds of currants, 1 pound of finely chopped pitted dates, 1 pound of thinly sliced citron, 1 tablespoon of grated orange rind, and 1½ teaspoons of grated lemon rind, and sift over it 1 cup of the flour mixture, tossing well together so as to enrobe the fruit thoroughly with the flour. Cream 1 pound of butter or other shortening; gradually adding 1 pound of brown sugar, and cream till very light and fluffy. Then add 12 well-beaten whole eggs, mixed with 4 squares of melted unsweetened chocolate and blend well. Stir in 1 cup of molasses, mixed with 1 cup of tart jelly, ¾ cup of orange juice, and 3 tablespoons of lemon juice. Add the flour gradually, beating well after each addition; then add the floured fruit. Turn into loaf pans which have been greased then lined with heavy white well greased paper, and bake in a very, slow oven (250° F.) until done. If in 8½-inch tube pans allow 4 to 5 hours; in 8 × 4 × 3-inch loaf pans 3 to 4 hours; and in 6 × 3 × 2½-inch loaf pans 2½ to 3 hours. If oven gets too hot, cover cakes with heavy white or brown paper or waxed paper during part of baking. This makes about 12½ pounds of Christmas Fruit Cake. If desired, sprinkle ⅓ pound of blanched, shredded almonds over tops of cakes before baking.

When cold, wrap in waxed paper and store in covered container. Chocolate fruit cake mellows quickly and keeps well for at least 6 to 7 weeks, if kept in a cool, dry dark place. This cake may be set aflame just before serving.

SPONGE CAKE   [2035]
(*Quick Method*)

Beat 2 whole eggs till very light; add ¼ teaspoon salt mixed with 1 cup sugar and beat well, adding while beating 1 teaspoon of vanilla. Scald ½ cup of rich sweet milk with 1 tablespoon of sweet butter; combine with first mixture then beat in gradually 1 cup of pastry flour sifted with 1 teaspoon of baking powder. Pour very quickly into a buttered, floured pan, and bake in a moderate oven (350°F.) 25 to 30 minutes. To dignify this dessert, serve with hot Butterscotch Sauce (No. 1969).

TIPSY SPONGE SQUIRE or TIPSY PUDDING   [2036]

Tipsy cake or pudding is a combination of sponge cake, almonds, sherry and soft custard. It is most attractive when the sponge cake is baked in a spring form or angel food pan. It should then be placed on a large deep platter. The almonds, blanched and split, should be studded closely over the top and sides of cake. Then pour sherry or madeira, over the whole cake and finally pour the soft custard (sauce) around or over the cake as preferred or split the cake and divide the wine and custard between two layers. The almonds may be toasted after blanching and splitting. Some recipes call for custard between the layers and whipped cream over the top. In this case, the almonds should be placed on top of the whipped cream.

The Soft Custard. Beat 4 egg yolks slightly; stir in 1/3 cup of sugar and a dash of salt. Now very slowly add 2 1/4 cups of hot, rich, scalded milk or better still, equal parts of sweet milk and sweet cream. Cook over hot water, stirring constantly, until thick. Remove from hot water; chill and flavor with 1/2 teaspoon of vanilla.

The Sponge Cake. Sift 1 cup of already once sifted cake flour and 1/4 teaspoon of salt three times. Beat 5 egg yolks until light and fluffy; add the grated rind and juice of half a lemon, and beat together until thick. Beat 5 egg whites until stiff but not dry; fold in 1 cup of sifted sugar, a little at a time, then fold in the egg yolks alternately with the flour mixture, a little at a time. Pour batter into ungreased tube pan and bake one hour in a slow oven (300–325° F.) Invert pan on cake rack for one hour, then remove cake from pan by lifting the pan as straight as possible.

WHITE FRUIT CAKE [2037]

Cream 1/2 pound butter with 1 pound sugar, and beat in 4 egg yolks. Cut 1 pound of blanched almonds in thin strips; cut fine 1/2 pound each of candied cherries, citron, and candied pineapple, and pick over 1 pound white raisins. Dredge the fruits with part of a pound of white flour, and add the remaining flour to the creamed mixture, alternating it with 1 cup sherry. Stir in 1/2 pound grated coconut and the floured fruit. Mix thoroughly, and add the 4 well beaten egg whites. Bake in a slow oven for about 4 hours, in a tube pan lined with greased brown paper.

> *This day, my Julie, thou must make,*
> *For mistress bride, the wedding cake;*
> *Knead out the dow, and it will be*
> *To paste of almonds turn'd by thee;*
> *Or kisse it thou, but once or twice,*
> *And for the bride cake, thou'll spice.*
> *—The Bride Cake (Herrick, seven-*
> *teenth century)*

COOKIES [2038]

Imagine, if you can, a group of ancient Egyptians gathered to honor their gods and goddesses by sacrificing an ox or perhaps a human being. Such sacrifices were expensive, however, and it was not always possible to find an ox or a human being to sacrifice when special favors were asked.

The Egyptians apparently did not have a great respect for the intelligence of their gods, for sometimes instead of sacrificing the ox or the human being, the priests would bring to the altar small cakes on which was the imprint of horns, symbolizing the ox, or which were cut to symbolize a man. The gods and goddesses were supposed to believe these were the real sacrifices and apparently they did do as much good. These are probably the first "cookies" recorded in history.

The Assyro-Babylonians offered such cakes to their horned moon goddess, Istelar, and the Greeks to Astarte and other divinities. The Greeks called these cakes *bous* (ox), an allusion to the ox-symbol marked on them, and from the accusative form of the noun, *boun*, it is suggested that the modern word *bun* is derived, though the character of the small cake, according to our modern conception, is quite different.

Diogenes Laertius (A. D. 200) a biographer of the early philosophers, when speaking of Empedocles (Greek philosopher 490–430 B. C.), told how he " . . . offered one of the sacred liba, called a *bouse*, made of fine flour and honey." Hescychius (sixth century) speaks of *bouen* and describes it as a kind of small cake with a representation of two horns marked upon it.

According to English historians, the first idea of cake in England was a small mass of dough little better than wheat flour and water, which was baked and eaten with ale and cheese. Shakespeare always spoke of cakes with disrespect, indicating that cakes of that day were not the delicious confections we know. In *Twelfth Night* he says, "Dost thou think, because thou art virtuous, there shall be no Cakes and Ale?" He evidently refers to Twelfth Night cakes which were merely a mixture of baked flour and water.

The term cookie has several possible sources. It may have been derived from the German word *kuchen* meaning to cook, or from the French Provencal *couque* meaning cake, or from the Latin *couquere* meaning to cook. In America, *Cookie* means a small sweet cake, usually crisp. To the English *Sweet Biscuits* means cookies, for to them the term *biscuit* seems to mean any small crisp, baked bread or cake, whether sweet or plain.

COOKIES—HINTS   [2039]

Cookies are easy to make, and have the advantage of keeping for a much longer time than most cakes. Properly stored, some cookies will keep several months, though varieties containing a high amount of fat or many nuts may eventually become rancid. Cookies containing fruit, honey or molasses, and cookies with a dry crisp texture have the best keeping qualities. However, like everything pertaining to cooking, certain rules must be followed.

Poor cookies may result from inaccurate measurements, poor materials, improper handling and incorrect baking. Inaccurate measurement is the most frequent cause.

Sugar in excess gives a waxy product and destroys or conceals the flavor of the other ingredients. *Not enough sugar* gives a flat tasting, uninteresting product with a crumbly, bread-like texture.

Excess fat makes the dough difficult to handle and may result in a cookie with a greasy texture and poor flavor. *Not enough fat* may result in a tough cookie with a dry texture.

Excess flour makes a dry, crumbly cookie and in some degree conceals the flavoring qualities of the other ingredients. *Not enough flour* makes a dough which is difficult to handle and apt to spread too much during the baking process. The cookie is apt to be porous and fragile.

Excess baking powder gives a bitter taste and produces a cookie which is too light and porous. In general, cookies take about half as much baking powder as cake; that is, from one-half to three-fourths of a teaspoon to the cup of flour.

Liquids may be varied in amount with less change in the finished product than any of the other basic ingredients. More liquid may be added to the rolled cookie dough and a drop cookie made from the same recipe; or less liquid may be used in a spread wafer and a rolled wafer made instead.

Variations in basic proportions will produce as many different effects as there are variations. Many are not displeasing, but all too frequently the result is a poor cookie. The right proportions depend on a good recipe to start with, plus accurate measurements.

Holiday cookies and cakes in which honey is used need about two weeks for ripening. They improve with age, provided they are stored in covered jars in a cool place. Regular fruit jars with rubber rings make good containers.

To outline Christmas Tree and Santa Claus Ginger Cookies with frosting, mix confectioner's sugar with a little cold water, using about 2 tablespoons of liquid to 1 cup of sugar. Stir until smooth and put it on with a pastry bag or a frosting gun using a tube with a small round hole.

In making Oatmeal Cookies, the flavor will be improved by toasting the uncooked oatmeal. For this, sprinkle a thin layer of flakes on a shallow pan and heat about 10 minutes in a slow oven.

Sugar sprinkled over the tops of cookies before putting them into the oven forms a sweet crust and makes a richer cookie.

As soon as cookies are baked, remove them from the baking sheets with a broad spatula and cool them on cake or cookie rack. This allows air to circulate and prevents sweating.

Before cutting icebox or refrigerator cookies wet the knife or cutter. You will then be able to cut cleanly, without ragged edges.

ALMOND COOKIES [2040]
Russian Lepeshki (Makes about 4 dozen cookies)

Cream 1 cup of butter or margarin with ½ cup of powdered or fine granulated sugar, and ½ teaspoon of salt. Then flavor with ½ teaspoon of almond and ¼ teaspoon of vanilla extract, mixing well. Work in 2 cups of pastry flour, which has been sifted twice, adding it a little at a time, and working well after each addition. Chill, then roll into balls the size of a small walnut, flatten them and arrange on a greased baking sheet. Press half of a split almond on each cookie, and bake in a slow oven (300–325° F.) 18 to 20 minutes, or until nicely browned.

BRAN ORANGE DROP COOKIES   [2041]
(*Makes about 4 dozen cookies*)

Combine ½ cup of whole bran, ½ of a large orange, ground, and ⅔ cup of sour milk; mix well and let stand while preparing remaining ingredients. Cream ½ cup of lard or other shortening until light; gradually add 1 cup of granulated sugar, and continue beating and creaming till thoroughly blended and light. Stir in 1 large egg, well beaten with ¼ teaspoon of almond extract. Add 2 cups of cake flour, sifted once, then resifted with ½ teaspoon of soda over the bran mixture and mix thoroughly. Continue beating for 4 or 5 minutes, then drop from the tip of a teaspoon onto a greased baking sheet; flatten slightly, with the tines of a fork and bake in a moderate oven (350–375° F.) about 18 to 20 minutes. When cold, ice with 1 cup of confectioner's sugar mixed with 1 tablespoon of creamed butter and 2½ to 3 tablespoons of orange juice. Store in a cool, dry place.

BREAD CRUMB CINNAMON COOKIES   [2042]
(*Makes about 2 dozen*)

Beat 3 eggs until very light and thick; gradually add 1 cup of sugar mixed with ¼ teaspoon of salt and beat until blended. Flavor with ¼ teaspoon of almond extract mixed with 1 teaspoon of vanilla extract, and blend thoroughly. Combine 2 cups of soft bread crumbs, dried in oven but not toasted, with ⅓ cup of finely chopped blanched almonds, and add to the first mixture. Press lightly but thoroughly to prevent air pockets and as evenly as possible into a shallow, 9-inch buttered pan, and bake in a slow oven (300° F.) for 25 or 30 minutes. Remove from oven; cool slightly and cut into small squares. When cold, store in a covered container between layers of wax paper.

CAJUN MACAROONS   [2043]
(*Makes 4 dozen 1½ inches in diameter*)

These should be baked a few days in advance of using. They will keep several months when stored in a closed tin in a cool, dry place.

Work ½ pound almond paste with a wooden spoon until smooth. Add 3 slightly beaten egg whites and blend thoroughly. Add ½ cup sifted pastry flour resifted with ½ cup each fine granulated sugar and ½ cup powdered sugar. Cover cookie sheets with bond paper, and drop the mixture onto them from the tip of a teaspoon. They may be shaped on the paper, or press through a cookie press, or a pastry bag and tube. Bake in a slow oven (300° F.) about 30 minutes. Lift the cakes from the paper with a spatula, while still warm.

Variations. Finely chopped or ground candied fruits may be added to the mixture before baking. Or the tops of the macaroons may be decorated before baking by placing in the center of each a nut half, a raisin (seedless, black or white), or a bit of candied fruit—such as a bit of angelica—cut fancifully, or by sprinkling with finely chopped nut meats. Again, the cakes may be decorated after baking by dainty frosting designs put on with a cake decorator or pastry tube.

CARROT COOKIES [2044]

Add ¼ teaspoon of baking soda to 1 cup of honey and blend thoroughly. Beat 2 eggs well, then beat in 1 cup of grated carrot, and work into the honey Sift 2 cups of pastry flour once, measure, add 2 teaspoons of baking powder, ⅓ teaspoon of salt and 1 teaspoon of powdered cinnamon, and gradually add to the first mixture, mixing well. Finally add alternately ½ cup of butter, melted to lukewarm, and 1 cup of chopped seedless raisins, mixed with 2 cups of rolled oats. Beat thoroughly, drop from a teaspoon onto a greased cookie sheet and flatten with the tines of a fork. Bake in a moderate oven (350° F.) for about 8 to 10 minutes, or until cookies are golden brown. Store between layers of waxed paper in an airtight container and in a dry place.

CHRISTMAS GINGERBREAD MEN COOKIES [2045]
(*Makes about 6 to 7 dozen*)

Note. The dough may be cut in the shape of Santa Clauses, donkeys, pigs, other animals, trees, angels, and so forth, to decorate the Christmas tree. The eyes, mouth, arm, may be made with a toothpick in the soft dough and the marks stay in right through the baking, but roll the toothpick along, otherwise the dough tears. Make a cardboard pattern, lay it on the rolled dough, cutting around the outline with a small, sharp-pointed knife, folding back the outside dough as you go along. With a broad pancake turner, transfer the figure to a buttered baking sheet.

Sift together 1 teaspoon salt, ¼ teaspoon of ground nutmeg, ½ teaspoon ground cloves, 1 tablespoon of ground cinnamon, 1 teaspoon of powdered ginger and 1 cup of previously sifted pastry flour into a large mixing bowl. Make a well in center, place in it 1 cup of shortening, and 1¼ cups of sugar, previously creamed together, and work sugar-shortening mixture into the flour with a pastry blender or two knives until it is fluffy and light. Add 1 large, well-beaten egg alternately with 1 cup of slightly warmed light molasses. Blend thoroughly. Now add gradually ⅓ cup of hot water, into which has been stirred 1⅛ teaspoons of baking soda, being sure the soda is thoroughly dissolved. *Don't beat,* but *stir*, to avoid bubbles. Now stir in 4 to 5 cups of twice sifted pastry flour, adding only about ½ cup at a time and stirring just to moisten the dough. The mixture should never be sticky. Altogether, about 5 cups of pastry flour usually works perfectly, but it may vary slightly. Chill the dough in refrigerator for at least 8 hours. Roll out a small portion at a time to about ⅛ inch in thickness on a lightly floured board. Bake in a moderate oven (350° F.) about 8 to 10 minutes. Place the cookies on a rack to cool and dry before adding the fancy decorations (eyes, mouth, and so forth) which may be colored. Ice with a seven-minute icing or uncooked confectioner's icing, making a little at a time to prevent the formation of crystals.

CITRON COOKIES [2046]

Cream ½ cup of butter or margarin until light and fluffy, then gradually add 1 cup of sugar and continue creaming until thoroughly blended. Beat in 2 fresh egg yolks, adding one at a time and beating well after each addition. Sift ½ cup of pastry flour once; measure, add 1 teaspoon of cream of tartar, ½ teaspoon of baking soda and ½ (scant) teaspoon of salt, and sift over the first mixture, mixing well. Now fold in 2 stiffly beaten egg whites flavored with ¼ teaspoon each of vanilla and almond extract, and add sufficient sifted pastry flour (about 1½ to 1¾ cups) to make a dough soft enough to roll out easily. Roll into a sheet ⅛ inch thick; cut with floured cutter.

Cut some candied citron into short narrow strips; arrange in flower design around small portions of chopped candied cherries; place the cookies on an oiled baking sheet, and bake about 8 to 10 minutes in a hot oven (400° F.). Store between layers of waxed paper in an airtight container in a cool, dry place.

CREAM CHEESE ALMOND COOKIES [2047]
(*Makes about 60 cookies*)

Note. A good way to use up stale bread is by making bread crumb cookies. They have a flavor and texture somewhat like macaroons.

Cream 6 tablespoons of butter until light; gradually add ⅔ cup of sugar, and continue creaming until sugar is thoroughly blended, then add ¼ cup of sieved cream cheese, and beat briskly till well blended. Beat 2 eggs, then beat in ¼ cup of blanched, chopped, then toasted almonds and add to the first mixture, mixing well. Sift 2 cups of pastry flour once, measure, return to sifter, add 2 teaspoons of baking powder and ½ teaspoon of salt and sift into a mixing bowl, then mix in the first mixture gradually. Drop from a teaspoon onto a greased baking sheet about 3 inches apart, flatten each cookie with a spatula, and bake in a moderate oven (350° F.) for 10 to 12 minutes, or until delicately browned. Remove at once from the oven, cool on cake rack, and when cold, store in a covered container between layers of waxed paper.

FIG PRESERVE COOKIES [2048]
(*Makes about 50 cookies*)

Mix and sift 3 cups of already once sifted pastry flour, ½ teaspoon salt and ½ teaspoon of soda into a mixing bowl. Cream ½ cup of butter until light, then add gradually ½ cup of sugar and continue creaming until thoroughly blended. Work in 2 well beaten eggs, combine flour mixture with the second mixture, and when thoroughly blended, stir in ⅓ cup of finely chopped and well drained fig preserves. Drop from teaspoon onto a buttered baking sheet about 2 inches apart to allow for spreading and bake in a moderate oven (350° F.) for about 10 to 12 minutes. Remove at once from the oven, cool on cake rack, and when cold, store in a closed container between layers of wax paper.

GINGER MOLASSES COOKIES JUNGLE [2049]
(*Makes about 60 cookies*)

Sift 2¼ cups of pastry flour; return to sifter and add 1 teaspoon of baking powder, 2 teaspoons of ground ginger, 2 teaspoons of baking soda and ½ teaspoon of salt, and sift into a mixing bowl. Bring 1 cup of light molasses to boiling point; remove from the fire, cool slightly, then stir in ½ cup of butter and cool to lukewarm. Stir in the flour mixture gradually, beating briskly after each addition until smooth. Cool, and when quite cold, place on a lightly floured board, and roll out as thinly as possible (about ⅛-inch). Cut into fancy animal or flower shapes, using fancy cookie cutters and dipping the cutter each time into flour. Arrange the cookies on a greased baking sheet as soon as cut, being careful not to handle them too much. Bake in a moderate oven (350° F.) until delicately browned, or for about 10 to 12 minutes. Store in a closed container between layers of wax paper.

GRAPEFRUIT LADYFINGERS [2050]

Proceed as indicated for Orange Ladyfingers (No. 2058), using 1 large, sound, clean grapefruit instead of 3 oranges, and ⅓ pound of sugar instead of ¼ pound.

HONEY BRANDY SPICED PAVÉS FRENCH STYLE [2051]

Boil 1½ pints of strained honey together with 1 pound of granulated sugar for 3 or 4 minutes, or until sugar is dissolved and the two well blended; stir in 2 teaspoons of ground cinnamon, 1 teaspoon of ground cloves and 1 oz. of potash (commercial and scant weight). Remove from the fire and stir in ¼ cup of heated brandy.

Sift 3 pounds of pastry flour, ½ teaspoon of salt, and 1 teaspoon of baking soda into a bowl; make a well in center and pour in the cooled honey-brandy mixture and ¾ cup of sweet butter, then work thoroughly to a smooth dough. Roll out thinly on a slightly floured board, lay neatly and evenly on a buttered baking sheet, and bake in a moderately hot oven (325-350° F.) until delicately browned. Cut while still hot into small squares, rounds, oblongs or triangles; cool and when cold, ice one portion of the cookies with vanilla icing, another with chocolate icing, and the remainder with orange icing. Store in an air-tight container between waxed paper, and store in a cool place.

Note. These delicious and attractive looking cookies or petits fours do not keep well. Candied citron, pineapple, orange or lemon peel, all finely chopped may be added to the dough before baking.

HONEY FRUIT BARS [2052]
(*Makes about 2 dozen*)

Cream ½ cup of butter until soft and smooth; gradually add ½ cup of granulated sugar; continue creaming until mixture is light and sugar thoroughly blended, then stir in 1 cup of strained, light honey alternately with 1 well beaten egg. Sift 2¾ cups of pastry once, measure, return to sifter and add 1 teaspoon of baking soda, ⅓ teaspoon salt, ¼ teaspoon each of ground cloves, cinnamon and ginger. Sift into mixing bowl over butter-honey mixture, and stir until thoroughly blended, adding, while mixing, about ½ cup of sour milk; now add ¼ cup of grated coconut mixed with ½ cup of seedless raisins previously plumped in boiling water then drained and well dried, also 1 cup of ground walnut meats. Mix well, spread the batter thinly, (about ¼ inch thick) on a generously buttered cookie sheet or a shallow pan, and bake in a moderate oven (350° F.) for 20 minutes. Cool to lukewarm, then cut into strips. Pack in a tight-fitting closed container, between layers of wax paper, and store in a cool, dry place.

LEMON LADYFINGERS [2053]

Proceed as indicated for Orange Ladyfingers (No. 2058), using 6 lemons instead of 3 oranges.

LIME LADYFINGERS [2054]

Proceed as indicated for Orange Ladyfingers (No. 2058), using 8 large limes and ⅓ pound of cut sugar instead of ¼ pound.

MOLASSES MINCEMEAT ALMOND COOKIES [2055]
CREOLE
(Makes about 40)

Break up a 9-ounce package of dehydrated mincemeat into small pieces in a small saucepan, add 1 cup of water, bring slowly to a boil, reduce the heat and cook gently until mixture reaches the consistency of pie filling, stirring frequently. Turn the mincemeat into a mixing bowl, and stir in ½ cup of butter, alternately with ½ cup of molasses. When thoroughly blended, stir in 1 well-beaten egg. Sift once 1½ cups of pastry flour, measure, return to the sifter, add ¾ teaspoon of soda, ½ teaspoon salt and ½ teaspoon of ground allspice powder, and resift into a mixing bowl containing ½ cup of shredded blanched almonds and mix, coating the almond shreds well. Gradually add the flour mixture stirring until smooth. Drop from the tip of a tablespoon on to a greased baking sheet having the cookies two inches apart, and bake in a hot oven (425° F.) about 10 minutes, or until delicately browned. Cool on a cake rack and when cold, store in a covered container between layers of wax paper.

NORMAND KISSES [2056]
(Makes about 2 dozen)

Add ¼ teaspoon salt and ¼ teaspoon each of vanilla and almond extract to 2 egg whites, and beat to a stiff foam. Gradually add ⅔ cup of fine granulated sugar, 1 tablespoon at a time and beat until stiff. Combine ½ cup of blanched and chopped almonds, ½ cup of finely chopped figs and 2 tablespoons of finely chopped citron with 3 tablespoons pastry flour, sifted with ⅛ teaspoon salt. When thoroughly mixed, fold in the beaten egg white. Drop by teaspoons on to a baking sheet covered with white paper, and bake in a moderate oven (350° F.) for about 18 to 20 minutes, or until delicately browned. Remove from the oven at once and top half of the kisses with a split almond half, and the remaining half with half a red maraschino cherry.

OUBLIÉS [2057]
French wafers (Makes about 3 pounds of wafers)

Cream 6 ounces of sweet butter with ½ pound of powdered sugar until very light; then, using a wooden spoon, cream in 2 egg yolks, adding one at a time and beat well after each addition alternately with ½ cup of dry white wine; beat briskly until thoroughly blended and fluffy; then fold in gently, but thoroughly, 2 stiffly beaten egg whites, alternately with 1 pound of pastry flour, previously sifted with 1 teaspoon of ground cinnamon and ½ teaspoon of salt. Beat steadily for 2 minutes, or until batter is light and of the consistency of heavy cream, adding more white wine as needed. Pour by tablespoons into a heated, buttered wafer iron, and cook from 1 to 1½ minutes. Remove immediately, and while still hot roll around the handle of a knife or a wooden spoon.

ORANGE LADYFINGERS   [2058]

Rub ¼ pound of cut sugar on the rind of 2 or 3 sound, clean oranges, then shred the rinds as thinly as possible and pass through the food chopper using the finest blade. Pound the sugar to a powder, then rub through a fine-meshed sieve into a mixing bowl. Cream ¼ pound of sweet butter until light and fluffy, then gradually add to it ¾ teaspoon of Curaçao liqueur alternately with 4 egg yolks, adding one at a time and beating well after each addition. When thoroughly blended, mix in the ground orange rind alternately with 8 tablespoons of pastry flour, sifted once, then resifted with ¼ teaspoon of salt; mix until smooth and fold in 4 stiffly beaten egg whites, beaten with a few grains of salt. Fill well-buttered ladyfinger molds with the batter; sprinkle each with a little fine granulated sugar, and bake 8 to 10 minutes in a very moderate oven (325° F.). When cool, store between layers of wax paper in an airtight container.

PEPPERNUTS   [2059]

Beat 5 eggs until very light, then slowly beat in 1 pound fine sugar and 10 tablespoons rich cream. Sift together 2 pounds flour, 1½ teaspoons each of ground cinnamon and cardamons, 1 teaspoon soda, and ½ teaspoon salt; add to the egg mixture together with ½ cup melted butter, to make a soft dough. Shape into small nuts or balls and bake on a greased cookie sheet until they are light brown in color—about 10 to 15 minutes.

PETITS FOURS LIEGEOIS BELGIAN STYLE   [2060]
Liège Cookies (Makes about 6 dozen)

Sift 1 cup of pastry flour; return to sifter, add ½ teaspoon of baking powder, ¼ teaspoon salt, ¼ teaspoon baking soda, and ¼ teaspoon of mace, and sift into a mixing bowl containing 1 teaspoon of finely grated lemon rind, ½ cup of chopped blanched almonds, ½ cup of seedless raisins, previously parboiled, drained and well dried, and blend thoroughly. Cream ⅓ cup of sweet butter until light; gradually add ½ cup of fine granulated sugar and 2 tablespoons of good brandy, and beat until thoroughly blended and fluffy, then work in 1 egg, well beaten with ¼ teaspoon of almond extract and 1½ tablespoons of cold light cream. Stir in the flour mixture gradually, beating until smooth after each addition. Drop from the tip of a teaspoon into 1½ cups of macaroon crumbs, which have been dried but not browned in a slow oven, tossing lightly to coat each drop, and placing these drops, as coated, on a buttered baking sheet. Top each with half a crystallized cherry and bake in a hot oven (400° F.) 10 to 12 minutes, or until pale brown. Cool on a cake rack, then store in a closed container between layers of wax paper.

POPPY SEED WAFERS [2061]

Sift 1 cup of cake flour into a bowl; stir in 1 cup of whole wheat flour, ½ generous teaspoon of salt, and 1 tablespoon of sugar; cut in 4 tablespoons of shortening with a pastry blender or two knives, then slowly add enough ice-cold water to give the dough the same consistency as pie dough; roll out paper-thin on a slightly floured board; sprinkle with poppy seeds, using as many or as few as desired. Mark into inch squares, then cut with a knife or a pastry wheel. Transfer the squares to a greased baking sheet with a spatula and bake in a very hot oven (425–450° F.) 3 or 4 minutes, or until brown. Cool and store in a covered tin.

Variations. Sesame seeds, caraway seeds, celery seeds, or other preferred seeds may be substituted for poppy seeds, if desired. These wafers are good slightly toasted, spread with cheese and served at cocktail time or with a green salad.

RATAFIA MACAROONS [2062]
(*Makes about 6½ dozen*)

These are made exactly like macaroons, but the paste must be a little softer, and they must be laid out in very small drops on a cookie sheet covered with white kitchen paper, then baked in a cool oven to a very pale color.

Ingredients. Three-quarters of a pound of blanched, ground sweet almonds, 1¼ pounds of powdered sugar, ¼ cup of sweet butter, ⅛ teaspoon salt and 6 to 8 egg whites.

Directions. Put all ingredients into a marble or porcelain mortar, and pound and rub at the same time into a smooth paste. When paste begins to stiffen and stands up in peaks it is ready. It is always wise to bake 2 or 3 ratafias before doing them all, to ascertain if the paste has been pounded enough.

Place the paste in a strong, dry pastry bag and press small dots, a little smaller than a silver quarter, on a baking sheet previously covered with white kitchen paper, having the ratafias or dots a good inch apart, and bake in a slow oven (250-275° F.) to a very pale color. Remove from oven, and immediately pull the ratafias from the paper. Place them on a pastry rack or an upturned large sieve, and let dry in a warm place. Store in an air-tight container in a cool, dry place.

SPRINGERLE [2063]

Beat 4 egg yolks until very light, sifting in 1 cup fine sugar during the process. Beat the whites stiff, and fold in 1 cup fine sugar. Then combine the two mixtures and add another 1¾ cups sugar, beating the whole until bubbles rise. Sift together 3½ cups flour, 3 teaspoons baking powder, and ½ teaspoon salt, and add slowly to the egg mixture, flavoring with the grated rind of 1 lemon. Add enough flour to make a stiff dough and chill for several hours. Roll out with a wooden *springerle* rolling pin, cut around the pictures, and bake the cookies on greased sheets (300° F.) for 30 to 40 minutes. When cool, remove from the pans.

CHOCOLATE ICING [2063—A]
(*For two 9-inch layer cakes*)

Cream ½ cup of butter until light and fluffy. Add gradually 2¾ cups of confectioner's sugar sifted with a pinch of salt. Next add 2 egg yolks one at a time, blending well after each addition. Then add 2 squares (2 oz.) unsweetened chocolate, previously melted over hot water, and 1 teaspoon of vanilla extract. Beat all thoroughly until very smooth and of right consistency to spread.

MOCHA ICING [2063—B]
(*For two 9-inch layer cakes*)

Cream ⅓ cup of butter until light and creamy. Add one-half of 4 cups sifted confectioner's sugar, gradually blending well after each addition. Then add 1 teaspoon of vanilla extract, a pinch of salt, 1 square melted over hot water unsweetened chocolate, and mix well. Now stir in remaining sugar alternately with about ⅓ cup of very strong coffee, beating well after each addition. Add more coffee if frosting is too thick to spread.

Chapter Sixteen

PIES AND PASTRIES

Pie has rightly been called "the great American dessert" and well it may be. Pie is not a new dessert, for away back in the time when Chaucer wrote The Canterbury Tales *he wrote of "hote pyes." Bacon was evidently fond of pie, for he wrote: "Mincing of meat in pies saveth the grinding of the teeth."*

In Irving's Sketch Book, *we find a description of a Christmas dinner in which the author said: "I was happy to find my old friend minced pie in the retinue of the feast," as though he might be speaking of a real friend.*

Pie must ever take a prominent place on the menu of every American household.

The town of Melun, Seine and Marne Department, famous throughout France in the last century for its delicious baked goods, elected its mayor on the basis of his cooking ability. Instead of an election, citizens held a baking contest and the winner became mayor of the town.

PIES AND PASTRIES

WHEN THE NATION WAS YOUNGER—FIFTY YEARS YOUNGER— the mixing bowl was a common kitchen utensil. It was a big yellow bowl; into it went flour and milk, sugar and yeast, fat and salt. But something more—the touch of the artist that produced the bread, the biscuits, the pies, the tarts. There was a quality and a flavor in those home-baked foods which the professional hostess and the modern cook would give much to recapture. Many believe that if this flavor could be identified, fixed, reproduced at will, the hostess would return to the mixing bowl.

Perhaps there is no type of cookery in which there are so many disappointing failures as in the making of bread and pastry, although it is very easy, if rules are followed. There are best stories, best plays, best babies, best shaped young ladies and best men—so why not best and easy pastry recipes? And my answer is in these few recipes, gathered from the kitchens of the country's best recipe-makers, tested and tasted by me during my long professional career of practical chef. But I say, no amount of mixing and blending can overcome inaccurate measurements. That is a chapter in itself. In the meantime, here are a few of my best tart recipes:

Tarts and Tortes should be used more frequently than they are, because they are both attractive and economical. As a rule they take less filling than pies but look like a larger portion. When fruits are expensive the wise hostess will make them "go farther" by using them in tarts rather than in pie fillings.

In making tarts or tortes, one may use cake crumbs, breadcrumbs, oatmeal crumbs, rice crumbs, and so forth. Cooked cream filling is usually the base. A fruit glaze made from fruit juice cooked to the "jell" stage, poured over the top prevents discoloration and adds to the appearance. Tart shells may be made of plain or puff paste and may be baked over inverted pie plates or muffin pans, if you are careful to have the surface pricked. They may also be baked in one pie plate, with another plate of the same size on top. Tarts and tortes if desired may be covered either with an ordinary meringue or a fancy one such as marshmallow. Because of its quality of puffing under the action of direct heat or flame, marshmallow makes a delicious and attractive topping for pastries, as well as puddings and other baked sweets.

In addition to the popular marshmallow topping, there are many other tempting and eye-appealing toppings, such as Apricot Cream, Honey, Berry, and so on. A topping, like the frosting on a cake, quite literally makes the tart, torte, kuchen, boulette, jelly ball, jelly roll, mille-feuille, strudel, log, charlotte, twist, checkerboard, pastry, fruit strip, napoleon, fluff, cobbler, blitz, sponge, fat rascals, petticoat tails, dundee, profiterolles, pistoles, as well as the innumerable list of short-cakes, and other fragile pastries.

PIE BAKING   [2065]

While in other countries "pie" may denote a substantial entrée of meat or fish having a top crust (such as "Beef and Kidney Pie"), to us the word definitely signifies a sweet pastry. Since this dessert is typically American, it certainly rates special attention.

The basis of these desserts is either a "plain" or "puff" pastry. Pies are usually made of the plain variety. Pastry is always made of flour, shortening, a liquid (usually water), salt and sometimes sugar or baking powder. The nature of the finished product depends upon the proportion of the various ingredients used, the temperature of each, the method of combining, the handling of the pastry and baking. *Tenderness* of pastry depends much upon the kind of flour, the amount of shortening and handling, while *flakiness* is determined more by the method of combining these ingredients. There are four points to remember in pastry making upon which food experts agree: (1) Use little water; (2) fold in as much air as possible; (3) handle lightly, and (4) put pastry into a hot oven (450° F.). The proportion of flour to shortening varies but is generally 3 or 4 to 1 by volume or 2 to 1 by weight. 1½ quarts (1½ pounds) of pastry flour with 1½ cups (¾ pound) shortening will give 6 pie shells or 3 2-crust pies. For less, reduce accordingly.

FLAKY PASTRY   [2066

To obtain a flaky pastry, the fat should be thoroughly chilled before being added to the flour. The aim is to have the fat evenly divided so that the mixture of flour and shortening resembles little pebbles the size of peas. It is important to keep fat cold during the mixing process. All tools should be chilled before using. Different methods are used such as pastry blenders, chopping knives, and working in the fat by hand. In the latter, it is best to work quickly because the heat of the hands may melt the fat. There is a knack about this method of mixing. The fat particles should be rubbed through the hands so that the fat is flattened between layers of flour, rather than being squeezed together. More air is incorporated in this way.

It is a great mistake to try to mix too great a quantity at one time. It is better to undermix than to overmix as overmixing makes the pastry tough. Furthermore, no amount of chilling after flour and fat have been blended will give as good results as having the fat thoroughly chilled before the mixing.

MEALY PASTRY   [2067]

This results when the shortening is soft so that it is partly dissolved in the mixing. When oils or semi-liquid fats are used, the pastry is of this type. However, it is possible to obtain the same results by blending a firm fat with flour in certain proportions; use the entire amount of shortening called for with half the required amount of flour and blend until the mixture is like coarse cornmeal; add the remainder of the flour and moisten with as little water as possible.

SHORT FLAKY PASTRY [2068]

A combination of the flaky and mealy pastries which is sometimes called "short-flaky" pastry may be obtained by this method: Mix half the shortening with all of the flour until thoroughly blended. Add remainder of shortening and mix to the "pebbly" stage as in Flaky Pastry (No. 2066). Add just enough water to combine.

ANNA'S BUTTER CRUST [2069]

Sift together 1¼ cups of flour, ½ teaspoon salt and ¼ teaspoon baking powder; cut in ½ cup plus 1 tablespoon of sweet butter until mixture resembles coarse meal. To 1 tablespoon of vinegar, add 3 blades of tarragon herb (dried tarragon herb may be used if fresh tarragon is not available) and 2 tablespoons of water; place in refrigerator and chill for 2 hours, then sprinkle the strained marinade over the flour-butter mixture; stir lightly with a fork to make particles hold together. Shape very lightly into a ball; place in a bowl; cover closely and chill thoroughly. This crust is especially appropriate for fruit pies.

Important. Under- rather than overmix. Chill dough before rolling.

CHEESE BISCUIT RINGS [2070]

Mix and sift together twice 2 cups of flour, 2 teaspoons of baking powder, ½ teaspoon salt and a pinch of powdered nutmeg. Work in 2 tablespoons of shortening, then ¼ pound (1 cup) grated cheese (any kind). Add ice-cold milk (about ¾ cup) to make a soft dough. Turn onto a floured board, knead for ½ minute, and roll out to about a ½-inch in thickness. Cut into biscuit rings with floured cutter, place on top of pie and bake in a hot oven (425° F.) until golden brown on top, or about 20 minutes.

CHEESE PIE CRUST [2071]

Sift 2½ cups of flour with ½ teaspoon salt. Cut in, using a pastry blender or two knives, 1½ cups of grated American cheese, ⅔ cup of shortening, working and cutting till mixture resembles coarse meal, then add enough ice-cold water (about ⅓ cup) to make particles hold together. Pat and chill thoroughly before rolling out ⅛ inch in thickness. Line an ungreased pie plate in the usual way, pour in the filling; adjust the top crust in the usual way; make a few slits on top for the escape of steam; brush with ice-cold water, milk or beaten egg yolk, and bake according to directions, i.e. 10 minutes in a very hot oven (450° F.) to set the pastry; then at 350° F., for about 25 minutes.

Note. Instead of mixing cheese into the dough, try the French pastry chefs' method: after the under crust has been fitted into the pie plate, sprinkle a thin layer of grated cheese over it, add the filling (fruit, fish, poultry, meat, game, vegetables, and so forth). Sprinkle another layer of grated cheese over the filling and adjust the top crust.

EGG YOLK PASTRY FOR PIE COVERING　　[2072]

Chop ¾ cup of any preferred shortening coarsely into 2 cups of flour which has been sifted with ½ teaspoon of baking powder and 1 scant teaspoon of salt, Mix 1 egg yolk with about 5 tablespoons of ice-cold water or milk (if for fruit pie, use fruit juice corresponding to fruit used), and add gradually to the dry mixture. Gather the dough together, roll out to ½-inch in thickness on a lightly floured board. Cut into rounds, squares, rings, etc., place on top of pie filling, brush with egg white, and bake in a hot oven (425° F.) until well-browned on top, or about 20 minutes.

HOT BISCUIT COVERING　　[2073]

Combine two cups of sifted flour with 2 teaspoons of baking powder, ½ teaspoon salt and a tiny pinch of nutmeg (optional), and sift into mixing bowl. Work in ⅓ generous cup of shortening with fork, finger tips, knives, or pastry blender; add about ⅔ cup of ice-cold milk or enough to make a soft dough. Turn to a lightly floured board, and knead gently for ½ minute, then pat or roll to ½-inch in thickness. Cut with floured cutter, place on top of pie filling and bake 15 to 20 minutes in a very hot oven (450° F.). Especially appropriate for fish, meat or poultry pies.

PARSLEY PASTRY COVER　　[2074]

Proceed as indicated for "Hot Biscuit Covering" (No. 2073), adding to the dough ⅓ cup of finely chopped parsely.

Variations. Substitute chopped watercress for chopped parsley. Substitute chopped green pepper for chopped parsley, or mix together the three preceding ingredients in equal parts. Substitute chopped, cooked spinach for chopped parsley.

PATTY SHELLS　　[2075]

Roll Paste I, II or III, (Nos. 2076, 2077 and 2078 respectively) to the thickness of a scant half-inch and with a fluted cookie cutter shape circles 2½ to 3 inches in diameter. With a smaller cutter, remove the centers from half the circles; brush the edges of the complete circles with cold water and lay the rings on top, pressing very gently to seal. Arrange on a baking sheet having the patty shells about an inch a part; chill then bake in a hot oven (425–450° F. from 15 to 18 minutes. Bake the small centers removed from the upper layers of the circles at the same time and use them as lids for the filled patties.

PUFF PASTE I CLASSIC STYLE   [2076]

Ingredients. ½ pound of butter, ½ pound of pastry flour, a dash of salt and 6 to 8 tablespoons of ice-cold water.

Directions. Wash butter, squeeze and fold until all water is extracted. Cut 2 tablespoons of butter into the sifted pastry flour, add cold water and knead the dough five minutes. Roll to a scant ¼-inch in thickness, keeping paste rectangular and corners square. Place remaining butter in center of lower half of dough, cover with upper half and fold right side under and left side over. Roll to a scant ¼-inch in thickness. Repeat this process four times. Put paste in a cold earthen bowl, cover with a napkin wrung out of cold water and chill in the refrigerator for at least an hour. Cut into desired shapes, place on paper-covered baking sheet and bake in a hot oven (450° F.) for five minutes; reduce heat to moderate (375° F.), and continue baking 25 to 30 minutes longer. To have a still more flaky crust, repeat the rollings six times instead of four.

PUFF PASTE II BOURGEOISE STYLE   [2077]

Knead ½ a pound of butter with 1 teaspoon of pastry flour to an even smooth paste. Place in refrigerator to chill well. Sift in a mixing bowl ½ pound of flour; make a well in center into which place 1 teaspoon of butter, 1 egg yolk, 1 teaspoon of vinegar and a pinch of salt. Mix thoroughly, adding while mixing 6 to 8 tablespoons of lukewarm water or enough to make a fairly soft dough. After working it for about 15 minutes, the dough should begin to leave your fingers and the board; if not, add a little more flour. Form the dough into a ball, wrap in cheesecloth and set in refrigerator for 25 minutes. Roll out on a lightly floured board and place bits of the chilled butter over the entire surface, pressing it down with the floured rolling pin. Now pull and fold the dough over the butter from all four corners; roll it out to about ½-inch in thickness and to an oblong shape, then turn the two ends evenly into the center, as you would fold the page of a book, and finally close the book or rather the dough; wrap it in cheesecloth before placing it in the refrigerator for 30 minutes. Repeat this operation 4 times, returning it after each rolling for a ½-hour rest in the refrigerator. Cut into desired shapes, place on paper covered baking sheet and bake in a hot oven (450° F.) for five minutes; reduce heat to moderate (375° F.), and continue baking 25–30 minutes longer. To have a more flaky crust, repeat the rollings six times instead of four.

PUFF PASTE III ITALIAN STYLE   [2078]

Sift ½ cup of pastry flour in a mixing bowl; cut in, as for pie, 1⅓ cups of washed butter as in Puff Paste I (No. 2076) until flour is all butter-dampened; roll out on a lightly floured board, into a ½-inch thick rectangle; wrap in a napkin wrung out of cold water and chill in refrigerator for 30 minutes. Meanwhile, combine 1½ cups of sifted pastry flour with ½ cup ice-cold water, 1½ tablespoons lemon juice and a scant half teaspoon salt and work until smooth and paste leaves sides of mixing bowl clean. Turn onto a lightly floured board and roll out into a square, a scant ½ inch thick. Place the chilled flour-butter mixture in the center of this square and fold, envelope-fashion, then roll out as thin as possible. Fold again as previously, and roll once more into a square. Chill 25 minutes. Repeat this 5 times, chilling 25 minutes each time. Wrap in a napkin wrung out of very cold water and chill in refrigerator overnight or longer, the longer the better, before shaping into desired form. Place on paper-covered baking sheet and bake in a hot oven (450° F.) for five minutes; reduce heat to moderate (375° F.) and continue baking 25 to 30 minutes longer. To have a more flaky crust, repeat six times instead of five.

Note. Use the puff paste for pie crust, napoleons, Sacher Torte, Linzer Torte, apple, or other fruit turnovers or dumplings, individual tartelets, large *tortes* (fruit, cream, sea food or other creamed food); as a base for canapés instead of bread, mille-feuilles pastry, finger pies, rings to be filled with cream, fruit, sea food or other food in cream, à la king, á la Reine; or as a crust for any fruit, fish, meat or game shortcake.

TART SHELLS   [2079]

Sift and measure 2⅓ cups pastry flour; add ¾ teaspoon salt, and sift again. No leavening agent, such as baking powder or yeast, is required. Cut ⅓ cup butter or other shortening into the flour with a pastry blender or two knives. When the mixture is of the consistency of coarse meal, add another ⅓ cup butter, and blend until the particles are the size of small navy beans. Add gradually about 5 tablespoons water, mixing the dough lightly with a fork. Roll out the pastry ⅛-inch thick on a slightly floured board. For 3-inch patty pans or individual tart tins, cut 5-inch rounds, and fit them into, or over the backs of the buttered pans. Bake 12 to 15 minutes in a very hot oven (450° F.). If fluted pans are used, fit the rounds of dough into the pans; press a second pan firmly into the first (over the pastry), and bake for 5 minutes in a very hot oven. Then remove the upper pan, and continue to bake until the shells are delicately browned. An attractively shaped tart may be made by fitting the rounds of dough over the backs of muffin tins, pricking the dough thoroughly to prevent puffing, and making about 7 pleats at regular intervals around the shell.

Note. The usual fillings for tarts are cooked, creamy mixtures, which are prevented from discoloring and hardening by a fruit glaze poured over the surface. The glaze is made from fruit juice cooked to the jellying stage.

Fresh fruit mixed with whipped cream or custard makes a dainty tart, especially delicious if you brush the inside of the shell with slightly melted marmalade, jam, or jelly. Or, spread 1 tablespoon sweetened cream cheese in the bottom of each tart shell, and top with sugared fresh or frozen berries.

WALNUT CRUMB CRUST   [2080]

Crush whole wheat flaked cereal to make 1 cup and mix in thoroughly ¼ cup granulated sugar and ½ cup ground shelled walnut meats. Stir in 1 unbeaten egg white and press into the bottom and sides of a 9-inch pie-plate. Bake 8 to 10 minutes in a moderate oven (350–375° F.). Cool before adding the desired filling. (For fruit or cream pies.)

ANGEL PIE   [2081]

Cook 1 cup of milk, with ½ cup of sugar, 2 tablespoons of flour, which has been moistened in a little of the (cold) milk, and ¼ teaspoon of salt in top of double boiler, but over direct flame, stirring constantly until thick. Strain through a fine sieve, and cool until it no longer steams. Fold in 3 egg whites, stiffly beaten with a few grains of salt, and flavored with ½ teaspoon each of vanilla and almond extracts. Turn preparation into a pre-baked, cooled pie shell, the bottom of which has been brushed with warmed jelly; cover with whipped cream, forced through a pastry bag using a fancy tube, and chill.

APPLE-COTTAGE CHEESE PIE   [2082]

Combine 2 lightly beaten eggs with ½ cup of sugar, ¼ teaspoon of salt, ½ cup of scalded thin cream and ¾ cup of rich milk and blend thoroughly; then beat in 1 cup of sieved cottage cheese flavored with 1 teaspoon of vanilla. Place 2 cups of sliced apples in a shallow saucepan with a few tablespoons of cold water and a pinch of salt; cover, and cook very gently until apples are tender. The apple should be rather dry and not broken; stir in gently ½ cup of sugar and arrange in a pastry-lined pie plate; sprinkle with ½ teaspoon of cinnamon mixed with ¼ teaspoon of nutmeg; pour cottage cheese mixture as evenly as possible over the apples and bake in a hot oven (450° F.) for 15 minutes; reduce temperature to 325° F. and continue baking for about 35 minutes, or until cheese custard is firm and a knife inserted in center comes out clean. Serve cold.

"A pie without cheese is like a kiss without a squeeze." The line, as we recall it, applies specifically to apple pie. But even so, the origin of the custom remains unexplained.

APPLE PAN DOWDY   [2083]

Line a deep dish with rich pastry. Fill with thinly sliced apples, sprinkle them with ½ cup sugar mixed with ½ teaspoon cinnamon and ¼ teaspoon each of salt and nutmeg. Mix ½ cup good black molasses with ¼ cup water and 3 tablespoons melted butter, and pour over the apples. Add a top crust, and bake until the crust is light and the apples tender. Remove from the oven, and chop apples and crust together with a chopper, adding more molasses and water if the pie seems dry. Return to the oven, and bake for an hour longer. Serve hot with butter and rich unsweetened cream.

APPLE PIE   [2084]

Line a 9 or 10 inch pie plate with unbaked pastry, and fill it with 3¾ cups pared, cored and sliced apples. Sprinkle over the fruit ½ cup granulated sugar mixed with ¼ teaspoon salt and ¼ teaspoon powdered cinnamon. Moisten with 1 tablespoon unstrained lemon juice and the grated rind of half a medium-sized lemon. Dot with 1 tablespoon butter, arrange the top crust in place, pushing it gently toward the center, and slash it to allow steam to escape. Press the edges of the crust together, and trim off any excess pastry. Bake in a very hot oven (450° F.) for 10 minutes to set the crust; then reduce the temperature to 350° F., and bake for 30 to 35 minutes longer.

BUTTERMILK RAISIN MERINGUE PIE   [2085]
(Sugarless)

Mix 7 tablespoons of pastry flour with ¼ teaspoon of salt and sift into top of double boiler; add 1 cup of white corn syrup, stir in 1½ cups of buttermilk and ¾ cup of seedless raisins, previously parboiled until plump, then well drained, and cook over hot water until mixture thickens, stirring constantly from the bottom of the pan; cover and continue cooking 5 minutes longer, stirring occasionally. Add part of the hot mixture to 3 beaten egg yolks, beat briskly, and return to the mixture in the pan; blend all thoroughly and continue cooking 3 minutes longer, stirring constantly; remove from hot water, stir in 3 tablespoons of lemon juice, also a few grains of nutmeg, and stir to mix well. Cool to lukewarm; pour into a pre-baked pie shell; cover with meringue made by beating 3 tablespoons of strained, light honey into 3 stiffly beaten egg whites with a few grains of salt, spread the meringue to edges of pie crust, and bake in a moderate oven (325° F.) for about 15 to 20 minutes, or until meringue is delicately browned. Cool.

CHERRY CHESS PIE [2086]

Pit 1 quart of sour cherries after first washing them quickly in cold water then draining well. Mix 2 tablespoons of flour, ½ teaspoon cinnamon, ½ cup of sugar, ⅓ cup of honey, a pinch of salt and 1½ tablespoons of melted butter or margarin. Stir in 3 well beaten eggs with a pinch of salt and add the cherries. Pour into an unbaked pie shell and bake in a hot oven (450° F.) for 12 minutes, to set the pie and crust; reduce the heat to 350° F. and continue baking for 20 minutes longer, or until set. Cool and serve with a whipped cream topping.

COFFEE RUM CHIFFON PIE [2087]

Mix together in top of double boiler and off the fire, 1 tablespoon of unflavored gelatin and 3 tablespoons of good rum. Let stand 5 minutes, then stir in ⅓ cup of fine granulated sugar, ¼ teaspoon of salt, ⅛ to ¼ teaspoon of powdered cinnamon, and 3 well-beaten egg yolks. Gradually, and a little at a time, add 1 cup of very strong coffee, beating briskly after each addition. When thoroughly blended, place over hot water and cook, stirring constantly until mixture coats the spoon heavily. Remove from hot water, and cool. When thoroughly cold, fold in 3 stiffly beaten egg whites, seasoned with a few grains of salt and flavored with ½ teaspoon vanilla. Sweeten with ⅓ cup of sugar. Beat until foamy. Pour as evenly as possible into a 9-inch pre-baked pastry shell and chill until firm. Serve cold topped with unflavored and unsweetened whipped cream forced through a pastry bag, using a fancy tube.

DEEP DISH BLUEBERRY PIE [2088]

Arrange a layer of blueberries in a deep pie plate, sweeten with sugar, sprinkle with flour, and dot with butter. Repeat until 3 cups of berries, ¾ cup sugar, and 1 tablespoon flour have been used. Pour over the fruit a mixture of ¼ cup water, ¼ cup sugar, a pinch of salt, and the juice of 1 lemon. Top with a crust of flaky pastry or with rich biscuit dough, and bake in a hot oven (400° F.).

FARMER'S NUT CREAM PIE [2089]

Beat 3 eggs till well blended; gradually beat in ½ cup of sugar and 1 cup of dark corn syrup alternately with ¼ cup of melted butter, which has been slightly cooled and mix thoroughly. Stir in ¼ teaspoon of salt, 1 teaspoon of vanilla, and 1 cup of coarsely chopped nut meats. Turn into an unbaked pie shell, and bake in a hot oven (450° F.) for 10 minutes; reduce heat to moderate (350° F.) and continue baking 30 minutes longer or until an inserted knife comes out clean. If served hot or warm, pass a pitcher of cold sweet cream; if cold, spread top with whipped cream forced through a pastry bag, using a fancy tube.

FRENCH APPLE SLICE PIE [2090]
(Original recipe)

This is just another version of the American apple pie.

Sift 2 cups of pastry flour; measure, return to sifter, add ½ teaspoon of salt and resift into a mixing bowl. Cut in ¾ cup of butter (using a pastry blender or two knives) until mixture resembles coarse meal. Beat 2 egg yolks slightly; add 7 tablespoons of sharp cider and 1 tablespoon of lemon juice and blend into the flour mixture, stirring only until a soft dough is formed. Roll out half the dough to about ⅛-inch in thickness on a lightly floured board and fit it in the bottom of a shallow baking dish, about 7 × 12 inches.

Peel, core and slice thin 8 apples; combine 1 cup of sugar, ¼ teaspoon of salt, 1 tablespoon of flour, ½ teaspoon of cinnamon and ½ teaspoon of nutmeg and blend thoroughly; add to the apple slices and toss gently so that all the slices are coated.

Arrange on the dough alternate layers of prepared apple slices, and seedless raisins, previously plumped in boiling water, then dried thoroughly and rolled in a very little flour, using in all, ¾ cup of raisins.

Roll out the second part of the dough to about ⅛-inch in thickness; cut several slits in it to allow for the escape of steam; adjust it over the filling and seal edges of crusts as for an ordinary pie. Bake in a moderate oven (350° F.), for about 50 minutes to one hour. Remove from the oven, cool, and when quite cold, ice with a thin confectioner's sugar icing.

FRENCH DEEP DISH APPLE PIE [2091]

Line a deep 9-inch pie pan with pastry, and set aside to chill while preparing the filling. Mix 6 cups thinly sliced tart apples with ½ to ¾ cups granulated sugar, ½ teaspoon freshly grated nutmeg, a pinch of ground cinnamon and 2 tablespoons flour. Toss thoroughly together in the mixing bowl. If the apples are not very juicy, sprinkle them with a little cold water mixed with equal parts of lemon juice. Fill the pastry-lined dish, and cover with the top crust, slashing it to allow the steam to escape. Brush with beaten egg yolk diluted with a little cold milk. Bake for 15 minutes in a very hot oven (450° F.); then reduce the heat to moderate (350° F.) and continue to bake for 25 minutes longer. If the crust seems to brown too quickly, cover it with a buttered paper until the last few minutes of baking. Serve with whipped cream.

LEMON CHIFFON PIE [2092]

Beat 4 egg yolks slightly, and add to them 5 tablespoons lemon juice, ½ cup granulated sugar, and the grated rind of half a lemon. Cook in the top of a double boiler until the mixture is thick, stirring constantly. Remove from the heat, and blend in ½ generous tablespoon granulated gelatin dissolved in ⅓ cup cold water. Cool.

Beat 4 egg whites until stiff but not dry, sweeten with ¼ cup granulated sugar, and gently fold this mixture into the first. Pour into a pre-baked pie shell, and place the pie in the refrigerator for 2 hours or more, until the gelatin has set. Serve with a topping of whipped cream prepared as follows: Beat ¾ cup heavy cream until stiff, adding a generous pinch of salt and ½ teaspoon each of finely grated lemon and orange rind, alternating with ¼ cup granulated sugar. Force the whipped cream mixture through a pastry bag using a fancy tube, either piping a rim of whipped cream around the edge, or covering the whole pie, as preferred. Dust the whipped cream with 1 tablespoon of finely chopped angelica and some ground blanched almonds.

LEMON CREAM PIE [2093]

Beat 4 eggs in the top of a double boiler with 1 cup granulated sugar. Add the grated rind of 1 large lemon, the unstrained juice of 2 lemons, and 4 tablespoons butter. Cook over hot water, stirring constantly, until so thick that the stirring spoon leaves its trace in the mixture. Remove from the heat, and cool to lukewarm. Coat bottom and sides of a pre-baked pastry shell with a purée of stewed apricots; then fill the shell with the lemon filling. Cover with a thick layer of unsweetened whipped cream forced through a pastry tube. Serve well chilled.

Variations. Substitute for the apricot purée currant jelly, or guava jelly.

MERINGUE CREAM PIE [2094]

Combine 2½ cups of crushed cornflakes with 2 tablespoons of flour, ⅓ cup of sugar and 2 tablespoons of butter, softened and flavored with

2 teaspoons of vanilla extract, press into a buttered pie plate, and fill with cream filling.

Cream Filling. Put in top of double boiler 1 cup of sugar, ¼ cup of cornstarch and ½ teaspoon of salt. Add 2 tablespoons of butter and 2 cups of cold milk, and stir until well-blended, then cook over hot water, stirring until thick. Remove from hot water and beat in 3 egg yolks, adding one at a time and beating briskly after each addition; return the pan to the hot water bath and cook until thick, stirring constantly from bottom of the pan.

Turn the cream mixture into the prepared pie crust, and cool to lukewarm. Cover the top with a meringue made with the stiffly beaten egg whites, a pinch of salt and 3 tablespoons of sugar. When stiff, pile over the filling; sprinkle over the meringue half a cup of crushed cornflakes, and brown delicately in a slow oven (300° F.). Cool.

MINCE PIE   [2095]

Three tablespoons chopped boiled lean beef; 3 tablespoons chopped beef kidney suet; ¾ pound chopped raw peeled cored apples; 3 tablespoons chopped seedless raisins ½ teaspoon salt; ½ teaspoon each chopped candied orange and lemon peel; 1 cup brown sugar; ⅛ teaspoon grated nutmeg; ⅔ teaspoon ground cinnamon; ⅛ teaspoon ground cloves; 1 cup cider.

Combine ingredients in the order given and simmer very gently for two hours placing an asbestos pad under the kettle to prevent scorching. Keep in tightly covered jar in a cool place until needed. As this mincemeat will keep six months it may be made in quantity.

The grated rind of 2 medium sized lemons added to the mixture before simmering is a great improvement. Brandy may be added before cooking but the flavor will evaporate, so try adding it with a syringe as suggested below.

Place this mellowed, ripened mixture between two crusts in the usual way and bake 10 minutes in a very hot oven (450° F.) to set the crust, then decrease heat to moderate (350° F.) and continue baking for 30 minutes longer. Serve hot, each portion topped with a slice of American cheese.

Variation brandied mincemeat. Combine in equal proportions brandy and straight apple cider, then inject 1½ to 2 ounces (about ¼ cup) of the mixture into the pie after it comes from the oven, using a drug store syringe for the purpose. This may sound strange but it works. Use a syringe made entirely of metal with a spout of approximately six inches. It is double acting, drawing the liquid in as well as forcing it out. Push the spout of the syringe through the crust at the edge of the pie plate where the top and bottom crusts are sealed, allowing the spout to penetrate to the center of the baked pie at which point the brandy and cider mixture is injected. Point the syringe down so that the liquor will not come in contact with the top crust, which would result in soaking it. The reason for diluting the brandy with the cider instead of injecting a lesser amount of straight brandy is that the larger volume of liquid gives more spread in the pie, thus allowing a more thorough penetration of the flavor. Much of the brandy will of course necessarily remain near the center; in other words, the first bite of each cut will carry the heaviest load of brandy. This is as it should be, as the flavor from the first bite will carry through the rest of the piece.

MOLASSES-PECAN PIE   [2096]
(A favorite of Abraham Lincoln)

Mix 3 well-beaten eggs with 1 cup of old-fashioned molasses, ½ cup of dark corn syrup, 1 teaspoon of vanilla and a pinch of salt. When thoroughly blended, beat in 2 tablespoons of melted butter. Coat 1 cup of chopped pecans with 1 tablespoon of flour, then stir into the first mixture. Pour evenly into an unbaked pie shell, bake in a moderate oven (350° F.) for about 40 minutes or until set. Cool.

NEW ENGLAND LEMON MERINGUE PIE   [2097]

Sift together 7 tablespoons cornstarch, 1 tablespoon flour, and 1¾ cups granulated sugar. Blend in 2 cups boiling water, stirring constantly until the mixture is smooth and creamy. Cook in top of double boiler for 5 minutes, then stir carefully into the hot mixture 4 beaten egg yolks, the grated rind of 2 lemons, 1 generous tablespoon butter, ¼ teaspoon salt, and ½ cup unstrained lemon juice. Continue to cook in the double boiler, stirring constantly, until the egg yolks are cooked and the mixture has become smooth and thick. Turn the filling into a pie shell already baked and cover with a meringue made as follows: Beat 5 egg whites until stiff, with ¼ scant teaspoon salt, sweetening with 8 to 10 tablespoons sugar added gradually. Continue to beat until the mixture is well blended.

Bake the pie in a slow oven (300° F.) until the meringue is delicately browned. Cool before serving.

PECAN EGGNOG PIE   [2098]

A favorite dessert for Christmas and the New Year. It should be made early in the day and well-chilled before serving.

Mix until thoroughly blended 1 cup of vanilla wafer crumbs, ¼ cup of softened butter and ¼ cup of very finely chopped pecans. Press onto bottom and sides of a buttered 9-inch pie plate and chill. Beat together 3 egg yolks, ¼ cup of sugar, ¼ teaspoon of grated nutmeg, and a generous pinch of salt. Gradually stir in 1 cup of scalded thin cream or undiluted evaporated milk, stirring briskly to prevent eggs from curdling and cook over hot water until mixture coats a metal spoon, stirring almost constantly. Combine ¼ cup of sherry wine and 1 tablespoon of unflavored, granulated gelatin. Let stand 5 minutes than add to the custard mixture, stirring briskly until gelatin is dissolved. Cool, then fold in very gently 3 stiffly beaten egg whites, sweetened with ¼ cup of sugar. Pour into the well-chilled wafer crumb crust; garnish with pecan halves; chill until firm and serve.

PECAN PIE   [2099]

Cream ⅓ cup of butter until light; gradually adding ½ cup of brown sugar and creaming until light and fluffy. Add 3 eggs, one at a time, beating well after each addition, also ¼ teaspoon of salt, 1 cup of dark corn syrup and ½ teaspoon of vanilla. Blend thoroughly, and finally stir in 1 cup of chopped slightly floured pecans. Line a 9-inch pie plate with pastry, crimping the edge, pour filling into it as evenly as possible, and bake in a hot oven (450° F.) for 10 minutes to set the pastry. Then reduce the heat to moderately slow (300–325° F.) and continue baking for about 30 minutes, or until a silver knife inserted in the center comes out clean.

Note. The filling browns very quickly. To avoid over-browning before filling is cooked, allow the oven door to remain open a minute when temperature is reduced, to make sure that heat is reduced at once. Watch closely for remainder of baking period.

PUMPKIN PIE I   [2100]

To the initiate, pumpkin pie is the first and most important of the pumpkin dishes. Indeed, the honorable history of New England's favorite "pie vegetable" is ample testimony to its perennial popularity. From earliest colonial days, squash and pumpkin have been as traditionally a part of the national diet as corn and cranberry sauce. The one-crust pumpkin pie that assumes such importance during the autumn season is really an open tart, what the French term a *flan*. But the culinary disputes that center around this truly American dessert arise less from etymological disagreement than from individual differences of opinion regarding proper ingredients and methods of baking.

Some cooks champion the cause of pumpkin pie filling made with egg whites or gelatin. Some vary the ordinary taste by adding a little cider, good brandy, or sherry to the custard. Often cream is substituted for part of the milk in a recipe to make a rich pumpkin pie, and ginger for at least part of the cinnamon and allspice that are most commonly and justly used. The variety and amount of spices mixed into the custard depend largely on the cook's preference. However, the following is a typical pumpkin pie recipe:

PUMPKIN PIE II [2101]

Line a 9-inch pie plate with pastry. Keep cool. Beat 4 egg yolks until lemon colored; combine with 1 cup of brown sugar, mixed with ½ teaspoon each of ground cinnamon, nutmeg and allspice. Blend until sugar is thoroughly dissolved, then add 2 cups sieved baked pumpkin mixed with ⅓ cup heavy cream and ¼ cup melted butter, stirred together until thoroughly blended. Beat 4 egg whites until stiff, sprinkle in 1 tablespoon of cornstarch, then fold into the pumpkin mixture. Pour into the prepared unbaked pastry shell and bake for 10 minutes in a hot oven (450° F.) to set the crust, then reduce the heat to moderate (350 °F.) and continue baking 20 to 25 minutes longer or until knife blade comes out clean when inserted. The following is optional but gives added flavor. When pie is thoroughly cold, pour over the entire surface ¼ cup strained honey mixed with ½ scant cup of finely chopped pecan meats.

RHUBARB PIE [2102]

Have ready pastry for a double crust pie. Sprinkle a little of 1½ cups of granulated sugar, mixed with 2 tablespoons of flour over lower crust to prevent soaking, and add remainder of measured sugar to 1 quart of cleaned, scraped tender rhubarb. Cut into inch pieces, and fill the pie; dot with 2 tablespoons of butter and top with the remaining pastry, pressing the edges of crust firmly together; make a few slashes in the top crust and bake in a hot oven (450° F.) for 15 minutes; reduce the heat to moderate (350° F.), and continue baking 25 minutes longer. Cool and serve with whipped cream or plain, sweet cream.

SHOOFLY PIE [2103]

Line a 7-inch pie plate with good pastry, and partly bake. Work lightly together, as for pastry, ¾ cup fine dry crumbs, ¼ cup flour, 1 teaspoon cinnamon, ¼ teaspoon nutmeg, ⅛ teaspoon ginger, and ¼ cup butter. Combine ¼ cup hot water, ¾ cup light molasses and 6 well-beaten eggs. Pour into the crust, and sprinkle the spiced crumb mixture over it. Bake in a quick oven (400° F.) until the pie is lightly browned; then reduce the heat to 325° F., and bake for 20 minutes longer.

STANDARD PIE PASTRY   [2104]
(*Makes 1 two-crust pie, 2 pastry shells, or 12 tart shells*)

Ingredients. Two and a half cups of sifted pastry flour, 1 teaspoon of salt, ¾ cup of cold shortening, 5 tablespoons (more or less) of water.

Directions. Mix once-sifted flour with salt and sift again. Cut in half of the shortening with two knives or a pastry blender until mixture looks like cornmeal. Cut in remaining shortening until particles are the size of a pea. At one side of the bowl, add 1 tablespoon of cold water and stir in as much of the flour mixture as the water will take up. Continue adding water, which should be very cold, 1 tablespoon at a time, until you have 4 or 5 balls of dough and some dry mixture left in the bowl. Press all together lightly with fingers and if all the dry flour is not taken up, add a little more cold water. Chill and roll.

Remember, the less the dough is handled, the flakier the pastry.

There is much to be said for fast work in mixing pastry. That is what our grandmothers meant when they said, for highest praise, "She has a light hand with pastry."

For the pastry shell, the dough should be rolled rather thin and draped over the underside of a pie plate. It should be pressed down firmly, any excess dough should be trimmed off at the edge of the plate with a sharp knife. The pastry should then be pricked all over with the tines of a fork. This prevents blistering by the steam which gathers during the baking process. A hot oven (450° F.) should be used and the shell should be just the right shade of color in ten to twelve minutes.

WALNUT-MAPLE SYRUP PIE   [2105]

Cream 1½ tablespoons of butter; gradually add 2 tablespoons of flour and continue creaming till well blended; then add 2 egg yolks, one at a time, beating well after each addition, alternately with 1 cup of maple syrup which has been mixed with ½ cup of cold water. Cook over direct flame or, if preferred, in top of double boiler, until thick and smooth, stirring constantly from the bottom of the pan. Remove from the fire; stir in ½ cup of nut meats, peeled and chopped fine. Cool to lukewarm, and pour into a pre-baked 8-inch pie shell. Top with a meringue and bake in a slow oven (300–325° F.) until meringue is nicely set and slightly browned. Cool before serving.

> *Did you ever have a party,*
> *In the days of long ago,*
> *Away back in the forest*
> *Where the sugar-maples grow?*

*If you have, you know the pleasure
That in "sugaring-off" is found
As you stir the maple sweetness
Round and 'round, 'round and 'round.*

*You know, life's a lot like maple sugar—
Weak, insipid at the start,
But the fires of time and trouble
Find the sweetness at the heart.*

*What's true of maple sugar
May be true of you and me!
The more we are fired and beaten
The finer-grained we'll be!*
                    —Evelyn R. Cheney (1845)

WASHINGTON'S GINGERBREAD CREAM PIE [2106]

Cream ⅓ cup of butter and 1 cup of old-fashioned molasses together until perfectly blended. Mix 1½ cups of cake flour, ½ teaspoon of soda, 1 teaspoon of baking powder, ½ teaspoon of salt, ¾ teaspoon of ground ginger, 1 teaspoon of ground cinnamon, ¼ teaspoon of ground cloves and sift together in a mixing bowl. Stir ½ cup of flour mixture into molasses mixture. Beat in 1 unbeaten egg; then add the remaining flour mixture, about half at a time, alternately with ½ cup of cold milk. Beat thoroughly with circular strokes. Pour into a generously-buttered and lightly floured 9-inch pie plate. Bake in a moderate oven (350° F.) for about 40 minutes. Remove from the pie plate. Cool. Split layer through center. Spread cream filling (see below) between layers. Sift powdered sugar over top.

Cream Filling. Soak 2 teaspoons of plain granulated gelatin in 2 tablespoons of cold water for 10 minutes. Combine ¼ cup of sugar, 2 tablespoons of cornstarch, and a pinch of salt in top of double boiler. Stir in ¼ cup of cold milk, and when thoroughly blended, add gradually, ¾ cup of scalded rich milk or equal parts of milk and thin cream. Cook over hot water for about 10 minutes, or until just beginning to thicken, stirring constantly. Add 1 large egg, which has been slightly beaten with 1 generous tablespoon of rum, then mixed with ½ cup of finely chopped mixed dried fruits, such as apricots, prunes, apples, pears, and so forth, in equal parts. Cook 2 or 3 minutes longer over hot water, stirring constantly from the bottom of the pan; remove from hot water; stir in gelatin, and cool quickly over cracked ice or ice water, stirring constantly. When firm enough, spread between layers of cold gingerbread and serve.

Golden as a fall sunset,
Light as a fleecy cloud,
Luscious as a sun-kissed berry—
That, my friend, is pie.
                    —Unknown.

APRICOT BOWKNOTS   [2107]
(Makes about 4 dozen small knots)

Dough. Soften 2 yeast cakes in ¼ cup of lukewarm water. Scald 1¼ cups sweet milk, then stir into it ½ cup of butter, ¼ cup of granulated sugar and 1½ teaspoons salt, cool to lukewarm and stir in the softened yeast. Gradually add 2 cups of twice-sifted pastry flour, stirring well, alternately with 2 eggs well-beaten with 2 teaspoons of finely grated lemon rind. When well blended, add 3 more cups (about) of sifted pastry flour, or enough to make a soft dough. Turn onto a lightly floured board and knead until smooth and satiny. Place the dough in a slightly greased pan; cover and set this pan in another pan containing hot (not boiling) water, and let rise until doubled in bulk, or about 1¾ hours. Punch down; cover again and let rest 10 minutes. Roll or pat out the dough under the hand to ½-inch in thickness; cut in pieces about 6 inches long; tie in knots; place on a greased baking sheet, and let rise 15 minutes. With finger tip, press down center of each bowknot; brush with melted butter, and fill hollows with apricot filling. For this put into a mixing bowl 1½ cups of finely chopped cooked, dried apricots, ¼ cup of apricot juice, ½ cup of granulated sugar, 1 tablespoon of unstrained lemon juice, ½ teaspoon of ground cinnamon, ¼ teaspoon of salt and ½ teaspoon of ground cloves. Mix thoroughly.

After filling the bowknots with the apricot filling, let rise in a warm place covered with cheesecloth until doubled in bulk, or about 30 minutes, then bake in a moderate oven (350–375° F.) 15 to 20 minutes. When cool, sprinkle lightly with confectioner's sugar.

BABA AU RHUM   [2108]
Cake with Rum

Sift 2 cups of cake flour with ⅓ teaspoon of salt; make a well in the center and put in 1 yeast cake which has been crumbled into ¼ cup of lukewarm milk; then, using a fork, cover the yeast mixture with a little of the flour and let it stand for 5 or 6 minutes. Now add 4 well beaten eggs, and using a wooden spoon, work all thoroughly together, adding a little more milk if too stiff. Knead for about 5 minutes; cover the bowl and let stand in a warm place for 30 minutes. Then add 6 tablespoons of melted butter, alternately with 1½ tablespoons of sugar, and work for another 4 minutes mixing in ⅔ cup of plumped, and dried seedless raisins. Butter a tube mold; half fill it with the dough, and let rise again until doubled in bulk, or up to the top of the mold. Bake in a moderate oven (350° F.) about 35 to 40 minutes. Remove at once from the oven and cool on a cake rack.

Boil together for 2 or 3 minutes ½ cup of cold water and 1¼ cups of sugar. Add a dash of salt, cool to lukewarm then stir in ½ cup of good rum and pour over the cake.

BLUEBERRY ROLL   [2109]
   (*Sugarless*)

Sift 2 cups of pastry flour once, return to sifter, add ½ generous teaspoon of salt, 1 tablespoon of baking powder and ⅛ teaspoon of powdered ginger, and sift again. Cut in 3 tablespoons of butter or shortening until mixture resembles coarse crumbs. Moisten with ¾ cup of milk. Turn mixture on to a lightly floured board; knead with a few strokes; roll out into an oblong shape about ⅛ inch thick and brush with melted butter. Combine 2 cups of clean, sound, quickly washed and dried blueberries with 1 tablespoon of lemon juice and ¼ cup of light corn syrup; spread on the dough and roll up like a jelly roll, sealing the ends well. Place smooth side up on a buttered baking pan; gash the top in 3 or 4 places, and bake in a hot oven (400° F.) about 25 minutes, or until delicately browned. Serve warm with plain cream, whipped cream, or raspberry or strawberry syrup.

BLUEBERRY TARTS   [2110]

Pile 2 cups washed, drained, dried, and chilled blueberries in 6 pre-baked tart shells (No. 2079). Soften a glass of currant jelly over hot water, and pour it over the berries. Then set the tarts in the refrigerator to chill; as the jelly hardens again, it will glaze the fruit and give it an attractive glossy appearance. Top with whipped cream.

Variation. Any other preferred berries may be substituted for blueberries.

BRANDIED PEACH JALOUSIES   [2111]

Roll out some puff paste (see No. 2076) as thinly as possible; cut in 3½ to 4 inch squares and arrange these on a baking sheet about an inch apart. Place on each square 2 tablespoons of sliced brandied peaches; wet the edges with cold water; cover with another square of puff paste and press gently but firmly to seal. Make a small slash in V-form in center of each square; brush tops with milk or egg yolk slightly beaten with equal amount of cold milk and bake in a hot oven (400° F.) for about 12 minutes, or until tops are delicately browned. Remove from oven, and while still hot, brush tops with liquid apricot marmalade. Cool before serving.

Variation. Any other fresh or preserved fruit may be substituted for the peaches, and a flaky pie crust (see No. 2104) may be used instead of puff paste.

BUTTER TARTS [2112]

Make a pastry, using 2 cups of pastry flour, sifted with ½ teaspoon of salt, ½ teaspoon of baking powder and ½ cup of butter or lard and moistening with ice water. Roll out thin on a floured board, cut into rounds and use to line muffin pans or tart tins.

Cream 2 tablespoons of butter, with 2 large eggs and 2 cups of brown sugar. When well blended and fluffy, add 1 cup of seedless raisins, parboiled until plump, then drained well dried and mixed with 1 cup of chopped nut meats. Fill the pastry lined pans with the mixture and bake in a slow oven (300° F.) until brown, about 20 minutes. Chill and serve topped with whipped cream.

CANNELONS PARISIENS [2113]

Cut strips of pastry, preferably puff paste (see Nos. 2076-77–79), about 16 inches long and 1 inch wide.

Wrap the strips closely and evenly around short thick sticks, which must be previously buttered and floured, and brush them over with beaten egg. Bake in a moderately hot oven (350° F.) until slightly browned. Take out the sticks, cool the pastry, and when quite cold, fill the cannelons with sweetened whipped cream, fruit, jam or jelly.

CINNAMON APPLE ROLY POLY PINWHEELS [2114]

Prepare a standard biscuit dough, flavoring it with ½ teaspoon of vanilla. Roll out as thinly as possible; spread with a little melted butter, then with 1½ cups of pared, cored diced apple mixed with 1½ cups of seedless raisins, previously plumped in boiling water then drained and dried, 1 teaspoon of powdered cinnamon and ¼ cup of granulated sugar. Roll up as for jelly roll; cut in 2-inch slices, place these on a greased baking sheet or in a shallow baking pan, pour in a scant ¾ cup of hot water, and bake 25 to 30 minutes in a hot oven (400° F.). Serve with unflavored and unsweetened whipped cream.

DATE TARTLETS [2115]

Rinse quickly, then drain and dry 2 cups of pitted dried dates; chop, then mix them with 2 teaspoons of grated lemon rind, 3 tablespoons of lemon juice, and 3 tablespoons of sugar dissolved in 2 tablespoons of rich, cold milk. When well blended, fill 6 individual unbaked tartlet shells (No. 2079); sprinkle tops with a little flour and dot with butter. Bake in a hot oven (400° F.) for 20 to 25 minutes. Cool, then top each tartlet with sweetened whipped cream.

FIG TARTLETS [2116]

Wash quickly ½ pound of dried figs. Drain and dry them, then cut off any stems. Place the figs in a saucepan, cover with boiling water, and simmer for 25 to 30 minutes. Drain, reserving the liquid; chop the figs, and boil down the fig juice to half its original volume; then add to it 2 tablespoons of sugar, 1 tablespoon of grated orange rind, and ½ teaspoon of grated lemon rind. Cool and when quite cold, fill 6 unbaked tartlet shells (No. 2079) and bake in a hot oven (400° F.) 20 minutes. Serve cold topped with whipped cream.

FROSTED APPLE DUMPLINGS or [2117] TURNOVERS

A dessert that is a favorite with almost everyone is the old-fashioned frosted apple dumpling. The trick in getting these dumplings to look just right is to roll the pastry square large enough to wrap around the apple without stretching the pastry. Moisten the edges of the pastry with water, so that they will cling together tightly when pressed around the apples. Basted with syrup while cooking, these dumplings are rich and juicy. Frost them while hot with a mixture of ½ cup of powdered sugar and 1½ tablespoons of cold water.

Make pastry as for pie (No. 2104), roll it out thinly into a large rectangle ⅛-inch thick and cut into six 6-inch squares.

Wash, peel and core (do not slice) 6 medium-sized cooking apples; place one in the center of each pastry square; fill center of each apple with brown sugar, and dot with a little butter or margarin, then sprinkle with cinnamon mixed with an equal amount of freshly grated nutmeg.

Bring the opposite corners of pastry square together over the top of the apple; moisten edges with cold water and seal; repeat with other corners. Prick pastry well with the tines of a fork; place in a baking pan or dish, and bake 15 minutes in a hot oven (425° F.), then lower the temperature to moderate heat (350° F.) and continue baking while basting with the following syrup:

Syrup. Combine 1 cup of sugar or corn syrup with ½ cup of cold water and 2 tablespoons of butter. Bake the apples 45 minutes altogether and baste with syrup every 10 or 15 minutes. When done, frost with powdered sugar and water as indicated above.

HONEY BRAN NUT KUCHEN [2118]

Sift ¾ cup of cake flour once; return to sifter, add 2½ teaspoons of baking powder and ⅓ teaspoon of salt, and sift again. Stir in ½ cup of rich, cold milk combined with 4 tablespoons of honey and 1 well beaten egg, alternately with 3 tablespoons of melted butter or margarin, mixing only to dampen the flour. Fold in 1½ cups of cereal bran flakes. Turn into a buttered 8 × 8 × 2 pan and top with the following mixture:

Combine in a saucepan 2 tablespoons of melted butter, 3 tablespoons of honey, ⅛ teaspoon of salt and ½ teaspoon of powdered cinnamon; mix thoroughly, then stir in ½ cup of chopped nut meats and cook and stir over a very gentle flame until mixture bubbles. Cool slightly; add 1 cup of bran flakes, mix lightly, and sprinkle over the top of batter, pressing the topping lightly into the batter. Bake in a moderate oven (375° F.) about 30 minutes. Serve warm or cold.

ICE CREAM TARTLETS [2119]

Bake 6 individual tartlet shells in the usual way (No. 2079). Cool, then place in each 1 generous tablespoon of canned, drained, crushed pineapple; fill up the shells with a scoop of any preferred ice cream; top with whipped cream forced through a pastry bag, and sprinkle blanched, toasted, chopped or shredded almonds over all.

A New York law, still on the statutes, states that no domestic animals except cats are to be allowed to remain in any pastry or bakery shops.

MADELEINES [2120]
(*Makes 2 dozen*)

Beat 4 egg yolks until light and fluffy; gradually add ¾ cup of sugar, and continue creaming and beating till sugar is dissolved. Now beat in 4 whole eggs, one at a time, beating briskly after each addition and adding with the last egg ½ teaspoon each of vanilla and almond extracts. Now, use a wire whip, beating steadily for 5 minutes or until mixture is very creamy. Then add gradually and gently 1 cup of sifted pastry flour with ¼ teaspoon of salt, alternately with 8 tablespoons of melted, lukewarm butter. Mix thoroughly. Butter some madeleine molds generously; fill them ⅔ full; place the filled molds on a baking sheet and bake in a moderate oven (350° F.) about 20 minutes, or until a nice golden color.

PARISIAN RASPBERRY TART [2121]
Tarte aux Framboises à la Parisienne

Combine 4 cups sifted flour, 3½ cups sifted powdered sugar, 1 pound blanched almonds, ground twice, using the finest blade of the chopper, 1 teaspoon ground cinnamon, 1 teaspoon baking powder, ¾ teaspoon salt and ½ teaspoon ground cloves. Cut 1 pound of butter into the mixture, until it is of the consistency of corn meal. Stir in with a wooden spoon 2 large whole eggs and 1 extra egg yolk, all slightly beaten. The resulting dough should be quite firm. Roll it out on a lightly floured board to a scant ¼-inch in thickness, and place in a large buttered tin. Spread over this uncooked shell raspberry jam flavored with a little Kirsch, and cut strips of dough to be placed criss-cross over the jam and around the edges. Brush the tart with a lightly beaten egg yolk, and bake in a moderate oven (375° F.) for 15 to 18 minutes or until the tart is a golden brown. Cool, then store in a cool, dry place. As the tart shell cools, it becomes very hard; but after it has been stored a while, it softens into a mellow, delicious dessert.

PROFITEROLLES AU CHOCOLAT [2122]
Little Puff Cakes with Chocolate Sauce

First Operation. (Pâte à Choux, or Puffed Paste) Combine and bring to a boil 1 cup of cold water, ½ cup of sweet butter, ¼ teaspoon of salt, and 1 teaspoon of sugar. When mixture boils violently, remove from the fire and add 1 cup of flour all at once and mix well. Return the pan to the fire and stir until the paste follows the spoon, or about 2 to 3 minutes. Remove from the fire, and add 5 eggs, one at a time, beating briskly and thoroughly after each addition. The paste should be smooth and shiny. Flavor with ⅛ teaspoon of orange flower water, or almond extract. Fill a pastry bag using a large plain tube and press small portions (the size of a walnut) on to a buttered baking sheet; brush the surface of each with a little cold milk or beaten egg yolk, and bake in a moderate oven (350° F.) for 12 to 15 minutes, or till the little mounds are well puffed. Remove from the oven and cool.

Filling: Crème Patissiere. Scald 1 cup of rich, sweet milk in top of double boiler; stir in ½ teaspoon of vanilla. Meanwhile combine and mix well ½ cup of pastry flour sifted with ⅛ teaspoon of salt, and a scant ½ cup of granulated sugar; stir this gradually into the hot milk, beating briskly and constantly until very smooth. Then add 3 egg yolks, one at a time, beating well after each addition, till mixture is shiny and smooth. Place over direct gentle flame and cook, stirring constantly, until mixture thickens and is smooth, and firm yet creamy.

The chocolate sauce. Break 5 squares of sweetened chocolate in a saucepan; add 1 teaspoon of sugar and ¾ cup of cold water. Cook, over direct flame stirring frequently, till sauce thickens, and is smooth.

Finale. Make a slit in each puff; fill with the cream filling; arrange on a cold dish or tray, and pour a little of the hot chocolate sauce over, almost entirely covering each puff. Cool before serving.

RED CURRANT STRIPS   [2123]
(*Makes 6 strips*)

Sift 1 cup of pastry flour once, measure, add ⅛ teaspoon salt and 4 tablespoons of fine powdered sugar and sift again into a mixing bowl. Cut in ½ cup of butter, creamed with 1 egg yolk and knead lightly to a smooth dough. Wrap in a damp cloth, and chill in refrigerator for ¾ of an hour; then pat and roll out to a scant ½-inch thick. Bake in a moderate oven (350° F.) for 25 minutes, or until done. Cool. Spread with sweet thick cream; cover the cream with 1 generous cup of fresh red currants, stemmed, washed and dried between towels, then top each strip with a meringue made of 2 egg whites stiffly beaten with a few grains of salt and a half teaspoon of grated orange rind, and sweetened with 4 tablespoons of sugar. Return to a very moderate oven (325° F.) and bake until meringue is delicately browned. Cool but do not chill. Serve for dessert or with afternoon tea or coffee.

ROTTERDAM ALMOND ROLLS or BANKET   [2124]

Cream 1 cup of butter or margarin until light; gradually add 2 cups of sifted pastry flour, and cut with pastry blender or two knives, till mixture looks like pebbles. Still using pastry blender or a fork, add from 4 to 6 tablespoons of ice water, sprinkling a little at a time over the flour-butter mixture. Roll out ⅛ of an inch thick.

Combine 2 cups of almond paste with 1 egg, which has been beaten previously with ¼ teaspoon of salt, 9 tablespoons of granulated sugar and ¼ teaspoon of lemon extract, mixing thoroughly. Form into three rolls each about 10 inches long by one inch thick. Roll each in a portion of the pastry; moisten ends and edges with water and seal. Bake in a hot oven (450° F.) for 25–30 minutes. When cold cut into slices ⅜ inch thick.

RUM PECAN TART FILLING   [2125]

Have ready 12 unbaked tart shells (No. 2079). Boil 1 cup brown sugar with ½ cup hot water for about 5 minutes or until the mixture has become a medium thick syrup; set aside to cool. Beat slightly 2 whole eggs in the top of a double boiler. Add 2½ tablespoons of flour which has been sifted with ⅛ teaspoon salt, and 1 cup of scalded rich milk. Set over hot water, and cook, stirring constantly, until the mixture is smooth and thick, about 15 minutes. Remove from the heat and stir in 2 tablespoons butter and half the brown sugar syrup, 1 teaspoon vanilla and 1 generous tablespoon good rum. Divide this filling among the tart shells; top each with ½ dozen pecan halves, pour the remaining syrup over the nuts, and bake the tarts in a very hot oven (450° F.) until they are delicately browned, about 12 to 15 minutes. Cool and decorate with whipped cream piped through a pastry bag using a fancy tube.

If desired use a meringue topping instead of the whipped cream. There are a number of other toppings, all tempting, all with eye-appeal: apricot cream topping, for example, or honey topping, or berry topping. Like the icing on a cake, topping is one of the most important parts of the tart.

SAVARIN GLACÉ AUX FRUITS MACÉRÉS   [2126]
Savarin with Vanilla Ice Cream with Marinated Fruits

Purchase a layer sponge cake and form it into a ring by pressing a ring mould down over it. Place on the serving platter on which it is to be served; and soak it with a light, rum-flavored sugar syrup.

Just before serving, pile the center high with vanilla ice cream covering this, in turn, with a mixture of fresh fruits in season, as berries or peaches or apricots cubed small and marinated in kirsch liqueur, then well drained.

Garnish with tufts of whipped cream forced through a pastry bag, using a rose tube.

SCHAUM TORTE   [2127]

Beat 6 egg whites with a wire whisk until stiff, then beat in 2 cups of sugar, ¼ cup at a time, adding with the last ¼ cup ¼ teaspoon of salt and beating thoroughly after each addition. Then beat in 1 teaspoon of vanilla mixed with 1 teaspoon of good white wine vinegar. Pour ⅔ of mixture into a buttered spring form; make small kisses dropped from the tip of a teaspoon with the rest of the mixture in the form of a circle on a tin, having this circle the same size and shape as the spring form. Bake 1 hour or longer in a very slow oven (275° F.). Cool and fill with whipped cream and strawberries.

SPICED PECAN MOLASSES TARTLETS   [2128]

Line 6 fluted individual tartlet molds with rich pastry and crimp the top into a rim. Cream ¼ cup of butter until light and fluffy; gradually add ¼ cup of brown sugar, alternately with 2 beaten egg yolks. Mix well ¼ cup of light molasses with ¼ cup of rich milk or thin cream, and add gradually to the first mixture, alternately with 1⅛ cups of pastry flour, sifted once, mixed with ¼ teaspoon of soda, ¼ teaspoon of ground cloves, ⅛ generous teaspoon of freshly grated nutmeg, and a very few grains of cayenne pepper, then mixed with ½ generous teaspoon of finely grated lemon rind. Half fill the pastry-lined molds with the mixture, top with 1 generous tablespoon of chopped nut meats, and bake in a hot oven (450° F.) for 8 minutes; then reduce the temperature to moderate (350° F.) and continue baking 15 minutes longer. Cool before serving.

From Pastry Cook to Prime Minister. Peter the Great wandering about Moscow saw a man hawking pies and cakes. Afterward this man became a pastry cook. Peter sought him out and made him his prime minister. As Prince Menshkoff he wielded tremendous power and became the richest subject in Europe.

TARTE AU CHOCOLAT AMANDINE [2129]
Chocolate Torte with Almonds

Line a pie plate with flaky pastry. Beat 5 egg yolks until light; gradually beat in ½ cup of sugar, alternately with ¼ cup of blanched, shredded, toasted and cooled almonds, mixing thoroughly. Beat 5 egg whites stiffly with a few grains of salt; gradually beat in ⅔ cup of cocoa, adding about 3 tablespoons at a time and beating well after each addition; then fold the egg white and cocoa mixture into the first mixture, blending well; turn into the prepared unbaked pastry shell, spreading evenly, and bake in a moderate oven (350° F.) for 25 to 30 minutes, or until crust is done and top nicely browned. Cool before serving.

TARTE A LA FERLUCHE [2130]
Raisin and Nut Tart

This delicious tart was originated during the days of the French régime in Canada, when trading with the Antilles was popular. Boil together 2 cups molasses, 1 cup water, 1 cup seeded raisins, and 1 cup brown sugar. Thicken with 6 tablespoons flour moistened with cold water to a smooth paste. Boil over a medium flame for 15 minutes to cook the flour, stirring constantly until the mixture is smooth and thick. Pour into pre-baked pastry tart shells (No. 2079), cool, and cover with chopped nuts (any kind except peanuts), or sprinkle with nutmeg. If a more elaborate tart is desired, add decoration with a border of whipped cream.

Quality is never born of haste or expediency.

VANOCKA   [2131]
Bohemian Christmas Twist

Work ½ cup of sweet butter into 4 cups of sifted pastry flour as for pie crust; add ½ cup of sugar, mixed with ⅓ teaspoon of salt and 1 teaspoon of grated lemon rind. Mix 1 crumbled yeast cake with 2 tablespoons of flour, 1 tablespoon of sugar and 3 tablespoons of ice-cold milk. Let stand until bubbling, and foamy, then add to flour mixture with 2 egg yolks beaten with 1 cup of cold, rich sweet milk. Knead the dough on a bread board for at least 20 minutes, the longer the better, adding while kneading ⅓ cup of seedless raisins, chopped fine, mixed with ¼ cup of blanched, finely chopped almonds, and 2½ tablespoons of finely chopped citron. When thoroughly blended, put the dough in a greased pan; cover, and let rise 2 hours in a warm place. Divide into nine parts; roll each into a strand about 14 inches long; make a braid with four of the pieces and put this first braid on a baking pan, covered with a sheet of greased paper. On this braid put another braid made with 3 pieces and finally the last one, using the two remaining pieces of dough. Brush with slightly beaten egg; let rise 1½ hours, in a warm place, covered with a light, clean cloth; brush again with slightly beaten egg and sprinkle the top with ⅓ cup of chopped nuts or almonds. Bake in a moderate oven (350° F.) about 1½ hours. Cool before slicing.

Chapter Seventeen

CANDY

Good living is an act of our judgment by which we grant a preference to those things which are agreeable to the taste above those that have not that quality.

—*Brillat-Savarin.*

CANDY

GIFT, DECORATION, FOOD—ALL THESE AT ONCE IS CANDY. A year-round favorite, it really comes into its own at Christmas, when it seems to be everywhere. It is the sweet that has tempted men and women since the days of ancient Egypt, since the glory of the Nile and the scarab. The Egyptians, of course, didn't use sugar for sugar refining was not yet known.

Nor was sugar itself to be known until about the third or the fourth century, when, according to legend, a cattle raiser of India discovered it accidentally, as a native of Africa had discovered butter. Neither of these was to realize the importance of his gift to men, and both were to disappear anonymously into that vast and strangely moving shade we call history. But before this, Indians, Africans and Egyptians had developed a taste for sweets which they satisfied with sweet herbs and condiments and honey.

And with these they continued to satisfy themselves, in the mass, through most of the centuries till now. They could do little else, for sugar was no common food, nothing to be idly eaten as a passing pleasure, to be squandered as a fancy for the tongue. As late as the seventeenth century, sugar was sold only through medical prescriptions, and reached a price equivalent to about $300 a pound. But even for that fabulous sum, the sugar was inferior in quality to any of the standard grades that we have today. And $300 worth of modern, highly refined sugar would last a whole family for years.

We need sugar, of course; we must have it, whether we get it concealed within the outward forms of other foods, or as white granules of sweetness, or temptingly prepared, as candy. We need sugar so badly that we in America consume every year from ten to twelve million tons of it—more than any other country. Perhaps we need more because we are an active energetic people, and the caloric value of sugar is high.

Probably because they are so active, children crave candy; and they should have it—in reasonable amounts, of course. But a good deal of the fun in candy for children—as well as for those many years beyond that class—is the making of it. There is a ritual to it, an anticipatory lingering, a fragrance sweet, delicious, pervading. And in the finished product there is not only pleasure, but the mark of a good cook.

Candy, however, cannot be just whipped up from any handy ingredients, cooked, and turned out on a plate to cool. Fine candy is no different from other fine foods in its demands for the best ingredients and the most careful preparation. Follow faithfully the directions in candy recipes—but don't always make the same types of candy. There is room for variety here as well as elsewhere. Learn the simple little tricks, such as tinting the candy with food colorings, and decorating the individual pieces with shredded coconut or nuts, or with a glaze.

CANDY TEMPERATURE CHART [2133]

Kind of Product	TEMPERATURE		STAGE	Reaction at stage attained
	Degrees Fahrenheit	Degrees Centigrade		
Syrup	230° to 234°	110° to 112°	Thread	The syrup spins a two-inch thread when dropped from a spoon.
Fondant Fudge Penuche	234° to 240°	112° to 115°	Soft ball	The syrup when dropped into very cold water forms a soft ball which flattens on removal.
Caramels	244° to 248°	118° to 120°	Firm ball	The syrup when dropped into very cold water forms a firm ball which does not flatten on removal.
Divinity Marshmallows Nougat Popcorn balls Salt water taffy	250° to 265°	121° to 130°	Hard ball	The syrup when dropped into very cold water forms a ball which is hard enough to hold its shape, yet plastic.
Butterscotch Taffies	270° to 290°	132° to 143°	Soft crack	The syrup when dropped into very cold water separates into threads which are hard but not brittle.
Brittle Glacé	300° to 310°	149° to 154°	Hard crack	The syrup when dropped into very cold water separates into threads which are hard and brittle.
Barley Sugar	320°	160°	Clear liquid	The sugar liquefies.
Caramel	338°	170°	Brown liquid	The liquid becomes brown.

ALGERIAN DATE CHEW [2134]

Split plump dates and remove the pits but do not separate the dates. Chop freshly toasted walnuts and almonds in equal parts and mix with just enough orange marmalade to make them adhere. Fill the dates neatly, roll in vanilla sugar and store between layers of wax paper in a tightly closed tin can. Keep in a dry, cool place.

ALMOND BRITTLE SQUARES [2135]

Place in a saucepan ½ cup of water and 2 cups of sugar with ⅛ teaspoon of salt and stir till sugar is dissolved. Cook without further stirring to the hard-crack stage (310° F.); remove from the fire and stir in 1 teaspoon of lemon extract or ½ teaspoon each of almond and lemon extracts. Sprinkle 2 cups of blanched and split almonds in a buttered tin and pour the boiling syrup over them. When cool mark into small squares with a sharp knife and break apart when cold. Store in an airtight container in a cool, dry place.

ALMOND CHOCOLATE PRALINE SQUARES [2136] FRENCH STYLE

Blanch, then toast ¼ pound of almonds until slightly toasted or browned. Put ½ pound of confectioner's sugar in a copper sugar boiler (not enameled, nor aluminum) without water and cook over a very gentle flame until lightly browned, stirring constantly with a wooden spoon; then stir in the prepared almonds, and when well blended, pour the whole on to an oiled marble slab or platter, spreading well. When cold, pound to a powder, or break into small pieces, put them through a food chopper three or four times, then rub through a fine-mesh wire sieve, and mix with sufficient chocolate, dissolved with as little warm water as possible to form a paste. Turn on to a cold platter or tin, spreading well. When cold, cut into small squares and dip each into melted dipping chocolate, placing each square on wax paper to set and dry. Store between layers of wax paper in an airtight container, and keep in a cool, dry place.

ALMOND KISSES I FRENCH BROWN STYLE [2137]

Blanch, chop and toast ⅔ cup of almonds. Combine in an enameled saucepan 1 pound of brown sugar, with 4 ounces of glucose, ⅛ teaspoon salt, 2 tablespoons butter and ½ cup of hot water, and cook to the firm ball stage (244–248° F.). Remove from the fire, and press the syrup against the sides of the pan by means of a wooden spoon, to give the candy a grained appearance. As soon as it becomes cloudy, stir in the prepared almonds, and when sufficiently firm, using a teaspoon, pile in small portions on an oiled marble slab. Let dry for about 25 minutes, then store between layers of wax paper in an airtight container, in a cool, dry place.

ALMOND KISSES II FRENCH WHITE STYLE [2138]

Proceed as indicated for Almond Kisses I (No. 2137) French Brown Style substituting white sugar for brown, and flavoring the syrup with ¼ teaspoon of vanilla extract, mixed with ⅓ teaspoon of almond extract.

BARLEY SUGAR TWIST I [2139]

Dissolve 2 pounds of sugar in 1 pint of cold water, and cook to the soft ball stage (234–240° F.). Stir in ½ teaspoon of strained lemon juice, and continue cooking to the hard crack stage (300° to 310° F.), then color with a few drops of yellow vegetable coloring. Remove from the fire, stir in a generous ½ teaspoon of lemon extract, and pour on to an oiled marble slab. When almost cold, cut into narrow strips of about 6 inches long and ½ inch wide; twist each strip into spiral form, and when quite cold, store in an airtight container.

BARLEY SUGAR TWIST II [2140]

Cook 1 pint of clarified sugar syrup (No 2150) to the hard crack stage, (300° to 310° F.). Stir in 1 teaspoon of strained lemon juice and 5 or 6 drops of lemon extract, then boil again until syrup just begins to attain a little color. Immediately stir in a tiny pinch of powdered saffron and pour at once on to an oiled marble slab. When almost cold, cut into pieces about 6 inches long and 1 scant inch wide, and twist them. Store in an airtight container.

Saffron is the dried stigma of the crocus; the most popular spice in the Mediterranean region, but the taste for it has to be acquired. It gives a beautiful orange-yellow color. Saffron is used in curry powder; the famous Bouillabaisse Marseillaise is flavored with it, as is Spanish rice.

BLACK WALNUT CRUNCHES [2141]

Place 6 cups of granulated sugar in a saucepan, add 1 tablespoon of butter, 2 tablespoons of molasses, ½ cup of cider vinegar, 2 cups of cold water and ¼ teaspoon of salt. Cook to the softcrack stage (290° F.), then stir very briskly for about half a minute, quickly stirring in 3 cups of finely ground black walnuts, 1 teaspoon of almond extract and ¾ teaspoon of orange extract. Turn into a buttered tin and when quite cold break into small pieces. Keep in a tightly closed tin, in a cool, dry place to prevent stickiness.

BRAZIL NUGGETS [2142]

Place ¼ cup each of thinly sliced Brazil nuts, seedless raisins which have been parboiled till plump, then drained and well dried, finely chopped figs, and shredded coconut in a generously buttered pan, spreading and mixing well. Place 2 cups of granulated sugar, 2 tablespoons of butter, ⅛ teaspoon of salt, ¼ cup of cider vinegar and ¼ cup of cold water in a saucepan and cook to the soft crack stage (290°F.). Add 1 teaspoon of lemon extract, or ½ teaspoon of mixed almond and lemon extracts, stirring well, and pour very carefully over the fruit and nut mixture. When quite cold, break in small pieces and store in an airtight container in a cool, dry place.

BURNT ALMONDS FRENCH STYLE [2143]

Blanch 1 pound of almonds and dry them thoroughly in a very slow oven (250° F.) leaving the oven door open. Put 1 pound of sugar, ¼ teaspoon salt and ¾ cup of cold water in a saucepan; stir until sugar is dissolved; bring to rolling boil, and when boiling fast, stir in the prepared almonds. Immediately lower the flame and cook very gently until almonds make a slight crackling noise. At once remove the pan from the fire and stir until syrup granulates, then turn the whole into a coarse enameled sieve, and stir in ¾ cup of hot water into which has been stirred ¾ pound of sugar. Let boil to the soft ball stage (234–240° F.). Now add the almonds, which should be lukewarm, and stir until well coated with the syrup. At the first inclination they show of sticking together, remove the pan from the fire and place them in the coarse sieve as before. The second coating of syrup is frequently colored and flavored according to taste. Store between layers of wax paper in an airtight container, in a cool, dry place.

CANDIED MINT LEAVES [2144

To candy mint leaves at home, select large, perfect mint leaves, wash and let drain until dry; then brush each leaf with slightly beaten egg white, sprinkle with granulated sugar and dry in a very slow oven (250° F.) having the door open. Store in a tin between layers of waxed paper and keep in a cool, dry place.

CHOCOLATE ALMONDS FRENCH STYLE [2145]

Blanch as many almonds as desired; dry them in a slow oven (250°F.) leaving the oven door open. When cold, dip each separately into melted dipping chocolate (No. 2153) placing them, as dipped, on an oiled marble slab or platter to set.

If desired, the almonds may be toasted and cooled before dipping. Or they may be dipped first into glacé sirup, then into dipping chocolate

CHOCOLATE FONDANT [2146]

This can be made by adding two squares of melted chocolate and 1 teaspoon vanilla to each pound of the white fondant. Both chocolate and vanilla are added while the lukewarm fondant is being beaten.

In reworking the fondant at a later date, warm the amount needed in a saucepan, and add whatever color or flavor is desired, stirring constantly with a wooden spoon, If, after warming, the fondant is too thick— it should be of the consistency of heavy cream—add a little sugar syrup. Since the fondant must never simmer or boil, the safest method of warming it is by putting it in the top of a double boiler, over hot (not boiling) water.

Note. Coloring and flavoring the fondant simply consists of adding the color desired—pink, violet, green or whatever is desired—and the flavor—peppermint, almond, vanilla, Crème de Noyau, Crème de Cacao, brandy, or any other preferred. The fondant must be lukewarm, and should be kneaded thoroughly after color and flavor are added. When the fondant has cooled, break it into pieces the size of a walnut, and shape it with the fingers into whatever form is desired. If you are using molds, pour the melted fondant into a pastry bag, and force it into the molds. A novel effect can be gained by filling the molds with two or three different colors and flavors, one above the other.

CHOCOLATE FUDGE SQUARES [2147]

Place 1 cup of brown sugar, 1 cup of granulated sugar, ¾ cup of sweet cold milk and 2 tablespoons of light corn syrup in a saucepan. Blend thoroughly, then stir in 2 squares (2 ounces) of unsweetened chocolate, mixing well. Place over a low flame and cook slowly, stirring constantly, until mixture boils; continue cooking, stirring occasionally, until mixture is at the soft-ball stage (236° F.); remove from the fire, stir in 3 tablespoons of butter or margarin and ⅛ teaspoon of salt. Cool to lukewarm (110° F.); stir in 1 teaspoon of vanilla and beat briskly until mixture thickens. Pour on to buttered or oiled platter or marble slab; cool, and when quite cold cut into small squares.

CHOCOLATE MARBLED FUDGE BARS [2148]

Follow recipe for Vanilla Fudge Squares (No. 2174), pour half of it into a buttered platter or marble slab. Sprinkle with ½ cup of chopped semi-sweet chocolate; cover with remaining fudge; top with additional chopped semi-sweet chocolate; cool and when quite cold cut in small bars.

CHOCOLATE MILK CARAMÉLS [2149]

Follow recipe for Milk Caramels (No. 2169), adding 4 squares of chocolate, shaved or cut small, to the mixture at the beginning of the cooking process.

CLARIFIED SUGAR SYRUP [2150]

Put into an enameled saucepan 3 pounds of sugar, ⅛ of a teaspoon of cream of tartar, 1 quart of cold water, 1 well-beaten egg white with the crushed shell, and ⅛ to ¼ teaspoon of salt. Stir until sugar is dissolved, and mixture thoroughly blended, using a rotary beater. Cook until reduced to a medium syrup, skimming well, then strain through a jelly-bag or fine muslin cloth, and when cold, bottle, cork and store until required. (Appropriate for water ices, preserves and candies.)

COCONUT FONDANT BALLS [2151]

Work into 1 cup of vanilla fondant (No. 2154) as much chopped, shredded coconut as possible without its becoming too stiff to mold. Roll into small balls, set aside to dry, then dip in melted fondant. Roll in chopped coconut before fondant coating becomes firm.

CREAM KISSES [2152]

Place 3 cups of sugar, 1 cup of cold water, 1 teaspoon of cider vinegar and ⅛ teaspoon of salt in a saucepan and stir until sugar is dissolved. Bring to boiling point and at once stir in ⅛ teaspoon of cream of tartar. Cook to the soft ball stage (240° F.), then very slowly pour in 1 cup of sweet, heavy, scalded cream and cook to the hard ball stage (254° F.). Pour at once into a generously buttered shallow pan, and when cool, add 1 teaspoon of vanilla extract mixed with ½ teaspoon of lemon extract, then pull until quite white. Cut into small cushions with scissors, and when cold, dip in melted dipping chocolate.

DIPPING CHOCOLATE [2153]

Melt at least 1 pound of dipping chocolate over warm, (not hot) water. Stir constantly until melted. Remove from heat and cool until almost cold. With a two-tined fork, or a regular chocolate dipping wire, dip the bonbons, almonds, nut meats, or patties or wafers into the chocolate quickly. Invert on boards (or a table) covered tightly with oil-cloth or with waxed paper. If the chocolate becomes too thick to be handled easily remelt over warm water.

FONDANT [2154]

Heat slowly in a large saucepan 6 cups granulated sugar and 2 cups cold water. Stir steadily only until the sugar is completely dissolved, then stop the stirring entirely. With a small brush moistened with water, or with a fork wrapped in a damp cloth, wash the inside of the pan down to the syrup's edge. Boil the syrup up once, and add either 1 tablespoon glucose or a pinch of cream of tartar. Still without stirring, continue to cook the syrup until the candy thermometer registers 240° F., or until a few drops tested in cold water form a soft ball. At that point remove the syrup immediately from the fire, and allow it to settle for 4 or 5 minutes, until the air bubbles have ceased rising. Pour the mixture on to a large wet platter to a thickness of 1½ inches, and set in a cool place. When its temperature has dropped to lukewarm, about 110° F., beat briskly with a wooden spoon.

Now work the mixture around, missing no part of it, until it becomes white. Then knead until perfectly smooth. Let the fondant stand for an hour covered with a towel which has been wrung out of cold water. At the end of this mellowing process, remove the towel, and knead the fondant again, so that it becomes creamy and smooth. Place it immediately in an airtight container until needed since air dries out fondant.

FONDANT—HINTS [2155]

Fondant is a creamy, smooth confection made of sugar, water and some acid substance such as glucose, cream of tartar, corn syrup or lemon juice. Its uses far surpass those of other candies because fondant not only forms the base of many delightful sweets, but is also used for coating nuts, fruits and other confections.

Because there are certain important rules involved in fondant making, all simple when they are understood, the standard recipe is given in much detail, with a list of hints.

Every particle of sugar should be melted before the syrup is allowed to boil. If this precaution is not taken and the sugar, being only partly dissolved, is allowed to boil, these crystals will not dissolve readily and will cause the syrup to grain.

The glucose or cream of tartar is used to prevent too rapid crystallization of the sugar and should be added after the sugar is dissolved.

Do not stir or *move* the pan after the mixture boils, or the syrup will become sugary.

Allow the syrup to "settle" before creaming the mass.

Add the desired coloring and flavoring to the lukewarm fondant at the beginning of the beating period, if desiring one flavor and color for the entire batch; otherwise, add the coloring and flavoring extract, liqueur, cordial, etcetera, to the fondant as it is used in various candies.

Allow the fondant to "ripen" for one hour before using it to make bonbons or candies.

Fondant used for coating confections should be melted in top of double boiler and over hot, not boiling water. It must be stirred gently but constantly.

The usual colors used in fondant are: white, pink, green, red and yellow.

The usual flavorings used in fondants are: peppermint, vanilla, wintergreen, spearmint, almond, lime, cinnamon, clove, or cordials, liqueurs, etc.

SHAPING FONDANT FOR MAKING BONBONS I [2156]

Take any quantity of fondant. Add any desired flavor, and color with vegetable coloring to the desired tint, then knead thoroughly until well blended. Break off small pieces of the fondant and shape or cut into balls, cubes, strips, patties, diamonds, or odd shapes, and let stand for several hours to dry. Chopped nuts and candied or crystallized fruits may be added to the fondant before it is shaped.

SHAPING BONBONS IN STARCH II [2157]

This is the process of shaping the bonbons with the aid of small molds. Fill a square wooden tray with fine, dry cornstarch, leveling it off even at the top. Press the molds into the starch as close together as possible. Now, warm a quantity of fondant in a saucepan over hot water or in top of double boilers and color and flavor to taste, stirring constantly with a wooden spoon. If too thick, a little stock syrup can be added while the fondant is hot; then fill the impressions made in the starch and let stand until cold. When quite cold, remove the fondants and brush them, removing all starch carefully.

ANOTHER METHOD OF SHAPING BONBONS III [2158

Another popular method of shaping fondant bonbons is to melt the fondant and run it into rubber mats (commercial). Prepare the fondant by warming a quantity in a small saucepan placed in a shallow pan of boiling water or in the top of a double boiler. Stir with a wooden spoon until it melts to the consistency of thick cream. If too firm to run smooth readily, reduce the consistency by adding a few drops of hot water or stock syrup. The fondant must not simmer or boil. When melted, pour into the rubber mat direct or through a paper icing bag. The impressions can be half-filled with one color, then filled up with another color.

LOLLYPOPS [2159]

Mix 1 cup of granulated sugar, ⅓ cup of light corn syrup, ⅔ cup of cold water and ⅛ teaspoon of salt, and stir till thoroughly blended. Cook over a low flame, stirring until mixture just begins to boil, then continue boiling without stirring until a few drops tested in cold water are very brittle (310° F. or hard crack stage). Be sure to wash away all crystals from sides of the pan with a damp cloth. Remove from the fire, stir in 6 or 8 drops of oil of peppermint, and a few drops of vegetable coloring.

Drop the syrup quickly from the tip of a tablespoon onto a flat, greased surface; press one end of a wooden skewer into edge of each lollypop, and when firm but still warm, loosen from surface to prevent cracking.

MAPLE FONDANT [2160]
(*Using maple sugar instead of granulated sugar*)

This fondant is cooked and tested in the same way as for Fondant (No. 2154), but usually requires longer beating to make it creamy. It makes delicious centers, which must be allowed to dry well before they are crystallized, dipped in melted fondant or melted chocolate.

MAPLE NUT FONDANT CREAMS [2161]

Pour melted maple fondant to the depth of an inch into a shallow buttered pan; cover with a layer of chopped nuts or chopped dried or candied fruits, or a mixture of the two and top with a layer of colored fondant. When cool, mark off into squares with a wet knife and break or cut apart when cold.

MARASCHINO BONBONS FONDANT [2162]
PARISIEN

Soak ¼ pound of gum arabic overnight in 1 cup of dry white wine. Then melt, and strain through a fine cloth or jelly-bag; stir in 1 cup of maraschino liqueur and enough confectioner's sugar to make a mass stiff enough to roll into balls the size of a large marble. Press half of a candied cherry into each ball. Dry on waxed paper. Then dip each ball into melted fondant or melted chocolate and set aside to dry thoroughly.

MARZIPAN I [2163]
(*Uncooked*)

Sift together ½ cup of confectioner's sugar and ½ cup of fine granulated sugar; add 2 cups of blanched, twice ground almonds alternately with 2 egg whites stiffly beaten with ¼ teaspoon of salt, blending well after each addition, and adding about ¾ teaspoon of any desired flavoring extract, a few drops of vegetable coloring to give the desired tint. Knead until smooth. If necessary, add a little more sugar to form a stiff paste. Allow mixture to stand for a few hours, then press small pieces of it into molds, or make into dainty shapes; or roll out and cut with small fancy cutters. This marzipan should be used at once as it does not keep well for any length of time.

MARZIPAN II [2164]
(Cooked, plain)

Dissolve 3 cups of granulated sugar in 1 cup of cold water in a saucepan, and stir in 5 cups of three-times ground blanched almonds. Cook gently, stirring constantly, until the mass will no longer adhere to the pan nor follow the spoon. Turn on to a marble slab, enamel table top, or baking sheet, and knead until smooth, adding flavoring extract and coloring to taste while mixture is still warm. Shape as desired.

The original confectioner was the apothecary, and practically all candies of the Middle Ages were medicines, such as mint and wintergreen lozenges.

MARZIPAN III FRENCH STYLE [2165]

Rub 4 cups of three-times ground blanched almonds into 1¼ lbs. of flavored fondant with a wooden spoon, blending thoroughly. Place 4 cups of granulated sugar and 2 cups of cold water in a saucepan, stir till sugar is dissolved, and heat slowly to the simmering point. Then stir in 1 tablespoon of glucose and boil, *without stirring* to the hard-ball stage (250° F.) or until it forms a hard ball when tested in cold water. Add the boiling syrup very quickly to the almond-fondant mixture and stir until the mass begins to harden. Then turn out onto a hard surface and knead until smooth. Flavor with any desired extract, liqueur or cordial, and color with vegetable coloring to the desired color. The flavoring and coloring should be done while mixture is still warm.

Note. This marzipan keeps well if wrapped first in waxed paper, then in a muslin cloth or doubled cheesecloth, and stored in an airtight tin box kept in refrigerator. If too hard when wanted, add a few drops of lukewarm water or better still, a few drops of cordial or liqueur and mix and knead well.

MARZIPAN PEARS [2166]

Mold yellow-tinted marzipan into the shape of a small pear, not larger than walnut size, making the stem and blossom ends with cloves. With a brush, apply diluted red coloring to one side of the pear.

MARZIPAN POTATOES [2167]

Shape like potatoes pieces (the size of small walnuts) of uncolored marzipan, making dents for the eyes with a small skewer or pick. Roll in cocoa mixed with equal parts of cinnamon, or cinnamon alone.

MARZIPAN STRAWBERRIES   [2168]

Shape marzipan (which may be tinted pink with vegetable coloring) into strawberries, let dry slightly, dip into beaten egg white, then roll in red sugar. Tuck green paper hulls into the tops.

MILK CARAMELS   [2169]

Place 2 cups of granulated sugar, 1 cup of light corn syrup and 1 cup of sweet milk in a saucepan, and blend well, then cook, stirring frequently, to the firm-ball stage (246–248° F.). Stir in very slowly 1 cup of scalded milk, ¼ cup of butter and ½ teaspoon of salt and cook again to the firm-ball stage, or until some of it tested in cold water is of the firmness desired in the finished caramel. Remove from the fire, stir in 1 teaspoon of vanilla extract and pour at once into a buttered pan or platter, marking in squares when cool.

PEANUT BRITTLE   [2170]

Cover the bottom of a generously buttered shallow pan with shelled, halved, toasted and cooled peanuts. Place 2 cups of granulated sugar or 1 cup of granulated and 1 cup of light brown sugar in a heavy skillet and heat gradually, stirring constantly with a wooden spoon, till sugars are melted to a light brown color. Pour at once over the peanuts and let stand till hard. Break into small pieces and store in an airtight container in a cool, dry place.

Moroccan youngsters of the seventeenth century were not allowed to eat candy because it was considered "Warriors' Food."

RUM HONEY CARAMELS   [2171]

Place in a saucepan 2 cups of granulated sugar, 2 cups of strained honey, 1 cup of glucose, and 1 cup of cold, rich milk; stir to blend well, and cook, over a low flame, stirring frequently, to the hard ball stage (255° F.). Gradually stir in 4 cups of scalded heavy cream, watching that the mixture never stops boiling gently, and stirring constantly. Add 2 tablespoons of sweet butter and 2 tablespoons of rum, mixed with 1 scant teaspoon of vanilla extract and cook again to the hard ball stage. Pour at once into a buttered or oiled pan; mark in small squares when almost cold, and when quite cold wrap each caramel in a piece of waxed paper. Store in a tightly closed tin in a cool, dry, dark place.

SALT WATER TAFFY [2172]

Dissolve 2 cups of sugar in 5 tablespoons of water; stir in 1 tablespoon of butter and ¼ teaspoon of salt. Cook, without stirring, to the soft-crack stage (290° F.); stir in 1 teaspoon of vanilla extract and ⅛ teaspoon of cream of tartar. Turn mixture into a buttered pan, and when cool enough to handle, pull until white. Stretch out in front of a batch-warmer or in front of the kitchen range, then cut in small pieces and wrap each in waxed paper. Store in a cool, dry place in an airtight container.

" . . . The fine arts are five in number: Painting, Music, Poetry, Sculpture, and Architecture, whereof the principal branch is CON-FECTIONERY. . . . "

—Anatole France.

SCOTCH BUTTERSCOTCH [2173]

Place in a large saucepan 6 cups of light brown sugar and 2 cups of cold water with ¼ teaspoon of salt and stir till sugar is quite melted. Gradually bring to a boil, stirring frequently; then as soon as boiling, stop stirring and add ⅛ teaspoon of cream of tartar. Cover the pan and allow to boil gently for 10 to 12 minutes. Remove the cover, and cook to the hard crack stage (310° F). Remove from the fire, stir in 1½ cups of melted salt butter and 2 teaspoons of lemon extract. When well blend-ed, pour between buttered candy bars, or into buttered shallow pan or pans, and when quite cold, cut with buttered scissors into small pieces and wrap each piece in waxed paper. Store in an airtight container in a cool, dry place.

VANILLA FUDGE SQUARES [2174]

Place 2 cups of sugar, ⅔ cup of heavy cream, 1 cup of milk, ¼ cup of light corn syrup and ¼ teaspoon of salt in a saucepan; blend well, and bring to a boil very slowly, stirring constantly; continue cooking, stirring occasionally, to the soft ball stage (234° F.). Remove from the fire; cool to lukewarm (110° F.); stir in 1 teaspoon of vanilla extract, beating steadily until mixture thickens and loses its gloss. Pour into a buttered platter or on to a marble slab to cool. When cold, cut in small squares.

Chapter Eighteen

GENERAL INFORMATION

Once women baked bread on a wood fire,
milked cows, churned butter, raised their
own vegetables, canned jar on jar of fruit,
cured their own meat . . . and didn't
consider it a feat.

But now they feel overworked and aggrieved
when they slice a tomato, bake a potato,
broil a chop, open a can of fruit cocktail,
and call it a meal!

Menu making today is a highly specialized
occupation. And the person who has that
job with its responsibilities must realize the
seriousness of it. Behind everything, of
course, is the homemaker, who must know
her refrigerator, buying, planning, family
preferences, leftovers and turnover.

METHODS OF COOKING [2175-76]

A PPLICATION OF HEAT IS THE MOST DIFFICULT STAGE OF THE
whole process of cookery. It is so easy to have the heat too
intense, or too low, to expose the food for too long or too short a time
to its action. We should look upon the application of heat as a continuation of nature's slow ripening process, a softening of tough fibres and a
development of pleasing flavors. For why do we cook at all except for
these reasons? Primitive man thought only that the food had a better
taste. He may have decided, too, that it was easier to masticate; but
we have learned that in some cases we may, with right methods of
cooking, make it easier to digest farther on in the alimentary canal.
Modern science carries us a step farther and teaches us that cooking
destroys lower organisms, such as harmful bacteria that may be present,
and even animal parasites in meats. We cook therefore, to improve the
appearance of food, to develop flavors, to render some foodstuffs more
digestible and to destroy micro-organisms.

Today we have at our command many different methods of cooking
our foods, which we will here pass briefly in review.

BRAISING [2177]

Braising is a method of cooking meat with vegetables and a small
amount of liquid in a closely covered pan, so gently that neither flavor
nor moisture is lost by evaporation.

The liquid may be animal juices, water, wine, vegetable or meat
stock or sometimes even a canned soup. It is a self-basting method, as
the steam and liquid which rise to the top of the pan or lid constantly
drop on to the food (often the less tender cuts of meat) subjected to this
method of cooking. Towards the end of the process, cooking wine or
other flavoring extract may be added. The amount of liquid used should
be barely sufficient to cover the meat. In this way the surrounding broth
is concentrated. Briefly, braising is a combination of stewing and baking
meat.

BROILING or GRILLING [2178]

Broiling or grilling has a decided advantage in flavor as well as in
nutritive value over meat which has been boiled for a long time, although
the latter may be tender and easily digested. Broiling is the most universal method of cooking. Broiling or grilling is a method cooking which
requires very much less time than roasting, boiling, or braising, because
intense heat is applied to comparatively small pieces of meat, fish, vegetables, game and fruits. It is really roasting on a smaller scale. A coating
of coagulated albumin forms on the outer surface of the food while the
albuminous material is gradually warmed and more slowly coagulated.
This method is usually applied to tender cuts of meat. A properly broiled
steak or chop is thickened in the center, but if badly broiled it is thin and
dry. It should be remembered that the evaporation depends upon the

extent of the surface of the meat, fish or game or poultry, and for this reason thinly cut steaks or chops become comparatively dry and shriveled in the center. Pouring melted fat over the meat checks evaporation almost completely, and in the case of large joints it prevents the external portion from becoming dry and indigestible before the albumin of the interior has coagulated.

APPROXIMATE TIME TABLE FOR   [2179]
BROILING
Preheat broiling oven and rack or pan at least 10 minutes

KIND OF FOOD	THICKNESS	RARE (Minutes)	MEDIUM (Minutes)
BEEF:			
Sirloin and Club Steaks	1 inch	10–12	14–16
	1½ inches	15–16	18–20
	2 inches	22–25	25–30
Porterhouse	1 inch	12–15	16–18
Top round or chuck steaks	1½ inches	18–20	22–25
	2 inches	25–28	28–30
Tenderloin steak	1 inch	6–7	8–9
	1½ inches	8–9	10–11
	2 inches	10–11	12–14
Hamburger Steak	¾ inch	5	7–8
LAMB:			
Loin or rib chops	1 inch	10–12	14–18
(double) or shoulder	2 inches	22–25	26–28
Steak	1 inch	10–12	14–16
	1½ inches	15–16	18–20
	2 inches	22–25	26–30
PORK:			
This method is rarely used.	. . . .	. . . . .	. . . . .
HAM:			
Sliced	¼ inch	. . . . .	12
	½ inch	. . . . .	16
	1 inch	. . . . .	22–25
BACON:			
Sliced	. . . .	. . . . .	3–4
LIVER:			
Beef, calf, lamb, mutton	¼ inch	3–4	5–6
pork	½ inch	6–7	8–9
	1 inch	8	12
KIDNEYS:			
Beef, lamb, mutton or pork	Proceed as indicated for liver.		
CHICKEN:			
Broilers	1 lb.	. . . . .	18–20
FISH:			
Filets, steaks or slices	¼ to ½ inch	. . . . .	7–10
	¾ to 1 inch	. . . . .	18–20–22
Whole, small	not split	. . . . .	6–7–9
Whole, medium	split	. . . . .	18–22

Broiled meat (any kind) generously brushed with lemon, lime or grapefruit juice, then seasoned to taste with salt and pepper before broiling gives a new taste experience. Split fish should be turned only once during broiling. Broil flesh side first then turn and cook skin side. Basting is obligatory for any kind of broiling.

DEEP FAT FRYING   [2180]

Deep fat frying is a process of cooking by which the heat is transmitted by the contact of the food with boiling fat, butter, lard, suet, oil, and not by radiation as in the case of roasting, broiling or grilling. The boiling point of fats is very much above that of water, and the vaporization of the latter is complete at 212° F. Heat between 300° and 500° F. may be required to vaporize the so-called volatile oils, but fats and oils used in cooking do not apply to this class, and when heated above 400° F., they turn dark brown or black and emit a disagreeable odor and smoke, leaving a non-volatile carbon residue.

The process of frying bears somewhat the same relation to boiling that the broiling of meat does, in that the heat employed is considerably greater. It is suddenly applied, and as a result the external surface of the food mass is coagulated and hardened before the juices in the interior have time to escape. Frying is less perfectly understood by cooks than almost any other method of preparing food, and the process, as usually carried out, results in very unwholesome products. The pans used are too shallow, and both food and fat are apt to become scorched. The fat may not be hot enough or may be too stale, if it has been used too often without being clarified. Clarification is an easy matter and fat should be clarified every time it is used.

Never allow fat to remain in the deep pan after using, clarify or strain it, then pour it into a clean can or jar for future use. (See No. 2181.)

The popular idea in regard to frying is that the fat used, whether butter (very expensive and seldom used), lard, oil or drippings, is simply for the purpose of preventing food from adhering to the pan or kettle. The best frying is done by completely immersing the food in a bath of fat or oil. The meat (or other food) is lowered in an open wire or netting basket into a deep pan which contains the heated fat, in which it is completely submerged. There is no danger of the fat soaking into the food if it is sufficiently hot and if the process is NOT continued too long, for the water amid the fibres of the food is *Boiling* and driving out steam *so rapidly* that *no fat* whatsoever can enter if the heat is maintained to the last moment. Fritters cooked in this way are light and puffy from the sudden expansion of the water which they contain into large bubbles of steam, and are consequently decidedly more digestible. Always fry bacon in its own fat.

HOW TO CLARIFY FAT AFTER USING   [2181]

Drop several slices of raw pared potatoes into the fat and let bubble up. Strain all through double or triple cheesecloth into pail, can or jar. The potatoes absorb odors and collect crumbs and leave the fat clear.

An accumulation of burnt food particles in the fat will cause excessive smoking and foaming and will shorten the frying life of the fat.

When the above method does not entirely clear the fat, it can be reconditioned by drawing it off into a separate container after it has cooled to a temperature below the boiling point of water (212° F.) and sprinkling the surface with cold water. As the water settles to the bottom it carries down the very fine particles of burnt foods that have been suspended throughout the fat. The clear fat can then either be poured from the sludge of burnt particles and water or the water and sediment can be drawn off from the bottom of the kettle.

The following approximate timetable for deep fat frying includes frying temperatures and times for a variety of deep fried foods.

APPROXIMATE TIMETABLE FOR DEEP FAT FRYING   [2182]

Important. Have food to be fried of standard (even) size. Preheat the fat before immersing the food. Use enough fat to completely cover the food.

The frying time will vary, depending on the size of the individual foods being fried, and also on the amount of food placed in the frying basket or frying kettle at one time. Naturally, large portions require longer frying than small ones. With an overload of cold food, the temperature of the fat may drop so low, that not only will longer time be needed for cooking, but also the food may become grease soaked, unappetizing and indigestible.

All deep fat fried food should, after cooking, be drained on soft (unglazed) crumpled paper as soon as removed from the hot fat.

KIND OF FOOD	TEMPERATURE	TIME (minutes)
CROQUETTES (any kind: fish, meat, fruit, vegetables, etc.)....................................	370–375° F.	2–3
CUTLETS (any kinds). Same as croquettes.		
DOUGHNUTS.....................................	370–375° F.	3–5
FISH FILETS.....................................	365–370° F.	3–5
FRENCH FRIED POTATOES		
Blanching....................................	367–370° F.	5–8
Browning....................................	385–390° F.	2–3
FRENCH FRIED ONIONS....................	345–355° F.	4–5–6
FRITTERS (fruit, meat, fish, vegetables, etc.)......	370–375° F.	3–5
OYSTERS.......................................	355–360° F.	1–3
SCALLOPS.....................................	355–360° F.	3–4
VEGETABLES		
Eggplant, cauliflower flowerets, asparagus, etc....	370–375° F.	5–6–7

PAN BROILING   [2183]

This method consists of cooking meat, fish, vegetables, game or even fruits in a skillet or frying pan, previously well heated, with very little or no fat. It is usually adopted for tender cuts of meat and fowl. The fire should never be too intense.

PAN FRYING [2184]

This method is the same as that of deep fat frying, except that the process is conducted in a skillet or a frying pan with a small or a large amount of fat, which, however, unless otherwise indicated, should never cover the food. The process is usually conducted over a medium fire or flame and the food is turned occasionally in order to brown it equally on both sides unless otherwise indicated.

POT ROASTING [2185]

Pot roasting is a method similar to braising except that the cooking may be on top of the range as well as in the oven. The meat or fish, game, or fowl or vegetable is usually seared, then placed in a covered kettle or Dutch oven, and the "braise" and liquid indicated added. See *Braising* (No. 2177). This process of cooking is a slow one and is usually applied to less tender cuts.

ROASTING [2186]

Really the process of roasting results in cooking the meat in a manner which is in some respects analogous to stewing; in fact, the interior portions of the meat are stewed in their own juices instead of in water. A coating of coagulated albumin forms upon the outer surface of the meat, fowl, game, and so forth, and this is produced by an intensive heat (searing) of 450 to 500 and even 550° F. to start. Then the temperature is reduced, and the process of roasting is allowed to continue until the meat is at the desired point of doneness. This method of cooking requires frequent bastings with the juices of the meat (which drip because of the intense heat); sometimes basting with other liquids is indicated. As in broiling or grilling, the outer coating prevents the evaporation of the juices of the food mass, which together with the extractive materials are retained and add flavor to it, as well as constituting juice or gravy.

Boned and rolled roast takes longer to cook than short or standing rib roast.

Roasting may be done at an even low temperature throughout the process or a hot oven may be used for searing after which the heat is reduced. Small roasts under six pounds need a longer time allowance per pound than do large ones.

If a meat thermometer is used, make a hole with a skewer through fat side and insert thermometer so that the bulb will be in the center of fleshy part of roast but NOT *touching* the bone.

APPROXIMATE TIMETABLE FOR   [2187]
ROASTING MEAT

Important. If the roast is not browned (seared) first, the oven should be moderate all the time, though a little hotter than is required to finish a roast that has been seared. The ideal temperature is 375° F. For rare beef allow 15 to 20 minutes per pound. For medium-rare, 18 to 20 minutes per pound. For well-done, 22 to 25 minutes per pound.

Veal, pork and poultry should always be well-done; otherwise they will be indigestible.

Never cover a roast during its cooking, and baste frequently, about every 15 minutes, with the drippings from the pan.

Gravy. If you estimate that you will need two cups of gravy, leave about *four* tablespoons of fat in the pan, pouring the rest off to use for frying later; add as much flour as there are tablespoons of fat in the pan and stir over a brisk flame, until the mixture is smooth and well browned. Then add 1½ cups of boiling water, mixed with ½ cup of Pique Seasoning; if a rich gravy is desired, use meat stock instead of water, but don't forget to add the Pique Seasoning, stirring until thick and smooth; season to taste, and strain through a finemeshed wire sieve into a heated sauceboat. This is plain, delicious beef gravy.

CUT OF MEAT	Minutes for searing	Oven (Searing) Temperature	Oven temperature after searing	Time per pound after searing
BEEF:				
Roast ribs	15–20	500° F.	325–350° F.	15–20
Roast tenderloin or filet of beef	12–15	450° F.	325–350° F.	10–12
Other meat cuts	12–15	450° F.	325–350° F.	12–15
LAMB AND MUTTON:				
Roast leg	15–20	475–500° F.	300–325° F.	20–22
Roast shoulder	15–20	450–475° F.	325–350° F.	20–22
Roast shoulder when boned	12–18	450–475° F.	325–350° F.	15–20
VEAL:				
Roast, stuffed	20–25	500° F.	350–375° F.	20–25
Roast leg	20–25	550° F.	350–375° F.	25–30
PORK HAM:				
Roast loin	20–25	550° F.	350–375° F.	25–30
Roast shoulder	20	500° F.	350–375° F.	25–30
Roast fresh ham................	20–25	550° F.	325–350° F.	30–35
Roast smoked ham (after boiling)	15–20	500° F.	325–350° F.	25–30

PRE-COOKED Ham: follow the directions on the label.

Before placing the roast in the oven, always preheat it to the desired degree. The most modern adjunct to meat cookery is the oven thermometer which has been designed to put into the meat (roast). When it reads 150° F., you will have a rare roast of beef or other meat; at 160° F., a medium roast and at 180° F. a well-done roast.

SEARING [2188]

In searing meat, the high temperature which is suddenly applied to the meat produces a firmer coagulation (a kind of caramelization of its outer layers) than occurs with any other method of cooking meat. Owing to this fact, the natural juices of the meat are almost completely retained. The heat should be strong when first applied and of shorter duration. Then the heat is reduced to prevent charring of the surface. This method enhances the flavor of the food to which it is applied, be it a tender or a tough cut. During the searing process the meat should always be basted, too, and turned frequently.

SIMMERING [2189]

This method implies cooking foods in liquid below the boiling point or from 180° F. up to 210° F. over direct heat. Simmering enhances flavor and softens tough cuts. When applied to fish it is called poaching.

APPROXIMATE TIMETABLE FOR [2190]
SIMMERING MEAT AND POULTRY

KIND OF MEAT	APPROXIMATE TIME PER POUND
Beef (depending on cut)	35–45 minutes
Mutton (leg)	25–30 minutes
Corned Beef	30 minutes
Ham	20–25 minutes
Poultry (depending on size and age)	20–30 minutes

STEAM ROASTING [2191]

Consists of cooking meat in the oven in a covered roaster, using indirect moist heat. A little liquid is sometimes indicated and poured into the pan to assure enough moisture for steam. It is a cross between roasting and braising. The steam self-bastes the meat, rendering it tender and flavorful.

STEWING [2192]

There are stews and stews—good, bad and indifferent! A stew can be a colorful, flavorful, mouth-watering dish, or it can be anemic, and utterly insipid—all depending on how it is handled and what goes into its making.

The French term for a stew is "Ragoût" (pronounced rag-oo). Typical ragoûts have larger pieces of meat than do goulashes and the vegetables are frequently used only as flavoring. Perhaps ragoût does sound more elegant than stew, but after all, it's not what is in the *name* that counts, but rather what is in the *stew*. In a stew, environment rules over heredity. The choice of vegetables is a wide one, but unfortunately, this choice is not exercised as it should be and as a consequence the general run of stews lack interest and variety.

Stewing differs from boiling in the fact that the juices of the meat, fish, poultry, game, or vegetables, or even fruits (compôte is a kind of stew) are dissolved in the heated liquid, usually water, unless otherwise indicated, whereas in boiling, the juices are kept from passing out into the liquid by the coagulation of the external surface of the food mass, which is usually first seared (in meat, fish, poultry and game), then immersed suddenly into boiling fluid. The proper temperature for stewing is between 135° F. and 160° F.

In thick stew, the juices dissolved in the water are eaten together with the cooked food, but in some instances, as in the making of beef tea and some soups, the aqueous solution only is used. Obviously the more the food is subdivided the greater the surface exposed to the solvent action of the liquid, hence, the thorough mincing of meat which is to be used in the preparation of beef tea. If such minced meat (in beef tea) has been soaked for a long time in cold water, a part of the albumen and the extractive materials are obtained in solution, but the meat which is left is colorless, tasteless, and unpalatable.

The manner in which stewing differs from other cooking processes is that instead of the meat itself surrounding and enveloping the juices, as it should when boiled, broiled, fried or roasted, in a stew we demand that the juices shall surround or envelop the meat to replace those juices which have passed out into the surrounding liquid. After the meat has been stewing for some time a scum containing a little coagulated albumin and more or less fat is usually seen floating on the surface. This is often removed by the cook in the preparation of beef tea and stew in order to make it more palatable and more agreeable to the eye, but its removal is at the expense of considerable nutritious material.

As both the solid substance of the meat and vegetables and the liquid materials which have been extracted from them are eaten together in the stew, this is an economical form of preparing food. Nothing is lost by evaporation, and nothing is thrown away except the bones.

SAUTÉEING   [2193]

Sautéeing is similar to pan frying, except that the food placed in the frying pan is jerked or shaken occasionally, and the pan tossed often to prevent the food sticking to the pan or burning, or scorching.

STEAMING   [2194]

Steaming is a cooking method mainly applied to vegetables, cereals, most tubers, also certain forms of puddings and desserts.

SHORT-BOILING   [2195]

Short-boiling, poaching, coddling, sometimes also called blanching or parboiling, is a method of cooking ordinarily applied to eggs and fish, especially fish filets. It is called "Court-Bouillon" in French culinary terms. Two different methods are used: Method No. 1, suitable for large pieces of fish such as salmon or large trout and Method No. 2 suitable for fish, fish filets or small whole fish such as trout, eel, or pike. Recipes will be found under *Sauces*.

OVEN TIMETABLE FOR BAKING OF [2196]
MEAT, FISH, AND SO FORTH

Baking is accomplished through cooking in a confined space, thus preventing the escape of the volatile products which are driven off in roasting. Consequently the food has a stronger and less delicate flavor than when roasted, but is *richer* in nutrient ingredients.

Very slow	250° F.	Moderately hot	375° F.
Slow	300° F.	Hot	400–425° F.
Moderately slow	325° F.	Very hot	450–500° F.
Moderate	350° F.	Extremely hot	500° F. up

CARVING [2197]
Art, Easily Acquired

Carving, like many other personal services, could not be done by a menial, but only by a person of a rank suitable to the guests. One recalls an English aristocratic magazine of fifty and some odd years ago—The Pall Mall Something or Other, as I remember it—the announcement of which said that it would be written "for gentlemen by gentlemen." Or, going farther back, one thinks of King Louis at Versailles whose morning breeches had to be held by a nobleman for the royal legs. Even now a lot of English offices—Ladies-in-Waiting who don't wait, Ladies of the Bed Chamber, who don't go to bed but stay up and play bridge—recall the earliest tradition.

So no wonder that carving was done for the English kings of the Middle Ages by noblemen of high degree. Edward IV, who lived in the Fourteen Hundreds, had four carvers-in-ordinary, with My Lord Willoughby as Carver-in-Chief. The royal servants included also my Lord of Buckingham, Cupbearer; Sir Richard Strangwicke, as Chief-Sewer (what he did, nobody knows); Sir Walter and eight other knights together with eight other squires as Knights of the Hall and extra Sewers; Sir John Malyvery as Painter, and with him a Ewerer and two Keepers of the Cupboard.

All of which and much more one can read in the contemporary account of how King Edward gave a great feast—he was as big-hearted as Ismail and it cost him nothing anyway—to celebrate the "inthronization" of Archbishop Nevill.

Anybody who reads of medieval meats will appreciate properly Chaucer's account of his Prioress whose manners were so refined that she never got gravy over her face or down her neck—

> *At meat she was well taught withall,*
> *She let no morsel from her lips to fall,*
> *Nor wet her fingers in her sauce too deep,*
> *Well could she carry a morsel and well keep*
> *That no drop fell upon her breast at all.*

But, of course, what we think of as "carving" in the modern sense only began when the Middle Ages gave way to the Age of Polite Living. A great gulf separates us from the people who lived in huge castles, or in wattled huts—in "halls" without glass windows, or on floors that were just bare earth covered with beaten rushes—and ate from a table that was called and was a "board."

Correct carving today is an art, which when mastered, is an accomplishment that adds greatly to the charm and grace of dining. It brings both genuine pleasure to the carver, and an abundancè of praise from the assembled guests.

In carving, as in everything else, there is a right and a wrong way, and invariably, the right way is the best and easiest. Do not take your carving duties as another one of those unnecessary evils—a task that must be performed regardless of results. Carving technique is not at all difficult but it requires a knowledge of how and where to cut. The best flavor of meats and fowl is emphasized when carved and served in an appetizing manner. For how distressing it is, when guests see a host hack and slash across one bone after another and bespatter the table with odds and ends. Such performance always dampens the appetite of those present.

What a pleasure it is to watch a carver, who separates the joints cleanly. When one carves with ease and grace, it immediately brings forth enthusiastic and favorable comment.

Good carving demands a knowledge of the structure of the meat to be carved; also the ability to judge thickness of tissue and placement of bones almost with the skill of a surgeon. The expert carver must also possess another attribute of a surgeon—a steady hand and ready confidence with a keen blade.

CARVING SETS [2198]

When buying a carving set, do not let beautiful handles, alone, intrigue you, but select one with steel that will satisfactorily hold an edge. The length of knives to be used for various cuts of meats and fowl is largely a matter of personal preference.

For *broiled steaks*, a 5½-inch to 6-inch blade is commonly used. The same type of knife is also used for other broiled or fried meats.

For *small game birds*, use a knife with a 6-inch or 6½-inch stiff blade.

For a *roast of* beef, leg of lamb, veal, and so forth, or for general carving, a knife with an 8-inch semi-flexible blade may be used.

For *turkey* or large roasts, use a knife with an 8½ to 10-inch semi-flexible blade.

All knives should be sharpened before they are brought to table; no one can carve satisfactorily without having a sharp knife. The same steel may be used for sharpening both short and long blades. A carving knife should never be actually immersed in water of *any* temperature. The ideal way is to wipe the entire blade with a warm, soapy cloth, then hold the blade, edge down, under the faucet for rinsing. Dry thoroughly before storing.

Caution. No matter how strongly tempted never cut a roast with a knife slicing toward the hand holding the fork. It is an exceptional carver whose knife never slips and you will find that a good carver *never* takes this chance.

Capon. A capon is carved somewhat like a turkey; that is, the legs should be separated from the body in similar fashion and the dark meat of the second joint put aside to be served with the filets which will be cut from each side of the breast. One should be able to carve four to five filets from each side of the breast of a capon.

Chicken. Same as capon. The only difference lies in the smaller size of the pieces. A *broiled* or *fried* chicken is usually served as it has been cut for cooking.

The *breast* of a roast chicken is cut from the breast bone at the front end of the carcass with a stroke in which the knife is at right angles to the chicken at the frontal bone and the cut is made from the breastbone toward the neck. The remaining breast may be removed by detaching it with the help of the prongs of the fork, and the knife without actually cutting it. This applies to any bird breast.

Duck. The leg joint of the duck is further under the body than the chicken's. Holding it firmly with the carving fork, force it gently but firmly away from the body, while exploring for the joint with a sharp knife. With a tender bird, when the flesh is separated from the body structure in cutting down, the leg will almost come away of itself. For the breast, follow directions given for chicken.

Wild Duck. Carve the same as the domestic, except that the breast may be carved either into filets or a whole (or half) breast served to a person.

Goose. Carve more or less like a capon, except that the legs are rarely served. It is most convenient to place the bird with the breast facing the carver. The breast is cut in moderately thick filets and immediately placed on a warm plate with gravy and a small quantity of dressing. Applesauce is usually served separately.

Grouse. A grouse is never carved, but split into two portions; or the breast may be carved the same as wild duck, allowing one breast (or half breast) for each serving. The legs are also served, if requested; they are, however, generally reserved for making a salmis.

Guinea Hen. Carved the same as chicken.

Partridge. Served whole, like pigeon, one to a person, or cut in half; or carve and serve the whole breast alone (never fileted), to a person.

Pheasant. The breast is rarely served whole, but fileted rather thick. The legs are seldom served. They may be used for a salmis.

Pigeons, Plover, Quail, Snipe, Squabs, and Teal Duck. Never carved, but may be split. They are usually served *as is* on toast which may be generously buttered then dipped in sherry or madeira wine.

Turkey. The turkey legs should be placed to the carver's right with the neck to his left. Usually turkey comes to the table resting on its back. The legs are removed in the same way as chicken legs, but the second joint is sliced into several pieces. The breast is cut into thin filets and not more than two filets are usually served to a portion with a slice of dark meat from the second joint, and a spoonful of stuffing. The wing tips and the drumsticks are never served, if it can be avoided except *en famille*, but are reserved for other purposes. If more than one side of the bird is needed, turn it on its side and remove the second leg; then turn it on its back again in order to slice filets from the breast.

Drumsticks of chicken, duck, goose, and turkey, and so forth, are improved if tendons are removed. These stringy tendons should therefore be removed *before cooking*. Do not cut off the feet until after the tendons are drawn to remove them: (a) Make a cut with a sharp knife on the inside of the leg, below the knee joint. (b) Separate the tendons of the leg, insert a metal skewer and pick up and pull each one out separately. (c) Then cut off the feet with the tendons hanging.

In general the muscles run lengthwise of the bird. Before starting to carve, tilt it slightly forward, so that the legs and wings are in a more accessible position to sever. Then remove the leg (both drumstick and thigh in one piece). To do this, only three cuts are necessary. Meanwhile, hold the bird by placing the fork astride the keel or breastbone. Make the first cut in front of the thigh, and cut deep, down to the pinion or joint which holds it to the backbone. The second cut should be back of the thigh to the pinion joint. These two cuts practically make a V. Thirdly, cut the skin between the leg and body so that it will not tear as the thigh is removed. All three cuts made, grasp the frilled drumstick in your fingers and turn it toward you when the entire leg should easily and quickly pull cleanly away from the socket joint. Of course, if the turkey is not thoroughly cooked, it may be necessary to force the leg away from the body with the knife to dislocate the joint. Lay the entire leg (drumstick and thigh) on a hot side platter. To separate the leg (drumstick) from the thigh, lay the browned side down, because the inside permits the joint to be more clearly seen and it is easier to sever the two with one clean cut right through the joint.

After the drumstick and thigh have been severed, turn them upright on the platter, so that the more appetizing looking brown side is on top.

Next, remove the wing. Here some carvers encounter difficulties because they fail to observe the fact that the joint that holds the wing to the shoulder is much closer to the body than the joint that holds the thigh to the backbone. Therefore, in removing the wing, first make one cut on the outside a little in front of the shoulder joint. The second cut forms another V. Then cut under the wing to sever it from the body, and as the joint is approached, turn the knife inward toward the front of the shoulder and cut deep so that the blade will strike right at the joint.

Now place the fork under the end of the wing and push out and forward. It should disjoint easily. Place the wing also on the side platter; again, it is easy to sever the upper and lower parts when cut from the inside (The tips of the wings should be removed before roasting, as there is little meat on them to eat, and they are good for flavoring soups and gravies or for the stock pot).

The "oyster," a small piece of dark meat, is a choice morsel which lies in the cavity of the back, or on each side of the backbone just above the thigh, ahead of the tail, and which the French call "the sot" or "sot l'y laisse," and which usually is reserved for the head chef in large restaurants. From the drumstick (if en famille), slice the dark meat in scant ¼-inch slices. These slices are made by holding the end of the drumstick upright in the left hand and cutting from the inside down through the ligaments or tendons if they have not been removed before cooking. In slicing the thigh, hold it flat on the same platter with the fork and cut in ¼-inch slices. These lengthwise sections are then cut across the grain at a 45 degree angle into two, three, or four pieces, depending on the size of the bird. *Do not* stop to do a clean job of the bone.

Some carvers leave the drumstick and thigh in one piece. To carve in this manner, hold the drumstick, slice the meat first from the thigh and then from the drumstick. It doesn't matter much which model you follow, but be sure to cut attractive-looking slices. Some carvers place the dark meat at one end of the small platter and the white meat at the other end. This is a matter of choice.

In carving the *Breast* or *White Meat,* hold the fork in the left hand and insert firmly astride the keel or breastbone, just beyond its highest point. Another way is to insert the fork through the rib section. Some people carve the breast parallel to the breastbone, but many prefer the former because one can carve more uniform and appetizing slices by using this angle across the grain. Whether to carve enough white meat to serve all plates, or to cut the breast as each plate is served, depends on the preference of the carver, but in any case you should follow the method that will insure hot meat for all and be in keeping with the type of dinner service. Usually cutting slices as each plate is served is the better procedure.

Fish. Always use a silver or a metal knife or spatula, called also palette. Be sure that as little bone as possible is served and that the flakes of fish are not broken.

Sole or Flounder and Similar Flat Fish. Cut down the middle of the fish from the head to the tail; then cut along the dorsal fringe of bones and from there all around the sole, cutting around the head and tail. Lift off the top two filets, and then the backbone, beginning at the tail and working towards the head, where it is broken off and laid aside. This gives access to the under side of the flat fish, which is then divided into two filets in exactly the same manner as the upper side.

Turbot. Cut a straight line in the middle of the flat fish from the head to the tail; then cut from each side of this center line a series of pieces (square or rectangular), each not over 2½ inches wide extending as far as possible towards the outer edges of the fish, and cutting as deep as the backbone will permit. If more portions are necessary, remove the backbone and repeat on the lower half exactly what was done on the upper half of the flat fish.

Salmon. This fish and similar ones are dissected somewhat like turbot above, by cutting a line from the head to the tail and cutting from each side of the line a series of pieces each about 2½ to 3 inches wide.

Trout (Brook). There are gourmets who consider the brain of a brook trout a great delicacy; hence, though some may question the practice, trout should be served whole and with head on

Shad. The shad being a very bony fish, the cook takes every precaution to pull out all the bones possible before cooking it, using tweezers to do it.

When a shad is served it is cut in fairly wide pieces, approximately 4 inches wide, right straight across the whole (from the back to the belly), as you would cut a steak. The fish cut in this way will show the remaining bones protruding from the pieces, and these bones may be pulled out with the aid of a clean side towel or paper napkin, if tweezers are not handy.

Smelts. Being small fish, they are usually served whole and fried. Or they may be split *à l'anglaise* in which case the bones are always taken out in the kitchen by splitting the fish from the top of the back down and removing the backbone.

Whitebait. Are never boned, being usually fried with heads and tails on.

Meats. Carving of the meat is easier than carving fowl or birds. When carving meat, the general rule is to cut across the grain to shorten the fibers and make the meat seem even more tender. If the man of the house is not a good carver and is inclined to be a bit nervous when guests are present, it is up to the hostess to help him out of his difficulties and draw the guests' attention to her and her conversation thus taking their eyes away from the nervous carver. It is the constant watching of his every movement that disconcerts the carver.

Carving meat and fowl, a fine art, was taught by Roman professors with the aid of *wooden models*, the parts of which were lightly fastened together so a pupil could separate them with a blunt knife.

Beef Tenderloin. Being boneless, beef tenderloin presents no problem in carving, except to cut even slices. The carver holds the meat with the fork grasped in his left hand. Beginning at the large end, the tenderloin is cut across in slices a little less than ½ inch in thickness.

Beef Tongue. The tongue should always be trimmed, removing the skin, and so forth, before bringing it to the table. It should be placed on the platter with the large end to the right and the rounded side away from the carver. The fork is inserted in the thick part and thin slices are cut slantwise down across the grain. About 3½ inches of the tip end should be served and sliced lengthwise, so as to get the greatest number of good-sized slices.

Brisket of Beef. Place on the platter with the round side away from you. Trim off excessive fat carefully and neatly. Make slices in rotation from three sides. Slices should be thin and at a slight angle. Carving in this way makes all the cuts across the grain.

Chateaubriand Steak. Few people know what a Chateaubriand steak is. And very few cooks prepare this dish properly, chiefly on account of the waste involved. Plain steaks are being served all over the States under the name of "Chateaubriand," but they bear scant resemblance to the steak named for the brilliant French writer and statesman, François René, Vicomte de Chateaubriand. The dish was first cooked in the year 1802 at the restaurant Champeaux, in the Place de la Bourse in Paris.

A real Chateaubriand steak is the center portion of a beef tenderloin, stuffed with a mixture of beef marrow, chopped shallots, tarragon and parsley. The profane wits of the kitchen thought that a good steak sent to the fire between two malefactor steaks was a fair parody of the title of Chateaubriand's book Génie du Christianisme. The filet or steak was cut so thick that by the ordinary method of cooking it might be burned on the surface whilst quite raw inside and therefore—although the original and authenic method is ignored nowadays—it was put upon the fire between two slices of beef which if burned could be thrown away. Thus only is the Chateaubriand steak properly cooked. As for carving, it is carved slightly on a slant. One slice is served to each person.

Crown Roast of Lamb or Pork. A crown roast of lamb or pork which has been prepared properly at the market is very easy to carve. In fact, the carver proceeds in much the same manner as in carving a pork loin roast. The carver steadies the crown roast by inserting the fork to the left between the ribs. He then makes the slices by cutting through the center between each two ribs. One chop and a portion of stuffing or vegetables that may be used to stuff the center of the crown are served to each person. A crown roast of lamb or pork is suitable for special occasions, and it lends itself to many garnishes and stuffings and may be served with a number of different accompaniments.

Ham. Boiled, roasted and braised ham are carved in the same way. The ham is held like the leg of lamb. Start slicing about 2 inches from where the bone protrudes and take one piece off. Then continue slicing diagonally towards the hand which is holding the bone and slice as far as possible. This is the most economical method of carving a ham, and when it is put away it has not been hacked to pieces. The carver should cut as deep as the bone and quite far around. The other side of the ham is then carved the long way, like the leg of lamb.

Leg of Lamb or Mutton. With the left hand grasp the leg by the bone with a clean towel. Hold it firmly on the platter on its edge, and cut thin slices diagonally (across the grain of the meat) away from the hand which is holding the bone. Then reverse the leg and cut long slices with level strokes along what was the bottom of the leg. Serve one slice with one taken from along the bone to each person.

Leg of Venison. Is carved like a leg of lamb or mutton.

Pork Loin. Cut straight across like a rack of lamb between the ribs. Serve one rib to one person.

Pork or Lamb Shoulder. Cut diagonally the flesh lying in the V of the shoulder bone in as many slices as possible, the strokes descending to the V. Grasp the shoulder bone with a clean towel and turn it up the other way. Quite a few slices can then be taken from the bottom part which is uppermost. *Mutton shoulder is carved the same, so is a shoulder of venison.*

Pot Roast. A blade pot roast contains at least a portion of one rib and a part of the blade bone. In the relatively long cooking period, the connective tissue, which binds the bones to the muscles, is softened to such an extent that these bones are loosened and may be slipped out easily, in which case it is just as well to remove them in the kitchen before the roast is brought to the table for carving. The carver then has only the task of making attractive servings from a boneless piece of meat. The chief problem in carving a blade pot roast, whether the bone is in or not, is to make attractive slices across the grain of the meat. There are several muscles, the fibers of which run in different directions and because of this, and because the bones may be in the roast, it is not possible to carve a slice parallel to the cut surface, such as one does in carving a rib roast. A very satisfactory method of carving a blade pot roast is to proceed as above.

Rib Roast (Roast Beef). This roast consists of from 3 to 6 ribs of beef. It is placed on the platter with the ends of the ribs to the left and the crust side uppermost. Very thin slices are cut horizontally from right to left across the grain at the thick end until the knife meets the bones. The first cuts are well done, and are served to the persons who prefer them. Roast beef can also be carved vertically—the ribs lying on the platter, but the first method is preferable in that the juice is retained in the meat instead of running off on the platter, and a slice which is as wide as the roast itself is more representative of the flavor of the meat as a whole. With a little practice the first method will prove the easier of the two, although in many American homes it is not popular. Practice carving with long even strokes, avoiding short sawing strokes. It is for this reason that a long-bladed knife is used for roast of beef or rib roast.

Rolled Boned Roast or Chicago Rolls. Beef, veal, lamb, mutton and pork breasts or shoulders are boned, sometimes stuffed, then rolled for roasts and are placed on the platter with the cut surface at right angles to the platter. The carver makes the slices by cutting from the top of the roast down to the platter and allowing each slice to fall back as it is made. Boned and stuffed breast or shoulder roasts are carved in the same manner, i.e., down through the meat and the stuffing to the platter. These rolled roasts are held together with kitchen string or skewers, which are removed by the carver as required.

Round Steak. As a rule the butcher cuts round steaks much thinner than porterhouse or sirloin, or club steaks, and in carving round steak, much wider portions are served. The individual portions usually are cut about 2 inches wide and 3 inches to 4 inches long. The natural divisions between the muscles may serve as a guide in carving round steak.

Saddle of Lamb, Mutton, Venison. The bone which runs through the saddle is the shape of a T, and the roast should be placed on the platter so that the T is upside down with the end of the roast diagonally towards the carver. Make a long cut the entire length of the backbone. Remove the meat from the bone by running the point of the knife underneath, close to the surface of the bone. Continue slicing the filets horizontally along the whole length of the saddle, starting at the center bone and continuing down to the fatty part which surrounds the under side of the saddle.

When the top of the saddle has been carved, turn the saddle upside down and carve the two filets which are to be found there, one on each side of the central bone. A slice from these filets, together with a portion from the top side of the saddle, should be served to each person. The saddle should *never* be carved crosswise in chunks.

Sirloin Steak. Is usually carved slightly on a slant, while *Porterhouse Steak* is usually first separated from the bone by cutting along the edge of the bone with the thin point of the knife. Then, beginning with the wide or bone end and following the grain of the meat, divide the steak into sections an inch or slightly more in width. In *Porterhouse Steak* and similar steaks, the tenderloin and the wider section of the steak are most tender and have the finest flavor and texture. For this reason steaks of this kind are usually carved in small sections and a serving of the finer quality meat with one less choice is given to each person with a bit of the crisp fat.

THE KITCHEN IS THE TEMPLE OF LIFE

So much there is that's lovely in a kitchen:
The silver water flowing to my hand,
The golden flame that answers to my fingers,
Row upon row of shining things that stand,
And wait my using in some mystery,
Ancient as Eden, new this very hour.
Here fragrance rises from a darkened cavern,
Strange mingling of flavor and of flour
From waving wheatfield and fruit laden trees.
Here ivory of eggs, and gleaming yolk
Pass through strange alchemy beneath my hands
Who make of them a strengthening for folk.
To the most dear. Beauty there is, and miracle,
Windows where roses nod, a bird's swift wing.
This is my kingdom, yea, my very temple,
Here may I serve and pray. Here may I sing.
—Catherine Cate Coblentz.

SEASONING [2199]

Any food, including desserts, needs seasoning. Certain seasonings "lift" certain foods, but in using them the cook must be careful neither to over-season nor under-season, but rather to obtain a delicious blend which will bring out the flavor of the predominant ingredient in the dish, be it a soup, a stew, a roast, or a dessert, and add an elusive aroma so subtle that even the gourmet hestitates to name it.

Flavor has been called "The soul of the food." It is flavor that makes all dishes, hot or cold, sweet or sour, enjoyable. Seasoning makes plain food, company food, and company food should always be the family food. It is not merely time or cooking skill which makes a jellied tomato consommé or a stew, or a soup, or a vegetable so good, but the spices and condiments, solids or liquids used in the seasoning.

It is difficult to put into words taste reactions regarding seasoning a food. What a cook, amateur or professional, needs is a dictionary of taste words. In mathematics there exist words to express any number from one into infinity, while to describe taste emotions, also infinite in their variety, we have but the loosest of definitions. We say a thing is sour, or sharp, or sweet, or bitter. But there are hundreds of shades of sourness, of sharpness, of sweetness, of bitterness.

Seasoning is to food what fragrance is to a flower. It is the elusive scent with many shades that raises the commonplace to the unusual. "Add salt to taste." This is perhaps the most commonly used phrase in every good cookbook, and this applies also to spices and condiments. Sometimes, of course, a definite amount of these important adjuncts is listed, but generally speaking this is left to the kitchen queen or king's taste.

Some cooks cook "by guess and by gosh" and still evolve just as appetizing dishes for their families or guests as do some fussy cooks who actually taste the food while preparing it in an effort to have it seasoned just right. We would expect the careful cooks to get the better results, but all too often they do not because their sense of taste plays peculiar pranks on them. There is the saltiness of food, for instance.

The cautious cook who adds a pinch of salt and then tastes with the tip of his or her tongue, is more likely than not to end up with the soup or stew so salty that everyone reaches for a glass of drinking water. The saltiness of food cannot be tested on the tip of the tongue. The food must be on the middle and sides of the tongue for one to tell whether or not it is perfectly salted.

The wise cook puts the food well into his or her mouth when sampling it for seasoning. And, if he or she is *really* wise, he or she leaves it there for some time, since the reaction of the taste buds to foods is sluggish. If a quick taste is taken, the food will not seem salty or spicy enough and more will be sprinkled on it. Then, when it is eaten it will be much too salty or too spicy.

A safe psychological rule for cooks to follow is to hold the food in their mouths for say, 15 seconds before deciding whether it needs more salt or other seasoning. If people would eat more slowly they would discover what food really tastes like.

The taste buds for sweets are located on the tip of the tongue. When sampling cooking to see if it has been sufficiently sweetened keep the sample at the front of the mouth, right on the tip of the tongue, for 15 seconds.

If that rule were followed when making salad dressing, it would be unduly sour. One should sample for sourness between the cheek and the side of the tongue. The tongue tip is blind to sourness, but the sides of the tongue have their "eyes" wide open for sour things.

Salad dressing will taste flat if sampled after eating something sweet. When different tastes or flavors follow one another closely, the last flavor is distorted just as a trick mirror distorts things. After tasting lemon pie filling, even sponge rubber would taste sweet.

This is why skilled professional cooks wisely rinse their mouth with lukewarm water between tasting foods. Many high caste Orientals also rinse their mouths with water between courses, that the lingering effects of the curried meat taste may not ruin a perfectly good salad or sweet. Try this some time; you may be pleasantly surprised to find that it helps you to cook better and to enjoy food more fully.

There are dozens of spices which American cooks seldom use because they do not know how to taste for them when preparing foods. But wonders can be worked with them by a person who has the imagination to try them and who also knows how to taste. However, until cooks learn how to taste—and to put some imagination into their food preparation —they are probably sensible if they accurately measure all spices and seasonings exactly as given in the recipe.

Do you know your herbs and spices? Here are a list of those most commonly utilized in cookery.

HERB AND SPICE CHART [2200]

Alder. Very bitter herb used for vermouth and in certain cordials as flavoring.

Allspice. Pill-size fruit of a West Indian tree; flavor resembles blend of nutmeg, clove and cinnamon, hence the name. Used in pickling, fruit preserving, flavoring meats, gravies, sauces and stuffings.

Angelica. A member of the mint family, it derives its name from its "angelical" virtues. Of distinctive, very delicate flavor. The leaves and stalks are candied, and often used as a decoration for cakes, pastries, and so forth and also for medicinal purposes.

Anise Seeds. Small seeds of herb grown in Southern Europe and Africa. Used in pickling, as flavoring for cakes, cookies and pastries and also as an ingredient in cordials and medicines. Latins add anise seeds to their soups, stews and boiled fish—a practice worthy of imitation.

Bay Leaves. This herb comes from trees growing abundantly in America, all more or less resembling the laurel. Bay leaves are used in soups, roasts, and stews, also as a part of the bouquet garni.

Borage. An erect rough European herb with blue flowers, used in beverages and medicines.

Camomile. A strong-scented bitter herb of the aster family, whose flowers are used as a tonic and beverage.

Capers. Also called "Mountain pepper," a caper, the size of a small pea, is the flower bud of a nasturtium-like plant, which grows in rambling patches along walls in the Mediterranean regions of Europe. Pungent and slightly bitter in taste, capers are dried, pickled in vinegar then used in salads, sauces and garnishes. Nasturtium seeds are sometimes sold as capers but in no way compare to the palatable genuine caper.

Caraway Seeds. Small oval "seeds" of an herb of the United States and Europe, caraway seeds are widely used in breads, cakes, vegetables, meats and gravies; also crushed in cottage cheese.

Cardamom Seeds. These brown seeds, found in small white pods resembling small orange pips taste like anise. Used in flavoring stewed fruits, breads, pastries, cookies, and pickles; also in liqueurs.

Cayenne Pepper. The hottest member of the pepper family, cayenne is the flesh of small red peppers grown chiefly in Africa, dried, then ground to a very fine powder. A few grains, or a dash are more than sufficient seasoning. Used in soups, stews, preserves, pickles, chutneys and sauces.

Celery Seeds. A seed-like fruit grown in Holland and France the celery seed is greatly used in pickling. It is also a flavoring for soups, fish, meats, game, sauces and potato salads. It is not the same as celery salt.

Chervil. A salad herb par excellence. This delicate green is like parsley in appearance but sweeter and more aromatic. Good for soups, stews, sauces, gravies, fish, meats, vegetables, and so forth.

Chili Pepper. Small elongated pods of a plant grown in California, Japan, Mexico, and so forth, the scarlet chili pods are seen in northern markets during the fall pickling season, but chili powder, made from this pepper or the green one, is packed in glass and sold the year round. Greatly used in tamales, chili con carne, pickling, and southern cuisine generally.

Chives. A member of the lily family, this perennial is allied to the leek and the onion. Chives contain a large amount of mustard oil which gives them their peculiar and delicate taste; widely used in soups, fish, meats, poultry, vegetables and salads. It is claimed that they stimulate the appetite, and help secrete the gastric juices by stimulating the digestive organs. The French call this herb "The beneficial *ciboulette* (chive) which cleans the blood." Chives are good in cottage and cream cheese; and added to scrambled eggs, they make that familiar breakfast specialty a distinctive dish. Excellent in sandwiches, too.

Cinnamon. Also called cassia, cinnamon is the thin aromatic bark of the cinnamon tree grown in India, China, Palestine, Italy, and so forth. When peeled off and cleaned it is known as "stick cinnamon." In earliest Colonial days cinnamon and sugar were mixed, put in a special big shaker called an "oomah" and used on waffles, pancakes, coffee cake and hot buttered toast. Fine in beverages, desserts, soups, fish, meat, pies, pastries, breads, and so forth.

Cloves. Cloves come from the Molucca Islands, generally known as the Spice Islands. They are also imported from the East and West Indies. The whole clove is the nail-shaped flower bud of the clove tree. Sold whole and in powder form, cloves are used to flavor soups, eggs, fish, meats, stuffings, sauces and gravies, pickles, chutneys, and so forth. French housewives have an ingenious way of eliminating cooking odors.

They sprinkle a bit of clove on the stove, or place a little burning clove on a special copper container and carry it from room to room. Oil of cloves is used in medicines, perfumes and cordials.

Coriander Seeds. Used the same way as cardamom seeds, these seeds are the dried fruit of a small plant, grown mainly in Morocco, China, Southern Europe and also in the United States. Used in cordial-making, candies, pickles, chutneys, as essential in gin making, in hot dogs, gingerbreads, frying batters, cookies, pound cake, biscuits, stuffings and even in mixed salads. Resembles small, white peppercorns and is sold both in whole and ground form.

Cumin. A member of the parsley group, this aromatic annual is good in meats, stews, cordials and liqueurs. In olden times, cumin mixed with honey was applied to black-and-blue marks from bruises. Among the ancients there was a superstition that cumin was a vexatious plant and that the farmer had to curse and abuse it while sowing the seeds if he wanted his crop to prosper and be abundant.

Curry Powder. Curry powder remains a generally misunderstood condiment. Unlike other spices it is not ground from any one herb or plant, but is a combination of more than fifteen different ingredients, all pounded to a powder and blended. This accounts for the wide range of variations in different curry powders available in this country. In India, the home of curries, every family has its own formula. The golden color of curry powder is due to turmeric. Used with chicken, lobster, shrimps, green bananas, mutton, lamb, eggs, and in pickles, and so forth. Curry powder is as good in summer as in winter.

Dill. Called *anet* in France and England, dill is another cousin of parsley, and can be used in many ways in cuisine. With new potatoes, add a few sprigs of dill when potatoes are about half done; add to crabmeat or salmon, and lamb or mutton, pickles, conserves, butters, vinegar, salads, tomatoes, and so forth. Aromatic and pungent, dill adds fragrance to cream or cottage cheese.

Fennel. Of the parsley family, the leaves and tender hollow stems are used in salads, boiled with fish; they may also camouflage medicines. The stalks are used raw—like celery stalks when well-iced. They add flavor to sauces. The seeds, of brownish tone, about $\frac{1}{4}$ inch long and concave, are used in soups and breads; with fruits, in pastries, and in infusions. Oil of fennel is used in medicine, cordials, liqueurs and perfumery.

Filé. A creole seasoning made from powdered sassafras, filé is the soul of New Orleans gumbos. This powder was originated by the Choctaw Indians in Louisiana, and is still prepared by members of the tribe.

Garlic. When you think of garlic, think of lilies whose relative they are. One of the oldest recorded seasonings, garlic may be eaten raw. For centuries garlic has been employed by superstitious people to ward off evil spirits—especially the legendary vampires. According to the old tales, vampires were the blood-sucking nocturnal reincarnations of the dead that rose from their graves at night and hunted the living by sucking their blood like the South American "vampire" bats of real life.

Garlic is widely used in French cuisine, in soups, stews, roasts, poultry, steaks, bread, stuffing, salad dressings, salads, pickles, chutneys, and so forth. Until the middle of the eighteenth century many Siberian villagers paid taxes in garlic: 15 bulbs for a man, 10 for a woman, 5 for a child.

Ginger. Ginger is regarded as the mystery plant by botanists for none of them can tell for a certainty just where this important spice plant had its origin. Some say Asia, some say Brazil, and all the dictionaries say that it is the pungent, spicy rootstock of a tropical plant. It is known however, that ginger was featured in Roman, Greek and Arabian as well as Chinese cooking even in the ages when its source of supply was kept a secret by the crafty traders. It was mentioned both in Sanskrit literature and in the Talmud. Its largest use in cookery is in the flavoring of cakes and cookies, then in beverages, in meat cookery, gravies, preserves, pickles, chutneys, candies, and so forth.

Horebound. This herb, also called "Hoarehound," is a whitish, bitter, perennial of the mint family used in candy making, beverages and medicines. Native of the south of Europe and the East and the United States.

Horseradish. A well-known perennial herbaceous plant which belongs to the order of the mustard family. It has a pungent watery juice. It possesses valuable antiscorbutic properties and is chiefly used as a condiment.

Hyssop. Belonging to the mint group, hyssop has medicinal qualities; the leaves as well as the blossoms are put into soups and salads. Spicy and hot, its mild bitterness helps to flavor fruit salads, beverages and confections.

Juniper. The dark-blue berries of a low evergreen tree with prickly leaves, widely used either whole or powdered with furred or feathered game. Due to its individual flavor a little goes a long way.

California juniper berries are often eaten by the Indians. Sometimes the fruits are ground and made into little cakes.

Lemon Balm. Also of the mint family, this plant is lemon-scented; the leaves are used as flavoring in fruit salads, sauces and hot beverages as well as in medicines. It is found in almost all parts of the United States and Mexico and the West Indies.

Lemon Berries. The red berries of a shrub often found on hillsides and growing among the sand dunes of southern California. They excrete an acid substance which when soaked in plain or charged water, makes an excellent beverage, as a substitute for lemonade, and for flavoring desserts, hot, cold and frozen.

Mace. An aromatic spice widely used in cookery, it is actually the lacy covering (orange-red in color) of the nutmeg.Used especially in preserving, flavoring fish, fish sauces, stuffings, and so forth.

Marigold. Sometimes known as "American cowslip," marigold has more than 25 different aliases. The leaves and stems are boiled and served in the same manner as spinach, and many people say that it is the equal of and even superior to spinach. In some parts of the country, the tender flower buds are picked and used as a substitute for capers. The flowers are also used as a food coloring.

Marjoram. Long ago the leaves of this mint perennial were used in scented waters. Now they are used for seasoning egg dishes, beef, pork and lamb and mutton, meat loaves, stuffings, mushrooms, soups, sauces, hamburgers and cheese dishes. Found all over the United States and Canada marjoram is often cultivated in kitchen window boxes as a pot herb.

Mint. What a world of pungent coolness is in store for those who have a mint patch tucked away in a shady corner of their yard or garden! Use its refreshing flavor in cooling drinks; in sauces, both for desserts and meats, especially mutton and lamb; as a garnish, whole or chopped; in frozen and chilled desserts; in vegetables, and in appetizers, cold or hot soups. Remember—just a dash of its tantalizing freshness is needed.

Cook a sprig or two of fresh mint with applesauce if you are seeking something tasty, yet inexpensive, to serve with lamb, goose and pork.

Mustard Seeds. The British mustard king, J. Colman, once said: "My fortune came not from the mustard people eat, but from the amount they leave on the side of their plate." The tiny white or black mustard seeds are widely used in pickling and come chiefly from California. In the South, mustard greens are cooked like spinach. The seeds are ground into powder and used for dry and prepared mustard. Its uses are well known.

Nasturtium. Flowers, stems, and leaves can be devoured literally. They have genuine eye-appeal when fresh, but when you've used the dried leaves you'll probably prefer to skim them out of the soups. The seeds are pickled, added to salads, green or fruit, and so forth.

Nutmeg. When you buy whole nutmeg and grate it, you get nutmeg. When you buy ground "nutmeg" maybe it's mostly mace, the not so good shell of the nut. This pit or kernel of the fruit of East Indies trees is widely used in cookery, almost from soup to nuts, including beverages.

Oregano. Oregano, the sage of Mexico, is an herb of velvety green leaf, its flavor a cross between sage and marjoram. It is a stock ingredient of chili powder, but use only a tiny pinch. Oregano gives a delightful, new, quite indescribable flavor when added to baked beans, stuffings, scrambled eggs, omelets, fish, pork, veal, beef, fish and meat loaves.

Paprika. The ground pod of sweet red pepper, from Turkey, Hungary and Spain. Paprika has such a mild flavor that it may be said to be more of a coloring or garnish than a true condiment. Many characteristic dishes secure their gay red or pink color from the lavish use of this pepper, as witness veal with paprika, or the famous Wiener schnitzel. It also lends its rich color to tomato catsups and other tomato condiments.

Parsley. This biennial is best known as a garnish, fresh or deep-fried, for almost any dish from soup to salad inclusive. It is also used as a seasoning. It is one of the best sources of vitamin A, an ounce supplying 30,000 units of that vitamin when cooked with other foods. When fresh and raw it is a large source of vitamin C and is high in iron, calcium, phosphorus, manganese and copper, all essential food minerals. Too many cooks look down on this humble green. But its history is by no means humble. Hercules wore a crown of parsley for special occasions. Horace had his banqueting hall decorated with parsley and roses, while

Anacreon called parsley the emblem of joy and festivity. *To keep parsley, mint or watercress fresh,* wash thoroughly, shake off excess water, place in a glass jar and keep in the refrigerator. The parsley and other greens will keep fresh for a week or more without becoming limp or slimy.

Peppers. Black and white peppers are made from the same berry, black pepper being ground from the whole fruit before it has fully ripened, while white pepper is obtained from the ripe fruit after the piquant hull has been removed. Nutmeg and mace are related in a similar manner, the mace coming from the outer shell of the nutmeg kernel. Ground black pepper, which is hotter than white pepper, is prepared from the dried immature berry of the pepper vine. Ground white pepper is made from the mature berry after the outer dark husk has been removed. Piperine, an alkaloid of pepper, stimulates perspiration, thus having a cooling effect on the body if a sufficient amount is eaten. For this reason, pepper is widely used in seasoning food in hot countries. Both black and white peppers are grown in the East Indies, southern India, French Indo-China and Siam.

Pique Seasoning. A meat-free liquid compound made of vegetable protein derivatives, water, salt, yeast, vegetable extract, spices and vegetable fat. Widely used in cooking as a flavor amplifier (it is a strong seasoning) its sole purpose is to emphasize the natural richness of the foods you cook. Pique Seasoning is concentrated and may be used sparingly in gravies, sauces, soups, meats, stews, goulashes, hashes, poultry, vegetables, fish and meat loaves, hamburgers, stuffings, game or cooked salad dressings. It is valuable for replacing the meat or vegetable stocks frequently demanded in good cuisine.

With absolutely no effort on the part of the cook, Pique Seasoning unobtrusively brings out hidden flavors in even the simplest dishes. To emphasize the robust flavors of mutton, beef or venison, a sauce containing this seasoning is almost traditional, as many chefs and cooks look upon Pique as the father of liquid condiments. It has aroma, body, character, flavor and tang.

For instant broth, bouillon or consommé, hot or cold, stir 1 teaspoon of Pique Seasoning into each cup of boiling or cold water. For gravies, 1 teaspoon of Pique Seasoning added to the pan after gravy has boiled 2 or 3 minutes, gives zest and enhances the natural flavor. For instant gravy, use 1 teaspoon of Pique Seasoning with 1 cup of vegetable water or stock to replace meat stock or milk in gravy recipe.

Poppy Seeds. Poppy seeds are imported from Holland and have a distinctive flavor but almost no fragrance. Some one who has counted them said there are 900,000 seeds to the pound. They are used mostly as a topping for cakes, rolls, yeast coffee cakes, cookies, confections, liqueurs and cordials.

Rosemary. The leaves of this evergreen mint, noted for its stimulating, refreshing fragrance are used to season chicken, lamb, pork, soups, sauces and fish stuffings or scattered over salads. There is an old legend about rosemary. When Mary hung the infant Jesus' clothes on a rosemary bush, it flowered at once.

It is said that rosemary never grows higher than Christ stood and that it is only supposed to live for 33 years. It has always been symbolical of good friendship and remembrance.

Rue. Nearly evergreen, rue's bitter leaves are used for seasoning and beverage-flavoring; it seasons salads; and is used in medicines. It is a small bushy herb used for its stimulating effects.

Saffron. Favorite flavoring and coloring for food in early England, saffron was so valuable and expensive that the nobles who grew it kept the special yard under lock and key. It is collected from the stigma of a variety of purple crocus which grows profusely in northern and southern Europe. That does not mean, however, that it is easily obtained, for it requires the stigmas of about 75,000 flowers to produce just one pound of saffron. The ancient Egyptians called it "The Blood of Thoth" and used it in religious ceremonies. They considered it a plant dedicated to the sun. Ladies of ancient Greece used it as a hair dye, the Babylonians as a perfume and cosmetic; the French, the Italians, and the Spanish use it as a flavoring in curries, sauces and rice.

Sage. Seers ages ago believed if a household prospered, the sage, with its swartly painted leaves, about it grew strong. Its a mint perennial, its most common uses are in stuffing, cheese, certain gravies and sauces, soups and meats, including game birds and venison, which, however, prefer the sagebrush, a shrubby plant of the aster family, abundant on the elevated plains of the western United States.

Salt. Common salt, formerly regarded as an elementary substance, is sodium chloride. Salt is important in nutrition. Trade between the Ægean and southern Russia was largely dependent upon salt, and salt was considered so vital that one of the oldest roads in Italy was called Via Salaria. Over this road the important commodity was carried from Ostia into the Sabine country.

Cakes of salt have been used for money in Abyssinia and Tibet. Marco Polo mentions its importance in his report on the financial system of the Mongolian emperors. As one might expect, much salt is obtained from the Great Salt Lake in Utah; the ocean water off California also yields great quantities of the commodity by evaporation. A daily portion of salt given as pay to Roman soldiers was often computed for money which was called "salarium." Hence the modern word "salary."

To eat salt with an Arab indicates to him the same responsibility of hospitality that we feel toward anyone who breaks bread with us. It is a tradition that the Arabs feel so strongly about salt that a robber who chances to fall over the family salt block as he enters the house to rob, will leave that house untouched. Salt was war material to the ancient Mayans. Quilted cotton jackets filled with salt were worn as body armor. It was as a result of looking for salt that one of Vermont's main industries (granite) was established. Montpelier (Vermont) citizens drilling for salt in 1827 gave it up as a bad job after striking layer upon layer of granite; later they decided to mine the granite!

"The Condiment of Condiments" thus Plutarch described salt. The Greeks at one time consecrated salt to the gods. In cookery, there is hardly anything that is not improved by a touch of salt which, however, should be used discreetly. A good cook will test a dish for seasoning and not depend entirely upon measurements.

While it is possible to live without salt, if a large amount of meat is eaten, most of us would find it difficult to take enough food to satisfy us if we had to do without it entirely. And seldom would we enjoy our meals in its absence. Of course, it is true that many of us use so much salt that we ruin our palate for other flavors. We all know men—and women —who shake the salt-shaker over food before they taste it. *This practice is an insult to the cook.* Taste first, and salt afterward if necessary, or if you think it is.

Sesame Seeds. Very difficult to acquire, sesame seeds are quite the most expensive of the spices when obtainable at all. Not much is imported nor is much grown, and of the amount grown, the native markets usually consume the greater part. In Persia (Iran) it is greatly used in bread. Sesame seeds are small honey-colored seeds from Turkey and the Orient, which give a nut-like flavor to breads and confections. Source of sesame oil.

Summer Savory. A hardy annual aromatic herb, the leafy top is used as a garnish; the leaves, chopped or powdered, are used in string beans, peas, salads, stuffings, hamburgers, meat loaves, croquettes, fruit, vegetable or vegetable juice cocktails.

Sweet Basil. Chiefly used as a seasoning for soups, stews, sauces, meats and poultry, basil is the potted plant often seen blossoming in windows and on fire escapes. It is the sacred household plant of India, and Italians think so much of it that the rustic lover hangs a sprig of basil over his ear when he goes a-courting. The clove-like, flowery tang has an especial affinity for tomatoes, cucumbers and squash.

Tarragon. Tarragon, the very badge of the gourmet, is never in the seedman's catalogues, yet it flavors our bottled capers and the green herb lends magical charm to salads, French dressing, omelets, aspics, mousses, to pickles, to vinegars, to mustard, to tartar sauce, to cocktail sauces, to ravigote, to compounded butter for fish and shell fish dishes, and chicken dishes, and is the very soul of Sauce Béarnaise. Tarragon herb is a European perennial plant allied to wormwood, cultivated in this country for its aromatic leaves.

Thyme. The Romans administered thyme as a certain remedy for melancholy spirits. The fairy tale of the Irish is that mounds of thyme are much liked by the fairies who choose aromatic flower beds for their hours of dancing. Thyme is one of the major herbs in flavor for stuffings, gravies, sauces, soups, meats, poultry, game meat, fish loaves, or "burgers." Thyme is a woody-based perennial with small gray leaves, a natural flavoring for rabbit and other wild game. Used also in pickles, chipped beef, in onion soup and scalloped onions.

Turmeric. The saliva-stirring aroma that greets the nostrils when you open a bottle of chow-chow is produced by one of the least known of the spices—turmeric. This musky-odored root spice is the neglected child of the spice family in the United States. Turmeric in the dried, unground state looks like pieces of thin twigs smeared with mustard, but the orange-yellow coloring is imparted by nature and not by the mustard spoon.

Because of its coloring properties, our frugal forefathers often used turmeric to give a rich appearance to light-tinted foods. Cakes, butter and cheeses often owed their egg yolk yellow to a pinch of this spice.

Vinegars. Lord Byron, it is said, during his lifetime drank gallons of vinegar in the unpoetic belief that it would keep his weight down. In European countries no salad was considered good if not seasoned with herbs. The Italians, for instance were so fond of burnet that they say:

> *"L'Insalata non e buon, ne bella*
> *Ove non e la Pimpinella."*

meaning that a salad is neither good nor nice if there is no burnet. To the French no salad was nice or good that was not seasoned with tarragon. The foundation of a fine French dressing, one that is the quintessence of simplicity, demands four basic flavorings: red or white wine vinegar; shallots, the delicate onion; garlic, the kitchen deity of all good cooks, and tarragon, so bittersweet it tempts the devil himself. Perhaps you believe that all vinegars are alike. A hundred times no! Vinegar skillfully made and aged can be as superior to the ordinary run as fine wines are to lesser vintages. And not only are there differences in qualities, there are differences in kinds. Good vinegar makes itself known to those who have a keen sense of smell and a discriminating palate. Quality vinegar has bouquet, the aroma of cider, wine or malt, according to the material of which it is made. Fine flavor too is dependent upon the quality of the vinegar's ingredients. Sourness or acidity, although essential to vinegar, is not its most desirable trait. It must possess flavor, aroma, mellowness, subtle strength. Don't get the impression that vinegars are only for the salad dressing. They serve as seasoners for all types of fine foods. Try vinegar with meats, fish, vegetables in sauces, stews, marinades for rabbit and venison, pickles, chutneys, and so forth. Add vinegar to a dish and you add flavor as surely as in the adding of spirits or vanilla.

Winter Savory. See "Summer Savory."

Woodruff, or Waldmeister, meaning "master of the forest" is grown in many American gardens as well as imported from Europe, and is chiefly used to perfume wine punch, champagne bowls, and similar beverages. Vodoo magic woodruff holds in leaf and flower. It is commended as most excellent "to open obstructions of the liver and spleen." Nourishing and restorative, but, more to the modern whim: "Put into wine woodruff makes a man merry."

Yerba Buena. A wild mint of great strength, which must be used with care. Add a miserly pinch to split pea soup or to the butter for basting the boiled potato, the squash purée, fruit salad or to "make" an afternoon tea.

The sameness of food, served day after day and month after month, has caused battles in homes, riots in institutions and rebellions in armies. A continued diet of bread and water is no worse than a prolonged existence on quail. Either one will get you in the end.

—G. Selmer Fougner.

FROZEN FOODS   [2201]
Fish

Seasonal and geographical limitations of menus used to be an inevitable fact of life just like death and taxes. But today even the most budget-minded homemaker can serve fresh-flavored sea food delicacies, any cut of meat or poultry, vegetables or fruits any day in the year, no matter where she lives. Science has crossed "out of season" off the food lists of the family, restaurant and institution menu. Arctic cold applied with the speed of light seals in the fleeting deliciousness of fresh ocean or fresh water fish. All cleaning and preparation are done before the quick freezing is applied. When the carton is opened the fish is ready to cook; meal preparation time is cut in half and there is no waste.

One of the principal reasons for advocating the selling of frozen fish *as* frozen fish is the fact that when it is defrosted prior to cooking, it loses a considerable portion of the food value due to leakage which is caused by the separation of the more soluble protein from the insoluble protein. It is advisable to handle frozen fish as frozen fish and retain them in the frozen condition until sold to the consumer, who should prepare them immediately for cooking. And properly frozen fish are fully as good as the best fresh fish, if honestly sold.

Thawing. Fish may be thawed completely, or only partially, before cooking. To thaw, place it in the refrigerator in the unopened container. Three-fourths of a pound requires about 6 to 10 hours. With slow thawing there is less leakage. Fish should be cooked *while still chilled* because it spoils quickly.

Cooking. Thawed fish may be cooked like any unfrozen fish. If the fish is cooked while still frozen, additional cooking time is, of course, required.

EGGS   [2202]

Frozen eggs *must* be thawed before they are used. Use the whites just as you would the whites of fresh eggs. Eggs may be thawed in the refrigerator, at room temperature in still air, in front of an electric fan, or by setting the container in cold water. Frozen eggs, particularly the yolks, should be used while they are still chilled.

Cooking. Thawed frozen egg whites may be used in any way in which unfrozen egg whites are used. They make just as good if not better meringues and angel cakes than do unfrozen egg whites.

It is customary to add sugar, honey, corn syrup, vinegar, or proteolytic enzymes to whole eggs and to egg yolks before freezing; therefore these eggs or egg yolks cannot be used in all recipes. When recipes call for them, allowance should be made for the sweetening or acid already in the eggs.

Egg yolks to which salt has been added are suitable only for making mayonnaise or salad dressings. Again, allowance must be made for the salt in the yolks.

VEGETABLES [2203]

Usually it is best to start cooking a vegetable while it is still frozen; however, stalk vegetables such as asparagus and broccoli may be thawed just enough to break the stalks apart, if not immersed in boiling water, particularly if they are to be cooked in a small amount of water by steaming or in a pressure saucepan. If they are to be slightly thawed, they should be left in the sealed package and thawed for not more than $1\frac{1}{4}$ hours at room temperature or for 4 hours in the refrigerator. This partial thawing shortens the total cooking time from 3 to 5 minutes. Solid blocks of leaf vegetables, such as spinach, may be cut in 1-inch cubes to insure uniform doneness. Vegetables such as peas, corn, green beans, and lima beans fall apart fairly quickly after starting to cook, so that it is not necessary to defrost them. As soon as these vegetables are partially thawed in cooking, it is advisable to break them apart gently with a fork to insure uniform cooking. In most methods of cooking corn on the cob it is necessary to thaw the cob before cooking. Otherwise it may be icy after the kernels are done. Partially thawed vegetables require a shorter cooking time than do the solidly frozen ones, less time is required for the water to return to the boil after they are added, and the cooked vegetables are more uniformly done. Completely thawed vegetables shrink while cooking and become less attractive. They also have a less desirable flavor and may have a lower ascorbic acid (vitamin C) content than do those cooked without being thawed or after partial thawing.

Dry-packed vegetables after removal from freezer storage may be kept in the icecube compartment of a refrigerator for from 5 to 7 days without significant loss of quality.

Cooking. No vegetables commonly frozen at home or at the locker plant are at present actually cooked before freezing, but beets, squash, baked beans and a few "ready-made" dishes are. Therefore, with the exception of these, all frozen vegetables require some cooking whether they are to be served hot or cold in a salad. In general, frozen vegetables are cooked by methods similar to those for fresh vegetables, except that frozen vegetables require only from $\frac{1}{2}$ to $\frac{1}{3}$ as long cooking as do the corresponding fresh ones. Care must be taken not to overcook frozen vegetables, because all of them have been partially precooked in preparation for freezing. It is almost impossible to give the exact cooking time for frozen vegetables, for that depends upon the variety, the maturity, the size of the vegetable pieces, upon the length of time the vegetable has stood between the garden and the blanching and temperature of the frozen vegetable when it is put on to cook. Only the amount that can be eaten at one meal should be cooked at a time. Holding a cooked vegetable and then rewarming it results in increased losses of vitamin C, as does also keeping it hot for any length of time (as for example in restaurants, over the steam table).

As the coloring in green vegetables is set by blanching and freezing, they can be satisfactorily cooked by some methods not satisfactory for fresh, green vegetables. The cook must be sure that they are cooked in such a way that her family likes the flavor, aroma, color, shape, and texture. She can usually help her family to develop a liking for the vegetables that are most health-giving.

Boiling. To cook in the least time, the water should be boiling and the cover, if one is used, should be hot when the vegetable is added. The water should be brought back to the boil in from 3 to 6 minutes, and then the heat should be reduced so that the water boils gently the rest of the period. *The time for cooking is counted after the water returns to the boil.* If a small amount of water is used so that no more than 1 or 2 tablespoonfuls are left at the end of the cooking period, the greatest amount of nutritive value is retained and the product is usually most palatable. The amount of cooking water needed depends upon the amount of frost present, the cooking time required, and the rate of evaporation which is determined by the rate of boiling, the size and shape of pan, and whether the pan is covered. One-fourth cupful of water is enough for many vegetables.

The heat should be high until the water returns to the boil and the vegetables are steaming. If the mass of vegetables has not broken apart by this time, it should be separated with a fork, the cover replaced, and the heat turned low to finish the steaming or boiling. If more than one package of frozen vegetables is to be cooked at one time, the cooking pan should be large enough in diameter to allow both packages to rest on the bottom of the pan; that is, one frozen block should not be placed on another. If frozen vegetables are cooked in as small an amount of water as ¼ cupful in a small covered pan, the greater portion of the vegetable is not immersed in water and is therefore cooked by steaming. This method keeps the solution of the flavor, the water-soluble vitamins, and the minerals into the cooking water to a minimum.

Steaming. Steaming in a standard type of steamer is a satisfactory way to cook some frozen vegetables, such as corn on the cob that has been thawed beforehand.

Pressure Saucepan. Cooking vegetables in a pressure saucepan results in a palatable product with a high vitamin retention. The possible exceptions in palatability are the green, so-called strong-juiced, vegetables, such as broccoli. Frozen vegetables, particularly the stalk vegetables, should be thawed enough to break them apart before they are placed in a pressure saucepan. Otherwise, because of the short cooking period at a high temperature, the center of the block may still contain ice crystals when the outside is done. The pan, including the cover, should be hot and the water boiling when the vegetable is added. At the end of the cooking time the pan should be placed immediately in cold water, the weight and then the cover removed as quickly as possible (within ¾ minute). Special care is needed to prevent overcooking any vegetables in a pressure saucepan and particularly frozen vegetables. The amount of water required is just enough to keep the vegetable from burning and, because of the frost in frozen vegetables, is about two-thirds as much as for fresh vegetables.

Double Boiler. Some vegetables, especially frozen squash, may be satisfactorily cooked in their own juices in a double boiler. Cut sweet corn is excellent when cooked in milk in the upper part of a double boiler, but peas and asparagus lose a little color and flavor.

Oven Cooking. Frozen corn on the cob is delicious when roasted for about 20 minutes in an oven at 400° F. The ears are brushed with melted, salt butter and roasted until done and slightly browned. The heat of the oven dries the corn so that it is less water-soaked than when cooked by other methods. Asparagus, peas, and probably other vegetables may be placed in a buttered casserole, with butter and salt added, and the covered dishes placed in an oven set at moderate (350° F.). Asparagus requires about 30 minutes to bake and peas 15 minutes.

Pan Frying. In pan frying, the frozen vegetable is added to about 2 tablespoons of melted fat in a heavy skillet. Salt is then added, the pan covered, and the vegetable cooked over moderate heat until done. At about two minute intervals, the cover should be lifted and the vegetable stirred. Corn and asparagus are good cooked this way. Asparagus should be cut into about ½-inch lengths and fried in small amounts for about 2½ minutes.

Deep-fat Frying. Defrosted corn on the cob is excellent when fried in deep fat. Some other vegetables, including cauliflower and asparagus, can be boiled, steamed, or cooked in a pressure saucepan, then dipped in a thin batter and fried in deep fat.

Other Ways To Serve Frozen Foods. Cooked frozen vegetables, like cooked fresh vegetables, may be served as cream soup, creamed vegetables, soufflés, fritters, timbales, casserole dishes, chop suey or salads. The directions for using cooked frozen vegetables in most dishes are the same as for using the corresponding cooked fresh vegetables.

GUIDE FOR COOKING TIME AND AMOUNT   [2204]
OF WATER FOR BOILING FROZEN
VEGETABLES

Note. This table is simply a guide based on 1-pound lots of vegetables added to boiling water and cooked in lightly covered pans. The cooking time varies with the variety, maturity, size of pieces, and method of preparation. If the smallest amount of water is used, the greater portion of the vegetable will be steamed rather than boiled. The time required for the water to return to a boil is from 3 to 6 minutes. Some prefer to use a large amount of water to heat the corn through quickly and thus help to prevent sogginess.

VEGETABLE (Approximately 2 cups)	AMOUNT OF WATER (Cups)	TIME OF BOILING AFTER WATER RETURNS TO BOIL (Minutes)
Asparagus	¼ to 1	5 to 10
Spears	¼ to ½	3 to 4
Cut in ½ lengths	¼ to 1	8 to 12
Beet greens	¼ to 1	10 to 15
Beans, green	¼ to 1	4 to 10
Broccoli	¼ to 1	3 to 6
Cauliflower	½ to 1	5 to 6
Corn, cut	¼ to ½	3 to 8
Corn on the Cob	Sufficient to cover well	3 to 8
Kale	¼ to 1	10 to 15
Lima beans	1 to 2	16 to 22
Mustard greens	¼ to 1	8 to 12
Peas	¼ to ¾	5 to 8
Soybeans	½ to 1	10 to 20
Spinach	¼ to ¾	4 to 8

TIMETABLE AND AMOUNT OF WATER FOR   [2205]
COOKING FROZEN VEGETABLES IN A
PRESSURE COOKER

VEGETABLE (About 2 cups)	AMOUNT OF WATER		APPROXIMATE TIME AT 15 POUNDS PRESSURE (Minutes)
	For 1 and 2 qt. saucepans (Cups)	For 3 and 4 qt. saucepans (Cups)	
Asparagus	⅙ to ¼	¼ to ½	0
Beet greens	⅙ to ¼	¼ to ½	¾ to 1
Beans, green	⅙ to ¼	¼ to ½	0 to 1
Broccoli	⅙ to ¼	¼ to ½	½ to 1
Cauliflower	⅙ to ¼	¼ to ½	½ to 1
Lima Beans	⅙ to ¼	¼ to ½	1½ to 2½
Peas	⅙ to ¼	¼ to ½	0 to ¼
Spinach	⅙ to ¼	¼ to ½	¾ to 1

FRUITS [2206]

Thawing. If frozen fruit is to be cooked before using, it need not be thawed. Berries for desserts are served while a little ice still remains in the fruit. The addition of cream will probably thaw the tissue still more. In this way the structure and the shape of the fruit are retained and leakage is kept low. Such fruits as peaches, apricots and apples require more thawing than berries.

Fruit for pie and cobblers must be thawed enough to spread, and fruit for shortcake, puddings and ice creams must be partially thawed. During thawing, fruit should be left in the unopened, original container.

The method of thawing depends on how soon the fruit is to be eaten. A one-pound package thaws in the refrigerator in from 5 to 6 hours. Fruit frozen in a water-tight package can be thawed in about forty-five minutes by standing it in a pan of cool water. If hot water is used, the fruit may heat above room temperature and darken and lose flavor. Peaches and apricots are particularly subject to darkening. The preferred method for these fruits is fairly rapid thawing in lukewarm water or in rapidly running cold water. A one-pound package of fruit thaws in from 3 to 4 hours at ordinary kitchen temperature. This time can be cut more than half by placing the package in front of an electric fan. From 6 to 10 hours are required if the package is placed in an ordinary household refrigerator. Partial thawing requires only about half of the time for complete thawing. In general, rapid thawing is best for fruits if they are not warmed in the process.

If the fruits have been packed in leak-proof packages, it is advisable to invert the packages while thawing. This results in more uniform color and flavor. All fruits darken and lose flavor soon after they are removed from the carton; therefore, they should be used immediately.

Fruits packed in sugar or syrup may be kept (after removal from freezer storage), in the ice-cube compartment of a refrigerator for from 10 to 15 days without significant loss of quality.

Cooking. In using frozen fruits, allowance should be made for the sugar added before the fruit was frozen. In some dishes no additional sugar is required. Frozen fruits lend themselves well to fruit juice for either pasteurization or for jelly-making because the freezing and thawing cause the fruit colors to dissolve in the juice and the cells of the fruit to break, thus releasing the juices. No heating of frozen fruit is necessary for the extraction of juice; therefore danger of overcooking and the extraction of bitter tannin is prevented. Strawberry and raspberry jams and preserves made from frozen berries that have been stored several months are as good as those made from fresh fruit during the berry season. They are superior to the jams and preserves made during the season and stored for several months.

TIMETABLE FOR COOKING FROZEN MEAT [2207]
(*From Minnesota Agricultural Experiment Station*)

Note. This table is merely a guide. The length of cooking depends on the proportion of fat and bone present, the shape, weight, and temperature of the meat, as well as the temperature of cooking. The best method to determine doneness is to insert a meat thermometer.

CUT	METHOD OF COOKING	DEGREE OF DONENESS	THAWED BEFORE COOKING Approximate Time	STARTED TO COOK IN FROZEN STATE Approximate Time
			Minutes per pound	Minutes per pound
Standing-Rib Roast	Roasting at 300° F.	Rare	18	43
		Medium	22	47
		Well-done	30	55
Rolled-Rib Roast	Roasting at 300° F.	Rare	28	53
		Medium	32	56
		Well-done	40	65
Pork Loin Roast Center Cut	Roasting at 350° F.	Well-done	30 to 35	50 to 55
Rib or shoulder end			40 to 45	50 to 55
Leg of Lamb	Roasting at 300° F.	Well-done	30 to 35	40 to 45
Beef Rump	Braising	Well-done	30 to 35	50
Porterhouse Steak				
1 inch thick	Broiling	Rare	8 to 10	21 to 33
1½ inches thick	Broiling	to	10 to 15	23 to 38
2 inches thick	Broiling	Medium	20 to 30	33 to 43
Beef Patties				
1 inch thick	Pan-broiling	Medium	10 to 12	16 to 18
Sausage Patties	Pan-broiling	Well-done	15 to 25	22 to 28

MEATS   [2208]

Thawing. Thin steaks, chops, and cutlets may be cooked without thawing but steaks as thick as 1½ inches should be either partially or completely thawed. Large roasts cook more uniformly if they are at least partially thawed otherwise the center may be raw and cold while the outside is well-browned. Ground meats should be *completely* thawed. Kidney fat which becomes rancid fairly quickly is better cooked while still frozen. It may be advisable for the same reason to cook, without thawing, pork that contains much fat.

A good way to thaw meat is to place it in the refrigerator without removing the wrapping. There is less drip than with more rapid thawing at room temperature.

Steaks weighing from 1 to 2 pounds thaw completely in the refrigerator in from 5 to 12 hours; a four-pound roast thaws in from 8 to 12 hours. Partial thawing requires about half as long. At room temperature meat thaws in about 2 hours per pound. Placing the meat in front of an electric fan decreases the time by more than half.

Cooking Thawed Meat. Thawed meats and fresh meats may be cooked in the same way. Solidly frozen roasts require from 12 to 25 minutes more cooking, per pound, than do thawed roasts. Since freezing tenderizes meat, less time may be required to cook some frozen meats.

Broiling Frozen Meat. Broiling is excellent for tender cuts of beef and lamb with large exposed surfaces, but is not suitable for pork and veal. Meat for broiling should be cut thick; steaks from 1 to 2 inches and lamb chops at least ¾ inch thick.

To Broil. Preheat the broiler rack, and rub over with fat. Place the meat on the rack in such a position that 2-inch thick meat is 3 inches from the source of heat. The temperature at the surface of the meat should be about 350° F. After the meat is brown on one side, salt it and turn by inserting the fork in the fat part of the meat. When brown on the second side, salt it and remove the meat to a hot platter. To broil a steak rare to medium: Broil a completely thawed 1-inch-thick steak from 8 to 10 minutes, a 1½-inch-thick steak from 10 to 15 minutes. If the steaks are broiled while still solidly frozen, the time is approximately doubled.

Pan-Broiling. Any meat that can be cooked by broiling can also be satisfactorily pan-broiled. To pan-broil: Preheat a heavy frying pan or skillet and rub fat over it. Place the meat in the hot pan without adding either fat or water. Brown it on both sides with high heat. Then reduce the temperature and continue cooking until done as desired. Pour off the fat as it accumulates during the cooking. Salt the steak, dot with butter, and serve on a heated platter.

Ground Meat (Hamburger). Ground meat patties may be broiled the same way.

Roasting. A tender cut is best for roasting, preferably at least 5 inches thick to prevent excess evaporation. To roast: Season the roast with mixed salt and pepper and pour any leakage over it. Insert a meat thermometer so that the bulb reaches the center of the largest muscle and does *not* rest on any fat or bone. Place the roast, fat side up, on a rack in a shallow pan. Do not add water and do not cover the pan.

Place beef, lamb, veal, and smoked pork in a low oven (300° F.), fresh pork in a moderate oven (350° F.). Roast to the desired degree of doneness. Baste with melted butter and hot water or beef stock. For rare beef, the thermometer should read 140° F.; for medium rare, 160° F.;

and for well done, 170° F. Lamb is roasted to 175° F. for medium, and to 180° F. for well done. Veal and pork should *always* be cooked until well done at 185° F.

A thawed, rolled-rib roast requires about 28 minutes a pound for rare, 32 minutes for medium-rare, and 40 minutes for well-done when the oven temperature is kept at 300° F.

Braising. The meat should be thawed and seasoned.

Stewing. The meat should be thawed.

The idea of frozen foods was fostered over 300 years ago by Lord Francis Bacon (1561–1626), English Statesman and scientist, who in his experiments tried to preserve meat with the aid of snow. The experiments ended when Lord Bacon caught a cold which proved fatal.

POULTRY THAWING   [2209]

All poultry except that for fricassée should be at least partially thawed. Whole chickens, ducks, turkeys, quail, and similar birds lose practically no juices on thawing because of their skin covering. Poultry for roasting should be completely thawed because the flesh near the bones has better flavor if it is completely done. A three-pound bird requires approximately 6 hours to defrost in a mechanical refrigerator. Larger birds require a shorter time per pound. Thawing only enough to remove the giblets and to stuff requires still less time. Since the fat in the body cavity tends to become rancid more quickly than does the surface fat, it may be advisable to remove the fat in the body cavity and keep it frozen until the beginning of the cooking.

Cooking. Thawed frozen poultry is cooked as is the unfrozen. If it is not completely thawed, additional cooking time is necessary. Like meat, the young tender birds can be cooked by dry heat and the older, less tender birds by moist heat. The less tender birds should be cooked at a simmering, not a boiling, temperature.

OTHER FOODS   [2210]

Milk, butter, cream, and cheese should be thawed completely and used as when fresh. Freezing retains more nutritive value than does any other method of food preservation; nevertheless, unless foods are carefully handled before freezing, some of their value may be lost in preparation. Foods when frozen require less cooking than when fresh, therefore they may be as high in nutritive value as when cooked fresh. Cooked frozen vegetables contain greater quantities of vitamins than do heated canned vegetables and considerably greater than cooked dehydrated vegetables.

No studies have been reported on the losses of vitamins during cooking of frozen meat, fish, poultry, or eggs.

TABLE OF MEASUREMENTS AND EQUIVALENTS OF MOST USED COMMON FOODS FOR MENU AND BUDGET MAKING [2211]

APPLE	Dried—1 pound = 5 cups. Double in bulk after cooking. Apple fresh, sliced or cubed—3 apples per pound.
APPLESAUCE	1 tablespoon = 1/2 ounce. 1/4 cup = 2 ounces. 1/2 cup = 4 ounces. 3/4 cup = 6 ounces. 1 cup = 8 ounces. 2 cups per pound.
APRICOTS	Dried, uncooked—1/4 cup = 1 1/3 ounces. 1/2 cup = almost 3 ounces. 3/4 cup = 4 ounces. 1 cup = 5 1/3 ounces. 3 cups = 1 pound. Dried, cooked—1/2 cup = 1 3/5 ounces. 3/4 cup = 2 2/5 ounces. 1 cup = 3 1/5 ounces. 1 pint = 6 2/5 ounces. 5 cups per pound.
ASPARAGUS	1 bunch = 1 pound.
BACON	Raw—medium strips = 30 slices. Wide strips = 15 slices per pound.
BAKING POWDER	1 ounce = 2 1/2 tablespoons.
BAKING SODA	1 ounce = 2 1/2 tablespoons.
BANANAS	Whole, unpeeled—3 bananas per pound. Peeled, sliced or cubed, 3 1/2 bananas per pound. Bananas, mashed, 1 cup = 8 ounces.
BARLEY	Pearl—2 cups = 1 pound.
BEANS	Navy and lima—2 2/3 cups per pound.
BLACKBERRIES	Fresh—1/4 cup = 2/3 ounce. 1/2 cup = 1 1/3 ounces. 3/4 cup = 2 ounces. 1 cup = 2 2/3 ounces. About 6 cups per pound.
BLUEBERRIES	Fresh—1/4 cup = 1 1/7 ounces. 1/2 cup = 2 2/7 ounces. 3/4 cup = 3 3/7 ounces. 1 cup = 4 4/7 ounces. 3 1/2 cups per pound.
BREAD CRUMBS	Day old—3/4 cup = 1 1/3 ounces. 1 cup = generous 1 3/4 ounces. 9 cups per pound. Day old, broken 1 cup = 1 3/4 generous ounces. 9 cups per pound. Toasted, sieved 1 tablespoon = 1/4 ounce. 1/4 cup = 1 ounce. 1/2 cup = 2 ounces. 3/4 cup = 3 ounces. 1 cup = 4 ounces. 4 cups per pound. Sandwich, 1 loaf = 36 to 40 slices 1/4 inch thick.
BUTTER	1 tablespoon = 1/2 ounce. 1/4 cup = 2 ounces. 1/2 cup = 4 ounces. 3/4 cup = 6 ounces. 1 cup = 8 ounces. 2 cups per pound.
CAKE CRUMBS	1/4 cup = 3/4 ounce. 1/2 cup = 1 1/2 ounces. 3/4 cup = 2 1/4 ounces. 1 cup = 3 ounces. 5 1/3 cups per pound.
CHEESE	American, grated—1/4 cup = 4/5 ounce. 1/2 cup = 1 3/5 ounces. 3/4 cup = 2 2/5 ounces. 1 cup = 3 1/5 ounces. 5 cups per pound. Cream cheese. 1 Tablespoon = 1/2 ounce. 1/4 cup = 2 ounces. 1/2 cup = 4 ounces. 3/4 cup = 6 ounces. 1 cup = 8 ounces. 2 cups per pound. Cottage cheese 1/4 cup = 1 3/4 ounces. 1/2 cup = 3 1/2 ounces. 3/4 cup = 5 1/4 ounces. 1 cup = 7 ounces. 2 2/7 cups per pound.
CHOCOLATE	Grated—1 Tablespoon = 1/3 ounce. 1/4 cup = 1 1/3 ounces. 1/2 cup = 2 2/3 ounces. 3/4 cup = 4 ounces. 1 cup = 5 1/3 ounces. 3 cups per pound. One pound = 16 squares. Chocolate, melted. 1 Tablespoon = 1/2 ounce. 1/4 cup = 2 ounces. 1/2 cup = 4 ounces. 3/4 cup = 6 ounces. 1 cup = 8 ounces. 2 cups per pound.
COCOA	1 Tablespoon = 1/4 ounce. 1/4 cup = 1 ounce. 1/2 cup = 2 ounces. 3/4 cup = 3 ounces. 1 cup = 4 ounces. 4 cups per pound.

TABLE OF MEASUREMENTS AND EQUIVALENTS OF MOST USED COMMON FOODS FOR MENU AND BUDGET MAKING   [2211]

COCONUT............... Shredded—1 Tablespoon = $\frac{1}{5}$ ounce. $\frac{1}{4}$ cup = $\frac{4}{5}$ ounce. $\frac{1}{2}$ cup = $1\frac{3}{5}$ ounces. $\frac{3}{4}$ cup = $2\frac{2}{5}$ ounces. 1 cup = $3\frac{1}{5}$ ounces. 5 cups per pound.

COFFEE................. Medium ground—$\frac{1}{4}$ cup = $\frac{6}{7}$ ounce. $\frac{1}{2}$ cup = $1\frac{5}{7}$ ounces. $\frac{3}{4}$ cup = $2\frac{4}{7}$ ounces. 1 cup = $3\frac{3}{7}$ ounces. About $4\frac{1}{2}$ cups per pound.

CORNMEAL............. Dry—$\frac{1}{2}$ cup = $2\frac{2}{3}$ ounces. $\frac{3}{4}$ cup = 4 ounces. 1 cup = $5\frac{1}{3}$ ounces. 3 cups per pound.

CORNSTARCH......... 1 Tablespoon = $\frac{1}{3}$ ounce. $\frac{1}{4}$ cup = $1\frac{1}{3}$ ounces. $\frac{1}{2}$ cup = $2\frac{2}{3}$ ounces. $\frac{3}{4}$ cup = 4 ounces. 1 cup = $5\frac{1}{3}$ ounces. 3 cups per pound.

CRACKERS............ Graham, Meal—$\frac{1}{4}$ cup = $\frac{7}{8}$ ounce. $\frac{1}{2}$ cup = $1\frac{3}{4}$ ounces. $\frac{3}{4}$ cup = $2\frac{5}{8}$ ounces. 1 cup = $3\frac{1}{2}$ ounces. About $4\frac{1}{2}$ cups per pound. About 40 crackers to the pound. Soda Crackers—About 75 to 85 per pound. Oyster Crackers—About 450 to 575 per pound.

CRANBERRIES......... Fresh—$\frac{1}{4}$ cup = $\frac{4}{5}$ ounce. $\frac{1}{2}$ cup = $1\frac{3}{5}$ ounces. $\frac{3}{4}$ cup = $2\frac{2}{5}$ ounces. 1 cup = $3\frac{1}{5}$ ounces. About 5 cups per pound.

CREAM................. Heavy—$\frac{1}{4}$ cup = 2 ounces. $\frac{1}{2}$ cup = 4 ounces. $\frac{3}{4}$ cup = 6 ounces. 1 cup = 8 ounces. A generous pint per pound. Sour Cream. Same as fresh. Whipped, almost double in bulk.

CREAM OF TARTAR... 1 Teaspoon = $\frac{1}{8}$ ounce. 1 Tablespoon = $\frac{3}{8}$ ounce. $\frac{1}{4}$ cup = $1\frac{1}{2}$ ounces. $\frac{1}{2}$ cup = 3 ounces. $\frac{3}{4}$ cup = $4\frac{1}{2}$ ounces. 1 cup = 6 ounces. $2\frac{2}{3}$ cups per pound.

CURRANTS............ Dried—1 Tablespoon = $\frac{1}{4}$ ounce. $\frac{1}{4}$ cup = 1 ounce. $\frac{1}{2}$ cup = 2 ounces. $\frac{3}{4}$ cup = 3 ounces. 1 cup = 4 ounces. 4 cups per pound.

DATES................. Dried—$\frac{1}{4}$ cup = $1\frac{3}{5}$ ounces. $\frac{1}{2}$ cup = $3\frac{1}{5}$ ounces. $\frac{3}{4}$ cup = $4\frac{4}{5}$ ounces. 1 cup = $6\frac{2}{5}$ ounces. $2\frac{1}{2}$ cups per pound.

EGGS................. Whole, medium—1 egg = 3 Tablespoons, about 2 ounces per egg—when unbeaten. 2 eggs, unbeaten = 4 ounces or $\frac{1}{4}$ cup. Egg white—1 = $\frac{1}{2}$ ounce. Egg yolk = 1 ounce per yolk.

EXTRACTS............. Flavoring—Any kind, 1 Tablespoon or 3 Teaspoons = $\frac{1}{2}$ ounce. $\frac{1}{4}$ cup = 2 ounces. $\frac{1}{2}$ cup = 4 ounces. $\frac{3}{4}$ cup = 6 ounces. 1 cup = 8 ounces. 2 cups per pound.

FIGS.................. Dried—$\frac{1}{4}$ cup = $1\frac{1}{3}$ ounces. $\frac{1}{2}$ cup = $2\frac{2}{3}$ ounces. $\frac{3}{4}$ cup = 4 ounces. 1 cup = $5\frac{1}{3}$ ounces. 3 cups per pound and about 25 to 30 figs per pound.

FLOUR................. Bread, unsifted—$\frac{1}{4}$ cup = $1\frac{3}{16}$ ounces. $\frac{1}{2}$ cup = $2\frac{3}{8}$ ounces. $\frac{3}{4}$ cup = $3\frac{1}{2}$ ounces. 1 cup = $4\frac{3}{4}$ ounces. $3\frac{1}{3}$ cups per pound. Bread, sifted. $\frac{1}{4}$ cup = a generous ounce. $\frac{1}{2}$ cup = $2\frac{1}{8}$ ounces. $\frac{3}{4}$ cup = $3\frac{3}{16}$ ounces. 1 cup = $4\frac{1}{4}$ ounces. $3\frac{3}{4}$ cups per pound. Cake, unsifted—same as sifted bread flour. Cake, sifted. 1 Tablespoon = $\frac{1}{4}$ ounce. $\frac{1}{4}$ cup = 1 ounce. $\frac{1}{2}$ cup = 2 ounces. $\frac{3}{4}$ cup = 3 ounces. 1 cup = 4 ounces. 4 cups per pound. Flour, graham, unsifted. $\frac{1}{4}$ cup = $1\frac{1}{7}$ ounces. $\frac{1}{2}$ cup = $2\frac{2}{7}$ ounces. $\frac{3}{4}$ cup = $3\frac{3}{7}$ ounces. 1 cup = $4\frac{4}{7}$ ounces. $3\frac{1}{2}$ cups per pound. Flour, pastry, unsifted. $\frac{1}{4}$ cup = $1\frac{1}{16}$ ounces. $\frac{1}{2}$ cup = $2\frac{1}{8}$ ounces.

TABLE OF MEASUREMENTS AND EQUIVA- [2211]
LENTS OF MOST USED COMMON FOODS
FOR MENU AND BUDGET MAKING

¾ cup = 3³⁄₁₆ ounces. 1 cup = 4¼ ounces. 3¾ cups per pound. Flour, pastry, sifted. 1 Tablespoon = ¼ ounce. ¼ cup = 1 ounce. ½ cup = 2 ounces. ¾ cup = 3 ounces. 1 cup = 4 ounces. 4 cups per pound. Flour, rye, unsifted. ¼ cup = 1 ounce plus 1 tablespoon. ½ cup = 2 ounces, plus 2 Tablespoons. ¾ cup = 3 ounces, plus 3 Tablespoons. 3⅞ cups = 1 pound.

GELATINE.............. Granulated—1 Tablespoon = ¼ ounce. ¼ cup = 1 ounce. ½ cup = 2 ounces. ¾ cup = 3 ounces. 1 cup = 4 ounces. 4 cups = 1 pound.

HOMINY................ Raw—1 Tablespoon = ⅜ ounce. ¼ cup = 1½ ounces. ½ cup = 3 ounces. ¾ cup = 4½ ounces. 1 cup = 6 ounces. 2⅔ cups = 1 pound.

HONEY................. Liquid—1 Teaspoon = ¼ ounce 1 Tablespoon = ¾ ounce. ¼ cup = 3 ounces. ½ cup = 6 ounces. ¾ cup = 9 ounces. 1 cup = 12 ounces. 1⅓ cups = 1 pound.

LEMON................. Gratings—1 Teaspoon = ⅛ ounce. 1 Tablespoon = ⅜ ounce. ¼ cup = 1½ ounces. ½ cup = 3 ounces. ¾ cup = 4½ ounces. 1 cup = 6 ounces. 2⅔ cups per pound. Lemon juice—1 Teaspoon = ⅙ ounce. 1 Tablespoon = ½ ounce. ¼ cup = 2 ounces. ½ cup = 4 ounces. ¾ cup = 6 ounces. 1 cup = 8 ounces. 2 cups = 1 pound. Lemon, whole. 3 to 5 lemons = 1 pound.

MACARONI............. 4 cups = 1 pound.

MEAT................. Chopped, raw—2 cups = 1 pound.

MARSHMALLOW....... 3¾ pieces = 1 ounce. 7½ pieces = 2 ounces. 15 pieces = 4 ounces. 30 pieces = 8 ounces. 60 pieces = 1 pound.

MILK.................. Evaporated—1 can = 14½ ounces net. ½ can = 7¼ ounces. ¾ can = 10⅞ ounces. 1⅔ cups per can. Milk, fresh—1 Teaspoon = ⅙ ounce. 1 Tablespoon = ½ ounce. ¼ cup = 2 ounces. ½ cup = 4 ounces. ¾ cup = 6 ounces. 1 cup = 8 ounces. 2 cups = 1 pound. Milk, malted—¼ cup = 1¼ ounces. ½ cup = 2½ ounces. ¾ cup = 3¾ ounces. 1 cup = 5 ounces. 3⅓ cups = 1 pound. Milk, powdered—½ cup = 2⅜ ounces. ¾ cup = 3½ ounces. 1 cup = 4¾ ounces. 3⅓ cups = 1 pound.

MOLASSES............. 1 Teaspoon = ¼ ounce. 1 Tablespoon = ¾ ounce. ¼ cup = 3 ounces. ½ cup = 6 ounces. ¾ cup = 9 ounces. 1 cup = 12 ounces. 1⅓ cups = 1 pound.

MUSTARD............. Dry—1 Tablespoon = ¼ ounce. 2 Tablespoons = ½ ounce. ¼ cup = 1 ounce. ½ cup = 2 ounces. ¾ cup = 3 ounces. 1 cup = 4 ounces. 2 cups = 8 ounces. 4 cups = 1 pound. Mustard seeds—1 ounce = 2½ Tablespoons.

NUTMEG.............. 1 ordinary nut = 2¾ Tablespoons.

NUTS .... See "Chart" (No. 2223)

OATS, rolled............. ½ pound = 2¾ cups. 1 pound = about 5½ cups.

OIL.................... ¼ cup = 1⅞ ounces. ½ cup = 3¾ ounces. ¾ cup = 5⅝ ounces. 1 cup = 7½ ounces. 2 cups = 15 ounces.

OLIVES................. 1 quart = about 60 to 70 olives

ONIONS................ 1 pound = 4 to 12 onions, according to size.

ORANGES.............. Whole, medium—About 2 oranges per pound. Orange gratings—1 Tablespoon = ⅜ ounce. ¼ cup = 1½

TABLE OF MEASUREMENTS AND EQUIVA- [2211] LENTS OF MOST USED COMMON FOODS FOR MENU AND BUDGET MAKING

	ounces. ½ cup = 3 ounces. ¾ cup = 4½ ounces. 1 cup = 6 ounces. 2⅔ cups = 1 pound. Orange juice— 1 Teaspoon = ⅙ ounce. 1 Tablespoon = ½ ounce. ¼ cup = 2 ounces. ½ cup = 4 ounces. ¾ cup = 6 ounces. 1 cup = 8 ounces. 2 cups = 1 pound.
OYSTERS..............	Shucked—1 quart = about 40 to 60 oysters, depending on size.
PARSNIPS..............	1 pound = about 3 to 5 parsnips, depending to size.
PEACHES..............	Dried—About double in bulk when cooked. 1 Tablespoon = ⅓ ounce. ¼ cup = 1⅓ ounces. ½ cup = 2⅔ ounces. ¾ cup = 4 ounces. 1 cup = 5⅓ ounces. 3 cups = 1 pound. Peaches, fresh—According to size 4 to 6 peaches = 1 pound. One bushel = about 45 to 50 pounds.
PEANUT BUTTER......	1¾ cups = 1 pound.
PEARS.................	Fresh—1 pound = 3 to 4 pears, according to size. 1 bushel = about 48 to 55 pounds.
PEAS...................	In pods—1 pound = 2 to 3 servings. 1 bushel = about 60 pounds.
PEPPER................	Whole, white—1 ounce = 4 scant tablespoons. Whole, black—1 ounce = 4½ tablespoons.
POTATOES.............	White—1 pound = about 4 to 5, according to size. 1 bushel = 60 pounds. Sweet or yams—1 pound = about 3 to 4, according to size. 1 bushel = 50 to 55 pounds.
PRUNES...............	Dried, whole, uncooked—1 Tablespoon = ⅖ ounce. ¼ cup = 1⅗ ounces. ½ cup = 3⅕ ounces. ¾ cup = 4⅘ ounces. 1 cup = 6⅖ ounces. 2½ cups = 1 pound. Prunes, dried, whole, cooked—pitted—4½ cups = 1 pound.
PUMPKIN..............	Cooked—¼ cup = 3¼ ounces. ½ cup = 6½ ounces. ¾ cup = 9¾ ounces. 1 cup = 13 ounces. 1 3⁄13 cups = 1 pound.
RAISINS...............	Seeded—1 Tablespoon = ⅖ ounce. ¼ cup = 1⅗ ounces. ½ cup = 3⅕ ounces. ¾ cup = 4⅘ ounces. 1 cup = 6⅖ ounces. 2½ cups = 1 pound. Raisins, seedless—1 Tablespoon = ⅓ ounce. ¼ cup = 1⅓ ounces. ½ cup = 2⅔ ounces. ¾ cup = 4 ounces. 1 cup = 5⅓ ounces. 3 cups = 1 pound.
RASPBERRIES.........	Fresh—3½ cups = 1 pound.
RICE..................	Uncooked—¼ cup = 2 ounces. ½ cup = 4 ounces. ¾ cup = 6 ounces. 1 cup = 8 ounces. 2 cups = 1 pound. Wild rice—Same as white rice. Rice, white, cooked—About double in bulk when cooked.
SALT..................	Table salt—1 Tablespoon = ½ ounce. ¼ cup = 2 ounces. ½ cup = 4 ounces. ¾ cup = 6 ounces. 1 cup = 8 ounces. 2 cups = 1 pound.
SHORTENING..........	Vegetable—Same as butter—Lard—Same as butter— Margarine—Same as butter.
SPICES................	General—1 Teaspoon = 1⁄12 ounce. 1 Tablespoon = ¼ ounce. ¼ cup = 1 ounce. ½ cup = 2 ounces. ¾ cup = 3 ounces. 1 cup = 4 ounces. 4 cups to a pound (approximate).
SPINACH..............	1 pound of uncooked spinach = about 2½ quarts.

TABLE OF MEASUREMENTS AND EQUIVALENTS OF MOST USED COMMON FOODS FOR MENU AND BUDGET MAKING [2211]

STABILIZER............	For pastry—1 Teaspoon = 1/8 ounce. 1 Tablespoon = 3/8 ounce. 1/4 cup = 1 1/2 ounces.
SUET....................	Chopped—1/4 cup = 5/8 ounce. 1/2 cup = 1 1/4 ounces. 3/4 cup = 1 7/8 ounces. 1 cup = 2 1/2 ounces. 6 2/5 cups = 1 pound
SUGAR..................	Brown—1 Tablespoon = 1/3 ounce. 1/4 cup = 1 1/3 ounces. 1/2 cup = 2 2/3 ounces. 3/4 cup = 4 ounces. 1 cup = 5 1/3 ounces. 3 cups = 1 pound. Sugar, confectioner's—1 Tablespoon = 2/7 ounce. 1/4 cup = 1 1/7 ounces. 1/2 cup = 2 2/7 ounces. 3/4 cup = 3 3/7 ounces. 1 cup = 4 4/7 ounces. 3 1/2 cups = 1 pound. Sugar, granulated—1 Teaspoon = 1/6 ounce. 1 Tablespoon = 1/2 ounce. 1/4 cup = 2 ounces. 1/2 cup = 4 ounces. 3/4 cup = 6 ounces. 1 cup = 8 ounces. 2 cups = 1 pound. Sugar, powdered—1 Tablespoon = 2/7 ounce. 1/4 cup = 1 1/7 ounces. 1/2 cup = 2 2/7 ounces. 3/4 cup = 3 3/7 ounces. 1 cup = 4 4/7 ounces. 3 1/2 cups = 1 pound.
SYRUP..................	Sugar—1 Teaspoon = 1/4 ounce. 1 Tablespoon = 3/4 ounce. 1/4 cup = 3 ounces. 1/2 cup = 6 ounces. 3/4 cup = 9 ounces. 1 cup = 12 ounces. 1 1/3 cups = 1 pound.
TAPIOCA................	1 Teaspoon = 1/12 ounce. 1 Tablespoon = 1/4 ounce. 1/4 cup = 1 ounce. 1/2 cup = 2 ounces. 3/4 cup = 3 ounces. 1 cup = 4 ounces. 4 cups = 1 pound.
WATER..................	Clear—1 Teaspoon = 1/6 ounce. 1 Tablespoon = 1/2 ounce. 1/4 cup = 2 ounces. 1/2 cup = 4 ounces. 3/4 cup = 6 ounces. 1 cup = 8 ounces. 2 cups = 1 pound.
WINE....................	Red or white—Same as for water.

EDIBLE NUTS—THEIR CHARACTERISTICS AND USES IN COOKERY [2212]

Food Value of Nuts. Nuts are a very concentrated food and are better used as an integral part of the menu rather than as supplement to an already adequate meal. Most nuts are extremely rich in fat. The starchy chestnut is the one exception.

In protein value, the different nuts range from less than 5 per cent to over 30 per cent. Although nut proteins are of good quality, the high fat content of most nuts makes them unsatisfactory as a substitute for meat or other sources of animal protein. Nuts may make a useful contribution to the protein of the diet, but under most circumstances it is better to consider them as a source of fat rather than of protein, and to use them interchangeably with other fatty foods, such as butter, margarin, oils, cream, chocolate and bacon or ham.

SELECTION AND CARE [2213]

If you buy nut meats rather than nuts in the shell, you'll save yourself considerable time, labor and storage space but nuts in the shell are cheaper and will stay fresh for a longer time. When the weight of the shell and the labor involved in cracking are considered, nuts purchased as kernels are probably cheaper per unit than are the same kind of nuts purchased in the shell. Some nuts with heavy shells, such as black walnuts and hickory nuts, are generally sold shelled (*See table giving the approximate weight of nuts in the shells needed to yield one pound or one cup (standard) of the shelled kernels*).

The flavor of nuts is largely dependent upon the oils which they contain, although in some nuts there are also specific flavoring substances. In most nut kernels the oils readily become rancid, and give the disagreeable flavor found in so-called stale nuts. Since it is easier to prevent the nut kernels from becoming rancid than it is to remove the rancid flavor, they should be kept in an air-tight container in a cool, dry, dark place. The container will also tend to protect the nuts from insects. Shelled nuts are now put up in vacuum-packed containers that help to prevent rancidity.

NUT PREPARATION AND PROCESSING   [2214]

Blanching is a means of removing the skin from kernels of almonds and other nuts that have a smooth surface. Peanut skins slip off easily after the nuts are roasted, and other nut kernels that have a tender skin, such as pecans, hickory nuts, butternuts, black walnuts and Persian (English) walnuts, do not need to be blanched for most uses. Only nuts with a smooth surface can be blanched satisfactorily.

TO BLANCH ALMONDS   [2215]

Pour boiling water over them and hold at simmering temperature (185° F.) for about 3 minutes (too long simmering will extract the flavor). Drain off the water. The skins will then come off easily when pressed with the thumb and forefinger at the pointed end of the nut. Spread the blanched and skinned kernels on absorbent paper and dry overnight at ordinary room temperature.

TO BLANCH BRAZIL NUTS AND FILBERT   [2216]
KERNELS

Prepare in an enameled or iron kettle (never aluminum) a lye solution, using two level tablespoons of granulated lye to each gallon of water. Heat to the boiling point, and immerse the kernels until the skins loosen. This will take from one to two minutes. Rinse and remove the skins while the kernels are still warm. Wash thoroughly in cold water and let dry overnight. If desired, the nuts may be polished with a dry soft cloth.

TO SHELL AND BLANCH CHESTNUTS   [2217]

Cut a gash on the flat side of the shell, cook the chestnuts in boiling water to cover for 15 minutes, (longer if the chestnuts be large); remove the shell and brown skin while hot. Or heat in a moderately hot oven (350° F.) for about 15 minutes, and remove shells and skins with a sharp knife.

SALTING AND ROASTING NUTS   [2218]

The flavor of some mild-flavored nuts, such as almonds, hickory nuts, Persian (English) walnuts and filberts may be developed by either roasting or frying. This makes them more desirable for use in such baked products as nut breads, cakes and cookies as well as puddings and confections. For ice creams and candies the addition of salt to the fried or roasted nuts is a further improvement.

For ½ pound of shelled and blanched almonds or of shelled, un-blanched, raw peanuts or filberts, allow one quart of fresh cooking oil. In a kettle adapted for deep-fat frying, heat the oil to a temperature of 300° F. or until a cube of bread browns in 5 or 6 minutes, or use a thermometer. Place the nuts in a sieve or a colander that is deep enough to prevent the nut kernels from floating over the top, and lower them into the hot fat. After 6 or 7 minutes, or as soon as the nut kernels are light brown, remove them from the fat. They continue to cook for a few minutes afterward. Spread them on absorbent paper, then while they are still hot, pat them gently with the paper to remove the excess of fat, and sprinkle with salt. Do not fry more than one kind of nut at a time, because some cook more rapidly than others.

Salt perfect halves of pecans, Persian (English) walnuts, or hickory nuts in just enough oil or butter to cover the surface of the nut kernels —about 2 tablespoons for one cup of nuts. Heat in a small frying pan over a very gentle flame, and stir and toss in the pan until hot. Avoid overcooking, because pecans darken after being removed from the fat. Drain on absorbent paper and sprinkle lightly with salt.

ROASTING PEANUTS AND SWEET   [2219]
ALMONDS

Spread the nuts with skins left on in a baking pan and heat them in a slow oven (300° F.), stirring occasionally. Too hot an oven will burn them and extract the flavor.

NUT LOAVES   [2220]

The standard mixture for a nut loaf includes in addition to the ground or chopped nuts (any kind), chopped vegetables, a cereal, bread crumbs, and a thick sauce for binder. It is desirable that at least one of the vegetables be celery, green pepper or carrots, to give crisp texture.

NUT CROQUETTES   [2221]

The mixture for *croquettes* is softer and more moist than for a loaf. To give this consistency, mashed potatoes, bean pulp, or some one of the cooked cereals form a suitable base.

Many other nuts as well as chestnuts give flavor and richness when used in the *stuffing* for poultry, game or meat. The mild-flavored nuts, especially almonds, are very good in creamed fish and meats, such as chicken, crab, tuna, shrimp or sweetbreads. Breast of chicken or chops may be dipped in a cover batter to which broken or shredded or ground almonds or pecans have been added, then fried in deep fat. Broken or coarsely chopped nuts may also be added to candied sweet potatoes or yams and to stewed dried fruits. Peanuts and chopped carrots may be cooked together.

NUT CHART AND CHARACTERISTICS   [2222]

Acorns (Quercus alba). Source: South and Pacific Coast. *Season:* Fall. *Shape, Color* and *Size:* Ovoid; light to deep green; ¾-inch across, 1 inch long. *Types:* The cow or basket; yellow chestnut; swamp, and so forth. *Process:* Raw, ground, blanched, paste. *Refuse:* 35.6%. *Place in the Menu:* As substitute for coffee, as meal for pancakes, and so forth. *Nutritive value:* Same as chestnuts.

Almonds (Amygdalus communis). Source: California, Morocco, Spain. *Season:* Fall. *Shape, Color, Size:* Elongated ovoid flattened at both ends; green and champagne; 1 inch (average). *Types:* (a) Papershell: Non-pareil, I.X.L. or Neplus, Peerless or Drake. (b) Hard Shell: Standard shell, Jordan, Valencia. *Process:* Raw, blanched, roasted, paste, confection. *Place in Menu:* Desserts, pastry, soufflés, liqueur, garnish, sauces, cakes, confections, macaroons, marzipan, and so forth. *As Purchased:* In the shell, salted, roasted, in paste. *Weight and Measures:* See Chart. *Refuse:* 64.8%. *Nutritive Value:* A pound of almonds is equal in nutritive value to 8.55 pounds of milk; 5.20 of eggs; 3.78 pounds of mutton and 9.18 of chicken. *Calories:* 3,030 per pound.

Beech Nuts (Fagus grandifolio) (Fagus Americana) (Fagus ferruginea). Source: Fagus Americana: Minnesota, Florida, Texas. *Season:* Fall, year round. *Shape, Color, Size:* Somewhat concave, kernel roundish; brownish; small, very sweet. *Type:* The American Beech. *Process:* Raw, blanched, roasted, candied. *Place in Menu:* Desserts, salads, confections, and so forth. *As Purchased:* In the shell, shelled, salted, candied, roasted, buttered, and so forth. *Weight and Measures:* See Chart. *Refuse:* 40.8%. *Nutritive value:* Same as almonds. *Calories:* 3,263 per pound.

Brazil Nuts (Alba Braziliana). Also called *Castanha da Para. Source:* Brazil, Malaya, Ceylon, Borneo, West Indies, Gold Coast. *Season:*

January, year round. *Shape, Color, Size:* Slanting crescent; black outside, *inside:* ivory snow; size varies from 3 to 8 inches in diameter enclosing from 14 to 28 "seeds." *Types:* One. *Process:* Raw, blanched, toasted, chips, roasted, paste, shredded. *Place in Menu:* Used in bread, cakes, cookies, candies, salads, appetizers, desserts, ice cream and certain main course dishes. *As Purchased:* In shell, shelled, buttered, shredded, chips, salted, roasted, candied, ground, and so forth. *Weight and Measures:* See Chart. *Refuse:* 49.6%. *Edible Portion:* 50.4%; 46-48 to the pound. *Nutritive Value:* Fat, 66.8%; mineral salts, 3.9%; vitamins A, B and C. *Calories:* 3,329 per pound.

Bullnuts (*Carya alba*). Also known as Mockernut, White-Heart Hickory Nut, and so forth. *Source:* Massachusetts, Nebraska, Florida, Texas. *Season:* Fall, year round. *Shape, Color:* Roundish, slightly oblong, hard shell; kernel nearly smooth, quite round, grayish or brownish, very sweet. *Type:* One. *Process:* Same as hickory nuts. *Place in Menu:* Same as hickory nuts. *As Purchased:* Mixed with other nuts, shelled or not. Same as hickory nuts. *Weight and Measures:* See "Hickory Nut" in Chart. *Nutritive Value:* Same as hickory nuts.

Butternuts (*Jaglans cinerea*). Also called "White Walnut," or "Oilnut." *Source:* Dakota, Kansas, Arkansas, Ohio, Georgia, in order of importance. *Season:* Fall. *Shape, Size:* Appears in clusters of 2 to 5; ridged, deeply furrowed, small. *Types:* One. *Process:* Same as almonds; very oily or fatty. *Place in Menu:* Do not keep; served in the fresh state, or used as ready-to-eat food same as almonds. *As Purchased:* Salted, toasted, paste. *Weight and Measures:* See Chart. *Refuse:* 86.4%. *Edible portion:* 13.6%. *Nutritive Value:* Oil: 61.2%; mineral salts: 3%; vitamins: A, B and C.

Cashew Nuts (*Indianis alba*). *Source:* India, West Indies, California (experimentation with promising success). *Season:* Fall, year round. Imported in sealed cans, and almost ready to use. *Shape, Color, Size:* Bent, light straw, about size of a peanut. *Types:* One. *Process:* Same as almonds. *Place in Menu:* Same as almonds. *As Purchased:* Salted, roasted, candied. *Weight and Measures:* See Chart. *Nutritive Value:* Same as almonds.

Chestnuts (*Castanea dentata*). *Source:* Italy, France, Spain, very little in America, from Mississippi and West Coast. *Season:* Winter (from October to beginning of spring). *Shape, Color, Size:* Round when in burr, sometimes 1, 2 or 3 seeds together in the burr. Size and quality vary according to the number in a burr or cell. *Types:* Various, according to origin. *Process:* Fresh, dried, flour, meal, paste, candied, and so forth. *Place in Menu:* Mixed with onions, Brussels sprouts, in purée, desserts, in syrup, brandied, roasted, boiled, preserved, glazed, and so forth. *As Purchased:* In the shell; shelled; when dried, by the pound, bag or barrel. *Weight and Measures:* See Chart. *Refuse:* fresh 16%; dried 24%. *Nutritive Value:* Fresh and cooked: 1,125 calories per pound; dried and cooked: 1,875 per pound. Very little fat. *Edible portion:* dried 76%; fresh 84%. Starch: fresh 42.1%; dried 74.2%. Vitamins A and B.

Chinquapin Nuts (*Castanea pumila*). *Source:* New Jersey, Pennsylvania, Indiana, Missouri, Florida, Texas, and so forth. *Season:* Winter.

Shape, Size: Shaped like chestnuts, they are smaller and each burr contains only one round, somewhat pointed nut or seed. *Types:* Several types are cultivated, each with little variance. *Process:* Same as chestnuts. *Place in Menu:* Various, according to origin. *As Purchased:* Same as chestnut. *Weight and Measures:* Same as the chestnut. *Nutritive Value:* Same as chestnut.

Chufa or *Earth Almond,* or *Earth Chestnut,* of which very little is known. Imported from China and widely used in Chinese cookery.

Cocoanut or *Coconut (Palmi alba). Source:* In almost every tropical country, especially India, Malay Peninsula, Puerto Rico, West Indies, etc. *Season:* Fall, also the year round. *Shape, Color, Size:* Elliptical; brown shell, snow white interior. Size: from a small to a large grapefruit. *Types:* One. *Process:* Domestic—long shred, medium shred, short shred. Partially domestic manufacture—(reprocessed) same shreds. Southern style, moist shredded coconut, prepared in hermetically sealed cans (a substitute for fresh grated coconut). *Place in Menu:* Used in desserts, pies, cakes, cookies, confections, garnish, and so forth. *As Purchased:* In the shell, shredded; in container hermetically sealed from ¼ pound up to 1 pound; in carton of 5, 25, 50 pounds; in tin of 10, 25, 60 and 70 pounds; in barrel from 120 up to 160 pounds. *Refuse:* fresh 48.8%; dried 24%; shredded, none. *Weight and Measures:* See Chart. *Nutritive Value:* Edible portion: fresh 84%; dried 76%; shredded 100%. Very much fat: fresh 50%; dried 55%; shredded 57.3%. Fuel value: fresh: 2,986 calories per pound; shredded 3,125 calories per pound.

Coco De Mer (Palmis alba). Source: Indian Ocean. Very little is known about this nut imported from the Seychelles Islands, which the natives believe is the "Forbidden Fruit" of the Garden of Eden.

Cola Nut or *Kola Nut (Cola acuminata). Source:* Africa, Central America, West Indies. *Season:* Fall. *Color, Size:* Chestnut, red and white; size of a walnut. *Types:* Several, but the most used is the *cola acuminata. Process:* Used whole as a food or distilled for several beverages and liqueurs. *Place in Menu:* On desserts, pies, cakes, confections, beverages, cordials, similar to tea or coffee. *As Purchased:* Shelled, candied, ground. *Weight and Measures:* By the pound. *Nutritive Value:* Astringent, slightly sweet, starchy, highly nutritive.

Filbert. (Corylus Americana) The wild filbert is called "Beaked Filbert." *Source:* Georgia, Tennessee, Kansas, Oregon (belongs to the oak family). *Season:* Fall; also all year round. *Shape, Color, Size:* Same shape, color and size as the hazelnut, though a trifle smaller. *Types:* Long and round from Italy and France; long from Turkey; round from Spain. *Process:* Same as almonds. *Place in Menu:* On desserts, with cocktails, pies, cakes, cookies, confections, salted, fried, as a garnish, in salads, meat, fish and game loaves, and so forth. *As Purchased:* In shell, shelled, buttered, salted, candied, ground, and so forth. *Weight and Measures:* See Chart. Refuse: 52.1%. *Edible portion:* 47.9%. *Nutritive Value:* Fat: 65.3%; Calories: 3,432 per pound.

Hazelnuts. (Corylus rostrata). Same specification as for filberts but a little larger. Domestic and imported. Sweet and easily cracked.

Litchi Nuts (Fructus alba). An imported Chinese nut, strawberry-like shape, containing a small kernel widely used in China, and of which very little is known up to now. Used in combination with food and certain desserts.

Macadamia Nuts (Australivus alba). Source: Native of Australia. Cultivated on a great scale in Hawaii and imported in this country after processing. *Season:* Fall, all year round. *Shape, Color, Size:* Round; pure white; moist and chewy resembling the flesh of a coconut; size of an overgrown hazelnut with 2 kernels in each cell, which is brown. *Types:* One. *Process:* Hard to crack; roasted, salted and vacuum-packed. *Place in Menu:* So far used as a tidbit, with cocktails, and in desserts; may be ingredient in food; its flavor is more delicate than the coconut. *As Purchased:* Roasted, salted, candied, buttered, dried, desiccated, ground, and so forth. *Weight and Measures:* Vacuum-packed jars in three sizes: ½ pound, 1 pound and 2 pounds. *Nutritive Value:* Not yet analyzed.

Peanuts (Arachis hypogaea). Family leguminosae. *Source:* Virginia, North Carolina, Tennessee. *Season:* Fall; all year round. *Shape, Color, Size:* Various shapes, round and elongated. Yellowish: kernel of the Virginia variety is large and long, while that of the Spanish variety is small and almost round. Spanish peanuts contain about 6% more oil than the domestic ones. *Types:* Several. Among the most popular are: Runner, Jumbo and Bunch, all domestic grown. *Process:* Dehydrated, roasted, desiccated, meal, steamed, roasted, buttered, sugared, and so forth. *Place in Menu:* Used in conjunction or combination with foods, meat especially, cereals, vegetables, meat and plain loaves, pies, cakes, cookies, confections, desserts, salads, and so forth. *As Purchased:* In shell, shelled, candied, glazed, buttered, salted, roasted, meal, peanut butter, and so forth. *Weight and Measures:* See Chart. *Refuse:* raw: 24.5%; roasted: 32.6%; Edible portion: raw 75.5%; roasted: 67.4%. *Nutritive Value:* Protein: raw 25.8%; roasted: 30.5%. Fat contents: raw: 38.6%; roasted 49.2.%. Calories: raw 2,560 per pound; roasted 3,177 per pound.

Pecan (Carya illinoensis) Hicoria pacan. *Source:* Texas, Oklahoma, Indiana, Iowa, Kansas, Alabama, all along the Gulf States. *Season:* Fall, all year round. Perhaps the best of all our hickory nut products. *Shape, Color, Size:* Oblong or olive-shaped, smooth, thin-shelled and pointed. Yellowish-brown. Different sizes, from 1¼ to 1¾ inches. By selection, many improved varieties have been developed, and large pecan orchards are being planted in the South. *Types:* Schley, Van Deman, Pabst, Mobile (long varieties) indicated by passing through opening 12/16-inch diameter, but not through opening 11/16-inch; deliveries all mixed up with the above types. *Process:* Salted, oil, roasted, candied, meal. *Place in Menu:* In conjunction with or adjunct to almost any kind of food; pies, cakes, desserts, confections, fruit cups, salads, cookies, and so forth. *As Purchased:* In shell, shelled, in tins of 1 pound, 5 pounds, 25 pounds. In bags, boxes and barrels. *Weight and Measures:* See Chart. *Refuse:* 53.2%; Edible portion: 46.8% *Nutritive Value:* Fat contents: 71.2%. Protein: 11.0%. Calories: 3,633 per pound.

Pignuts (Carya glabra). Same characteristics as hickory nuts, to which family they belong, but the kernel is oval or pear-shaped, slightly compressed, nearly smooth. The shell is sometimes heavy. The kernel is rather small and sweet, certain species are slightly bitter and are used in place of bitter almonds in confections and certain desserts and liqueurs and cordials. In great favor in Pennsylvania.

Pistachio Nuts (Pistakion edulis). Source: Syria, Iran, Egypt, Arabia, Turkey, West Indies (small amounts), and California. *Season:* Year round. *Shape, Color, Size:* Bean-shape, green, white and pink (the last color being artificially produced), bean size. *Types:* One. *Process:* Salted, roasted, candied. *Place in Menu:* Cocktail snacks, candies, ice cream, pastries, cakes, cookies, liqueur and cordials. *As Purchased:* In shell (seldom), shelled, colored, candied, confections, and so forth, in tins, from 1 pound up to 25 pounds. *Weight and Measures:* See Chart. *No refuse.* Edible portion 100%. *Nutritive Value:* Protein: 22.6%. Fat: 54.5%. Calories: 3,010 per pound.

Pine Nuts or Pinon Nuts. (Pinus edulis). Source: Colorado and south and west of Mexico at altitudes of 5,000 to 7,000 feet. *Season:* Every other fall. *Shape, Color, Size:* Nearly as thick as wide, slightly flattened; brownish, about ½ inch long by ¼ inch wide. *Types:* Several. In fact almost all the seeds from pine are edible, but Colorado seeds are the most prized. *Process:* Same as almonds or any other nuts. *Place in Menu:* In combination with cooked or raw foods, as a snack, in desserts, pies, pastries, cakes, ice cream, candies, and so forth. *As Purchased:* By the pound in tins of 1 up to 10 pounds. Salted, roasted, buttered, confections, pastries, salads, glazed, cookies, and so forth. *Weight and Measures:* Sold by the pound. Refuse: (when sold in package, unshelled): 40.6%. Edible portion: 59.4%. When shelled: 100% edible portion. *Nutritive Value:* Protein: 14.6%. Fat: 61.9%. Calories: 3,364 per pound.

Walnuts (Black) (Juglans nigra). Source: California (producing almost our entire supply). Oregon. Indigenous to Persia. *Season:* Fall; all year round. *Shape, Color, Size.* The fruit is nearly round, yellowish green, roughly dotted, 1½ to 3 inches in diameter. The nut within is dark, rough, very hard or bony, nearly round, only slightly compressed, and 1¼ to nearly 2 inches in diameter. A 4-celled kernel. *Types:* Several with trade names such as Chase, Ehrhardt or Placentia Perfection or Fancy, Concord, Eureka, Franquette, Mayehe, Payne, and so forth. Parisienne, Mayette, and Franquette are representatives of varieties having the best quality. *Process:* Salted, glazed, roasted, meal, butter, pickling (immature ones only), catsup, sauces, etc. *Place in Menu:* In conjunction with or adjunct to almost any kind of cooked, baked or roast foods, salads, breads, cakes, cookies, pies, fillings, frostings, candies, as a nibble, or a garnish. *As Purchased:* Salted or roasted in tins of 1 up to 25 pounds or in shell in boxes or bags. *Weight and Measures:* See Chart. *Refuse:* 74.1%. Edible portion: 25.9%. *Nutritive Value:* Protein: 27.6%. Fat: 56.3%. Calories: 3,105 per pound.

Walnuts, English (a misnomer) *(Juglans regia).* Have the same characteristics as black walnuts. In reality they are grafted from the

Persian walnuts. The nuts are small, thin-shelled, and sweet. Another walnut, the *Juglans kindsii*, is found in Central California and has the same characteristics as the English or Persian walnut; the same uses and the same, or almost the same nutrient properties.

Mixed Nuts. Assorted nuts and mixed nuts are sold by weight as follows: 35% walnuts, 25% almonds; 20% Brazils; 10% filberts or hazelnuts; 10% pecans. Free from hulls or other foreign material they conform in every respect to specifications covering grades and varieties indicated above.

General Remarks Concerning All Nuts. Freshness is one of the first factors to consider in purchasing nuts, whether in the shell or shelled. If nuts are not properly stored, they become rancid because of their high fat content, also dry out and shrink because of loss of moisture. Experts judge nuts by these characteristics: Flavor, cleavage, or cracking quality. *Percentage* of kernel. *Appearance and Size.* Size of nut and quality do not always run parallel because often the small or medium size nut has the best flavor.

Nut Preparation. Almonds are easily shelled by a twist of the fingers.

Brazil Nuts. If nuts are steamed a few minutes before cracking, the kernel can be easily removed.

Filberts. Strike gently with hammer in center of rounded side, or use a nut cracker.

Peanuts. Same as for almonds.

Pecans. To remove nut meats whole, cover nuts with boiling water and let stand until cold.

Walnuts, Black or English. To remove nut meats whole, strike with hammer or similar utensil or tool in center of rounded side half way between joining of the two halves.

To Chop Nuts. Place nuts in wooden bowl and chop with vegetable chopping knife.

To Grind Nuts. Use regular vegetable grater, meat chopper or special nut meat chopper.

To Slice Nuts. A sharp knife is all that is needed.

To Shred Nuts. A vegetable shredding knife is best, but any sharp knife will do.

To Remove Brown Skin Covering From Nut Meats. Cover the meats with boiling water and let stand 5 minutes in a covered dish. Drain, then quickly rub off the skins with the fingers. A small, sharp knife may be needed on Brazil nuts.

NUT CHART FOR WEIGHT AND MEASURE [2223]

KIND	HOW PURCHASED	WEIGHT	MEASURE BY CUPS
ALMONDS			
Hard shell	In shell	One pound	= 1 cup meats
Soft shell	In shell	One pound	= 2 cups meats
Jordans	Meats	One pound	= 3 cups meats
Valencias	Meats	One pound	= 3 generous cups
Salted	Meats	One pound	= 3½ cups meats
BUTTER	Glass jar	Five ounces	= ⅓ cup meats
BRAZIL NUTS	In shell	One pound	= 1½ cups meats
BUTTERNUTS	In shell	One pound	= ½ cup meats
CASHEW NUTS	Salted	One pound	= 4 cups meats
CHESTNUTS	In shell	One pound	= 2 cups meats
COCONUT			
Shredded	Bulk	One pound	= 6 cups
Shredded	Paper carton	One ¼ pound	= 1⅓ cups
Shredded	Paper carton	One ½ pound	= 2⅔ cups
Shredded	Tin can	Four ounces	= 1½ cups
Shredded	Tin can	Ten ounces	= 3½ cups
Whole	In shell	One average nut	= 2 cups chopped
FILBERTS	In shell	One pound	= 3½ cups meats
Shelled	Meats	One pound	= 3½ cups meats
HICKORY	In shell	One pound	= 1 cup meats
PEANUTS			
Jumbo	Salted	One pound	= 3 cups meats
Spanish	Salted	One pound	= 3⅓ cups meats
Roasted	In shell	One pound	= 2½ cups meats
Peanut butter	Glass jar	Six and one-half ounces	= ¾ cup
PECANS			
Paper shell	In shell	One pound	= 2 cups meats
Hard shell	In shell	One pound	= 1 cup meats
Meats	Meats	One pound	= 3½ cups meats
PINENUTS	Meats	One pound	= 4 cups meats
PISTACHIOS	In shell	One pound	= 2 cups meats
WALNUTS (English)			
Hard shell	In shell	One pound	= 1⅓ cups meats
Soft shell	In shell	One pound	= 1⅔ cups meats
Halves	Meats	One pound	= 4½ cups meats
Halves	Tin can	Eight ounces	= 2 cups meats
Broken pieces	Meats	One pound	= 3 cups meats
WALNUTS (Black)	In shell	One pound	= ⅔ cup meats
Shelled	Meats	One pound	= 4 cups meats

Before a noble was executed at Cleopatra's command, she granted him a "last meal" of any food he desired. Many of the condemned, therefore, ordered certain nuts which grew a thousand miles away and required three months to obtain.

BISCUITS, BREAD, MUFFINS AND ROLLS

TERMS USED IN BAKING AND THEIR MEANING [2224]

Baking. Cooking in a dry heat.

Batter. Several ingredients beaten together to form a semiliquid mixture suitable for baking or cooking.

Bread. The sound product made by baking a dough consisting of a leavened or unleavened mixture of ground grain and/or other clean, sound, edible farinaceous substance, with potable water, and, with or without, the addition of other edible substances.

Buns. Small cakes or breads, generally round or oval in shape and frequently spiced.

Cake. Leavened flour mixtures with egg, fat and sugar added.

Caramel. A syrup made from scorched sugar used for coloring food products.

Caraway Seed. A highly aromatic seed used whole for flavoring rye bread of certain types. Also used in cooking.

Corn Bread. A bread prepared from corn meal, with flour, sugar, lard (or substitute), and baking powder.

Crullers. Ring-shaped cakes of dough, usually sweetened and fried brown in smoking fat.

Crumb. The soft inner part of the loaf as distinguished from the crust.

Crust. The outside of a loaf of bread. It is formed by the intense baking heat and consequent drying of the surface. This drying and a certain chemical change in the starch are known as caramelization. In the crust the gluten has hardened or gummed and the starch has changed into a more digestible form.

Currant Buns. Buns with currants added.

Dough. A name given to the unbaked product resulting when flour, water, yeast, salt, and other ingredients are combined by mixing.

Dough Mixer. A machine for mixing ingredients. It should be kept thoroughly cleaned.

Doughnuts. A sweet, round dough composition with center cut out, fried in deep fat.

Dredge. To sprinkle, as with pepper and salt, or rub in, as with flour, etc.

Fermentation. A chemical change in organic substances caused by micro-organisms.

Fermentation Period. The period elapsing between the time dough is mixed and the time it is sent to the oven.

Flour. Bolted grain meal.

Gems or Muffins. Hot breads made from white flour, graham, or corn meal and baked in gem pans. Usually eggs are added.

Gluten. That constituent of wheat flour dough which enables the dough to expand and thus retain the fermentation gases. Two elements of flour, distinct from each other in a dry state, unite upon the addition of water to form gluten.

Grits. Grains, as of wheat, corn, or oats, coarsely ground.

Hominy. Cracked Indian corn from which the outer husk has been removed.

Hops. The cured, kiln-dried blossoms of the hop vine, a perennial, climbing plant cultivated in Europe and on the Pacific coast for its blossom. The flavoring element is known as lupulin and can be extracted by boiling 10 or 15 minutes.

Icing. A glazing or coating of sugar, usually mixed with white of egg and suitable flavoring, and applied to cakes. Sometimes called frosting.

Ingredients. A general term describing the factors that constitute a substance. For example, ingredients of bread include flour, water, yeast, salt, sugar, shortening, and in some instances milk, hop tea or malt.

Leaven. A piece of old dough used as a ferment in making bread by the left-over process.

Loaf. The characteristic shape of the bread after it has been molded and the baking process is completed.

Make-up Period. The length of time between end of fermentation period and time molded and panned dough is placed aside for raising.

Molding. Shaping bread into forms suitable for baking.

No-time Dough. A straight dough that has no fermentation period. As soon as the dough is mixed it is molded and panned and then placed in a warm place for proofing.

Oven. The closed, insulated section of a stove in which bread is baked.

Pastries. Food preparations such as cakes, pies, jelly rolls, lady fingers, cookies, plum duff, etc. Sugar, butter, eggs, baking powder and extracts are generally employed in their preparation. Also a short paste, as for pie crusts.

Poppy Seed. The seed of the black or white poppy. Contains about 50 per cent oil. Used for enriching rolls and loaves of Vienna style bread.

Protein. A complex constituent of foods that builds body tissues and muscle. Lean meats, fish, eggs, peanuts and soy beans contain a complete protein. Cereals, peas, beans and lentils have an incomplete protein.

Scald. As applied to flour, potatoes, etc., to submerge or wet with water at a temperature of 160° F. or more, which is sufficient to dissolve the bands of the starch cells and expose the individual grains composing it to the action of the yeast plant.

Short-time Dough. A dough which, by reason of increased amount of leavening agent and/or temperatures of mixed dough or fermentation, requires a shorter fermentation period than usual.

Shortening. Lard, butter, or other fats or oils mixed in bakery prodducts to make them more friable, richer and more crumbly in texture.

Slack Dough. A dough that contains more water or other liquid than is required to make a dough of the proper consistency. It has a tendency to flatten out and to stick to the hands or the mixer.

Sponge. A dough that contains part of the flour, part of the water, all or part of the yeast and all, part, or none of the other ingredients to be used in making baked products.

Sponge and Dough Process. A process resulting from the combining of a fermented sponge with the remainder of the ingredients to be used and mixing same. A sponge and dough necessitates at least two mixing periods, that is, the mixing of the sponge ingredients and the mixing of the fermented sponge with the other ingredients to form the sponge and dough.

Stiff Dough. A dough that contains less water or other liquid than is required to make a dough of proper consistency. It is hard to handle, especially when hand-mixed. Generally used to overcome deficiencies in flour.

Straight Dough Process. A process whereby a dough is obtained by mixing together at one time all the ingredients to be used.

Temperature. "The degree or intensity of sensible heat." A condition that pertains to heat or cold; that is, the relative degree of each. This is one of the most important factors in bread making and must be taken into consideration in connection with the yeast, water, dough, sponge, fermentation development or retardation, bake ovens, etc.

Unfermented Bread. This includes all breads made without yeast, such as aerated bread, crackers, baking powder biscuits, etc.

METHODS OF MIXING AND THE RISING [2225] OF HOMEMADE BREAD

The Sponge. Local tradition and taste peculiarity determine the character of many homemade breads. New England has its steamed Boston brown and its extra crusty spider corn bread, made in an old-fashioned frying pan. The South has its batter bread, sometimes baked according to Chief Justice Marshall's family recipe. The "Tall-Corn Belt" smacks its lips over fresh corn bread (and many sections recall pioneer days with hoe cakes no longer baked on the blade of a hoe). But the entire nation of homemakers unites in making the palate-proved favorite, old-fashioned white bread.

In the last few decades "store breads" have almost entirely replaced home-baked bread, particularly in urban communities. But the era of Wednesday and Saturday bread making has not entirely passed; America's private kitchens, especially in rural districts where "rising time" does not weigh so heavily on the housewife's conscience, still regularly witness the sacred rites of bread making.

The "makings" are simple—white flour, water, salt, yeast, and sometimes milk instead of, or mixed with, water. Although the methods have differed, that formula has been used for ages by bakers, both at home and in shops. Yet the domestic entrepreneur among her ingredients today, in spite of gas, electric or coal stove ovens, really has no more assurance of success than did her greatgrandmother. Bread making is a skill, and its results are the logical outgrowth of the cook's deftness in mixing, kneading, letting rise and baking.

A warm bowl receives the sifted flour and salt. The yeast is creamed separately in warm water. Then the skilled housewife pours the yeast into a hollow made in the flour, stirs in enough flour to make a thick batter, sprinkles a little more on top, and sets the sponge in a warm place to rise, always covered with a dry, clean, light cloth. When the sponge has risen and bubbled, she mixes in the rest of the flour and enough warm water or milk to make a soft dough. She flours a board and flours her hands. The dough is ready for the kneading, the process that thoroughly distributes the yeast, breaks up the bubbles, and works the leavening gas evenly through the dough to make a fine-grained bread.

The covered dough is set aside again in a warm place until it is twice its original size or bulk, and has little cracks all over the surface, after which it is ready for a second light kneading before being shaped into loaves and put in greased tins.

If the homemaker is especially wise, she will know that new baking tins should be baked blue in the oven before they are consecrated to their use.

Baking requires as meticulous care as mixing and kneading. The bread should continue to rise for fifteen minutes after being placed in the hot oven; then it should begin to brown. After twenty minutes of browning (or thereabouts, according to directions), the oven's heat must be reduced. The last fifteen minutes fill the kitchen with that new-baking smell which is sweeter than the aroma of Elysium's finest flowers. Then the crusty loaves are taken from the oven and allowed to cool. The baking is done. The bread is ready for the waiting family and guests.

Yeast breads must be allowed to take their time; never make them in a hurry. Unless you have experimented you cannot realize the difference in the flavor, volume, tenderness and texture between a bread dough allowed to rise slowly and gently and a dough quickened by the use of too much yeast or heat.

For normal plain homemade yeast breads, four to six hours should be allowed from mixing time to serving time; one cake of yeast should be allowed to 3 to 6 cups of flour; the room temperature should be around 80 to 85° F. Many kitchens, during the working day, have this as a steady temperature, but if your kitchen is drafty or really cool, place the bowl containing the yeast dough in a bowl of warm water, about 90° F. (the same temperature as the milk you heat for rennet custard) during the rising period. But do not set it over a too-hot oven or on a very hot radiator, or you will never realize the goodness of yeast bread.

BISCUITS—HINTS [2226]

Butter always gives a characteristic flavor that most gourmets find palatable. If the cost f butter is prohibitive, it is possible sometimes to use half butter and half other fat.

The shortening in biscuit dough is cut into the flour mixture with a fork, two knives or a pastry blender until the mixture resembles coarse meal, or it may be blended in with tips of the fingers. It is important to have the mixture cool. If it is warm the fat melts and melted fat makes less tender products. Flakiness and tenderness depend upon the shortening being distributed in very thin layers between the layers of flour. This is best accomplished when cold fat is used.

Generally biscuit dough which is stirred up in a few minutes is the best. Just enough milk, fruit juice or even water to hold the mixture together nicely, should be added quickly. The dough then is put on a floured board and patted out or kneaded only two or three times to make it smooth enough to handle.

All hot breads, such as biscuits, should be served as soon as they come out of the oven if they are to be at their best.

In making biscuits the flour is sifted before measuring. It is then combined with the salt and baking powder and sifted again so that baking powder and salt are evenly distributed in the flour.

The quality of baking powder biscuits is determined largely by the kneading of the dough. The least possible handling (stirring for drop biscuits, just enough to moisten the ingredients and then dropping the dough on a baking sheet) produces tender, crisp biscuits.

The same dough spread on a board, cut and baked, produces even, crusty, flat biscuits. Dough which receives 15 to 18 strokes of kneading produces tall, light, flaky, tender biscuits. Too much kneading results in tough, flat, close-grained biscuits because the gluten in the flour is developed to the point of toughness. Some of the leavening is lost. Folding and rolling the dough several times produces flakier biscuits than kneading it on the board. The less flour added to the dough on the rolling board the better.

Biscuit dough may be varied many ways. Try adding grated cheese . . . or a couple of tablespoons of minced parsley, minced cress, minced onion . . . or chopped pimiento . . . or substitute one-half cup of hot mashed potatoes for a half cup of the flour in the basic recipe . . . or use tomato, spinach, beet or any other kind of juice as the liquid in making biscuit. Cut biscuit dough in rounds or with a doughnut cutter; or cut into pie-shaped wedges, squares, diamonds or any fancy shape desired.

To reheat biscuits put them into a wet paper bag, tie up tightly and place in a moderate oven.

To a biscuit, add sugar, fruit, jam or candied citrus peel—and you have a quick and good dessert. Add cheese—and you have a salad accompaniment or an afternoon snack.

Baking powder biscuits should be placed two-thirds to an inch apart on the baking pans. This gives them room for expansion during rising and baking.

To make tasty tea biscuits add chopped candied fruit or peel to your regular biscuit dough. The fruit may be placed inside or on top of the mixture before it is baked. Candied ginger, too, may be used.

To make biscuits for breakfast or after-school snacks, sprinkle a sugar and cinnamon mixture generously over the top of them before placing in the oven. Watch them disappear.

Cut an extra pan of biscuits when baking and place in the refrigerator; cover with wax paper and the next morning you can slip them into your oven while preparing breakfast. A real treat with no precious minutes lost in preparation.

When baking biscuits for tea time, by way of variety press into center of each a sugar dot which has been dipped in fruit juice, marmalade, jam or preserve.

Biscuits need a hot oven and naturally the smaller they are the quicker they will bake. As soon as they are out of the oven they should be served, so that the butter will melt when they are split and buttered.

The best amount of shortening or butter for biscuits is two level tablespoons for each cup of flour. Do not be stingy; even three tablespoons will do no harm.

You may add a half cup of cut seedless or seeded raisins before milk is added. Cheese added to a biscuit mixture should be finely grated or sieved or added to flour with shortening.

For shortcakes and dumplings, increase shortening to five level tablespoons and add one-quarter cup sugar to each two cups flour. To prepare shortcakes (old-fashioned), divide dough in half and pat into two rounds to fit pie pan, individual tartlet molds or shallow pan. Butter and put other half on top. After baking, the two rounds, or what have you, can be separated easily.

Sprinkle poppy seeds over baking powder biscuits. First brush with slightly beaten egg whites.

Too much has been said, too many jests have been repeated about the bride's biscuits. The considerate bride will experiment in private, keeping any unfortunate results a secret between herself and the ashcan; but, in the meantime, there is no reason why she may not serve hot bread, since most good biscuit recipes cannot fail, if followed to the letter, with special attention to oven temperature (450° F. hot oven) for 12–15 minutes.

Brown biscuits may be made by spreading the rolled biscuit dough with melted butter and then with brown sugar. Roll up like a jelly roll and cut in one-inch slices. Place in a buttered pan and bake in a quick oven (425° F.) for 12 to 15 minutes. Serve as hot as possible.

Add one cup mashed bananas to any biscuit recipe, using two cups whole wheat flour, and adding raisins or nuts. You have a delicious little cake to eat with stewed fruit, or for breakfast, especially on Sunday.

AFTERNOON TEA MOLASSES-NUT BISCUITS [2227]

Approximately 8–10 biscuits. Oven temperature: 400° F.
Baking time: 15 minutes

3 tablespoons melted butter	2 cups sifted bread flour
½ cup molasses	3 teaspoons baking powder
¼ teaspoon cinnamon	½ teaspoon salt
½ cup pecans	¼ cup shortening
	¼ cup milk

Combine melted butter, molasses and ground cinnamon and put ½ tablespoon in eight muffin pans. To the flour add baking powder and salt and sift once. Cut in the shortening to make a coarse grained mixture; then add cold milk gradually, and stir it rapidly. Turn out on lightly floured board and knead about 25 seconds. Roll into an oblong 6 × 12 inches. Spread with remaining molasses mixture and sprinkle with chopped nuts. Roll up from the long side and cut roll into 1½-inch lengths. Place cut side down in greased muffin pans. Bake in a hot oven as directed.

AMERICAN CHEESE BAKING POWDER BISCUITS [2228]

Approximately 24 biscuits. Oven temperature: 450° F.
Baking time: 10–12 minutes

2 cups sifted bread flour	2 tablespoons shortening
2 teaspoons baking powder	1 cup grated American cheese
⅝ teaspoon salt	¾ cup milk (about)

To the flour add baking powder and salt and sift together. Cut in shortening and cheese, then add milk gradually until dough is soft. Turn dough onto floured board and knead 25 seconds. Roll out ¼-inch in thickness and cut with floured biscuit cutter. Bake on ungreased baking sheet in a hot oven as directed.

Very fine to serve hot with a green salad.

BAKING POWDER BISCUIT—STANDARD RECIPE [2229]

Approximately 15 biscuits. Oven temperature: 450° F.
Baking time: 12 to 15 minutes

2 cups sifted bread flour	½ teaspoon salt
3 teaspoons baking powder	¼ cup shortening
	¾ cup milk (about)

To the flour add the baking powder and salt and sift together. Cut in shortening with two knives or pastry blender until the consistency of coarse corn meal. Stir in the milk to make a soft dough; then turn dough out on slightly floured board and knead for ½ minute. Roll out to about ½ inch in thickness. Cut in 2-inch rounds with floured biscuit cutter and bake on ungreased pan in a hot oven as directed.

BAKING POWDER DROP BISCUITS [2230]

Number varies with size of biscuits dropped

Proceed as indicated for Standard Baking Powder Biscuit Recipe (No. 2229), having the dough slightly softer (⅞ to 1 cup milk). Drop from teaspoon or tablespoon onto ungreased baking sheet and bake 12 to 15 minutes in a hot oven (450° F.).

BRAN BUTTERMILK BISCUITS [2231]

Approximately 1 dozen biscuits. Oven temperature: 450° F.
Baking time: 12–15 minutes

Add ½ cup breakfast bran to ¾ cup of buttermilk and let stand while assembling other ingredients:

1½ cups sifted bread flour	½ teaspoon soda
1 teaspoon baking powder	⅓ cup shortening
¾ teaspoon salt	Buttermilk mixture

To the flour add baking powder, salt and soda and sift again. Cut in the shortening until mixture resembles fine meal; then add the buttermilk-bran mixture and mix until the dough follows the wooden spoon around the bowl. Turn out onto lightly floured board and knead lightly for about 20 seconds. Roll out one-half inch thick and cut with floured biscuit cutter. Bake on a lightly greased baking sheet in a hot oven as directed.

Should you like them a little sweet, you may add to the dry ingredients before sifting, 1 tablespoon of sugar. Should you prefer to use sweet milk instead of buttermilk, omit soda and increase baking powder to 3 teaspoons.

BUTTERMILK BISCUITS [2232]

Approximately 1½ dozen biscuits. Oven temperature: 450° F.
Baking time: 12 minutes

2 cups sifted bread flour	¾ cup buttermilk
2 teaspoons baking powder	½ teaspoon salt
¼ cup shortening	¼ teaspoon soda

To the flour, add baking powder, salt and soda. Sift once. Cut in shortening until mixture resembles coarse meal. Make a depression in center and add buttermilk; mix lightly with fork to make a soft dough. Toss and knead dough on lightly floured board until smooth (about half a minute). Roll out dough ½-inch thick; cut with floured biscuit cutter; place on ungreased baking sheet and bake in a hot oven as directed. Serve warm with butter, jam, marmalade or preserves.

CHEESE BISCUITS [2233]

Cheese biscuits are no more than the usual baking powder biscuit with a teaspoon of cheese and butter melted together and placed on top of each one before baking. Or add 1 cup grated cheese to flour blended with shortening. These biscuits require no butter when served, and this also recommends them for passing with salads at late suppers or whenever something piquant and dainty is needed to accompany a dish.

A good suggestion is to cream equal amounts of butter, cream cheese, and a few ground nut meats and drop by spoonfuls on top of biscuit rounds. Chill in refrigerator a few hours. Bake 12 to 15 minutes in a hot oven (450° F.).

COTTAGE CHEESE BISCUITS COUNTRY STYLE [2234]

Approximately 12 biscuits. Oven temperature: 450° F.
Baking time: 10–12 minutes

1 cup cottage cheese, sieved	2 tablespoons butter, softened
2 tablespoons thin cream	2 cups sifted bread flour
1 egg, beaten	½ teaspoon salt
A pinch of ground thyme	4 teaspoons baking powder

Cream together cottage cheese, butter, egg and cream. Combine the flour with salt, ground thyme and baking powder. Make a hole in the flour mixture and damp in the cottage cheese mixture. Gradually blend, starting from the center and bringing down the flour mixture from the edge, making a soft dough. Turn out on lightly floured board, knead 30 seconds, then roll out to ½ inch in thickness. Cut with floured biscuit cutter; place on ungreased baking sheet, and bake in a hot oven as directed. Serve warm.

CREAM CHEESE BISCUITS [2235]

Approximately 18 small biscuits. Oven temperature: 425° F.
Baking time: 15 minutes

This recipe is quite different from No. 2233, the cream cheese being mixed into the dough before baking. For a variation, you may add a heaping tablespoon of chopped almonds or mixed candied fruit when kneading the dough. Then these rich biscuits become a real sweetmeat.

No baking powder used.

1 cup sifted bread flour	1 three-ounce package cream cheese
½ teaspoon salt	½ cup butter

Add salt to the flour; then sift twice. Add cream cheese, creamed or sieved with the butter and blend thoroughly. Toss upon lightly floured board and knead 30 seconds. Shape into a flat cake and roll out to ¼ inch in thickness. Cut with floured biscuit cutter; place on ungreased baking sheet and bake in a hot oven as directed. Serve warm.

CURRIED BISCUITS [2236]
Dropped Biscuits

Approximately 18 small biscuits. Oven temperature: 425° F.
Baking time: 12 minutes

Exceedingly fine with lamb cooked in any style, shortcakes made of left-over meat, etc.

1 cup sifted bread flour	1 generous teaspoon curry powder
1½ teaspoons baking powder	2 generous tablespoons butter
½ teaspoon salt	½ cup sweet milk (about)

To the flour add baking powder, salt and curry powder, and sift twice. Cut in the butter to a coarse-grained meal and add the milk. (The original recipe requires coconut milk, so if you have some on hand you may use it.) Blend to a soft dough and drop by spoonfuls onto a greased baking sheet. Bake in a hot oven as directed. Serve hot. Split the hot biscuits, butter generously and fill with a mixture of creamed meat, poultry, mushrooms, etc.

DATE AND NUT BISCUITS [2237]

Approximately 14 biscuits. Oven temperature: 450° F.
Baking time: 12–15 minutes

Make Standard Baking Powder Biscuits No. 2229. After stirring in the milk, add ½ cup each of chopped dates and nut meats previously floured. Bake in very hot oven as directed.

ENGLISH TEA BISCUITS [2238]

Approximately 15 biscuits. Oven temperature: 450° F.
Baking time: 12–15 minutes

2 cups sifted bread flour	½ cup rich milk (about)
1½ teaspoons baking powder	1 rounded teaspoon grated orange rind
½ generous teaspoon salt	1 egg yolk, beaten
5 tablespoons butter	4 tablespoons orange juice (about)

Melted butter

To the flour add baking powder and salt and sift twice. Cut in the butter until mixture is as fine as corn meal. Remove about ⅓ of the dough from the mixing bowl and set aside. Into the remaining two-thirds, gradually stir just enough (about ½ cup) milk to make a soft but not sticky dough. Toss onto lightly floured board; knead about 30 seconds, then roll out to ½-inch in thickness.

Into the third part set aside, stir the grated orange rind, mixed with the egg yolk and orange juice (just enough to make a soft dough). Roll this third part upon a lightly floured board to ½ inch in thickness and place in center of the plain biscuit dough. Fold ends over to cover the yellow third of dough, envelope-style, then roll out to ½ inch in thickness. Cut with floured biscuit cutter, place on ungreased baking sheet and brush tops with melted butter. Bake in very hot oven as directed. Serve hot. These delicious biscuits are very popular in England and are usually served for afternoon tea with jam, marmalade or jelly.

HONEY BISCUITS—FARMER'S STYLE   [2239]

Approximately 1 dozen biscuits. Oven temperature: 450° F.
Baking time: 12–15 minutes

Make Standard Baking Powder Recipe No. 2229. Bake as directed. When done, quickly split biscuits in two and spread lower halves with strained honey and upper halves with butter. Put halves together and let stand a few minutes so that the flavor permeates the biscuits.

MARYLAND BEATEN BISCUITS   [2240]

Approximately 2½ dozen biscuits. Oven temperature: 350° F.
Baking time: 35–40 minutes

No leavening of any kind is used in these biscuits which when made in the old-fashioned method will keep perfectly fresh for almost a week. Preferably Winter wheat should be used, although any kind will serve. The dough should be wrapped in a clean towel and beaten mercilessly for a half hour with a hatchet, stick, flat iron or solid rolling pin—hard work, but it's what "makes" the biscuits. Down in Maryland, every Saturday morning about 8 a.m. one can hear the thump, thump, as the folks start beating their biscuit dough. Almost every family has a biscuit block, similar to meat blocks seen in butcher shops, only a little smaller. When the dough is beaten out flat, it is folded up again and again and beaten for 25 to 30 minutes, until you can hear the dough snap and crackle. Then it is made into small, round biscuits, the wrist gives them a little push to dent the top and they are pricked with the tines of a floured fork and baked for a long time in a moderate oven.

Here is a modernized method for these delicious biscuits:

2 cups sifted bread flour
½ teaspoon salt

Ice water or chilled milk (as little as possible)
1 tablespoon leaf lard

Add salt to flour and rub in the lard with the hands. Add the iced liquid (water or milk, or equal part of each) to make a very stiff dough, kneading all the time. Wrap the stiff dough in a strong, clean, dry towel and beat hard with either a hatchet, a heavy stick or flat-iron, for 25–35 minutes or more, the time depending on the snapping and crackling of the dough. Cut into small biscuits and prick tops with the tines of a fork dipped in flour. Place on ungreased baking sheet, and bake in a moderate oven as directed. Serve hot or cold, usually the latter.

MASHED POTATO BISCUITS   [2241]

Approximately 1½ dozen biscuits. Oven temperature: 400° F.
Baking time: 12–15 minutes

1 cup cold mashed potatoes
1 cup sifted bread flour
3 tablespoons baking powder

1 scant teaspoon salt
2 tablespoons butter
½ cup cold milk

To the flour add baking powder and salt and sift once. Work in the butter (a little more butter will make the biscuits richer); add the potatoes and blend thoroughly, being careful not to leave any lumps. Then add enough cold milk to make a soft dough. Toss upon a lightly floured board and knead a few seconds (about 12 to 15). Roll out the dough lightly to about ½ inch thickness. Cut with biscuit-cutter and bake on ungreased baking sheet in a hot oven as directed. Serve warm.

NEW ENGLAND HASTY PUDDING   [2242]
BISCUITS

Approximately 2½ dozen biscuits. Oven temperature: 400° F.
Baking time: 20 minutes

Prepare a Hasty Pudding (Corn Meal Mush) as follows:

1 cup granulated corn meal
1½ cups boiling water

½ cup cold water
¼ teaspoon salt

Make a paste of the corn meal and cold water, stirring until there are no lumps. Pour gradually into the rapidly boiling water, slightly salted, stirring until mixture is thick. Place in top of double boiler and cook over hot water for from 2 to 2¾ hours, stirring frequently from the bottom of the pan.

For the biscuits follow these directions:

4 cups of thick, lukewarm Hasty Pudding	1 tablespoon melted butter
1 yeast cake	½ teaspoon ground cinnamon
½ cup lukewarm water	½ teaspoon ground ginger
1 egg, well-beaten	½ cup molasses
	4½ to 5 cups sifted bread flour

Dissolve the yeast cake in lukewarm water; add to the lukewarm Hasting Pudding and mix well. Then stir in the combined beaten egg, butter, spices and molasses. Stir briskly, taking care that there are no lumps. Add enough flour to make a stiff dough. Knead well. Let rise overnight, in a cool place, covered with a towel.

Next day toss onto a lightly floured board; roll out ½ inch in thickness; place on ungreased baking sheet and let rise to twice its bulk. Bake in a hot oven for 10 minutes; brush biscuits with milk, and bake 10 minutes longer until delicately brown. Serve hot.

NEW ORLEANS SHRIMP BISCUITS   [2243]
Approximately 1 dozen biscuits. Oven temperature: 450° F.
Baking time: 12–15 minutes

Prepare a batch of Standard Baking Powder Biscuits No. 2229 and bake in the usual way, making the biscuit a little larger and thinner than usual. Place on half of the biscuits 2 or 3 tablespoons of creamed shrimps; cover with another biscuit and serve covered with white sauce sprinkled with grated cheese.

PEANUT BUTTER BISCUITS   [2244]
Approximately 12 biscuits. Oven temperature: 350° F.
Baking time: 12–15 minutes

2 cups sifted bread flour	1 tablespoon butter
4 teaspoons baking powder	3 generous tablespoons peanut butter
½ teaspoon salt	2 whole eggs, well-beaten
1 tablespoon granulated sugar	Cold milk to make a soft dough

Add baking powder, salt and sugar to the flour and resift twice. Cut in the butter and peanut butter to a coarse meal, then stir in the beaten eggs and enough cold milk to make a soft dough. Blend well, then toss upon lightly floured board and knead 20 seconds. Roll out to ½ inch in thickness and cut with floured biscuit-cutter. Place on ungreased baking sheet, close together, brush tops with beaten egg yolk, and bake in a moderate oven as directed.

PINWHEEL TEA BISCUITS   [2245]
Approximately 1 dozen biscuits. Oven temperature: 450° F.
Baking time: 12 minutes

1½ cups sifted bread flour	3 tablespoons butter
½ generous teaspoon salt	1 egg yolk, beaten and mixed with ½
3½ teaspoons baking powder	cup milk
	Melted butter

To the flour add salt and baking powder and resift twice. Add butter and mix with tips of fingers. Add beaten egg yolk to milk and stir into the mixture. Mix lightly. Turn out on lightly floured board and knead for 30 seconds, or until smooth. Roll about ¼ inch in thickness; spread with softened, but not melted, butter (peanut butter will give a nutty flavor). Roll up like a jelly roll. Cut in 12 equal slices and bake in muffin pans in a very hot oven as directed.

SOUR CREAM BISCUITS—COUNTRY STYLE   [2246]

Approximately 12 biscuits. Oven temperature: 450° F.
Baking time: 12–15 minutes

Note. ¼ cup chopped seedless raisins, dates or figs can be mixed with the flour, in which case a little more liquid may be needed.

2 cups sifted bread flour	1 tablespoon lard
¾ teaspoon salt	1 cup light sour cream
3 teaspoons baking powder	½ teaspoon soda

To the flour add salt, baking powder and sift once into mixing bowl. Rub in the lard with finger tips dipped in flour; stir in combined light sour cream and soda, then mix with a fork. If too dry, add a few spoonfuls of milk until dough is soft enough to be handled easily. Place on lightly floured board, roll into a smooth sheet about ¾ inch thick; cut with floured biscuit cutter; place close together on a greased baking sheet so they almost touch and bake in a very hot oven as directed. Serve warm.

Half of this recipe makes the old-fashioned shortcake if baked in a 9-in pie pan.

SWEET POTATO BISCUITS—SOUTHERN   [2247]
METHOD

Approximately 16 small biscuits. Oven temperature: 450° F.
Baking time: 15–20 minutes

1 cup sifted bread flour	2 generous tablespoons butter
3 teaspoons baking powder	1 cup mashed sweet potatoes, cold
¾ teaspooon salt	Enough cold milk to make a soft dough

Combine flour, baking powder and salt and sift into mixing bowl. Cut in butter, rubbing it in with tips of the fingers. Add sweet potatoes, then enough milk to make a soft dough (the amount will vary from 2 to 4 tablespoons according to moisture of potatoes). Turn dough upon lightly floured board and knead 30 seconds. Pat lightly into a sheet ½ inch thick. Cut with floured biscuit-cutter about 2¼-inches in diameter. Place biscuits on lightly oiled baking sheet and bake in a very hot oven as directed.

These crusty biscuits should be served very hot, split and spread with butter.

WATERCRESS BISCUITS [2248]

Approximately 1 dozen biscuits. Oven temperature: 450° F.
Baking time: 12–15 minutes

Color is one of the tests in selecting cress. It should be green, and a deep green at that, all through the bunch. It should look crisp and even lively. To be kept that way until it is used, it needs to be washed right away in icy-cold water, wrapped in a wet towel and placed in the refrigerator. It must be hidden from light and air.

Watercress has a past as well as a present. Ancient recipes made frequent reference to the green herb. It was believed that this green, eaten with vinegar, would cure a deranged mind. This gave rise to a Greek proverb, "Eat cress and get more wit." There may be something to this notion. At any rate it is rich in minerals and vitamins A and C. Fresh cress munched while drinking is rumored to keep the drinker sober.

2 cups sifted bread flour	½ generous cup chopped watercress
3 teaspoons baking powder	5 tablespoons shortening
½ teaspoon salt	¾ cup milk (about)
A few grains of cayenne pepper	½ teaspoon onion juice

To the flour add baking powder, salt and cayenne pepper and sift together. Chop cress very fine and press very gently in a dry clean towel, just enough to remove excess moisture, and blend into the flour mixture as thoroughly as possible. Cut in shortening with two knives or pastry blender; combine onion juice and milk, add to flour mixture, using enough to make a soft dough. Roll out on a lightly floured board to ½-scant inch in thickness; cut with floured biscuit-cutter and place on an ungreased baking sheet. Bake in a very hot oven as directed.

Very fine with almost any salad, fish, meat, poultry, etc.

BREADS—HINTS [2249]

Young growing bodies need the energy and nourishment provided by bread. Keep their natural appetite for bread alive by serving a variety of breads. Choose different breads when you buy or bake—serve different breads from meal to meal—put two or three kinds of bread on the same tray or plate—and watch your family sit up and take notice.

Thousands of women have, without realizing it, fallen into the "one bread habit." It is an easy habit to break. Frequent change and a variety of breads heighten interest in the whole meal.

Bread should be cooled thoroughly before it is stored. In hot weather, especially, each loaf should be inspected daily—for mold. The bread box also should be cleaned and aired frequently and kept in as cool a place as possible.

If you haven't time to make regulation patty shells, cut bread in two-inch slices, hollow out the center, and then fry in deep fat until a golden brown, or place in the oven until crisp and brown. A splendid substitute.

How did that dark, moist bread receive its name? Napoleon, on one of his campaigns had been given the coarse bread with his dinner. The little Corporal had sniffed at it and had then remarked scoffingly, "Bon pour Nickel." Nickel was his horse. Thereafter the bread, through local corruption of the French words, came to be known as "pumpernickel."

The Arabs say that wheat and other grains, including millet, rye (doura) and barley (oats are unknown except in a very limited region in Syria) came down from heaven in seven mandeels or handkerchiefs, and that it must always be respected since Allah took so much trouble to keep it clean and pure from all defilement. All who know the life of the East have listened with reverence to the cry of the breadseller going his early round. "Allah Karim!" is his cry. "God is merciful." Bread is recognized as His special gift—it is life—El Aish. It is not treated as ordinary food. There was a time not so long ago when bread could not be sold. It must always be given or exchanged—gift for gift.

To freshen dry bread or rolls, moisten with cold water and place in a hot oven until thoroughly heated, or in a paper bag in the oven for a few minutes.

Summer calls for diligent cleaning and airing of bread and cookie jars and boxes, since these foods mold easily when it's hot.

When making bread remember it should be kneaded until perfectly smooth and so elastic that any indentation made with the finger will fill up again instantly.

Often a crust forms on rising dough. To avoid that spread a little fat over the dough and cover it with a dry clean cloth.

To keep yeast fresh press into bottom of cup or bowl, invert and place in a saucer containing a little cold water.

To prevent corn bread from sticking to pan, grease well, then sprinkle with sifted corn meal.

Corn bread, that simplest of all fare, but, alas, seldom prepared as it should be, is also known under different "aliases" or disguises—"johnny cake," "corn pone," "bumble puppy" or "hush puppies," etc.

Brush your loaf of bread with melted shortening to get a fine even brown crust. By the way, do you know that a one-pound loaf of bread will make fifteen slices?

When compressed yeast is used in bread, if potato water should be used for the liquid instead of milk, it will remain moist much longer.

Graham bread takes its name from Sylvester Graham, Suffield, Connecticut, temperance lecturer, who preached vegetarianism as well as temperance in the early nineteenth century.

When removing homemade bread or rolls from the oven dip a piece of waxed paper in butter and rub the tops. It gives a luster to the crusts, making them appear more tempting.

If you have trouble with bread molding in hot weather, wrap it securely in waxed paper and store in the refrigerator.

Butter slices of bread and cut off the crusts, then cut the slices into half inch cubes. Toast these quickly on a baking sheet in a hot oven and serve piping hot at breakfast time to "dunk" into soft cooked eggs.

Fine breads, perhaps, are the best test of good cooking. They require quick, accurate workmanship and a dash of imagination to lift them from the commonplace. A fine cook goes about her mixing and baking with an endless zest. Such cooks are bold, creative artists, blending everyday staples into tender-textured, crisply-browned culinary master-pieces—with as skilled a hand as an orchestra leader's.

Toasted corn bread is tasty with creamed meats, fish or vegetables. Toast on both sides.

Bread is economical because it gives a high return in calories and some protein (energy-giving and body-building elements) for what it costs.

Dry bread crumbs are used as a topping for scalloped dishes, for coating croquettes and in place of all or part of the flour in steamed puddings, muffins, unbaked pie shells, etc.

The safest place for bread in warm humid weather is in a cool dry place. In average weather, the keeping of bread is not a problem unless it is kept too tightly sealed from the air.

Coarse bread crumbs fried in butter make an acceptable garnish for any vegetable or for alimentary pastes.

If you get crumbled food, as croquettes, ready some time before frying, scatter crumbs on a board and set the croquettes, or whatever, on these. And how they take it!

"Soft bread crumbs" means crumbs from soft or fresh bread out of the inside of the loaf, no crust included. They may or may not be soaked in water, milk or other liquids, but usually only dry bread is soaked. For Brown Betty, the bread should be grated; for bread puddings or dishes for which crumbs are soaked, you may break in very small pieces unless the recipes state otherwise.

To make buttered crumbs, melt 1/4 cup of butter or substitute and stir in one cup of bread crumbs, mixing gently over low heat until butter is absorbed and crumbs delicately browned. Such buttered crumbs are used as a filling, a topping, for scalloped dishes or "au gratin dishes" when combined with grated cheese.

Save the bread for crumbs in a paper bag; keep it tied and hanging so that the air can circulate through it rather than in the bread box or a closed jar where it soon becomes moldy. *Don't store away* buttered pieces of bread as the butter becomes rancid and the taste is far from pleasing. For fine, dry crumbs, put bread in a cloth bag and roll on board with rolling pin. Sift and re-roll the coarse crumbs. Crumbs of this type may be kept days before using. If you use grinder, fasten a large paper or cloth bag over the end to catch all of the crumbs.

Whether a little sugar goes into your corn bread or not is a matter you must decide. Experiments show that small amounts of sugar encourage browning without adding apparent sweetness.

Slice crust off one loaf of bread. Slice thin, butter generously, put together in loaf form again. Place in steamer and put in low oven for an hour. Serve very hot. You have here a delicious, rich bread.

Kneading of bread will take from three to five minutes. To test, cut the dough with a sharp knife and if there are no large bubbles the knead-ing has been sufficient. The hands may be greased or floured; this de-pends largely upon the natural warmth of the hands. The time for kneading bread may be cut by lifting the dough—baker fashion—and dropping it on the surface to break the bubbles.

ALSATIAN ONION BREAD [2250]

Approximately 15 individual breads or biscuits. Oven temperature: 450° F. Baking time: 12–15 minutes

Coarsely chop 2 cups onions, and fry in ¼ cup of lard until soft and transparent but do not allow to brown, stirring almost constantly. Season to taste with salt and freshly ground black pepper and turn mixture into a shallow baking pan. Keep warm.

2 cups sifted bread flour	¼ cup lard or other shortening
3 teaspoons baking powder	¾ cup cold milk (about)
½ teaspoon salt	

To the flour add baking powder and salt and sift again. Cut in shortening as you would for baking powder biscuit, that is until mixture is of the consistency of coarse corn meal. Stir in the milk to make a soft dough. Turn dough out on lightly floured board and knead for ½ minute or so. Roll out to ½ scant inch in thickness and spread the sheet over the onions in the pan. Over the dough pour the following mixture:

Beat together 1 cup thin sour cream (or 1 cup evaporated milk soured with 2 tablespoons of good vinegar) and 3 egg yolks. Season highly with freshly ground black pepper and salt and bake in a very hot oven as directed. To serve, cut into squares the size of biscuits, or spoon out if preferred.

This delicious bread is usually served with roast meat or fowl, like Yorkshire pudding.

BAKING POWDER BRAN BREAD [2251]
Quick Method

Makes 1 loaf. Oven temperature: 350° F. Baking time: 1 hour

2 cups sifted bread flour	½ cup seedless raisins (or nuts)
2 teaspoons baking powder	1 egg, well beaten
1 teaspoon soda	⅔ cup molasses
1 scant teaspoon salt	3 tablespoons melted shortening
2 cups all-bran	1½ cups sour milk

Brush a loaf pan with shortening and set aside. To flour add baking powder, soda and salt and sift together; stir in the all-bran, mixing well.

Beat egg, molasses, melted shortening and sour milk together, add the raisins. Combine with flour mixture and stir thoroughly. Turn dough into greased loaf pan, having the sides higher than the center. The pan should be only two-thirds full. Let stand about 15 minutes to mellow and ripen. Bake in a moderate oven as directed. Remove from oven, invert upon a rack, let cool before slicing very thin.

BAKING POWDER NUT BREAD [2252]
Quick Method
Makes 1 loaf. Oven temperature: 350° F.
Baking time: 1 hour

In making this easy and quick nut bread, two points should be kept in mind. First, the dough must stand fifteen minutes in the pan before being baked. Second, the baked loaf must be allowed to cool before it is sliced. This will require several hours standing upon a rack. You may vary the bread by using half whole wheat or graham flour and half bread flour. Brown sugar may replace the white sugar.

2⅔ cups sifted bread flour	1 cup chopped dates
4 teaspoons baking powder	1 whole fresh egg, well-beaten
½ generous teaspoon salt	½ cup granulated sugar
1 cup broken nut meats	1 cup fresh, cold milk

To the bread flour add baking powder and salt and sift together. Add the broken nut meats and shredded dates, incorporating well in the flour mixture. To the beaten egg add the sugar and beat till sugar is dissolved and mixture is fluffy and creamy. Then pour in the cold milk, beating well. Add this to the flour mixture, stirring only until thoroughly blended. Turn batter in a buttered loaf pan; let stand 15 minutes to mellow and ripen, and bake in a moderate oven as directed. When well cooled, slice very thin.

BANANA BREAD [2253]
Makes 1 loaf. Oven temperature: 350° F.
Baking time: 1¼ hours

What is called the "Quick loaf bread" is very familiar to many homemakers, who use it at tea-time, as afternoon snacks for school children, or as a sandwich spread for the lunch-box. In technique, such "quick breads" are mixed as is a muffin.

½ scant cup of shortening	½ teaspoon salt
1 scant cup sugar	½ teaspoon baking soda, dissolved in
2 eggs, well-beaten	2 tablespoons sour milk
2 cups sifted bread flour	1 cup mashed, sieved bananas (about 3)

Cream shortening; add sugar slowly, creaming until fluffy. Now add the eggs and beat well. Combine flour, salt and baking soda (dissolved in sour milk) and add to shortening mixture, alternately with bananas. Beat briskly for a minute or two. Turn batter into a greased loaf pan, and bake in a moderate oven as directed. Cool before cutting.

BOHEMIAN BREAD (HOUSKA) [2254]
Pronounced Hoska

Makes 3 loaves. Oven temperature: 400–350° F
Baking time: 40–45 minutes

1 cake of compressed yeast
2 tablespoons sugar
2 cups milk, scalded
8 cups (2 quarts) bread flour, sifted
1¼ teaspoons salt
¼ teaspoon ground mace
1 cup lard or other shortening
3 eggs, well-beaten
1 cup seedless raisins, parboiled, drained
½ cup chopped blanched almonds

Make a sponge with crumbled yeast, 2 tablespoons sugar, ½ cup milk and 2 tablespoons sifted flour. Mix well and allow to rise until doubled in bulk. Sift remainder of bread flour once, add salt and mace and sift together three times; cut in shortening. Add remainder of sugar to remainder of milk; stir into mixture. When dissolved, add the eggs, blending well, and turn this into the yeast sponge. Combine parboiled, drained and dried raisins with almonds and sift over them 2 tablespoons of flour; combine with flour sponge mixture. Allow to rise until double in bulk. Divide dough into three even sections and divide each section into three even strips. Make one braid out of each three strips and place in greased loaf pans. Let rise to double its bulk and bake in a hot oven (400° F.) for 15 minutes. Reduce heat to moderate (350° F.) and continue baking 20–25 minutes longer.

BOSTON BROWN BREAD I [2255]
A Companion to Baked Boston Beans

Makes 3 loaves. Steaming time: 3 hours. Oven temperature: 250° F.
Baking time: 25–30 minutes

Note. The loaves which are not used at once should be wrapped in waxed paper and stored in bread box and then resteamed in the molds until hot.

1 cup corn meal, sifted
2 cups whole wheat flour
2 teaspoons baking soda
1½ teaspoons salt
½ cup seedless raisins, parboiled
¾ cup molasses
2 cups buttermilk or sour milk

Combine corn meal and whole wheat flours with baking soda and salt and sift together; stir in parboiled, drained and dried raisins. Blend well. Combine molasses and milk and add to flour mixture, mixing thoroughly. Steam in three well-greased covered one quart molds, filled ⅔ full, to allow for expansion, for 3 hours. Uncover and bake in a very slow oven as directed.

BOSTON BROWN BREAD II [2256]
Yeast Method

Makes 2 loaves. Steaming time: 4 hours. Baking time:
250° F. for 5 hours

For this special homemade bread, it is wise to weigh the flours.

½ lb. corn meal	1¼ teaspoons salt
1 cup boiling water	¾ ounce yeast
1 cup molasses	½ lb. graham flour
½ lb. whole wheat flour	

Scald the corn meal by pouring the boiling (really boiling) water over it. Add molasses and salt and blend well. When lukewarm add the crumbled yeast, then the combined graham and whole wheat flours. Toss upon a lightly floured board and knead lightly. Place in large greased bowl and allow to rise six hours, at room temperature, covered with a light towel. Knead again until glossy; cut into two loaves of equal weight; place in high round molds and let rise again for about 30 minutes. Cover tightly and steam for 4 hours or place molds in several inches of hot water and bake in a 250° F. oven for 5 hours. Delicious, and keeps moist several days.

BRAIDED BREAD—COUNTRY STYLE [2257]

Makes 3 braids. Oven temperature: 375° F.
Baking time: 30 minutes

2 compressed yeast cakes	½ scant cup sugar
¼ cup lukewarm water or milk	1 teaspoon salt
1 cup milk, scalded	2 whole fresh eggs, beaten
¼ cup butter	5 cups sifted bread flour

Crumble yeast cakes into lukewarm milk. Stir in the cup of scalded milk; add butter, sugar and salt and cool to lukewarm, stirring well. To the flour, add the yeast mixture, using enough flour to make a thick batter. Then, add beaten whole fresh eggs and beat briskly. Turn out on lightly floured board and knead until satiny. Place the dough in greased bowl, cover with a light dry towel and let rise until double in bulk (about 2 hours). When light, divide in half and cut each half of dough into three equal pieces. Roll each piece until about eight inches long; cross three of the rolls in the center, braid to each end and fasten. Place on greased baking sheet. Braid remaining rolls. Place on top of first braid; cover and let rise until doubled in bulk. Brush with beaten egg yolk and sprinkle with rock sugar. Bake as directed.

BRAN BREAD—HOME METHOD [2258]
A Light and Tender Bran Bread

Makes 1 pan serving 6. Oven temperature: 375° F.
Baking time: 20 minutes

¼ cup butter or margarine	1 cup bread flour, sifted
¾ cup sugar	½ cup yellow corn meal, sifted
3 eggs, unbeaten	2 teaspoons baking powder
3 cups of bran	½ generous teaspoon salt
1½ cups milk	1 scant cup seedless raisins, parboiled

Cream fat; add sugar gradually and continue creaming until mixture is light and fluffy; add eggs, one at a time (beating briskly after each addition) alternately with the bran. To the flour and corn meal add baking powder and salt, and sift together; then add gradually to first mixture alternately with milk and floured raisins. Pour batter into greased shallow pan to ⅓ inch and bake in moderate oven as directed. Serve hot. Raisins may be omitted. To parboil raisins, place in a pan, cover with boiling water and allow to simmer 8 to 10 minutes; drain, then dry in folded towel.

BRAN HONEY BREAD [2259]

Makes 1 loaf. Oven temperature: 375° F.
Baking time: 1¼ hours

A long and interesting story could be told about honey, one of the oldest sweets known to mankind. Centuries ago it was held in high esteem by peoples of all races. The Old Testament describes the ideal living place as one "flowing with milk and honey." Romans and Greeks referred to honey as a "food fit for the gods."

The Norsemen wrote about the wonders of honey. As a food it is a delight to people, young and old, of many lands. Just as the honey-bee intrigues the imagination of artists, writers, poets and scientists of every land, this nectar-sweet liquid, of more-or-less pronounced flavor, compels the interests of every connoisseur of foods.

Honey has many uses in cookery, particularly in making bread, cakes, cookies and confections. Many Old World Christmas cakes, breads and cookies using honey are extremely popular, and have a most remarkable lasting quality, because baked foods made with honey will keep moist longer than those made with sugar. Honey has much the same consistency as molasses and may be used in place of it, measure for measure, in bread, gingerbread, steamed puddings, brown bread, etc. It contains less acid than molasses, so use one teaspoon of baking powder for each quarter teaspoon of soda in substituting honey for molasses.

Honey contains some water. This affects the amount of liquid used in a recipe when honey is substituted for sugar. The liquid must be reduced, however, more than the difference between the water content of the honey and sugar and also according to the proportion of honey used. For example, if medium-thick honey is sub itituted for *one-half the sugar* in cake or quick-bread recipes, reduce the liquid *one-fourth*. If honey is substituted for *all the sugar*, reduce the liquid *one-half*. If ʰoney is very thin or very thick, this proportion may have to be altered.

In making honey cakes and quick breads, mix the honey with the liquid called for in the recipe and bake at the lowest temperature possible. This prevents loss or change of flavor of the honey and also avoids too rapid browning.

As to the care of honey in the home, always store it, particularly comb honey, in a warm place, and *never* in the refrigerator, as low temperatures make honey crystallize or become cloudy, and high temperatures make it turn dark and browner. To liquefy a jug or jar of honey which has become solid or crystallized, set in a dish of moderately hot (140° F.) water—not higher, or it will lose its flavor. Honey, which is a summer-made sweet, needs warmth in winter, too, so just keep it on the kitchen shelf, or the dining-room buffet.

Other Uses. Many homemakers have learned that the distinctive flavor of honey makes a delicious sandwich filling when creamed with butter and mixed with chopped nuts or grated orange peel, or used in combination with cream cheese, peanut or almond butter, or chopped dried fruits.

Substituting honey for half the sugar in hard sauce, or serving it as a sauce for ice cream and other desserts, produces results appealing to most palates. A good frozen dessert may be made with a cup of honey dissolved in two cups of water, to which the juice of half a medium-sized lemon is added. The mixture may be frozen like ordinary ice cream if it is done rapidly; or it may be chilled and hardened by the addition of finely powdered ice, which is stirred in gradually until the mixture is of the proper consistency.

Honey and half-honey jellies add distinction to a breakfast table and honey custards and puddings appeal as much to the healthy member of the family as to the invalid. Sweet potatoes and other vegetables candied with honey are a wholesome variation and half a cup of honey poured over a baking ham enhances both its flavor and appearance. In making candies like fondant, nougat and caramels, honey is often substituted for corn syrup. Now for the recipe:

Beat 1 egg, adding gradually ¼ cup brown sugar alternately with ½ cup honey and melted butter, margarine or lard. Stir in 1 cup of bran, blending well. Sift 2½ cups of bread flour once, measure, then add ¾ teaspoon baking soda, 2 teaspoons baking powder and 1 scant teaspoon salt. Sift together over 1 cup of chopped figs (stems removed) and ½ cup chopped nut meats (either pecans, walnuts, peanuts, hazelnuts or Brazil nuts). Next stir the flour mixture into the egg-sugar-honey-butter mixture, alternately with 1½ cups of cold milk. Blend thoroughly, then pour into a greased loaf pan and bake as directed. Cool before slicing.

BRAN RAISIN BREAD [2260]

Makes 1 loaf. Oven temperature: 350° F.
Baking time: 1 hour

The two varieties of raisins with which most of the homemakers are familiar are the Thompson and the Muscat. The Thompson raisin grows without seeds and the Muscat, while it contains seeds when harvested, usually reaches the home with the seeds removed, except for fruit which is left on the stems and sold at holiday time. Both raisins are made from grapes by the same sun-drying process. Because of the high flavor of seeded raisins they are preferred by many for various types of baking and cooking.

There are two main reasons for using raisins. One is that their luscious taste and texture "make common foods uncommonly good"; and the other is that their nutritional value is extremely high. This combination of values puts raisins away up on the "Must" list of foods to be kept handy on the pantry shelf.

Although raisins are appropriate and appreciated all the year-round, winter, when fresh fruits are less available and more limited, is a fine time for their greater use. And no matter how inexpensive the package, raisins always remain a luxury food because of the quality they give to any baked or cooked dish to which they are added.

As a winter sauce or breakfast fruit, figs, dates and raisins could be more widely used. Each and all of these are particularly wholesome and high in food and calorie value as well as full of taste.

Practically all foods shrink during the cooking process but the dried fruits are a notable exception. The following figures show how much a pound of the different dried fruits swell and will help you in deciding how much to use:

Dried apricots, figs, prunes and raisins double in weight; dried peaches and pears are almost tripled, and dried apples absorb enough water to make their cooked bulk five times the original weight.

There are so many ways of using raisins that homemakers will have no difficulty in thinking up raisin dishes. Seedless raisins may be added whole, by the cupful to almost any recipe for bread, cake, candy, cookies, muffins and puddings. They are also good in stuffing for meat or poultry and in meat and dessert sauces. The fruity flavor of raisins, perhaps more than anything else, makes them very zestful in sauces. For raisins provide a sauce fit for a gourmet—one which gives tone and contrast to roast poultry, baked meats, etc. They should be cut with the scissors, however, before being added to a thin, light cake batter or to icing. Put them sliced on the breakfast table in a pretty bowl and let the children, and grown ups, sprinkle them on the cereal before adding the sugar and cream. And don't forget the raisins in the old stand-by custards and puddings—be it bread, cottage, or rice—of which the family is apt to tire if they are not dressed up a bit. One should not need to hunt for the raisins! Be liberal.

1 egg, well-beaten
¼ cup molasses or honey
¼ cup sugar
1 cup buttermilk or sour milk
2 tablespoons shortening, melted, cooled
2½ cups sifted bread flour

2 teaspoons baking powder
1 generous teaspoon salt
½ teaspoon baking soda
½ cup chopped, seedless raisins, parboiled
1 cup bran

To the egg, add molasses, sugar, buttermilk or sour milk, shortening and bran and blend thoroughly. Let stand until most of the moisture is taken up (about 15 minutes). To the flour, add baking powder, salt and soda and sift together. Add to the first mixture, reserving 2 tablespoons to blend with chopped raisins, added last. Stir only until flour disappears; turn into a greased loaf pan, lined with greased or waxed paper on bottom only. Bake in a moderate oven as directed. Cool before slicing.

BROWN NUT BREAD I   [2261]
Using Brown Sugar

Makes 2 loaves. Oven temperature: 325° F.
Baking time: 1 hour or more

2 cups brown sugar
2 whole fresh eggs, beaten
1 cup sour milk
¾ teaspoon baking soda
1 teaspoon water, warm

1¾ cups graham flour
¾ teaspoon salt
1 teaspoon baking powder
1¾ cups sifted bread flour
1 cup broken nut meats

To the eggs add brown sugar gradually, beating well after each addition, then stir in sour milk to which has been added the baking soda, dissolved in the warm water. Combine all the dry ingredients and sift once. Add to the first mixture gradually, stirring briskly until mixture is smooth, adding last the broken nut meats (any kind desired). Turn dough into greased loaf pans, and bake in a slow oven as directed.

BROWN NUT BREAD II   [2262]
Using Molasses

Makes 1 loaf. Oven temperature: 325° F.
Baking time: 1 hour or more

Molasses-making and the production of sugar is older than the Bible. Hindu mythology indicates that the first molasses and sugar were produced in India. Other ancient writings refer to that country's "honey-bearing" reeds. The prophet Jeremiah in the Bible speaks of "incense from Sheba and the sweet cane from a far country." History is vague regarding how cane spread into the Mesopotamian Valley. Yet by the fifth century A.D. it was growing there abundantly. By the tenth century the manufacture of crude sugar and molasses was large enough to attract traders from many distant lands. In the thirteenth century

Marco Polo found the Chinese making sugar and molasses by open-kettle methods. Today cane is grown in a wide tropical and subtropical belt that encircles the world.

It was in 1750 that the first cane, as introduced in America, was planted in New Orleans. Today molasses is used principally for flavor rather than as a sweetening.

About molasses Dr. James A. Tobey says: "People used to take pink pills. Now they take foods rich in iron, which drive away their languor and give them the rosy glow of good health. Anemia, or a deficiency of red blood, is easy to prevent and yet too many persons suffer from this malady. It is estimated, in fact, that fully half of our child population is anemic in some degree, and that numerous adults are similarly afflicted.

"When bread and molasses was a favorite food and was served at every meal, there was much less nutritional anemia than exists today. The reason was because plain old-fashioned molasses is an outstanding source of the type of iron that the body can best use for making red blood. The old custom of dosing the family with sulphur and molasses in the spring served to cure the anemia that often developed during the winter. It was the molasses that did it, not the sulphur, which made the mixture sharp and disagreeable, but merely passed through the body. The best old-fashioned molasses sold today never contains sulphur."

When molasses is eaten with bread, even more iron is utilized. Bread contains a little iron itself, but more significant is the fact that white bread made with milk is fairly high in calcium and phosphorus, which help the body to assimilate its food-iron. (Molasses, which is made from sugar cane, is of course not the only food that will help to prevent anemia, although it is probably the least expensive. Other foods high in available iron are liver, raisins, egg yolk, dried apricots, figs, prunes, red meats, and whole wheat bread.) Along with iron, these excellent foods also contain small amounts of copper, which aid in producing hemoglobin in the blood. Since the blood carries oxygen to the muscles and other body tissues, good red blood likewise helps to prevent fatigue.

In using molasses as a flavoring, remember it has sweetening power. In cookery a *cupful of high-grade molasses furnishes about the same sweetening contained in three-quarters of a cup of granulated sugar.* When substituting molasses for sugar, take into account that *a cupful of molasses carries about 2½* fluid ounces of liquid into the formula and compensation should be made, especially in baking recipes, *by decreasing the water, milk or other liquid ingredient accordingly.*

In baking, the soda neutralizes the acid in the molasses, thereby providing the leavening gas. This action is similar to the effect obtained by using sour cream, buttermilk or sour milk with soda. It aerates and raises cakes and bread and controls the spread and spring of cookies.

1½ cups graham flour	1½ cups fresh milk
¾ cup sifted bread flour	⅓ cup molasses
½ teaspoon salt	¼ cup broken nut meats

1½ teaspoons baking soda

Combine flours, salt and baking soda and sift together. Add fresh cold milk to molasses, blending well, and stir into the flour mixture. Last, stir in the nut meats. When smooth, pour batter into a greased loaf pan and bake in a very moderate oven as directed. Let cool before slicing.

CARAWAY BREAD [2263]

Makes 2 loaves. Oven temperature: 350° F.
Baking time: 45 minutes

3½ cups sifted bread flour	1½ cups cold milk
1 tablespoon baking powder	1 whole fresh egg, well beaten
½ scant cup granulated sugar	1 cup seedless raisins
1 teaspoon salt (scant)	1 tablespoon caraway seeds
1 tablespoon melted lard or butter	

To the flour add baking powder and salt and sift together, sifting a little over the parboiled, drained and dried seedless raisins. Combine the eggs with milk and sugar; then stir into flour mixture, blending well, and adding the floured raisins alternately with caraway seeds and melted lard or butter. Knead a few seconds, then allow to stand for about 30 minutes. Divide the dough between two greased loaf pans; let stand 20 minutes in a warm place before baking in a moderate oven as directed. Let cool before slicing. You may stir into the dough or the milk mixture ½ to ¾ teaspoon of vanilla extract.

CHEESE SHORTBREADS [2264]
Appropriate with Any Kind of Salad

Makes about 50 tiny balls. Oven temperature: 400° F.
Baking time: 8–10 minutes

¾ lb. American cheese, grated	A pinch of cayenne pepper
¾ cup butter, creamed	1½ cups bread flour, sifted twice with
½ scant teaspoon salt	

Blend grated cheese with creamed butter thoroughly, using a wooden spoon; then blend in the flour with salt and cayenne pepper. Roll into small balls one inch in diameter. If mixture becomes too soft, put in refrigerator to chill. Place the balls on an ungreased cookie sheet and bake in a hot oven as directed until delicately brown. Serve warm.

CHRISTMAS BREAD [2265]

Makes 2 loaves. Oven temperature: 350° F.
Baking time: 40 minutes (about)

1 9-oz. package dry mincemeat	¾ cup fine granulated sugar
½ cup water	4 teaspoons baking powder
2 cups bread flour, sifted twice	1 scant teaspoon salt
1 cup all-wheat flour (unsifted)	1 whole egg, slightly beaten
1 cup cold rich milk	

Break the mincemeat in small pieces into a saucepan, add the water and cook, stirring it constantly, until lumps are thoroughly broken and dissolved. Bring to a brisk boil and boil for 3 minutes, as indicated on the package of mincemeat, or until mixture is practically dry. Cool. Combine sifted bread flour and all-wheat flour with sugar, baking powder and salt and mix together. Mix well the slightly beaten egg with the milk and add to the flour mixture, beating vigorously to make a smooth dough. Then fold in the mincemeat thoroughly. Pour dough into two greased loaf pans and bake in a moderate oven as directed. Preferably served cool, although it may be eaten warm, if desired.

CORN BREAD—TENNESSEE MANNER   [2266]

Serves 6–8. Oven temperature: 425° F.
Baking time: 18–20 minutes

1 cup bread flour, sifted	¾ cup bran flakes
½ cup corn meal, sifted	1 whole fresh egg, well-beaten
3 tablespoons granulated sugar	1 cup milk
1 tablespoon baking powder	3 tablespoons melted butter
½ teaspoon salt	

To the mixed flour and corn meal add sugar, baking powder and salt and sift together. Stir in the bran flakes. Combine beaten egg and cold milk and add to dry ingredients, stirring just enough to blend. Melt butter in a shallow square pan (8 × 8 inches); add the butter to the batter; pour the butter into pan and bake in a very hot oven as directed. Serve hot in squares with plenty of butter.

CORN BREAD—KENTUCKY MANNER   [2267]
Using Whole Sweet Kernels

Serves 6. Oven temperature: 425° F.
Baking time: 30 to 35 minutes

1 cup bread flour, sifted	2½ teaspoons baking powder
2 teaspoons sugar	2½ cups scraped sweet corn kernels
1¼ teaspoons salt	1 whole fresh egg, well-beaten
¼ cup shortening, melted	

To the flour add sugar, salt and baking powder and sift together over the corn, mixing thoroughly. Stir in egg alternately with melted shortening—no liquid is necessary, the moisture being given by the scraped corn. Turn into a generously greased shallow pan (8 × 8 inches) and bake in a very hot oven as directed. Serve hot with plenty of butter.

CORN BREAD—FARMER'S METHOD [2268]
Very Rich and Mellow Bread

Serves 6–8. Oven temperature: 425° F.
Baking time: 18–20 minutes (about)

4 cups white corn meal	1 cup evaporated milk
2 cups boiling water	1 cup hot water
4 whole fresh eggs, well-beaten	2 teaspoons salt
¼ cup bacon or ham drippings	

Pour boiling water over meal and stir well. To the eggs add combined drippings, evaporated undiluted milk, hot water and salt; blend well; then mix thoroughly with white corn meal. Turn batter into two greased shallow pans (8 × 8 inches). Bake one pan in a very hot oven as directed, and while this is being served bake the other pan in the same way. Serve with plenty of butter and molasses.

DATE BREAD [2269]

Makes 1 loaf. Oven temperature: 350° F.
Baking time: 50–55 minutes

2 cups chopped dates	1 cup boiling water
1 teaspoon baking soda	1 teaspoon vanilla extract
1 tablespoon butter	1 cup sugar
½ teaspoon salt	½ cup chopped pecans
1 egg	1½ cups bread flour, sifted twice
½ teaspoon baking powder	

Sprinkle soda over dates; add boiling water. Let stand until cool. Beat egg with salt, sugar, butter, nuts and vanilla extract; then mix well with the dates and water. To the flour add baking powder and sift together; add to first mixture and blend thoroughly. Turn batter into a generously greased loaf pan, and bake in a moderate oven as directed. Allow to cool before slicing.

DATE MOLASSES YEAST BREAD [2270]
Keeps Moist for Several Days

Makes 3 loaves. Oven temperature: 350° F.
Baking time: 55 minutes (about)

3 cakes compressed yeast	1½ cups lukewarm milk
¼ cup lukewarm water	1½ cups lukewarm water
½ cup molasses	4 tablespoons melted butter or margarine
1½ teaspoons salt	3 cups quartered pasteurized dates
10 to 12 cups entire-wheat flour	

Dissolve yeast cakes in the quarter-cup lukewarm water and combine with molasses, salt, milk and the 1½ cups lukewarm water, melted butter or margarine and dates. Mix slightly to blend. Beat in the entire wheat flour until mixture is of the consistency to knead, and knead about five minutes, or until dough is elastic and does not stick to the board, which should be lightly floured. Cover with a light, dry cloth; let stand in a greased pan, placed over warm water to rise until doubled in bulk. Toss upon lightly floured board, kneading lightly for about a minute; then form into three loaves. Transfer the loaves to well-greased loaf pans; cover and let rise again until doubled in bulk. Bake in a moderate oven as directed or until firm in the center and brown on top. Rub over with butter after baking. Let cool before slicing.

DATE NUT BREAD [2271]
Using Baking Powder

Makes 1 loaf. Oven temperature: 350° F.
Baking time: 1¼ hours

½ lb. dates, chopped	1 teaspoon salt
1 cup boiling water	1 whole egg, well beaten
¼ cup butter, margarine or lard	2½ cups bread flour, sifted
1 scant cup sugar	2½ teaspoons baking powder

½ cup chopped nut meats (any kind)

Parboil chopped dates in the boiling water for 3 or 4 minutes; stir in shortening, sugar and salt; blend well and allow to cool. When cold, stir in the beaten egg, alternately with flour, mixed with baking powder. Sift a little over the chopped nut meats and add them alternately with the flour mixture, blending thoroughly. Turn dough into generously greased loaf pan and bake in a moderate oven as directed. Let cool before slicing.

DUTCH APPLE BREAD [2272]

Makes 1 loaf. Oven temperature: 350° F.
Baking time: 55 minutes

½ cup butter	1 teaspoon baking soda
1 cup sugar	½ teaspoon ground cinnamon
1 egg, well-beaten	1 cup peeled, sliced apples, packed solid
2 cups bread flour, sifted twice	½ cup sweet milk
½ teaspoon salt	¼ cup chopped raw cranberries

Cream butter; add sugar and cream well, then add egg. To the flour, add salt, soda and cinnamon and sift together over apple and cranberries. Mix well and add to first mixture, alternately with cold milk, stirring thoroughly. Turn batter into generously greased loaf pan, and bake in a moderate oven as directed. Let cool before slicing.

FIG BREAD   [2273]

Makes 1 loaf. Oven temperature: 350° F.
Baking time: 1 hour (about)

2½ cups bread flour, sifted	1¼ cups of dried figs, coarsely chopped
4 teaspoons baking powder	1½ cups cold milk
½ teaspoon salt	2 whole eggs, well-beaten
½ cup sugar	¼ cup lard or butter, melted

Combine flour with baking powder, salt and granulated sugar and sift over chopped figs. Blend well, so as to coat figs with flour mixture to prevent their falling to bottom of bread. Combine eggs with cold milk and add to flour-fig mixture, mixing thoroughly, adding as you go along the melted lard or butter. Turn dough into generously greased loaf pan. Let stand 25 minutes to mellow and ripen, and bake in a moderate oven as directed. Let cool before slicing.

FRENCH BREAD STYLE   [2274]

Makes 1 long loaf. Oven temperature: 400° F.
for 15 minutes, then 375° F. for 30 minutes

1 cake compressed yeast	1¾ cups lukewarm water
2 teaspoons sugar	1 teaspoon salt
	6 cups bread flour, sifted

Rub yeast and sugar together until liquid. Add lukewarm water and salt. Make a hollow in the center of the flour. Add liquid mixture and mix to form a smooth elastic dough, starting from center and gradually reaching the edge. Rub or brush with butter and let stand until dough has doubled in bulk, over a pan containing hot (not boiling) water. Now toss upon lightly floured board, and knead slightly. Return to the pan or mixer and let rise again. Shape into a loaf about 15 inches in length and three inches in height and place on lightly floured baking sheet. Brush again with butter and let rise until doubled in bulk. Bake in a hot oven as directed. Ten minutes before bread is done brush with the following mixture:

1 tablespoon cornstarch	1 tablespoon sugar
	2 tablespoons cold water

HOMEMADE BREAD   [2275]
Yeast Method

Makes 2 loaves. First rising time: 2 hours, or until double in bulk.
Second rising time: 1 hour, or until double in bulk.
Oven temperature: 450°–350° F.
Baking time: 55–60 minutes

The recipe for two large loaves calls for six to seven cups of bread flour, one pint liquid (milk, milk and water or water and powdered milk), a little sugar, a little salt and, last but not least, yeast. For the very short process two cakes compressed yeast to the pint of liquid is the rule and the bread will be mixed and baked in three to four hours. One cake of yeast produces bread in five to six hours, and one-fourth to one-half yeast cake, by the overnight rising method, which some homemakers may find more convenient.

Follow the directions carefully if you are making bread for the first time; experienced bread-makers will of course vary the recipe to suit themselves.

2 cups (one pint) milk, scalded	2 cakes compressed yeast
2 tablespoons granulated sugar	¼ cup lukewarm water
1½ teaspoons salt	6 to 7 cups sifted bread flour

3 tablespoons melted shortening

Add sugar and salt to the scalded milk; cool to lukewarm. Crumble yeast cakes in a large mixing bowl; add the lukewarm water, stirring until dissolved; stir in the warm milk mixture.

Sift in 4 cups of the bread flour (also called all-purpose flour) in two installments, stirring to smoothness; add the melted shortening and 2 more cups of the flour.

Stir until the dough leaves the sides of the mixing bowl using a bit more flour if needed.

Turn upon a lightly floured board; knead until smooth, elastic and bubbled under the surface, using as little of the reserved flour as possible. The kneading time is five to eight minutes. Form the dough into a ball; place in a greased mixing bowl and brush over the top to prevent cracking. Cover with a dry cloth; put upon a rack over hot (not boiling) water; keep in a warm place till doubled in bulk and very light and fragrant. The time may vary from one and one-half to two hours with the temperature, draft and unforeseen conditions.

Cut down the dough; divide into two equal parts (it is always wise to weigh the dough); knead each one for a minute; shape into loaf form; brush with melted shortening; place in greased loaf pans. Again cover; place over hot water; let rise till very light and doubled in bulk. The time varies from forty to sixty minutes.

Place the loaves in a very hot oven (450° F.); in fifteen minutes reduce the heat to moderately hot; or, place in a steady moderate oven (350° F.), and bake until brown and shrunken from the sides of the pans. Remove from the pans to racks. When quite cold store in a fresh, well aired bread box.

Important. If a soft crust is desired, brush the molded loaves with melted butter before setting them to rise; then brush the baked loaves with butter after removing them from the pans.

Smells delicious, looks delicious, is delicious!

HOMEMADE RYE BREAD [2276]

Makes 2 loaves. Oven temperature: 350° F.
Baking time: 55–60 minutes

Use recipe for No. 2275, substituting 3 cups rye flour for 3 cups bread flour. Proceed as indicated.

By way of variety, you may add raisins, currants, shaved almonds or nuts, or any two in combination, to the bread dough before the final folding. You can play games with any variety of fruits, too—blueberries, preserved pineapple, raisins with poppy seeds. The procedure is general: Roll out the dough, brush with melted butter, spread with the desired mixture, roll up tight, cut into slices of ¾ inch to an inch, place cut side down on greased pans; let rise until light and bake in a moderate oven as directed.

How about turning your bread dough into pecan or cinnamon rolls? Or spreading it with a layer of mincemeat over which brandy or rum has been poured and cinnamon and sugar sprinkled?

HOMEMADE WHOLE WHEAT BREAD [2277]

Makes 2 loaves. Oven temperature: 350° F.
Baking time: 55–60 minutes

Use recipe for No. 2275, substituting 3 cups of *unsifted* whole wheat flour for 3 cups of bread flour. Bake as indicated.

HOMEMADE WHOLE WHEAT HONEY [2278] BREAD

Yeast Method. No Sugar Used

Makes 2 loaves. Oven temperature: 350° F
Baking time: 1 hour (about)

1 cup boiling water	2 cups unsifted whole wheat flour
4 tablespoons honey	¾ cup lukewarm water
½ cup lukewarm water	2¼ teaspoons salt
2 cakes compressed yeast	3 tablespoons shortening, melted
3½ cups *unsifted* whole wheat flour	

Place the boiling water in large mixing bowl; stir in honey. Dissolve yeast cakes in the ½ cup lukewarm water, then add to water-honey mixture (which has been cooled to lukewarm) alternately with the 2 cups of whole wheat flour. Blend this sponge well. Cover and let rise to double its bulk over hot water. When raised, cut it down and add combined ¾ cup lukewarm water, salt and melted shortening, alternately with the remaining 3½ cups of flour. Blend thoroughly. Knead until smooth and elastic. Place in greased bowl; brush with melted shortening and let rise to double in bulk. Remove dough from the bowl; knead a few minutes, then let rise but not quite double in bulk this time. Divide into two equal parts; shape into loaves and brush with melted shortening. Place upon slightly greased baking sheet, and bake in a moderate oven as indicated. Let cool before slicing.

HONEY BRAN BREAD [2279]

Makes 1 loaf. Oven temperature: 400° F.
Baking time: 1 hour (about)

½ cup bran flour
1 cup graham flour
1 cup bread flour, sifted
4 teaspoons baking powder
1 whole fresh egg, well-beaten
½ teaspoon salt
1 cup sweet milk
⅓ cup honey
½ cup chopped walnuts or raisins

Combine all dry ingredients and sift together over chopped nut meats or raisins. Blend thoroughly. Combine milk, honey and egg and beat briskly, then stir into dry mixture, blending well. Pour batter into greased loaf pan and bake in a hot oven as directed. Cool before slicing.

HUSH PUPPIES [2280]
Southern Corn Bread or Corn Pones

Serves 6

Embodied in the title of this bread recipe is a most interesting story. Years ago (in some sections it is still the custom) the Negroes of Tallahassee, Florida, that quaint southern capital, would congregate on warm fall evenings for cane grindings. Some of them would feed the sugar cane to a one-mule treadmill while others poured the juice into a large kettle where it was boiled to sugar. After their work was completed they would gather around an open fire over which was suspended an iron pot in which fish and corn pones were cooked in fat.

The Negroes were said to have a certain way of making these corn pones which were unusually delicious and appetizing. While the food was sizzling in the pot the Negroes would engage in rather weird conversations, spell-binding each other with "tall" stories of panther and bear hunts. On the outer edge of the circle of light reflected by the fire would sit their hounds, their ears pricked for strange sounds and their noses raised to catch a whiff of the savory odor of the frying fish and pones. If the talking ceased for a moment a low whine of hunger from the dogs would attract the attention of the men and subconsciously a hand would reach for some of the corn pone which had been placed on a slab of bark to cool. The donor would break off a piece of the pone and toss it to a hungry dog, with the command, "Hush, puppy!"

The effect of this gesture on the hounds was always instantaneous and the Negroes attributed the result to the remarkable flavor of what eventually became known as "The Tallahassee Hush Puppy."

2 cups fine corn meal, sifted
2 teaspoons baking powder
1 teaspoon salt

1½ cups milk
½ cup water
1 extra large onion, chopped fine

Sift the first three ingredients together. Combine milk and water and stir in, alternately with the onion. Add more corn meal (sifted) as may be necessary to form a soft but workable dough. With the hands dipped in flour, mold pieces of dough into pones (oblong cakes, about 5 inches long, 3 inches wide and ¾ of an inch thick). Fry in deep hot fat or oil until well browned on all sides. Serve hot.

INDIVIDUAL SHIRRED SPOON BREAD   [2281]
Southern Method

Serves 6. Oven temperature: 375° F.
Baking time: 20 minutes (about)

2 cups corn meal
1½ cups (about) boiling water
1½ tablespoons butter or margarine
1¾ teaspoons salt

3 cups buttermilk
1 teaspoon baking soda
1 egg yolk, well-beaten
2 whole fresh eggs, well-beaten

Add enough boiling water to the corn meal to make it the consistency of thick mush. Then stir in the butter or margarine and salt, alternately with combined buttermilk, soda, egg yolk and whole eggs. Fill 6 generously greased individual, shirred-egg dishes and bake in a moderately hot oven as directed. Serve hot. A fine bread for breakfast or luncheon, formal or informal.

IRISH RAISIN BREAD   [2282]
Called Also "Irish Soda Bread"

Makes 1 small round loaf. Oven temperature: 350° F.
Baking time: 40 minutes

This quick bread, sweetened with raisins or currants and flavored with caraway seeds if desired, takes its name from the soda used with buttermilk or sour milk as the leavening agent. Most recipes for the small round loaf call for ½ teaspoon of baking soda to neutralize the acidity of one cup of buttermilk; but when the milk is *rather sour*, the addition of a little baking powder gives a lighter loaf.

2 cups bread flour, sifted
1½ teaspoons baking powder
½ generous teaspoon salt

¼ teaspoon baking soda
½ cup seedless raisins (or currants), cut
1 tablespoon caraway seeds

1 cup buttermilk (about)

Combine the flour, baking powder, salt and soda, and sift together over the washed, dried, cut raisins (or currants) and caraway seeds.

Blend thoroughly. Stir in enough buttermilk to make a soft dough. Turn dough upon a scantily floured board and knead lightly until smooth and not sticky (about a minute). Shape the dough into a round loaf; place in a greased round pan. With a knife cut a cross on the top and bake in a moderate oven as indicated or until loaf is brown and shrinks from sides of pan. Should the loaf be very thick in the center, bake a few minutes longer. Let cool before cutting. The bread should sound hollow when tapped with the knuckles and may be rolled loosely in a clean cloth and tilted on end to cool.

JEWISH TWISTED BREAD [2283]
Overnight Rising Bread

Makes 2 twists. Oven temperature: 350° F.
Baking time: 45–50 minutes

½ cake compressed yeast	1 tablespoon granulated sugar
1 cup lukewarm water	8 cups (2 quarts) bread flour, sifted
2 teaspoons salt	1 cup sweet milk, lukewarm

Crumble half yeast cake into lukewarm water and add salt and sugar. Sift flour into a large deep bowl; make a depression in the center of the flour and pour in the yeast mixture mixed with the milk. Stir with a wooden spoon to make a dough; turn out on a lightly floured board and knead until smooth and velvety. Return to greased bowl; brush top with melted butter or oil, cover the bowl and let stand in a place free from draughts until morning. Then divide the dough in half (I advise weighing it) and shape into two twisted loaves. Allow to rise for about 40 minutes, or until almost doubled in bulk, and bake in a moderate oven as directed.

JEWISH MATSOS CRIMSEL [2284]

Serves 6. Frying time until delicately brown all over in deep fat

3 matsos, soaked in cold water	¼ cup grated blanched almonds
12 tablespoons (6 ozs.) sugar	1 teaspoon grated lemon rind
3 well beaten whole fresh eggs	1 tablespoon goose fat
1 cup apples (or prunes) chopped	

Press the soaked matsos until quite dry. Cream together sugar and eggs, then add the soaked pressed matsos, alternately with remaining ingredients, except the chopped fruit. Roll this dough out into circular pieces about the size of a tea cup saucer. Spread the chopped fruit on the dough, covering with another piece of dough. Pinch the edges firmly after brushing with water. Roll in matsos meal and fry in deep hot fat until delicately browned all over. Serve warm, sprinkled with sugar mixed with cinnamon.

The true orthodox Jewish cookery reflects centuries of Jewish culture. It is based on the rituals of the religion itself. Jewish cookery is noteworthy not only because of its strict adherence to the Mosaic laws, but because its development through the ages has produced many tasty and interesting dishes. In the orthodox kitchen, only animals that have been killed in the Kosher way can be used. Blood as well as pork is prohibited and in the Kosher method of slaughtering, the animal is bled almost entirely. To make sure that no blood remains, all meat is soaked in cold water for one-half hour and in salted water for one hour before it is prepared as food.

NUT RAISIN BREAD [2285]
With Bread Flour

Makes 1 loaf. Oven temperature: 300° F.
Baking time: 1¼ hours (about)

3½ cups bread flour, sifted
¾ teaspoon salt
4 teaspoons baking powder
¾ cup fine granulated sugar

1 whole fresh egg, well-beaten
1 cup sweet milk, cold
1 cup seedless raisins, parboiled
¾ cup finely chopped walnut meats

Combine flour with salt, baking powder and sugar and sift over raisins (washed, parboiled, thoroughly drained and dried) mixed with finely chopped walnut meats. Mix thoroughly. Combine beaten egg with cold milk; beat well, and gradually stir into the flour-raisin-nut mixture, stirring just enough to moisten the dry ingredients. Turn into a greased loaf pan, lined with waxed paper, and bake in a slow oven as directed, or until bread is brown and slightly shrunken from the pan. Cool and slice very thin.

ORANGE BREAD I [2286]
Yeast Method

Makes 2 loaves. Oven temperature: 350° F.
Baking time: 1 hour

1 cake compressed yeast
1 cup lukewarm water
1 cup orange juice (unstrained)
Grated rind of 2 medium-sized oranges
2 tablespoons butter, melted

1 teaspoon salt
2 tablespoons granulated sugar
1 egg yolk, well-beaten
4 cups bread flour, sifted twice
Melted butter for tops

Crumble yeast cake into lukewarm water; mix well then stir in orange juice and grated rind, salt, sugar and beaten egg yolk. Beat briskly until well blended. Gradually stir in the flour, mixing thoroughly after each addition. Place upon lightly floured board and knead for one minute. Turn the dough into a greased mixing bowl; cover; and let rise to double its bulk, over hot water. Now cut down the dough and knead a half minute. Divide dough into two equal parts; shape into loaves; place in greased lined loaf pans and allow to rise to double in bulk. Brush tops with melted butter and bake in a moderate oven as directed. Serve warm and thinly sliced.

ORANGE BREAD II   [2287]
Baking Powder Method

The syrup

Cut rinds of two large oranges; place in small saucepan, cover with cold water, and simmer for 10 minutes. Drain; cover again with cold water, bring to the boiling point, and let simmer slowly for 10 minutes longer, or about 20 minutes. Drain and put rind through food chopper, using the finest blade. Return to a small saucepan; add ½ cup sugar and ½ cup cold water. Stir until sugar is dissolved; then bring to the boiling point and simmer slowly until a thick syrup is formed and chopped rinds become semi-transparent. Remove from the fire, and let cool.

The dough

2½ cups bread flour, sifted	½ cup unstrained orange juice
1 tablespoon baking powder	1 teaspoon unstrained lemon juice
½ generous teaspoon salt	3 tablespoons melted butter or lard
½ cup fine granulated sugar	The orange rind syrup, well-cooled
2 whole fresh eggs, well-beaten	Melted butter for top

To the flour add baking powder, salt, sugar, and sift together. Combine beaten eggs, unstrained orange and lemon juice, melted butter or lard (or any other desired shortening) and last the orange rind syrup. Blend thoroughly, using a rotary beater. Skim off the foam; then add gradually to the flour mixture, blending thoroughly after each addition. Let stand 10 minutes before turning into greased loaf pan; brush with melted butter and bake one hour in a moderate oven (350° F.). Allow to cool before slicing.

I would not strain orange or lemon juice used in pastry, bread or cookies. To do so means that only the water-soluble material of the orange or lemon is used and there is nutrient value, notably vitamin A and iron, in the suspended particles of pulp which are discarded. In fact, the decrease in the use of whole fruit as a result of the greater convenience of orange juice represents to my mind and to that of dietitians some loss of nutritive value.

RAISIN BREAD [2288]
Yeast Method

Makes 1 loaf. Oven temperature: 400° F.
Baking time: 45 minutes (about).
First rising: 50 minutes. Second rising: 2½ hours.
Third rising: 1 hour

1 cup sweet milk, scalded, cooled	⅓ cup dark brown sugar, sifted
1 cup compressed yeast	¾ generous teaspoon salt
1 tablespoon granulated sugar	1 whole fresh egg, well-beaten
1¼ cups bread flour, sifted	1 cup chopped seedless raisins
2 tablespoons shortening	2 cups whole wheat flour

Scald milk and cool to lukewarm. Crumble yeast cake into a little lukewarm water, and stir into lukewarm milk, alternately with sugar. Add bread flour gradually and beat hard until very smooth. Cover the sponge; set over a pan containing hot water, and let rise for fifty minutes, or until light with large bubbles on the surface.

Cream shortening and brown sugar well, add beaten egg and salt and beat until smooth, then stir in the light yeast mixture called a sponge. Beat well until smooth, then stir in the whole wheat flour, mixed with raisins. Turn dough out upon a lightly floured board and knead until all stickiness disappears and the dough is elastic, using a little more whole wheat flour if needed. Place dough in a large greased bowl; cover; set in a warm place or over a pan of hot water and let rise again (second rising) until doubled in bulk. Mold quickly into one long, or two short, loaves; place in a well greased loaf pan (or two smaller pans); cover; let rise again (third rising) in a warm place or over hot water until doubled in bulk. Bake in a hot oven as directed or until brown on top and the loaf, tapped on the bottom, gives forth a hollow sound. Cool, uncovered, before slicing. If you bake in two loaf pans, bake for about 40 minutes.

SALLY LUNN BREAD [2289]
Yeast Method

Makes 2 loaves. Oven temperature: 350° F.
Baking time: 50 minutes (about)

4 cups bread flour, sifted	½ cup lukewarm water
1 teaspoon salt	2 whole fresh eggs, beaten slightly
1 cup milk, scalded, cooled to lukewarm	1 cake compressed yeast
2 tablespoons granulated sugar	

To the flour add salt and sift together. To the lukewarm milk add eggs and blend well. Crumble yeast cake into the lukewarm water and let stand 4 or 5 minutes, then stir into the milk mixture, gradually, with the flour and salt mixed with sugar. Beat vigorously for a few minutes.

Cover; set the bowl over hot water and allow to rise to double its bulk. Cut down the dough, toss upon lightly floured board and knead until smooth, elastic and not sticky to the hands. Shape into two loaves; brush with melted butter, place in greased, floured loaf pans and let rise to double in bulk. Bake in a moderate oven as directed. Serve hot, cut into squares or slices, with plenty of butter.

SALT-RISING BREAD [2290]

*Makes 2 loaves. Oven temperature: 375° F. for ten minutes,
then 350° F. for 25 minutes. Total time: 35 minutes*

Here is a real old-time family recipe for "salt-risin' bread"—the kind that many Americans remember from their childhood.

The sponge and dough require a higher temperature (115° F.) than yeast mixtures. The "starter" should be kept at a constant temperature for an active mixture. The home-made salt-rising bread is not so light as yeast bread; it is moist and crumbly.

1 cup sweet milk, scalded	1½ teaspoons salt
1 tablespoon granulated sugar	¼ cup white corn meal

Scald milk; remove from heat and stir in sugar, salt and white corn meal; turn into 2-quart jar or pitcher, cover and set in pan of water, hot to the hand (110 to 115° F.).

Let stand in a warm place 6 to 7 hours, or until it ferments; when gas escapes freely, stir in, in order named:

1 cup lukewarm water (100° F.)	2 tablespoons shortening
1 tablespoon granulated sugar	2¼ cups bread flour, sifted

Beat thoroughly. Return jar to hot water bath (115° F.) and let rise until sponge is very light and full of bubbles. Turn sponge into warm, greased large mixing bowl, and gradually stir in 2¼ cups bread flour, sifted, or just enough to make a stiff dough, or until smooth after kneading a few minutes.

Divide in half, shape into loaves, place in generously greased loaf pans. Brush with melted butter; cover and let rise in warm place until two and one-half times its original bulk. Bake in moderately hot oven to set the dough, then at moderate heat as directed. Let cool before slicing.

SPOON BREAD [2291]

*Serves 6 generously. Oven temperature: 400° F.
Baking time: 20–25 minutes*

2 cups sweet milk	1 teaspoon salt
1 cup white corn meal, sifted	½ lb. butter
1 tablespoon brown sugar	6 egg yolks, well-beaten
6 egg whites, stiffly beaten	

Heat sweet milk to the scalding point; gradually and very slowly stir in the corn meal with brown sugar and salt and stir briskly from the bottom of the pan, gradually adding the butter. After cooling, add beaten egg yolks a little at a time, beating vigorously the while; then fold in the stiffly beaten egg whites. Turn into a generously buttered soufflé dish or light earthenware casserole and bake in a hot oven as directed. Serve sizzling hot.

SWEDISH COFFEE RINGS   [2292]

Makes about 4 dozen rings. Oven temperature: 350° F.
Baking time: 7 or 8 minutes

2 cups bread flour, sifted   ½ teaspoon salt
⅓ cup fine granulated sugar   ½ cup butter, creamed
                 1 whole fresh egg, well-beaten

Sift together the flour, fine granulated sugar (or equivalent of powdered sugar) and salt; add the butter creamed with beaten egg, and when well blended, turn onto a lightly floured board, shape into a long roll and cut off very small pieces. Roll each piece with the palm of the hand, lightly floured, into a pencil-like roll, about ⅛ inch in diameter. Cut off 5 or 6 inch lengths and shape into a circle. Place circles on a lightly greased baking sheet and bake in a moderate oven as directed or until delicately browned.

VIENNA BREAD   [2293]
Yeast Method

Makes 2 small loaves or several fancy shapes.
Oven temperature: 425° F.
Baking time: 25 to 30 minutes

3¾ cups bread flour, sifted twice   1 teaspoon granulated sugar
1 generous teaspoon salt   1 cup sweet milk, lukewarm
2 tablespoons butter (no substitute) 1 whole fresh egg, well beaten
1 cake compressed yeast   Melted butter for tops

Add salt to flour and sift together. Cream yeast and sugar thoroughly, then add milk and beaten egg mixing well; then mix with flour mixture. The dough should be very smooth. Cover; place over a pan of hot (not boiling) water, and let rise one hour. Knead on lightly floured board until smooth, elastic and not sticky; shape into two small loaves or into several fancy shapes; place on generously buttered baking sheet; let rise 15 minutes and bake in a quick oven as directed. Brush tops with melted butter and let cool before slicing.

YEAST POTATO BREAD [2294]

Makes 3 loaves. Oven temperature: 350° F.
Baking time: 1 hour (about)

Boil 2 medium-sized peeled potatoes in 1 quart of water until they can be mashed into the water. This is the water to be used in the making of this bread which remains moist several days.

1 quart potato water	8 to 10 cups bread flour, sifted
1 cup milk	5 tablespoons granulated sugar
¼ cup lard or butter	2 tablespoons salt
2½ cakes compressed yeast	

To the mashed potato water, boiling briskly, add milk and lard or butter; then set where it will be lukewarm. Sift flour, sugar and salt together into large mixing bowl. Make hole in center and add potato water to which has been added the crumbled yeast cakes, soaked in ½ scant cup lukewarm water. Mix just enough of the flour into the center to make a light sponge, beating it well to prevent lumping. Then stir in the rest of flour to the smooth stage. Brush top with lard or butter; cover and allow to rise until double in bulk. Knead down and when smooth, elastic and not sticky, return to the greased mixing bowl; brush with lard or butter and allow to rise to double in bulk. Cut down; knead a short minute; form into three loaves; place loaves in greased loaf pans and let rise again to double in bulk. Brush tops with melted shortening and bake in a moderate oven as directed or until brown and bread leaves sides of pans. Let cool before slicing.

BUNS—HINTS [2295]

According to old custom, the Scottish bride is carried over the threshold of her new home. She is met on the other side by the groom's mother or some other female relative who breaks a currant bun over her head. A miss is considered an unlucky omen.

Buns are surprisingly simple to make. They are merely a variation of the standard yeast bread recipe. Like any yeast bread, these buns are most successful if the home baker will follow the rules for handling this type of bread. The most common mistake made by home bakers is permitting the dough to become hot. This results in killing the yeast plants and it follows that the dough will not be properly leavened.

A second point is to have a correct, even temperature for baking. Too low heat will give a product too light and porous in texture, while too high a temperature may result in uneven baking or burning of the buns. The correct temperature is about 400° to 425° F.

Towards the end of the eighteenth century in Bath, England, a young girl, Sally Lunn, sold her buns night and morning on the city streets. They were so delicious that they were named after her and the recipe came to America soon afterwards.

The American version of the hot cross bun probably comes from England. In the old days a hot cross bun was hung in the chimney place on Good Friday and left there throughout the year to bring good luck by preventing evil spirits from coming down the chimney to ruin bread baking and cause other domestic troubles. Today we do not think about good luck in connection with these delicious buns except perhaps to appreciate the good luck that lets us enjoy them!

There used to be an old English superstition (and maybe there still is) that on Easter Day the sun danced or leaped as it came up above the horizon, and our forefathers used to get up very early on Easter morning to catch him at it. Unfortunately the Devil always put a hill in the way, and so nobody ever got a chance to see the miracle. Of all the old legends there couldn't be one easier to believe, for if ever the sun were inclined to dance, it would undoubtedly be on an Easter morning, which is, beyond all question, the gayest holiday of the whole year. Naturally, it calls for the gayest fare.

Everybody whose grandmother came to these shores from Russia, or Ireland, or Italy, or Hungary, or France, or from most anywhere else, is going to enjoy the Easter lamb, or the Easter cakes, or the Easter loaf, or the Easter bun. All the same, one of these recipes may find a place on the Easter table, too.

BUNS [2296]
Yeast Method

Makes 1½ dozen buns. Oven temperature: 400° F.
Baking time: 12 to 15 minutes

1 whole fresh egg, well-beaten	¾ teaspoon sugar
½ yeast cake	3 additional tablespoons sugar
1¼ cups lukewarm water	1 teaspoon salt
3 tablespoons lard or other shortening	3½ to 4 cups bread flour, sifted

Beat egg and add half of the water in which yeast and the ¾ teaspoon sugar have been dissolved. Let stand ½ hour. Mix together salt, lard or other shortening and remaining sugar and water and add to first mixture. Blend thoroughly. Put about half of the flour into the liquid mixture and beat thoroughly, then add more sifted bread flour until dough is stiff enough to be handled, keeping dough softer than bread dough. Brush dough with shortening; place it in a generously greased mixing bowl and let rise to double its bulk. Knead down and let rise again or make into buns after first rising. Cut with floured biscuit cutter, then press flat and lay on a generously greased pan at least 1 to 1½ inches apart according to size. Brush top and set in a warm place to rise. It will probably take 2 to 2½ hours. Bake in a hot oven as directed or until golden brown.

Bad planning as to the time table can be as disastrous as bad planning in the menu itself. Including in the same course a dish requiring a hot oven and another which takes slow cooking can produce a small panic in the kitchen when each begins to stalemate the other. A failing common to all disorganized cooks lies in planning such things as biscuits, buns or muffins to be served piping hot with some dish like egg timbales or chicken soufflé—the first needing a hot-as-blazes oven and the eggs and chicken dish taking very slow heat.

CINNAMON BUNS [2297]
Yeast Method

As cinnamon buns became more and more popular, home bakers as well as professionals experimented with the original recipes and changed them about a bit to conform to their own ideas and taste. As a result, today there are two schools of thought among cinnamon bun gourmets. One insists that the buns should be made with currants, following traditions; the other argues enthusiastically that seedless raisins give the buns a certain subtle flavor which is lacking when they are made with currants. The latter faction points out that since the cinnamon bun was not a creation, but rather a series of departures from a baked product that started out as something else, it is perfectly all right to improve it still further by using seedless raisins.

The conservative school, however, points to an old recipe for what many claim is the perfect cinnamon bun. Here it is:

½ cup shortening	5 cups bread flour, sifted
1 cup scalded milk	½ cup melted butter
1 teaspoon salt	1 cup brown sugar
¾ cup granulated sugar	2 tablespoons of cold milk
2 yeast cakes	1½ teaspoons cinnamon
2 whole fresh eggs, well beaten	½ cup currants

Add shortening to hot milk. Add salt and sugar and dissolve thoroughly. Cool to lukewarm, then crumble in the yeast cakes. When dissolved, stir in beaten eggs, then the flour. Knead till smooth and elastic and allow to rise until double in bulk. Combine ¼ cup of the butter, ½ cup of the brown sugar and the milk (2 tablespoons). Mix well and spread on bottom of pan. Roll dough to ¼-inch thick, and spread with remaining butter and sugar mixed with the cinnamon, and the currants which have been washed, then sponged dry. Roll as for jelly roll and cut in one-inch slices. Place cut side down in pan over the butter-brown-sugar and milk mixture and allow to rise to double in bulk; brush with melted butter and bake in a hot oven as directed.

While fanciers of the Philadelphia sticky cinnamon bun say that the buns have been popular "as long as they can remember" and the name of the chef who first thought of adding cinnamon to the other ingredients and giving it a distinctive taste is lost to culinary history, there are many theories as to how the bun originated in this country.

One of the most logical of these theories is advanced by the Department of Nutrition, American Institute of Baking, which believes that when the Dutch sailed into the New World they brought with them a recipe for spice cakes which was very popular in 1623 and which Philadelphians later changed to cinnamon buns. The old recipe reads as follows:

. . . To make excellent spice cakes, take halfe a pecke of very fine Wheat-flower, take almost one pound of sweet butter, and some good milke and creame mixt together, set it on the fire, and put in your butter, and a good deale of sugare, and let it melt together; then straine Saffron into your milke a good quantity; then take seven or eight spoonful of good Ale barme, and eight egges with two yelkes and mixt them together, then put your milke to it when it is somewhat cold, and into your Wheat-flower put salt. Aniseedes bruised, Cloves and Mace, and a good deale of Cinamon; then worke all together good and stiffe, that you neede not worke in any Wheat-flower after; then put in a little rose water cold, then rub it well in the thing you knead it in, and worke it thoroughly; if it be not sweet enough, scrape in a little more sugar and pull it all in pieces, and hurle in a good quantity of Currants, and so worke all together againe, and bake your Cake as you see cause in a gentle warme oven. . . .

When in a hurry, here is a quick bun which is really good if the directions are followed:

CINNAMON NUT RAISIN BUNS [2298]
Quick Baking Powder Method

Makes about 10 buns. Oven temperature: 475° F.
Baking time: 12 minutes (about)

Preliminary preparation for the pan:

½ cup brown sugar	A pinch salt
½ cup butter	½ cup broken pecans

Combine these ingredients and mix well; spread in bottom of shallow pan; then lay the cinnamon slices on top, cut side down.

Dough:

4 cups bread flour, sifted twice	4 tablespoons melted butter
2½ tablespoons baking powder	½ cup seedless raisins, parboiled,
1½ teaspoons salt	sponged
8 tablespoons shortening	½ cup chopped pecan meats
1½ cups sweet cold milk	1½ teaspoons ground cinnamon
½ cup brown sugar	

Add baking powder and salt to the flour (be sure to use 2½ tablespoons baking powder) and sift together in a mixing bowl; cut in shortening, then stir in the milk slowly and gradually, mixing well. Toss mixture upon a lightly floured board and roll out to ¼ inch thickness. Brush with melted butter. Combine well dried raisins, pecan meats, cinnamon and brown sugar and dust over flat dough; and roll it up like a jelly roll. Cut into 1¼ inch slices; lay them in prepared shallow pan, cut side down. Bake in a very hot oven as directed. Then ring the bell!

HOT CROSS BUNS   [2299]

Makes 2 dozen buns. Oven temperature: 425° F.
Baking time: 20 minutes

¼ cup shortening	¼ cup lukewarm water
1 cup boiling water	2 whole fresh eggs, unbeaten
½ cup granulated sugar	1 cup seedless raisins or currants
1 teaspoon salt	¼ cup shredded citron or orange peel
1 cup sweet milk, scalded	¾ teaspoon ground cinnamon
1½ cakes compressed yeast	4 cups bread flour, sifted twice

Put the shortening, boiling water, sugar, salt and scalded milk in large mixing bowl; stir well; then let cool to lukewarm. Add the yeast, which has been dissolved in the lukewarm water. Blend well. Add unbeaten whole eggs one at a time, beating well after each addition, alternately with mixed raisins and citron, and the flour, which was sifted, the last time over the fruit with the cinnamon. Blend thoroughly, then knead for a half minute on floured board, adding more sifted bread flour if necessary. When smooth, place dough in a greased bowl; cover and let rise to double in bulk over hot water. Cut down the dough; place on lightly floured board, cut off small pieces and form them into balls. Place balls on a greased baking sheet; allow to rise until double in bulk (about one hour or more) and bake in a very hot oven as directed until brown. Remove from oven; brush with melted butter and when cold mark a cross with white icing on the top.

For Icing. To 1 tablespoon hot water add sifted confectioner's sugar until thick and flavor to taste with either vanilla, lemon or almond extract. Or, just before removing from the oven, brush with sugar and water and fill the cross with the above icing.

There may be doubts about how to entertain for Christmas and what sort of a party to give on New Year's and whether Thanksgiving dinner should be in the middle of the day or at night, but surely everybody will agree that Easter breakfast is the gayest and most completely satisfactory occasion imaginable.

Of course those righteous souls who rise early and go to church deserve an especially fine breakfast waiting their return, but even the lazy and the unregenerate can appreciate, although they may not merit, a perfectly grand meal with which to begin the day. Easter breakfast ought to be so good and so bountiful that no more food is needed till tea time.

The early Fathers of the Church undoubtedly knew how to work up to a dramatic climax—the lean, gray days of Lent and the emotions of Good Friday and Holy Saturday all leading up to the joy bells of Easter with a breakfast featuring Hot Cross Buns.

STICKY BUNS—PENNSYLVANIA DUTCH [2300] METHOD I
Baking Powder Method

Makes 10 large buns. Oven temperature: 425° F.
Baking time: 25 minutes

This method results in a cluster and should be turned out in one cake and separated as needed.

Preliminary preparation—skillet or baking pan:

Cream 4 tablespoons of butter and ½ cup brown sugar by stirring them together in a bowl until creamy and fluffy. Spread this all over the bottom and sides of skillet or baking pan.

Dough:

3 cups bread flour, sifted	1 teaspoon salt
6 teaspoons (2 tablespoons) baking powder	4 tablespoons butter
	1 whole fresh egg, well beaten
2 tablespoons granulated sugar	¾ cup sweet cold milk

To the flour add baking powder, granulated sugar and salt and sift together. Stir to mix thoroughly. Add butter and cut it into small pieces with two knives or pastry blender. Then completely work in butter with lightly floured hands. Combine well-beaten whole egg with milk and pour slowly into the mixture, stirring with a large wooden spoon. There should be just enough liquid to make a dough. If a little more liquid is necessary, add a very little milk. Now knead slightly about ½ minute. Roll out on a lightly floured board into an oblong 20 inches by 9 inches wide, keeping corners as square as possible and edges of dough straight.

Spread:

3 tablespoons butter, softened	1 teaspoon ground cinnamon
1 cup brown sugar	¾ cup seedless raisins, parboiled, sponged

Spread butter over the dough. Over butter sprinkle combined brown sugar and ground cinnamon, then distribute prepared raisins as evenly as possible over the whole.

Now roll dough like a jelly roll. Cut with a sharp knife into pieces each about 2 inches long. Place the cut pieces of rolled dough in the prepared skillet or pan, cut side up and let stand 15 minutes, covered with a light, dry cloth. Bake in a hot oven as directed. Remove pan or skillet from oven and immediately turn the buns upside down on a large platter. Be careful in turning the buns out, because of the hot brown sugar.

STICKY BUNS—PENNSYLVANIA DUTCH   [2301]
METHOD II
Yeast Method

Makes about 16 buns. Oven temperature: 425° F.
Baking time: 20–25 minutes

This method results in a cluster and should be turned out in one cake and separated as needed.

Preliminary Preparation. Same as for Recipe No. 2300 above.

Dough:

2 cups scalded sweet milk	1 cake compressed yeast
1½ teaspoons salt	¼ cup lukewarm water
¼ cup granulated sugar	6 cups (about) bread flour, sifted twice

Cool scalded milk to lukewarm; add salt, granulated sugar and yeast cake which has been dissolved in the lukewarm water and blend well. Gradually add the flour, beating briskly after each addition, using enough flour to make a soft dough which can be handled easily. Knead dough until smooth, elastic and not sticky. Place dough in a generously greased mixing bowl; cover with a light, clean, dry towel and let rise over hot water until it trebles in bulk. Toss upon lightly floured board and roll into a sheet ¼ inch thick and spread with the following mixture:

Spread:

4 tablespoons butter, softened	1¾ teaspoons ground cinnamon
1½ cups brown sugar	1 generous cup seedlees raisins

Spread softened butter over the dough. Over butter sprinkle combined brown sugar and cinnamon; then cover with raisins (or currants) which have been parboiled, drained and thoroughly dried between two towels.

Roll the dough as for jelly roll. Cut with a sharp knife into pieces about 2 inches long. Place the cut pieces of rolled dough in the prepared skillet or pan, cut side up and let stand, covered with a clean cloth, until light and almost double in bulk. Bake in a hot oven as directed until delicately brown. Remove pan or skillet from oven and immediately turn the buns upside down on a large platter. Be careful in turning the buns out because of the hot brown sugar.

The first dunker on record appears to be the Danish Lord of Fres who in A.D. 1160 commented on the tastiness of bread dipped in ale.

MUFFINS, GEMS AND JOHNNY CAKES—   [2302]
HINTS

Quick mixing of dry and liquid ingredients is the secret of obtaining light muffins. *Stir* only until all the flour is moistened. The batter may look lumpy, but it is ready for the pans.

A muffin is a gem and a gem is a muffin. The only difference is that old-time recipes used a heavy muffin pan, which was then, and still is, called a "gem pan." Otherwise the ingredients of muffins are the same as for gems.

Knobs or peaks on top of muffins and long narrow holes inside may indicate that the batter has been stirred too long.

When filling gem or muffin pans, leave one of the small sections empty and fill with water—the gems or muffins will never scorch.

All muffins or gems need a moderately hot oven and will take from twenty to twenty-five minutes to bake, depending on their size. If you like a crisp crust, use the old-fashioned iron gem pans for baking them.

Muffin or gem batter should *not be beaten*. The flour should be *stirred* with the liquid only enough to dampen the flour so that no dry flour is visible around edges of the bowl.

Muffins made partly with cooked cereal will not be heavy if the cereal is first worked into the flour by means of the finger tips.

Try buttermilk muffins. If you don't have buttermilk on hand, you can sour sweet milk by adding one tablespoon of vinegar to each cup of milk used.

Bread flour may be used to replace part of the corn meal called for in corn muffins; if more corn meal than flour is used, the finished muffin will resemble corn bread somewhat in texture and taste. When the amount of flour exceeds the meal, the product is more like regular muffins. Either white or yellow corn meal may be used according to preference; the use of sugar is also a matter of taste.

Use canned unsweetened pineapple juice instead of milk in making muffins. Top each muffin, before baking, with a small lump of sugar dipped in the fruit juice or with a cube of the canned fruit sprinkled with sugar.

Top the corn muffins, before baking them, with uncooked diced bacon. Bake for 15 minutes in a hot oven; then place the muffins under the flame of the broiling oven and let the bacon crisp. Fine for breakfast, luncheon, afternoon snacks and supper.

Drop a teaspoon of peanut butter in each muffin pan, over which pour batter. This gives muffins a delightful nutty flavor.

Speaking of peanut butter, try substituting ⅓ cup of peanut butter or one-half cup of grated cheese for the regular shortening.

Left-over biscuits and muffins make fine foundations for luncheon dishes. Scoop out the inside crumbs, brush generously with melted butter, then fill with a creamed vegetable, meat, fish or chicken mixture. Bake about 10 minutes in a moderately hot oven (350° F.). Serve as hot as possible. Muffins not eaten at Sunday supper may be sliced, toasted and buttered for Monday breakfast.

Try glazing your muffins. First brush the muffins with slightly beaten egg white; then sprinkle with poppy seeds. Watch them disappear.

In graham muffins one-half graham flour replaces one-half the white flour.

A bran muffin is, at breakfast, a bran muffin—and very good too. Add a crushed banana to the mixture. Cake can't beat it.

For afternoon tea, little rice muffins may be neatly hollowed out and filled with some of your newly made strawberry or raspberry jam or marmalade. Have the muffins hot, of course.

For the simplest bran muffins, part of the flour may be replaced with bran, from ⅓ to ⅔ as a rule, and the amount of liquid increased to supply the additional moisture the bran makes necessary.

For date muffins, add ½ cup finely cut dates to dry ingredients.

Use odd bits of jelly, jam, peanut butter, apple butter and all the gamut of fruit butters by putting one teaspoonful into center of muffin after it is partly baked. It will not go to bottom nor make muffins or gems fall. Do not remove pan from oven. Work quickly.

AFTERNOON CHOCOLATE MUFFINS [2303]
These Are More Cup Cakes than Muffins

Makes about 1 dozen muffins. Oven temperature: 375° F.
Baking time: 20 minutes

2 squares chocolate, unsweetened	¼ teaspoon vanilla extract
½ cup sweet milk	½ cup cold milk
2 egg yolks, well-beaten	1 scant teaspoon baking soda
1 cup granulated sugar	1¼ cups bread flour, sifted twice
3 tablespoons butter	2 egg whites, stiffly beaten

Put broken chocolate in top of double boiler; add ½ cup milk and place over hot water. Stir until chocolate is dissolved and mixture is smooth; stir in the beaten egg yolks, a little at a time, beating well after each addition and stirring constantly until smooth. Remove from hot water, stir in sugar, butter and vanilla extract. Blend till sugar is dissolved; then gradually add second ½ cup of milk in which soda has been dissolved, adding alternately with the flour. Lastly fold in the stiffly beaten egg whites. Pour batter into greased muffin pans, and bake.

BANANA BRAN MUFFINS [2304]

Makes 6 large or 12 small muffins. Oven temperature: 375° F.
Baking time: 30 minutes

Someone has said that in the days of Alexander the Great bananas were called "The fruit of the wise men." That may or may not be a true statement. However, modern scientists are sure that bananas are a fine source of vitamins, essential minerals and energy-giving substances. And, furthermore, bananas are available the year round at low cost. They are always picked green and ripened off the tree. When partially ripe, they are yellow with green tips and at that stage may be classed as a vegetable, for they must be cooked to be really edible. When the green tip disappears, they may be eaten raw but do not yet have the sweetness and aromatic flavor that is distinctive. When brown flecked, they have reached eating perfection and are so digestible that they are often given to infants.

Note. This recipe calls for diced or sliced bananas. This makes a somewhat stiffer batter than usual for muffins.

1 cup bread flour, sifted	1 whole egg, well-beaten
½ teaspoon salt	1 cup unsifted bran
¾ teaspoon baking soda	2 tablespoons buttermilk or sour milk
2 tablespoons shortening	3 bananas (2 cups finely diced or very
¼ cup granulated sugar	thinly sliced)

Add salt and baking soda to flour and sift together. Cream shortening and sugar well. Combine beaten egg, unsifted bran and buttermilk or sour milk well and stir in the bananas. Mix again; then add to combined flour mixture and creamed shortening, stirring only enough to dampen all the flour. Turn batter into generously greased muffin pans, ⅔ full, and bake in a moderate oven as directed. Serve hot with plenty of butter.

You may substitute one cup bread flour, whole wheat flour, or corn meal for bran, if desired.

BLACKBERRY MUFFINS [2305]

Makes about 14 small muffins. Oven temperature: 400° F.
Baking time: 20 minutes (about)

1½ cups bread flour, sifted	1 whole egg, well-beaten
3½ teaspoons baking powder	¾ generous cup sweet cold milk
¾ teaspoon salt	3 tablespoons melted butter
¾ cup carefully-washed, hulled, drained blackberries	

Add baking powder and salt to the flour and sift together. Combine beaten egg with cold milk and melted butter and add to flour mixture, alternately with blackberries, stirring only enough to dampen the flour. Turn batter into greased muffin pans and bake in a hot oven as directed. Serve hot.

BLUEBERRY BRAN MUFFINS [2306]

Makes 16 medium muffins. Oven temperature: 400° F.
Baking time: 25 minutes

The ease with which muffins can be mixed and dropped into greased pans for the oven recommends them to busy homemakers over biscuits that need rolling and cutting preparatory to baking. Also the standard muffin recipe permits wider variation for breakfast use than those for some other hot breads. Part of the flour may be replaced by whole wheat flour, oatmeal, bran or corn meal, for example. Something may be added, such as fresh berries, raisins, dates or nuts.

1 cup bran, unsifted	1 whole fresh egg, well-beaten
1 cup sweet cold milk	1 cup bread flour, sifted twice
2 tablespoons shortening	3 teaspoons baking powder
¼ cup granulated sugar	½ scant teaspoon salt

½ generous cup fresh blueberries, washed, sponged

Pour cold milk over the unsifted bran, let stand 5 minutes to soak and absorb almost all the milk. Cream shortening and sugar; beat in the egg; then stir in the bran mixture alternately with flour mixed with salt and baking powder and sifted over the blueberries. Stir just enough to dampen the flour mixture or until it disappears. Turn into greased muffin pans ⅔ full and bake in a hot oven as directed, until muffins are brown and slightly shrunken from sides of pans. Serve very hot with plenty of butter.

Blueberry gems are made in the same manner, except that the batter is turned into heavy iron muffin pans.

BLUEBERRY MUFFINS [2307]
Master Recipe

Makes 1 dozen muffins. Oven temperature: 375° F.
Baking time: 20–25 minutes

2 cups bread flour, sifted twice	2 tablespoons melted butter
2 tablespoons granulated sugar	1 whole egg, well beaten
1 tablespoon baking powder	½ cup sweet cold milk
½ teaspoon salt	1 cup washed, sponged blueberries

Mix ½ cup of the flour lightly with the blueberries, let stand 10 minutes. Add sugar, baking powder and salt to remaining flour and sift three times. Combine egg and milk and add to flour mixture alternately with floured blueberries. Turn batter into generously buttered muffin pans and bake in a moderate oven as directed until tops are brown and muffins shrunk from edges of pans. Serve very hot and with plenty of butter.

BRAN MUFFINS [2308]
Master Recipe

Makes 8 large or 12 small muffins. Oven temperature: 400° F.
Baking time: 25–30 minutes

2 tablespoons butter	¾ cup sweet cold milk
¼ cup granulated sugar	1 cup bread flour, sifted with
1 whole fresh egg, well beaten	2½ teaspoons baking powder, and
1 cup bran	½ generous teaspoon salt

Cream butter and sugar; gradually add egg, then beat briskly until mixture is fluffy. Stir in bran, dampened with milk, and let stand 5 minutes, or until moisture is taken up, then add combined flour, baking powder and salt, sifted together, and stir until flour is dampened, no more, no less. Turn batter into generously buttered muffin pans and bake until muffins are brown and leave sides of pans, in a hot oven as directed. Serve as hot as possible.

BRAN RAISIN MUFFINS [2309]

Makes 10 large muffins. Oven temperature: 375° F.
Baking time: 25 minutes

For the simplest bran muffins, part of the flour in the recipe is replaced with bran (from ⅓ to ⅔, as a rule) and the amount of liquid increased to supply the additional moisture the bran makes necessary. Brown sugar or molasses is preferred to white sugar as the sweetening agent.

1 cup sweet milk	¾ cup seedless raisins, parboiled,
1 cup bran	sponged
2 tablespoons shortening	1 cup bread flour, sifted with
¼ cup dark brown sugar	1 tablespoon baking powder, and
1 whole fresh egg, well beaten	⅛ teaspoon salt

Pour milk over bran and let stand 5 minutes. Cream shortening and brown sugar; then add the egg, beating briskly until thoroughly blended. Add bran-milk mixture, mixed with seedless raisins which have been parboiled, drained and well sponged. Over this sift combined bread flour, baking powder and salt and blend just enough to moisten flour. Mixture will look lumpy, but do not attempt to stir out the lumps. Fill generously buttered muffin pans ⅔ full; bake in a moderately hot oven as directed or until firm, brown and shrunken slightly from the pans. Serve hot with plenty of butter.

BUTTERMILK MUFFINS [2310]

Makes about 1½ dozen muffins. Oven temperature: 400° F.
Baking time: 20 minutes

4 cups bread flour, sifted twice	1 scant teaspoon baking soda
3 tablespoons corn meal	2 whole fresh eggs, well beaten
1 tablespoon salt	1 tablespoon brown sugar
	3 to 3½ cups buttermilk

Add corn meal, salt and soda to flour. Beat eggs with brown sugar into buttermilk, then add to dry ingredients, gradually, stirring just enough to dampen flour mixture. Pour batter into generously greased muffin pans and bake in a hot oven as directed until muffins are brown and leave sides of pans. Serve very hot with plenty of butter, jam or marmalade.

CORN MUFFINS   [2311]
Master Recipe

Makes 1 dozen muffins. Oven temperature: 375° F.
Baking time: 25–30 minutes

2 cups bread flour, sifted twice	½ teaspoon salt
2 tablespoons granulated sugar	1 cup sweet milk (about)
1 tablespoon baking powder	1 whole fresh egg, well beaten
1 cup corn meal (white or yellow)	4 tablespoons melted shortening

Add sugar, baking powder and salt to flour and sift into a warm bowl containing the corn meal and mix well. Combine milk, egg and melted shortening, blend well and pour over flour mixture all at once, then stir just enough to dampen flour. Fill greased muffin pans ⅔ full and bake as directed or until muffins are brown and have shrunk from sides of pans. Serve hot with butter, jam or marmalade.

ENGLISH MUFFINS   [2312]
Yeast Method

Makes about 10 muffins. Hot greased griddle.
Baking time: 15 minutes (about)

1 cup scalded milk	1 teaspoon granulated sugar
2 tablespoons butter	¼ cup milk, lukewarm
½ generous teaspoon salt	1 yeast cake
3½ to 4 cups bread flour, sifted	

To the scalded milk add butter, salt and sugar. Stir well and let cool to lukewarm. Crumble yeast cake into lukewarm milk, stir until dissolved, then stir into first mixture. Gradually stir in flour (enough to make a thick batter). Turn batter into a greased mixing bowl; brush top with melted shortening; cover and allow to rise over hot (not boiling) water until doubled in bulk. Knead a half minute over lightly floured board; roll batter into ¾-inch thickness; let rise on board, covered with a dry towel, until doubled in bulk and cut into 3-inch rounds. Bake on a hot, greased griddle about 15 minutes, turning often. When cool, split, toast and butter generously. Serve as hot as possible.

GINGERBREAD MUFFINS [2313]

Makes 1 dozen large muffins. Oven temperature: 350° F.
Baking time: 25 minutes

½ cup each butter and lard mixed	1½ teaspoons baking soda
¼ cup brown sugar	1 teaspoon cinnamon
¼ cup granulated sugar	1 teaspoon ginger
1 whole fresh egg	¾ teaspoon salt
1 cup molasses	1 cup hot water
3 cups bread flour, sifted twice	½ teaspoon ground cloves

Cream thoroughly butter and lard with brown and granulated sugars. Blend in the beaten egg alternately with the molasses. To the flour add baking soda, cinnamon, ginger, salt and ground cloves and sift together over first mixture. Stir in alternately with just enough hot water to dampen the dry mixture. Turn batter into warm, buttered muffin pans (⅔ full) and bake until muffins are brown and leave sides of pans, in a moderately hot oven as directed. Serve very hot with plenty of butter. For afternoon tea, bake in small muffin pans which will yield 1½ dozen muffins.

JOHNNY CAKES I [2314]
American Original Recipe

Makes about 2 dozen cakes. Oven temperature: 375° F.
Baking time: 15–20 minutes

"Johnny Cake" is said to come from "Journey Cake," so-called because in the days of Daniel Boone no man left the settlements without his sack of corn meal, the prime ingredient of "Johnny Cake."

This is a sophisticated recipe; but for the authentic Johnny Cake a griddle is used and cakes are baked until browned on both sides and eaten with an abundance of sweet butter.

Rich Johnny Cakes baked in buttered iron skillet:

2 cups water-ground white corn meal	Cold sweet milk
1 teaspoon salt	2 whole fresh eggs, well-beaten
Boiling water	2 tablespoons butter

Combine white corn meal with salt, mixing well; pour onto it rapidly boiling water to make a thick paste and when slightly cooled, thin with enough milk beaten with the eggs to give a smooth, soft pancake consistency. Lastly stir in melted, cooled butter. Pour batter into a very hot, well greased skillet all at once and bake in a moderate oven as directed until brown on top. Bubbles form similarly to those appearing on pancakes made on a hot griddle.

To Serve. Turn the big cake upside down upon a hot, round platter, spread generously with butter and serve in wedges at once.

For the original recipe, bake upon a hot, generously greased griddle until brown on both sides. You may omit the eggs, but cakes will be less tender. Down South the batter is dropped upon a greased baking sheet by spoonfuls and baked in a hot oven (400° F.) for about 15 to 20 minutes, until brown.

Another method in great favor in the Middle West is the following:

JOHNNY CAKES II   [2315]

Serves 12. Oven temperature: 425° F.
Baking time: 25 minutes

1 cup water-ground white corn meal   ½ teaspoon salt
¼ cup bread flour, sifted   2 whole eggs, well-beaten
1½ teaspoons baking powder   ½ cup sweet milk
             4 tablespoons melted butter

Mix and sift dry ingredients. Combine beaten eggs and milk and pour over dry ingredients; stir until smooth and lastly stir in melted butter. Pour batter into a well greased baking pan, about ¾ of an inch in thickness, and bake in a hot oven as directed. Serve hot, cut in wedges, with plenty of butter.

POTATO FLOUR MUFFINS   [2316]
English Method

Makes about 10 muffins. Oven temperature: 400° F.
Baking time: 20 minutes (about)

In this fine recipe only potato flour is used, and enough additional moisture is furnished by a very little cold water and strictly fresh eggs.

3 egg yolks, beaten until creamy   ½ generous cup potato flour, sifted
½ scant teaspoon salt   1 generous teaspoon baking powder
1 tablespoon granulated sugar   3 egg whites, stiffly beaten

Combine creamed egg yolks, salt, sugar and cold water and beat briskly. Add baking powder to potato flour and sift over first mixture. Stir just enough to dampen evenly, gradually folding in the stiffly beaten egg whites (about 25 strokes). Pour batter into hot, buttered muffin pans and bake in a hot oven as directed until muffins are brown and leave sides of pans. Serve hot with plenty of butter, jam, jelly, marmalade, honey, maple syrup, molasses or preserves.

SALLY LUNN MUFFINS   [2317]

Makes 18 small muffins. Oven temperature: 400° F.
Baking time: 25–30 minutes

Toward the end of the eighteenth century in Bath, England, a young girl, Sally Lunn, sold her buns, muffins and home-made breads night and morning on the city streets. They were so delicious that they were named after her and the recipe came to America soon afterwards.

½ cup lard or butter or half and half
½ cup granulated sugar
3 whole fresh eggs, well-beaten
½ generous teaspoon salt

1 cup rich sweet milk, cold
2 cups bread flour, sifted twice
4 teaspoons baking powder

Cream shortening until smooth and fluffy. Gradually add sugar and cream until thoroughly blended. Combine eggs with milk and beat gradually into creamed mixture. To the flour add baking powder and salt and sift over first mixture; stir just enough to dampen evenly. Fill hot, buttered (*not greased*) muffin pans ⅔ full, and bake in a hot oven as directed until muffins are delicately brown and separate easily from sides of pans. Serve at once with butter, jam, jelly, marmalade or preserves.

GINGERBREAD [2318]

Ginger is regarded as the mystery plant by the Sherlock Holmeses of the botanical world, for none of them can tell for a certainty just where this important spice plant had its origin. Some say Asia, some say Brazil, but however indefinite its background, its popularity as a seasoner has been known from prehistoric times. Today, in a cold, thirst-quenching drink such as ginger ale or in appetizing and aromatic gingerbread, this spice is among the most useful and widely employed seasoners. *To ginger* means to put spirit into and that is exactly what the ginger root does to anything with which it comes in contact, be it candy or preserves. Wise old kings of the Orient nibbled ginger properly boiled in honey. Great-grandmama kept a little stone jar of candied ginger on the pantry shelf. Today we are losing track of the fine practice of "gingering" our food.

Add a few snips of candied or preserved ginger to a fruit cocktail, to a salad—zingo! Every taste bud snaps into strict attention. Like that little cup of black coffee, the morning eye-opener, ginger has the power to waken you. Put the bite of ginger into a soufflé, either the ground ginger or preserved, and the dish begins to sing.

AFTERNOON TEA (OR DESSERT) GINGERBREAD [2319]

Serves 6 generously. Oven temperature: 350° F.
Baking time: 35 long minutes

½ cup butter
1 cup brown sugar
½ cup molasses
1 cup sweet milk
1 whole fresh egg, well beaten
2½ cups bread flour, sifted

1 teaspoon cinnamon
½ generous teaspoon ginger
¼ teaspoon allspice
¼ teaspoon cloves
¼ teaspoon salt (generous)
1 teaspoon baking powder

1 teaspoon baking soda

Cream butter until fluffy; gradually add brown sugar and continue creaming until thoroughly blended. Stir in molasses mixed with sweet milk and beaten egg until thoroughly blended. To the flour add all the remaining ingredients and sift twice, the last time over the first mixture. Beat all together for three or four minutes until smooth. Pour into a generously greased, shallow, square pan and bake in a moderate oven as directed. Serve with whipped cream or chocolate sauce for dessert; or hot with butter for afternoon tea.

APPLE SAUCE GINGERBREAD   [2320]

Serves 6 generously. Oven temperature: 350° F.
Baking time: 40–45 minutes

6 tablespoons butter or lard	1 teaspoon baking soda
⅓ cup light brown sugar	¼ teaspoon cloves
1 whole fresh egg, well beaten	1 teaspoon cinnamon
¼ cup molasses	½ teaspoon ginger
1¾ cups bread flour, sifted	½ scant teaspoon salt

⅔ cup strained thick apple sauce

Cream butter or lard until fluffy; gradually add light brown sugar and continue creaming until mixture is light and creamy. Combine egg and molasses and add to creamed mixture. To the flour add the remaining dry ingredients and sift twice, the last time over creamed mixture. Beat briskly, gradually adding the apple sauce. Mixture should be very smooth and thoroughly blended. Turn into a greased square, shallow pan, and bake in a moderate oven as directed. Serve warm. Top may be spread with softened cream cheese.

OLD-FASHIONED GINGERBREAD   [2321]
Called Also "Hot Water Gingerbread"

Serves 6 generously. Oven temperature: 350° F.
Baking time: 35 minutes

½ cup brown sugar	1½ teaspoons baking soda
¼ cup butter	1 generous teaspoon ginger
¼ cup lard	1 teaspoon cinnamon
1 egg, well-beaten	½ teaspoon salt
1 cup New Orleans molasses	½ teaspoon cloves
2½ cups bread flour, sifted	1 cup hot water

Cream sugar and mixed fats together until fluffy; add egg and beat briskly to blend thoroughly. Gradually add molasses, mixing well. To the flour add all the remaining ingredients, except hot water, and sift together over first mixture. Mix thoroughly, adding the hot water gradually. Then beat for 1 or 2 minutes or until batter is smooth and free from lumps. Turn batter into a square, shallow, greased pan, and bake in a moderate oven as directed until firm in center. Cut into squares and serve warm or cold.

POPOVERS—HINTS [2322]

Popovers, feather light, are a treat whenever served, for breakfast, luncheon, dinner, afternoon tea or evening party. And they are versatile, too.

From a standard recipe can be made many variations. But popovers, even more than biscuits and muffins, must be so hot that they burn your fingers when you break them open. They must be baked long enough to have a deep brown crust and be thick enough to prevent falling when they are removed from the pans. The inside, however, should not be too dry lest the flavor be entirely lost.

Those are the standards for real popovers. The question is how to meet them. First of all, follow the recipe and *sift your flour before measuring*. After the batter is mixed, make sure that it is about the consistency of heavy cream. Not all eggs are of the same size; if they are small, your batter may be a little too thick. In this case add a little more milk.

Heavy iron muffin pans are best for popovers and gem pans are very handy. In order to promote the rising of the batter, the pans should be heated before they are generously greased. The full time for baking given in the recipe should be allowed and it will *not hurt* the popovers to stand in the closed oven for five or even 10 minutes after it is turned off.

A very hot oven is required at the start; then when the batter is set, the temperature is lowered and the baking continued for an average of 40–45 minutes all together.

For large popovers to be used as patty shells and filled with a creamed mixture, it's better to use individual custard cups.

Next to iron pans and gem pans, earthenware pans, custard cups or glass pans are better than agate or tin for baking popovers. The use of earthenware or glass pans gives the bottom of popovers a glazed appearance.

Popovers will always double when baked; so when pouring batter, fill only ⅔ full *or less*.

Although popovers have a reputation for trickiness, they are the easiest of hot breads to make and bake. The heat of the oven has a great deal to do with success or failure. It must be hot enough to generate the steam that leavens the batter. Once the popovers have risen and popped, the heat is reduced (unless otherwise indicated) to moderate to drive out all moisture and bake the little breads until they hold their shape.

The reason why the cold batter is poured into sizzling hot iron, custard cups or glass cups is to provide more steam than cold cups. No baking powder or soda is needed in any popover recipe; steam is the raising agent.

Never cover hot baked popovers with a napkin lest they become soggy.

Yorkshire pudding is made from the same mixture. Always make a slit in each popover to allow steam to escape.

CHEESE POPOVERS [2323]

Makes 8 popovers. Oven temperature: 450–475° then 350° F.
Baking time: 40–45 minutes

1 cup bread flour, sifted twice	1 cup sweet milk
½ scant teaspoon salt	1 cup grated cheese
1 whole fresh egg, well-beaten	A few grains of cayenne pepper

Make pans very hot; then grease or butter generously. Sift salt with flour. Combine egg with milk, mix well and gradually add to the flour mixture, beating briskly until smooth. Add cayenne pepper. Into each greased hot pan, spoon 1 tablespoon of batter, then 1 teaspoon grated cheese, then 1 tablespoon of batter, and again cheese, repeating until pans are ⅔ full. Set in a very hot oven as directed and bake 30 minutes; reduce oven temperature to moderate and continue baking 10 to 15 minutes longer until popovers have risen and are delicately brown. Serve very hot.

Handkerchiefs inscribed with recipes for bread and cake baking were carried by fashionable belles of seventeenth-century England.

RICH POPOVERS [2324]

Makes 8 large popovers. Oven temperature: 450–350° F.
Baking time: 40–45 minutes

3 whole fresh eggs, well beaten	1 cup bread flour, sifted twice
½ cup of sweet milk	½ generous teaspoon salt
½ cup thin cream	A generous pinch of nutmeg

2 tablespoons melted butter

Combine well-beaten eggs with milk and cream (you may use undiluted evaporated milk instead of thin cream) and beat with rotary beater until thoroughly blended. Add salt and nutmeg to flour and sift over egg-milk mixture. Beat until smooth and as thick as heavy cream, adding the melted butter while beating. Fill sizzling hot generously buttered custard cups up to ⅔ full and bake in a hot oven and then in a moderate oven as directed until popovers are almost double in size and delicately browned. Immediately make a slit in each and serve at once with butter, jam, jelly, marmalade, preserves, etc.; or split in two and use as patty shell for creamed fish, meat, poultry or vegetables.

The famous monument called the "Uneven Dozen," in Sucre, Bolivia, was built with money collected from bakers who were fined for not selling a "baker's dozen" (13 pieces to the dozen).

RYE MEAL POPOVERS   [2325]

Makes 8 popovers. Oven temperature: 425–350° F.
Baking time: 40–45 minutes

⅓ cup bread flour, sifted   ⅔ cup rye meal, unsifted
½ scant teaspoon salt   1 cup sweet milk
                    2 whole eggs, well-beaten

Add salt to the flour and sift over rye meal. Blend thoroughly. Combine milk and well-beaten eggs and beat with rotary beater until well mixed. Pour all at once over flour mixture and beat briskly for 2 or 3 minutes, or until smooth and free from lumps. Fill hissing hot, buttered, iron gem pans or custard cups ⅔ full and bake 20 to 25 minutes in a very hot oven as directed, reducing heat to moderate and continue baking about 15 to 20 minutes longer until popovers are puffed and brown. Immediately make a slit in top for escape of steam and serve at once with plenty of butter, jam, jelly, marmalade or preserves.

SUNDAY POPOVERS   [2326]
A Sunday Breakfast Dish

Makes 8 popovers. Oven temperature: 450–350° F.
Baking time: 40–45 minutes

The thoughtful homemaker with an eye to good nutrition and her mind on the food budget will serve eggs in some form regularly, and winter meals are in particular need of a "lift." She may serve eggs either coddled, scrambled, in omelets or poached for her breakfast menu, but here is a delicious and tempting way to serve this concentrated food— for after milk and meat, it's eggs!

Make your favorite popover recipe. As soon as baked, cut an opening in the top of each popover and fill with scrambled eggs, either plain or country method (that is, scrambled with canned tomato). Serve at once topped with one or two crisp slices of bacon. You may omit the bacon and replace the top of popover. Serve steaming hot, bearing in mind that the best scrambled eggs must be rather moist.

WHOLE WHEAT POPOVERS   [2327]

Makes 8 popovers. Oven temperature: 450–350° F.
Baking time: 40–45 minutes

½ cup bread flour, sifted   2 whole fresh eggs, well-beaten
½ teaspoon salt   1 cup rich milk
½ cup unsifted whole wheat flour   2 teaspoons melted butter

Add salt to sifted flour and sift over unsifted whole wheat flour. Blend thoroughly. Combine eggs, milk and melted butter and beat until thoroughly blended. Pour all at once over flour mixture and beat with rotary beater until smooth. Pour batter into hissing hot custard cups and bake 25 minutes in a very hot oven as directed; reduce heat to moderate and continue baking about 15 minutes longer until popovers are puffed and delicately browned. Make a slit in top for escape of steam and serve at once with plenty of butter, jam, jelly, marmalade, honey, maple syrup or molasses.

Homemakers of Reykjavik, the Iceland capital which is named for its hot springs, often use the hot flowing earth near-by for baking their bread.

ROLLS—HINTS   [2328]

Browning once wrote: "Now we shall arbitrate? Ten men love what I hate, shun what I follow, slight what I receive; ten who in ears and eyes match me: we all surmise, they this thing, and I that; whom shall my soul believe?" And his appeal may be applied quite as well to the problems of bread-making, appetite and taste as to those of philosophy, ethics, or morals. *Chacun à son goût!*—the pot should think twice before calling the kettle black.

As there is no one article of food that enters so largely into our daily fare as bread, no degree of skill in preparing other articles can compensate for lack of knowledge in the art of making good, palatable and nutritious bread, rolls, etc.

The first thing required for making wholesome bread, rolls, etc., is the utmost cleanliness; the next is the soundness and sweetness of all the ingredients used; and in addition there must be attention and care through the whole process.

An almost certain way of spoiling dough is to leave it half-made and allow it to become cold before it is finished.

Never allow the bread to remain in the pan, or on a pine table to absorb the odor of wood.

When any recipe calls for baking powder and you do not have it, you can use one level teaspoonful of soda to two of cream of tartar. When making rolls either with baking powder or soda and cream of tartar (cream of tartar is a wholesome fruit product made from fine, ripe grapes—it has been known for generations as the finest baking-powder ingredient), the oven should be prepared first; the dough handled quickly and put into the oven immediately.

The flavor of rolls is influenced considerably by the shaping and baking. A small roll with a large proportion of crust, like a finger roll, will taste altogether different from a product made from the same dough into large rolls baked close together in a pan and so having little crust.

Various flavorings may be added to rolls by using poppy seeds, anise, caraway seeds, crystal salt and so on.

Sweet rolls are similar to plain, but they are richer, having more shortening, eggs and usually more sugar and flavoring.

To freshen stale rolls or biscuits, put them into a steamer for ten minutes, then dry off in a hot oven (425–450° F.); or dip each roll for an instant in cold water and heat them crisp in the oven. You also may use a double boiler for steaming rolls or biscuits. Reheated rolls or biscuits should always be served immediately.

Yeast dough, stored in the refrigerator, keeps well several days and permits the baking of hot rolls at will. Because the dough may develop an off-flavor, it should not be stored longer than three days before being baked. Stirring down the dough daily helps to drive off the gas and slow up yeast growth. When wanted, the dough is taken from the refrigerator, kneaded and shaped into rolls of the desired size and kind; they are allowed to rise until double in bulk before being baked in a very hot oven. The remaining dough is greased on top, placed in a smaller bowl, covered with waxed paper and returned to the refrigerator.

The choice of a tested simple recipe with concise, easy-to-follow directions is the initial step for a beginner; next comes careful reading and study of the recipe to gain a clear understanding of the process from first to last. Then practice will make perfect.

When decorating the rolls with poppy seeds, spread just a little unbeaten white of egg on top of the rolls before sprinkling on the seeds. After baking, the seeds will remain on the rolls.

For most rolls, a moderately hot oven (400° F.) should be used. The time of baking will be from 15 to 20 minutes, depending upon the size of the rolls.

You can make cinnamon rolls from light bread dough. After letting them rise, just before putting them in the oven, pour an uncooked filling of one cup brown sugar and ½ cup cream over them. It really makes them delicious.

In Elizabethan days every Englishman carried a knife in his belt for cutting his bread and meat in case the host failed to provide one.

BUTTER FLAKE ROLLS [2329]
Yeast Method

Makes about 3 dozen rolls. Oven temperature: 400° F.
Baking time: 18–20 minutes

2 cakes compressed yeast	1 teaspoon salt
2 tablespoons granulated sugar	½ cup butter, melted, not hot
2 tablespoons dark brown sugar	5 cups (about) bread flour, sifted twice
1½ cups sour milk or buttermilk, luke-warm	½ teaspoon baking soda

Crumble yeast cake into mixing bowl; add both sugars; mix well, then pour sour milk or buttermilk over mixture. Blend and let stand 15 minutes. Then add salt and melted butter. Add soda to the flour and sift over first mixture. Beat briskly until smooth and free from lumps. Turn into greased mixing bowl; brush top with butter; cover with a dry cloth and set the bowl over hot water. Let rise until very light (about 40 minutes). Empty the bowl onto lightly floured board and roll out as thin as possible with floured rolling pin. With a brush, spread a thin coat of flour over the thin sheet of dough and cut into strips 2 inches wide. Cut strips into squares; brush with melted butter, and set in a warm place, covered with a dry towel to rise until very light (10–12 minutes). Bake in a hot oven as directed. Rolls separate in layers easily and require no butter. Serve warm or cold.

BUTTER ROLLS—FRENCH METHOD [2330]
Yeast Method

Makes 24 rolls. Oven temperature: 400° F.
Baking time: 20 minutes

2 cakes compressed yeast
1 tablespoon granulated sugar
¼ cup milk, lukewarm
1 scant teaspoon vanilla extract

3 egg yolks, well-beaten
1½ cups bread flour, sifted twice
½ scant cup butter
½ scant cup granulated sugar

¼ cup finely chopped nut meats (any kind)

Dissolve yeast cakes and sugar (the tablespoon) in lukewarm milk which has been scalded and cooled. Add vanilla and beaten egg yolks and blend thoroughly. Cut flour into butter and combine with the first mixture. Form into a ball; place the ball in a cheesecloth and put in pan of cold water. Let stand from ¾ to 1 hour. Remove from the cloth. Shape into balls, the size of an egg and roll in mixed sugar and finely chopped nut meats. Twist. Place on greased baking sheet and allow to rise for 20 minutes. Then bake in a hot oven as directed. Serve cold.

In the fifteenth century, Diaprun or Diaprunum, a concoction of Damson plums, violet seeds, grated ivory (yes ivory), sandalwood and other odd ingredients, was a favorite afternoon bread which was eaten with wine, also sweetened with odd ingredients. It must have been hard on stomach linings!

BUTTERMILK POPPY SEED DINNER [2331]
ROLLS
Yeast Method

Makes 2 dozen rolls. Oven temperature: 400° F.
Baking time: about 20 minutes

2 yeast cakes
¼ cup granulated sugar
1½ cups buttermilk, lukewarm
½ cup melted butter, not hot

5 cups bread flour, sifted twice
1 scant teaspoon baking soda
Melted butter
1 scant teaspoon salt

¼ cup poppy seeds

Crumble yeast cakes into mixing bowl; add granulated sugar and buttermilk; stir until dissolved, adding while stirring the melted (not hot) butter. To the flour add salt and soda and sift over liquid mixture. Stir well until smooth, adding while stirring half of the poppy seeds. Place in greased mixing bowl; cover with a light, clean, dry cheesecloth, and let rise to double its bulk (about 30 minutes). Cut down; shape into balls the size of a small egg; brush with melted butter; sprinkle with remaining poppy seeds and let rise again until double in bulk (about 15 minutes), on greased pan. Bake in a hot oven as directed. Serve warm or cold. (You may omit poppy seeds.)

CHEESE ROLLS [2332]
Yeast Method

Makes 25 small rolls. Oven temperature: 450° F.
Baking time: 7 to 8 minutes

¼ cup granulated sugar	½ yeast cake
1¼ teaspoons salt	3 tablespoons lukewarm water
¼ cup butter	2¾ cups bread flour, sifted twice
1 cup sweet milk, scalded	Melted butter and grated cheese

Dissolve sugar, salt and butter in scalded milk. Cool to lukewarm after blending thoroughly. Add yeast dissolved in lukewarm water and beat vigorously. Stir in enough flour slowly to form a soft ball that can be handled easily. Put in a greased mixing bowl; cover with a light, clean, dry cloth and keep in a warm place to raise until doubled in bulk. Toss lightly onto floured board and roll out ⅓-inch thick. Butter generously, then sprinkle with ¼ inch grated cheese after dividing dough in two equal parts. Roll out each half in rounds like pie crust, until ¼ scant inch thick. Spread with a little cold butter then cut each round like a pie into 4 pieces. Roll each piece from the center, forming rolls about 3 inches long, pointed at one end and large at the other. Arrange far apart on generously greased baking sheet and brush with beaten egg yolk. Let rise until double in bulk and bake in a hot oven as directed. Serve hot.

In the early eighteenth century little strips of salted hard cheese were sold to New York City theater audiences who could eat them or throw them at the actors. They did both.

CINNAMON ROLLS [2333]
Baking Powder Method

These little rolls look like muffins, but are called rolls in restaurants. Make baking powder biscuits by Recipe No. 2229. Roll out and cut one small biscuit, the size of the bottom of a muffin pan, place in bottom of generously buttered muffin pan; shape with fingers to resemble a small bottom pie crust. Brush generously with butter, then sprinkle with cinnamon to taste. Fill hollow with a little strained honey; top with a bit of butter, and place another small biscuit on top. Spread second biscuit with softened butter, then with cinnamon and bake in a hot oven as directed. When removed from muffin pans, each little roll will be in one well-formed piece, extra tender and light.

For variations you may add chopped almonds, nut meats, seedless raisins, chopped figs or dates. You may brush tops with cold milk, egg yolk or cream before baking.

CLOVER LEAF ROLLS [2334]
Waldorf Method

This is a combination of yeast and baking powder method. The dough will keep in refrigerator for several days.

½ cup cooked hot potatoes, riced
½ cup lard
2 cups sweet milk, scalded
½ cake compressed yeast

½ cup granulated sugar
4 cups bread flour, sifted twice (about)
1 teaspoon baking powder
½ teaspoon baking soda

1 teaspoon salt

Cook potatoes until tender and rice them. Add lard while potatoes are warm. Heat milk, cool to lukewarm and crumble in the yeast, stirring until dissolved; add to potato mixture. To the flour add baking powder, soda, salt and sugar and sift together; gradually add to liquid mixture; turn dough into greased mixing bowl; brush with lard; cover with a light, clean, dry cloth and let rise until doubled in bulk (about one hour) in a warm place or over hot (not boiling) water. Cut dough down, add more flour if needed to make a stiff dough; brush top with melted lard to prevent a crust from forming.

Place in refrigerator and keep overnight. When used, knead for a minute or so on lightly floured board; shape into small rolls and bake in moderate oven as directed. Serve hot or cold.

Everyone knows that an artistic presentation can turn a drab, everyday affair—whether it be a movie or a meal—into a delightful experience. One intangible ingredient in such artistry is "high-lighting." Following is a second method for a quick and easy recipe for "highlighting" menus with the ever popular Clover Leaf Rolls.

DINNER ROLLS [2335]
Yeast Method—Refrigerator

Makes 2½ dozen rolls (about). Oven temperature: 400° F.
Baking time: 18–20 minutes

2 cups sweet milk, scalded
¼ scant cup granulated sugar
¾ teaspoon salt
1 generous tablespoon shortening

1 cake compressed yeast
2 tablespoons lukewarm water
1 whole fresh egg, well-beaten
3½ cups bread flour, sifted twice

Ice water for tops

Scald milk; combine with sugar, salt and shortening. Cool to luke-warm. Meanwhile crumble yeast cake in lukewarm water, adding 1 generous teaspoon of the sugar; stir well until dissolved and add to luke-warm milk mixture. Add egg and stir in half of the flour. Beat thoroughly until smooth, then beat in the remaining flour, and as much more as can be stirred in *without kneading*. Brush surface with melted shortening. Set in refrigerator covered tightly. When ready to bake, turn out on a lightly floured board and invert so that both sides are covered with flour. Take off small pieces the size of an egg and roll out to the thickness to make the type of roll desired, *i.e.:* Parker House, Clover Leaf, etc. When rolls have been shaped, place them on a greased baking sheet, let rise until *very light* (refrigerator rolls take a longer time for rising than those which have not been chilled to 45° F. or lower). Sprinkle with a little ice water and bake in a hot oven as directed. Serve warm or cold.

EMERGENCY CINNAMON RAISIN ROLLS [2336]
Baking Powder Method

Makes about 1 dozen rolls. Oven temperature: 350° F.
Baking time: 20–25 minutes

2 cups bread flour, sifted twice
½ generous teaspoon salt
1 tablespoon granulated sugar, or
1 tablespoon dark brown sugar, rolled
¾ teaspoon cinnamon
4 teaspoons baking powder

⅓ cup shortening
1 whole fresh egg, well-beaten
⅓ cup sweet cold milk
1 generous tablespoon softened butter
2 tablespoons sifted brown sugar
1 teaspoon cinnamon

½ generous cup parboiled, sponged seedless raisins

To the flour add salt, sugar, the ¾ teaspoon cinnamon and baking powder and sift into mixing bowl. Rub in shortening as for pie with a fork or pastry cutter. Combine egg and milk and stir into flour mix-ture to make a soft dough. Turn dough out on a lightly floured board and roll out into an oblong sheet a scant ½ of an inch thick.

Spread quickly and lightly with softened butter; then sprinkle with sifted brown sugar mixed with remaining powdered cinnamon and pre-pared raisins. Roll dough up like a jelly roll from the long side of the oblong. Cut down in slices ½ inch thick and place cut side down and *close together* on greased baking sheet. Bake in a moderate oven as directed. Serve warm or cold.

You may brush one side with a thin sugar icing as soon as removed from oven. Warm slices are much more delicate than cold ones. May be reheated in a covered pan in a hot oven (400° F.) for 5 minutes, if not iced.

PARKER HOUSE ROLLS [2337]

Makes 2 dozen small rolls. Oven temperature: 450° F.
Baking time: 12 to 14 minutes

1 cup sweet milk, scalded	½ cake compressed yeast
¼ cup granulated sugar	¼ cup lukewarm water
1½ scant teaspoons salt	2¾ cups bread flour, sifted
¼ cup butter	Melted butter for tops

Dissolve sugar, salt and butter in scalded milk. Cool to lukewarm. Add crumbled yeast dissolved in lukewarm water and beat vigorously. Add flour slowly and only just enough to make a ball that can be handled easily. Put in a greased bowl, cover and keep in a warm place to rise until it doubles in bulk. Toss lightly on slightly floured board and roll to the thickness of ⅓ inch. Cut the dough in rounds with a biscuit cutter. Brush one-half of each round with melted butter, dip knife handle in flour and make a deep crease across the middle of each roll. Fold over and place in a row in a generously greased baking pan. Brush with melted butter and let rise until double their bulk. Bake in a very hot oven as directed until delicately brown. Serve warm.

In 1626 Louis XIII of France became so fond of gingerbread that his courtiers carried it around for him in ornamental cases.

PENNSYLVANIA CINNAMON PECAN ROLLS [2338]
Yeast Method

Makes about 2 dozen rolls. Oven temperature: 350° F.
Baking time: 25 minutes

Ever since the thirteen families of Crefelders and Mennonites arrived on the Concord at Philadelphia in 1683, the Pennsylvania Dutch have been noted for their food, and many of their recipes which have come down through the years represent a superior type of regional cookery whose fame has spread throughout the country. They were the first gourmets in America and the first dining club in the New World was organized in 1732 in Philadelphia, a city which became and remains a center for good food.

As early as 1725, Dutch farmers were building the huge Conestoga wagons with the typical boatlike curves of the wagon bodies hanging low in the middle which were later to be seen in increasing numbers as pioneers pushed their way westward. Loaded with food and grain for the Philadelphia markets, the Dutch farmers brought with them hearty appetites and a taste for the wholesome and even lavish fare of their kitchens. They were accustomed to good food, for there has never been a more tireless preserver, pickler, curer, spicer, canner or baker than the Dutch housewife. Very little escaped her expert touch; she got in the habit centuries ago of loading every table so liberally with "sweet and sours" that over the years it became a fixed tradition of hospitality for her to put on the table, especially for guests, precisely seven sweets and seven sours.

Often she would serve afternoon coffee with Cinnamon Pecan Rolls which were made as follows:

1½ cakes compressed yeast
½ cup lukewarm water
2 cups sweet milk, scalded, cooled to lukewarm
4 egg yolks, well-beaten
1¼ teaspoon salt
½ cup butter, melted

¾ cup granulated sugar
4½ to 5 cups bread flour, sifted twice
Melted butter (not too hot) for spreading
2 tablespoons granulated sugar
2 tablespoons brown sugar
1½ to 2 teaspoons powdered cinnamon
1 cup chopped pecan meats

Butter for tops

Dissolve yeast cakes in water and stir until dissolved. Stir in the milk, alternately with 2 cups of the flour. Beat briskly; cover with a light, dry towel and set over a pan containing hot (not boiling) water to rise until mixture bubbles and is half doubled in bulk; beat in the egg yolks with salt, butter and ¾ cup of granulated sugar.

Mix well and let rise until doubled in bulk, after adding the remaining sifted flour, or enough to make a stiff dough that can be handled and kneaded easily. When doubled in bulk, knead down until smooth, elastic and not sticky. Put in a greased mixing bowl; brush with melted butter; cover with a dry cloth and place over a pan of hot (not boiling) water until it rises. Then cut it down with your hands and allow to rise again to double in bulk.

Knead lightly (about ½ minute); roll out until dough is ¼ inch thick; spread with melted butter, then with granulated sugar, and sprinkle brown sugar on top of granulated sugar. Over the brown sugar sprinkle powdered cinnamon, adding more if desired. Now take one end of the dough and roll up like a jelly roll. With a sharp knife cut slices about an inch wide.

Grease a baking pan generously; sprinkle with a thin layer of granulated sugar, and over this spread pecan meats. Arrange the slices over the nuts; brush tops with melted butter to prevent hardening and allow to rise until doubled in size, in a warm place and covered with a dry towel. Bake in a moderate oven as directed. Remove from oven, let stand a few minutes, then turn upside down on a hot platter, thus getting a thick syrup with pecans on top of slices.

POTATO WATER FEATHER ROLLS [2339]
Pennsylvania Dutch Recipe—Yeast Method

Makes about 2½ dozen rolls. Oven temperature: 400° F.
Baking time: 20 minutes

Note. The potato water used in this recipe is that saved from potatoes cooked before.

1 cake compressed yeast	1¾ teaspoons salt
½ cup lukewarm potato water, strained	2 cups lukewarm potato water, strained
½ cup butter or lard	5 cups bread flour, sifted twice
2 tablespoons granulated sugar	Melted butter for tops

Add crumbled yeast cake to the ½ cup of lukewarm potato water and stir until dissolved. Cream butter or lard with combined sugar and salt, stir into the remaining 2 cups of potato water, and when thoroughly blended stir in the yeast mixture. Blend well; then gradually add the flour, beating vigorously after each addition, until mixture is smooth and dough begins to leave the wooden spoon (about 5 or 6 minutes). Cover with a clean, dry towel; place pan over hot (not boiling) water and let rise until doubled in bulk. Then knock the dough down with your hands and let rise until it is again doubled in bulk. Place a spoonful of dough in each generously greased muffin pan, slightly warmed. Work quickly so as not to release air bubbles, handling as little as possible. Place muffin pans away from drafts in a warm place, covered; allow to rise again until doubled in bulk or dough fills the pans. Bake in a hot oven as directed. Serve warm with either jam, jelly, marmalade or preserves, as well as plenty of butter.

REFRIGERATOR CLOVER LEAF ROLLS   [2340]
Modern Yeast Method

Makes about 2½ dozen rolls. Oven temperature: 425° F.
Baking time: 12–15 minutes.
Sponge standing: 30 minutes. First rising time: 2 hours (about).
Chilling time in refrigerator: 2–3 days.
Second rising time: 1 hour (about)

1 cake compressed yeast	1 scant teaspoon salt
¼ cup lukewarm water	1 whole fresh egg, well-beaten
¼ teaspoon granulated sugar	1⅓ cups sweet milk, scalded, cooled
¼ cup shortening	5 cups (about) bread flour, sifted twice
¼ cup granulated sugar	2 or 3 tablespoons melted butter for tops

Crumble yeast cake into lukewarm water and stir until dissolved; stand in a warm place for 30 minutes (this is called sponge). Blend shortening, sugar and salt in mixing bowl; stir in combined egg and milk and add to the yeast sponge. Blend thoroughly; then stir in flour enough to make a dough that can be easily kneaded. Turn upon a slightly floured board and knead until smooth, elastic and not sticky, adding a little more flour if needed. Form into a large ball; cover; put over a pan containing hot (not boiling) water and let stand until doubled in bulk and very light. Knead dough again, about half a minute; brush with butter; place in a greased bowl; cover with waxed paper; secure with a string or still better with a rubber band and store in refrigerator. Every day knead the dough half a minute to drive off the gas.

When ready to make the rolls, knead the dough slightly, pinch off very small pieces and roll into balls an inch in diameter. Place 3 balls in each buttered muffin pan, having the pan one-half full. Brush with melted butter; cover with a light, clean, dry cloth; let rise in a warm place until doubled in bulk. Bake in a very hot oven as directed. Serve warm or cold.

In 1467 the Earl of Leicester created a bread sauce which he called "saucealiper."

SOUR CREAM ROLLS—MIDWEST METHOD [2341]
Yeast Method

Makes about 3 dozen rolls. Oven temperature: 400° F.
Baking time: 18 minutes

1 cake compressed yeast	3 tablespoons granulated sugar
¼ cup lukewarm water	1¾ generous teaspoons salt
2 cups heavy dairy-made sour cream, scalded	¼ generous teaspoon baking soda
	5 cups (about) bread flour, sifted twice

Melted butter for tops

Crumble yeast cake into lukewarm water and stir until dissolved. To the sour cream add sugar, salt and soda; stir; cool to lukewarm; add yeast mixture; blend thoroughly; then stir in half of the flour, and stir briskly until smooth Add enough of the remaining flour to make a soft dough, easy to knead; turn out on lightly floured board and knead for 5 minutes, or until dough is smooth, satiny, elastic and does not stick to the hands. Roll out ½-inch thick; cut into small rounds with floured cutter or pinch off pieces the size of a small egg and shape into desired form; place close together on well-greased baking pan or sheet; brush with melted butter; cover with light cloth and allow to rise until doubled in bulk (about 2 hours), in a warm place or over hot water. Bake in a hot oven as directed until delicately browned. Serve warm or cold.

Note. Buttermilk plus 3 tablespoons of melted shortening may be used instead of sour cream.

In 1794 patrons of New York's only hostelry, the City Hotel, had to bring their own vegetables, their own bread and pay extra for having vegetables cooked.

YEAST COFFEE RING [2342]

Serves 6 generously. Oven temperature: 400–300° F.
Baking time: 20 minutes

1 cup rich sweet milk, scalded	¼ cup warm water
¼ cup butter	4½ cups bread flour, sifted
½ cup granulated sugar	Softened butter
1 teaspoon salt	Sugar, cinnamon, and nutmeg to taste
1 yeast cake	Raisins or currants

To the hot milk add sugar and salt and after mixing let cool to lukewarm. Dissolve the yeast cake in lukewarm water and add to milk; then stir in the flour. Allow to rise in a warm place until doubled in bulk. Toss on lightly floured board and knead a half-minute. Roll out about ¼-inch thick. Spread generously with softened butter; then sprinkle with mixed sugar and spices. Shape in ring, and place on buttered baking sheet; cover with a clean, light cloth and let rise until doubled in bulk. Bake immediately for 10 minutes in a hot oven; reduce the heat to moderate and continue baking 10 minutes longer. Remove from the oven and again brush with softened butter. Let cool and serve lukewarm.

YEAST COFFEE RAISIN TWIST [2343]

Makes 1 large twist. Oven temperature: 400–350° F.
Baking time: 40–45 minutes

1½ cups rich sweet milk, scalded	1 quart (4 cups) bread flour, sifted
1 yeast cake	1 teaspoon salt
⅓ cup granulated sugar or equal parts of granulated and brown sugar, or all brown sugar	½ teaspoon ground ginger
	½ teaspoon ground nutmeg
	½ teaspoon ground cinnamon
¼ cup butter, melted	⅔ cup seedless raisins

Wash raisins, scald, and let stand in hot water for 15 minutes. Scald rich milk and cool to lukewarm. Crumble yeast cake into sugar and stir until dissolved. Then add to lukewarm milk with melted butter, 2 cups of the flour, salt and spices. Beat briskly, add remaining 2 cups of flour and mix well. Turn dough onto lightly floured board and knead gently until smooth, elastic, velvety and not sticky. Now add raisins, thoroughly dried, kneading them into the dough. Place dough in a generously greased bowl, brush with melted lard or butter and cover with a light, dry cloth. Let rise in a warm place 2½ to 3 hours or till doubled in bulk.

Now divide dough into two equal parts and from one part make four strips of even length and thickness. Braid them and lay them on a greased and lightly floured baking sheet. From ⅔ of the remaining dough, make three thinner strips, braid them and place on top of the first braid. From remaining dough make two small strips, twist them together and lay on top of the two braids. Cover with a light, dry cloth, let rise in a warm place ¾ hour longer, or until doubled in bulk, and bake 15 minutes in a hot oven. Reduce heat to moderate and bake 25 minutes longer. Serve warm or cold with jam, jelly, marmalade, preserves, honey or maple syrup.

YEAST COFFEE STREUSEL CAKE   [2344]

Approximately 2 coffee loaf cakes. Oven temperature: 375° F.
Baking time: 25 minutes

2 yeast cakes	3 whole eggs, beaten
1 tablespoon granulated sugar	¾ teaspoon salt
4 to 4½ cups bread flour, sifted	1 cup scalded milk, cooled to lukewarm
6 tablespoons lard, melted	¾ cup lukewarm water
½ cup granulated sugar	Streusel

Dissolve yeast cakes by crumbling them in mixed lukewarm milk and water to which has been added the tablespoon granulated sugar; add 3 cups of flour and beat until smooth. Now add melted lard alternately with eggs, remaining sugar and balance of bread flour sifted with the salt, making a moderately soft dough. Toss upon lightly floured board and knead lightly (about 30 seconds). Place in greased bowl, brush with a little melted butter, cover with a dry towel and let rise to twice its bulk (about 2 hours). Now divide the dough in half, spreading each half in a pan 8″ × 11″, pressing into corners. Let rise about 1 hour, covered, in a warm place. Brush tops with beaten egg yolk diluted with half a tablespoon of milk; sprinkle with *streusel* and a little cinnamon to taste, and bake in a moderately hot oven as directed.

Streusel top dressing:

1 cup bread flour	1 cup sugar
	½ cup butter

Work all together with fingers thoroughly and sprinkle over top of cakes before baking.

There is a certain satisfaction—even a thrill—in making things with your own hands. There is nothing that quite equals a warm, light, cozy kitchen and the rich smell of bread baking.

TOAST   [2345]

BACON CHEESE TOAST   [2346]

(Appropriate for breakfast, light luncheon or supper)

Remove crusts from as many slices of bread as required. Place a thin piece of American cheese on each slice; then add one or two slices of bacon and place under the flame of the broiling oven until bacon is brown and cheese melted. Serve bubbling hot. Worcestershire or mixed mustard will add a suggestion of Welsh rabbit.

BUTTERSCOTCH TOAST   [2347]

(Appropriate for breakfast, afternoon tea or coffee or evening snack)

Toast narrow strips of day-old bread on one side. Spread untoasted side with a mixture of equal parts of butter (or margarine) and dark brown sugar creamed together as for hard sauce. Toast under the flame of the broiling oven until hot and bubbly. Serve at once.

Variation. Add a little grated lemon or orange rind to butter and brown sugar mixture.

King Arthur is said to have invented the round table so no one of his knights could feel he was sitting "at the foot of the table."

CINNAMON TOAST   [2348]

(Appropriate for breakfast, especially Sunday, afternoon tea or coffee)

Cinnamon toast is perfect for tea, but alas, it is seldom we find it really good.

Toast bread slices on one side only. Have ready a mixture of 1 cup soft brown sugar and 2 (or more) tablespoons ground cinnamon. Butter bread slices on the untoasted side, spread with a thick layer of sugar-cinnamon mixture and place under broiler a good 5 inches below the flame. Let it toast very, very slowly until the sugar is melted and bubbling and the bread delicately browned and crisp, but not burned on the edges. Remove from the oven at once, cut in strips and serve as quickly as you can run with it to the table.

Further Suggestions. Remove crusts, since they may burn; increase cinnamon to taste (some like up to 4 tablespoons); put small bits of butter on top of cinnamon-sugar mixture.

FRENCH GRIDDLE TOAST   [2349]
Serves 6

(Appropriate for breakfast, light luncheon or supper)

Beat 3 strictly fresh eggs slightly; add 2 tablespoons of granulated sugar and ⅓ teaspoon salt. Strain into a shallow dish. Cut 6 half-inch slices of one loaf day-old bread; remove crusts. Dip slices of bread in the egg-milk mixture, turning them until liquid is well absorbed. Brown both sides on a hot, well-greased griddle or frying pan. Remove to hot plate and sprinkle lightly with fine powdered sugar. Serve with jelly, jam, marmalade, preserves, honey or maple syrup.

In 1880 Czar Alexander II of Russia was nearly killed by a bomb in his great winter palace in St. Petersburg (Leningrad today). The guards searched the thousand-odd rooms, but did not find the anarchist.

However, they did discover, in an unused boudoir on an upper floor, a peasant and his cow and several loaves of bread. Both of them had lived there a number of years.

FRENCH TOAST [2350]
Serves 6

From the standpoint of genuine goodness as well as for economy, French toast stands as one of America's favorite breakfast and luncheon dishes. For breakfast it may be served plain to accompany bacon and eggs or fried liver and bacon, and often it is used as the main part of the meal with jam, marmalade, honey, maple syrup, etc. The preparation is very simple and it is an excellent way to utilize stale bread. In France French toast is called *pain perdu* ("lost bread") and is very popular as a dessert.

Allow one slice of bread for each serving. For six servings beat 3 fresh eggs slightly and add 1 cup of rich sweet milk, or half milk and half thin cream (undiluted evaporated milk may be used); season with ½ teaspoon salt, a fresh grating of nutmet (this is a "must") and a dash of white pepper, and 1 teaspoon of granulated sugar. Dip each slice of bread (toasted or not) into mixture, being careful not to get the bread sodden as it will break, and brown on both sides in plenty of hot butter. Serve, well-drained on a folded napkin. Sprinkle freely with confectioner's sugar, if served for dessert or breakfast.

For a luncheon or supper dish, unsweetened French toast will be just the thing. Use any left-over piece of fish, carefully boned, chicken, meat, ham or cheese minced. Spread one slice of the bread with any one of these, cover with another slice; dip in egg-milk mixture (unsweetened) and brown as for French toast, *i.e.* on both sides until delicately browned. Seasonings, will of course, depend upon the filling of these sandwiches. Serve as hot as possible.

MELBA TOAST [2351]

This paper-thin toast may be served as a side dish with almost any kind of soup and salad; or spread with butter, cream cheese, jam, jelly, ground cooked fish (carefully boned), meat, poultry or game. It may be served hot or cold. To make it, you need a stale loaf of bread—the staler the better.

Slice bread, white preferably, as thinly as possible and remove the crusts. Cut either in two or four pieces; arrange on a dry baking sheet and bake in a very slow oven (250° F.) until pieces are evenly browned and crisp on both sides. This toast may be made in large quantity and stored in a dry, cool place in an airtight container.

Lunches were carried to meetings in handkerchiefs or small leather bags by members of our first Continental Congress.

MILK TOAST [2352]
Serves 1

(Old-fashioned Method)

Trim the crusts from 2 or 3 slices of bread and toast very dry. Spread with butter while hot. Bring 1½ to 2 cups of rich milk (or half-milk and half-cream) to a boil. Cream 2 tablespoons of butter with 1 tablespoon of flour and drop by small pieces into the simmering milk. Season to taste, and dip each slice of toast into the milk mixture. Quickly lay the toast in a soup plate, and pour the boiling, seasoned milk over it. With old-fashioned milk toast, made as above, it is the rule to serve a small jug of boiling thin cream (or undiluted evaporated milk). Very nourishing.

Chapter Twenty

ICE CREAM DESSERTS

" . . . It is easy to conceive of a gold mine
or oil well worth five million dollars, but
how many ideas would bring such a
fabulous price? Yet that is the sum which
hard-headed American business men are
reported to have paid for the secret of
freezing with heat . . . "

—L. P. De G.

GENERAL INFORMATION

THERE ARE THREE GENERAL TYPES OF ICE CREAM: FRENCH ICE cream, which is a rich egg yolk custard and heavy. American ice cream, which is a less rich custard with or without flour or cornstarch, and cream or cream and milk. Philadelphia ice cream, which is a thin cream, or cream and milk and no eggs.

MAKING ICE CREAM—FUNCTIONS OF INGREDIENTS USED

The most important ingredients used in ice cream making are:

Milk, which gives body to the mixture, the solid substances in milk holding air bubbles and preventing crystallization. The milk should always be scalded.

Evaporated milk, which may be substituted for sweet milk for richness, having the same properties and action as sweet milk. It is not necessary to scald it before using.

Condensed milk, giving the same results as sweet and evaporated milk, plus richness of texture and certainty of sweetness.

Cream, which gives richness, smoothness, since its butter fat contents prevent crystallization.

Eggs, acting as a binder, leavening, thickening, stabilizer, and giving texture as well as flavor.

Sugar, giving sweetness and at the same time preventing crystallization.

Gelatine, acting as a stabilizer, and holding ice crystals apart.

Marshmallows, acting like gelatine, being a gelatine themselves.

Flavorings, have no effect on the freezing.

Fruits, being solids, retard the freezing process, and thus should not be added until the mixture is half solid or half frozen.

Nuts, acting in the same manner as fruits.

Starch, be it flour or cornstarch, is a stabilizer because it holds the ice crystals apart.

Milk should always be scalded to reduce its water content and concentrate its protein. Evaporated and condensed milk used in ice cream making need not be scalded for the simple reason that their protein has already been concentrated during the manufacturing process, the butter fat is evenly distributed or emulsified.

The amount of sugar should be carefully measured as too sweet a mix will delay the freezing.

Cream should be added when half beaten, or to a fluffy texture, the consistency of boiled custard.

Gelatine and marshmallows should be always dissolved.

Ice cream to be smooth, that is, free of crystals, must be frozen quickly, so the control should be set in the coldest position, and, as soon as the mixture is frozen, the control should be turned back to normal, lest the ice cream become too hard.

An important point to be remembered is that all the ingredients used in ice cream making should be chilled thoroughly before combining them.

If water is used in the recipe, the mixture should be beaten when it is frozen to a stiff mush, as this will break up any crystals that may have formed.

HOW TO USE A HAND FREEZER   [2355]

There are many patterns of ice cream freezers that are well constructed and inexpensive. They are sold by the size, a No. 2-quart freezer giving you two quarts of the frozen cream or ice.

See that the crank is oiled and the whole apparatus clean. Have ready cracked ice and rock salt, usually in the proportion of 1 part salt to 3 parts of cracked ice (snow may be used). Shavers or mallet or machines come for cutting the ice, but it is easy to pound or crack it in a strong bag or burlap. Set the freezer can in place, which should be well-chilled, put around it the ice and coarse rock salt alternately, shaking down and packing firmly. Have the ice cream mixture cool, pour it in, having the can not more than ¾ full, to allow for expansion. Put on the lid, cover with ice and salt, wait 5 short minutes, and begin to turn the crank. Open and stir down once or twice, being careful to keep out the salt, lest the cream mixture may be spoiled. Now take out the crank before the cream mixture is too stiff. Pack the cream firmly down in the can, or mold, if desired (see "How to mold ice cream"). See that the melted water is removed from the pail, put in more ice and rock salt, and leave for at least two hours.

If ice cream is granular, too much salt was used in freezing, or the can was too full, or the crank was turned too rapidly. The turning of the crank should be slow and steady to insure a smooth, fine-grained mixture. After frozen to a mush (about 10 minutes) crank should be turned more rapidly until it turns with difficulty, showing that mixture is frozen solid. After packing the finished product, cover with newspapers or heavy carpet.

HOW TO USE A REFRIGERATOR   [2356]

Most desserts such as mousses, parfaits, and in fact almost all frozen desserts, which merely require packing in salt and ice, can be easily made in a mechanical refrigerator without stirring. But, as there are many different makes of this useful apparatus, it is wise to always consult the booklets issued by manufacturers for exact information about using each make of mechanical refrigerator. However, whatever the make, you should be always certain that the temperature of the refrigerator is sufficiently low for freezing. The motor may be set correctly for proper and correct refrigeration, and yet, not low enough for freezing desserts. A temperature control feature obviates any disappointment and allows temporary adjustment.

HOW TO WHIP EVAPORATED MILK [2357]

Pour the indicated quantity of evaporated milk into top part of double boiler. Heat with the lid off over boiling water until hot. Add to the hot milk granulated gelatine, which has been soaked in cold water (see table of proportions below). Stir until dissolved. Pour into chilled bowl and chill until icy cold before whipping. Whip until stiff with rotary egg beater; then sweeten to taste or as directed.

Important. Do not remove the film of milk solids that forms on top of the hot milk. It will whip up just like the rest of the milk.

The bowl should be large, from 3½ to 5½ inches, according to amount of milk to be whipped.

If you use a cooking thermometer, you will find that the temperature of the milk is about 150° F. when sufficiently heated, but not boiled, and about 45° F. when thoroughly chilled.

Follow this table for proportions of milk, gelatine and water. Soak the gelatine in the cold water for 5 minutes:

MILK	GELATINE	WATER
½ cup	¼ teaspoon	1 teaspoon
¾ cup	½ teaspoon	2 teaspoons
1 cup	½ teaspoon	2 teaspoons
1½ cups	¾ teaspoon	3 teaspoons

Another simple method for whipping evaporated milk is as follows: Place an unopened can of evaporated milk in the freezing compartment of refrigerator for at least one long hour. Empty into a well-chilled bowl and whip. This takes but a few minutes. Or, pour a can of evaporated milk into one of the ice trays of the electric refrigerator and set the control for quick freezing. When partly frozen, that is when in a mush, whip in the ordinary way.

There is yet another method similar to the one mentioned at the beginning of this section, but without the use of gelatine, and which is as follows:

Pour the amount of evaporated milk called for into top part of a double boiler and heat over boiling water to scalding point. Do not discard the film of milk solids that forms on top of the hot milk. It will whip up just like the rest of the milk; stir it in, then chill the milk by placing it in a pan containing either cracked ice or very cold water. Then chill in refrigerator and whip in the usual way; or, place the unopened can of evaporated milk into a saucepan and cover with very cold water. Boil 5 long minutes, after boiling actually begins. Cool in running cold water, chill and whip in the usual way. *The main point to remember in whipping evaporated milk is that the milk must be thoroughly chilled*, either in refrigerator or the can placed in a large bowl and surrounded and covered with cracked ice.

HOW TO WHIP TOP OF RICH MILK [2358]

By taking the cream from the top of a bottle of rich fresh milk, which has stood for 48 hours, adding ¼ teaspoon lemon juice and beating with a rotary beater for two or three minutes, the thrifty homemaker can have a perfect bowl of whipped cream with no thought of failure. Whipped cream made like this, and added to any recipe, calling for whipped cream either for refrigerator or hand freezer ice cream, eliminates any fear of crystallization.

HOW TO USE GELATINE TO ADVANTAGE IN FROZEN DESSERTS   [2359]

Gelatine, which we use so much today, is very useful, may be purchased in all sorts of flavors, and is used to stiffen many other desserts besides the simple, clear, chilled jellies. Gelatine has become a practical necessity in every home kitchen, as it combines well with almost any kind of cooked or raw food with the exception of fresh pineapple which contains an enzyme (derived from the Greek word "en," meaning "in," and "zyme," meaning "yeast"; or together "in yeast"), which prevents gelatine from setting. If you wish to combine fresh pineapple with gelatine, always scald the pineapple, both fruit and juice. When using canned pineapple this is not necessary, as the pineapple has already been cooked.

ICES   [2360]

The word "Frappé" is French, meaning *"chilled"* or iced. The mixture thus prepared has the coarsest texture of all the frozen desserts, resembling coarse rock salt, and is used chiefly as a frozen mass in punch bowls, etc.

Ices, Water or Fruit Ices desserts, are similar to sherbets. They are made of water mixture (or fruit mixture) of coarser grain than a sherbet. Nothing but juices and flavored water and syrup are used. Ices are more granular than the sherbets, and are usually served in well-chilled sherbet glasses. A hand freezer or refrigerator tray may be used in all of the following recipes.

APRICOT ICE   [2361]

For effect, you may serve ices in orange cups, if desired.

2 cups boiling water   1 cup apricot juice
½ cup granulated sugar   2 tablespoons unstrained lemon juice

Add sugar to boiling water, and cook for 5 minutes. Add apricot juice and unstrained lemon juice, stir well and cool. Freeze either in refrigerator or hand freezer as indicated for Parfaits No. 2436. Serve in chilled sherbet or punch glasses.

BLUEBERRY ICE MAINE STYLE   [2362]

1 pint blueberries   1 cup boiling water
1 cup granulated sugar   ½ cup unstrained lemon juice
½ tablespoon granulated gelatin   1 egg white, stiffly beaten
½ cup cold water

Sprinkle a little of the sugar over the well-washed blueberries and force through a sieve. There should be 1 cup of juice. Add cold water to juice making 1½ cups of liquid. Soak gelatine in 2 tablespoons of cold water; add boiling water to which has been added the granulated sugar. Now combine blueberry juice mixture, add lemon juice and stir in the stiffly beaten egg white. Freeze in either refrigerator tray, or hand freezer, following the directions (Nos. 2355-2356), accordingly. Serve in chilled sherbet glasses.

CHERRY ICE [2363]

2 No. 2 cans sour pitted red cherries ½ cup unstrained lemon juice
¼ cup granulated sugar 1 tablespoon granulated gelatine
1 egg white, stiffly beaten

Drain cherries and measure 2 cups of the cherry juice, then boil for 5 minutes. Soak granulated gelatine in lemon juice for 5 minutes. Chop 2 cups of the cherries and stir in the softened gelatine mixture, then add to the hot cherry syrup. Stir well. Cool. When cold rub mixture through a sieve, and pour into freezing trays of refrigerator. When frozen to a mush, turn mixture into a large bowl and beat well, using an egg beater, folding in at the same time the stiffly beaten egg white and the remaining whole cherries. You may mold, or place in refrigerator tray and freeze until firm (about 3 hours) stirring every 30 minutes until set. Delicious.

You may use equal amounts of sour cherries and maraschino cherries if desired.

CIDER ICE [2364]

1 quart cider ½ cup unstrained lemon juice
1 cup unstrained orange juice 1 cup granulated sugar

Combine all the above ingredients and stir until sugar is thoroughly dissolved. Freeze in hand freezer, using equal parts of ice and rock salt. Serve in chilled orange cups or in red apple cups. Very appropriate for Thanksgiving Day.

CITRUS FRUIT ICE [2365]

1¾ cups cold water 1 cup each of orange juice and grapefruit
¾ cup granulated sugar juice
2 tablespoons of lemon juice

Boil water and sugar and all the fruit rinds for 5 minutes. Strain; chill, then add orange and grapefruit juice. Freeze to a mush in either refrigerator tray or hand freezer. Serve in chilled parfait glasses.

COFFEE ICE FRENCH METHOD   [2366]

Grind enough roasted coffee so as to have 5 tablespoons (more if a stronger mixture is desired) place in a hot saucepan, and pour over 2 cups of boiling milk; cover and allow to infuse for 20 minutes. Strain through a fine muslin cloth; add 1 cup of sugar syrup made of equal parts of water and granulated sugar. Chill, then freeze to a solid mush in hand freezer, using 3 parts ice and 1 part of rock salt. Serve in chilled sherbet glasses. topped with a rosette of whipped cream.

CRANBERRY ICE   [2367]
(*Very appropriate for Thanksgiving or Christmas*)

Have ready 1 pint of fresh cranberries, washed and cooked 10 minutes in 1¼ cups of water, or long enough to soften the berries, and force through a sieve. Cool while preparing the following mixture:

1 teaspoon granulated gelatine	¼ cup orange juice
¼ cup cold water	½ cup granulated sugar
⅓ cup white corn syrup	2 tablespoons lemon juice
	¼ scant teaspoon salt

Sprinkle gelatine over cold water and allow to soak for 5 minutes. Bring corn syrup and sugar to the boiling point, stirring often, then add the soaked gelatine, stir and cool slightly. Combine this with sieved cranberries, orange and lemon juice and salt. Stir well, and allow to chill. Freeze in refrigerator tray, stirring every 15 minutes. Then freeze to a smooth mush. Serve in chilled, scalloped paper cases alongside of the roast.

GRAPE JUICE ICE   [2368]

3 cups cold water	2 cups bottled grape juice
1½ cups granulated sugar	¼ cup lemon juice
⅛ teaspoon salt	Grated rind of half orange

Make a sugar syrup with water and sugar, boiling it for 5 long minutes; remove from fire and add grape juice, salt and grated orange rind. Cool, then add lemon juice. Chill, then freeze to a mush, in hand freezer, using 6 parts of ice and 2 parts of rock salt. Serve in sherbet glasses which have been chilled.

HONEYDEW MELON ICE   [2369]

1 large honeydew melon	⅛ teaspoon salt
Juice of a large lemon	¾ cup sherry wine
2 cups cold water	1 egg white stiffly beaten, or
1 cup granulated sugar	½ cup heavy cream, whipped
	Mint leaves

You may serve the ice either in the scooped honeydew, in scooped red apples, or in chilled orange basket.

Peel or scoop out melon; force pulp through a sieve, and sprinkle over lemon juice. Stir well. Make a sugar syrup with cold water, sugar and salt, allowing it to boil 5 minutes. Cool slightly, and add sieved honeydew pulp mixture and sherry wine. Stir well, then fold in either the stiffly beaten egg white or the whipped heavy cream. Freeze in refrigerator tray until firm, that is, to a rather solid mush, stirring every 30 minutes.

LIME ICE [2370]

2 cups cold water
⅔ cup granulated sugar
½ cup unstrained lime juice

A few drops green vegetable coloring
2 egg whites, stiffly beaten
A few grains salt

Make a sugar syrup with water and sugar, and allow to boil for 10 minutes. Add unstrained lime juice; cool, then add enough green vegetable coloring to attain the desired hue. Freeze to a mush in refrigerator tray; remove from refrigerator and scoop into a well-chilled bowl, then beat with rotary egg beater until mixture is very light. Then, fold in the stiffly beaten egg whites and salt; return to freezing tray and allow to freeze for 3 to 4 hours. Serve in well-chilled sherbet glasses, topping each glass with a crystallized mint leaf.

LEMON ICE [2371]

Make a syrup with 2 cups of granulated sugar and 4 cups of cold water, allowing it to boil for 5 minutes. Remove from the fire, cool slightly, add ¾ cup of lemon juice and freeze in hand freezer, using 3 parts of ice and 1 part of rock salt. Serve in well-chilled sherbet glasses, or in orange baskets, if desired.

MINT ICE [2372]
(*Very appropriate to serve with lamb or mutton course*)

1 quart cold water
2 cups granulated sugar

Juice of two medium-sized lemons
3 tablespoons dried mint leaves
A few drops of green vegetable coloring

Make a sugar syrup with water and sugar and allow to boil for 5 long minutes. Quickly pour over crushed mint leaves. Allow to infuse while cooling, then strain, and add lemon juice and a few drops of green vegetable coloring. Freeze either in refrigerator, or in hand freezer, using 3 parts of ice and 1 part of rock salt. Mold, if desired, into small paper cases, using a teaspoon, dipped in hot water, or serve in small chilled sherbet cups.

ORANGE ICE [2373]

It may seem strange, but I seldom strain orange juice, used in cooking, either for hot, cold or frozen dish. To do so, means that only the water-soluble material of the fruit is used, and I have learned while studying for my degree of dietitian, that there is a good deal of nutrient food value, notably vitamin A and iron, in the suspended particles of pulp which are discarded. The result, especially when a clear crystal product is desired, may not be clear enough, yet it is advisable to leave the pulp, or at least, if straining is wanted, to use a coarse strainer.

2 cups granulated sugar	2 cups orange juice
4 cups cold water	¼ cup lemon juice

Grated rind of 2 oranges

Make a syrup with cold water and sugar, and allow it to boil for 5 long minutes. Cool slightly, then add orange and lemon juice and grated orange rind. Cool, strain and freeze in hand freezer, using 3 parts of ice and 1 part of rock salt. Serve in chilled orange baskets, or in chilled sherbet glasses.

PINEAPPLE ICE [2374]

¼ cup granulated sugar	½ can canned crushed pineapple
½ cup cold water	1 egg white, stiffly beaten
½ cup cold water	3 tablespoons granulated sugar

¼ cup lemon juice

Combine the ¼ cup granulated sugar and first ½ cup of cold water, stir until sugar is dissolved, and boil for 3 long minutes. Cool to lukewarm, then stir in the second ½ cup cold water, combined with lemon juice, crushed pineapple and half of its juice, and stir well. Freeze to a mush either in refrigerator, or in hand freezer (if latter method is used, use 3 parts ice and 1 part of rock salt). Remove from refrigerator, or hand freezer when mushy; break up with a fork, and add, folding gently the stiffly beaten egg white, into which has been folded the 3 tablespoons of granulated sugar. Return to refrigerator, or hand freezer, and freeze until firm, but not icy. Serve in orange cups, or chilled sherbet glasses.

RASPBERRY ICE [2375]

Several methods are used to make this refreshing and delicious ice which are as follows:

4 cups cold water	2 cups of raspberry juice
1⅔ cups granulated sugar	2 tablespoons lemon juice

Make a sugar syrup with cold water and sugar, and allow it to boil for 5 minutes; cool, then add raspberry juice, made from enough mashed (raw) raspberries, then squeezed through a fine muslin, then add lemon juice and strain again. Freeze in hand freezer, using 3 parts of ice and 1 part of rock salt. Serve in either orange baskets, or in chilled sherbet glasses.

STRAWBERRY ICE [2376]

Strawberries must be fresh. In general, the freshness is indicated by the firmness and perfume. Berries that are not fresh, or are over-ripe take on a dull, lustreless appearance. They are sometimes shrivelled or shrunken, and very likely, wet or leaky. Damaged and leaky strawberries can usually be traced by a stained box.

When buying strawberries, or in fact any kind of berries, look for the berries which have a fresh, clean, bright appearance, with a full solid red color throughout. It should be free from moisture, dirt and trash, and the cap should always be attached to the berry.

In washing strawberries do not allow the faucet (cold water faucet) play on them. Put them into a bowl of cold water and then lift them out of the water with fingers somewhat apart to act as strainer. The sand and soil on the berries will settle to the bottom of the bowl. It is for that reason that you should not pour the water off the berries. Unless they are quite dirty, two such rinses are usually sufficient. Then allow them to drain, placing them into a colander. Do not keep berries too long in refrigerator, their flavor and perfume will suffer. This applies to any kind of berries.

1½ cups granulated sugar	2 cups strawberry juice
4 cups cold water	2 tablespoons lemon juice
¼ teaspoon salt	½ teaspoon grated lemon rind

Make a syrup with water and sugar, and let it boil 5 long minutes. Cool slightly, then add remaining ingredients. Chill, then freeze in hand freezer, using equal parts of ice and rock salt. Serve in chilled sherbet glasses.

ICE CREAM [2377]

Recipes and formulas have been adapted to serve an average family of six persons, unless otherwise indicated.

APRICOT ICE CREAM I [2378]
(Hand freezer)

¾ cup granulated sugar	2 cups heavy cream, whipped
¾ cup cold water	1½ cups canned, drained cut apricots
¼ teaspoon salt	3 egg whites, stiffly beaten

Make a sugar syrup with granulated sugar and water, and let it boil for 5 minutes. Carefully and very slowly pour this hot syrup over stiffly beaten egg whites to which salt has been added. Beat until cool, then fold in whipped cream, alternately with cut apricots. Freeze in hand freezer, using 3 parts ice and one part rock salt. Pack or mold and let stand in salt and ice for at least 2 hours before serving.

Any kind of fruit, canned or fresh may be prepared in the same way, if desired.

APRICOT ICE CREAM II   [2379]
(*Refrigerator tray*)

This delicious fresh apricot ice cream may be served with apricot sauce, if desired.

1 lb. fresh apricots	½ cup evaporated milk, chilled
1 cup boiling water	¼ cup granulated sugar
½ cup granulated sugar	Grated rind of ½ lemon
1 cup heavy cream, whipped	4 drops almond extract

Wash fresh apricots and cook with boiling water, over a very low flame for 10 minutes; then add the ½ cup granulated sugar, stirring gently until dissolved, and cook 10 minutes longer, or until fruit is soft, but not overdone. Put fruit and juice through a sieve; measure 1 cup and set aside the remaining cup to be used as a sauce, placing it in refrigerator. Now, add to the first cup the whipped cream, combined with the chilled evaporated milk, grated lemon rind and almond extract. Freeze in refrigerator tray for 1 hour; then fold or stir from bottom and sides of the tray, smooth and return to refrigerator to freeze for 3 more hours, or until firm. Serve with a side dish of the reserved cup of apricot puree, which may be sweetened to taste, if desired.

Try, after freezing for 1 hour, and just when folding and stirring to break up crystal sugar, adding 1 dozen blanched, shredded almonds, simmered for 5 minutes with equal parts of cold water and lemon juice, just enough to cover almonds. The mixture is then allowed to infuse until cold, then drained and the almonds only added to the cream mixture. The liquid may be set aside and used for either dessert or a sauce foundation, or a beverage foundation. This will add a very delicious flavor and render the cream a little crunchy.

To serve: You may scoop up balls of the ice cream, roll in coconut, or crumbled macaroons, or rice krispies, and what not, such as coarsely ground nut meats, which may be tinted, or into chocolate shots, etc.

BAKED ALASKA   [2380]

A solid frozen brick of ice cream is needed for this recipe. Furthermore, the ice cream should not contain water ice, it should be made of milk or cream. Here is how to operate:

Cover a bread board or an oven plank with a piece of wax or white paper. Place a layer of sponge or pound cake cut 1 inch thick on the paper, and then place the ice cream on the cake. The cake should extend about ½ generous inch beyond the ice cream all around. Cover completely with a thick coating of meringue made by beating 4 egg whites to a stiff consistency, then folding in gradually ¾ cup confectioner's sugar. This will make enough meringue for 1 quart ice cream. Remember, the meringue should be light and dry. Dust well with powdered sugar and set the whole in a very hot oven (450–475, and even 500° F.) for just enough to delicately brown. Slip the ice cream, thus browned, onto a chilled platter and serve at once.

Individual baked Alaskas are made by placing slices of very solid ice cream on rounds or squares of sponge or pound cake; then topped with meringue made as indicated above, and set in very hot oven or under the flame of the broiling oven to brown quickly. Like the large ones they should be served at once.

Both large or individual baked Alaskas may be sprinkled with coarsely ground nut meats (any kind) just before setting in the oven.

Here a few words are necessary as to how to make a good meringue, which are often a puzzle to the homemaker.

INSTRUCTIONS ABOUT MERINGUES   [2381]

Meringues are easy to make, and delicious cold and frozen desserts may be made out of them. The shell should be tender, opaque, and the interior should be almost dry and free from much of the stickiness which makes a meringue hard. If the egg whites are not beaten enough before the sugar is added, the mixture will not get stiff to keep its peaks and to shape well, even with much beating later. The meringue will be sticky and runny. Then the sugar is added gradually, a small amount at a time. Folding in the sugar may be made over gently simmering water; this will help to drive out part of the moisture naturally present in the egg white, to set a little, and also to dissolve the sugar granules.

Meringues and their kindred creations, filled with whipped cream or ice cream, are a favorite dessert throughout the year. They have a great advantage as they may be prepared in advance, and be adapted to all sorts of menus without any danger of "left-overs."

Usually 8 egg whites and 1 lb. powdered sugar are used for meringue dessert. The whites are whipped very stiff and while being whipped about ⅓ of the sugar is gradually incorporated. The balance of the sugar is folded in gradually with a wooden spoon. Care must be taken not to overwork the meringue. They are baked on a wooden board, previously moistened, and baked in a slow oven (275° F.) for about one hour. With a spatula remove them carefully to wire rack while hot, open side up, and when cold place them in proof box until completely dry. Thereafter, they are put back into the oven for a very short time to give them just a light yellow color.

The filling and garnish is, of course, entirely left to your own taste. Ordinarily, two shells are placed together, filled with whipped cream

("Meringue Chantilly") or ice cream ("Meringue Glace"), crushed berries, fruit ice, or whipped flavored gelatine, or any of the variety of creams.

Kisses are meringues baked in very small mounds, shaped either by a spoon, or pastry bag, ordinarily the size of a large walnut. They may be filled like large meringue. For large shells, which will be filled with ice cream, mousse, parfait mixture, any of the numerous cream desserts, etc., the meringue mix is shaped on the moistened board by means of pastry bag with a large plain tube, baked, cooled and filled.

BANANA ICE CREAM   [2382]
(Hand freezer)

To a quart of ice cream (No. 2421 Vanilla Ice Cream, French method), omitting vanilla, add the following mixture:

4 bananas, skinned, scraped, then sieved   1 generous tablespoon lemon juice
¼ scant teaspoon salt

Freeze in hand freezer, using 3 parts ice and 1 part rock salt. Pack or mold in ice and salt and let stand 2 hours before serving.

BISCUIT TORTONI I   [2383]
(Refrigerator tray)

This kind of frozen dessert is not an ice cream, but rather a mousse, yet it is so popularly called and classified with ice cream that the author has deemed necessary to class it here. There exist several methods of preparing this delicious sweetmeat, which will be found below:

1 cup heavy cream, whipped   ½ cup sieved dried macaroons
¼ cup powdered sugar   Paper cups and macaroons, sieved
2 teaspoons sherry wine   1 egg white, stiffly beaten

Add, or rather fold, powdered sugar gradually into the whipped cream, then fold in the stiffly beaten egg white, alternately with sieved macaroons and sherry wine. Pack in individual paper cups, sprinkle top with sieved macaroon crumbs and set in tray of refrigerator to freeze until firm. Do not stir.

BISCUIT TORTONI II   [2384]
(Hand freezer or refrigerator)

2 cups thin cream or undiluted evapo-   ⅛ teaspoon salt
    rated milk   ½ cup granulated sugar
1 cup dried macaroons, sieved   ⅓ cup good sherry
2 cups heavy cream, whipped

Combine thin cream or undiluted evaporated milk and allow to stand for 1 hour; then add salt, sugar and sherry wine (more or less according to taste), and freeze to a mush (about 1 hour) in hand freezer, using 3 parts ice and 1 part rock salt. Then add whipped cream; mold and pack in equal parts of ice and rock salt, allowing to stand 3 hours. You may use the refrigerator tray if desired. You may place the mixture in individual paper cups, top with a small pinch of sieved dried macaroons, and freeze in refrigerator for 3 hours.

BURNT ALMOND ICE CREAM [2385]
(Refrigerator tray or hand freezer)

¾ cup granulated sugar	¼ teaspoon salt
1 quart thin cream	1 teaspoon vanilla extract
½ lb. browned almonds, chopped	

Combine and stir until dissolved, the sugar, thin cream, salt and vanilla extract; then stir in the browned chopped almonds which have been blanched before browning. Freeze in refrigerator tray, stirring once when mixture is mushy, for 3 hours.

BUTTERMILK ICE CREAM [2386]
(Hand freezer)

½ cup hot water	2½ cups buttermilk
¾ cup granulated sugar	½ generous teaspoon grated lemon rind
Finely chopped rind of ½ orange	½ cup strained pineapple juice, canned
⅛ teaspoon salt	

Make a sugar syrup with water and sugar, and let it boil for 5 minutes. Cool slightly and add chopped orange rind, lemon rind and strained pineapple juice (canned) and salt. Freeze in hand freezer, using 3 parts ice and 1 part rock salt until mixture is to a mush. Then add buttermilk, stir well and pack.

BUTTERSCOTCH ICE CREAM [2387]
(Hand freezer)

2 cups scalded rich milk	¼ teaspoon salt
1 tablespoon flour	2 teaspoons vanilla extract
1 cup brown sugar	1 quart undiluted evaporated milk, or
2 tablespoons butter	half milk and half heavy cream
1 whole egg, slightly beaten	

Cook sugar with butter in a heavy skillet or saucepan until melted and allow to boil 1 long minute. Add to scalded milk, stirring well. Beat slightly the whole egg with salt and flour, the flour added a small amount at a time, and pour milk over egg mixture, slowly, stirring constantly. Cook over boiling water, for 10 minutes, stirring constantly for 5 minutes, then occasionally for the remaining 5 minutes. Should custard have a curdled appearance, it will disappear in freezing. Cool, and when cold add undiluted evaporated milk or half milk and heavy cream and vanilla extract. Strain through a fine sieve, and freeze in hand freezer, using 3 parts ice and 1 part rock salt. Pack or mold in 4 parts ice and 1 part rock salt.

BUTTERSCOTCH PECAN ICE CREAM [2388]
(Refrigerator tray or hand freezer)

1½ cups granulated sugar
2 cups fresh milk
2½ tablespoons butter
3 egg whites, stiffly beaten

3 egg yolks, slightly beaten
⅛ teaspoon salt
1 teaspoon vanilla extract
1 pint heavy cream

1 cup chopped pecans

Caramelize half the sugar by putting it in heavy shallow pan or skillet. Melt over moderate heat, stirring constantly until melted to a light brown syrup; add the milk and when the caramel is well-dissolved, stir in the remaining sugar mixed with butter and slightly beaten egg yolks. Cook over hot water, until mixture coats a spoon, stirring constantly. Cool, add salt, vanilla extract and the stiffly beaten egg whites mixed with whipped cream. Freeze to a mush in refrigerator tray or about 1 hour; remove from tray, stir in chopped pecans, return to tray and freeze for 3 long hours. You may use hand freezer, using 3 parts ice and 1 part rock salt, freezing until mushy, then adding the chopped pecans. Pack or mold in 4 parts of ice and 1 part of rock salt.

CARAMEL ICE CREAM [2389]
(Hand freezer or refrigerator tray)

⅓ cup granulated sugar
1 cup milk scalded
⅛ teaspoon salt

1 cup undiluted evaporated milk,
  whipped
2 egg yolks, slightly beaten
2 tablespoons granulated sugar

1 teaspoon vanilla extract

Caramelize the ⅓ cup granulated sugar in the usual way. When browned, stir in the scalded milk. Turn mixture into top of double boiler and cook over boiling water until sugar crystals are completely dissolved, or about 5 minutes, stirring occasionally. Add salt and 2 tablespoons to beaten eggs, mix well, and pour milk-caramel slowly over the egg mixture, stirring and beating alternately and constantly. Return to double boiler and cook until mixture coats a spoon, stirring constantly. Chill. Add whipped undiluted evaporated milk (see "How to Whip Evaporated Milk" No. 2357). Pour creamy mixture in refrigerator tray and freeze until mushy, or about 1 hour. Remove from refrigerator and beat well, using a wire whisk. Return to refrigerator tray and freeze 3 hours.

CHOCOLATE ICE CREAM I [2390]
(Hand freezer or refrigerator tray)

Important. When chocolate is used in cookery, it should be melted over hot water, as too high a temperature changes the flavor. Instead, it may be cut in pieces, to which a little cold water may be added and the two stirred together over a gentle fire until a smooth thick syrup results. If cocoa is used to replace chocolate in any kind of dessert requiring chocolate, it should be blended with the sugar or flour used in the recipe. When it is used as a foundation for a beverage, cold water should be added and the mixture stirred over a very gentle flame until smooth and thick. The cold milk, or whatever liquid indicated, may then be added as it is for chocolate. When the mixture begins to foam, while being heated over a gentle flame, it should be beaten with an egg beater in order to prevent a scum from forming over the top. By this method either cocoa or chocolate can be made with only one saucepan. In preparing chocolate, it is well to remember that it tends to burn easily.

1¼ cups granulated sugar	2 cups scalded milk
1 tablespoon all-purpose flour	2 squares bitter chocolate
¼ generous teaspoon salt	2 cups heavy cream
2 whole eggs, slightly beaten	1 tablespoon vanilla extract

Combine and mix well the melted chocolate, sugar, flour and salt, then beat in the slightly beaten whole eggs. Pour the hot scalded milk over the egg mixture, slowly and gradually, stirring briskly while pouring. Cook over hot water until mixture is thickened; cool, and strain through a muslin, then add heavy, unwhipped cream, and freeze in hand freezer, using 3 parts ice and 1 part rock salt. Pack or mold using 4 parts ice and 1 part rock salt.

CHOCOLATE ICE CREAM II [2391]
(Hand freezer or refrigerator tray)

1 square bitter chocolate	½ teaspoon vanilla extract
⅔ cup sweetened condensed milk	½ cup of heavy cream, whipped to
⅔ cup hot water	custard-like consistency with
	⅛ teaspoon salt

Melt chocolate over hot water; add condensed milk and cook, stirring constantly for about 5 minutes until mixture thickens. Then, stir in hot water. Chill, and add vanilla extract (¼ teaspoon almond extract may be substituted for vanilla extract, if desired). Lastly fold in the heavy cream whipped to a custard-like consistency. Freeze in refrigerator tray until mushy, or about 1 hour; then remove from refrigerator and scrape mixture from bottom and sides of pan, beat until smooth. Return to refrigerator tray and continue freezing for 3 hours.

CHOCOLATE MARSHMALLOW ICE CREAM [2392]
(*Refrigerator tray*)

2 squares bitter chocolate, grated then
    melted over hot water
1 cup fresh scalded milk
16 marshmallows, cut small

¼ scant teaspoon salt
4 tablespoons granulated sugar
1 cup undiluted evaporated milk
1 tablespoon lemon juice

½ teaspoon ground cinnamon

To the chocolate melted over hot water, add scalded milk, slowly and gradually, stirring constantly, until mixture is thoroughly blended. Add marshmallows, cut small with scissors, dipped in flour, salt and sugar, and place over hot water, heating slowly, while stirring constantly, until marshmallows are dissolved and sugar melted, then chill. When cold, fold in the whipped undiluted evaporated milk to which has been added lemon juice and ground cinnamon. Freeze in refrigerator tray without stirring for 3½ hours. To serve: With a tablespoon dipped in hot water, rapidly cut egg shapes from the frozen ice cream, and arrange, crown-like on a well-chilled platter. Fill center of the ring with Raspberry whipped cream made as follows:

1¼ cups raspberries

1 cup powdered sugar

1 egg white

Put all the above ingredients in a mixing bowl, and beat with a wire whisk until stiff enough to hold its shape, or about 25 minutes. Pile lightly or force through a pastry bag with a large fancy tube, in center of the ice cream ring. You may dust the whip with shredded blanched almonds, or crumbled dry macaroons, if desired.

COFFEE ICE CREAM I [2393]
(*Hand freezer*)

In this recipe extra strong coffee liquid is used, yet it is still the custard method.

1 cup milk (cold)
¼ cup extra strong coffee liquid
3 egg yolks, slightly beaten
⅛ teaspoon salt

1 cup granulated sugar
3 cups undiluted evaporated milk or thin
    cream

Scald cold milk with coffee, and add half the sugar. Combine slightly beaten egg yolks with the remaining ½ cup granulated sugar and slowly add to scalded milk-coffee mixture, stirring rapidly until mixture is thoroughly blended. Cook over hot water until mixture thickens, stirring almost constantly. Remove from hot water, cool slightly, then add 1 cup of the undiluted evaporated milk or thin cream, and allow to stand for half an hour, to mellow and cool. Then strain through double cheese-cloth; add remaining milk or thin cream and freeze in hand freezer, using 3 parts ice and 1 part rock salt. Pack or mold in 4 parts ice and 1 part rock salt and let stand 2 hours before serving.

COFFEE ICE CREAM II   [2394]
(*Refrigerator tray*)

Using granulated gelatine, no cream, and grape nuts cereal.

1 teaspoon granulated gelatine	½ cup grape nuts cereal
1 cup extra strong cold coffee liquid	1 cup undiluted evaporated milk,
½ cup granulated sugar	whipped to custard-like consistency

½ teaspoon vanilla extract

Soak, or rather sprinkle gelatine over cold coffee, and allow to stand 5 minutes, then heat, stirring constantly until gelatine is dissolved and coffee is up to the boiling point; then add granulated sugar and cook over a low flame for 5 short minutes, stirring frequently. Strain through a double cheesecloth. Chill. Combine slightly whipped undiluted evaporated milk and grape nuts, and add to chilled coffee mixture; then stir in the vanilla extract. Freeze in refrigerator tray for 1 hour, or until mixture is mushy, then scrape bottom and sides, and beat until smooth. Return to refrigerator tray, and freeze for 3 hours.

EGGNOG ICE CREAM   [2395]
(*Refrigerator tray*)

6 egg yolks, beaten until thick	6 egg whites, stiffly beaten
½ cup granulated sugar	¼ teaspoon salt
4 tablespoons (more or less) sherry	1 cup heavy cream whipped stiff

Nutmeg

Beat egg yolks until thick, then add sugar gradually and continue beating until sugar is thoroughly blended. Set in refrigerator while beating egg whites until stiff with the salt. Then fold egg yolk mixture with stiffly beaten egg whites, adding gradually the sherry wine (rum or brandy may be stubstituted, if desired). Lastly fold in the heavy cream beaten stiff. Freeze in refrigerator tray, without scraping or stirring, for 4 hours. When ready to serve, sprinkle over each serving a small pinch of ground nutmeg, or still better a grating from a whole nutmeg.

FLAMING ICE CREAM SAUCE   [2396]
(*Serve 1*)

½ brandied peach, sliced	Sugar to taste
½ brandied apricot, sliced	1½ teaspoons brandy
4 brandied pitted cherries	1 small round of sponge cake cut the size
¼ teaspoon curacao liqueur	of a biscuit

1 scoop vanilla ice cream

Heat the combined brandied fruits in a small frying pan. Add curacao, then sprinkle with sugar. Stir gently, but do not allow to boil, simply heat. Then pour brandy over mixture and touch it with a match. Place round of sponge cake, or any other kind of cake, cut the size of a biscuit, using a biscuit cutter, on dessert plate; top with ice cream and pour the fruit over it. Serve at once. This may be prepared right on the table, if desired. Variations to the above may be made by using any kind of canned or fresh fruit.

HALLOWEEN ICE CREAM CLOWN   [2397]
(*Serve 1*)

For children's Halloween party.

Put a scoop of ice cream in an ice cream cone, invert on round cooky, features from gumdrops and make a ruff with whipped cream put on through pastry bag and tube.

MACAROON ICE CREAM   [2398]
(*Hand freezer*)

1 cup macaroon crumbs	1 teaspoon almond extract
½ cup confectioner's sugar	1 quart cream (heavy)
¼ scant teaspoon salt	

Combine all the above ingredients. Stir well, and freeze in hand freezer, using 3 parts ice and 1 part rock salt, until firm. Pack or mold in 4 parts ice and 1 part rock salt.

MAPLE WALNUT ICE CREAM   [2399]
(*Refrigerator tray*)

1 cup maple syrup	3 egg whites, stiffly beaten
3 egg yolks, slightly beaten, with	1 cup heavy cream, beaten to a custard-
¼ teaspoon salt	like consistency
1 teaspoon vanilla extract	½ cup chopped, skinned walnuts

Place maple syrup in upper part of double boiler, and heat, but do not boil, over hot water. Then, stir in the slightly beaten egg yolks until well-blended. Cook, stirring constantly, over hot water, until mixture thickens. Remove from water, and add vanilla extract. Chill. When cold, fold in the stiffly beaten egg whites, alternately with the heavy cream, which has been beaten to a custard-like consistency. Freeze in refrigerator tray, to a mushy consistency, or until a layer is frozen 1 inch from sides of tray; remove from refrigerator and scrape and stir from bottom and sides of tray. Then beat until smooth, incorporating at the same time the chopped, skinned walnut meats. Return to refrigerator and freeze for 3 hours.

MARRON GLACÉ ICE CREAM [2400]
(Home method, using hand freezer)

Prepare marrons (chestnuts) as follows:

Shell chestnuts, using about 1 lb., by cutting a ½-inch slit or gash on the flat side. Put chestnuts in a heavy pan; add ½ teaspoon of oil or butter to each cup of chestnuts. Shake over the fire for 5 minutes, then set in a moderate oven (350° F.) for 5 minutes longer. Remove from oven and remove the shells and skins, while still hot, using a sharp knife. Place shelled, skinned chestnuts in a pan, cover with boiling, salted water, and cook gently for 15 to 20 minutes, or steam for 45 minutes. Rice, that is, put through ricer while hot.

5 egg yolks, slightly beaten with	3 cups milk, scalded
1½ cups granulated sugar, and	¼ cup pineapple syrup
½ teaspoon salt	2 cups undiluted evaporated milk

1½ cups boiled chestnuts, riced

Pour hot scalded milk over sugar-egg mixture very slowly, stirring rapidly and constantly. Cook over hot water, until mixture thickens, stirring constantly. Strain through double cheesecloth. Cool. Add undiluted evaporated milk, alternately with pineapple syrup and riced cooled chestnuts. Freeze in hand freezer, using 3 parts ice and 1 part rock salt, until firm and solid. Pack or mold in 4 parts ice and 1 part rock salt for 2 hours.

You may use the same amount of chestnuts, prepared as follows: Shell chestnuts as indicated above, blanch with enough water to cover, then allow to simmer until nearly tender, or about 35 minutes. Drain and place in a thin sugar syrup made by boiling 1 cup sugar with 2¼ cups water for ten minutes, which may be flavored with 1 teaspoon vanilla extract, maraschino, etc., for each quart of water. In this case use ½ teaspoon. Simmer chestnuts in syrup for 1 hour, lift chestnuts, drain and cool. Then put through ricer. If using this method, omit the pineapple syrup.

Prepared in this way, the chestnuts are then called marrons, in French. They may be preserved, by boiling down the syrup until quite thick, and pouring it boiling over prepared chestnuts, which have been placed in sterilized jars to overflowing, then sealing while hot.

MINT ICE CREAM [2401]
(Refrigerator tray)

1 cup fresh milk, scalded	1 egg yolk
¼ cup granulated sugar	1 teaspoon granulated gelatine
1 tablespoon all-purpose flour	2 tablespoons cold water
¼ teaspoon salt	1½ cups heavy cream, whipped stiff
1 teaspoon peppermint flavoring extract	Green vegetable coloring

Stir half of the sugar into hot scalded milk. Add salt and flour which has been stirred in a little water, and cook over hot water for 15 minutes, stirring almost constantly. Beat egg yolk with remaining ¼ cup sugar, and very slowly pour the milk mixture over it, stirring rapidly and constantly for 2 long minutes, or until mixture coats the spoon. Add gelatine which has been soaked in cold water for 5 minutes, and stir until entirely dissolved. Cool slightly, add green vegetable coloring. Chill; fold stiffly beaten heavy cream into creamy mixture, then add the peppermint extract (not oil of peppermint). Freeze in refrigerator tray until mushy, then scrape bottom and sides, and beat until smooth. Return to refrigerator tray, freeze again until a little stiff, or about 30 minutes, and repeat the scraping and stirring; then, freeze for 3 hours.

MOCHA ICE CREAM   [2402]
(*Hand freezer*)

To a preparation of Vanilla Ice Cream, selecting your favorite recipe, substitute extra strong coffee for milk. Freeze as indicated.

NEAPOLITAN ICE CREAM   [2403]
(*Hand freezer*)

A sort of Tutti-Frutti ice cream which is very appropriate for special parties. The flavor is a mingling of caramel nuts and candied fruits. A very rich ice cream.

1 quart thin cream, heated	½ cup chopped pecans
½ cup granulated sugar, caramelized	¼ cup chopped candied cherries
2 egg yolks, slightly beaten	¼ cup chopped candied pineapple

¼ teaspoon salt

To the heated cream (not boiled, nor scalded) add caramelized sugar, and stir until thoroughly dissolved; then slowly pour in the slightly beaten egg yolks, stirring rapidly until mixture is well-blended. Then stir in salt. Cool, and freeze in hand freezer using 3 parts ice and 1 part rock salt until mushy. Add pecans and candied fruit, stir, and continue freezing until firm and solid. Pack or mold using 4 parts ice and 1 part rock salt for 2½ hours.

ORANGE ICE CREAM I   [2404]
(*Refrigerator tray*)

An economical ice cream in which sugar is substituted by sweetened condensed milk and sugar contained in orange juice.

⅔ cup sweetened condensed milk	⅛ teaspoon salt
½ cup orange juice	3 drops orange extract
2 teaspoons grated orange rind	1 cup heavy cream, whipped to a custard-like consistency

Combine sweetened condensed milk, orange juice and grated orange rind, salt and orange extract. Mix well and chill. Fold in the heavy cream, whipped to a custard-like consistency and freeze in refrigerator tray until mushy (about 40 minutes), remove from refrigerator, scrape bottom and sides, then beat until smooth. Return to refrigerator and freeze for 2½ hours.

ORANGE ICE CREAM II [2405]
(Hand freezer)

1 cup undiluted evaporated milk	¼ teaspoon salt
1 cup heavy cream	2 cups orange juice

⅓ cup (more or less) granulated sugar

Combine milk and heavy cream, add slowly to orange juice, stirring constantly, stir in salt and sugar, adding more or less sugar, according to sweetness of orange juice. Chill, then freeze in hand freezer, using 3 parts ice and 1 part rock salt, until firm. Pack or mold in 4 parts ice and 1 part rock salt. A fine result if served with a side dish of crushed berries (any kind) sweetened to taste.

PEACH ICE CREAM I [2406]
(Hand freezer)

¾ cup fresh peach pulp	1½ cups undiluted evaporated milk,
¾ cup granulated sugar	whipped to custard-like consistency
Juice of ½ lemon	

Put fresh peach through ricer, collecting juice and pulp. There should be ¾ cup. Add sugar, stir, then stir in the lemon juice. Freeze in hand freezer, using 3 parts ice and 1 part rock salt, until mushy; then add whipped milk, and freeze until firm. Pack or mold in 4 parts ice and 1 part rock salt.

PEACH ICE CREAM II [2407]
(Refrigerator tray)

Very economical method.

½ cup peach jam	⅛ teaspoon salt
½ cup undiluted evaporated milk	3 or 4 drops almond extract

¾ cup heavy cream, whipped to a custard-like consistency

Add evaporated milk to peach jam and stir until blended, add salt and almond extract, then fold in the heavy cream whipped to a custard-like consistency. Freeze in refrigerator tray until mushy; remove from refrigerator, scrape bottom and sides, then beat until smooth. Return to refrigerator and freeze for 3½ hours.

PEACH MELBA [2408]
(*Home method*)

For each serving take a round of sponge cake; place on it a scoop of Vanilla Ice Cream and top with a preserved or canned peach. Pour over a tablespoon or two of Melba sauce, garnish with small rosettes of whipped cream, forced through a pastry bag with a fancy tube.

Melba Sauce I

1 cup canned or fresh raspberries   ¼ cup granulated sugar

Rub berries through a sieve to remove the seeds; add sugar and cook to a heavy syrup, stirring frequently to prevent scorching.

Melba Sauce II

1 cup of pulp and juice of fresh raspberries, rubbed through a sieve to remove the seeds   ½ cup granulated sugar
⅛ teaspoon salt
1 small glass jar currant jelly   ½ tablespoon arrowroot or corn-starch
1 tablespoon cold water
¼ teaspoon lemon juice

Combine currant jelly, sugar and pulp and juice of berries. Place over direct flame and bring to boiling point (210° F.). Add salt, arrowroot or cornstarch, and cook, stirring constantly, until mixture thickens and becomes clear. Strain through double cheesecloth. Cool.

Pears may be prepared in this delicious way.

PEPPERMINT ICE CREAM [2409]

Substitute mint flavoring (not oil of peppermint) for vanilla to your favorite Vanilla Ice Cream recipe, and color to the desired hue, using green vegetable coloring. Freeze and pack as directed.

Hollowed-out melon shells (cantaloupe, honey-dew or watermelon) make perfect ice cream dishes. They may also be used for mousses, parfaits or sherbets. Pineapple shells are pretty and appealing, too.

PINEAPPLE ICE CREAM [2410]
(*Hand freezer*)

2 cups crushed canned pineapple (juice and pulp)   ½ cup granulated sugar
⅛ teaspoon salt
2½ cans undiluted evaporated milk, or thin cream

Combine pineapple and undiluted evaporated milk, stir and allow to stand 30 minutes. Strain, through double cheese cloth, add sugar and freeze in hand freezer, using 3 parts ice and 1 part rock salt until solid. Pack or mold in 4 parts ice and 1 part rock salt for 1 hour.

PISTACHIO ICE CREAM I [2411]
(Hand freezer)

If you follow the directions exactly, you will have a pistachio ice cream which will be mellow, and light.

1 cup blanched ground pistachio nuts	1 quart heavy cream
1 generous teaspoon heavy cream	1 tablespoon spinach juice, or a few drops
1 scant teaspoon grated lemon rind	of green vegetable coloring
¾ cup granulated sugar	8 egg yolks, slightly beaten

Grind the pistachio nut meats three times, combine with the teaspoon of cream, more or less, and grated rind of lemon. Mix to a paste, adding more cream if necessary, so as to obtain a soft, yet solid paste. Place this paste in a large saucepan, or still better in top of a double boiler, and pour all at once, the slightly beaten egg yolks with the sugar. The flame should be low, the water in bottom of double boiler up to boiling point. Stir continually, while cooking until mixture is thoroughly blended, then, gradually pour in the unbeaten heavy cream, stirring constantly. Bring to the boiling point, and cook until mixture coats the spoon. Remove from hot water and strain through double cheesecloth. Cool, add either spinach juice or vegetable coloring to the desired hue, and freeze in hand freezer, using 3 parts ice and 1 part rock salt, until solid. Pack or mold in 4 parts ice and 1 part rock salt.

This is the French method of making Pistachio ice cream. In it you have the full flavor of the nuts, plus the entire nutrient power, plus delicateness, fineness and mellowness.

PISTACHIO ICE CREAM II [2412]
(Short method)

To your favorite vanilla ice cream recipe, omit vanilla, add 1 teaspoon almond extract, ¼ cup ground pistachio nuts and a few drops of vegetable coloring. Freeze as directed.

RAISIN NUT ICE CREAM [2413]
(Short cut. Hand freezer)

Put 1 cup washed, sponged seedless raisins through food chopper, alternately with 1 cup nut meats (any kind), and add to your favorite Vanilla Ice Cream recipe before freezing. The recipe should be a hand freezer one, as in the refrigerator the mixture would require too much scraping.

RASPBERRY ICE CREAM [2414]
(*Hand freezer*)

The pressed juice of raspberries, red currants or blackberries makes a cooling and refreshing beverage or "shrub" when added to some effervescent water. Aside from making delicious desserts, raspberries are very popular for ice cream.

Their chemical composition is approximately that of strawberries.

2 quarts fresh raspberries
2 cups granulated sugar
¼ scant teaspoon salt

3 pints thin cream, or equal amount of undiluted evaporated milk (3 cups)

Wash, hull and coarsely crush the raspberries, sprinkle with sugar and salt, and allow to stand for 2 hours in a warm place. Then mash again, strain. Freeze chilled thin cream or undiluted evaporated milk to a soft mush, then gradually add raspberry juice and continue freezing, using 4 parts ice and 2 parts rock salt, until firm and solid. Pack or mold in 3 parts ice and 2 parts rock salt for 2 hours to mellow.

SPUMONE ICE CREAM [2415]
(*Hand freezer or refrigerator tray*)

1½ cups fresh milk, scalded
⅔ cup granulated sugar
2 tablespoons cornstarch
⅛ teaspoon salt
½ cup fresh cold milk
3 egg yolks slightly beaten with

1 egg white
2 egg whites stiffly beaten with a little of the sugar
1 teaspoon vanilla extract
1 cup heavy cream, whipped to a custard-like consistency

⅓ cup cocoa

Stir in the hot scalded milk the sugar, reserving 2 tablespoons. Combine and blend cornstarch, salt and ½ cup of milk, add to the scalded milk and cook, stirring constantly, until mixture coats the spoon. Add then the slightly beaten egg yolks and egg white, slowly and gradually, stirring briskly and constantly. Return to hot water and continue cooking for 5 short minutes. Remove from hot water, cool then chill. When thoroughly chilled, add stiffly beaten egg whites combined with heavy cream, which has been whipped to a custard-like consistency with the vanilla extract. Freeze in refrigerator tray until mushy; remove from refrigerator, scrape bottom and sides, then beat in the cocoa. Return to tray and freeze for 3 hours.

STRAWBERRY ICE CREAM I [2416]
(*Hand freezer*)

Important. All the different methods of making ice cream with raspberries may be applied to strawberries, substituting strawberries for raspberries.

3 cups thin cream or undiluted evaporated milk
⅛ teaspoon salt

Syrup from canned strawberries
Sugar as necessary
Red vegetable coloring

Flavor thin cream or evaporated milk with enough syrup to make it
sweet according to taste, adding more sugar if necessary. Add salt and a
few drops of red vegetable coloring and freeze in hand freezer, using 5
parts ice and 2 parts rock salt until solid. Pack or mold in 4 parts ice and
1 part rock salt.

STRAWBERRY ICE CREAM II   [2417]
(Refrigerator tray)

1 cup sweetened condensed milk
½ cup cold water

1½ cups crushed strawberries
1 cup heavy cream, whipped stiff

⅛ teaspoon salt

Combine and mix sweetened condensed milk and water thoroughly.
Add crushed fresh ripe strawberries, which have been washed, picked
over, hulled. Stir in gently but thoroughly the heavy cream whipped
stiff with the salt, and freeze in refrigerator tray until mushy; remove
from refrigerator, scrape bottom and sides, beat 2 minutes, or until
smooth, and return to refrigerator tray to freeze for 3 hours. You may
add ½ teaspoon vanilla extract to the whipped cream before stirring in
the whipped heavy cream, if desired.

STRAWBERRY ICE CREAM III   [2418]
(Hand freezer or refrigerator tray)

A strawberry ice cream which has just the piquancy that it deserves
and fit to be served in the form of flowers. The thing to do is to freeze
slowly in the usual way until almost completely frozen (hard mush),
then fill fruit and flower molds and freeze an hour longer, if refrigerator
tray is used; and if hand freezer is used, pack in 4 parts ice and 1 part
rock salt for 1 hour.

2 cups fresh ripe strawberries, washed,
picked over, hulled, crushed, then
sieved through a coarse strainer to
remove the seeds.
¼ scant teaspoon salt

2 teaspoons lemon juice
½ cup granulated sugar
¾ cup orange juice
1 pint heavy cream, mixed with
2 tablespoons confectioner's sugar

To the strawberry pulp and juice, add salt, lemon juice, granulated
sugar and orange juice. Let stand 30 minutes to ripen, stirring frequently,
with the vessel in a warm place. Then add unwhipped heavy cream into
which has been stirred the confectioner's sugar. Chill. Freeze in hand
freezer, using 3 parts ice and 1 part rock salt, and turning slowly until
mixture is solid. Pack or mold as indicated above.

TUTTI FRUTTI ICE CREAM   [2419]
(*Hand freezer or refrigerator tray*)

1 cup orange pulp, cut into small pieces
¼ cup drained maraschino cherries cut into small pieces
2 bananas, peeled then mashed
½ cup drained crushed pineapple
2 tablespoons lemon juice

1 teaspoon granulated gelatine
1 tablespoon cold water
¾ cup undiluted evaporated milk, whipped as for recipe No. 2357
¼ cup blanched finely chopped almonds
¾ cup granulated sugar

Combine all the fruit with sugar. Stir well and add gelatine which has been softened in cold water and dissolved over hot water. Fold in the whipped undiluted evaporated milk (whipped stiff) and freeze in hand freezer, using 3 parts ice and 1 part rock salt until mushy, then add chopped almonds, and freeze until solid. Pack or mold in 4 parts ice and 1 part rock salt. If using refrigerator tray, freeze to a mush, remove from refrigerator, scrape bottom and sides, then beat in the chopped almonds until smooth. Return to refrigerator and freeze for 3½ hours.

VANILLA ICE CREAM I   [2420]
(*American method. Hand freezer or refrigerator tray*)

2 cups scalded milk
1 tablespoon flour
1 cup granulated sugar
2 egg yolks, slightly beaten

¼ teaspoon salt
1½ teaspoons vanilla extract
1 quart thin cream, or undiluted evaporated milk

Combine flour, sugar and salt, and add to slightly beaten egg yolks; then slowly, while stirring briskly and constantly, pour scalded milk over egg mixture. Turn this into top of double boiler, and cook over hot water 10 minutes, stirring constantly, until custard coats the spoon. Strain through double cheesecloth while hot; cool, chill, and freeze in hand freezer, using 3 parts ice and 1 part rock salt, until solid. Pack or mold in 4 parts and 1 part rock salt.

VANILLA ICE CREAM II   [2421]
(*French method. Hand freezer or refrigerator tray*)

2 cups rich milk, scalded
4 egg yolks, slightly beaten
½ cup granulated sugar

1 cup heavy cream, unwhipped
1 generous teaspoon vanilla extract
⅛ generous teaspoon salt

Combine sugar and salt, and add slightly beaten egg yolks, beating gently until sugar is dissolved and mixture is thoroughly blended. Pour rich scalded milk over, slowly, while stirring briskly and constantly. Turn creamy custard into top of double boiler and cook, over simmering water, stirring constantly, until mixture coats the spoon. Strain through double cheesecloth, cool, then chill. Add unwhipped heavy cream and vanilla, and freeze in hand freezer, using 3 parts ice and 1 part rock salt, until solid. Pack or mold in 4 parts ice and 1 part rock salt. For refrigerator tray, see note in previous recipe.

MOUSSES [2422]

Mousse, means "MOSS" in French and so-called because of its spongy consistency. The original basic foundation is sweetened and flavored whipped heavy cream. To this may be added sieved cooked or raw fruit, and flavoring or flavorings. A little gelatine may be added as a stabilizer. These delicate desserts are the simplest to freeze in the automatic refrigerator because of their richness. Here, too, the sweet cordials and sweet dessert wines may be used either alone or in conjunction with flavoring extracts. The mixture should be well combined, then poured into the trays, and stirred or not, according to directions, only once after the mixture has been frozen to a mush, operating as for ice cream.

Mousses are seldom served in chilled glasses. They may be packed in large or individual molds or frilled or scalloped paper cups. Or, the refrigerator tray may be lined with home made or purchased ice cream, the center filled with whipped cream, or undiluted evaporated milk, sweetened and flavored to taste, or combined with chopped candied or crystallized fruit, or any kind of nut meats. The tray is then unmolded on a chilled platter, or on an ice block and served at once, after being allowed to freeze 2 to 3 hours.

Packed in large or individual plain or fancy molds, mousses afford attractive desserts for formal or informal functions. All these are left to the imagination of the homemaker, according to her budget, or the occasion.

APRICOT MOUSSE [2423]
(Refrigerator tray)

1 cup heavy cream, whipped stiff	¼ cup granulated sugar
2 egg whites, stiffly beaten	½ scant teaspoon salt
1 can apricots, drained then sieved	½ teaspoon almond extract
2 tablespoons ground almonds	

Combine gently, stiffly beaten egg whites and heavy cream whipped stiff. Combine sieved apricot pulp (no juice), sugar, salt and flavoring extract and blanched ground almonds; then add to combined egg whites and heavy cream. Blend well, but gently. Turn mixture into refrigerator tray and freeze 4 hours without stirring. You may substitute apple sauce, or apricot marmalade for canned apricots if desired. You may also use fresh apricot pulp.

BRANDY MOUSSE   [2424]
(*Refrigerator tray*)

1 cup heavy cream, whipped stiff
⅓ scant cup powdered sugar

⅛ generous teaspoon salt
1 tablespoon good brandy

2 egg whites, stiffly beaten

Fold into the stiffly whipped heavy cream, the powdered sugar and
salt, then gently fold in the stiffly beaten egg whites, to which has been
added the brandy. Freeze in refrigerator tray, scraping once when mixture begins to mush, or about 20 minutes, then continue freezing for 4
hours.

Rum, Madeira wine, or any other liqueur, according to taste, may be
substituted for the brandy.

BURNT ALMOND MOUSSE   [2425]
(*Refrigerator tray or hand freezer*)

Any other kind of nut meats may be substituted for almonds, if
desired. In the following recipe undiluted evaporated milk, whipped
stiff is suggested. The creamy preparation may be packed in hand
freezer, using equal parts of ice and rock salt. But do not churn.

½ cup granulated sugar, caramelized
½ cup boiling water
1 teaspoon granulated gelatine
1 tablespoon cold water

1½ cups undiluted evaporated milk
    whipped (see recipe No. 2357)
1 teaspoon vanilla extract
¼ cup blanched, roasted almonds

Place sugar into a heavy skillet, over a gentle flame and cook, stirring
constantly until sugar is golden brown and melted. Then add boiling
water, and let simmer until mixture is thoroughly blended, stirring
occasionally. To this, add gelatine, softened in the cold water, alternately
with ½ cup of the cold milk. Cool until mixture is thickened, and fold
in the remaining cup of undiluted evaporated milk, whipped stiff, and
the vanilla extract. Freeze in refrigerator tray or in mold, using hand
freezer pail, until mixture is mushy; then add almonds, beat and scrape
at the same time for 2 minutes, then continue freezing for 3½ hours.

CHANTILLY MOUSSE   [2426]
(*Refrigerator tray*)

This mousse requires no stirring at all, and if meringues— small or
broken ones—are not on hand, they may be purchased for a few cents,
or you may substitute crumbled macaroons, if desired.

1 cup heavy cream, whipped stiff
¼ cup powdered sugar
⅛ teaspoon salt

½ teaspoon vanilla extract
1 egg white, stiffly beaten
1 cup, broken small, macaroons or
    meringues

To the stiffly whipped heavy cream, add powdered sugar and salt and whip again to blend sugar and salt thoroughly. Fold in stiffly beaten egg white, to which has been added the vanilla extract, alternately with the broken meringues (see meringues, recipe No. 2381) or broken macaroons. Mold either in large or individual molds, plain or fancy, and set in refrigerator tray for 3 hours.

CHERRY MOUSSE [2427]
(Refrigerator tray or hand freezer)

You may use the hand freezer pail if desired, using equal parts ice and rock salt, stirring once after 30 minutes of packing, but do not churn.

1 No. 2 can red pitted cherries	½ cup granulated sugar
2 teaspoons granulated gelatine	1 tablespoon lemon juice
2 tablespoons cold water	⅛ teaspoon salt
1 cup heavy cream, whipped to a custard-like consistency	

Reserve a few whole cherries to garnish the mousse when unmolded. Rub the remaining cherries through a coarse sieve. Heat cherry pulp and juice to the boiling point; add gelatine which has been softened in cold water. Stir, then add sugar and lemon juice, and chill. When well-chilled, stir in the whipped cream, and freeze in refrigerator tray until mushy, then scrape bottom and sides, then beat for 2 minutes. Return to refrigerator and continue freezing for 3 hours. A fine mousse for Valentine's Day.

CHOCOLATE MOUSSE [2428]
(Hand freezer or refrigerator tray)

2 squares bitter chocolate, melted over hot water	2 generous teaspoons granulated gelatine, soaked in
½ cup powdered sugar	3 tablespoons cold water
1 cup scalded fresh milk	¾ cup granulated sugar
¼ teaspoon salt	1 teaspoon vanilla extract
2 cups heavy cream, whipped stiff	

To the melted chocolate, add powdered sugar and stir until well blended, then, gradually pour over the hot scalded milk, stirring constantly. Place over a gentle flame and allow to come to the boiling point. Do not allow to boil. Remove from the fire and stir in the soaked gelatine, alternately with the granulated sugar and vanilla extract. Strain through a single cheesecloth or a fine strainer. Chill until mixture begins to thicken, then beat, using rotary egg beater until mixture is light. Lastly fold in the stiffly whipped cream with the salt. Mold, and freeze in refrigerator tray for 3 hours.

COFFEE MOUSSE   [2429]
(Refrigerator tray or hand freezer)

½ tablespoon granulated gelatine	4 egg yolks and
2 tablespoons cold water	1 egg white, beaten together
1 cup very strong black coffee	3 tablespoons good brandy
1 teaspoon vanilla extract	2 cups heavy cream, whipped stiff
¼ teaspoon salt	1 cup granulated sugar

Soak gelatine in cold water. Stir in very hot coffee to which has been added the sugar, and which has been boiled for 5 minutes or to a syrupy consistency. Pour over slightly beaten egg yolks and egg white, beaten together while hot, stirring briskly and constantly from bottom of saucepan to prevent curdling. Strain through double cheesecloth. Cool. Add vanilla and good brandy, then fold in the stiffly beaten heavy cream with the salt. Pour into mold or individual paper cases. If desired, and when using a large mold, you may pack in hand freezer pail, using equal parts ice and rock salt and allow to stand 2½ to 3 hours. If using refrigerator tray, freeze, if in paper cases, for 2½ hours, if large mold, freeze for 4 hours.

CURAÇAO MOUSSE   [2430]
(Refrigerator tray)

Any other kind of liqueur may be substituted, if desired. Follow the directions as indicated for recipe No. 2424, Brandy Mousse, using the same amount of ingredients, but substituting curaçao liqueur for brandy.

OLD-FASHIONED COFFEE MOUSSE   [2431]
(Hand freezer)

1 pint heavy cream	½ teaspoon vanilla extract
4 tablespoons powdered sugar	⅓ cup very strong black coffee
	⅛ teaspoon salt

Combine unwhipped heavy cream, sugar, vanilla extract and salt. Chill thoroughly, then whip stiffly, setting the bowl in a pan of ice water, removing the froth, as it rises, and placing it over a fine sieve. When no more froth will rise, turn the drowned whip carefully into a wet mold, adjust the cover, bind the edges with a strip of muslin dipped in melted butter, and bury in equal parts of ice and rock salt for 3 hours.

PEACH MOUSSE   [2432]
(Hand freezer pail or refrigerator tray)

This very economical and really delicious mousse requires 4 good sized fresh peaches, gelatine and undiluted evaporated milk, whipped.

⅔ cup granulated sugar
2 cups, peeled, sliced peaches
½ teaspoon granulated gelatine
1 tablespoon cold water
⅛ cup evaporated milk

⅔ cup warm water
½ teaspoon salt
1 tablespoon cornstarch
2 egg yolks, beaten thick
1 teaspoon vanilla extract

⅔ cup undiluted evaporated milk, whipped (Recipe No. 2357)

Sprinkle sugar over sliced peaches and let stand for 30 minutes, then force through a sieve, using a coarse one. Soak granulated gelatine in cold water for 5 minutes. Combine ⅓ cup undiluted evaporated milk and warm water, and scald in the usual way, and pour over the softened gelatine. Then add salt and cornstarch which have been mixed with enough cold water to form a smooth, thin paste. Cook, over hot water, stirring constantly, until mixture coats the spoon; then pour creamy mixture over thickly beaten egg yolks; return to double boiler and cook few minutes longer, or until mixture is thick. Chill. When cool, fold in the sieved peach pulp and juice, alternately with the whipped undiluted evaporated milk. Freeze either in hand freezer pail, using equal parts ice and rock salt for 2½ to 3 hours, or in the refrigerator tray, either molded or right into the tray. If small molds are used, freeze for 2 to 2½ hours; if large mold or mixture is frozen right into the tray, freeze for 3½ to 4 hours.

PINEAPPLE MOUSSE   [2433]
(Refrigerator tray or hand freezer)

In the following recipe, canned pineapple juice is used. If you use fresh pineapple juice, have it boiled first before stirring in the granulated gelatine.

1 teaspoon granulated gelatine
1 tablespoon cold water
2 tablespoons boiling water
¼ teaspoon salt

2 tablespoons lemon juice
½ cup granulated sugar
2 cups heavy cream, whipped stiff
1 cup syrup from canned pineapple

Soak granulated gelatine in cold water; dissolve in boiling water and add to canned pineapple syrup combined with lemon juice and sugar. Then, heat mixture to the boiling point, strain while hot; chill until mixture begins to congeal, and beat until light. Lastly fold in the stiffly whipped heavy cream. Freeze in refrigerator tray, molded or unmolded, for 3½ to 4 hours. You may freeze, that is pack, after molding in hand freezer pail, using equal parts ice and rock salt, for 3 hours.

STRAWBERRY MOUSSE   [2434]
(Hand freezer pail or refrigerator tray)

Of course, the amount of sugar may be less or more, according to sweetness of the berries.

| 1 cup strained strawberry pulp and juice | ¼ teaspoon salt |
| 1 teaspoon lemon juice | 1 pint heavy cream, whipped stiff |

¾ cup powdered sugar

Combine fresh strawberry pulp and juice, which have been strained through a fine sieve, lemon juice, powdered sugar (more or less) and salt. Mix thoroughly and chill. Then fold in the stiffly whipped heavy cream and freeze 3½ to 4 hours in refrigerator tray, or 3 hours in hand freezer pail (when molded).

VANILLA (or other flavorings) MOUSSE   [2435]
(*Hand freezer or refrigerator tray*)

| 1 cup heavy cream whipped stiff | ⅛ teaspoon salt |
| ¼ scant cup powdered sugar | ½ generous teaspoon vanilla extract |

1 egg white, stiffly beaten

Fold into the stiffly whipped heavy cream, the powdered sugar, salt and vanilla extract; then fold in the stiffly beaten egg white. Freeze.

PARFAITS   [2436]

Parfait, which means "perfect" in English, differs from ice cream in that it is less cold and more creamy, which makes this French creation more delicate. The name "PARFAIT," which used to apply exclusively to "Coffee Parfait," has become very popular in America. Sometimes parfaits are called "Bombes" when their composition is of only one kind of flavoring, their preparation is similar to the bombes, which consist of a thick creamy mixture, in which the same amount of whipped cream is incorporated, before being frozen.

Parfaits may be molded or served in special chilled glasses. They are much appreciated because they do not require special treatment, and are classed among the light ice creams. They may be made with almost any kind of fruit, canned, fresh or dried, as well as with almost any kind of sweet cordials or liqueurs or dessert wines. Whiskey, however, is not recommended.

To freeze a parfait in mechanical refrigerator, pack in tray, or mold and place in tray and freeze until firm, or about 2½ hours. To freeze in hand freezer pail, fill mold or molds to overflowing. Cover with buttered paper, then with buttered muslin or cheesecloth around the rim, to prevent salt water from entering into the creamy mixture; or rub butter around rim of the mold or molds, and let stand for about two hours if in small molds, and 3 to 3½ hours if large molds. Use equal parts of ice and rock salt, over and around the molds, turning off the salt water as it accumulates, before it reaches the top of the molds.

In almost every parfait recipe, the basic foundation is a sugar syrup cooked to the indicated stage or degree, egg whites, cream or undiluted whipped evaporated milk, flavoring, and in some granulated gelatine is used as a stabilizer.

ANGEL PARFAIT [2437]

¾ cup water
⅔ cup granulated sugar
3 egg whites, stiffly beaten

¼ scant teaspoon salt
2 cups (1 pint) heavy cream, whipped
  stiff
1 scant teaspoon vanilla extract

Stir sugar into water and boil until syrup spins a thread when dropped from tip of spoon. Immediately pour in a fine stream on to stiffly beaten egg whites, beating briskly and constantly until mixture is cool. Lastly fold in the stiffly whipped heavy cream with salt and vanilla extract. Freeze as directed for recipe No. 2436.

APRICOT PARFAIT [2438]

In the following recipe dried cooked apricots are used. The binding is made with cornstarch added to the custard, and undiluted evaporated milk, whipped stiff, adds smoothness, since its butterfat and solid substances hold air bubbles and prevent crystallization.

16 dried, cooked apricots, sieved
⅓ cup evaporated milk, diluted with
⅔ cup hot water
1 tablespoon cornstarch
A little cold water
2 egg yolks, stiffly beaten

⅔ cup granulated sugar
¼ teaspoon salt
½ teaspoon granulated gelatine
1 tablespoon cold water
⅔ cup undiluted evaporated milk,
  whipped stiff
4 to 5 drops almond extract

Wash dried apricots, rinse, add ½ cup cold water, and let soak overnight, after cutting into small pieces. Cook to a mush, and put through a sieve. Combine ⅓ cup undiluted evaporated milk and hot water in a double boiler, stir in the cornstarch which has been mixed with a little cold water, then stir in the thickly beaten egg yolks with the granulated sugar. Cook over hot water until mixture coats the spoon, stirring constantly. Then, add gelatine which has been soaked in 1 tablespoon cold water and continue cooking until gelatine is dissolved. Pour through a double cheesecloth, then over sieved apricots and mix thoroughly. Chill. Add stiffly whipped undiluted evaporated milk (see recipe No. 2357) to which has been added the salt and almond extract. Freeze.

CHOCOLATE PARFAIT [2439]
(Hand freezer pail or refrigerator tray)

½ cup water
½ cup granulated sugar
¼ teaspoon salt
1 scant teaspoon granulated gelatine

2 tablespoons cold water
2 egg yolks, well-beaten
1 cup heavy cream, whipped stiff
1½ teaspoons vanilla extract
2 squares bitter chocolate

Boil the ½ cup water, sugar and salt until syrup spins a thread when dropped from the tip of a spoon. Then stir in the grated bitter chocolate which has been melted over hot water, and immediately pour chocolate syrup in a fine stream on to well-beaten egg yolks, beating briskly and constantly. Then add granulated gelatine which has been soaked in the 2 tablespoons of cold water, and continue beating until gelatine is dissolved. Cool, stirring occasionally. Fold in stiffly whipped heavy cream and vanilla extract. Freeze.

COFFEE PARFAIT   [2440]
(*Hand freezer pail or refrigerator tray*)

1½ cups rich milk, scalded
1½ cups extra strong coffee liquid
4 egg yolks beaten with

¼ scant teaspoon salt, and
½ generous cup granulated sugar
½ teaspoon vanilla extract

¼ scant cup of good rum

Scald milk, remove from the fire and combine with strong coffee liquid. Place egg yolks in a saucepan with salt and sugar and beat mercilessly until thoroughly blended and almost white. Then pour hot milk mixture in a fine stream into beaten egg yolk mixture, beating briskly and constantly. Return this mixture to the fire, and cook, stirring constantly, until mixture coats the spoon. Strain through double cheesecloth. Fill a melon mold to overflowing with the creamy mixture and freeze, either in hand freezer pail or refrigerator tray, until mushy. Then add and stir in the vanilla extract combined with the rum (curaçao liqueur, or brandy may be substituted for rum, if desired), and continue freezing until solid, or about 2½ hours or longer, according to size of mold. Unmold on to a chilled serving platter, and garnish with plain whipped cream forced through a pastry bag with a fancy tube.

GOLDEN PARFAIT   [2441]
(*Hand freezer pail or refrigerator tray*)

¾ cup granulated sugar
⅓ cup boiling water
3 egg yolks, beaten until light

⅛ teaspoon salt
2 cups heavy cream, whipped stiff
1¾ teaspoons vanilla extract

Make a sugar syrup with water and sugar, cooking it until it threads (230° F.), that is, spins a thread from tip of a spoon. Immediately pour in a fine stream on to beaten light egg yolks, beating briskly and constantly until mixture is cool. Chill, then fold in stiffly whipped heavy cream and vanilla extract, and freeze.

MAPLE PARFAIT   [2442]
(*Hand freezer pail or refrigerator tray*)

⅔ cup hot maple syrup
4 whole eggs, slightly beaten

1 pint heavy cream, whipped stiff
¼ teaspoonful salt

Pour in a fine stream on to the slightly beaten whole eggs, the hot maple syrup, beating briskly and constantly. Return mixture to double boiler and cook, stirring constantly, until mixture coats the spoons. Cool, then add stiffly whipped heavy cream with the salt. Freeze.

MARRON GLACÉ PARFAIT [2443]
(Hand freezer pail or refrigerator tray)

¼ cup water
⅔ cup granulated sugar
6 egg yolks, thickly beaten
1 cup marrons, cut in small pieces (See recipe No. 2400, Marron Glacé Ice Cream.)

3 generous teaspoons vanilla extract
2 cups heavy cream, whipped stiff

Make a sugar syrup with water and sugar, stir until sugar is dissolved, bring to the boiling point, and let boil for 5 long minutes without stirring, or until syrup spins a thread from tip of the spoon. Immediately pour in fine stream over the thickly beaten egg yolks, while beating briskly and constantly. Return to double boiler and cook, over hot water, stirring constantly until mixture coats the spoon. Remove from hot water and beat until cold. Then, add cooked marrons, as indicated for recipe No. 2400, which have been cut in small pieces and soaked in the vanilla extract for at least 30 minutes after being cooked and drained. Do not add the vanilla extract remaining in the bowl, reserve it for other use, if any, because the chestnuts will have absorbed the greater part of it. Fold in the stiffly whipped heavy cream, and freeze.

If fresh chestnuts are not available, or are out of season use dried ones, or you may substitute chopped nuts, or macaroon crumbs.

MOCHA PARFAIT (French method) [2444]
(Hand freezer only)

Place in a mixing bowl 8 egg yolks with ¼ teaspoon salt and ¼ cup cold water, and using rotary egg beater, beat the eggs until almost white. Then, continuing beating, pour in fine stream 1 cup of extra strong coffee liquid which has been heated to the boiling point. Beat rapidly and constantly, while adding gradually ½ generous cup of powdered sugar. Cook, over hot water, stirring constantly until mixture begins to coat the spoon. Remove from the fire, and stir in rapidly and briskly 1½ to 2 bitter chocolate squares, melted over hot water. Chill, then fold in 2 cups heavy cream stiffly whipped with 1½ teaspoons vanilla extract. Mold; bury in equal parts of ice and salt and let stand for 2 long hours. This parfait should be mellow and very light. Unmold onto a chilled platter, and decorate with small rosettes of whipped cream, forced through a pastry bag with a small fancy tube; or spoon into chilled parfait glasses, and top with whipped cream, also forced through a pastry bag.

RASPBERRY PARFAIT   [2445]
(*Hand freezer pail or refrigerator tray*)

2 pints fresh raspberries	2 egg whites
1 cup granulated sugar	⅛ generous teaspoon salt
2 teaspoons lemon juice	1 cup heavy cream, whipped stiff

Wash, drain, and rub fresh raspberries through a sieve. Sprinkle over the sieved raspberries the granulated sugar and lemon juice, and let stand 30 minutes. Strain through a double cheesecloth, and bring the raspberry juice to a boil. Let boil until syrup spins a thread when dropped from the tip of a spoon. Immediately pour in a fine stream onto stiffly beaten egg whites, while beating briskly and constantly, until cold and mixture holds its peaks. Then fold in the stiffly whipped heavy cream with the salt, and freeze.

Important. You may, if desired, proceed thus: To the sieved raspberries add ¾ cup of the sugar and lemon juice. Beat egg whites with the salt and remaining ¼ cup of granulated sugar, a small amount at a time. Then fold in this meringue, alternately with the stiffly whipped cream into the strained raspberry juice, blending thoroughly. Freeze as indicated above. This method, called the meringue method, eliminates cooking of the syrup. Yet, the smoothness is not the same.

STRAWBERRY PARFAIT   [2446]
(*Hand freezer pail or refrigerator tray*)

Proceed exactly as indicated for recipe No. 2445, Raspberry Parfait, substituting fresh strawberries for raspberries. Freeze as directed.

SHERBETS   [2447]

Sherbet originated in Turkey where it is very popular. In a sherbet there is a very large proportion of liquid or fruit juice, hence special treatment is required to keep the texture solid and smooth. Beaten egg whites, marshmallow and gelatine are used most as stabilizers. As in ice cream, parfaits, ices and mousses, there is no limit to the varieties of sherbets.

Like refrigerator ice cream, sherbets should be stirred once, or twice while freezing, before they get too hard and after they are about half frozen or mushy. They should be scraped up from the sides and bottom of the tray, or molded with a large spoon and then returned to the refrigerator tray to continue freezing until solid. If they are stirred too soon, they will infallibly return to their original liquid state. If they freeze too hard, it will be difficult to stir them to a very smooth mush without beating so hard that the air which was included with the stabilizer—whipped cream, beaten egg whites, marshmallows or gelatine—is irredeemably lost. This operation is not required when using a hand crank freezer.

The mixture should be thoroughly chilled for this saves time in freezing. Whichever method of freezing is used, hand freezer or refrigerator tray, the mold or tray should not be more than ¾ full, as the constant stirring during the freezing process beats in air, causing the mixture to increase in bulk.

The reason that the freezing process takes longer in a refrigerator tray than in the hand freezer is because of the temperature of the ice chamber. (26 to 30° F.)

Sherbets are usually served in special sherbet glasses, always chilled before filling, yet they may be molded in large or individual molds. Seldom is a sauce served with a sherbet. The sherbet may be served either as an appetizer, a digestive or a dessert. If served to help digestion, this should be done immediately after the roast, and it should be eaten very slowly. For this purpose, sherbets have no equal.

Almost any sherbet, as well as water or fruit ice, may be made into a delicious flavored beverage, especially when the mixture is made with a syrup base. And, any water or fruit ice may be made into sherbets by the addition of two stiffly beaten egg whites or 1½ teaspoons of granulated gelatine which has been soaked in cold water and dissolved over hot water or steam.

You may color almost any kind of sherbet to the desired hue, using vegetable coloring.

CHAMPAGNE SHERBET I   [2448]
(*Hand freezer only*)

Very appropriate for a dinner party of 12 people, and to be served right after the roast. For 6 servings, use half of the ingredients and serve in chilled sherbet glasses.

½ cup granulated sugar	¼ teaspoon salt
1 cup water	1 pint dry champagne, chilled
Grated rind of ½ lemon	Juice of 1 lemon
Grated rind of 1 orange	Juice of 4 oranges
1 (extra) pint dry champagne, chilled	

Make a sugar syrup with sugar and water, and boil until syrup spins a thin thread when dropped from the tip of a spoon; then stir in the lemon and orange rinds and salt. Let stand 10 long minutes. Then stir in the previously chilled pint of champagne, juices of lemon and orange. Stir, chill, then freeze in hand freezer, using 5 parts ice and 1 part salt, until mushy. Stir and add the second pint of chilled champagne, stirring constantly. Pack and allow to stand in 6 parts ice and 1 part rock salt for 1 hour. Serve in chilled sherbet glasses.

A less expensive method is the following:

CHAMPAGNE SHERBET II   [2449]
(*Hand freezer only*)

1½ cups water	Juice of 2 oranges
¾ cup granulated sugar	¼ teaspoon salt
Grated rind of ½ orange	1 pony brandy (about 1½ tablespoons)
Juice of 2 lemons	½ cup chilled champagne

Make a sugar syrup with the water and sugar, and cook until syrup spins a thread when dropped from the tip of a spoon. Remove from the fire and add grated orange rind and the fruit juices. Strain through a double cheesecloth. Chill. When well-chilled, combine syrup mixture with the chilled pint of champagne and freeze, using 5 parts ice and 1 part rock salt, until almost solid. Pack, using equal parts of ice and salt, for 1 hour, and when ready to serve, stir in the combined pony of brandy and the ½ cup of chilled champagne. Serve in sherbet glasses.

CITRUS SHERBET   [2450]
(*Hand freezer or refrigerator tray*)

The following sherbet, in great favor on the Pacific Coast as well as in Florida, if prepared as indicated, is one of the most digestive and delicious of the sherbet family. You may use blood oranges, if a beautiful color effect is desired.

3 cups granulated sugar	¼ scant teaspoon salt
3 cups water	Juice of 3 oranges
Grated rind of 1 orange	Juice of 3 lemons
3 bananas, sieved	3 egg whites, stiffly beaten

Make a sugar syrup with sugar, water and grated rind of 1 orange. Boil for 5 minutes. Chill. Add banana pulp (sieved) combined and thoroughly blended with the fruit juices and salt. Then, fold in the stiffly beaten egg whites. Freeze either in refrigerator tray, without stirring, for 3 hours, or in hand freezer, using 3 parts ice and 1 part rock salt until almost solid. Pack, remove dasher, and let stand 1 hour, using equal parts of ice and salt. Serve in chilled sherbet glasses.

CRANBERRY SHERBET   [2451]
(*Hand freezer only*)

1 lb. fresh cranberries	¼ scant teaspoon salt
2 cups water	Juice of a medium-sized lemon
1¼ cups granulated sugar	Grated rind of 1 orange
1 cup orange juice	2 egg whites, stiffly beaten

Cook washed, picked over cranberries and water for 10 minutes, or until berries pop. While hot rub through a fine sieve. There should be 2 cups of juice, if not add enough hot water to compensate. To the still hot cranberry juice add sugar and stir until dissolved. Boil once, remove from the fire, and strain through a double cheesecloth. Then, add orange juice, salt, lemon juice and grated rind of 1 orange. Fold in stiffly beaten egg whites and freeze in hand freezer, using 6 parts ice and 1 part rock salt, turning crank slowly and steadily to insure smooth fine grained mixture. Freeze until almost solid. Remove dasher, let the water run, and pack in 4 parts ice and 1 part rock salt for 1 hour. Serve in chilled sherbet glasses.

GRAPE JUICE SHERBET [2452]
(Hand freezer or refrigerator tray)

1 cup of grape (fresh) juice
1 cup boiling water
½ cup granulated sugar
⅛ teaspoon salt
1 teaspoon gelatine (granulated)
1 tablespoon cold water
2 cups milk, chilled

Make a sugar syrup of boiling water and sugar and boil for 5 short minutes. Remove from the fire and add gelatine which has been soaked for 5 minutes in cold water, and stir until mixture is well-blended. Strain. Cool and chill. Lastly add combined fresh grape juice and chilled milk. Freeze, if using hand freezer, with 3 parts ice and 1 part rock salt, for 1½ to 2 hours. Pack, using 5 parts ice and 1 part rock salt, for 1 short hour to mellow and ripen. If using refrigerator tray, freeze, without stirring for 3 hours. Serve in chilled sherbet glasses.

LEMON SHERBET [2453]
(Hand freezer or refrigerator tray)

2 cups water
¾ cup granulated sugar
1 teaspoon grated lemon rind
2 teaspoons granulated gelatine
4 tablespoons cold water
⅛ teaspoon salt (generous)
⅓ cup lemon juice
2 egg whites, stiffly beaten

Combine water, sugar and grated lemon rind; bring to the boiling point, then let simmer for 10 minutes. Remove from the fire and stir in the granulated gelatine which has been soaked in cold water; add the salt, stir, then strain through double cheesecloth and chill. When well chilled stir in the lemon juice, and freeze as indicated for recipe No. 2452, Grape Juice Sherbet, until mushy. Then stir well and fold in the stiffly beaten egg whites and freeze again until creamy mixture begins to solidify, and stir again to break up the ice crystals. Return to freezer or tray, and continue freezing until solid. Serve in chilled sherbet glasses.

LEMON MILK SHERBET [2454]
(Hand freezer or refrigerator tray)

1 quart milk
1½ cups granulated sugar
¼ teaspoon salt
2 teaspoons granulated gelatine
¾ cup lemon juice

Soak gelatine in ½ cup of cold milk and dissolve over hot water. When thoroughly dissolved, add to remaining milk; then add combined lemon juice, sugar and salt. Mix thoroughly, then freeze as indicated for recipe No. 2452, Grape Juice Sherbet. Serve in well-chilled sherbet glasses.

You may substitute buttermilk for fresh milk if desired.

LIME SHERBET [2455]
(Refrigerator tray only)

This fine sherbet is very appropriate for roast lamb instead of the traditional mint jelly or sauce.

⅔ cup granulated sugar
1½ cups water
1 teaspoon granulated gelatine
1 tablespoon cold water

4 drops green vegetable coloring
Juice of 5 fresh limes, strained or not
2 egg whites, stiffly beaten
⅛ generous teaspoon salt

Combine sugar and water and stir until sugar is thoroughly dissolved; bring to the boiling point and let simmer for 10 minutes. Then add the granulated gelatine, which has been soaked in cold water, and stir until gelatine is dissolved. Cool, then chill. Stir in 4 drops of green vegetable coloring, alternately with the lime juice (strained or unstrained). Freeze in refrigerator tray until mushy; remove from refrigerator and beat until fluffy, folding in at the same time the stiffly beaten egg whites and salt. Return to tray, and freeze again for 30 minutes, beat again, return to tray and freeze for 2½ hours. Serve in chilled sherbet glasses.

MINT SHERBET [2456]
(Hand freezer or refrigerator tray)

To a Lemon Ice (No. 2371), add 4 tablespoons bruised mint leaves to the boiling syrup. Strain and freeze as directed. A delicious side dish to hot or cold lamb, or any kind of cut or assorted cold cuts.

ORANGE MILK SHERBET [2457]
(Hand freezer only)

¾ cup undiluted evaporated milk or heavy cream, unwhipped, but thoroughly chilled
1 cup granulated sugar

⅛ generous teaspoon salt
½ cup hot water
1 cup orange juice
1 tablespoon lemon juice
1 teaspoon grated orange rind

Chill milk in refrigerator or a pan of chopped ice. Boil sugar, salt and water for 5 minutes, beginning after boiling point is reached. Remove from the fire and add orange and lemon juice and grated rind of orange. Let stand for 10 minutes, then chill. Pour chilled mixture into chilled cream or evaporated milk and freeze in hand freezer, using 4 parts ice and 1 part salt, until solid but not too hard. Serve in chilled sherbet glasses, orange cups, or cantaloupe halves.

Variations Using Orange Milk Sherbet

With Peaches and Strawberries. Arrange sliced peaches (fresh or canned) and strawberries in chilled sherbet glasses. Sprinkle over with minced maraschino cherries, green or red, and set in refrigerator until needed. Just before serving, fill the glasses with orange milk sherbet.

With Pineapple and Strawberries. Mix ⅔ cup, each, fresh shredded pineapple and strawberries, cut in quarters. Sprinkle with ¼ cup powdered sugar. Cover and let stand in a cold place (refrigerator) for 2 long hours—the longer the better. When ready to serve, put mixture in equal parts in 6 sherbet glasses, which have been chilled, and cover with orange milk sherbet. You may top with a rosette of unsweetened whipped cream or undiluted evaporated milk, if desired.

PINEAPPLE MARASCHINO CHERRY SHERBET [2458]
(Hand freezer or refrigerator tray)

2 teaspoons granulated gelatine	1 cup pineapple juice
¼ cup cold water	½ cup canned crushed pineapple
½ cup granulated sugar	2 tablespoons lemon juice
1¾ cups water	¼ scant teaspoon salt

½ cup quartered maraschino cherries (red or green)

Soak granulated gelatine in the ¼ cup cold water for 5 minutes. Make a syrup of sugar and remaining 1¾ cups of water, bring to the boiling point, and allow to boil gently for 5 minutes. Remove from the fire, cool a little, then stir in the combined pineapple juice, crushed pineapple, lemon juice, salt and quartered maraschino cherries. Chill. Freeze in either hand freezer or refrigerator tray as indicated for recipe No. 2452, Grape Juice Sherbet, without stirring until solid, but not too hard. Serve in chilled sherbet glasses, orange cups or cantaloupe halves, also chilled.

PINEAPPLE SHERBET [2459]
(Hand freezer or refrigerator tray)

1 cup granulated sugar	1½ tablespoons cold water
3 cups boiling water	2 cups canned crushed pineapple
1 teaspoon granulated gelatine	Juice of 1 lemon, rind of half
¼ teaspoon salt	2 egg whites stiffly beaten

Boil sugar and boiling water for 5 long minutes. Add granulated gelatine which has been softened in cold water, and stir until thoroughly dissolved. Cool, then combine with crushed pineapple, lemon juice and rind, mix well and stir in, very gently, the egg whites stiffly beaten with the salt. Freeze either in hand freezer or refrigerator tray, until solid and without stirring. If hand freezer is used, use 4 parts ice and 1 part of rock salt. Serve either in chilled sherbet glasses, orange cups, cantaloupe halves or in paper cases.

RASPBERRY MILK SHERBET I   [2460]
(Hand freezer only)

A very economical way of making this refreshing frozen dessert when raspberries are out of season is to use canned raspberries, operating as follows:

1 cup canned raspberries	⅛ teaspoon salt
2 cups chilled milk	Juice of 1 lemon
½ cup granulated sugar	1½ teaspoons vanilla extract

Force canned raspberries through a sieve. Add chilled milk, sugar, salt, lemon juice and vanilla extract. Blend thoroughly, and freeze as indicated for recipe No. 2452, Grape Juice Sherbet, until solid but not too hard. Serve in chilled sherbet glasses, or chilled orange cups or cantaloupe halves.

You may use fresh raspberries, if desired.

RASPBERRY SHERBET II   [2461]
(Hand freezer or refrigerator tray)

This recipe results in a rich, nourishing frozen dessert. The creamy mixture should be stirred, when mushy, or about 30 minutes after being placed in the tray, and 15 minutes after being churned in the hand freezer.

1½ cups granulated sugar	1 tablespoon lemon juice
1 tablespoon corn syrup	1 quart fresh raspberries
⅔ cup boiling water	½ cup heavy cream, whipped stiff
2 egg whites stiffly beaten	¼ scant teaspoon salt

Cook sugar, corn syrup and boiling water until syrup spins a fine thread (238° F.). Immediately pour in a fine stream over stiffly beaten egg whites which have been salted, while beating briskly and constantly. Then add lemon juice combined with fresh raspberries, which have been forced through a sieve, alternately with the stiffly whipped heavy cream. Freeze either in hand freezer, or refrigerator tray, until mushy; scrape bottom and sides, then beat for 1 short minute and continue freezing until solid, but not too hard. Serve according to fancy. A good suggestion is to serve this sherbet in fresh scooped yellow apples. The effect is really tempting.

STRAWBERRY SHERBET   [2462]
(*Hand freezer or refrigerator tray*)

2½ cups strawberry pulp and juice   ⅛ teaspoon salt
¾ cup granulated sugar   2 egg whites, stiffly beaten

Combine strawberry pulp and juice with sugar and salt, and chill for 1 long hour; then freeze as indicated for recipe No. 2452, Grape Juice Sherbet, until mushy. Stir in the stiffly beaten egg whites, and continue freezing until solid, but not too hard. Serve in chilled sherbet glasses or orange cups or cantaloupe halves.

Chapter Twenty-One

PRESSURE COOKERY

" . . . *We may live without poetry, music and art,*
We may live without conscience, and live without heart;
We may live without friends; we may live without books;
But civilized man cannot live without cooks!

****

He may live without books—what is knowledge but grieving?
He may live without hope—what is hope but deceiving?
He may live without love—what is passion but pining?
BUT where is the man that can live without dining?

—*Owen Meredith.*

S AVE FUEL. DON'T WASTE IT IN YOUR KITCHEN. MAKE EVERY bit of heat cook for its keep. With either an electric or gas range, always start your cooking as quickly as possible by turning the heating unit or burner on high. Then when the food begins to cook, reduce the heat to a point that will maintain a cooking temperature. See that all gas burners are properly adjusted to burn with a clear blue flame at the right height. A yellow flame means you're wasting fuel. The gas company will adjust them on request.

Remember that gently boiling water is just as hot as water that boils vigorously, so don't waste fuel by boiling water at full speed. Use flat-bottom pans that are the same size or slightly larger than the heating unit. Pans that are too small waste heat. Always cover the container in which water is heated.

One of the best methods to save fuel is to cook foods in a pressure cooker, and it is better to have two of them than only one.

Along with the gnomes, elves and fairies of childhood myths has vanished the "like-mother-used-to-make" fable. Unloyal though is may seem, doubts have hovered for some time over the minds of many of us as to just how good mother's cooking was, compared to the modern variety! You see, cooking has been reduced to such a scientific basis that nearly every cook can make "the eatin'est victuals" ever tasted, in a pressure cooker. Few of us have sighed for the "good old days" as far as cooking is concerned. And why should we? The modern cook doesn't have to make her own cheese before she can bake Bill's favorite cheesecake. Too, she knows that an egg is an egg as long as it is fresh—and not too fresh for an angel food cake! Yesterday's cooks advised the use of brown-shelled eggs because "they taste richer."

Gone are the days when food was hung in the well for cooling. Gone, too, are the days when milk cans flanked the brook's edge. Correct temperatures, measuring and the right proportions mean perfect results, especially in a pressure pan cooker. We even have fats for frying which don't smoke or smell up the house. Instead their mild odors urge the appetite on to new strides. It would be interesting to know who is responsible for the change in cooking. Was it a henpecked husband or a discouraged bride who decided that there must be some way to take the guessing out of cooking? Anyhow, no matter what knowing old Solomon it was, cooking in the modern pressure cooker is something for which to be thankful. Not only does it save fuel, but also time, patience and dishes to wash—and money, too. Keeping within a budget is a key to happiness.

A FEW DO'S AND DON'TS IN PRESSURE COOKERY [2464]

DO purchase a pressure cooker branded by a well-known manufacturer, and see to it that a direction booklet accompanies the purchase, giving the directions as to its uses, how to handle it, and the whys and wherefores.

DO start cooking over high heat, except in the case of dried foods such as vegetables, beans, peas, lentils, macaroni, noodles, spaghetti and the like cereals, rice, etc., which should be always started over low heat.

DO always prepare your food as if it were to be cooked in the ordinary way—that is, cleaning, paring, cutting, washing, etc.

DO always reduce pressure at once, when cooking time is up, thus preventing overcooking.

DO reduce heat once pressure is built up.

DO set the timer for time required for cooking.

DO cook frozen vegetables as you would fresh ones, remembering, however, that a shorter cooking time is required.

DO always tilt the lid of a pressure cooker toward you when removing it so that any steam left is directed away from the face.

DO always wash a pressure cooker in fairly hot soapy water after use; and keep uncovered after drying thoroughly.

DON'T leave your kitchen when cooking in a pressure cooker. If you have to go to open the door or answer the telephone, remove the pressure cooker from the heat, and when you come back, return it to the heat.

DON'T try to remove the lid until pressure has subsided. This is very important, as it may cause serious steam burns.

DON'T become alarmed if water bubbles on lid of your pressure cooker, this is excess steam which has condensed and dripped from the vent pipe.

DON'T fill the pan to more than two-thirds with the liquid and solid, to prevent clogging the steam outlet and to leave room for expansion and steam outlet.

DON'T start cooking in a pressure cooker unless lid is tight and well adjusted.

HOW TO STUDY A RECIPE   [2465]

A recipe is a bit of experience handed down for us to make useful. Some one experimented at some time long ago, perhaps failed at first, tried again, finally succeeded, and passed on the result by word of mouth to others. There were doubtless good cooks long before there were printed or written recipes. Some recipes, however, have been handed down from Roman times, and recipes were printed as early as the fifteenth century. Modern recipes are much more accurate than the old, as you may see if you have opportunity to read some old cook book.

In using a recipe, follow its directions exactly. Notice the proportions and read twice carefully the directions for combining the ingredients, noting those points that are most important, especially in pressure cooking. Have the whole process well in mind before you begin work. Read carefully the instructions in a small booklet always given with each cooker. Do not let it be necessary to refer to the printed page at every move you make. This is poor technique.

When the use of a recipe is preceded by some simple experiment that makes the basic principle clear, it is much easier to use the recipe with intelligence. When you are no longer a novice you may take liberties with a recipe, even a new one, scanning it with a critical eye, and perhaps giving it a cool welcome. It may not be new at all! For this is the secret of recipes: There are really only a few, and the key to their use is the recognition of the old in a new garb. Each kind of prepared dish has one, or two, or three basic forms or mixtures. Learn these, and then with experience you will become inventive and make your own variations.

TEMPERATURE OF STEAM [2466]
(Provided air has been driven from cooker)

5 pounds of steam pressure equal	228° F.
10 pounds of steam pressure equal	240° F.
15 pounds of steam pressure equal	250° F.
20 pounds of steam pressure equal	259° F.
25 pounds of steam pressure equal	267° F.

ALTITUDE CORRECTIONS TO TIME TABLES [2467]

Note. *The table below shows the number of pounds pressure that should be added to the pressure given above.*

ELEVATION ABOVE SEA LEVEL	BOILING POINT OF WATER	EXTRA POUNDS PRESSURE ADDED TO PRESSURE COOKER TIME TABLE OF TEMPERATURE OF STEAM BY POUND
2,000 feet	212° F. below	0 pound
3,000 feet	208° F. above	1 pound
4,000 feet	206° F. above	2 pounds
5,000 feet	204° F. above	3 pounds
6,000 feet	202° F. above	3 pounds
7,000 feet	201° F. above	4 pounds

PRESSURE COOKER CHART FOR FRESH VEGETABLES [2468]

KIND OF VEGETABLE	PRELIMINARY PREPARATION	AMOUNT OF LIQUID (Water, stock or wine)	MINUTES AFTER STEAM IS AT 15 POUNDS	RE-DUCE PRES-SURE
ARTICHOKE (*Globe*)	Remove imperfect leaves; trim stem; soak, head down, in salted lukewarm water; drain; place in cooker, heads up; add salt and pepper to taste. When done, serve hot with hollandaise, cream or butter sauce, or cold with French dressing or vinaigrette	½ cup of stock or water, salted and peppered.	8–10 minutes (according to size)	At once
ARTICHOKE (*Jerusalem*)	Rub in a towel with coarse salt or peel thinly; slice or cut in uniform pieces or halves if medium-sized. When done, mash or serve as is, with parsley or plain butter, or cold with French dressing or vinaigrette. If mashed, season like mashed potatoes.	⅓ cup of meat stock or water, salted and peppered.	10 minutes	At once
ASPARAGUS (*Tips*)	Scrape and cut tough portion. Tie in portion bundles. When done, drain well and serve hot with hollandaise, cream or butter sauce. If large, cook 3 minutes longer. If served cold, serve with French dressing, mayonnaise or vinaigrette.	¼ cup of water, salted.	2 minutes	At once
ASPARAGUS (*Tough part*)	For cream soup	⅓ cup of water, salted.	5 minutes	At once
BEANS (*Green, Frenched*)	Wash quickly, drain, cut into strips, and when done, drain and season with parsley butter or cream sauce.	¼ cup salted water.	½ to 1 minute	At once
BEANS (*Green and cut in lozenges*)	Wash, string, cut into lozenges, and when done season with butter, salt, pepper and nutmeg to taste. Toss with chopped parsley.	¼ cup salted water.	1 minute	At once
BEANS (*Green, whole*)	Wash, string, cook, and when done season with butter, chopped chives or parsley, salt, pepper and nutmeg.	¼ to ⅓ cup of salted water.	3 minutes	At once

PRESSURE COOKER CHART FOR [2468]
FRESH VEGETABLES

KIND OF VEGETABLE	PRELIMINARY PREPARATION	AMOUNT OF LIQUID (Water, stock or wine)	MINUTES AFTER STEAM IS AT 15 POUNDS	RE-DUCE PRES-SURE
BEANS (*Wax or yellow, Frenched, cut or whole*)	Proceed as for green beans, either Frenched, cut into lozenges or whole, following directions for each kind of bean. Either green or yellow may be served in salad form, when cold.	⅓ cup of salted water.	Follow directions for each kind of green beans.	At once
BEANS (*Soy in pod and shelled*)	Wash carefully and blanch the unshelled soy beans 5 minutes. Drain; cook in shells; drain and toss in cream, brown, tomato or butter sauce, highly seasoned with salt, pepper, clove and mace to taste. May be served cold (pods or shelled) in salad form.	½ cup of salted water in pods. ⅓ cup of water shelled.	1½ minutes in pods. Same shelled.	At once
BEETS (*Diced*)	Wash; scrub; dice, peel or not, and when done season with butter, salt, pepper and nutmeg to taste, or toss in orange juice, sour cream or lemon butter. If served cold, serve in salad form with equal parts of diced, cooked potatoes.	¼ cup of water or orange or grapefruit juice.	5 minutes	At once
BEETS (*Sliced*)	Wash, scrub, peel, slice, and when done sauté in butter. Season to taste with salt, pepper, cloves and chopped parsley. If served cold, add to green salad, or toss in sour cream for salad, appetizer or relish.	¼ cup of cold water.	7 minutes	At once
BEETS (*Whole, small and young*)	Wash, scrub, do not peel; leave 2 inches of stem. When done, slip skins and sauté in butter, or as Harvard beets, or with hot mayonnaise.	½ cup of slightly salted water.	10–12 minutes, depending on size.	At once
BEETS (*Greens*)	Wash thoroughly, discard spoiled leaves and stems, if old; if young leave them on. Coarsely chop. When done, season with salt, pepper, nutmeg and grated onion, then butter generously. If served cold, serve in salad form.	¼ cup of slightly salted water.	3 minutes	At once

PRESSURE COOKER CHART FOR FRESH VEGETABLES　　　　[2468]

KIND OF VEGETABLE	PRELIMINARY PREPARATION	AMOUNT OF LIQUID (Water, stock or wine)	MINUTES AFTER STEAM IS AT 15 POUNDS	RE-DUCE PRES-SURE
BEETS (*Large*)	Cook as indicated for whole, small and young beets. When done, slice or dice and serve in cream, cheese, egg or hot mayonnaise sauce. Or cool and add sliced or diced to green salad.	½ cup of slightly salted water.	20 minutes	At once
BROCCOLI	Same as asparagus, which see.			
BRUSSELS SPROUTS	Wash in lukewarm, salted water after removing wilted leaves and part of stems. When done, serve plain and seasoned with salt, pepper and nutmeg; butter generously. Or mash like potatoes, or spinach. Or sauté in butter until slightly brown, together with bread croutons.	¼ cup of salted water.	1½ to 2 minutes	At once
CABBAGE (*Shredded, new*)	Discard wilted leaves, wash in slightly salted lukewarm water; drain. When done, butter and season with salt and plenty of black pepper, or bacon sauce, cream, sour, or cheese sauce, pan-fried or cook with raisins, au gratin, etc.	¼ cup water or ⅓ cup of milk.	2 minutes	At once
CABBAGE (*Wedges, new*)	Discard wilted leaves, quarter or cut in wedges; wash in salted, lukewarm water. Drain and squeeze gently. When done, season with salt and plenty of black pepper and a dash of clove to taste, and toss in melted butter, or serve very hot with egg sauce, caper sauce or tomato sauce.	⅓ cup of slightly salted water.	4 minutes	At once
CABBAGE (*Whole, new*)	Discard wilted leaves, soak in lukewarm, slightly acidulated water for 25 minutes, to dislodge insects or sand. When done, cut in wedges or quarters and serve with sour-sweet, tomato, ham or bacon sauce.	½ cup of slightly salted water or cider.	10 minutes	At once
CABBAGE (*Old*)	Requires 2 minutes additional time on each form above. When done, serve as new on each form.			

PRESSURE COOKER CHART FOR FRESH VEGETABLES [2468]

KIND OF VEGETABLE	PRELIMINARY PREPARATION	AMOUNT OF LIQUID (Water, stock or wine)	MINUTES AFTER STEAM IS AT 15 POUNDS	RE-DUCE PRES-SURE
CABBAGE (*Red*)	Same preparation as green or white cabbage on each form, except that apple, pared, cored, and chopped or quartered is added in equal parts.			
CARDOON (*Stalks*)	The stalks are cooked like cabbage after being washed, dried and diced and are served in cream, tomato, brown, or mushroom sauce.			
CARDOON (*Leaves*)	The leaves are cooked and seasoned like beet greens.			
CARROTS (*Sliced or diced*)	Wash, scrape, slice or dice small. When done, toss in parsley or chive butter; and salt, pepper, nutmeg or clove to taste. Anise seeds in buttered carrots add the umph to the dish. They keep their vitamin C. A few chopped, blanched almonds are also very good. Or serve creamed, scalloped, mashed or breaded and fried in deep fat; in croquettes, mashed and mixed with butter, or soufflé; when mashed, curried, in ring mold, with rice in loaf, honeyed, etc.	¼ cup of slightly salted water, or orange or grapefruit juice, or sugared water.	2½ minutes	At once
CARROTS (*Strips*)	Wash, scrape, cut into strips like French fried potatoes (about 2-inch). When done, drain and French fry in deep fat. Or roll in bread (sieved) crumbs, then in beaten egg, and deep fry. Or serve in cream, tomato, egg or mushroom sauce.	⅓ cup slightly salted water and sugared water.	1½ minutes	At once
CARROTS (*Young, whole*)	Scrape, wipe with a damp cloth. When done, toss in parsley and chive butter, or deep fry, or pan-fry, or serve in sour or sweet cream sauce.	½ cup of sugared water also slightly salted.	3 to 3½ minutes	At once
CAULIFLOWER (*Flowerets*)	Wash in slightly acidulated lukewarm water and let stand 15 minutes. When done, toss in parsley butter and season to taste with salt, pepper and nutmeg. Or roll in sieved cracker or bread crumbs, then in beaten egg, and deep-fry; or serve with hollandaise, hot mayonnaise or cream sauce to which has been added a little grated orange rind; or in custard, au gratin, etc.	⅓ cup of water slightly salted and 1 tablespoon grated onion.	1½ minutes	At once

PRESSURE COOKER CHART FOR FRESH VEGETABLES   [2468]

KIND OF VEGETABLE	PRELIMINARY PREPARATION	AMOUNT OF LIQUID (Water, stock or wine)	MINUTES AFTER STEAM IS AT 15 POUNDS	RE-DUCE PRES-SURE
CAULIFLOWER *(Stalks)*	Cook like celery, which see.			
CAULIFLOWER *(Whole, medium)*	Wash in slightly acidulated water and let stand 15 minutes, to draw out sand and foreign matter. When done, sprinkle with tiny bread croutons fried in butter, or with browned bread crumbs in fat mixed with equal parts of hard-cooked, chopped eggs, or hollandaise, cream, egg or curry sauce; or cover with cheese sauce and brown in broiling oven; or scalloped, in casserole with tomato au gratin, or sautéed in anchovy butter or with lemon butter sauce, etc.	¼ cup of slightly salted water with 1 whole clove, 3 strips of lemon peel and 1 bay leaf.	4 to 5 minutes	At once
CAULIFLOWER *(Whole, large)*	Same as for medium, allowing 1 minute longer steaming.			
CAULIFLOWER *(Stalks)*	Same as cardoon, which see.			
CAULIFLOWER *(Leaves)*	Same as beet greens.			
CELERY *(Stalks, sliced or diced and scraped)*	Same as cardoon, which see.			
CELERY *(Stalk or whole, braised)*	Trim neatly each stalk or whole root or bunch; cut off leaves and root. Halve or quarter, according to size. When done, place in buttered baking pan, cover with meat gravy, then with a buttered paper, and braise in a moderate oven (350–375° F.) for 30 minutes; remove paper and continue braising 10 minutes longer.	⅓ cup slightly salted water, 1 bay leaf, 1 clove, 3 sprigs parsley.	4 minutes	At once

PRESSURE COOKER CHART FOR FRESH VEGETABLES [2468]

KIND OF VEGETABLE	PRELIMINARY PREPARATION	AMOUNT OF LIQUID (Water, stock or wine)	MINUTES AFTER STEAM IS AT 15 POUNDS	RE-DUCE PRES-SURE
CHARD (*Swiss, leaves*)	Same as beet leaves.			
CHARD (*Swiss, stalks*)	Same as celery stalks. When done, serve on a platter with the stalks in the center, surrounded by a ring of chopped chard leaves. Rhubarb chard served in this manner with its red stalk pieces provides a festive and unusual, as well as delicious, vegetable to put before guests.			
CHICORY	Same as beet greens.			
COLLARDS	Same as beet greens.			
CORN (*Cob, small*)	Husk; remove silk and bad spots. When done, serve with melted or plain hard butter.	¼ cup of water, slightly salted.	3½ minutes	At once
CORN (*Cob, large*)	Same as small, allowing 1½ minutes longer, and serving in the same way.			
CORN (*Cut*)	Prepare same as on the cob, then scrape or cut close to the cob. Serve in custard, pan-fried, O'Brien style, creamed, curried, etc.	¼ cup of water.	1 minute	At once
CUCUMBER (*Green, diced or sliced*)	Wash large cucumbers, peel, dice or slice; scallop with a fork before slicing. When done, drain and serve with cream-caper sauce, cream (sweet or sour) sauce, pan-fried, au gratin, scalloped, stewed, in pancakes, etc.	¼ cup of slightly salted water.	1 minute	At once
CUCUMBER (*Whole, ripe*)	Wash, dry, leave whole. When done, drain; halve lengthwise, scoop inside and stuff. Or cut in inch-thick slices; and after draining, serve with parsley butter, sour cream or sweet cream sauce, hollandaise, or hot mayonnaise.	¼ cup of slightly salted water.	2½ minutes	At once
DANDELIONS	Same as beet greens.			

PRESSURE COOKER CHART FOR FRESH VEGETABLES　　　[2468]

KIND OF VEGETABLE	PRELIMINARY PREPARATION	AMOUNT OF LIQUID (Water, stock or wine)	MINUTES AFTER STEAM IS AT 15 POUNDS	RE- DUCE PRES- SURE
DASHEENS	Same as potatoes—that is, peeled, cooked, mashed, riced, fried baked, etc.			
EGGPLANT (*Sliced or diced*)	Wash, dry, slice in ½-inch slices, pare or not. When done, pan-fry, scalloped, soufflé, baked with tomatoes, pie, mashed like potatoes, rolled in seasoned flour and French fried, à la Creole, fried in batter, etc.	¼ cup of slightly salted water.	⅓ minute	At once
EGGPLANT (*Whole for stuffing*)	Wash, dry. When done, halve lengthwise and stuff according to taste with bread, meat, sausage or ham stuffing, adding the scooped parts to the stuffing. Bake. Serve with or without sauce.	⅓ cup of slightly salted water.	4 to 5 minutes	At once
ENDIVE (*Whole*)	Trim, wash, dry, then cook. When done proceed as for braised celery, which see; or serve with cream, mushroom or tomato sauce.	⅓ cup of slightly salted water.	4 minutes	At once
ESCAROLE	Same as beet greens, which see.			
GREENS—Kale, Beets, Purslane, Mustard, Turnip, Fiddleheads, Spinach, Celery Leaves, Radish Tops, etc.	Same as beet greens.			
KALE	Wash, remove tough stems; cook. When done serve like beet greens, also with vinaigrette, French dressing, scalloped, with salt pork or bacon, in ring mold, soufflé, etc.	¼ cup of slightly salted water and a few slices of onion and 1 bay leaf.	4 minutes	At once
KOHLRABI (*Sliced*)	Wash carefully, scrubbing lightly; remove leaves; leave peel on, cook. When done serve au gratin, parsley, cream, egg, or brown sauce.	¼ cup of slightly salted water.	2 to 3 minutes	At once

PRESSURE COOKER CHART FOR FRESH VEGETABLES [2468]

KIND OF VEGETABLE	PRELIMINARY PREPARATION	AMOUNT OF LIQUID (Water, stock or wine)	MINUTES AFTER STEAM IS AT 15 POUNDS	RE-DUCE PRES-SURE
KOHLRABI (*Whole*)	Wash carefully; remove leaves, leave peel on, and cook. When done, cube and serve like the slices after peeling. Or cut a slice on top; scoop inside pulp, and stuff with your favorite stuffing, then bake, having kohlrabi close together in baking pan.	½ cup of slightly salted water.	7 to 8 minutes	At once
LEEKS (*Whole*)	Wash, trim green leaves and roots, tie in small bundles like asparagus, and cook. When done, drain well and serve with cream, hollandaise, Béchamel, egg, or mushroom sauce. If served cold, serve like asparagus (French dressing, vinaigrette, sour cream dressing, etc).	¼ cup of water and 1 blade of garlic and 1 large bay leaf.	3 to 3½ minutes	At once
MARROW VEGETABLE	Same as kohlrabi, which see.			
MUSHROOMS (*Sliced*)	Peel, slice caps and stems. DO NOT WASH. Then cook. When done, serve in sweet or sour cream, Béchamel, parsley or chive sauce; or scallop, in pie, au gratin, baked, deviled, sautéed, in omelets, in macaroni, spaghetti or noodles, in rice, with peas, in fritters creamed in spinach ring, stewed, etc.	¼ cup of slightly salted water.	1 minute	At once
MUSHROOMS (*Whole, caps*)	Peel, remove stems and cook. When done, stuff, broil, en brochette, under bell, stewed in sherry, bake, sautéed in anchovy butter, brandied, deviled, on toast, with cream, Béchamel, brown or tomato sauce, etc.	⅓ cup of slightly salted water.	2 minutes	At once
OKRA(*Sliced*)	Wash, remove stems and cut into ½ to ¾ inch slices. When done, use in soup, stewed, creamed, in tomato sauce, fried, Creole style, fritters, in rice, macaroni, spaghetti, parsley or chive sauces, etc.	¼ cup of slightly salted water and 1 small clove of garlic.	1½ to 2 minutes	At once

PRESSURE COOKER CHART FOR FRESH VEGETABLES [2468]

KIND OF VEGETABLE	PRELIMINARY PREPARATION	AMOUNT OF LIQUID (Water, stock or wine)	MINUTES AFTER STEAM IS AT 15 POUNDS	RE-DUCE PRES-SURE
OKRA (*Whole*)	Prepare as above, but do not slice. Cook, and when done, serve stewed in tomato juice, in cream, pan-fry, and add to any kind of stew before serving.	¼ cup of slightly salted water.	3 to 3½ minutes	At once
ONIONS (*Sliced*)	Peel, slice, discarding the first and last slice, then cook. When done, serve with parsley, caper, egg, cream, mushroom or tomato sauce; scalloped, with macaroni, spaghetti, noodles, rice, beans, French fried in batter, short-cake, pie, glazed, en casserole with tomatoes, soufflé, etc.	¼ cup of slightly salted water.	3 minutes	At once
ONIONS (*Small, silver or white*)	Peel, cook. When done, serve in sweet or sour cream sauce, clari-fied butter, parsley butter, Bé-chamel, mushroom or tomato sauce, pies, shortcakes, dump-lings, glazed, broiled, skewered, scalloped, baked, caramelized, smothered, on toast with al-monds, in cheese sauce, etc.	¼ cup of salted water with 1 bay leaf and, if desired, a small clove of garlic.	5 to 6 minutes	At once
ONIONS (*Large Bermuda or Spanish, whole*)	Peel. Cook. Drain well. Scoop and stuff, mashed and buttered, browned around a roast, baked, stuffed or not, soufflé, braised in white wine, pudding with nut meats, cream, horseradish or tomato sauce, casserole with bacon, with sage and giblet sauce, etc.	½ cup of salted water with bay leaf garlic and parsley.	9 to 10 minutes	At once
ONIONS (*Green*)	Trim, wash, drain and cook. When done serve on toast with melted butter, parsley, chive, cream, horseradish, tomato or egg sauce. Cold with mustard dressing, French dressing, may-onnaise, sour cream dressing, or vinaigrette, etc.	¼ cup of salted water and nutmeg.	1½ minutes	At once

PRESSURE COOKER CHART FOR FRESH VEGETABLES [2468]

KIND OF VEGETABLE	PRELIMINARY PREPARATION	AMOUNT OF LIQUID (Water, stock or wine)	MINUTES AFTER STEAM IS AT 15 POUNDS	RE-DUCE PRES-SURE
PARSNIPS (*Sliced*)	Scrape; wipe with damp cloth. Cook. When done, drain, and serve creamed, drawn or parsley butter with grated orange rind, in cream, Béchamel or tomato sauce, browned, scalloped, glazed or caramelized, patties, puffs, fritters, croquettes, stewed, au gratin, etc.	¼ cup of slightly salted water with 2 cloves and bay leaf.	2½ to 3 minutes	At once
PARSNIPS (*Whole*)	Scrape, wipe with damp cloth and cook. When done, halve, remove cores, and pan fry, broil, glaze, caramelize, bake in cream, tomato juice or mushroom soup, stuff, roast alongside meat roast, etc.	½ cup of cold water with bay leaf and garlic.	10 to 12 minutes depending on size and age.	At once
PEAS (*Green, fresh, shelled, small*)	Shell. Do not wash; add half of the washed, drained and stringed pods and cook. When done, drain and serve with parsley, drawn butter, cream (sweet or sour), soufflé, with small, whole onions, chopped watercress, in omelet, with cooked cucumber cubes, with cooked, diced carrots, à la Creole, with cubed rutabagas (cooked), in baked tomato cups, onion cups, green pepper cups, etc.	¼ cup of slightly salted water, with or without a few sprigs of mint leaves, parsley and thinly sliced onion.	1½ minutes	At once
PEAS (*Green, fresh, shelled and large*)	Same preparation and cooking and serving as the small one, allowing 1½ to 2 minutes longer (3 minutes in all) than for small fresh peas. The pods, diced carrots (raw) may be added to large peas; the time of cooking is the same.	¼ cup of water.	3 minutes	At once
PEAS (*Pods*)	Wash thoroughly, snap off stems (ends) and cook. When done, serve in purée (mashed) patties, soufflé, creamed, soup, buttered, timbales filled with green peas, croquettes, fritters, with sautéed mushrooms, etc.	¼ cup of water, a few mint leaves, onion slices and a blade of garlic, water well salted.	1 minute	At once

PRESSURE COOKER CHART FOR FRESH VEGETABLES [2468]

KIND OF VEGETABLE	PRELIMINARY PREPARATION	AMOUNT OF LIQUID (Water, stock or wine)	MINUTES AFTER STEAM IS AT 15 POUNDS	REDUCE PRESSURE
POTATOES (*White, sliced for mashing*)	Peel, wash, drain, and cook. When done, drain and mash exactly like boiled potatoes. Serve also in patties, croquettes, fritters, soufflé, pan fried, creamed, buttered, etc.	½ cup of salted water.	1 minute	At once
POTATOES (*White, quartered*)	Peel, wash, drain, and cook. Drain. Serve with parsley butter, drawn butter, cream sauce, mushroom sauce, pan-fried, browned around the roast, German fried, with cooked sauerkraut, etc. May also be mashed.	½ cup of salted water.	4 to 5 minutes	Gradually
POTATOES (*White, small, peeled or not whole*)	Wash well. Dry. Cook. When done, peel or not as desired. If peeled, may be rolled in butter, then in chopped parsley or chives, browned in butter or deep fat, placed around the roast a few minutes before it is done, quartered and French fried, creamed, scalloped, etc.	½ cup of cold, salted water.	8 minutes	Gradually
POTATOES (*White, large, peeled or not, whole*)	Same as above. **Note.** If steamed 10 minutes, may be baked, stuffed, sliced, then broiled.	¾ cup of cold, salted water.	15 to 20 minutes	Gradually
POTATOES (*Sweet or yams*)	Same as White Potatoes on each form.			Gradually
PUMPKIN (*In wedges*)	Wash. Dry. Do not peel if young, but do so if old and seems tough. Cut in wedges of about 3 or 4 inches. Cook. Drain well; mash and serve as a side dish, or in pies. May be served with potato as a whip, browned as a vegetable. If underdone, may be French fried, sautéed, glazed, diced in sweet or sour cream, sliced and broiled, scalloped, etc.	⅓ cup of slightly salted water.	10 to 12 minutes, according to tenderness.	At once
ROMAINE	Same as Greens, which see.			

PRESSURE COOKER CHART FOR FRESH VEGETABLES   [2468]

KIND OF VEGETABLE	PRELIMINARY PREPARATION	AMOUNT OF LIQUID (Water, stock or wine)	MINUTES AFTER STEAM IS AT 15 POUNDS	RE-DUCE PRES-SURE
RUTABAGAS (*Swedish turnip, also called Lapland turnip, or Yellow turnip—sliced*)	Scrub; wash; dip in boiling water or not, pare and again wash quickly. Cook same as potato slices, or if quartered, like quartered potatoes. May be prepared in all the different methods as the white potato, the yam or the sweet potato on each form.			
SALSIFY (*Also called erroneously "Oyster plant," whole*)	Wash and scrub well; drop into acidulated water (1 scant tablespoon of lemon juice or vinegar to each quart of cold water) to prevent discoloring. Cool. When done, may be sliced and deep fried, cut in French fried potato style and deep fried, or rolled in batter and deep fried. May be creamed, buttered, mashed and made into a cream soup, chopped and made in croquettes, patties, cream, Béchamel, hollandaise, mousseline sauces, chopped very fine (not mashed) and made in soufflé, etc.	½ cup of salted water and 2 teaspoons of lemon juice.	12 to 15 minutes	At once
SAUERKRAUT	Well drained and gently squeezed. Cook; drain again; season with salt, pepper and bacon or ham drippings, onion juice. May be mixed with tomato juice, made into patties and fried, mixed with cooked apples, with slices of frankfurters, garnished with liver dumplings, with boiled small onions, timbales, pot pie, chopped fried onions, etc., as a main or side dish or with link sausages or sausage patties in winter.	¼ cup of unsalted water or white wine with ⅓ cup of grated raw potatoes or 2 peeled chopped raw apples and 1 teaspoon caraway seeds.	4 minutes	Gradually
SORREL	Same as Greens, which see.			
SPINACH	Same as Greens, which see.			
SUCCOTASH	Cook corn separately (on the cob or cut). Cook fresh lima beans (not the dry kind) separately. Combine both and mix with cream or cream sauce, highly seasoned.	Lima beans ¼ cup of water.	2 minutes	At once

PRESSURE COOKER CHART FOR FRESH VEGETABLES [2468]

KIND OF VEGETABLE	PRELIMINARY PREPARATION	AMOUNT OF LIQUID (Water, stock or wine)	MINUTES AFTER STEAM IS AT 15 POUNDS	RE-DUCE PRES-SURE
SQUASH (*Acorn, halved*)	Scrub, wash, halve and seed, then cook. Drain excess of water, reserving for soup, season with butter, salt and pepper. Or form in patties, croquettes, cutlets, and deep fry after rolling in crumbs and egg, twice. Soufflé, au gratin, fritters, mashed with nut meats, timbales, mixed with curried rice and baked, en casserole with pineapple, squash and pea fritters, whipped with cream sauce, etc.	½ cup of salted water or meat stock.	8 to 10 minutes	At once
SQUASH (*Hubbard, wedges*)	Scrub gently, wash, do not peel, cut in wedges and cook. When done, remove the pulp, mash, season and return to shell. Sprinkle with buttered bread or cracker crumbs and grated cheese in equal parts and brown under flame of broiling oven. Or add to pulp, equal parts of crushed, drained pineapple, and proceed as above.	½ cup of salted water or meat stock.	12 to 15 minutes	At once
SQUASH (*Summer, whole*)	Wash, peel or not. Cook. When done, halve, remove seeds and fibers, and season with salt, pepper and nutmeg and melted parsley, chive or plain melted butter.	⅓ cup of salted water or meat stock.	2 to 3 minutes	At once
SQUASH (*Italian zucchini, sliced*)	Wash well. Dry. Slice. Do not peel. Cook. When done, season with salt, pepper, nutmeg and butter. Or dip in batter and deep fry; or roll in bread crumbs and pan-fry in butter.	¼ cup of salted water or meat stock.	½ minute	At once
SQUASH (*Italian zucchini, whole*)	Wash, dry, leave whole and cook. When done, slice and French fry. Or halve, remove seeds and fibers, stuff, cover with crumbs and cheese and bake till brown. For a main dish stuff with cooked, chopped chicken livers, creamed ham, chicken, turkey or dried beef.	½ cup of salted water or meat stock.	5 to 7 minutes	Gradu-ally

PRESSURE COOKER CHART FOR FRESH VEGETABLES [2468]

KIND OF VEGETABLE	PRELIMINARY PREPARATION	AMOUNT OF LIQUID (Water, stock or wine)	MINUTES AFTER STEAM IS AT 15 POUNDS	RE-DUCE PRES-SURE
STRING BEANS	See BEANS.			
TOMATOES (*Juice for cocktail or soup—cut*)	Wipe, do not peel, cut in eighths or quarters (according to size) and using ripe tomatoes without a blemish. Cook. When done, strain through a fine-meshed wire sieve (not a cloth, lest you get only colored water); season to taste with salt, pepper, a dash of nutmeg or clove, and chill thoroughly for cocktail or use at once for soup.	No water at all	⅓ of a minute	At once
TOMATOES (*Stewed, cut*)	Prepare as above. Season; add extra a little chopped parsley or chives. Or reduce a little over a bright flame and use as a filling for omelet, pie timbale, spaghetti, macaroni or noodles. Or rub through a sieve and make a soufflé. **Note.** You may omit the water or stock, if tomatoes are soft.	½ cup of salted water or meat stock, plus 1 bay leaf, tied with 6 sprigs of parsley and 1 sprig of thyme. Also add 1 tablespoon of grated onion.	¾ of a minute	At once
TOMATOES (*Stewed, whole*)	Wipe, peel. Leave whole, and cook. Drain excess of juice, and serve with parsley, chive, onion, drawn butter, as a side dish with any kind of main dish.	¼ cup of meat stock for flavor, plus 1 bay leaf, 6 sprigs parsley 1 sprig thyme, 1 tablespoon grated onion and 1 slice of garlic.	1 to 1½ minutes	At once

PRESSURE COOKER CHART FOR FRESH VEGETABLES [2468]

KIND OF VEGETABLE	PRELIMINARY PREPARATION	AMOUNT OF LIQUID (Water, stock or wine)	MINUTES AFTER STEAM IS AT 15 POUNDS	RE-DUCE PRES-SURE
TRUFFLES (*Sliced, whole*)	Brush with a soft brush; wash quickly. Do not peel. Cook. When done, slice and use for garnish, or roll in butter, which should be clarified. Or chop and use in sauce, in omelet, stuffings, meat loaves, patties, etc.	¼ cup dry white wine.	2 minutes	At once
TURNIPS (*White, diced or sliced or quartered, if small, for mashed or stewed*)	Peel, halve and dice or slice, or quarter. Cook. Drain excess of liquid and season with salt, pepper, nutmeg, parsley or chives or both. Or fry in butter; glaze like onions and carrots. Or cook with equal parts of scraped, diced, sliced or quartered carrots to remove the bitterness of the tuber. May be mashed like potatoes, made in croquettes, patties or cutlets; cooked with a little onion, sliced, in custard, puffs, turnovers, en casserole with spinach, glazed or caramelized, French fried, etc. **Important.** Never salt turnips while they are cooking. It extracts their sweetness.	¼ cup of unsalted water or meat stock.	4 to 5 minutes	At once
TURNIPS (*White, whole*)	Wash thoroughly. Peel or not. Cook in unsalted water or meat stock. When done, drain, cool slightly and peel. Carefully scoop the pulp inside and combine with your favorite stuffing, or with cooked peas, string beans, succotash, spinach, creamed carrots, sausage meat, or any leftover cooked meat, fish, poultry or game. Cover with buttered bread or cracker crumbs and bake till brown.	⅓ cup of unsalted water or meat or poultry stock.	18 to 21 minutes, depending on size and age.	Gradually
TURNIPS (*Yellow*)	See Rutabagas.			
WAX BEANS	See Beans.			

INDEX

Abalone, 224
Abatis d'Oie, 528
Acorn Squash, Baked, 730
  Squash, Pressure Cooked, 1174
  Squash Rings, 730
  Squash, Sausage Stuffed, 729
Acorns, 1026
Afternoon Tea Menu, 84
Aglio, Macaroni all', 754
Aiglefin, a fish, 200
Aigrettes d'Anchois, 4
  au Parmesan, 4
Aioli Sauce, 558
A l'Americaine, Filets of Sole (Flounder),
  252
A la Mode, Beef, 319
A la Reine, Cream of Chicken Soup, 124
  Galantine de Capon, 488
  Onions, 693
  Poached Eggs, 181
A la (Title), *see* under proper names.
Alaska, Baked, 1122
  Dab, a fish, 203
Albacore, Great, a fish, 220
Ale Bowl, Wassail, 52
  Soup, 105
Alewife, 202
Alexandra Consommé, 115
Algerian Date Chew, 968
All-Bran Dumplings, 95
Allumettes, Sweet Potatoes, 712
Almond(s), 1026
  Blanching, 1024
  Blanket, 960
  Brandy Sauce, Clotted, 891
  Brittle Squares, 968
  Burnt, 971
  Burnt, Ice Cream, 1125
  Burnt, Mousse, 1140
  Butter I, 550
  Butter II, 550
  Chocolate, 971
  Chocolate Pralines, 969
  Chocolate Sauce, 890
  Chocolate Torte, 962
  Cookies, 925
  Cream Cheese Cookies, 928
  Cream Cheese Sandwich, 843
  Cream of Lettuce Soup, 105
  Cream Pudding, Fluffy, 872
  Cream Sauce, 890
  Creamed Chicken Ragoût, 512
  Egg Dumplings, 785
  Fritters, 859

Almond(s), Kirsch Hard Sauce, 896
  Kisses I, 969
  Kisses II, 969
  Mayonnaise Dressing, 835
  Minted Mutton Soup, 105
  Molasses Mincemeat Cookies, 931
  Pancakes, 798
  Sausage Stuffing, 789
  Soufflé, 859
  Soup, Cream of Buttermilk, 121
  Sweet, Roasting, 1025
  See also Sandwiches
Alsatian Coquillage Doughnuts, 780
  Halibut Steak, 264
  Onion Bread, 1052
Amandine Asparagus, 600
  Broccoli, 617
  Cauliflower Soufflé, 633
  Celery, 636
  Crême, 865
  Dried Beef, 432
  Filets of Sole (Flounder), 251
  Noodles, 759
  Poached Eggs, 176
  Potato Soufflé, 709
  Spinach Soufflé, 723
  Steamed Cabbage au Gratin, 626
  Tarte au Chocolat, 962
  Trout (Brook), 298
  Trout (Brook) Delices d'Annecy, 301
Ambassador Trout (Lake), 299
  Trout Sauce, 299
Americaine, Lobster à l', 265
American Artichokes, 596
  Beet Soup, 108
  Black Bean Soup, 109
  Cheese, *see* Sandwiches and Sandwich
    Fillings
Anchovy, the, 7–9
  Aigrettes, 4
  Artichoke Dressing, 8
  Béarnaise Sauce, 8
  Birds (Wild), Larding, 9
  Broccoli Dressing, 8
  Butter, 8, 550
  Canapé Fingers, 5
    Lozenges, 6
    Nantais, 6
    Odette, 6
    Patricia, 7
    Rounds, 6
    à la Royale, 7
    à la Statler, 9
  Eclairs, 27

Anchovy, Fowl, Larding, 9
  Fritots in Pyramid, 9
  Game Larding, 9
  Hollandaise Sauce, 8
  Larding with, 9
  and Liver Mold, 451
  Meat, Larding with, 9
  Oyster Dressing, 8
  Ravigote Sauce, 8
  Remoulade Sauce, 8
  Roasts, Larding, 9
  Salad Dressing, 8
  Seasoning, 8
  see also Sandwiches and Sandwich
    Fillings
Andalouse Consommé, 115
  Mushrooms à l', 682
Angel Food Cake, 909
  Failures, 908–909
Angel Parfait, 1145
  Pie, 943
Angels on Horseback, 9
Anguilla, a fish, 196
  au Vert Bruxelloise, 250
Annabelle, Peaches, 882
Anna's Butter Crust, 939
Appetizers, 3–45
  Fillings, 852–856
Apple(s):
  Baked, Belmont, 860
    with Sausage Cores, 456
  Chopped, in Salads, 811
  Cinnamon Roly Poly Pinwheels, 956
  Cottage Cheese Pie, 943
  Duff, 860
  Dumplings, Frosted, 957
  Ginger Soup, 107
  and Ham Pie, 416
  Pan Dowdy, 944
  Pancake, 797
  Pie, 944
  and Pork Pie, 401
  and Prune Stuffing, 794
  Pudding, Steamed, 887
  Raisin Cake, 911
  with Roast Ham, 423
  and Sausage, 456
  Slice Pie, French, 946
  Soup Polish Style, 106
  in Sour Cream Sauerkraut, 719
  Spareribs, Stuffing, 409
  Turnovers, Frosted, 957

Apple(s), Waffles, 805
  see also Salads; Sandwiches; Sandwich
    Fillings
Applesauce, Acorn Squash Rings, 730
  Cake, Michigan, 919
  Gingerbread, 1092
Apricot Bowknots, 954
  Cream Cheese Sandwich, 844
  Ice, 1116
  Ice Cream I, 1121
  Ice Cream II, 1122
  Mousse, 1139
  Parfait, 1145
  Trifle, 860
  Upside-Down Cakes, 911
  See also Salads; Sandwiches
Arabian Mocha, 67
Arctic Cooler, 67
Ardennaise, Veal Kidneys, 447
Argenteuil Consommé, 115
Aristotle's Lantern, Shellfish, 232
Arizona Baked Frijole Beans Piman, 606
Arm Pot Roast, 312
  Roast, Veal, 348
  Steak, 312
    Beef, 312
    Pork, 394
    Veal, 348
Armenian Coffee, 68
  Eggplant, 655
  Lentil Soup, 135
  String Beans, 727
Armenonville Jellied Chicken Loaf, 513
  Sauerkraut, 718
  Stuffed Radishes, 39
Aromatic Tea Russian Manner, 83
Arrow-Toothed Halibut, 201
Arroz con Polla Castillane, 492
Artichokes, 593
  American, 596
  Bottom Pompadour Manner, 24
  Cocktail, 32
  Dressing Anchovy, 8
  à la Favorite, 594
  (Globe), Boiled, 596
    à la Calabrese, 595
    Knickerbocker, 595
    Mother's, 595
    à la Ninon, 596
    Pressure Cooked, 1162
  (Jerusalem), 596
    Boiled, 597
    Creamed, 597
    French Fried, 597

Artichokes, (Jerusalem), à la Lyonnaise, 598
  Mashed, 598
  and Mushroom Pancakes, 598
  Pressure Cooked, 1162
  à la Provençale, 594
Asparagus, 598
  Amandine, 600
  Au Gratin, I, 601
  Au Gratin, II, 602
  Bearnaise Sauce, 600
  Buca Lapi, 600
  Cold, 600
  Creamed, in Toast Rings, 603
  Custard, 601
  Flemish Style, 600
  Franconville, 601
  French Fried, 603
  German Style, 600
  Italian Style, 600
  and Olives au Gratin, 602
  Patty, 600
  Pie, 602
  Polish Style, 600
  à la Pompadour, 603
  Pressure Cooked, 1162
  Salad, Jellied, 813
  Soufflé, 603
  Soup, Cream of, 120
  Spanish Style, 600
  Tip Omelet, 599
Asperges des Pauvres Vinaigrette, 10
Aspic, 10–12
  Coating Jelly, Madeira Wine, 543, 572
    Port Wine, 39, 581
    Sherry, 41
  Cucumber Cottage Cheese, 652
  Fish, 266
  Grapefruit, Annette, 824
  de Homard en Bellevue, 266
  Lamb Tongues in, 466
  Madeira, 543
  Poached Eggs in, I, 177
  Poached Eggs in, II, 177
  Shrimp in, 289
  Smoked Beef Tongue in, 466
  Stuffed Eggs in, 187
  Tomato, Plaza, 45
  Turkey, Supper, 540
  See also Gelatin; Jelly
Au Gratin:
  Asparagus, I, 601
  Asparagus, II, 602
  and Olives, 602

Au Gratin, Brains, 430
  Brussels Sprouts, 620
  Cabbage Amandine, Steamed, 626
  Cabbage and Celery, 622
  Cauliflowered, Smothered, 635
  Celery, Gastronome, 638
  Creamed Leeks, 670
    Variations, 670
  Creamed Parsnip, 694
  Cucumbers, 652
  Deviled Creamed Noodles, 757
  Deviled Mushrooms, 681
  Eggs, 160
  Eggplant, 656
  d'Epinards Jeanette, 722
  Kohlrabi, 668
  Macaroni, 755
  Okra, 687
  Onions, 692
  Potato, 708
  Succotash, 735
  String Beans, 727
  Whitefish Filets, 305
Aurora Abalone, Shellfish, 224
Aurore Consomme, 114
Auvergnate, Cassolettes of Lentils à l', 671
  Chestnut Soup, 113
Avocado Crabmeat Cocktail, 32
  Fish Cocktail, 33
  Lobster Cocktail, 33
  Omelet au Curry, 167
  Sandwich Filling, 852
  Scallop Cocktail, 33
  Shrimp Cocktail, 33
  See also Salads

Baba au Rhum, 954
Bacon, Broiling, 984
  Cheese Toast, 1107
  Crumbs, 96
  and Kale, 664
  and Lima Beans Casserole, 611
  and Mushrooms on Toast, 682
  and String Beans, 726
  and Tomato Sandwich, Hot, 848
  Waffles, 806
  see also Sandwiches
Baked Acorn Squash, 730
  Alaska, 1122
  Apples Belmont, 860
  Apples and Sausage, 456
  Beans, *see* Beans, Baked
  Bluefish Creole, 235

Baked Carp, Breaded, 236
  Carrots, French, 630
  Chick-Peas, 606
  Codfish, Stuffed, Rhode Island Style, 237
  Crabmeat-Stuffed Eggplant, 655
  Cucumbers, Stuffed, 651
  Custards, 870
  Eggs San Sebastian, 153
  Frijole Beans Piman, 606
  Ham Gourmet, 411
  Hamburger-Stuffed Pumpkin, 714
  Liver and Onions, 449
  Onion Rings, 690
  Onions, Liver-Stuffed, 689
  Onions, Stuffed, 690
  Pork Chops Charcutière, 395
    Double Stuffed, 396
    Florentine, 395
    Hawaii, 395
    Normande, 396
  Potatoes, 702
  Potato, Stuffed, 702
  Potato Soubise, 703
  Pumpkin, Fluffy, 716
  Pumpkin, Whole, 715
  Shad, Planked, Sherry Netherland, 238
  Shad Roe Plantation, 237
  Shad Rouennaise, 236
  Steak, Spanish, Baroness, 314
  Sausages, Link, 456
  Sweet Potatoes, 703, 710
  Sweetbreads, Larded, Creole, 461
  Tomatoes, Curried, 736
  Turkey Roll, 539
  Veal, 353
Baking Chart, Cake, 902–909
  Failures, Cake, 902–909
  Fish, 191, 192, 233
  Pie, 938
  Potatoes, 703
  Sour Milk in, 80
  Terms, 1035–1037
Baking Powder Dumplings, 96
Balaos, a fish, 201
Balls, Bread Crumb, 96
  Burger, with Marjoram, 97
  Chicken Forcemeat, 98
  Codfish, 243
  Corn Meal, 748
  Egg, 100
  Marrow, 102
  Matzoth, 102

Balls, Pimiento Butter, 645
  Pork, 434
  Potato, Bavarian, 344
    Cheese, 707
  Veal, Curried, 354
    Swiss, 359
  See also Burgers
Baltimore Oyster Fricassee, 279
  Terrapin, 297
Banana Blanc Mange, 861
  Bran Muffins, 1084
  Bread, 1053
  Fluff, Sweet Potato and, 711
  Ice Cream, 1124
  Jellied, en Chartreuse, 877
  Lamb Curry with, 379
  Pancakes, 799
  Salad, 811, 812; *see also* Salads
  Sauce, Foamy, 892
  Trifle, 861
Barbecued Beef, Short Ribs, 314
  Ham, Fresh, Virginia, 396
    Slices, 412
  Lamb, Leg, 373
  Sauce, 396, 439
Bar-Le-Duc Dressing, 830
Barley Soup, 106
  Soup, Cream of, 120
  Sugar Twist I, 969
  Sugar Twist II, 970
Baron of Lamb Brabançonne, 374
Baroness, Spanish Steak, 314
Barquettes of Beef Marrow, 12
Barracuda, 193
Bars, Chocolate Marbled Fudge, 972
  Honey Fruit, 930
Bass, a fish, 193
  California, 193
  Channel, 208
  Reef, 209
  Rock, 194
  Striped, 193
  Sun, 218
  White, 193
Bastard, a fish, 199
Bastard Halibut, 201
Basting a Roast, 343
  Sauce for Shellfish, 262
Batter, Cardoons Fried in, 628
  Frying, 30
  Frying, I, for Fritters, 568
  Frying, II, for Fritters, 568
  Frying, III, 569
  Frying, IV, 569

Batter, Frying, for Eggplant, 656
  Frying, Royal, 159
  Italian, 29
Bavarian Cream, 873
  Potato Balls, 344
  Sauerbraten, 343
Bay Salts Oysters, 230
  Scallops, 231
Bayou Creamed Green Peas, 697
Beaming Scallops, 231, 232
Beans, 604–606
  Baked, 605
    Boston, 608
    Boston Croquettes, 608
    Breton, 608
    Canned, 605
    Home-Baked, 606
    Italian, 610
    Suggestions, 605
  Dried, Hopping John, 610
  Frijole, Piman, 606
  Hints, 605
  Lima, Bacon Casserole, 611
    Cassoulet à la Toulousaine, 388
    Creamed Fresh Lima, 609
    Deviled, 609
    French, 609
  and Onion, 689
  Red Kidney, Casserole Bercy, 611
  Soup, Black, I, 109
    Black, II, 109
    Black, country Style, 110
    Black, Fermière Style, 110
    Black, Grandmother's, 110
    Black, Guatemala Style, 110
    Cream of, 121
  Soy, Pressure Cooked, 1163
  Sprouts, *see* Sprouted Soybeans
  String, *see* String Beans
  Wax, Pressure Cooked, 1163
Bearnaise Sauce, 559
  Sauce, Anchovy, 8
  Sauce Variations, 559
  Tounedos à la, 346
Beaten Biscuits, 1045
Beating Eggs, 149
Béchâmel, Boiled Goose Oyster Stuffing,
    527
  Sauce, 119
  Stuffed Eggs à la, 187
Beech Nuts, 1026
Beef, 312–346
  Arm Pot Roast, 312
  Bourgeoise, 319

Beef, Bourguignonne, 314
  Brains, 427
  Braised Filet of, 325
    Hot Pot, 326
    Oxtail, 327
  Brisket, 312
    Corned, 312
    with Sauerkraut, 328
  Broiling, 984
  Bubble and Squeak, 330
  and Cabbage, Fried, 330
  Carbonade of, Flamande, 331
  Chart, 312–313
  Chateaubriand of, 338
  Chicago Roll, 325
    Boiled Larded, 324
  Chili con Carne, 332
    Frijoles, 332
  Chipped, *see* Beef, Dried
  Chop Suey, 315
  Chuck, 312
  Corned, and Cabbage, 334
    Cold, 334
    and Fowl Succotash, 335
    Sandwich, Hot, 849
    See also under Corned Beef *and pp.*
      333–334
    Soufflé, 335
  Croquettes, 373
  en Daube, 316
  Dried, 427
    Amandine, 432
    Creamed with Poached Eggs, 432
    Egg Pie, 433
    Hints, 431
    Noodle Ring, 433
    Shortcake Creole, 433
    See also Sandwich Fillings
  Filet of, with Bearnaise, 346
    Braised, 325
    Chipolata, 336
    Garibaldi, 337
    au Marsala, 337
    Mignon, 338
    à la Richmond, 338
    Stefanie, 339
  Flank, 312
  Garofolato al Roma, 341
  Goulash Hungarian Style, 316
    Transylvanian Style, 317
  Grenadins of, 356
  Hamburger Celestine, 340
    à la Creole, 341
    and Onion Rings, 339

Beef, Heart, 310, 427
  Loaf, 441
  Potroast, 442
  Rice Raisin Stuffing, 442
  Kidneys, 310, 427
    Chop Suey, 445
    Creole, 445
    Pie, 321
  Liver, 427, 449; *see also* Liver
  Loaf, 318
  Marrow Barquettes, 12
    Canapés, 23
  Mironton, 320
  à la Mode, 319
  Neck, 312
  and Oyster Pie, 321
  Pie, 324
  Plate, 312
  Pot Roast à la Romane, 341
  Raw, Canapes, 15
  Roast, Standing, Method I, 342
    Standing, Method II, 343
    with Yorkshire Pudding, 342
    Roasting, 342, 988
  Rolled (Olives), 326
  Sauerbraten, 343
  Schmor Braten, 345
  Shank, 312
  Short Loin, 313
  Short Ribs, 312
    Barbecued, 314
  Slices, Stuffed, 345
  Soup, Clear, 140
  Spiced Dutch Pot Roast, 344
  Steak, Arm, 312
    Baked Spanish, 314
    Blade, 312
    Chez-Soi, 322
    Chuck, Pepper, 340
    Club, Broiled, 328
    on Horseback, 322
    Minute, Broiled, 329
    Salisbury, 343
    Porterhouse, Marchand de Vin, 329
      Marrow, 329
    Sirloin, la Pérouse, 336
      Soufflé French Style, 323
    Strips, Chinese, 333
    Swiss, 345
    See also Steak
  Stew, 323
    Under Crust, 324
  à la Strogonoff, 324
  Sweetbreads, 310, 428

Beef, Tails, 428
  Tongue, 311, 428
    Boiled, 465
    Braised Fresh, 465
    Jardiniere, 465
    Smoked, in Aspic, 466
      Cumberland Sauce, 466
      Sauce Piquante, 467
      Sweet Sour, 467
  Tournedos of, 338
    à la Bearnaise, 436
  Tripe, 428
Beer, 44–50
  Bishop, Tavern, 51
  Bowl, Wassail, 53
  Flip, Waldorf, 51
  Gravy, 358
  in Shandygaff, 51
  Soup, 105
  Syllabub, 50
Beet(s), 613
  Boiled, 614
  Buttered, 615
    Variation, 615
  Celery, Apple Mold Salad, 814
  Cold, 613
  Hints, 613
  Hors d'Oeuvres, 614
  Mashed, 615
  in Orange Sauce, 614
  Pressure Cooked, 1163–1164
  in Salad, 614
  Savory Whole, 615
  Soup, 107
    American, 108
  in Sour Cream, 613
  in Spicy Sauce, 614
  Tops, Cooked, 615
    in Salads, 615
Belgian Coffee, 71
Bell Peppers, *see* Green Peppers
Bellevue, Lobster, 266
Belmont Baked Apples, 860
  Minced Chicken, 515
Benedict Eggs, 157
  Oysters, 279
Benedictine Crabs, 244
Bercy Kidney Beans Casserole, 611
  Butter, 550
  Lamb Chops, 377
  Sauce, 584
Bernardine Egg Souffle, 165
Bernhardt, Sarah, Scallops, 244
  Veal Cutlets, 363

Berry Tarts, 955
  Waffles, 808
Beurre Noir, Skate Wings au, 291
Beverages, 47–86
Biarritz, Lamb Cutlet Casserole, 380
  Lobster, 267
Big-eyed Herring, 202
Big-Jawed Sucker, a Fish, 217
Bigos, Polish, 625
Birds, Veal, Hungarian Style, 359
  Veal, à la Rossini, 360
  Wild, Larding with Anchovy, 9
  See also Poultry
Biscuit(s)
  Baking Powder, 1041
  Beaten, 1045
  Bran Buttermilk, 1042
  Buttermilk, 1042
  Cheese, 1041, 1043
  Cottage Cheese, 1043
  Cream Cheese, 1043
  Curried, 1044
  Date and Nut, 1044
  Drop, 1042
  English Tea, 1044
  Hasty Pudding, 1046
  Hints, 1039–1040
  Honey, 1045
  Mashed Potato, 1046
  Molasses-Nut, 1041
  Peanut Butter, 1047
  Pinwheel Tea, 1047
  Rings, Cheese, 939
  Shrimp, 1047
  Sour Cream, 1048
  Sweet Potato, 1048
  Watercress, 1049
Biscuit Tortoni I, 1124
Biscuit Tortoni II, 1124
Bishop, Tavern Beer, 51
Bisque, Tomato, 367
Black Bean Soup I, 109
  Soup II, 109
    Country Style, 110
    Fermière Style, 110
    Grandmother's, 110
    Guatemala Style, 110
Black Bonita, a fish, 195
  Butter, Brains in, 429
    Shirred Eggs with, 185
  Champagne Velvet, 51
  Drum, a fish, 196
  Eyed Peas Pot Likker, 607
  Grouper, 199

Black Bonita, Salmon, 195
  Sea Bass, 193
  Truffles, Newburg Sauce, 579
  Walnuts, 1030, 1031
    Crunches, 970
Blackberry Duff, 861
  Muffins, 1085
Blackfish, 194, 199
Blackjack, 223
Blade Pot Roast, 312
  Roast, Veal, 348
  Steak, Beef, 312
  Veal, 348
Blanc Mange, Banana, 861
Blanchaille, a fish, 222
Blanching, *see* Short-Boiling, 990
Blanching Nuts, Almonds, 1024
  Brazil Nuts, 1024
  Chestnuts, 1025
  Filberts, 1024
Blanket, Rotterdam Almond, 960
Blanquette of Veal, 349
  à la Weimar, 350
Bleu, Trout (Brook) au, 300
Blinis, 12, 15
Blond Roux, 584
Blossoms, Pumpkin, Fried, 715
  Squash, 729
Blowfish, 207
Blue Cat, a fish, 195
Blue Crabs, 227
Blue Herring, 202
Blue Perch, 194
Blue Point Oysters, 230
Blue Sunfish, 194
Blueback Herring, 202
  Salmon, 209
  Trout, 219
Blueberry Bran Muffins, 1085
  Cake, 912
  Flummery, 862
  Ice, 1116
  Muffins, 1086
  Pie, Deep Dish, 945
  Roll, 955
  Sauce, 890
  Soufflé, 862
  Tarts, 955
    Variations, 955
  Waffles, 806
Bluefin Tuna, 220
Bluefish, 194
  Creole, Baked, 235
  Grilled, 261

Bluegill, a fish, 194
Blue-Headed Suckër, a fish, 217
Boar Grunt, a fish, 199
Boca Colorado, a fish, 200
Bohemian Bread, 1054
  Christmas Twist, 963
  Potato Dumplings, 784
  Rye Bread Soup, 110
Bohemienne, Lobster, 267
  Sauce, 267, 585
Boiled:
  Artichokes (Globe), 596
    Jerusalem, 597
  Beef Tongue, 465
  Beets, 614
  Broccoli, 617
  Cardoons, Divers Sauces, 628
  Carlton Dressing, 839
  Celery Knob Hollandaise, 636
  Chard Greens, 641
  Chicago Roll (Beef), Larded, 325
  Cucumber, 651
  Custards, 870
  Dressing, 838
  Fish, 191, 233, 234
  Goose Oyster Stuffing Bechamel, 527
  Ham, 412
  Lamb Tongues Paysanne, 465
  Leeks, Sauces, 669
  Lentils, 671
  Lobster, 265
  Macaroni, 753
  Mackerel Dinner, 271
  Leg of Mutton, 386
  Noodles, 756
  Parsnip, 694
  Pumpkin, 715
  Rice, Near East, 769; see also Rice
  Salsify with Sauces, 716
  Spinach, Sour Cream, 721
  Sour Cream Dressing, 839
  String Beans Magic, 726
  Tongue, 465
  Turnips, 742
  Waltham Dressing, 839
Boiling, Short, 990
Boiler (Poultry), 481
Bolognese, Spaghetti alla, 760
Bombes, 1144
Bonbons Method I, 975
  Method II, 975
  Method III, 975
  Maraschino Parisien, 976
Bonitos, 194, 195, 220

Bonne Femme, Filets of Sole (Flounder), 253
  Lamb Chops, 378
  Mussels, 273
  Petits Pois, 698
Bordelaise, Mussels, 274
  Onions à la, 692
Borecole, 663
Bortsch, 107
  Polonaise, 108
Boston Baked Beans, 608
  Baked Bean Croquettes, 608
  Brown Bread, I, 1054
  Brown Bread II, 1055
  Cinnamon Cream, 862
  Haddock Dinner, 263
  Mackerel, 204
  Oyster Fricassee, 279
Bottom Round Steak, 313
Bouchots, Shellfish, 229
Bouillabaisse Marseillaise, 234
  Style Whitefish, 305
Bouillon, 90
    See Court Bouillon
Boulangère Poached Eggs, 177
Boulevardier, Shirred Eggs, 185
  Trout (Brook), 299
Bourdaloue Poached Eggs, 177
Bourgeoise, Beef, 319
  Celery Knob, 638
  Egg Patties, 162
  Sauce, 302, 585
Bourgogne Style Snails, 294
  Variation, 294
Bourguignonne, Beef, 314
  Brains à la, 429
  Chicken Sauté, 507
  Coq à la, 510
  Trout (Brook), 300
Bouquets, 233
Bowback, a fish, 223
Bowfin, a fish, 194, 199
Bowknots, Apricot, 954
  Polish, 783
Bowl, Spicy Cider, 63
Brabançonne, Baron of Lamb, 374
  Veal Kidneys, 447
Bracken Fern, 662
Braided Bread, 1055
Brain(s), 427, 429
  Au Beurre Noir, 429
  Au Gratin, 430
  Beef, 427
  in Black Butter, 429

Brain(s), à la Bourguignonne, 429
  Calf, 427
  Fritters, 430
  Grilled, 431
  Lamb, 427
  Mushroom Dumplings, 430
  Mushroom Stew, Red Wine, 429
  in Popover Cases, 431
  Pork, 427
  à la Poulette, 431
Braised (Braising), 983
  Baby Ducks, 520
  Beef Filet, Madeira Sauce, 325
  Beef Hot Pot, 326
  Capon, Stuffed, 486
  Celery, 637
  Ducklings, Chestnuts, 520
  Ham in Red Wine, California, 413
    in Red Wine, French, 413
  Hot Pot English Style, 326
  Leeks Bourgeoise, 669
  Lettuce, 675
  Liver, 450
  Leg of Mutton, French, 387
    Provençale, 388
  Oxtail, 327
  Pork Chops Creole, 397
  Sweetbreads Bonne Maman, 461
    Old Style, 462
  Veal Roll, 350
Bran Banana Muffins, 1084
  Blueberry Muffins, 1085
  Bread, 1056
    Baking Powder, 1052
    Honey, 1056, 1068
    Raisin, 1058
  Buttermilk Biscuits, 1042
  Dumplings, 95
  Muffins, 1086
    Raisin, 1087
  Nut Honey Kuchen, 958
  Orange Drop Cookies, 926
Brandade de Morue I, (Salt Cod), 238
  de Morue II, (Fresh Cod), 240
  de Morue Ménagère, 239
Brandied Ham-Walnut Stuffing, 792
  Mincemeat, 948
  Peach Jalousies, 955
    Variations, 956
Brandy, Cherry, Raspberry Sauce, 891
  Ginger Sauce, 890
  Hard Sauce, 896
  Honey Spiced Pavés, 930
  Mousse, 1140

Brandy, Sauce, Clotted Almond, 891
Braten, Schmor, 345
Brazil Nuggets, 970
Brazil Nut(s), 1026, 1031
  Blanching, 1024
  Chips, 13
Brazilian Chocolate, 54
  Mocha I, 68
  Mocha II, 68
Bread, Apple, Dutch, 1064
  Banana, 1053
  Bohemian, 1054
  Boston Brown, I, 1054
  Boston Brown, II, 1055
  Braided, 1055
  Bran, 1056
    Baking Powder, 1052
    Honey, 1056
    Raisin, 1058
  Brown Nut, I, 1059
  Brown Nut, II, 1059
  Caraway, 1061
  Christmas, 1061
  Coffee Rings, 1075
  Corn, Farmer's, 1063
    Kentucky, 1062
    Southern, 1068
    Stuffing, 790
    Tennessee, 1062
  Crumb Balls, 96
    Cinnamon Cookies, 926
    Dumplings, 784
    Omelet, 153
  Date, 1063
  Date Molasses Yeast, 1063
  Date Nut, 1064
  Fig, 1065
  French, 1065
  Hints, 1049–1052
  Homemade, 1037–1039
  Homemade White, 1065
  Honey Bran, 1068
  Irish Raisin, 1069
  Lost, 878
  Mixing, 1037–1039
  Nests, Scrambled Eggs in, 184
  Nut, Baking Powder, 1053
  Nut Raisin, 1071
  Onion, 1052
  Orange, I, 1071
  Orange, II, 1072
  Pancakes, 798
  Pulled, 104
  Rising, 1037–1039

Bread, Rye, 1067
Salt-Rising, 1074
Sally Lunn, 1073
Sauce, 559
Soup, 110
Soup, Bohemian Rye, 110
Spoon, 1069, 1074
Sticks, 96
Twisted, 1070
Vienna, 1075
Whole Wheat, 1067
Whole Wheat Honey, 1067
Yeast Potato, 1076
Breaded Carp, Baked, 236
Chops, Egg Coating, 152
Sweetbreads, 462
Bream, a fish, 194
Breast of Capon Drouant, 487
Chicken, Sauté Chasseur, 496
Ducklings Marquise, 521
Guinea Hen Adelina Patti, 532
Connoisseur, 532
Creole, 532
Genievre, 533
Lamb, 370
Lamb, Roast Stuffed, 384
Breton Baked Beans, 608
Breton Cabbage, 623
Bride's Cake, 912
Bridge Canapés, 14
Brigue, a fish, 193
Brisket, Beef, 312
Brisket, Beef, Corned, 312
Brisket of Beef with Sauerkraut, 328
Brisling, a fish, 211
Brittle, Peanut, 978
Brittle Squares, Almond, 968
Broadbill Swordfish, 218
Broccoli, 615
Amandine, 617
Boiled, 617
Creamed, au Gratin, 618
Divers Sauces, 618
Dressing,
Anchovy, 8
à la Drouant, 617
Hints, 616
Italian Style, 617
alla Milanese, 618
Pressure Cooked, 1164
Soufflé, 618
in Stuffed Tomatoes, 739
Brochet, a fish, 207

Brochette, Definition, 373
Chicken Liver, 450
Eggplant and Tomato, 657
Lamb, 369
Lamb Kidneys, 446
Sweetbreads, 462
Broiled Corn Picnic Fashion, 645
Cucumbers, 651
Duckling, 522
Fish, 191
Steak, Club, 328
Minute, O'Brien, 329
Porterhouse, Marchand de Vin, 329
Porterhouse, Marrow, 329
Tomato Sandwich, 848
Broiler, 482
Broilers, Oven Cooked, 515
Broiling, 983
Fish, 233
Pan Methods, 986
Sausage, 455
Time Table, 984
see also under names of foods.
Brook Sucker, a fish, 217
Brook Trout, 219, 298
Broth, 90
Broth, Chicken, Parisian, 113
Broth, Short, *see* Court Bouillon
Brown Bread, Boston, I, 1054
Bread, Boston, II, 1055
Butter Sauce, 559
Flour, 559
Nut Bread I, 1059
Nut Bread II, 1059
Potatoes, Hashed, 705
Pumpkin, 715
Rice, 768
Roux, 584
Sauce I, 560
Sauce II, 560
Sauce, III, 560
Stock, 91, 92
Sugar Hard Sauce, 896
Tomato Sauce, 561
Brûlot, Café, Creole Manner, 69
Brûlot, Louisiana Petit, 74
Brunoise, Definition, 96
Brunswick Stew of Old Dixie, 494
Brunswick Stew Maryland, 493
Brussels Sprouts, 619
Boiled, 619
with Chestnuts, 620
Chez Nous, 620
Crumb Sauce, 620

Brussels Sprouts, French Fried, 621
  Gourmet, 621
  au Gratin, 620
  Pressure Cooked, 1164
  Steamed, 619
Bruxelloise, Anguilles au Vert, 250
Bubble and Squeak, 330
Buca Lapi Asparagus, 600
Bucards, Shellfish, 225
Bucco, Osso, 357
Buckingham, Scrambled Eggs, 183
Buckled Skate, a fish, 214
Buckwheat Cakes, 798
  Cakes, Variations, 799
  Doughnuts, 780
Budapest Calf's Feet, 13
Buffalo Crabs, 227
  Fish, 195
Bull Frogs, 228
  Redfish, 209
  Trout, 220
Bull-head, 195
Bullnuts, 1027
Buns, Cinnamon, 1078
  Cinnamon Nut Raisin, 1079
  Hints, 1076
  Hot Cross, 1080
  Sticky, I, 1081
  Sticky, II, 1082
  Yeast Method, 1077
Burger Balls with Marjoram, 97
  Fried Egg, 168
  Hominy Croquettes, 752
  and Hominy, Squares, 751
  Rice, Mexican, 769
  Stuffing Loaf, 790
  Turkey Stuffing, 789
  See also Balls; Hamburgers
Burnt Almonds, 971
  Ice Cream, 1125
  Mousse, 1140
Burnt Chicken Princess, 495
Butt, Ham, and Sauerkraut, 417
  Pork, 393
Butter(s)
  Almond, I, 550
  Almond, II, 550
  Anchovy, 8, 550
  Balls, Pimiento, 645
  Bercy, 550
  Black, Brains in, 429
  Black, Shirred Eggs with, 185
  Brown, Sauce, 559
  Caviar, 550

Butter(s), Chivry, 550
  Cinnamon, Russian, 552
  Clarified, 563
  Compounded (Creamed), 549
  Crayfish, 551
  Crust, Anna's, 939
  Flake Rolls, 1097
  Garlic, 551
  Green, 551
  Herring, 551
  Horseradish, 551
  Lobster, 551
  Kneaded, 551
  Maître d'Hôtel, 573
  Marchand de Vin, 552
  Meuniere, 575
  Mustard, 551
  Nutmeg, Russian, 552
  Paprika, I, 552
  Paprika, II, 552
  Parsley, 573
    Kohlrabi, 667
    Mustard Variation, 573
  Peanut, *see* Peanut Butter, 852
  Roe, 552
  Rolls, 1098
  Sauce, Drawn, 567
  Sauce, Lemon, 572
  Shallot, 553
  Shrimp, 553
  Smoked Salmon, 552
  Snail, 294
  Tarragon, 553
  Tarts, 956
  Tomato, I, 553
  Tomato, II, 553
  Truffle, 553
  Vegetable, 553
Buttered Beets, 615
  Beets, Variation, 615
  Carrots, with Nuts, 629
  Cinnamon Fern, 662
  Hot Cabbage, 623
  Kale, 664
  Noodles, French, 757
  Ostrich Ferns, 661
  Rum Punch, 62
Buttermilk, 75, 80, 1125
  Almond Soup, Cream of, 121
  Biscuits, 1042
  Bran Biscuits, 1940
  Cornmeal Waffles, 806
  Griddle Cakes, 799
  Muffins, 1087

Buttermilk, Raisin Meringue Pie, 944
　Rolls, 1098
Butternuts, 1027
Butterscotch, Candy, 979
　Hard Sauce, 897
　Ice Cream, 1125
　Pecan Ice Cream, 1126
　Sauce, 891
　Toast, 1108

Cabbage, 621
　and Beef, Fried, 330
　à la Bretonne, 623
　Celery, 622
　and Celery au Gratin, 622
　Chinese, 622
　Corned Beef and, 334
　Hints, 622
　Hot Buttered, 623
　Hungarian, 624
　　Stuffed, 624
　Irish Colcannon, 625
　Koldolma, 625
　Leaves, Stuffing, Burger, 789
　　Stuffing, Epicure, 791
　Polish Bigos, 625
　Pressure Cooked, 1164
　Red, and Chestnuts, Casserole, 626
　　German, 623
　　Pressure Cooked, 1165
　for Salad, 622
　Savoy, French Style, 626
　Soup, Sour Cream, 121
　Steamed, au Gratin Amandine, 626
　Stuffed, 627
　　Madras, 627
　See also Salads
Cabellerote Snappers, a fish, 215
Cabillaud, a fish, 196
Cabinet Pudding, 863
Cacciotora, Chicken, 497
Cachicato, a fish, 200
Cactus, Pear, 827
Caen, Tripe à la Mode de, 472
Café Brûlot Creole Manner, 69
　Crème Fromage au, 865
　Diable, 69
　Diabolique Creole Manner, 69
　Eggnog Southern Manner, 70
　Épicé, 70
　Essence, 70
　Expresso, 70
　Flamand, 71
　Gloria, 71

Café Brûlot Creole Manner, au Lait, 71
　Mazagran, 72
　Mexicain, 72
　Royal, 71
　Syrien, 72
　Turque, 72
　Viennois, 71
Cajun Macaroons, 926
Cake, Apple Raisin, 911
　Applesauce Michigan, 919
　Angel Food, 909
　Baking Chart, 902–909
　Baking Failures, 902–909
　　Angel Food, 908–909
　　Layer Cakes, 902–908
　　Pound Cakes, 902–908
　　Sunshine Cakes, 908–909
　Blueberry, 912
　Bride's, 912
　Cheese, 913
　Chocolate, 913
　Coffee Custard, 914
　　Streusel, 1107
　Dobos, 914
　　Chocolate Filling for, 915
　　Icing, 915
　Egg Shortcake, 164
　Frozen Honey Fruit, 916
　Fruit, Frozen, 916
　　White, 921
　Hartford, 917
　Honey, 925
　Ice Cream, 917
　'Lection, 917
　Little Puff, 959
　Maraschino Cherry, 918
　Marble Loaf, 918
　Mocha Sponge, 919
　Raisin, Pioneer Salt Pork, 920
　Refrigerator Cheese, 920
　with Rum, 954
　Spice, 921
　Spiced Chocolate Fruit Creole, 921
　Sponge, 922
　Tipsy Sponge Squire, 922
Cakes, Buckwheat, 798
　Buckwheat, Variations, 799
　Crab, Maryland, 272
　Fish, 234
　Griddle, *see* Griddle Cakes, 795
　Puffs, Green Corn, 648
Calabrese, Artichokes, 595
Calas, 781

Calf's Brains, 427
  Feet, 427, 434, 437
    Budapest, 13
    Vinaigrette, 435
  Head, 351
    Grill Provençale, 352
    Soup I, 110
    Soup II, 111
    en Tortue, 352
    à la Vinaigrette, 352
  Heart, 427
  Kidneys, 427
  Liver, 310, 427, 449; see also under
    Liver
  Sweetbreads, 310, 428
  Tongue, 428
Calico Salmon, 209
California
  Bass, a fish, 193
  Dressing, 830
  Herring, 202
  Prune Whip Crunch, 863
  Veal Rolls, 352
Callista Clams, 225
Callos à la Catalana, 470
  Madrilena, 471
Cambridge Sauce, 561
Camembert Cheese, see Sandwich Fill-
  ings
Camille Canapés, 15
Campania, Spaghetti alla, 761
Canadian Clam Pie, 240
  Pea Soup, 112
Canapés, 5
  Anchovy Fingers, 5
    Lozenges, 6
    Nantais, 6
    Odette, 6
    Patricia, 7
    à la Royale, 7
    Rounds, 6
  Aristocrates, 14
  Beef Marrow, 23
  pour Bridge, 14
  Camille, 15
  Cannibal, 15
  Caviar, Leur Façon, 16
    Caviar Ma Façon, 16
    Sa Façon, 16
    Voisin, 15
  de Crevettes Creole, 17
  Fillings, 852–856
  Finnan Haddie, 19–20
  Flamands, 17

Canapés, Flemish, 17
  de Foie Gras, 17
    Goose Liver Pâté, 17
  de Haddock Fumé, 19–20
  Ham I, 20
  Ham II, 21
  Ham III, 21
  Ham Fried, 21
  Herring Roe, 21
  de Homard I, 20
  de Homard II, 20
  d'Huitres, 20
  de Jambon I, 20
  de Jambon II, 21
  de Jambon III, 21
    en Beignets Frits, 21
  Laitances de Hareng, 21
  Lobster I, 20
  Lobster II, 20
  Lorenzo, 22
  Marquis, 22
  Mephisto, 23
  Meurice, 23
  à la Möelle de Boeuf, 23
  Monte Cristo, 24
  Oyster, 20
  Richardin, 24
  Shrimp Creole, 17
  à la Statler, 9
Canard à la Paillard, 519
  au Sang, 522
Candied Carrots, 629
  Mint Leaves, 971
  Sweet Potatoes, 710
Candy, 965–979
  Temperature Chart, 968
Canned Corn Cream Style, 646
  Corn on the Cob, 645
  Fiddlehead Fern, 662
  Ostrich Fern, 662
Cannelons Parisiens, 956
Cannibal Canapés, 15
Cantaloupe, see under Salad
Cape Cod Fish Sauce, 262
  Grilled Codfish, 261
  Oysters, 230
  Sandwich, (Crabmeat), Hot, 848
Caper Dressing, 836
Caper-Hollandaise Sauce, 561
Capitone, a fish, 196
Capon, 481, 485–486, 490
  Braised Stuffed, 486
  Breast of, Drouant, 487
  Curry, à l'Indienne, 487

Capon, Galantine de, à la Reine, 488
　　Mousse, 488
　　Norfolk, 486
　　Roast, Alexandre Dumas, 489
　　Stuffed, with Raisins, 489
　　Stuffing, Ham-Walnut Brandied, 792
　　　　Olive, 793
　　　　Pecan, 794
Caracas Poached Eggs, 178
Caramel Ice Cream, 1126
Caramel Soup Coloring, 92
Caramels, Milk, 978
　　Milk, Chocolate, 972
　　Rum Honey, 978
Caraway Bread, 1061
Carbonade of Beef Flamande, 331
Cardinal, Lobster, 268
Cardoon(s), 628
　　Boiled, Divers Sauces, 628
　　Cooking of, 628
　　Fried in Batter, 628
　　Pressure Cooked, 1165
　　in Salad, 628
　　in Soup, 628
　　in Stews, 628
Caribbean Style Tamales, 45
Carlton Dressing, Boiled, 839
Carmen, Filets of Sole, 253
Carp, 195, 217, 236
　　Baked Breaded, 236
　　in Red Wine, 241
Carrelet, a fish, 198
Carrot(s), 628
　　Apple, and Cabbage Salad, 814
　　Au Gratin Gastronome, 638
　　Baked, 630
　　Boiled, 629
　　Buttered, with Aniseed, 629
　　　　with Nuts, 629
　　Candied, Nutmeg on, 629
　　Cookies, 927
　　Creamed, Nuts in, 629
　　Custard Cups, 631
　　à la Cyrano, 630
　　Flamandes, 630
　　Fritters, 631
　　Glazed, 632
　　Hints, 629
　　Juice, 631
　　Mint Leaves, 629
　　and Potato Fritters, 706
　　Pressure Cooked, 1165
　　Riced, 630
　　in Salad, 812

Carrot(s), Sandwich Filling, 853
　　Seasoning, 629
　　Shoestring, 632
　　Soufflé, 631
　　Vichy, 631
　　Whole, 629
Caruso, Potato Salad, 817
　　Spaghetti alla, 761
Carving, 991–999
　　Sets, 992
Casanova Sauce, 561
Cashew Nuts, 1027
Casino Clams, 241
　　Oysters, 279
Casserole
　　Chicken, Henrietta, 497
　　　　Metropole, 498
　　　　Newlywed, 498
　　　　and Sweet Potatoes, 508
　　Curried Rice with Mushrooms, 681
　　Deviled Mushrooms Au Gratin, 681
　　Eggplant, 656
　　Eggs Charcutière, 158
　　Frankfurter, Creole, 440
　　　　and Onion, 440
　　Ham, Bourgeoise, 418
　　　　and Rice, 419
　　Kidney Beans Bercy, 611
　　Lamb Cutlet Biarritz, 380
　　　　Hearts en, 443
　　Lentils, à l'Auvergnate, 671
　　Lima Beans and Bacon, 611
　　Red Cabbage and Chestnuts, 626
　　Scalloped Cucumbers, 653
　　Yellow Turnips en, 743
Cassolettes, Fricassee Frogs' Legs in, 259
　　of Lentils à l'Auvergnate, 671
Cassoulet à la Toulousaine, 388
Castillane, Guinea Hen à la, 533
Catfish, 195
Cauliflower, 632
　　Au Gratin, Smothered, 635
　　Boiling, 633
　　Country Style, 633
　　Curried, 634
　　Custard, 633
　　French Fried, 634
　　Leaves, 633
　　Lemon Butter, 635
　　Pressure Cooked, 1165–1166
　　à la Romane, 634
　　Souffle Amandine, 633
　　Soup, Cream of, 122

Cavalla, a fish, 195, 203
Caviar, 15, 218
  Butter, 550
  Canapés Leur Façon, 16
    Ma Façon, 16
    Sa Façon, 16
    Voisin, 15
  Dressing, 836
  Horseradish Dressing, 836
  See also Sandwiches
Cayenne Pepper, 1002
Ceci, 604; *see also* Chick-Peas
Cecile, Shirred Eggs, 185
Celeriac, 636; *see also* Celery Knob
Celery, 635
  Amandine, 636
  Boiled, 636
  Braised, 637
  Cabbage, 622
  and Cabbage au Gratin, 622
  Centerpiece, 37
  and Chestnuts, Creamed, 638
  Cranberry, Grape Salad, 824
  Crispness, 636, 812
  Custard Cups, 637
  Fritters, Curried, 637
  au Gratin Gastronome, 638
  Hints, 636
  Juice, 636
  Knob, 636
    Boiled, Hollandaise, 636
    Bourgeoise, 638
    Creamed, 639
    au Gratin Gastronome, 638
    Mashed, 639
  Pressure Cooked, 1166
  Root, 636, *see also* Celery Knob
  Sauce, 562
  Soup, Cream of, 122
  Stewed, 640
  Stuffed, 42
  Stuffing, 790
  Stuffing, Roast Goose, 529
  Tops, Dry, 636
  see also Salads
Celestine, Chicken, 498
  Eggs, 158
  Hamburger, 340
  Veal Ring Soufflé, 365
Cendrillon Consomme, 115
Cereals, 747
Cero, a fish, 202
Certified Milk, 76
Chablis, Spring Chicken Sauté au, 517

Chafing Dish, Brandade de Morue, 239
  Burnt Chicken Princess, 496
  Liver Terrapin in, 455
  Sweet Potatoes Imperial, 712
  Sweet Potatoes Royal, 713
  Sweetbreads Melba, 464
Chain Pickerel, 206
Chainside, a fish, 194
Chambertin Sauce, 562
Champagne Sherbert I, 1149
Champagne Sherbet II, 1150
Champagne Velvet, Black, 51
Champeaux, Chicken aux, 499
Channel Bass, 193, 196, 208
Channel Catfish, 195
Chantilly Mousse, 1140
Charcutière Baked Pork Chops, 395
Charcutière, Baked Shad Roe, 237
Charcutière, Eggs Casserole, 158
Chard, 640
  Croquettes, 641
  Greens, Boiled, 641
  Pressure Cooked, 1167
  Ring with Mushrooms, 641
    Variation, 642
  Soufflé, 642
  Swiss Style, 642
Charleston Shrimp Pie, 290
Charlotte, Filets of Sole, 253
Charlotte, Pineapple, Monte Carlo, 882
Charlotte Royal, 863
Chart, Beef, 312–313
  Broiling, 984
  Cake Baking, 902–909
  Candy Temperature, 968
  Deep Fat Frying, 986
  Frozen Meat, 1016
  Frozen Vegetables, Boiling, 1014
  Frozen Vegetables, Pressure Cooking, 1014
  Herb and Spice, 1001–1009
  Lamb, 370–371
  Fish, 193–224
  Nut, Characteristics, 1026–1031
  Nut, Weights and Measures, 1032
  Pork, 393–394
  Poultry, 481–484
  Pressure Cooker, 1162–1176
  Pressure Cookery, Altitude Corrections
    for, 1161
  Roasting, 988
  Shellfish, 224–233
  Variety Meats, 427
  Veal, 348–349

Chartreuse, Jellied Bananas, 877
Chasseur, Kidney, Veal or Lamb, 448
Chasseur Sauce, 571
Chasseur, Veal Cutlets, 362
Chateaubriand Steak, 313, 338, 997
Chatelaine, Sauce, 544, 585
Chatelaine, Turkey Grill, 544
Cheese, American, *see under* Sandwiches,
    Sandwich Fillings
  Bacon Toast, 1107
  Balls, Potato, 707
  Biscuit Rings, 939
  Biscuits, 1041, 1043
  with Brussels Sprouts, 619
  Cake, 913
  Cake, Refrigerator, 920
  and Chive Floats, 97
  Cottage, 75
    Biscuits, 1043
    and Marmalade Sandwich, 843
    Mold, 865
    Omelet, 155
    and Raisin Sandwich, 843
    Sandwich Filling, 854
  Cream, Almond Cookies, 928
    and Almond Sandwiches, 843
    and Apricot Sandwich, 844
    Biscuits, 1043
    Dressing, 831
    and Jelly Sandwich, 844
    and Pineapple Sandwich, 844
    see also Salads
  Creamed, Celery Stuffing, 42
  Custard Pie, Onion, 691
  Custard, Tomato Stuffing, 739
  Egg Dressing, 832
  Eggs in White Wine with, 166
  Head, Jellied Sour, 400
  and Hominy Timbales, 752
  and Lentil Loaf, 671
  and Macaroni Custard, 754
  Nests, Potato, 707
  Nutritional Values, 75
  Parmesan, Aigrettes, 4
  Parmesan, Grated, 760–762
  Parmesan, *see also* Sandwich Fillings
  Popcorn, 97
  Popovers, 1094
  Pot, Dressing, 840
  Pot, Schnitzelbank, 41
  Pie Crust, 939
  Pie, Curried Onion, 690
  Pie, Tomato, 740
  Ricotta, Lasagna al', 765

Cheese, Rolls, 1099
  Roquefort, Celery Stuffing, 42
  Roquefort, Dressing, French, 832
  Roquefort, Dressing, Mayonnaise, 838
    Sandwiches, 843–845
  Sauce, 562
    Variation I, 562
    Variation II, 562
    Variation III, 562
    Variation IV, 562
  Scrambled Eggs with, on Toast, 183
  Shortbreads, 1061
  Soufflé, 188
  Soufflé, Tomato, 740
  Sticks, 97
  Swiss, *see* Sandwiches
  Waffles, 806
  in Water, 28
  see also Sandwiches and Au Gratin recipes
Cherna, a fish, 199
Cherry Brandy Raspberry Sauce, 891
  Cake, Maraschino, 918
  Chess Pie, 945
  Hard Sauce, 897
  Ice, 1117
  Imperial, 864
  Mousse, 1141
  Sauce, 562
  (Maraschino) Pineapple Sherbet, 1153
  See also Salads
Cherrystone Clams, 225
Chesapeake Oysters, 230
Chess Cherry Pie, 945
Chestnuts, 1027
  Blanching, 1025
  Braised Ducklings with, 520
  Brussels Sprouts with, 620
  and Celery, Creamed, 638
  Ice Cream, 1131
  Marrons, 866, 1131
  Potted Stuffed Squabs, 536
  and Red Cabbage Casserole, 626
  Sea-Chestnuts, 232
  Shelling, 1025
  Soup Auvergnate, 113
    Cream of, 123
  Stuffing, 790; *See also* Marrons
Cheveux d'Ange, Consommé, 115
Chew, Algerian Date, 968
Chez Nous Brussels Sprouts, 620
Chez-Sci Beefsteak, 322
Chicago Roll Boiled Larded, 325
Chicken, 490–492
  Arroz con Polla, 492

Chicken, Breast Sauté Chasseur, 496
Broiling of, 984
Broth Parisian, 113
Burnt Princess, 495
Cacciotora, 497
Casserole Henrietta, 497
 Metropole, 498
 Newlywed, 498
Celestine, 498
aux Champeaux, 499
Chop Suey, 315
Chow Mein, 401
Cintra, 500
Cloister Style, 500
Cold Dishes, 514
Consommé, 141
à la Creole, 500
Croquettes, 480
Curry Napal, 512
Custard Cubes, 97
Dumplings, 517
in Egg Soufflé, 165
Excelsior, 501
Forcemeat Balls, 98
Fritters Grand'mere, 501
in Half Mourning, 501
Hodge Podge, 513
Liver en Brochette, 450
 Curry, 451
 Macaroni with, 755
 and Mushrooms on Toast, 451
 with Wild Rice, 774
 See also Sandwiches
Loaf, Cold, 510
 Jellied, 513
à la Maryland, 502
Minced, Belmont, 515
Mousse, 502, 514
and Mushroom Pie, 502
Pancakes, Netherland, 801
Pie, 480
Pies, Granny Lee's, 512
Poached, 516
in the Pot, 503
Ragoût, Almond Cream, 512
with Rice, 492
Risotto Piemontaise, 505
Roast Spring, en Casserole, 516
Roasting, 480
Salad 812
 Tuxedo Park, 506
See also Sandwiches
Sandwich Filling I, 853
 Filling II, 853

Chicken, *See also* Sandwich Fillings and
 Sandwiches
Sauce, Milk, 502
Sauté Bourguignonne, 507
 au Chablis, Spring, 517
 Jambalaya, 507
 Mushrooms and Olives, 508
Soufflé, Southern, 508
Soup, Cream of, 123
 Cream of, à la Reine, 124
Stew Hungarian Style, 356
Stock, 480
Stuffing, 504
 Celery, 790
 Ham-Walnut Brandied, 792
 Onion, 793
 Pecan, 794
Sweet Potatoe Casserole, 508
Tartar Style, 509
Tettrazini, 509
Timbale, 517
Waffles, 807
Chick-Peas, 604
Baked, 606
Chicory, Pressure Cooked, 1167
Chiffon Pie, Coffee Rum, 945
 Lemon, 947
Chiffonade, Dressing, 831
 Garnish, 98
Chili con Carne, 332
 con Frijoles, 332
 Green Tomatoes, 332
Chili Sauce, 748
Chincoteague Oysters, 230
Chinese Cabbage, 622
 Fried Pumpkin, 714
 Steak Strips, 333
Chinook Salmon, 209
Chinquapin, a fish, 206
Chinquapin Nuts, 1027
Chipolata Filet of Beef, 336
 Duckling, Menagere, 523
Chipped Beef, *see* Beef, Dried
Chips, Potato, 710
 Parsnip, Saratoga, 695
 Saratoga, 710
Chive(s), 1002
 and Cheese Floats, 97
 Creamed Spinach with, 721
Chivey, a fish, 223
Chivry Butter, 550
Chocolate, 53–54, 1127
 Almonds, 971
 Praline Squares, 969

Chocolate, Brazilian, 54
  Cake, 913
  Cream Roll, 913
  Dipping, 973
  Eggnog Plain, 54
  Filling for Dobos Cake, 915
  Fondant, 971
  French, 56
  Fruit Cake Spiced, 921
  Fudge Squares, 972
  Hard Sauce, 897
  Ice Cream I, 1127
  Ice Cream II, 1127
    Shake, 55
  Iceberg, 54; Iced, 57
  Icing, 934
  Malted Milk, 55
  Marbled Fudge Bars, 972
  Marshmallow Ice Cream, 1128
  Milk Caramels, 972
  Minted, 57
  Mousse, 1141
  Muffins, 1084
  Omelette, 864
  Parfait, 1145
  Pot de Crème au, 883
  Sauce, Almond, 890
    French, 893
    and Little Puff Cakes, 959
  Soda, 55
  Soufflé, 864
  Syrup, 55
  Torte with Almonds, 962
  Waffles, 807
Chops
  Breaded, Egg Coating, 152
  Broiling, 984
  Kidney, Veal, 348
  Lamb, 370
  Lamb, see Lamb Chops
  Loin, Pork, 393
    Lamb, 370
    Veal, 348
  Mutton, see Mutton Chops
  Pork, see Pork Chops
  Rib, Lamb, 370
    Pork, 393
    Veal, 348
  Shoulder, Lamb, 370
  Sirloin, Lamb, 371
  Veal, 347
    en Papillotes, 361
    Paprika, 361
    à la Rosalind, 361

Chop Suey, 315
  Beef, 315
  Beef Kidney, 445
  Dessert Sauce, 801
  Veal Heart, 443
Choucroute Garni, 397
Choupiquel, a fish, 194, 199
Chow Mein, 315
  Chicken, 401
  Liver, 452
  Pork, 401
  Turkey, 541
  Veal, 401
Chowder, Clam, Mass. Bay, 129
  Clam, New England, 129
  Codfish, 131
  Corn, 118
  Crabmeat and Corn, 132
  Cream Sauce in, 119
  Hudson River, 132
  Lobster, 133
  Vegetable, 142
Christmas Bread, 1061
  Gingerbread Men Cookies, 927
  Hard Sauce, 897
  Twist, Bohemian, 963
Chruszczik, 783
Chub, a fish, 203
Chuck of beef, 312
Chuck Steak Dinner, Pepper, 341
Chufa, 1028
Chutney Dressing, French, 831
  Mayonnaise, 835
Cider, 58–59
  Bowl, Spicy, 63
  Cooler, 59
  Cup I, 60
  Cup II, 60
  Cup III, 60
  Cup, English, 62
  Frappé, 60
  Fruit Punch, Normande, 61
  Hard, 59
  Ice, 1117
  and Lemon Cooler, 61
  Mulled, 62
  and Orange Cooler, 61
  and Pineapple Cooler, 61
  Punch, Peach, 62
    Punch, Thanksgiving, 63
  Sauce, smoked meat, 563
    for Pancakes, 804
  Sweet, 59
  Wassail, 61

Cigarette Fish, 223
Cimanda, a fish, 203
Cinnamon, 1002
  Apple Roly Poly Pinwheels, 956
  Bread Crumb Cookies, 926
  Buns, 1078
  Butter, Russian, 552
  Cream, Boston, 862
  Fern, 662
    Buttered, 662
  Honey Sauce, 893
  Nut Raisin Buns, 1079
  Pecan Rolls, 1102
  Raisin Rolls, 1101
  Rolls, 1099
  Toast, 1108
Cintra, Chicken, 500
Citron Cookies, 928
Citrus Fruit Ice, 1117
  Sherbet, 1150
Clam(s), 225
  Casino, 241
  Chowder, Mass. Bay, 129
    New England, 129
  Epicure, 242
  Fritters, 242
  Griddle Cakes, Curried, 799
  Juice Cocktail, 35
  Omelet, 153
  Pie, Canadian, 240
  Sauce, Lemon, 295
    Onion, 295
  Soufflé Club Style, 243
  Steamed, 295
Clambake, New England Kitchen, 277
Clarified Butter, 563
  Sugar Syrup, 972
Clarifying Fat, 985
  Stock, 94
Clear Beef Soup, 140
  Consommé, 141
  Turtle Soup, 130
Clementine, Lamb Chops, 378
Cloche, Mushrooms sous, 684
Cloister Style Chicken, 500
Clotted Almond Brandy Sauce, 891
Clover Leaf Rolls, 1100
  Refrigerator, 1104
Club Dressing, 831
  Sandwiches, *see* Sandwiches, Three-
    Decker
  Steak, 313, 328, 984
  Style Stuffed Celery, 42
Coalfish, 207

Coating Jelly
  Madeira Wine Aspic, 572
  Port Wine Aspic, 39, 581
  Sherry Aspic, 41
Cobia, a fish, 195
Cock-a-Leekie Soup, 114
Cocktail, Artichoke, 32
  Clam Juice, 35
  Crabmeat, Avocado, 32
    Knickerbocker Manner, 33
  Cranberry Juice, 33
  Fish Avocado, 33
    Raw, 36
  Grapefruit Mint, 34
  Honey, 34
  Lobster, 34
    Avocado, 33
  Melon Ball, 34
  Orange Juice, 33
  Oyster, Pickled, 35
  Raspberry, 33
  Sauce, I, 563
  Sauce, II, 563
  Sauce, III, 564
    Epicure, 34
    Fish, 36
    Horseradish Cream, 35
    Oyster, 36, 579
    for Shellfish, 34
  Scallop, Avocado, 33
  Shrimp, Avocado, 33
  Strawberry Juice, 33
  Tomato, Frozen, 33
Coco de Mer, 1028
Cocoa, 53–54, 1127
  Eggnog, 56
  Spiced, 58
  Syrup, 56
Coconut, 1028
  on Dessert Salads, 812
  Fondant Balls, 973
  Hard Sauce, 897
  Milk, 564
Coddled Eggs, 154
Coddling, *see* Short-Boiling, 990
Codfish, 196
  Baked Stuffed, 237
  Balls, 243
  Chowder, 131
  Creamed, in Potato Ring, 248
  Fresh, 240
  the Green, 207
  Grilled, Cape Cod Style, 261
  Omelet, 154

Codfish, Salt, 238
  Scramble (Fresh Cod), 240
  Scramble (Salt Cod), 238
  Steak Portuguese Style, 243
  Waffles, 807
Codling, 201
Coeur au Vin, 443
Coeurs d'Artichauts Pompadour, 24
Coffee, 63–67
  Armenian, 68
  Belgian, 71
  Brazilian Mocha I, 68
    Mocha II, 68
  Café Brûlot Creole Manner, 69
    Diable, 69
    Diabolique Creole Manner, 69
    Eggnog Southern Manner, 70
    Épicé, 70
    Expresso, 70
    Gloria, 71
    au Lait, 71
    Mazagran, 72
    Royal, 71
  Cream, a dessert, 865
  Cream, Imperial, 74
  Custard Cake, 914
  Essence of, 70
  Float, 72
  Frosted, 73
  Ice, a dessert, 1118
  Ice Cream I, 1128
  Ice Cream II, 1129
  Iced, a drink, 73
  Making, Drip Pot Method, 66
    Percolator Method, 66
    Pot Method, 66
    Vacuum Method, 67
  Mexican, 72
  Mousse, 1142
    Old-Fashioned, 1142
  Parfait, 1146
  Raisin Twist, 1106
  Ring, 1105
  Rings, 1075
  Rum Chiffon Pie, 945
  Sauce, for desserts, 891
  Shake, 73
  Streusel Cake, 1107
  Syrian, 72
  Turkish, 72
  See also Mocha
Coho Salmon, 210
Cola Nut, 1028
Colcannon, 625

Cold Chicken Loaf, 510
  Corned Beef, 334
  Ham Platter, 414
  Platter, 40
Cold-Water Method for Iced Tea, 83
Cole Slaw I, 815
  Creamy II, 815
  and Beet Ring Marinette, 813
  Swiss Cheese Sandwich, 844
Colette Poached Eggs, 178
Collards, Pressure Cooked, 1167
Colorado, a fish, 209
Colorado Trout, 219
Coloring, Caramel, 92
  Fondant, 972
  Soup, 91
  Whipped Cream, 917
  Whipped Evaporated Milk, 917
Columbia River Salmon, 209
Colys, 353
Compounded Butters, 549–554
Concarneau, Filets of Sole, 254
Conde, Pears, 882
Condensed Milk, Definition, 75
  Mayonnaise, 834
Conger Eel, 197
Connecticut Succotash, 733
Consommé, 90, 140
  Alexandra, 115
  Andalouse, 115
  Argenteuil, 115
  à l'Aurore, 114
  Cendrillon, 115
  aux Cheveux d'Ange, 115
  Chicken, 141
  Clear, 141
  Eggs Poached in, 152
  Ivan, 116
  Lorette, 116
  Madrilène, 115, 136
  Midinette, 116
  Mille Feuilles, 116
  Murat, 117
  Nana, 117
  Olga, 117
  Paulette, 117
  Saint Quentin, 117
  with Vermicelli, 115
Connoisseur, Breast of Guinea Hen, 532
Convent Style Liver, 453
Cookies, 923–934
  Almond, 925
  Bran Orange Drop, 926
  Bread Crumb Cinnamon, 926

Cookies, Carrot, 927
  Citron, 928
  Fig Preserve, 929
  Gingerbread Men, 927
  Ginger Molasses, 929
  Hints, 924
  Honey, 925
  Oatmeal, 925
Cooking Methods, 983
Cooler, Arctic, 67
  Cider, 59
  Cider and Lemon, 61
  Cider and Orange, 61
  Cider and Pineapple, 61
Coon Oysters, 230
Copper-nosed Bream, a fish, 194
Copper-Nosed Sunfish, 217
Coq à la Bourguignonne, 510
Coquelet au Corton, 511
Coquette, Poached Eggs, 178
Coquillage Doughnuts, Alsatian, 780
Coquilles St. Jacqueline, 244
  St. Jacques, 232, 244
  Sarah Bernhardt, 244
Corn, 642
  Boiling, 644
  Bread, Farmer's, 1063
    Kentucky, 1062
    Southern, 1068
    Stuffing, 790
    Tennessee, 1062
  Broiled, Picnic Fashion, 645
  Canned, Cream Style, 646
  Chowder, 118
  on the Cob, 648
  on the Cob, Canned, 645
  Crab Meat Chowder, 132
  Custard Pie, 646
  Egg Scramble, 155
  Fritters, 646
  Green Pepper-Stuffed Tomatoes, 739
    Cake Puffs, 648
    Roasted, 645
    Tamales, 45
  Hints, 644
  Husks, for Tamales, 44, 45
  Meal, 747
    Balls, 748
    Buttermilk Waffles, 806
    Dumplings, 98, 328
    Fritters, 749
    Mush, 1046
    Noodles, Southern, 759
    Polenta, 750

Corn, Meal, Pudding, Old-Fashioned, 749
    Ring Luncheon, 749
    Soufflé Dinner, 748
  Muffins, 1088
  O'Brien, 646
  Oysters, 646
  Pone, 607, 1068
  Pressure Cooked, 1167
  Pudding, 647
  Puffs, Curried, 648
  Roast, 648
  Scallop, 647
  Soufflé, 645, 647
  Soup, Cream of, 124
  Squaw, 645, 647
  Waterless Method of Cooking, 644
Corned Beef, 333–334
  Brisket, 312
  and Cabbage, 334
  Cold, 334
  Fowl Succotash, 335
  Sandwich, Hot, 849
  Soufflé, 335
Corned Pork Shoulder, 398
Cornets d'Abondance, 25
Corton, Coquelet au, 511
Côtelettes à la Victime, 390
Cotoros, a fish, 200
Cottage Cheese, 75
  Apple Pie, 943
  Aspic, Cucumber, 652
  Biscuits, 1043
  Marmalade Sandwich, 843
  Mold, 865
  Omelet, 155
  Raisin Sandwich, 843
  Sandwich Filling, 854
  see also Sandwich Fillings, 852–856
Cottonfish, 194, 199
Cotton Picker's Turnip Delight, 742
  Mashed Fluffy, 743
  Black Bean Soup, 110
Country Style Onion Omelet, 173
Couronnes de Concombre en Gelée, 25
Court Bouillon, 300
  I, 564
  II, 564
  III, 564
  Lobster, 268
  Salmon, Hollandaise, 286
  see also Short-Boiling, 990–991
Cove Oysters, 230
Coventry Style Liver, 453
Crab(s), 227

Crab(s), Benedictine, 244
  Cakes, Maryland, 272
  Creamed, on Waffles, 804
  à la Creole, 246
  Epicurean Friars Style, 245
  à la Maylie, 246
  Mousse, 514
  Soft-Shell, 227, 301
    Grilled Creole Style, 262
    Newburg, 248
Crab-Eater, a fish, 195
Crabmeat Cocktail, Avocado, 32
  Cocktail Knickerbocker, 33
  and Corn Chowder, 132
  Creamed, Sandwich, Hot, 848
  Crunches, 26
  Dewey, 247
  Extender, for, 292
  Louisette, 247
  Omelet à la Newburg, 155
  Paste Celery Stuffing, 42
  Puffs, 291
  Ravigote, 248
  Remick, 26
  Sandwich Filling, 853
  See also Sandwiches
  Stuffed Baked Eggplant, 655
Cracker Dumplings, 784
Crackers, Parsley, 104
  Puffed, 104
Craig Flounder, 198
Cranberry Dressing, 836
  Grape, Celery Ring Mold, 824
  Ice, 1118
  Juice Cocktail, 33
  Raw, in Salads, 811
  Sherbet, 1150
  Stuffing, 791
Craplach, 101
Crappie, a fish, 206
Cravo, a fish, 204
Crayfish Butter, 551
Cream, 75
  Almond Sauce, 890
  of Asparagus Soup, 120
  of Barley Soup, 120
  Bavarian, 873
  of Bean Soup, 121
  Boston Cinnamon, 862
  of Buttermilk Almond Soup, 121
  Canned Corn, Style, 646
  of Cauliflower Soup, 122
  of Celery Soup, 122
  Cheese, *see under* Cheese, Cream

Cream, of Chestnut Soup, 123
  of Chicken Soup, 123
    Reine Façon Bourgeoise, 124
  of Cucumber Soup, 125
  Coffee, a dessert, 865
  of Corn Soup, 124
  Desserts, Definition of, 874
  Dressing I, 831
  Dressing (Foamy) II, 831
  of Giblet Soup, 125
  Ginger, a dessert, 875
  Gold, a dessert 875
  Gravy, 565
  Gravy, for Sausage, 459
  Imperial Coffee, 74
  of Kidney Soup, 125
  Kisses, a candy, 973
  of Lettuce Soup, 126
  Lettuce Soup Amandine, 105
  Maple Nut Fondant, 976
  Mashed Pea Pods in, 698
  of Mushroom Soup, 126
  of Pea Pods Soup, 127
  Pie, Farmer's Nut, 946
    Gingerbread, Washingston's, 953
    Lemon, 947
      Variations, 947
    Meringue, 947
  Pudding, Fluffy Almond, 872
  of Pumpkin Soup, 127
  Roll, Chocolate, 913
  Sauce in Chowders, 119
    Medium, 118
    Thick, 118
    Thin, 118
  Soups, 118–128
  Soups, Delicate, 119
  Sour, 79
    and Beets, 613
    Bortsch, 107, 108
    of Cabbage Soup, 121
    Cubed Veal in, 353
    Dressing, 838
    Dressing, Boiled, 839
    Horseradish Sauce, 587
    Salad Dressing, 812
    Sauerkraut in, 719
      with Apples, 719
      with Spinach, 721
  Spanish, 873
  of Spinach Soup, 128
  Sweetness of, 80
  Thin, How to Whip, 916
  of Tomato Soup, 128

Cream, Whipped, How to Color, 917
  Jelly Dressing, 841
Creamed Artichokes, Jerusalem, 597
  Asparagus in Toast Rings, 603
  Broccoli au Gratin, 618
  Butters, 549
  Carrots, Nuts in, 629
  Celery and Chestnuts, 638
    Knob, 639
  Cheese Celery Stuffing, 42
  Chicken Ragoût, Almonds, 512
  Codfish in Potato Ring, 248
  Cucumber Slices, 652
  Dried Beef, Poached Eggs, 432
  Eggs in Spinach Ring, 156
  Finnan Haddie Delmonico, 249
  Green Peas, Bayou, 697
  Ham in Rice Border, 414
  Hamburger Sandwich Filling, 854
  Hominy, 751
  Kohlrabi, 667
  Leeks au Gratin, 670
    Variations, 670
  Lettuce, 675
  Lima Beans, Fresh, 609
  Macaroni, 754
  Mushrooms, 680
  Noodles au Gratin, 757
  Parsnip au Gratin, 694
  Pea Pods, 697
  Potatoes, 702
    Old Fashioned, 704
  Spinach with Chives, 721
  Tuna Sandwich, Hot, 849
Crema, Macaroni alla, 754
Crème Amandine, 865
  Fromage au Café, 865
  aux Marrons, 866
  de Neige, Sauce, 895
  Pot de, au Chocolat, 883
  Vichyssoise, 123
Creole, Beef Kidney, 445
  Bluefish, Baked, 235
  Café Brûlot, 69
  Café Diabolique, 69
  Chicken à la, 500
  Crabs à la, 246
    Grilled Soft-Shell, 262
  Custard, Sweet Potato, 712
  Cake, Chocolate Fruit, 921
  Dried Beef Shortcake, 433
  Guinea Hen, Breast of, 532
  Hamburgers à la, 341
  Ham Steaks, 420
  Lamb Chops, 378

Creole, Liver, 452
  Okra, 686
  Omelet, 156
  Pig, Roast Suckling, 407
  Pork Chops, Braised, 397
  Rice, 768
    way of cooking, 247
    in Stuffed Tomatoes, 739
    Sauce New Orleans, 565
    West Indies, 565
  Sausage Meat Patties, 459
  Sausage Noodle Ring, 759
  Shrimp Canapés, 17
  Sprouted Soybeans, 612
  Tripe, 470
  Veal Ragoût, 365
Crêpes, 796, 866–869
  à la Francaise, 801
  Helena, 866
  Lisette Meringuées, 867
  Nantaises, 867
  Suzette, 801, 866, 868
Crevettes, shellfish, 233
Crimsel, Matsos, 1070
Croaker, a fish, 193
Crocus, a fish, 196
Crooked Neck Squash, Glazed, 730
Croquettes, 373
  Boston Baked Bean, 608
  Chard, 641
  Chicken, 480
  Dominicaines, 26
  Fish, 234
  Frying, Deep Fat, 986
  Ham and Egg, 160
  Hominy and Burger, 752
  Lentil, 672
  Nut, 1026
  Onion, 692
  Oyster, Dominican, 26
  Potato and Spinach, 709
  Rice, I, 770
  Rice, II, 770
Crosnes, 649
  Boiled, 649
  in Salads, 649
Croustades, 19
  Rice, 771
Croûtons, 99
  Dumplings, Fried, 785
  Hominy, 101
Crovens, a fish, 213
Crown Roast, Frankfurter, 436
  Lamb, 370, 375

Crown Roast, Lamb, Variations, 376
    Pork, 398
    Spareribs, 409
    Veal, 348
Crullers, 781
Crumb Balls, 96
    Bread, *see* Bread Crumb
    Cinnamon Cookies, 926
    Sauce, Brussels Sprouts, 620
    Walnut Crust, 943
Crumbs, Bacon, 95
Crumpets, 781
Crunches, Black Walnut, 970
Crust, Pie, Cheese, 939
    Pie, Anna's Butter, 939
    Walnut Crumb, 943
    See also under Pie
Cubes, Chicken Custard, 97
    Royal Custard, 105
Cubed Veal in Sour Cream, 353
Cucumber(s), 649
    Au Gratin, 652
    Baked Stuffed, 651
    Boiled, 651
    Broiled, 651
    Cooking of, 650
    Cottage Cheese Aspic, 652
    Creamed Slices, 652
    Dressings, 650, 831
        Hot, 839
    Fluted, in Salad, 811
    Fritters, 652
    Hints, 650–651
    Nasturtium Leaves on, 651
    Pressure Cooked, 1167
    Rings in Jelly, 25
    See also Salad
    Sauce, 296, 650–651
    Sautéed, 653
    Scalloped, 653
    Sliced, 650
    Slices, Stuffed, 27
    Soup, Cream of, 125
    Sour Cream, 651, 653
    Wilted, 651
Cumberland Dressing, 836
    Sauce I, 566
    Sauce II, 566
    Snacks, 27
Cup, English Cider, 62
    Cider, I, 60
    Cider, II, 60
    Cider, III, 60
    Onion, Peas in, 699

Cup, Orange-Cherry, 411
Curaçao Mousse, 1142
Currant Strips, Red, 960
    Jelly Dressing, 831
    Jelly Gravy, 565
Curried Avocado Omelet, 167
    Biscuits, 1044
    Cauliflower, 634
    Celery Fritters, 637
    Chopped Meat in Stuffed Tomatoes, 739
    Clam Griddle Cakes, 799
    Corn Puffs, 648
    Eggs, Hard-Cooked, with Noodles, 157
    Scrambled, with Lobster, 157
    Lamb with Bananas, 379
        Kidneys, 445
        Stew, 372
    Onion Cheese Pie, 690
    Potato Nockerln (Dumplings), 99
    Rice with Mushrooms, 681
        Waffles, 808
    Sausage and Onion Shortcake, 459
    Tomatoes, Baked, 736
    Veal Balls, 354
Curry, Beans, Canned Baked, 605
    of Capon à l'Indienne, 487
    Chicken Liver, 451
    of Chicken Napal, 512
    Dressing, 832
    Lobster Risotto Crown, 268
    of Mutton, 389
    of Rice, 768
    Sauce, Cocoanut Milk for, 564
    Sauce I, 566
    Sauce II, 567
    Sauce III, 567
    Skate Wings, 292
    Soybeans, Sprouted, 612
    of Turkey Wild Rice, 539
Cushion, Lamb, 371
    Pork, 394
    Roast, Veal, 348
Custard(s), 869
    Asparagus, 601
    Baked, 869, 870
        Browning, 869
    Boiled, 869, 870
    Cake, Coffee, 914
    Cauliflower, 633
    Cheese, Stuffed Tomatoes with, 739
    Cubes, Chicken, 97
        Royal, 105
    Cups, Carrot, 631
        Celery, 637

Custard, Delicate, 870
  Firm, Creamy, 870
  French, Rich, 870
  Hints, 869
  Macaroni and Cheese, 754
  Orange, 881
  Pies, 869
    Corn, 646
    Onion Cheese, 691
  as Sauces, 871
  Soft, 870, 871
  Sweet Potato, Creole, 712
  Turnip, 743
Cutlet(s), Fish, 234
  Frying, Deep Fat, 986
  Orange Sauce, 894
  Lamb, Casserole Biarritz, 380
  Mutton, à la Soyer, 390
  Veal, 348
    Chasseur, 362
    a la D'Aremberg, 362
    à la Sacher, 363
    Sarah Bernhardt, 363
    Sevillana, 363
    Smitana, 364
Cutthroat Trout, 219
Cyrano, Carottes à la, 630

Dab, a fish, 196, 203
Dagouret, Red Wine Sauce, 583
Dame Simone, Stuffed Lettuce, 677
Dandelion Greens Farmer's Style, 663
  Pressure Cooked, 1167
  Wilted, 663
D'Aremberg Veal Cutlets, 362
Dasheens, Pressure Cooked, 1168
Date(s)
  Chew, Algerian, 968
  Bread, 1063
  Hard Sauce, 897
  Molasses Yeast Bread, 1063
  and Nut Biscuits, 1044
  Nut Bread, 1064
  Tartlets, 957
  See also Salads
  See also Sandwich Fillings
Daube, Beef en, 316
Dauphinoise, Lentils à la, 672
Deep Dish Apple Pie, French, 946
  Dish Blueberry Pie, 945
  Fat Frying, 985
    Time Table, 986
  Fried Pumpkin Blossoms, 715
  Sea Scallops, 231

Deglacé, 578
Delmonico, Cherry, 823
  Creamed Finnan Haddie, 249
  Potatoes, 704
  Steak, 313
Demi-Glace Sauce, 567
Desserts, 859–889
  Cakes, 901–923
  Cookies, 924–934
  Cream, Definition, 874
  Frozen, Gelatin, 1116
  Gingerbread, 1091
  Jelly, Definition, 874
  Mousses, 1139–1144
  Pies, 937–953
  Pastries, 954–963
  Ice Creams, 1113–1138
  Parfaits, 1144–1148
  Sauces, *see* Sauces, Dessert
  Sherbet, 1148–1155
  Waffles, 804
  See also Cream; Crême; Crêpes; Custard; Doughnuts; Duff; Fritters; Gelatin; Jelly; Meringues; Pies; Pudding; Sponge; Soufflé; Tarts; Tortes; Trifles; *and names of* Individual Ingredients
Deviled Grilled Guinea Hen, 533
  Herring, 249
  Lamb Kidneys, 446
  Lima Beans, 609
  Mushrooms au Gratin, 681
  Noodles au Gratin, 757
  Pig's Feet, 435
  Tomatoes, 737
Dewey, Crab Meat, 247
Diabolique, Cafe, Creole, 69
Dickens, Veal and Ham Pie, 364
Dieppoise Mussel Omelet, 169
Dietetic Egg, 158
Dill Slices, Stuffed, 28
Dinner Rolls, 1100
Dipping Chocolate, 973
Dixie Brunswick Stew, 494
Dobos Cake, 914
  Icing, 915
  Chocolate Filling for, 915
Dog Salmon, 209
  Snappers, a fish, 215
Dogfish, 194, 199
Dollardee, a fish, 194
Dolly Warden Trout, 219
Dolmas, 44
  (Hot or Cold), 376

Dominican Oyster Croquettes, 26
Don Gasper, Mushrooms, 683
Dore Pike, 207
Dory Pike, 207
Double Sirloin Steak la Pérouse, 336
Doughnuts, 779, 782
  Alsatian Coquillage, 780
  Buckwheat, 780
  Deep Fat Frying, 986
  Filled, 782
  Gingerbread, 782
  Hints, 779
  Lemon, 783
  Raised, 783
Drawn Butter Sauce, 567
Drawn Poultry, 481
Dredge, Definition, 1035
Dressed Poultry, 481
Dressing, Artichoke, 8
  Broccoli, 8
  French, 830
    Variations, 812, 830–833
  Mayonnaise, 834
    Variations, 834–838
  Meat & Poultry, *see* Stuffing
  Oyster, 8
  Salad, 830–841; *see also* Salad Dressings
Dried Beef, *see* Beef, Dried
Drop Biscuits, 1042
  Cookies, Bran Orange, 926
Drouant, Broccoli à la, 617
Drum, a fish, 196, 213
  Fresh Water, 206
  Red, 208
Dry Milk, 76
Dublin Pond Trout, 219
Dubrovnik, Spinach Entree, 721
Duchesse Potatoes, 706
Duck(s), 483, 518
  à la Bearnaise, 519
  in Its Own Blood, 522
  à la Bourgeoise, 519
  Braised Baby, 520
    in White Wine, 519
  en Chausson, 519
  a l'Italienne, 519
  Mock (Lamb), 371
  au Navets, 519
  with Olives, 524
  Potted, à la Creole, 519
  Stew Hungarian Style, 356
  Stuffing, 526–527
    Giblet, 791
    Olive, 793

Duck(s), and Rice Dinner, 524
  Roast à l'Orange, 525
  Roasting, 526
Ducklings, Braised, 520
  Breasts of, Marquise, 521
  Broiled, 522
  Chipolata Menagere, 523
  Montmorency, 523
Duff, Apple, 860
  Peach, 881
  Plum, 883
Dumas, Roast Capon Alexandre, 489
Dumplings, 783
  All-Bran, 95
  Apple, Frosted (Dessert), 957
  Baking Powder, 96
  Brain and Mushrooms, 430
  Bread Crumb, 784
  Chicken, 517
  Cornmeal, 98, 328
  Cracker, 784
  Crouton, Fried, 785
  Egg-Almond, 785
  Farina, 100
    Fried, 785
  Floats, 100
  Fluffy, 785
  Ham, 786
  Hungarian, 317
  Lithuanian, 787
  Liver, 102
    Moderne, 786
  Meat, 786
  Milk (Dessert), 880
  Nutmeg, 103
  Parsley, 787
  Philadelphia, 140
  Potato, Bohemian, 784
    Curried, 99
  Salmon, 787
  Tomato Juice, 788
  Watercress, 788
Dungeness Crabs, 227
Dutch Apple Bread, 1064
  Banana Pancakes, 799
  Nanies, 799
  Spiced Pot Roast, 344
  Potted Veal Steak, 358
Duxelles, Mushroom, 339
Dweller Clams, 225, 226

Easter Cross, 195
Eastern Hard Crabs, 227
Echinus, a shellfish, 232

Eclairs d'Anchois, 27
Edible Nuts, 1023
  Wild Greens, 662
Eel, 196
  Back, *see* Flounder, 198
  Conger, 197
  in Green Herbs Brussels, 250
  Gulper, 203
  Pout, a fish, 203
  Sand, 197
  Stew, 250
Egg(s), 143–188
  Almond Dumplings, 785
  Asparagus & Spinach Salad, 813
  Avocado & Roquefort Cheese, 822
  Balls, 100
  Beating, 149
  Benedict, 157
  Burger Luncheon, Fried, 168
  Casserole Charcutière, 158
  Celestine, 158
  Cheese Dressing, 832
  Chocolate Omelette, 864
    Soufflé, 864
  Coating for Breaded Chops, 152
  Cookery Rules, 151
  Dietetic, 158
  Digestibility of, 146
  Dressing, 836
  and Dried Beef Pie, 433
  Flakes, 100
  Florida, 158
  Fried, with Noodles, 758
    Sandwich, 849
  Scotch Style, 168
  Fritters à la Milanaise, 159
    à la Royale, 159
  Frozen, 1010
  au Gratin Celia, 160
  and Ham, Croquettes, 160
    in Denver Sandwich, 849
  Methods of Cooking, 146, 150, 151
  Meringues, 879, 1123–1124
  Mollet, 160
  Noodles, Fried, Chinese Style, 758
    Homemade, 758
    Ring, 757
  Omelet, *See under* Omelet
  Ox Eyes, 161
  Pancake Turnovers, 169
  Patties Bourgeoise, 162
  Pie French Style, 161
  Planked, in Nest My Way, 175

Egg(s), Poached, 152, 176
  Amandine, 176
  in Aspic I, 177
    II, 177
  Boulangère, 177
  Bourdaloue, 177
  Caracas, 178
  Colette, 178
  Comte Potocki, 180
  Coquette, 178
  à la Frissac, 179
  Leeks, Lemon Butter, 670
  Lucette, 179
  Mongole, 179
  Mornay, 179
  Ninon, 180
  Parmentier, 180
  Potato Nests Jacqueline, 180
  à la Reine, 181
  in Rice Ring, 181
  Rodriquez, 181
  à la Rotonde, 182
  with Sausage Cakes, 458
  Strasbourgeois, 182
  à la Suissesse, 182
  Suzanne, 182
  and Potato Scallop, 162
  Ramekins Florentine, 162
  Renversés, 163
  Yvonne, 163
  Rice Patties in Watercress, 164
  Ring Parisienne, 164
  Sauce I, 568
  Sauce II, 568
  Salad, *see* Sandwiches
  Sausage, English, 166
  Scrambled, 152
    in Bread Nests, 184
    à la Buckingham, 183
    with Cheese on Toast, 183
  Scrambled, Milanaise, 184
  Scrambled, and Sausages, 456
  Scrambled, Spanish Style, 184
  Shirred, 184
    au Beurre Noir, 185
    Boulevardier, 185
    Cecile, 185
    à l'Estragon, 186
    Midinette, 186
    Tetrazzini, 186
  Short Cake, 164
  Soufflé Bernardine, 165
  Stew, Mother Kate Turner's, 165

Egg(s), Stuffed, 42, 152
  in Aspic, 187
  à la Béchamel Suprême, 187
  Filling No. 1, 42
  Filling No. 2, 42
  Filling No. 3, 43
  Filling No. 4, 43
  Filling No. 5, 43
  Filling No. 6, 43
  Filling No. 7, 43
  Filling No. 8, 43
  Squiggled, 183
  and Tomato Jelly Luncheon, 741
  à la Tripe, 166
  in White Wine with Cheese, 166
  Yolk Garnish, 152
    Pastry Pie Covering, 940
  See also Sandwich Filling
Eggnog, Café, Southern, 70
  Cocoa, 56
  Chocolate, Plain, 54
    Fluffy, 54
  Ice Cream, 1129
  Pecan Pie, 949
  Sauce, 892
Eggplant, 654
  Armenian Style, 655
  Baked Crabmeat Stuffed, 655
  Casserole, 656
  French Fried, 657
  Fried in Batter, 656
  au Gratin, 656
  Hints, 654
  Pressure Cooked, 1168
  à la Romaine, 657
  Soufflé, 657
  Steak, Grilled, 658
    Variations, 658
  and Steak Sandwich, Hot, 850
  Stuffing, Burger, 789
  and Tomato en Brochette, 657
Eggs, Sea, shellfish, 232
Elbot, a fish, 201
Elder Blossom Pancakes, 800
Emincé of Chicken Belmont, 515
Endive, Pressure Cooked, 1168
English Cider Cup, 62
  Egg Sausage, 166
  Mutton Chops, 389
  Muffins, 1088
  Plum Pudding, 871
  Tea Biscuits, 1044
  Walnuts, 1030, 1031
Eperlans, a fish, 214

Épicé, Café, 70
Epicure Clams, 242
  Cocktail Sauce, 34
    Variation (a), 35
    Variation (b), 35
    Variation (c), 35
  Scallop, 287
  Stuffing, 791
Epicurean Friars, Crabs, 245
Equivalents & Measurements, 1019–1023
Erenacca Skate, a fish, 214
Esaü Potage, 135
Escargots à la Bourguignonne, 294
Escarole, 812
  Pressure Cooked, 1168
Escallop of Veal with Sorrel, 355
Escalopes de Veau à l'Oseille, 355
Escoffier Potato Salad, 818
Essence, Café, 70
Espada, a fish, 218
Espagnole, Sauce, 587
Estragon, Shirred Eggs à l', 186
Evaporated Milk, 75
  Whipped, 80, 916, 1115
  How to Color, 917
Excelsior, Chicken, 501
Expresso, Café, 70
Extender for Crabmeat, 292

Fairmaid, a fish, 208
Fall Herring, 202
Farina Dumplings, 100
  Fried, 785
Farmer's Nut Cream Pie, 946
Fasnachts, 783
Fat, Deep, Frying, 985
  How to Clarify, 985
Fathead, a fish, 209
Favorite, Artichoke, à la, 594
Feet, 427, 434
  Calf's, 427, 434
    Vinaigrette, 435
    in White Wine Jelly, 437
  Lamb's, 369, see also pp. 434–437
  Pig's, 427, 434
    Baked Granny's Way, 434
    Deviled, 435
    Pickled, 436
    St. Menehould, 437
    in Wine Jelly, 436
  Sheep's, 427, 434
    Mutton Trotters au Gratin Melbourne, 435

Feet, Sheep's, Mutton Trotters, Ravigote, 436
  in White Wine Jelly, 437
Feather Potato Water Rolls, 1103
Ferluche, Tarte à la, 962
Fermière Black Bean Soup, 110
  Petits Pois à l'Etuvée, 699
Fern, Bracken, 662
  Cinnamon, 662
    Buttered, 662
  Fiddlehead, 661
    Canned, 662
  Ostrich, Buttered, 661
Fiddler Crabs, 227
Fig Bread, 1065
  Imperatrice, 871
  Preserve Cookies, 929
  Tartlets, 957
  Waffles, 808
  see also Sandwich Fillings
Figaro, Lobster, 269
Filberts, 1028
  Blanching, 1024
Filé Powder, 495
Filet
  of Beef with Bearnaise, 346
    Braised, 325
    Chipolata, 336
    Garibaldi, 337
    au Marsala, 337
    Mignon, 313, 338
      à la Richmond, 338
      Stéfanie, 339
    Roast Pork, 405
  of Sole (Flounder) Amandine, 251
    Ambassador Hotel, 252
    à l'Américaine, 252
    Bonne Femme, 253
    Carmen, 253
    Charlotte, 253
    Concarneau, 254
    Cordon Bleu, 254
    Jacqueline, 255
    Jeanine, 255
    Marguery, 256
    Meunière, 256
    Mornay, 257
    Nadine, 257
    St. Malo, 257
    St. Raphael, 258
    Valenciennes, 258
    Whitefish, au Gratin, 305
Filled Doughnuts, 782

Filling, Tart, Rum Pecan, 960
  Chocolate, for Dobos Cake, 915
  Canapes, see Sandwich Fillings
Fingers, Anchovy Canapés, 5
Fines Herbes Liver, 453
  Omelet aux, 170
  Sauce, 453
Fine-scaled Sucker, a fish, 217
Finnan Haddie, 198, 200
  Canapés, 19–20
  Creamed, Delmonico, 249
  in Milk, Poached, 282
Fish, 189–224, 233–306
  Aspic, 266
  Baking, 191, 192, 233
  Boiling, 191, 233, 234
  Broiling, 191, 233, 984
  Cakes, 234
  Chart, 193–224
  Chop Suey, 315
  Cleaning, 234
  Cocktail, Avocado, 33
    Raw, 36
    Sauce, 36
  Croquettes, 234
  Cutlets, 234
  in Egg Soufflé, 165
  Essence, 580
  Filets, Deep Fat Frying, 986
    see also Filet
  Frozen, 233, 1010
  Frying, 233, 234
  Fumet, Parisian, 580
  Gefuellte, Cold, 261
  Gefuellte, Hot, 261
  Grilled, 261
  Jelly, 266
  and Milk superstition, 254
  Mousses, 514
  Pan-Frying, 192
  Paste Celery Stuffing, 42
  Poached, 191
  Roe, see Caviar and Sandwich Fillings
  Salad, 813
  Salt, 234
  Sauce, 192
    Cape Cod, 261
  Short Broth for Boiling, see Court-Bouillon
  Smoked, 234
  Stuffing, Epicure, 791
  Stock, 92
Flakes, Egg, 100
Flaky Pastry, 938

Flaky-Short Pastry, 939
Flamand, Café, 71
Flamande, Carbonade of Beef, 331
Flaming Ice Cream Sauce, 1129
Flamingo Snapper, a fish, 215
Flank, Beef, 312
  Steak, 312
Flannel-Mouthed Sucker, 217
Flatfish, 203
Flemish Asparagus, 600
  Beef and Oyster Pie, 321
  Canapés, 17
  Carrots, 630
  Pancakes, 800
Fletan, a fish, 201
Flip, Waldorf Beer, 52
Float, Coffee, 72
Floating Island, 872
Floats, Cheese and Chive, 97
  Dumpling, 100
Flour, How to Brown, 559
Florentine Baked Pork Chops, 395
Florida Eggs, 158
Flounder, 198, 251
  Summer, 251
  Winter, 251
Flounder, Filet of, Amandine, 251
  Ambassador Hotel, 252
  à l'Américaine, 252
  Bonne Femme, 253
  Carmen, 253
  Charlotte, 253
  Concarneau, 254
  Cordon Bleu, 254
  Jacqueline, 255
  Jeanine, 255
  Marguery, 256
  Meunière, 256
  Mornay, 257
  Nadine, 257
  St. Malo, 257
  St. Raphael, 258
  Valenciennes, 258
Flowers, Zucchini Squash, 729
Fluff, Banana and Sweet Potato, 711
  Sauce, Orange, 894
Fluffy
  Almond Cream Pudding, 872
  Avocado Omelet au Curry, 167
  Dumplings, 785
  Mashed Potato Spinach, 721
  Pumpkin, Baked, 716
  Rum Sauce, 892
  Turnips, Mashed, 743

Fluke, a fish, 198
Flummery, Blueberry, 862
Foamy Banana Sauce, 892
Fondant, 973
  Balls, Coconut, 973
  Chocolate, 971
  Coloring, 972
  Flavoring, 972
  Hints, 974
  Maple, 976
    Nut Creams, 976
  Maraschino Bonbons, 976
Fondue de Tomates, 585
Forcemeat Balls, Chicken, 98
  Stuffing, Lamb, 385
  for Turkey Galantine, 542
Four-Spotted Flounder, 198
Fowl, *see* Poultry
  and Corned Beef Succotash, 335
Framboise à la Nina, 873
Franconville, Asparagus, 601
Frankfurter(s), 437
  Barbecue Sauce for, 439
  Barbecued with Bacon, 438
  Caraway Cabbage, 438
  Casserole Creole, 440
  Crown Roast, 439
  in Golden Jackets, 439
  and Kale Dinner, 665
  with Lentils, 672
  and Onion Casserole, 440
  Platter, 440
Frappé, 1116
  Cider, 60
French
  Apple Slice Pie, 946
  Beans, String, 726
  Bean Soup, Black, 109
  Bean Soup, Cream of, 121
  Bread, 1065
  Calf's Head Soup, 111
  Chestnut Soup, Cream of, 123
  Chocolate, 56
  Chocolate Sauce, 893
  Deep Dish Apple Pie, 946
  Dressing, 811, 812, 830
    Variations, 830–833
      Bar-Le-Duc, 830
      Breslin, 830
      California, 830
      Chiffonade, 831
      Chutney, 831
      Club, 831
      Cream Cheese, 831

French, Dressing, Variations, Cream I,
831
  Cream (Foamy) II, 831
  Cucumber, 831
  Currant Jelly, 831
  Curry, 832
  Egg-Cheese, 832
  Honey, 832
  Mint, 832
  Roquefort Cheese, 812, 832
  Vinaigrette, 832
  Waldenstein, 832
  Wilmot, 833
Egg Pie, 161
Fried
  Artichokes, Jerusalem, 597
  Asparagus, 603
  Brussels Sprouts, 621
  Cauliflower, 634
  Eggplant, 657
  Kohlrabi, 667
  Okra, 686
  Pepper Rings, Green, 659
  Onions, 691, 986
  Pancakes, 800
  Potatoes, 703, 986
  Sweet Potatoes, 711
Fritto Misto, Potato, 704
Griddle Toast, 1108
Grunt, a fish, 199
Hard Sauce, 897
Lamb Chops, 372
Lima Beans, 609
Little Pot, 139
Mutton, Braised Leg of, 387
Noodles, Buttered, 757
Pancakes, 801
Peas, Green, 698
Peas, Stewed Green, 699
Petits Pois à la, 698
Potato Fritto Misto, 704
Toast, 1109; see also Pain Perdu
Tomato Fritters, 737
Veal Stew, 349
Wafers, 931
Fresh Water Drum, a fish, 206
Freshwater Herring, 202
Friar's Friandises Platter, 27
Fricassée Fowl, 480
  Frogs' Legs, 259
  Mackerel, 271
  Oyster, Baltimore, 279
  Oyster, Boston, 279

Fried Beef and Cabbage, 330
  Crouton Dumplings, 785
  Egg Burger Luncheon, 168
  Eggs Montfermeil, Stuffed, 168
  Egg Noodles, 758
    Chinese, 758
  Egg Sandwich, 849
  Eggs Scotch Style, 168
  Farina Dumplings, 785
  French, see under French Fried
  Frogs' Legs, 259
  Ham Canapés, 21
    Sandwich, 849
  Pig's Knuckles, 398
  Pumpkin Blossoms, 715
  Pumpkin, Chinese, 714
Frigate, a fish, 203
Frijole Beans, Baked, 606
  Chili con Carne con, 332
Frimsel Soup, 134
Frissac, Poached Eggs, 179
Fritots, Anchovy, 9
Fritter(s), Almond, 859
  Batter I, 568
  Batter II, 568
  Brain, 430
  Carrot, 631
  Chicken, Grand'mere, 501
  Clam, 242
  Corn, 646
  Corn Meal, 749
  Cucumber, 652
  Curried Celery, 637
  Deep Fat Frying, 986
  à la Milanaise, 159
  Okra, I, 687
  Okra, II, 687
  Oyster, 280
  Parsnip, 695
  Potato and Carrot, 706
  à la Royale, 159
  Salsify, 717
  Squash, I, 731
  Squash, II, 731
  Tomato, 737
  Turkey, 542
Fritto Misto, 28
  Potato Batter, 704
  Sea Food, 292
Frogs, 228
  Legs Fricassée en Cassolettes, 259
    Fry My Way, 259
    Gourmet, 260
    Mornay, 260

Fromage de Cochon, 399
  Crème, au Café, 865
Frosted Apple Dumplings, 957
  Coffee, 73
  Raspberry Cocktail, 33
Frost Fish, 198, 223
Frozen Fish, 233
  Foods, 1010–1018
  Fruit Cake, 915
  Fruits, 1015
  Honey Fruit Cake, 916
  Meats, 1016–1018
    Chart, 1016
    Cooking Time Table, 1016
  Poultry, Thawing, 1018
  Tomato Cocktail, 33
  Vegetables, Boiling Chart, 1014
    Pressure Cooker Chart, 1014
Fruit(s)
  Cake, Frozen, 915
    Frozen, Honey, 916
    Spiced Chocolate, 921
    White, 923
  Frozen, 1015
  Honey Bars, 930
  Juices, in Salad Dressing, 811
  Marinated, with Ice Cream, 961
  Peels, Candied, in Salads, 811
  Punch à la Normande, 61
  Salad Toppings, 811
  Syrup, 797
Fruited Ham Steak, 415
Frumets, Sausage Meat, 458
Fry, Mixed, 28, 704
  Mixed Sea Food, 292
  Oyster, 280
  Smelt, Canadian, 292
  Whitebait, 304
  Whiting, 305
Fryer, poultry, 482
Frying
  Batter, 30
  Batter I for Fritters, 568
  Batter II for Fritters, 568
  Batter III, 569
  Batter IV, 569
    for Eggplant, 656
    Royal, 159
  Deep Fat, 985
    Chart, 986
  Fish, 192, 234
  Pan, 987
Fudge Bars, Chocolate, 972
  Squares, Chocolate, 972

Fudge Squares, Vanilla, 979
Fumet, Fish, Parisian, 580

Gaff-Topsail Pompano, a fish, 208
Galantine de Capon à la Reine, 488
  Turkey, à la Paderewski, 542
  de Volaille Armenonville, 513
Galapagos Mullet, 205
Game, Larding with Anchovy, 9
Garbanzos, 604, 606
Garibaldi Filet of Beef, 337
Gardner Island Oysters, 230
Garlic Butter, 551
  in Cream Sauce, 119
  in Green Salad, 813
  Macaroni with, 754
  Soup Madrilene, 134
Garofolato al Roma, 341
Garni, Choucroute, 397
Garnish, Chiffonade, 98
  Egg, 152
  Sandwich, 842
  for Soup, 94–105
    Popcorn, 123
Garnished Sauerkraut, 397
Gaspereau Herring, 202
Gasperou, a fish, 196
Gaspergou, a fish, 206
Gaspe Salmon, 210
Gastronome, Celery au Gratin, 638
Gefuellte Fish, Cold, 261
  Hot, 261
Gelatin, 873–875
  Apple, Rosita (Molded), 821
  Desserts: Cream, 873
    Frozen, 1116
    Sponge, 873
    Whip, 873
  Fruit, 812
  Mayonnaise, 835
  see also Jelly; Aspic
Gems, *see* Muffins
Genievre, Guinea Hen Breast, 533
German Style Asparagus, 600
  Red Cabbage, 623
Giant Crabs, 227
Gibbed Smelts, 292
Giblets, Goose, 528
  Gravy I, 569
    II, 569
  Pie, Goose, 528
  Preparation of, 478
  Soup, Cream of, 125
  Stuffing, 791

Ginger
  Ale, in Shandygaff, 51
    Peach, Grape Mold Salad, 827
  Brandy Sauce, 890
  Cream, 875
  Molasses Cookies Jungle, 929
  Soup, Apple, 106
  see also Sandwich Fillings
Gingerbread, 1091
  Applesauce, 1092
  Cream Pie, Washington's, 953
  Doughnuts, 782
  Hot Water, 1092
  Men, 927
  Muffins, 1089
  Old-Fashioned, 1092
  Waffles, 807
Glacé, Marron, Parfait, 1147
Glancefish, 204
Glazed Carrots, 632
  Crooked Neck Squash, 730
  Ham, Baked, 415
    Loaf Raisin Sauce, 416
  Parsnip Slices, I, 694
    II, 694
  Turnips, 743
Glazing Ham, 415
Globe Artichokes, *see* Artichokes, Globe
Gloria, Café, 71
Glut Herring, 202
Gnocchi, 763
  Piemontese, 764
  alla Romana, 763
Goat(s)
  Milk, 77
    and Vichy Water, 77
  Roast, 78
Goeyduck Clams, 225
Goggle-eye Bass, 194
Gold, Cream, 875
  Perch, 194
Golden Carp, 195
  Parfait, 1146
  Trout, 219
Goose, 483, 525–527
  Boiled, Oyster Stuffing, 527
  Giblets, 528
    Pie, 528
  How to Buy, 526
  Jellied, 528
  Liver Pâté Canapes, 17
  Roast, Celery Stuffing, 529
    Milanaise, 530
    Prune Stuffing, 530

Goose, Roasting, 526
  Smoked, 531
  Stuffing, 526–527
    Celery, 529
    Giblet, 791
    Milanaise, 530
    Olive, 793
    Oyster Bechamel, 527
    Prune, 530
  Stew Hungarian Style, 356
Gooseberry Trifle, 876
Goulash, 316
  Beef, Hungarian, 316
    Transylvanian, 317
  See also Stew *and* Stewing, 980
Gourd-Seed Sucker, a fish, 217
Gourmet Brussels Sprouts, 621
  Frogs' Legs, 260
  Grilled Lobster, 262
  Honey Cake, 916
  Turtle Pie, 303
Grand Ear Shell, a shellfish, 224
Grand Rock Clams, 225
Grand'mere Chicken Fritters, 501
Grandmother's Black Bean Soup, 110
Granny Lee's Chicken Pies, 512
Grape(s), Juice Ice, 1118
  Juice Sherbet, 1151
  Leaves, in Dolmas, 376
  See also Salads
  Sponge, 876
Grapefruit Jelly, 878
  Ladyfingers, 929
  Mint Cocktail, 34
  see also Salads
Grass Pickerel, 206
Grass Porgies, 208
Gratin, *see* Au Gratin
Gravy, Beer, 358
  Cream, 565
    for Sausage, 459
  Currant Jelly, 565
  Duck and Rice Dinner, 524
  Giblet, I, 569
    II, 569
  Stock, 93
  Wine, 414
  see also Sauces
Grayling, a fish, 198
Gray Grunt, a fish, 199
Great Lakes Trout, 219
Great Albacore, 220
Greffels, 782
Greek Mussels and Sauce, 275

Green
  Butter, 551
  Cod, 196
  Corn Cake Puffs, 648
    Tamales, 45
  Dressing, 836
  Noodles, Homemade, 758
  Peas, Creamed, Bayou, 697
    French Style, 698
    Good Woman Style, 698
    Niçoise, 698
    Stewed, French Style, 699
    See also under Peas
  Peppers, 658
    Chuck Steak Dinner, 341
    and Onion Ragout, 693
    Rings, French Fried, 659
    See also Sandwiches
    Smothered, Lyonnaise, 659
      Variations, 659
    Stuffed, 659
      Burger, Stuffing, 789
      Crab Meat Stuffing, 660
      Epicure, Stuffing, 791
      Meat Stuffing, 660
      Mexican Style, 660
      Poultry Stuffing, 660
      Slices, 28
  Salad, 812
    Garlic in, 813
    Tomato Chili con Carne, 332
Greens, 660
  Chard, Boiled, 641
  Dandelion, Farmer's Style, 663
    Wilted, 663
  Pressure Cooked, 1168
  Turnip, 742
    Cotton Picker's Delight, 742
  Wild, 662
  Zucchini Vines and Leaves, 729
Greenland Halibut, 201
Greenland Turbot, a fish, 221
Greenport Oysters, 230
Grenadins of Beef, 356
  of Lamb, 356
  of Mutton, 356
  of Veal Parisienne, 355
Grenouilles, frogs, 228
Grèque, Tomatoes à la, 818
Griddle Cakes, 795, 797
  Buttermilk, 799
  Curried Clam, 799
  Peach, 802
  Soy Flour, 803

Griddle Toast, French, 1108
Grill, Lamb Mixed, 380
  Mackerel, 272
  Sausage and Fruit, 457
  Shad Roe, 288
  Turkey, Chatelaine, 544
Grilled Bluefish, 261
  Brains, 431
  Calf's Head Provençale, 352
  Codfish Cape Cod Style, 261
  Eggplant Steak, 658
    Variations, 658
  Fish, 261
  Guinea Hen à la Diable, 533
  Hamburgers, Onion Rings, 339
  Lobster Gourmet, 262
  Mushroom Caps, 681
  Soft-Shell Crabs Creole, 262
  Sweet Potatoes, 711
  Tomato Slices, 737
    Variations, 738
  Tripe, 470
Grilling, 983
Grindle, a fish, 194, 199
Grooved Shrimp, 232
Grouper, a fish, 199
Grunt, a fish, 199–200
Guacamaia, a fish, 200
Guachanche, a fish, 193
Guatemala Black Bean Soup, 110
Guava Soufflé Havanaise, 876
Gudlax, a fish, 204
Guinea Fowl, see Guinea Hen
Guinea Hen, 484, 531
  Breast of, Adelina Patti, 532
    Connoisseur, 532
    Creole, 532
    au Genievre, 533
    à la Castillane, 533
  Grilled Baby, à la Diable, 533
  Roast, 534
Gulper Eel, 203
Gulyas, 316
Gumbo, Oyster, 134
Gumbo Filé Powder, 495

Habitant Pea Soup, 112
Haddie, Finnan, see Finnan Haddie
Haddo Salmon, 209
Haddock, 198, 200
  Boston Style, 263
  Jerusalem, 204
  Young, 212
Hake, a fish, 201, 224

Half-Beak, a fish, 201
Half Mourning, Chicken in, 501
Halibut, 201, 221
  Little, 221
  Soup, 132
  Steak Alsatian Manner, 264
    Miramar, 263
Hallowe'en Ice Cream Clown, 1130
Ham, 393, 410–424
  and Apple Pie, 416
  Baked, 411
    in Rye Crust, 417
  Boiled, 412
  Braised in Red Wine:
    California, 413
    French, 413
  Broiling, 984
  Butt and Sauerkraut, 417
  Canapés I, 20
    II, 21
    III, 21
    Fried, 21
  Casserole Bourgeoise, 418
  Chop Suey, 315
  Creamed, in Rice Border, 414
  Croquettes, 373
  Dumplings, 756
  and Egg Croquettes, 160
    in Denver Sandwich, 849
    Soufflé, 165
  Fresh, 393
    Roast, 404
  Fried, Sandwich, 849
  Glazed Baked, 415
  Hot Pot, 418
  Loaf, Glazed, Raisin Sauce, 416
    Upside-Down, 424
  Mousse I, 418
    II, 419
  and Onion Stuffing, 792
  Platter, Cold, 414
  and Rice Casserole, 419
  Roast, with Apples, 423
  Roast, Fresh, 404
  Roasting, 988
  Sandwich Filling, Spicy, 856
  and Sausage Pie, 423
  Shank, 394
  Slices, Barbecued, 412
  Soufflé, 421
  Spinach Shortcake with, 723
  Steak, 410
    Baked in Milk, 420
    Creole, 420

Ham, Steak, Epicure, 421
  Fruited, 415
  Gourmet, 421
  Montmorency, 422
  Moscovite, 422
  and Swiss Cheese Sandwich, 845
    Hot, 849
  Tenderloin, Prune Sauce, 423
  and Veal Pie à la Dickens, 364
  Virginia, Barbecued Fresh, 396
    Roast, 424
  and Waffles, 804
  Walnut Brandied Stuffing, 792
  see also Sandwiches and Sandwich
    Fillings
Hamburger(s), 340, 373
  Celestine, 340
  à la Creole, 341
  and Egg, 340
  Grilled, Onion Rings, 339
  and Mushroom, 340
  Potatoes in, 703
  Sandwich, 850
  Sandwich Filling, 854
  Steak, Broiling, 984
  Stuffed Pumpkin, Baked, 714
  and Tomato, 340
  See also Burgers; Balls
Hammer Oysters, 231
Hammer-headed Shark, 213
Hard-Boiled Eggs, see Hard-Cooked
    Eggs
Hard-Cooked Eggs, 152
  with Noodles, 157
Hard Sauces, 896–898
  Almond Kirsch, 896
  Brandy, 896
  Brown Sugar, 896
  Butterscotch, 897
  Cherry, 897
  Chocolate, 897
  Christmas, 897
  Coconut, 897
  Date, 897
  French, 897
  Lemon, 898
  Melba, 898
  Mocha, 898
Hard-Shell Clams, 225
Hard-Shell crabs, 227
Hare-Lipped Sucker, a fish, 217
Hartford Cake, 917
Harvest-Fish, 224

Hash, Mulligan, 401
  Poker, 401
  Veal Tongue, 467
Hashed Brown Potatoes, 705
Hasty Pudding, 1046
  Biscuits, 1046
Havanaise, Guava Soufflé, 876
Havraise, Salmon Mousse, 286
Hawaii, Baked Pork Chops, 395
Hayo Salmon, 209
Hazel Nuts, 1028
Head, *see* Calf's Head; Lamb's Head
Head Cheese, 399
  Jellied Sour, 400
Health Omelet, 173
Heart(s), 427, 441
  Beef, 310, 427
    Loaf, 441
    Potroast, 442
    Stuffed with Rice, 442
  Calf, 427
  Lamb, 427
  Lamb, en Casserole, 443
  Mutton, 427
  Pork, 427
  Veal, Chop Suey, 443
    Stew, 443
Heel of Round, Veal, 348
Helena, Crêpes, 866
Henrietta, Chicken Casserole, 497
Herb Chart, 1001–1009
  Green, Eels in, 250
  Omelet aux Fines, 170
  and Spices, 1001–1009
Hermit Crabs, 228
Herring, 202
  Butter, 551
  Deviled, 249
  Filets in White Wine, 38
  Potted, 283
  Roe Canapés, 21
  Stew, Polish, 283
Hickory Nut, 1027
Highback, a fish, 223
Hind Shank, Beef, 312
Hochepot, 134
Hock, Pork, 394
Hodge Podge Chicken, 513
Holia Salmon, 209
Hollandaise
  Boiled Celery Knob, 636
  Caper Sauce, 561
  Sauce I, 569
  Sauce II, 570

Hollandaise, Sauce III, 300, 570
  Sauce Anchovy, 8
  Sauce, Kohlrabi, 668
  Sauce Suprême, 300
Holy Cross, a fish, 195
Homard Lobster, 229
  en Bellevue, Aspic de, 266
Homemade Bread, 1037–1039, 1065
  Egg Noodles, 758
  Green Noodles, 758
Hominy, 101, 747, 1036
  and Burger Croquettes, 752
  Burger Squares, 751
  and Cheese Timbales, 752
  Creamed, 751
  Croutons, 101
  with Sherry, 752
Honey, 1056–1057
  Biscuits, 1045
  Bran Bread, 1056, 1068
    Nut Kuchen, 958
  Brandy Spiced Pavés, 930
  Cake(s), 925
    Frozen Fruit, 916
    Gourmet, 916
  Cinnamon Sauce, 893
  Cocktail, 34
  Cookies, 925
  Dressing, 832
  Fruit Bars, 930
  Nut Sauce, 893
  Rum Caramels, 978
  See also Sandwich Fillings
  Soufflé, 877
  Sponge Lemon Pudding, 877
  and Tomatoes, Sliced, 736
  Whole Wheat Bread, 1067
Honeydew Melon Ice, 1118
Hoopid Salmon, 210
Hopping John, 610
Hops, 1036
Horns of Plenty, 25
Horned Guinea Fowl, 484
Horned Pout, a fish, 195
Hors d'Oeuvres, 1–45, 614
Horse Mackerel, 203, 220
Horse Mussels, 229
Horseback, Beefsteak on, 322
Horseradish Butter, 551
  Cream Cocktail Sauce, 35
  Dressing, 836
    Caviar, 836
  See also Sandwich Fillings
  Sauce, Sour Cream, 587

Hot Biscuit Pie Covering, 940
  Buttered Cabbage, 623
  Buttered Rum Punch, 62
  Cross Buns, 1080
  Cucumber Dressing, 839
  Dogs, *see* Frankfurters
  Pot, Ham, 418
    Mutton, Lancashire, 391
  Sandwiches, *see* Sandwiches, Hot
  Water Gingerbread, 1092
Houska, 1054
"How to," *see under names of processes*
Hubbard Squash, Baked, 715
  Boiled, 715
  Pressure Cooked, 1174
  Whipped, 732
Hudson River Chowder, 132
Humpback, a fish, 223
Humpback Salmon, 209, 210
Hungarian Beef Goulash, 316
  Cabbage, 624
  Cabbage, Stuffed, 624
  Dumplings, 317
  Lentils, 672
  Sauerkraut, 718
  Turnips, 743
  Veal Birds, 359
    Chops Paprika, 361
    Stew, 356
Hunter Sauce, 571
Hush Puppies, 1068

Ice Cream, 1121
  Apricot, I, 1121
  Apricot, II, 1122
  Banana, 1124
  Biscuit Tortoni, 1124
  Buttermilk, 1125
  Butterscotch, 1125
    Pecan, 1126
  Cake, 917
  Caramel, 1126
  Chocolate, I, 1127
  Chocolate, II, 1127
    Marshmallow, 1128
  Clown, Halloween, 1130
  Coffee, I, 1128
  Coffee, II, 1129
  Eggnog, 1129
  Hand Freezer Method, 1114
  Ingredients Used, 1113
  Macaroon, 1130
  Maple Walnut, 1130
  Marron Glacé, 1131

Ice Cream, Mint, 1131
  Mocha, 1132
  Orange, I, 1132
  Orange, II, 1133
  Neapolitan, 1132
  Peach, I, 1133
  Peach, II, 1133
  Peppermint, 1134
  Pineapple, 1134
  Pistachio, I, 1135
  Pistachio, II, 1135
  Raisin Nut, 1135
  Raspberry, 1136
  Refrigerator Method, 1114
  Sauce, Flaming, 1129
  Shake, Chocolate, 55
  Spumoni, 1136
  Strawberry, I, 1136
  Strawberry, II, 1137
  Strawberry, III, 1137
  Tartlets, 958
  Tortoni, Biscuit, 1124
  Tutti Frutti, 1138
  Vanilla, I, 1138
  Vanilla, II, 1138
    Savarin with Fruits, 961
Iceberg, Chocolate, 54
Ices, 1116
  Apricot, 1116
  Blueberry, 1116
  Cherry, 1117
  Cider, 1117
  Citrus Fruit, 1117
  Coffee, 1118
  Cranberry, 1118
  Grape Juice, 1118
  Honeydew Melon, 1118
  Lemon, 1119
  Lime, 1119
  Mint, 1119
  Orange, 1120
  Pineapple, 1120
  Raspberry, 1120
Iced Chocolate, 57
  Coffee, 73
  Tea, Cold-Water Method, 83
Imperatrice, Figs, 871
Imperial, Cherries, 864
  Coffee Cream, 74
  Sweet Potatoes, 712
Inconnu Salmon, 210
India Curry of Capon, 487
Indian Dressing, 840
Indienne, Potage à l', 137

Intoxicated Loin of Pork, 400
Irish Colcannon, 625
   Pompano, 208
   Raisin Bread, 1069
   Soda Bread, 1069
   Stew, 377
Irradiated Milk, 76
Island, Floating, 872
Italian Asparagus, 600
   Baked Beans, 610
   Batter, 29
   Broccoli, 617
   Ham and Sausage Pie, 423
   Veal Stew, 357
Ivan Consommé, 116
Ivory Sauce, for Chicken, 516

Jaboncilla, a fish, 199
Jack Crevalle, a fish, 195
   Pike, a fish, 207
   Salmon, 207
   White, a fish, 205
Jackets, Potatoes in, 702
Jackfish, 195, 206
Jacqueline, Filets of Sole, 255
   Poached Eggs, 180
Jalousies, Brandied Peach, 955
   Variations, 956
Jambalaya, Chicken Sauté, 507
Jardiniere Beef Tongue, 465
   Sauce, 571
   Vegetable, in Stuffed Tomatoes, 739
Jeanine, Filets of Sole, 255
Jelly, Apricot (Molded), 821
   Coating, Wine Aspic, 572
   Cream Cheese Sandwich, 844
   Current, Dressing, 831
   Desserts, Definition of, 874
   Dressing, Whipped Cream, 841
   Fish Aspic, 266
   Grapefruit, 878
   Gravy, Current, 565
   Lemon, 878
   Madeira Wine (Dessert), 886
   Orange, 878
      Ring (Molded) Salad, 827
   Pig's Feet in, 436
   Port Wine (Dessert), 886
      Aspic Coating, 39, 581
   See also Gelatin
   See also Sandwiches
   Sherry Wine (Dessert), 886
      Aspic Coating, 41

Jellied Asparagus Salad, 813
   Bananas en Chartreuse, 877
   Chicken Loaf, 513
   Goose, 528
   Madrilène, 136
   Sour Head Cheese, 400
   Tomato & Egg Luncheon, 741
   Molded Tomato Surprise, 819
   Tongue, 465
   Veal Loaf, 356
Jerusalem Artichokes, *see* Artichokes, Jerusalem
Jerusalem Haddock, a fish, 204
Jewish Kraplach, 101
   Gefuellte Fish, 261
   Matsos Crimsel, 1070
   Twisted Bread, 1070
Johnny Cakes I, 1089
Johnny Cakes II, 1090
   Hints, 1083
Jolt-Head Porgies, a fish, 208
Jordan Trout, 219
Jug o'Rum Frogs, 228
Juice, Carrot, 631
   Fruit, in Salad Dressing, 811
   Onion, 689
   Tomato, Dumplings, 788
Jumbo Shrimp, 233
Jumping Clams, 225
June Sucker, a fish, 217
Juniper, a fish, 201

Kabab, Shish, 385
Kale, 663
   and Bacon, 664
   Buttered, 664
   Cooking, 664
   Creole Style, 664
   and Frankfurter Dinner, 665
   Pressure Cooked, 1168
   Ring, 665
   Scalloped, 666
   Smothered, 666
      Variations, 666
   Steamed, 666
Kamloop Trout, 219
Kampfer's Crabs, 227
Kebab, Kebob, *see* Kabab
Kentucky Corn Bread, 1062
   Corn and Egg Scramble, 155
   Roast Suckling Pig, 408
Kernnerly's Salmon, 209
Kern River Trout, 219
Kidney Beans, Casserole, 611

Kidney(s), 310, 427, 444–449
  Beef, 427
  Beef, Chop Suey, 445
    Creole, 445
  and Beef Pie, 321
  Broiling, 984
  Calf, 427
  Chop, Veal, 348
  Lamb, en Brochette, 446
    Chasseur, 448
    Curried, 445
    Deviled, 446
    Montagnards, 447
    Polonaise, 448
    Stew, 446
  Pork, 427
  and Roast Loin of Lamb, 383
  Scalding, 445
  Sheep's, 427
  Soup, Cream of, 125
  Veal, Ardennaise, 447
    Brabançonne, 447
    Chasseur, 448
    Polonaise, 448
King Crabs, 227
  Mackerel, 203
  Salmon, 209
Kingfish, 202
Kirsch Almond Hard Sauce, 896
Kisses, Almond, I, 969
  Almond, II, 969
  Cream, 973
  Meringue, 1124
  Normand, 931
Kisutch Salmon, 210
Kitchen Clambake, New England, 277
Kneaded Butter, 551
Knickerbocker Artichokes, 595
Knoedel, Matzoth, 102
Knuckles, Pig's, 398
Kohlrabi, 666
  Boiled, 667
  Brown Parsley Butter, 667
  Country Style, 667
  in Cream, 667
  French Fried, 667
  au Gratin, 668
  Hollandaise Sauce, 668
  Pressure Cooked, 1168–1169
Kola Nut, 1028
Koldolma, 625
Kraplach, 101
Kuchen, Honey Bran Nut, 958
Kyack Herring, 202

Lac de Marbre Trout, 210
Ladyfingers, Grapefruit, 929
  Lemon, 930
  Lime, 931
  Orange, 932
Laevis Skate, 214
Laguipere Sauce, 571
Lait, Café au, 71
Lake Herring, 202
  Shrimp, 233
  Tahoe Trout, 219
  Trout, 298
Laker Trout, 220
Lamb(s), 367–386
  Barbecued, 373
  Baron Brabançonne, 374
  Brains, 427
  Breast, 370
    Roast Stuffed, 384
  Brochettes, 369
  Broiling, 984
  Chart, 370–371
  Chops, 370
    Bercy, 377
    Bonne Femme, 378
    Breading, 372
    Clementine, 378
    French, 372
    Loin, 370, 372
    Minted, 372
    en Papillotes, 378
    à la Paysanne, 378
    Rib, 370
    Shoulder, 370
    Sirloin, 371
    Soubise, 379
    Stuffed, Deviled Ham, 373
    Stuffed, Liver Paste, 373
  Croquettes, 373
  Crown Roast, 370, 375
    Variations, 376
  Curry with Bananas, 379
  Cushion, 371
  Cutlet Casserole, 380
  Facts About, 367
  Feet, 369
  the Fell, 372
  Garnish, Lime Gelatine, 372
    Mint Gelatine, 372
  Grenadins of, 356
  Grill, Mixed, 380
Lamb's Head, 369
  Heart(s), 369, 427
    en Casserole, 443

Lamb, Hints, 372–373
  Kidneys en Brochette, 446
    Chasseur, 448
    Curried, 445
    Deviled, 446
    Montagnards, 447
    Pie, 321
    Polonaise, 448
    Stew, 446
  Leg, 371
    Barbecued, 373
    Boiled, Stuffed, 386
    Roast of, Venison, 382
  Lights, 369
Lamb Liver, 310, 449; *see also under* Liver
  Loaves, Meat, 373
  Loin Roast, 371
    with Kidneys, 383
  Mock Duck, 371
  Neck, 372
  Noisettes, 368
  and Parsley Pinwheels, 381
  Patties, 373
  Pocket, 370
  Pot Pie, 381
  Rack, 368
  Relishes for, 372
  Riblet, 370
  Roast, 372
  Roasting, 988
  Saddle, Roast, 384
  Sandwich, Hot, 850
  Shank, 371
  Shoulder, 371
    Stuffing, 793
  Sirloin Roast, 371
  Steak, 371
    Minute, 371
  Stew, Curried, 372
    Grease, to Remove, 372
    Hungarian Style, 356
    Irish, 377
    Oriental Touch, 373
    Parisienne, 382
    Potato Crust, 372
  Stuffing, Forcemeat, 385
    Mint, 792
    Shoulder, 793
  Sweetbreads, 310, 428
  Tongue, 311, 369
    in Aspic, 466
    Boiled, 465
Lancashire Mutton Hot Pot, 391
Landlocked Salmon, 210

Lane Snappers, fish, 215
Lantern, Aristotle's, a shellfish, 232
Laperouse Sauce, 571
Larded Sweetbreads, Breaded, 462
Larding with Anchovy, 9
Lasagna al' Ricotta Cheese, 765
Lasagne, 763
Lauia, a fish, 200
Lawyer, a fish, 194
Layer, a fish, 199
Layer Cakes, Reasons for Failures, 902–908
Leaven, 1036
Leaves, Grape, in Dolmas, 376
'Lectin Cake, 917
Lee's, Granny, Chicken Pies, 512
Leeks, 668
  Boiled, Sauces, 669
  Creamed, au Gratin, 670
    Variations, 670
  French Method, 817
  au Gratin Gastronome, 638
  and Poached Eggs on Toast, 670
  Pressure Cooked, 1169
  à la Vinaigrette, 10
Left-Over Meat Filling, 856
Leg of Lamb, 371
  Lamb, Barbecued, 373
    Venison, Roast, 382
Leg of Mutton, Braised, French, 387
  Provençale, 388
Legs, Frog, *see* Frogs' Legs
Lekai Salmon, 209
Lemon
  Butter Cauliflower, 635
    Sauce, 572
  Clam Sauce, 295
  Chiffon Pie, 947
  and Cider Cooler, 61
  Cream Pie, 947
    Variations, 947
  Doughnuts, 783
  Hard Sauce, 898
  Honey Sponge Pudding, 877
  Ice, 1119
  Jelly, 878
  Juice, on String Beans, 726
  Ladyfingers, 930
  Meringue Pie, New England, 949
  Milk Sherbet, 1151
  Sherbet, 1151
Lemon Fish, 195
Lemon Sole, a fish, 203

Lentils, 670
  Boiled, 671
  Cassolettes à l'Auvergnate, 671
  and Cheese Loaf, 671
  Croquettes, 672
  à la Dauphinoise, 672
  with Frankfurters, 672
  Hungarian Style, 672
  Mecklenburg Style, 673
  Pie, 673
  Puree, 673
  Ramekins, 673
  Relish Parisienne, 37
  Soup Armenian Style, 135
  and Walnut Loaf, 674
Leopard Frogs, 228
Lepeshki, Russian, 925
Lettuce, 674
  Braised, 675
  Creamed, 675
  Cups, 17
  Leaves, Cooked, 812
  Royale, 675
  Soup, Almond Cream, 105
    Cream of, 126
  Stewed, à la Romaine, 676
  Stuffed à la Dame Simone, 677
  Tomato, and Cucumber Salad, 817
  Varieties, 674
  see also Sandwiches
Liège Cookies, 932
Lights, 310
  Lamb's, 369
Lima Beans, 606
  and Bacon Casserole, 611
  Cassoulet à la Toulousaine, 388
  Creamed Fresh, 609
  Deviled, 609
  French, 609
Limande, a fish, 203
Lime Ice, 1119
  Ladyfingers, 931
  Sherbet, 1152
  Water, 79
Lisette, Crêpes, Meringuées, 867
Litchi Nuts, 1029
Lithuanian Dumplings, 787
Little Halibut, 201
  Head Porgies, a fish, 208
  Neck Clams, 225
  Pot, French, 139
  Puff Cakes, 959
  Redfish, 209

Liver(s), 310, 427, 449–455
  and Anchovy Mold, 451
  Baked, Stuffed Onions, 689
  and Onions Delmonico, 449
  Beef, 427; (*May be used in all Liver
    recipes in this index section.*)
  Braised, 450
  Broiling, 984
  Calf, 310, 427, 449; (*May be used in all
    Liver recipes in this index section.*)
  Chicken (*May be used in all Liver
    recipes in this index section.*)
    Chicken, en Brochette, 450
    Curried, 451
    Chicken, Macaroni with, 755
    Chicken, & Mushrooms, 451
    Chicken, Wild Rice, 774
  Chow Mein, 452
  Covent Style, 453
  Creole, 452
  Dinner Coventry Style, 453
  Dumplings, 102
    Moderne, 786
  Fines Herbes, 453
  Lamb, 310; (*May be used in all Liver
    recipes in this index section.*)
  Loaf French Style, 453
    Viennese, 454
  Mutton, 310; (*May be used in all Liver
    recipes in this index section.*)
  and Onions, Baked, 449
  Pâté Goose Canapes, 17
  Pork, 427
  See also Sandwich Fillings
  Sheep's, 427, *see* Liver, Mutton
  Soufflé, 454
  Terrapin in Chafing Dish, 455
  and Wild Rice, 775
Liverwurst and Swiss Cheese Sandwich,
  845
Loaf, Beef, 318
  Beef Heart, 441
  Burger Stuffing, 790
  Chicken, Cold, 510
    Jellied, 513
  Ham, and Onion, 792
    Upside-Down, 424
  Lentil and Cheese, 671
    and Walnut, 674
  Liver, French, 453
    Viennese, 454
  Nut, 1025
  Poultry Meat, 480
  Prune (Molded), 829

Loaf, Sweetbread, Gastronome, 462
  Veal, Jellied, 356
Lobster, 229
  à l'Américaine, 265
  Bellevue, 266
  Biarritz, 267
  Bohemienne, 267
  to Boil, 265
  Butter, 551
  Canapés I, 20
  Canapés II, 20
  Cardinal, 268
  Chowder, 133
  Cocktail, Avocado, 33
    Gourmet, 34
  Court-Bouillon, 268
  Curry Risotto Crown, 268
  Figaro, 269
  Grilled, Gourmet, 262
  How to Eat, 264, 265
  à la King, 290
  Mousse, 514
  Newburg I, 269
  Newburg II, 269
  Puffs, 291
  Purée Celery Stuffing, 42
  Sauce, 572
  Thermidor, 270
  in Veal Cutlets, 362
  oin Chops, Lamb, 370
  Chops, Pork, 393
    Veal, 348
  of Lamb, & Kidneys, 383
    Pork, 394
    Roast, Lamb, 371
    Veal, 348
  Short, Beef, 313
Lollypops, 975
London Celery Centerpiece, 37
Long-Eared Sunfish, 217
Long-Headed Trout, 219
Long Island Duck, 518
Long-Nosed Sucker, a fish, 217
Lorette Consommé, 116
Lost Bread, 878
Lost Salmon, 209
Lote, a fish, 203
Louise Sauce, 572
Louisette, Crab Meat, 247
Louisiana Petit Brûlot, 74
Lozenges, Anchovy Canapés, 6
Lucette, Poached Eggs, 179
Lung, *see* Lights
Lunn, Sally, Bread, 1073

Lurid Oysters, 230
Lyonnaise, Artichokes, Jerusalem, à la, 598
  Beans, String, 728
  Peppers, Green, Smothered, 659
    Variation, 659
  Sauce, 572
Lynnhaven Oysters, 230

Macadamia Nuts, 1029
Macaroni, all' Aglio, 754
  Boiled, 753
  and Cheese Custard, 754
  alla Crema, 754
  and Egg Scallop, 162
  with Garlic, 754
  au Gratin, 755
  Mushrooms, Chicken Livers, 755
  Pie, 755
  Soufflé Ring, 756
  alla Tita Ruffo, 754
Macaroon(s), Cajun, 926
  Ice Cream, 1130
  Ratafia, 933
Mackerel, 203, 213
  Boiled Dinner, 271
  Filets in White Wine, 37
  Fricassée Fisherman, 271
  Grill, 272
  Horse, 220
  King, 203
  Salt, Preparation of, 271
Mackinaw Trout, 219
Madeira Aspic, 543
  Mushroom Sauce, 572
  Wine Aspic Coating Jelly, 572
    Jelly (Dessert), 886
  Sauce, 573
Madeleines, 958
Madras Stuffed Cabbage, 627
Madriléne Consommé, 115
  (Jellied), 136
Mad Tomcat, a fish, 195
Maine Shrimp Puffs, 291
  Succotash, 732
Maître d'Hôtel Butter, 573
Mako, a fish, 213
Maltaise Sauce, 573
Malted Milk, Chocolate, 55
Mama Suzy Turner's Molded Pudding, 879
Manchego Snappers, a fish, 215
Mangrove Snappers, a fish, 215

Maple Fondant, 976
  Nut Fondant Creams, 976
  Parfait, 1146
  Syrup-Walnut Pie, 952
  Walnut Ice Cream, 1130
Maquereaux Marinés Au Vin, 37
Maraschino, Bonbons Fondant, 976
  Cherry, Cake, 918
    Pineapple Sherbet, 1153
Marble Cake, Loaf, 918
Marbled Fudge Bars, 972
Marchand de Vin Butter, 329, 552
  Sauce, 573
  Steak, 329
Margaret Grunt, a fish, 199
Marguery, Filets of Sole, 256
Marguery Sauce, 574
Marigold, 1004
Marinades, 574
  Marinade I, 574
  Marinade II, 575
  Marinade III, 575
Marinated Filets of Mackerel, 37
  Fruits, with Ice Cream, 961
  Veal Loin Portuguese, 357
Marinière, Mussels, 276
Mariposa, a fish, 204
Marjoram Burger Balls, 97
  Dumplings, 97
Marlin, a fish, 205
Marmalade and Cottage Cheese Sandwich, 843
  See also Sandwiches
Marmite, Petite, 139, 503
Marquise, Breasts of Ducklings, 521
Marrons, Chestnuts, 1131
  Crème aux, 866
  Glacé Ice Cream, 1131
  Glacé Parfait, 1147
  See also Chestnuts
Marrow Balls, 102
  Beef Barquettes, 12
    Canapés, 23
  Broiled Steak with, 329
  Vegetable, Pressure Cooked, 1169
Marsala, Filet of Beef au, 337
  Veal al, 366
  Veal Scalopini au, 366
Marseillaise Bouillabaisse, 234
  Shrimp à la, 290
Marshmallow Chocolate Ice Cream, 1128
Martinique Creole Rice, 768
Maryland Brunswick Stew, 493
  Chicken à la, 502

Maryland Crab Cakes, 272
  Terrapin, 298
Marzipan I, 976
  Marzipan II, 977
  Marzipan III, 977
  Pears, 977
  Potatoes, 977
  Strawberries, 978
Mashed Artichokes, Jerusalem, 598
  Beets, 615
  Celery Knob, 639
  Fluffy Turnips, 743
  Pea Pods in Cream, 698
  Potatoes, 702, 704, 706
    Biscuits, 1046
    with Spinach, 721
  Squash and Potato, 730
  Sweet Potatoes, 703, 711
Massachusetts Bay Clam Chowder, 129
  Succotash, 733
Match Stick Potatoes, 707
Matsos (or Matzoth)
  Balls, 102
  Crimsel, 1070
  Knoedel, 102
Mattituck Oysters, 230
Matto Wacca Herring, 202
Maylie, Crabs à la, 246
Mayonnaise, 811, 812, 833–838
  Almond Dressing, 835
  Caper Dressing, 836
  Care of, 833
  Caviar Dressing, 836
  Caviar Horseradish, 836
  Chutney Dressing, 835
  with Condensed Milk, 834
  with Cooked Base, 835
  Cranberry Dressing, 836
  Cream Dressing, 835
  Cumberland Dressing, 836
  Egg Dressing, 836
  with Gelatine, 835
  Green Dressing, 836
  Horseradish Dressing, 836
  Olga's Dressing, 837
  Olive Dressing, 837
  Piquante Dressing, 837
  Red Dressing I, 837
  Red Dressing II, 837
  Roquefort Cheese, 838
  Russian Dressing I, 837
  Russian Dressing II, 837
  Russian Dressing III, 837
  See also Sandwich Fillings

Mayonnaise, for Shrimp, 289
  Sour Cream Dressing, 838
  Thousand Island I, 838
  Thousand Island II, 838
  Victory Dressing, 838
Mazagran Coffee, 72
McKay's Sunfish, 217
Meal Corn, *see* Corn Meal
Mealy Pastry, 938
Measurements and Equivalents, 1019–1023
Meats, 307–424
  Balls, Spaghetti with, 762
  Cakes with Poached Eggs, 458
  Chopped, for Stuffing Tomatoes, 739
  Dumplings, 786
  in Egg Soufflé, 165
  Frozen, 1016–1018
    Cooking Time Table, 1016
  Ground, 373
  Larding with Anchovy, 9
  Loaf, Potatoes in, 703
  Loaf, Poultry, 480
  Mousse, 514
  Patties, Creole, 459
  Quality of, 309
  Red, 309
  Roasting, Time Table, 988
  See Sauces, Meat, Fish, etc.
  Simmering, 989
  Smoked, Prune Sauce for, 582
  Variety, 425–473
    Chart, 427
  Waffles, 807
  White, Definition, 309
  See also Beef, Calf, Ham, Lamb, Mutton, Pork, Veal
Mecklenburg Style Lentils, 673
Melba, Cantaloupe, 823
  Hard Sauce, 898
  Peach, 1134
  Sauce, 893
  Sauce I, 1134
  Sauce II, 1134
  Sweetbreads, 464
  Toast, 103, 1109
Melon Ball Cocktail Epicure, 34
Melon, Honeydew, Ice, 1118
Melon à l'Orientale, 879
Ménagère, Brandade de Morue, 239
  Duckling Chipolata, 523
  Sauce, 523
Menhaden, a fish, 211

Meringue(s), 1123–1124
  Chantilly, 1124
  Cream Pie, 947
  Glacé, 1124
  Hints, 879
  Kisses, 1124
  Pie, Buttermilk Raisin, 944
    Lemon, 949
  Rice Pudding, 885
Meringuées, Crêpes Lisette, 867
Merlan, a fish, 223
Merluche, a fish, 201
Mero, a fish, 199
Methods of Cooking, 983
Metropole, Chicken Casserole, 498
Meunière Butter, 575
  Filets of Sole (Flounder), 256
  Shad Roe, 288
  Trout, 301
Mexican Burger Rice, 769
  Coffee, 72
Miami Style Red Snapper, 284
Michigan Applesauce Cake, 919
Midinette Consommé, 116
  Shirred Eggs, 186
Mignon, Filet, 313, 338
Milanaise
  Broccoli, 618
  Minestrone, 136
  Risotto alla, 772
  Roast Goose, 530
  Scrambled Eggs, 184
Milk, 74–81
  Beer Syllabub, 50
  Caramels, 978
    Chocolate, 972
  Certified, 76
  Chocolate Malted, 55
  Cocoanut, 564
  in Coffee, 66, 78
  Condensed, 75
    Mayonnaise, 835
  Cooking with, 78
  Dry, 76
  Dumplings (Dessert), 880
  Evaporated, 75
    Whipped, Coloring, 917
    Whipping, 80, 916, 1115
  Finnan Haddie Poached in, 282
  and Fish Superstition, 254
  Fresh, Whole, 75
  Goat's, 77
    and Vichy Water, 77

Milk, Ham Steak Baked in, 420
  Irradiated, 76
  Lemon Sherbet, 1151
  Not Fattening, 76
  Orange Sherbet, 1152
  Pasteurized, 75
  Pasteurizing at Home, 80
  Raspberry Sherbet, 1154
  Sauce, Chicken, 502
  Scalding, 79
  Shake, Mocha, I, 57
  Shake, Mocha, II, 57
  Skim, 75
  Sour, 8, 78
    in Baking, 80
  Souring, 78
  Soy, 612
  in Tea, 78
  Toast, 1110
  Top, Whipping, 1115–1116
  Tripe and Onions in, 473
  Wild Rice in, 775
Milk-Fed Crabs, 227
Mille Feuilles Consommé, 116
Mince Pie, 948
  Brandied Mincemeat, 948
Minced Chicken Belmont, 515
Mincemeat, Brandied, 948
  Molasses Almond Cookies, 931
  Plum Pudding, Steamed, 887
Minestrone Milanaise, 136
Mint, 1005
  Dressing, 832
  Ice, 1119
  Ice Cream, 1131
  Leaves, Candied, 971
  Leaves, in String Beans, 726
  Sauce for Meat I, 576
  Sauce for Meat II, 576
  Sauce, Salad, 812
  Sherbet, 1152
  in Spinach, 721
  Stuffing, 792
  See also Salads
Minted Chocolate, 57
  Lamb Chops, 372
  Mutton Almond, Soup, 105
Minute Steak, 313
  Lamb, 371
  O'Brien, Broiled, 329
Miramar, Halibut Steak, 263
Mironton, Beef, 320
  Sauce, 320
Missouri Sucker, a fish, 217

Mixed Fry, 28
  Potato Batter, 704
  Sea Food, 292
Mixed Grill, Lamb, 380
Mitred Guinea Hen, 484
Mocha, Arabian, 67
  Brazilian, I, 68
  Brazilian, II, 68
  Dessert Sauce, 893
  Hard Sauce, 898
  Ice Cream, 1132; Icing, 934
  Milk Shake I, 57
  Milk Shake II, 57
  Parfait, 1147
  Rum Sauce, 894
  Sponge Cake, 919
  Sponge Dessert, 880
  See also Coffee
Mock Duck, 371
  Hollandaise Sauce, 570
  Turtle, 352
    Soup, 136
Mode, Beef à la, 319
Molasses, 1059–1060
  Date Yeast Bread, 1063
  Ginger Cookies Jungle, 929
  Mincemeat Almond Cookies, 931
  Nut Biscuits, 1041
  Pecan Pie, 949
    Tartlets, Spiced, 961
Molded Pudding, Mama Turner's, 879
Mollet, Eggs, 161
Mondongo, 471
Mongole, Poached Eggs, 179
Monsieur Pique's Egg Pancake Turn-
    overs, 169
Montagnards, Lamb Kidneys, 447
Monte Cristo Canapés, 24
Monterey Halibut, 201
  Mackerel, 203
Montfermeil, Fried Stuffed Eggs, 168
Montmorency Dessert Sauce, 895
Moonfish, 204
Mornay, Filets of Sole, 257
  Frogs' Legs, 260
  Poached Eggs, 179
  Sauce, 576
    Home Style, 576
Moro Crabs, 228
Morton Clams, 225
Morue, Brandade de, Ménagère, 239
  Brandade de, I, 238
  Brandade de, II, 240
Moscovite, Squabs, 537

Mother Turner's Egg Stew, 165
Mother Poulard's Omelet, 171
Moules, Shellfish, 229
Mousseline Sauce, 577
Mousse, 286, 514, 1139
  Apricot, 1139
  Brandy, 1140
  Burnt Almond, 1140
  Capon, 488
  Chantilly, 1140
  Cherry, 1141
  Chicken, 502
  Chocolate, 1141
  Coffee, 1142
    Old-Fashioned, 1142
  Cold, 419
  Curaçao, 1142
  Ham, I, 418
  Ham, II, 419
  Peach, 1142
  Pineapple, 1143
  Salmon (Cold), 287
    (Hot), Havraise, 286
  Spinach, 722
  Strawberry, 1143
  Tongue, 467
  Vanilla, 1144
Mud Catfish, 195
  Sunfish, 218
Mudfish, 194, 199
Muffins, 1083–1091
  Banana Bran, 1084
  Blackberry, 1085
  Blueberry, 1086
  Bran, 1086
    Raisin, 1087
  Chocolate, 1084
  Corn, 1088
  English, 1088
  Gingerbread, 1089
  Hints, 1083
  Potato Flour, 1090
  Sally Lunn, 1090
Mulled Cider, 62
Mullet, 205
  Plantation Style, 272
Mulligan Hash, 401
Mulligatawny Soup, 137
Murat Consommé, 117
Mush, Corn Meal, 1046
  Pioneer, 750
Mushroom(s), 677
  à l'Andalouse, 682
  and Artichoke Pancakes, 598

Mushroom(s), and Bacon on Toast, 682
  under Bell, 684
  and Brain Stew Red Wine, 429
  Caps, Grilled Fresh, 681
  Chard Ring, 641
    Variation, 642
  Chicken Livers, on Toast, 451
  and Chicken Pie, 502
  with Curried Rice, 681
  Creamed, 680
  Deviled, au Gratin, 681
  Duxelles, 339
  à la Don Gasper, 683
  Macaroni with, 755
  Olives, Chicken Sauté, 508
  Omelet with Sherry, 169
  and Onion Shortcake, 682
  and Oyster Pie, 280
  à la Poulette, 683
  Pressure Cooked, 1169
  Saint Germain, 684
  Sauce, 577
    Madeira, 572
    with Wine, 577
  Sautéing, 680
  and Shrimp à la King, 289
  Soufflé, 684
  Soup, Cream of, 126
  sous Cloche, 684
  Steaming, 680
  Stewed in Red Wine, 685
  Stock, 577
  on Toast, Canadian, 685
Muskellunge, 205, 206, 207, 273
Mussel(s), 229, 272
  Bonne Femme, 273
  Bordelaise, 274
  Cocktail, 35
  Greek Manner, 275
  à la Henri Pullig, 275
  How to Eat, 274
  Marguery Sauce, 574
  Marinière, 276
  à la Newburg, 276
  Omelet Dieppoise, 169
  à la Provençale, 277
  Puffs, 291
  Sauce, 274
    Greek, 275
Mustard Butter, 551
  Dressing, 840
  Greens, 1005
  Pickles, Liquid from, 812
  Sauce I, 577

Mustard, Sauce, II, 578
Mutton, 386–391
  Chop Suey, 315
  Chops, English, 389
  Croquettes, 373
  Curry of, 389
  Cutlets à la Soyer, 390
  Grenadins of, 356
  Heart, 427
  Hot Pot Lancashire, 391
  and Kidney Pie, 321
  Leg, Stuffed Boiled, 386
    Braised, French, 387
    Provençale, 388
  Liver, 310
  Oyster Stuffing, 386
  Pancakes, Scotch, 802
  Roasting, 988
  Roast Saddle, 384
  Soup, Almond Minted, 105
  Stew Hungarian Style, 356
  Sweetbreads, 310
  Tongue, 311
  Trotters au Gratin, 435
  Trotters Ravigote, 436
Muttonfish, 217
Mutton-Snapper, 217

Nadine, Filets of Sole (Flounder), 257
Nana Consommé, 117
Nanies, Dutch, 799
Nantaises, Crêpes, 867
Nantua Sauce, 578
Napoli Style Ravioli, 764
Napolitan Pizza, 738
Nassau Grouper, a fish, 199
Nasturtium Leaves on Cucumbers, 651
Navets, Duck aux, 519
Neapolitan Ice Cream, 1132
Near East Boiled Rice, 769
Neck, Beef, 312
Negro Salmon, 210
Neige, Sauce Crème de, 895
Nest, Eggs, Planked in, 175
Nests, Bread, Scrambled Eggs in, 184
  Potato Cheese, 707
    Poached Eggs in, 180
  Rice, I, 770
  Rice, II, 771
Netherland Chicken Pancakes, 801
Netted Carpet Clams, 225
Newburg, Crabmeat Omelet, 155
  Lobster, I, 269
  Lobster, II, 269

Newburg, Mussels à la, 276
  Sauce, 578
  Soft-Shell Crabs, 248
New England Clambake, 277
  Clam Chowder, 129
  Hake, a fish, 201
  Lemon Meringue Pie, 949
  Liver Dumplings, 102
  Succotash, 733
Newlywed, Chicken Casserole, 498
New Mexico Curried Veal Balls, 354
New Orleans Chicken Sauté, 507
  Creole Sauce, 565
  Pigeon Pie, 534
Niçoise, Green Peas, 698
Nina, Framboise à la, 873
Ninon, Artichokes (Globe), 596
  Poached Eggs, 180
Nockerln, 99
Noisettes, Lamb, 368
Noodle(s), 748
  Amandine, 759
  Boiled, 756
  Buttered, French, 757
  Corn Meal, Southern, 759
  Egg, Fried, 758
    Fried, Chinese Style, 758
    Homemade, 758
    Ring, 757
  and Egg Scallop, 162
  au Gratin, Deviled, 757
  Green, Homemade, 758
  Ring and Sausage Creole, 759
  and Sausage Dinner, 457
  Spinach, Border, 415
  Viennese, 759
Norfolk Capon, 486
Normand Kisses, 931
Normande, Baked Pork Chops, 396
  Cider Fruit Punch, 61
Nuggets, Brazil, 970
Nut(s), 1026–1030
  Brazil, Chips, 13
  Bread, Baking Powder, 1053
    Brown I, 1059
    Brown II, 1059
  in Carrots, Buttered, 629
  in Carrots, Creamed, 629
  Chart, Characteristics, 1026–1031
    Weight and Measure, 1032
  Cream Pie, Farmer's, 946
  Croquettes, 1026
  and Date Biscuits, 1044
    Bread, 1064

Nut(s), Edible, 1023
  Grape, and Date Salad, 824
  Honey Bran Kuchen, 958
    Sauce, 893
  Loaves, 1025
  Maple Fondant Creams, 976
  Meats, *See also* Sandwich Fillings
  Preparation, 1024–1031
  Raisin Bread, 1071
    Cinnamon Buns, 1079
    Ice Cream, 1135
    Tart, 962
  Roasting, 1025
  Salting of, 1025
  See also Sandwiches
Nutmeg, Butter, Russian, 552
  in Brussels Sprouts, 619
  Dumplings, 103
  Tea, 84

Oatmeal Cookies, 925
  Waffles, 807
O'Brien, Minute Steak, 329
  Corn, 646
Ocean-Perch, a fish, 209
Ocean Pout, a fish, 203
Oeil de Perdrix, a fish, 205
Oeufs à l'Oeil de Boeuf, 160
Oeufs Frits à l'Écossaise, 168
Offshore Cod, 196
Oil, Olive, 29
Okow, a fish, 207
Okra, 686
  Creole, 686
  French Fried, 686
  Fritters I, 687
  Fritters II, 687
  au Gratin, 687
  Pressure Cooked, 1169–1170
Old-Fashioned Belgian Coffee, 71
  Applesauce Cake, 919
  Corn Meal Pudding, 749
  Gingerbread, 1092
  Plum Sauce, 894
  String Beans, 727
Old Plymouth Succotash, 734
Olga Consommé, 117
  Dressing, 837
Olive(s)
  and Asparagus au Gratin, 602
  and Chicken Sauté, 508
  Dressing, 837
  Duck with, 524
  Green Salad, 813

Olive(s), Oil, 29
  Ripe, 812
    in Salad Dressing, 811
  Rolled Beef, 326
  Sauce, 352
  Sauce I, 579
  Sauce II, 579
  Squabs with, 537
  Stuffing, 793
Omelet, 152, 170
  Asparagus Tip, 599
  Avocado, au Curry, 167
  Bread Crumb, 153
  Chocolate, 864
  Clam, 153
  Codfish, 154
  Cottage Cheese, 155
  Crabmeat, à la Newburg, 155
  Creole, 156
  Filling, 170
  aux Fines Herbes, 170
  Mascotte, 170
  à la Mère Poulard, 171
  Mushroom, with Sherry, 169
  Mussel, Dieppoise, 169
  Onion, Country Style, 173
  Puffed, 174
  à la Romaine, 173
  Rum, Aflame, 885
  Santé, 173
  Sea Urchin, 288
  des Sports, 174
  Soufflé, 174
  Soufflé, Parsley, 173
Onion(s), 687
  Baked Stuffed, 690
  and Beans, 689
  à la Bordelaise, 692
  Bread, 1052
  Cheese Custard Pie, 691
  Cheese Pie, Curried, 690
  Clam Sauce, 295
  Croquettes, 692
  Cups, Peas in, 699
  Frankfurter Casserole, 440
  French Fried, 691
  Glazed, 689
  au Gratin, 692
  and Ham Stuffing, 792
  Hints, 689
  Juice, 689
  and Liver, Baked, 449
  and Mushroom Shortcake, 682
  Omelet Country Style, 173

Onion(s), and Pepper Ragout, 693
  Pressure Cooked, 1170
  à la Reine, 693
  Rings, Baked, 690
    Grilled Hamburgers, 339
  See also Sandwiches
  Sauce, 579
  Sausage Shortcake Curry, 459
  Scalloped Tomatoes with, 738
  Soufflé, 693
  Soup au Gratin, 138
  Stuffed, 689
    Baked Liver, 689
  Stuffing, 793
    Burger, 789
    Epicure, 791
  and Tripe, 468, 473
  Tripe, and Oysters, 473
Opah, a fish, 204
Open-Mouther Grunt, a fish, 200
Oquassa Trout, 219
Orange, see also Salads
  Bran Drop Cookies, 926
  Bread I, 1071
  Bread II, 1072
  Cherry Cups, 411
  and Cider Cooler, 61
  Custard, 881
  Custard Dessert Sauce, 894
  Fluff Dessert Sauce, 894
  Ice, 1120
  Ice Cream I, 1132
  Ice Cream II, 1133
  Jelly, 878
  Juice Cocktail, 33
  Juice, in Mint Sauce, 812
  Ladyfingers, 932
  in Louisiana Petit Brûlot, 74
  Milk Sherbet, 1152
    Peaches & Strawberries, 1153
    Pineapple & Strawberries, 1153
  Roast Duck with, 525
  Salad, 811
  Sauce, Beets in, 614
Oregano, 1005
  Clams, 225
Oregon Charr Trout, 220
Orientale, Melon à l', 879
Osso Bucco, 357
Ostrich Ferns, Buttered, 661
  Canned, 662
Ouananiche Salmon, 210
Oubliés, 931
Oursins, shellfish, 232

Outside Clams, 225
Oven Cooked Broilers, 515
Ox Eye Eggs, 161
Oxtail, 327
  Braised, 327
  Soup, 138
Oyster Plant, 1173
Oyster(s), 230, 277–279
  Angels on Horseback, 9
  Bay Oysters, 230
  and Beef Pie, 321
  Benedict, 279
  Canapés, 20
  Casino, 279
  Cocktail, Pickled, 35
  Cocktail Sauce, 36, 579
  Corn, (Mock), 646
  Crabs, 227
  Croquettes, Dominican, 26
  Deep Fat Frying, 986
  Dressing, Anchovy, 8
  Fricassée Baltimore, 279
    Boston, 279
  Fritters, 280
  Fry, 280
  Gumbo, 134
  à la King, 290
  Marguery Sauce, 574
  and Mushroom Pie, 280
  opening, 281
  Onions, and Tripe, 473
  Pilote, 281
  à la Rockefeller, 38
  Stew, 282
  Stuffing, 793
    Boiled Goose Béchamel, 527
    Mutton, 386
  and Turkey Fritters, 542
    Scallop, 544

Paderewski Turkey Galantine, 542
Paillard, Canard à la, 519
Pain Perdu, 878
Pale Flounder, 198
Palmer House Clam Juice Cocktail, 35
Palukaluka, a fish, 200
Pan, Broiling, 986
  Dowdy, Apple, 944
  Frying, 987
    Fish, 192
    Sausage, 455
Pancake(s), 795, 866–869
  Almond, 798
  Apple, 797

Pancake(s), Banana, 799
  Bread, 798
  Buckwheat, 798
  Buckwheat, Variations, 799
  Elder Blossom, 800
  Flemish, 800
  French, 801
  French Fried, 800
  Hints, 797
  Mushroom & Artichokes, 598
  Netherland Chicken, 801
  Pineapple, 797
  Potato, 707
  Rice, 802
  Russian, 12
  Scotch Mutton, 802
  Sourdough, 803
  Syrup, Fruit, 797
  Turnovers, Egg, 169
Panned Porgies, 282
Pannequets aux Amandes, 798
Papillotes, Lamb Chops en, 378
  Pompano en, 282
  Veal Chops en, 360
Paprika Butter I, 552
  Butter II, 552
  Veal Chops, 361
Parboiling, see Short-Boiling, 990
Parfait(s), 1144
  Angel, 1145
  Apricot, 1145
  Chocolate, 1145
  Coffee, 1146
  Golden, 1146
  Maple, 1146
  Marron Glacé, 1147
  Mocha, 1147
  Raspberry, 1148
  Strawberry, 1148
Pargo Colorado, a fish, 215
  Colorado al Vera Cruz, 285
  Porgies, a fish, 208
  Prieto, a fish, 215
Parisian,—en,—enne:
  Cannelons, 956
  Chicken Broth, 113
  Egg Ring, 164
  Fish Fumet, 580
  Grenadins of Veal, 355
  Lamb Stew, 382
  Raspberry Tart, 959
  Turnips à la, 744
Parker House Rolls, 1102
Parmentier, Poached Eggs, 180

Parmesan Cheese, Aigrettes, 4
  Grated, 760–762
  See also Sandwich Fillings
Parrot-Fish, 200
Parsley, 1005
  Butter, 573
    Kohlrabi, 667
    Mustard Variation, 573
  Crackers, 104
  Dumplings, 787
  and Lamb Pinwheels, 381
  Omelet Soufflé, 173
  Pastry Cover, 940
    Variations, 940
  Sauce, 580
Parsnip(s), 694
  Boiled, 694
  Chips, Saratoga, 695
  Creamed, au Gratin, 694
  Fritters, 695
  au Gratin Gastronome, 638
  Pie, 695
  Pressure Cooked, 1171
  Puffs, 695
    Variation, 695
  Slices, Glazed, I, 694
    Glazed, II, 694
Pastry, Egg, Pie Covering, 940
  Flaky, 938
  Mealy, 938
  Pie, Standard, 952
  Short Flaky, 939
Pasteurized Milk, 75
Pasteurizing Milk at Home, 80
Patates Douces dans Coquille d'Oranges,
    711
Pâté de Foie Gras, 17–19
  de Foie Gras, Imitation, 453
  Froid de Volaille, 510
  Goose Liver Canapés, 17
Patti, Adelina, Breast of Guinea Hen,
    532
Patty(ies), Asparagus, 600
  Egg, 162
  Egg & Rice, in Watercress, 164
  Shells, 940
  Squash, I, 731
  Squash, II, 731
  See also Hamburger, Sausages
Paugy Porgies, a fish, 208
Paulette Consommé, 117
Pavés, Honey Brandy Spiced, 930
Paysanne, Lamb Chops à la, 378

Peach(es)
  Annabelle, 882
  Cider Punch, 62
  Duff, 881
  Griddle Cakes, 802
  Ice Cream I, 1133
  Ice Cream II, 1133
  Jalousies, Brandied, 955
  Jalousies, Brandied, Variations, 956
  Melba, 1134
  Mousse, 1142
  Poached in White Wine, 881
  See also Salads
  See also Sandwich Fillings
  with Sherbet, 1153
Peanut(s), 1029, 1031
  Brittle, 978
  Butter Biscuits, 1047
  Butter, 852. *See also* Sandwiches
    See also Sandwich Fillings
  Roasting, 1025
Pearl Hen, 484, 531
Pear Nina Lenclos, 828
Pears Condé, 882
  See also Salads
Pea(s), 696
  Black-Eyed, Pot Likker, 607
  Crabs, 227
  Green, Creamed, Bayou, 697
    and Egg Scallop, 162
    French Style, 698
    Good Woman Style, 698
    Niçoise, 698
    in Onion Cups, 699
    Stewed French Style, 699
  Pods, Creamed, 697
    Mashed, in Cream, 698
    Pressure Cooked, 1171
    Soup, Cream of, 126
  Pressure Cooked, 1171
  Purée, Split, 699
  Soup, Canadian, 112
    Split, 141
  Split, Sausage, 699
  Cooked in Vichy Water, 697
Pea-Lip Sucker, a fish, 217
Pecan(s), 1029, 1031
  Butterscotch Ice Cream, 1126
  Cinnamon Rolls, 1102
  Eggnog Pie, 949
  Molasses Pie, 949
    Tartlets, Spiced, 961
  Orange, Banana Salad, 826
  Pie, 957

Pecan(s), Rum Tart Filling, 960
  Stuffing, 794
Peconic Oysters, 230
Pelerines, scallops, 231
Pennsylvania Dutch Succotash, 733
Pepper, Cayenne, 1002
  Chuck Steak Dinner, 341
  Pot, 469
    Philadelphia, 139
Peppers, Bell, 658, *see* Green Peppers
  Green, 658; *see under* Green Peppers
  Sweet, 658
Peppermint Ice Cream, 1134
Peppernuts, 932
Perch, a fish, 206
  Ocean, 209
  Red, 209
  Red-Eye, 194
  Sand, 218
  White, 213
Permit Pompano, a fish, 208
Pérouse, Double Sirloin Steak, 336
Pershing, General, Squabs, 535
Pescado, a fish, 209
Petite Marmite, 139
  of France, 503
Petits Fours, Honey Brandy Spiced
    Pavés, 930
  Liègeois, 932
Petits Pois, 697
  Bonne Femme, 698
  à l'Etuvée (Fermière), 699
  à la Française, 698
  à la Niçoise, 698
"Petticoat Tails," 920
Petoncles, scallops, 231
Philadelphia Pepper Pot, 139
  Pepper Pot, 469
Picareau Blanc, 205
Pickerel, 206, 207
  Muskellunge, 205
Pickle Sauce, for Tongue, 466
Pickled Oyster Cocktail, 35
  Pig's Feet, 436
  Sauce, 580
Pickles, Mustard, Liquid of, 812
Picnic, Pork, 394
Pie(s), Dessert: *see separate listing for*
    Meat, etc., Pies
  Angel, 943
  Apple, 944
    Cottage Cheese, 943
    French Deep Dish, 946
    Slice, French, 946

Pie(s), Baking, 938
  Buttermilk Raisin Meringue, 944
  Cherry Chess, 945
  Coffee Rum Chiffon, 945
  Covering, Biscuit, 940
    Cheese, 939
    Egg Yolk Pastry, 940
  Custard, 869
  Farmer's Nut Cream, 946
  Lemon, Chiffon, 947
    Cream, 947
      Variations, 947
    Meringue, New England, 949
  Meringue Cream, 947
  Mince, 948
    Brandied Mincemeat, 948
  Molasses-Pecan, 949
  Pecan, 950
    Eggnog, 949
  Pumpkin, I, 950
  Pumpkin, II, 951
  Rhubarb, 951
  Shoofly, 951
  Walnut-Maple Syrup, 952
  Washington's Gingerbread Cream, 953
Pie(s), Meat, etc.: *see separate listing for*
    Dessert Pies
  Apple and Ham, 416
  Asparagus, 602
  Beef, 324
    Dried, and Egg, 433
    and Kidney, 321
    and Oyster, 321
  Chicken, Granny Lee's, 512
    and Mushroom, 502
  Clam, Canadian, 240
  Corn Custard, 646
  Crust, *see under* Crust
  Curried Onion Cheese, 690
  Egg, French Style, 161
  Goose Giblet, 528
  Lamb Pot, 381
  Lentil, 673
  Macaroni, 755
  Onion Cheese Custard, 691
  Oyster, and Beef, 321
    and Mushroom, 280
  Parsnip, 695
  Pastry, Standard, 952
  Pigeon, New Orleans, 534
    Pot, 536
  Pork, and Apple, 401
    and Sweet Potato, 402
    Tamale, 403

Pie(s), Sausage and Ham, 423
  Shrimp, Charleston, 290
  Tomato, 738
    Cheese, 740
  Turkey, 544
  Turtle, Gourmet, 303
  Veal and Ham, Dickens, 364
Piemontaise, -ese, Chicken Risotto, 505
  Gnocchi, 764
  Polenta à la, 750
  Sauce, 586, 750
Pig, Suckling, Roast, 406
  Creole, 407
  Kentucky, 408
Pigeon(s), 483, 534
  General Pershing, 535
  Pie, New Orleans, 534
  Pot Pie, 536
  Potted Chestnut-Stuffed Squabs, 536
  Squabs Moscovite, 537
    with Olives, 537
    on Toast, 537
  Stuffing, Wild Rice and Sausage, 795
Pignuts, 1030
Pig's Feet, 393, 427
  Baked, 434
  Deviled, 435
  Pickled, 436
  St. Menehould, 437
  in Wine Jelly, 436
Pig's Knuckles, 398
  see also Pork
Pike, a fish, 207
Pilchard, a fish, 211
Pilgrim Scallops, 232
Pilot, Fish, 223
  Shark, 213
Pilote, Oyster, 281
Piman Baked Frijole Beans, 606
Pimiento, Butter Balls, 645
  Whip, 104
Pineapple, Charlotte Monte Carlo, 882
  and Cider Cooler, 61
  and Cream Cheese Sandwich, 844
  Ice, 1120
  Ice Cream, 1134
  Maraschino Cherry Sherbet, 1153
  Mousse, 1143
  Pancake, 797
  for Salads, 811
  Sherbet, 1153
  with Sherbet, 1153
  see also Salads; Sandwiches
Pine Nuts, 1030

Pinon Nuts, 1030
Pintade, a Guinea Hen, 484
Pintado, a fish, 202
Pinwheel(s), Cinnamon Apple Roly Poly, 956
  Lamb and Parsley, 381
  Tea Biscuits, 1047
Pioneer Mush, 750
  Salt Pork Raisin Cake, 920
Piquante, Dressing, 837
  Sauce, 580
Pique Seasoning, 1006
Pique's Egg Pancake Turnovers, 169
Pistachio Ice Cream I, 1135
  Ice Cream II, 1135
  Nuts, 1030
Pizza, Napolitan, 738
  Rustica, 423
Plank cooking, 175
Planked Eggs in Nest My Way, 175
  Shad, Baked, 238
Plantation Baked Shad Roe, 237
Plantation Style Mullet, 272
Plate, Beef, 312
Plaza Tomato Aspic, 45
Pleated Horse Mussels, 229
Plum, Duff, 883
  Pudding, English, 871
    Mincemeat, Steamed, 887
    Surrey, 887
  Sauce, Old-Fashioned, 894
Plymouth (Mass.) Succotash, 733
Poached
  Chicken, 516
  Eggs, 152, 176
    Amandine, 176
    in Aspic I, 177
    in Aspic II, 177
    Boulangère, 177
    Bourdaloue, 177
    Caracas, 178
    Colette, 178
    Comte Potocki, 180
    Coquette, 178
    à la Frissac, 179
    and Leeks on Toast, 670
    Lucette, 179
    Mongole, 179
    Mornay, 179
    Ninon, 180
    Parmentier, 180
    in Potato Nests Jacqueline, 180
    à la Reine, 181
    in Rice Ring, 181

Poached, Eggs, Rodriguez, 181
    à la Rotonde, 182
    Strasbourgeois, 182
    à la Suissesse, 182
    Suzanne, 182
  Finnan Haddie in Milk, 282
  Fish, 191
  Peaches in White Wine, 881
Poaching, see Short-Boiling, 990
Pocket, of Lamb, 370
  Veal, Roast, 348
Pods, Pea, Creamed, 697
  Cream Soup, 127
Pois, Petits, 697
  Bonne Femme, 698
  à la Francaise, 698
  à la Niçoise, 698
Poisson Blanc, 223
Poisson Lune, 204
Poivrade Sauce, 581
Poker Hash, 401
Polenta, à la Piemontese, 750
  Romana, 750
Polish Apple Soup, 106
  Asparagus, 600
  Bigos, 625
  Bortsch, 108
  Bow Knots, 783
  Herring Stew, 283
Polla, Arroz con, Castillane, 492
Pollock, 207, 208
Polonaise, Bortsch, 108
  Cucumber, 816
  Kidneys, Veal or Lamb, 448
Pomegranate West Coast, 829
Pompadour, Artichoke Bottom, 24
  Asparagus, 603
Pommes Soufflées, 706
  de Terre Allumettes, 707
  de Terre Copeaux, 710
Pompano, a fish, 208, 283
  California, 224
  en Papillotes "La Louisiane," 282
Pone, Corn, 607
Popcorn, Cheese, 97
  as Soup Garnish, 123
Popover(s), 1093–1095
  Cases, Brains in, 431
  Cheese, 1094
  Hints, 1093
  Rich, 1094
  Rye Meal, 1095
  Sunday, 1095
  Whole Wheat, 1095

Poppy Seed Wafers, 933
  Variations, 933
Porbeagle, a fish, 213
Porgies, 206, 208
  Panned, 282
Pork, 391–410
  and Apple Pie, 401
  Arm Steak, 394
  Balls, 434
  Bladder, Chicken in, 501
  Brains, 427
  Butt, 393
  Chart, 393–394
  Chops:
    Baked, Charcutiere, 395
      Florentine, 395
      Hawaii, 395
      Normande, 396
      Stuffed Double, 396
    Braised, Creole, 397
    Loin, 393
    Rib, 393
  Chop Suey, 315
  Chow Mein, 401
  Cooking of, 392–394
  Croquettes, 373
  Crown Roast, 398
  Cushion, 394
  Filet, Roast, 405
  Ham, 393; *see also* Ham
    Fresh, 393
    Shank, 394
  Heart, 427
  Hock, 394
  and Kidney Pie, 321
  Kidneys, 427
  Liver, 427, 449
    see also Liver
  Loin, 394
    Intoxicated, 400
    Roast "Frenched," 404
  Picnic, 394
  Pig's Feet, 393, 427
    See also Pig's
  Roasting, 988
  Salt, Raisin Cake, 920
  Salt, and String Beans, 726
  Sandwich, Hot, 850
  Sausages, 427–428
  Shoulder, 394
    Corned, 398
  Smoked, 411
  Soufflé, 402
  Spareribs, 394

Pork, Stew, 402
  Hungarian Style, 356
  and Sweet Potato Pie, 402
  Tails, 428
  Tamale Pie, 403
  Tenderloin, 394, 403
  Tongues, 311, 428
Porter Punch, 51
Porterhouse Steak, *see* Steak, Porter-
  house
Portuguese Codfish Omelet, 154
  Codfish Steak, 243
  Jelly (Dessert), 886
  Marinated Veal Loin, 357
Port Wine Jelly, Aspic Coating, 39, 581
Potato(es), 700
  Baked, 702
    Soubise, 703
    Stuffed, 702
  Baking, 703
  Balloons, 706
  Balls, Bavarian, 344
  Cakes, 703
  and Carrot Fritters, 706
  Cheese Balls, 707
    Nests, 707
  Chips, 710
  Creamed, 702
    Old Fashioned, 704
  Delmonico, 704
  Duchesse, 706
  Dumplings, Bohemian, 784
  Dumplings, Curried, 99
  and Egg Scallop, 162
  French Fried, 703
  Fritto Misto, 704
  Flour Muffins, 1090
  au Gratin, 708
  in Hamburger, 703
  Hashed Brown, 705
  in Haste, 704
  Hints, 702
  in their Jackets, 702
  Mashed, 702, 703, 706
    Biscuits, 1046
    with Spinach, 721
  Mashing, 702
  Match Sticks, 707
  in Meat Loaf, 703
  Nests, Poached Eggs in, 180
  Pancakes, 707
  Pressure Cooked, 1172
  Ricing, 702
  Ring, Creamed Codfish in, 248

Potato(es), Salad, Raw Carrot in, 629
  Scallop, 708
    Cheese Variation, 708
    Meat Variation, 708
    Mushroom Variation, 708
    Vegetable Variation, 708
    Village Style, 708
  Shoe Strings, 707
  in their Skins, 702
  Soufflé Amandine, 709
  and Spinach Croquettes, 709
  Spirals, 709
  and Squash Mashed, 730
  Sweet, *See* Sweet Potatoes
  and Walnut Croquettes, 709
  Water Feather Rolls, 1103
  Yeast Bread, 1076
Potage, Esaü, 135
  à l'Indienne, 137
Pot Cheese Dressing, 840
Pot, Chicken in the, 503
Pot de Crème au Chocolat, 883
Pot-au-Feu, 140
Pot Likker, Black-Eyed Peas, 607
Potocki, Comte, Poached Eggs, 180
Pot Pie, Lamb, 381
  Pigeon, 536
Pot Roast, Arm, 312
  Beef Heart, 442
  Blade, 312
  à la Romane, 341
  Sour, 343
  Spiced, 344
Pot Roasting, 987
Potted
  Duck à la Creole, 519
  Herring (Fresh), 283
  Stuffed Squabs with Chestnuts, 536
  Veal Steak Dutch Style, 358
Poulard, Omelet à la Mère, 171
Poularde, Excelsior, 501
  en Petit Deuil, 501
  à la Tartare, 509
Poule, d'Inde, 484
  de Numidie, 484
Poulet du Cloître, 500
Poulette, Mushrooms à la, 683
  Sauce, 581
Poultry, 475–545
  Boiler, 481
  Broiler, 482
  Capon, 481, 485–486, 490
    See also under Capon
  Chart, 481–484

Poultry, Chicken, 481, 482, 490–492
    See also under Chicken
  to Divide, 479
  Drawn, 481
  Dressed, 481
  Duck, 483, 518
    See also under Duck
  Fowl, 481
    Larding with Anchovy, 9
    Stuffing, 791
  Fricassée, 480
  Frozen, 481
    Thawing, 1018
  Fryer, 482
  Goose, 483, 525–527
    See also under Goose
  Guinea Hen, 484, 531
    See also under Guinea Hen
  Hints, 479–480
  and Kidney Pie, 321
  Meat Loaf, 480
  Milk-Fed, 481
  Pigeons, 483, 534–537
    See also under Pigeons
  Preparation, 478–479
  Roaster, 482
  Simmering, 989
  Squabs, *see* Pigeons
  Turkey, 484, 537–545
    See also under Turkey
Pound Cakes, Failures, 902–908
Pout, Eel, 203
  Ocean, 203
Pralines, Almond Chocolate, 969
Prawn(s), à la King, 290
  Puffs, 291
Pressure Cookery, 1157–1176
  Chart, 1162–1176
  Frozen Vegetables, 1013
    Chart, 1014
Presumpscot River Salmon, 210
Princess, Burnt Chicken, 495
Profiterolles au Chocolat, 959
Provençale, Artichokes, à la, 594
  Calf's Head Grill, 352
  Braised Leg of Mutton, 388
  Mussels à la, 277
  Sauce, 585
  Sausage à la, 457
  Snails à la, 295
Prune and Apple Stuffing, 794
  Loaf (Molded), 829
  Sauce, for Smoked Meat, 423, 582
  Stuffing, Roast Goose, 530

Prune, Whip Crunch, California, 863
Pudding, 883
  Almond Cream, Fluffy, 872
  Apple, Steamed, 887
  Cabinet, 863
  Corn, 647
    Meal, 749
  Honey Sponge Lemon, 877
  Molded, Mama Turner's, 879
  Plum, English, 871
    Steamed Mincemeat, 887
    Surrey, 887
  Rice, Meringue Topped, 885
  Tipsy, 922
  Yorkshire, 342
Puff(s)
  Cakes with Chocolate Sauce, 959
  Corn, Curried, 648
  Parsnip, 695
    Variation, 696
  Paste I, 941
    Paste II, 941
    Paste III, 942
  Salsify, 717
  Shrimp, Maine Style, 291
Puffed
  Crackers, 104
  Omelet, 174
Pulled Bread, 104
Pullig, Mussels à la Henri, 275
Pumpkin, 713
  Baked, Fluffy, 716
    Hamburger Stuffed, 714
    Whole, 715
  Boiled, 715
  Blossoms, Deep Fried, 715
  Browned, 715
  Fried Chinese, 714
  Pie I, 950
    Pie, II, 951
  Pressure Cooked, 1172
  Soup, Cream of, 127
Pumpkinseed, a fish, 218
Punch
  Cider, Fruit, à la Normande, 61
    Peach, 62
    Thanksgiving, 63
  Porter, 51
  Rum, Hot Buttered, 62
  Tea, 84
Purée, Lentil, 673
  Split Pea, 699
  Spinach, Saint Mandé, 723

Quahaug Clams, 225
Quatog Clams, 225
Quin Scallops, 231
Quinnat Salmon, 209
Quohog Clams, 225

Rack, Lamb, 368
Racoon Perch, 206
Radishes
  Roses, 811
  Stuffed, 39
Ragoût, *see* Stewing, 989
  Chicken, Creamed, & Almonds, 512
  Onions and Pepper, 693
  of Veal Creole, 365
Raiado, a fish, 215
Raie (Skate), 214
Rainbow Abalone, a shellfish, 224
Rainbow Trout, 219
Raised Doughnuts, 783
Raisin(s), 1058
  Apple Cake, 911
  Bread, 1073
    Bran, 1058
    Irish, 1069
  Buttermilk Meringue Pie, 944
  Cinnamon Nut Buns, 1079
    Rolls, 1101
  Coffee Twist, 1106
  Cottage Cheese Sandwich, 843
  Nut Bread, 1071
    Ice Cream, 1135
    Tart, 962
  Sauce, 582
  in Sauce for Capon, 489
  Sauerkraut with, 719
  Waffles, 808
Ramekins
  Egg, Florentine, 163
    Renversés, 163
    Yvonne, 163
  Lentil, 673
  Sausage Meat, 460
Rarebit, 44
Raspberry Cherry Brandy Sauce, 891
  Cocktail, 33
  Ice, 1120
  Ice Cream, 1136
  Milk Sherbet I, 1154
    Sherbet II, 1154
  Parfait, 1148
  Sauce, 894
  Tart, Parisian, 959

Ratafia Macaroons, 933
Ravigote, Crab Meat, 248
  Sauce, 582
    Anchovy, 8
Ravioli, 763
  Napoli Style, 764
Razor Clams, 225
Recipe, How to Study, 1160
Red
  Cabbage & Chestnuts Casserole, 626
    German, 623
  Currant Fritters, 884
    Strips, 960
  Dressing I, 837
    Dressing II, 837
  Drum, a fish, 196, 208
  Grouper, a fish, 199
  Hot, _see_ Frankfurters
  Kidney Beans Casserole Bercy, 611
  Meats, 309
  Snapper Miami Style, 284
    Vera Cruz Style, 285
  Wine, 85
    Carp in, 240
    Sauce, 583
      Dagouret, 583
Red-Eye Bass, 194
  Mullet, 205
  Perch, 194
Redfish, 196, 208, 209
  Little, 209
Reef Bass, 209
Refrigerator Cheese Cake, 920
  Clover Leaf Rolls, 1104
Relish, Lentil, 37
Remick Sauce, 583
Remoulade Sauce, 509
  Anchovy, 8
Rhode Island Baked Stuffed Cod, 237
Rhubarb, Chard, 640
  Pie, 951
Rhum, Baba au, 954
Rib(s), Chops, Lamb, 370
  Chops, Pork, 393
    Veal, 348
  Short, Beef, 312
  Roast, Standing, beef, 313
    Veal, 348
Ribbed-Carpet Clams, 225
Riblets of Lamb, 370
  Veal, 349
Rice, 766
  Arroz con Polla, 492
  Boiling Method, 767

Rice, Border, 769
  Brown, 768
    How to Cook, 768
  Cakes, Calas, 781
  Chicken with, 492
  Chinese Style, 766
  Cooked in Hard Water, 767
  Creole, 768
    with Crabs, 247
    in Stuffed Tomatoes, 739
  Croquettes I, 770
  Croquettes II, 770
  Curried with Mushrooms, 681
  Curry of, 768
  Double Boiler Style, 767
  and Duck Dinner, 524
  and Egg Patties, 164
  and Ham Casserole, 419
  How to Cook, 766–767
  Mexican Burger, 769
  Mold, Southern, 886
  Near East Boiled, 769
  Nests I, 770
  Nests II, 771
  Pancakes, 802
  Pudding, Meringue Topped, 885
  Reheated Rice, 767
  Ring, Poached Eggs in, 181
  Risotto, 505
  Saffron, 773
  Valentienne, 771
  Waffles, 808
    Curried, 808
  Wild, 773, 768
    with Chicken Livers, 774
    How to Cook, 768
    in Milk, 775
    with Turkey, 539
Riced Carrots, 630
Rich Johnny Cake, 1089
  Popover, 1094
Richardin, Canapés, 24
Richmond, Filet Mignon à la, 338
Ricing Potatoes, 702
Ricotta Cheese, Lasagne al', 765
Ring(s), Shaped:
  Beet, & Cole Slaw, 813
  Cauliflower Soufflé Amandine, 633
  Chard, with Mushrooms, 641
    Variation, 642
  Cheese Biscuit, 939
  Coffee, 1105
    Swedish, 1175
  Corn Meal, Luncheon, 749

Ring(s), Egg Noodle, 757
  Egg, Parisienne, 164
  Kale, 665
  Macaroni Soufflé, 756
  Noodle, and Sausage Creole, 759
  Potato, Codfish in, 248
  Rice, Poached Eggs in, 181
  Veal, Soufflé, Celestine, 365
Rings, Slice:
  Green Pepper, French Fried, 659
  Onion, Baked, 690
  Squash, Apple Sauce, 730
Ripe Olives, 812
Risotto, 505
  alla Milanaise, 772
  Chicken, Piemontaise, 505
  Crown Curry Lobster, 268
Rivvles, 787
Roast(s); *see also under* Roasting
  Beef, 312–313, 342
    Arm Pot, 312
    Blade Pot, 312
    Chuck, 312
      Arm, 312
      Blade, 312
      à la Romane, 341
      Sour, 343
      Spiced, 344
    Standing, Method I, 342
    Standing, Method II, 343
    Standing, Rib, 313
    Yorkshire Pudding, 342
  Capon Alexandre Dumas, 489
  Chicken en Casserole, 516
  Corn, 648
  Duck à l'Orange, 525
  Goat, 78
  Goose Celery Stuffing, 529
    Milanaise, 530
    Prune Stuffing, 530
  Guinea Hens, 534
  Ham, Fresh, 404
    Virginia, 424
  Lamb, 371
    Breast, Stuffed, 384
    Crown, 370, 375
      Variations, 376
    Leg of, Venison, 382
    Loin, & Kidneys, 383
    Saddle of, 384
  Larding with Anchovy, 9
  Mutton, Saddle of, 384
  Pig, Suckling, 406
    Creole, 407

Roast(s), Mutton, Kentucky, 408
  Pork Filet, 405
    Loin of, "Frenched," 404
  Turkey, 540
  Veal, Arm, 348
    Blade, 348
    Crown, 348
    Loin, 348
    Loin of, Beer Gravy, 358
    Pocket, 348
    Rib, 348
    Round, 349
    Rump, 348, 349
Roaster, poultry, 482
Roasting, 987; *see also under* Roasts
  Beef, 342
  Chart, 988
  Duck, 526
  Goose, 526
  Meat, Time Table, 988
  Nuts, 1025
  Pot, 987
  Steam, 989
Robert, Tomato, 819
Robbins Island Oysters, 230
Rochelaise Sauce, 584
Rock Bass, 194
  Clam, 226
  Cod, 196
Rockefeller, Oysters à la, 38
Rodriguez, Poached Eggs, 181
Roe, Butter, 552
  See also Caviar
  Herring Canapés, 21
  See also Sandwich Fillings
  Shad, 212
    Baked, 237
    Baked, Plantation, 237
    Grill, 288
    Meunière, 288
    Sturgeon's, 218
Roll; (*see also* Rolled; Rolls)
  Blueberry, 955
  Chocolate Cream, 913
  Stuffed Spinach, 724
  Turkey, Baked, 539
  Braised Veal, 350
Rolled; (*see also* Roll; Rolls)
  Beef "Olives," 326
Rolls; (*see also* Roll; Rolled)
  Veal, Shoulder, 349
  Butter, 1098
    Flake, 1097
  Buttermilk, 1098

Rolls, Cheese, 1099
  Cinnamon, 1099
    Pecan, 1102
    Raisin, 1101
  Clover Leaf, 1100
    Refrigerator, 1104
  Hints, 1096–1097
  Parker House, 1102
  Potato Water Feather, 1103
  Rotterdam Almond, 960
  Sour Cream, 1105
  Sweet Potato, 713
  Veal, California, 352
Roly Poly Pinwheels, Cinnamon Apple,
  956
Romaine, Lettuce Stewed, 676
  Pressure Cooked, 1172
Roman Omelet, 173
  Style Eggplant, 657
Romana, Gnocchi alla, 763
  Polenta, 750
  Vitello al Marsala, 366
Romane, Cauliflower, 634
  Pot Roast à la, 341
Roncos, a fish, 199
Roquefort Cheese
  Avocado, and Egg Bowl, 822
  Celery Stuffing, 42
  Dressing, French, 812, 832
    Mayonnaise, 838
  See also Sandwich Fillings
Rosalind, Veal Chops à la, 361
Roses d'Hiver Armenonville, 39
Roses, Radish, 811
Rossini, Veal Birds à la, 360
Rotonde, Poached Eggs, 182
Rotterdam Almond Rolls, 960
Rouennaise, Baked Shad, 236
Rough Abalone, a mollusk, 224
  Dab, a fish, 203
Round, Beef, 312
  Steak, 312
    Bottom, 313
    Top, 313
    Veal, 349
  Veal, Heel of, 348
    Roast, 349
Roux, 557, 584
  Blond, 584
  Brown, 584
Royal(e), Anchovy Canapés, 7
  Batter, Frying, 159
  Charlotte, 863
  Coffee, 71

Royal(e), Custard Cubes, 105
  Lettuce, 675
Rum, Cake with, 954
  Coffee Chiffon Pie, 945
  Honey Caramels, 978
  Mocha Sauce, 894
  Mousse, 1140
  Omelette Aflame, 885
  Pecan Tart Filling, 960
  Punch, Hot Buttered, 62
  Sauce, Fluffy, 892
Rump Roast, Veal, 348, 349
Russian Aromatic Tea, 83
  Cinnamon Butter, 552
  Dressing I, 837
  Dressing II, 837
  Dressing III, 837
  Lepeshki, 925
  Nutmeg Butter, 552
  Pancakes, 12
Rusty Dab, a fish, 203
Rutabaga, 742
  Pressure Cooked, 1173
Rye Bread, 1067
  Bread Soup, Bohemian, 110
  Meal Popovers, 1095

Sabayon, 886
  Variations, 886
Sabayon Sauce, 892, 895
Sacher, Veal Cutlet, 363
Sacramento Salmon, 209
Saddle of Lamb, Roast, 384
Saddle of Mutton, Roast, 384
Saffron Rice, 775
Sage Stuffing I, 794
  Stuffing II, 795
Saint Germain, Mushrooms, 684
  Jacqueline Scallops, 244
  Jacques Scallops, 244
  Malo, Filets of Sole, 257
  Mandé, Spinach Purée, 723
  Quentin, Consomme, 117
  Raphael, Filets of Sole, 258
Salad, 811–829; *see also* Salad **Dressing**
  Apple & Cream Cheese Balls, 820
  Apple, Dates, & Almonds, 820
  Apple Gelatin Rosita, 821
  Apricot Jelly (Molded), 821
  Apricot Orange Cheese, 821
  Asparagus (Jellied), 813
  Asparagus & Green Olives, 813
  Asparagus, Spinach, & Eggs, 813
  Avocado, Date, & Orange, 822

Salad, Avocado, Egg and Roquefort
  Cheese Bowl, 822
 Avocado, Grapefruit, & Mint, 822
 Banana, 811
  Balls in Basket, 822
  Date and Walnut, 822
  Orange, and Canteloupe, 823
 Beets in, 614
 Beet, Celery and Apple Molds, 814
 Beet Ring and Cole Slaw, 813
 Cabbage for, 622
  Bowl, 814
  Carrot, and Apple, 814
  and Pineapple, 814
 Caesar, 815
 Cantaloupe Nellie Melba, 823
 Cardoons in, 628
 Cherry Delmonico, 823
 Cherry and Pineapple Wheel, 823
 Chicken, 812
 Chicken, Tuxedo Park, 506
 Cole Slaw, 815
 Cranberry, Grapes & Celery, 824
 Crosnes in, 649
 Cucumber, 815
  Baskets, 816
  Cream Cheese, 816
  Horseshoe, 816
  Polonaise, 816
  Tomato, and Lettuce, 817
 Fish, 813
 Grapes, Dates, and Nuts, 824
 Grape Maria, 824
 Grapefruit Aspic Annette, 824
  Cherry & Celery, 825
  Mint Ring, 825
  Rainbow, 825
 Green, Egg Yolk in, 152
 Green, Garlic in, 813
 Greens, Dressing, 812
 Leeks French Method, 817
 Making Hints, 811
 Orange, 811
  Banana, and Pecan, 826
  Cream Cheese Ring, 826
  Ring Jelly (Molded), 827
 Peach and Cream Cheese, 827
 Peach, Grape, and Ginger Ale, 827
 Pear Cactus, 827
 Pear French Style, 828
 Pear Nina Lenclos, 828
 Pineapple Collette, 828
 Pineapple Gloria, 829
 Pineapple Golden Glow, 829

Salad, Pomegranate West Coast, 829
 Potato, 817
  Caruso, 817
  Escoffier, 818
  Rachel, 818
  Raw Carrot in, 629
 Prune Loaf (Molded), 829
 Tomato Basket Beatrice, 818
  Basket Emily, 819
  à la Grèque, 818
  Porcupine, 819
  Robert, 819
  Surprise (Jellied), 819
 Salmagundi, 40
 Salsify, 716
 Spinach, Raw, 812
 Vegetable, 812
 Watercress, 820
Salad Dressings, 830–841, 1001, see also
  Salad
 Anchovy, 8
 Bar-le-Duc, 830
 Boiled, 838
 Boiled Carlton, 839
 Boiled Waltham, 839
 Breslin, 830
 California, 830
 Caper, 836
 Caviar, 836
 Caviar Horseradish, 836
 Chiffonade, 831
 Chutney, French, 831
 Chutney, Mayonnaise, 835
 Club, 831
 Cranberry, 836
 Cream, I, 831
 Cream (Foamy), II, 831
 Cream Cheese, 831
 Cucumber, 831
 Cucumber, Hot, 839
 Cumberland, 836
 Currant Jelly, 831
 Curry, 832
 Egg, 836
 Egg-Cheese, 832
 French, 830
  Variations: See under French Dressing
 Green, 836
 Honey, 832
 Horseradish, 836
 Indian, 840
 Mayonnaise, 833, 834
  Almond, 835
  Condensed Milk, 834

Salad Dressings, Mayonnaise, Cooked
    Base, 835
    Cream, 835
    Gelatine, 835
    See also under Mayonnaise
Mint, 832
Mustard, 840
Olga's, 837
Olive, 837
Piquante, 837
Pot Cheese, 840
Red, I, 837
Red, II, 837
Roquefort, French, 832
Roquefort, Mayonnaise, 838
Russian, I, 837
Russian, II, 837
Russian, III, 837
Sour Cream, 812, 838
Sour Cream, Boiled, 839
Suzette's, 840
Sweet Sour, 840
Thousand Island, I, 838
Thousand Island, II, 838
Victory, 838
Vinaigrette, 832
Waldenstein, 832
Whipped Cream Jelly, 841
Wilmot, 833
Salami and Swiss Cheese Sandwich, 845
Salema, a fish, 213
Salisbury Steak, 343
Sally Lunn Bread, 1073
Sally Lunn Muffins, 1090
Salmagundi, 39
Salmagundi Salad, 40
Salmon, 209, 210
    Black, 195
    Club Sandwich, Hot, 850
    Court-Bouillon, Hollandaise, 286
    Dumplings, 787
    Mousse (Cold), 287
    Mousse Havraise (Hot), 286
    Pike, 205, 207
    Smoked, Butter, 552
    Trout, 219
    White, 223
Salsify, 716
    Boiled, with Sauces, 716
    Fritters, 717
    Pressure Cooked, 1173
    Puffs, 717
    Salad, 716
    Scallop, 717

Salt, 100, 1007
    Cod, 238
    Fish, 234
    Mackerel, 271
    Pork and String Beans, 726
    Pork Raisin Cake, 920
    Rising Bread, 1074
    Water Taffy, 979
Salting Nuts, 1025
Samp, 752
Sand Boy, a fish, 197
    Crabs, 228
    Clams, 225
    Dab, a fish, 203
    Eel, 197
    Fish, 224
    Launce, a fish, 197
    Shark, 213
Sandwiches, 841–856
    Cheese, 843–845
        Cottage, and Marmalade, 843
        Cottage, and Raisin, 843
        Cream, and Almond, 843
        Cream, and Apricot, 844
        Cream, and Jelly, 844
        Cream, and Pineapple, 844
        Swiss, and Coleslaw, 844
        Swiss, and Ham, 845
        Swiss, and Liverwurst, 845
        Swiss, and Salami, 845
    Filling, 851–856
        See also Sandwich Fillings
    Garnishings, 842
    Hot, 848–851
        Bacon and Tomato, 848
        Cape Cod (Crabmeat), 848
        Corned Beef, 849
        Denver, 849
        Egg, Fried, 849
        Ham and Swiss Cheese, 849
        Ham, Fried, 849
        Hamburger, 850
        Lamb, 850
        Pork, 850
        Salmon Club, 850
        Steak and Eggplant, 850
        Tomato, Broiled, 848
        Tongue, 851
        Tuna, Creamed, 849
        Turkey, 851
        Western, 851
    Three-Decker, 845–848
        Almond-Marmalade, 846
        Almond-Pineapple, 846

Sandwiches, Three-Decker, Apple-Peanut Butter and Pineapple, 846
  Apricot-Ham, 846
  Bacon-Chicken and Anchovies, 846
    Chicken Livers & Tomato, 847
    Chicken-Green Pepper & Tomato, 847
    Green Pepper & Tomato, 847
    Onion & Tomato, 847
    Marmalade & Banana, 846
  Caviar-Onion & Tomato, 847
  Cheese-Ham and Tomato, 846
  Chicken-Bacon and Tongue-Tomato, 847
  Chicken-Nut Meats and Jelly-Lettuce, 847
  Chicken Salad and Ham-Tongue, 848
  Crab Meat Mayonnaise-Tomato and Egg Salad-Cress, 848
  Crab Meat-Raw Spinach and Egg Salad-Lettuce, 848
  Salmon Club, Hot, 850
Sandwich Fillings, 851–856
  See also Sandwiches
  Anchovy & Parmesan Cheese, 852
  Apple & Peanut Butter, 852
  Avocado, 853
  Beef, Dried, and American Cheese, 854
  Carrot, 853
  Cheese, American, and Nut, 852
  Cheese, Cottage, 854
  Cheese, Roquefort & Camembert, & Ham, 856
  Chicken, I, 853
  Chicken, II, 853
  Crab Meat, 853
  Egg Mayonnaise, 854
  Fig and Date, 854
  Fish Roe Mayonnaise, 854
  Ginger and Date, 855
  Ham and Mayonnaise, 855
  Ham, Spicy, 856
  Hamburger, Creamed, 854
  Honey Nut, 855
  Liver and Egg, 855
  Peach and Nut Meats, 855
  Peanut Butter, Fluffy, 855
  Texas, 856
  Tongue and Horseradish, 856
Sang, Canard au, 522
San Pedro Mariposa, 204
San Sebastian Baked Eggs, 153
Santé Omelet, 173

Saratoga Chips, 710
  Parsnip Chips, 695
Sardines, 211
  Filets in White Wine, 38
Saucer-Eye Porgies, 208
Sauces, Dessert
  See separate listing for Fish, Meat, Poultry, Vegetable, etc., Sauces
  Almond Cream, 890
  Banana, Foamy, 892
  Blueberry, 890
  Brandy Ginger, 890
  Butterscotch, 891
  Cherry Brandy Raspberry, 891
  Cider, for Pancakes, 804
  Chocolate, Almond, 890
    French, 893
    for Little Puff Cakes, 959
  Chop Suey, 891
  Coffee, 891, *see also* Mocha Sauces
  Crème de Neige, 895
  for Crêpes Helena, 867
    Suzette, 868
    See also under Crêpes
  Custards as, 871
  Eggnog, 892
  Hard, *see* Hard Sauce
  Honey, Cinnamon, 893
    Nut, 893
  Ice Cream, Flaming, 1129
  Melba, 893
    Melba, I, 1134
    Melba, II, 1134
  Mint, for Salad, 812
  Mocha, 893
  Montmorency, 895
  Orange, Custard, 894
    Fluff, 894
  Plum, Old-Fashioned, 894
  Raspberry, 894
  au Rhum Mousseuse, 892
  Rum Mocha, 894
  Fluffy, 892
  Sabayon, 892, 895
  Strawberry, I, 895
    Strawberry, II, 896
Sauces, Fish, Meat, Poultry, Shellfish, Vegetable, etc., 554–590
  Aioli, 558
  Barbecue, 396, 439
  Bearnaise, 559
    Anchovy, 8
    Variations, 559
  Bechamel, 119

Sauces, Bercy, 584
  Bohemienne, 267, 585
  Bourgeoise, 302, 585
  Bread, 559
  for Broccoli, 618
  Brown, I, 560
    Brown, II, 560
    Brown, III, 560
    Butter, 559
    Tomato, 561
  Burnt Chicken Princess, 495
  Cambridge, 561
  for Cardoons, 628
  Casanova, 561
  Celery, 562
  Chambertin, 562
  Chasseur, 571
  Chatelaine, 544, 585
  Cheese, 562
    Variation I, 562
    Variation II, 562
    Variation III, 562
    Variation IV, 562
  Cherry, 562
  for Chicken, Cintra, 500
    Cloister, 500
    Timbale, 517
  Chili, 748
  Cider, 563
  Clam, Onion, 295
    Lemon, 295
  Cocktail, I, 563
    Sauce II, 563
    Sauce III, 564
  Cream, in Chowders, 119
    Medium, 118
    Tettrazini, 509
    Thick, 118
    Thin, 118
  Creole, New Orleans, 565
    West Indies, 565
  Crumb, Brussels Sprouts, 620
  Cumberland I, 566
    Sauce II, 566
  Curry, for Capon, 487
    Cocoanut Milk for, 564
    Sauce I, 566
    Sauce II, 567
    Sauce III, 567
  Demi-Glace, 567
  Drawn Butter, 567
  Epicure Cocktail, 568
  Espagnole, 587
  Fines Herbes, for Liver, 453

Sauces, Fish, 192
  Cape Cod, 262
  Hollandaise I, 569
    II, 570
    III, 300
  Caper, 561
  Anchovy, 8
  Suprême, 300
  Hunter, 571
  Ivoire, for Chicken, 516
  Jardiniere, 571
  Laguipere, Bourgeoise, 571
  Laperouse, 571
  for Lasagna al' Ricotta Cheese, 765
  for Leeks, Boiled, 669
  Lemon Butter, 572
  Lobster, 572
  Louise, 572
  Lyonnaise, 572
  Madeira, 573
    Mushroom, 572
  Making, 557
  Maltaise, 573
  Marchand de Vin, 573
  Marguery, 574
  Melba, for Sweetbreads, 464
  Ménagère, 523
  Milk, for Chicken, 502
  Mint, I, 576
    Sauce, II, 576
  Mironton, 320
  Mornay, 576
  Mousseline, 577
  Mushroom, 577
  Mussel, 274
    Greek, 275
  Mustard, I, 577
    Sauce II, 578
  for Mutton Pancakes, 802
  Nantua, 578
  Newburg, 578
  Olive, 352
    Sauce I, 579
    Sauce II, 579
  Onion, 579
  for Onions, Stuffed, 690
  Orange, Beets in, 614
    Pie, New Orleans, 535
  Parsley, 580
  Pickle, for Tongue, 466
  Pickled, 580
  Piemontese, 586
    for Polenta, 750
  Pigeon, General Pershing, 536

Sauces, Piquante, 580
  Poivrade, 581
  Poulette, 581
  Provençale, 585
  Prune, for Smoked Meat, 582
  Raisin, 582
  Ravigote, 582
    Anchovy, 8
  Red Wine, 583
    Dagouret, 583
  Remick, 583
  Remoulade, Anchovy, 8
  Rochelaise, 584
  à la Romaine, 582
  Salsify with, 716
  for Shellfish, 34
  for Shellfish, Basting, 262
  Smitane, 586
  Soubise, 586
  Spaghetti, 760
    alla Bolognese, 760
    alla Campania, 761
    alla Caruso, 761
    alla Fiorentina, 762
    with Meat Balls, 762
  Spanish, 587
  Spicy, Beets in, 614
  Stocks for, 557
  for String Beans, 127, 725
  for Tagliatelli, 764
  Tartare, I, 588
    Sauce II, 588
  Tomato, 367, 588
  Tongue, 465
  Trout, Ambassador, 299
  Velouté, 589
  Venison, 588
  White, 590
  White Wine, 590
  Wine Dealer, 573
  Wow Wow, 330
Sauerbraten Bavarian Style, 343
Sauerkraut, 717
  Armenonville, 718
  Brisket of Beef with, 328
  Garnished, 397
  Ham Butt and, 417
  Hungarian, 718
  Pressure Cooked, 1173
  with Raisins, 719
  Shepherd's, 719
  in Sour Cream, 719
    Variation with Apples, 719
  Woodsman's, 720

Sauger Pike, a fish, 207
Sausage(s), 427–428, 437, 455–460
  Almond Stuffing, 789
  and Apples, 456
  Baked with Apples, 456
  in Blankets, 457
  Broiled, and Scrambled Eggs, 456
  Broiling, 455
  Cakes, Poached Eggs, 458
  Creole, Noodle Ring, 759
  English Egg, 166
  Fruit Grill, 457
  and Ham Pie, 423
  Hints, 456
  Link, 456
    Baked, 456
    Parboiling, 456
    Scallop, 458
  Meat Frumets, 458
    Piscalleria, 459
    Ramekins, 460
  and Noodle Dinner, 457
  & Onion Shortcake Curry, 469
  Pan-Frying, 455
  Patties, 456
    Cream Gravy Creole, 459
  Pigs in Hay, 456
  Pork, 456
  à la Provençale, 457
  Sautéed with Prunes, 456
  Smoked, 428
  Split Pea, 699
  Stuffed Acorn Squash, 729
  Summer, 428
  and Wild Rice Stuffing, 795
Sauté(ed)
  Chicken Breast, Chasseur, 496
  Chicken, Bourguignonne, 507
  Chicken, Jambalaya, 507
  Chicken, Mushrooms & Olives, 508
  Cucumbers, 653
  Larded Sweetbreads, Breaded, 462
Sautéeing, 990
Savarin Glacé aux Fruits Macérés, 961
Savarin with Vanilla Ice Cream with
    Marinated Fruits, 961
Savory, Summer, 1008
  Whole Beets, 615
  Winter, 1009
Savoy Cabbage French Style, 626
Sawbelly, a fish, 202
Scalding, Kidneys, 445
  Milk, 79
  Starches, 1036

Scaled Ling, a fish, 194, 199
Scallop(ed); *see also* Escallop
  Corn, 647
  Cucumbers Casserole, 653
  Egg and Potato, 162
    Variations, 162
  Kale, 666
  Potato, 708
    Cheese Variation, 708
    Meat Variation, 708
    Mushroom Variation, 708
    Vegetable Variation, 708
    Village Style, 708
  Salsify, 717
  Sausage Links, 458
  Tomatoes with Onions, 738
  Turkey and Oyster, 544
Scallop(s), sea, 231
  Cocktail, Avocado, 33
  Deep Fat Frying, 986
  Epicure, 287
  des Gourmets, 260
  Saint Jacqueline, 244
  Saint Jacques, 244
  à la King, 290
  Sarah Bernhardt, 244
  Stew, 287
Scalopini, Veal, Marsala, 366
Scarlet Sunfish, 218
Schaum Torte, 961
Schmor Braten, 345
Schnitzel, Wiener, 366
Schnitzelbank Cheese Pot, 41
Schoodic Lake Salmon, 210
Scotch Beef and Kidney Pie, 321
  Butterscotch, 979
  Fried Eggs, 168
  Mutton Pancakes, 802
  Oatmeal Waffles, 807
Scramble, Codfish (Fresh), 240
  Codfish (Salt), 238
  Corn and Egg, 155
Scrambled Eggs, 152
  in Bread Nests, 184
  à la Buckingham, 183
  with Cheese on Toast, 183
  with Lobster, Curried, 157
  Milanaise, 184
  Spanish Style, 184
Scrapple, 408
  Tuna, 302
Scrod, 196, 211, 212
Scup Porgies, 208
Scuppang Porgies, 208

Seasoning, 554, 999
  Anchovy, 8
Sea Bob, 233
  Chestnuts, 232
  Eel, 197
  Eggs, 232
  Hedgehog, 232
  Trout, 219, 221, 298
  Urchins, 232, 288
  Wolf, 193
Seapure Oysters, 230
Searing, 989
Seawanhaka Oysters, 230
Sebago Salmon, 210
Seed, Poppy, Wafers, 933
  Variations, 933
Seeds, Squash, 729
Sergeant Fish, 195
Sevillana, Veal Cutlets, 363
Shad, a fish, 212
  Baked Planked, 238
  Boning, 237
  Cooking, 237
  of Lake Champlain, 223
  Roe, 212
    Grill, 288
    Meunière, 288
    Plantation, Baked, 237
  Rouennaise, Baked, 236
  Stuffing, 238
  Taylor, 202
Shake, Chocolate Ice Cream, 55
  Coffee, 73
  Mocha Milk, I, 57
  Mocha Milk, II, 57
Shallot Butter, 553
Shandygaff, 51
Shank, Hind, Beef, 312
  Lamb, 371
  Veal, 349
Shark(s), 213
  Fins, 213
  Pilot, 213
Sheep's Feet, 427
  Feet, St. Menehould, 437
  Kidneys, 427
  Liver, 427
  Tails, 428
  Tongues, 428
Sheepshead, 196, 213
  Perch, 206
Shellfish, 224–233; (*See also individual* names)
  Basting Sauce, 262

Shellfish, Chart, 224–233
  Cocktail Sauce for, 34
  in Egg Soufflé, 165
  Haddock, 200
Shells, Patty, 940
  Tart, 942
Shepherd's Sauerkraut, 719
Sherbet(s), 1148
  Champagne, I, 1149
  Champagne, II, 1150
  Citrus, 1150
  Cranberry, 1150
  Grape Juice, 1151
  Lemon, 1151
  Lemon Milk, 115
  Lime, 1151
  Mint, 1152
  Orange Milk, 1152
  Pineapple, 1153
    Maraschino Cherry, 1153
  Raspberry, 1154
  Raspberry Milk, 1154
  Strawberry, 1155
Sherry Aspic Coating Jelly, 41
  Mushroom Omelet, 169
  Netherland Baked Planked Shad, 238
  Wine Jelly (Dessert), 886
Shirred Eggs, 184
  au Beurre Noir, 185
  Boulevardier, 185
  Cecile, 185
  à l'Estragon, 186
  Midinette, 186
  Tetrazzini, 186
Shish Kabab, 385
Shoestring, a fish, 196
  Carrots, 632
  Potatoes, 707
Shoofly pie, 951
Short Boiling, 990
  Broth, *see* Court Bouillon
  Flaky Pastry, 939
  Loin, Beef, 313
  Ribs, Beef, 312
    Barbecued, 314
Shortbreads, Cheese, 1061
Shortcake, Egg, 164
  Mushroom and Onion, 682
  Spinach, with Ham, 723
Shoulder Chops, Lamb, 370
  Lamb, 371
  Pork, 394
  Rolled, Veal, 349

Shrimp(s), 17, 232
  in Aspic, 289
  Biscuits, 1047
  Butter, 553
  Canapés Creole, 17
  Cocktail, Avocado, 33
  Creamed, on Waffles, 804
  Marguery Sauce, 574
  à la Marseillaise, 290
  Mousse, 514
  and Mushroom à la King, 289
  Paste Celery Stuffing, 42
  Pie Charleston Style, 290
  Puffs Maine Style, 291
  in Stuffed Tomatoes, 739
Shrub, beverage, 1136
Sierra, a fish, 202
Sild, a fish, 211
Silver Bass, 193
  Fish, 201
  Hake, 201
  Trout, 219
Silversides, 222, 304
Simmering, 989
  Meat and Poultry, 989
Singapore Mutton Curry, 389
Sirloin, 313
  Lamb Chops, 371
  Roast, Lamb, 371
  Steak, 313
    Broiling, 984
    la Pérouse, 336
    Veal, 348
Skate, a fish, 214
  Wings au Beurre Noir, 291
  Wings Curry, 292
Skim Milk, 75
Skipjack, a fish, 195, 222
Slaw, *see* Cole Slaw
Smear Dab, 203
Smelts, 214
  Fry Canadian Style, 292
  Gibbed, 292
Smitana, Veal Cutlets, 364
Smitane Sauce, 586
Smoked Beef Tongue, Sauce Piquante, 467
  Fish, 234
  Goose, 531
  Meat, Prune Sauce for, 582
  Pork, 411
  Salmon Butter, 552
  Sausages, 428

Smothered
  Cauliflower au Gratin, 635
  Green Peppers Lyonnaise, 659
    Variation, 659
  Kale, 666
    Variations, 666
  Lettuce, 676
Snake Pickerel, a fish, 207
Snappers, a fish, 215, 284
  Red, Miami Style, 284
  Vera Cruz Style, 285
Snails, 293–294
  Bourgogne Style, 294
    Variation, 294
  Butter, 294
  à la Provençale, 295
Snowy Grouper, a fish, 199
Sockeye Salmon, 210
Soda, Chocolate, 55
Soft-shell Clams, 225
  Crabs, 227, 301
    Grilled, Creole Style, 262
    Newburg, 248
Soho, a fish, 204
Sole, 251
  Filet of, Amandine, 251
    Ambassador Hotel, 252
    à l'Américaine, 252
    Bonne Femme, 253
    Carmen, 253
    Charlotte, 253
    Concarneau, 254
    Cordon Bleu, 254
    Jacqueline, 255
    Jeanine, 255
    Marguery, 256
    Meunière, 256
    Mornay, 257
    Nadine, 257
    St. Malo, 257
    St. Raphael, 258
    Valenciennes, 258
  Lemon, 203
Sorrel, Escallop of Veal with, 355
  Pressure Cooked, 1173
Soubise, Baked Potato, 703
  Lamb Chops, 379
  Sauce, 586
Soufflé, Almond, 859
  Asparagus, 603
  Beef, 323
  Blueberry, 862
  Broccoli, 618
  Carrot, 631

Soufflé, Cauliflower Ring Amandine, 633
  Chard, 642
  Cheese, 188
  Chicken, Southern, 508
  Chocolate, 864
  Clam, 243
  Corn, 645, 647
    Meal, Dinner, 748
  Corned Beef, 335
  Egg, Bernardine, 165
  Eggplant, 657
  d'Epinards au Lait d'Amandes, 723
  Guava, Havanaise, 876
  Ham, 421
  Honey, 877
  Liver, 454
  Macaroni, Ring, 756
  Mushroom, 684
  Omelet, 174
  Onion, 693
  Parsley Omelet, 173
  Pommes, 706
  Pork, 402
  Potato Amandine, 709
  Spinach, Amandine, 723
  Spinach, Plain, 724
  Squash, 731
  Succotash, 735
  Tomato Cheese, 740
  Tuna, 302
  Turkey, 545
  Turnip, 744
  Veal Ring Celestine, 365
Soup(s), 87–142
  Ale, 105
  Apple, Ginger, 106
    Polish, 106
  Barley, 106
  Bean, Black, I, 109
    II, 109
      Country Style, 110
      Fermière Style, 110
      Grandmother's, 110
      Guatemalan, 110
  Beef, Clear, 140
  Beer, 105
  Beet, 107
    American, 108
  Bohemian Rye Bread, 110
  Bortsch, 107
  Bouillon, 90
    See also under Bouillon
  Bread, 110
  Broth, 90; *See also* Broth

Soup(s), Calf's Head, Recipe I, 110
  Recipe II, 111
  Cardoons in, 628
  Chowder, *See* Chowder
  Classification of, 90
  Cock-a-Leekie, 114
  Cold, 90
  Coloring, 91
    Caramel, 92
  Consommé, 90, 114–117
    See also under Consommé
  Cream, 118–128
    Asparagus, 120
    Barley, 120
    Bean, 121
    Buttermilk Almond, 121
    Cauliflower, 122
    Celery, 122
    Chestnut, 123
    Chicken, 123
      A la Reine, 124
    Corn, 124
    Cucumber, 125
    Delicate, 119
  Giblet, 125
    Kidney, 125
    Lettuce, 126
    Lettuce, Almond, 105
    Light, 90
    Mushroom, 126
    Pea Pods, 127
    Pumpkin, 127
    Spinach, 128
    Tomato, 128
  Frimsel, 134
  Garlic, 134
  Garnish(es), 94–105
    Egg Yolk, 152
    Hints, 95
    Popcorn, 123
  Halibut, 132
  Heavy, 90
  Hochepot, 134
  Jellied, 90; *see also under* Jellied
  Lentil, 135
  Madrilène, 136
  Minestrone, 136
  Mock Turtle, 136
  Mulligatawny, 137
  Mutton, Almond Minted, 105
  Onion, au Gratin, 137
  Oxtail, 138
  Oyster Gumbo, 134
  Pea, Split, 141

Soup(s), Pepper Pot, 139
  Petite Marmite, 139
  aux Pois à l'Habitant, 112
  Pot-au-Feu, 134, 140
  Sour Cream Cabbage, 121
  Spring, 142
  Stocks, 90
    see also Stock
  Summer, 90
  Tomato, 142
  Turtle, Clear, 130
Soupfin, 213
Sour Cream, and Beets, 613
  Cream Biscuits, 1048
    Bortsch, 107
    Cabbage Soup, 121
    Cucumber in, 653
    Cucumbers in, 651
    Dressing, 838
    Dressing, Boiled, 839
    Horseradish Sauce, 587
    Rolls, 1105
    Salad Dressings, 812
    Sauerkraut in, 719
      with Apples, 719
    Smitane Sauce, Russian, 586
    with Spinach, 721
    Veal, Cubed, in, 353
  Milk in Baking, 80
  Pot Roast, 343
  Sweet Dressing, 840
  Sweet Tongue, 467
  Veal Stew Home Style, 359
Sourdough, 803
  Pancakes, 802
Sourgrass, *see* Sorrel
Southern Cafe Eggnog, 70
  Cauliflower Soup, 122
  Chicken Soufflé, 508
  Corn Bread, 1068
    Meal Noodles, 759
  Fleece, 187
  Rice Mold, 886
  Vegetable Chowder, 142
Soy Flour Griddle Cakes, 803
  Milk, 612
Soybean(s), Dried, 605
  Meal, 605
  Sprouted, 605
    Creole, 612
    Curry, 612
Spaghetti, 760–763
  See also Noodles
  alla Bolognese, 760

Spaghetti, Border, 415
  alla Campania, 761
  alla Caruso, 761
  Cooking, 760
  alla Fiorentina, 762
  with Meat Balls, 762
  Sauces, 760–763
Spanish, Style Asparagus, 600
  Cream, 873
  Eggs, Scrambled, 184
  Mackerel, 203, 204
  Sardines, 211
  Sauce, 587
  Steak, Baked, Baroness, 314
Spareribs, Apple Stuffing, 409
  of Beef, 312
  Crown Roast, 409
  Pork, 394
Spearing, 222, 304
Speckled Cat, 194, 199
  Trout, 219
Spice(d)(y)
  Cake, 921
  Chart, 1001–1009
  Cider Bowl, 63
  Cocoa, 58
  Fruit Cake, Chocolate, 921
  Pavés, Honey Brandy, 930
  Peach Salad, 827
  Pot Roast Dutch Style, 344
  Sauce, Beets in, 614
  Tartlets, Pecan Molasses, 961
  Tea, 84
Spider Crabs, 227
Spinach, 720
  Asparagus, Egg Salad, 813
  Creamed, with Chives, 721
  and Egg Scallop, 162
  Entree Dubrovnik, 721
  Flavorings for, 721
  au Gratin Jeanette, 722
  Hints, 721
  Mint in, 721
  Mousse, 722
  Noodle Border, 415
  Potato Croquettes, 709
  with Potato, Mashed, 721
  Pressure Cooked, 1173
  Purée Saint Mande, 723
  Raw, see also Sandwiches
  Ring, Creamed Eggs in, 156
  Roll, Stuffed, 724
  Salad, 812
  Shortcake with Ham, 723

Spinach, Soufflé Amandine, 723
  Soufflé, Plain, 724
  Soup, Cream of, 128
  with Sour Cream, 721
  Swiss Style, 642
  Tarts, 724
  Timbales, 724
Spiny Bristles, 232
Spirals, Potato, 709
Split Pea Purée, 699
  Sausage, 699
  Soup, 141
Sponge, Bread, 1037
  Cake, 922
  Cake, Mocha, 919
  Grape, a dessert, 876
  Honey, Lemon Pudding, 877
  Mocha, a dessert, 880
  Squire Cake, Tipsy, 922
Spoon Bread, 1069, 1074
Sportive Omelet, 174
Spotted Trout, 219
Sprat, a fish, 211
Spring Herring, 202
  Chicken Sauté, Chablis, 517
  Soup, 142
Springerle, 934
Sprouted Soybeans, 605
  Creole, 612
  Curry, 612
Sprouts, Brussels, See Brussels Sprouts
Spumone Ice Cream, 1136
Squabs, see Pigeons
Squares, Almond Brittle, 968
  Almond Chocolate Praline, 969
  Chocolate Fudge, 972
  Hominy Burger, 751
  Vanilla Fudge, 979
Squash, 728
  Acorn, Baked, 730
    Pressure Cooked, 1174
    Rings, Apple Sauce, 730
    Sausage Stuffed, 729
  Blossoms, 729
  Crooked Neck, Glazed, 730
  Fritters I, 731
  Fritters II, 731
  Hints, 729
  Hubbard, Baked, 715
    Boiled, 715
    Pressure Cooked, 1174
    Whipped, 732
  Patties I, 731
  Patties II, 731

Squash, and Potato Mashed, 730
  Seeds, 729
  Soufflé, 731
  Summer, 728
    Pressure Cooked, 1174
    Steaming, 730
  Vine, 729
  Winter, 729
  Zucchini, Flowers, 729
    Pressure Cooked, 1174
Squaw-Corn, 645
Squeteague, a fish, 221
Squiggled Eggs, 183
Squirrel, in Brunswick Stew, 494
Standing Beef Roast, Method I, 342
  Method II, 343
  Rib, 313
Starry Flounder, 198
Steak(s)
  Arm, Beef, 312
    Pork, 394
    Veal, 348
  Baked Spanish, Baroness, 314
  Blade, Beef, 312
    Veal, 348
  Broiling, 984
  Chuck, 312
  Club, 313, 328
  Codfish, 243
    Pepper, 341
  Chateaubriand, 313, 997
  Delmonico, 313
  Eggplant, Grilled, 658
    Variations, 658
  and Eggplant Sandwich, Hot, 850
  Filet Mignon, 338
    à la Richmond, 338
    Stefanie, 339
  Flank, 312
  Halibut, Alsatian Manner, 264
    Miramar, 263
  Ham, 410
    Baked in Milk, 420
    Creole, 420
    Epicure, 421
    Gourmet, 421
    Montmorency, 422
    Moscovite, 422
  on Horseback, 322
  Lamb, 371
  Marchand de Vin, 329
  Minute, 313
    O'Brien, 329

Steak(s), Porterhouse, Broiled, 329
    Marchand de Vin, 329
    with Marrow, 329
  Round, 312
    Bottom, 313
    Top, 313
    Veal, 349
  Salisbury, 343
  Sirloin, 313
    La Pérouse, 336
    Veal, 348
  Strips, Chinese, 333
  Swiss, 345
  T-Bone, 313
  Tenderloin, 313
  Tuna, 303
  Turtle, 304
  Veal, 347, 348
    Potted Dutch Style, 358
Steamed Apple Pudding, 887
  Cabbage au Gratin Amandine, 626
  Clams, 295
  Kale, 666
  Mincemeat Plum Pudding, 887
Steamers, Clams, 227
Steaming, 990
Steam Roasting, 989
Steelhead Trout, 219
Stéfanie, Filet Mignon, 339
Stew, Beef, 323
  Brain and Mushroom, in Red Wine, 429
  Brunswick, Old Dixie, 494
    Maryland, 493
  Chicken, Hungarian Style, 356
  Duck, Hungarian Style, 356
  Eel, 250
  Egg, 165
  Goose, Hungarian Style, 356
  Heart, Veal, 443
  Herring, Polish, 283
  Kidney, Lamb, 446
  Lamb, 372
    Hungarian Style, 356
    Irish, 377
    Parisienne, 382
  Mutton, Hungarian Style, 356
  Oyster, 282
  Pork, 402
    Hungarian Style, 356
  Scallop, 287
  Tripe, 473
  Turkey, Hungarian Style, 356

Stew, Veal, Creole, 365
   French, 349
   Hungarian, 356
   Italian, 357
   Sour, 359
Stewed Celery, 640
   Green Peas French Style, 699
   Lettuce à la Romaine, 676
   Mushrooms in Red Wine, 685
   Tomatoes, 739
Stewing, 989
Sticks, Bread, 96
Sticky Buns I, 1084
   Buns II, 1082
Sting Ray, 214
Sting (Skate), 214
Stock, Brown, 91, 92
   Chicken, 480
   Clarifying, 94
   Fish, 92
   Gravy, 93
   Mushrooms, 577
   for Sauce, 557
   Soup, six kinds, 90
   Veal, White, 93
   Vegetable, 93
   Velouté, 589
Stockfish, 196
Stone Crabs, 228
Strasbourgeois, Poached Eggs, 182
Strawberries, with Sherbet, 1153
Strawberry Ice, 1121
   Ice Cream I, 1136
      Ice Cream II, 1137
      Ice Cream III, 1137
   Juice Cocktail, 33
   Mousse, 1143
   Parfait, 1148
   Sauce I, 895
      Sauce II, 896
   Sherbet, 1155
Streusel, 911
   Coffee Cake, 1107
String Beans, 725
   à l'Armenienne, 727
   with Bacon, 726
   Boiled, Magic, 726
   Boiling, 726
   Creole, 727
   and Egg Scallop, 162
   Frenched, 726
   au Gratin, 727
   Hints, 725
   à la Lyonnaise, 728

String Beans, Old-Fashioned, 727
   Pressure Cooked, 1162
   with Salt Pork, 726
   Sauce for, 725
   Sweet-Sour, 726
Striped Bass, 193
   Grunt, a fish, 199
   Lake Bass, 193
   Marlin, 205
   Mullet, 205
   Tuna, 220
Strips, Red Currant, 960
Strogonoff, Beef à la, 324
Stuffed (*See also* Stuffing)
   Acorn Squash, 729
   Beef Slices, 345
   Cabbage, 627
      Hungarian, 624
      Madras, 627
   Capon, Braised, 486
      with Raisins, 489
   Celery Club Style, 42
   Codfish, Baked, 237
   Cucumbers, Baked, 651
      Slices, 27
   Dill Slices, 28
   Eggs, 42, 152
      Filling No. 1, 42
      Filling No. 2, 42
      Filling No. 3, 43
      Filling No. 4, 43
      Filling No. 5, 43
      Filling No. 6, 43
      Filling No. 7, 43
      Filling No. 8, 43
      in Aspic, 187
      à la Béchamel Suprême, 187
      Montfermeil, Fried, 168
   Green Peppers, Crab Meat, 660
      Meat Stuffing, 660
      Mexican Style, 660
      Poultry Stuffing, 660
      Slices, 28
      Variations, 659
   Lamb, Breast of, Roast, 384
   Lettuce à la Dame Simone, 677
   Mutton, Leg of, Boiled, 386
   Olive, Green, Salad, 813
   Onions, 689
      Baked, 690
      Baked Liver, 689
   Pork Chops, Baked, 396
   Pumpkin, Baked, 714
   Radishes Armenonville, 39

Stuffed, Spinach Roll, 724
  Tomatoes, 739
    Broccoli, 739
    with Cheese Custard, 739
    Chopped Meat, Curry, 739
    Corn and Green Pepper, 739
    Creole Rice, 739
    Vegetable Jardiniere, 739
Stuffing, 526–527, 788. *See also* Stuffed
  Almond Sausage, 789
  Burger Loaf, 789
  Capon, Ham-Walnut Brandied, 792
    Olive, 793
    Pecan, 794
  Celery, 790
    Roast Goose, 529
  Chestnut, 790
  Chicken, 504
    Celery, 790
    Ham-Walnut Brandied, 792
    Olive, 793
    Onion, 793
    Oyster, 793
    Pecan, 794
  Corn Bread, 790
  Cranberry, 791
  Duck, Giblet, 791
    Olive, 793
  Fish, Epicure, 791
  Fowl, Giblet, 791
  Giblet, 791
  Goose, Celery, 529
    Giblet, 791
    Milanaise, 530
    Olive, 793
    Oyster Bechamel, 527
    Prune, 530
  Ham and Onion, 792
  Ham-Walnut Brandied, 792
  Lamb Forcemeat, 385
    Mint, 792
    Onion, 793
  Milanaise, 530
  Mint, 792
  for Mutton, Oyster, 386
  Olive, 793
  Onion, 793
  Oyster, 793
    Boiled Goose Bechamel, 527
  Pecan, 794
  Prune and Apple, 794
    Roast Goose, 530
  Sage, I, 794
  Sage, II, 795

Stuffing, Shad, 238
  Spareribs with Apple, 409
  Turkey, Almond Sausage, 789
    Burger, 789
    Chestnut, 790
    Corn Bread, 790
    Cranberry, 791
    Ham-Walnut Brandied, 792
    Olive, 793
    Oyster, 793
    Pecan, 794
  Veal Cushion, Onion, 793
  Wild Rice and Sausage, 795
Sturgeon, a fish, 218
Sturgeon's Roe, 218, *see* Caviar
Succotash, 732, 735
  Connecticut, 733
  Corned Beef and Fowl, 335
  au Gratin, 735
  Maine, 732
  Massachusetts, 733
  New England, 733
  Plymouth (Mass.), 733, 734
  Pressure Cooked, 1173
  Soufflé, 735
  Tomatoes Stuffed with, 736
Sucker, a fish, 217
Suckling Pig, Roast, 406
  Roast, Creole, 407
  Roast, Kentucky, 408
Suet Dumplings, 140
Sugar Syrup, Clarified, 972
  Twist, Barley, I, 969
    Barley, II, 970
Suissesse, Poached Eggs, 182
Summer Flounder, 198, 251
  Sausages, 428
  Savory, 1008
  Squash, 728
    Pressure Cooked, 1174
    Steaming, 730
Sunday Popovers, 1095
Sunfish, 217
  Bass, 194
Sunshine Cakes, Failures, 908–909
Suprême Hollandaise Sauce, 300
Surf Clams, 225
Surf-Fish, 206
Surrey Plum Pudding, 887
Suzanne, Poached Eggs, 182
Suzette, Crêpes, 801, 866, 868
  Trifle, 889
Suzette's Dressing, 840
Sweet Almonds, Roasting, 1025

Sweetbread(s), 310, 428, 460–463
  Baked Larded, 461
  Beef, 310, 428
  Braised, Bonne Maman, 461
    Old Style, 462
  Breaded Sautéed Larded, 462
  Brochette of, 462
  Calf, 310, 428
  Lamb, 310, 428
  Loaf Gastronome, 462
  Lyonnaise, 463
  Melba, 464
  Mutton, 310
Sweet Peppers, 658
Sweet Potato(es) Allumettes, 712
  Baked, 703, 710
  and Banana Fluff, 711
  Biscuits, 1048
  Candied, 710
  Chicken, Casserole, 508
  Custard Creole, 712
  French Fried, 711
  Grilled, 711
  Imperial, 712
  Mashed, 703, 711
  and Pork Pie, 402
  Pressure Cooked, 1172
  Rolls, 713
  Royal, 713
  Sour Dressing, 840
  String Beans, 726
  Tongue, 467
  Waffles, 808
  Whipped, 713
Sweet Water Crabs, 227
Swiss Chard, 640
  Cheese, *see under* Cheese, *and also* Sandwiches
  Eggs, Poached, 182
  Steak, 345
  Veal Balls, 359
Swordfish, 218, 295
Syllabub, Beer, 50
Syrian Coffee, 72
Syrup, Chocolate, 55
  Cocoa, 56
  Fruit, 797
  Sugar, Clarified, 972

Tadpole, a fish, 195
Taffy, Salt Water, 979
Tagliatelli, 764
Tails, Beef, 428
  Petticoat, 920

Tails, Pork, 428
  Sheep, 428
  Veal, 428
Tamale(s), 44
  Caribbean Style, 45
  Green Corn, 45
  Pie, Pork, 403
Tarhonia, 317
Tarragon, *See also* Estragon
  Butter, 553
  Shirred Eggs with, 186
Tartare Sauce I, 588
  Sauce II, 588
Tartar Style Chicken, 509
Tart(e)(s)
  See also Tartlets; Torte
  Blueberry, 955
    Variations, 955
  Butter, 956
  au Chocolat Amandine, 962
  à la Ferluche, 962
  Filling, Rum Pecan, 960
  Fillings, Description, 943
  aux Framboises à la Parisienne, 959
  Raisin and Nut, 962
  Raspberry, Parisian, 959
  Shells, 942
  Spinach, 724
Tartlets, Date, 957
  Fig, 957
  Ice Cream, 958
  Spiced Pecan Molasses, 961
Tasting, Correct Method, 1000
Tavern Beer Bishop, 51
Taylor Herring, 202
  Shad, 202
T-Bone Steak, 313
Tea, 81–84
  Afternoon, 84, 1044
  Biscuits, English, 1044
  Biscuits, Pinwheel, 1047
  Iced, Cold-Water Method, 83
  Nutmeg, 84
  Punch, 84
  Russian Aromatic, 83
  Spiced, 84
Tenderloin, Pork, 394, 403
  Beef, Steak, 313
    Broiling, 984
Terrapin, 296
  Baltimore, 297
  Liver, in Chafing Dish, 455
  Maryland, 298
Tête Pressée, 399

Tettrazini, Chicken, 509
  Cream Sauce, 509
  Shirred Eggs, 186
  Turkey, 545
Thanksgiving Cider Punch, 63
Thawing Frozen Poultry, 1018
Thermidor, Lobster, 270
Thick-shelled Clams, 225
Thin Cream, How to Whip, 916
Thousand Island Dressing I, 838
  Dressing II, 838
Three-Decker Sandwiches, *see* Sandwiches, Three-Decker
Thresher, a fish, 213
Thunder-Pumper, a fish, 196
Tiger Shark, 213
Timbale(s), Chicken, 517
  Hominy and Cheese, 752
  Spinach, 724
  Tuna Fish, 303
Time Tables, *See also* Charts
  Baking of Meat, Fish, etc., 991
  Broiling, 984
  Frozen Meat, Cooking, 1016
  Frying, Deep Fat, 986
  Roasting Meat, 988
  Simmering Meat and Poultry, 989
Tinker, a fish, 203
Tipsy Pudding, *see* Tipsy Sponge Squire, 922
Tivela Clams, 225
Toast, Bacon Cheese, 1107
  Butterscotch, 1108
  Cinnamon, 1108
  French, 1109
    Griddle, 1108
  Garlicked, 451
  Melba, 103, 1109
  Mushrooms on, 685
  Milk, 1110
  Squabs on, 537
Tobacco Skate, a fish, 214
Tomato(es), 735
  Aspic Plaza, 45
  Bacon Sandwich, Hot, 848
  Baked, 736
    Curried, 736
  Bisque, 367
  Broiled, Sandwich, 848
  Butter I, 552
  Butter II, 553
  Canned, 736
  Cheese Pie, 740
    Soufflé, 740

Tomato(es), Cocktail, Frozen, 33
  Deviled, 737
  Eggplant en Brochette, 657
  Fritters, French, 737
  Green, Broiled, 736
    in Chili con Carne, 332
  Hints, 736
  Jelly and Egg Luncheon, 741
  Juice Cocktail Georgia Manner, I, 36; II, 36; III, 36
  Dumplings, 788
  Pie, 738
  Pressure Cooked, 1175
  See also Salads
  See also Sandwiches
  Sauce, 367, 585, 588
    Brown, 561
  Scalloped, with Onions, 738
  Slices, Grilled, 737
    Grilled, Variations, 737
    with Honey, 736
  Soup, 142
    Cream of, 128
    Eggs Poached in, 152
  Stewed, 736, 739
  Stuffed, 739
    Broccoli, 739
    Cheese Custard, 739
    Chopped Meat with Curry, 739
    Corn and Green Pepper, 739
    Creole Rice, 739
    Shrimps, 739
    with Succotash, 736
    Vegetable Jardiniere, 739
  Stuffing, Burger, 789
    Epicure, 791
  Torte Piemontese, 741
Tongue(s), 311, 464–468
  Beef, 311, 428
    Boiled, 465
    Braised Fresh, 465
    Jardiniere, 465
    Smoked, in Aspic, 466
      Sauce Piquante, 467
    Sweet Sour, 467
  Boiled, 465
  Calf's, 428
  Lamb, 311, 369
    in Aspic, 466
    Boiled, 465
  Mousse, 467
  Mutton, 311
Tongue, Pork, 311, 428
  See also Sandwiches

Tongue, *See also* Sandwich Fillings
  Sandwich, Hot, 851
  Sauce, 465
  Sheep's, 428
  Veal, 311
    Hash, 467
Top Round Steak, 313
Toro, a fish, 195
Torte(s), 937
  Chocolate, with Almonds, 962
  Schaum, 961
  Tomato, Piemontese, 741
Tortoni, Biscuit, 1124
  Biscuit, II, 1124
Tortue, Calf's Head en, 352
Totuava, a fish, 193
Toulousaine, Cassoulet, 388
Tournedos à la Bearnaise, 346
  of Beef, 338
Tourteaux, clams, 225
Trading Clams, 225
Transylvanian Beef Goulash, 317
Tree Oysters, 230
Trifle, 888
  Apricot, 860
  Banana, 861
  Gooseberry, 876
  Suzette, 889
Tripe, 311, 428, 468–473
  à la Catalana, 470
  à la Creole, 470
  Eggs à la, 166
  Grilled, 470
  à la Lorraine, 471
  à la Madrilena, 471
  Maître d'Hôtel, 471
  à la Mode de Caen, 472
  and Onions (Milk), 468, 473
  Onions, and Oysters, 473
  Stew, 473
Trotters, Mutton, au Gratin, 435
  Ravigote, 436
Trout, 198, 219, 298–301
  Brook, 298
    Amandine, 298
    au Bleu, 300
    Boulevardier, 299
    Bourguignonne, 300
    Delices d'Annecy Amandine, 301
    Meunière, 301
  Lake, 219–220, 298
    Ambassador, 299
    Home Style, 301

Trout, Sauce, Ambassador, 299
    Bourgeoise, 302
  Sea, 219, 221–222, 298
Truffle Butter, 553
Truffles, Pressure Cooked, 1176
Truite au Bleu, 300
Tuna, 220
  Cooking, 302
  Creamed, Sandwich, Hot, 849
    on Waffles, 804
  Scrapple, 302
  Soufflé, 302
  Steak, 303
  Timbales, 303
Tunny, 220, *See* Tuna
Turbot, a fish, 214, 221
Turkey, 484, 537–545
  Aspic Supper, 540
  Chow Mein, 541
  Curried, with Wild Rice, 539
  Fritters, 542
  Galantine à la Paderewski, 542
  Grill Chatelaine, 544
  Hints, 538
  and Oyster Fritters, 542
    Scallop, 544
  Pie, 544
  Roast, 540
  Roasting, 538
  Roll, Baked, 539
  Sandwich, Hot, 851
  Soufflé, 545
  Stew Hungarian Style, 356
  Stuffing, Almond, 789
    Burger, 789
    Chestnut, 790
    Corn Bread, 790
    Cranberry, 791
    Ham-Walnut Brandied, 792
    Olive, 793
    Pecan, 794
  Tetrazzini, 545
Turkish Coffee, 72
Turner, Mama Suzy, Molded Pudding, 879
  Mother Kate, Egg Stew, 165
Turnips, Boiled, 742
  Cotton Picker's Mashed Fluffy, 743
  Custard, 743
  Glazed, 743
  au Gratin Gastronome, 638
  Greens, 742
    Cotton Picker's Delight, 742
  Hungarian, 743

Turnips, à la Parisienne, 744
  Pressure Cooked, 1076
  Soufflés, 744
  White, 741
  Yellow, 742
    en Casserole, 744
    Pressure Cooked, 1173
Turnovers, Apple, Frosted, 957
  Brain and Mushroom, 430
  Pique's Egg Pancake, 169
Turque, Café, 72
Turtle(s), 296
  Mock, 352
  Pie Gourmet, 303
  Soup, Clear, 130
    Mock, 136
  Steaks, 304
Tutti Frutti Ice Cream, 1138
Tuxedo Park Chicken Salad, 506
Twist, Barley Sugar, I, 969
  Barley Sugar, II, 970
  Bohemian Christmas, 963
Twisted Bread, 1070

Uccelletti Scappati (veal), 751
Urchins, Sea, 232, 288
Upside-Down Cakes, Apricot, 911
  Ham Loaf, 424

Valenciennes, Filet of Sole, 258
Valentienne, Rice, 771
Vancouver Clams, 226
Vanilla Fudge Squares, 979
  Ice Cream I, 1138
  Ice Cream II, 1138
    Savarin with Marinated Fruits, 961
  Mousse, 1144
Vanocka, 963
Variety Meats, 425–473
  Chart, 427
Veal, 346–367
  Baked, 353
  Balls, Curried, 354
    Swiss, 359
  Birds Hungarian, 359
    à la Rossini, 360
  Blanquette of, 349
    à la Weimar, 350
  Chart, 348–349
  Chops, 347
    Loin, 348
    en Papillotes, 360
    Paprika, 361

Veal, Rib, 348
  à la Rosalind, 361
  Chop Suey, 315
  Chow Mein, 401
  Croquettes, 373
  Cubed, in Sour Cream, 353
  Cushion Stuffing, Onion, 793
  Cutlet(s), 348
    Chasseur, 362
    à la D'Aremberg, 362
    à la Sacher, 363
    Sarah Bernhardt, 363
    Sevillana, 363
    Smitana, 364
  Escallop, with Sorrel, 355
  Grenadins of, Parisienne, 355
  Ham Pie à la Dickens, 364
  Heart Chop Suey, 443
    Stew, 443
  Heel of Round, 348
  Kidney(s), Ardennaise, 447
    Brabançonne, 447
    Chasseur, 448
    Chop, 348
    Pie, 321
    Polonaise, 448
  Loaf, Jellied, 356
  Loin, Marinated, 357
  Mock Turtle Soup, 136
  Quality of, 347
  Ragoût Creole, 365
  Riblets, 349
  Ring Soufflé Celestine, 365
  Roast(s), 988
    Arm, 348
    Blade, 348
    Cushion, 348
    Crown, 348
    Loin, 348
      Beer Gravy, 358
    Pocket, 348
    Rib, 348
    Round, 349
    Rump, 348, 349
  Roll, Braised, 350
  Rolled Shoulder, 349
  Rolls, California, 352
  Scalopini au Marsala, 366
  Shank, 349
  Steaks, 347
    Arm, 348
    Blade, 348
    Potted, Dutch Style, 358
    Round, 349

Veal, Steaks, Sirloin, 348
  Stew Creole, 365
    French, 349
    Hungarian, 356
    Italian, 357
    Sour, 359
  Stock, 93
  Tails, 428
  Tongue, 311
    Hash, 467
  Uccelletti Scappati, 751
  Vitello, Marsala Romana, 366
Vegetable(s), 591–744, 1162–1176
  Butter, 553
  Chowder, 142
  Deep Fat Frying, 986
  Frozen, 1011–1014
    Boiling Chart, 1014
    Pressure Cooking, 1014
  Jardiniere, 739
  Marrow, 1169
  Salads, 812
  Stock, 93
Velouté Sauce or Stock, 588
Venison Sauce, 588
  Mock Ham, Chasseur, 421
Vera Cruz, Red Snapper, 285
Vermicelli Consommé, 115
Vichy Carrots, 630
  Water & Goat's Milk, 77
    Peas Cooked in, 697
Vichyssoise, Crème, 123
Victory Dressing, 838
Vienna Bread, 1075
Viennese Coffee, 71
  Liver Loaf, 454
  Noodles, 759
Vinaigrette, 590
  Calf's Head à la, 352
  Dressing, 832
Vine Leaves, 376
  Squash, 729
Vinegars, 1009
Virginia Barbecued Fresh Ham, 396
  Calf's Head Soup, 110
  Ham Roast, 424
Vitello al Marsala Romana, 366
Voisin Canapes de Caviar, 15

Wafers, French, 931
  Poppy Seed, 933
    Variations, 933
Waffles, 803–808
  Apple, 805
  Bacon, 806

Waffles, Basic Recipe, 805
  Berry, 808
  Blueberry, 806
  Buttermilk Cornmeal, 806
  Cheese, 806
  Chicken, 807
  Chocolate, 807
  Codfish, 807
  Dessert, 804
  Fig, 808
  Gingerbread, 807
    and Ham, 804
  Hints, 804
  Leavened, 804
  Meat, 807
  Oatmeal, 807
  Raised, 804
  Raisin, 808
  Rice, 808
  Rice, Curried, 808
  Sweet Potato, 808
Walla Walla Salmon, 209
Waldenstein Dressing, 832
Waldorf Beer Flip, 52
Wall-Eyed Herring, 202
Wall-Eyed Pike, 207
Walnut(s)
  Banana, and Date Salad, 822
  Black, 1030, 1031
    Crunches, 970
  Croquettes, Potato and, 709
  Crumb Crust, 943
  English, 1030, 1031
  Grated, in Salads, 811
  Ham Brandied Stuffing, 792
  and Lentil Loaf, 674
  Maple Ice Cream, 1130
  Maple Syrup Pie, 952
Waltham Dressing, Boiled, 839
Wassail Ale Bowl, 52
  Beer Bowl, 53
  Cider, 61
Washington Clams, 225
Washington's Gingerbread Cream Pie, 953
Watercress, 813, 820, *See also* Salads
  Biscuits, 1049
  Dumplings, 788
  Nests, Egg and Rice Patties in, 164
Watermelon Supreme, 889
Wax Beans, *See* Beans, Wax
Weakfish, 219, 221, 222, 298
Weimar, Blanquette of Veal à la, 350
Welsh Rarebit, 856

West Indian Creole Sauce, 565
  Lamb Curry, 379
Western Sandwich, 851
Whale, a fish, 222
Whey, 78
Whip, 873
  California Prune, Crunch, 863
  Pimiento, 104
Whipped Cream, Coloring, 917
  Cream Jelly Dressing, 841
  Hubbard Squash, 732
  Sweet Potatoes, 713
Whipping Evaporated Milk, 80, 916,
    1115
  Thin Cream, 916
  Top Milk, 1115–1116
White Bass, 193
  Fruit Cake, 923
  Grunt, a fish, 199
White Hake, a fish, 201
  Meats, 309
  Pike, 205
  Sauce, 590
  Sea Bass, 193
  Stock, 93
  Wines, 85
  Wine Sauce, 590
Whitebait, 222, 304
  Fry, 304
Whitefish, 223
  Bouillabaisse Style, 305
  Filets, au Gratin, 305
Whiting, 201, 202, 223, 224
  Fry, 305
Whole Wheat Bread, 1067
  Honey Bread, 1067
  Popovers, 1095
Wiener Schnitzel, 366
Wiener, *see* Frankfurters
Wild Greens, Edible, 662
Wild Rice, 768, 773
  with Chicken Livers, 774
  and Liver, 775
  in Milk, 775
  and Sausage Stuffing, 795
  with Turkey, 539
Wilmot Dressing, 833
Wilted Dandelion Greens, 663
Window Pane, a fish, 221

Wine Dealer Sauce, 573, 590
  Steak, 329
Wine(s), *see also under individual names*
  Cooking with, 85
  gravy, 414
  How to Drink, 85
  Madeira, Aspic Coating Jelly, 543, 572
    Jelly (Dessert), 886
  Mousse, 1140
  Port, Aspic Coating Jelly, 39, 581
    Jelly (Dessert), 886
  Sherry, Aspic Coating Jelly, 41
    Jelly (Dessert), 886
  Red, 85
    Carp in, 241
    Mushrooms Stewed in, 685
  Sauce, Madeira, 573
  Sauce, Red, 583
    Dagouret, 583
  Sauce, White, 590
  White, 85
    Eggs in, with Cheese, 166
    Mackerel Filets in, 37
Winnonish Salmon, 210
Winter Carp, 195
  Flounder, 198, 251
  Savory, 1009
  Squash, 729
Wisconsin Salmon, 210
Woodsman's Sauerkraut, 720
Wow Wow Sauce, 330

Yams, *see also* Sweet Potatoes
  Pressure Cooked, 1172
Yellow Perch, 206
Yellow Turnips, en Casserole, 744
  Pressure Cooked, 1173
Yellowfin, 220
  Trout, 220
  Tuna, 220
Yoghurt, 76
Yorkshire Pudding, 342

Zabaglioni, 886
  Variations, 886
Zucchini; *See also* Squash
  Flowers, 729
  Pressure Cooked, 1174
  Vines and Leaves, 729